W9-CNM-217

Antique Trader™

Antiques & Collectibles

2003 PRICE GUIDE

"KIS-ME"

KIS-ME GUM CO.

edited by **KYLE HUSFLOEN**

Published by

Antique Trader, a division of

An F&W Publications Company

700 East State Street • Iola, WI 54990-0001
715-445-2214 • 888-457-2873
www.krause.com

Please call or write for our free catalog of publications.
Our toll-free number to place an order or obtain a free catalog is 800-258-0929
or please use our regular business telephone 715-445-2214.

ISBN: 0-87349-480-6

Printed in the United States of America

A WORD TO THE READER

Another year has flown by and we are all getting adjusted to antiquing in the new Millennium. To help guide you through the complexities of this ever-growing and changing marketplace we are pleased to offer our all-new *Antique Trader Antiques & Collectibles Price Guide 2003*. This, our nineteenth annual edition, builds on our tradition of producing timely and informative price guides since 1970.

We have always prided ourselves on preparing a reference offering the most detailed and accurate listings available on a broad spectrum of antiques and collectibles. This year we again have made that our chief goal, and you'll find included here over 18,000 individual listings highlighted with over 5,500 black and white photographs, many more pictures that appear in comparable guides. Also, to add interest and appeal, we provide a special 16-page full-color supplement of choice pieces selected from our listings. In addition to the photographs, many of our ceramics and glass categories also include a sketch of a signature or trademark found on those pieces. Brief introductory notes to many of our categories will also prove of value to readers. Altogether this means that you, the reader, whether collector, dealer or appraiser, will get the biggest bang for your buck with the *Antique Trader Antiques & Collectibles Price Guide 2003*.

In every edition of our annual price guide we include extensive pricing sections on major segments of collecting such as Ceramics, Glass and Furniture but we go well beyond just those areas. As the world of collecting continues to expand and become even more diversified we work to keep up with all the latest trends. We track a variety of new collecting areas and then select several new topics to include in each new edition. New categories you will find in this 2003 edition include Chess Collectibles, Cold War Collectibles, Children's Records, Sonja Henie Memorabilia, Pennants and Travel Maps. We also have special sections on Jazz and Pop Music recordings and collectibles in our "Pop Culture Collectibles" category, Billiards Collectibles (see Sports Collectibles) and Tea Serving Accessories (see Kitchenwares). Greatly expanded listings are also included for Circus Collectibles, Sheet Music and Trade Cards as well as extensive listings of Model Kits and Squeeze Toys in our "Toys" category. We feel that this wide diversity of subjects, as well as great coverage of other traditional collecting

fields provides collectors, dealers and appraisers with an invaluable reference tool sure to be of lasting value.

Our editors and staff always work diligently to ensure the most accurate and up-to-date information possible, and we work to produce a detailed Index and other cross-referencing to assist you in looking up your special piece. We also take pride in working with a large number of Special Contributors whose expertise provides invaluable insights. I want to offer all these people a special word of thanks for their time and efforts. You will also find them listed on a separate page according to their collecting specialty.

When using this price guide, I'm sure you'll appreciate the vast amount of detailed information we provide. However, you need to keep in mind that this book should be used as only a guide to establishing pricing. We draw our pricing information from various sources including auctions, private sales, advertisements and special experts, but any number of factors can effect what a specific item may sell for in a specific market. Condition, rarity and general market demand are always key factors, but regional interest and even the general economic conditions should also be factored in. We provide such detailed descriptions of items included in our guide because we feel that the better informed you are about a specific piece the better you can understand the price noted. Keep in mind that in general the values listed here are *retail replacement values*, that is, a price you might expect to pay if you found a comparable piece on the general market. What you might actually buy or sell an item for depends on the factors listed above as well as your general knowledge and, of course, luck. Remember that dealers can generally offer you only fifty percent or less of the "retail" value for an item since they must figure in a profit margin and display and marketing costs.

Antique Trader Antiques & Collectibles Price Guide basically follows an alphabetical format in most of our categories. However, we have arranged some larger categories together, including Ceramics, Furniture and Glass. These are separated into their own sections with the different subcategories arranged alphabetically within those sections. You can check our comprehensive Index at the back of the guide if you have a question about where to locate a special item you may have.

Please remember that although our descriptions, prices and illustrations have been double-checked and every effort has been made to ensure accuracy, neither the editor, publisher nor contributors can assume responsibility for any losses that might be incurred as a result of consulting this guide, or of typographical or other errors.

A great many of our photographs are provided by our Special Contributors, but we also draw from other sources including photographers, dealers, auction houses, galleries and private collectors. Below I will list these in alphabetical order.

The following photographers contributed images to this edition: E.A. Babka, East Dubuque, Illinois; Stanley L. Baker, Minneapolis, Minnesota; Johanna Billings, Danielsville, Pennsylvania; Herman C. Carter, Tulsa, Oklahoma; Susan N. Cox, El Cajon, California; Ruth Eaves, Marmora, New Jersey; Susan Eberman, Bedford, Indiana; Charles Hippler, Monticello, Illinois; Robert G. Jason-Ickes, Olympia, Washington; Dorothy Kamm, Port St. Lucie, Florida; Vivian Kromer, Bakersfield, California; Mark Moran, Rochester, Minnesota; Louise Paradis, Sparta, Wisconsin; and Rich Penn, Waterloo, Iowa.

For other photographs, artwork, data and permission to photograph in their shops, we sincerely express appreciation to the following auctioneers, galleries, museums, individuals and shops: Albrecht Auction Service, Vassar, Michigan; Alderfers, Hatfield, Pennsylvania; American Social History and Social Movements, Tucker, Georgia; Jay Anderson Antiques, Wabasha, Minnesota; Auction Team Koln, Cologne, Germany; Autopia Advertising Auctions, Woodinville, Washington; Mannie Banner, So. Bloomfield, Michigan; Carol Berk, Bethesda, Maryland; Brookside Antiques, New Bedford, Massachusetts; The Burmese Cruet, Montgomeryville, Pennsylvania; The Cedars - Antiques, Aurelia, Iowa; Charlton Hall Galleries, Columbia, South Carolina; Frank Chiarenza, Newington, Connecticut; Christie's, New York, New York; Cincinnati Art Galleries, Cincinnati, Ohio; Les and Irene Cohen, Pittsburgh, Pennsylvania; Collector's Auction Service, Oil City, Pennsylvania; Collector's Sales & Services, Pomfret Center, Connecticut; Copake Country Auction, Copake, New York; Daniel Auction Company, Sylvester, Georgia; DeFina Auctions, Austenburg, Ohio; William Doyle Galleries, New York, New York; DuMouchelles, Detroit, Michigan; Early Auction Company, Milford, Ohio; John Fontaine Gallery, Pittsfield, Massachusetts; Garth's Auctions, Delaware, Ohio; Glass-Works Auctions, East Greenfield, Pennsylvania; Glick's Antiques, Galena, Illinois; Green Valley Auctions, Mt. Crawford, Virginia;

Guyette & Schmidt, West Farmington, Maine.

Also to Vicki Harmon, San Marcos, California; the Gene Harris Antique Auction Center, Marshalltown, Iowa; Kenneth S. Hays & Associates, Louisville, Kentucky; the late William Heacock, Marietta, Ohio; Norman Heckler & Company, Woodstock Valley, Connecticut; Henry/Peirce Auctions, Homewood, Illinois; Don Hoffmann, Aurora, Illinois; International Rose O'Neill Club, Branson, Missouri; International Toy Collectors Association; Athens, Illinois; Jackson's Auctioneers & Appraisers, Cedar Falls, Iowa; Bev and Ray Jaeger, St. Louis, Missouri; Jerry's Antiques, Davenport, Iowa; James Julia Auctions, Fairfield, Maine; Greg Kowles, Winona, Minnesota; Peter Kroll, Sun Prairie, Wisconsin; G. and V. Kranz, Rochester, Minnesota; Lang's Sporting Collectibles, Raymond, Maine; Leland's Auctions, New York, New York; Joy Luke Galleries, Bloomington, Illinois; J. Martin, Mt. Orab, Ohio; Mastronet, Inc., Oakbrook, Illinois; Russ McCall Auctioneers, Onawa, Iowa; Randall McKee, Kenosha, Wisconsin; McMasters Doll Auctions, Cambridge, Ohio; Dr. James Measell, Marietta, Ohio; The Miniature Lamp Collectors Club, Northville, Michigan; Mom's Antique Mall, Oronoco, Minnesota; Monsen & Baer Auctions, Vienna, Virginia; William Morford Auctions, Cazenovia, New York; Pacific Glass Auctions, Sacramento, California; Past Tyme Pleasures, San Ramon, California; David Rago Arts & Crafts, Lambertville, New Jersey; Jane Rosenow, Galva, Illinois; Skinner, Inc., Bolton, Massachusetts; Slawinski Auction Company, Felton, California; Sotheby's, New York, New York; Stanton's Auctioneers, Vermontville, Michigan; Temple's Antiques, Eden Prairie, Minnesota; R. and K. Townsend, Rochester, Minnesota; Treadway Gallery, Cincinnati, Ohio; Lee Vines, Hewlett, New York; Mary M. Wetzel-Tomalka, Mishawaka, Indiana; C. Williams, Rochester, Minnesota; Dannie Woodard, Weatherford, Texas; Woody Auctions, Douglass, Kansas; and York Town Auctions, York, Pennsylvania.

We hope everyone who consults the *Antique Trader Antiques & Collectibles Price Guide 2003* will find it the most up-to-date and informative guide to this ever-changing world of collecting.

The staff of this guide welcomes all letters from readers, especially those of constructive critique, and we make every effort to respond personally.

- Kyle Husfloen, Editor

SPECIAL CONTRIBUTORS
2003 ANNUAL PRICE GUIDE

AVIATION COLLECTIBLES
Jim Trautman
R.R. 1
Orton, Ontario, Canada LON 7N0
e-mail: trautman@sentex.net

BANKS, STILL & MECHANICAL
Richard D. Friz
P.O. Box 472
Peterborough, NH 03458
(603) 563-8155
e-mail: joshdickmad@monadnet.com

CAT COLLECTIBLES
Cat Collectors
P.O. Box 150784
Nashville, TN 37215
(615) 297-7403
Web site: www.catcollectors.com

CHILDREN'S BOOKS
Kerra Davis
925 Bud St.
Blackshear, GA 31516
(912) 449-6494

COMPACTS & VANITY CASES
Roselyn Gerson
P.O. Box 40
Lynbrook, NY 1 1 563
Photos by Alvin Gerson
(516) 593-8746
Fax: (516) 593-0610
e-mail: compactldy@aol.com

BLADE BANKS, CHARACTER
BABY FEEDING DISHES,
CHILDREN'S WHIMSICAL
& WHISTLE CUPS
& TOOTHBRUSH HOLDERS
Deborah Gillham
47 Midline Ct.
Gaithersburg, MD 20878
e-mail: dgillham@erols.com

CHILDREN'S BOOKS
Kerra Davis
925 Bud St.
Blackshear, GA 31516
(912) 449-6494

CIRCUS COLLECTIBLES,
COLD WAR COLLECTIBLES
Jim Trautman
R.R. 1
Orton, Ontario, Canada LON 7N0
e-mail: trautman@sentex.net

COFFEE GRINDERS
Mike White
P.O. Box 483
Fraser, CO 80442
(970) 726-0448
e-mail: mwhite483@rkymtnhi.com
Web site: rkymtnhi.com/grinder

GRANITEWARE
Mari Ellen Furth-Vanderlinde
P.O. Box 57
E.Vassalboro, ME 04935
(207) 923-3660
e-mail: vinnysmef@aol.com

KITCHENWARES

Egg Timers, Pie Birds

Ellen Bercovici
5118 Hampden Lane
Bethesda, MD 20814
(301) 652-1140
e-mail: bercovici@erols.com

Kitchen Utensils

Paul Smith
1307 Baldwin
Harlan, IA 51537
e-mail: harlannet.com

Napkin Dolls, Reamers, Tea Serving Accessories

Bobbie Zucker Bryson
1 St. Eleanoras Lane
Tuckahoe, NY 10707
(914) 779-1405
e-mail: Napkindoll@aol.com

Co-author of *Collectibles For The Kitchen, Bath & Beyond - Second Edition*, Krause Publications

LIGHTING DEVICES

Aladdin Lamps
Thomas Small
201 Hemlock Lane
Meyersdale, PA 15552
e-mail: koko@shol.com

Fairy Lamps
Jim Sapp
Fairy Lamp Club & Newsletter
(703) 971-3229
e-mail: sapp@erols.com
Web site: www.fairylampclub.com

Kerosene Lamps & Lighting
Catherine M.V. Thuro
Toronto, Ontario, Canada

Dennis Hearn
Radio City Station
P.O. Box 1555
New York, NY 101 01 -1 555
Web site: www.Oillamp.com

Miniature Lamps
The Miniature Lamp Collectors Club
Night Light, newsletter
Bob Culver
38619 Wakefield Ct.
Northville, MI 48167-9060
(248) 473-8575
e-mail: rculver107@aol.com

Tiffany Lamps
Carl Heck
Box 8416
Aspen, CO 81612
(970) 929-8011
Web site: www.carlheck.com

LIPSTICK HOLDER LADIES
Ellen Bercovici
5118 Hampden Lane
Bethesda, MD 20814
(301) 652-1140
e-mail: bercovici@erols.com

FRATERNAL ORDER COLLECTIBLES, PLANT WATERERS & POLITICAL ITEMS
Bobbie Zucker Bryson
1 St. Eleanoras Lane
Tuckahoe, NY 10707
(914) 779-1405
e-mail: Napkindoll@aol.com

PENNANTS
Jim Trautman
R.R. 1
Orton, Ontario, Canada LON 7N0
e-mail: trautman@sentex.net

POP CULTURE COLLECTIBLES
Michael J. Goldberg
823 S.E. 25th Ave.
Portland, OR 97214
(503) 238-1977
e-mail: emjaygee@inetarena.com

RADIOS
Harry Poster
P.O. Box 1883
S.Hackensack, NJ 07606
(201) 794-9606
Fax: (201) 794-9553
e-mail: hposter@worldnet.att.net

RECORDS

Children's 45 rpm - Bonus Play
Michael J. Goldberg
823 S. E. 25th Ave.
Portland, OR 97214
(503) 238-1977
e-mail: emjaygee@inetarena.com

Children's 78 rpm
Peter Muldarin
173 W. 78th St.
New York, NY 10024
(212) 362-9606
e-mail: kiddie78s@aol.com
Web site: www.kiddierekordking.com

SCIENTIFIC INSTRUMENTS
Dr. Robert J. Elsner
29 Clubhouse Lane
Boynton Beach, FL 33436-6056
(561) 736-1362
rjelsner@aol.com

Specialist in antique barometers and nautical instruments; member: National Association Watch & Clock Collectors; featured on national live TV: FX Collectors program; listed in Mahoney's Antique & Collectors Resource Directory, Heights Antique and Auction House, owner & director

SEWING ADJUNCTS
Beth Pulsipher
Prairie Home Antiques
240 N. Grand
Schoolcraft, MI 49087
(616) 679-2062

SHEET MUSIC, TRADE CARDS
Kerra Davis
925 Bud St.
Blackshear, GA 31516
(912) 449-6494

SONJA HENIE MEMORABILIA

Ann J. Bates
5660 Keefe Rd.
Land o'Lakes, WI 54540
e-mail: ajb@newnorth.net

SPACE AGE COLLECTIBLES

Dana Cain
5061 S. Stuart Ct.
Littleton, CO 80123
(303) 347-8252
dana.cain@worldnet.att.net

Joe Fex
5061 S. Stuart Ct.
Littleton, CO 80123
Joefex @ aft. net

Jim Trautman
R.R. 1
Orton, Ontario, Canada LON 1N0
(519) 855-6077
e-mail: trautman@sentex.net

SPORTS COLLECTIBLES, BILLIARDS

Brad Morris, New Deco, Inc.
23123 Sunfield Dr.
Boca Raton, FL 33433
(800) 543-3326
Fax: (561) 488-9743
e-mail: newdeco@mindspring

STEREOSCOPES & STEREO VIEWS

Jim Trautman
R.R. 1
Orton, Ontario, Canada LON 1 N0
(519) 855-6077
e-mail: trautman @ sentex

TOY SOLDIERS

Henry Kurtz, Ltd.
163 Amsterdam Ave. No. 136
New York, New York 10023
(212) 642-5904
Fax: (212) 874-6018

TRAVEL MAPS, TOYS - PLAYSETS & TOY SOLDIERS

Jim Trautman
R.R. 1
Orton, Ontario, Canada LON 1N0
(519) 855-6077
e-mail: trautman@sentex.net

TRAYS, SERVING & CHANGE

Richard A. Penn
Pennyfield's Publishing
Box 1355
Waterloo, IA 50704-1355

WESTERN CHARACTER COLLECTIBLES, LONE RANGER

Laura M. Zucker
451 Greenville Ave.
Johnston, RI 02919
(409) 232-3648
e-mail: Mssz@aol.com

WORLD'S FAIR (1939-40) COLLECTIBLES

Richard D. Friz
P.O. Box 472
Peterborough, NH 03458
(603) 563-8155
e-mail: joshdickmad @ monadnet.com

CERAMICS

American Painted Porcelain

Dorothy Kamm
P.O. Box 7460
Port St. Lucie, FL 34985-7460
(561) 465-4008
e-mail: dorothykamm@usa.net

Flow Blue

Vivian Kromer
1 1 800 Shanklin St.
Bakersfield, CA 93312
(661) 588-7768

LuRay Pastels

Joe Zacharias
1233 Moultrie Ct.
Raleigh, NC 27615-6032
(919) 848-6966

McCoy

Craig Nissen
P.O. Box 223
Grafton, WI 53024-0223
(414) 377-7932
e-mail: McCoyCN@aol.com

Noritake

Tim Trapani
145 Andover Pl.
West Hempstead, NY 1 1 552

Purinton Pottery

Sharon Dahlhauser
212 N. Jones
Algona, IA 50511
(515) 295-5499
e-mail: csdahl@rconnect.com

Royal Bayreuth & R.S. Prussia

Mary McCaslin
6887 Black Oak Court, East
Avon, IN 46123
(317) 272-7776
e-mail: maryjack@indyrrcom

Royal Copenhagen

Ellen Bercovici
5118 Hampden Lane
Bethesda, MD 20814
(301) 652-1140
e-mail: bercovici@erols.com

Shelley China

Mannie Banner
6412 Silverbrook W.
W. Bloomfield, MI 48322-1034

Willow Wares

Jeff Siptak
The Willow Review
P.O. Box 41312
Nashville, TN 37204
Willowware@aol.com

International Willow Collectors
503 Chestnut St.
Perkasie, PA 18944
www.willowcollectors.org

GLASS

Amberina & Crown Milano

Louis O. St. Aubin, Jr.
Brookside Antiques
New Bedford, MA
Brooksideartglass@aol.com

Carnival Glass

Bruce Dooley
2571 - 7th Ave.
Sweetwater, NJ 08037
(609) 965-2535

Depression Glass

Debbie & Randy Coe
1240 SE 40th Ave.
Hillsboro, OR 97123

Animals, Cambridge, Consolidated, Duncan & Miller, Fenton, Fostoria, Fry, Heisey, Imperial, Morgantown, New Martinsville, Paden City, Westmoreland

Neila & Tom Bredehoft
10217 Stickle Rd.
St. Louisville, OH 43071-9753

Milk Glass

Frank Chiarenza
National Milk Glass Collecters Society
80 Crestview
Newington, CT 06111-2404
(860) 666-5576

Pattern Glass

Randall McKee
(262) 657-6958

Nancy Smith
Lamplight and Old Glass
P.O. Box 6192
Grand Rapids, MI 49506
(616) 942-0645

Iris Cottage Interiors
Andrea & Alan Koppel
Rt. 295 & County Rt. 5
P.O. Box 254
Canaan, NY 12029
(518) 781-4379

Tim Timmerman
11 655 S.W. Allen Blvd., #31
Beaverton, OR 97005
(U.S. Coin pattern)

ADVERTISING ITEMS

Roberts Turkey Brand Bill Hook

Bill hook, "Roberts Turkey Brand Corned Meats," celluloid w/metal wire hook, round disk printed w/a central image of a Tom turkey within a ring & outer border w/advertising, early 20th c. (ILLUS.)............. **$83**

Bill hook, "Walker Products," hanging-type, oval celluloid button printed in color w/pictures of various canned products, on a long metal hook holder, 2 x 6 1/2".......... **66**

Blotter, "Smith Brothers Chewing Gum," rectangular printed in black & white w/bearded logo heads of the brothers & pictures of the products, dated 1913, unused, 4 x 9 1/2" **55**

Sunoco/Sun-Heat Furnace Oil Blotter

Blotter, "Sunoco/Sun-Heat Furnace Oil," rectangular, Disney theme showing Mickey Mouse sleeping in an easy chair near a window showing winter scene, marked "For Winter days, it's hard to beat The Warmth and Comfort of - Sun-Heat Furnace Oil," dealer information at bottom, dated 1939, minor bends, soiling & wear, 3 1/4 x 6" (ILLUS.) **358**

Blotter, "The Aetna Powder Company," long rectangular form w/the company name spelled out in large sticks of dynamite against a white ground, unused, 4 x 9 1/4" (some fly specks).............................. **44**

7Up Six-bottle Tin Carrier

Bottle carrier, "7Up," tin, six-bottle size, high arched overhead handle, oblong side band in silver printed in red & dark blue "You Like It - It Likes Your" w/logo, 5 1/4 x 7 1/2", 9 1/2" h. (ILLUS.) **69**

Bottle carrier, "Pepsi-Cola," stamped aluminum, high arched strap handle "Drink Pepsi-Cola" trimmed in red, 4 3/4 x 8 1/2", 10 1/2" h. **95**

Winchester Shotgun Shell Box

Box, "Winchester Ranger Loaded Shot Shells," cardboard, colorful design w/an orange ground w/wording in dark orange & black w/a scene of a hunting dog on point, empty, 2 1/2 x 4", 4" h. (ILLUS.) **61**

Early California Box Label

Box label, "California Poppy Brand Oranges," lithographed paper, colorful design of California poppies on a white ground w/wording in red & blue, ca. 1900, 10 1/2 x 11" (ILLUS.)................................. **578**

Bread plate, "Coon Chicken Inn," ceramic, round, white w/a red, pink & black caricature of a black man's face at the top, a dark blue dotted border band, made by Inca Ware, 5 1/2" d. (scattered tiny knife nicks) **165**

Brush, "Chas. P. Shipley Saddlery Co.," premium item, oblong wood handle in yellow w/black prints including two vignettes, red rim band, new & unused in original box, 2 x 7" **33**

Crescent Trailways Bus Pin

Bus driver's pin, "National Trailways Bus System - Crescent Trailways - 186," die-cut painted metal, shield-shaped w/the upper portion in red, white & blue enamel w/the lower portion w/a silvery finish, double screw post mounts, minor overall wear, 2 3/8 x 2 9/16" (ILLUS.) **143**

Early Aviation Celluloid Button

Button, "Aviation Contest - Los Angeles - Jan. 1910," celluloid, large size w/a color panoramic scene of early airplanes, balloons & dirigibles flying above a large crowd of spectators, information on a large white flying banner, easel back stand, 6" d. (ILLUS.)... **358**

Clark's Mile-End Spool Calendar

Calendar, 1886, "Clark's Mile-End Spool Cotton," girl seated under Oriental parasol above January page showing advertising, framed 20 x 30" (ILLUS.) **650**

Calendar, 1886, "Hood's Sarsaparilla Calendar," large profile bust portrait of a pretty young Victorian girl w/blonde hair wearing a flower-trimmed white bonnet w/blue ribbons, advertising date pad across the bottom, 4 3/4 x 7" (slight crease) **77**

Calendar, 1888, "Hood's Sarsaparilla," die-cut paperboard, young girl's head portrait wearing blue bonnet, full pad, 9 3/4"............. **180**

Calendar, 1891, "Aetna Insurance Co.," port scene w/mountain beyond, full pad, matted & framed, image 6 1/2 x 9 1/2" (glass cracked) **25**

1891 Simmons Hardware Calendar

Calendar, 1891, "Simmons Hardware Co.," rectangular, cardboard w/paper pad, wood frame, portrait of young woman w/"Simmons Hardware Co. - St. Louis, Mo. - J.I.C. Horse Nails - Finished and Pointed and Made From Best Norway Fillets," 13 x 16 1/2" (ILLUS.)...................... **225-325**

Calendar, 1892, "Hood's Sarsaparilla," round, eight children w/various sewing projects surround complete calendar pad, 7 3/4" d. **85**

Calendar, 1893, "John Hancock Insurance," horse-drawn carriage w/building beyond, full calendar, matted & framed, image 12 1/2 x 16" **45**

Calendar, 1893, "Prudential Insurance Co.," round w/girl holding insurance policy surrounded by months of the year, 9" d. **75**

Calendar, 1894, "Prudential Life Insurance Co.," April, May & June sheet on the diagonal shows girl w/hand at mouth & halo of flowers, 6 x 6" **45**

Calendar, 1894, "Prudential Life Insurance Co.," July, August & September sheet on the diagonal showing boy in billed cap, 6 x 6" **40**

Rare & Early U.M.C. Calendar

Calendar, 1894, "Union Metallic Cartridge Co. (The)," long rectangular form w/color scene of a mother hunting dog & her pups w/an open package of the cartridges, partial date pad, excellent condition, 14 x 28 1/4" (ILLUS.) **5,005**

Calendar, 1895, "Consumers Brewing Co.," elegant woman in blue dress & hat, full pad, framed, image 14 1/2 x 19" (water staining & soiling) **400**

Calendar, 1895, "Edward Heuer Bottler," waitress beside large bottle surrounded by flowers, full pad, matted & framed, image 12 x 19" **975**

Calendar, 1895, "Winchester Cartridges," large rectangular form w/an upper color scene of two hunters in a winter landscape beside a dead bear, the small date pad in the center above a small landscape of hunters at a rocky lake shore, partial date pad, based on artwork by A.B. Frost, 14 1/4 x 26 1/2" (both bands pinned to matte board, tack holes, missing piece, small tears) **935**

Calendar, 1896, "F.L. Ober Brewing Co.," die-cut, dog holding monthly calendar sheets in front of palm trees, framed, image 9 1/2 x 17" **350**

Calendar, 1897, "Hood's Sarsaparilla," die-cut paper, pretty child in lilac hat, October pad, 4 1/2 x 7" (top corner bent & facial creasing) **38**

Calendar, 1897, "Lorenz Schmidts' Estate Mt. Carbon Brewery," paper, girl w/dog at her feet, December sheet only, framed, image 15 x 19 1/2" **350**

Calendar, 1898, "F.A. Poth & Son Brewers," paper, hunter & dog pausing to look at billboard, full calendar, framed, image 20 1/2 x 30" **800**

1898 Hood's Coupon Calendar

Calendar, 1898, "Hood's Coupon Calendar," top of cover w/a color bust picture of a pretty golden-haired child in a circle framed by white daisies on a pale blue ground, unused condition, 4 1/2 x 7" (ILLUS.) **100-150**

Listers Bone Fertilizers Calendar

Calendar, 1898, "Listers Animal Bone Fertilizers," Dutch farm scene, full pad, framed, 18 1/2 x 29" (ILLUS.) **175**

Calendar, 1898, "Louis Bergdoll Brewing Co.," Bavarian couple on royal carpet flanked by men w/flagons, full pad, framed, image 20 x 27" **1,000**

Calendar, 1898, "Oriental Brewery," boating scene w/logo & lettering above, framed, image 19 1/2 x 27 1/2" (minor creases) **1,100**

Calendar, 1898, "Prospect Brewing Co.," inset of three children w/floral border, framed, image 16 x 20 1/2" (minor creasing & soiling) **1,100**

First National Bank Calendar

Calendar, 1899, "First National Bank," pictures sailing ship, "First National Bank, Moravia, NY" in red, full pad (ILLUS.) **230**

Calendar, 1899, "Geo. Ringler & Co. Brewers," paper, girl wrapping herself in American flag, 12 calendar sheets below, framed, image 16 x 24"............................. **2,500**

Calendar, 1899, "John Kress Brewing Co.," U.S. fleet leaving for war in shield w/eagle atop, framed w/metal strips, full pad, 30 x 32"... **700**

Calendar, 1899, "Keystone Brewery," barmaid enticing fellow w/beer, Otto Eyring above, February pad, framed, image 15 1/2 x 30"..................................... **900**

Calendar, 1899, "Lauer Brewing Co.," paper, girl w/upheld tray serving drinks to three men, full pad, framed, image 17 x 22 1/2"... **900**

Calendar, 1899, "Muhlenberg Brewing Co.," paper, girl presenting seasons greetings, Lager Beer & Porter, April pad, framed, image 15 x 19".................................. **900**

Winchester Ammunition Calendar

Calendar, 1899, "Winchester Ammunition," lithographed rectangular form w/a large color top scene of hunters in a rocky winter setting w/a large bear in the distance, a bottom color scene of a hunter & dogs in an open field, partial date pad, some creases, 14 1/4 x 27" (ILLUS.) **1,650**

Calendar, 1900, "DuPont," battle scene of Santiago, Cuba, full pad, matted & framed, 14 x 28"... **495**

Calendar, 1900, "DuPont," tall narrow rectangular form w/a large upper color scene of a naval battle viewed from a battleship, full date pad at bottom, both bands, 14 x 28 1/4" (minor creases, minor stain at bottom left) **358**

Calendar, 1900, "Jno C. Stocker Brewer," girl behind fence surrounded by knotted rope, September sheet, framed, image 16 x 22".. **750**

Calendar, 1900, "United States Fidelity Guaranty Co.," cardboard, shield-shaped, children in uniform & portrait inserts, April pad, framed, image 16 x 20" **300**

Calendar, 1901, "Daisy & Sentinel Air Rifles," paper, child holding rifle, full pad, rare, framed, image 15 1/2 x 22 1/2".......... **3,200**

Calendar, 1901, "Lipton's Teas," embossed paper, girl w/cup of tea surrounded by months, floral ground, framed, image 10 x 12".. **55**

Calendar, 1901, "Olympia Beer," six individually matted cards picturing women surrounded by flowers, framed, image 10 x 13".. **500**

Calendar, 1902, "Berdoll's Beer," elderly man & woman w/glass of beer, circular logo in upper corners, framed, image 16 1/2 x 22"... **400**

Calendar, 1902, "John Hancock Life Insurance Co.," company name & year above girl asleep beside large dog, two rows of months below, 8 1/2 x 10 1/2"....................... **185**

Bemis Bros. Bag Co. Calendar

Calendar, 1903, "Bemis Bros. Bag Co.," rectangular, lithographed cloth, red w/white & yellow lettering, center w/white circle depicting head of a buffalo in black & white & surrounded by a circle of white dots, flanked by torches above bags & marked above "Animals that Are Hunted," Bemis Bros. Bag Co., St. Louis, Missouri, each page features different animal & colors, ca. 1903, 11 x 16" (ILLUS.)..................................... **450-650**

Plate-shaped Fairbanks Calendar

Calendar, 1903, "Fairbanks Fairy Soap," die-cut cardboard in a round plate shape w/gently scalloped rim, wide blue border band w/gold banded trim enclosing months, center color scene of a lovely young fairy maiden w/flowing hair seated on blossoming branches, based on art by Paul Moran, 9 1/2" d. (ILLUS.) **33**

Hazard Smokeless Powder Calendar

Calendar, 1903, "Hazard Smokeless Powder - The Trophy Winner," color scene at the top w/a dog & youth walking home w/his rifle & dead game, titled "Return of the Hunters," dark grey ground w/gold & white wording, partial date pad, some scuffs around edges, 3 1/2 x 6 1/4" (ILLUS.).. **495**

Calendar, 1903, "John C. Stocker Brewer," elegant woman seated in ornate gold chair, February sheet, framed, image 14 1/2 x 19".. **550**

Calendar, 1903, "Pabst Extract," paper, babies from all nations holding calendar sheets, stork at bottom, framed, image 11 x 28" **375**

Calendar, 1903, "Weisbrod & Hess Brewery," vignettes of parks, seashore scenes, display of products, etc., full pad, framed, image 20 x 28"................... **1,050**

Early DuPont Powder Calendar

Calendar, 1904, "DuPont Powder Co.," a large color image at the top of a group of hunters waiting on a railroad depot platform w/a young black boy holding the collar of one of the hunting dogs, deep maroon background w/"DuPont" in large gold letters, partial calendar pad at bottom (ILLUS.).. **3,080**

1904 Youth's Companion Calendar

Calendar, 1904, "Youth's Companion," fold-out die-cut cardboard printed in color, left & right panels w/scenes of birds in blossoming branches, center scene of a young family standing under blossoming trees, minor blemishes mostly on reverse, 12 x 21" (ILLUS.) **187**

Libby, McNeil & Libby Calendar

Calendar, 1905, "Libby, McNeil & Libby Corned Beef," little girl in front of pink flowers, corned beef can beside calendar below, 11 x 16 1/2" (ILLUS.)............................. **45**

Calendar, 1906, "Connecticut General Fire Insurance Co.," general on horseback carrying document, full pad, matted & framed, 13 1/2 x 19 1/2" (stains & creases) 70

Calendar, 1906, "Dode Meeks Company Livestock," diamond-shaped w/a round center color print of a pretty lady in a large red-feathered hat & a red gown, small date pad at the bottom, framed, overall 11" sq. 154

Calendar, 1906, "Frank Coe's Fertilizer Co.," pictures three lads at field's edge w/plow & fence, full pad, 9 x 13" 35

Calendar, 1906, "Grand Rapids Brewing Co.," paper, little girl in red shawl & bonnet w/open book, pad missing, framed, image 9 1/2 x 14 1/2" 550

Calendar, 1906, "Horrigan Supply Company," large central color bust portrait of a pretty lady w/brown hair wearing a choker necklace & a low-cut deep red gown, black & white wording & small pictures of pumps around the sides, small partial date pad at bottom, bands w/wrinkles, 15 x 20" 259

Calendar, 1907, "Adam Scheidt Brewing Co.," man standing beside two women in sailor attire, floral border, full pad, framed, 21 x 29 1/2" 600

Calendar, 1907, "Harrington & Richardson Arms Co.," wintry scene w/running mountain man, full pad, framed, 14 x 27" 2,000

Calendar, 1907, "Hudson County Consumers Brewing Co.," pictures factory scene surrounded by hops & wheat, logo upper right, framed, image 12 x 17" (pad missing) 900

Calendar, 1907, "Mathie Brewing Co.," die-cut cardboard, cherub & flowered beauty in gondola, full pad, framed, 14 1/2 x 15 1/2" 1,300

Calendar, 1907, "P Barbey & Son Brewers," cardboard, oval image of girl in fur-trimmed jacket flanked by logo, May pad, framed, 19 1/2 x 24" 975

Calendar, 1907, "West End Brewing Co.," paper, girl at table sampling brew w/factory out window, full pad, framed, image 16 x 23 1/2" 600

Calendar, 1908, "Adloff & Hauerwaas Breweries," die-cut cardboard, fishing scene w/brewery inset below, full pad, matted & framed, image 13 x 20" 1,250

Calendar, 1908, "Ballantine's Breweries," cardboard, brewery inset at top, decorative border, December sheet framed, image 12 1/2 x 20" 320

Calendar, 1908, "David Stevenson Brewing Co.," Uncle Sam toasting residents of New York above factory inset, framed, image 19 1/2 x 28" 2,300

Calendar, 1908, "Deering Harvesting Machines," shows hunter & two bird dogs, 1908 stamped over two rows of six months each at bottom, no pad 160

Calendar, 1908, "DeLaval Cream Separators," oval image of girl & cow, yellow lettering above, calendar never opened, framed, 17 1/2 x 24 1/2" 650

Dr. Miles Remedies Calendar

Calendar, 1908, "Dr. Miles Remedies," child holding a rose, "H.H. Alley & Co. Druggist...," calendar never opened, minor edge wear (ILLUS.) 50

Calendar, 1908, "Lion Brewery," lion w/front paws on barrel surrounded by factory insets, no pad, framed, image 13 x 16 1/2" 220

Calendar, 1908, "Parmenter & Polsey Fertilizer Co.," paper, bust-portrait of elegant girl in oval surrounded by fancy border, full pad, 13 1/2 x 21" 375

Calendar, 1908, "SP Lapcevic Steamship Agent," die-cut w/embossed cowgirl & vignettes of horses, full pad, framed, 11 x 21" 550

Calendar, 1909, "Collins Celebrated Bread," diagonal version w/product name above girl in bonnet w/holly leaves, full pad, 8 x 8" 25

Calendar, 1909, "Geo. Zett Brewery," embossed die-cut cardboard, two children in hay surrounded by puppies, framed, 20 x 20" 1,000

Calendar, 1910, "E. Robinson's Sons Pilsner," oval image of girl w/roses above product & factory insets, matted & framed, image 11 x 22" 350

Calendar, 1910, "Independent Brewing Co.," paper, girl in elegant dress & bonnet holding basket of flowers, framed, image 14 1/2 x 19 1/2" 475

United States Separator Calendar

Calendar, 1910, "United States Cream Separator," girl in profile w/cows beyond, Vermont Farmer Machine Co. below, March/April pad, framed 20 x 30" (ILLUS.).. 200

Calendar, 1911, "Collins Baking Co.," child on edges, full pad 130

Calendar, 1911, "Fleischmann's Yeast," pocket-type, celluloid cover, pictures lady w/long hair, calendar & product name on reverse, 2 x 3" 26

Calendar, 1911, "Orange Candy Kitchen," die-cut cardboard, little boy playing violin while kittens play, matted & framed, 15 x 19" 100

Calendar, 1912, "Lykens Brewing Co.," mother & child w/dog walking across creek on a board, full pad, framed, image 16 1/2 x 23" 300

Calendar, 1912, "Penn Beer," paper, girl in green & black outfit & hat, Consumers Brewing Co., full pad, framed, image 16 x 31" 400

Calendar, 1913, "Ebling Brewing Co.," paper, factory scene w/casino & restaurant in foreground, full pad, framed, image 21 x 28 1/2" 500

Calendar, 1913, "Ebling Brewing Co.," paper, factory scene w/casino & restaurant in foreground, full pad, framed image 21 x 28 1/2" 500

Calendar, 1914, "Lowell Fertilizer Co.," paper, girl seated in profile w/bouquet of roses, full pad, framed, image 14 1/2 x 21 1/2"... 95

Calendar, 1914, "New England Fertilizer Co.," paper, girl seated in window sill w/flowers in background, full pad, framed, image 15 x 23"...................................... 75

Calendar, 1914, "Rieger & Gretz Brewing Co.," bust-length portrait of a girl in wide-brimmed hat, logo upper left, full pad, framed, 16 1/2 x 22" 450

Winchester 1914 Calendar

Calendar, 1914, "Winchester," large rectangular color image of a hunter & dogs stalking through an autumn field of corn shocks at sunset, full date pad, dry-mounted, bands missing, 15 1/4 x 30 1/4" (ILLUS.)............................... 528

Calendar, 1915, "Bernheimer & Schwartz Pilsner Brewing Co.," large brewery image, lettering above, full pad, framed, image 20 1/2 x 29"................................. 800

Calendar, 1915, "Crown Beer," paper roll-down, girl holding rose, crown logo in each corner, full pad, 10 x 34"...................... 305

Calendar, 1915, "DeLaval Cream Separators," product name above boy giving calf pan of milk, scrolled courtesy panel below, full pad 1,500

Stunning 1915 Winchester Calendar

Calendar, 1915, "Winchester," tall rectangular form w/large color image at the top showing a large condor-like bird attacking a white mountain goat, brand in large red letter at bottom above the partial date pad, picture based on artwork of Lynn Bogue Hunt, bands pinned to mat, roll creases, 15 1/4 x 30 1/4" (ILLUS.) 1,155

Calendar, 1916, "Geo. Ringler & Co. Brewers," factory image w/bottle insets below, store inset above, March pad, framed, image 13 1/2 x 19" 650

Weed Chains Advertising Calendar

Calendar, 1916, "Weed Chains," four colorful vignettes of women in hats above full calendar, minor wear, small edge tear 13 1/2 x 34" (ILLUS.) 550

Calendar, 1917, "Peters," a tall rectangular format w/most of the page decorated w/a color scene of two hunting dogs in a field of corn shocks, small partial date pad at the bottom flanked by panels of advertising, based on artwork by G. Muss Arnolt, professionally mounted & framed, 13 5/8 x 27 1/8" (wrinkles from being rolled up) 550

Calendar, 1918, "DeLaval Cream Separators," product name above girl standing w/horse, courtesy panel at right, full pad, framed 12 x 24" 695

Calendar, 1918, "James V. Cardi Italo - American Bread Co.," features bakery w/baker serving customers, full pad, 15 x 21 1/2" 75

Calendar, 1920, "Chevrolet Motor Cars," green w/white lettering & lined border, farm scene w/car & family above, full pad, 16 x 31" 145

Calendar, 1920, "Globe Feeds," pictures children & chicks, full pad............................. 110

Calendar, 1920, "Sharples Separator," tall rectangular form w/a large color top picture of a young girl giving her little brother a drink from a pot, their mother in the background walking into a porch w/the separator, complete calendar pad, top band, 12 x 22" (minor tears & creases in upper right) 237

Union Oil Company Pocket Calendar

Calendar, 1921, "Union Oil Company of Arizona," celluloid, pocket-type, colorful image of yellow & black early convertible auto & service station marked "Union Oil Company," logos on reverse, minor wear & light bends, 2 3/8 x 3 3/4" (ILLUS.) 198

Calendar, 1922, "Sunshine Biscuits," girl in yellow & pink gown w/brown stole ready for an evening out, June sheet, 9 x 15" (worn)... 50

Texaco Advertising Calendar

Calendar, 1922, "Texaco," "The Texas Company Petroleum & Its Products"

surround star logo atop calendar, full pad, 25 x 13" (ILLUS.) 185

Calendar, 1922, "U.S. Cartridges," a tall narrow form w/a very long upper color picture of a standing, growling brown bear holding a crate of the product in a snowy landscape, only January date page, 15 x 35 1/2" (wrinkles due to rolling up, few splits, top band glued to mat board top & bottom) 468

Calendar, 1922, "Western & Southern Life Insurance," shows girl in bonnet w/flowers, two rows of six months each below, 9 x 9" 21

Dramatic 1923 Winchester Calendar

Calendar, 1923, "Winchester" tall rectangular form, a tall full-color picture at the top w/a brand in red above a panoramic mountainous landscape w/a hunter perched high on a craggy rock, based on artwork by Phillip R. Goodwin, a large partial date pad at the bottom, top band pinned to mat board, a minute pin hole, 13 3/4 x 25 5/8" (ILLUS.).............................. 990

1924 Snyder Restaurant Calendar

Calendar, 1924, "Thos. C. Snyder - Restaurant - Confectionary - Ice Cream - Fruit," large color scene at the top of Little Red Riding Hood & the wolf, large partial date pad across bottom, great colors, band at top, 12 x 21" (ILLUS.) 242

Calendar, 1925, "Sherwood's Confectionary and Grocery," rectangular aluminum mount w/a printed label w/a black & white scene of American Indians on horseback titled "The Buffalo Hunt," partial date pad across the bottom, 7 x 9 1/2" **110**

Calendar, 1928, "Hudson's Bay Company," long horizontal rectangular format w/a color image on the left of two trappers getting ready to climb into a canoe, nice landscape scene titled "Starting a Canoe Trip" by artist Phillip R. Goodwin, text in red & black on the right side includes "We Want Your Raw Furs" above the company name, w/original mailing envelope, 6 1/2 x 11 1/2" **468**

Calendar, 1928, "Iroquois Brewery," profile of young Native American squaw w/feathers & beads in her hair, full pad, framed, image 13 1/4 x 27 1/2" **850**

Tyee Tackle 1928 Calendar

Calendar, 1928, "Tyee Tackle," rectangular, printed in color w/a large image of a pretty lady getting ready to fish standing on the right, landscape in background, small dated pad in lower left corner, includes a 1927 California game laws booklet w/same advertising, calendar 12 x 16 1/2", 2 pcs. (ILLUS. of calendar) **605**

Calendar, 1929, "Western Cartridge Co.," pointer sitting in chair, original mailing promo price still attached, full pad, 14 x 27" **600**

Calendar, 1931, "U.S. Shot-Shells & Cartridges," titled "Opportunity," man beside dog w/dead game, full pad, framed, 16 x 31 1/2" **650**

Calendar, 1935, "Royal Style Ale," Indian princess picking water lilies, Globe Brewing Co., full pad, framed, image 14 x 28" **425**

Trucking Company Calendar

Calendar, 1937, "Waldron & Solberg, Algona, Iowa - Independent Jobber," die-cut tin, the upper section w/a billboard behind a 1930s tanker truck all in white, dark blue, red & green, a long narrow paper calendar pad below, minor scratches, thin paint at center, few small bends, missing stand tabs on back, 4 3/8 x 6" (ILLUS.) **61**

Calendar, 1938, "Hercules Powder Company," tall narrow rectangular form, a long color scene at the top showing interior of medieval chemist's shop w/a young pretty female alchemist kissing the forehead of a handsome young man in front of an open window, titled "The Alchemist," based on art by N.C. Wyeth, partial date pad, minor cracks from being rolled up, bright colors, 11 3/4 x 30 1/2" **77**

Calendar, 1940, "Hood's Milk," pictures happy baby face w/bottle, October pad, 10 x 14" **35**

Calendar, 1942 "Burlington Railroad," rectangular, image of "Silver King" at top last page w/three months printed on main poster, missing the previous months (heavy crease side to side at top, rip at top right side, minor edge creases & tears) **83**

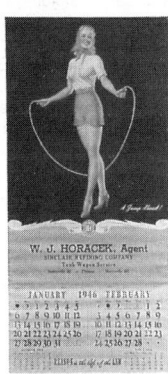

Sinclair Gasoline Calendar

Calendar, 1946, "Sinclair Gasoline," full pad, image of beautiful girl w/jump rope wearing purple shorts, yellow sweater & red head scarf, titled "A Jump Ahead!" by Earl Moran, minor rolls, 16 x 33 1/2" (ILLUS.) **110**

Calendar, 1947, "Gilmore Gasoline," red lion logo, 7 x 17" **19**

Calendar, 1947, "Jno C. Stocker Brewer," girl behind fence surrounded by knotted rope, September sheet, framed, image 16 x 22" **750**

Calendar, 1949, "Royster Fertilizers," baby girl w/segmented wooden doll, signed "Charlotte Becker," full pad, 4 3/4 x 8" **16**

Calendar, 1950, "Great Northern - Streamlined Empire Builder," a large color portrait at the top of Tom Dawson, a famous early mountain man & explorer, a vignette of two train engines just above the date pad, w/both bands, 16 x 33 1/2" **77**

1950 Hair Dressing Calendar

Calendar, 1950, "Pinol Tar-mange Sham-poo - Southern Rose Hair Dressing," tall rectangular form w/a large color picture at the top showing a young fisherman standing in a stream & holding up a net w/a large fish, a scowling young woman w/fishing rod standing beside him in the water, scene titled "Happy Ending," based on artwork by J.F. Kernan, advertising section below w/small date pad flanked by color images of the products, 17 x 35" (ILLUS.) **121**

Calendar, 1953, "TWA Airline," rectangular, six double-sided pages, each w/a different month & picture from around the world (minor edge & surface wear, light rolls at top) **33**

Calendar, 1955, "John Deere," wildlife book, full pad **25-35**

Coca-Cola Wall Calendar

Calendar, 1972, "Coca-Cola," tin, button-style wall calendar, complete pad w/cover, light wear, 8 x 19 1/4" (ILLUS.) **523**

Calendar, 1979, "Ruger Firearms," 30th Anniversary, scene of hunting moose in a canoe, full pad.. **65**

Calendar, 1980, "Campbell's Soup," paper........ **10**

See's Candies Candy Hammer

Candy hammer, "See's Candies," cast-brass w/silvered finish, embossed wording on side, 3 1/2" l. (ILLUS.)............................ **24**

Chalkboard, "Robin's Best - America's Finest Flour," upright rectangular easel-back style, the top section w/a color image of a flour sack & red & yellow wording on a black ground, lower black ground divided by white horizontal lines, wording in top bands reads "Specials Today - Robin's Best Flour...," wording in bottom section in white & yellow reads "and don't forget Robin's Best Flour," 14 x 21 1/4" (very minor surface & edge wear, few small scatches) **303**

Clicquot Club Clock

Clock, "Clicquot Club," electric, round w/center image of young boy wearing fur-trimmed parka holding large green bottle, black Arabic numerals & black-tipped hands, Telechron, ca. 1940s, composite case repainted, metal plate installed near hanging hole, 15" d. (ILLUS.) **495**

Electric Light-up Coppertone Clock

Clock, "Coppertone," electric, square plastic & metal light-up model, two-sided, the white ground w/a large full color image of the Coppertone girl & her dog, the boxed clock dial in the upper right, slogan in black in the bottom right "Don't Be A Paleface," 8 x 36", 36" h. (ILLUS. of one side) **1,760**

Fisk Tires Clock

Clock, "Fisk Tires," desk-type, electric, clock w/"Time to Re-Tire - Get Fisk," little boy logo at bottom, mounted in black rubber tire w/airplane on it, tire is hardened & out of round, clock missing stand-up support bracket & adjuster knob, appears to keep good time, 6 1/4" d. (ILLUS.) **187**

Hastings Piston Rings Electric Clock

Clock, "Hastings Piston Rings," electric, round w/plastic domed cover, white ground w/black Arabic numerals w/wording in the top center above the red, white & black Hastings Piston man logo, works, minor wear, retention ring missing tabs, 14 3/4" d. (ILLUS.) **176**

Clock, "Lucky Strike," key-wind, wooden schoolhouse-style case w/octagonal top w/wood graining surrounding the brass bezel opening to the round dial w/Roman numerals around a red center dot reading "R.A. Patterson Tob. Cos. - Lucky Strike," short drop below w/gilt-trimmed glass door over the pendulum, late 19th - early 20th c., original key, chimes, 12 1/4" w., 19" h. **660**

Motorola Radio Neon Clock

Clock, "Motorola Radio For Home and Car," neon spinner-type, white face w/blue Arabic numerals & red lettering, keeps good time, repainted case, wear to reverse glass, minor wear & rust to face, 1 1/2" d. (ILLUS.) **550**

Nesbitt's Orange Electric Clock

Clock, "Nesbitt's Orange," electric, backlighted metal & plastic w/domed plastic cover, black Arabic numerals & orange dots form dial, central logo design in black, white & orange in a bold geometric design, two bottles & oranges shown in the lower left, very minor nicks & wear to reverse face, Canadian origin, working, 16 1/4" d. (ILLUS.) **495**

Phillips 66 Light-up Electric Clock

Clock, "Phillips 66 Tires - Batteries," electric, round plastic light-up type w/'double-bubble' dial cover, white background, large company shield-shaped logo in black, white & red in the center w/black wording above & below, an outer ring of Arabic numerals, sweep seconds hand, light not working, 15" d. (ILLUS.) **688**

Price's Milk Neon Clock

Clock, "Price's Milk," neon w/glo-dial, chrome-plated case, black face w/blue border, white hands & Arabic numerals, keeps good time, minor wear to reverse glass detail, hands may have been repainted, 14 1/2" d. (ILLUS.)............................ **523**

Pepsi Electric Wall Clock

Clock, "The Light Refreshment - Pepsi," electric, round wire grill-form background mounted w/large gold teardrops serving as numbers, the white round center printed w/a gold sunburst & wording in black w/a red, white & blue Pepsi bottle cap, white openwork dial hands, ca. 1950s, very minor wear & scratches, minor paint loss & bends to hands, 17 1/4" d. (ILLUS.).. **171**

Time Oil Company Electric Clock

Clock, "Time Products - Time Tested," electric, round metal w/glass dial cover, white dial w/blue, orange & white logo in the center & blue Arabic numerals around the sides, very minor scattered nicks & wear, 14 1/2" d. (ILLUS.)............................... **303**

Clock, "Whistle," electric, back-lighted metal & plastic w/plastic domed cover, round w/blue Arabic numbers & dots with musical notes around the outside border of the dial, blue, orange & white design in center w/a large musical note printed w/"Thirsty? - Just Whistle," orange printing just below center reads "Sparkling Orange Goodness," sweep seconds hand, 14 1/2" d. (frosty dirty look w/some tiny flecks).. **231**

Coaster wagon, "Buster Brown Shoes," rectangular red metal bed w/rounded corners, rubber-rimmed red solid metal wheels, black handlebar, white band on sides w/wording in red, original paint & decals, 15 x 36", 15" h. (some scuffs, scratches & paint chips, one hub cap missing).. **550**

Counter display, "Chiclets Gum," cylindrical tin counter-top holder for loose packages of Chiclets gum, color stripes around the outside show different flavors of the gum including "Charcoal" **127**

Adams Chewing Gum Display Box

Counter display box, "Adams Tutti Frutti Chewing Gum," counter display box of cardboard printed in color w/a large rectangular bust image of Lillian Russell, advertising in white on red around the edges, intact w/glass inside, minor scuffs & edge tear, 4 1/4 x 10", 1 1/4" deep (ILLUS.).. **242**

Full Hickman's Silver Birch Gum Box

Counter display box, "Hickman's Silver Birch Chewing Gum - 5¢," counter display box full & complete w/20 packages, original slip cover top w/wording in green & red against a white birch bark ground, a bluebird in one corner, near mint, 4 1/2 x 6 1/2" (ILLUS.) **688**

Counter display box, "Sen Sen Chewing Gum," cardboard display box, fine overall condition, includes some original packages, 3 x 3 1/2", 4" h. **44**

Counter display box, "Walla-Walla Peppermint Chewing Gum," cardboard box printed in red & pale green on cream, low rectangular form, 4 x 6" (minor scuffs) **55**

Rare Belding Spool Cabinet

Counter display cabinet, "Belding Silk," walnut, wording on ornate crestrail centered by a clock dial, thirty drawers w/curved glass fronts on upper drawers, mirrors center door at top, ca. 1890, 17 x 34", 45" h. (ILLUS.) **2,400-2,800**

Rare Humphreys' Specific Cabinet

Counter display cabinet, "Humphreys' Veterinary Specifics," walnut, front-opening w/heavily embossed composition panel w/a profile of a horse, scarce version reading "Humphreys' Veterinary Homeopathic Specifics," dated 12/14/87, 10 x 21", 34" h. (ILLUS.) **5,000-6,000**

GE Man Jointed Display Figure

Counter display figure, "General Electric," large jointed wood figure of the GE Man in a band major uniform, painted in red, white, gold, black & pink, early 20th c., 19" h. (ILLUS.) **880**

Howard Johnson Pie Man Display

Counter display figure, "Howard Johnson," plaster composition figure of pie man walking toward the fair carrying a stack of pies, good old repaint, 6 x 27", 42" h. (ILLUS.) **358**

Early Kessler Football Display Figure

Counter display figure, "Kessler" rubber composition standing figure of an early football player holding a ball & wearing a green, red, gold & white uniform, original paint, 11 x 18", 46" h. (ILLUS.) **385**

Counter display figures, "Wanna Pop," cast plaster model of small seated Pug dog on a square base, brand name in black on front of base, cast overall w/holes for inserting the lollipops, retains most of its paint, 5 1/4 x 6 3/4", 7" h. (a few dings & abrasions) **226**

Cricket clicker, "John Deere," celluloid w/white ground & black wording w/brown deer leaping over a red-handled plow, reads "I Chirp For The John Deere Plow Co. - Omaha, Neb." (ILLUS.) **743**

Baltimore Enamel Novelty Door Push

Door push, "Baltimore Enamel & Novelty Co.," rectangular, porcelain on metal, green w/black & white letters reading "Please Close Door - The Baltimore Enamel & Novelty Co.," ca. 1910, 2 3/4 x 4" (ILLUS.) **125-175**

Tom's Toasted Peanuts Jar

Counter display jar, "Enjoy Tom's Toasted Peanuts - Delicious," cylindrical clear glass w/inset domed cover, red knob & blue wording on sides, appears unused, 7 x 10 1/2" (ILLUS.) **55**

Dr. Caldwell's Door Push

Door push, "Dr. Caldwell's Syrup Pepsin," rectangular, porcelain on metal, black & yellow, reads "Push - You Can Depend on Dr. Caldwell's Syrup Pepsin - The Family Laxative," ca. 1920s, 3 3/4 x 6 3/8" (ILLUS.) **150-200**

Squirrel Brand Peanut Jar

Counter display jar, "Squirrel Brand Salted Peanuts," clear glass squared jar w/metal lid printed in brown, tan & red w/a center picture of a squirrel, 5 1/2" sq., 9" h. (ILLUS.) **77**

Rare John Deere Cricket Clicker

Ex-Lax Door Push

Door push, "Ex-Lax," rectangular, porcelain on metal, blue, white, yellow & red, product package in center marked "For Relief of Constipation - Ex-Lax - the Chocolated Laxative," top marked "Pull" & bottom w/"Get Your Box Now!," ca. 1920s, 4 x 8" (ILLUS.) **150-225**

Pinkerton's Detective Agy. Door Push

Door push, "Pinkerton's National Detective Agency," rectangular, porcelain on metal, black w/white letters reading "Member of The Jewelers' Security Alliance - For Protection Against Burglary - Sneak Theft - Holdup - Pinkerton's Nat. Detective Agency - Detective Agents for the Alliance" w/red & white oval image of reclining dog, ca. 1920, 3 3/8 x 7 1/4" (ILLUS.) **325-400**

Pinkertons Detective Agy. Door Push

Door push, "Pinkertons Nat. Detective Agency," rectangular, porcelain on metal, blue w/white lettering reading "Member of The Jewelers' Security Alliance for Protection Against Burglary - Pinkertons Nat. Detective Agency - Detective Agents for the Alliance," w/brown & white oval image of reclining dog, ca. 1900, 3 3/8 x 7 1/4" (ILLUS.) **400-500**

Door push bar, "Sunbeam Bread," heavy steel, an oblong color image of a loaf of bread in white, blue & red w/a color image of the Sunbeam girl, dark blue mounting strips at the ends, reads "Sunbeam - Batter Whipped," 8 3/4 x 26 1/2" (minor edge wear, scratches & flecks) **248**

Rainbo Bread Door Push & Handle

Door push w/handle, "Rainbo Bread," steel blue bar w/attached oval sign in blue w/yellow & red border bands, white letters in center reading "Rainbo is good Bread," w/vertical blue steel bar & attached metal handle, light scratches, 8 1/2 x 26 1/2" (ILLUS.) **231**

Rare Kis-Me Gum Paper Fan

Fan, "Kis-Me Gum," folding paper forming a circle, wooden sticks, wording printed in black, appears unused, 10" d. open (ILLUS.) **523**

King Midas Flour Scoop

Flour scoop, "King Midas Flour," lithographed tin w/white ground & orange wording on outside of bowl, slight wear, 1 3/4 x 4" (ILLUS.) **165**

Anchor Stove Miniature Frying Pan

Frying pan, "Anchor Stove and Range Co. - Louisville, KY - New Albany, Ind.," miniature cast-iron piece w/silvered finish, 2 3/4 x 3 1/2" (ILLUS.) **35**

Kanotex Aviation Gasoline Globe

Gas pump globe, "Kanotex Aviation," single lens, airplane image on bottom of lens, tiny surface scratches, 13 1/2" d. (ILLUS.) **2,200**

Gum package, "Sterling Cinnamon Gum," full pack of five sticks of gum, blue & white label, 1/2 x 3/4 x 3" **72**

Yellow Cab Driver's Hat

Hat, "Yellow Cab," yellow naugahyde cap w/black wording, woven vent band & black bill, some embroidery missing, size 7 3/8 (ILLUS.) **110**

Borden's Products Hat Badge

Hat badge, "Borden's," porcelain, oval, dark blue ground w/white border band & brand name in large white letters, minor wear & scratches, paint chip above one letter, screw posts appear to be replaced, 1 3/4 x 2 3/4" (ILLUS.) **33**

Yellow Cab Operator's Hat Badge

Hat badge, "Yellow Cab," die-cut metal, squared silvered metal form w/stepped edges, round yellow enameled center w/black wording, outer ring band incised w/"Yellow Cab Co. of Virginia - Operator - 284," double screw post, 1 3/4 x 2 1/4" (ILLUS.) **77**

Jar, "Roundup Coffee," 1 lb. clear glass jar in wide cylindrical form w/rounded base & shoulder, stippled upper & lower sections w/smooth center band w/a paper label printed in blue, gold, white & red, white metal screw-on lid, made for the Round Up Grocery Company of Spokane, Washington, 4 x 6" **121**

Jigsaw puzzle, "Baby Ruth Candy Bar," rectangular cardboard puzzle w/a color scene of a young boy & girl w/their dog, seated on the ground under a large orange umbrella w/each eating a candy bar, a large bar & the label shown in the foreground, professionally framed & matted, puzzle glued down, image 5 1/2 x 7" **77**

License plate tag, pharmacist, die-cut metal, outline of a mortar & pestle w/"RX" in white & "Registered Pharmacist" below, screw-mount, unused condition, 3 x 5" **99**

Ceresota Flour Tin Match Box Holder

Match holder, "Ceresota Flour," hanging holder, die-cut embossed lithographed tin, a color image at the top of a young boy cutting a large loaf of bread, a rectangular compartment for a box of matches at the bottom, printed w/the company logo & "Ceresota Prize Bread Flour of the World," overall bright color w/some tiny scrapes, near mint, 2 1/4 x 5 1/2" (ILLUS.) **440**

Early Cast-iron Figural Match Holder

Match holder, "Compliments of Wm. A. Weber Wholesale Cigar Dealer," cast-iron model of a turtle opening to hold matches, fine original finish, slight traces of surface rust, 3 1/4 x 5 1/4" (ILLUS.).......... **451**

General Store Match Holder

Match holder, "General Merchandise - O.H. Thundale - Harmony, Minn.," stamped metal w/black finish & gold lettering, holds box of wooden matches, some rusting, 3 1/4 x 6" (ILLUS.)................................ **70**

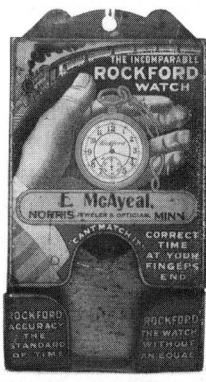

Rare Rockford Watch Match Holder

Match holder, "Rockford Watch," hanging holder, color-printed metal, an upright rectangular form w/scalloped top w/hanging hole, red ground printed at the top w/a small steam train above a large hand holding a watch, white & black wording, reads at top "The Incomparable Rockford Watch" (ILLUS.) **1,400**

B.P.O.E. Match Safe

Match safe, "B.P.O.E." (Benevolent & Protective Order of Elks), brass w/silver plate, rectangular, embossed fraternal symbols & marked "Cervus Alles," ca. 1910, 1 1/2 x 2 3/4" (ILLUS.).................. **125-175**

Beach Wickham Grain Co. Match Safe

Match safe, "Beach Wickham Grain," metal & celluloid, rectangular, lithograph of horse head above "At Your Service," reverse marked "Compliments of Beach Wickham Grain Co. - Board of Trade - Chicago," three match heads shown in upper right corner, litho by Whitehead & Hoag, ca. 1900, 1 3/8 x 2 1/4" (ILLUS. of both sides) **150-200**

Blatz Beer Match Safe

Match safe, "Blatz Beer," brass, rectangular, embossed floral decoration at corners, center marked "Blatz Brewing Co. - Milwaukee - U.S.A.," ca. 1910, 1 1/2 x 2 3/4" (ILLUS.) **150-225**

DeLaval Figural Match Safe

Match safe, "DeLaval Cream Separator," plated & painted metal miniature cream separator in black & silver, unused in original cardboard box w/a picture of a lady using the separator on the front, dated 1908, box 4 x 6 3/4" (ILLUS.).................... **918**

Harley Davidson/Merkel Match Safe

Match safe, "Harley-Davidson - Merkel Motorcycle," metal, rectangular, paper insert
reads "There's No Match - to the - Harley-
Davidson - or - Merkel Motor Cycles -
Sold by South Side Cycle Co., St. Louis,
MO.," holds book matches, ca. 1930's,
1 1/2 x 2 1/2" (ILLUS.) **75-125**

Keen Kutter Match Safe

Match safe, "Keen Kutter," aluminum, flip-
out-type, Simmon's Hardware, St. Louis,
Missouri, ca.   1893,   1 1/4 x 1 1/2"
(ILLUS.) **75-125**

Liquor Dealer Match Safe

Match safe, metal w/paper, rectangular,
novelty-type, reads "You Can't Find A
Match For - John B. Gahn - Dealer in
Wines, Liquors & Cigars," ca. 1910,
made in Austria, 1 3/8 x 2 1/2" (ILLUS.) .. **85-125**
Match safe, "Rosa de Valle Cigars," flat
rectangular safe w/celluloid portrait insert
in tiger stripe-plated safe, fine colors, appears unused, 1 5/8 x 2 1/2" (ILLUS.) **165**

Two Sharples Match Holders

Match safe, "Sharples Separator Co.,"
hanging holder, color-printed metal, long
rectangular form w/arched scalloped top
& bottom, color scene of cows in pasture
above a woman seated at the cream separator, holder reads "Tubular Cream
Separator - The Sharples Separator Co.
- West Chester, Pa...." (ILLUS. left) **230**
Match safe, "Sharples Separator Co.,"
hanging holder, color-printed metal, long
rectangular form w/arched scalloped top
& bottom, color scene of cows in pasture
above a mother & young daughter operating the separator, reads "The Pet of the
Dairy - Tubular Cream Separators - The
Sharples Separator Co. - West Chester,
Pa...." (ILLUS. right) **260**

Stewart Stoves Match Safe

Match safe, "Stewart Stoves & Ranges," silver metal & celluloid, rectangular, front
w/logo in center marked "Stewart Stoves
& Ranges," w/"The Fuller-Warren Co.
Milwaukee, Wis." marked below, reverse
w/color lithographed image of Eros &
Psyche, Litho by Whitehead & Hoag, ca.
1905, 1 1/2 x 2 7/8" (ILLUS. of both
sides) **175-250**

World Automatic Injector Match Safe

Match safe, "World Automatic Injector," metal & celluloid, rectangular, lithograph depicts injector on cover, American Injector Company, Detroit, Michigan, litho by Whitehead & Hoag, ca. 1905, 1 3/8 x 2 1/2" (ILLUS.) **125-200**

Lee Overalls Neckerchief

Neckerchief, "Lee Overalls," red cloth square printed in white w/pictures of buildings & vignette scenes of people wearing the jeans, ca. 1920, near mint, 23" sq. (ILLUS.)... **33**

Pioneer Club Dealer Necktie

Necktie, "Famous Pioneer Club - Downtown Las Vegas, Nevada," black rayon decorated w/iridescent colors showing card, dice & the head of a cowboy, worn by a casino dealer, ca. 1950s, appears unused, 4 x 52" (ILLUS.) **88**

Early Celluloid Pocket Notebook

Notebook, "Berg's Pure Ingredient Guanos Bone Manures," celluloid pocket-type, rectangular cover printed in color w/a comical man wearing a sandwich board advertisement, dated 1903, unused, 2 1/2 x 5" (ILLUS.)... **66**

Cash's Woven Names Paperweight

Paperweight, "Cash's Woven Names," cast iron, upright flat form on round base, front cast w/a standing man in a barrel & "Mark'em - I didn't," for clothing tags, traces of original paint, 2 1/4" d., 4 3/4" h. (ILLUS.)... **250**

Rare Cupid Cigars Paperweight

Paperweight, "Cupid Cigars," cast metal w/a seated figural Cupid on the top resting on a tapering rectangular base w/embossed wording including "Jno. W. Loves 'Cupid' Cigars," minute edge crack at base, 2 1/2 x 4", 4" h. (ILLUS.)...................... **259**

Feronia Cigars Paperweight

Paperweight, "Feronia Cigars," rectangular clear glass w/rounded corners, paper label glued to bottom w/gold & red wording on white, shows brand name & "James F. Martin, Inc. - Peekskill, N.Y. - Phone 88," mirrored back, 2 1/2 x 4 1/4" (ILLUS.)............. **44**

Havana Plantation Cigars Paperweight

Paperweight, "Havana Plantation" cigars, cast metal oval form cast in relief w/a long cigar, embossed wording reads "Havana Plantation - A.A. Arnold. Mfr.," 1 1/2 x 4" (ILLUS.)... **83**

Husky Refining Company Paperweight

Paperweight, "Husky Refining Company," heavy cast-metal w/bronzed finish, a model of a standing husky on a flaring rectangular platform base w/advertising across the front, original felt on base, minor wear, 2 3/8 x 3 7/8", 4 3/8" h. (ILLUS.)... **55**

Lion Oil Company Paperweight

Paperweight, "Lion Oil Company," brass, figural lion on rectangular base, minor wear to base, 1 1/2 x 2 3/4 x 3 3/4" (ILLUS.) **77**

Palmer House Cigars Paperweight

Paperweight, "Palmer House Key West Cigars," round w/a colorful label centered by a red & gold crown, slight foxing on upper edges, 3" d. (ILLUS.)............................. **55**

Richfield Paperweight - Pen Holder

Paperweight, "Richfield," a bronzed metal square platform w/beveled edges & the brand name at the front supporting a pen holder & a standing figure of an early airplane pilot, 7" h. (ILLUS.)............................... **160**

Valvoline Oil Paperweight

Paperweight, "Valvoline Cylinder and Lubricating Oils," rectangular thick glass backed by paper advertising w/a black, white & green sketch of a can on the left w/black wording on the right, ca. 1920, very minor scratches, 2 5/8 x 4" (ILLUS.)...... **121**

White Eagle Advertising Paperweight

Paperweight, "White Eagle Refining Company," molded plaster model of a perched white eagle on a thick oblong base, well-detailed, dated 1924, light to moderate overall wear, 6 1/8" h. (ILLUS.)..... **209**

Pennant, "Old Dutch Cleanser," cloth, downward pointed long triangular form, dark red ground w/a small section of green at the tip, partial can of the product shown at the center, reads "Safest for Porcelain and Enamel - There's nothing like it," 15 3/4 x 26" (moderate wear)............ **121**

Eversweet Toiletry Pin Tray

Pin tray, "Eversweet - A Daily Toilet Necessity - For Refined People," rectangular w/flanged scalloped w/rounded fluted corners, rectangular color center scene of a scantily clad standing young lady reaching up to red roses, printed design of jewels along two sides, 3 1/2 x 5" (ILLUS.)............................... **254**

Success Manure Spreader Pin Tray

Pin tray, "'Success' Manure Spreader," rectangular lithographed tin, wording in red around the flanged border, center color scene of farmer using the spreader, a few scuffs, 3 1/4 x 4 3/4" (ILLUS.).............. **105**

Pinback button, "Dead Shot Smokeless Powder," celluloid w/color image of a wounded falling duck, black wording around the edges, bright colors, 7/8" d. **66**

DuPont Smokeless Powder Button

Pinback button, "DuPont Smokeless Powder," color center picture of a grouse in an autumn landscape, black border band w/white wording, by Whitehead & Hoag, 1 1/4" d. (ILLUS.)... **110**

Polarine & Red Crown Gas Pinback

Pinback button, "Polarine and Red Crown Gasoline - Standard Oil Company," celluloid, round w/white & pale yellow ground w/red & blue wording, very minor wear & surface scratches, 1 1/2" d. (ILLUS.) **143**

Remember the Belle Pinback Button

Pinback button, "'Remember The Belle' - Best Nickel Cigar," cream ground w/gold wording & color bust portrait of a long-haired maiden, 1 3/4" d. (ILLUS.) **66**

Pitcher, "Crawford Cooking-Ranges," printed flow blue design, Sampson Bridgwood & Sons, ca. 1885, 8" h. **250**

Plate, "Crawford Cooking-Ranges," ceramic w/printed flow blue design, Sampson Bridgwood & Sons, ca. 1885, 10" d............... **125**

Angelus Marshmallows Pocket Mirror

Pocket mirror, "Angelus Marshmallows," oval, celluloid, cupid standing on square base marked "Angelus Marshmallows" playing horn & holding box also marked "Angelus Marshmallows," Rueckheim Bros. & Eckstein, Chicago, Illinois, ca. 1900, 1 3/4 x 2 3/4" (ILLUS.) **125-175**

Angelus Marshmallows Pocket Mirror

Pocket mirror, "Angelus Marshmallows," oval, celluloid, scene of a dark-haired & a blond cupid leaning on box marked "Angelus Marshmallows," Rueckheim Bros. & Eckstein, Chicago, Illinois, ca. 1900, 1 5/8 x 2 3/8" (ILLUS.) **95-150**

Kern Barber Supply Co. Pocket Mirror

Pocket mirror, "August Kern Barber Supply Company," round, celluloid, center w/image of barber chair marked "America" & border w/"August Kern Barber Supply Co. - Saint Louis, MO.," ca. 1910, 2" d. (ILLUS.) **125-175**

Checkers Popcorn Pocket Mirror

Pocket mirror, "Checkers Popcorn," round, celluloid, an image of a red & white checkered box marked "Checkers" w/"Eat - Eat - Eat" above & "A Nice Prize in Each Package - Shotwell Mfg. Co. Chicago" below, ca. 1910, 2 1/4" d. (ILLUS.)..................................... **125-175**

Cracker Jack Pocket Mirror

Pocket mirror, "Cracker Jack," round, celluloid, dark blue w/white, red & blue package in center below "The More You Eat - The More You Want." w/"Look At The Cracker Jack On The Other Side - Rueckheim Bros. & Eckstein, Chicago" at the bottom, ca. 1897, 2" d. (ILLUS.)....... **175-225**

Garland Stoves Pocket Mirror

Pocket mirror, "Garland Stoves," oval, celluloid, colorful lithograph by Whitehead & Hoag depicts the production plant below logo marked at top "Largest Makers of Stoves and Ranges in the World" w/"Where They - Are Made" flanking logo w/"Garland Stoves and Ranges," ca. 1910, 1 3/4 x 2 3/4" (ILLUS.) **175-225**

H.S. & B. Company Pocket Mirror

Cascarets Pocket Mirror

Pocket mirror, "Cascarets," round, celluloid, image of cupid on chamber pot above "Cascarets - Did It - They Work While You Sleep" & "All Going Out - Nothing Coming In," Sterling Remedy Company, Chicago, Illinois, ca. 1910, 2" d. (ILLUS.)............................... **95-135**

Pocket mirror, "H.S. & B Co.," oval, celluloid, white w/blue circular band marked "Cutlery - & Tools," center blue band centered by dark blue shield form flanked by gold scrolls, center marked "O - V - B" in white letters under gold letters reading "Our Very Best," below banner marked "H.S. & B. Co.," Cruver Mfg. Co., Chicago, Illinois, ca. 1910, 1 3/4 x 2 3/4" (ILLUS.) **125-175**

Horlick's Malted Milk Pocket Mirror

Pocket mirror, "Horlick's Malted Milk," round, celluloid, colorful lithograph of young girl in long dress & white apron standing next to brown cow, white border marked "The Diet For Infants, Invalids And Nursing Mothers - The Original Malted Milk - Ask For Horlick's - Avoid Substitutes," litho by Whitehead & Hoag, ca. 1900, 2" d. (ILLUS.) **100-175**

J.I. Case Company Pocket Mirror

Pocket mirror, "J. I. Case," oval, celluloid, white w/image of eagle atop a world globe marked "J. I. Case Threshing Machine Company Incorporated - Racine, Wis. - U.S.A.," ca. 1900, 1 3/4 x 2 3/4" (ILLUS.) **225-300**

Mennen's Talcum Pocket Mirror

Pocket mirror, "Mennen's Talcum Powder," oval, celluloid, depicts container decorated w/pink & gold florals, marked "Mennen's Flesh Tint Talcum" in gold & flanked w/pink & gold floral decoration, gold top, gold lettering at bottom reads "A Pink Powder Not A Rouge," Gerhard Mennen Co., Newark, New Jersey, ca. 1910, 1 3/4 x 2 3/4" (ILLUS.) **125-175**

Mennen's Talcum Pocket Mirror

Pocket mirror, "Mennen's Toilet Powder," oval, celluloid, decorated w/bouquet of purple violets & green leaves w/image of man w/mustache on lower leaf, marked at bottom "Use Mennen's Violet Talcum Toilet Powder," Gerhard Mennen Co., Newark, New Jersey, ca. 1910, 1 3/4 x 2 3/4" (ILLUS.) **125-175**

Morton's Salt Pocket Mirror

Pocket mirror, "Morton's Salt," round, celluloid, white w/blue & white product package depicted filling salt shaker, reads "An Every Meal Necessity - Morton's Salt - Makes Food Taste Better," litho by Parisian Novelty, ca. 1900, 2" d. (ILLUS.) **125-175**

New King Snuff Pocket Mirror

Pocket mirror, "New King Snuff," rectangular w/rounded corners, celluloid, ivory w/center image of brown jar w/tan & yellow label below reading "The New King Snuff," Weyman-Bruton Company, Nashville, Tennessee, litho by Pilgrim Spec. Co., Malden, Massachusetts, ca. 1915, 1 3/4 x 2 3/4" (ILLUS.) **75-125**

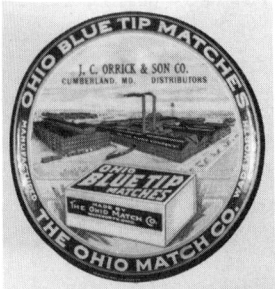

Ohio Match Company Pocket Mirror

Pocket mirror, "Ohio Blue Tip Matches," round, celluloid, dark blue border w/white letters reading "Ohio Blue Tip Matches - The Ohio Match Co." & "J.C. Orrick & Son Co. - Cumberland, MD. Distributors" above scene of factory w/white & blue product package below, Ohio Match Company, Wadsworth, Ohio, ca. 1900, 3 1/2" d. (ILLUS.) **175-225**

Old Reliable Coffee Pocket Mirror

Pocket mirror, "Old Reliable Coffee," round, celluloid, colorful lithograph of man wearing red jacket & brown hat, one elbow resting on can, marked "Old Reliable Coffee - Always Good," litho by Bastian Bros., ca. 1910, 2" d. (ILLUS.) **75-125**

Parry Carriage Mfg. Co. Pocket Mirror

Pocket mirror, "Parry Manufacturing Company," colored lithograph scene of factory by Bastian Bros., marked "Parry Man-

ufacturing Company - The Largest Carriage Factory In The World - Indianapolis, Ind." above & "Our Goods Are Sold By - John Theroff, Donnellson, Iowa," ca. 1910, 1 3/4 x 2 3/4" (ILLUS.). **175-225**

Peninsular Stove Pocket Mirror

Pocket mirror, "Peninsular Stove Company," oval, celluloid, lithograph scene of factory by Bastian Bros., Peninsular Stove Company, Detroit, Michigan, ca. 1910, 1 3/4 x 2 3/4" (ILLUS.) **225-275**

Queen Quality Shoes Pocket Mirror

Pocket mirror, "Queen Quality Shoes," oval, celluloid, brown w/image of woman w/long brown curls, brown bonnet w/filmy tie under chin, marked at bottom "Queen Quality - Shoes," A.M. Farwell & Company, Franklinville, New York, ca. 1900, 1 3/4 x 2 3/4" (ILLUS.) **100-175**

Pocket mirror, "Remington Typewriters," round, celluloid, red w/white sawtooth border, lithographed image of typewriter in center w/white lettering above reading "To Save Time is to Lengthen Life - Standard" & "Remington Typewriter," below, litho by Parisian Novelty Company, ca. 1915, 3 1/2" d. (ILLUS.)............................ **150-200**

Scott-Wilkerson Pocket Mirror

Pocket mirror, "Scott-Wilkerson Ambulance Service," round, celluloid, scene of antique vehicle w/trees in background, marked at bottom "Scott-Wilkerson Superior Ambulance Service - Memphis, Tenn.," ca. 1915, 3 1/2" d. (ILLUS.) **125-175**

Studebaker Pocket Mirror

Pocket mirror, "Studebaker," oval, celluloid, lithograph scene of automobile production plant by Bastian Bros., marked "Studebaker Vehicle Works - Largest in the World - South Bend, Ind. U.S.A.," ca. 1900, 1 3/4 x 2 3/4" (ILLUS.) **200-250**

Pocket mirror, "Thompson's Ice Cream," round, depicts colorful bust of Andy Gump w/"Thompson's Unexcelled Ice Cream" around edge & "Andy Gump - for President" flanking the figure **231**

Travelers Insurance Pocket Mirror

Pocket mirror, "Travelers Insurance Company," oval, celluloid, depicts approaching train engine w/skyline in background, "The Travelers Insurance Company - Hartford, Conn." in red letters above & "The Railroad Men's Reliance" in red lettering below, ca. 1900, 1 5/8 x 2 3/8" (ILLUS.) **125-175**

Victor Victrola Pocket Mirror

Pocket mirror, "Victor Victrola," rectangular w/rounded corners, celluloid, lithograph

by Parisian Novelty shows logo in upper left corner opposite "Have You A Victrola In Your Home," image of phonograph center right opposite "This is a Victrola XI - $100 - Mahogany or Oak - Other Styles $15 to $200 - We Will Demonstrate It and Play Any Music You Wish to Hear," dealer information at bottom, ca. 1910, 1 5/8 x 2 3/4" (ILLUS.) **175-225**

Victory Bicycles Pocket Mirror

Pocket mirror, "Victory Bicycles," oval, celluloid, black w/gold trim, centered by large V & "Victory" on red band, "Chicago" above w/"Bicycles - Tires - New York" below & "Edwards & Christ Co. - Detroit - Cleveland - Philadelphia - Newark" around edge, Parisian Novelty Co., ca. 1900, 1 3/4 x 2 3/4" (ILLUS.) **150-200**

Early Hawaiian Travel Postcard

Postcard, "See Hawaii - Matson Navigation Co. - San Francisco - Honolulu - Direct to Volcano," stylized color landscape in blue, red & orange w/a guitar-playing native woman in the foreground & a steamship & smoking volcano in the distance, wording in red & white, 3 1/2 x 5 1/2" (ILLUS.) **66**

Buster Brown Throw Rug

Rug, "Buster Brown Shoes," round nylon throw rug, dark blue border band w/yellow stars, center logo image of Buster & Tige in red, white, blue, brown & yellow against a yellow ground, "Buster Brown" in red under the image, overall light soiling, 54" d. (ILLUS.) **347**

Sack rack w/string holder, "Carey Bro. & Grevenmeyer," quarter-round wood framework w/slots for sacks & ball-shaped pierced iron string holder at the top, yellow stenciled wording on the side, 8 x 16", 20" h. **350-425**

The Gales Bicycle Score Keeper

Score keeper, "The Gales Bicycle," trapezoidal cardboard printed w/the design of a safety bicycle, the wheels turning to show "Points" & "Games" through small round holes, advertising in black wording between frame of bicycle reads "'The Gales' - Wins The Game - The Highest Grade...," 3 x 4 1/2" (ILLUS.) **55**

Sewing kit, "Stevens Firearms," cylindrical tin w/a thimble lid, made for ladies, printed w/a cream ground & black & red wording centered by a target & crossed rifles, early 20th c., 1 x 2 3/4" (some wear) **165**

Socony-Mobil Ship's Flag

Ship's flag, "Socony - Mobil," double-sided rectangular nylon, printed w/a flying red Pegasus logo above a red band w/black bands at the top & bottom edges, no wording, canvas & rope mountings, some wrinkles, 37 x 65" (ILLUS.) **55**

Columbia Brewing Shoe Brush

Shoe brush, "Columbia Brewing Co. - Tacoma, Wash.," rectangular wooden top w/rounded ends, premium item, ca. 1910, 2 x 8" (ILLUS.) **66**

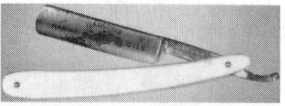

Richfield Spray Gun

Spray gun, "Richfield - New Rapid-Atomizing Spray-Gun - Insect Spray - Surface Spray," tubular metal shaft w/plunger handle printed in red, white & blue bands w/yellow, blue & white wording, plain metal cylindrical tank w/screw-on cap, few small scratches, minor wear on plated tank, 13 1/2" l. (ILLUS.) **110**

Gargoyle Marine Oils Razor

Straight razor, "Gargoyle Marine Oils," long bone handle w/hinged steel blade etched w/gargoyle logo & wording, soiling, some rust spotting on blade, early 20th c., 9" l. (ILLUS.) **165**

String holder, "Chase & Sanborn's Canister Teas," rectangular lithographed tin sign in white w/dark green lettering, a wire cage string holder fitted at the top center edge, 10 x 13" **350-425**

Hambone Cigars String Holder

String holder, "J.P. Alley's Hambone Sweets 5¢ - Above All Five Cent Cigars - Finest Quality," embossed die-cut two-sided, colorful decoration centered by a comic pilot flying an airplane & smoking a cigar all on a white ground, 7" d. (ILLUS.)........ **44**

String holder, "King Midas," die-cut rectangular metal sign w/orange & white wording on dark blue reading "Buy King Midas - The Highest Priced - Flour - In America - Worth All It Costs," arched opening at the bottom holds a tall cone of string, ca. 1910, 20" w., 13 1/2" h. **1,400-1,550**

String holder, "La Touraine Coffee," nearly square die-cut metal sign w/white & yellow printing on dark blue on both sides, a color picture of a package of the product in the center, each side w/a cut-out post to hold a string cone, reads "La Touraine - Fresh Roasted - Ground To Order - The Perfect Coffee - W.S. Quinby Company - Boston - Chicago," ca. 1910, 20 1/4" w., 17" h... **3,700-4,000**

String holder, "Red Goose," die-cut metal in the silhouetted shape of a red goose printed in white w/"Red Goose Shoes," sign suspends a wire frame holding a tall cone of string, two-sided, ca. 1910, 29" h.. **2,200-3,000**

7Up Advertising Table Lamp

Table lamp, "7Up," a one quart soda bottle mounted on a round wood base forming the lamp, fitted w/a large cylindrical paper shade printed w/the red & black 7Up logo, ca. 1950, 15 x 24" (ILLUS.).................. **209**

5/A Horse Blankets Thermometer

Thermometer, "5/A Horse Blankets," round, yellow metal w/paper face, black numbers & black diamond shape in center marked "We've Got 'Em - You Want 'Em - 5/A Horse Blankets," & marked along bottom near frame "Standard Thermometer and Electric Company, Peabody, Massachusetts, Pat. May 8, 1888," 9 1/4" d. (ILLUS.) **175-225**

Barrel Remodeling Co. Thermometer

Thermometer, "Barrel Remodeling Company," round, metal w/paper face, black numbers, image of barrel in center over "Barrel Remodeling Co. - Barrels Bought and Sold - Kansas City, Mo.," litho by The American Art Works, Coshocton, Ohio, ca. 1900, 9 1/4" d. (ILLUS.) **150-200**

Thermometer, "Barrows Implement Company," painted aluminum, rounded top, white ground decorated at the top w/a red & black tractor above advertising w/the thermometer below, an International Harvester logo at the bottom, 3 3/4 x 13 1/4"...... **176**

Thermometer, "Bireley's," lithographed tin, long rectangular form w/rounded corners, a dark gold ground printed in blue, white & orange w/a large orange bottle of the drink & half an orange & leaves & blossoms at the bottom, reads "Got a Minute? Enjoy Bireley's - It's Different - Non-Carbonated," 4 1/2 x 15 3/4" (mercury is separated).. **220**

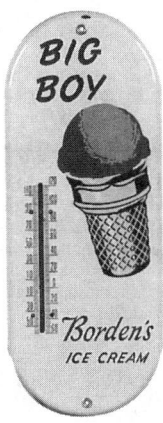

Borden's Ice Cream Thermometer

Thermometer, "Borden's Ice Cream," porcelain, wide oval form w/a white background, a small glass thermometer in the lower left, printed w/large blue letters at the top "Big Boy" above a color image of a strawberry ice cream cone, "Borden's Ice Cream" in blue at the bottom, small chip at top above grommet, 6 x 15" (ILLUS.) **798**

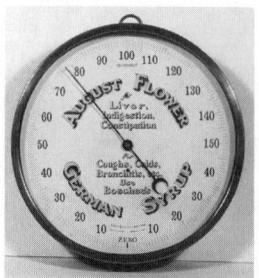

Boschee's Syrup Thermometer

Thermometer, "Boschee's August Flower German Syrup," round, yellow metal w/paper face, black numbers, center w/yellow lettering outlined in black reading "August Flower for Liver, Indigestion, Constipation - for Coughs, Colds, Bronchitis, etc. - Use Boschee's German Syrup," ca. 1900, 9 1/2" d. (ILLUS.)....... **175-225**

Thermometer, "dpm Flavor Guard Meats - Marysville, California," round lithographed metal, dark yellow ground w/red numbers & wording, ca. 1950s, 12" d. **66**

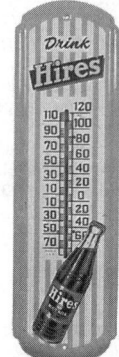

Hires Root Beer Thermometer

Thermometer, "Drink Hires," tin, oblong w/a light blue & white striped background & lettering in yellow & black at the top, a large glass thermometer down the center & a colored bottle of Hires at the bottom, moderate overall nicks, scratches & wear, 8 x 27" (ILLUS.).................................... **154**

Large Pepsi-Cola Thermometer

Thermometer, "Drink Pepsi-Cola - Ice-Cold," round metal-framed w/glass lens, large center red, white & blue Pepsi logo w/black numbers around the border, unused condition, ca. 1951, 12" d. (ILLUS.).. **1,100**

Dominion Royals Tire Thermometer

Thermometer, "Drive Safely - Ride On Dominion Royals," porcelain, rectangular w/rounded top, small glass thermometer mounted at center right, black & white wording at top & bottom w/large black & white tire in the center all on a dark orange ground, very minor surface & edge wear, chips & flecks, 10 x 30" (ILLUS.) . **550-750**

EX-LAX Thermometer

Thermometer, "EX-LAX," porcelain on metal, blue, black w/red & white bands at top & bottom, reads "EX-LAX - the chocolated laxative - keep 'regular' with EX-LAX - Prescriptions - Drugs - Toilet Articles," ca. 1920s, 8 x 36" (ILLUS.)..... **200-250**

Hills Bros. Coffee Thermometer

Thermometer, "Hills Bros. Coffee," porcelain, long rectangular form w/rounded
top, dark red ground w/white wording,
large image of Arab man in yellow robe
drinking from cup, dated 1915,
8 3/4 x 21" (ILLUS.)..................................... **908**

Thermometer, "Keen Kutter - Simmons
Hardware Company," metal on wood,
long rectangular form in dark yellow
w/black numbers around the front-
mounted glass thermometer, Keen Kut-
ter red logo at the top, 1 3/4 x 7 1/4" **176**

NR & Tums Thermometer

Thermometer, "NR (Nature's Remedy) Lax-
ative & Tums," rectangular, porcelain on
metal, top marked "NR - All Vegetable
Laxative - Come In - If You Get It Here It's
Good" & marked at the bottom "Tums -
Quick Relief for Acid Indigestion," black &
red w/white lettering, ca. 1920, 7 x 27"
(ILLUS.) **225-300**

Thermometer, "Oldsmobile - Boise Auto
Company - Boise, Idaho," round metal
w/domed cover, the Arabic numerals in
white on white ground, red arrow & red
Oldsmobile logo at top w/the name & address of the dealer in the bottom half,
12" d. (some minor paint flakes at the
bottom edge) **495**

Thermometer, "Orange Crush," porcelain,
wide oval shape, white ground printed
w/a large bottle on the right, small thermometer on the left, wording in orange at
top & bottom reads "From Natural Orange Juice - Naturally it Tastes Better,"
6 x 15" (chip in bottom around mounting
hole).. **132**

Orange Crush Thermometer

Thermometer, "Orange Crush," round
metal w/a dark orange background
w/white wording & black numbers, 12" d.
(ILLUS.)... **132**

OshKosh Overalls Thermometer

Thermometer, "OshKosh Overalls," rectangular, metal, red & yellow w/"OshKosh
B'gosh - Work Wear" at the top & "The
World's Best Overall - Union Made" at the
bottom, ca. 1920, 10 x 25 1/2" (ILLUS.).. **475-600**

Red Seal Dry Battery Thermometer

Thermometer, "Red Seal Dry Battery," porcelain, long narrow rectangular form w/rounded ends, dark blue ground w/white border, a large red, white & blue picture of the battery above the black & white thermometer w/glass tube, white wording at the bottom reads "The Guarantee Protects You," ca. 1915, chipping at top mounting hole, touch-up to bottom of thermometer, 7" w., 27" h. (ILLUS.) 275

Tobacco Importers Thermometer

Thermometer, "Sternemann Bros. & Hayden, Importers of Tobacco - Milwaukee, Wis.," long figural model of a tobacco leaf w/advertising at the top above the mounted glass thermometer, glass tube probably replaced, one metal bracket missing, 5 1/2 x 23 3/4" (ILLUS.) 259

Department Store Thermometer

Thermometer, "The Emporium Department Store," rectangular wood w/rounded top & slightly curved edges, painted white w/blue lettering reading "The Emporium Department Store - Dyersville's Leading Merchants Over 40 Years - Complete Head to Foot Outfitters for Men - Women - and - Children," ca. 1920, 9 x 21" (ILLUS.) 125-175

Trico Wiper Blades Thermometer

Thermometer, "Trico Wiper Blades," glass & metal fan-shaped design w/a white ground, black lettering at the edge & a red arch over red & black wording, soiling, rust & pitting, 15" w., 9" h. (ILLUS.) 143

Valvoline Oil Thermometer

Thermometer, "Valvoline," round metal housing & frame w/glass domed front, dark yellow ground w/dark green numbers along the border w/a large green & white picture of a can of oil w/red & white wording "Ask For The World's First Motor Oil - Valvoline," red gauge, 12" d. (ILLUS.) 220

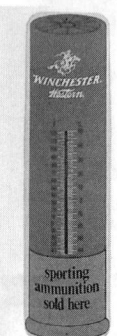

Winchester Ammunition Thermometer

Thermometer, "Winchester Western - Sporting Ammunition Sold Here," tall rectangular form designed to resemble a large shotgun shell in red w/a dark gold bottom section, the glass thermometer up the center, red wording at top & black wording at the bottom, very minor edge wear, 7 1/2 x 26 3/4" (ILLUS.) 121

Thermometer, "Winston," tall rectangular form w/rounded corners, yellow background w/the glass thermometer in the upper right, black wording at upper left reads "How good it is" above a color image of an open cigarette pack, 5 3/4 x 13 1/2" (couple of small nicks).............. **33**

Rare Early Aunt Jemima String Toy

Toy, "Aunt Jemima Pancake Flour," die-cut cardboard, string-climbing type w/a small rectangular package of flour at the top suspending a string w/an early image of Aunt Jemima climbing the string, printed in red, white & black, early 20th c., rare (ILLUS.).. **7,590**

Round Oak Stoves Toy Sad Iron

Toy, "Round Oak," sad iron, cast iron, miniature size w/stove name on the sides, 1 3/4 x 3 3/4", 2 1/2" h. (ILLUS.) **95**

Advance Rumley Oil Pull Watch Fob

Watch fob, "Advance Rumley Oil Pull," metal, embossed tractor, marked on oval base "Oil Pull," leather strap, Advance Rumley, LaPorte, Indiana, by F. H. Noble & Co., ca. 1910, 1 5/8 x 1 1/2" (ILLUS.) **225-275**

Saddle-shaped Watch Fob

Watch fob, "Hamley & Co.," stamped brass model of a saddle on a leather strap, marked "The Roundup," from Pendleton, Oregon, 1 1/2 x 3" (ILLUS.) **110**

John Deere Watch Fob

Toy truck, "Bell Telephone," painted cast iron w/red wheels & white rubber tires, Hubley, aging to tires, few nicks & rust spots, 4" l. (ILLUS.) **165**

Hubley Bell Telephone Truck

Watch fob, "John Deere," oval, enameled metal w/brown running deer logo against blue ground, leather strap, ca. 1910, 1 1/2 x 1 3/4" (ILLUS.) **175-225**

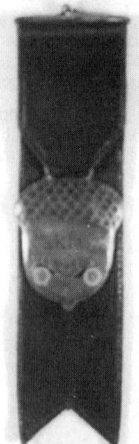

Rare John Deere Watch Fob

Watch fob, "John Deere," oval metal medallion w/a black enamel ground & a silvered metal leaping deer & plow logo, on original leather strap (ILLUS.) **880**

Watch fob, "Magnolia Gasoline/Motor Oil," round, cloisonné, blue center w/green petaled flower & "Motor Oil" & reading around border "Magnolia Gasoline," by Robbins Co., 1 5/8" d. (professional repair in border) **242**

Oakland Automobiles Watch Fob

Watch fob, "Oakland Automobiles," enameled green & red acorn shape on leather strap, image of an antique auto & marked "Oakland," by Whitehead & Hoag, Newark, New Jersey, ca. 1910, 1 1/4 x 5" (ILLUS.) **275-350**

Old Dutch Cleanser Watch Fob

Watch fob, "Old Dutch Cleanser," round enameled metal w/Dutch girl image in blue & white on yellow background, braided leather strap, Cudahy Packing Company, by Green Duck Co., Chicago, Illinois, ca. 1910, 1 1/4 x 1 3/4" (ILLUS.). **125-175**

Sterling Silver Bank Watch Fob

Watch fob, "Western National Bank," marked sterling silver, scroll-trimmed medallion-form w/a profile bust of a Native American chief on the front & the advertising for the Ft. Worth, Texas bank on the back, original leather strap, fob 1 1/2" w. (ILLUS. of both sides) **110**

Combination Watch Fob - Cigar Cutter

Watch fob, "Woodward's Pool Parlor," combination fob & cigar cutter, oblong nickel plate over brass w/an embossed image of horse head & bridle on one side & wording on the other, well detailed, 1 1/2 x 1 3/4" (ILLUS. of both sides) **160**

Watch fob, "Y-B Cigars," key-shaped simulated mother-of-pearl celluloid frame w/single fold-out knife blade, white w/blue lettering, appears unused, 7/8 x 2" **66**

ARCHITECTURAL ITEMS

In recent years the growing interest in and support for historic preservation has spawned a greater appreciation of the fine architectural elements which were an integral part of early building, both public and private. Where, in decades past, structures might be razed and doors, fireplace mantels, windows, etc., hauled to the dump, today all interior and exterior details from unrestorable buildings are salvaged to be offered to home restorers, museums and even builders who want to include a bit of history in a new construction project.

Carved Eagle Building Ornament

Building ornament, carved eagle, pine, made of three pieces of wood, supposedly one of several that came off exterior of a courthouse, ca. 1860, 12 x 36", 40" h. (ILLUS.) **$10,000**

Arts & Crafts Leaded Glass Door

Door, oak & leaded glass, Arts & Crafts style, upper half of leaded glass comprised of stylized red rose on long stem w/green leaves, textured colorless glass ground segmented by stylized Art Nouveau leading, oak frame w/a Gothic-style interior arch, the lower half framed by six vertical boards joined by exposed butterfly joints, original medium brown finish, ca. 1905, 28" w., 77 3/4" h. (ILLUS.) **633**
Door, pine, tongue & groove joinery on a two-paneled door w/wrought-iron HL hinges, New England, 18th c., old surface, 28 1/4" w., 74 1/2" h. **374**

Pair of G. Poillerat Doors & Lunette

Doors, parcel-gilt wrought-iron doors, each decorated w/an arrow pointed upward, topped by lunette, by Gilbert Poillerat, ca. 1945, 4' 2 1/2" w., door 6' 6 1/2" h., lunette 28 3/4" h., pr. (ILLUS.) **34,500**
Fanlight, painted wood & metal, metal sash bars, swags & rosettes, painted white, New England, early 19th c., 42" w., 23" h. (wear, paint loss) **863**

Cherry Victorian Fireplace Mantel

Fireplace mantel, cherry, Victorian, w/applied & carved decoration, center shelf at top w/turned supports, large center beveled mirror flanked by two small beveled mirrors behind small shelves w/tendril supports, egg-and-dart decoration along mantel edge above raised center panel flanked by applied carving & turned supports on either side of fireplace opening, original finish, ca. 1890, 14 x 60", 96" h. (ILLUS.).. **3,600**

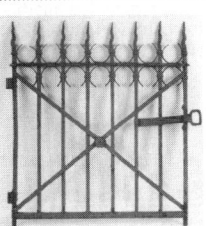

Painted Iron Gate

Gate, iron, composed of eight square spindles w/tapering flame tops joined by semi-circular elements, further embellished by crossed bars centering a rosette, old green paint, American, late 19th c., 35" w., 38" h. (ILLUS.) **633**

Gate, painted wood, constructed w/arched & carved cross stretchers joined by slender dowels, wrought-iron latch & pintles, weathered yellow paint, 19th c., 38 1/2" w., 36 1/2" h. (wear) **1,035**

Gate, painted wood, wrought-iron latch & strap hinges, curve-topped end posts w/molded cross rails, weathered white paint, 19th c., 31" w., 28" h. (wear) **403**

Gates, wrought iron, Continental style in rectangular shape w/urn-shape scrolling design, 19th c., 68" w., 82 1/2" h., pr. **1,232**

Raymond Subes Gates

Gates, wrought iron, interlocking loops & geometrical design, by Raymond Subes, ca. 1925, 5' 71/2" w., 5'2 3/4" h., pr. (ILLUS.) **11,500**

Louver, painted wood, diamond-shaped frame, weathered blue paint, 19th c., 28 x 33 1/2" **1,610**

Louver, painted wood, Gothic-style, the crest mounted w/three pinnacles over double-arched framed louvered panels, traces of red & white paint, 19th c., 36" w., 91" h. (wear, cracks) **633**

Louis XVI-style Marble Mantel

Mantel, gilt-bronze mounted marble fireplace mantel, Louis XVI-style, 12" x 5'8", 45" h. (ILLUS.) **7,200**

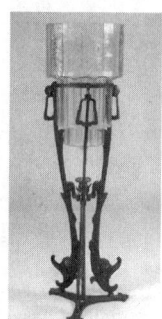

One of a Pair of Eagle Ornaments

Ornaments, cast-iron eagles w/spread wings perched on rectangular base w/"1918" in raised numerals, from Boston

Navy Yard, old verdigris finish over gilt, American, 13" h., 30 1/4" l., pr. (ILLUS. of one) **2,070**

Cast-iron Architectural Posts

Posts, cast iron, baluster-form posts w/decorative rosette, scroll & swirl elements, gadrooned ball finial, painted terra-cotta red, American, late 19th c., 42 1/2" h., pr. (ILLUS.) **345**

Shutters, painted wood, arched louvered Gothic design, touches of weathered green paint, 19th c., 18 1/4" w., 65" h., pr. (wear) **1,380**

ART DECO

Interest in Art Deco, a name given an art movement stemming from the Paris International Exhibition of 1925, continues to grow today. This style flowered in the 1930s and actually continued into the 1940s. A mood of flippancy is found in its varied characteristics - zigzag lines resembling the lightning bolt, sometimes steps, often the use of sharply contrasting colors such as black and white and others. Look for prices for the best examples of Art Deco design to continue to rise. Also see JEWELRY, MODERN.

Unusual Art Deco Aquarium

Aquarium, glass & bronze, floor model, the aquarium in a stepped & paneled form molded in translucent yellow glass, decorated w/six panels of stylized flowers, set into a bronzed metal tripod stand, three enameled green handles, the legs terminating in stylized dolphins, central light fixtures, tri-part base, dark patina, Europe, ca. 1925, slight chips in glass, some wear, overall 41 1/2" h. (ILLUS.).... **$2,415**

ART NOUVEAU

Art Nouveau's primary thrust was between 1890 and 1905, but commercial Art Nouveau productions continued until about World War I. This style was a rebellion against historic tradition in art. Using natural forms as inspiration, it is primarily characterized by undulating or wave-like lines and whiplashes. Many objects were made in materials ranging from glass to metals. Figural pieces with seductive maidens with long, flowing hair are especially popular in this style. Interest in Art Nouveau remains high, with the best pieces by well known designers bringing strong prices. Also see JEWELRY, ANTIQUE.

Frankart Sailor Boy Figure

Figure of a boy, cast metal, walking boy wearing a sailor suit & carrying a toy sailboat under his arm, painted gold on a stepped metal black base, Frankart, Inc., 3 1/4 x 3 3/4", 7 1/4" h. (ILLUS.) **65**

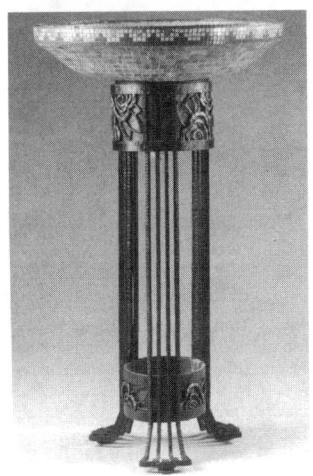

Rare Art Deco Glass & Iron Fountain

Fountain, mosaic glass & wrought iron, the top basin inlaid w/a geometric arrangement of mosaic glass tiles in shades of light & aquamarine blue & gold, raised on an iron stand w/wide bands of pierced stylized foliage at the top & bottom between the three tall legs composed of slender square rods, iron attributed to Raymond Subes, France, ca. 1930, 26 1/2" d., 42" h. (ILLUS.) **6,900**

Lamp, electric table model, spelter w/bronze tone finish, figure of scantily clad woman w/flowing hair stands on rectangular base next to satin glass teardrop-shaped floral shade, style number 183, 5 1/2 x 11 x 12") **165**

Model of Airedale, cast brass, marked on bottom "Moulds Brass Foundry," 1 x 1 5/8", 2 1/2" h. **55**

Gilt Metal Art Nouveau Inkstand

Inkstand, cast spelter w/gold paint, ornate scroll-cast form w/two capped inkwells w/milk glass liners, flared collars around each well above the projecting scroll pen rest, arched base & feet, overall cast flowers & leaves, 3 1/4 x 6 3/4", 3 1/4" h. (ILLUS.).. **$145**

Art Nouveau Owl Letter Holder

Letter holder, cast iron, pierced upright undulating sides centered by a perched owl flanked by pine boughs, gilt finish, base numbered "6643," 3 x 7 1/2", 5" h. (ILLUS.)... **125**

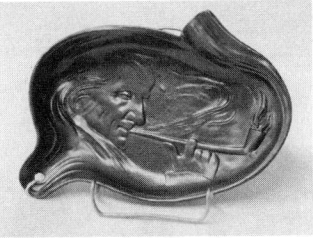

Art Nouveau Cast Pipe Tray

Pipe tray, cast spelter w/bronzed finish, undulating oblong shallow dish cast w/a swirling profile of a man smoking a long pipe, numbered on base "70," early 20th c., 5 1/2 x 7 1/4" (ILLUS.).................................... **55**

AUDUBON PRINTS

John James Audubon, American ornithologist and artist, is considered the finest nature artist in history. About 1820 he conceived the idea of having a full color book published portraying every known species of American bird in its natural habitat. He spent years in the wilderness capturing their beauty in vivid color only to have great difficulty finding a publisher. In 1826 he visited England, received immediate acclaim, and selected Robert Havell as his engraver. "Birds of America," when completed, consisted of four volumes of 435 individual plates, double-elephant folio size, which are a combination of aquatint, etching and line engraving. W. H. Lizars of Edinburgh engraved the first ten plates of this four volume series. These were later retouched by Havell who produced the complete set between 1827 and early 1839. In the 1840s, another definitive work, "Viviparous Quadrupeds of North America," containing 150 plates, was published in America. Prices for Audubon's original double-elephant folio size prints are very high and beyond the means of the average collector. Subsequent editions of "Birds of America," especially the chromolithographs done by Julius Bien in New York (1859-60) and the smaller octavo (7 x 10 1/2") edition of prints done by J. T. Bowen of Philadelphia in the 1840s, are those that are most frequently offered for sale.

Anyone interested in Audubon prints needs to be aware that many photographically-produced copies of the prints have been issued during this century for use on calendars or as decorative accessories, so it is best to check with a print expert before spending a large sum on an Audubon purported to be from an early edition.

Arctic Fox

Arctic Fox - Plate CXXI, hand-colored lithograph on wove paper by J.T. Bowen, 1847, framed, 17 1/8 x 24 3/4", mat stain, foxing, losses at sheet edges, remains of tape hinges (ILLUS.) **$2,300**

Belted Kingfisher

Belted Kingfisher - Plate 77, hand-colored etching, engraving & aquatint by R. Havell, 1830, 20 3/4 x 26", slight foxing, staining (ILLUS.) **11,500**

Black Vulture or Carrion Crow

Black Vulture or Carrion Crow - Plate CVI, hand-colored etching, engraving & aquatint by R. Havell, 1830, framed, 26 1/8 x 38 3/4", slight damage (ILLUS.)... **4,887**

Blue-winged Teal

Blue-winged Teal - Plate CCCXIII, hand-colored etching, engraving & aquatint by R. Havell, 1836, 14 3/4 x 20 1/2", some damage (ILLUS.) **11,500**

Boat-tailed Grackle - Plate CLXXXVII, hand-colored etching, engraving & aquatint by R. Havell, 1834, 20 1/2 x 25 5/8", slight damage **8,625**

Brown Pelican

Brown Pelican - Plate CCCCXXI, hand-colored etching, engraving & aquatint by R. Havell, 1838, 25 1/2 x 38 5/8" (ILLUS.).. **16,100**

Carolina Pigeon

Carolina Pigeon - Plate 17, hand-colored etching, engraving & aquatint by R. Havell on paper, framed, 26 7/8 x 30 3/4", mat stain, tear, minor soiling (ILLUS.)...... **14,950**

The Cougar. Male.

Cougar (The). Male. - Plate XCVI, hand-colored lithograph by J.T. Bowen, 1846, 18 1/8 x 25", some tears (ILLUS.).............. **2,587**

Great American Cock Male

Great American Cock Male - Plate I, hand-colored etching & engraving by W.H. Lizars, retouched by R. Havell, Jr., 1829, 25 1/4 x 37 1/2", slight damage (ILLUS.). **23,000**

Great White Heron

Great White Heron - Plate CCLXXXI, hand-colored etching, engraving & aquatint by R. Havell, 1835, framed, 25 5/8 x 38", some minor damage (ILLUS.).. **46,000**

Hooping Crane

Hooping Crane - Plate CCXXVI, hand-colored etching, engraving & aquatint by R. Havell, 1834, 25 7/8 x 38 3/4", some slight damage (ILLUS.).............................. **57,500**

Meadow Lark

Meadow Lark - Plate CXXXVI, hand-colored etching, engraving & aquatint by R. Havell, 1832, 26 x 38 3/4", some minor damage (ILLUS.) **27,600**

Summer or Wood Duck

Summer or Wood Duck - Plate 391, chromolithograph by J. Bien, New York, 1860, framed, 26 3/8 x 39 3/4", minor soiling, tape stains (ILLUS.) **3,450**

Summer Red Bird

Summer Red Bird - Plate 44, hand-colored etching, engraving & aquatint by R. Havell, Jr., printed & colored by R. Havell Sr., 1828, 12 3/8 x 19 5/8", some minor damage (ILLUS.) **5,175**

White-headed Eagle

White-headed Eagle - Plate 31, hand-colored etching, engraving & aquatint by

R. Havell, 1828, 25 5/8 x 38 1/8", some tears, foxing, rippling (ILLUS.) **14,950**

AUTOMOBILES

Austin Healey, 1967 Sprite, two-door convertible, red w/black top & black vinyl seats, four-speed transmission, radio, heater & white-wall tires, 34,535 miles **$3,300**

Jaguar E-type 4.2-litre series II Roadster, 1970, finished in black w/black interior, wire wheels, some parts rebuilt & replaced, everything works but the clock (ILLUS. below) **26,880**

Lincoln Town Car "Le Panache," 1993, black leather interior w/gold trim, full black vinyl top w/moonroof, white sidewall tires, 106,050 miles (ILLUS. below) ... **6,050**

AUTOMOTIVE COLLECTIBLES

Mobil Ashtray w/Figural Pegasus

Jaguar E-type Series II Roadster

Lincoln "Le Panache" Town Car

Ashtray, "Mobil," round metal ribbed ashtray w/curved extension mounted w/figural Pegasus logo, original felt base, minor nicks & wear to base, 3 3/4 x 4 x 5 1/2" (ILLUS.) **385**

Attendant's hat, "Gulf," dark blue cloth w/woven blue border band & orange braid above black plastic visor, orange & blue Gulf cloth logo patch on front, size 7 1/4, original packing paper inside **297**

Mobilgas Hat with Badge

Attendant's hat, "Mobilgas - Mobiloil," tan cloth hat w/black plastic rim band & bill, die-cut enameled company badge on front w/Pegasus logo & wording in red & blue, size 6 7/8, very minor wear & soiling on hat, moderate nicks & scratches on badge (ILLUS.).. **275**

Attendant's hat, "Texaco," dark green material w/green woven border band & braid cord above black plastic bill, white, red, green & black Texaco cloth logo patch on front, size 7 3/8 (minor wear & fading) **209**

Effecto Auto Finishes Color Wheel

Auto finish color display, "Effecto Auto Finishes," figural spoked wheel, metal rim w/wood inner, spokes display various finish colors, Pratt & Lambert, minor bends to tin signs on each side, some flaking & chips on spokes, 25" d. (ILLUS.) **385**

Badge, "Mobil/Socony Vacuum," nickelplated w/red & blue painted detail, large pin/clasp, die-cut five-point shield form, w/"1939 - Clinic Member - Socony - Vacuum," 2 x 2 1/8" (minor scratches)................ **242**

Shell Plastic Bank

Bank, "Shell," plastic, double-sided yellow shell-shaped w/red letters reading "Shell," 2 x 4 x 4" (ILLUS.) **138**

Shell Gasoline Pump-form Bank

Bank, "Shell Premium Gasoline," molded plastic bank, model of a gas pump in red & green w/sticker labels in red, white & yellow, very minor soiling, hose tip broken off, heat-stamped on the back "Mankato Oil Co.," 1 1/4 x 1 7/8", 4 5/8" h. (ILLUS.)... **264**

Banner, "Gargoyle - Mobiloil," long narrow lithographed canvas banner, a red ground w/a red & white Gargoyle logo at the left end & a white & red can of the product at the right end, "Mobiloil - Make the chart your guide" in white letters in the center, 24 x 117" (minor soiling & wear, one grommet torn, couple of small holes).. **495**

Oilzum Ink Blotter

Blotter, "Oilzum," rectangular, white & yellow w/black images of checkered flags & sprint cars, top reads "1951 Oilzum Champions," dealer information at bottom, 3 3/8 x 6 1/4" (ILLUS.) **39**

Havoline Oil Bottle Rack

Bottle rack, "Havoline Wax Free Oil," rectangular metal framework w/raised center section & conforming porcelain side signs in black, white & red, chips at mount holes, 19 x 29 1/2", 22 1/2" h. (ILLUS.) **825**

Mobiloil Bottle Rack

Bottle rack, "Mobiloil," composed of two porcelain signs bolted to a steel frame w/original green paint, the small sign at the top reads "Property of Vacuum Oil Company," the larger sign w/the image of a large red gargoyle in the center, black & red letters reading "Authorized Service - Genuine Gargoyle - Mobiloil," tiny edge flecks on signs, 20 3/4 x 25 x 30" (ILLUS.) **1,870**

Shell Motor Oil Bottle Rack

Bottle rack, "Shell Motor Oil," metal rectangular rack designed to hold eight one quart bottles, w/attached yellow porcelain sign, black letters reading "Shell Motor Oils - S.A.E. Numbers" w/list of various oils, rack w/overall wear, bends & rust, sign 5 1/4 x 6 3/8" (ILLUS.) **187**

Early Model T Auto Horn

Car horn, iron & tin, for a Model T Ford, the iron frame & mount w/a trumpet-form horn w/tin mouth, working, early 20th c., 8 1/2" l., overall 8" h. (ILLUS.) **169**

Mohawk Gasoline Lighter

Cigarette lighter, "Mohawk Gasoline," pocket-type, metal w/cloisonné die-cut image of American Indian head w/feather & marked "Mohawk," Penquin brand, 3/8 x 1 1/4 x 2 1/4" (ILLUS.) **242**

K C Pistons Figure

Figure, "K C Pistons," yellow & black smiling figural, nodder/bobber-type, base marked "Let Casey Go to Bat For You," in original box, 7" h. (ILLUS.) **154**

Mobilgas-Mobiloil First Aid Kit

First aid kit, "Flying Red Horse - Mobilgas-Mobiloil First Aid Kit," flattened rectangular tin w/a dark blue lid printed in the center w/a large red flying Pegasus logo w/white wording at the top & bottom & a red banner w/blue wording, features the Good Housekeeping seal of approval, denting & wear on lid, 3 x 3 1/2" (ILLUS.)...... **209**

Frontier Gasoline Globe

Gas pump globe, "Frontier - Rarin' To Go" w/black & red image of man on rearing horse, single Gill body lens, minor edge soiling (ILLUS.).. **3,080**

Hudson Gasoline Globe

Gas pump globe, "Hudson Regular," single globe lens, black, white & red w/image of tank truck marked "Hi-Octane Gas - Hudson Oil Company," chipping at mounting hole areas & below w/material loss, 13 1/2" d. (ILLUS.)... **880**

Gas pump globe, "Sinclair Power-X - The Super Fuel," white glass in original Capco frame, green & red wording, from original deteriorated box, 13 1/2" w...................... **270**

Texaco Gas Pump

Gasoline pump, w/round Texaco glass & metal glove, w/"Fleckenstein Visible Gasometer Co., Pat. July 4, 1916" (ILLUS.)... **2,640**

Rare Early American Oil Gas Pump

Gasoline pump, "American Oil Pump and Tank Co.," cast iron, sheet metal & glass, front slides up & down to expose pumping mechanism, glass tank at top, completely restored, one BB hole in glass tank, 17" d., 99" h. (ILLUS.)....................... **2,365**

Early Atlantic Gasoline Pump

Gasoline pump, "Atlantic," tall upright red metal casing w/rounded top & stepped sides w/two porcelain name plates above the meter dial on each side & the name in red lettering in white stripes down the front, back name insert cracked, well restored, 15 x 28", 79" h. (ILLUS.) **1,540**

Chevron Gasoline Pump Sign

Gasoline pump sign, "Chevron Gasoline," die-cut tin, round top, white w/red & blue letters reading "Chevron Supreme Gasoline," red, white & blue chevron logo at base, overall surface scratches, rubs & nicks, paint loss at bottom tip of logo, 11 x 13 3/4" (ILLUS.)...................................... **303**

Douglas Blend Gasoline Pump Sign

Gasoline pump sign, "Douglas Blend Gasoline," rectangular, white w/red & blue lettering, left side w/wing atop a red heart, wear, 10 x 14" (ILLUS.) **550**

Socony Motor Oil Pump Sign

Gasoline pump sign, "Socony Motor Oil," curved circular porcelain, white shield form in center, edged in red w/blue letters reading "Socony - Motor Oil - Standard Oil Co. of New York," white letters "SO - N - Y" on blue around border, small chip at bottom, tiny edge & surface flaws, 15" d. (ILLUS.)... **1,073**

Union Oil Company Badge

Hat/uniform badge, "Union Oil Company," cloisonné five-point shield-shape, blue top w/"Union Oil Company" above red & white stripes, by Whitehead & Hoag, small repair in white at bottom center, minor cracks, 1 3/4 x 1 3/4" (ILLUS.) **798**

Union 76 Inkwell & Pen

Inkwell w/fountain pen, "Union 76," Bakelite w/logo etched into lid, minor wear to gold paint, inkwell 3 x 3 1/4 x 4", the set (ILLUS.) **55**

Mobil License Plate Attachment

License plate attachment, "Mobil," die-cut embossed tin, red Pegasus logo, overall light soiling, wear, scratches, 4 1/2 x 6 1/4" (ILLUS.) **77**

License plate attachment, "Motorola Auto Radio," oval, embossed tin, yellow & red, marked on red banner at top "Drive Safely" w/black letters reading "Motorola Auto Radio" in black letters in center, 4 5/8 x 4 3/4" (minor scratches & rubs) **143**

Ice Cream License Plate Attachment

License plate attachment, "Peacock Ice Cream," rectangular, white, red & black, image of smiling Indian w/crown on head indicating a World Series championship & marked "Follow the Indians - Peacock Ice Cream," nicks & scratches, some paint thinning, 4 3/4 x 9 7/8" (ILLUS.) **220**

Pioneer Club License Plate Attachment

License plate attachment, "Pioneer Club," die-cut aluminum, image of man smoking cigarette & wearing red neckerchief & white cowboy hat, the hat marked "The Famous" & white letters across bottom reading "Pioneer Club - Downtown Las Vegas, Nevada," surface & edge wear, dings, 7 3/8 x 10 5/8" (ILLUS.) **275**

Tydol License Plate Attachment

License plate attachment, "Tydol Motor Oil," die-cut embossed tin "Running Man," scattered nicks & wear, 4 1/2 x 6 5/8" (ILLUS.) **121**

Die-Cut Tin License Plate Attachment

License plate attachment, "Washington Chief," die-cut tin, a long narrow rectangular plaque w/slits for mounting, a red, white & blue circle w/arched panel at the top on the upper right end reads "New Polyform - Washington Chief," the plaque below in red & blue w/white wording reads "It's Great To Be An American!," very minor nicks & wear, 4 7/8 x 10" (ILLUS.) **143**

Nourse Motor Oil Sign

Lubrication sign, "Nourse Motor Oil," double-sided tin, image of warrior in center below "Guaranteed Motor Oil," blue border w/white letters reading "Nourse - Business is Good," w/original clamp, overall wear, scratches & paint loss, 6 1/2 x 8 1/2" (ILLUS.) **385**

Lubrication sign, "Pennzoil," rectangular, double-sided tin, yellow w/logo & "Pennzoil" in center, upper left corner reads "Supreme Pennsylvania Quality" w/"Safe Lubrication" in lower right corner, 3 7/8 x 9 1/2" (scratches, nicks & wear) **121**

Shell Household Memo Pad Holder

Memo pad holder, "Shell," metal holder w/cardboard backing, full paper pad & slot to hold household bills, receipts, etc., together w/pencil w/Super Shell & Golden Shell logos, minor wear & soiling, 5 1/4 x 8" (ILLUS.) **110**

Gilmore Lion Head Mileage Card

Mileage card, "Gilmore Motor Oil," rectangular, cardboard, red & yellow, image of lion head on left w/"Gilmore Lion Head Motor Oil - The Most Highly Filtered Motor Oil in America," reverse w/mileage chart for California cities from Los Angeles, minor edge & surface wear, 2 1/2 x 4 1/8" (ILLUS.) **39**

Motor oil can, "Shell," cylindrical w/pouring spout, yellow w/red letters reading "Shell Handy Oil" w/image of auto & logo at bottom, additional graphics & text on reverse, 3 1/2 oz. (minor scratches & wear) **231**

Conoco Motor Oil Can Rack

Motor oil can rack, "Conoco," painted steel, two porcelain red & blue company logo signs at the top, arched top bar over wide cylindrical body fitted w/slots for oil cans, complete w/18 empty one-quart cans, rack repainted, some fading on signs, cans range from good to fair condition, overall 43" h., the group (ILLUS.)....... **770**

Esso Oil Figural Oil Containers

Motor oil containers, "Esso," yellow figural plastic Esso Happy character forming the container w/a pointed spout top w/small white cap, in original countertop point of purchase display box, complete w/blue, yellow, white & red marquee, 20 containers, 5 3/4" h., the group (ILLUS.) **250-300**

Name badge, "Conoco," nickel-plated brass, Art Deco design, rectangular frame w/fanned top w/the Conoco logo beside "Conoco" in red enamel letters, encloses original celluloid insert over the name typed on paper, 1 1/4 x 2 3/8" (chip to first "C," minor scratches of plating) **220**

Oil dispenser, "Union Oil Company," 1 pt. , copper w/swingspout....................................... **110**

Early Bowser Oil Pump

Oil pump, "Bowser Self Measuring Oil Pump," wood & metal, wooden casing encloses the oil pump & bulk oil tank, ca. 1900-12, restored, 21 3/4 x 29 3/4", 50 1/2" h. (ILLUS.).. **468**

Mobil/General Petroleum Pen Holder

Pen holder, "Mobil/General Petroleum," desk-type, five-point shield form w/figural Pegasus logo, 15-year service award, brass plate not engraved w/name of recipient, pen missing, 4" h. (ILLUS.) **303**

Pin, "Texaco," shield-form, cloisonné logo & small diamond on detailed 10k gold base, marked "Appreciation Award - Twenty-Five Years," 5/8 x 5/8" (minor wear)................ **66**

Texaco Star Club Award Pin

Pin, "Texaco - Star Club - New York District," round award pin, gold-filled pin w/white, red, green & gold enameled company logo in the center, embossed letter in gold border band, 1/2" d. (ILLUS.)... **259**

Union 76 Pinback Button

Pinback button, "Union 76," round celluloid, orange w/Minute Man logo & "I'm Fast!," soiling, light surface scratches, dimple dent at center, 2 1/4" d. (ILLUS.) **149**

Bardahl Rack Topper

Rack topper, "Bardahl," die-cut tin, man in black opening his jacket to reveal can marked "Bardahl," w/"Try it!" on right, wear & some rust, 10 x 10" (ILLUS.)............. **220**

Goodrich Radiator Grille Attachment

Radiator grille attachment, "Goodrich," porcelain, circular, yellow center marked "Goodrich - Tourist," the white border marked "Safety - First," minor edge wear, chip & scratches, 4 x 5" (ILLUS.) **303**

Chevron Gas Transister Radio

Radio, "Chevron," transister-type, model of a rectangular gas pump w/AM radio tuner dial where the pump numbers would be, front w/label "Chevron Custom" & logo, made in Hong Kong, ca. 1950s, 2 1/2 x 4" (ILLUS.) **110**

Road map, "Marland Road Map of North Central United States," three-fold printed paper in white, red, pink & grey, the three panels showing a continuous lakeside resort landscape w/people camping, ca. 1920s, 9 x 12" (minor wear at folds, corners & edges) **341**

Road map, "Official Road Map of California - Washington - Oregon - Union Oil Company of California," two-fold color-printed paper, the top of the two panels w/a rectangular color scene of a period gas station w/a roadster being serviced by attendants in red, blue, green, black & white, wording below in dark blue & red on white, dated 1926, 8 x 9 3/8" (very minor edge discoloration, small edge bumps) **385**

Shell Motor Road Guide

Road map, "Shell Motor Oil - Gasoline Motor Road Guide - Roxana Petroleum Corp., St. Louis, Missouri," three-fold color-printed paper, the cover of the three panels w/a continuous color landscape scene of an early gas station w/autos & couple playing golf in the foreground, Shell logos in gold & red, wording in red & dark blue, edge & fold wear, minor scattered soiling, 9 x 12" (ILLUS. of cover) **413**

Unusual Mobil Safety Award

Safety award, "Mobil Oil," a brass model of a ship's wheel on an oval platform base, the glass face includes a thermometer & humidity indicator, 1955, some soiling & scuffs, 4 1/2" d., 4 1/2" h. (ILLUS.) **55**

Sales award pin, "Texaco," sterling silver, star-shaped w/scroll trim on the lower half & set w/a pearl below the star, star centered by a green "T," Balfour maker's mark, 1/2" d. **303**

Union 76 Salt & Pepper Shakers

Salt & pepper shakers, "Union 76," ceramic, gas pump shape w/logo at center, dealer information at bottom, minor crazing, 3 1/2" h., pr. (ILLUS.) **385**

Scale-tool, "Valvoline Oil Company," flat stainless steel bar etched w/numbers & w/a bolted-on swiveling arm w/etched wording, w/original leather pouch, ca. 1920-40, 5 3/4" l. (minor tool wear, pouch worn & soiled) **33**

Service pin, "Wasatch (Refining Company) 5 Years," round gilt-metal w/a central bust profile of a Native American chief, red enameled band w/brand name, other wording embossed in outer ring, single screw back, 5 /8" d. **413**

Service station map rack, "Cities Service Road Maps - For People - Going - Places!," painted tin, upright five-tiered rack in dark green w/a yellow, white & green company logo at the top & other wording in white, two hanging holes near the top, 7 x 8 1/4", 19 1/4" h. (overall minor to moderate nicks, scratches, rubs & dings, few small rust spots, some adhesive residue) **220**

Old Shell Soap Dispenser

Soap dispenser, "Shell," heavy cast metal w/silvered finish, a deep rounded octagonal covered container swiveling in a metal mount, the Shell logo riveted on the cover, minor overall wear, new wood stand, 6 1/2" w. (ILLUS.) **468**

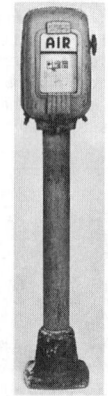

Early Eco Tireflator Pump

Tire air pump, "Eco Tireflator," painted metal & glass, a heavy iron base supporting the round red-painted pedestal & top meter compartment w/a glass dial cover below the word "Air," original condition w/overall paint loss, early 20th c. (ILLUS.) **721**

Early Michelin Tires Stand

Tire stand, "Michelin Tires," die-cut tin, an upright panel outlining the Michelin man beating a large drum, heavy metal rack for tire, in dark blue, gold & white, fold-out supports, ca. 1920s, moderate peppering, nicks, scratches & overall edge wear, rusty on back, 10 x 19 x 20 1/4" (ILLUS.).. **1,540**

AVIATION COLLECTIBLES

Recently much interest has been shown in collecting items associated with the early days of the "flying machine." In addition to relics, flying adjuncts and literature relating to the early days of flight, collectors also seek out items that picture the more renowned early pilots, some of whom became folk-heroes in their own lifetimes, as well as the early planes themselves.

Airplane model, Coca-Cola premium, series entitled "America's Fighting Planes," color cardboard, different designs by artist Snyder Heaslip, first issued in 1941-45, meant to be cut-out & hung, 72 card set, 13 x 15", each card average value of $45, mint complete set **$1,000**

Ashtray Stand with DC-3

Ashtray stand, floor-model, chromed metal, a large model of a DC-3 at the top above a round disk tray on a round pedestal & domed round base, late 1930s-1940s, 30" h. (ILLUS.) **225**

Air Stories Magazine of 1937

Book, "Air Stories - The First Air Story Magazine!," Volume 3, No. 7, Spring 1937, cover story titled "The Phantom Pirate of Jungle Skies," cover art of woman pilot &

man shooting at a pursuing plane, pulp-type magazine (ILLUS.) 25

Aircraft Spotters' Guide Book

Book, "Aircraft Spotters' Guide," Part 1, 1942, shows three silhouette positions of each aircraft, includes the U.S. Great Britain, Netherlands, Germany, Japan, Italy, Russia & France, cover in dark blue & orange shows London at night, excellent condition (ILLUS.) 50

Book, "Austin of the Air Force - Illustrated," by Dan Senseney, story of two buddies who enlist in the U.S. Air Force, Signal Books, New York, 1962 10

Book, "Fifty Years Fly Past - From the Wright Brothers to the Comet Jet," by Geoffrey Dorman, The Comet was one of the first jet passenger liners, Forbes Robertson, Ltd., Publishing, London, England, 1951 20

Book, "Of Flight & Life," by Charles Lindbergh, 1948, w/dust jacket 32

Book, "The Impact of Airpower," by Eugene M. Emee, Office of Civil Defense Mobilization, describes use of aircraft in in wartime & how new jets may effect future wars, D. Van Nostrand Company, 1959 35

Book, "The Red Knight of Germany - The Story of Baron Von Richthofen - Germany's Great War Bird," by Floyd Gibbons, Garden Publishing Co., New York, New York, story & photos of World War I ace, his aircraft on the cover, hardcover, 380 pp., 1927 75

Brochure, N.A.T. Airline, 1920s, colorful 38

Early Jupiter Rex Flight Certificate

Certificate, "Jupiter Rex," a scroll issued to each airline passenger who crossed the Equator, issued by Pan American Airways for flight from Africa to South America, includes details on the flight & w/a gold seal, framed, 10 12 x 13 1/2" (ILLUS.) 450

Cigarette cards, Lambert & Butler Tobacco Company, "Empire Air Routes," each color card features a different airplane, 1936, the set 150

Commemorative set, coin & stamp commemorating the first nonstop trans-Atlantic flight on June 14-15, 1919, made by Capt. John Alcock & Lt. Arthur Whitten Brown from Newfoundland to Ireland, issued on the 50th anniversary in 1969, includes first day cover & coin showing the aircraft, in leather case, the set 75

Royal Canadian Air Force Figure

Figure of Royal Canadian Air Force flyer, papier-maché, standing in uniform, sent to girlfriends, wives & mothers during World War II, wearing a blue uniform w/name of airbase on the base, in good condition (ILLUS.) 80

Flight schedule, TWA schedule for USA - Europe - Africa - Asia, for August 1 - September 29, 1951, for Chicago, Illinois, photo of Chicago skyline on cover 25

1951 TWA Flight Schedule

Flight schedule, TWA schedule for USA - Europe - Africa - Asia, for June 1 - July 30, 1951, for Paris, France, photo of Joan of Arc statue in Paris on cover, 4 x 9" (ILLUS.) 25

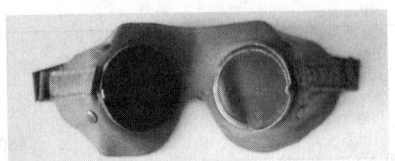

World War II Air Crew Goggles

Goggles, World War II air crew-type, plain green or brown w/head strap (ILLUS.) **20**

Luggage labels, Caspair, Ltd., Kenya, East Africa, "The Colonial Airlines," 1940s, each **5**

Luggage labels, Mohawk Airlines, "The Route of the Air Chiefs," shows Mohawk chief in headdress, 1950s, each **4**

Luggage labels, Pan American Airways System, each features an Art Deco design image of a man & woman passenger & porter, 1920s-30s, each **20**

Magazine, "Mechanix Illustrated," March 1949, cover story "Air War Over the North" by Major General K.P. McNaughton, focuses on the Starfighter Squadron stationed in Alaska **15**

Magazine, "Popular Science," December 1953, cover story on the newest American fighter, the F-100 Super Sabre, aircraft on the cover **8**

Toronto Star Weekly Magazine

Magazine, "Toronto Star Weekly Magazine," weekly newspaper magazine usually featuring a Royal Canadian Air Force feature & cover art, various issues 1940-45, full cover & magazine, each (ILLUS. of one) **15**

Map, Western Airline Wood Route, 1950s, large **1,500**

Avro Arrow Aurora Model Kit

Model kit, "Avro Arrow CF-105," Aurora, from Famous Fighters series, fine box cover artwork, 1960, mint in box (ILLUS.) **75**

Revell Scorpion Model Kit

Model kit, "Northrop F-890 Scorpion," Revell, cover art shows plane on a snow-covered airfield, 1950s, mint in box (ILLUS.) **50**

Model kit, "Spirit of St. Louis Miniature Model Kit," premium for Kellogg's, 1956, 2 x 3" **80**

Movie poster, "Aviator," starring Edward Everett Horton, Warner Brothers, 1929, one-sheet, 27 x 41" **150**

Movie poster, "The Spirit of St. Louis," starring James Stewart, Warner Brothers, 1957, one-sheet, 27 x 41" **125**

Paint-by-numbers kit, World War I aircraft - SE-5 & Baron Von Richthofen flying in the clouds, 1950s, 10 x 14" **25**

Pin, brass, model of the Spirit of St. Louis, 1927, rare **100**

Pin, "Captain Hawks' Sky Patrol," brass, in the shape of an airplane propeller w/raised portrait of Hawks in the center, Post Cereal premium, 1935-37 .... **45**

KLM Flying Junior Pin

Pin, oblong metal w/blue enamel, "KLM Flying Junior," center embossed image of the 747 Jumbo jet, given to young flyers, 1 3/4" l. (ILLUS.) **4**

Pin, silver wings, Bond Bread premium, back pictures the Fleetster Transport aircraft, 1930s **35**

Pinback button, Beech-Nut Gum premium, photo of the Beech-Nut Autogiro, 1931, 1 3/4" d. **75**

Pinback button, commemorates the 75th Anniversary of the first powered flight in Canada of the Silver Dart on February 23, 1909, 1909-1984, 2 1/4" d. **10**

Pinback button, photo button of Commander Richard E. Byrd, commander of the first flight over the South Pole, shown wearing hat & goggles, 1 1/4" d. **60**

Pinback button, picture button of 1930s aviator Stanislaw Hausner, picture w/his aircraft, 1 1/2" d. **65**

Pinback buttons, a set illustrating early aviators including Loma Worth, Woman Stunt Pilot, 70 in the set, each **25**

Plaque, bronze, relief portrait of Charles Lindbergh, copyright by Louis L. Leach, South Carolina, ca. 1927, 10 1/4 x 13 1/4" **173**

Plate, china, commemorates Charles Lindbergh's transatlantic flight, 1927, manufactured for Golden Glow, full-color portrait of "Lucky Lindy" in the center, sold in stores, 8 1/2" d. **40**

Playing card deck, Braniff International Airlines, complete deck.. **25**

Playing card deck, TWA airline premium, promotes DC-3 flights, back describes the Lindbergh Line Shortest - Fastest - Coast to Coast, top shows Charles Lindbergh, 1940, complete deck in top condition **225**

Postcard of Knoxville Airport

Postcard, linen-type, Municipal Airport, Knoxville, Tennessee (McPhee Tyson Airport), pictures a DC-3 airliner of the Capital Airlines, control tower in background, 3 1/2 x 5 1/2", 1948 (ILLUS.).............. **15**

Postcard of New Lions Bridge

Postcard, linen-type, New Lions Bridge, Vancouver, B.C., three aircraft overhead, motorboat & sailboat below, early 1930s, 3 1/2 x 5 1/4" (ILLUS.) **15**

Royal Canadian Air Force Program

Program, "Annual Air Force Ball - Station Toronto," Ontario, February 23, 1951, first annual Royal Canadian Air Force event, paper covers, 4 1/4 x 6 1/4" (ILLUS.).. **80**

Ring, "Clipper Ring," brass ring showing a Pan-American Clipper high above a glove w/the Pan-Am logo, Quaker Cereal premium, 1930s **50**

Schedule, basketball schedule of the Philadelphia 76ers, 1976-77 schedule, back features advertisement for TWA - Official Airline of the Sixers, front cover shows crowd cheering the team on, 2 1/2 x 3 3/4" **10**

Sheet music, "Lindy, Lindy," ca. 1927 .... **15**

Store poster, "Chesterfield Cigarettes - Meet Steve Canyon - NBC TV Show," cardboard, pictures Steve Canyon in his flight suit smoking a Chesterfield, 1950s, 21 x 22".. **125**

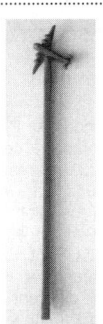

1950s Airline Swizzle Stick

Swizzle stick, plastic, red w/a small four-engine plane at the top, came in various color w/name of airline down the side, 1950s, value depends on whether the airline is still flying (ILLUS.) **3-10**

Tapestry, machine-woven, commemorating Lindbergh's flight from New York to Paris, ca. 1927, 18 1/2 x 55" **125-150**

Cracker Jack Aviation Card

Trading cards, Cracker Jack prize, each card w/a different painting of an aircrafts including the Martin Mars, Republic Lancer & The Blackburn Botha, 1940s, set of 50, 2 1/2 x 3", the set (ILLUS. of one)... **350**

Card from the "Famous Air Pilots" Set

Cards from "Freedom's War" Set

Trading cards, "Famous Air Pilots," premium from Heinz Company, color image of pilot on each, No. 3 features Capt. Eddie Rickenbacker, World War I ace, back of card w/details on the pilot, 1935, 6 x 8" album & 25 different cards, complete in good condition (ILLUS. of one) **100**

Trading cards, "Freedom's War," Topps series featuring different aircraft & scenes of World War II & the Korean War, 1950, 203 cards in set, each 2 1/16 x 2 5/8", the set (ILLUS. of three) **450**

Card from Topps "Wings" Set

Trading cards, "Wings," Topps series, each card pictures a different painting of an aircraft, 1954, set of 200, 2 5/8 x 3 3/4", complete mint set (ILLUS. of one) **550**

BANKS

Original early mechanical and cast-iron still banks are in great demand with collectors. Their scarcity has caused numerous reproductions of both types and the novice collector is urged to exercise caution. The early mechanical banks are especially scarce and some versions are seldom offered for sale but, rather, are traded with fellow collectors attempting to upgrade an existing collection. Numbers after the bank name in mechanical banks refer to those in John Meyer's Handbook of Old Mechanical Banks. However, another book Penny Lane—A History of Antique Mechanical Toy Banks, *by Al Davidson, provides updated information and the number from this new volume is indicated in parenthesis at the end of each mechanical bank listing.*

In past years, our standard reference for cast-iron still banks was Hubert B. Whiting's book Old Iron Still Banks, *but because this work is out of print and a well illustrated book,* The Penny Lane Bank Book—Collecting Still Banks *by Andy and Susan Moore pictures and describes numerous additional banks, we will use the Moore numbers as a reference after the name of each listing. Other newer books on still banks include* Iron Safe Banks *by Bob and Shirley Peirce (SBCCA publication),* The Bank Book *by Bill Norman (N),* Coin Banks by Banthrico *by James Redwine (R), and* Monumental Miniatures *by Madua & Weingarten (MM). We will indicate the Whiting or other book reference number, with the abbreviation noted above, in parenthesis at the end.*

The still banks listed are old and in good original condition with good paint and no repair unless otherwise noted. An asterisk (*) indicates this bank has been reproduced at some time.

Cards from "Power for Peace" Set

Trading cards, "Power for Peace," each card pictures a different aircraft or other atomic weapon, Bowman, 1954, set of 96, 2 1/2 x 3 1/4", complete mint set (ILLUS. of part) **300**

Card from Skybirds Set

Trading cards, "Skybirds," National Chicle set, each w/a different painting of an aircraft, early 1940s, 108 cards in set, depending on rarity & condition, each card (ILLUS. of one) **20-125**

Mechanical

Acrobat - 1 - w/blue base, swinging acrobat causing the clown to spin & the coin to fall, designed by Edward Morris of Boston, pat. Feb. 8, 1883, 7 1/4" l. (PL 1) **$5,800**

Afghanistan Bank - 2 - bear (Russia) & lion (England) pivot at gates to city of Aria in Herat Province, black & green w/gilt trim, ca. 1885 (PL 3).................................. **4,500**

"(I) Always Did 'Spise a Mule - 4 -" boy on bench facing mule, red version, rarer white plus white version known, by J. E. Stevens Co., 10" w., PL 250 .... **3,500**

Artillery Bank (Rectangular Trap) - 6 - soldier shoots cannon into block house, bronzed finish, Shepard Hardware, 1892, PL 11 .... **2,000**

Atlas - "Money Moves the World" - 8 - white metal figure & wooden globe that spins, gilt & silver, 8 1/4" h. (PL 13) **5,175**

Bad Accident - 9 - man riding in cart pulled by donkey w/boy hiding behind cat-tail plant, J. & E. Stevens, multicolored, PL 20 .. **4,500**

Bill E. Grin - 15 - bust of clown, turns eyes, sticks out tongue, white face, black eyebrows, red lips, J. & E. Stevens, 1915 (PL 33)... **4,500**

Bird on Roof - 16 - bronzed finish, J. & E. Stevens, patented on March 5, 1878 (PL 36)... **5,500**

Bismark Bank - 193 - name embossed on side, figure of pig w/pop-up Bismark figure, reflects outrage of Americans when Bismark prohibited importing pork from the U.S. to Germany, red, black & gold, J. & E. Stevens, ca. 1883-84 (PL 37) **10,000**

Boy Robbing Bird's Nest - 20 - a.k.a. Tree Bank, multicolored, J. & E. Stevens, ca. 1906 (PL 51)... **10,000**

Boy Scout Camp - 21 - tent w/boy, tree w/owl & two other figures, mulitcolored, PL 52 .... **20,000**

Boys Stealing Watermelons - 22 - doghouse w/dog, two boys stealing watermelons, Kyser & Rex, multicolored, ca. 1885-95, 7" w. (PL 53)............................ **5,000**

Buffalo - "Butting Buffalo" - 26 - buffalo w/boy & raccoon in tree stump, mulitcolored, Kyser & Rex (PL 90) **8,500**

Bull Dog Bank - 63 - seated, coin on nose, brown & red, rare white varient known, J. & E. Stevens, 1880 (PL 64) **4,500**

Bull Dog Savings Bank - 62 - dog springs toward man, clockwork mechanism, red & gold, Ives, Blakeslee & Co., 1878, PL 65 ... **6,500**

Cabin - 33 - cabin w/man standing in doorway, red & black w/yellow walls, pivoting man kicks coin through roof, J. & E. Stevens (PL 93)... **2,200**

Calamity - "Football" - 34 - three football players, brass finish, J. & E. Stevens, 1904, PL 94 .... **30,000**

Calumet Baking Powder, tin & lithographed paper label, can of baking powder w/baby's head on top above "Thank You," patented in 1924, 5" h. (PL 97)........... **110**

Chief Big Moon - 42 - Indian seated in front of teepee holding fish w/flipping frog and pond, J. & E. Stevens, 1899, PL 108 .... **6,000**

Circus Ticket Collector - 48 - man standing by barrel, detailed buttons on lapel, head is two-part casting, a.k.a. Money Barrel, multicolored, Judd Mfg. Co., ca. 1879 (PL 115)... **3,000**

Clown, Harlequin & Columbine - 119 - after coin is inserted between figure of Harlequin & clown, press lever on right & the two figures reverse themselves, causing figure of Columbine to spin & coin to go into the bank, multicolored, J. & E. Stevens, pat. Nov. 13, 1877 but cast ca. 1907 .... **16,000**

Clown on Bar - 50 - cast iron & tinplate, figure of clown suspended on crossbar above deep rectangular latticework base, C.G. Bush, ca. 1880, extremely rare (PL 126)... **74,000**

Clown on Globe - 49 - w/turning & flipping mechanism, red & orange outfit, blue sphere & tan base, J. &. E. Stevens, 1890, PL 127 .... **2,500**

Creedmoor Bank - 53 - figure w/cape & trousers, firing rifle at tree stump & nodding head, color variations in clothing, J & E Stevens Co., ca. 1877 (PL 137)............. **2,000**

Darktown Battery - 56 - three black baseball figures - pitcher, catcher, & batter, multicolored, known in rarer white player version, J. & E. Stevens, ca. 1888, PL146 .... **3,500**

Darky and Watermelon (Football Bank) - 92 - place coin in the football & pull figure's right leg back until it locks; press lever on figure's back & he kicks the football dropping coin into bank, J. & E. Stevens, ca. 1888, PL 147, extremely rare **354,500**

Dinah - 58 - aluminum variation, bust of black woman, places coin in mouth, "Dinah" cast on back, red, white & black, John Harper, Ltd., England, 1911 (PL154) **400**

Ding Dong Bell - 60 - lithographed tin & wood upright shadowbox-style w/figures of children on fence, by well & ringing bell, Weeden Mfg. Co., ca. 1888, extremely rare (PL 155)................................. **74,000**

Eagle & Eaglets - 75 - bending mother eagle & rising young, w/bellows that simulate birds chirping, grey, white & yellow, green grass version known, J. & E. Stevens, ca. 1883, PL 165 .... **4,500**

Elephant & Three Clowns on Tub - 88 - red blanket, the elephant's trunk knocks the coin into the base & the mounted clown turns, multicolored, J. & E. Stevens, 1883 (PL 170) **5,500**

Elephant - Jumbo on Wheels - 86 - red & grey paint, attributed to J. & E. Stevens, ca. 1883 (PL 284) **5,500**

Ferris Wheel - 91 - conversion of chain-driven toy, wheel w/six gondolas each carrying two male riders, base w/clockwork motor, coin-slot & on/off lever, red, green, yellow & silver, Hubley, ca. 1930-40, PL188 .... **12,000**

Football Bank - 93 - player w/goal posts, blue, bronze & black paint, John Harper, Ltd., England, 1895 (PL 191) **2,500**

"Freedman's Bank" - 98 - wood, metal, cloth, after winding the spring in rear of bank, place coin on table by figure's left hand & press lever; figure will turn his head from side to side as he scoops coin into slot on top of table & raises his right hand to his face & thumb to his nose, moving each finger independently; then he lowers his hand & shakes his head, historically important, Jerome Secor, ca. 1880, PL 198, extremely rare **321,500**

Frog Bank (Two Frogs) - 99 - two frogs, one lying on back, one sitting, w/opening mouth, green & yellow, J. & E. Stevens, ca. 1882 (PL 200) **7,000**

Frog on Round Lattice Base - 102 - foot operation opening mouth & eyes, green & brown lattice base, variation known w/yellow lattice base, J. & E. Stevens, ca. 1870s, PL 204 .... **3,000**

Germania Exchange Bank - 106 - lead & cast iron, goat holding stein standing on beer keg, J. & E. Stevens, ca. 1894, extremely rare (PL 211) **55,200**

Giant - 107 - standing giant w/club, a.k.a. Giant That Jack Killed, bronzed finish, Judd Mfg. Co. (PL 212) **22,000**

Girl in Victorian Chair - 108 - w/dog in lap, black, red & yellow paint, W.S. Reed, ca. 1880 (PL 216) **9,000**

Girl Skipping Rope - 109 - multicolored, J. & E. Stevens, ca. 1890, extremely rare (PL 217) **55,000**

Goat, Frog & Old Man (Initiating 2nd Degree) - 114 - bearded old man on goat facing frog, similar action to Initiating, 1st Degree bank, black, yellow & green paint, Mechanical Novelty Works, 1880s (PL 220) **10,000**

Hall's Excelsior - 118 - cast iron & wood, considered the first cast-iron mechanical bank, string-pull mechanism, building w/pop-up monkey in roof, paper "Cashier" label, multicolored, J. & E. Stevens, ca. 1869 (PL 228) **750**

Hen & Chick - 121 - hen opens mouth & her chick pops up to deposit the coin, w/bellows making "clucking" sound, red, silver & bronze paint, J. & E. Stevens, 1901 (PL 236) **5,500**

Hindu - 122 - bust of man wearing turban, red, yellow, blue & white paint, Kyser & Rex, 1882 (PL 239) **5,000**

Hoop-La Bank, clown w/hoop, barrel & dog, multicolored, name on side of base, John Harper, Ltd., England, 1895, PL 245 .... **4,500**

Humpty Dumpty - 127 - clown figure depicts well-known pantomime G. L. Fox, w/moving arm, tongue & eyes, multicolored, Shepard Hardware, 1884 (PL 248)... **8,500**

Initiating Bank (The) - "First Degree" - 130 - goat butting black man w/frog, black, red & yellow paint, Mechanical Novelty Works (PL 258) **14,000**

Jolly Nigger - 132 - red shirt, moving arm, tongue & rolling eyes, J. & E. Stevens, patented on March 14, 1882, 1880s-1930s, many variations (PL 275) **4,500**

Jonah & the Whale - 139 - on pedestal w/small boat at whale's tail, multicolored, Shepard Hardware, ca. 1880s, extremely rare (PL 283) **55,000**

Jonah & the Whale - 138 - Jonah in boat w/whale in water, multicolored, Shepard Hardware, pat. July 15, 1890, pedestal base version much rarer (PL 282) **14,000**

Kiltie Bank, Scotsman w/blue & red plaid sash & hat, John Harper, Ltd., England, 1931 (PL 290) **3,500**

Leap Frog Bank - 143 - two boys play leap frog near fence & tree stump, one boy leaps over the other to hit a lever which causes the coin to fall into the tree, multicolored, Shepard Hardware, 1890, PL 292 .... **5,500**

Lion Hunter - 148 - hunter aiming rifle at lion, moving head, & rearing lion, J. & E. Stevens, 1911, PL 301 .... **15,000**

Lion & Two Monkeys - 147 - monkey drops coin into lion's mouth while baby monkey jumps up tree stump to watch, multicolored, Kyser & Rex, pat. July 17, 1883, (PL 300) **4,000**

Magic Bank - 153 - building w/cashier holding tray, red, black & cream paint, J. & E. Stevens, 1886 (PL 311) **3,500**

Magician Bank - 154 - magician holding top hat w/table, multicolored, J. & E. Stevens (PL 315) **5,000**

Mammy & Child - 155 - mammy feeding child laying across lap, multicolored, Kyser & Rex, 1884 (PL 318) **8,500**

Mason Bank - 156 - Irish hod carrier working w/Italian bricklayer, multicolored, Shepard Hardware, patented in 1887, PL 321 .... **15,000**

Mikado Bank - 159 - magician holds two hats down on table, Kyser & Rex, ca. 1886, extremely rare (PL 326) **123,500**

Monkey & Coconut - 163 - seated monkey w/coconut in lap, w/moving hand, mouth & eyes, & opening coconut, brown, green & orange paint, J. & E. Stevens, ca. 1886 (PL 332) **260,000**

Mosque - 168 - rotating gorilla figure inside building & hand crank at side, black paint, Judd Mfg. Co, ca. 1875 (PL 340) **2,600**

Motor Bank - 228 - trolley w/keywind mechanism, black, red & white paint, Kyser & Rex, 1889 (PL 341) **20,000**

Mule Entering Barn - 169 - multicolored, J. & E. Stevens, marked "Pat'd. Aug. 30, 1880" (PL 342) **2,000**

New Bank - Building & Guard - 174 - building w/soldier in doorway, orange & black paint, J. & E. Stevens, 1870s, PL 357 ...... **2,000**

North Pole - 175 - base features dog sled w/three figures, flag on top of gold globe, multicolored, J. & E. Stevens, 1910 (PL 360) **8,000**

Octagonal Fort (Fort Sumter) - 7 - cannon pointing at fort , grey, black & red paint, ca. 1890 (PL 363) **6,000**

Old Woman in the Shoe - 242 - woman raises her arm & boy leans forwards to deposit coin, W.S. Reed, ca. 1883, PL 367, extremely rare **426,000**

Organ Bank (Boy & Girl) - 178 - form of a portable barrel organ, w/hand-turned mechanism causing the monkey to drop a coin into the top, and tip his cap, the boy & girl to dance & the bell to ring, multicolored, Kyser & Rex, ca. 1882, PL 368 .. **7,000**

Organ Grinder & Dancing Bear - 181 - key-wind mechanism, multicolored, Kyser & Rex, 1890s (PL 372) **10,000**

Owl - 182 - turning head mechanism, grey, black & yellow paint, J. & E. Stevens, ca. 1880 (PL 375).. **2,000**

Owl w/Book - 184 - w/coin-slot in book under wing causing the eyes to move, Kilgore, 5 3/4" h. (PL 373) **1,035**

Paddy & His Pig - 185 - Irish figure holding pig in his lap, multicolored, J. & E. Stevens, ca. 1885, PL 376 .... **9,000**

Panorama Bank - 186 - house w/opening in front to reveal lithographed pictures mounted on wooden wheel which moves when coins are deposited, blue, red & white paint, J. & E. Stevens & Co., pat. March 7, 1876 (PL 377).............................. **8,500**

Peg Leg Beggar - 188 - w/off-white face, drop coin in slot in the hat & beggar nods his head in thanks, black & white paint, Judd Mfg. Co., ca. 1875 (PL 380).............. **3,500**

Pelican - 189 - w/baseball player inside beak, various versions w/different figures, bronzed bird w/multicolored figure, J. & E. Stevens - Trenton Lock & Hardware, ca. 1878 (PL 381)...................... **800**

Pig in Highchair - 194 - cast w/floral & foliate motifs, the pig lifts tray, swallows the coin & moves his tongue, nickel plated, J. & E. Stevens, pat. Aug. 24, 1897, 6" h., PL 390 .... **2,000**

Pistol Bank - 209 - nickeled finish, Richard Elliot Co., 1909 (PL 391) **3,500**

Trick Pony - 196 - pony lowers head to deposit the coin in the trough trap door which opens & closes to receive the coin, red, brown, black & yellow paint, Shepard Hardware (PL 484) **1,200**

Professor Pug Frog's Great Bicycle Feat - 201- Mother Goose reading w/frog riding bicycle & clown holding large basket, multicolored, J. & E. Stevens, ca. 1886 (PL 400)... **12,500**

Pump & Bucket - Registering - 202 - water pump & bucket on base, red, green & gold, ca. 1892 (PL 401) **5,000**

"Punch & Judy" - 203 - figures in theater setting, embossed name on front, multicolored, Shepard Hardware, ca. 1884, PL 404 .... **9,500**

Rabbit - 205 - large standing rabbit on rectangular base, bronzed finish, attributed to Lockwood Mfg. Co., 1890s (PL 406)...... **1,700**

Reclining Chinaman - 45 - the figure w/moving arms showing his arms & saluting, multicolored, J. & E. Stevens, ca. 1885 (PL 410).. **9,000**

Red Riding Hood - 208 - girl seated on bed w/grandmother, multicolored, W.S. Reed Co or J. & E. Stevens, ca. 1880, extremely rare (PL 412) **96,000**

Roller Skating Bank - 211 - two figures skating around rink, two have fallen & one stands, attributed to Kyser & Rex, multicolored, ca. 1890s, extremely rare (PL 417)... **156,500**

Rooster - 212 - on base, w/moving head & beak, black & red paint, Kyser & Rex, ca. 1880-90 (PL 419)................................ **5,000**

Santa Claus - 214 - Santa drops coin down chimney, red, white & gold paint, Shepard Hardware, ca. 1889 (PL 428) **4,500**

Speaking Dog - 69 - seated girl w/large dog, rectangular coin trap, multicolored, J. & E. Stevens, ca. 1885 (PL 447) **6,000**

Sportsman - "Fowler" - 97 - hunter standing pointing rifle w/bird ready to be launched below, multicolored, J. & E. Stevens, ca. 1892, extremely rare (PL 449)... **60,550**

Stump Speaker, standing figure w/carpetbag, w/moving arm & opening mouth & carpetbag, multicolored, Shepard Hardware, ca. 1896, PL 453 .... **4,000**

Tabby Bank - 223 - cat sitting on egg w/protruding head of chick, grey & yellow w/blue base, ca. 1887 (PL 454) **1,200**

Tammany Bank (Little Fat Man) - 224 - moving head & arm, various color variations, J. & E. Stevens, pat. Dec. 23, 1873, PL 455 .... **500**

Teddy and the Bear - 226 - Teddy Roosevelt shoots the bull's-eye, raises his head & the bear pops out of the brown tree, green base, J. & E. Stevens, ca. 1907, PL 459 .... **3,500**

Toad on Stump - 103 - (PL 475) **575**

Trick Dog Bank (six-part base) - 71 - clown w/hoop, barrel & dog, multicolored, Hubley, patented July 31, 1888, produced through 1906 (PL 481)..................... **1,100**

Uncle Sam w/Satchel & Umbrella - 231 - coin is dropped into open satchel, w/moving hand & mouth, red, white, blue & gold, Shepard Hardware, PL 493 .... **8,500**

William Tell - 237 - figure firing rifle at boy w/apple on head, into the tower & strikes the bell, multicolored, J. & E. Stevens, ca. 1896 (PL 565) **4,000**

World's Fair Bank - 244 - the Indian chief appears after lever is pushed, then hands Columbus a peace pipe as Columbus salutes, w/"Columbus" cast into base, "World's Fair Bank" cast on front, gold & silver, J. & E. Stevens, 1893, PL 573 ...... **3,000**

Zig Zag Bank, cast iron, tin, papier-maché & cloth, tall flat backplate topped w/wizard's face & cap, coin dropped in hat & activates jack-in-the-box at the base, patented in 1889, extremely rare (PL 575) . **189,500**

Zoo Bank - 245 - building w/lion & bear at windows & monkey in cupola, red, black & green paint, Kyser & Rex, ca. 1894 (PL 576)... **3,000**

Pottery

Model of a cottage, w/blue & green sponge decoration w/black details, Staffordshire, 3 3/4" h. (minor flakes) **220**

Redware Pottery Bank

Model of a dresser, redware, two over three drawers w/applied yellow glazed rosettes, chips, applied feet are missing, 4 x 7", 6 3/4" h. (ILLUS.)............................... **248**

Still

537 Bull, cast-iron figure of bull on oblong base, traces of brown paint on underside, 5 7/8" l. **193**

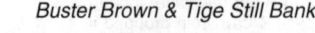

Silver Building Still Bank

Building, cast-iron, building w/small reeded dome, sides pierced w/windows, original silver paint & "Bank" embossed on roof, 3" h. (ILLUS.).. **65**

Buster Brown & Tige Still Bank

Buster Brown & Tige, cast iron, Tige sits next to hatted Buster Brown figure, traces of original paint, 5 1/4" h. (ILLUS.)................. **325**

Clown Still Bank

Clown, cast iron, standing clown in pointed hat, traces of original paint, 6 1/4" h. (ILLUS.)... **350**

Combination Safe Still Bank

Combination safe, cast iron & stamped steel, decorated w/images of boy, dog & angel, worn black & gold paint, unpainted combination dial, 3 7/8" h. (ILLUS.)................. **80**

Grey Elephant Still Bank

Elephant, cast iron, standing elephant w/head down, original grey paint, 2 x 2 7/8 x 4 1/4" (ILLUS.)............................... **185**

Elephant Still Bank

Elephant, cast iron, w/upraised trunk, tusks, old gold paint over red, 4" h. (ILLUS.) **120**

Horse Still Bank

Horse, cast iron, w/horseshoe embossed on side marked "Good Luck," original worn paint, 1 1/4 x 4 1/4 x 4 3/4" (ILLUS.) **225**

House, cast iron & stamped steel, two-story house on rectangular base w/"Twelfth Street Bank" & "Save for a Home," w/key, 3 3/4" l. **125**

Victorian House Still Bank

House, cast iron, Victorian style building w/tile roof, gable windows, widow's walk & turret, original paint, 4 1/4" h. (ILLUS.) **120**

Lion Still Bank

Lion, cast iron, standing male lion w/gold paint & red mouth & eyes, 2 1/4 x 5 1/4 x 6 1/4" (ILLUS.) **185**

Pig Still Bank

Pig, cast iron, advertising "Decker's - Iowana," gold painted surface, 4 1/4" l. (ILLUS.) **110**

Rearing Horse Still Bank

Rearing horse, cast iron, black painted horse w/red mouth & nostrils, white eyes & silver-painted hooves on rectangular base, 2 3/4 x 6 3/4 x 7 1/2" (ILLUS.) **115**

"Security Safe Deposit" Still Bank

Safe, cast iron, combination safe, w/"Security Safe Deposit" embossed on front & stylized floral forms on top & sides, worn black paint, marked on bottom "Patented Feb. 15, 1881 - March 1, 1887," 4" h. (ILLUS.) **80**

Safe, cast iron, patented Aug. 17, 1897, made by J.E. Stevens Co., Cromwell, Connecticut, original gold painted surface, top & sides w/floral & scroll decorations, 5" h. **125**

Pierced Safe Still Bank

Safe, cast iron, w/pierced scroll decoration on sides & top, bottom is marked "Patom [in a horseshoe] - Patented June 2, 1986," 3 1/4" h. (ILLUS.) **100**

Treasure Chest Still Bank

Treasure chest, stamped steel w/copper finish, decorated w/images of crossed pistols, cutlass & pirate head, w/sliding tray in front for depositing coins, 3 1/8 x 3 3/4 x 4" w/tray closed (ILLUS.).......... 39

Turret, cast iron, two pierced wings attached to cylindrical body, domed lid w/finial, original worn paint, 3 1/2" h. 48

Alphabet - 1604 - cast iron, 26 facets w/letter on each, American-made, 3 7/8" d. 1,500

Andy Gump - 217 - cast iron, multicolored, seated figure reading newspaper, Arcade Mfg. Co., 1928, 2 7/8 x 4 3/8" h............ 700

"Andy Gump Savings Bank" - 219 - lead, plain finish, General Thrift Products, ca. 1920s, 5 3/4 x 5 3/4"............................ 650

Apple - 1621 - cast iron, w/twig, three leaves & bumblebee on apple, Kyser & Rex Co., 1882, 5 1/4" w., W. 299 1,200

Automobile - Yellow Cab - 1493 - cast iron w/steel wheels, orange & black, Arcade Mfg. Co., 1921, 7 7/8" l., 4 1/4" h., W. 158 750

Baseball on Three Bats - 1608 - cast iron, "American and National League Ball" & "Official League Ball," silver & red paint, Hubley Mfg. Co., 1914, 5 1/4" h. (W. 220)..... 800

Baseball Player - 18 - cast iron, brown & red paint, A.C. Williams Co., 1909-34, 5 3/4" h. (W. 10)... 300

Baseball Player - 20 - cast iron, gold paint, A.C. Williams Co., 1909, 5 3/4" h. (W. 10)..... 154

Battleship - Battleship Maine - 1439 - cast iron, "Maine" painted on side, white on green waves, J. & E. Stevens Co., 1901, 10 1/4" l., 6" h., W. 143 4,500

Battleship - Battleship "Maine" (large) - 1441 - cast iron, "Maine" embossed on side, black w/gold trim, Grey Iron Casting Co., 1897-1903, 6 5/8" l......................... 1,200

Battleship - Battleship Oregon (large) - 1452 - cast iron, grey w/red trim, J. & E. Stevens Co., 1898-1906, 6" l., 4 7/8" h. (W. 144)... 1,500

Battleship - Battleship Texas - 1439 variant - cast iron, "Texas" painted on side, white, J. & E. Stevens Co., 1901, 10 1/4" l., 6" h., W. 143 2,400

Bean Pot - 951 - cast iron, "Nickel Register" w/bail handle, good red paint & nickel plate, American-made, 3 7/16" d., 3" h. 319

Bear - Bear Stealing Pig - 693 - American-made, original gold paint, scarce, pristine, 5 1/2" h. 1,430

Bear - "Teddy" Bear - 698 - cast iron, "Teddy Bear" embossed on sides, Arcade

Mfg. Co., 1910-25, 3 7/8" l., 2 1/2" h. (W. 331).. 175

"Billiken" - 80 - cast iron, gold & red, name on base, embossed "Billiken Shoes Bring Luck" across chest, A.C. Williams Co., 1909, some paint wear, 4 1/4 x 2 1/2" 110

"Billiken" on Throne - 73 - cast iron, A.C. Williams Co., gold & red, 1909, 3 1/8" w., 6 1/2" h. (minor paint wear) 55

Billy Bounce - 15 - cast iron, "Give Billy a Penny" on chest, silver clothing w/red cap & bow tie & flesh-colored face, Hubley Mfg. Co., 1906, 4 11/16" h. (W. 22) 450

Black Man - Darkey (Sharecropper) - 173 - cast iron, w/toes visible on one foot, black painted w/red trim, A.C. Williams Co., 1901, 5 1/2" h. (W. 18)............................ 250

*Black Woman - Aunt Jemima (Mammy with Spoon) - 168 - cast iron, blue, red & silver paint, A.C. Williams Co., 1905-30, 5 7/8" h., (W. 17) 350

Black Woman - Aunt Jemima (Mammy with Spoon) - 169 - cast iron, slot between legs, American-made, 5 7/8" h. 363

*Black Woman - Mammy with Hands on Hips - 176 - cast iron, blue kerchief w/white dots, red blouse & white scarf, long white dress, Hubley Mfg. Co., 1914-46, 5 1/4" h. (W. 20)...................................... 121

Boss Tweed (Tammany Tiger) - 110 - cast iron, "Savings Bank" on front, "Tiger" on back, black paint, American-made, ca. 1873, 3 7/8" h. (W. 318) 600

Boy with Large Football - 10 - cast iron, red & silver paint, Hubley Mfg. Co., 1914, 3 1/4" w., 5 1/8" h. (W. 11)......................... 1,200

*Buffalo - Buffalo - 560 - cast iron, small, gold paint, Arcade Mfg. Co. 1920-25 & A.C. Williams Co. 1920s-34, 4 3/8" l., 2 3/8" h. (W. 208) 110

* Building - 1876 Bank - 1011 - cast iron, no date, H.L. Judd Mfg. Co., 1895, 2 3/16 x 3 x 3 3/8" (W. 388) 297

Building - Boston State House - 1210 - cast iron, blue & red w/gold dome, Smith & Egge Mfg. Co., late 1800s, 3 1/2" sq., 5 1/8" h. (W. 271) 4,000

Colonial House Still Bank

*Building - Colonial House (House with Porch) - 992 - cast iron, A.C. Williams Co., 1910-34, repainted in green & copper, 2 3/4 x 3 7/8 x 4" h., W. 404 (ILLUS.).. 70

Building - Columbia - 1069 - cast iron, white or gold paint, Administration Building at Columbian Exposition, Kenton Mfg. Co., ca. 1893-1904, 3 1/2" sq., 4 1/2" h. (W. 431) 550

Building - Columbia - 1070 - cast iron, large trap, white or gold paint, Administration Building at Columbian Exposition, Kenton Mfg. Co., ca. 1893-1913, 4 1/4" sq., 5 3/4" h. (W. 430) 750

Building - Columbia - 1077 - cast iron, white or gold paint, Administration Building at Columbian Exposition, Kenton Mfg. Co., ca. 1893-1904, 5 1/2" sq., 7" h. (W. 429) 700

Building - Columbia Bank - 1073 - cast iron, white or gold paint, Administration Building at Columbian Exposition, Kenton Mfg. Co., ca. 1893-1913, 7" sq., 8 3/4" h. (W. 428) 600

Building - Domed Mosque "Bank" - 1176 - cast iron, combination door, gold or bronze finish, Grey Iron Casting Co., 1903-28, 3 1/8 x 5 1/8 x 5 1/8" h., (W. 417) 1,100

Building - Domed Mosque "Bank" - 1178 - cast iron, gold paint, Grey Iron Casting Co., 1903-28, 2 15/16 x 3 1/8 x 3 1/8" h., W. 415 198

Building - "Flat Iron Building Bank" - 1159 - cast iron, silver finish, Kenton Mfg. Co., 1904-13, 4 3/4 x 6 1/8 x 8 1/4" h. (W. 410) 550

Building - "Home Bank" (Crown) - 1232 - cast iron, white w/blue trim, J. & E. Stevens Co., patented 1872, 3 1/4 x 4 5/16 x 5 1/4" h. 15,000

Building - Home Savings - 1201 - cast iron, red w/black roof, embossed "Property of the Peoples Savings Bank, Grand Rapids, Mich." over doorway, four coin slots, American-made, 6 1/4 x 8 1/8 x 10 1/2" h... 1,500

Building - Independence Hall - 1244 - cast iron, tan & red paint, Enterprise Mfg. Co., 1875, 6 1/4 x 6 11/16 x 8 7/8" h. (W. 358).. 1,000

Building - Independence Hall Tower - 1202 - cast iron, gilded, Enterprise Mfg. Co., 1876, 3 7/8" sq., 9 1/2" h. 1,200

Building - Palace - 1116 - cast iron, ornate building w/tower, double stairway & colonnaded front, japanned w/gold trim, Ives, 1885, 5 x 8 x 7 1/2" h., W. 433 2,200

Building - Quadrafoil [sic] House - 1003 - cast iron, gilt trim & green roof, Stevens, Wing Mfg. Co. & Arcade Mfg. Co. 1902-13 & Kenton Mfg. Co., ca. 1904-26, 2 x 2 1/4 x 3 1/8" h. (W. 356) 176

Building - San Gabriel Mission - 957 - lead pattern, silver finish, American-made, 2 9/16 x 3 3/4 x 4 11/16" h. 350

Building - Tower Bank - 1208 - cast iron, smooth sides, John Harper Ltd., England, 1902-11, 3 7/8" sq., 9 1/4" h. 363

Building - Tower Bank - 1208 var. - cast iron, brick sides, John Harper Ltd., England, 1902-11, 3 7/8" sq., 9 1/4" h. 385

Building - Trader's Bank of Canada (The), cast iron, three-story building, silver finish, embossed "Colborne St." on front & "Yonge St." on sides, 8 1/2" h.................... 1,500

Building - Victorian House - 1142 - cast iron, nickeled finish, J. & E. Stevens Co., 1892, 2 1/2 x 3 1/4 x 4 1/2" h. (W. 352) 325

Building - Woolworth Building - 1042 - cast iron, small version, gold paint, Kenton Mfg. Co., 1915, 1 1/4 x 1 9/16 x 5 3/4" h. 193

Building - Alamo - 1187 - cast iron, gilt paint, Alamo Iron Works, U.S., 1930s, 1 7/8 x 2 3/4 x 3 3/8" 400

Building - "Bayside National Bank of New York," white metal w/golden finish, 2 3/8" h. (R 542) 231

Building - Century of Progress - 1064 - cast iron, Arcade, model of Chicago World's Fair building in white w/a blue roof, 1934, 4 1/2 x 7" 1,200

Building - "Chemung Canal Trust," white metal w/golden finish, 4" h. (R 549) 83

Building - "Easton National Bank," white metal w/silvered finish, 3 1/4" h. (R 975) 83

Building - "First Federal Savings," white metal w/bronzed finish, 4 5/8" h. (R 680) 33

Building - "First National Bank of Amarillo," white metal w/golden bronzed finish, 4" h. (R 602) 160

Building - French Cottage - lithographed tin, Stevens & Brown, ca. 1870 600

Building - "Heritage County Bank," white metal w/golden finish, 4 3/8" h. (R 631) 116

Building - Jarmulowsky Bldg. - 1086 - cast iron, brass finish, name embossed on all four sides, J. & E. Stevens, 2 1/8 x 5 x 17 3/4" 5,200

Building - John Brown Fort - 1185 - cast iron, grey paint, U.S., 2 3/4 x 2 11/16 x 3"..... 400

Building - Lighthouse - 1115 - cast iron, black w/red tower, U.S. 1891, 5 1/2 x 5 1/2 x 10 1/4" 550

Building - "Petersburg Savings and American," white metal w/bronzed finish, 3 1/4" h. (R 681) 88

Building - "Southwestern Savings & Loan," white metal w/bronzed finish, 3 7/8" h. 149

Building - "Staten Island Savings Bank," white metal w/bronzed finish, 5 1/2" h., R 704 (ILLUS. left with Exchange Bank, top of next page) 242

Building - Swiss Cottage, lithographed tin, Stevens & Brown, ca. 1870 550

Building - "Syracuse Savings Bank," white metal w/bronzed finish, 5 5/8" h. (R 707) 132

Building - "The Security Bank & Trust of Lawton," white metal w/antiqued bronze finish, 3 1/8" h. (R 695) 77

Building - "Virginia Mutual Savings," white metal w/bronzed finish, 4" h. (R 714) 110

Building - "Waterbury National Bank," white metal w/bronzed finish, 2 3/4" h. (R 716) 72

Building - "Wilmington Mutual Savings and Loan," white metal w/bronzed finish, 2 1/2" l. (R 718) 138

Building - "Exchange Bank of St. Augustine," white metal w/bronzed finish, 5 1/2" h., R 578 (ILLUS. center, top of next page) 132

Group of Three Building Still Banks

Building - "Lawn Savings," white metal w/bronzed finish, 3 1/8" h., R 646 (ILLUS. right with Exchange Bank).................. **88**

New England Church Still Bank

Building - New England Church - 986 - cast iron, green roof, white w/gold spire & window trim, American-made, 4 x 7 1/2 x 7 1/2" (ILLUS.)............................. **495**

Buster Brown & Tige - 241 - cast iron, gold paint w/red trim, A.C. Williams Co., 1910-32, 5 1/2" h., W. 2 .... **484**

Camel - Camel (large) - 767 - cast iron, A.C. Williams Co., ca. 1917-20s, 6 1/4" l., 7 1/4" h., W. 201 .... **300-350**

Camel - Camel (small) - 768 - cast iron, Hubley Mfg. Co. & A.C. Williams Co., ca. 1920-30s, 3 7/8" w., 4 3/4" h......................... **400**

"Campbell Kids" - 163 - cast iron, gold paint, A.C. Williams Co., 1910-21, 3 1/4" h.. **250**

"Captain Kidd" -38 - cast iron, w/shovel beside tree, American-made, 1901, 5 1/2" h., W. 38 (replaced screw).................. **182**

Cat - Cat with Ball - 353 - cast iron, greenish paint w/yellow ball, American-made, 5 5/8" l., 2 1/2" h. **297**

Cat - Cat with Bow - 364 - cast iron, seated, gold paint, Grey Iron Casting Co., 1922, 2 7/8" w., 4 3/8" h. (slight paint wear)........... **341**

Cat - Kitty Bank - 349 - cast iron, kitten w/ribbon at neck, white w/pink ribbon, Hubley Mfg. Co., 1930s-1946, 4 3/4" h., W. 335 (very slight paint wear)......................... **94**

Cat - Seated Cat with Soft Hair - 366 - cast iron, black, Arcade Mfg. Co., ca. 1910-29, 2 7/8" l., 4 1/4" h. (W. 248) **325**

Charlie McCarthy - 206 - white metal w/moveable wooden jaw, seated figure, Vanio, 1938, 5 1/2" h................................... **225**

Clown - 211 - cast iron, standing figure w/pointed hat, gold paint, A.C. Williams Co., 1908, 6 3/16" h. (W. 29) **150**

Clown with Crooked Hat - 210 - cast iron, American-made, worn gold, white & red paint, 2 1/4" w., 6 3/4" h., W. 28 .... **605**

Cross - 1628 - cast iron, black finish, American-made, 4 5/8" l., 9 1/4" h. **850**

Dog - Wirehaired Terrier - 422 - cast iron, seated w/one leg forward, brownish white

w/black spots, Hubley, 1920-40, 5 3/4" h. (some paint wear)... **176**

Devil - Two-Faced Devil (Devil Head Toy Bank) - 31 - cast iron, A.C. Williams Co., 1904-12, 4 1/4" h. (W. 41)........................... **650**

Dog - Boston Bull - 413 - cast iron, seated, Hubley Mfg. Co., 1930s-40, 5 5/8" l., 4 3/8" h., W. 114 (replaced screw) **264**

Dog - Boston Bull Terrier - 421 - cast iron, standing, black & white paint, Vindex Toys, ca. 1931, 5 3/4" l., 5 1/4" h.................. **231**

Dog - Bulldog, Seated - 396 var. - cast iron, marked "Made in Canada," ca. 1928, 3 7/8" h., W. 102 .... **131**

Dog - Fido - 417 - cast iron, white & black w/red collar, Hubley Mfg. Co., "1914,"-46, 5" h. (W. 337)... **94**

Dog - Spaniel with Trap - 418 - cast iron, standing, black & white paint, Hubley Mfg. Co., 1930s, 6" l., 3 3/4" h. (W. 109) **165**

Dolphin - 33 - cast iron, boy in boat w/"Dolphin" on side, Grey Iron Casting Co.(?), 1900(?), 4 1/2" h...................................... **450**

Donkey (large) - 500 - cast iron, grey overall w/brown saddle, A.C. Williams Co., ca. 1920s, pristine, 6 1/4" l., 6 13/16" h., W. 197 .... **343**

Donkey (small) - 499 - cast iron, gold & red paint w/some wear, Arcade Mfg. Co. 1913-32 & A.C. Williams Co. 1910-34, 4 5/8" l., 4 1/2" h. (W. 198)...................... **60**

Dreadnought Bank - 1314 - cast iron, embossed "United We Stand," w/clasped hands & English flags, Sydenham & McOustra, England, ca. 1915, 7 1/2" l., 7" h. (W. 363).. **450**

Duck - 630 - cast iron, w/wings spread, white w/orange bill & feet, on grassy mound base, Hubley Mfg. Co., 1930s, 4 3/4" h., W. 324 (slight paint wear) **55**

Dutch Boy on Barrel - 180 - cast iron, red, green, yellow & white paint, Hubley Mfg. Co., 1930s, 5 5/8" h., W. 36 (some paint chipping)... **55**

Eggman (The) - 108 - cast iron, caricature of Wm. H. Taft, golden bronze painted w/black trim, Arcade, ca. 1908, 4 1/8" h....... **500**

Elephant - Hoover & Curtis - 463 - cast iron, names of 1928 Republican candidates embossed on side of white elephant, Hubley, 1928, 3 3/8 x 4 3/4" **550**

Elephant - Elephant with chariot & clown (small) - 465 - cast iron, Hubley, ca. 1906, 7" l... **800**

Elephant - Circus Elephant - 462 - cast iron, seated animal wearing child's straw hat w/ribbon, Hubley Mfg. Co., 1930-40, 3 7/8" h.. **300-330**

Elephant - McKinley-Roosevelt - 453 - cast iron, embossed portraits of Republican candidates on sides, American-made, 1900, 3 1/2" l., 2 1/2" h........................ **700**

Elephant - Elephant with Bent Knee - 447 - cast iron, grey finish, Kenton Mfg. Co., 1904, 4 7/8" l., 3 1/2" h.............................. **450**

Football Player - 11 - cast iron, bronzed finish, A.C. Williams Co., 1910-31, 5 7/8", (W. 12) **450**

Foxy Grandpa (Grandpa Bank) - 320 - cast iron, w/screw, silver paint, Wing Mfg.

Co. 1900 & Hubley Mfg. Co. 1920s, 5 1/2" h. (W. 23) 350

Gen. Sheridan on Base - 50 - cast iron, officer astride rearing horse, good gold paint, Arcade Mfg. Co., 1910-25, 2 3/8 x 4" base, 6" h. (W. 88) 550

General Butler - 54 - cast iron, man in the form of a frog reads "Bonds & Yachts for Me - For the Masses This is $1,000,000," J. & E. Stevens Co., 1884, 6 1/2" h., W. 294 2,000-2,500

Globe - Globe on Arc - 789 - cast iron, dark blue & gold, Grey Iron Casting Co., 1900-03, 5 1/4" h. 286

Golliwog - 85 - cast iron, red, blue & black paint, John Harper Ltd., England, 1910-25, 6 3/16" h. (W. 3) 250

Goose - "Red Goose Shoes" - 610 - cast iron, red body w/yellow bill & feet, Arcade Mfg. Co., ca. 1920s, very good, 3 3/4" h. 385

Heater - Space Heater (Bird) - 1087 - cast iron, six-sided upright heater w/openwork design of Bird of Paradise, Chamberlain & Hill, England, ca. 1892, 4" sq., 6 1/2" h. (W. 320) 117

Heater - Ace heater (Flowers) - 1094 - cast iron, England, ca. 1890, 3 7/8 x 4 1/8 x 6 1/4" h. 176

Horse - Good Luck Horseshoe - 508 - cast iron, shown w/Buster Brown & Tige, Arcade Mfg. Co., 1908-32, 4 3/4" l., 4 1/2" h. (W. 83) 300

Humpty Dumpty - 42 - cast iron, seated on tall chimney-like wall, red, white & brown, American-made, 1930s, 5 1/2" h 550

Indian - Indian Bust of Chief Dowagiac, white metal w/bronzed finish, name embossed at front base, 6 3/8" h. (R 13) 138

Indian - Indian Bust of Chief Shawmut, white metal w/bronzed finish, 6 5/8" h. (R 53) 33

Indian - The Indian Family - 224 - cast iron, busts of Indian chief, squaw, & papoose, bronzed finish, J.M. Harper Co., 1905, 3 5/8" h. (W. 289) 650

Indian - Two-Faced Indian (Indian Toy Bank) - 215 - cast iron, turnpin, chief in full headdress, bronzed finish w/silver trim, A.C. Williams Co., 1901-06, 3 3/4" w., 4 5/16" h. 750

Indian - Indian with Tomahawk - 228 - cast iron, red, brown & tan paint, Hubley Mfg. Co., 1915-30s, 5 7/8" h. (W. 39) 900

Lion - Lion on Wheels - 760 - cast iron, gilt paint, A.C. Williams Co., 1920s, 4 5/8" l., 4 1/2" h., W. 95 350

Lion with Tail Right Still Bank

*Lion - Lion, Tail Right -755 - cast iron, Arcade Mfg. Co. 1910-13 & A.C. Williams Co. 1905-31, original gold paint, 4 7/8" l., 4" h. (ILLUS.) 85

*Mary & Little Lamb - 164 - cast iron, white w/red trim, American-made, 1902, 4 3/8" h. (W. 1) 650

Mascot - 3 - cast iron, boy standing on baseball, bronze & red paint, "American and National League Ball," Hubley Mfg. Co., 1914, 5 13/16" h. 1,200

Mascot, "Alabama Crimson," model of elephant standing & leaning on football, white metal w/bronzed finish, 6 1/8" h., R 63 (ILLUS. bottom row, right, with Auburn Tigers) 72

Various Mascot Still Banks

Mascot, "Auburn Tigers," model of recumbent tiger on large football, white metal w/golden finish, 4 1/8" h., R66 (ILLUS. top row, left) 33

Mascot, "Bevo - Texas," model of bull-headed football player, white metal w/bronzed finish, no base plate, 5 3/4" h. (R 102) 77

Mascot, "Clemson Tiger," model of tiger standing & leaning on football, white metal w/golden bronzed finish, 6 3/8" h. (unlisted) 99

Mascot, "Georgia Bulldogs," model of bulldog standing & leaning on football, white metal w/bronzed finish, 6" h. (R 72 var.) 72

Mascot, "Iowa Hawkeyes," model of hawk in football uniform, white metal w/bronzed finish, no base plate, 5 1/2", R 75 (ILLUS. top row, far right w/Auburn Tigers) 28

Mascot, "Oregon State," model of beaver standing & leaning on football, white metal w/bronzed finish, 6" h. (R 97) 187

Mascot, "Save with Torchy," model of standing torch figure leaning on a piggy bank, white metal w/bronzed finish, 6 1/2" h., R 286 (ILLUS. bottom row, left with Auburn Tigers) 72

Mascot, "St. Louis Cardinals," model of cardinal in baseball uniform holding bag & leaning on large baseball, white metal w/golden finish, 6 1/2" h. (R 101) 127

Mascot, "UCLA Bruins," model of bear standing & leaning on football, white metal w/bronzed finish, 6 1/2" h., R 84 varient (ILLUS. top row center w/Auburn Tigers) 110

Mascot, "Wisconsin Badgers," model of badger standing & leaning on football, white metal w/bronzed finish, 6 1/4" h., R

104 (ILLUS. bottom row, center, w/Auburn Tigers) **99**

Mermaid - 34 - cast iron, girl seated in boat, gold paint, Grey Iron Casting Co.(?), 1900(?), 4" l., 4 9/16" h. (W. 5) **400**

Mickey Mouse Playing Mandolin - 203 - white metal, Mickey seated on large drum, painted, Arthur Shaw & Co., England, 1934, 4 11/16" h. **350**

Monkeys - Three Wise Monkeys - 743 - cast iron, embossed "See, Hear & Speak No Evil" on base, A.C. Williams Co., 1910-12, excellent, 3 1/4" x 3 1/2" **250**

Mutt & Jeff - 157 - cast iron, bronze-colored paint, A.C. Williams Co., 1912-31, 3 1/2" x 4 1/4" h., W. 13 .... **250**

Owl - 597 - cast iron, orange & white, Vindex, 1930, pristine, 2 1/2" w., 4 1/4" h. (W. 203)........................ **400**

***Pershing - Gen. Pershing - 150 -** bronze electroplated cast iron, bust of the general, Grey Iron Casting Co., patented 1918, 7 3/4" h. (W. 312)......................... **150**

Pig - Pig (small) - 623 - cast iron, standing, white paint, Arcade, 1910-32, 2 x 4", W184 (slight paint wear)................... **132**

Policeman - 182 - cast iron, blue & black paint, Arcade Mfg. Co., 1920-34, 5 1/2" h. (W. 9) **600**

Possum - Billy Possum - 563 - cast iron, "Possum & Taters" on base, golden bronze paint w/black trim, J.M. Harper Co., 1908, 4 3/4" l., 3" h.......................... **450**

Rabbit - Rabbit Standing beside small Office Building, white metal w/bronzed finish, marked "Coast Federal Savings," 5 1/8" h. (R 561)........................ **242**

Rabbit - Seated Rabbit (small) - 568 - cast iron, Arcade Mfg. Co., 1910-20s, 3 5/8" h. (W. 96)......................... **171**

Record Player - "Sunny Suds" Record Player - 824 - brass, model of early upright cabinet-type w/wording "Save For Your Sunny Suds," American-made, early 20th c., 4 1/2" h. **110**

***Recruit (Cutie) - 40 -** cast iron, white body & blue pants, John Harper, Ltd., England, ca. 1918, 6 1/8" h. (worn paint) **451**

Reindeer - Large Reindeer (Elk) - 737 - cast iron, red paint, A.C. Williams Co., 1910-35, 5 1/4" l., 9 1/2" h. **150**

Rhino - 721 - cast iron, black w/gold horn, Arcade Mfg. Co., 1910-25, very good, 2 5/8" h. , 5" l. (W. 252).................. **300**

Roosevelt, Franklin D. - Roosevelt ("New Deal") - 148 - cast iron, bust of Roosevelt, Kenton Mfg. Co., 1933-36, 5" h. **125**

Roosevelt, Theodore - "Teddy" - 120 - cast iron, bust of Roosevelt on pedestal base, A.C. Williams Co., 1919, 3 1/2" w., 5" h. **242**

Rooster - Polish Rooster - 541 - cast iron, black & white w/red topknot, yellow legs, American-made, 5 1/2" h. (W. 186).......... **800**

Rumpelstiltskin -75 - cast iron, "Do You Know Me" on feet & base, red w/gold trim, American-made, 1910s, 2 5/16" w., 6" h. (W. 49)........................ **200**

Safe bank - Grant bust, cast iron, figural bust of General Grant at top of safe, black, J.M. Harper, 1903...................... **450**

Safe bank - Washington bust, cast iron, figural bust of George Washington at top of safe, black, J.M. Harper, 1903.................. **450**

Safe - "Children's Safe Deposit," cast iron, raised wording on door w/raised scrolls, short rounded feet, 4 1/8" h. (ISB 191)........................ **88**

Safe - Hexagonal Door, cast iron & tin, large door knob, raised on short legs, 4" h., ISB 308 var. (slight surface rust on door) **116**

Safe - "Save Your Pennies," cast iron, pierced scroll door w/wording, on short legs, 3 1/2" h. (ISB 260) **204**

Security Safe Deposit Bank

Safe - "Security Safe Deposit," cast iron, raised wording around central dial knob, zig-zag border band, black w/gold trim, 5 7/8" h., ISB 40 (ILLUS.).................... **308**

Security Safe Home Deposit Bank

Safe - "Security Safe Home Deposit," cast iron & tin, two dials on door w/raised wording around five-point star, 6 3/4" h., ISB 230 (ILLUS.) **143**

Safe - "Sport," cast iron, raised word above embossed scene of young boy & begging dog on door, black w/gold trim, 3" h. (ISB 290)........................ **83**

Safe - "Star Safe," cast iron & tin, large knob & wording on door, 3 1/2" h. (ISB 113)........................ **50**

Safe - Watch Dog safe - cast iron, large embossed reclining dog on the door, no wording on the door, on small feet, Stevens, 6" h........................ **460**

Sailor (large) - 29 - cast iron, saluting & holding oar, silver & blue uniform w/flesh-colored face, Hubley Mfg. Co., 1905-15, 5 5/8" h. (W. 16)......................... **250**

Santa Claus - Santa - 56 - cast iron, missing removable wire tree (value could double w/tree intact), Ives(?), ca. 1890s, 7 1/4" h., W. 31 750

Santa Claus - Santa Claus - 59 - cast iron, standing figure in old-fashioned red suit, Wing Mfg. Co. ca. 1900 & Hubley Mfg. Co. 1906, 5 7/8" h. (W. 30) 450

Santa Claus - Santa "Save & Smile" - 60 - cast iron, hanging-type, black w/red cap, England, 7 1/4" h. 850

Santa Claus - Santa with Tree - 61 - cast iron, red, white & green paint, Hubley Mfg. Co., 1914-30, 5 7/8" h. (W. 32)............. 400

Satchel - 1268 - heavy steel, model of carpetback bronzed finish, American-made, 2 1/2 x 3 3/8 x 5 3/4" 127

Shell Bank (1 1/2 Inch) - 1420 - World War I deactivated artillery shell, Ferrosteel Mfg. Co., 1919, 8 1/16" h. (W. 385)................. 50

Ship - Indiana Paddle Wheeler - 1442 - cast iron, black w/red trim, patented by Robert J. Sellentine, 1896, 7 1/8" l. 850

Ship - Fortune Ship - 1457 - cast iron, embossed "When My Fortune Ship Comes In" on deck, yellow & brown, Brighton, England, 5 3/8" l., 4 1/8" h. (W. 249) 1,500

Ship - Gunboat - 1462 - cast iron, pull toy-type, black & white paint, Kenton Mfg. Co.(?), ca. 1910, 8 1/2" l., 2 3/4" h. with mast, W. 145 600

Ship - Steamboat (6 holes) - 1461 - cast iron, sidewheeler w/sidewheel pierced w/six holes, silver w/black trim, American-made, 8 1/8" l., 2 11/16" h. (W. 150)... 1,000

Soldier - Doughboy - 48 - cast iron, World War I soldier, brown & tan paint, Grey Iron Casting Co., 1919, 7" h. (W. 40) 500

*Soldier (Minuteman) - 44 - cast iron, standing soldier w/rifle, Hubley Mfg. Co., 1905-06, 6" h. (W. 15)................................ 450

Soldier - Officer (Cadet) - 8 - cast iron, blue paint w/gold stripes, Hubley Mfg. Co., 1905-15, 5 3/4" h. (W. 7) 650

Songbird on Stump (Bird Toy Bank) - 664 - cast iron, gold paint, A.C. Williams Co., 1912-20s, 4 3/4" h. (W. 209)........................ 350

Statue of Liberty - 1164 - cast iron, worn gold paint, A.C. Williams Co., ca. 1910-early 1930s, 2 1/4" sq., 6 1/16" h. (W. 269).. 83

Statue of Liberty - 1166 - cast iron, green paint, Wing Mfg. Co. ca. 1900 & Kenton Mfg. Co. 1911-1932, 3 3/8 x 3 7/16 x 9 5/8" h. (W. 268)............................. 2,000

Stove - Mellow Stove - 1363 - cast iron, cylindrical model of stove, Liberty Toy Co., 3 9/16" h... 44

Taft-Sherman - 109 - cast iron, "Smiling Jim" & "Peaceful Bill" mask of each presidential candidate back-to-back, bronzed finish, J.M. Harper, 1908, 2 3/4" w., 4" h. (W. 314)... 500

Tank - "Tank Savings Bank" - 1417 - cast iron, model of a WW I tank, Ferrosteel, ca. 1919, 9 1/2" l., 4" h. 250

Turkey - Large Turkey - 585 - cast iron, black & red paint, A.C. Williams Co., 1905-12, 4" w., 4 1/4" h. (W. 194)................. 600

U.S. Mailbox - U.S. Mail - 836 - cast iron, small combination trap, silver & red paint, some paint wear, Kenton Mfg. co., 3 x 3 1/2 x 4 3/4" h. 77

Washington, George - Washington, Tall Bust - 153 - cast iron, Grey Iron Casting Co., late 1920s, 3 7/8" w., 8" h...................... 525

Wisconsin War Eagle - 678 - cast iron, horizontal cylinder on tiny feet, the end embossed w/a large perched eagle & wording "Wisconsin's Historic Eagle - Old Age," ca. 1880, 2 7/8" h. 407

Tin

Bokar Coffee Advertising Tin Bank

Advertising-type, "Bokar Coffee," upright coffee tin-form, black ground w/white panel, red & black wording, 1 1/2 x 2 1/8", 4" h. (ILLUS.)............................ 18

Conoco Motor Oil Can Tin Bank

Advertising-type, "Conoco Germ Processed Motor Oil," miniature oil can in white & green w/red, white & green printing, 2" d., 3 1/2" h. (ILLUS.)............................ 45

Harold Lloyd, semi-mechanical, model of actor's head & shoulders w/mouth that opens so that tongue protrudes & eyes roll, Selhumer & Strauss, Germany, 1925, 5 1/2" h. (PL 234) .... 1,000+

Tin Mailbox Bank

Mailbox, miniature model printed in red, white & blue, made in Japan, 1 1/4 x 1 3/4", 2 3/4" h. (ILLUS.) **25**

BARBERIANA

Razor Blade Banks

Barber, "Looie" found in right handed & left handed versions, 7" h. **$85-100**

"Tony" Razor Blade Bank

Barber, "Tony," Ceramic Arts Studio, 4 3/4" h. (ILLUS.) **90-100**

Barber Chair Razor Blade Bank

Barber chair, large, 5 3/4" h. (ILLUS.) **125-150**

Cleminson Barber Head Blade Bank

Barber head, Cleminson, different colors on collar, 4" h. (ILLUS.) **30-35**

Common Barber Pole

Barber pole, common, made in Japan, usually reads "Blades" on front but could have other words (ILLUS.) **15-25**

Barber Pole Razor Blade Bank

Barber poles, red & white (various designs), 6" h. (ILLUS. of one) **25-35**

Barbershop Quartet Razor Blade Bank

Barbershop quartet, "The Gay Blades," 5 1/4 x 4 1/4" (ILLUS.) **75-100**

Bell-Shaped Cleminson Blade Bank

Bell-shaped, man shaving, Cleminson, 3 1/4" h. (personalized $45-55) (ILLUS.)... **25-35**

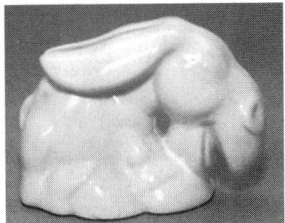

Donkey Razor Blade Bank

Donkey, ceramic, Listerine, 1936, 2 1/4" h. (ILLUS.) **20-30**

Elephant Razor Blade Bank

Elephant, ceramic, Listerine, 1936, 2 1/2" h. (ILLUS.) **25-35**
EverReady, resembles a treasure chest, top reads "For Old Blades," 1 3/4" h. **35-40**

Frog Razor Blade Bank

Frog, ceramic, Listerine, 3" h. (ILLUS) **15-25**

Green & Yellow Frog Razor Blade Bank

Frog, "For Used Blades" on front base, found in green & yellow, made in Japan, 3" h. (ILLUS.) **60-70**

Decora Ceramics Blade Bank

Grinding stone, by Decora Ceramics Ins., reads "For Dull Ones," 2 3/4" h. (ILLUS.) **80-100**

House-shaped Blade Bank

House, tin, by Twinplex, "Home for Aged Blades," on front, "Dull House" on roof, 2 1/4" (ILLUS.) **125-150**
Metal Gem Blades, looks like a book or ledger, reads "Record Shaves" on the cover, top contains slot & reads "File Old Blades Here," 1 7/8" h. **30-40**
Ocean Spray Cranberry Sauce, 2 5/8" h. **35-45**
Palmolive Shaving Soap, handy box for used razor blades, 2" h. **35-40**

Razor Bum Blade Bank

Razor Bum, poem imprinted on front, 8" h. (ILLUS.) **85-100**

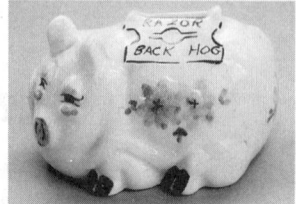

Razor Back Hog Bank

Razor Back Hog, by Bayet Pottery of California, 2 1/2" h. (ILLUS.) **55-65**

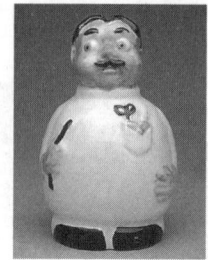

Roly Poly Barber

Roly poly barber, California Cleminsons, 5" (ILLUS.) **65-75**

Sheraton Hotels Paper Envelope

Sheraton Hotels, paper envelope for used blades to protect maids' fingers from being cut when emptying trash, w/drawing of maid w/bandage on finger & "Please!

put used Razor Blades in this cup," 4 1/4" h. (ILLUS.) **10-15**

U.S. Deck Paint Sample Tin

U.S. Deck Paint sample tin, top contains slot for used razor blades w/"This label safeguards sharp buyers" & "This slot safeguards dull blades," 2 1/4" h. (ILLUS.) **40-50**
Vault, Click Modern Bakelite, 2 1/4" h. **25-35**
Wolfs Head Motor Oil, 3 1/2" h. **30-40**

BASEBALL MEMORABILIA

Baseball was reputedly invented by Abner Doubleday as he laid out a diamond-shaped field with four bases at Cooperstown, New York. A popular game from its inception, by 1869 it was able to support its first all-professional team, the Cincinnati Red Stockings. The National League was organized in 1876 and though the American League was first formed in 1900, it was not officially recognized until 1903. Today, the "national pastime" has millions of fans and collecting baseball memorabilia has become a major hobby with enthusiastic collectors seeking out items associated with players such as Babe Ruth, Lou Gehrig, and others who became legends in their own lifetimes. Though baseball cards, issued as advertising premiums for bubble gum and other products, seem to dominate the field there are numerous other items available.

Advertisement, "Tuxedo Tobacco," full color lithograph w/a large color bust portrait of Christy Mathewson on the right & advertising & a picture of a tin of tobacco on the left, yellow background w/red border & red & black wording, 1912, a few abrasions & very slight border chipping, 11 x 20 3/4" (ILLUS. below) **$9,620**

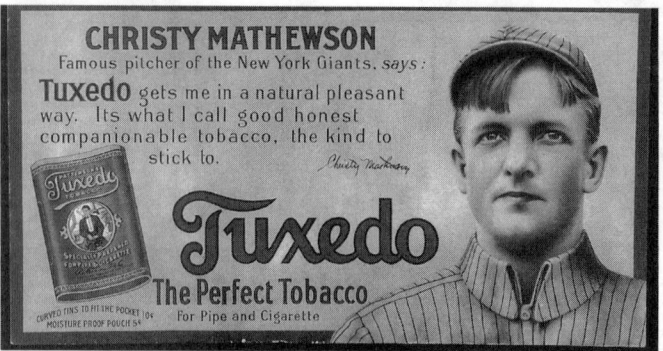

Early Mathewson Tobacco Sign

Baseball, 1921 New York Giants team-signed, Official National League model, signed in black ink by 27 members of the team, very good condition **12,502**

Baseball, 1925 Washington Senators team-signed, Official American League model, signed in black ink by 27 members of the team, excellent to mint **2,300**

Baseball, 1938 Brooklyn Dodgers team-signed, Spalding ball signed in black ink by 17 members of the team including Babe Ruth, very good condition **2,922**

Baseball, 1942 Pittsburgh Pirates team-signed, Official National League model, signed in various shades of ink by 21 members of the team including Honus Wagner, near mint **1,392**

Baseball, 1956 Brooklyn Dodgers team-signed, Official National League model, signed in blue ink by 29 members of the team, near mint **2,657**

Baseball, 1961 New York Yankees team-signed, DeBeer & Son Official League Baseball, signed by 19 members of the team, near mint **3,780**

Baseball, 1969 New York Mets team-signed, Official National League model, signed in blue ink by 32 members of the team, near mint **2,195**

Baseball, 1975 Cincinnati Reds team-signed, Official National League model, signed in black ink by 26 members of the team, near mint **2,094**

Baseball, Carlton Fisk's record setting 328th home run ball, August 17, 1990, hit during the second game of a double-header at Arlington Stadium, later inscribed by Fisk to umpire Durwood Merrill, included a letter of authenticity from Merrill **2,132**

Baseball, Casey Stengel-signed, Official National League model, signed in black ink "Best Wishes - Casey Stengel," slightly light, excellent **843**

Baseball, multi-autographed, including Joe Jackson, Babe Ruth, Ty Cobb & Ray Chapman, Official American League model, signatures in fair to excellent condition, probably late teens **10,189**

Baseball cap, Lou Boudreau game-worn cap, black & red Cleveland Indians model, signed by Boudreau under the bill, 1940s **1,236**

Very Rare Babe Ruth Rookie Card

Baseball card, Babe Ruth, 1915 M101-5 Sporting News #151, rookie card for Babe Ruth, grade 8, near mint (ILLUS.) .. **60,439**

Baseball card, Carl Yastrzemski, 1963 Fleer #8, mint **900**

Baseball card, Clark Griffith, 1911 Gold Border T205 card w/color portrait of Clark Griffith, American Tobacco Company, grade 8 .... **2,839**

Baseball card, Don Mattingly, rookie card, 1984 Topps Tiffany #8, mint **633**

Baseball card, Jackie Robinson, 1955 Tops #50, near mint **1,813**

Rare Joe Jackson Rookie Card

Baseball card, Joe Jackson, 1909 E90-1 American Caramel card, rookie card for Jackson, strong colors & well focused, corners rounded, light surface wrinkles in the border, very good condition (ILLUS.) .. **5,420**

Baseball card, Joe Jackson, 1915 Cracker Jack #103, half-length batting pose of Jackson on a red ground, grade 6 .... **8,733**

Baseball card, Mickey Mantle, 1951 Bowman #253, very good to excellent **2,132**

Goudey 1933 Napoleon Lajoie Card

Baseball card, Napoleon Lajoie, 1933 Goudey #106, omitted from the 1933 set & actually printed in 1934 in limited numbers & sent only to card collectors requesting it, condition 8 .... **40,679**

Baseball card, P.T. Somers, 1887 N172 Old Judge card w/photo of P.T. Somers in a pitching pose, near mint **1,180**

Baseball card, Pete Rose, 1968 Topps #230, mint **805**

Baseball card, Roberto Clemente, 1955 Topps #164, near mint **4,934**

Baseball card, Roy Campanella, 1953 Bowman #46, mint **7,216**

1964 Topps Sandy Koufax Card

Baseball card, Sandy Koufax, 1964 Topps #200, condition 9 (ILLUS.) **1,834**

Very Rare 1948 Satchel Page Card

Baseball card, Satchel Page, 1948 Leaf #8, part of a very rare post-war series of cards, condition 7 (ILLUS.) **12,641**

Baseball card, Super Stars - Harmon Killebrew, Willie Mays, Mickey Mantle, 1968 Tops #490, mint **928**

Baseball card, Ted Williams, 1957 Topps #1, near mint.. **1,668**

Baseball card, Walter Johnson, T206, color half-length portrait of Johnson, back w/Old Mill advertising, near mint **7,464**

Baseball card, Willie Mays, 1953 Topps #244, near mint **7,464**

Baseball card, Yogi Berra, 1949 Bowman #60, mint **3,364**

Baseball glove, pre-war store model Martin DiHigo split fingered model, facsimile signature of the player, faint traces original silver highlighting (checking on reverse, tear at the inner heel) **743**

Rare Mantle & Maris Bobbin' Heads

Bobbin' head dolls, Mickey Mantle & Roger Maris, molded plastic w/life-like faces, great color & original paint & gloss, Mantle doll w/slight chip on rear of neck, early 1960s, the pr. (ILLUS.) **1,600**

DeWitt's 1877 Base Ball Guide

Book, "DeWitt's Base Ball Guide - 1877," yellow paper cover w/black print & a wood cut of an early pitcher, very minor imperfections (ILLUS.)................................. **1,558**

Rare Book About Ted Williams

Book, "The Splendid Splinter - The Story of How the Sportswriters Tried to Chop up the Splinter for Firewood," by Ted Blood, 1960, Exposition Press, hardcover, complete w/dust jacket (ILLUS.)........................ **1,091**

Bracelet, 1978 World Series umpire model presented to Frank Pulli, National League umpire, top section w/a design of a baseball inset w/curved bands of tiny diamonds & the raised wording "World Series 1978," flanked by the logo initials of Los Angeles & New York, 18k gold, near mint... **1,392**

Rare 1870 Baseball Carte de Visite

Carte de visite, photo montage of the 1870 Forest City Base Ball Club team of Rockford, Illinois, the name under each player, marked on the back "G.W. Barnes, Photographer - Rockford, Ill." (ILLUS.)............. **4,478**

1915 Boston Red Sox Commemorative

Commemorative, oversized natural leather piece irregularly cut & printed w/a central oval team photo of the 1915 Boston Red Sox World Series Champion team surrounded by several shots of individual players, printed under the center picture "Red Sox - World Champions - 1915," minor tears, 32 x 39" (ILLUS.) **3,061**

High school yearbook, 1949 Commerce High School, Mickey Mantle's high school & year of graduation, white covers w/blue printing "1949 - Bengal Tales," includes various photos of Mantle as a student, Commerce, Oklahoma (moderate wear)... **991**

Jersey, child's store model, "Lou Gehrig" in blue across the front of the white flannel shirt, the number "4" on the back & w/the Empire label in the collar, 1935 (wear, some light staining & fabric loss on the number)... **373**

Jersey, Denny Galehouse St. Louis Browns 1941-42 game-worn jersey, white flannel w/zipper front, black & red team name across the front & "11" on the back, labeled, size 44 (use wear) **5,640**

Lithograph, "Union Prisoners at Salisbury, N.C.," large color view of Civil War Union soldiers playing a game of baseball at the Confederate prison camp in Salisbury, North Carolina, many figures shown in the panoramic landscape, by Goupil & Co., New York, New York, 1863, framed, print 27 1/2 x 42 1/2" (professionally cleaned).. **22,412**

Notepad, blue cover w/double color-printed cartoon of Ted Williams, titled "Sports Oddities - Ted Williams" above notes about his career, complete & unused, 1951, 5 3/8 x 8 7/8" (slight natural cover discoloration) **304**

Pencil, mechanical advertising-type, mottled green & mottled white celluloid, printed in red "Compliments of Fred Stone Rice-Stix Dry Goods Co.," also w/a black & white oval reserve w/portraits of Dizzy & Daffy Dean separated by the red wording "Dizzy and Paul Dean Shirts," around

the reserve is printed "Sole Distributors of Dizzy and Paul Dean Shirts," 1935 .... **2,839**

Photograph, 1927 original wire photo showing Babe Ruth signing his 1927 Yankees contract while Jacob Ruppert & Ed Barrow look on, this contract made Ruth the highest paid baseball player in the history of the game to that time, 6 1/2 x 8 1/2" **1,091**

Photograph, black & white action shot of Ray Chapman of Cleveland during the 1918 season fielding a ground ball, 7 x 10" **373**

Photograph, original black & white wire photo of Lou Gehrig as he stretches to catch a throw during 1935 spring training, 6 x 8" (minor creases & restored scrape)...... **460**

Fine Early Ty Cobb Photograph

Photograph, Ty Cobb photographed by Charles Conlon, oversized image showing Cobb in a pensive mood, shown wearing a Detroit Tigers uniform, Conlon border notations on the left edge, ca. 1915-16, 7 3/4 x 9 1/4" (ILLUS.) **3,980**

Scarce Joe DiMaggio Promotional Pin

Pinback button, "Joe DiMaggio TV Club - Buitoni Macaroni," red print on white w/black & white face of DiMaggio in the center, premium from the late 1940s children's show, "The Buitoni Show," host of the program, ca. 1948, near mint (ILLUS.).. **1,201**

Pinback button, large button w/a dark blue background & color bust portrait of Babe Ruth w/the white wording "Ask me," Texaco premium, ca. 1935, near mint, 3" d........ **452**

Pinback button, souvenir-type, "Champions -1929 - Cubs Team," long oval w/printed photo of the Chicago Cubs team, issued following their capture of the National League pennant, 2 3/4" l........... **886**

Pocket   watch,   presentation-type, presented to Honus Wagner in 1908 on the occasion of "Honus Wagner Day" in Pittsburgh, open-faced 18k gold minute repeating Jules Jurgensen watch w/engraved monogram on back & inscription on the inside, in original fitted, velvet-lined presentation case w/maker's card **29,079**

Postcard, real photo-type, team group shot of the St. Paul Gophers, "World's Colored Champions," shows all members of this early black baseball team that disbanded after only one season, 1909 (minor surface spots, small crease, corner wear) **1,497**

Poster, advertising-type, "Fatima Cigarettes," large black & white team photo of the 1915 Boston Red Sox team including Babe Ruth, name of team members under photo & color picture of pack of cigarettes in the lower right corner, reads across the bottom "Red Sox Ready To Do Battle For World's Championship," 12 x 18" (fold lines) **2,990**

Poster, "Hassan Cigarettes," long full-color poster used to promote the 1912 Hassan T202 Triple Folder set, shows a color portrait of Christy Mathewson flanked by vertical baseball bats & a pack of cigarettes above & below, one of three known, framed, 15 x 35" (some very subtle professional restoration) **50,511**

Very Rare Early Press Pin

Press pin, 1911 Philadelphia Athletics World Series pin, blue-enameled top pin w/"Press" suspending a wide blue ribbon printed in white "World's Series Shibe Park Philadelphia 1911," suspends a rounded scalloped medal w/a blue enamel border band w/gold wording "American Base Ball Club of Philadelphia," centering a design of an elephant above a pair of crossed bats & ball over "Athletics," extremely rare, near mint (ILLUS.) **14,920**

Press pin, 1912 New York Giants World Series, blue enamel bar at top w/"Press" suspending a wide blue ribbon printed in gold "World's Series Brush Stadium Polo Grounds New York 1912," suspending a flat round gilt medallion cast in low-relief w/a batter & the phrase "New York Giants vs. Boston Red Sox," excellent condition .. **6,412**

Press pin, 1913 New York Giants World Series, rounded slightly scalloped brass pin w/a circle & crossbar in blue enamel

w/gold lettering reading "Worlds - 'Giants' - Series," center half-round reserves, one w/crossed bats above the other w/"1913," mint **3,980**

Press pin, 1938 All Star Game, white celluloid printed in red "Press - All Star Game - Crosley Field - Cincinnati 1938" w/the "C" & star Cincinnati Reds logo in the center, 1/2" d. (slight cracking, some fading) **1,600**

Print, advertising-type, "The Boston Club Cigars and Tobacco," advertising at top above a large black & white image of a baseball game in progress, titled below image "Opening Game of the Boston Base-Ball Club," by John A. Andrews & Co., 1889, framed, 20 x 24" (areas of toning, slight border chips) **3,061**

Print, long black & white photographic print of the 1917 Chicago White Sox, shown standing in Comiskey Park w/the stadium crowd in the background, titled across the top "Comiskey's Champion White Sox - 1917," matted & framed, 17 x 38" **3,705**

Rare 1888 Cincinnati Game Program

Program, "1888 Cincinnati Base Ball Club," eight-fold style w/the cover printed in yellow, red, white & black centered by a bust portrait of Tony Mullane, scorecard for an American Association game between Cincinnati & Brooklyn, partially scored in pencil, excellent condition, 4 x 6 1/4" (ILLUS.) **1,091**

Program, 1914 World Series, Philadelphia Athletics, cover design in pink, red, white & black features four performing elephants, 24 pp., excellent condition **2,415**

Program, 1920 Cleveland Indians World Series, red, black, grey & brown, large graphic of a Native American chief shooting an arrow, reads "Read The Pink Press - Best For Live Sports - World Series Official Score Card - Price 10¢," also in bottom panel "The Cleveland Base Ball Co. - Visitors To The City Ask anybody in Cleveland about Euclid Beach - The Humphrey Co.," 12 pp., unscored (near mint) **5,182**

Program, 1923 New York Yankees World Series, grey ground printed in red, black & white, centered by large oval black & white bust photos of Miller Huggins &

John McGraw, the team managers, printed across the top "Yankees vs Giants - 1923" (slight vertical fold, some minor staining on back)... **900**

Program from First All Star Game

Program, 1933 All Star game, from first All Star game held in Chicago in conjunction w/the 1933 Century of Progress Exposition, cover printed in red, white, blue & black w/a head photo of Louis Comiskey at the top flanked by the title above a large baseball-shaped ad reading "always a hit - Blue Valley Butter - finer flavor," near mint, beware of reproductions (ILLUS.)... **3,289**

Shaving mug, occupational, porcelain w/the name of the original owner in gold above a pair of crossed baseball bats over a baseball, ca. 1890s (very slight wear).. **1,780**

1920s Babe Ruth Sheet Music

Sheet music, "Along Came Ruth," by Irving Berlin, originally published in 1914 but did not relate to Ruth or baseball, re-released in the 1920s w/the black & white oval portrait of Ruth w/a facsimile signature, 6 pp., slight pencil notations at top, two very small stains, some areas of tape residue on back cover (ILLUS.)..................... **417**

Stadium seats, two-seat unit from the original Yankee Stadium, blue slatted backs, seats & cast-iron arm rests, all original hardware, numbers "10" & "9" on the backs **3,376**

Stock certificate, Philadelphia Athletics American Association, dated July 23, 1889, signed by various officers.................... **805**

Store display sign, "Draper & Maynard Sporting Goods," color-lithographed cardboard, three-section, the large

center section w/a view of the factory over a grouping of baseball mitts, bats & masks, on the left panel a grouping of small photos of members of the 1911 American League Champion Philadelphia Athletics & on the right a grouping of the members of the 1911 National League Champion New York Giants, 1912, overall 22 x 46" (some professional restoration)............................ **22,412**

Store display sign, "The Peach Gloves," color lithograph w/a large scene of various noted players of the early 20th c. in action poses in a baseball stadium w/a high fence w/advertising in the background beside bleachers, last name of each player near his foot, ca. 1910, matted & framed, 19 1/2 x 29 3/4".................. **35,187**

Rare Early Advertising Poster with a Baseball Theme

Store poster, "Old Judge Cigarettes," color lithographed elaborate design w/numerous color vignettes of players of the era in action, the large central ring enclosing a color scene of a baseball stadium, ca. 1888, professionally restored, framed, poster 27 x 28" (ILLUS.)............................ **29,832**

Store sign, "Schafer Beer," color-printed self-framed cardboard, large central color group shot of the 1955 Brooklyn Dodgers, brown frame w/gold liner printed w/name of the beer in a red oval at the top & printed on the lower gold liner w/"World Champion Brooklyn Dodgers," 13 x 20 3/4" (minor flaws) **1,760**

Store sign, "Sugar Crisp" color-printed cardboard, large bust portrait of Leo Durocher holding a copy of the "Sugar Crisp Baseball Facts and Fun Book," his name above his head on a white background, wording at right reads "Get this Great Baseball Book - Only 15¢ and 2 boxtops from Sugar Crisp," early 1950s, 23 x 28" **675**

Ticket stub, 1933 All-star Game, Comiskey Park, All Star American-National League Ball Game, July 6, 1933, printed in red, black & white (slight vertical tear at top, slight corner crease) **1,497**

Trolley car signs, "Lucky Strike Cigarette," color-printed cardboard, each long rectangular sign w/a dark green background & the large red dot logo on the left side, a color image of an early baseball player in action on the right under his name, includes Paul Waner, Bob Grove, Lloyd Waner, Harry Heilman & Tony Lazzeri, bright colors & near mint, 1928, each 10 1/2 x 20 1/2", set of 5............................ **22,413**

Vending machine, baseball card & bubble gum, large cast-metal red-painted upper section w/view windows for baseball cards flanking the gumball holder, fully operational, on a repainted black iron post & round foot, 1950s, 42" h. **2,415**

BASKETS

The American Indians were the first basket weavers on this continent and, of necessity, the early Colonial settlers and their descendants pursued this artistic handicraft to provide essential containers for berries, eggs and endless other items to be carried or stored. Rye straw, split willow and reeds are but a few of the wide variety of materials used. The Nantucket baskets, plainly and sturdily constructed, along with those made by specialized groups, would seem to draw the greatest attention to this area of collecting.

Berry basket, stave & wire construction, two swing handles, 3 3/8 x 4 1/2"................ **$385**

"Buttocks" basket, finely woven splint w/38 ribs, bentwood handle, miniature size, 4 7/8" l., 2 5/8" h. **550**

"Buttocks" basket, tightly woven w/twenty ribs, natural light brown patina, 7" x 6 1/4" h. **165**

Gathering basket, round, woven splint w/dry natural finish, woven foot on base, shaped bentwood handle, 17 1/2" d., 16" h. **110**

"Melon" Basket

"Melon" basket, woven splint, 28-rib construction, five dark-stained bands, bentwood handle, 5 1/4 x 11" (ILLUS.)................ **523**

Melon basket, woven splint, twenty ribs w/old natural brown finish, 14" w., 13" h. **110**

Miniature basket, rectangular, woven splint, bentwood handle, 3 1/4 x 3 7/8" **220**

Miniature Woven Splint Basket

Miniature basket, woven splint ribbed basket w/bentwood handle, American, late 19th/early 20th c., 5 1/2" sq. (ILLUS.)............ **173**

Nantucket Basket w/Swing Handle

Nantucket basket, woven cane & splint w/round wooden bottom & bentwood swing handle, 9 1/2" d., 6" h., pieced repair at handle post (ILLUS.)............................ **485**

Nantucket basket, woven wicker, round w/thick wrapped rim & fixed arched bentwood handle, painted red, 19th c., 9 1/2" d., 8" h. w/handle **2,760**

Storage basket, cov., Pennsylvania round coil woven storage basket w/round fitted lid over cylinder-shaped body, ca. 1895, 17" d., 9" h. **157**

Storage basket, finely woven cane, squatty bulbous base w/fitted domed cover, painted green, New England, 19th c., 4 3/8" h. (wear) **1,725**

Utility basket, woven splint, round w/single wrapped rim, fixed bentwood handle, painted salmon, New England, 19th c., 10 1/2" d., 5 1/2" h. (paint wear) **518**

Utility basket, woven splint, rectangular w/two double rows of blue painted ribs, carved rigid bentwood handle, New England, 19th c., 11 1/2 x 16 1/4", 15 1/4" h. (breaks)............................... **288**

Wall basket, woven splint, rectangular form w/carved loop handle, painted green, early 19th c., 9 3/4 x 11 1/2", 7 1/2" h. **2,300**

Wall basket, woven splint w/wooden base, rectangular, two punched iron strap hangers on the extended back, painted yellow, early 19th c., 4 x 10 1/2", 7" h. (imperfections) **2,415**

BELLS

Ornate Carved Oriental Gong

Gong, an ornately carved mahogany arched frame, the pierced & scroll-carved crest centered by a large grotesque mask, stylized dragons at the bottom sids, narrow bottom rail w/trestle feet on replaced wheels, round bronze gong, probably China, original finish, ca. 1890, 48" w., 44" h. (ILLUS.) **$1,200**

Meneely Bell Foundry Steeple Bell

Steeple bell, bronze, cast at The Meneely Bell Foundry, West Troy, New York, 1875, in original iron & wood frame mount, 30 3/4" d. at base (ILLUS.) **3,500**

1860 Meneely Foundry Steeple Bell

Steeple bell, bronze, cast at The Meneely Foundry, West Troy, New York, 1860, complete, at least 30" d. at base (ILLUS.).. **1,750**

Finely Cast Buckeye Foundry Bell

Steeple bell, bronze, cast by C.W. Coffin at The Buckeye Bell Foundry, Cincinnati, Ohio, 1845, fully marked in three panels separated by cherubs at work & play, also a band of flowers & scrolls & a border band, 25 1/2" d. at base (ILLUS.) **4,500**

Hy Stuckstede Bell Co. Steeple Bell

Steeple bell, bronze, cast by The Hy Stuckstede Bell Co., St. Louis, Missouri, ca. 1881 (ILLUS.) **2,000**

BLACK AMERICANA

Over the past decade or so, this field of collecting has rapidly grown and today almost anything that relates to Black culture or illustrates Black Americana is considered a desirable collectible. Although many representations of African-Americans, especially on 19th and early 20th century advertising pieces and housewares, were cruel stereotypes, even these are collected as poignant reminders of how far American society has come since the dawning of the Civil Rights movement, and how far we still have to go. Other pieces related to this category will be found from time to time in such categories as Advertising Items, Banks, Character Collectibles, Kitchenwares, Signs and Signboards, Toys and several others. For a complete overview of this subject see Antique Trader Books' Black Americana Price Guide *with a special introduction by Julian Bond.*

Almanac, "Anti-Slavery Almanac - 1840," Volume 1, No. 5, published by the American Anti-Slavery Society, New York & Boston, combines usual almanac information w/stories on slavery outrages & anti-slavery agitation, 46 pp., 4 3/8 x 7 3/8" (soil & wear to wraps, one page missing, some soil & foxing) **$55**

Autograph, Booker T. Washington TLS, 1903, on Tuskegee Normal and Industrial Institute letterhead, good content, one page, folded in half (slight browning & soil) **135**

Book, "A Brave Black Regiment - History of the 54th Regiment of Massachusetts Volunteer Infantry, 1863-1865," by Luis F. Emilio, Boston Book Company, first edition, 1891, maps & illustrations, hard covers, 410 pp. (spine somewhat loose, pages a bit browned) **853**

Book, "The Negro American Family - A Social Study made by Atlanta University under the patronage of the Trustees of the John F. Slater Fund," The Atlanta University Press, 1908, first edition, edited by

W.E. B. DuBois, grey paper cover, 156 pp., 6 x 9" (some paper missing along cover edges, hole through back cover, dark stain in corner, soil) 28

Book, "The Story of the Lord's Dealings with Mrs. Amanda Smith, the Colored Evangelist," autobiography, introduction by J.M. Thoburn, recounts her travels around the world, illustrated, Meyer & Brother, Chicago, 1893, first edition, hard cover w/stamped gold portrait of Amanda Smith, 506 pp. (some cover wear, spine tight, paper slightly browned) 198

Book, "Who's Who in Colored America," edited by Joseph J. Boris, 1927, published by WWICA, Inc., New York, 1927, brown hard covers, hundreds of biographical sketches, illustrated, 333 pp., 7 3/4 x 11" 88

Booklet, "The Negro in the Abolitionist Movement," by Herbert Aptheker, International Publishers, orange paper covers, 1941, 48 pp., 5 1/4 x 7 3/4" (covers slightly soiled & browned)................................. 14

Slave Branding Iron

Branding iron, antebellum slave branding iron bearing initials "E.F." (ILLUS.) **1,100**

Broadside, "Monster Mass Meeting sponsored by Negro Democratic Club," October 23, 1931, Vaux Hall, New Jersey, single sheet, 6 x 8 3/4" (folded, corners torn, browning) 45

Broadside-playbill, printed paper, long narrow sheet announcing "73rd Performance!...Uncle Tom's Cabin...," presented at the Boston Museum, 1853, 7 1/2 x 19 1/2" (top corner clipped, creases, folds & slight stain) 253

Brochure, Black Panther Party, front cover w/photo, inside contains one big illustrated page of buttons & other items for sale, back cover w/illustration of Panther handing out papers, open 11 x 17" (browning) 56

Carte de Visite of Former Slaves

Carte de visite, photo titled "Lerning (sic) is Wealth," part of a series by Chas. Paxson published to support the education of former slaves, shows the former slave children, Rebecca, Charley & Rose, seated reading w/an older black man, probably Private Gordon, 1864, slight browning & foxing (ILLUS.) 145

Diploma, Tuskegee Institute, 1929, engraved document w/embossed seal, 16 x 20" (some creases, light edge wear) 58

Document, estate appraisal listing 14 slaves, Bourbon County, Kentucky, 1853, two pages front & back on lined paper (some soil & minor damage) 99

Document, estate appraisal, listing names & prices of 28 slaves, from Garrard County, Kentucky, dated February 28, 1812, front & back of two pages (creased & folded, some ink blots)................................. 83

Document, IOU for boarding slaves, from an estate in Yancy County (sic), North Carolina, 1835, half sheet of paper (bottom torn, folded, minor damage)...................... 55

Document, will, Madison County, Kentucky, 1836, allows eight slaves to keep their property, two pages front & back, folded into four (some small spots, holes & tears, some browning) 132

Doll, Golliwog, velveteen face, hands & feet, applied felt eyes & mouth, inked nose, golden crepe paints, red braid trim, yellow checked shirt stitched-on, removable grey & white checked wool jacket, England, 1930s, 20" h. (some soil)............... 460

Doll, lady, oil-painted cloth, dark brown painted head, shoulders & lower arms, flat face, black-painted eyes & nose, white accents, no wig, red print bandanna sewn-on, blue cloth legs, red-painted shoes, print dress, early 20th c., 15 1/2" h.. 748

Dolls, nut head Mammy w/twins, painted features, looped plush hair, whisk broom body, original commercial assemblage, pink print dress, twin black babies in green print organdy outfits, early 20th c., 12" h. 633

Caricature Figure of a Black Woman

Figurine, bisque, tall elongated standing caricature of a black woman, her hair pulled into three lobes, her eyes wide open & mouth agape, wearing a corset & blossoms, holding a large club in hand at her side & holding up a sign w/the other reading "Votes for Women," indistinct mark on base, Germany, ca. 1910, 7 1/2" h. (ILLUS.) **1,093**

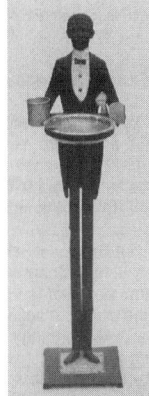

Black American Folk Art Figure

Folk art figure, metal figure of a black man w/elongated legs, in butler's uniform holding a cigarette holder, match holder & ashtray, square base, early 20th c., 34 1/2" h. (ILLUS.) **784**

Rare Color-printed Ceramic Jar

Jar, stoneware, wide cylindrical body w/rounded shoulder to a wide cylindrical short neck w/molded rim, decorated w/full color transfer prints w/scenes of Uncle Tom & Eva reading on one side & a scene of Uncle Tom being whipped on the other, probably English, ca. 1860, one small chip at bottom, signs of use, 3" d., 3" h. (ILLUS.) **627**

Martin Luther King License Plate

License plate, memorial-type, "In Memoriam - Martin Luther King, Jr. - 'I Have A Dream' - 1929-1968," white w/brown & black , a bit of soil, some scratches & tiny rust spots, 5 3/4 x 11 1/2" (ILLUS.) **55**

World War I Era Patriotic Print

Lithograph, full-color interior scene showing a black mother & her children admiring the picture of their father-husband in his World War I uniform, service star in the window, titled at bottom "True Blue," E.G. Renesch, Chicago, 1919, 16 x 20" (ILLUS.) **363**

Pamphlet, "M Is For Mississippi and Murder," issued by the NAACP, New York, November 1955, describes various atrocities in Mississippi, seven pages, 5 1/4 x 8 1/2" (pencil marks on cover & page 3, faint browning) **44**

Photo Portrait of Booker T. Washington

Photograph, bust portrait of Booker T. Washington, photo by Scurloch, cream-colored matte, early 20th c., browning around edges, overall 11 1/2 x 15 1/2" (ILLUS.) **231**

Pinback button, "March on Boston - Desegregate Schools - Stop Racist Attacks," celluloid, black on white, 2 1/4" d. **20**

Rare Anti-Slavery Stoneware Pitcher

Pitcher, cov., milk, salt glaze stoneware, footed ovoid shape fitted w/a pewter rim & hinged cover, loop handle w/head thumb rest, pale green sides molded in high-relief on one side w/a slave auction w/sign reading "Auction this Day - A Prime Lot of Healty Negroes," a black man being sold while woman & children cry, the reverse w/a scene of Simon Legree chasing Eliza & her baby across the frozen river, base marked "Ridgway & Abington, Hanley - January 1, 1853," 6" h. (ILLUS.) **1,705**

"Great American Minstrels" Poster

Poster, "Great American Minstrels" chromolithograph of Neil O'Brien w/character portrait & "Oscar F. Hodge Presents Neil O'Brien - Great American Minstrels" at top & quote "Think twice befo' yo' speak: An' then talk to yo'self" at bottom, framed & glazed, 14 1/2 x 22 1/2" (ILLUS.) **748**

Poster, "Kidnapped," large black & white photo of Bobby Seale at a microphone, at bottom in small type are two black panthers flanking the words "Bobby Seale...Chairman, Black Panther Party," 24 x 30" (some soil & water spots on back) **55**

Negro American League Poster

Poster, Negro American League Baseball game poster, titled "Baseball Plus Variety Acts...," game between the New York Black Yankees & the Indianapolis Clowns at Bowen Field in Bluefield, WV, 1946, printed in red, green, blue & black, heavy soil, browning & upper left corner torn, 14 x 22" (ILLUS.) **341**

Poster, "The NAACP Says 'Protect Your Family' - Register and Vote," New York State Conference, 11 x 14" (some browning along edges, small tear on bottom corner) **61**

Program, "Negro Youth Fighting for America - 5th All-Southern Negro Youth Conference," April 1942, Tuskegee Institute, Alabama, photos on the blue & white cover, 8 1/2 x 11" (folded, soiled along creases) **61**

Scrap book, "Official Souvenir Scrap Book - World's Heavyweight Champion - Joe Louis," half-length photo of Louis in boxing trunks on the cover, election promo for Mayor Richard W. Reading of Detroit, photos & stories on Louis w/ads for Reading, 1939, 48 pp., tan cover & sepia ink, 7 x 10" (some cover soil & spine worn) **176**

Early "Jimmy Crow" Sheet Music

Sheet music, "Jimmy Crow," dramatic caricature of a black man dancing on the cover, published by Atwill's Music Saloon, New York, ca. 1860, black & white, 4pp., 10 1/2 x 13 1/2" (ILLUS.) **105**

Sheet music, "Oh! Susanna!," crude caricature of a black man at the top above the lyrics, ca. 1900, words in dialect, decorative printed border, thin white paper, 6 1/4 x 8 3/4" (fragile, edges folded up) **99**

Sheet music, "The Dawn of Freedom," composed by M.B. Ladd, Philadelphia, personally inscribed, 1864, 10 1/8 x 13 1/4" (only slight browning, some soil on cover, binding fragile) **110**

Stereo view card, Booker T. Washington, formal portrait of Washington seated in a studio chair, Presko Binocular Company, Chicago, grey curved mount, 1912 (minor signs of dampness, pictures somewhat scuffed) **135**

Token, bronze, anti-slavery, image of kneeling woman slave in chains, reads "Am I Not A Women and a Sister - United States of America - Liberty 1838," 1 1/8" d. (wear) **55**

BOOK ENDS

Archway & Roses Book End

Bronzed metal, archway-form w/square, reeded pillars flanking a central panel cast w/roses in a vase, 6" h., pr. (ILLUS. of one) **$125**

Bronzed Boot Book End

Bronzed metal, child's boot w/tulip cutout on side, rests on spelter base w/gadrooned edge, bright copper finish, 3 1/4 x 7 x 7 1/4", pr. (ILLUS. of one) **90**

Book End with Minerva Profile

Cast iron, arched backplate cast w/a profile portrait of the goddess Minerva, goldtone finish, 4" h., pr. (ILLUS. of one) **59**

Kissing Oriental Couple Book End

Cast iron, arched fan-shaped back w/bold relief-cast figures of seated Oriental couple kissing, bronzed finish, 5" h., pr. (ILLUS. of one) **110**

Book End with Angelus Scene

Cast iron, gently arched back cast in relief w/a peasant couple standing & praying, based on the painting "The Angelus," goldtone finish, Model No. 74, 5" h., pr. (ILLUS. of one) **98**

Sailing Galleon Book End

Cast iron, gently arched upright cast w/a galleon under full sail on rough seas, copper-flashed finish, 5" h., pr. (ILLUS. of one)... **85**

Grazing Horse Book End

Cast iron, model of a horse, standing wearing saddle w/head down grazing, goldtone finish, marked on back "S200," 4 1/2" h., pr. (ILLUS. of one)........................... **125**

Sailing Ship Book End

Cast iron, model of a sailing ship representing the USS Constitution, three-masted openwork design, on rectangular base cast w/waves, goldtone finish, 5 1/2" h., pr. (ILLUS. of one).. **78**

Spanish Galleon Book End

Cast iron, model of a Spanish galleon w/a pierced design, bronzed finish, 8 1/2" h., pr. (ILLUS. of one).. **85**

Airedale Book End

Cast iron, model of an airedale, standing, gold-painted finish, marked on back "PAL Copr. 1929" & a "C" in a triangle in a circle, 5 3/4" h., pr. (ILLUS. of one)................... **125**

Book Ends with Double Scotties

Cast iron, model of two Scottish terriers each on blocks of wood, goldtone finish, 6 1/2" h., pr. (ILLUS.) **60**

Abraham Lincoln Book End

Cast iron, rectangular book ends w/relief decoration of head of Abraham Lincoln in profile on back plates, goldtone finish, 7 1/4" h., pr. (ILLUS. of one).............................. **95**

Cast iron, tall upright back cast in relief w/a Viking ship under sail on rough seas, bronzed finish, 5 3/4" h., pr. **78**

Windmill Scene on Silvered Book End

Cast iron, the arched upright cast in low-relief w/a landscape w/windmill & sailboat flanked by reeded columns, silvered finish, back marked "Ye Old Mill - 902," 5 1/4" h., pr. (ILLUS. of one)............................ **95**

Old Fisherman Book End

Cast iron, the flat upright cast in relief w/a seated old fisherman wearing hat & slicker, smoking a pipe & reading a paper, marked on back "Cape Cod Fisherman - Copyright 1930" & a "C" in a triangle in a circle, 5 1/2" h., pr. (ILLUS. of one) **45**

Book End with Windmill Landscape

Cast iron, upright back w/shaped cartouche-form sides w/leaves & berries enclosing an oval reserve w/a windmill & tree landscape, goldtone finish, 6 3/4" h., pr. (ILLUS. of one)... **49**

Scottish Terrier Book Ends

Spelter, model of a Scottish terrier, weighted base, silvered finish, 5" h., pr. (ILLUS.) **65**

Goldtone Spelter Eagle Book End

Spelter, model of an eagle, spread-winged bird on a plinth w/"1776" on the front & "Colonial Virginia" on the back, on a rectangular onyx base, goldtone finish, 7" h., pr. (ILLUS. of one) **69**

Dutch Boy & Girl Book Ends

Spelter, standing figures of Dutch boy & girl in traditional garb, rounded rectangular base & back plate, goldtone finish, 3 3/4 x 5 1/4 x 5 1/2", pr. (ILLUS. on one)..... **125**

BOTTLES

Bitters

(Numbers with some listings below refer to those used in Carlyn Ring's For Bitters Only.)

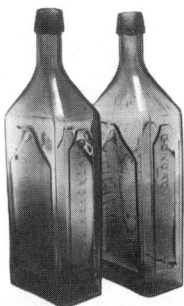

Two Rare Allen's Bitters Bottles

Allen's (William) Congress Bitters, semi-cabin w/pointed side panels, applied sloping collar mouth, smooth base, ca. 1855-70, amber, 10 1/2" h. (ILLUS. right) **$2,640**

Allen's (William) Congress Bitters, semi-cabin w/pointed side panels, applied sloping collar mouth, smooth base, ca. 1855-70, deep bluish emerald green, 10 1/2" h. (ILLUS. left) **2,860**

Allen's (William) Congress Bitters, semi-cabin w/pointed side panels, applied sloping collar mouth, smooth base, ca. 1855-70, unlisted deep olive green, 10 1/2" h. **5,280**

Rare Baker's Orange Grove Bitters

Baker's - Orange Grove - Bitters, square w/ropetwist corners, applied sloping collar mouth, smooth base, ca. 1865-75, greenish citron, 9 3/8" h. (ILLUS.) **8,800**

Bennet's Wild Cherry Stomach Bitters - Chenery, Souther & Co. Sole Agents San Francisco, Cal., square, applied top, ca. 1871, orangey red amber, fifth...... **1,540**

Bohlin's (Dr.) Norman Bitters, square w/beveled corners, tooled top, ca. 1890, clear, fifth **242**

Bourbon Whiskey Bitters, barrel-shaped, ten rings above & below center band, light strawberry puce, 9 3/8", G-101 (small flake on rim) **330**

Bourbon Whiskey Bitters, barrel-shaped, ten rings above & below center band, plum puce, 9 3/8" (G-101) **495**

Bourbon Whiskey Bitters, barrel-shaped w/rings above & below center band, applied top, smooth base, cherry puce, crude (couple of flat flakes off lip).................. **220**

Brown's Celebrated Indian Herb Bitters - Patented 1867, figural Indian Queen, rolled lip, light yellowish amber w/areas of pure yellow, 12 1/8" h. **2,200**

Brown's Celebrated Indian Herb Bitters - Patented 1867, figural Indian Queen, rolled lip, medium light amber, 12 1/8" h. **770**

Brown's Celebrated Indian Herb Bitters

Brown's Celebrated Indian Herb Bitters - Patented Feb. 11 1867, figural Indian Queen, rolled lip, shaded golden amber, 12 1/8" h. (ILLUS.) 770

Brown's Celebrated Indian Herb Bitters - Patented Feb. 11 1867, figural Indian Queen, shaded yellowish amber w/areas of yellow, rolled lip, 12 1/8" h. 1,045

Brown's Celebrated Indian Herb Bitters - Patented Feb. 11, 1868, figural Indian Queen, rolled lip, bright yellowish amber w/a touch of green, 12 1/8" h. 990

Brown's Celebrated Indian Herb Bitters - Patented Feb. 11, 1868, figural Indian Queen, rolled lip, shaded dark & light amber, 12 1/8" h. 688

Rare California Herb Bitters Bottle

California Herb Bitters - Pittsburgh PA - G.W. Frazier, square w/paneled sides, applied sloping collared mouth, smooth base, medium amber, ca. 1865-75, 9 3/8" h. (ILLUS.) 3,850

Rare Celebrated Eagle Bitters Bottle

Celebrated Eagle Bitters - St. Louis - Lange & Bernecker, square w/arched paneled sides & beveled corners, applied sloping collar mouth, smooth base, bright medium orangish red, 9" h. (ILLUS.) 3,410

Scarce Cundurango Bitters Bottle

Cundurango, square w/two inset side panels, short neck w/applied lip, ca. 1872-80, Western, medium bluish green, crude w/manufacturing flaw (ILLUS.) 1,210

Damiana Bitters - Baja California - Manuf'r Lewis Hess (around shoulder), round w/paneled sides, applied sloping double collar mouth, smooth base, ca. 1875-85, deep aqua, 11 1/2" h. 105

Doyle's - Hop - Bitters - 1872, around sides of sloping shoulder, square w/paneled sides w/raised clusters of hop berries & leaves, applied sloping double collar mouth, smooth base, ca. 1872-80, yellow amber, 9 7/8" h. 303

Drake's (S T) - 1860 - Plantation - X - Bitters - Patented - 1862, cabin-shaped, four-log, applied sloping collar mouth, ca. 1862-70, amber, 10" h. (D-110) 132

Drake's (S T) - 1860 - Plantation - X - Bitters - Patented - 1862, cabin-shaped, four-log, applied sloping collar mouth, ca. 1862-70, yellowish amber, 10" h. (D-110) 1,870

Drake's (S T) - 1860 - Plantation - X - Bitters - Patented - 1862, cabin-shaped, four-log, applied sloping collar mouth, ca. 1862-70, yellowish green, 10" h. (D-110).. 2,420

Drake's (S T) - 1860 - Plantation - X - Bitters - Patented - 1862, cabin-shaped, six-log, golden honey amber, 10" h. (D-105) 132

Electric Bitters (on front & back labels), square, 100% intact labels, ex-Ring collection, light amber, pt. 88

Fish (The) Bitters - W.H. Ware, Patented 1866, figural fish, applied top, bright amber, 11 1/2" h. 264

Fish (The) Bitters - W.H. Ware, Patent 1866 - W.H. Ware Patent 1866 (on bottom), figural fish, tooled lip, deep tobacco amber, small crack from lip into neck, 11 3/4" h. (ILLUS.) 110

Flint's (Dr.) - Quaker Bitters - Providence, R.I., rectangular, applied top, 90% of original paper label showing a Quaker, aqua, 9 1/2" h. 550

Globe Bitters Byrne Bros & Co. New York - Globe Bitters Manufactured Only by Byrne Bros & Co. New York, cylindrical w/stepped, ringed neck & applied mouth, smooth base, ca. 1870, light amber, 10 3/4" h. 1,650

Greeley's Bourbon Bitters, barrel-shaped, ten rings above & below center band, burnt chocolate puce, 9 3/8" h. (G-101) 358

Greeley's Bourbon Bitters, barrel-shaped, ten rings above & below center band, crude, grape puce amber, 9 3/8" h. (G-101) 550

Greeley's Bourbon Bitters, barrel-shaped, ten rings above & below center band, medium amber, 9 3/8" h. (G-101) 385

Greeley's Bourbon Bitters, barrel-shaped, ten rings above & below center band, medium grape puce, 9 3/8" h. (G-101) 605

Greeley's Bourbon Whiskey Bitters, barrel-shaped, ten rings above & below center band, applied mouth, medium plum amber, 9 3/8" h. (G-102) 715

Hall's Bitters - E.E. Hall New Haven - Established 1842, barrel-shaped, applied mouth, smooth base, medium golden amber, 9 1/8" h. 264

Hall's Bitters - E.E. Hall New Haven - Established 1842, barrel-shaped, applied mouth, smooth base, medium to deep amber, 9 1/8" h. 275

Hall's Bitters - E.E. Hall New Haven - Established 1842, barrel-shaped, applied square collar top, smooth base, bright canary yellowish green, 9 1/8" h. 605

Hartwig Kantorowicz (around base), bulbous squatty spherical base tapering to a tall neck, smooth base w/deep kick-up, reddish amber, 7 3/4" h. 330

Dr. Henley's Bitters in a Rare Color

Henley's (Dr.) Wild Grape Root - IXL (in oval) Bitters, cylindrical w/tall neck & applied mouth band, smooth base, deep bluish green aqua, ca. 1870, 12 1/8" h. (ILLUS.).. 2,420

Henley's (Dr.) Wild Grape Root - IXL (in oval) Bitters, cylindrical w/tall neck & applied square collar, smooth base, deep aqua, ca. 1870, qt., 12 1/8" h. 165

Front & Back of Herkules Bitters

Herkules Bitter - AC (monogram) - 1 Quart, ball-shaped, tooled mouth, 99% original paper label on back panel, deep green, 7 1/2" h. (ILLUS.)............................... 1,760

Hertrichs Bitter, Einziger Fabrikant, Hans Hertrich Hof Gesetzlich Geschutzt, footed ball-shaped w/tall ringed neck, applied mouth, smooth base, olive green, 8 3/4" h. 550

Hibernia Bitters, square w/beveled corners, applied top, golden amber, ca. 1886-90, fifth (very light open surface bottle on back) 110

Holtzermann's Patent Stomach Bitters (on roof), cabin-shaped, four-roof, tooled mouth, complete paper label reading "Holtzermann's Stomach Bitters" above barrel, ca. 1880-1895, reddish amber, 9 3/4" h. 770

Holtzermann's Stomach Bitters (on paper label), cabin-shaped, four-roof, tooled mouth, ca. 1880-1895, sample size, no label, amber, 4" h. 220

Hostetter's (Dr. J.) Stomach Bitters, square w/beveled corners, short neck w/applied sloping collar mouth, ca. 1860-70, very crude mouth, medium olive amber, fifth... 242

Hostetter's (Dr. J.) Stomach Bitters - L & WI (on base), square w/beveled corners, short neck w/applied sloping collar mouth, ca. 1860-70, bright citron, fifth 176

Hostetter's (Dr. J.) Stomach Bitters - W. MCG & Co. (on base), square w/rounded shoulder, applied sloping collar mouth, 85% original front & back labels, yellow w/olive tone, 9" h. 935

Hubble & Co. (Geo. C.), tall rectangular semi-cabin shape, short neck & applied mouth, dark aqua (some wear) 176

Rare Light Green Lacour's Bitters

Lacour's Bitters - Sarsapariphere, cylindrical w/sunken side panels & ringed rim & base, applied mouth, ca. 1866-79, light green, small pressure ding on shoulder, very minor area of stain, 9 3/8" h. (ILLUS.).. 4,180

Langley's (Dr.) - Root & Herb - Bitters - 99 Union St. - Boston, cylindrical w/short neck & flattened applied mouth, ca. 1855-65, light greenish blue, 7" h. 154

Lippman's Great German Bitters - Savannah, Georgia, square w/beveled corners, applied top, bright yellowish olive, long drip on inside of neck, open bubble on one panel, fifth (light interior haze)........ 1,045

Lippman's Great German Bitters - Savannah, Georgia, square w/beveled corners, applied top, dark amber, fifth................ 440

Loveridge Wahoo Bitters Bottle

Loveridge (E. Dexter) Wahoo Bitters - (design of eagle & arrow) - E. Dexter Loveridge Wahoo Bitters - DWD Patd XXX 1863 (on shoulder), square semi-cabin w/paneled sides, applied mouth, smooth base, medium amber, 10 1/4" h. (ILLUS.) **880**

Rare Early Western Bitters Bottle

Lyons & Co. (E.G.) Manufacturers San (backward 'n') F Co, square w/short neck & applied square collar, light pastel green, small bruise on back right base corner (ILLUS.)... **5,060**

Mack's Sarsaparilla Bitters - Mack & Co. Prop'rs San Francisco, square w/beveled corners, applied top, ca. 1884-87, golden amber (tiny bit of stain) **303**

Marshall's Bitters - The Best Laxative and Blood Purifier, square w/beveled corners, tooled top, ca. 1900, amber, fifth (minor interior haze) **77**

McKelvy's - Stomach Bitters - Pittsburgh PA, square w/paneled sides & rounded shoulder, applied sloping collar mouth, smooth base, rare medium cobalt blue, 9" h. (minor bruise inside lip) **13,750**

Moffat (Jno.) - Phoenix Bitters - New York - Price 1$, rectangular w/rolled out lip, pontil, dark tobacco amber approaching black, ca. 1835-55, 5 1/2" h. (ILLUS. top of next column)... **1,925**

National Bitters, figural ear of corn, "Patent 1867" on base, applied mouth, bright golden yellow, 12 1/2" h. (slight roughness around mouth) **770**

Rare Jno. Moffat Phoenix Bitters

National Bitters, figural ear of corn, "Patent 1867" on base, applied mouth, smooth base, medium amber, ca. 1870, 12 1/2" h. **523**

National Bitters, figural ear of corn, "Patent 1867" on base, applied mouth, smooth base, bright golden amber to medium golden apricot, ca. 1870, 12 1/2" h. **715**

National Bitters, figural ear of corn, "Patent 1867" on base, applied mouth, smooth base, deep cherry puce, ca. 1870, 12 1/2" h. **1,870**

National Bitters - Patent 1867, figural ear of corn, "Patent 1867" on base, applied mouth, deep golden yellow, 12 1/2" h. **1,980**

Rare Early OK Bitters Bottle

OK Bitters, cylindrical w/a tall neck & crude applied top, heavily whittled, ca. 1870, medium bluish aqua (ILLUS.).................... **6,160**

Old - Homestead - Wild Cherry - Bitters - Patent, cabin-shaped, scalloped shingles on four-sided roof, applied sloping collar mouth, ca. 1865-80, bright amber, 9 3/8" h. **495**

Old Sachem - Bitters - and - Wigwam Tonic, barrel-shaped, ten-rib, applied mouth, smooth base, ca. 1855-70, bright apricot, 9 1/4" h. **880**

Petzold's (Dr.) Genuine German Bitters Incept. 1862 - Patented 1884 (around shoulder) oval w/twenty side ribs, tooled mouth, medium golden amber 10 1/2" h. **121**

Purdy's Cottage Bitters, rectangular, applied top, smooth base, amber, 9 1/2" h.... **3,080**

Red Jacket Bitters - Bennett, Peters & Co., square w/beveled corners, applied top, medium amber, fifth (small radiating potstone on side) **198**

Richardson's (S.O.) Bitters - South Readings - Mass, rectangular w/beveled edges & wide rounded shoulder w/short neck & flared lip, open pontil, very crude, aqua **165**

Roback's (Dr. C.W.) - Stomach Bitters - Cincinnati, O., barrel-shaped, applied sloping collar mouth, red iron pontil, ca. 1855-65, amber, 9 7/8" h. (some light inside stain) **523**

Roback's Stomach Bitters - Rare Color

Roback's (Dr. C.W.) - Stomach Bitters - Cincinnati, O., barrel-shaped w/rings above & below center band, applied sloping collar mouth, smooth base, crude, ca. 1860-70, dark olive green, 10" h. (ILLUS.) **3,300**

Sazerac Milk Glass Bitters Bottle

Sazerac Armotic Bitters (on base) - monogram in ring on shoulder, cylindrical w/tall lady's leg neck & applied rim ring, ca. 1870s, milk glass, 10 1/4" h. **385**

Sazerac Armotic Bitters (on base) - monogram in ring on shoulder, cylindrical w/tall lady's leg neck & applied rim ring, ca. 1870s, light golden olive, 10" h. **440**

Sazerac Armotic Bitters (on base) - monogram in ring on shoulder, cylindrical w/tall lady's leg neck & applied rim ring, ca. 1870s, yellowish olive green, 10 1/4" h. (tiny flakes on lip) **1,540**

Schroeder's Bitters - Louisville, KY, round w/lady's leg neck, "Ky. G. W. Co." on base, applied top, yellowish amber, 11 3/4" h. **303**

Suffolk Bitters Figural Pig Bottle

Suffolk Bitters - Philbrook & Tucker Boston, figural pig, applied double collar mouth, smooth base, medium amber to bright golden amber, ca. 1870, 10 1/4" l. (ILLUS.) **935**

Swain's (C.H.) - Bourbon Bitters, square w/beveled corners, applied sloping collar top, crude, very deep amber **176**

Swain's (C.H.) - Bourbon Bitters (embossed on three sides), square w/beveled corners, applied sloping collar top, very crude, amber **264**

W.C. Bitters (on shoulder) - Brobst & Rentschler Reading, PA, barrel-shaped w/three rings above & below center band, tooled mouth, smooth base, amber shading to lighter amber in shoulders, 10 1/2" h. **605**

Wahoo - & - Calisaya - Bitters - Jacob Pinkerton - Y!! - O.K. - I.M. - Y!!!, semi-cabin w/paneled sides, applied sloping collar mouth, ca. 1865-75, yellowish amber, 10 3/8" h. **1,320**

Extremely Rare Wheeler's Bitters

Wheeler's - Berlin - Bitters - Baltimore, hexagonal, applied mouth, graphite pontil, bright emerald green, 9 1/2" h. (ILLUS.) **15,400**

Figurals

Barrel, milk glass, tall form w/three staves around top & three around bottom, oval label panel on reverse, Europe, ca. 1900, 11" h. **303**

French Bust of Gambeth Bottle

Bust of Gambeth, clear, tooled mouth, pontil, France, ca. 1900, 11 1/8" h. (ILLUS.)....... **165**

Hand pointing upward, medium yellowish olive green, on a rectangular base w/paneled sides embossed "W. Zeige & Sohn Berlin - Marke - Feigelinger," applied mouth, smooth base, Germany, ca. 1915-25, 10 3/4" h. **94**

Helmet w/plume, clear, embossed "1" in star on front & "Haselhorst - Dresden" on smooth base ground lip, Germany, ca. 1910, 3 3/8" h. **198**

French Hot Air Balloon Bottle

Hot air balloon, clear, diamond lattice design w/"Ballon Captif - 1878," pontiled base w/"Depose," France, ca. 1900, missing original stopper, 9" h. (ILLUS.)...... **1,155**

Joan of Arc, clear, standing figure, pontil, "Depose" embossed on side of base, tooled mouth w/ground interior, France, ca. 1900, 13 5/8" h. (stopper missing)... **72**

Monument, deep cobalt blue, tall slender cologne-type w/rolled lip, smooth base, somewhat crude, U.S., ca. 1875, 8 1/8" h... **495**

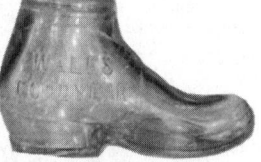

Glass Advertising Shoe Bottle

Shoe, clear, embossed on the side "Wales - Goodyear," ground lip, smooth base, U.S., ca. 1910, 2 1/8" h. (ILLUS.) **121**

Flasks

Flasks are listed according to the numbers provided in American Bottles & Flasks and Their Ancestry by Helen McKearin and Kenneth M. Wilson.

Blown-glass, clear w/opalescent looping, attributed to South Jersey, 8 1/4" h. (tiny pots stones)... **275**

Blown-glass, Nailsea type, fiery opalescent w/pink & cobalt looping, 7 1/4" h. (chipped pontil) **110**

GI-21 - Washington bust (facing right) below "Fells," "Point" below bust - Washington Monument in Baltimore without statue above "BALTo," sheared mouth, pontil, amethystine, qt. (some minor exterior wear)... **1,120**

GVI-2 - Baltimore Monument above "Balto." - Sloop sailing to the right w/"Fells" above & "Point" below, vertically ribbed edges, sheared lip, pontil, medium mottled yellowish green, 1/2 pt. (overall dullness) **1,568**

Fine Early Chestnut Flask

Chestnut, mold-blown, twenty broken ribs swirled to the right, sheared lip, pontil, greenish aqua, Midwestern, 6 1/2" h. (ILLUS.).. **880**

GI-1 - Washington bust below "General Washington" - American Eagle w/shield w/seven bars on breast below an arch of nine 5-point stars, standing on oval w/inner band of 18 large pearls, edges w/horizontal beading w/vertical medial rib, sheared mouth, pontil, bright deep aqua, pt. (interior bubble bursts, slight interior resident, some minor exterior wear).......... **1,456**

GI-10 - Washington bust below "G. Washington" - American Eagle below eleven stars & standing on oval frame w/liner band of 15 small pearls, sheared mouth, pontil, greenish aqua, pt................................. **338**

GI-112 - "Louis Kossuth" above full-faced bust of Kossuth in uniform above crossed flags - Frigate sailing left flying flags above "U.S. Steam Frigate Mississippi S. Huffsey," "Ph. Doflein Mould Maker Nth.5t St 84" on base, calabash, applied sloping collar, pontil, bluish aqua, qt. **303**

Kossuth Calabash in a Rare Color

GI-113 - "Kossuth" above bust - Tall tree in foliage, calabash-style, smooth edges, crudely applied top, open pontil, light olive green, qt. (ILLUS.)...................... **935**

GI-114 - Classical draped bust of Byron facing right - Classical draped bust of Scott facing left, tooled lip, pontil, yellowish amber, 1/2 pt. **242**

GI-121 - Columbia bust facing left below thirteen small six-pointed stars - American Eagle w/shield w/nine vertical bars above "B & W" in script below, vertically ribbed edges, aqua, pt. **440**

GI-14 - Washington bust below "General Washington" - American Eagle w/shield w/seven bars on breast, head turned to right, "E Pluribus Unum" in semicircle above, vertically ribbed edges w/"Adams & Jefferson July 4, A.D. 1776" & "Kensington Glassworks Philadelphia," sheared lip, pontil, aqua, pt. (pinhead in-making lip bruise)............................. **303**

GI-26 - Washington bust - American Eagle w/shield w/eight vertical & two horizontal bars on breast, head turned to right, slightly inward rolled mouth, pontil, aqua, qt. **202**

GI-26 - Washington bust - American Eagle w/shield w/eight vertical & two horizontal bars on breast, head turned to right, slightly inward rolled mouth, pontil, greenish aqua, qt. **246**

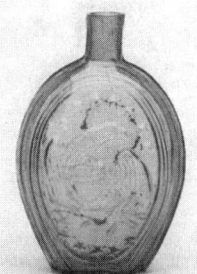

Washington-Eagle Flask in Rare Color

GI-26 - Washington bust - American Eagle w/shield w/eight vertical & two horizontal bars on breast, head turned to right, sheared mouth, pontil, small flat flake inside mouth, medium yellowish green, qt. (ILLUS.) **1,232**

GI-28 - Washington bust below "Albany Glass Works," "Albany NY" below bust - full-rigged ship sailing to right, vertically ribbed edges, applied double collared mouth, pontil, aqua, pt. (some light interior haze)...................... **280**

GI-32 - "Washington" above bust, uniform without bars on lapel - "Jackson" above bust, sheared lip, pontil, yellow amber w/slight olive tone, pr. **242**

GI-33 - "Washington" above bust facing left - "Jackson" above bust facing left, bars on lapels of coats missing, sheared mouth, pontil, yellowish olive, pt. **246**

GI-34 - Washington bust portrait obverse - Jackson bust portrait reverse, Coventry, Connecticut Glass Works, sheared mouth, pontil, light yellowish amber, 1/2 pt. (slightly week impression) **336**

Rare Washington-Taylor Flask

GI-38 - Washington bust below "The Father of His Country" - Taylor bust, "Gen. Taylor Never Surrenders, Dyottville Glass Works, Philad.a.," applied square collar mouth, smooth edges, smooth base, medium yellow shading to copper, qt. (ILLUS.) **1,540**

GI-39 - Washington bust below "The Father of His Country" - Taylor bust below "Gen Taylor Never Surrenders," smooth edges, sheared mouth, pontil, bright bluish green, qt.. **2,464**

GI-42 - Washington bust below "The Father of His Country" - Taylor bust below "A Little More Grape Captain Bragg, Dyottville Glass Works, Philad.a," smooth edges, sheared lip, open pontil, aqua, qt. **99**

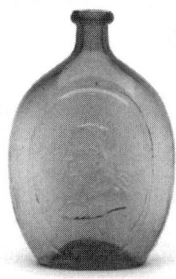

Rare Lockport Washington Flask

GI-47 - Washington bust below "The Father of His Country" - plain reverse, applied collar mouth, pontil, medium bluish green, some minor scratches on reverse, qt. (ILLUS.) **1,456**

GI-48 - Washington bust below "The Father of His Country" - blank oval on reverse, medium to light emerald green, pt. **2,640**

GI-65 - "General Jackson" surrounding bust - American Eagle w/shield on oval frame, "J.T. & Co." below frame, thirteen small five-pointed stars above eagle, horizontal beading w/vertical medial rib, sheared mouth, pontil, aqua **1,064**

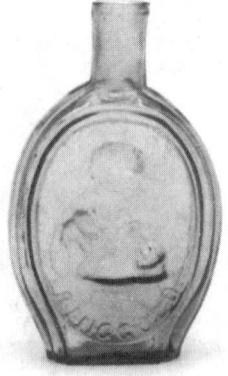

Taylor - Ringgold Flask

GI-71 - Taylor bust (facing left) w/"Rough and Ready" below - Ringgold bust (facing left) w/"Major" in semicircle above bust & "Ringgold" below bust, heavy vertical ribbing, light amethyst, two small fissures on medial rib, interior oil-treated, pt. (ILLUS.) **616**

GI-72 - Taylor bust (facing left) w/"Rough and Ready" below - Ringgold bust (facing left) w/"Major" in semicircle above bust & "Ringgold" below bust, heavy vertical ribbing, sheared mouth, pontil, aqua, pt. **101**

Rare Taylor - Monument Flask

GI-73 - Taylor bust facing left below "Genl. Taylor" - Washington Monument, Baltimore without statue, "Fells Point" above & "Balto" below, sheared lip, pontil, amethystine, pt. (ILLUS.) **825**

GI-74 - Taylor bust, facing right, w/"Zachary Taylor" above & "Rough & Ready" below - "Corn For the World" above cornstalk, vertically ribbed edges, sheared neck, pontil, aqua, pt. (small shallow flake on inside of mouth, exterior high point wear) **168**

GI-80 - "Lafayette" above bust & "T. S." & bar below - "De Witt Clinton" above bust & "Coventry C-T" below, corrugated edges, sheared lip, pontil, medium yellow amber w/olive tone, pt. **1,017**

GI-80 - "Lafayette" above bust & "T. S." & bar below - "De Witt Clinton" above bust & "Coventry C-T" below, corrugated edges, sheared lip, pontil, brilliant yellow amber, pt. **1,870**

GI-84 - "Lafayette" above bust & "T. S." & bar below - Masonic arch, pillar & pavement w/Masonic emblem inside arch, horizontal corrugated edges, horizontal rib at base, sheared mouth, pontil, bright light yellowish green w/olive tone, 1/2 pt... **4,200**

GI-85 - "Lafayette" above bust & "Covetry (sic) - C-T" below - French liberty cap on pole & semi-circle of eleven five-pointed stars above, "S & S" below, fine vertical ribbing, two horizontal ribs at base, sheared lip, pontil, yellowish olive, pt. **1,100**

Lafayette - Liberty Cap Flask

GI-86 - "Lafayette" above bust & "Coventry - C-T" below - French Liberty cap on pole & semicircle of eleven five-pointed stars above, "S & S" below, fine vertical ribbing, two horizontal ribs at base, sheared mouth, pontil, medium yellowish olive, 1/2 pt. (ILLUS.) **952**

GI-90 - Lafayette bust facing right below "General La Fayette," "Republican Gratitude" in border band - American Eagle facing left w/shield below "E. Pluribus Unum" & above oval reserve w/twenty-one pearls & "T.W.D.," border band w/"Kensington Glass Works Philadelphia,"sheared lip, open pontil, strong strike, aqua, pt. **385**

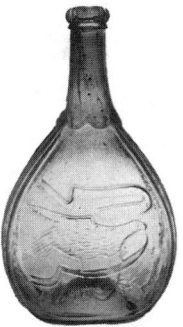

Rare Franklin-Dyott Flask

GI-94 - Franklin bust below "Benjamin Franklin - Where Liberty Dwells There Is My
Country" - Dyott bust below "T.W. Dyott,
M.D. - Kensington Glass Works Philadelphia," ribbed edges, sheared lip, pontil,
tiny cooling crack on shoulder, golden
amber, pt. (ILLUS.) **2,530**

GII-141 - American Eagle w/pennant in beak
& in talons above monument w/scroll ornament flanking a small oval at top supported by a gallery of 22 narrow ribs over
a panel enclosing a six-striped flag flying
to right above a narrow plain base frame
- Indian standing facing right & shooting
arrow at flying bird, small dog & bare stylized tree at far left above a scrolled frame
enclosing four small oval petals around a
pearl, smooth edges & base, applied
mouth band, medium aqua, qt. (some mi-
nor interior haze) **413**

American Eagle Calabash Flask

GII-143 - American Eagle w/plain shield in
talons & pennants in beak, calabash-
form, four-flute edges, aqua, hint of inte-
rior stain, qt. (ILLUS.) **143**

GII-19 - American Eagle on horizontal flag-
swagged pole - morning glory vine, applied double collar mouth, pontil, bluish
aqua, pt. **385**

GII-20 - American Eagle w/little detailing,
head turned to the right, spread-winged &
standing upright on thick legs, within the
arched panel sides obverse & reverse,
narrow vertical medial rib, sheared
mouth, pontil, deep aqua, pt. **4,480**

GII-24 - American Eagle facing left w/ribbon
above head w/random ribbing, two

arched rows of four-point stars at top, arrows & olive branch in talons above bottom oval frame enclosing an elongated
eight-point star - Large conventionalized
floral medallion above an oval frame enclosing an elongated eight-point star,
horizontally corrugated edges, sheared
mouth, pontil, pale bluish green, pt.
(small burst bubble on vase) **146**

Double Eagle Flask

GII-26 - American Eagle above stellar motif
obverse   &   reverse,   horizontally
corrugated edges, plain lip, open pontil,
pale blue, small open bubble on side, 1/2
pt. (ILLUS.) **385**

GII-32 - American Eagle in large oval medallion obverse & reverse, overall heavy vertical ribbing except for medallions,
sheared mouth, pontil, greenish aqua, pt.
(shallow flake at top of mouth) **476**

GII-33 - American Eagle below four stars in
small oval panel on an overall vertically
ribbed body - "Louisville Ky Glassworks"
in oval panel on ribbed body, vertically
ribbed edges, applied double collared
mouth, smooth base, aqua, 1/2 pt. (some
light inside haze) **179**

GII-41 - American Eagle & shield facing left
below twenty-six rays & above an oval reserve bordered w/tiny pearls - Large leafy
tree, vertically ribbed edges, sheared
mouth, pontil, aqua., pt. (some light inte-
rior haze spots) **179**

GII-48 - American Eagle facing left w/shield
on breast above a plain oval panel -
Furled American Flag w/nineteen stars
below "Coffin & Hay." & above "Hammon-
ton," oval border panels, sheared lip,
pontil, ca. 1830, deep aqua, qt. **264**

GII-61 - American Eagle below "Liberty" - inscribed in four lines "Willington - Glass
Co - West Willington - Conn," smooth
edges, bright yellowish olive, qt. **532**

GII-61 - American Eagle below "Liberty" - inscribed in four lines "Willington - Glass
Co - West Willington - Conn," smooth
edges, applied sloping collar mouth,
smooth base, deep forest green, qt. **728**

GII-61 - American Eagle below "Liberty" - inscribed in four lines "Willington - Glass
Co - West Willington - Conn," smooth
edges, medium reddish amber, qt. **825**

GII-62 - American Eagle below "Liberty" - inscription in five lines "Willington - Glass -
Co - West, Willington - Conn.," smooth
edges, medium olive green, pt. **303**

GII-62 - American Eagle below "Liberty" - inscription in five lines "Willington - Glass - Co - West, Willington - Conn..," smooth edges, light emerald green, pt. **605**

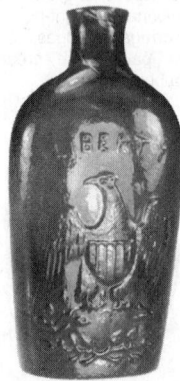

American Eagle-Willington Flask

GII-63 - American Eagle below "Liberty" - inscription in five lines "Willington - Glass - Co - West Willington - Conn..," smooth edges, olive green, 1/2 pt. (ILLUS.) **242**

GII-63 - American Eagle below "Liberty" - inscription in five lines "Willington - Glass - Co - West Willington - Conn..," smooth edges, applied double collared mouth, smooth base, bright golden yellowish amber w/olive tone, 1/2 pt. **308**

GII-64 - "Liberty" above American Eagle w/shield facing left on leafy branch - "Willington - Glass - Co - West Willington - Conn," smooth sides, applied double collared mouth, smooth base, yellowish olive, pt. **504**

GII-70 - American Eagle lengthwise obverse & reverse, vertically ribbed edges, sheared mouth, pontil, medium to deep yellowish olive, pt. (minor highpoint wear) **269**

GII-73 - American Eagle w/head turned right & standing on rocks - Cornucopia w/produce & X to the left, vertically ribbed edges, sheared mouth, pontil, forest green w/heavier olive striations across eagle, pt. **532**

GII-81 - American Eagle above oval inscribed "Granite - Glass Co." obverse - reverse the same except inscription "Stoddard - NY," narrow vertical edge rib, sheared mouth, pontil, yellowish olive, minor mouth roughness, pt. (ILLUS.) **101**

GII-86 - American Eagle above oval obverse & reverse, vertically ribbed edges, sheared lip, pontil, medium yellowish amber, 1/2 pt. **154**

GII-95 - American Eagle above oval & w/head on long neck turned to right, obverse & reverse, w/"Pittsburgh, Pa." in oval on obverse, narrow vertical rib on edges, unusual applied top, aqua, 1/2 pt. **88**

GIII-14 - Cornucopia with Produce & curled to right - Urn with Produce, vertically ribbed edges, sheared mouth, pontil, bluish emerald green, 1/2 pt. **1,008**

Sapphire Blue Cornucopia-Urn Flask

GIII-16 - Cornucopia with Produce & curled to right - Urn with Produce & w/"Lancaster. Glass.Works N.Y.," vertically ribbed edges, crudely sheared mouth, pontil, sapphire blue, pt. (ILLUS.) **5,040**

Rare Cornucopia - Urn Flask

GIII-17 - Cornucopia with Produce & curled to right - Urn with Produce, sheared lip, vertically ribbed edges, emerald green, pt. (ILLUS.) **660**

GIII-8 - Cornucopia with Produce & large pearl at left - Urn with Produce, vertically ribbed sides, sheared mouth, pontil, bright bluish green w/yellow tone, 1/2 pt. **476**

Double Eagle Flask

GIV-1 - Masonic Emblems - American Eagle w/ribbon reading "E Pluribus Unum" above & "P" (old-fashioned J) below in oval frame, sheared inward rolled mouth, pontil, light to medium bluish green, pt. (slight exterior wear)............................. 246

GIV-18 - Masonic Arch, pillars & pavement w/Masonic emblems - American Eagle without shield on breast, plain oval frame below "KCCNE" inside, smooth edges w/single rib, sheared mouth, pontil, light yellowish olive, pt............................. 235

GIV-21 - Masonic Arch, pillars & pavement w/Masonic emblems - American Eagle w/oval frame below, smooth edges w/single vertical rib, sheared mouth, pontil, medium yellowish olive, pt. 258

GIV-24 - Masonic Arch, pillars & pavement w/Masonic emblems - American Eagle grasping large balls in talons & without shield on breast, plain oval frame below, smooth edges w/single medial rib, sheared mouth, pontil, yellowish olive amber, 1/2 pt. (some minor exterior wear)... 336

GIV-27 - Masonic Arch, pillars & pavement w/Masonic emblems & radiating triangle enclosing the letter "G" - American Eagle w/"NEG Co" in oval frame below, vertically ribbed edges, tooled lip, pontil, bluish aqua w/olive neck striations, pt. 303

Masonic Star & Eye of God Flask

GIV-43 - Masonic six-point star w/eye of God in center all above "A D" - six-point star w/arm in center all above "GRJA," sheared lip, vertical edge ribs, bright amber, pt. (ILLUS.) 523

Masonic Arch & Zanesville Eagle Flask

GIV-32 - Masonic arch, pillars & pavement enclosing Farmer's Arms w/sheaf of rye & implements - American Eagle & shield facing right below "Zanesville" & above oval frame enclosing "Ohio" above "J. Shepard (S reversed) & Co.," tooled mouth, pontil, deep reddish amber, pt. (ILLUS.) 1,155

GIV-37 - Masonic Arch w/Farmer's Arms, sheaf of rye & farm implements within arch & "Kenington Glass Works Philadelphia" around edge - American Eagle facing right on oval w/27 small pearls & "T.W.D.," tooled mouth, pontil, aqua, pt....... 253

GIV-43 - Masonic six-point star w/eye of God in center all above "A D" - six-point star w/arm in center all above "GRJA," vertical edge ribs, sheared mouth, pontil, medium yellowish amber w/olive tone, pt. (some high point wear & scratches) 308

Rare Olive Green Scroll Flask

GIX-10a - Scroll w/two eight-point stars, a small one in upper space & medium sized one in mid-space obverse - seven-point star reverse, vertical medial rib, applied mouth, red iron pontil, dark olive green w/yellow tone, pt. (ILLUS.)............... 1,100

GIX-11 - Scroll w/six-point stars, a small one in upper space & medium sized one in lower space obverse & reverse, vertical medial rib, sheared lip, pontil, moonstone, pt. (small shallow chip off inside of lip) 688

GIX-11a - Scroll w/two eight-point stars, obverse & reverse, tooled lip, pontil, light to medium bluish green, pt............................... 798

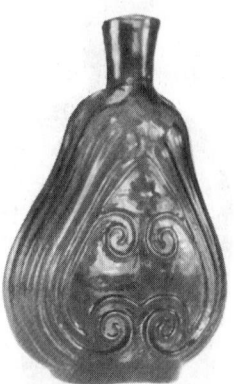

Amber Scroll Flask with Stars

GIX-14 - Scroll w/six-point star above seven-point star obverse & reverse, vertical medial rib on edge, tooled lip, pontil, medium amber, pt. (ILLUS.) **605**

GIX-14 - Scroll w/six-point star above seven-point star obverse & reverse, vertical medial rib on edge, tooled lip, pontil, medium yellowish green, pt. **825**

GIX-18 - Scroll w/large inverted heart-shaped framed formed by medial & inferior scrolls, star w/scalloped edge above medial scroll - Similar obverse w/no bead on neck, sheared lip, pontil, medium sapphire blue, pt. (several chips off outside of lip, small bruise inside lip) **2,145**

GIX-2 - Scroll w/large inverted heart-shaped frame formed by medial & inferior scrolls & containing a large six-point star w/a similar star above frame, sheared lip, open pontil, medium apple green, qt. **688**

Rare Moonstone-colored Scroll Flask

GIX-2 - Scroll w/large inverted heart-shaped frame formed by medial & inferior scrolls & containing a large six-point star w/a similar star above frame, sheared lip, open pontil, moonstone w/amethystine tint, qt. (ILLUS.) **908**

GV-10 - "Railroad" above horse-drawn cart on rail & "Lowell" below - American Eagle lengthwise & 13 five-point stars, vertically ribbed edges, sheared mouth, pontil, yellowish olive, 1/2 pt. **364**

GV-3 - "Success to the Railroad" around embossed horse pulling cart - similar reverse, sheared mouth, open pontil, light yellow amber, pt. **420**

GV-5 - "Success to the Railroad" around embossed horse pulling cart - similar reverse, sheared mouth, pontil, vertically ribbed edges, medium yellowish green, pt. (tiny flake on medial rib) **336**

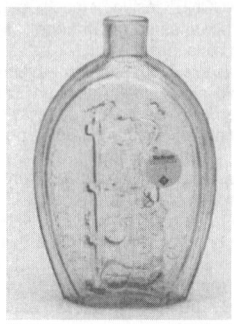

Aqua Success to the Railroad Flask

GV-5 - "Success to the Railroad" around embossed horse pulling cart - similar reverse, sheared mouth, pontil, vertically ribbed edges, aqua, pt. (ILLUS.) **840**

GV-6 - "Success to the Railroad" around embossed horse pulling cart obverse & reverse, w/"Success" above scene, sheared mouth, pontil, yellowish olive, pt. **392**

GV-7 - Horse pulling loaded cart obverse & reverse, no inscription, sheared mouth, tubular pontil, olive green, pt. (slight exterior high point wear) **784**

GV-7a - Horse pulling loaded cart obverse, no inscription - American Eagle lengthwise, applied mouth, open pontil, golden to reddish amber, pt. **242**

Eagle-Railroad Yellow-Olive Flask

GV-8 - "Success to the Railroad" around embossed horse pulling cart - large American Eagle w/head turned left & holding a shield w/seven vertical & two horizontal bars on breast, seventeen large five-pointed stars surround eagle, three vertical edge ridges w/heavy medial rib, sheared mouth, pontil, yellowish olive, pt. (ILLUS.) **364**

GV-9 - Horse pulling loaded cart & no inscription - Large American Eagle with shield lengthwise, no stars, sheared mouth, pontil, deep forest green, pt............. **157**

GV-9 - Horse pulling loaded cart & no inscription - Large American Eagle with shield lengthwise, no stars, sheared mouth, pontil, deep yellowish olive, pt. (some minor exterior wear, slightly weak impression) **168**

GVI-2 - Baltimore Monument above "Balto." - Sloop sailing to the right w/"Fells" above & "Point" below, vertically ribbed edges, sheared lip, pontil, medium pinkish amethyst, 1/2 pt. (shallow flake off lip) **1,925**

Rare Baltimore Monument Flask

GVI-2 - Baltimore Monument above "Balto." - Sloop sailing to the right w/"Fells" above & "Point" below, vertically ribbed edges, sheared lip, pontil, deep olive green, 1/2 pt., tiny cooling crack on edge (ILLUS.)..... **4,730**

GVI-4 - "Baltimore" below monument - "Corn For The World" in semicircle above ear of corn, smooth edges, applied square collared mouth, smooth base, aqua, qt............. **123**

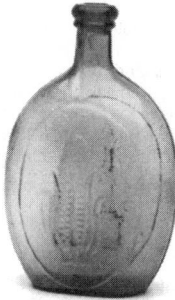

Rare Colored Corn for the World Flask

GVI-4 - "Baltimore" below monument - "Corn For The World" in semicircle above ear of corn, smooth edges, applied double collar mouth, smooth base, golden yellow w/apricot tone some interior residue, small burst bubble on shoulder, qt. (ILLUS.) **1,344**

GVI-4 - "Baltimore" below monument - "Corn For The World" in semicircle above ear of corn, smooth edges, short applied slop-

ing collared mouth, smooth base, medium plum puce, qt. (large burst bubble with small bruise on shoulder, some exterior high point wear) **2,688**

GVIII-10 - Sunburst w/twenty-nine triangular sectioned rays, center raised oval w/"Keen" reading from top to bottom on obverse & reverse, sheared mouth, pontil, bright medium yellowish olive, 1/2 pt. (mold slightly underblown at base)................ **532**

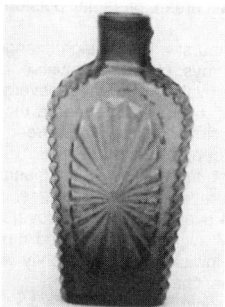

Early Yellowish Olive Sunburst Flask

GVIII-16 - Sunburst w/twenty-one triangular sectioned rays obverse & reverse, sheared & tooled lip, pontil, medium yellowish olive, 1/2 pt. (ILLUS.)........................... **672**

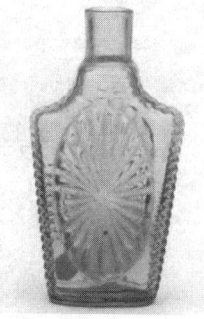

Twenty-four Ray Sunburst Flask

GVIII-2 - Sunburst w/twenty-four triangular sectioned rays obverse & reverse, sheared mouth, pontil, potstone w/no radiating, some minor interior haze, pale green, pt. (ILLUS.)... **504**

Clear Sunburst Flask

GVIII-26 - Sunburst w/sixteen rays obverse & reverse, ray converging to a definite point at center & covering entire side of flask, horizontally corrugated edges, plain lip, open pontil, clear w/light grey hue, light overall interior haze, pt. (ILLUS.) **308**

GVIII-5 - Sunburst w/twenty-four rounded rays obverse & reverse, horizontal corrugated edges, inward rolled mouth, pontil, bright forest green, pt. (small potstone in neck) **784**

GVIII-8 - Sunburst w/twenty-eight triangular sectioned rays, obverse & reverse, center raised oval w/"KEEN" on obverse & w/"P & W" on reverse, sheared mouth, pontil, medium to deep forest green, pt. (weak letter embossing) **504**

GVIII-8 - Sunburst w/twenty-eight triangular sectioned rays, obverse & reverse, center raised oval w/"KEEN" on obverse & w/"P & W" on reverse, sheared mouth, pontil, yellowish olive, pt. (slightly weak impression, shallow pontil chip) **560**

GX-14 - "Murdock" in semi-circle - "& - Cassel" in two straight lines, beneath rectangular band of heavy diagonal ribbing & below that a wider band of heavy vertical ribs extending to the base - "Zanesville" in semi-circle & "Ohio" in straight line, below ribbing similar to obverse, vertically ribbed edges w/narrow medial rib, sheared mouth, pontil, pale bluish green, pt. (mouth roughness, small chip at top of mouth) **672**

GX-15 - Summer Tree - Winter Tree, smooth edges, applied double lip, smooth base, mottled citron, pt. (some interior stain & scratches, medial rib crack) **420**

Summer Tree - Winter Tree Flask

GX-19 - Summer Tree - Winter Tree, sheared mouth, smooth edges, pontil, aqua, qt. (ILLUS.) **110**

GX-4 - Cannon framed by "Genl Taylor Never Surrenders" - Grapevine frame around "A Little More Grape Capt Bragg," vertically ribbed sides, medium greenish aqua, pt. **495**

GX-4 - Cannon framed by "Genl Taylor Never Surrenders" - Grapevine frame around "A Little More Grape Capt Bragg," vertically ribbed sides, sheared mouth, pontil, bright light green, pt. (weak impression) **616**

GX-8 - Sailboat (sloop) w/pennant on waves - eight-point star w/three-pointed ornaments, vertically ribbed sides, pontil, aqua, 1/2 pt. **154**

GXI-17 - Prospector w/tools & cane, slender figure w/small head, standing on oblong frame - American Eagle w/pennant above oval frame, applied mouth, smooth base, light to medium yellowish green, pt. **908**

GXI-46 - "For Pike's Peak" above prospector w/tools & cane, short & stocky figure w/tiny hands & feet - Hunter at left shooting stag at right, stocky figure w/tiny hands & feet & large head, smooth base, applied mouth, deep ice blue, qt. **550**

GXI-9 - "For Pike's Peak" above prospector w/tools & cane standing on oblong framed w/"Old Rye," American Eagle w/pennant above frame w/"Pittsburgh, PA.," smooth edges, aqua, pt. (hint of interior haze) **121**

Union-Clasped Hands & Eagle Flask

GXII-13 - Clasped hands above oval w/"L.F. & Co." all inside shield w/"UNION" above - American Eagle above frame w/"Pittsburgh Pa.," smooth base, applied mouth, amber, qt. (ILLUS.) **550**

GXII-19 - Clasped hands above oval enclosing "LF & CO," all inside shield w/"Union" above - American Eagle above oval frame enclosing "Pittsburgh, PA," applied mouth band, smooth base, deep aqua, pt. **220**

GXII-19 - Clasped hands above oval enclosing "LF & CO," all inside shield w/"Union" above - American Eagle above oval frame enclosing "Pittsburgh, PA," applied mouth band, smooth base, orangish amber, pt. **523**

Clasped Hands - Union Flask

GXII-25 - Clasped hands above oval w/"Old Rye" all inside shield below "Union" - American Eagle w/shield & pennant in beak inscribed "A & DHC," above cartouche panel w/"Pittsburgh, PA," aqua, pt. (ILLUS.) **99**

GXII-31 - Clasped hands above oval, all inside shield - American Eagle above oval, banded lip, smooth base, lime green w/green stripe down the front, 1/2 pt. **605**

GXII-31 - Clasped hands above oval, all inside shield - American Eagle above oval, banded lip, smooth base, brilliant yellow citron, 1/2 pt. **825**

GXII-33 - Clasped hands above oval all inside shield w/"Union" above shield - American Eagle above shield-shaped frame, round collar just below plain lip, medium amber, 1/2 pt. **198**

GXII-38 - Clasped hands above oval, all inside shield w/"Union" above - large cannon & American flag, applied mouth band, smooth base, bluish aqua, qt. (interior needs cleaning) **220**

GXII-40 - Clasped hands above oval w/"FA & Co.," all inside shield w/"Union" above - Small cannon & large American flag, applied mouth band, smooth base, aqua, pt. **154**

GXIII-12 - Soldier standing on patch of ground holding rifle & pointing to drum above bevel-edged narrow rectangular bar inscribed "BALT. MD." - Ballet dancer on patch of ground holding tambourine above bevel-edged narrow rectangular bar inscribed "Chapman," sheared mouth, pontil, aqua, pt. **179**

GXIII-16 - Horseman in full-dress uniform on high-stepping steed riding to right, saber held erect - Large hound walking right, applied double collar mouth, smooth base, straw yellow w/olive tone, qt. **715**

Amber Jockey - Hound Flask

GXIII-17 - Horseman wearing cap & short tight coat on a racing horse w/flying tail - Hound walking to the right, medium yellow amber, pt. (ILLUS.) **364**

GXIII-21 - "Flora Temple" above figure of a horse over "Harness Trot 219 3/4," plain reverse, flask-form w/applied handle, applied mouth w/ring, smooth base, strawberry puce, pt. **448**

GXIII-29a - "Will You Take A Drink (w/small floral design)" & "Will A (picture of a duck) Swim,?" - plain reverse, applied mouth w/ring, smooth base, deep bluish aqua, 1/2 pt. **1,008**

GXIII-35 - Sheaf of Grain w/rake & pitchfork crossed behind sheaf - "Westford Glass Co., Westford Conn," smooth edges, dark reddish amber, 1/2 pt. **253**

GXIII-36 - Sheaf of Grain w/rake & pitchfork crossed behind sheaf & five-pointed star centered between rake & pitchfork handles - "Westford Glass Co., Westford, Conn.," applied double collared mouth, smooth base, medium yellowish olive, pt. **179**

GXIII-4 - Hunter facing left wearing flat-top stove pipe hat, short coat & full trousers, game bag hanging at left side, firing gun at two birds flying upward at left, large puff of smoke from muzzle, two dogs running to left toward section of rail fence - Fisherman standing on shore near large rock, wearing round-top stove pipe hat, V-neck jacket, full trousers, fishing rod held in left hand w/end resting on ground, right hand holding large fish, creel below left arm, mill w/bushes & tree in left background, calabash-style, edges w/wide flutes, large open pontil, applied top, deep bluish green, qt. **330**

GXIII-4 - Hunter facing left wearing flat-top stove pipe hat, short coat & full trousers, game bag hanging at left side, firing gun at two birds flying upward at left, large puff of smoke from muzzle, two dogs running to left toward section of rail fence - Fisherman standing on shore near large rock, wearing round-top stove pipe hat, V-neck jacket, full trousers, fishing rod held in left hand w/end resting on ground, right hand holding large fish, creel below left arm, mill w/bushes & tree in left background, calabash-style, edges w/wide flutes, large open pontil, applied top, deep wine, qt. **880**

GXIII-44 - Sheaf of grain on crossed rake & pitchfork below arched leafy stems - Eight-point star, calabash-style, vertically ribbed edges, open pontil, applied top, medium to deep aqua, qt. **110**

Rare Topaz Baltimore-Sheaf Flask

GXIII-51 - Anchor w/fork-ended pennants inscribed "Baltimore" & "Glass Works" - Sheaf of Grain w/rake & pitchfork crossed behind sheaf, smooth edges, long neck w/sheared mouth, topaz, 1/2 pt. (ILLUS.) **5,040**

Rare Blue Anchor-Sheaf Calabash

GXIII-52 - Anchor between fork-ended pennants inscribed "Baltimore" & "Glass Works" - Sheaf of Grain w/crossed rake & pitchfork, calabash-form, applied double collared mouth, pontil, bright sapphire blue, spider crack on left of sheaf, interior stain in lower portion, some wear to impression, qt. (ILLUS.) **2,576**

Amber Anchor-Phoenix Flask

GXIII-53 - Anchor w/fork-ended pennants inscribed "Baltimore" & "Glass Works" on obverse - Phoenix rising from flames on rectangular panel inscribed "Resurgam" on reverse, applied square collared mouth, smooth base, golden amber, pt. (ILLUS.) **616**

GXIII-53 - Anchor w/fork-ended pennants inscribed "Baltimore" & "Glass Works" on obverse - Phoenix rising from flames on rectangular panel inscribed "Resurgam" on reverse, applied square collared mouth, smooth base, bright apricot topaz w/puce striations, pt. (small sand grain hairline, small shallow slip on side of mouth ring, tiny bruise on base) **840**

GXIII-54 - Anchor w/fork-ended pennants inscribed "Baltimore" & "Glass Works" on obverse - Phoenix without crest rising from flames on rectangular panel inscribed "Resurgam" on reverse, applied collared mouth, smooth base, smooth edges, mottled yellowish amber, pt. (two small flakes on side of base) **308**

GXIII-58 - Anchor w/fork-ended pennants inscribed "Spring Garden" & "Glass Works" - three-quarter view of log cabin, smooth edges, round collar, aqua, pt. **143**

GXIII-6 - Hunter facing left, wearing wide-brimmed hat w/high peaked crown, short coat, trousers & hunting boots firing gun straight ahead at two birds in flight at right, small dog running toward bush & rail fence at right - Fisherman standing on low bank, dressed similar to hunter, creel at left side, rod held in left hand & curving to left above head, line w/fish on end hanging to left & caught in left hand well above fish, rock & bush to left bank, calabash-form, light greenish aqua, qt. **154**

GXIII-60 - Anchor w/upper banner enclosing "Spring Garden" & lower banner enclosing "Glassworks" above long narrow panel - Log Cabin & leafless tree above a long narrow panel, applied double collared mouth, smooth base, orangish amber, pt. (small bruise at corner of base) **504**

GXIII-8 - Sailor dancing a hornpipe on an eight-board hatch cover, above a long rectangular bar - Banjo player sitting on a long bench, smooth edges, applied double collared mouth, smooth base, bright golden amber, 1/2 pt. (some light exterior wear) **392**

Sailor-Banjo Player Variant Flask

GXIII-8 variant - Sailor dancing a hornpipe on an eight-board hatch cover, above a long rectangular bar w/"Chapman" - Banjo player sitting on a long bench above a long rectangular bar, smooth edges, sheared mouth, open pontil, deep aqua, 1/2 pt. (ILLUS.) **258**

GXIII-9 - Sailor dancing a hornpipe on an eight-board hatch cover, above a long rectangular bar - Banjo player sitting on a long bench above a long rectangular bar inscribed "BALT. MD.," smooth edges, applied double collared mouth, pontil, pale greyish blue, 1/2 pt. **157**

GXIV- 3 - "Traveler's Companion" arched above & below star forms by a circle of eight small triangles - Sheaf of Grain w/rake & pitchfork crossed behind, applied mouth band, smooth base, deep bluish aqua, pt. **264**

GXIV-4 - "Traveler's Companion" above & below eight-point star - "Lancaster Erie Co., N.Y." above & below eight-point star, applied double collar mouth, smooth base, medium bluish green, pt. **1,925**

GXV-17 - "Ravenna Glass Works" in three
lines on obverse - plain reverse, smooth
edges, applied collared mouth w/ring,
iron pontil, aqua, pt. (some light interior
stain spots) **476**

Inks

Rare Early Free-blown Ink Bottle

Bulbous, deep yellowish olive, free-blown
squatty rounded body tapering to a short
sheared mouth, pontil scar, small burst
bubble on base, some minor scratches,
possibly Stoddard glasshouse, Stoddard,
New Hampshire, 1846-60, 2 1/8" d., 2" h.
(ILLUS.) **1,344**

Carter's Cathedral Master Ink Bottle

Cathedral, master-size, six Gothic arch
panels w/three embossed at the bottom
"CA - RT - ER," cobalt blue, ABM lip,
smooth base marked "Carter's," ca.
1920, 6 1/4" h. (ILLUS.) **253**
Cone-shaped, aqua, embossed "Dovell's
Patent" on side, rolled lip, ca. 1900 .... **55**
Cone-shaped, greenish citron, embossed
"Carter's 1897 - Made in USA" on base,
rolled lip, 2 1/2" h. **143**

Green Cone-shaped Ink Bottle

Cone-shaped, medium green, rolled lip,
pontil, ca. 1850, 2 5/8" h. (ILLUS.) **242**
Cone-shaped, medium yellowish olive,
sheared mouth, pontil, New England,
1840-60, 2 1/8" d., 2 3/8" h. **269**

Wood's Ink Bottle in a Rare Color

Cone-shaped, pale green, marked "Wood's
Black Ink Portland," inward rolled mouth,
rough pontil, 1840-60, 2 1/4" d., 2 5/8" h.
(ILLUS.) **1,904**

Unlisted Herron's Ink Bottle

Cylindrical, aqua, rounded shoulder to narrow neck w/inward rolled mouth, pontil,
embossed "Herron's Ink - Newville,Pa.,"
some faint interior haze, ca. 1840-60,
2 1/2" d., 3 3/8" h. (ILLUS.) **1,680**

Rare Small Harrison's Ink Bottle

Cylindrical, deep sapphire blue, "Harrison's Columbian Ink," inward rolled
mouth, pontil, ca. 1850, 2 1/8" d., 2" h.
(ILLUS.) **2,128**
Cylindrical, low w/wide shoulder & central
short neck, yellowish olive, tooled mouth,
pontil, embossed around sides "Perine
Guyot," France, 1840-60, 1 7/8" d., 2" h.
(pinhead flake on a letter) **156**

W.E. Bonney Master Ink Bottle

Cylindrical, master size, aqua, barrel-shaped w/ring bands, embossed "W.E. Bonney," applied sloping collar mouth w/spout spout, smooth base, 1870-90, 7 1/4" h. (ILLUS.) **364**

Fine Harrison's Master Ink Bottle

Cylindrical, master size, cobalt blue, "Harrison's Columbian Ink," applied mouth, pontil, ca. 1850, 7 1/4" h. (ILLUS.) **1,375**

Cylindrical, master size, cobalt blue, "Harrison's Columbian Ink," applied mouth, pontil, ca. 1850, 5 3/4" h. **1,705**

Cylindrical, master size, dark puce, embossed "Cowles' Ink" on shoulder, neck w/applied double collar mouth w/pour spout, smooth base, 1860-80, 9" h. **532**

Unusual Mold-blown Ribbed Inkwell

Cylindrical, mold-blown, medium violet blue, 24 fine ribs around the sides w/flat shoulder & flared ground mouth, smooth base, Boston & Sandwich Glass Co., 1820-40, 1 7/8" d., 1 7/8" h. (ILLUS.) **1,344**

Cylindrical w/12 sides, bright green, rounded shoulder & inward rolled mouth, pontil, original stained paper label reading "No. 2 Stand. - Gaubert's Steel Pen Ink. Black - Manufactured by -

Alonzo Gaubert - No. 10, Arch Row, Augusta, ME.," 2" w., 2" h. (some interior ink residue) **616**

Scarce Green Harrison's Ink Bottle

Eight-sided w/central neck, bright yellowish green, inward rolled lip, pontil, embossed "Harrison's Columbian Ink," ca. 1845-55, 2 1/8" w., 1 3/4" h. (ILLUS.) **672**

Eight-sided w/central neck, medium yellowish amber w/olive tone, embossed wording around sides "Farleys - Ink," sheared mouth, pontil, probably Stoddard, New Hampshire, 1846-60, 1 7/8" w., 1 7/8" h. (pinhead flake on base).. **952**

Figural, model of a turtle shell w/upright neck spout, clear glass, ground mouth, smooth base, possibly America or England, 1860-80, 4" w., 2" h.............. **224**

Igloo-form w/side neck, bright bluish green, ground mouth, smooth base, 85% original paper label reading "Superior - Writing Fluid - H.B. Foster - Concord, N.H.," 1860-80, 2" d., 2" h. **616**

Rare Domed Igloo Ink Bottle

Igloo-form w/side neck, golden amber, high domed form w/ground mouth, smooth base, some mouth roughness & flat chip on side of mouth, 1860-80, 1 7/8" d., 1 7/8" h. (ILLUS.)........................... **672**

Igloo-form w/side neck, sapphire blue, high domed form w/ground mouth, smooth base, 1860-80, 1 7/8" d., 2" h. (tiny flake on edge of base) **1,008**

Rare Log Cabin Ink Bottle

Log cabin-shaped, clear, central chimney neck w/tooled mouth, smooth base, ca. 1870, 2 3/8" h. (ILLUS.) **853**

Pitkin-type, dark yellowish olive, squared w/beveled corners & 36 fine ribs swirled to the left, disk mouth, pontil, probably Pitkin Glassworks, Manchester, New Hampshire, 1783-1830, 2 1/4" w., 1 3/4" h. (small burst bubble on one corner) **3,080**

Very Rare Early Pitkin Inkwell

Pitkin-type, deep yellow olive, squatty melon ribbed-form, 28 vertical ribs, tooled mouth, pontil, probably Pitkin Glass Works, Manchester, Connecticut, 1783-1830, 2 7/8" d., 1 5/8" h. (ILLUS.) **8,960**

Pitkin-type, medium yellowish olive, cylindrical w/36 ribs swirled to the left, tooled disk mouth, pontil, 1 1/2" h. **633**

Square, yellowish green free-blown form w/low tooled & flared mouth, pontil, 1800-30, 1 7/8" w., 2" h. **308**

Teakettle-type fountain inkwell w/neck extending up at angle from base, bright golden yellow, eleven-sided w/cut & polished panels, ground mouth w/brass collar & cap, ground pontil, probably England, 1830-60, 3 3/16" w., 2" h. (some minor roughness around ground top) **476**

Teakettle-type fountain inkwell w/neck extending up at angle from base, bright medium plum amethyst, vertically ribbed & paneled sides, ground mouth, smooth base, probably England 1830-60, 3 1/2" w., 2" h. **308**

Sapphire Blue Teakettle Inkwell

Teakettle-type fountain inkwell w/neck extending up at angle from base, bright medium sapphire blue, octagonal, ground mouth, smooth base, probably England, 1830-60, no brass collar or cap, 3 5/8" w., 2 1/16" h. (ILLUS.) **280**

Teakettle-type fountain inkwell w/neck extending up at angle from base, cobalt blue, double-font style, twelve-sided pyramidal form w/stopper for upper font, ground mouth, smooth base, probably England, ca. 1830-60, 3 1/4" w., 4" h. (no brass collar or cap) **728**

Teakettle-type fountain inkwell w/neck extending up at angle from base, cobalt blue, paneled barrel shape w/raised rings, ground mouth, smooth base, American, 1830-60, 3 1/16" w., 2 1/4" h. (ground mouth roughness, tiny bruise on top) **392**

Teakettle-type fountain inkwell w/neck extending up at angle from base, cobalt blue w/gilt floral trim, octagonal w/cut panels, ground mouth w/brass collar & cap, smooth base, probably England, 1830-60, 3 1/4" w., 1 7/8" h. **336**

Rare Blue Barrel-shaped Inkwell

Teakettle-type fountain inkwell w/neck extending up at angle from base, cornflower blue, barrel-shaped w/thin rings at the top & base, ground mouth, smooth base, 1830-60, 3 1/4" w., 2 1/8" h. (ILLUS.) **840**

Teakettle-type fountain inkwell w/neck extending up at angle from base, fiery opalescent, conical sides w/molded blossom head on top, embossed & painted leaf & flower decoration in blue, red, green & gold around the sides, ground mouth, smooth base, probably France, 1830-60, 3 1/4" w., 2 3/8" h. **476**

Teakettle-type fountain inkwell w/neck extending up at angle from base, fiery opalescent, rounded ten-paneled inverted acorn form w/a molded flowering vine around the sides painted in green, red & blue, ground mouth w/brass collar & cap, smooth base, Boston & Sandwich Glass Co., 1830-60, 3 1/2" w., 2 1/2" h. **364**

Rare Benjamin Franklin Inkwell

Teakettle-type fountain inkwell w/neck extending up at angle from base, figural, cobalt blue bust of Benjamin Franklin, ground mouth w/brass collar, smooth base, France, ca. 1830-60, no brass lid, 4 1/2" l., 2 3/4" h. (ILLUS.) **2,016**

Teakettle-type fountain inkwell w/neck extending up at angle from base, light opaque lime green, inverted acorn-form molded w/six lobes & six large acanthus leaves, ground mouth w/brass collar & cap, smooth base, probably England, 1830-60, 3" l., 2 1/2" h. **476**

Teakettle-type fountain inkwell w/neck extending up at angle from base, medium amethyst, paneled barrel shape w/raised rings, ground mouth, smooth base, American, 1830-60, 3" w., 2 1/4" h. (minor mouth roughness) **1,232**

Paneled Teakettle Inkwell

Teakettle-type fountain inkwell w/neck extending up at angle from base, medium green, eight-sided, ground lip, smooth base, original brass neck ring, ca. 1880, 2 1/8" h. (ILLUS.).................... **688**

Very Rare Miniature Teakettle Inkwell

Teakettle-type fountain inkwell w/neck extending up at angle from base, miniature, sapphire blue, octagonal w/cut & polished panels & neck, ground mouth w/metal collar & cap, smooth base, probably England, 1830-60, 2" w., 1 1/8" h. (ILLUS.).. **3,080**

Rare Opaque Blue Teakettle Inkwell

Teakettle-type fountain inkwell w/neck extending up at angle from base, opaque robin's-egg blue, pressed inverted acorn-form w/a leaf & eye design, ground mouth, smooth base, probably France, 1830-60, 3 1/2" w., 2 3/4" h. (ILLUS.) **504**

Unusual Turtle-form Inkwell

Turtle-form, base band below domed top w/band of edge scalloped below an embossed bird design, light bluish green, ground mouth, smooth base, American, 1860-80, 2 1/4" d., 1 1/2" h. (ILLUS.)............ **896**

Turtle-form, paneled sides, aqua, embossed letters on panels "J - & - I - E - M," ground lip, smooth base, ca. 1880, 1 3/4" h. **33**

Paneled Turtle Bottle in a Rare Color

Turtle-form, paneled sides, deep emerald green, embossed letters on panels "J - & - I - E - M," ground mouth, smooth base, ca. 1860-80, 2 1/4" w., 1 5/8" h. (ILLUS.).. **2,688**

Turtle-form, paneled sides, medium sapphire blue, embossed letters on panels "J - & - I - E - M," ground mouth, smooth base, ca. 1860-80, 2 1/4" w., 1 3/4" h. **1,568**

Turtle-form, paneled sides, yellowish green, embossed letters on panels "J - & - I - E - M," ground mouth, smooth base, ca. 1860-80, 2 1/4" w., 1 1/2" h. (some light interior haze)............................ **3,360**

Twelve-sided w/central neck, master size, deep emerald green, "Jones' Empire Ink N.Y.," applied mouth, iron pontil, ca. 1850, 5 7/8" h. **4,730**

Rare Ross's Excelsior Ink Bottle

Twelve-sided w/central neck, master-size, medium emerald green, "Ross's Excelsior Ink," applied mouth, pontil, insignificant flake on side of lip, ca. 1850, 7 3/8" h. (ILLUS.).. **4,620**

Umbrella (8-panel cone shape), golden amber, inward rolled mouth, smooth base, 75% original paper label reading "Thaddeus David & Co.," American, 1860-70, 2 1/2" w., 2 5/8" h. **123**

Rare 12-Panel Umbrella Ink Bottle

Umbrella-type (12-panel cone shape), bright golden amber, inward rolled mouth, tubular pontil scar, New England, 1840-60, 1 7/8" w., 2 1/8" h. (ILLUS.)............ **840**

Umbrella-type (8-panel cone shape), dark olive green, inward rolled mouth, tubular pontil scar, probably New England, 1840-60, 2 1/4" w., 2 3/8" h...................................... **308**

Umbrella Ink in Rare Amber Color

Umbrella-type (8-panel cone shape), medium orangish amber, inward rolled mouth, tubular pontil scar, 1840-60, 2 1/4" w., 2 1/4" h. (ILLUS.) **1,064**

Umbrella-type (8-panel cone shape), bright dark green, inward rolled mouth, pontil, w/90% of original stained paper label reading "Jet Black Record Ink - Frankfort Village," American, 1840-60, 2 1/4" w., 2 3/8" h. (some interior ink residue) **952**

Octagonal Umbrella Ink Bottle

Umbrella-type (8-panel cone shape), bright light yellow w/a slight olive tone, tooled collared mouth, smooth base, 1860-80, two tiny flakes on mouth, 2 3/4" w., 2 1/2" h. (ILLUS.) **532**

Umbrella-type (8-panel cone shape), deep golden amber, inward rolled mouth,

pontil, probably New England, ca. 1840-60, 2 5/8" w., 2 5/8" h. **258**

Umbrella-type (8-panel cone shape), light blue, rolled lip, pontil (minor interior stain)........ **55**

Umbrella-type (8-panel cone shape), light green, sheared lip, large base pontil **44**

Umbrella-type (8-panel cone shape), light to medium emerald green, rolled lip, pontil, crude **90**

Umbrella-type (8-panel cone shape), medium yellowish olive, sheared mouth, pontil, probably New England, 1840-60, 2 1/4" w., 2 5/8" h. **280**

Umbrella Ink in a Scarce Color

Umbrella-type (8-panel cone shape), yellowish olive, inward rolled mouth, pontil, 1840-60, 2 1/4" w., 2 3/8" h. (ILLUS.) **560**

Medicines

Alexander's Silmaeau, flattened fiddle-shape w/tall bulbed neck & tooled mouth, pontil, ca. 1845-55, medium sapphire blue, 6 1/4" h. (overall milky interior stain)...... **550**

Brant's Indian Pulmonary Balsam, octagonal w/applied top, smooth base, medium aqua, 6 1/2" h. **22**

Carter's Spanish Mixture, cylindrical, applied sloping double collar mouth, iron pontil, ca. 1845-55, deep yellowish olive green, 8" h. **578**

Celery Compound Bottle

Celery Compound - Compound (superimposed on bunch of celery), square semi-cabin w/paneled sides, tooled mouth, smooth base, ca. 1890, yellow w/olive tone, 10" h. (ILLUS.)............................ **176**

Rare Covert's Balm of Life

Covert's (I.) - Balm of Life, rectangular w/beveled corners, applied sloping collar mouth, open pontil, ca. 1835-55, deep olive green, 6" h. (ILLUS.) **2,585**

DeVincent (Dr.) Magic Cough Cure - San Francisco, rectangular w/paneled sides, applied top, aqua, 7" (light interior dirt) **330**

Howe's (Stewart D.) Arabian Tonic Blood Purifier - New York, rectangular w/paneled sides, applied top, smooth base, aqua, 10 1/2" h. **264**

Indians (The) Panacea, cylindrical w/domed label panel on reverse, applied sloping double collar mouth, pontil, ca. 1835-55, deep green w/hint of yellow, 8" h. **5,280**

Jayne's (Dr. D.) Alterative 242 Chestnut St. Phila., rectangular w/inset front panel, rounded shoulders & short neck w/applied rolled lip, smooth base, aqua, 7 1/2" h. (some scratches) **22**

Log Cabin - Cough and Consumption - Remedy, three-sided w/flat back, tooled lip, smooth base marked "Pat. Sept.6.87," medium amber, ca. 1890, 6 3/4" h. **198**

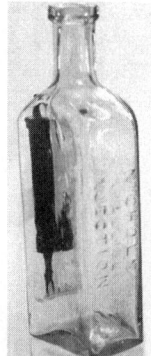

Nichol's Infallible Injection w/Injector

Nichol's Infallible Injection, rectangular, applied rim band, rare original metal injector attached to side, very crude, some minor interior haze, 7 3/4" h. (ILLUS.) **110**

Rare Wm. Radam's Bottle

Radam's (Wm.) - (design of man beating a skeleton) - Registered Trade Mark Dec. 13, 1887 (in shield below) - Germ, Bacteria or Fungus Destroyer, square w/rounded shoulder & short neck w/plain sheared lip, smooth base, aqua, 10 1/2" h. (ILLUS.) **715**

Raspail's (Dr.) Specific Cordial, oval base w/gently flared sides, tall tapering shoulder & applied rim band, smooth base, crude, aqua, 9" h. **176**

Reed's Gilt (1878) Edge Tonic, square w/applied mouth, smooth base, ca. 1870-80, amber, 8 5/8" h. **220**

Rheumatic Trade Mark Syrup

Rheumatic (motif of tree) Trade Mark - Syrup 1882 - R.S. Co. Rochester. N.Y., square w/paneled sides, applied sloping collar mouth, smooth base, some light outside dullness, spot of roughness under lip edge, ca. 1880, medium amber, 9 3/4" h. (ILLUS.) **165**

Smith's Green Mountain Renovator

Smith's - Green Mountain - Renovator - East Georgia, VT, tall octagonal form w/applied sloping collar mouth, iron pontil, ca. 1845-55, deep yellowish amber w/hint of olive, 7 1/8" h. (ILLUS.).......... **2,695**

Sparks Perfect Health (below Trade Mark) - bust of man - for Kidney & Liver Diseases, Camden, N.J., rectangular w/beveled corners, tooled mouth, smooth base, ca. 1880-95, cleaned, yellow amber, 9 1/2" h. **209**

Starkweather's Hepatic Elixir

Starkweather's (J.) Hepatic Elixir - Upton, Mass., six-sided, applied sloping collar mouth, pontil, ca. 1845-55, greenish aqua (ILLUS.)... **132**

U.S.A. Hosp. Dept. Bottle

U.S.A.- Hosp. Dept., cylindrical w/rounded shoulder & applied double collar mouth, smooth base, ca. 1860-70, medium yellowish olive green, 9 1/2" h. (ILLUS.) **578**

U.S.A.- Hosp. Dept. (on shoulder), cylindrical w/tooled mouth & smooth base, ca. 1860-75, medium cobalt blue, 7 3/8" h. (few spots of inside haze).............................. **605**

University Free Medicine Philadelphia, six-sided, applied mouth, pontil, ca. 1845-55, bluish aqua, 4 7/8" h. (some light interior stain) **143**

Wakelee Cameline, rectangular, tooled rim, bright cobalt blue, 5" h. (minor scratches) **523**

Warner's Safe Diabetes Remedy

Warner's Safe Diabetes Remedy (below) 16 oz., oval w/rounded shoulder & short neck w/tooled rim, bright light yellowish green, 9 1/2" h. (ILLUS.) **550**

Warner's Safe Kidney and Liver Remedy (motif of safe) - Rochester, N.Y., - 16 Fl. Oz. (on shoulder), oval, tooled mouth, smooth base, late 19th c., olive green **605**

Warner's Safe Rheumatic Cure (motif of safe) - Rochester, N.Y., oval, tooled mouth, smooth base, late 19th c., dark amber, 9 1/2" h. **154**

Wishart's (L.Q.C.) - Pine Tree Tar Cordial, Phila. - Patent (design of pine tree) 1859, square w/beveled corners, applied sloping collar, smooth base, ca. 1859-70, light Lockport green, 9 1/2" h. (in-the-making chip under applied collar)................. **220**

Wishart's (L.Q.C.) - Pine Tree Tar Cordial, Phila. - Patent (design of pine tree) 1859, square w/beveled corners, applied sloping collar, smooth base, medium emerald green, 7 1/2" h. **259**

Wishart's (L.Q.C.) - Pine Tree Tar Cordial, Phila. - Patent (design of pine tree) 1859, square w/beveled corners, applied sloping collar, smooth base, ca. 1859-70, dark yellowish green, 9 1/2" h. **358**

Wishart's (L.Q.C.) - Pine Tree Tar Cordial, Phila. - Patent (design of pine tree) 1859, square w/beveled corners, applied sloping collar, smooth base, ca. 1859-70, dark emerald green, 9 1/2" h. **358**

Very Rare Wood's Elixir

Wood's (Dr. J.S.) Elixir, Albany , N.Y., rectangular w/deeply cut corners & tombstone shoulders, applied sloping collar mouth, iron pontil, ca. 1845-55, deep bluish green, tiny flake on front panel, 8 3/4" h. (ILLUS.) 5,390

Yerba Santa (in cross) - San Francisco, California, rectangular w/paneled sides, tooled mouth, crude, deep bluish aqua, 8 1/2" h. (partially open bubble on shoulder) 121

Mineral Waters, Sodas & Sarsaparillas

Adirondack Spring - Westport, N.Y., cylindrical w/applied sloping double collar mouth, smooth base, ca. 1865-80, bluish emerald green, qt. 264

Arctic Soda Water Works - M. R. Desa Prop. (in slug plate) - Honolulu HI, cylindrical w/tooled blob top, aqua 55

Artesian Spring Co. "AS" (monogram) Ballston N.Y. - Ballston Spa "AS" (monogram) Mineral Water, cylindrical w/applied sloping double collar, smooth base, ca. 1865-75, medium emerald green, pt., 7 5/8" h. 121

Beard's Mineral Water Bottle

Beard's Mineral Water - F & B Boston, tapering cylindrical w/applied blob top, smooth base, ca. 1860, medium bluish green, 7" h. (ILLUS.) 71

Rare Early Dubuque Mineral Water

Belcher & Co. Dubuque - Excelsior Mineral Waters, tapering cylindrical w/applied blob mouth, iron pontil, ca. 1850, small chip off top of lip, some case wear, deep cobalt blue, 7 1/2" h. (ILLUS.) 1,430

Brennan & Graham - Stuebenville (errant "O"), cylindrical w/tapering shoulder & tall neck w/applied top, iron pontil, very crude, light aqua 198

Champion Spouting Spring - Saratoga. N.Y. - Champion Water, cylindrical w/applied sloping double collar mouth, smooth base, ca. 1865-80, amber, pt. (potstone in neck w/several stress cracks) 413

Scarce Chemung Spring Water Bottle

Chemung - Spring Water (design of Native American) - Trade Mark - Bottled at the spring - This Bottle is Loaned - and Never Sold, cylindrical w/rounded shoulder & short neck w/tooled lip, smooth base, ca. 1885-1900, golden yellow amber, 1/2 gal. (ILLUS.) 660

John Clarke New York Pint Bottle

Clarke (John) - New York (on front), cylindrical w/applied sloping double collar mouth, pontiled base, ca. 1845-55, deep olive green, pt. (ILLUS.) 440

Clarke & White - (C) - New York, cylindrical w/applied sloping double collar mouth, smooth base, ca. 1855-65, deep olive green, qt. 83

Clarke & White - New York, cylindrical w/applied sloping double collar mouth, pontil, ca. 1860-75, dark to medium moss green, pt. 55

Clarke & White - New York, cylindrical w/applied sloping double collar mouth, pontil, ca. 1860-75, medium yellowish olive green, qt. 121

Clarke & White - New York, cylindrical w/applied sloping double collar mouth, smooth base, periods after "White" & "York," very crude, ca. 1860-75, deep emerald green, pt. 99

Congress & Empire Spring Co. Bottle

Congress & Empire Spring Co. - C (inside frame) - Saratoga, N.Y., cylindrical w/applied sloping double collar mouth, smooth base, ca. 1870, deep bluish green, pt. (ILLUS.) 633

Congress & Empire Spring Co - C - Saratoga, N.Y. - Congress - Water, cylindrical w/applied sloping double collar mouth, smooth base, bluish green, ca. 1860-75, qt. 61

Congress & Empire Spring Co. Columbian Water Saratoga, N.Y., cylindrical w/applied double collar mouth, smooth base, emerald green, ca. 1870, pt. (several open bubbles) 688

Congress & Empire Spring Co. - Hotchkiss' Sons - C - New-York - Saratoga, N.Y. - Congress Water, cylindrical w/applied sloping double collar mouth, smooth base, ca. 1865-75, emerald green, qt. 83

Congress & Empire Spring Co. - Hotchkiss' Sons - C - New-York - Saratoga, N.Y., cylindrical w/applied sloping double collar mouth, smooth base, ca. 1865-75, bright yellowish green, pt. 175

Congress & Empire Spring Co. - Hotchkiss' Sons - C - New-York - Saratoga, N.Y., cylindrical w/applied sloping double collar mouth, smooth base, ca. 1865-75, root beer amber, crude, qt. 385

Congress & Empire Spring Co. - Hotchkiss' Sons - E - New York Saratoga, N.Y., cylindrical w/applied double collar mouth, smooth base, ca. 1865-75, yellowish golden amber, pt. (very minor iridescent bruise on lip) 165

Congress & Empire Spring Pint

Congress & Empire Spring Co. - Hotchkiss' Sons - E - New York Saratoga, N.Y., cylindrical w/applied double collar mouth, smooth base, ca. 1865-75, medium reddish amber, pt. (ILLUS.) 413

Eureka Spring Co. Bottle in Stand

Eureka Springs Co. - Saratoga, NY, ten-pin form w/applied top, in original upright pronged silver plate stand marked "Saratoga Club House - G.M. Co." & an anchor, dark green (ILLUS.) 550

Excelsior Spring - Saratoga, N.Y., cylindrical w/applied sloping double collar mouth, smooth base, ca. 1870-80, emerald green, qt. 99

Excelsior Spring - Saratoga, N.Y., cylindrical w/applied sloping double collar mouth, smooth base, ca. 1870-80, deep lime green, qt. 165

Franklin Spring Mineral Water Bottle

Franklin Spring - Mineral Water - Ballston Spa - Saratoga Co. N.Y., cylindrical w/applied sloping double collar mouth, smooth base, ca. 1865-75, emerald green, pt. (ILLUS.) 523

Gettysburg Katalysine Water, cylindrical w/tall neck & applied sloping double collar, ca. 1865-80, yellowish green, qt., 9 5/8" h. 88

Geyser Spring - Saratoga Springs - State of New York - The Saratoga Spouting Spring, cylindrical w/applied sloping double collar, smooth base, ca. 1865-75, deep bluish aqua, qt.......................... 77

Gilbert (B.) Yreka, cylindrical w/tooled blob top, "G" in circle on base, California, 1890-98, crude, aqua.......................... 264

Hawaiian Soda Works Honolulu T.H., cylindrical w/crown top, initials of the Pacific Coast Glassworks on the base, ca. 1900, aqua 44

Highrock Congress Spring- 1767- (design of a rock), C. & W. Saratoga N.Y., cylindrical w/applied sloping double collar mouth, smooth base, medium yellowish amber, ca. 1865-75, pt. 231

Highrock Congress Spring- 1767- (design of a rock), C. & W. Saratoga N.Y., cylindrical w/applied sloping double collar mouth, smooth base, golden amber, ca. 1865-75, qt.......................... 358

Highrock Congress Spring (design of a rock), C. & W. Saratoga N.Y., cylindrical w/applied sloping double collar, smooth base, ca. 1865-75, light to medium teal blue, pt. 495

Highrock Congress Spring Bottle

Highrock Congress Spring (design of a rock), C. & W. Saratoga N.Y., cylindrical w/applied sloping double collar, smooth base, ca. 1865-75, teal blue, pt. (ILLUS.) 523

Honolulu Soda Water Co. Ltd. T.H., cylindrical w/tooled blob top, light greenish aqua.......................... 55

Log Cabin - Sarsaparilla - Rochester, N.Y., three-panel front w/flattened back, "Pat. Sept. 6th 1887" on base, applied mouth, ca. 1890, deep amber, 9" h. (ILLUS. top of right column) 187

Log Cabin Sarsaparilla Bottle

Lynch & Clarke New York, cylindrical w/applied sloping double collar mouth, pontil, yellowish olive amber, ca. 1830-40, pt. 468

M.R. - Sacramento, tapering cylindrical w/applied blob mouth, iron pontil, ca. 1850, tiny flake on edge of base, cobalt blue, 7 1/2" h. 660

Middletown Healing Springs Bottle

Middletown Healing Springs, Grays & Clark, Middletown, Vt., cylindrical w/tall neck & applied sloping double collar mouth, smooth base, ca. 1865-75, medium yellowish amber, qt. (ILLUS.)..................... 83

Missisquoi - A - Springs, cylindrical w/applied sloping double collar mouth, smooth base, ca. 1865-80, medium bluish green, qt. 94

Missisquoi - A - Springs, cylindrical w/applied sloping double collar mouth, smooth base, ca. 1865-80, yellowish olive green, qt. 105

Norris (C.) A & D.H.C. - City Bottling Works Detroit, Mich., cylindrical tapering to applied blob mouth, smooth base, ca. 1870, medium cobalt blue, 7 1/2" h. (some stains)..................... 83

Oahu Soda Works Aiea, Oahu - Bottle Not Sold, cylindrical w/tooled blob top, aqua (hint of stain) 55

Oak Orchard Acid Springs, Address G.W. Merchant, Lockport, N.Y. (around shoulder), cylindrical w/applied sloping double collar mouth, smooth base, ca. 1865-75, deep bluish green, qt., 9" h. **110**

Oak Orchard - Acid Springs - H.W. Bostwick - Agt. No. 574 - Broadway, New York, cylindrical w/applied sloping double collar mouth, embossed on smooth base "Glass From F. Hitchins Factory - Lockport, N.Y.," medium teal bluish green, qt. **187**

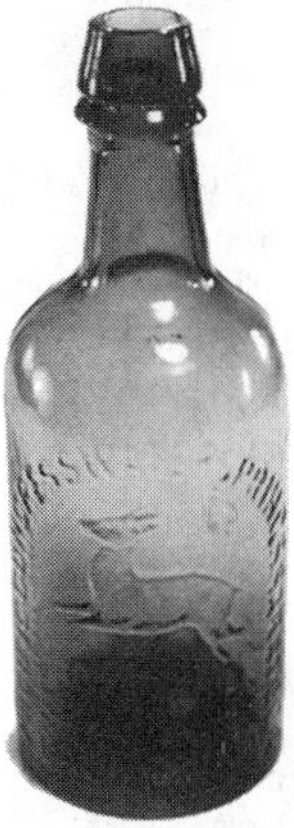

Fine Pacific Congress Springs Bottle

Pacific Congress Water Springs - Saratoga - California (arched & surrounding a running deer) - Pacific Congress Springs (on reverse), cylindrical w/rounded shoulder & tall neck w/double applied sloping collar, smooth base, bright medium green (ILLUS.) **1,760**

Pacific Soda Works Co. Ltd. Honolulu T.H., cylindrical w/crown top, ca. 1900, light greenish aqua **55**

Pavilion & United States Spring Bottle

Pavilion & United States Spring Co. - P - Saratoga N.Y. - Pavilion Water, cylindrical w/applied sloping double collar mouth w/original wire closure, smooth base, ca. 1860-80, deep tobacco amber, pt. (ILLUS.) **485**

Pavilion & United States Spring Co. - Saratoga, N.Y. - Pavilion Water - Aperient, cylindrical w/rounded shoulder & applied sloping double collar mouth, smooth base, ca. 1865-80, deep emerald green, pt. **275**

Pioneer Soda Works - Smith & Bryan Co. - Reno, Nevada, cylindrical w/tooled blob top, early 20th c., light lime-aqua **303**

Roussel's Mineral Water - Manufactured in Silver, cylindrical w/tapering shoulder & neck w/applied sloping color, facsimile silver medal on the back, graphite pontil, emerald green (some scratches) **165**

Saratoga A Congress Pint Bottle

Saratoga - A - Congress (in slug plate) - Carl H. Schultz - N.Y., cylindrical w/applied sloping double collar mouth, smooth base, ca. 1855-65, medium bluish green, small flake on edge of collar, pt. (ILLUS.) **743**

Saratoga - A - Spring Co NY, cylindrical w/applied sloping double collar mouth, smooth base, ca. 1855-65, emerald green, pt. **154**

Saratoga A Spring Co. Bottle

Saratoga - A - Spring Co NY, cylindrical w/applied sloping double collar mouth, smooth base, ca. 1855-65, yellowish olive, pt. (ILLUS.) **605**

Saratoga (design of star) Spring, cylindrical w/tall neck & applied double collar

mouth, smooth base, ca. 1865-75, full of
seed bubbles, medium amber, qt..................... **99**

Saratoga (Star) Spring Variant

**Saratoga (design of star) Spring (back-
ward "S"),** cylindrical w/tall neck & applied double collar mouth, smooth
base, ca. 1865-75, medium yellowish
amber, qt. (ILLUS.)... **132**

Rare Saratoga Highrock Spring Bottle

**Saratoga Highrock Spring (motif of rock)
Saratoga, N.Y.,** cylindrical w/applied
sloping double collar, smooth base, ca.
1865-75, medium emerald green, pt.
(ILLUS.)... **1,320**

**Smith & Kelly's Soda and Mineral Wa-
ters,** cylindrical w/tapering shoulder &
neck w/applied sloping collar, iron pontil,
deep green **231**

**Spring Soda Water Works Co. Waialua
Oahu,** cylindrical w/crown top, em-
bossed orchid on base, ca. 1900, aqua.......... **44**

**Star Soda Water Works (above five-point
star) Honolulu T.H.,** cylindrical w/crown
top, ca. 1900, bluish aqua **121**

**Star Spring Co. (design of star) Saratoga,
N.Y.,** cylindrical w/applied double collar
mouth, smooth base, ca. 1865-75, deep
olive, amber, pt. (ILLUS. top of right
column).. **187**

**Star Spring Co. (design of star) Saratoga,
N.Y.,** cylindrical w/applied sloping double
collar mouth, smooth base, ca. 1865-75,
deep reddish amber, pt., 7 3/4" h.................. **209**

Star Spring Co. Saratoga Bottle

Sun Rise Soda Water Works Honolulu,
cylindrical w/applied blob top, light to me-
dium bluish aqua **88**

Fine Sutton Root Beer Bottle

Sutton (I.) & Co Covington, KY, twelve-
sided cylindrical w/sloping neck to applied flat rim, iron pontil, ca. 1845-55, co-
balt blue, 8 1/4" h. (ILLUS.) **1,760**

**Syracuse Springs - D - Excelsior A.J. De-
lator - New York,** cylindrical, applied
sloping double collar mouth, smooth
base, ca. 1870, yellowish amber, 1/2 pt.
(some outside stain).. **743**

**This Bottle - is The Property of - The
Southern Mineral Water Company - Atlanta, GA. - and Must Not Be Sold,** cylindrical w/rounded shoulder & short neck
w/tooled lip, smooth base, ca. 1885-95,
aqua, 1/2 gal. **132**

Tonopah Soda Works Nev., cylindrical
w/tooled blob top, 1902-05, light lime-
aqua (minor areas of stain)............................. **825**

**Townsend's (Dr.) - Sarsaparilla - Albany,
N.Y.,** square w/beveled corners & applied sloping collar, ca. 1845-55, bright
bluish green, 9 1/2" h..................................... **468**

**Townsend's (Dr.) - Sarsaparilla - Albany,
N.Y.,** square w/beveled corners & applied sloping collar, ca. 1845-55, bright
green, 9 1/2" h. **468**

**Townsend's (Dr.) - Sarsaparilla - Albany,
N.Y.,** square w/beveled corners &

applied sloping collar, smooth base, ca. 1845-55, medium Lockport green, 9 7/8" h. (very minor interior lip flake)........... **121**

Townsend's (Dr.) - Sarsaparilla - Albany, N.Y., square w/beveled corners & applied sloping collar, smooth base, ca. 1845-55, dark Lockport green, 9 7/8" h. **176**

Townsend's (Dr.) - Sarsaparilla - Albany, N.Y., square w/beveled corners & applied sloping collar, smooth base, ca. 1845-55, bright 7-Up green, 9 7/8" h. **187**

Tweddle's Celebrated Soda or Mineral Waters- Courtland Street - 38 New York, cylindrical w/applied sloping collar mouth, pontil, ca. 1845-55, medium bluish green, 7 1/2" h. (some minor stain) **330**

Twichell - T - Philada., cylindrical tapering to a wide applied top, smooth base, light green (scratches & light pitting)........................ **33**

Vermont Spring - Saxe & Co. - Sheldon. Vt., cylindrical w/a tall tapering neck & applied sloping double collar mouth, smooth base, deep emerald green, ca. 1870-80, qt. **66**

Washington Spring Bottle with Bust

Washington Spring Co. (bust of Washington) Ballston Spa N.Y. - C, cylindrical w/rounded shoulder, applied sloping double collar mouth, smooth base, emerald green, ca. 1865-75, faint iridescent bruise inside lip, pt. (ILLUS.)........................ **660**

Washington Spring - Saratoga - N.Y., cylindrical w/rounded shoulder, applied sloping double collar mouth, smooth base, ca. 1865-75, emerald green, pt. **253**

Weston (G.W.) & Co. Saratoga. N.Y., cylindrical w/applied sloping double collar mouth, pontil, medium yellowish olive amber, ca. 1860, pt. ' **220**

Poisons

Amber, rectangular, embossed skull & crossbones, tooled top, 2 1/2" h....................... **55**

Cobalt blue, cylindrical w/overall embossed diamond lattice design, tooled lip, smooth base, rectangular stopper w/points & "Poison," ca. 1890-1910, 5 1/2" h. **143**

Rare Canadian Poison Bottle

Cobalt blue, square w/beveled corners, tooled mouth, smooth base, "Contents 4 Fl. Oz." on shoulder above large heart enclosing "The J.E. Hartz Co. Limited Toronto" above rows of small hearts, rows of small hearts on sides, ca. 1890-1910, 5" h. (ILLUS.) **825**

Owl Drug Company Poison Bottle

Cobalt blue, triangular w/rounded shoulder & tooled mouth, marked "Poison - (molded design of owl on mortar & pestle) - The Owl Drug Co.," 8" h. (ILLUS.) **440**

Emerald green, six-sided w/fine horizontal ribbing in panels & "Poison" in alternating panels, tooled top, 5 1/2" h. **55**

Olive green, six-sided w/embossed skull & crossbones panels alternating w/"Vorsicht - Gift" on panels, ABM lip, "250" on smooth base, Germany, ca. 1920-30, 6 7/8" h. (pinhead flake on base corner) **121**

Whiskey & Other Spirits

Ale, "Dr. Cronk Gibbons & Co. Superior Ale - Buffalo, N.Y.," applied mouth, iron pontil, ca. 1850, brilliant emerald green, 6 5/8" h. **495**

Ale, "Swan Brewery Co. - X. X. X. Ale" (in circle enclosing a swimming swan) - "This Bottle Never Sold by the Co" (on reverse), cylindrical w/sloping shoulder & tall neck w/applied top, smooth base, Western U.S., dark yellowish olive (ILLUS. top of next page) **1,650**

Rare Western Ale Bottle

Beer, "Bay View Brewing Co., Seattle, Wash." in circle, cylindrical w/applied mouth, medium forest green, pt. 660

Beer, "Buffalo Brewing Co. - Sacramento, Cal" in circle around a horseshoe, cylindrical w/applied top, dark amber, pt. 44

Beer, "Buffalo Brg. Co. - Sacramento" (w/other wording), cylindrical, applied top, dark reddish amber, qt. 110

Beer, "Celery Beer - Keller Candy Company - Distributors - Oakland, Cal." in circle, cylindrical w/applied top, amber, qt. 110

Beer, "Honolulu Brewing Co. - Honolulu H.T.," cylindrical w/blob top, ca. 1890, aqua, qt. 77

Beer, "Los Angeles Brew Co." below American eagle & shield, cylindrical w/applied top, dark amber, qt. (some interior stain) 33

Beer, "P.B. - Milwaukee" in circle, cylindrical w/tooled top, crude, bright golden amber, pt. 22

Beer, "Peterson (H.A.) Watsonville, Cal.," cylindrical tapering to a tall neck w/tooled rim, medium amber, qt. 66

Beer, "Proll (J.) Bottling Works US Lager SF Cal," cylindrical tapering to tall neck w/original porcelain & wire stopper, crude, amber, qt. 330

Beer, "Rainier Beer Brewing and Malting Co. Seattle," cylindrical w/crown top, dark green, 1/2 pt. 132

Beer, "Schmiel (Wm.) San Jose California," cylindrical tapering to a tall neck w/original porcelain & wire stopper, amber, qt. 55

Beer, "Seal Rock Bottling Co. - John Kroger - San Francisco, Cal.," cylindrical w/tooled top, medium amber, 1/2 pt. 99

Beer, "Sebastapol Bottling Works - Cal," cylindrical w/tooled top, amber, pt. 33

Beer, "Standard Bottling Co. - S.F.," cylindrical w/tooled top, dark reddish amber, pt. (very light staining) 33

Beer, "Sunset Bottling Co. (over monogram) San Francisco, Cal.," cylindrical tapering to a tall neck w/tooled rim, light to medium golden amber, qt. 44

Beer, "Tons (John) - over monogram - Stockton, Cal.," applied top, bright yellow w/some green, qt. 110

Beer, "U.S. Bottling Co. - John Fauser & Co. - San Francisco," cylindrical w/tooled top, reddish amber, pt. 33

Beer, "Wonder Bottling Co. - W. Noethig - Sacramento, Cal.,v cylindrical w/tooled top, amber, pt. 44

Rare Landsberg's Brandy Bottle

Brandy, "Landsberg's Pure Blackberry Brandy - 1876 - A. Heller & Bros. New York," square w/arched sides w/embossed spread-winged eagles above recessed panels framed by a chain-like designs, band of stars around base of neck, applied sloping collar mouth, smooth base, deep bluish aqua, 11 1/4" h. (ILLUS.) 4,510

Brandy, "Livingston's Pure Blackberry Brandy - Distilled From The Berry," cylindrical w/tall neck & applied top, star on base, ca. 1877-84, bright golden amber, sixth 1,100

Case gin, square tapering form, embossed "Blankenheym & Nolet," applied shoulder seal w/a key design, tooled top, dark yellowish green, 10 3/4" h. 66

Case gin, square tapering form, embossed "Meder & Zoon" w/swan design, applied clear shoulder seal w/"W.P.," tooled top, clear, 9 1/2" h. 143

Case gin, square tapering form, "Genuine Hollands Geneva" (on paper label), embossed "Daniel Visser & Zonen Schiedam" on back, dark green (flat chip on base) 121

Cosmopoliet Dutch Case Gin

Case gin, square tapering form, marked "Cosmopoliet (design of standing man) J.J. Melchers WZ - Schiedam," applied sloping collar mouth, smooth base, Holland, ca. 1880-95, deep olive green, 9 1/2" h. (ILLUS.) 132

Case gin, square tapering form w/cobalt blue applied seal on shoulder embossed "Daniel Visser & Zonen Scheidam," clear, 11" h. 413

Gin, "Bininger (A.M.) & Co. No. 19 Broad St. N.Y. - Old London Dock - Gin," square w/beveled corners & applied top, smooth base, reddish amber, qt. 413

Gin, "Bininger (A.M.) & Co. No. 338 Broadway - Old London Dock - Gin," square w/beveled corners & applied top, smooth base, dark yellowish green, qt., 9 3/4" h. 187

Gin, "London Jockey - Club House - Gin" w/design of jockey on horse, square w/rounded shoulder & short neck w/applied sloping collar, smooth base, ca. 1855-70, reddish amber, fifth (small open bubble on one shoulder) 303

London Jockey Club House Gin

Gin, "London Jockey - Club House - Gin" w/design of jockey on horse, square w/rounded shoulder & short neck w/applied sloping collar, smooth base, ca. 1865-75, deep olive green, small partial open bubble on one corner, 9 3/8" h. (ILLUS.) 385

Rare London Jockey Club House Gin

Gin, "London Jockey - Club House - Gin" w/design of jockey on horse, square

w/rounded shoulder & short neck w/unusual crude laid-on top, smooth base, light bluish green, tiny bleeding potstone, crude, 9 5/8" h. (ILLUS.) 770

Gin, "Old Tom Longchamp's London Cordial Gin," square w/beveled corners & rounded shoulder & short neck w/applied sloping collar, smooth base, yellowish olive green, 9 3/4" h. 330

Schnapps, "Melcher's (J.J.) - Aromatic Schnapps - W.Z. Schiedam," square, applied top, smooth base, light emerald green 110

Schnapps, "Udolpho Wolfe's Aromatic Schnapps, Schiedam," rectangular w/beveled corners, applied sloping collar mouth, dark olive amber, 9 3/8" h. 66

Schnapps, "Udolpho Wolfe's Aromatic Schnapps, Schiedam," rectangular w/beveled corners, applied sloping collar mouth, smooth base, ca. 1885-90, bright yellowish green, 9" h. 165

Schnapps, "Udolpho Wolfe's Aromatic Schnapps, Schiedam," rectangular w/beveled corners, applied sloping collar mouth, dark amber w/olive tone, graphite pontil, 9 3/8" h. 209

Spirits, free-blown, bulbous cylindrical body tapering to a tall neck w/applied string lip & applied seal w/"W. Oakley - 1789," open pontil, England, olive amber, 5" d., 10 7/8" h. 1,965

Spirits, free-blown onion-form w/tall neck & applied string lip, pontilled base, applied seal w/design of a fox beneath a baron's coronet, England, ca. 1700-10, olive green, half-size, 4 1/8" d., 5 1/8" h. (short crack from lip into neck, minor outside stain) 2,310

Rare Early English Seal Bottle

Spirits, free-blown onion-form w/tall neck & applied string lip, pontilled base, applied seal w/"I. Smith -1706," olive amber, England, early date, 5 1/8" d., 6 5/8" h. (ILLUS.) 7,700

Spirits, mold-blown demijohn, cylindrical w/tall neck & applied sloped rim, heavily whittled & crude, bright yellowish emerald green, 15" h. 110

Spirits, mold-blown demijohn, cylindrical w/tall neck & applied sloped rim, improved pontil, heavily whittled & many bubbles, dark olive green, 16" h. 121

Early Zanesville Spirits Bottle

Spirits, mold-blown, globular, tall neck w/rolled rim, twenty-four ribs swirled to the right, pontil, bright yellow w/a hint of olive, Zanesville, Ohio, ca. 1820s (ILLUS.) **3,080**

Whiskey, "Bennet & Carroll - No. 120 Wood St. - Pitts. PA," chestnut flask-shaped, applied rim band, iron pontil, brilliant golden amber, 8 1/2" h. **1,100**

Whiskey, "Bininger (A.M.) & Co. - No. 19 Broad St. - New York," cylindrical w/wide sloped shoulder to short neck w/applied double collar mouth & small strap handle, smooth base, yellowish amber, ca. 1855-65, 8" h. **523**

Whiskey, "Blake's (G.O.) Bourbon Co. KY - Moore, Reynolds & Co. - Sold Agents for Pacific Coast," applied top, 1875-80, medium to deep amber, fifth (couple open surface bubbles) **990**

Whiskey, "Booth & Co. [large anchor motif] - Sacramento" (in circle on front), tooled top, clear **303**

Rare E.G. Booz Old Cabin Whiskey

Whiskey, "Booz's (E.G.) Old Cabin Whiskey - 120 Walnut St. Philadelphia" on roof, "1840 - E.G. Booz's Old Cabin Whiskey" on sides, cabin-shaped, applied sloping collar mouth, smooth

base, golden amber, ca. 1855-70, 7 1/2" h. (ILLUS.) **3,740**

Whiskey, "Bottled by Samuel Brothers & Co. Louisville, KY - San Francisco, Cal" beside monogram in shield flanked by "O - K," square w/tall neck & applied top, bright golden orangish amber **495**

Whiskey, "Boulevard OK Bourbon - S.F. Cal." in oval belt w/buckle around "Buneman & Martinoni Sole Agents," applied top, light smoky amber, fifth **440**

Whiskey, "Boulevard OK Bourbon - S.F. Cal." in oval belt w/buckle around "H. Buneman Sole Agent," applied top, light olive amber, fifth (tiny ding on base) **253**

Whiskey, "Chesley (W.) Sacramento, Cal.," late pumpkinseed flask-form w/rolled rim, 1890s, clear, pt. (small open bubble, hint of haze) **110**

Whiskey, "Chestnut Grove Whiskey, C.W.," chestnut flask-shaped w/applied neck handle, applied mouth, pontil, 95% original paper labels, amber, 9 1/2" h. **253**

Whiskey, "Clark's (G.H.) Bourbon Co KY Whiskey - Moore Reynolds & Co Sole Agents For Pacific Coast," cylindrical w/tall neck & applied top, bright golden amber **2,090**

Whiskey, "Clinch & Co. (Bottled by) - [below monogram] - Dealers in Wines & Liquor - Grass Valley, Cal.," cylindrical w/a tall neck & tooled top, clear, fifth **33**

Rare J.F. Cutter Bourbon Variation

Whiskey, "Cutter (J.F.) Extra Old Bourbon" centering a star in shield flanked by "Trade Mark," cylindrical w/tall neck w/applied top, bright yellowish green (ILLUS.) **1,870**

Whiskey, "Cutter (J.H.) Old Bourbon A.P. Hotaling & Co. Sole Agents" below crown, cylindrical w/tall neck & applied top, 1877-80, dark amber, fifth (small potstone on back bottom panel) **990**

Whiskey, "Cutter (J.H.) Old Bourbon - A.P. Hotaling & Co. Sole Agents," cylindrical w/tall neck & applied top, 1877-80, dark amber, fifth (tiny nick off side collar) **303**

Whiskey, "Cutter (J.H.) - Old Bourbon" above barrel design, "C.P. Moorman Manufacturer Louisville, KY" at bottom, tooled top, late 19th c., clear, fifth (ping on left side) **132**

Whiskey, "Cutter (J.H.) - Old Bourbon" above barrel design, "Milton J. Hardy & Co. Manufacturers Louisville, KY" at bottom, applied top, late 19th c., dark amber, fifth (cleaned) **253**

Whiskey, "Cutter (R.B.), Louisville, KY," ovoid w/applied mouth & handle, large rough pontil, 8 1/2" h. **358**

Whiskey, "Cutter's (R.B.) Pure Bourbon," ovoid body w/applied mouth & handle, pontil, ca. 1855-65, deep cherry puce, 8 1/2" h. (some scratching on back) **495**

Whiskey, "Forest Lawn - J.V.H." in circle on shoulder, spherical body w/tall neck & applied mouth, iron pontil, ca. 1855-65, forest green, 7 1/2" h. (open bubble on shoulder) **715**

Whiskey, "Gaines (W.A.) Old Crow Whiskey, The Arcade, Cheyenne, Wyo.," rectangular flask-shaped w/neck screw threads, amethystine, half pint (tiny flash on lower back, small open bubble) **121**

Whiskey, "Gayen (J.T.) - Altona," figural cannon, applied top, smooth base, crude, amber **1,650**

Rare Griffith Hyatt & Co. Whiskey

Whiskey, "Griffith Hyatt & Co. - Baltimore," arched panel on front, bulbous ovoid shape tapering to neck w/applied mouth & applied handle, open pontil, ca. 1860-70, medium to deep pure olive green, very crude, 7 1/8" h. (ILLUS.) **1,320**

Whiskey, "Gruenberg (M.) & Co. San Francisco [in band around] Old Judge KY Bourbon," cylindrical w/tall neck & applied top, air-vented at the shoulder, fine yellowish amber, ca. 1880, fifth **495**

Whiskey, "Harris (Adolph) & Co. - San Francisco" in circle around a deer head, tooled top, 1902-06, amber, fifth **440**

Whiskey, "Kane, O'Leary & Co. - 221 & 223 Bush Street S.F." in square slug plate, applied top, 1881-83, medium amber, fifth **1,320**

Whiskey, "Kerrigan & Leslie Cheyenne, Wyo." in ring around "The Arcade," rectangular pocket-flask shaped w/tooled screw top, clear, 1/2 pt **154**

Whiskey, "Lilienthal and Co. Distillers" w/embossed crown in circular slug plate, coffin flask-form, amber, 1885-90, pt. (a large & small open bubble, slight interior haze) **825**

Lilienthal & Miller Whiskey Bottles

Whiskey, "Lilienthal & Co. S.F.," banded flask-form w/single roll applied collar, light golden amber, 1878-82, 1/2 pt. (ILLUS. left) **3,080**

Whiskey, "Miller's Extra Trade Mark [above shield] - E. Martin & Co. Old Bourbon," flask-shaped w/applied mouth & smooth base, ca. 1875-80, deep olive, 7 1/2" h. .. **1,045**

Whiskey, "Miller's Extra Trade Mark [above shield] - E. Martin & Co. Old Bourbon," flask-shaped w/applied mouth & smooth base, ca. 1875-80, bright golden olive, 7 1/2" h. (ILLUS. right with Lilienthal bottle) **1,760**

Whiskey, "Moore (Jesse) & Co. Louisville KY." below motif of antlers & in ring around "G.H. Moore Old Bourbon & Rye" above "Moore, Hunt & Co. Sole Agents" at bottom, cylindrical w/double applied collar mouth, bright golden amber, fifth **209**

Whiskey, "Old Bourbon Castle Whiskey - F. Chevalier & Co., Sole Agents," cylindrical w/tall neck & tooled lip, dark amber, 12" h. **231**

Whiskey, "Old Gilt Edge - [crown & OK] - Bourbon -Wichmann & Lutgen Sole Agents San Francisco," cylindrical w/thin neck & small applied top, amber, fifth **660**

Whiskey, "Old Gilt Edge - OK - Bourbon - Wichman Lutgen & Co." in circle on front, applied top, late 1890s, clear, fifth **231**

Whiskey, "Patent" on shoulder, cylindrical w/tall neck & applied top, graphite pontil, sparkling light blue **143**

Rare Pharazyn Indian Queen Bottle

Whiskey, "Pharazyn (H.) - Phila - Right Secured," figural Indian Queen, rolled-in lip, smooth base, golden amber, 12 3/8" h. (ILLUS.) **1,430**

Whiskey, "Phoenix [motif of spread-winged phoenix] Bourbon - Naber, Alfs & Brune," flask-form w/tooled mouth & smooth base, clear, pt. (slight haze) **121**

Whiskey, "Phoenix Old [motif of spread-winged phoenix above] Bourbon - Naber, Alfs & Brune SF Sole Agts," cylindrical w/tall neck & applied top, amber **1,210**

Whiskey, "Pride of Kentucky Old Bourbon Livingston & Co Sole Agents," cylindrical w/tall neck & applied top, dark amber **2,860**

Whiskey, "Provis (Wm.) Fine Liquors Grass Valley," cylindrical w/tall neck & tooled top, amber, fifth **209**

Whiskey, "Roth & Co. - 214 & 216 Pine St. - San Francisco" in circle on front, flask-shaped w/double roll collar w/tooled top, "3" on base, 1880-85, amber **209**

Whiskey, "Roth & Co. [monogram] - San Francisco," cylindrical w/tall neck & applied top, reddish amber (tiny ding on lower back) **220**

Whiskey, "Roth & Cosan - San Francisco" in circle on front, tooled top, ca. 1900, clear, fifth (cleaned) **66**

Rare S.H.M. Superior Bourbon Bottle

Whiskey, "S.H.M. - Superior Trade Mark [over fleur-de-lis design] - Old Bourbon," cylindrical w/tall neck & applied top, 1874-78, Western U.S., amber, fifth (ILLUS.) **5,060**

Whiskey, "Spears (Wm. H.) Old Pioneer Whiskey [above design of walking bear over] A. Fenkhausen & Co Sole Agents SF," cylindrical w/tall neck & applied top, medium amber (small bleeding potstone on back)... **715**

Whiskey, "Spruance Stanley & Co. [inside horseshoe] Wholesale [above sun rays] Liquor Dealers San Francisco Cal," star on base, cylindrical w/tall neck & applied sloping double collar mouth, smooth base, ca. 1895, golden amber, 11 5/8" h. **110**

Whiskey, "Spruance Stanley & Co. [inside horseshoe] Wholesale [above sun rays] Liquor Dealers San Francisco Cal," cylindrical w/tall neck & applied sloping

double collar mouth, smooth base, ca. 1895, clear, 11 5/8" h. **176**

Whiskey, "Spruance Stanley & Co. [inside horseshoe] Wholesale [above sun rays] Liquor Dealers San Francisco Cal," cylindrical w/tall neck & applied sloping double collar mouth, smooth base, ca. 1895, rare dark amber, 11 5/8" h. **1,320**

Whiskey, "Standard Old Bourbon Whisky - Weil Bros S.F. Sole Agents" in square slug plate, large tooled top, ca. 1880, amber, fifth **468**

Teakettle Old Bourbon Bottle

Whiskey, "Teakettle Old Bourbon" around design of teakettle, cylindrical w/tall neck & tooled lip, medium amber (ILLUS.) **1,650**

Whiskey, "Van Bergen & Co. (N.) Gold Dust Kentucky Bourbon" inside ring centered by standing horse, further wording around outside of ring, cylindrical w/tall neck & applied top, bluish aqua, fifth **825**

Wharton's Whiskey with Handle

Whiskey, "Wharton's Whiskey 1850 Chestnut Grove," flask-shaped w/tall neck pulled into spout, applied handle, "Whitney Glass Works Glassboro, N.J." on base, amber, 10" h. (ILLUS.) **550**

Whiskey, "Wharton's Whiskey 1850 Chestnut Grove," flask-shaped w/tall neck pulled into spout, applied handle, "Whitney Glass Works Glassboro, N.J." on base, golden yellowish amber, 10" h. **935**

BOXES

Band box, cov., oval, wallpaper-covered cardboard, the paper covering depicting Holt's New Hotel, New York City, the cover w/New York City Hall, pink & white on a blue ground, early 19th c., 14 1/2 x 18 1/4", 12" h. (damage) **$1,380**

Band box, cov., wallpaper-covered, deep oval sides w/fitted flat cover, decorated w/light yellow (darkened) paper w/white, pink & brown floral designs, interior lined w/newspaper, label reading "Warranted Nailed Band Boxes, made by Hannah Davis, Jaffrey" (New Hampshire), 10 1/2" l., 5 1/2" h. (some wear) **1,485**

Band box, cov., wallpaper-covered, oblong w/worn but colorful paper w/green, yellow, white & brown diamonds, lines & foliage scrolls, 5 1/4 x 7", 3 1/8" h. (wear) **440**

Bentwood box, cov., oval, Harvard-type finger construction, original black paint w/red & mustard stripes on lid & base & "R.G.A." in gold on lid, 6 1/4" l. (minor wear, paint is finely alligatored) **7,150**

Bible box, grain-painted wood, nearly square top w/a hinged lid, gilt linear decoration on the side, American, 19th c., 10 1/4 x 11 3/4", 3 1/2" h. **805**

Bride's box, cov., oval, bent or steamed pine or fir, orginal floral rosemaled decoration in rose motif w/painted inscription in German around top, woven lap construction on sides, ca. 1850-60, 10 x 18", 8" h. **950**

Bride's box, cov., oval, old red & yellow tulips & foliage w/star on the lid, black ground, wire staples at seams, 8 1/2 x 13", 5" h. (split in lid) **1,485**

Polychrome Bride's Box

Bride's box, cov., pine, oval bentwood w/laced seams, original paint w/brown bands & black reserves w/polychrome floral decoration on sides & full-length stylized figure of woman on lid, minor age cracks & insect damage, 17 1/2" l. (ILLUS.) **1,320**

Stenciled Pine Dresser Box

Dresser box, cov., pine, domed top w/leather hinge on rectangular box w/rounded sides ending in bracket-shaped feet, painted green w/gilt stenciling of fruit compote on lid, stag & star on sides, early 19th c., 4 x 8", 5 3/8" h. (ILLUS.) **575**

Glass box, cov., circular inverted thumbprint box w/hinged lid, ormolu feet & bands where lid meets body, golden amber w/applied sapphire blue serpent on lid, body decorated w/small enameled flowers & green leaves, 4 3/8" d., 4 5/8" h. **225**

Glass box, cov., cylindrical body tapering in where it meets hinged lid, cobalt blue w/white enameled leafy scroll decoration on lid & body, ormolu looped feet & bands around base of body & where lid & body meet, 4 3/4" d., 4" h. **195**

Glass box, cov., cylindrical box w/hinged lid, sapphire blue decoration w/white enameled rose, green & blue leaves, orange bug on lid, leaves & another orange bug on body, two brass ring handles at sides, brass band at top & bottom of body & around base of lid, 5" d., 5" h. **325**

Glass box, cov., cylindrical cobalt blue, body w/white dot decoration around base, hinged lid decorated w/blue violets & green leaves, 3 1/4" d., 3 1/4" h. **145**

Glass box, cov., egg-shaped w/hinged lid, swirl pattern, entire box flashed in lavender, metal bands where lid meets body, 3 3/4" d., 6 1/2" h. **150**

Glass box, cov., ruby-colored, cylindrical body on ormolu feet, hinged lid decorated w/enameled white & blue flowers & blue & yellow butterfly, 5 1/2" d., 6" h. **295**

Regency Jewelry Box

Jewelry box, cov., rosewood & mother-of-pearl inlaid coffin shape w/hinged lid, opening to fitted interiors w/lift-out tray over a body in conforming shape, resting on bun feet, England, Regency period, 9 x 12", 7" h. (ILLUS.) **252**

Neoclassical Mahogany Knife Boxes

Knife boxes, cov., mahogany, Neoclassical style, serpentine fronts w/silver fittings, slant-lid tops w/shell inlay, string inlay at edges, each on three shaped feet, English, early 19th c., 8 1/2 x 11", 15" h., age split, pr. (ILLUS.) **3,738**

Miniature box, cov., sterling silver, hinged lid topped w/polychrome figure of peacock, engraved on side "B. Cormel," 1 1/8 x 1 5/8 x 2" **295**

Miniature box, cov., sterling silver, in the form of a bunt cake mold, 1 1/8 x 1 3/4" **125**

Patch box, cov., glass, round cobalt blue body, hinged lid decorated w/white flowers w/orange centers, metal bands where lid meets body, 2" d., 1 1/2" h. **115**

Star Inlaid Storage Box

Storage box, cov., mahogany, dovetailed construction, the lift-top lid decorated w/exotic wood star inlay at center & star points at corners, the lid interior w/ripple molding, the body w/two half-drawers, banding & escutcheon w/contrasting inlay, American, 19th c., 10 x 13 x 20", age cracks (ILLUS.) **805**

Storage box, cov., oval, bent pine w/original dark blue background, rosemaled designs on lid & sides, lapped construction, Scandinavian, ca. 1850-60, 8 x 15", 7" h. **800**

Painted Storage Box on Ball Feet

Storage box, cov., rectangular box on ball feet, original red paint w/decoration in yellow, green, gold & black of eagle & banner w/"Hannah Miller" on lid, pheasants w/cornucopia on front, birds kissing on one side, birds apart on other side, interior lined w/worn orange paper, 4 5/8 x 9", 4 3/4" h. (ILLUS.) **12,100**

Storage box, curly maple, rectangular, dovetailed construction, w/sliding lid, signed, 5 x 10 5/8", 3 3/4" h. **275**

Top hat box, wallpaper-covered cardboard, molded in the form of a large top hat, the paper covering w/yellow & white flowers on scrolled & foliate shaded blue ground, early 19th c., 13" l., 10 1/2" h. (minor losses) **1,495**

BREWERIANA

Beer is still popular in this country, but the number of breweries has greatly diminished. More than 1,900 breweries were in operation in the 1870s, but we find fewer than 40 major breweries supply the demands of the country a century later, although micro-breweries have recently sprung up across the country.

Advertising items used to promote various breweries, especially those issued prior to Prohibition, now attract an ever growing number of collectors. The breweriana items listed are a sampling of the many items available. Also see Antique Trader Advertising Price Guide.

Olympia Beer Cloth Banner Sign

Banner, "Olympia Beer," velvet-like fabric suspended on a wooden hanging stick & cord, red ground w/lettering in gold & white above a color horseshoe logo at the bottom, gold border, ca. 1940s, minor overall crackling to gold, 10 1/2 x 11" (ILLUS.) **$50**

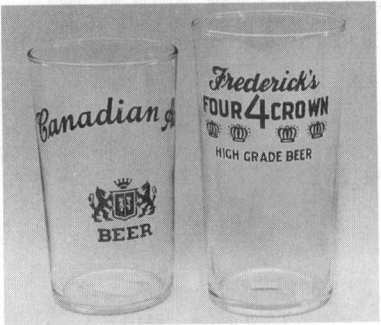

Canadian Ace & Frederick's Glasses

Beer glass, clear cylindrical form enameled in red & blue "Canadian Ace - Beer" w/logo, Chicago, Illinois (ILLUS. left) **44**

Beer glass, clear cylindrical form enameled in red "Frederick's Four 4 Crown - High Grade Beer," Chicago or Thornton, Illinois (ILLUS. right with Canadian Ace glass) **110**

Beer glass, clear cylindrical form, etched "Buffalo Brewing Co. - Sacramento, Cal. - Buffalo Lager," w/horseshoe & grain logo **185**

Beer glass, clear cylindrical form, etched "Fox Lake Beer," Fox Lake, Wisconsin **95**

Beer glass, clear cylindrical form, etched "Kurth's Columbus," Columbus, Wisconsin **60**

Hamm's & Hillsboro Pale Glasses

Beer glass, clear tall cylindrical form enameled in blue "Hamm's - Cultra-Floyd Co.," w/eagle logo, distributor glass (ILLUS.left).. **72**
Beer glass, clear tall cylindrical form enameled in red "Hillsboro Pale Beer - Hillsboro, Wisconsin," w/logo (ILLUS.right with Hamm's glass) **53**
Beer glass, clear wine glass-form w/flaring bowl on knopped stem, etched "Compliments of Tulz Bros. - Kansas City, MO" **230**

Elder Brau & Old Dutch Tumblers

Beer glass, "Elder Brau," clear glass cylindrical form, gold wording, Arizona (ILLUS. left)... **336**

Two Early Detroit Beer Tumblers

Beer glass, "Koppitz-Melchor Brewing Co.," clear glass cylindrical form w/gold rim band & white printing reading "Koppitz-Melchor Brewing Co. (below logo w/"Pale Select") - Detroit, U.S.A." (ILLUS. left) **45**
Beer glass, "Mundus West Side," clear glass cylindrical form w/white printing reading "Mundus West Side Brewery Co. - Detroit, Mich." w/logo at the top (ILLUS. right).. **32**
Beer glass, "Old Dutch," clear glass cylindrical form w/red wording reading "Pennsylvania Best - Old Dutch - Happy

Holiday" (ILLUS. right w/Elder Brau glass).. **36**

Old Reading & Schepps Beer Glasses

Beer glass, "Old Reading Pale Reserve," clear glass cylindrical form w/red & white wording (ILLUS. left)...................................... **256**
Beer glass, "Schepps Xtra Beer," clear glass cylindrical form w/red & blue design & silver rim band, Dallas, Texas (ILLUS. right) **40**

Two Early Beer Tumblers

Beer glass, "Utah Brau," clear glass cylindrical form w/white wording reading "The Standard Brewerys (over eagle logo) - Utah Brau - & Standard Malt Extract," Chicago (ILLUS. left) **253**
Beer glass, "Zang Brewing Co.," clear glass cylindrical form w/white wording reading "P.H. Zang (below logo) - Denver, Colo. - The G.A. Lammers Bottling Co." (ILLUS. right) **77**
Calendar, 1957, "Simon Pure Beer - Old Abbey Ale," long rectangular paper w/rectangular color print at top of dogs playing poker, advertising at the center above the full date pad, 18 x 27 1/2" **33**
Calendar, 1968, "Horlacher Brewing Company - Allentown, Pennsylvania," tall rectangular color print at the top of a lovely blonde reclining & riding a surfboard on a large wave, advertising & full date pad below, 16 x 33" (minor edge wear & tears, tape repair on back, scattered field soiling & wear) **33**
Decanter set: flattened moon-shape decanter & six small barrel-shaped mugs; ceramic, molded designs of German peasants in color costumes, the decanter w/a large molded floral wreath & ball stopper, Budweiser set, CS31 Coracao set, color variation, the set (ILLUS top of next page.).. **690**

Budweiser Coracao Decanter Set

Door push, "Stegmaier's Beer," long rectangular lithographed tin, gold ground w/a large grey shield at the top printed in white & black "We Serve Stegmaier's Gold Medal Beer," a bottle & can of the beer in color at the bottom, appears unused, minor face dirt, hole scratched, 3 1/2 x 8" **94**

Silver Spring Brewery Barrel End Label

Label, "Silver Spring Brewery," paper barrel end label, round w/center image of uniformed fireman holding glass below "The Life Saver," in white letters, blue border w/red letters reading "Silver Spring Brewery Ltd - Victoria, B.C.," yellow oval at each side reading "6 Doz." & "Quarts," framed under glass, ca. early 1900s, minor wrinkles, 13 x 16" (ILLUS.) **99**

Mug, "Budweiser," ceramic, color logo of the "Budman" w/"Hero No. 1" below, white ground (ILLUS. third from left w/other newer Bud mugs below) **50**

Mug, "Budweiser," ceramic, figural commemorative w/gold Budweiser logo & "New Hampshire" (ILLUS. far left w/other newer Bud mugs below).................................... **46**

Mug, "Budweiser," ceramic, footed tapering cylindrical form, view of the Brew House above "Budweiser" in red, gold band trim (ILLUS. far right w/other newer Bud mugs below)... **33**

Budweiser Clydesdale Mugs

Mug, "Budweiser," ceramic, slender tapering cylindrical shape, color printed Clydesdales & wagon design, Ceramarte CS12 (ILLUS. far left w/other Clydesdale mugs) **176**

Mug, "Budweiser," ceramic, tapering cylindrical shape, color printed Clydesdales & wagon design, made in U.S.A. (ILLUS. second from left w/other Clydesdale mugs) **36**

Mug, "Budweiser," ceramic, tapering cylindrical shape, color printed Clydesdales & wagon design, made in U.S.A. (ILLUS. third from left w/other Clydesdale mugs)......... **36**

Various Newer Budweiser Mugs

Ceramarte Ceramic Collector Mugs

Mug, "Budweiser," ceramic, tapering cylindrical shape, color printed Clydesdales & wagon design, made in U.S.A. (ILLUS. far right w/other Clydesdale mugs).................. **36**

Mug, ceramic, cylindrical w/molded design of men on a barrel against a dark blue ground, Ceramarte (ILLUS. far left above)........ **33**

Mug, ceramic, cylindrical w/tapering rim, heavy angled handle, relief-molded scene of man loading a beer wagon, tan & brown glaze, Ceramarte (ILLUS. far right with men & barrel mug above).................. **22**

Mug, ceramic, tapering cylindrical form, arched front panel w/molded men & woman at a tavern table decorated in color against a dark blue ground, tan ground, Ceramarte (ILLUS. second from left with men on barrel mug above).............. **138**

Mug, ceramic, tapering cylindrical form, arched white center reserve enclosing a red & green emblem marked "Aspen," tan & gold-trimmed background, Ceramarte (ILLUS. second from right with men on barrel mug above) **44**

Two Ceramarte Bayazzo Mugs

Mug, ceramic, tapering cylindrical form, large molded front reserve in color showing musician in tavern scene on a dark blue ground, beaded border bands & iridized tan top & base bands, Ceramarte Bayazzo series, color variation (ILLUS. left) **38**

Mug, ceramic, tapering cylindrical form, large molded front reserve in color showing musician in tavern scene on a dark blue ground, beaded lower border band & thin blue band & iridized tan top & base bands, Ceramarte Bayazzo series, color variation (ILLUS. right)...................... **74**

Mug, ceramic, tapering cylindrical form, large molded front reserve in cream trimmed in brown showing musician in tavern scene on a dark blue ground, beaded lower border band over dark blue band, Ceramarte Bayazzo series, color variation (ILLUS. right with other rare coloration variation)... **110**

Ceramarte Mugs with Rarer Colors

Mug, ceramic, tapering cylindrical form, large molded front reserve in pastel colors showing musician in tavern scene on a white ground, beaded lower border band & iridized tan top & base bands, Ceramarte Bayazzo series, color variation (ILLUS. left) **200**

Golden Eagle & North Pacific Mugs

Mug, pottery, barrel-shaped, "Golden Eagle Brewery - Caramel Malt Beer," deep red wording on the cream ground, possibly from Pennsylvania, pre-Prohibition (ILLUS. left) **282**

Mug, pottery, cylindrical w/tapering rim, "North Pacific Brewing Co. - Astoria, Oregon," deep reddish brown wording & shield logo w/stag, pre-Prohibition (ILLUS. right with Golden Eagle mug) **555**

Mug, pottery, "Franziskaner - Chicago, ILL.," dark blue wording & figural logo on a cream ground, pre-Prohibition **176**

Mug, pottery, "Prosit 1900! - M.K. Goetz Brewing Co. - St. Joseph, MO," blue & brown wording w/brown vignette of Cavalier drinking, cream ground w/blue base band, pre-Prohibition **231**

Two Wurzburger Beer Mugs

Mug, "Wurzburger Hofbrau," miniature, ceramic, Budweiser product, label in green, black & yellow (ILLUS. left) **17**

Mug, "Wurzburger Light Beer," miniature, ceramic, Budweiser product, label in dark blue (ILLUS. right) **61**

Mugs, "Budweiser," ceramic, stacked cylindrical mugs w/embossed logo on top one & embossed wording on lower one reading "Pick A Pair of 6-Paks - Buy Bud," tan glaze, pr. (ILLUS. second from left w/other newer Bud mugs, page 122) **52**

Salinas Brewing Company Plate

Plate, "Salinas Brewing Company," ceramic, round plate w/tightly scalloped rim, center printed w/a brown & white horse head against a white ground bordered in dark brown, made by the Sterling China Company for a California company, dated 1904, 9" d. (ILLUS.) **55**

Centlivre's Nickel Plate Beer Poster

Poster, "Centlivre's Nickel Plate Beer," rectangular, color lithograph scene of railcar interior, man & woman seated at table w/glasses & bottles, waiter standing nearby, white border reads "Centlivre's Nickel Plate Bottled Beer - Manufactured By C. L. Centlivre Brewing Co. - Fort Wayne, Ind.," image of bottle in lower right corner, oak frame, 26 3/4 x 31" (ILLUS.) **440**

Rare Iroquois Brewery Sign

Sign, "Iroquois Brewery," embossed die-cut porcelain, detailed bust profile of Native American chief in headdress, finely hand-painted & artist-signed, no factory mounting on back, some edge chips in face region, probably pre-production sample, 17 1/4 x 19 1/2" (ILLUS.) **4,840**

Lucky Lager Embossed Tin Sign

Sign, "Lucky Lager," embossed tin, tall narrow rectangular form, large amber bottle w/red & white label against pale blue ground, name at top in dark blue & white w/"Ice Cold" in white at the bottom, early 1950s, minor scattered field & edge wear, 17 1/2 x 43 1/2" (ILLUS.) **495**

Sign, "Mabel Black Label Beer," die-cut cardboard easel-back type, an upright tapering rectangular backboard w/a color image of a man & woman carrying a cartoon & case of beer, other figures in background, advertising to right side w/image of beer can at lower right, minor wear at edges & corners, ca. 1960s, 21 x 28 1/2" **50**

Miller High Life Mirror Sign

Sign, "Miller High Life," surface-applied mirror sign, long rectangular form w/a dark blue ground & large white wording, a color image of the Miller Girl on crescent moon at the left, visible wear to text, cardboard backing, easels torn off, 4 x 8" (ILLUS.).. **303**

National Brewing Co. Stamp Holder

Stamp holder, "National Brewing Co., San Francisco, Cal.," flat celluloid sleeve printed in blue w/a racing cowboy holding up a bottle of beer, red lettering, top reads "The Best in the West," 1 1/2 x 2 1/2" (ILLUS.) **110**

Stein, "Bud Natural Light," miniature pottery, white ground w/blue, red, gold & white logo label (ILLUS. right, next column)............ **180**

Stein, "Busch," miniature pottery, white ground w/blue, gold & white Busch mountain logo label (ILLUS. left, next column)........ **180**

Two Miniature Pottery Steins

Stein, ceramic, Budweiser Blue Delft series, large country-style four-petal red blossom flanked by green three-leaf sprigs, colored leaf band borders, iridescent gold ground, CS12 (ILLUS. second from left with other Blue Delft steins below).......... **276**

Stein, ceramic, Budweiser Blue Delft series, large red & dark blue blossom on an upright leafy stem in blue & green, zigzag blue & white borders, 1976 wording, CS12 (ILLUS. second from right with other Blue Delft steins below) **100**

Stein, ceramic, Budweiser Blue Delft series, large red & dark blue blossom w/a yellow center on a curved dark blue stem w/green & blue leaves & red buds, blue & white zigzag borders, CS12 (ILLUS. far right with other Blue Delft steins below) **151**

Stein, ceramic, tall cylindrical form, Budweiser Blue Delft series, stylized red & blue blossom w/diamond-shaped petals, blue & white leaf band borders, CS12 (ILLUS. far left below)........................... **250**

Stein, cov., glass & metal, clear cylindrical paneled sides, pewter lid & thumbrest w/porcelain inset w/color logo for "Primator - Garden City Brewery - Chicago, Ill.," pre-Prohibition (ILLUS. far left top of next page) **40**

Stein, cov., glass & metal, clear cylindrical paneled sides, pewter lid & thumbrest w/porcelain inset w/color logo for "Prima - Independent Brewing Assoc.," Chicago, Illinois, pre-Prohibition (ILLUS. second from left w/other glass steins)................... **40**

Budweiser Delft Blue Steins

Glass & Pewter Advertising Steins

Stein, cov., glass & metal, clear cylindrical paneled sides, pewter lid & thumbrest w/porcelain inset w/color logo for "Rienzi - Old German Brew," w/color scene of couple seated at a table, Chicago, Illinois, pre-Prohibition (ILLUS. second from right w/other glass steins) **142**

Stein, cov., glass & metal, clear cylindrical paneled sides, pewter lid & thumbrest w/porcelain inset w/color logo for "Bavarian Brew - Special Brew - White Eagle Brewery, Chicago,Ill.," pre-Prohibition (ILLUS. far right w/other glass steins) **180**

Stein, cov., pottery, swelled tall cylindrical form w/hinged pointed pewter lid, "Budweiser" molded above relief design of horses & wagon, 1981 Holiday model, CS50 .... **913**

Stein, cov., pottery, tall tapering cylindrical form w/hinged pointed pewter lid, Budweiser series, red, white, blue & yellow printed design showing Soldier Field in Chicago, reads "Chicago - 1982 - Our Kind of Town - Soldier Field," white background **380**

Stein, pottery, Budweiser German Cities series, full color coat-of-arms over "Stuttgart," CS16 (ILLUS. far right with other German Cities steins below) **185**

Stein, pottery, Budweiser German Cities series, full color coat-of-arms over "Frankfurt," CS16 (ILLUS. far left below) **227**

Stein, pottery, Budweiser German Cities series, full color coat-of-arms over "Heidelburg," CS16 (ILLUS. second from left with other German Cities steins below) **278**

Stein, pottery, Budweiser German Cities series, full color coat-of-arms over "Munchen," CS16 (ILLUS. second from right with other German Cities steins below) **350**

Stein, pottery, cylindrical w/angled handle, Budweiser series, "Bud Girl" in red & white framed by blue scrolls on a grey ground, Ceramarte-made, CS21 .... **400**

Stein, pottery, cylindrical w/rounded handle, Budweiser series, "Bud Girl" scene on tan ground, U.S. variation **13**

BUTTER MOLDS & STAMPS

Acorn stamp, round, deeply carved image of acorn surrounded by oak leaves, coggle edge, one-piece carved handle, 4" d. (ILLUS. bottom row, right, w/various butter stamps, top next page) **$385**

Cow stamp, round, delicately carved figure of cow, soft mellow finish, threaded inserted handle, 4 1/8" d. (ILLUS. top row, right, w/various butter stamps, next page)...... **880**

Cow stamp, round, image of cow standing on wavy grass beneath leafy branch, 4 5/8" d. (case has age crack)......................... **83**

Cow stamp, w/a flower overhead, coggled rim, one-piece handle, old, worn surface, 4 1/4" d. (some worm holes)........................... **468**

Budweiser German Cities Steins

Various Butter Stamps

Deer stamp, round, crosshatched design of deer walking beneath blazing sun, zigzag border, lightly scrubbed surface, 4" d. **550**

Double-sided stamp, lollipop style, w/scratch-carved designs of star flower, arrow & diamonds on one side, flowers, sunrise & "BU" on other, long, rounded handle, scrubbed finish w/traces of yellow, 3 1/2" d. (ILLUS. middle row, second from left, w/various butter stamps) **385**

Double-sided stamp, round, w/carved eagle & shield surrounded by deeply carved stars & initials "MS" on one side, the other side w/potted flower design, lightly scrubbed surface, 4 1/2" d. (ILLUS. top row, left, w/various butter stamps) **825**

Eagle stamp, militant looking eagle figure w/shield & arrows, crosshatched neck & incised border lines, one-piece carved handle, 4 5/8" (minor edge damage & ink stains) **193**

Eagle stamp, round, carved eagle design in coggled border, 3 5/8" d. (ILLUS. right w/sheaf of wheat stamp, bottom next page) **550**

Eagle stamp, round, carved eagle on laurel branch, coggled rim & one-piece carved handle, 4 1/2" d. (ILLUS. middle row, second from right, w/various butter stamps) **578**

Eagle stamp, round, crosshatched design of spread-winged eagle & sun, one-piece handle, old, scrubbed surface, 4 5/8" d. (edge chips) **358**

Eagle stamp, round, design of spread-winged eagle w/shield, leaf border, 4 1/4" d. **358**

Pennsylvania Butter Stamp

Floral stamp, lollipop style, carved hexagonal compass flower in coggled border, chamfered handle w/hole for hanger, Pennsylvania, small age split, 9 3/8" l. (ILLUS.) **770**

Floral stamp, lollipop style, carved stylized leaves & flower bud w/coggled double rim, long tapering handle w/rounded edge, age crack stabilized w/wooden pegs, 7 1/2" l. (ILLUS. bottom row, center, w/various butter stamps) **248**

Floral stamp, round, w/ stylized thistle-like flower, 4 1/4" d. **105**

Flower stamp, semicircular, w/design of thistle-like flower, inset nailed handle, dark patina, 7" l. (age crack, minor wear) **440**

Heart stamp, round, crosshatched design of heart surrounded by leaves, one-piece handle, 4 1/2" d. (minor age crack) **275**

Heart stamp, semicircular shape, w/carved, crosshatched heart & foliage design, soft, worn finish, threaded handle, 7" l. (ILLUS. right, w/tulip stamp, next page) **660**

Heart stamp, semicircular, w/crosshatched design of heart & leaves, scrubbed surface, inset pegged handle, 6 7/8" l. **688**

Leaf stamp, lollipop style, chip carved quatrefoil leaf design, handle w/cut-out hole, 3 5/8" d. (ILLUS. middle row, far left, w/various butter stamps) **715**

Multi-design Butter Stamp

Multi-design stamp, rectangular w/eight different individual carved designs, varnish finish, 5 1/2 x 11" (ILLUS.) **138**

Partridge stamp, round, delicately carved partridge in coggled border, threaded inserted handle, lightly scrubbed surface, 4 1/8" d. (ILLUS. top row, center, w/various butter stamps) **798**

Pineapple stamp, semicircular, w/image of pineapple in center, scrubbed surface, inset nailed handle, 7" l. **440**

Pomegranate stamp, round, stylized pomegranate w/coggled rim, lightly scrubbed surface, one-piece carved handle, 4 1/2" d. (ILLUS. middle row, far right, w/various butter stamps) 193

Sheaf of wheat stamp, rectangular, w/image of sheaf of wheat flanked by leaves, 4 1/2" l. 138

Sheaf of wheat stamp, semicircular shape, carved decoration of sheaf of wheat & leaves, 6 3/8" l. (ILLUS. left, w/eagle stamp, bottom of page)................................. 523

Sheaf of wheat stamp, semicircular, w/carved sheaf of wheat design, back has scrubbed surface, threaded handle, 7" l., age cracks (ILLUS. right, w/thistle stamp)... 220

Sheaf of wheat stamp, semicircular, w/carving of sheaf of wheat flanked by leaves, inset handle (softly worn from use) 248

Sheaf of wheat stamp, semicircular, w/design of sheaf of wheat, inset pegged handle, two holes in top, possibly for second print, scrubbed surface, 6 7/8" l...................... 303

Starflower stamp, lollipop style, carved star flower w/ridged edges, long handle, 4" d. (ILLUS. bottom row, left, w/various butter stamps)... 660

Strawberries Butter Stamp

Strawberries stamp, round, carved strawberries & leaves, ringed rim, threaded handle, old refinishing, 3 1/2" d. (ILLUS.) 440

Swan stamp, figure of swimming swan, incised border lines, one-piece carved handle, 4 1/8" d. (age crack & old ink stains) 358

Thistle & Wheat Butter Stamps

Thistle stamp, semicircular, w/carved crosshatched thistle design, old, lightly worn surface w/good patina, threaded handle, 7" l. (ILLUS. left) 440

Tulip stamp, rectangular, design of tulip & stars on raised panel w/notched edge, dark patina, 4 3/4" h. (inset handle missing, age crack) 303

Tulip & Heart Butter Stamps

Tulip stamp, semicircular shape, w/carved tulip decoration, soft worn finish, threaded handle, 7" l. (ILLUS. left)........................... 633

CANDLESTICKS & CANDLEHOLDERS

Also see Antique Trader Books Lamps & Lighting Price Guide.

Candleholder, wrought iron, a tall cylindrical shaft w/a candle ejector knob & angled rim handle, set on a disk drip pan base raised on three short legs w/penny feet, early, 9 1/2" h. **$495**

Candlestick, Bennington pottery, tall ringed columnar shaft on a flaring round foot, mottled brown Flint Enamel glaze w/some dark green, mid-19th c., 8" h. 825

Candlestick, blown glass, clear, tall cupped socket w/original pewter insert & bulbed bottom attached w/a wafer to the tall hollow standard w/applied rings applied to a heavy disk foot, probably Pittsburgh, ca. 1820-30, 9 1/8" h. 2,475

Candlestick, pressed flint glass, Petal & Loop patt., the petal-form socket attached by a wafer to the loop design base, attributed to the Boston & Sandwich Glass Co., deep cobalt blue, 7" h. (few tiny flakes on foot edge) 1,760

Candlesticks, Battersea enamel, tall cylindrical socket w/flaring flattened rim above a tall slender ringed standard & domed paneled foot, decorated w/dark blue enameling & white enamel panels all highlighted w/gilt & colored florals, England, 18th c., 9" h., pr. (chips on bobeches & small flake on one stick)........ 2,530

Candlesticks, brass, octagonal bases & ring turned columns w/circular rosettes around centers, both retain original push ups, both marked "Good Luck" on the

Wheat & Eagle Butter Stamps

bases w/faint horseshoe stamps, Victori-
an, 12 1/2" h., pr. **275**
Candlesticks, brass, octagonal scalloped
stepped bases, paneled baluster stems,
soldered two-piece construction,
9 5/8" h., pr. **825**
Candlesticks, pressed flint glass, a petal
socket above a figural dolphin standard
on a double-step square base, canary
yellow, Boston & Sandwich Glass Co.,
mid-19th c., 10" h., pr. (one w/tiny chip on
tip of dolphin tail, & tiny spall on corner of
base) **1,430**
Candlesticks, pressed flint glass, hexago-
nal tulip-form socket on a ringed stem &
hexagonal base, canary yellow, Boston &
Sandwich Glass Co., mid-19th c.,
7 1/4" h., pr. (normal mold roughness) **330**
Candlesticks, pressed flint glass, jade
green petal socket attached w/a wafer to
a reeded columnar milk white shaft
w/square foot, mid-19th c., some mold
roughness, 9" h., pr. **2,090**
Candlesticks, pressed flint glass, petal
socket attached w/a wafer to a ribbed columnar standard w/a stepped square
base, canary yellow, attributed to Boston
& Sandwich Glass Co., ca. 1840-60,
9 1/2" h., pr. **770**
Girandoles, cast brass & marble, a
stepped white marble base w/brass trim
supporting a cast figure of a standing Victorian lady in an exotic bloomer outfit, a
slender shaft at the back topped w/down-
scrolled leaves centering a candle socket, each leaftip hung w/a long triangular
glass prism, good patina w/areas of orig-
inal gilding, mid-19th c., 15" h., pr. **220**

CANS & CONTAINERS

B.B. shot, "Selby B.B. Split Shot," small celluloid disk, the top in cold w/blue & white
lettering, 1 1/2" d. **$150**

Princine Baking Powder Tin

Baking powder, "Princine Baking
Powder," 1/2 lb. tin, cylindrical w/side
strap handle, red ground w/white & gold
wording, round center picture of a smiling
lady holding a package of the product,
full, unopened, dated 1916, 3 x 3"
(ILLUS.) **88**

Watkins Baking Powder Trial Size Tin

Baking powder, "Watkins Baking Powder -
Purity Guaranteed," trial size, cylindrical
w/an orange & red ground w/red & white
wording, half-length color image of a
1930s woman holding plate of biscuits,
2 x 3 1/4" (ILLUS.) **59**
Baking soda, "Royal Baking Soda," 1/8 lb.
sample tin, red ground w/white wording &
center circle w/color picture of the tin,
1 1/2 x 2 1/2" **33**

Instant Postum Beverage Tin

Beverage, "Instant Postum - A Beverage,"
sample size, cylindrical w/a printed black
& white label w/small red circle in lower
half, top w/sketch of a table set for break-
fast, 1 1/2 oz., 2 x 3 1/2" (ILLUS.) **44**

Decorated Biscuit Tin

Biscuit tin, steel, tapering cylindrical vase-
like shape w/straight handles at sides,
decorated w/scene of two collies &
children, primarily in shades of gold,
orange & brown, 5 1/4 x 5 1/4", 13" h.
(ILLUS.) **445**

Colorful Biscuit Tin

Biscuit tin, steel, w/embossed polychrome scenes of children at play, made by Gray Dunne & Co., Glasgow, 2 1/4 x 4 3/4 x 6 1/4" (ILLUS.) **425**

Blasting caps, "Hercules No. 6," small cylindrical form w/pry-off lid, dark gold w/black printing, the flat lid centered by a sketch of Hercules, the side reads "Twenty-five Blasting Caps - No. 6," 1 1/2 x 1 5/8" (minor scrapes)........................ **132**

German Chocolate Tin

Chocolate tin, steel, in the form of a German inn w/dormers & chimney, brass bell on side, polychrome embossed decoration of tile roof, architectural details & woman giving treats to boy & girl at door, made by Heinrich Haeberlein, Nuremberg, 3 1/8 x 5 5/8 x 8" (ILLUS.) **225**

Gibson Girl Cigarettes Tin

Cigarettes, "Gibson Girl," flat rectangular form, dark ground printed w/a color image of a seductive standing Gibson-like girl wearing a long black dress w/pink rose trim & smoking a cigarette, red, black & white logo at top left, slight wear, 3 x 3 1/4" (ILLUS.) **275**

Between the Acts Cigar Tin

Cigars, "Between The Acts Little Cigars," flat rectangular w/the embossed lid printed in red, white & black w/a seated gentleman smoking a cigar in each lower corner, tax stamp dated 1909, bright, 3 x 5 1/2", 1" h. (ILLUS.) **55**

Old Seneca Stogies Tin

Cigars, "Old Seneca Stogies," color image of a Native American chief's face framed by red & white wording against a gold ground, some rim wear, good color, 4 x 5 1/2" (ILLUS.)... **264**

Orcico Cigar Tin

Cigars, "Orcico," oblong lift-top tin, decorated w/a colorful image of a Native American chief w/landscapes flanking him, printing in orange & brown, dated 1919, 4 x 6", 5 1/2" h. (ILLUS.) **385**

Possum Cigars Tin with Gold Ground

Cigars, "Possum Cigars - 3 for 5¢ - 'Am Good and Sweet,'" large cylindrical size in dark gold w/brown reserves w/white & red wording around a color image of a white possum, slight wear, 5 x 5" (ILLUS.) **396**

Possum Cigars Tin with Contents

Cigars, "Possum Cigars - 'Am Good and Sweet,'" large cylindrical size in red w/black & white wording around a color image of a white possum, full & w/original insert rim sign reading "Possum - 3 for 10¢ - Extra Mild - Extra Good," strong colors, 5 x 5" (ILLUS.) **421**

Cigars, "Red Dot Junior Cigar," flat rectangular tin, a radiating design of alternating gold & white rays centered by a red dot w/a head of a pretty woman, writing in red on gold, 2 3/4 x 4 3/4" **50**

Cleaning powder, "Gold Dust Scouring Cleanser," cylindrical w/a dark reddish orange ground w/the black Twins at the top above the wording in white, unopened, 3 x 4 1/2"... **55**

Acme Coffee Tin

Coffee, "Acme Brand Coffee," 1 lb. tin, front w/a large oval w/the brand name framed by coffee berries & printed in red, blue & gold w/the lower half in white polka dots on red, the reverse w/another oval w/a coffeepot & cup & saucer w/"Home Coffee," 4 x 6" (ILLUS. of two sides) **66**

American Home Brand Coffee Tin

Coffee, "American Home Brand Fresh Roasted Coffee," 1 lb. tin, colorful paper label printed in red, white & blue w/a color scene of large home on one side & a large cup of coffee on the other, very clean, 4 x 6" (ILLUS.).. **83**

Arabian Coffee Tin

Coffee, "Arabian Coffee," 1 lb. tin, screw-on lid, red background w/white & gold lettering, a bust profile of an Arab drinking coffee, dated 1929, a few scrapes & dings, 4 1/4 x 6" (ILLUS.)... **330**

Ghiradelli Cocoa Tin

Cocoa, "Ghiradelli Cocoa," 1lb. tin, tall cylindrical form w/paper label, orange background w/large red wordings surrounding a spread-winged eagle above the company monogram, unopened, 3 1/4 x 6 1/2" (ILLUS.) **77**

Betsy Ross Coffee Tin

Coffee, "Betsy Ross Brand Coffee," 1 lb. tin, colorful label w/a white ground printed w/dark blue & red wording, central diamond-shaped logo, 4 x 6" (ILLUS.) **55**

Coffee, "Bunker Hill Coffee," 1 lb. tin, pry-off lid, red ground w/large white wording above & below a central square reserve w/a color image of the Bunker Hill Monument, 4 1/4 x 5 3/4" (slight blemishes & dings, minor fading) **88**

Campbell Coffee Four Pound Tin

Coffee, "Campbell Brand Coffee," 4 lb. tin, lift-off lid, bail handle, dark yellow ground w/red & brown wording above & below a vignette of a group of Arabs w/camels, a few scratches, 7 3/4 x 8" (ILLUS.) **66**

Caswell's Three Pound Coffee Tin

Coffee, "Caswell's Coffee," 3 lb. tin, tall cylindrical form w/pry-off lid, a center oval reserve w/a black & white profile portrait

of a lovely long-haired woman, gold on yellow wording & scrolled reserve around the portrait against a black & gold spiral band background, dated 1924, several small dings & scrapes, 5 1/4 x 9" (ILLUS.) **154**

Coffee, "Country Club Coffee," 1 lb. tin, screw-off lid, a dark blue over black background, gold lettering at the top & light blue & gold at bottom, a color center reserve showing a country club clubhouse, few minor scrapes, 4 x 6" **193**

Coffee, "Demi-Tasse Coffee," 1 lb. tin, wide brown bands at the top & bottom printed w/large white lettering, a wide central gold band decorated w/silhouetted figures of walking people & mules, 4 1/4 x 6" (minor dings & scrapes, hole in top) **65**

5th Ave. Brand Coffee Tin

Coffee, "(Fifth) 5th Ave. Brand Coffee," 1 lb. tin, cylindrical w/pry-off lid, label printed in gold, dark brown, light brown & cream, front w/center monogram of The O'Donohue Knight & Gage Company, producers of the brand, 4 x 6" (ILLUS.) **66**

Fine Fort Pitt Coffee Tin

Coffee, "Fort Pitt Coffee," cylindrical, printed in color w/the brand name around a vignette of an early fort, in red, white, black & gold, 4 1/4" d., 5 1/2" h. (ILLUS.) **470**

Galt House Blend One Pound Tin

Coffee, "Galt House Blend Coffee," 1lb. tin, paper label printed in white, red, gold & light blue on a dark blue ground, color scene of the Galt House Hotel in the center, dated 1908, bright colors, 4 1/4" d., 5" h. (ILLUS.)................................. **495**

Coffee, "Glendora Brand Coffee," sample tin, cylindrical w/pry-off lid, dark blue ground printed w/white & gold w/blue & gold wording, gold bands around top & bottom, 2 x 3 1/4"............................... **47**

Ideal Brand Coffee Tin

Coffee, "Ideal Brand Coffee," 1 lb. tin w/screw-on lid, white ground printed w/red, dark blue & gold wording w/a color image of a large early percolator on a round tray w/two cups of coffee, slight wear, 4 x 6" (ILLUS.)...................................... **143**

Matchless Coffee One Pound Tin

Coffee, "Matchless Coffee," 1 lb. tin, fitted flat cover, a dark green ground w/thin

gold & red bands at the top & bottom, red & gold & black & gold wording flanks a central image of a long leafy branch of coffee blossoms & beans, minor color fading, several small dents on back, 4 x 6" (ILLUS.) **215**

Mi-Lady Coffee Deluxe Tin

Coffee, "Mi-lady Coffee Deluxe," cylindrical, lithograph w/a central oval reserve in color showing a pretty woman wearing black from the back & looking at herself in a hand-held mirror, orange background w/black & white wording w/thin blue top & base bands, dated 1921, minor dings & scrapes around the sides, 4 1/4 x 6" (ILLUS.).. **242**

Mister Donut Coffee Tin

Coffee, "Mister Donut Exclusive Blend Coffee," 1 lb. tin, key-wind lid, red & black ground w/black, red & white wording & a brown & white Mister Donut carton, 3 1/2 x 5" (ILLUS.).. **275**

Coffee, "Parke's Newport Coffee," 1 lb. tin, color label in red, white & blue w/central color scene of the factory, 4 1/4 x 6"............. **303**

Parke's Newport Coffee Tin

Coffee, "Parke's Newport Coffee," 3 lb. tin, color label in red, white & blue w/color central scene of the factory, 6" d., 8" h. (ILLUS.) **358**

Coffee, "Planters House Brand Coffee," 1 lb. tin, pry-off lid, red ground w/white wording & a rose & white scene of a large hotel, minor dings & rust spots, 4 1/4 x 5 3/4" **275**

Serv-Us Coffee Tin

Rare Roaster To Customer Coffee Tin

Coffee, "Roaster To Customer," 2 1/2 lb. tin, cylindrical w/paper label, one side w/color image of an early delivery truck, reverse has image of black Mammy & reads "Blue Ribbon Products Co. Coffee," minor scratches & scuffs, 5 1/4 x 7 1/4" (ILLUS. of front) **578**

Coffee, "Royal Dutch Coffee," 1 lb. tin, screw-off lid, red & white large wording w/a background design of a royal shield & a branch of coffee beans, a band of pearl-like bead bands at the rim & base, 4 x 6 1/4" (minor fading, few scrapes & dings) **66**

Strong-Heart Coffee Tin

Coffee, "Strong-Heart Brand Coffee," 1 lb. tin, pry-off lid, yellow ground w/black print, a center oval reserve w/a color bust portrait of a Native American chief, minor scrapes & dings, 4 1/4 x 5 3/4" (ILLUS.) **264**

Coffee, "Swell Blend Chautauqua Brand Coffee," 1 lb. tin, pry-off lid, decorated w/a large dark blue shaped panel enclosing gold & white wording around a center oval reserve showing a steamship, 4 x 6" (minor scuffs & dings) **215**

Royal Quality Steel Cut Coffee Tin

Coffee, "Royal Quality Steel Cut Coffee," 1 lb. tin, lithographed design w/a white ground & a red, blue & gold central coat-of-arms, wording in blue, red & gold, 4 x 6" (ILLUS.) **69**

Coffee, "San Marto Coffee," 1 lb. tin, screw-on lid, gold ground w/bold red wording, the front w/an image of a knight on horseback, the back w/a shield emblem, 4 x 6" (minor fading) **220**

Coffee, "Serv-Us Coffee," 1 lb. tin, screw-on lid, red ground w/white & blue wording, blue-trimmed white cup & saucer of coffee at bottom, excellent condition, 4 x 6" (ILLUS. top of next column) **77**

Rare Large Turkey Coffee Tin

Coffee, "Turkey Brand Coffee," 3 lb. tin, tall cylindrical form w/red wording on tan ground w/central brown & red picture of a large turkey, minor dents & scuffs, 5 1/2 x 10 3/4" (ILLUS.) **1,650**

Coffee, "Twin Ports Steel Cut Coffee," 1 lb. tin, screw-on lid, white label w/a large oval reserve w/the brand name in blue above a color scene of a large steamship, other wording in red & blue below w/a blue band around the bottom, dated 1923, 4 x 6" (scrapes & dings) **171**

Condom, "Sheik - Reservoir End," flat rectangular form, orange ground w/a white vignette of a racing Arab sheik on horseback above wording in dark blue & w/a pale yellow narrow band, full, 1 5/8 x 2 1/8" **33**

Buffalo Crank Pin Grease Tin

Crank pin grease, "Buffalo Crank Pin Grease," 3 lb. tin w/wire bail handle, pry-off lid, yellow ground w/lid & sides decorated in black w/a vignette of a standing buffalo w/wording above & below, text on reverse, very minor dings, dents & paint wear, 5 1/4" d. (ILLUS.) **402**

Gasoline additive, "Speedoline," flattened upright hand-soldered tin w/a screw-on cap, black & white label, the front w/brand name & advertising centered by a sketch of a speeding early race car, ca. 1920, 2 1/2 x 4", 7" h. **72**

Gunpowder, "DuPont Superfine Gunpowder," 1/2 lb. tin, flattened oval upright form, inside thread cap, red tin w/a black & tan paper label w/minor blemishes, early, 1 3/8 x 3 7/8", 4 1/4" h. **44**

DuPont Gunpowder Tin

Gunpowder, "DuPont Superfine Gunpowder - Wilmington, Delaware," 1 lb. tin, flat-sided w/small top neck w/cap, ca. 1880, 1 1/2 x 4 x 5 3/4" (ILLUS.) **187**

Gunpowder, "Hercules Black Sporting Powder," 1/2 lb. flattened ovoid flask-

form in orange w/an oval tin lithographed label in blue, orange & white centered by an image of Hercules, belt loop intact, 3 1/4 x 6" **71**

Early Imperial Powder Tin

Gunpowder, "Imperial Power...," large cylindrical form w/a domed top w/a small round threaded neck, dark red ground printed in black, lithographed by B.W. Thayer, Boston, 3" d., 3 3/4" h. (ILLUS.) **187**

Indian Rifle Gunpowder Tin

Gunpowder, "Indian Rifle Gunpowder," 1/2 lb., red upright flattened oval form w/small screw cap, the front & back w/colorful paper labels centered by a picture of a Native American hunter stalking game, 1 x 3 3/4", 4 1/4" h. (ILLUS.) **204**

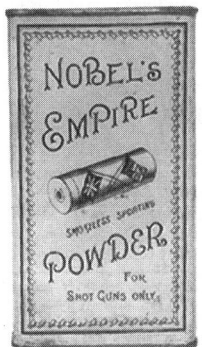

Nobel's Empire Powder Tin

Gunpowder, "Nobel's Empire Smokeless Sporting Powder - For Shot Guns Only," lithographed tin flat upright rectangular form, label in black & white w/an image of a shotgun shell, 3 1/2 x 6" (ILLUS.) **264**

Orange Extra Sporting Powder Tin

Gunpowder, "Orange Extra Sporting - Laflin & Rand Powder Co. - New York U.S.A.," 1 lb. tin, flattened upright rectangular form, orange background w/a large circle on the front printed w/a large black & red-striped flag w/gold wording enclosed by a gold wreath, ca. 1900, excellent condition, 4 x 6" (ILLUS.) **94**

Whale Amber Harness Dressing Tin

Harness dressing, "Whale Amber Harness Dressing," shallow round form w/the cover in blue on white, a central scene of a large whale among icebergs, wording around border reads "Blackens - Softens - Waterproofs and Preserves the Leather - Unexcelled For Hoofs," many dents, dirty, 5 1/4" d., 1 1/2" h. (ILLUS.) **99**

Bradshaw's 3 Bears Honey Tin

Honey, "Bradshaw's 3 Bears Honey," 5 lb. tin, cylindrical w/pry-off lid, cartoon design of Papa, Mama & Baby bear in and around a large white tree w/green leaves against a golden ground, wording in black & white, dated 1949, 5 x 5 3/4" (ILLUS.) **55**

Imitation milk, "SMA Imitation Milk," cylindrical w/pry-off lid, grey ground w/small yellow wording centered by a round color bust portrait of a pretty blond baby, dated 1929, 4 1/4 x 4 3/4" (few scuffs & scrapes) **66**

Old Faithful Lighter Fluid Tin

Lighter fluid, "Old Faithful Lighter Fluid," flattened upright metal oiler-style tin, lead spout w/plastic cap, red & black graphics show geyser & crowd, 4 oz., 4 3/4" h. (ILLUS.) **143**

Lighter fluid, "Shell Lighter Fluid," flattened upright metal oiler-style tin, screw-on cap w/upright lead spout, orange background w/yellow wording & Shell logo, 3 1/2 oz., 4 7/8" h. (light dent on front, few tiny nicks, some fading) **110**

General Petroleum Lubricant Tin

Lubricant, "General Petroleum Corporation," cov. cylindrical metal 5 lb. tin w/bail handle, green w/white letters, front marked "General Lubricants - General Petroleum Corporation - Lubricant - Grade Medium - A Pure Lubricating Compound," text on reverse, minor overall wear, dings & soiling, partial contents (ILLUS.) **413**

Scarce Power-lube Lubricant Tin

Lubricant, "Power-lube Lubricant - The Powerine Company - Denver, Colorado," 1 lb. tin, yellow ground w/rectangular dark blue panel w/yellow wording & yellow & blue stalking tiger, overall heavy wear, scratches & dings, partial contents, 4 1/2" h. (ILLUS.) **578**

Texaco Home Lubricant Tin

Lubricant, "Texaco," flattened upright metal oiler-style 4 oz. tin, lead spout & cap, green w/white rectangular area at top marked "Texaco Home Lubricant" w/logo below, text on reverse, no contents, soiled overall, fading & push dents on both sides, 4 oz. (ILLUS.) **440**

Scarce Blakely Motor Oil Tin

Motor oil, "Blakely Special 10-30 Heavy Duty Motor Oil," 1 qt. tin, red ground w/yellow & silver wording, a center color image of a race car & checkered yellow &

black flag, text on reverse panels, Arizona-based company, full, very light flat spot on front, few scattered nicks & dings, scarce (ILLUS.) **468**

Grand Champion Two Gallon Oil Tin

Motor oil, "Grand Champion," 2 gal. tin, upright rectangular form w/top strap handle & screw-on cap on spout, colorful scene of cartoon-style race cars & drivers racing around a track w/a large red banner across the top w/the brand name in large white letters, minor scratches & wear overall, one heavy scratch on back (ILLUS.) **226**

Jay-Bee Motor Oil Underseat Tin

Motor oil, "Jay-Bee Motor Oil," 1 qt. rectangular underseat-style tin, loop bail handle at center of flat top w/straight & angled spouts w/screw-on caps, orange background w/white wording centering the company logo, manufacturer's name in small black wording at the bottom, hand-soldered, very minor nicks, scratches & rubs, 2 3/4 x 5 3/4", 4 3/4" h. (ILLUS.) **358**

Unusual Mobiloil Conical Tin

Motor oil, "Mobiloil," tall slender conical 2 1/2 gal. tin, small spout at top, white ground w/thin red border bands, black wording & a red gargoyle logo, foreign-made, probably pre-1931, overall soiling & scuffs, rusting & dents, 11" d., 21" h. (ILLUS.).. **226**

Motor oil, "Oilzum Motor Oil," 1 qt. tin, white ground w/triangular orange company logo w/man's head, blue band w/white wording near base, small blue wording at bottom reads "Choice of Champions" (minor dents, nicks & dings, yellowing) **83**

Spinner Motor Oil Tin

Motor oil, "Spinner Motor Oil," cylindrical 1 qt. tin, yellow & red, both sides w/image of top & marked "Spinner Motor Oil - 35¢ - Top Oil Co. Lubrock, Tex.," punched at bottom, minor nicks & rubs (ILLUS.) **231**

Zephyr Motor Oil Tin

Motor oil, "Zephyr Motor Oil - Guaranteed 100% Paraffine Base," 1 qt. tin, dark orange background w/white angled band w/brand name in orange, other wording in dark blue, dark blue base band w/manufacturer's name & address in white, full, very minor nicks & dings (ILLUS.)..................... **99**

Watkins Nutmeg Tin

Nutmeg, Watkins Nutmeg tin, steel, rectangular, in orange, black & white, w/"Watkins Nutmeg - The Best in Spices" on front, 1 1/2 x 2 1/2 x 3 3/4" (ILLUS.)................. **15**

Signal Outboard Motor Oil Tin

Outboard motor oil, "Signal Outboard Motor Oil," 1 qt. tin, wide black & yellow bands printed w/yellow, black & red wording centered by a red & white racing outboard motor, full w/factory seal & full tab on top, reverse w/text & stoplight logo, very minor nicks & dings (ILLUS.) **253**

Liberty Brand Oyster Tin

Oysters, "Liberty Brand Fresh Oysters," 1 gal. tin, white background printed w/red & black wording, a gold image of The Statue of Liberty w/"Liberty Brand - Fresh Oysters - packed by Ivens and Hudson, Rock Hall, MD," in the lower right in front of a red disk, minor blemishes & scrapes, 6 1/2 x 7 1/2" (ILLUS.) **215**

Shedd's Peanut Butter Tin

Peanut butter, "Shedd's Peanut Butter," steel, tapering cylindrical 5 lb. pail w/wire swing handle, gold, white, red & green colors, cartoonish drawings of elves & circus animals on sides, w/triangular sign w/"Shedd's Peanut Butter," 6 x 6 1/4" (ILLUS.) **14**

Extremely Rare Large Peanuts Tin

Peanuts, "The Planters Mother's Brand Salted Peanuts," 10 lb. tin, yellow background w/red & black wording & a central color reserve showing a young mother & child (ILLUS.).. **12,430**

Early Alaska Salmon Tin

Salmon, "Sailor's Brand Alaska Pink Salmon," lithographed color paper label w/the head of a sailor on one side & a large salmon on the other, small tear on shoulder of sailor, other minor tears, early, 3 x 4 1/2" (ILLUS. of both sides) **231**

Watkins Petro-Carbo Salve Tin

Salve, "Watkins Petro-Carbo Salve" tin, stamped steel, cylindrical, in red, black & white, w/image of J.R. Watkins in circle on the front & "Made by the Makers of Watkins Liniment - Phenol 11 Grains Per Ounce" in border on lid, 2" h., 4 1/2" d., worn surface (ILLUS.) **10**

Shoe polish, "Whittemore's Brown New Era Shoe Polish," flattened round form, the lid printed in white, dark brown & black, center bust portrait of a man, full & unused, 3 1/2" d. **44**

Spice, "A & P Sultana," tall cylindrical tin w/fitted cap, pale yellow ground printed in black w/name & a bust portrait of an elderly lady above "Take Grandmother's Advice - Use A&P Spices," excellent condition, 3 1/4 x 7 1/4" **33**

Spice, "Busy Biddy Pure Spices - Ground Allspice," upright narrow rectangular tin w/the front printed in red, white & black w/a center circle w/a color picture of a native carrying a basket of spices, a hen logo on the side, 2 x 3" **77**

Pretty Iris Spice Tin

Spice, "Iris Brand Marjoram," 2 oz. tin, flattened upright rectangular form, pry-off lid, dark ground w/a large blue & yellow iris w/green leaves w/wording in gold, white & black, red top & bottom trim bands, 2 1/4 x 3 1/4" (ILLUS.) **121**

Sugar Container

Sugar container, steel, cylindrical container, dark bluish background w/beige & grey image of workers in cane fields w/ox cart & "Sugar" on front, bottom marked "Tindeco," 5 x 5 3/4" (ILLUS.)........................... **15**

Syrup, "Bar-None Brand Imitation Maple Syrup," 5 lb. tin, upright rectangular form, printed w/a rectangular panel w/wording in red & black & a center scene of a cowboy on rearing horse w/mountains in the distance, all on a gold ground, dark brown border, no cap, 3 x 5", 7" h. **88**

Cute Cadette Talc Tin

Talcum powder, "Cadette Talc," cylindrical tall form w/tall cap printed in color to represent an army cadette in uniform, w/contents, Cadette Products Corp., Rutherford, New Jersey, 2 1/4 x 7 1/4" (ILLUS.) **154**

Talcum powder, "Colgate's Baby Talc," tall slender flattened oval form, white ground w/blue lettering centered by an oval reserve w/a color portrait of a cute baby holding a can of the product, gold shoulder & cap, 2 1/4 x 6" (minor surface scratches & a small ding) **110**

Royal Rose Talcum Powder Tin

Talcum powder, "Royal Rose Talcum Powder," tall slender oval form w/round cap, tan ground printed w/pale background stripes of pink & green roses w/a large red rose in the foreground, from Canada, excellent condition, 2 1/4 x 6" (ILLUS.) **143**

Egyptian Bouquet Talc Tin

Talcum powder, "Watkins Egyptian Bouquet Talc," upright embossed tapering

square form w/small round cap, colorful Egyptian vignettes on each side (ILLUS. of two sides) **204**

Bagley's Wild Fruit Tobacco Tin

Tobacco, "Bagley's Wild Fruit Flake Cut Tobacco" tin, steel, rectangular, dark blue background w/reddish & yellow printing & design on sides & worn lid, 3 1/4 x 3 3/4 x 6" (ILLUS.) **90**

Belfast Cut Plug Tobacco Tin

Tobacco, "Belfast Cut Plug" tin, steel, rectangular, dark background w/"Belfast Cut Plug - Smoke or Chew" & "United Cigars" emblem in beige on sides & lid, 3 1/4 x 6 3/4 x 6" (ILLUS.) **70**

Tobacco, "Bishop's Move Tobacco," horizontal pocket tin, rectangular w/rounded corners, lid printed in red & white on a black ground w/a chess queen & bishop on a checkered board, printed in white across the bottom edge "A Unique Blend of Rare Quality," slight wear, 2 1/4 x 3 1/4" **44**

Tobacco, "Buckingham Cut Plug Smoking Tobacco," large cylindrical tin, pry-off cover, brightly printed wording in gold, blue & red on a dark brown ground, 5 x 5" **44**

1920s Hi-Plane Tobacco Pocket Tin

Tobacco, "Hi-Plane Smooth Cut Tobacco,"
vertical pocket tin, red ground w/white &
blue wording & a flying 1920s airplane,
excellent condition, 3 x 4 1/2" (ILLUS.) **132**

Unopened Hi-Plane Tobacco Tin

Tobacco, "Hi-Plane Smooth Cut Tobacco,"
vertical pocket tin, red ground w/white
wordings & image of 1950s airplane, full
& unopened, 3 x 4 1/2", 1" deep (ILLUS.) **215**

Honeymoon Tobacco Pocket Tin

Tobacco, "Honeymoon Rum-Flavored Tobacco," vertical pocket tin, red ground
w/gold & white wording, center circle w/a
young man seated on a crescent moon
looking up at the face of a young woman,
3 x 4 1/2", 1" deep (ILLUS.) **198**

Old English Pipe Tobacco Tin

Tobacco, "Old English Curve Cut Pipe Tobacco" tin, steel, rectangular, w/image
of ca. 1800 gentleman smoking pipe in
cartouche on side, red, white & black,
2 3/4 x 3 3/4 x 4 3/4" (ILLUS.) **40**

Pilot Cigarette Tobacco Tin

Tobacco, "Pilot Cigarette Tobacco,"
cylindrical w/screw-on lid, decorated w/a
small flying plane spelling out the word
"Pilot" in white above red wording
"Cigarette Tobacco" & a red dot w/the
price, all on a light tan ground,
4 1/2 x 4 1/2" (ILLUS.) **55**

Tobacco, "Sweet Burley," store bin, yellow
& red, marked "Light - Sweet Burley - To-
bacco," minor dings, 8 1/2 x 10 3/4" **215**

Van Bibber Pipe Tobacco Tin

Tobacco, "Van Bibber Sliced Plug Pipe Tobacco" tin, steel, rectangular w/rounded
corners, gold background w/red, brown &
white detail, picture of period gentleman
in ornately bordered circle on lid next to
product name, 3/4 x 2 3/4 x 4 1/2", sig-
nificant wear to surface (ILLUS.) **45**

Edmondsons Toffee Tin

Toffee tin, "Edmondsons Red Seal Toffee"
tin, steel, in the form of a leather valise
decorated w/stylized leaves, poppies & a
winged lion in deep red, forest green,
burnt orange & gold, real leather strap
handle, 3 3/4 x 8 x 9 5/8" (ILLUS.) **445**

Old Town Typewriter Ribbon Tin

Typewriter ribbon, "Old Town," shallow round form, the lid w/a color design of an Art Deco lady wearing a long red gown, her arms raised over her head, the sides of her gown swirl up in blue on one side & green on the other all against a black ground, reads around the top "Pure Silk Typewriter Ribbon" & across the bottom "An 'Old Town' Ribbon," new unused condition, 2 1/2" d. (ILLUS.) 55

CAROUSEL FIGURES

When master artisans of the past two centuries carved these beautiful creatures they little knew that what were to them mere seats on an amusement ride would become highly sought after collectibles. Whether called folk art, fine art, or more accurately splendid examples of industrial design at its finest, these appealing animals recall a time of simpler joys, when a leap onto a prancing pony presaged a gallop into a land of childhood fantasies. Collectors of carousel figures recapture some of those memories and preserve an important part of our popular cultural history. For those who wish to ride the ever-cycling menagerie the following information is provided by www.mycarousel.com.

Bothman Carousel Donkey

Donkey, prancing, many layers of old crazed paint, head & neck removed & reattached w/heavy springs to achieve a nodding action, large-eyed gentle expression, twin lions' heads at pommel, peek-a-boo in mane, ca. 1900, Bothman, Germany, seam separation, 36" body (ILLUS.) **$4,900**

Charles Looff Carousel Giraffe

Giraffe, inner row figure, park paint w/expressive face, tasseled headstall, jeweled breastband, high spoonback saddle, stamped on underside "Made by Looff, Riverside, RI," ca. 1906, Charles Looff, rare in sound condition, 46" l., 43" h. (ILLUS.) **14,000**

Charles Looff Carousel Goat

Goat, prancing position, mellowed old paint, expressive face, nice fur detail, classic checkerboard blanket, jeweled headstall & harness, ca. 1895-1900, Charles Looff, repair to right front hoof, 60" h., 56" l. (ILLUS.) **26,000**

Spillman Carousel Horse

Horse, animated jumper, park paint, needs moderate restoration, tasseled headstall & flipped back saddle blanket, breast band & blanket have simple groove enhancements, ca. 1918, Spillman, 52" l., 36" h., 32" chest-to-rump (ILLUS.) .. **2,300**

Philadelphia Toboggan Co. Carousel Horse

Horse, jumper, compact body, sweet faced, mounted on porcelain barber chair stand, ca. 1920s, Philadelphia Toboggan Company, remnants of old paint & moderate seam separation, 45" l., 42" h., 30" body (ILLUS.) **4,500**

Anderson Carousel Horse

Horse, jumper, double seated, good condition w/old nicely patinated, possibly original paint, deeply carved floral motifs on body, large carved girth buckle, Anderson's trademark flower (Scarlet Lychnis) carved on headstall, appropriate metal ears & glass eyes, name "Tim" painted on neck scroll, ca. 1900, Anderson, England, 72" l., 48" h., 42" body (ILLUS.) **3,800**

Charles Parker Carousel Jumper

Horse, jumper in racing position, professionally restored by Gary Franklin, not painted but stained to show woodgrain, old hunting prints, untamed expression, deeply carved mane, bobtail, fringed blanket & jeweled breastband & headstall, soulful setter dog face on cantle, Leavenworth period, ca. 1920, Charles Parker, 55" l., 28" h., 34" body (ILLUS.) **2,970**

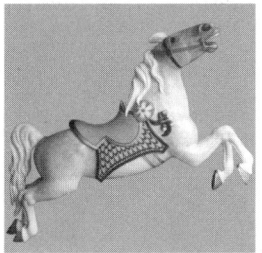

Restored Philadelphia Toboggan Co. Jumper Horse

Horse, jumper, last operated on PTC Number 17 at Ghost Town in Glen, Moosic, Pennsylvania, professionally restored, large-eyed gentle expression, flower w/three buds carved in deep relief at shoulder, h.p. in acrylics to a pale dappled rosy grey body w/sage green, bronze grey, golden brown, orange & gold trappings, ca. 1907, Philadelphia Toboggan Company, 54" h., 65" l., 41" body (ILLUS.) **8,000**

Charles Looff Jumper Horse

Horse, jumper, last operated on the Whalom Park Carousel, Lunenberg, MA, dismantled April 2000, professionally restored & h.p. in artist oils by Sandy Paul, pink, blue, tearose & gold, subtly dappled pale grey horse, sweet face & simple trappings of its early period, natural horsehair tail, ca. 1880, Charles Looff carousel factory, Brooklyn, NY, 56" l., 47" h., 35" body (ILLUS.) **4,900**

Parker Tucked-head Carousel Horse

Horse, jumper, professional restoration, very large Wild West motif, tightly tucked head, high & deeply carved peek-a-boo mane, fringed triple saddle blanket, eagle feathers hanging from a buckled breast-band, lariat, pistol & mountain lion saddle cantle, h.p. acrylics, creamy white w/rose, teal & gold trappings, ca. 1912, Charles Parker (ILLUS.) **11,500**

Herschell-Spillman Carousel Horse

Horse, jumper, professionally restored by Joe Daley, animated, tucked head, double blanket, keyhole girth, hatching on girth flap & under blanket, metal horseshoes, h.p. in artist oils, mahogany bay w/pink, turquoise & tan trappings, ca. 1915-20, Herschell-Spillman, 52" l., 33" h., 33" body (ILLUS.) **2,700**

Allen Herschell Carousel Horse

Horse, jumper, professionally restored & h.p., dappled dark rose · bay w/trappings in terra-cotta, brown & gold, tightly tucked head, "Trojan Horse" mane, double saddle blanket w/set-in jewels & painted scrollwork, tasseled headstall w/bridle fan pinned by jeweled keeper, gold color metal shoes, ca. 1925, Allen Herschell, 57" l., 39" h., 35" body (ILLUS.) **6,050**

Spillman Jumper Carousel Horse

Horse, jumper, professionally restored & h.p. in artist oils, bright bay pinto w/forest green, denim blue & gold trappings, animated "stargazer," double saddle blankets w/fringe, armored breastband, jeweled headstall & gold

colored metal shoes, ca. 1918, Spillman (ILLUS.) **3,600**

Spillman Tucked-head Carousel Horse

Horse, jumper, professionally restored & h.p. in oil glazes, warm light golden brown w/dark green, light green, saddle tan & burgundy trappings, tucked head, roached mane, rippled flipped back saddle blanket & jeweled breastband, tassel on browband, headstall fan pinned w/jeweled keeper, ca. 1916, Spillman, 53" l., 42" h., 36" body (ILLUS.) **4,100**

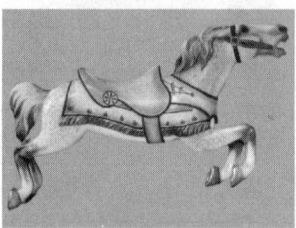

Spillman Tossed-head Horse

Horse, jumper, professionally restored & h.p. in oils, soft dappled cocoa w/golden brown, rose pink & gold trappings, tossed head, wild expressions, rippling mane, fringed saddle blanket & breastband decorated w/incised carvings, jeweled headstall, gold colored metal shoes, ca. 1920, Spillman, 55" l., 38" h., 35" body (ILLUS.) **4,620**

Dentzel Tucked-head Carousel Horse

Horse, jumper, rare closed-mouth, tucked head, deeply carved mane, tournament trappings in burgundy, Nile green and gold, restored by Gary Franklin, h.p. in artist oil by Sandy Paul to dappled chestnut w/flaxen mane & tail, oil glazing for brilliance & depth of color, last operated on the Storytown (Great Escape) amusement park in Lake George, New York, ca.1920, carved by Daniel Miller, William Dentzel,

Philadelphia, Pennsylvania, 52" l., 49" h.,
36" body (ILLUS.) **10,900**

Dentzel Carousel Horse

Horse, jumper, restored by Linda Lima,
raised head, kind face, painted in dapple
rose grey w/soft pink, teal, silver, gold &
rust trappings, ca. 1915, Daniel Muller,
hairline seams due to age, 52" l., 47" h.,
38" body (ILLUS.) **6,500**

Charles Looff Carousel Horse

Horse, jumper, striped w/remnants of old
paint, solid construction, graceful swan
neck, unusual leg position, hundreds of
multi-colored glass jewels, simply carved
trappings, gentle expression, layered
mane w/split forelock framing the large
eye, carved horseshoes, ca. 1885, Looff,
60" l., 59" h., 50" body (ILLUS.) **16,000**

Stein & Goldstein Jumper

Horse, jumper, wood, stocky w/prominent
saddle cinch ring & buckle, double saddle
blankets w/fringe, feathered medicine
charm depending from bedroll behind
cantle, feathered breastband, more
feathers slipped through a bezel on the
headstall, deeply carved bidirectional
mane, carved horseshoes, ca. 1920,
Stein & Goldstein, sound condition,
stripped to bare wood, miner seam separations corrected, 48" l., 49" h., 40" body
(ILLUS.) **9,900**

Charles Carmel Carousel Horse

Horse, outside row jumper, from Maple Leaf
Village Carousel, Canada, professionally
restored to apricot buckskin w/black
points & deep rose, cream, green & gold
trappings, large w/elegant head carriage,
beautifully detailed mane, tucked fore-
legs & extended rear legs, unusual
fringed, draped blanket tied w/tasseled
cords, jeweled breastband w/curved tasseled lappets, similar jewels & tassels on
the breeching, jeweled keeper on headstall, Charles Carmel, 44" body, 66" over-
all length (ILLUS.)...................................... **11,000**

Herschell Jumper Carousel Horse

Horse, outside row jumper, head-up &
turned out "Stargazer," triple blankets,
jeweled saddle, bridle & blanket, last operated by Lee's Rides, NC, ca. 1920s,
Allen Herschell, in primer paint but needs
restoration, 54" l., 50" h., 37" chest-to-
rump (ILLUS.) **2,400**

Charles Dare Carousel Horse

Horse, outside row jumper, older professional restoration by Betty Jean Rukows-
ki, from steam track machine, friendly
face, martingale straps, breast medallion, twin dolphins carved on floating birdback saddle, handpainted, soft pale grey
w/deep blue, blue-green, leather brown,
gold & silver trappings, ca. 1890s,
Charles Dare, exhibits stress separation,
50" l., 50" h., 35" rump-to-chest (ILLUS.) .. **2,700**

Stein & Goldstein Standing Horse

Horse, outside row stander, professionally restored to light grey w/natural leather trappings accented w/red & gold, dramatic "straining at the bit," carved fish scale blanket, breastband w/chain appendage evolving into a plastron, carved scimitar attached to saddle, fringe trimmed lappets depending from cantle, ca. 1912-1915, Stein & Goldstein (ILLUS.)............. **20,000**

Dentzel Stander Carousel Horse

Horse, outside row stander, stripped, repair to left rear ankle, powerful striding pose, original brass fixtures & jewels, ca. 1890, Gustav Dentzel, minor cracks, 55" l., 62" h. (ILLUS.)... **15,000**

Horse, prancer, last operated Braddock Heights, Maryland, stripped w/indication of old paint, solid construction w/seam separation, scalloped breastband, breeching display w/triangular lappets & fleur-de-lis, saddle blanket displays incised lozenge pattern, ca. 1900 Karl Muller, Germany, 54" x 55", 36" body **3,500**

Dentzel Prancing Carousel Horse

Horse, prancing position, professionally restored & h.p. to medium dapple grey, sweet faced mare, deeply layered mane, golden brown painted faux leather saddle & burgundy blanket, intricate painted

knotwork pattern on blanket & breastband, carved shoes, ca. 1900, Dentzel, 50" l., 55" h., 36" body (ILLUS.) **10,000**

Spillman Tucked-head Horse

Horse, professionally restored & h.p., faintly dappled cream, tucked head w/kind expression, windswept mane, trappings in various shades of green w/gold fringe, carved yellow rose w/two leaves tucked under the pommel, jeweled headstall, ca. 1928, Spillman, 55" l., 46" h., 39" body (ILLUS.).. **4,400**

Marcus Illions Carousel Horse

Horse, second row jumper, from "Supreme" style carousel, professionally restored to a cream color w/red, green, blue & gold trappings, gold leaf mane, alert yet gentle expression, jeweled & tasseled lappets depending from breastband & breeching, square cinch ring ties girth to saddle, ca. 1915, Marcus Illions, 41" l., 48" h., 38" body (ILLUS.)... **10,000**

Horse, stander, partially stripped, classic sweet face "Arabian" w/tournament trappings, unusual saddle configuration, double breastband, flipped back saddle cloth with tassel, eagle head cantle, ornately carved headstall, carved horseshoes, ca. 1918, Dentzel, sound condition, 62" l., 58" h., 50" body **18,000**

Charles Looff Stander Horse

Horse, stander, professionally restored & painted to a medium dapple grey w/burgundy, blue & gold trappings, long mane, extended forelock frames the large eyes, unusual breastband & breeching composed of dozen amulets containing clear glass jewels, classic female profile on cantle, carved horseshoes, ca. 1891, Looff, 50" body (ILLUS.) **17,050**

M.C. Illions Stander Horse

Horse, stander, stripped w/traces of old paint, elegant "Feltman Period" stander w/pensive face, jeweled headstall, richly carved full flowing mane, long extending peck-a-boo forelock, winged chimera on chest, birdback saddle & long flowing jeweled tassels depending from breeching, carved horseshoes, natural horsehair tail, ca. 1900, M.C. Illions, 52" l., 54"., h. 42" body (ILLUS.) **17,500**

Dentzel Stander Carousel Horse

Horse, stander, sweet face, flowing mane, jeweled headstall & birdback saddle, h.p. in artist's oils a dark dappled grey w/soft burgundy & sage green trappings, carved shoes, natural horsehair tail, professional restoration by Sandy Paul & Gary Franklin, ca. 1885, Dentzel, 43" l., 49" h., 36" body (ILLUS.) **8,300**

Carmel "Stargazer" Carousel Horse

Horse, standing stargazer, sound condition, old park paint w/great patina, lifted head & lolling tongue, sweeping bidirectional mane, fringed trappings w/hundreds of Borelli jewels, Charles Carmel, 45" body (ILLUS.) **18,000**

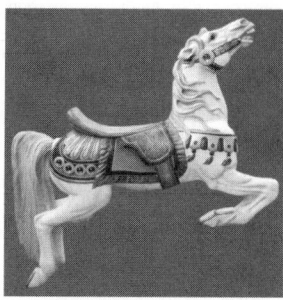

Charles Looff Stargazer Horse

Horse, stargazer jumper, professionally restored by Gary Franklin & h.p. by Sandy Paul to a creamy white w/gold, burgundy & claret trappings, displaying prominent muscle structure, half armored trappings, deeply fringed saddle blanket, tassels depending from breastband lappets, rose pink glass jewels, saddle faux finished to resemble tooled leather, carved horseshoes, ca. 1905 Looff, 48" l., 42" h., 35" (ILLUS.) **8,250**

Outside Galloping Carousel Horse

Horse, unusual "two-faced" outside galloping example w/wide girth strap & bridle, image of a lion face on body of horse & "Michael" on neck, w/original mounting board & brackets, made at the Savage Carousel Manufacturing Co., Burton on Trent, England, ca. 1885, 72" l., 45 1/2" h. (ILLUS.) **5,052**

Pair Thummel Carousel Horses

Horses, prancers, nearly identical pair, professionally restored by Sandy Paul &

Gary Franklin, h.p. in artist's oils, pale dappled chestnut w/English red & dusty green trappings, attentive expressions, scalloped breastbands, saddle cantles in the form of eagle wings & shoulders, trappings enhanced w/painted arabesques & florals, ca. 1900, Thummel, Germany, 48" l., 51" h., 33" body (ILLUS.) **18,000**

Herschell-Spillman Carousel Rooster

Rooster, trotting, fine feather detail, simple saddle & girth, stripped w/remnants of old paint, ca. 1902, Herschell-Spillman, minor restoration needed to repair slight seam separation, 48" l., 41" h. (ILLUS.) ... **3,900**

CAT COLLECTIBLES

Alarm clock, large Garfield clock w/bells on top, Sunbeam... **$30**
Andirons, cast iron, in the form of black cats w/glass eyes..................................... **300-500**
Ashtray, ceramic, in the form of a pipe w/cat sitting on stem, pipe is red clay w/brown glaze, tabby wears red bow, cold paint accents **45-50**
Bank, ceramic, Kliban cat w/red tennis shoes **35**
Bench, cast iron, decorated w/figures of cats on the ends, early 20th c., no rust **250**
Compact, faux ivory, contains solid perfume, Estée Lauder **275**
Cruets, ceramic, oil & vinegar cruets in the form of red clay male & female cats, the female w/closed painted white eyes in the shape of a "V" (for "vinegar") & the male w/wide open green eyes in the shape of an "O" (for "oil"), the pr. **60**
Dealer sign, Cats Meow Village retail sign **65**
Drawing, Maine Cat original drawing by Clare Turlay Newberry, children's author/illustrator, w/artist signature **350**
Greeting card, cut-out figure of kitten wearing card w/"Have a VERY Nice Birthday" attached by ribbon around its neck, Norcross **5**
Model of cat, ceramic image of scared cat, by Sylvac, English, 6" (comes in variety of colors, dull finish).. **70**
Model of cat, ceramic, large cat in crouching position w/stylized orange/red body w/brown face & ears, matte finish, Brayton Laguna, late 1950s or early 1960s.. **250-350**
Model of cat, ceramic, w/fur accents **20**
Model of cat, ceramic, white w/black spots, orange bow, green eyes, marked "Japan" in red, 4 1/2" **30**
Model of cat, ceramic, winking cat, Royal Haeger, 20".. **75**

Model of cat, cold-painted bronze, Austrian, 1 1/2" h., 2 1/2" l. (moderate paint loss in spots) **110**
Model of cat, crying, ceramic, white w/colored eyes, nose & mouth, clear overglaze, marked "Made in Czechoslovakia"....... **40**
Model of cat, glass, Murano **85**
Model of cat, most in carnival glass, some in satin & milk glass, Fenton, label attached, 10 1/2" h., 5 3/4" w., price depends on age & color.............................. **100-225**
Model of cats, ceramic, figures of Puff & Muff, Kay Finch, each................................... **75-90**
Perfume candle, Elizabeth Arden **21**
Planter, ceramic, in the form of a cat & kitten, pink & green accents, Hull **45**
Plate, ironstone-type ceramic, h.p. image of Puss in Boots, made in Austria (large chips)... **60**
Print, block print of black cats, signed, dated 1959 .... **95**
Print, of kitten, by Florence Kroger, 1940s **18**
Purse, mahogany, Enid Collins Sophistikits box-style, w/image of three cats decorated w/plastic "jewels," by Collins of Texas, 1967.. **80**
Salt & pepper shakers, bisque, stylized sitting cats, black matte finish w/red coldpainted flowers on heads, 1960s **27**
Scarf, silk, figures of Chessie & kittens & daddy Peake, used as advertising for Chesapeake Railroad **45**
Stringholder, ceramic, in the form of a cat, w/string & scissors, Fitz & Floyd **75**
Stuffed animal, cat w/rhinestone eyes & collar, JeeBee Creation, 1950s-60s **60**
Wall hanging, metal, set of three brown cats w/gold collars in graduated sizes of 13 1/5", 14 1/2" & 20", marked "Sexton USA".. **55**
Wall pocket, in the form of a Siamese cat & pink basket, Japanese (black ink mark), ca. 1950s... **55**
Wine bottle, Zeller Schwarze Katz bottle w/plastic gold cat on it, German, 1972 .... **35**

CERAMICS

ALSO SEE: Antique Trader Ceramic Price Guide, 3rd Edition.

American Painted Porcelain

During the late Victorian era American artisans produced thousands of hand-painted porcelain items, including tableware, dresser sets, desk sets, and bric-a-brac. These pieces of porcelain were imported and usually bear the marks of foreign factories and countries. To learn more about identification, evaluation, history, and appraisal, the following books and newsletter by Dorothy Kamm are recommended: American Painted Porcelain: Collector's Identification & Value Guide, Comprehensive Guide to American Painted Porcelain, *and Dorothy Kamm's* Porcelain Collector's Companion.

Berry spoon holder, pierced handles, decorated w/two clusters of blackberries, light blue border, burnished gold rim & handles, marked "Bavaria," ca. 1894-1914, 4 5/8 x 10" **$45**

Bonbon Box with Peacock Decor

Bonbon box, cov., round, low domed cover decorated w/a conventional design of three intertwined peacocks, baby blue base, burnished gold rims & feet, opal luster interior, marked "T&V Limoges - France," 1892-1907 (ILLUS.) **95**

Small Footed Bowl

Bowl, 5 1/2" d., 2 3/4" h., pedestal foot, decorated w/a conventional border in moss, yellow, orange & burnished gold on an ivory ground, dark green base, burnished bold rim & band, marked w/"La Seynie - P and P - Limoges - France," 1903-17 (ILLUS.) **50**

Butter dish, cover & liner, decorated on the domed cover & dished base w/clusters of pink roses & greenery on a pale pink & green ground, burnished gold rim & handle, signed "R.O. BRIGGS, AUSTIN, IL (?)," marked w/crowned double-headed eagle & "MZ - Austria," 1884-1909 .... **75**

Butter tub, round, decorated w/forget-me-nots on an ivory ground, burnished gold rim & handles, signed "Tossy," marked "T & V - Limoges - France," ca. 1892-1917 (no pierced insert) **50**

Cake plate, pierced rim handles, scalloped edge, decorated w/a four-panel design w/conventional-style flowers in each panel, burnished gold border outlines, dotted grounds & rim, signed w/illegible cipher & marked "HR - Charlotte - Bavaria," ca. 1887+, 9 1/8" d. **75**

Celery dish, long narrow shallow boat-form w/squared ends, decorated w/a border design of daisies & leaves on a pastel polychrome ground, ivory center, signed "Weiler," 1900-20, 5 3/4 x 12 3/4" (ILLUS. below) **60**

Chocolate cup & saucer, decorated w/yellow primrose on a shaded yellow brown ground, burnished gold rims, cup base & handle, signed "A. Brown," marked "Haviland - Limoges - France," ca. 1894-1931 .... **35**

Chocolate pot, cov., decorated w/cluster of pink roses on a pastel polychrome ground, burnished gold knob & handle, signed "M.H. Dorothy," marked "GDA - France," ca. 1900-41 .... **175**

Coffeepot, cov., decorated w/a conventional-styled dandelion design, burnished gold rims, spout interior, upper lip & handles, signed "M. Lamour," marked "J. & C. Bavaria," ca. 1902, 10" h. **225**

Morning Glory-decorated Compote

Compote, 8 7/8" d., 4 1/4" h., open, wide shallow round flaring bowl raised on a flaring pedestal base, the interior decorated w/a cluster of pink & white morning glories, rim & foot decorated w/bands of conventional pink butterflies, burnished gold rim & foot, signed "CL April 13th, 188(1)," marked "CFH" (ILLUS. of interior) **200**

Celery Dish with Daisy Border

Decorated Creamer & Covered Sugar

Cracker & cheese dish, decorated w/a conventional Chinese-style floral design, an opal lustre ground, burnished gold borders & rims, illegible signature, marked w/a wreath & star & "R.S. Tillowitz - Silesia," ca. 1920-38, 8 1/2" d................. **110**

Creamer & cov. sugar bowl, each w/a tapering cylindrical form, the base decorated w/a conventional blue & green floral border on a burnished gold band, ivory ground, burnished gold lips, spout, rims & handles, signed "Helen Hurley," 1900-20, pr. (ILLUS. top of page) **55**

Cup & Saucer with Celtic Border

Cup & saucer, cylindrical cup w/angled handle, decorated w/a conventional Celtic border design in celadon, light blue border, ivory center & interior, burnished gold rims & handle, signed "L.E.S.," marked w/a crown in double circle & "Victoria Austria," 1900-20, the set (ILLUS.)......... **35**

Cup & saucer, tapering cylindrical cup w/angled handle, decorated w/a conventional blue floral garland border design, burnished gold rims & handle, signed "Jane Bent Telin," marked "Favorite Bavaria,"1910-25, the set (ILLUS. bottom of page) **40**

Fern pot, decorated w/pink wild roses on a graduated green ground, signed "B.E. Miehling 99," marked "Elite" in a shield & "Limoges - France," 1899, 7 1/2" d., 4 3/4" h. **200**

Handkerchief box, cov., decorated w/peach-tinged yellow roses on a pastel polychrome ground, signed "WSO - 1913," marked "D. & Co. - France," 5 1/4" sq., 3" h. **75**

Honey dish, on three ball feet, decorated w/pink clover & wheat sheaves, light grey border, white enamel trim, burnished

Cup & Saucer with Floral Border

gold rim, marked "Bavaria," ca. 1891-1914, 7 1/8" d. **40**

Ice cream bowl, decorated w/a winter scene w/burnished gold border & rim, signed "F.L. Hey," marked "CFH - GDM," ca. 1920-30, 6 3/4 x 10 5/8", 2 3/16" h **115**

Lobster or shrimp salad bowl, decorated w/border clusters of seashells & seaweeds, white enamel trim, pale polychrome ground colors on exterior, burnished gold rim, marked "H and Co. - Limoges - France," ca. 1888-1896, 7 3/4 x 10 1/2" **125**

Mayonnaise bowl & underplate, decorated w/clusters of forget-me-nots on a pale blue border, ivory ground, burnished gold rims & feet, signed "AG," marked "Stouffer," 1906-1914, bowl 4 1/2" d., underplate 5 7/16" d., 2 pcs. **30**

Mug, decorated w/colorful yellow & yellowish red gooseberries on a polychrome ground, marked w/a crown & two shields w/"Vienna - Austria," ca. 1900-15, 4 3/4" h. **65**

Mug, decorated w/colorful yellow & yellowish red gooseberries on a polychrome ground, marked w/a crown & two shields "Vienna Austria," 1900-15 .... **65**

Napkin ring, half moon-shape, decorated w/a purple columbine on an ivory ground, ca. 1880-1915, 2 1/2" w. **25**

Olive dish, ring-handled, decorated w/heliotrope w/etched & burnished gold border & burnished gold handle, marked "T & V - Limoges - France," ca. 1892-1907, 7 3/8" d. **50**

Perfume with Honeysuckle Decor

Perfume bottle w/original gold stopper, ovoid body w/a short neck & large ball stopper, decorated w/a conventional design of honeysuckle in matt bronze greens, outlined in burnished gold, on a matt pale green ground, burnished gold lip & stopper, signed "M.L. Cushman" & "CFH/GDM," 1882-1890, 4 3/4" h. (ILLUS.) **85**

Perfume bottle w/original gold stopper, squatty bulbous base tapering to a tall slender cylindrical neck, decorated around the lower body w/daisies & leaves on an ivory ground, burnished gold rim &

Perfume Bottle with Daisy Decoration

stopper, marked w/a wreath & "O. & E.G. - Royal - Austria," 1898-1918, 4 3/4" h. (ILLUS.) **75**

Pin Tray with Moth Decoration

Pin tray, oval, decorated w/a border design of four blue & burnished gold moths, connected by a burnished gold & black band, ivory ground, burnished gold rim, signed "E. Arrindell - 1-2/18," marked w/a crown & double-headed eagle & "MZ - Austria," 1918 (ILLUS.) **50**

Pitcher, 5 3/4" h., lemonade-type, decorated w/clusters of purple grapes on an ivory ground, antique green beaded handle & border band at top, ca. 1900-16 .... **225**

Coupe Plate with Cornucopias

Plate, 6 3/4" d., coupe-style, decorated w/a border design of pink roses in burnished gold cornucopias, interspersed on a pink band, ivory ground, burnished gold rim & banding, marked w/a crown & scepter & "Silesia," ca. 1900-20 (ILLUS.) **25**

Plate Decorated with Pansies

Plate, 7 3/4" d., round w/lightly scalloped rim, decorated w/multi-colored pansies & greenery & burnished gold scrolls, ivory center, lavender rim border, burnished gold rim band, signed "BS" & marked "J&C - Louise - Bavaria," ca. 1902+ (ILLUS.) **50**

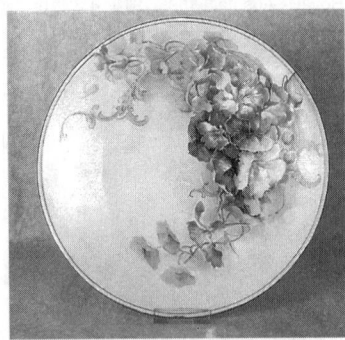

Plate with Well-painted Nasturtiums

Plate, 8 3/4" d., decorated w/orange nasturtiums, green leaves & light green scrolls accented w/gilded dots, burnished gold border band & rim, signed "G. Leykauf - 1908," marked "J.P.L. - France" (ILLUS.) **275**

Powder puff box & pin tray, round box w/domed cover & gold scroll loop finial, oblong lobed tray, each decorated w/a conventional dark bluish violet floral & pale green leaf border design w/burnished gold rims & vines outlined in black, on a pale pecan background, ivory ground, burnished gold finial, pin tray marked "GDA - France," box marked "T&V Limoges - France," 1900-20, tray 4 1/2 x 5 5/8", box 4 7/8" d., the set (ILLUS. below) **100**

Punch cups, decorated w/clusters of forget-me-nots, opal lustre interiors, burnished gold stems & rims, marked w/"Royal," a wreath & "O. & E.G.," 1898-1918, 4" h., set of 5 .... **125**

Pretty Painted Relish Pot

Relish pot, cov., ovoid body w/small inset domed cover w/gold loop handle, gold side handle, decorated w/a conventional design of fruits & flowers in polychrome colors, yellow enamel accents, baby blue ground, burnished gold rim & handles, signed "L Hogue," marked in a circle "K&L - Germany," 1915-30, 3 5/8" h. (ILLUS.) **30**

Salt dips, cauldron-shaped, decorated w/pink roses on a pale blue & yellow ground, burnished gold rims & ball feet, signed "P. Putzki," marked w/a crown double-head eagle & "MZ - Austria," ca. 1884-1909, set of 6 .... **120**

Salt & Peppers with Blue Insects

Powder Puff Box & Pin Tray

Salt & pepper shakers, tapering square form w/domed gold top, white ground decorated w/a conventional design of blue-winged insects, burnished gold tops, 1905-20, 3" h., pr. (ILLUS.) **35**

Sandwich tray, double pierced handles, decorated w/a polychrome conventional design, burnished gold rim & handles, marked w/a crown & crossed scepters w/"Rosenthal - Bavaria," 1908-25, 10" l. **85**

Sherbet, decorated w/daisies on an ivory ground, mother-of-pearl lustre interior, burnished gold border, rim & foot, signed "M. Paddock," marked "Epiag - Czechoslovakia," ca. 1920-39, 3 1/8" h. **35**

Soup plates, flanged rim decorated w/three clusters of seashells & seaweeds on a very pale polychrome ground, burnished gold rims, signed "ALB," marked "H. & Co. - Haviland - Limoges - France," 1876 - 1879, 9" d., pr. **50**

Sugar shaker, decorated w/Art Nouveau-style florals & squiggling border band in burnished gold, burnished gold pierced top, signed "E.C.R.," ca. 1905-15, 2 3/4" d., 4 1/2" h. **50**

Toast set: plate & cup; 9 3/16 w. plate decorated w/conventional-style strawberries on an ivory ground, opal lustre cup interior, burnished gold borders, rims & handle, ca. 1925-30, 2 pcs............................... **60**

Toothpick holder, decorated w/double violets on a pastel ivory & green ground, burnished gold rim, signed "Wats" & "Pitkin & Brooks Studio," marked "T & V - Limoges - France," 1903-10, 2 3/4" h................. **30**

Art Deco Design Painted Vase

Vase, 7 7/8" h., bulbous baluster-form w/wide flared neck, decorated w/two Art Deco-style floral panels in lustre & burnished gold, gold center band & base & neck bands, signed "M.D.P. 1920," marked w/a shield & "Thomas" (ILLUS.).......... **85**

Arequipa

Dr. Philip King Brown established The Arequipa Sanitorium in Fairfax, California, in the early years of the 20th century. In 1911 he set up a pottery at the facility as therapy for his female tuberculosis patients since he had been impressed with the success of the similar Marblehead pottery in Massachusetts.

The first art director was the noted ceramics designer Frederick H. Rhead who had earlier been art director at the Roseville Pottery.

In 1913 the pottery was separated from the medical facility and incorporated as The Arequipa Potteries. Later that year Rhead and his wife, Agnes, one of the pottery instructors, left Arequipa and Albert L. Solon took over as the pottery director. The corporation was dissolved in 1915 and the pottery closed in 1918 although the sanitorium remained in operation until 1957.

Bowl, 6 1/2" d., 2 1/4" h., wide flat bottomed form w/squatty bulbous incurved sides w/a wide flat mouth, embossed w/eucalyptus branches under a dark matte green & blue glaze, stamped mark, incised "KH - 11".. **$880**

Rare Miniature Arequipa Vase

Vase, 3 1/2" h., 2 1/2" d., miniature, simple ovoid body w/closed rim, decorated in squeezebag w/a rim band of holly leaves & red berries against a matte, mottled greenish blue ground, by Frederick Rhead, white & brown glaze mark (ILLUS.).. **6,325**

Early Arequipa Squatty Vase

Vase, 4 1/4" h., 7" d., footed wide squatty bulbous form w/the wide shoulder tapering to a short flared neck, enamel-decorated w/a plant w/white berries against a semi-matte greyish blue ground, rare early mark, incised "AP - 1911" (ILLUS.)....... **660**

Bauer

The Bauer Pottery was moved to Los Angeles, California from Paducah, Kentucky, in 1909, in the hope that the climate would prove beneficial to the principal organizer, John Andrew Bauer, who suffered from severe asthma. Flowerpots, made of California adobe clay, were the first production at the new location, but soon they were able to resume production of stoneware crocks and jugs, the mainstay of the Kentucky operation. In the early 1930s, Bauer's colorfully glazed earthen dinnerwares, especially the popular Ring-Ware pattern, became an immediate success. Sometimes confused with its imitator, Fiesta Ware (first registered by Homer Laughlin in 1937), Bauer pottery is collectible in its own right and is especially popular with West Coast collectors. Bauer Pottery ceased operation in 1962.

Bowl, batter, Ring-Ware, large $75-100
Casserole, w/holder, Ring-Ware, 5 1/2" h. 60-75
Cookie jar, pastel Kitchenware.................. 100-150
Cup & saucer, Monterey Moderne patt......... 20-30
Custard cup, Ring-Ware 15-25
Gravy boat, Monterey patt. 30-40
Gravy boat, Monterey patt. 30-40
Jug, ball-shape, La Linda patt...................... 40-50
Mixing Bowl, speckled, 1950s, 6" h. 15-20
Oil Jar, #122, 20" h.................................. 750-100
Plate, chop-type, Ring-Ware, 15" d. 75-100
Plate, luncheon-type, Ring-Ware.................... 20-25
Refrigerator set, stacking, Ring-Ware,
   4 pcs. 250-350
Shakers, La Linda patt., old style 20-25
Sugar bowl, Monterey patt............................. 20-25
Teapot, Ring-Ware, 6 cup capacity........... 100-150
Vase, 8" h., Billy-type 50-75

Berlin (KPM)

The mark, KPM, was used at Meissen from 1724 to 1725, and was later adopted by the Royal Factory, Konigliche Porzellan Manufaktur, in Berlin. At various periods it has been incorporated with the Brandenburg sceptre, the Prussian eagle or the crowned globe. The same letters were also adopted by other factories in Germany in the late 19th and early 20th centuries. With the end of the German monarchy in 1918, the name of the firm was changed to Staatliche Porzellan Manufaktur and though production was halted during World War II, the factory was rebuilt and is still in business. The exquisite paintings on porcelain were produced at the close of the 19th century and are eagerly sought by collectors today.

Bowl, handled oblong form, decorated in a
   colorful floral design w/a gilt edge, underglaze-blue K.P.M. mark, ca. 1890,
   11 1/4" l. $173
Cabinet cup, painted w/a military figure
   seated before a brick wall, w/a battle
   waging in the background, within gilt borders, blue sceptre mark, impressed letters & numbers, mid-19th c., 4 3/4" h........... 345
Cabinet plate, octagonal w/reticulated rim,
   the center w/a color portrait of Frederick
   the Great, 19th c., 9 1/8" w. 230
Figure group, depicting a peasant couple
   w/an infant, late 19th c., 12" h. (minor
   losses) 374
Figure group, depicting two bacchantes &
   a goat, decorated in color, 19th c., 8" l.
   (repairs).. 173
Plaque, rectangular, h.p. landscape scene
   w/a farm girl, impressed K.P.M. mark,
   late 19th - early 20th c., giltwood frame,
   4 x 5 3/4" 1,610
Plaque, "Rose de Mai," signed, titled &
   stamped in lower right "Wagner,"
   stamped & titled on verso, 5 x 7" (ILLUS.
   top next column) 2,576
Plaque, oval, bust portrait of a young bru-
   nette beauty facing right, wearing a grey
   shift w/a red sash, a bundle of wheat at
   the lower left, late 19th - early 20th c., impressed monogram & sceptre mark, art-
   ist-signed, 6 5/8 x 8 7/8" 4,600

Berlin Porcelain Plaque

Plaque, rectangular, h.p. scene of an Arab
   maiden in colorful attire standing next to
   a fountain & looking off to the left w/one
   hand shielding her eyes, titled "Expecta-
   tions," artist-signed, w/raised gilt trim, ca.
   1900, unframed, 6 x 9" 3,450
Plaque, oval, bust portrait of a young girl
   w/short wind-blown dark hair, head
   turned to one side, wearing a locket &
   open-collared blouse & shawl, impressed
   mark & sceptre, late 19th c., 6 3/4 x 9"...... 1,495
Plaque, rectangular, "September Morning,"
   painted in a soft palette in the Art Nouveau
   style w/a young nude lady standing &
   bathing in a highland lake w/mountains in
   the distance, early 20th c., impressed
   sceptre & monogram mark, various
   ciphers, in a black frame, 7 1/2 x 9 7/8" 2,875
Plaque, rectangular, finely painted w/a
   scene of a Renaissance lady standing
   before a church door, a rosary & book of
   prayers in her right hand, late 19th c., impressed sceptre & monogram mark, titled, w/paper label & signed by F. Wagner, in a giltwood frame, 6 7/8 x 10".......... 3,680
Plaque, rectangular, bust portrait of a young
   peasant woman turned to the side w/her
   smiling face turned to the viewer, her
   blonde hair braided atop her head, wearing a colored scarf & white blouse, impressed "KPM" & sceptre, ca. 1900,
   7 1/2 x 10".. 2,875
Plaque, rectangular, painted w/a figural
   scene w/a woman kneeling by a small girl
   holding a water ewer, impressed mark, in
   a giltwood frame, 19th c., 7 1/2 x 10"........ 3,680
Plaque, oval, allegorical bust portrait of
   "Beauty," a young woman facing right
   wearing a low-cut gown, her long brown
   hair flowing over her shoulders, impressed sceptre mark & K.P.M., 19th c.,
   framed, 8 1/2 x 10 1/4" 8,050
Plaque, oval, a half-length portrait of a seated gypsy girl, her long dark hair under a
   gold coin-trimmed cap, leaning on one elbow & looking left, blue sceptre & K.P.M.
   mark, late 19th c., 10 3/4" h....................... 3,900
Plaque, rectangular, "La Fiammetta," half-
   length portrait of a young maiden looking
   left, a laurel wreath in her long brown
   hair, wearing a white, blue & gold-
   trimmed gown, impressed marks, artist-
   signed, late 19th c., 12 1/2" h..................... 7,200

"Return from His First Voyage" Plaque

Plaque, rectangular, polychrome enamel interior scene of a sailor & family sitting around a table entitled "Return from His First Voyage," impressed "K.P.M." mark, 19th c., giltwood frame, 10 x 12 1/2" (ILLUS.) **9,200**

Plaque, rectangular, three-quarter length portrait of a young maiden standing in the dark & shielding a candle w/one hand, the light reflecting back on her face & body, titled "Gute Nacht," after Hom, artist-signed, late 19th c., impressed mark & sceptre, 8 x 13".. **2,875**

Plaque, rectangular, porcelain, full figure portrait of young dark-haired girl in field of flowers, after Marowsky, titled "Ophelie" ornate scrolled leafy frame, early 20th c., impressed "KPM" sceptre mark & dimensions, 8 x 13 1/4" **6,900**

Plaque, oval, porcelain three-quarter portrait of young girl w/long dark hair pulled to one side & over her shoulder, floral background, artist-signed, late 19th c., impressed "KPM - 6" & sceptre mark, 13 1/2" h... **13,800**

Plaque, rectangular, painted w/a scene of a young woman in Mideastern attire standing beside a well & leaning on a jug, palm trees in the background, impressed sceptre mark & K.P.M., late 19th c., giltwood frame, 11 1/4 x 13 1/2".............................. **7,475**

Plaque, rectangular, scene of a Greek maiden w/a water jug, artist-signed, ca. 1900, giltwood frame, 10 x 15 1/2" **6,900**

Plaque, rectangular, a half-length portrait of a standing young maiden wearing a white long-sleeved loose robe, her hand held to her throat & her eyes looking heavenward, a long curly brown hair hanging loose, tall slender green leafy stems w/large feathery lavender blossoms behind her, artist-signed, impressed marks, late 19th c., 10 3/4 x 16"............................. **7,800**

Plaque, rectangular, a scene of a young woman wearing a tightly wrapped classical off-the-shoulder gown standing & holding a mandolin in front of her, a dark tropical landscape behind her, artist-signed, late 19th c., 11 1/4 x 19" **11,400**

Plaques, rectangular, one depicting a pair of peasant girls seated among ruins w/a large basket of grapes, one counting change in her hand, the second scene of two young boys & a seated dog w/a basket of fruit & one eating slices, after Murillo, late 19th c., 10 x 12 1/2", pr................. **13,800**

Portrait plates, 10 3/4" d., each depicting Napoleon or ladies or gentlemen of his court, gilt-beaded borders w/gilt & cobalt band, ca. late 19th c., artist-signed & titled in red enamel, underglaze-blue beehive mark, set of 12..................................... **7,475**

Berlin Urn

Urns, cov., square base w/flared foot below wide ovoid body, two ring handles w/lion's head masks, decorated w/h.p. & gilded multicolored foliage, domed cover w/blossom finial, late 19th c., 8 1/2" h., pr. (ILLUS. of one)...................................... **1,035**

Vase, 10" h., pâte-sur-pâte, square-form handles w/scrolled ends, stylized gilt foliage designs around the pate-sur-pate cartouche of a child w/fruit basket on one side, enameled floral reserve on the other side, KPM mark, late 19th c................... **5,175**

K.P.M. Gourd-shaped Vase

Vase, 14" h., double gourd form, one side decorated w/figural reserves, reverse w/foliate spray, turquoise ground (ILLUS.).. **633**

Vases, cov., 17" h., a round stepped base below the ringed tapering pedestal supporting the tall tapering ovoid body molded around the shoulder w/gadrooning and around the base w/a band of serpents & acanthus leaves, upright looped shoulder handles, the domed cover w/a berry finial, white ground w/heavy gold trim, the sides decorated on the front w/a colored scene of an amorous couple in 18th c. costume & on the back w/a floral bouquet. also trimmed in pink & green, blue sceptre & iron-red orb marks, late 19th c., pr. **5,750**

Vegetable tureen, cov., oval, decorated in tones of lavender & green w/flower-filled urns & scrolls, 1850-70, 14" l. **460**

Boch Freres

The Belgian firm, founded in 1841 and still in production, first produced stoneware art pottery of mediocre quality, attempting to upgrade their wares through the years. In 1907, Charles Catteau became the art director of the pottery and slowly the influence of his work was absorbed by the artisans surrounding him. All through the 1920s wares were decorated in distinctive Art Deco designs and are now eagerly sought along with the hand-thrown gourd-form vessels coated with earth-tone glazes that were produced during the same time. Almost all Boch Freres pottery is marked, but the finest wares also carry the signature of Charles Catteau in addition to the pottery mark.

Box, cov., low rectangular form w/rounded corners, decorated w/crossed bands of stylized flowers in turquoise, sapphire blue, yellow & black on a crackled ivory ground, brass hinge & border, base w/circular stamp "Boch F La Louvière," brass stamped "France," ca. 1920s, 4 x 5 1/2", 1 1/2" h. **$288**

Boch Freres Charger & Vases

Charger, large round form w/flanged rim, decorated in the center w/a large grazing antelope, the border band w/round geometric devices, in sapphire blue, turquoise green & black on a crackled ivory ground, marked "D943 - Ch. Catteau - 22p C K," ca. 1920s, 14 1/2" d. (ILLUS. center) **1,150**

Boch Freres Pottery Lamp Base

Lamp base, bulbous ovoid body tapering to a short flared neck w/lamp fittings, inscribed w/stylized vines & fruits descending from the shoulder in shades of yellow, brown & blue against an oatmeal ground,

glossy glaze, marked "Keramis - Made in Belgium," ca. 1928, crazing, 24 1/4" h. (ILLUS.) **316**

Vase, 7" h., bulbous ovoid body tapering sharply to a small neck, decorated w/a repeating floral design of yellow blossoms, bluish green leaves & burgundy berries on branches, on a sapphire blue ground, separated by bands of blue, green, orange & black, circular stamp mark "Boch F La Louvière," ca. 1920s (crazing) **920**

Vase, 8 1/2" h., ovoid body tapering to a tall slender & slightly tapering neck, decorated w/three stylized flowers & leaves in a basket w/double swag, repeated in three sections, divided by border of multiple ovals, in yellow, orange, sapphire blue & light blue on an ivory crackled ground, circular mark "Boch F La Louvière," Belgium, ca. 1920s **403**

Two Boch Freres Vases

Vase, 8 3/4" h., footed ovoid body w/the swelled shoulder tapering to a wide, short flared neck, decorated overall w/large stylized yellow blossoms & leafy vines in yellow, turquoise, sapphire blue, orange & pale green w/blue borders on a crackled ivory ground, partial stamp "Keramis - Made in Belgium - 31," ca. 1920s (ILLUS. right) **690**

Vase, 8 3/4" h., low footring supporting a wide bulbous cylindrical body w/a wide rounded shoulder centering a thick molded rim band, decorated w/a wide center band featuring a continuous row of large upright stylized penguin-like birds in black against a yellow ground, black borders at the base & top, signed & stamped "Ch. Catteau - Keramis - Made in Belgium - Grès Keramis - 1059 C," ca. 1928-29 .... **6,600**

Vase, 9" h., wide ovoid body w/a wide rounded shoulder centering a short cylindrical neck, decorated w/a continuous band of large grazing antelope in sapphire blue, turquoise, bluish green & black on a crackled ivory ground, marked "Boch F La Louvière - D943 - 13 - 1291," ca. 1925 (ILLUS. left with flower-decorated vase) **1,265**

Vase, 9 1/4" h., very wide bulbous ovoid body tapering to a short cylindrical neck, decorated w/symmetrical stylized floral reserve in sapphire blue, bluish green & orange on a crackled white ground, stamped "Keramis - Made in Belgium - D60 - R V Larouche Belge - 1293," ca. 1920s **805**

Vase, 9 1/2" h., bulbous ovoid body tapering to a tiny cylindrical neck, decorated w/a white central band painted w/large stylized black bears against a white band w/narrower brown upper & lower bands trimmed w/black banding & zigzag lines, signed & stamped "Ch. Catteau - D. 1487 - Keramis - Made in Belgium - Grès Keramis - 996 C"... **5,100**

Vase, 10 1/2" h., flat-bottomed wide ovoid body w/a small cupped neck, decorated w/large brown & black flying bats against a greenish grey sky w/dark grey clouds, design 1378, signed & impressed "D. 1378 - Ch. Catteau - Keramis - Made in Belgium - Grès Keramis - 1053 C.," ca. 1929 (drilled)...................................... **3,840**

Boch Freres Vase with Sunbursts

Vase, 10 1/2" h., simple ovoid body tapering to a flat molded mouth, decorated w/four large repeating stylized swirled sunburst flowers in sections separated by a wavy line w/alternating oval dots, in turquoise, yellow & sapphire blue on an ivory crackled ground, turquoise border bands, stamped & signed "Boch F La Louvière - D889 - CT - K 899," ca. 1920s (ILLUS.)........ **575**

Vase, 10 1/2" h., simple ovoid form w/a footring & rim ring, decorated w/wide color vertical bands of stylized tulips & flowers w/leaves in yellow, sapphire blue, green & brown on an ivory crackled ground, sapphire blue bands, marked "Keramis - Made in Belgium - D2779 - 9 - 899," ca. 1920s **690**

Vase, 11" h., simple ovoid form tapering to a small flat mouth, decorated around the sides w/large black flamingos running the full length of the sides against a mottled yellowish green ground, signed & stamped "C.Catteau - D. 979 - Keramis - Made in Belgium - Grès Keramis - 987," ca. 1925 .... **9,000**

Vase, 11 1/8" h., ovoid body tapering slightly to a wide short neck w/molded rim, the upper portion decorated w/a wide band featuring large stylized oblong black & white bird-like creatures against a mottled dark grey ground, a wide lower band w/a lattice design in light brown & black, a narrow crosshatch band around the rim, signed & stamped "Ch. Catteau - D. 1025 - Keramis - Made in Belgium - 967 - Grès Keramis," ca. 1925.......................... **10,200**

Vase, 12" h., large wide ovoid body tapering gently to a wide, short cylindrical neck, decorated w/stylized flowers & leaves in pinks, sapphire blue, yellow, brown & grey on a pale yellow ground, bordered w/a ring of small blossoms & leaves & sapphire blue bands, marked "Keramis - Made in Belgium - 2243 - 909," ca. 1920s (crazing) **805**

Vase, 12 1/8" h., wide ovoid body tapering to a short rolled neck, decorated w/a wide central band featuring a continuous design of large stylized black & white owls against a tan ground, white dash & solid thin bands above & below the center band, black bands around the top & base, signed & stamped "Ch. Catteau - D. 1060 - Keramis - Made in Belgium - Grès Keramis - 914 C," ca. 1925 .... **5,760**

Catteau-designed Boch Freres Vase

Vase, 12 1/4" h., ovoid body tapering slightly to a short, flaring molded neck, decorated w/a wide center band w/a continuous row of large white stylized bird-like creatures against a black ground w/thin brown lines, white upper & lower bands w/thin brown scalloped designs, signed & stamped "Ch. Catteau - D 1026 - Boch Frs. - La Louvière - Made in Belgium - Fabrication Belgique - Grès Keramis - 911 C," ca. 1925 (ILLUS.) **6,600**

Vase, 12 1/2" h., stoneware, tall simple ovoid form w/a thick short rolled neck, a wide central band decorated in black & cream w/a row of large stylized birds, the upper & lower bands in black w/cream fishscale designs, designed by Charles Catteau, signed "Ch. Catteau - D. 1026A" & incised "Gres Keramis" w/wolf mark & "Keramis - Made in Belgium," original retailer's sticker, ca. 1925.............................. **3,300**

Boch Freres Antelope Vase

Vase, 13 1/2" h., wide ovoid body tapering to a wide cupped neck, decorated w/a wide central band of stylized antelope in dark blue & black grazing on blue & green grass at the bottom & w/leaves & geometric designs around the top, against a crackle-glazed white ground, signed & stamped "Ch. Catteau - Boch Frs. - La Louvière - Made in Belgium - Fabrication Belgique - 911," ca. 1924 (ILLUS.).. **6,000**

Vase, 16" h., tall baluster-form w/a cylindrical short neck, decorated w/a wide band of gazelle in dark blue, purple & black among stylized foliage against a creamy white ground, the neck & lower body w/overall geometric ring designs in matching colors, designed by Charles Catteau, signed "Ch. Catteau - D. 943," stamped "Keramis - Made in Belgium - 24," inscribed "762" **3,300**

Vase, 19 1/4" h., large ovoid form w/a heavy rolled rim, the body painted w/large stylized exotic birds among large rounded blossoms & leafy branches w/berries in greenish yellow on a dark brown ground w/black base & rim bands, designed by Jules-Ernest Chaput, signed, ca. 1930 .... **12,000**

Large Boch Freres Floral Vase

Vase, 19 1/2" h., large, tall ovoid form tapering to a tiny neck w/deeply rolled rim, wide vertical bands of stylized creamy white blossom clusters & green scrolls alternating w/narrow creamy white zigzag stripes, stamped & signed "Ch. Catteau - D. 1003 - Boch Frs. - La Louvière - Made in Belgium - Fabrication Belgique - Grès Keramis - 961 - V.," ca. 1925 (ILLUS.)....... **6,000**

Vases, 11 1/2" h., ovoid body tapering to a short cylindrical neck w/molded rim, decorated w/two large stylized standing birds w/extended wings among leafy vines, in sapphire blue, blue, bluish green & pale green on an ivory crackled ground, striped border bands, stamped "Keramis - Made in Belgium - D4507," ca. 1920s, pr. (ILLUS. left & right with charger).............. **920**

Canton

This ware has been decorated for nearly two centuries in factories near Canton, China. Intended for export sale, much of it was originally inexpensive blue-and-white hand-decorated ware. Late 18th and early 19th century pieces are superior to later ones and fetch higher prices.

Bowl, 9" d., round, w/scalloped edge, blue & white design... **$523**

Bowl, 8 1/4 x 10", lobed shape, orange peel glaze, ... **330**

Container, cov., round w/two wire bale handles, lid w/flat wafer finial, 6 3/4" d., 3 1/4" h.. **990**

Creamer, "bullnose" spout w/flared rim, orange peel glaze, 3 3/4" h. **220**

Creamer, helmet-shaped, w/Oriental hooked crosses on foot & molded swirls on branch handle, 4 1/8" h. (ILLUS. second from left, below) **578**

Creamer, squat body w/high handle, 3 1/4" h.. **220**

Fruit basket & undertray, oval gently flaring basket w/reticulated sides, on a matching undertray w/reticulated edges, 19th c., 10 1/4" l., 3 3/4" h., 2 pcs. (minor edge chips).. **805**

Pitcher, 6" h., bulbous body w/high, thin handle w/molded fan end & exaggerated slope to spout, orange peel glaze.................. **880**

Platter, 13 x 16", octagonal w/dark slate blue & white decoration (some firing imperfections in glaze)...................................... **330**

Platter, 14 x 17 1/2" rounded octagonal shape, medium blue decoration of a bridge, pagodas & an island, orange peel glaze **495**

Platter & strainer, 13 3/4 x 17 1/8", deep oval form, oblong w/canted corners, 19th c., 2 pcs. (minor glass irregularities, color variations) **978**

Serving dish, square w/lobed corners, orange peel glaze, 8 1/2" sq. **440**

Sugar bowl, cov., cup-shaped w/double, intertwined handles w/ applied decorative ends, fruit finial, 3 7/8" d., 4 1/2" h., minor flakes on foot (ILLUS. second from right, below).. **523**

Canton Porcelain Pieces

Teapot, cov., canister-shaped body & intertwined, reeded handle w/ornate, applied floral ends, fruit finial, straight spout, 5 1/2" h., some rim flakes (ILLUS. far left, bottom previous page) 908

Teapot, cov., cylindrical body tapering in at top, intertwined handle w/decorative ends, fruit finial on lid, curved spout, 6 3/4" h. (ILLUS. far right, bottom previous page) 578

Tureen, cov., rectangular w/rounded corners, flared base, the cover decorated w/a leaf-shaped knop, boar's head handles, 19th c., 13" l., 8 1/2" h. (minor small firing cracks) 1,955

Warming dish, cov., high base w/blue & white design on interior, lid has fruit finial, 9 3/8" d., 5" h. 660

Water bottle, ovoid, w/long neck, white ground w/hint of blue, darker blue design of buildings w/hills, 7 5/8" h., short hairlines at lip (ILLUS. center, bottom previous page) 688

Catalina Island Pottery

The Clay Products Division of the Santa Catalina Island Co. produced a variety of wares during their brief ten-year operation. The brainchild of chewing-gum magnate, William Wrigley, Jr., owner of Catalina Island at the time, and his business associate D. M. Retton, the plant was established at Pebbly Beach, near Avalon in 1927. Its two-fold goal was to provide year-round work for the island's residents and building material for Wrigley's ongoing development of a major tourist attraction at Avalon. Early production consisted of bricks and roof and patio tiles. Later, art pottery, including vases, flower bowls, lamps and home accessories were made from a local brown-based clay and, about 1930, tablewares were introduced. These early wares carried vivid glazes but had a tendency to chip readily and a white-bodied, more chip-resistant clay, imported from the mainland, was used after 1932. The costs associated with importing clay eventually caused the Catalina pottery to be sold to a California mainland competitor in 1937. These wares were molded and are not hand-thrown but some pieces have hand-painted decoration.

Ashtray, fish laying on side $30-40
Bowl, flower-type, fluted, 10 x 15", 2" h. 75-100
Candleholder, footed, 4" h. 25-40
Cup & saucer, Rope patt. 5-10
Shot glass, nude figure, "þBottoms Up" 25-30
Sugar bowl, Rope patt. 30-50
Vase, 7" h., Conch shell patt. 40-50

Chinese Export

Chinese Export Armorial Bowl

Bowl, 9 1/4" d. , armorial, octagon-form rim decorated w/alternating panels of birds, flowers & shells, center w/arms of Mercer, ca. 1755 (ILLUS.) **$1,064**

Pair of Chinese Export Bowls

Bowls, 9 3/4" d., "Tobacco Leaf" patt., wide rim, overall vibrant painted overlapping leaf & floral spray design, ca. 1800, pr. (ILLUS.) 2,576

Mug, cylinder shape w/applied twig handle, blue enamel bands & Batten coat of arms , ca. 1790, 5 1/2" h. 728

Plates, 9 1/4" d., honeycomb border interspersed w/pictures of duck & woman, the center w/scene of women w/parasol & group of ducks, in Chinese Imari palette, ca. 1735, pr. 2,912

Platter, 13 3/8 x 16 1/8", blue Nanking patt., oblong w/cut corners, 18th c. (rim chips) 575

Chinese Export Punch Bowl

Punch bowl, armorial, footed, rounded flared sides decorated w/arms of Campbell the Duke of Argyll and motto "NE OBLIVISCARIS, VIX EA NOSTRA VOCO" & chinoiserie cartouche, chain design rim, ca. 1770 (ILLUS.) 2,688

Sauce tureen, cov., blue Fitzhugh patt., footed squatty bulbous oval form w/flared rim & low domed cover w/a large blossom finial, entwined lapped end handles, 19th c., 8 1/4" l., 5 1/2" h. 920

Tureen, cov., blue Fitzhugh patt., high-footed large deep bulbous oval body w/an upright rim band supported a tapered domed cover w/large blossom finial, entwined lapped end handles, 19th c., 14" l., 11 1/4" h. 2,645

Covered Tureen with Underplate

Tureen w/underplate, cov., oblong, footed, in Claerbout design in rust, blue & green on white ground, ca. 1790, 9 1/2 x 14", 9 1/2 h. (ILLUS.).. **1,904**

Chinese Export Vase

Vase, baluster form, cylindrical neck w/flaring lip, decorated in famille verte w/scenic panels, late 19th c., 21 1/2" h. (ILLUS.).. **448**

Warming plate, blue Nanking patt., octagonal shape w/picture of a man w/an umbrella walking across bridge, flowers on wide edge, 9 1/4" d... **385**

Clarice Cliff Designs

Clarice Cliff was a designer for A. J. Wilkinson, Ltd., Royal Staffordshire Pottery, Burslem, England when they acquired the adjoining Newport Pottery Company whose warehouses were filled with undecorated bowls and vases. About 1925 her flair with the Art Deco style was incorporated into designs appropriately named "Bizarre" and "Fantasque" and the warehouse stockpile was decorated in vivid colors. These hand-painted earthenwares, all bearing the printed signature of designer Clarice Cliff, were produced until World War II and are now finding enormous favor with collectors.

Note: Reproductions of the Clarice Cliff "Bizarre" marking have been appearing on the market recently.

Bowl, 5" d., 3" h., footed flared cylindrical form, Autumn Crocus patt., a yellow band on the inside rim, the exterior w/blue, orange & purple flowers, ca. 1930s (minor glaze scratches)... **$345**

Bowl, 6 1/4" d., octagonal flanged rim on the rounded body, Woodland patt., stylized landscape w/trees in orange, green, black, blue, purple & yellow, marked............ **550**

Bowl, 6 1/2" d., 3" h., "Bizarre" ware, footed deep slightly flaring sides, Crocus patt., the sides divided into two horizontal bands of color w/a band of small crocus blossoms along the upper half, in orange, blue, purple & green, stamped mark **550**

Bowl, 8" d., 3 3/4" h., "Bizarre" ware, deep gently rounded sides tapering to a footring, Original Bizarre patt., a wide band of blocks & triangles around the upper half in blue, orange, ivory & purple, purple band around the bottom section, marked..... **650**

Bowl, 8" d., 4 1/4" h., "Bizarre" ware, octagonal, h.p. w/Original Bizarre patt., large crudely painted bands of maroon, dark orange & dark blue diamonds above an ochre base band, ink mark **1,100**

Bowl, 9" d., deep rounded sides, the upper half w/a wide band in polychrome featuring large stylized cottages w/pointed orange roofs beneath arching trees, lime green banding, marked **800**

Bowl, 9 1/2" d., 4 1/2" h., orange, green & blue h.p. poppies... **600**

Butter dish, cov., "Bizarre" ware, Crocus patt., a wide shallow base w/low, upright sides fitted w/a shallow, flat-sided cover w/a slightly domed top & flat button finial, the top decorated w/purple, blue & orange blossoms on an ivory ground, marked, 4" d., 2 3/4" h. **550**

A Variety of Clarice Cliff Patterns

Butter dish, cov., "Bizarre" ware, short wide cylindrical body w/an inset cover w/large button finial, Secrets patt., decorated w/a stylized landscape in shades of green, yellow & brown w/red-roofed houses on a cream ground, marked, 4" d., 2 5/8" h. (ILLUS. left) **550**

Cracker jar, cov., "Bizarre" ware, Blue Chintz patt., stylized blue, green & pink blossom forms w/blue border band **1,800**

Cracker jar, cov., "Bizarre" ware, bulbous barrel shape w/large side knobs to support the arched woven wicker bail handle, wide flat mouth w/a slightly domed cover centered by a large ball finial, Gayday patt., decorated w/a wide band of large stylized flowers in orange, rust, amethyst, blue & green above a lower band in orange on a cream ground, the cover w/an orange finial & yellow band, 5 7/8" d., 6 1/4" h. (ILLUS. right w/butter dish) **975**

Delecia Citrus Cracker Jar & Vases

Cracker jar, cov., "Bizarre" ware, squatty kettle-form w/side knobs supporting the swing bail handle, Delecia Citrus patt. (ILLUS. right)... **1,400**

Cup & saucer, "Bizarre" ware, Autumn Crocus patt., Athens shape................................... **300**

Demitasse set: cov. coffeepot, six demitasse cups & saucers, creamer & open sugar bowl; "Bizarre" ware, Fantasque patt., decorated w/a stylized tree on one side, the other w/stylized hollyhocks, small chips to one saucer, 15 pcs. (ILLUS. of part, top next page) **3,200**

"Bizarre" Demitasse Set

Dinner service: four dinner plates, thirteen luncheon plates, fifteen soup bowls, eight fruit plates, seven appetizer plates, four dessert plates, seven cups & saucers, cov. sugar, creamer & serving bowl; Biarritz patt., the square plates w/deep rounded wells, the creamer & sugar w/upright flattened round shapes, each decorated w/concentric bands in black, maroon, taupe, gold & yellow on a cream ground, ca. 1929, marked, the set **1,150**

Figures, "Bizarre" ware, flat cut-outs, comprising two groups of musicians & two groups of dancing couples, all highly stylized & glazed in reddish orange, yellow, lime green, cream & black, printed factory marks, ca. 1925, 5 5/8 to 7" h., 4 pcs. . **29,000**

Jam pot, cov., Blue Firs patt., flat-sided round form on small log feet, domed cover w/flat round knob, stylized landscape w/trees, marked, 4 1/4" h. **900**

Lemonade set: 8" h. tankard pitcher & four cylindrical tumblers; each decorated in an abstract geometric pattern in orange, blue, purple, green & yellow, marked, the set **1,100**

Pitcher, 5 3/4" h., "Fantasque" line, Melon patt., wide conical body w/solid triangular handle, orange & thin black bands flanking a wide central band of stylized melons in yellow, blue, green & orange, marked, ca. 1930 (tiny glaze nicks at rim & base, faint scratch in lower orange band).. **875**

Pitcher, 6 7/8" h., "Bizarre" ware, flaring cylindrical body w/a wide rim & wide arched spout opposite an angled handle, Secrets patt., decorated w/a stylized landscape in shades of green, yellow & brown w/a red-roofed house on a cream ground, stamped mark.. **900**

Pitcher, 7" h., 7" d., "Bizarre" ware, tapering cylindrical body w/flat rim & wide pointed spout, flattened angled handle from rim to base, Sliced Fruit patt., wide band of abstract fruit in yellow, orange & red, stamped mark.. **1,800**

Pitcher, 9 1/4" h., "My Garden" patt., wide rim tapering to a flared base w/embossed flowers ornamenting the handle in orange, green & brown on a light tan ground, post-1936 .... **288**

Pitcher, 9 3/4" h., 7 3/4" d., jug-type, "Bizarre" ware, Isis shape, Summerhouse patt., decorated w/trees & gazebos in yellow, green, purple, red & blue against an ivory ground, marked **3,900**

Lotus Pitcher in Delecia Citrus Pattern

Pitcher, 12" h., "Bizarre" ware, Lotus shape, ringed ovoid body tapering to a wide cylindrical neck, heavy loop handle, Delecia Citrus patt., large stylized red, yellow & orange fruits around the top w/green leaves & streaky green on a cream ground (ILLUS.).............................. **2,200**

Pitcher, 12" h., jug-type, "Bizarre" ware, Trees & House patt., ovoid w/molded narrow rings, decorated w/wide bands of orange & black flanking a wide central band w/green-roofed houses & black & orange trees, marked, ca. 1930 .... **1,265**

Plate, 7 3/4" d., Broth patt., predominantly orange w/bubbles & orange, purple & blue cobwebs (few glaze scratches) **230**

Plate, 9" d., "Bizarre" ware, Blue Chintz patt., decorated w/stylized flowers in green, blue & pink against an ivory ground, marked.. **650**

Plate, 9 3/4" d., Forest Glen patt., a stylized cottage in a woodland scene in orange, ivory & green, die-stamped "Clarice Cliff - Newport Pottery - England" **950**

Sugar shaker, Autumn patt., sharply pointed conical form w/rows of small holes pierced around the top, decorated in pastel autumn colors, marked, 5 1/2" h........... **1,200**

Sugar shaker, "Bizarre" ware, Crocus patt., sharply pointed conical form, decorated w/blue, purple & orange crocus flowers, marked, ca. 1930, 5 5/8" h. (chips on base)... **460**

Sugar shaker, "Bizarre" ware, flattened egg-shaped body set on two tiny log-form feet, Crocus patt., banded body w/a central row of stylized crocus blossoms, in yellow, blue, orange & purple, stamped mark, 2 1/2" w., 5" h... **750**

Tumbler, Sunray patt., conical form, polychrome decoration of a stylized sun, orange banding, marked, 3" h. **600**

Vase, 5 1/4" h., "Bizarre" ware, Shape No. 341, squatty bulbous chalice-form, Delicia Citrus patt.,, bright fruits on a creamy ground (ILLUS. left w/cracker jar).................. **900**

Vase, 8" h., "Bizarre" ware, Shape No. 362, ovoid upper body above a heavy ringed & waisted base, Delecia Citrus patt., brightly painted fruits on a cream ground (ILLUS. center w/cracker jar)..................... **1,200**

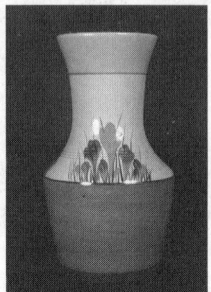

Crocus Pattern Vase

Vase, 8" h., "Bizarre" ware, Shape No. 386, swelled cylindrical base below the angled shoulder & tall gently flaring neck, Crocus patt., a yellow rim band & brown bottom section below a cluster of colorful crocus blossoms on a cream ground (ILLUS.) **1,500**

Clewell Wares

Though Charles W. Clewell of Canton, Ohio, didn't operate a pottery, he is responsible for a category of fine art pottery through his development of a unique metal coating placed on pottery blanks obtained from Owens, Weller and others. By encasing objects in a thin metal shell, he produced copper- and bronze-finished ceramics. Later experiments led him to chemically treat the metal coating to attain the bluish green patinated effect associated with copper and bronze. Although he produced metal-coated pottery from 1902 until the mid-1950s, Clewell's production was quite limited for he felt no one else could competently recreate his artwork and, therefore, operated a small shop with little help.

Bowl-vase, a small footring supporting a wide bulbous body w/a short widely flared rim, fine bronzed & verdigris patina, incised "Clewell 417-2-G," 5 1/4" d., 4 1/2" h. **$495**

Vase, 3 3/8" h., bulbous body w/short molded rim, brown patina on upper half w/crusty green patina below, marked "Clewell" (minor scuffs) **252**

Vase, 4 5/8" h., bulbous ovoid shouldered body tapering to cylindrical neck w/flaring rim, green over brown patina, base incised "Clewell 466" (patina polished away in small spots about the shoulder) **224**

Small Slender Clewell Vase

Vase, 6 1/2" h., a wide round base tapering to a slender waisted body, deep red patina w/pale green patina band around the base, small glaze chips around base (ILLUS.) **287**

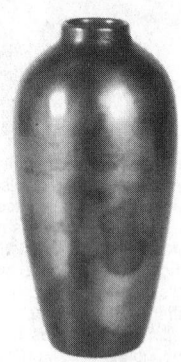

Clewell Vase with Shiny Patina

Vase, 7" h., simple ovoid form tapering to a small flat mouth, overall shiny coppery patina, signed, light scratches & wear (ILLUS.) **374**

Clewell Vase with Original Patina

Vase, 7 1/4" h., round foot below the bulbous lower body tapering to tall trumpet-form sides, even dark bronze original patina, signed (ILLUS.) **287**

Clewell Vase with Shaded Patina

Vase, 7 1/2" h., 3 1/2" d., ovoid body w/the rounded shoulder centering a small flaring neck, dark green verdigris shaded to dark reddish bronze patina, incised "Clewell - 351 - 215" (ILLUS.)...................... **1,725**

Clewell Vase with Dark Green Patina

Vase, 7 1/2" h., 3 3/4" d., ovoid body w/the rounded shoulder centering a small flaring neck, overall shaded dark green to lighter green verdigris patina, couple of small patina flakes near base, incised "Clewell - 351- 6" (ILLUS.) **920**

Vase, 7 3/4" h., bulbous base tapering to tall cylindrical neck w/flared rim, early 20th c., inscribed "Clewell 293-29" **575**

Clewell Vase No. 463

Vase, 8 1/2" h., broad-shouldered tapering ovoid body w/a small, short rolled neck, No. 463, some surface glaze flaws & flaking (ILLUS.).. **431**

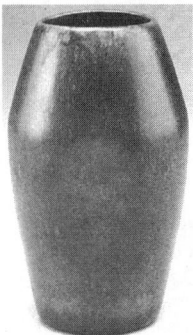

Ovoid Clewell Vase

Vase, 8 1/2" h., 5" d., simple ovoid form tapering to a flat rim, deep reddish bronze & verdigris patina, pea-sized colored spot near base, incised "Clewell - 60- 215" (ILLUS.).. **978**

Vase, 9" h., 4 1/2" d., tall slender tapering urn-form body w/a flattened shoulder centering a short rolled neck flanked by small angled handles, bronze & verdigris patina, incised "C.W. Clewell - 520-220" (few patina chips on base).......................... **1,125**

Clewell Vase No. 305-6

Vase, 10" h., tall baluster-form body, fine bronzed patina, No. 305-6, signed (ILLUS.).. **862**

Vase, 11 1/4" h., 8 1/2" d., a large gently flaring cylindrical body w/a wide angled shoulder centering a low squatty neck, verdigris finish, signed................................ **2,760**

Clifton Pottery

William A. Long, founder of the Lonhuda Pottery, joined Fred Tschirner, a chemist, to found the Clifton Art Pottery in Newark, New Jersey in 1905. Crystal Patina was their first art pottery line and featured a subdued pale green crystalline glaze later also made in shades of yellow and tan. In 1906 they introduced their Indian Ware line based on the pottery made by American Indians. Other lines which they produced include Tirrube and Robin's-egg Blue. Floor and wall tiles became the focus of the production after 1911 and by 1914 the firm's name had changed to Clifton Porcelain Tile Company, which better reflected their production.

Clifton Pottery Humidor

Humidor, cov., Indian Ware, cylindrical w/inset cover w/large knob handle, dark brown ground w/black stylized geometric designs, two chips at rim (ILLUS.) **$109**

Pitcher, 7" d., wide squatty bulbous body tapering to a wide slightly rolled rim w/low arched spout, D-form loop handle, cream ground incised & painted w/stylized geometric black flying birds **176**

Vase, 6" h., wide bulbous tapering ovoid body w/a small cylindrical neck w/flared rim, bold Greek key-style Native American designs in deep brick red outlined in cream against a black ground, incised mark **275**

Vase, 6 1/2" h., tall slender tapering cylindrical body w/a tiny cylindrical neck, the body in green & tan crystalline glaze decorated overall w/a silver overlay design of stylized blossoms & long tendrils arranged as oblong reserves up the sides & around the neck, incised mark **1,430**

Vase, 8" h., 11" d., Native American design, "Homolobi," large squatty bulbous body centered by a wide, short cylindrical neck, decorated w/large repeating S-scroll design & borders in black on a terra cotta ground, incised "Clifton 233" & titled (typical glaze flaking) **495**

Clifton Native American-style Vase

Vase, 9 1/2" h., Native American form vessel w/a wide squatty bulbous base centered by a wide cylindrical neck, incised & painted w/geometric designs in black, cream, tan & dark brown, incised mark (ILLUS.) **330**

Vase, 9 1/2" h., 4 1/2" d., ovoid form tapering to a short cylindrical neck, Crystal Patina, mottled creamy white & greenish yellow glaze, incised "Clifton - 158" **385**

Vase, 10" h., 7" w., a gently flaring cylindrical lower body below a wide shoulder centering a tall cylindrical neck, long pointed angled handles from the rim to the shoulder, Crystal Patina glaze, incised mark **495**

Cowan

R. Guy Cowan opened his first pottery studio in 1912 in Lakewood, Ohio. The pottery operated almost continuously, with the exception of a break during the war, at various locations in the Cleveland area until it was forced to close in 1931 due to financial difficulties.

Many of this century's finest artists began with Cowan and its associate, the Cleveland School of Art. This fine art pottery, particularly the designer pieces, are highly sought after by collectors.

Many people are unaware that it was due to R. Guy Cowan's perseverance and tireless work that art pottery is today considered an art form and found in many art museums.

Book ends, figural, model of a ram, black, thick rectangular base w/slanted top, Shape No. E-3, designed by Waylande Gregory, 7 1/2" h., pr. **$2,500**

Book ends, model of a stylized horse, back legs raised in kicking position, black, designed by Waylande Gregory, Shape No. E-1, 9" h., pr. **2,500**

Cowan Bust and Vases

Bowl, miniature, 2" d., footed, flared body, Shape No. 514, mark No. 5, orange lustre 60

Bowl, 10" d., 2 1/2" h., Egyptian blue, Shape No. B-12 75

Bowl, 3 x 10 x 11 1/2", leaf design, ivory & green, designed by Waylande Gregory 125

Bowl-vase, green & gold, Shape No. B-4, 11" 300

Bust, "Colonial Head," stylized angular bust portrait w/long wavy hair, on a rectangular plinth, overall peach crackled glaze, by Waylande Gregory, circular mark, 7" w., 14" h. (ILLUS. at right, bottom previous page) 3,656

Candelabrum, "Pavlova," porcelain, two-light, Art Deco style, a footed squatty tapering central dish issuing at each side a stylized hand holding an upturned cornucopia-form candle socket, the center fitted w/a figure of a nude female dancer standing on one leg w/her other leg raised, her torso arched over & holding a long swirled drapery, Special Ivory glaze, stamped mark, 10" l., 7" h. (chip under rim of one bobeche) 400

Candleholders, footed, designed by R. G. Cowan, ivory, Shape No. 811, 2 3/8" h., pr. 50

Candleholders, semi-circular wave design, white glaze, Shape No. 751, 4 3/4" h., pr. 125

Cowan Figural Nude Candlestick

Candlestick, two-light, large figural nude standing w/head tilted & holding a swirling drapery, flanked by blossom-form candle sockets supported by scrolled leaves at the base, matte ivory glaze, designed by R.G. Cowan, Shape No. 745, 7 1/2" w., 9 3/4" h. (ILLUS.) 1,200

Candlesticks, curled form, royal blue, 1 1/2" h., pr. 125

Candlesticks, w/loop handle, green, Shape No. 781, 4" h., pr. 75

Charger, round, decorated in the center w/a large stylized leaping horse & rider surrounded by smaller figures of stylized dogs, birds, horse & flowers w/greenery, glossy glaze w/multicolored animals in

Schreckengost-designed Charger

light shades of blue, yellow, gree & brown on an oatmeal-colored ground, green scallop inner border, designed by Viktor Schreckengost, ca. 1930s, crazing, 11 1/2" d. (ILLUS.) 978

Charger, octagonal, hand-decorated by Thelma Frazier Winter, 13 1/4" 1,200

Console bowl, footed, low rounded sides w/incurved rim, orange lustre, Shape No. 567-B, 2 3/4 x 9 3/4" 45

Console set: 6 1/2 x 10 1/2 x 17" bowl & pr. of candleholders; footed bowl w/figural bird handles, lobed sides, designed by Alexander Blazys, Shape No. 729, mottled blue glaze, the set 550

Decanter w/stopper, figural Queen of Hearts, seated figure holding scepter & wearing crown, Oriental Red glaze, designed by Waylande Gregory, Shape No. E-5, 10 1/2" h. 950

Figurine, Russian peasant, "Tambourine Player," white crackle glaze, designed by Alexander Blazys, Shape No. 757-760, 9" h. 1,000

Flower frog, figural, Art Deco nude scarf dancer, No. 35, ivory glaze, signed, 7 1/4" h. 400

Flower frog, figural, an Art Deco dancing nude lady leaning back w/one leg raised & the ends of a long scarf held in her outstretched hands, overall white glaze, impressed mark, 7 1/2" h. 300

Lamp, w/fittings, moth decoration, blue, 13" h., overall 22" h. 350

Lamp base, Art Deco style, angular, green, designed by Waylande Gregory, Shape No. 821, 8 3/8" h. 200

Model of a ram, Oriental Red glaze, designed by Edris Eckhart, 3 1/2" h. 250

Vase, 4 3/4" h., bulbous body w/horizontal ribbing, wide cylindrical neck, mottled turquoise glaze, Shape No. V-30 80

Vase, 4 3/4" h., waterfall, designed by Paul Bogatay, maroon, hand-decorated, Shape No. V-77 1,000

Vase, 5" h., fan-shaped, designed by R.G. Cowan, golden yellow, Shape No. V-801 70

Vase, 6 1/4" h., 5 1/4" d., bulbous ovoid body tapering to a tiny molded mouth, decorated overall w/small stylized fish, seaweed & bubbles in light green sgrafitto on an emerald green ground, small interior rim repair, circular mark & "Cowan" (ILLUS. center with bust, page 164) 1,069

Vase, 8" h., 8" d., wide bulbous body w/narrow molded rim, embossed w/a band of stylized leaves and covered in a Persian blue crackled glaze, Shape No. V-61, impressed mark 950

Vase, 8 1/2" h., bulbous ovoid form decorated w/relief-molded squirrel & foliage, designed by Waylande Gregory, green, Shape No. V-19 850

Vase, 11 3/4" h., blue lustre, Shape No. 691-C 250

Vase, 12 1/4" h., footed bulbous body tapering to wide cylindrical neck, green crystalline glaze, designed by Arthur E. Baggs, Shape No. V-47 2,500

Vases, 11 1/4" h., 8" w., Chinese-style pillow form, each w/an oval paneled platform base supporting a large reclining molded phoenix bird below the large flattened, ribbed & fanned vase, crackled green glaze, small manufacturing bruise on base of one, circular mark, pr. (ILLUS. left with bust) 1,350

Dedham & Chelsea Keramic Art Works

This pottery was organized in 1866 by Alexander W. Robertson in Chelsea, Massachusetts, and became A. W. & H. Robertson in 1868. In 1872, the name was changed to Chelsea Keramic Art Works and in 1891 to Chelsea Pottery, U.S.A. About 1895, the pottery was moved to Dedham, Massachusetts, and was renamed Dedham Pottery. Production ceased in 1943. High-fired colored wares and crackle ware were specialties. The rabbit is said to have been the most popular decoration on crackle ware in blue.

Since 1977, the Potting Shed, Concord, Massachusetts, has produced quality reproductions of early Dedham wares. These pieces are carefully marked to avoid confusion with original examples.

Bowl, 8" d., 3" h., footed wide & deep rounded form w/flat rim, Rabbit patt., blue ink stamp (ILLUS top of next column.) **$633**

Large Dedham Rabbit Bowl

Bowl, 8" d., 3" h., footed wide rounded form, Rabbit patt., blue ink stamp (ILLUS. top row, far left, below) 506

Cup & saucer, extra large coffee-size, Rabbit patt., blue ink stamp, 5" d., 3" h., the set (ILLUS. center, bottom row with bowl, below).. 338

Cups & saucers, tea-size, Rabbit patt., blue ink stamp, saucer 6" d., set of 6 (ILLUS. bottom row, far left with bowl, below).. 1,238

Unusual Chelsea Keramic Jar

Jar, cov., oval flattened 'pilgrim flask'-form, raised on four wide rounded tab feet, small scroll side handles, the flattened & domed cover w/a fanned finial, a molded oval side scene base on a printed image by L. Knauss showing a little girl feeding geese under a glossy dark teal blue glaze, the border, feet & cover in glossy green, modeled by Hugh Robertson, stamped Chelsea Keramic Art Works mark, 10 1/2" w., 9 1/4" h. (ILLUS.)............ 1,840

Variety of Dedham Crackleware Pieces

Medallion, oval, molded w/a scene of a trumpeting postboy riding a horse & viewed from behind, based on an image by J.E. Kelly, covered in a forest green glaze, by Hugh Robertson, incised "HCR - James Kelley," w/a rare catalog "American Decorative Tiles 1870-1930" which includes the piece, medallion 4 x 4 3/4".. **844**

Pitcher, 5" h., 5 1/4" d., "Night and Day" design, blue ink stamp (ILLUS. top row, far right with bowl, bottom previous page) **619**

Pitcher, 7 3/4" h., tall rectangular tapering form w/a squared stepped rim spout & square loop handle, incised w/a Greek key border & geometric linear border at the rim, handle & base, glossy green glaze later painted w/birds & nest in a flowering tree, impressed Chelsea Keramic Art Works mark, ca. 1885 ... **800-1,000**

Plate, 8 1/2" d., luncheon size, Grape patt., blue ink stamp, bruise to table ring (ILLUS. bottom row, second from right with bowl, bottom previous page)................ **141**

Plate, 8 1/2" d., luncheon size, Turkey patt. (ILLUS. top row, second from right with Rabbit bowl, bottom previous page)..... **100-200**

Plate, 10" d., Dolphin patt., early mark............ **844**

Plates, 6" d., bread & butter size, Rabbit patt., restoration to small chip on rim of one, blue ink mark, set of 6 (ILLUS. bottom row, second from left with bowl, bottom previous page) **619**

Plates, 8 1/2" d., luncheon size, Horse Chestnut patt., blue ink mark, pr. (ILLUS. bottom row, far right with bowl) **309**

Plates, 8 1/2" d., luncheon size, Rabbit patt., blue ink mark, short, tight line in one, set of 6 (ILLUS. top row, second from left with bowl, bottom previous page) **844**

Miniature Dedham Robertson Vase

Vase, 2 3/4" h., 2" d., miniature, simple ovoid form w/flat mouth, dripping ox-blood, green & blue mottled glaze, by Hugh Robertson, short opposing firing lines in rim, Dedham mark (ILLUS.) **575**

Chelsea Keramic Bottle-form Vase

Vase, 6 1/2" h., 4" d., footed bottle-form, squatty bulbous body tapering to a tall cylindrical neck, unusual oxblood & slate grey glaze, stamped Chelsea Keramic Art Works mark (ILLUS.) **1,725**

Chelsea Keramic Pilgrim Vase

Vase, 6 3/4" h., 4" w., flattened upright rectangular flask-form w/rounded flat borders & a small spout neck, embossed on the side panel w/a scene of an elderly bearded pilgrim walking through a landscape, panel w/a deep teal blue glossy glaze, the border w/an olive green glossy glaze, by H. Robertson, short, tight opposing lines at the rim, small stilt pull chip on the back, stamped "CKAW - HCR" (ILLUS.)........ **731**

Fine Lustre Glazed Dedham Vase

Vase, 7 1/2" h., 4" d., ovoid body tapering to a tall, wide cylindrical neck, fine experimental lustered oxblood glaze, by Hugh Robertson, Dedham mark (ILLUS.)............ **4,313**

Dedham & Chelsea Keramic Vases

Vase, 7 1/2" h., 5" d., wide baluster-form w/short cylindrical neck, experimental example by Hugh Robertson, covered in a superior mirrored oxblood dripping glaze, incised "Dedham Pottery - HCR" (ILLUS. left, above) **1,980**

Chelsea Keramic Pilgrim Flask Vase

Vase, 7 1/2" h., 6 1/4" w., flattened round pilgrim flask-form on four peg feet, tapering to a short cylindrical neck, the sides incised w/pine boughs & flowers under a speckled amber glossy glaze, by George Ferrety, stamped mark & artist-signed (ILLUS.) **1,495**

Vase, 8" h., 3" d., slender tall ovoid form, experimental fine mirrored oxblood glaze, by Hugh Robertson, incised Dedham Pottery mark **605**

Vase, 8 1/4" h., 3 1/2" d., slightly flaring cylindrical body w/a wide angled shoulder tapering to a short cylindrical neck, fine oxblood "orange peel" semi-matte glaze, unsigned Chelsea Keramic Art Works (ILLUS. center with experimental vase, above) **1,760**

Vase, 8 1/2" h., 5 1/4" h., Chinese bronze-shaped, squared, tapering double-lobe form embossed in the side panels w/flowers or geometric designs resembling decorated bronze, overall white crackled glaze, Dedham rabbit ink stamp (ILLUS. right with experimental vase, above) **550**

Large Chelsea Keramic Pillow Vase

Vase, 11" h., tall flattened ovoid pillow-form body on knob feet, tapering to a flared scalloped mouth, the sides embossed w/scrolls & overall flowers, butterflies & bees, mottled glossy green glaze, artist-signed, Chelsea Keramic Art Works mark (ILLUS.) **633**

Flow Blue

Flow Blue ironstone and semi-porcelain was manufactured mainly in England during the second half of the 19th century. The early ironstone was produced by many of the well known English potters and was either transfer-printed or hand-painted (Brush stroke). The bulk of the ware was exported to the United States or Canada.

The "flow" or running quality of the cobalt blue designs was the result of introducing certain chemicals into the kiln during the final firing. Some patterns are so "flown" that it is difficult to ascertain the design. The transfers were of several types: Asian, Scenic, Marble or Floral.

The earliest Flow Blue ironstone patterns were produced during the period between about 1840 and 1860. After the Civil War Flow Blue went out of style for some years but was again manufactured and exported to the United States beginning about the 1880s and continuing through the turn of the century. These later Flow Blue designs are on a semi-porcelain body rather than heavier ironstone and the designs are mainly florals. Also see Antique Trader Pottery & Porcelain Ceramics Price Guide, 3rd Edition.

ABBEY (George Jones & Sons, ca. 1900)
Beeker, 3 1/2" d., 4" h. $100
Bowl, 8" d., 4 1/2" h. 550
Bowl, 9" d., 4 1/2" h. 600
Hot water pot, 6" h. 125
Punch bowl, 10 1/2" d., 6" h. 750
Shredded wheat dish, 6 1/4" l., 5" w. 150

ABBEY (Petrus Regout Co., Maastricht, Holland, date unknown)
Farmer's cup & saucer, oversized, cup
   5" d., 4" h. & saucer, 8" d. 165

ABERDEEN (Bourne & Leigh), ca. 1900, Floral,
Butter pat, 3 1/2" d. 40

ACME (Sampson Hancock & Sons, ca. 1900)
Plate, 9" d., five-sided.. 150

Acme Plate

Plate, 9" d., scalloped (ILLUS.) 125

ADDERLEY (Doulton & Company, ca. 1886), Floral
Vegetable bowl, open, round, 8 1/2" d.,
   2 3/4" h. 195

ALASKA (W.H. Grindley & Company, ca. 1891)
Bowl, berry, 5" d... 40
Creamer, 5 1/4 h. 200
Plate, 10" d., scalloped....................................... 115
Platter, 14" l. 300
Soup plate w/flanged rim, 9" d. 90

ALBANY (Johnson Bros., ca. 1900)
Plate, 8" d... 65
Tea cup & saucer, cup, 2 1/2" h., 3 1/2" d,
   saucer, 6" d.. 115

ALBANY (W.H. Grindley & Company, ca. 1899)
Butter pat, 3 1/2" d. 45
Plate, 6 1/2 d.. 50

Albany Platter

Platter, 14 1/2" l. (ILLUS.).................................... 275

ALTHEA (Podmore, Walker & Company, ca. 1834-1859)
Coffeepot, cov., 11" d. 1,200
Creamer, 6" h. 300
Sugar, cov., footed, two-handled, 7" h. 475
Tea cup & saucer, cup, 4" d., 2 1/2" h.,
   saucer, 5 3/4" d.. 165

ALTON (W.H. Grindley & Company, ca. 1891)
Platter, 18" l. 550

AMOUR (Societé Céramique, Dutch, ca. 1865)

Armour Footed Compote

Compote, footed, two-handled, 10" d.
   (ILLUS.).. 575

ANDORRA (Johnson Bros., ca. 1901)

Andorra Vegetable Bowl

Vegetable bowl, open, round, 9 1/2" d.
   (ILLUS.).. 165

ANEMONE (Lockhart & Arthur, ca. 1855)
Plate, 10 1/4" d... 135
Platter, 16" l. 525

ARGYLE (W.H. Grindley & Company, ca. 1896)
Platter, 16" l. 450
Platter, 18" l. 575

ASHBURTON (W.H. Grindley & Company, ca. 1891)
Plate, 9" d... 90
Plate, 8" d... 75
Platter, 12" l. 175
Platter, 14" l. 295
Platter, 16" l. 425
Platter, 18" l. 550
Sauce ladle, 7" l. 295
Plate, 10" d... 115

ATALANTA (Wedgwood & Company, ca. 1900)

Atalanta Platter

Platter, 14" l. (ILLUS.) 295

BALTIC (W.H. Grindley & Company, ca. 1891)
Gravy boat, 7" l. 125
Plate, 10" d. 100

BEAUFORT (W.H. Grindley & Company, ca. 1903)

Beaufort Underplate

Underplate, for cov. butter, two-handled,
    9" d. (ILLUS.) 125

BELMONT (J.H. Weatherby & Sons, ca. 1892)
Plate, 9" d. 75
Plate, 10" d. 95

BLUE DANUBE, THE (Johnson Bros., ca. 1900)
Creamer, 4" h. 200
Plate, 10" d. 95
Soup bowl, open, 9" d. 80
Sugar, cov., 5" h. 275
Tea cup & saucer 100

BLUEBELL (Dillwyn-Swansea, Welch, ca. 1840)
Syrup pitcher w/pewter lid, 8 1/2" h 800

BOUQUET (Henry Alcock, ca. 1895)

Bouquet Vegetable Dish

Vegetable dish, cov., footed, 12" l. (ILLUS.)..... 300

BRAZIL (W.H. Grindley & Company, ca. 1891)

Brazil Sugar Bowl

Sugar bowl, cov., 5" h. (ILLUS.) 250

BRITISH SCENERY (Davenport & Company, ca. 1856)
Charger, 13" d. 350

British Scenery Platter

Platter, 19" l. (ILLUS.) 750
Vegetable bowl, oval, 10" l., 3 1/2" h. 400

BURMESE (Thomas Rathbone & Company, ca. 1912)
Serving dish, rectangular, pierced, two-
    handled, 13 1/2 l., 9" w. 375

CALICO (Warwick China Company, American, ca. 1900, aka Daisy Chain)

Calico Tankard

Pitcher, 7 1/2" h., 9" w. (ILLUS.) 275

CAMBRIDGE (Alfred Meakin, ca. 1891)
Platter, 14" l. 325
Relish dish, oval, 8 1/2" l. 145

CANNISTER (Unknown, marked "Germany," ca. 1891)
Canister, cov., marked "Sugar," 6" d., 8" h. 225
Spice jar, cov., 5" h. 75

CASHMERE (Francis Morley, ca. 1850)
Plate, 10 1/2" d. 250
Underplate, 8" d. 175

CECIL (F. Till & Son, ca. 1891)
Bone dish, crescent-shaped 65
Plate, 6" d. 50

CHINESE (Thomas Dimmock, ca. 1845)
Tea set: cov. teapot, oversized cov. sugar & creamer; Primary body shape, teapot 9" h., the set 2,800

CHRYSANTHEMUM (Myott, Son & Co., ca. 1907)
Platter, 14" l. 400

CLARENCE (W.H. Grindley & Co., ca. 1900)
Platter, 16" l. 450

CLAYTON (Johnson Bros., ca. 1902)
Chamber set: pitcher & bowl, chamber pot, shaving mug & small water pitcher; the set 2,500
Platter, 16" l. 450
Soup plate w/flanged rim, 9" d. 95
Vegetable dish, open, oval, 9" l. 165
Wash set: pitcher & bowl, chamber pot, toothbrush holder & shaving mug; the set.. 2,000

CLYTIE (Wedgwood & Co., Ltd., ca. 1908)
Plate, 10" d., w/turkey design........................... 175
Platter, 19" l., w/turkey design 1,000

COLONIAL (J. & G. Meakin, ca. 1891)
Butter pat, 3 1/2" d. 45
Vegetable bowl, open, oval, 9" l. 125

CONWAY (New Wharf Pottery, ca. 1891)

Conway Vegetable Bowl

Vegetable bowl, open, 9 1/2" d. (ILLUS.)......... 195

DAISY (Burgess & Leigh, ca. 1897)

Daisy Soup Plate

Soup plate w/flanged rim, 9" d. (ILLUS.) 95

DELFT (Minton, ca. 1893)

Delft Oyster Plate

Oyster plate, 10" d. (ILLUS.)............................. 300

Delft Platter

Platter, 14" l. (ILLUS.) 325

DERBY (W.H. Grindley, ca. 1891)
Plate, 9" d... 85

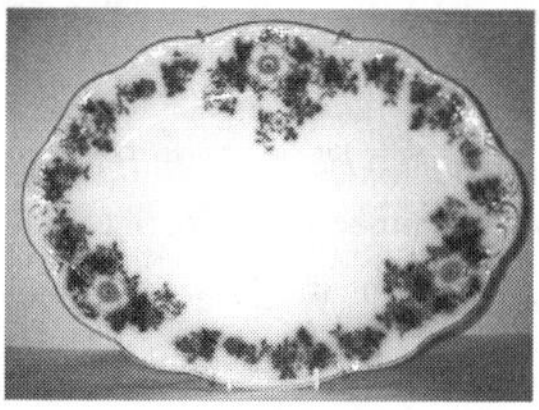

Derby Platter

Platter, 14" l. (ILLUS.) 295
Soup plate w/flanged rim, 9" d. 85
Vegetable dish, cov., 12" l., 7" h. 275

DOT FLOWER (Unknown, ca. 1840)

Dot Flower Creamer

Creamer, 5" h. (ILLUS.) 275

EGERTON (Doulton & Co., Ltd., ca. 1905)
Cheese dome w/underplate, half-stilton, very unusual, dome 8" w., 6" h., under-plate, 10" d. 325

Plate, 8 1/2" d. 65
Plate, 9 1/2" d. 90
Platter, 12" l. 165
Platter, 16" l. 400
Platter, 18" l. 500
Soup plate w/flanged rim, 10 1/2" d. 100

Egerton Covered Vegetable

Vegetable dish, cov., 13" w., 6 1/2" h.
  (ILLUS.) 375
Plate, 10 1/2" d. 100

ENGLISH ROSE (Unknown, ca. 1891)

English Rose Soup Plate

Soup plate w/flanged rim, 9" d. (ILLUS.) 90

FAIRY VILLAS III (W. Adams & Sons, ca. 1891)

Plate, 8" d. 75
Platter, 16" l. 450
Plate, 10 1/4" d. 125

FLORA (Thomas Walker, ca. 1845)

Flora Plate

Plate, 10 1/2" d. (ILLUS.) 200

FLORIDA (Ford & Sons, ca. 1891)

Plate, 10 1/4" d. 100

Florida Platter

Platter, 17" l. (ILLUS.) 500
Vegetable dish, cov., 12" w., 7" h. 300

GAINSBOROUGH (Ridgways, ca. 1905)

Creamer, 4" h. 200
Sugar, cov., 5" h. 275

GERANIUM (Doulton & Co., ca. 1890s)

Bowl, heavily gilded, scalloped, footed,
  10" l. 400

GIRONDE (W.H. Grindley, ca. 1891)

Gironde Gravy Boat

Gravy boat, 6 1/2" l. (ILLUS.) 125
Plate, 10 1/4" d., 14-sided 100

GLOIRE DE DIJON (Doulton & Co., ca. 1895)

Gloire de Dijon Pitcher

Pitcher, belonging to pitcher/bowl wash set
  (ILLUS.) 275

GRACE (W.H. Grindley, ca. 1897)

Butter pat, 3 1/2" d. 45
Platter, 16" l. 375

GRECIAN SCROLL (T.J. and J. Mayer, ca. 1850)

Grecian Scroll Teapot

Teapot, 10" h. (ILLUS.) 695

HADDON (W.H. Grindley, ca. 1891)

Butter pat, 3 1/2" d. 45
Butter w/insert, cov. 325
Plate, 9" d. 90
Platter, 12" l. 175
Vegetable bowl, cov., round, 11" d.,
 6 1/2" h. 300
Vegetable bowl, open, oval, 9" d. 165
Plate, 10" d. 100

HEATH'S FLOWER (Thomas Heath, ca. 1830)

Heath's Flower Plate

Plate, 9 1/2" d., 12-sided (ILLUS.) 165

HOLLAND (Johnson Bros., ca. 1891)

Gravy boat, 6 1/2" l. 125
Soup bowl, open, 8" d. 85
Vegetable dish, cov., footed, 12" l.,
 6 1/2" h. 275

HONC (Petrus Regout, ca. 1858)

Honc Bedpan

Bedpan (ILLUS.) 1,000

IVANHOE (Wedgwood & Co., ca. 1900)

Plate, 9 1/2" d. 125

Ivanhoe Plate

Plate, 10 1/2" d. (ILLUS.) 150

IVY (Davenport Potteries, ca. 1820-60)

Ivy Platter

Platter, 22" l., w/meat well (ILLUS.) 875

JENNY LIND (Arthur Wilkinson Ltd., Royal Staffordshire Pottery, ca. 1895)

Cup & saucer, cup 3 1/2" d., saucer
 5 3/4" d. 100
Plate, 6" d. 55

KENWORTH (Johnson Bros., ca. 1900)

Berry bowl, 5" d. 45

Kenworth Plate

Plate, 10" d. (ILLUS.) 100
Soup bowl, open, 9" d. 80

KNOX (New Wharf Potteries, ca. 1891)

Plate, 7" d. 48
Tea cup & saucer, cup 4" h., 3 1/2" d., sau-
 cer 6" d. 125

KYBER (W. Adams & Co., ca. 1891)

Plate, 9" d. 85

LABELLE (Wheeling Pottery, ca. 1900)

Charger, 13" d. 450

Labelle Portrait Plate

Portrait plate, 13" d., Lovely Ladies
 (ILLUS.) 495

LaBelle Ring-handled Dish

Ring-handled dish, 11" l., 10 1'2" w. (ILLUS.)... **325**

LAKEWOOD (Wood & Sons, ca. 1900)
Butter pat, 3 1/2" d. **60**
Tea cup & saucer, cup 4" h., 3 1/2" d., saucer 6" d. **110**

LORNE (W.H. Grindley, ca. 1900)
Bowl, berry, 5" d. **45**
Platter, 12" l. **165**

MANHATTAN (Henry Alcock, ca. 1900)
Bowl, berry, 5" d. **45**
Butter dish w/insert, cov. **325**
Cake plate, two-handled **175**
Plate, 8" d. **55**
Plate, 9" d. **95**
Platter, 14" l. **275**
Platter, 16" l. **400**
Soup plate w/flanged rim, 9" d. **90-95**
Tea cup & saucer **100**

Manhattan Covered Sugar

Tea set: teapot, sugar & creamer; the set (ILLUS. of sugar) **1,100**
Vegetable dish, cov., footed............................. **300**

MARIE (W.H. Grindley, ca. 1891)

Marie Pitcher

Pitcher, 7" h. (ILLUS.) **275**
Plate, 10 1/4" d. **100**

MARLBOROUGH (W.H. Grindley, ca. 1891)
Butter pat, 3 1/2" d. **45**

Marlborough Graduated Pitchers

Pitcher, 6" h. (ILLUS. right) **225**
Pitcher, 8" d. (ILLUS. middle) **325**
Pitcher, 10" h. (ILLUS. left) **400**

Marlborough Open Vegetable Bowl

Vegetable bowl, open, oval, 9" l. **165**

MARTHA WASHINGTON (Unknown, English, ca. 1900, aka Chain of States)

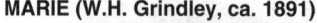

Martha Washington States Plate

Plate, 9" d. (ILLUS.)... **150**

MEISSEN (F. Mehlem, ca. 1891)
Vegetable bowl, open, 10" d. **165**

MELBOURNE (W.H. Grindley, ca. 1891)
Bowl, berry, 5" d. **45**
Butter pat, 3 1/2" d. **45**
Cake plate, 12" d., two-handled **165**
Plate, 6" d. **50**
Plate, 8" d. **70**
Plate, 9" d. **90-95**
Plate, 10" d. **125**
Platter, 14" l. **275**
Platter, 16" l. **200-375**
Platter, 18" l. **495**
Soup tureen, cov., oval, footed, 14" l., 7 1/2" h. **650**
Vegetable bowl, cov., oval **300**
Vegetable bowl, open, round **200**

MELROSE (Doulton & Co., ca. 1891)
Platter, 20" l. **600**
Plate, 10 1/4" d. **90**

MIKADO (A.J. Wilkinson, ca. 1896)
Plate, 10 1/2" d. 100
Platter, 18" l. 600
Soup plate w/flanged rim, 10 1/2" d. 100

MILTON (Poutney & Bristol, ca. 1890s)
Plate, 9" d. 90
Platter, 18" l. 575
Sauce boat w/ladle & underplate, cov.,
   oval, footed 425
Plate, 10" d. 115

MONGOLIAN (F. & W., Unidentified Manufacturer, mid-to-late Victorian)
Charger, 14" d. 400
Gravy boat, footed 195

MONTANA (Johnson Bros., ca. 1900)
Plate, 9" d. 85

MORNING GLORY (Elsmore/Forster, ca. 1853-71)
Cup & saucer, handless 195

MURIEL (Upper Hanley Potteries, ca. 1895)
Platter, 14"l. 325

NANKIN (Mellor, Venables & Co. or Thomas Walker, ca. 1845)
Tea set: Primary body style, teapot, over-
   sized cov. sugar, creamer, 6 handless
   cups & saucers, 6 9" d. plates; the set 3,200

NON PAREIL (Burgess & Leigh, ca. 1891)
Cake plate, 11" d., handled 395

NON PAREIL (Middleport Potteries, ca. 1891)
Butter pat 50
Platter, 16" l. 475
Soup plate w/flanged rim, 9" d. 95

NORMANDY (Johnson Bros., ca. 1900)
Bowl, berry, 5" d. 45
Butter pat, 3 1/2" d. 45
Plate, 9" d. 95-120
Soup plate w/flanged rim, 10" d. 115

OLD CURIOSITY SHOP (Ridgways, ca. 1910)
Platter, 16" l. 450
Vegetable bowl, open, oval, 10" l. 195

ORCHID (John Maddock & Sons, Ltd., ca. 1896)
Platter, 16" l. 375
Platter, 18" l. 475

ORIENTAL (Samuel Alcock, ca. 1840)
Plate, 9 1/2" d. 150
Platter, 16" l. 600
Underplate, two-handled w/reticulated tab
   handles, 13" d. 450
Plate, 10 1/2" d. 200

ORMONDE (Alfred Meakin, ca. 1891)
Plate, 8" d. 65
Plate, 10 1/4" d. 100

PAISLEY (Mercer, ca. 1890)

Paisley Platters, Bone Dishes, Gravy

Bone dish, crescent-shaped (ILLUS. lower
   left) 60
Gravy boat (ILLUS. lower right) 125
Platter, 20" l. (ILLUS. upper right) 650
Relish dish, 9" l. 125
Soup tureen, cov., round 675

PEKIN (Johnson Bros., ca. 1891)
Plate, 10" d. 90

PLYMOUTH (New Wharf Pottery, ca. 1891)
Plate, 8" d. 85
Plate, 10" d. 100
Tea cup & saucer 100

POPPY (Doulton & Co., ca. 1902)
Jardiniere, 10" h. 650

PORTMAN (W.H. Grindley, ca. 1891)
Platter, 14" l. 225

QUEBEC (Paul Utzchneider, ca. 1891)
Plate, 10" d. 85

RALEIGH (Burgess & Leigh, ca. 1906)
Gravy boat, 6 1/2" l. 125

REBECCA (George Jones, ca. 1900)
Plate, 9" d. 125

REEDS & FLOWERS (Unknown, ca. 1855)
Soup plate w/flanged rim, 10 1/2" d. 200

REGENT (Johnson Bros., ca. 1910)
Plate, 8" d. 65
Plate, 9" d. 90
Platter, 18" l. 575
Tea cup & saucer 100
Tea set: cov. teapot, sugar & creamer; the
   set 1,000
Plate, 10" d. 100

ROSEVILLE (John Maddock & Sons, ca. 1891)
Celery dish, 11" l. 175

SCINDE (J&G Alcock, 1840)
Jam jar w/attached tray, w/lion's head han-
   dles, only one of its kind 6,000
Platter, 18" l. 750
Teapot, primary body style, 9" h. 900

SEVILLE (New Wharf Pottery, ca. 1891)
Plate, 10" d. 115

SHANGHAI (W.E. Corn, ca. 1900)
Plate, 10" d. 100

SHUSAN (F. & R. Pratt & Co., ca. 1855)
Plate, 10 1/2" d. 195

SLOE BLOSSOM (Wm. Ridgway & Co., ca. 1830)
Waste jar, part of dresser set 1,500
Water pitcher, 7 1/2" h. 475

SPINACH (Brushstroke, maker unknown)
Waste bowl, 5" d. 125

SYRIAN (W.H. Grindley, ca. 1892)
Chamber pot, cov., 11" w., 7" h. 325

TOKIO (Johnson Bros., ca. 1900)
Plate, 9" d. 95

TULIP (Copeland & Garrett, ca. 1845)
Fruit compote, footed, 10" d., 6" h. 875

TURKEY (Cauldon, Ltd., ca. 1905)
Plate, 10 1/2" d. 200

TURKEY (Doulton & Co., ca. 1900)
Serving set: 22" l. platter, 12 10 1/2" d.
   dinner plates; the set 3,000

TURKEY (Ridgways, ca. 1900)
Turkey set: platter, 22" l, & 12 dinner plates,
   10" d.; the set **3,200**

VERMONT (Burgess & Leigh, ca. 1895)
Sauceboat w/underplate, 9" l., 5" h. 275

VIRGINIA (John Maddock & Sons, ca. 1891)
Platter, 16" l. 450

WATER NYMPH (Josiah Wedgwood, ca. 1872)
Bowl, footed, 8" d., 5" h. 295

WATTEAU (Doulton & Co., ca. 1900)
Oil lamp, converted to electric, 26" h............. **2,200**
Plate, 10 1/2" D. 150

WAVERLY (John Maddock & Son, ca. 1891)
Platter, 16" l. 425

WENTWORTH (J. & G. Meakin, ca. 1907)
Butter pat, 3 1/2" d. 40
Plate, 10" d. 90
Vegetable bowl, cov., 12" l., 6 1/2" h. 250

Fulper Pottery

The Fulper Pottery was founded in Flemington, New Jersey, in 1805 and operated until 1935, although operations were curtailed in 1929 when its main plant was destroyed by fire. The name was changed in 1929 to Stangl Pottery, which continued in operation until July of 1978, when Pfaltzgraff, a division of Susquehanna Broadcasting Company of York, Pennsylvania, purchased the assets of the Stangl Pottery, including the name.

Book ends, figural, each molded as a large spread-winged eagle perched atop a large thick rectangular platform w/an embossed American shield at the front, Cucumber green matte Crystalline glaze,

rectangular ink stamp, 7 1/2" w., 9" h., pr.
(restoration to beak & neck of one) **$1,069**

Fulper Liberty Bell Book Ends

Book ends, model of the Liberty Bell in mounting, Verde Antique crystalline glaze, rectangular ink mark & paper label, 4" w., 7 1/4" h., pr. (ILLUS.) 690
Bottle, footed bulbous base tapering to tall cylindrical neck w/flat rim, embossed salamander at base of neck, Cat's Eye flambé glaze, rectangular ink mark, 8" h., 4" d. 1,800
Bowl, 10" d., 4" h., wide low cushion form w/the wide shoulder centered by a wide, low cylindrical neck, rich Flemington Green flambé glaze over a mustard yellow ground, rectangular ink mark............... 1,013
Bowl, 11 1/2" d., a small, low cylindrical foot supporting a wide wide rounded & cupped blossom-form bowl w/wide ribs around the exterior & a lightly scalloped & pointed rim, exterior w/multi-toned green crystalline glaze, pale yellow interior, incised vertical mark (minor flakes on foot)...... 231
Bowl w/flower frog, 7 1/4" d., 5" h., "Vaz-bowl," a wide flat-bottomed compressed squatty form on tiny feet, a ringed shoulder w/a flattened rim, the center w/a tall waisted three-legged flower frog, Blue Wisteria & Mirrored Green glaze,

Fulper Vaz-bowl and Small Vases

rectangular ink mark, Pan-Pacific & original Fulper paper labels (ILLUS. left) 518

Center bowl, wide flat bottom w/low incurved sides, embossed fish design covered in a green & Butterscotch flambé glaze, rectangular ink mark, 11" d., 3" h. ... 1,125

Console bowl, a very wide shallow form w/rounded incurved sides, raised on three short peg legs, dark green crystalline matte glaze, stamped vertical mark, 10 1/2" d. (minor flakes) 523

Flower frog, figural, standing full figure Egyptian by John Kunzman, green & turquoise flambé glaze, rectangular ink stamp & "Made by John Kunzman, 1909," 7 1/2" h. (two small chips & bruise to base) 788

Incense burner, cov., wide squatty bulbous body on four tiny feet & w/four tiny squared buttresses around the shoulder, the low neck w/a domed, pierced cover, matte green crystalline glaze, rare, early, unmarked 5" d., 4" h. (bruise to lip interior, restoration to chip) 1,069

Jug, inverted pear-shaped body w/flared foot, the wide shoulder w/short cylindrical neck & spout w/molded rims, loop handle from shoulder to rim, blue, green & ivory flambé glaze, one of three known, rectangular ink mark, 7" d., 9 3/4" h. (chip to base, mostly under foot) 2,588

Rare Fulper Lamp Base & Shade

Lamp, table model, an 18" d. domical pottery shaded in Chinese blue flambé glaze w/bands of triangular & almond-shaped caramel slag glass segments flanking green slag eyebrow segments around the rim, raised on a matching pottery base w/a knopped standard & widely flaring squatty bulbous base, original porcelain sockets, invisible repair to shade, rectangular ink & Vasecraft marks, 18" h. (ILLUS.) 10,350

Pipe holder, figural, modeled at the front w/a fox (?) lying on a snag log w/a large & smaller cylindrical upright log forming holders behind, match striker section to one side of the base, overall Mahogany glossy glaze, unmarked, 6 1/2" w., 3 1/4" h. (repair to fox ears & largest log) 900

Urn, a small foot supporting a wide, deep urn-form body w/an angled shoulder tapering to a short flared neck, upright pierced square handles at the edge of the shoulder, fine frothy blue to Famille Rose flambé glaze, inked racetrack mark, 8" d., 9 1/2" h. 1,575

Vase, 3 3/4" h., 6" d., low squatty bulbous lower body centering an upright short wide neck w/incurved mouth, fine green to Chinese Blue flambé glaze, rectangular Prang mark 366

Vase, 4" h., 5" d., nearly spherical melon-lobed form, green & Chinese Blue flambé glaze, ink racetrack mark (ILLUS. right with vaz-bowl) 633

Vase, 5" h., 7 1/4" d., a wide half-round lower body below a wide angled shoulder centered by a short, wide cylindrical neck, frothy Flemington Green flambé glaze, rectangular ink mark (ILLUS. center with vaz-bowl) 431

Vase, 6" h., 9" d., squatty bulbous form, the wide shoulder tapering to molded rim, Mirrored Black flambé glaze, ink racetrack mark 619

Fulper Vase with Wisteria Matte Glaze

Vase, 6" h., 9" d., wide footed squatty bulbous form w/a wide rounded shoulder centered by a small rolled neck, frothy Wisteria Matte glaze, minor grinding chip on base of footring, mark obscured by glaze (ILLUS.) 863

Vase, 6 1/4" h., 3 1/4" d., footed squatty bulbous base tapering to a tall cylindrical body w/a bulbed neck w/a flat rim, Rose Famille glaze, experimental, squat rectangular ink mark & "121 - McConnell" 1,463

Vase, 7" h., a flaring pedestal base supporting a large spherical body tapering to a tiny flared neck, the upper body in cream shading to a striped cream, blue & green drip glaze & mottled blue pedestal, impressed mark 286

Fulper Vase with Frothy Blue Glaze

Vase, 7" h., 4 1/2" d., swelled cylindrical body w/a narrow angled shoulder & wide short rolled neck w/short buttress handles from rim to shoulder, lustered frothy turquoise glaze over a matte blue ground, obscured racetrack mark (ILLUS.) 978

Squatty Bulbous Fulper Vase

Vase, 7 1/4" h., 7 1/4" d., wide squatty bulbous form w/the wide rounded upper body centering a short, small molded neck, frothy Wistaria Matte glaze, mark obscured by glaze (ILLUS.) 978

Vase, 8 1/2" h., 8 1/2" d., squatty bulbous body w/a wide shoulder attached to the short flaring neck w/four arched short handles, turquoise & Moss to Rose flambé glaze, raised racetrack mark 2,588

Squatty Bulbous Fulper Vase

Vase, 8 3/4" h., 11" d., footed squatty wide bulbous body w/a wide shoulder centering a short flared neck, Mirror Black glaze, raised racetrack mark & perfect paper label (ILLUS.) 1,955

Vase, 9" h., 2 1/2" d., very slender tall baluster-form w/a tiny flared neck, Butterscotch flambé glaze, inked racetrack mark 309

Vase, 9 1/2" h., large ovoid body w/a narrow rounded shoulder centering a short, wide cylindrical neck w/closed rim flanked by pierced squared handles from the rim to the shoulder, green crystalline glaze, incised vertical mark 605

Vase, 9 1/2" h., tapering wide foot supporting a wide slightly flaring cylindrical body flanked by low angled & ribbed buttress handles part way up the sides, a dark blue over caramel drippy glaze, impressed mark 550

Vase, 9 1/2" h., 5" d., "Fool's Cap" tall corseted form, overall Flemington Green flambé glaze, rectangular inked mark 675

Vase, 9 3/4" h., 6 1/2" d., bulbous baluster-form, fine Leopard's Skin pale green crystalline glaze, inked racetrack mark 675

Vase, 10" h., wide baluster-form w/a wide cylindrical neck w/flaring rim, brown, blue & cream flambé glaze, incised vertical mark (drill hole in base) 320

Vase, 10" h., 10" d., bulbous ovoid body w/the round shoulder centering a short cylindrical neck, overall Chinese Blue flambé glaze, raised racetrack mark (minor scratches near rim) 1,913

Vase, 12" h., 4 1/2" d., tall slender baluster-form body w/a rounded shoulder to the small flared neck, Butterscotch flambé glaze, inked racetrack mark 619

Vase, 12" h., 7" d., simple ovoid body tapering to wide cylindrical neck w/flaring rim, frothy Rouge Flambé glaze, raised racetrack mark 731

Vase, 12" h., 7 1/2" d., tall baluster-form body w/heavy loop handles arching from the neck rim down to the shoulder & along the sides, fine Mirrored Green, Mahogany & Ivory flambé glaze, rectangular ink mark 1,350

Rare & Early Tall Fulper Vase

Vase, 12 3/4" h., 5 1/4" d., Vasekraft, tall cylindrical lower body below four small buttress projections supporting a narrow flaring shoulder below the tapering cylindrical neck molded w/pointed panels, speckled cafe-au-lait glaze, long hairline from rim, few glaze chips on base, rare & early, rectangular ink mark (ILLUS.) 1,265

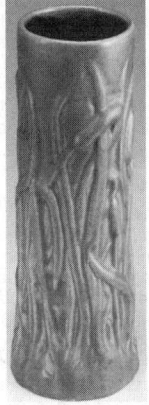

Tall Fulper Vase with Cattails

Vase, 13" h., 4 3/4" d., tall slightly waisted cylindrical form, embossed w/tall cattails under a Cucumber Matte crystalline glaze, rectangular mark, shown in Paul Evans pottery book (ILLUS.)....................... **5,750**

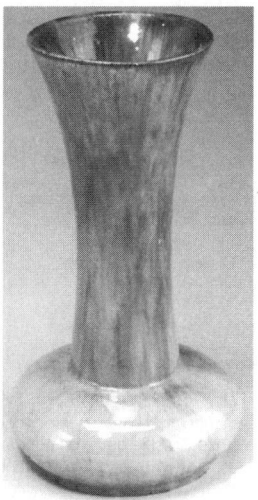

Tall Trumpet-form Fulper Vase

Vase, 13" h., 5 1/2" d., low squatty bulbous base w/a wide shoulder to the tall trumpet-form neck, overall Cat's Eye to blue flambé glaze, impressed racetrack mark, early (ILLUS.) **1,955**
Vase, 13" h., 12" d., Roman Urn-form, a large bulbous ovoid body tapering to a short cylindrical neck & molded rim, the shoulder mounted w/four small C-scroll handles, Mirror Black crystalline glaze, incised racetrack mark (restoration to handles, tight lines in rim, several short scratches) **788**
Vase, 15" h., 8" d., tall classical urn-form, the angled shoulder mounted w/two upright inwardly scrolled handles, Mirror Black to Copperdust Crystalline glaze, paper label & "MR" in red (glaze chip on one handle).. **1,575**
Vase, 16" h., 5" d., tapering cylindrical shouldered body w/molded rim, Cat's Eye flambé glaze, incised racetrack mark.. **2,813**
Vase, 17" h., 8" d., floor-type, tall swelled cylindrical form tapering to a short cylindrical neck, Chinese blue & brown mirror flambé glaze, rectangular ink mark (drilled hole in bottom) **1,688**
Wall pocket, spearpoint-form Pipes of Pan design w/a cluster of tapering tubes forming the upper body, Cucumber green matte glaze, rectangular ink mark, 4 3/4" w., 10 1/2" l.. **450**

Gallé Pottery

Fine pottery was made by Emile Gallé, the multi-talented French designer and artisan, who is also famous for his glass and furniture. The pottery is relatively scarce.

Gallé Lion Candlestick

Candlesticks, figural, in the form of a seated roaring lion wearing a crown that forms the socket, a large shield at the front decorated w/a thistle, other floral decoration, in grey, black & red on a light blue ground w/gilt trim, signed, late 19th c., repairs, 8" h., pr. (ILLUS. of one)........... **$575**
Dish, foliate-shaped bowl, the interior painted in naturalistic colors w/wild flowers in front of a shore landscape, gilded rim, base w/red stamp mark, late 19th c., 10 1/4" w. (restored) **316**

Gallé Pottery Seated Cat

Model of cat, seated w/head turned facing the viewer, bulging eyes w/smiling expression, glazed in white & decorated w/scattered ringed dots & heart-like devices, signed, ca. 1890, 13" h. (ILLUS.) **3,600**

Gallé Cat with Flowers & Stripes

Model of cat, seated w/head turned facing the viewer, bulging eyes w/smiling expression, glazed in white & decorated w/pale lavender bands & reddish orange & green floral clusters, a painted neck chain w/a locket holding a dog portrait, minor chips to paws & one ear, ca. 1895, 12 3/8" h. (ILLUS.) **5,700**

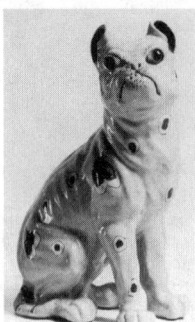

Rare Gallé Pottery Dog

Model of dog, seated Boston Terrier-like animal facing the viewer, open front legs, bulging eyes & angry expression, painted in white w/scattered ringed dots & heart-like devices, signed, ca. 1890, 12 5/8" h. (ILLUS.) **6,000**
Model of owl, faience, molded in full relief, perched owl w/glass eyes, glazed in shades of grey & amber on russet base, inscribed **3,737**

Gaudy Welsh

This is a name for wares made in England for the American market about 1830 to 1860, with some examples dating much later. Decorated with Imari-style flower patterns, often highlighted with copper lustre, it should not be confused with Gaudy Dutch wares whose colors differ somewhat.

Mug, Grape variant in cobalt, green, orange & lustre, 3 3/4" h. **$193**
Serving tray, Tulip variant in cobalt, orange, yellow, green & lustre, molded handles, 9 1/4" l. (light stains on back) **138**
Soup plate, Oyster patt. in cobalt, orange, unusual teal green & lustre, 10 1/4" d. (minor enamel wear) **83**
Teapot, cov., bulbous body, short fluted foot, flattened domed lid, molded feet, handle, spout & finial, Columbine patt. in orange, cobalt, pink & green w/lustre in band around body & lid, 8" h. **275**
Teapot, cov., bulbous lobed body tapering to flaring base w/fluted rim, w/molded acanthus leaves & flower finial, C-scroll handle, Vine patt. in orange, cobalt, green & lustre, 7" h. (damaged rim flange, chip on lid) **220**

Gonder

Lawton Gonder founded Gonder Ceramic Arts in Zanesville, Ohio in 1941 and it continued in operation until 1957.

The firm produced a higher priced and better quality of commercial art potteries than many firms of the time and employed Jamie Matchet and Chester Kirk, both of whom were outstanding ceramic designers. Several special glazes were developed during the company's history and Gonder even duplicated some museum pieces of Chinese ceramic. In 1955 the firm converted to the production of tile due to increased foreign competition and by 1957 their years of finest production were over

Increase price ranges as indicated for the following glaze colors: red flambé - 50 percent, antique gold crackle - 70 percent, turquoise Chinese crackle - 40 per cent, white Chinese crackle - 30 per cent.

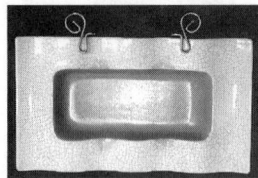

Gonder Rectangular Ashtray

Ashtray, rectangular w/wavy wide edge, Chinese White Crackle glaze on edges & brown on interior, no mold number (ILLUS.) **$75-100**
Ashtray, square, Mold No. 805, 9 1/4" w. **20-40**
Ashtray, "S" swirl design, Mold No. a 408, 2 1/2 x 10" **25-35**
Basket, shell shape w/overhead handle, Mold No. 674, 7 x 8" **25-50**
Bell, figural "Sovereign Bonnet Lady," Mold No. 800, 3 1/2" h. **50-75**
Book end, model of horse, Mold No. 582, 10" h. **100-125**

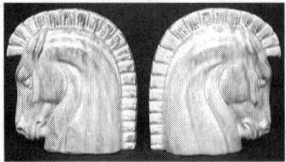

Trojan Horse Head Book Ends

Book ends, model of Trojan horse head, mottled green glaze, Mold No. 220, 7 1/2" h., pr. (ILLUS.) **100-150**
Candleholders, model of dolphin, Mold No. 561, 2 1/4 x 5", pr. **40-60**

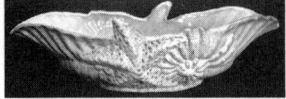

Shell-shaped Console Bowl

Console bowl, oblong shell-molded w/pointed ends & starfish molded at the sides, speckled brown on yellow glaze, Mold No. 500 (ILLUS.) **100-125**
Console set: 5 x 12" bowl & pr. of 6 1/2" h. candleholders; crescent moon shape, Mold Nos. J-55 & J-56, the set **60-70**
Console set: 16" l. bowl & pr. of candleholders; "Banana Boat" bowl, Mold Nos. 565 & 567, the set **75-100**

Cornucopia-vase, w/leaf design, Mold No. J-61, 9" h... **50-60**

Gonder Slant-top Ewer

Ewer, bulbous base tapering to a tall slanted top w/pointed spout & integral handle, Mold 410, Chinese Turquoise Crackle glaze (ILLUS.) **75-100**
Figure group, pair of chair bearers w/chair, Mold No. 765, 12 1/2" h. **100-150**
Figure of Oriental mandarin, Mold No. 755, 8 3/4" h. **50-75**
Lamp, model of Trojan horse head, 8 1/2" h. ... **20-35**

Gonder Model of an Elephant

Model of elephant, stylized standing animal w/greenish brown glaze & ivory trim, Mold 108 (ILLUS.) **400-500**
Model of panther, standing, Mold No. 205, 12" h.. **30-50**
Pitcher, 6 1/2" h., squatty bulbous base, cylindrical neck w/flared rim, zigzag handle, Mold No. E-73 & E-373.............................. **25-35**
Planter, bulbous body w/tab handles, decorated w/relief-molded flowers, Mold No. H-83, 5 1/2" h. **50-60**
Planter, model of Chinese sampan (junk), Mold No. 550, 10" l................................... **10-25**

Gonder La Gonda Pattern Teapot

Teapot, cov., upright rectangular form, LaGonda patt., creamy yellow glaze, Mold 914 (ILLUS.) **50-75**

TV lamp, figural "Comedy & Tragedy Mask," Mold No. 519, 6 1/2 x 10"......................... **75-100**

Gonder Oriental-style Vase

Vase, squared Oriental-style w/angular neck handles, pale green glaze, Mold 537 (ILLUS.)... **50-75**
Vase, 5 x 5" sq., flared, leaf decoration, Mold No. 384.. **25-35**
Vase, 7" h., pinched leaf design, Mold No. E-372.. **15-30**
Vase, 7 1/2" h., basketweave w/knothole design, Mold No. 867................................ **30-50**
Vase, 6 x 8", model of starfish, Mold No. H-79 .... **15-25**
Vase, 8 1/2" h., flat leaf design, Mold No. H-78 .... **15-30**
Vase, 8 1/2" h., relief-molded double leaf form w/berries, Mold J-70 .... **35-50**
Vase, 6 1/2 x 9", model of stylized horse w/wings, Mold No. 553 .... **10-25**
Vase, 9 1/2" h., model of fawn head, Mold No. 518... **75-100**
Vase, 10" h., Art Deco free form design, Mold No. 636.. **80-100**
Vase, 10" h., square form w/impressed flower design, Mold No. 688......................... **50-75**
Vase, 11 1/2" h., blades of grass design, Mold No. 861.. **40-60**
Vase, 12" h., footed ovoid body w/small rim handles, decorated w/relief-molded flowers & leaves.. **50-75**
Vase, 13" h., trellis w/flowers design, Mold No. 863... **50-75**

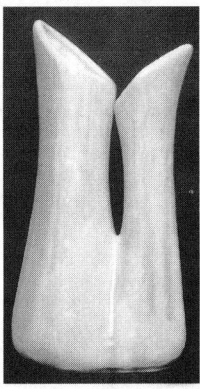

Double Cylindrical Form Vase

Vase, 6 1/2 x 13", double, tall slender cylindrical forms joined at triangular form base, slanted rim, mottled green glaze, Mold No. 868 (ILLUS.) **150-200**

Vase, 15 3/4" h., leaves & twigs design, Mold No. 599 .... **100-150**

Gouda

While tin-enameled earthenware has been made in Gouda, Holland since the early 1600s, the productions of modern factories are attracting increasing collector attention. The art pottery of Gouda is easily recognized by its brightly colored peasant-style decoration with some types having achieved a "cloisonné" effect. Pottery workshops located in, or near, Gouda include Regina, Zenith, Plazuid, Schoonhoven, Arnhem and others. Their wide range of production included utilitarian wares, as well as vases, miniatures and large outdoor garden ornaments.

Small Gouda Handled Vase

Vase, 4 1/4" h., 3 3/4" d., footed bulbous ovoid body w/a ringed neck & small loop handles at the sides, decorated w/stylized designs in dark yellow, brown, white, beige & black, marked "Benda Gouda Holland" (ILLUS.) **$110**

Unique Gouda Pottery Vase

Vase, 13" h., a round flared foot supporting a wide squatty bulbous body w/integral handle at each side curving up to form a high rounded continuous handle, the flattened shoulder centered by a bulbed neck, decorated w/Art Nouveau stylized iris blossoms in purple, blue, green & taupe w/a glossy glaze, marked "Made in Zuid, Holland" & house mark, small nick (ILLUS.) **920**

Vases, 11 1/4" h., ovoid body tapering to a flared rim, decorated w/geometric & stylized foliage designs in blue, yellow, orange & green on a mottled greyish green ground, blue painted & impressed marks (minor base chips) **518**

Grueby

Some fine art pottery was produced by the Grueby Faience and Tile Company, established in Boston in 1891. Choice pieces were created with molded designs on a semi-porcelain body. The ware is marked and often bears the initials of the decorators. The pottery closed in 1907.

Bowl, 4" d., low squatty bulbous form w/incurved sides, incised w/short vertical leaves around the sides, dark green matte glaze, artist-initialed, impressed mark & partial paper label **$990**

Bowl, 5 1/2" d., low wide form w/flaring rounded sides & a wide incurved rim, exterior w/dark blue matte glaze, impressed mark & two paper labels **935**

Grueby Bowl with Square Rim

Bowl, 7 1/2" w., 3 1/2" h., deep rounded sides curving up to a wide square rim, tooled & applied overlapping pointed leaves around the exterior under a smooth speckled ochre matte glaze, glossy green interior glaze, by Wilhelmina Post, minute nick on edges of some leaves, small glaze miss on side, stamped mark (ILLUS.) **2,300**

Wide & Shallow Grueby Bowl

Bowl, 8" d., 2 1/2" h., wide flat bottom below low incurved sides & wide flat rim, speckled matte green glaze w/mineral deposits, glaze bubbles on side, signed (ILLUS.) **575**

Rare Grueby Papyrus Bowl-vase

Bowl-vase, wide squatty bulbous form w/the wide shoulder centered by a short rolled neck, tooled & applied papyrus design under a fine oatmealed matte green glaze, by Wilhelmina Post, minor glaze flakes on base, 10" d., 5" h. (ILLUS.) **10,925**

Grueby Jardiniere by W. Post

Jardiniere, slightly tapering ovoid form w/a wide & low rolled rim, tooled & applied up the sides w/long, wide leaves, frothy matte green glaze, by Wilhelmina Post, few minor glaze nicks, stamped mark, 10 1/2" d., 6" h. (ILLUS.).............................. **5,175**

Large Grueby Jardiniere

Jardiniere, wide bulbous body w/a narrow rounded shoulder & wide, low rolled rim, molded w/continuous wide pointed leaves up the sides alternating w/blossoms on thin stems, green matte glaze, impressed mark, artist-signed, minor rim repair, 9" d. (ILLUS.) **2,310**

Paperweight, figural, oblong model of a large scarab beetle, matte bluish grey glaze, Grueby Faience stamped mark, 2 3/4 x 4".. **563**

Paperweight, figural, oblong model of a large scarab beetle, matte greenish brown glaze, Grueby Faience stamped mark, 2 3/4 x 3 3/4" (small glaze flake on front).. **731**

Vase, 3" h., miniature, bulbous ovoid body w/a thin shoulder centered by a flattened flaring neck, thick dark green matte glaze, impressed mark............................... **1,045**

Squatty Bulbous Grueby Vase

Vase, 5" h., 5 1/2" d., footed wide squatty bulbous body w/a wide shoulder tapering to a short, wide flaring neck, tooled & applied w/wide arched & pointed leaves around the lower body alternating w/stems below large yellow blossoms around the rim, circular mark (ILLUS.)..... **12,650**

Vase, 6 1/4" h., 5" d., bulbous nearly spherical bottom below a wide cylindrical ringed neck, speckled bluish grey matte glaze, Grueby Pottery stamped mark (touch-up to rim nick) **900**

Vase, 6 3/4" h., 7 1/4" d., very wide ovoid body w/a closed rim, molded in low-relief w/tall wide leaves alternating w/slender stems w/tiny yellow & orange buds around the rim, leathery matte green glaze, circular mark & incised "RE," by Ruth Erickson... **28,125**

Vase, 7" h., 3" d., cylindrical body w/an inset footring & shoulder centered by a low rolled neck, thick oatmealy matte glaze, Grueby Faience stamp mark **956**

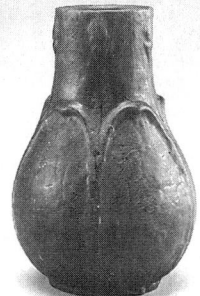

Grueby Vase with Leaves & Buds

Vase, 7" h., 5" d., narrow footring below bulbous ovoid body tapering to a short cylindrical neck, the sides tooled w/wide tapering leaves alternating w/thin stems topped by buds, oatmealy dark green matte glaze, partially obscured mark, remnant of paper label, touch-up to rim nick (ILLUS.) **2,760**

Vase, 7 1/4" h., 4 1/2" d., ovoid body tapering to a cylindrical neck w/flat rim, tooled w/a band of tall, wide leaves, matte green glaze, Grueby Faience stamped mark & "ERF," by Ellen Farmington (minor nick to one leaf edge) **2,925**

Vase, 7 1/4" h., 4 3/4" d., simple ovoid form tapering to a flat rim, molded around the sides w/wide rounded leaves alternating w/stems & blossoms, buds reaching to the rim, leathery matte green glaze, stamped circular Faience mark w/"LEM"... **2,813**

Vase, 7 1/4" h., 7 3/4" d., squatty bulbous body w/a wide shoulder centered by a wide cylindrical neck, tooled & applied around the body w/a band of large overlapping upright leaves, fine leathery matte green glaze, pottery stamp & "WP - 6- 8" (restoration to rim, touch-ups to leaf edges) **2,813**

Vase, 7 1/4" h., 10" d., squatty bulbous shouldered body w/a short flaring neck, the sides applied w/wide pointed overlapping leaves, pulled leathery matte glaze, circular stamp mark (touch-ups to minor flecks on leaf edges & invisible restoration to rim chip).. **9,000**

Vase, 7 3/4" h., 4" d., ovoid body w/floriform rim, applied broad leaves alternating w/flower buds, leathery matte green glaze, circular Faience mark **4,219**

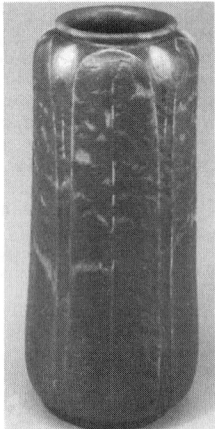

Tall Waisted Grueby Vase with Buds

Vase, 9 1/2" h., 4 1/4" d., tall gently waisted cylindrical form rounded at the bottom & the shoulder, short, wide molded mouth, tooled & applied w/full-length rounded leaves alternating w/stems topped w/yellow buds, fine frothy matte green glaze, by Wilhelmina Post, circular mark & "WP - 322 - 11.20.5" (ILLUS.)............................. **6,900**

Grueby Bottle-form Vase

Vase, 9 1/2" h., 5 3/4" d., bottle-form, a wide bulbous base w/a wide flattened shoulder centering a tall cylindrical neck w/slightly flared rim, the base molded & applied w/an overlapping band of wide rounded leaves, fine organic matte green glaze, touch-up to edge & rim, stamped mark & "190" (ILLUS.).................................. **5,175**

Rare Grueby Vase with Jonquils

Vase, 10" h., large bulbous ovoid body w/a wide shoulder & short flaring neck, unusual decoration w/three sets of sculpted & applied jonquils, the flowers in red, green & yellow on green leafy stems against a fine suspended green matte background, by Marie Seaman, impressed mark (ILLUS.) **46,000**

Vase, 10 1/4" h., 8" d., footed wide ovoid body w/short flaring neck, molded w/wide leaves alternating w/buds, curdled matte green glaze, circular Grueby Faience stamp & "AL - 100" (four opposing hairlines, drilled hole at base, few minor glaze nicks to edges, glaze chip to base) .. **2,588**

Vase, 11" h., 5 1/4" d., tall ovoid body w/slightly flared & pinched rim, decorated w/relief-molded daffodils in profile in yellow, red & blue on long slender green leaves outlined in yellow, leathery matte green glaze, circular Grueby paper label & paper label from Geo. W. Benson Art Shop, Buffalo, incised "RE," by Ruth Erickson (small chip to inner rim, color run to one flower) **21,375**

Very Rare Grueby "Kendrick" Vase

Vase, 12" h., 8" d., "Kendrick" design, tall gourd-form w/low incurved rim, sides & rim tooled w/long pointed leaves in a fine pulled & leathery matte green glaze, chip to base, few small chips on leaftips, circular mark (ILLUS.) **51,750**

Vase, 13 3/4" h., a narrow footring supporting the tall tapering & waisted cylindrical body, molded w/tall overlapping tapering leaves around the sides, some leaftips showing the clay body, heavy matte green glaze, faint round impressed mark, attributed to Ellen R. Farrington, ca. 1902.. **7,475**

Large Ovoid Grueby Vase

Vase, 13 3/4" h., 9" d., large bulbous ovoid body tapering to a cylindrical neck w/flat rim, tooled & applied around the lower half w/overlapping bands of broad rounded leaves below alternating blossoms & tall buds, fine leathery matte green glaze, circular "Faience" mark, w/letter from Grueby family member, through whose family it descended, restoration to inner rim chip (ILLUS.).. **8,625**

Rare & Unusual Tall Grueby Vase

Vase, 17 1/2" h., 8 1/2" d., large bottle-form w/squatty bulbous base & tall slender cylindrical neck w/flaring rim, tooled & applied small quatrefoils around the rim, broad pointed leaves around the lower body, fine leathery green matte glaze, No. 133A, stamped mark & paper label (ILLUS.).. **57,500**

Unusual Grueby Wall Pocket

Wall pocket, bulbous ovoid form w/flat arched backplate, the front tooled & applied w/broad ribbed, rounded overlapping leaves, leathery matte green glaze, enlarged hanging holes, unmarked, 5 3/4" w., 7" h. (ILLUS.)................................ **1,840**

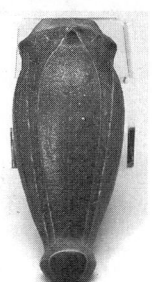

Grueby Wall Pocket with Leaves

Wall pocket, long ovoid body molded w/long pointed leaves up to the flared rim, w/a molded bulbed bottom tip, thick oatmealy matte green glaze, unmarked, 3 1/2" w., 8 1/2" l. (ILLUS.) **3,738**

Hampshire Pottery

Hampshire Pottery was made in Keene, New Hampshire, where several potteries operated as far back as the late 18th century. The pottery now known as Hampshire Pottery was established by J. S. Taft shortly after 1870. Various types of wares, including Art Pottery, were produced through the years. Taft's brother-in-law, Cadmon Robertson, joined the firm in 1904 and was responsible for developing over 900 glaze formulas while in charge of all manufacturing. His death in 1914 created problems for the firm and Taft sold out to George Morton in 1916. Closed during part of World War I, the pottery was later reopened by Morton for a short time and manufactured white hotel china. From 1919 to 1921, mosaic floor tiles became the main production. All production ceased in 1923.

Low Hampshire Bowl in Mottled Blue

Bowl, 5 1/4" d., 2 1/4" h., wide flattened bottom below the squatty bulbous sides tapering to a wide flat mouth, the sides molded w/wide low arches alternating w/triple grooves, mottled dark blue matte glaze, two opposing rim cracks, signed (ILLUS.).. **$288**

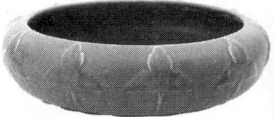

Hampshire Bowl with Trilliums

Bowl, 9" d., wide flat bottom below low incurved sides & a wide mouth, molded
around the sides w/large stylized trillium
blossoms, matte green glaze w/cream
showing through, marked (ILLUS.) 460

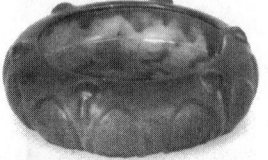

Hampshire Pottery Low Bowl

Bowl, 10" d., 3" h., a wide flat-bottomed
round form w/low incurved sides molded
w/a band of rounded lily pads alternating
w/buds on stems, dark green matte
glaze, signed, glaze miss on rim, tight
line from rim (ILLUS.) 345

Hampshire Green Bowl-Vase

Bowl-vase, wide squatty bulbous form
w/the wide shoulder centered by a low
rolled rim, heavy matte green glaze,
Model No. 136, inscribed mark, chip on
glaze drip (ILLUS.) 258
Bowl-vase, wide squatty bulbous base be-
low sharply tapering incurved sides w/a
wide, flat rim, the sides incised w/a wide
band of linear & scrolled repeating design, mottled matte green glaze, ink
stamp on base, ca. 1910, 4 1/2" d.,
2 3/4" h. 690
Chamberstick, deep tricorner base w/in-
folded sides centering a cylindrical socket w/flared rim, high loop handle at the
back, dark green glossy glaze, im-
pressed mark, 7" w., 3 1/2" h. 253

Hampshire Pottery Chamberstick

Chamberstick, round dished base tapering
to a cylindrical standard w/a wide rolled
socket rim, a round loop handle near the
base, mottled blue glaze, impressed
mark, two chips, firing lines in base rim
(ILLUS.) 115

Hampshire Matte Green Ewer

Ewer, footed squatty bulbous lower body tapering to cylindrical sides w/a high
arched spout opposite & high arched &
looped handle, matte green glaze, 8" h.
(ILLUS.) 431
Ewer, wide squatty bulbous form w/the wide
shoulder centered by a short slender
neck w/a wide inwardly folded tricorner
rim, round loop handle from back of rim to
base of neck, shaded dark brown, green
& gunmetal glossy glaze, impressed
mark, 6" h. 143

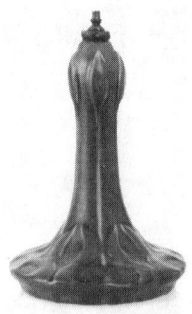

Unusual Hampshire Lamp Base

Lamp base, a thick rounded flaring base
molded w/pointed leaves & tapering to a
slender standard molded w/buds on
stems, matte green glaze, missing socket
& wiring, 12" h. (ILLUS.) 1,380
Lamp base, a wide round cushion foot
molded in relief w/five repeating tulips, a
tall tapering slender shaft molded w/the
stems below a bulbed top w/the electric
socket, matte green glaze, marked on the
base, ca. 1910, 11" h. (wear to lamp fit-
tings) 920

Hampshire Lamp Base with Tulips

Lamp base, tall gently flaring cylindrical form w/rounded shoulder to a wide flat mouth, molded up the sides w/broad pointed tulip leaves alternating with blossoms around the rim, dark matte green glaze, signed, several burst bubbles, small grinding chip on base, w/patinated rim ring (ILLUS.)................................... **1,150**

Lamp base, wide flared disk foot tapering to a tall slender trumpet-form body w/a wide rounded shoulder centered by the electric fittings, embossed w/twining lily pads around the sides, smooth olive green glaze, verdigris patina on the fittings, stamped "Hampshire Pottery - 0018," 7" d., 16" h. **1,013**

Hampshire Pottery Large Urn-Vase

Urn-vase, a bulbous base tapering to a tall slightly tapering cylindrical neck flanked by slender angled & pierced handles from high on the neck to the shoulder, embossed Greek Key design bands around the upper neck & the lower body, matte green glaze, light abrasion to the base, stamped "Hampshire Pottery - 88," 9" d., 15" h. (ILLUS.) **1,913**

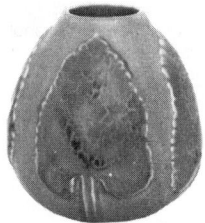

Miniature Hampshire Vase

Vase, 3 1/2" h., miniature, bulbous ovoid body tapering to a small flat mouth, embossed around the sides w/large pointed upright leaves, matte brown glaze, marked (ILLUS.).. **690**

Vase, 3 3/4" h., miniature, bulbous ovoid form tapering to a tiny mouth, the sides molded w/wide pointed & veined leaves up the sides, green & brown matte glaze, impressed mark, experimental glaze............ **715**

Vase, 4 1/4" h., simple ovoid form w/a rounded shoulder centering a short, small rolled neck, lightly molded arched panel-style leaves up the sides, mottled

green matte glaze, impressed mark, experimental glaze **413**

Vase, 4 1/2" h., bulbous tapering ovoid form w/a very wide flat mouth, incised around the rim w/a wavy band of stylized leaves & blossoms, dark green matte glaze............. **605**

Hampshire Moss Green Vase

Vase, 4 1/2" h., wide ovoid body tapering to a wide, flat mouth, overall dark moss green matte glaze, raised mark (ILLUS.) **517**

Vase, 4 3/4" h., flat-bottomed ovoid body w/a rounded shoulder centered by a short rolled neck, light vertical panels covered w/an overall dark blue matte glaze, impressed mark **286**

Vase, 5" h., a flat-based wide bulbous ovoid body w/a rounded shoulder tapering to a wide trumpet neck, overall mottled multi-toned greyish blue matte glaze, impressed mark **605**

Vase, 6" h., an oblong boat-shaped base w/pulled-out tapering end handles looping up & connecting asymmetrically to a slender cylindrical neck which tapers up from the lower body, green matte glaze, impressed mark **660**

Vase, 6" h., slightly flaring cylindrical form w/a rounded shoulder tapering slightly to a wide flat mouth, good green matte glaze, incised mark **385**

Vase, 6 3/4" h., 3 3/4" d., gently tapering cylindrical form w/a wide rounded shoulder centering a flat mouth, embossed around the shoulder w/broad stylized green leaves on a blue ground, incised mark **825**

Hampshire Handled Blue Vase

Vase, 7" h., a squatty bulbous bottom tapering sharply to a cylindrical body w/a narrow neck & molded small rim flanked by two small shoulder handles, matte blue glaze, impressed mark, clay bubbles on side of base (ILLUS.) **460**

Vase, 7" h., simple swelled cylindrical form w/a closed rim, fine slightly mottled dark blue matte glaze w/black highlights, impressed mark (hard-to-find hairline) **275**

Hampshire Vase with Molded Leaves

Vase, 7" h., wide ovoid body tapering to a wide flat mouth, the sides molded w/a band of wide pointed leaves alternating w/stems & buds, dark green matte glaze, impressed mark (ILLUS.) **1,092**

Vase, 7 1/2" h., elongated ovoid body w/an inverted rim, mottled matte green glaze, by Cadmon Robertson, impressed marks..... **575**

Hampshire Vase with Lightning Decor

Vase, 7 1/2" h., simple ovoid form w/small loop handles at the center sides, a molded band at the base & rim, each issuing creamy white lightning-like bars all against a matte green ground, impressed mark (ILLUS.) **575**

Vase, 7 1/2" h., wide gently swelled cylindrical form w/a closed rim, overall dark matte blue glaze w/bold crackled design, impressed mark **605**

Hampshire Vase with Wave Band

Vase, 7 3/4" h., slightly swelled cylindrical form tapering to a short flared neck, a narrow embossed band of repeating wave-like scrolls around the shoulder, dark green matte glaze, signed (ILLUS.)....... **575**

Ovoid & Tall Hampshire Vases

Vase, 8" h., wide ovoid body w/a wide low rolled rim, molded w/broad overlapping & slightly swirled leaves, unusual blue & green suspended matte glaze, impressed mark & paper label (ILLUS. right) **1,495**

Vine-handled Hampshire Vase

Vase, 8 1/2" h., ovoid body tapering to a flaring neck, vine-form open handles on each side connecting to long molded spearpoint leaves down the sides, matte green glaze, signed, light line in one handle (ILLUS.) **748**

Vase, 9" h., wide ovoid form tapering to a wide, flat mouth, overall dark brown matte glaze, raised mark................................. **605**

Tall Ovoid Hampshire Green Vase

Vase, 11" h., round dished foot w/a slender stem supporting a tall ovoid body w/a molded flat mouth, green matte glaze, impressed mark, small firing line, light crazing (ILLUS.) **460**

Vase, 12" h., a tall gently swelled cylindrical form w/a narrow rounded shoulder & wide cylindrical neck w/flat rim, fine dark blue matte glaze, impressed mark **1,045**

Vase, 12" h., tall slender swelled cylindrical form w/a narrow shoulder to the short rolled neck, overall multi-toned blue matte glaze, impressed mark **990**

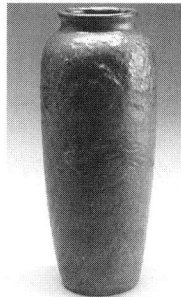

Very Large Blue Hampshire Vase

Vase, 12 1/4" h., 5" d., tall slender ovoid body tapering to a short rolled neck, very thick frothy blue & bluish green matte glaze, green spot on side, stamped mark (ILLUS.) **1,725**

Vase, 15" h., wide squatty bulbous base tapering to a tall & slightly tapering cylindrical neck flanked by long slender angled & pierced handles, a narrow geometrical dash band around the top of the neck & a wider matching band around the lower body, green matte glaze, impressed mark (ILLUS. left with broad ovoid blue vase, previous page) **2,070**

Harker Pottery

Harker Pottery was in business for over 100 years (1840-1972) in the East Liverpool area of eastern Ohio. One of the oldest potteries in Ohio, it advertised itself as one of the oldest in America. The pottery produced two lines that are favorites of collectors: ovenware under the BakeRite and HotOven brands and Cameoware. However, Harker also produced many other lines as well as Rockingham reproductions, souvenir items and a line designed by Russel Wright that are gaining popularity with collectors. Harker was marketed under dozens of backstamps in its history.

The Harker Pottery was established in East Liverpool, Ohio, in 1840 by Benjamin Harker, Sr. In 1890 the pottery was incorporated as the Harker Pottery Company. By 1911 the company had acquired the former plant of the National China Company and in 1931 Harker purchased the closed pottery of Edwin M. Knowles in Chester, West Virginia.

Harker's earliest products were yellowware and Rockingham-glazed wares produced from local clay. After 1900 whiteware was made from imported materials. Perhaps their best-known line is Cameoware, deco-rated on solid glazes with white "cameos" in a silhouette fashion.

There were many other patterns and shapes created by Harker over the years. In 1972 the pottery was closed after it was purchased by the Jeanette Glass Company.

BakeRite, HotOven

Harker was one of the first American potteries to produce pottery that could go from the oven to the table. Most of this ware, made from the late 1920s to 1970, features brightly colored decals that are popular with collectors today. Prices vary depending upon the decal pattern. Among the most popular designs are Amy, Colonial Lady, Countryside, red and blue Deco Dahlia, Fireplace, Ivy, Lisa, Mallow, Monterey, Oriental Poppy, Petit Point, Red Apple and Tulips.

Au gratin/casserole, cov. **$25-35**
Batter bowl, w/pouring lip **40-50**
Batter jug, cov., Ohio shape **30-40**
Batter set, two batter jugs, lifter & utility plate, the set **100-150**
Bean pot, Calico Tulip patt., w/original wire rack **65**

Various Petit Point Pattern Pieces

Bean pot, individual, Petit Point patt. (ILLUS. top row, center front) **8-10**
Bowl, 6" d., Red Apple I patt., Zephyr shape (ILLUS. front row, second from right w/casserole, above) **20**
Bowl, 9" d., Petit Point Rose patt. **15**
Butter dish, cov., Petit Point patt., 1 lb. **40**
Butter tray, cov. **30-50**
Cake/pie lifter **10-20**
Casserole, cov., Petit Point patt., Zephyr shape (ILLUS. top row, left w/bean pot, above) **35**
Casserole, cov., stacking-type **10-20**
Cheese bowl, cov. **30-40**
Cheese tray, Zephyr shape **15-20**
Coffeepot, cov., Petit Point patt, Zephyr shape, no brewer (ILLUS. top row, right w/bean pot, above) **50**
Coffeepot, cov., w/basket **65-80**
Condiment jar, cov., individual **10-15**
Condiment set, three jars in a holder, the set **50-60**
Cookie jar, cov., Modern Age shape **25-30**
Cookie jar, cov., Zephyr shape **40-50**
Cup & saucer, jumbo size **20-30**
Custard cup, individual **8-10**
Custard cup set, six cups in a rack, the set .. **60-75**
Grease jar, cov., D'Ware shape **20-25**
Grease jar, cov., Hi-Rise shape **15-25**
Hot plate, Petit Point Rose patt. **40**
Mixing bowl, medium **15-20**
Mixing bowl, Petit Point patt., large **25-50**

Mixing bowl, Petit Point patt., medium (ILLUS. middle row, center w/bean pot, previous page) 20
Pie baker 15-25
Pie plate, Amy patt. 16
Pie plate, Petit Point Rose patt. 15
Pitcher, jug-type, Arches patt. 20-30
Pitcher, jug-type, Hi-Rise shape 50-125
Pitcher, jug-type, Regal shape 25-40
Plate, dinner, Petit Point patt. (ILLUS. middle row, right w/bean pot, previous page) 15
Rolling pin 75-125
Rolling pin, Petit Point patt. (ILLUS. front left w/bean pot, previous page) 125
Rolling pin, Silhouette patt. 115
Salad fork or spoon, Petit Point patt., each (ILLUS. front row, right w/bean pot, previous page) 20
Salt & pepper shakers, Hi-Rise shape, pr.... 15-25
Scoop 50-150
Syrup pitcher, cov., Ohio shape 15-25
Tea tile, octagonal, Petit Point patt. (ILLUS. top row, center back, previous page) 25
Teapot, cov., w/basket 65-85
Utility bowl, Petit Point patt., Zephyr shape, 3" d. (ILLUS. middle row, left, previous page) 8
Utility plate, Calico Tulip patt., Virginia shape, 12" w. 28
Utility plate, Virginia shape 10-25

Cameoware

Created in the early 1930s and based on a European process, the sky blue ware with its white design that seems to be etched into the surface is Harker's most widely collected pattern. The process was first tried by Bennett Pottery but when Bennett closed, the Cameoware line was taken over by Harker. After the blue intaglios met with great success, Harker also made pink, which was much less popular and rare today, and yellow, which never went into full production. Because of its rarity and its bright contrast to the blue engobe, the yellow ware is highly prized and highly priced today. Prices given are for pink or blue. Yellow prices are almost double or more, depending upon the item.

In addition, Harker also manufactured a line of blue and pink intaglio ware for Montgomery Ward with the name "White Rose." Not so common as the design called "Dainty Flower," White Rose has its own devoted fans.

Ashtray, Dainty Flower patt., Swirl or Zephyr shape, each 5

Cameoware Pieces

Ashtray, Modern Age shape, blue Dainty Flower patt., (ILLUS. far left).............................. 20
Au gratin/casserole, cov., Zephyr shape...... 25-45
Berry/salad set, serving bowl & six individual dishes, the set.................................... 40-50
Bowl, cereal, Shellware shape....................... 8-10
Bowl, salad, Pear patt., Swirl shape (ILLUS. front center w/ashtray)................................... 8-10

Cake/pie lifter 15-20
Casserole, cov., square, blue.............................. 65
Coffeepot or teapot, cov., each 30-50
Cookie jar, cov., blue Dainty Flower patt., Zephyr shape (ILLUS. far right w/ashtray, below).. 50
Creamer 10-25
Cup & saucer, Swirl shape, blue 16
Custard cup 8-10
Demitasse cup & saucer 25-30
Fork or spoon, each.................................... 15-20

A Variety of Dainty Flower Pieces

Fruit dish, blue Dainty Flower patt., Virginia shape (ILLUS. top, far right) 5
Gravy boat 30-35
Grease jar, cov., D'Ware shape 15-30
Grease jar, cov., Hi-Rise shape 10-25
Mixing bowl 25-45
Pitcher, jug-type, Hi-Rise shape 75-150
Pitcher, jug-type, round 30-50
Pitcher, jug-type, square 30-50
Plate, 6" d., Swirl shape 5-8
Plate, 6" sq., blue Dainty Flower, Virginia shape (ILLUS. top row, far left w/fruit dish, above)... 8
Plate, 7" d., luncheon, blue Dainty Flower patt., Swirl shape (ILLUS. back row, left w/ashtray, above)...................................... 10
Plate, 7" sq., Zephyr shape 12-15
Plate, 9" d. 12-15
Platter, oval, plain...................................... 15-35
Platter, rectangular.................................... 20-40
Rolling pin, blue or pink 100-125
Salt & pepper shakers, D'Ware shape, pr. .. 20-25
Salt & pepper shakers, Dainty Flower patt., Hi-Rise shape, stained, pr. (ILLUS. top row, center front w/fruit dish, above)................. 6
Salt & pepper shakers, Hi-Rise shape, perfect, pr. 25-30
Salt & pepper shakers, Modern Age shape, pr.. 10-20
Soup plate, flat rim, square........................... 10-15
Sugar bowl, cov... 10-25
Tea tile 20-30
Utility plate, blue Dainty Flower patt., Virginia shape, 12" w. (ILLUS. back row, center w/fruit dish, above)............................... 25
Vegetable bowl, blue Dainty Flower patt., Virginia shape (ILLUS. bottom w/fruit dish, above).. 20

Imari

This is a multicolor ware that originated in Japan, was copied by the Chinese, and imitated by the English and European potteries. It was decorated in overglaze enamel and underglaze-blue. Made in Hizen Province and Arita, much of it was exported through the port of Imari in Japan. Imari often has brocade patterns.

Bowl, 10" d., 4 1/2" h., fluted paneled design, decorated in rust red & cobalt blue, ca. 1875.. **$336**

Imari Shallow Dish

Bowl or charger, round, shallow form w/raised rim, alternating panels of floral motifs & landscapes, all in traditional colors, around central panel in blue & white, late 19th c., 12" d. (ILLUS.)........................... **420**

Charger, round w/scalloped edge, decorated w/center cartouche of floral design surrounded by fan-shaped panels, cobalt blue, rust & green w/gilt decorations, ca. 1860, 14 1/2" d., repair to rim (ILLUS. between vases, below) **308**

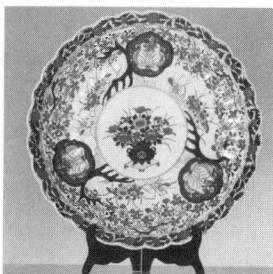

Imari Porcelain Charger

Charger, scalloped reeded rim, floral spray & medallion decorations, 1860, 18 1/2" d. (ILLUS.)... **840**

Vases, ovoid body decorated w/cartouches painted w/cranes & other birds, molded rim on narrow neck, pedestal base, ca. 1880, 15 3/4" h., pr. (ILLUS. left & right of vase, below) **616**

Jugtown Pottery

This pottery was established by Jacques and Juliana Busbee in Jugtown, North Carolina, in the early 1920s in an attempt to revive the skills of the diminishing North Carolina potter's art as Prohibition ended the need for locally crafted stoneware whiskey jugs. During the early years, Juliana Busbee opened a shop in Greenwich Village in New York City to promote the North Carolina wares that her husband, Jacques, was designing and a local youth, Ben Owen, was producing under his direction. Owen continued to work with Busbee from 1922 until Busbee's death in 1947 at which time Juliana took over management of the pottery for the next decade until her illness (or mental fatigue) caused the pottery to be closed in 1958. At that time, Owen opened his own pottery a few miles away, marking his wares "Ben Owen - Master Potter." The pottery begun by the Busbees was reopened in 1960, under new management, and still operates today using the identical impressed mark of the early Jugtown pottery the Busbees managed from 1922 until 1958.

Bowl, 7 1/4" d., 4 1/2" h., a footring supporting a deep rounded bowl w/slightly flared rim, Chinese blue glaze, circular stamp mark (three small glaze misses on interior).. **$825**

Bowl, 13" d., redware w/a yellow slip-decorated chicken, impressed mark, 20th c......... **165**

Vase, 3 1/2" h., simple ovoid body tapering to a small flat mouth, mottled & streaky glossy brown glaze, impressed mark............ **121**

Vase, 4" h., 3" d., simple ovoid form tapering to a small flat mouth, Chinese Blue glaze w/mottled dark brown, circular mark... **825**

Imari Charger Flanked by Imari Vases

Vase, 5 1/4" h., 4" d., narrow footring below the bulbous ovoid body tapering to a small flat mouth, overall Chinese Blue glaze mottled w/deep red & white, circular stamp mark **770**

Vase, 6 1/4" h., 7" d., bulbous body w/wide shoulder tapering to short neck w/flat rim, Chinese Blue glaze, impressed circular mark **1,463**

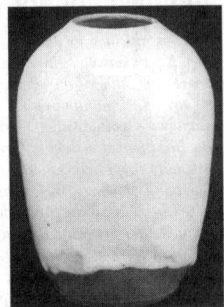

Jugtown Vase with White Drippy Glaze

Vase, 6 1/2" h., 4 1/4" d., ovoid body tapering to a small flat mouth, dripping white semi-matte glaze over a brown clay body, circular stamp mark (ILLUS.) **495**

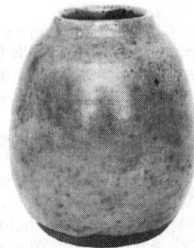

Egg-shaped Jugtown Vase

Vase, 7" h., ovoid egg-shaped body tapering to a flat mouth, embossed w/two medallions, mottled light blue glaze w/clay band showing around the base, bruise on rim, short firing line in base of neck, stamped mark (ILLUS.) **288**

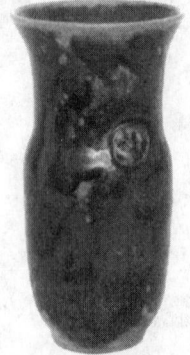

Jugtown Chinese Translation Vase

Vase, 8" h., slightly ovoid body tapering to a wide flaring neck, unusual Chinese translation form in dark red & blue mottled glazes (ILLUS.) **698**

Liverpool

Liverpool is most often used as a generic term for fine earthenware products, usually of creamware or pearlware, produced at numerous potteries in this English city during the late 18th and early 19th centuries. Many examples, especially pitchers, were decorated with transfer-printed patriotic designs aimed specifically at the American buying public.

Liverpool Masonic Jug

Pitcher, 10 5/8" h., creamware, jug-form, black transfer-printed design on buff ground of "The Mason's Arms" on front, reverse w/a verse "Masonic Secrets" & various Masonic emblems, area under spout decorated w/oval panel of Freemasons in fanciful architectural landscape beneath the script monogram "W.&D.C.," & area under handle decorated w/dividers & a square encompassing the letter "G" within a triangle, ca. 1800 (ILLUS.) ... **$3,300**

Pitcher, 11" h., jug-form, creamware w/black transfer-printed decorations w/color enamel trim, one side w/an oval reserve centering a portrait medallion of "John Adams President of the United States" surrounded by symbolic figures of Plenty w/a cornucopia of fruit, Justice w/her scale & Cupid, the other side w/a yellow sailing ship flying a red, white & blue American flag & pennant on a green sea above the name "John Adams," an American eagle above a cartouche w/initials under the spout, floral design at the base of the handle, a floral swag border at the neck, w/gold trim, early 19th c. (imperfections) **16,100**

Pitcher, 9 1/2" h., presentation pitcher w/Masonic transfer scenes on all sides in black w/gold foliage & detail, "W.P." & "Success to Delemere" (some wear) **880**

Pitcher, 10" h., jug-form, creamware decorated w/a black transfer-printed design w/color enamel trim, one side w/a Masonic panel, the other w/a sailing ship in brown & black w/yellow masts & flaying a red, white & blue American flag & pennant, on a green sea, a cartouche w/initials & the American Eagle under the spout, early 19th c. (imperfections) **1,725**

Liverpool Creamware Punch Bowl

Punch bowl, 10" d., creamware, round sides tapering out at top, footrim, black transfer-printed design of bust portrait of Benjamin Franklin or George Washington on front & back, the sides decorated w/pastoral landscapes, the interior w/a three-masted ship in full sail flying the American flag, various trophies around the rim, ca. 1790-1800, chip to footrim, some scratching to interior (ILLUS.).......... **1,800**

Longwy

This faience factory was established in 1798 in the town of Longwy, France and is noted for its enameled pottery which resembles cloisonné. Utilitarian wares were the first production here but by the 1870s an Oriental style art pottery that imitated "cloisonné" was created through the use of heavy enamels in relief. By 1912, a modern Art Deco style became part of Longwy's production and these wares, together with the Oriental style pieces, have made this art pottery popular with collectors today. As interest in Art Deco has soared in recent years, values of Longwy's modern style wares have risen sharply.

Longwy Floral Cup & Saucer

Cup & saucer, decorated w/overall vibrant colored stylized flowers, ink stamp marks, rim chips on both pieces, cup 2 1/4" h., the set (ILLUS.)................................ **$67**

Art Deco Longwy Tile

Tile, square, decorated in bold colors w/a stylized Art Deco woman in a garden, a deep brick red ground w/the woman in white, purple, white & black w/a yellow & white landscape w/purple, pink, white & black trees, marked "Longwy France Primavera," 8" w. (ILLUS.)........................... **400-425**
Vase, 11 3/4" h., flared neck on a round flattened body raised on an oval foot, the exterior w/turquoise blue crackle glaze, base w/a green ink stamp mark "Primavera Longwy France," after 1913.................... **230**
Vase, 12 1/2" h., tapering ovoid body w/everted lip, molded w/a mythological ram & bird w/two female nudes amid a stylized landscape, covered in ivory, turquoise blue, cobalt blue, purple & black glaze, green printed mark "Primavera - Longwy - France," ca. 1925....................... **2,587**
Vase, 22" h., ten sided melon-form body w/stepped tapering neck & circular foot, molded w/stylized teal & pink berries on black vines reserved on a crackled ivory ground, sawtooth border at neck & cobalt glazed rim & foot, ca. 1925, printed "Societe Des Faienceries - Longwy - France" .. **2,300**

LuRay Pastels

LuRay Pastels, made by The Taylor, Smith & Taylor Co. of Chester, West Virginia from 1938 until 1961, was a line available in four colors - Windsor Blue, Surf Green, Persian Cream and Sharon Pink. No one original color seems to be more desirable than the others. A fifth color, Chatham Gray, ran from 1949 until 1952. Collectors refer to the early-shaped A/D sets as "Chocolate Sets." Decal-decorated LuRay sets were produced but are very rare. No known examples of the handleless sugar, 7" mini platter or gray salad bowl have been found with the LuRay backstamp. An asterisk (*) indicates an older original mold shape.

After-dinner chcolate cup, gray **$75-100**

Original Style After-Dinner Chocolate Service

After-dinner chocolate cup, four original colors, each (ILLUS. front)........................... **20-25**
After-dinner chocolate pot, cov., four original colors, each (ILLUS. back, above) .. **135-175**
After-dinner individual sugar bowl, cov., four original colors, each (ILLUS. right, above)... **40-65**
After-dinner individual creamer, four original colors, each (ILLUS. left, above) **35-55**
After-dinner saucer, four original colors, each (ILLUS. front), above........................... **7-12**
After-dinner saucer, gray **15-25**

LuRay Bowls

Bowl, 5" d., fruit, four original colors, each
(ILLUS. front) **5-8**
Bowl, 5" d., fruit, gray **10-16**
Bowl, 6 1/4" d., grapefruit, rare, four original
colors, each (ILLUS. left w/fruit bowl).... **350-400**
Bowl, 36's bowl (oatmeal), four original col-
ors, each **50-75**
Bowl, 36's bowl (oatmeal), gray................. **250-300**
Bowl, coupe soup, flat, four original colors,
each (ILLUS. right w/fruit bowl) **15-20**
Bowl, coupe soup, flat, gray **30-40**
Bowl, cream soup, four original colors, each.. **65-85**
Bowl, lug soup (tab cereal), four original col-
ors, each **15-20**
Bowl, lug soup (tab cereal), gray.................... **40-50**
Butter dish, cov., four original colors, each .. **50-75**
Butter dish, cov., gray **150-225**
Cake plate, 11" d., four original colors, each .. **50-75**

LuRay 10" Calendar Plate

Calendar plate, 8", 9" or 10" d., each
(ILLUS. of 10" d) **35-65**
Calendar plate, 8", 9" or 10" d., yellow,
each **85-100**
Casserole, cov., four original colors, each
.... **125-175**

Modern Style "Chocolate Set"

"Chocolate set" A/D creamer*, four original colors, each (ILLUS. left) **350-400**
"Chocolate set" A/D cup*, four original col-
ors, each (ILLUS. front) **75-100**

"Chocolate set" A/D pot*, cov., four origi-
nal colors, each (ILLUS. back) **1,000-1,500**
"Chocolate set" A/D saucer*, four original
colors, each (ILLUS. front)......................... **25-35**
"Chocolate set" A/D sugar bowl*, cov.,
four original colors, each (ILLUS. right) . **400-500**
Chop plate, four original colors, 15" d.,
each **30-40**
Chop plate, gray, 15" d............................... **300-350**
Coaster (nut dish), four original colors,
each.. **65-85**

Compartment (Grill) Plate

Compartment (grill) plate, four original col-
ors, each (ILLUS.) **25-30**
Compartment (grill) plate, gray **100-125**
Cream soup saucer, four original colors,
each **20-25**
Creamer, four original colors, each................ **10-15**
Creamer, gray **30-45**
Egg cup, double, four original colors, each .. **15-25**
Egg cup, double, gray.................................... **75-100**
Epergne (flower vase), four original colors,
each **125-150**

Various LuRay Jugs

Jug, juice, four original colors, each (ILLUS.
left)... **175-225**
Jug, water, flat, four original colors, each
(ILLUS. right, above)..................................... **75-95**
Jug, water, footed*, four original colors,
each (ILLUS. center, above)................... **100-125**
Mixing bowl, four original colors, 7" d.,
each.. **125-175**
Mixing bowl, four original colors, 8 3/4" d.,
each.. **125-175**
Mixing bowl, four original colors, 10 1/4" d.,
each.. **125-175**

Luray Muffin Cover & Plate

Muffin cover, four original colors, each
(ILLUS. w/an 8" plate)............................ **175-225**
Pepper shaker, four original colors, each **10-15**
Pepper shaker, grey **20-30**
Pickle (celery) dish, four original colors,
each **35-45**
Plate, 6" d., four original colors, each **4-6**
Plate, 6" d., grey **8-12**
Plate, 7" d., four original colors, each **10-15**
Plate, 7" d., grey **20-30**
Plate, 8" d., four original colors, each **20-25**
Plate, 8" d., grey (ILLUS. w/muffin cover) **40-50**
Plate, 9" d., four original colors, each **10-15**
Plate, 9" d., grey **20-30**
Plate, 10" d., four original colors, each **15-20**
Plate, 10" d., grey **30-40**
Platter, 7" l., mini size, four original colors,
each **200-250**
Platter, 11 1/2" l., four original colors, each .. **15-20**
Platter, 11 1/2" l., grey **45-65**
Platter, 13" l., four original colors, each **15-25**
Platter, 13" l., grey **45-65**
Relish dish, four-part, four original colors,
each **125-175**
Salad bowl, four original colors, each **50-75**
Salad bowl, grey **300-400**
Salt shaker, four original colors, each........... **10-15**
Salt shaker, grey... **20-30**
Sauceboat, four original colors, each **30-40**
Sauceboat, w/fixed stand, four original col-
ors, each **35-50**
Sugar bowl, cov., four original colors, each .. **15-20**

LuRay Sugar Bowls

Sugar bowl, cov., grey (ILLUS. left) **45-60**
Sugar bowl, cov., handleless, four original
colors, each (ILLUS. right) **75-125**
Tea cup, four original colors, each **7-12**
Tea cup, grey **15-25**
Tea saucer, four original colors, each **3-5**
Tea saucer, grey **7-10**
Teapot, cov., curved spout, four original col-
ors, each **75-95**
Teapot, cov., curved spout, grey **300-400**
Teapot, cov., flat spout*, four original colors,
each **150-200**
Tidbit tray, three-tier, four original colors,
each **95-125**

Two-tier Tidbit Tray

Tidbit tray, two-tier, four original colors,
each (ILLUS.).. **65-85**
Tidbit tray, two-tier, grey **150-200**

LuRay Tumblers

Tumbler, juice, four original colors,
3 1/2" h., each (ILLUS. left) **45-65**
Tumbler, water, four original colors,
4 1/4" h., each (ILLUS. right, above).......... **65-85**
Vase, bud, four original colors, each........... **250-350**
Vase, urn-type, four original colors, each... **250-350**
Vegetable bowl (baker), oval, four original
colors, each **20-25**
Vegetable bowl (baker), oval, grey............... **50-65**
Vegetable bowl (nappy), round, four origi-
nal colors, each.. **20-25**
Vegetable bowl (nappy), round, grey........... **50-65**

Lustre Wares

*Lustred wares in imitation of copper, gold, silver and
other colors were produced in England in the early 19th
century and onward. Gold, copper or platinum oxides
were painted on glazed objects which were then fired,
giving them a lustred effect. Various forms of lustre
wares include plain lustre with the entire object coated
to obtain a metallic effect, bands of lustre decoration
and painted lustre designs. Particularly appealing is the
pink or purple "splash lustre" sometimes referred to as
"Sunderland" lustre in the mistaken belief it was con-
fined to the production of Sunderland area potteries.
Objects decorated in silver lustre by the "resist" process, wherein parts of the objects to be left free from lustre decoration were treated with wax, are referred to as
"silver resist."*

*Wares formerly called "Canary Yellow Lustre" are
now referred to as "Yellow-Glazed Earthenwares."*

Copper
Pepper pot, cov., bulbous body on short
foot w/round base, waisted neck tapering
to domed lid w/finial, decorated w/light
rust band w/pink lustre foliage & blue ber-
ries, 4 1/8" h. **$165**
Pitcher, ribbed body, scrolled handle &
molded fan spout, white neck w/red,
green & pink lustre strawberries, base
has a starch blue band, 4 1/2" h. **55**
Salt, open, squat bulbous body on flared
foot w/round base, ring rim on top, decorated w/blue band of pink lustre foliage &
pale yellow berries, 2" h. (minor interior
wear) **110**

Silver & Silver Resist
Tea service: cov. teapot, cov. sugar bowl,
milk jug & three larger jugs; teapot, sugar
bowl, milk jug & larger jug in silver lustre
w/floral decoration, another jug w/enamel
floral decoration in blues & reds on cream

ground beneath silver-lustre neck, spout & handle, & one copper lustre jug w/spout in form of bear's head & dolphin form handle, decorated w/red, yellow, pink & green flowers & leaves on blue ground; Staffordshire, ca. 1820, tallest jug 8 7/8" h., the set (chips, hairline, restuck handle) **1,560**

Sunderland Pink & others

Pitcher, 8 1/2" h., softpaste, satyr head spout, pink lustre h.p. w/pink queen's roses in blue, green & orange, w/a scene of three sailing ships, verse & "David & Elizabeth Buchannan" (minor flaking, in-the-making hairline on handle) **1,320**

Pitcher, 8" h., Sunderland lustre pitcher w/dark red transfer of ship, verse & two sailors w/"Mariners Arms," h.p. enamel in red, green, yellow & blue (spout has minor wear) **770**

Marblehead

This pottery was organized in 1904 by Dr. Herbert J. Hall as a therapeutic aid to patients in a sanitarium he ran in Marblehead, Massachusetts. It was later separated from the sanitarium and directed by Arthur E. Baggs, a fine artist and designer, who bought out the factory in 1916 and operated it until its closing in 1936. Most wares were hand-thrown and decorated and carry the company mark of a stylized sailing vessel flanked by the letters "M" and "P."

Book ends, square upright slant-fronted form, the face incised w/panels enclosing a view of ships under full sail, a different view on each, midnight blue matte glaze, impressed mark & paper label, ca. 1916, 5 3/8" h., pr. (hairline).................................. **$690**

Marblehead Two-color Bowl

Bowl, 2 1/2" h., wide squatty flaring form w/a wide tapered shoulder & a wide flat mouth, molded around the shoulder w/a triangular linear design, matte brown on a green ground, impressed mark, by Hannah Tutt, early 20th c. (ILLUS.) **1,725**

Marblehead Lotus Leaf Bowl

Bowl, 8 1/4" d., 3 1/4" h., a small footring supporting a deep rounded bowl w/molded overlapping lotus leaves below the

widely flaring flattened rim, speckled blue glaze, lighter speckled blue interior, impressed mark, minute rim fleck (ILLUS.) **402**

Pink-glazed Marblehead Bowl

Bowl, 8 3/4" d., 3" h., small round base below widely flaring slightly rounded sides w/a wide flat rim, speckled dark pink matte glazed exterior & lighter pink interior, unmarked (ILLUS.) **431**

Marblehead Squatty Bowl

Bowl, 8 3/4" d., 4" h., wide rounded incurved sides to a wide flat mouth, speckled matte brown glaze on exterior, celadon green & oxblood glossy interior glaze, stamped mark (ILLUS.) **805**

Bowl-Vase with Geometric Band

Bowl-vase, bulbous tapering form w/a wide flat mouth, carved around the top w/a geometric block design in dark brown against a matte green speckled ground, by Arthur Baggs, one-inch bruise, small rim hairline, illustrated in Paul Evans pottery book, marked, 5" d., 3 3/4" h. (ILLUS.).. **6,325**

Bowl-vase, a wide bulbous upper body w/wide closed rim, tapering sharply to a cylindrical base, overall lavender matte glaze, impressed mark, 5 1/2" d. **770**

Bowl-vase, wide gently flaring rounded cylindrical form w/a wide closed rim, matte green ground, incised w/a wide rim band in darker green of stylized blossoms w/twisted stems forms panels around the sides, marked & artist-initialed, ca. 1916, 6 1/2" d., 4 3/4" h. **6,900**

Bowl-vase, wide squatty spherical form tapering to a closed rim, fine speckled ochre matte glaze, impressed mark, 6 1/2" d., 5" h. **1,265**

Flaring Marblehead Bowl-Vase

Bowl-vase, cylindrical waisted lower body below widely flaring sides w/a flat rim, yellow matte exterior & teal green matte interior, impressed mark, 8 1/2" d., 5" h. (ILLUS.) **518**

Marblehead Squatty Humidor

Humidor, cov., squatty bulbous form w/incurved low sides & inset cover w/large knob handle, the cover painted w/a narrow ochre band of leaves, dark blue matte ground, stamped mark, 6" d., 4" h. (ILLUS.) **1,750**

Vase, 3" h., 4" d., bulbous nearly spherical lower body w/a rounded shoulder centering a wide, swelled cylindrical neck w/closed rim, incised around the body w/four stylized geometric panels in dark olive brown against a green ground, marked, ca. 1908 (imperfection in the making) **1,265**

Vase, 3" h., 4 1/4" d., low squatty wide bulbous form tapering sharply to a rolled rim, ringed sides, smooth green & charcoal matte glaze, incised "winged M" mark **440**

Vase, 3 1/2" h., miniature, small wide bulbous ovoid body tapering to a short flared neck, matte greyish green ground w/a linear band at the rim connecting eight stylized trees around the sides in brown matte glaze w/round blue foliage, by Hannah Tutt, marked, ca. 1912 .... **6,900**

Vase, 3 1/2" h., miniature, small wide slightly tapering cylindrical form w/a closed rim, unusual very dark blue matte glaze, impressed mark **385**

Vase, 3 1/2" h., 3 1/2" d., miniature, simple ovoid body tapering slightly to a wide flat mouth, speckled grey ground painted around the rim w/a stylized band of two-tone greyish blue flying geese, stamped ship mark **1,688**

Miniature Blue Marblehead Vase

Vase, 3 3/4" h., miniature, swelled cylindrical form tapering slightly to a wide flat mouth, speckled matte blue glaze, impressed mark (ILLUS.) **460**

Vase, 4" h., 4" d., bulbous base tapering to a wide, short cylindrical neck, matte deep blue ground w/incised rim band & stylized geometric border on neck in dark green, by Arthur Baggs, factory mark & artist-initialed **2,415**

Vase, 4 3/8" h., 3 7/8" d., a wide mouth on a cylindrical body, green ground decorated w/a blue linear band at the rim w/eight repeating stylized flowers w/multiple trailing stems in two shades of matte blue, by Hannah Tutt, marks & artist-signed, ca. 1912 .... **4,888**

Vase, 5" h., cylindrical w/rounded base & shoulder w/a short rolled rim, medium blue semi-gloss glaze, cipher & paper label **259**

Vase, 5" h., small footring supporting a widely flaring trumpet-form body, overall brown matte glaze, impressed mark **550**

Dark Blue Marblehead Vase

Vase, 5" h., wide baluster-form w/a wide, short flaring neck, overall dark matte blue glaze, impressed mark (ILLUS.) **345**

Vase, 5" h., 3 1/4" d., swelled cylindrical body w/a wide, flat rim, "watermelon rind" glaze, slightly iridescent finish on a textured ground in rich green, stamped mark & paper label, ca. 1908 .... **1,093**

Vase, 5 1/8" h., 3 1/4" d., a wide flat mouth on a swelled tapering cylindrical body, grey ground decorated w/a blue linear rim band w/five repeating stylized flowers w/trailing stems in three shades of matte blue, by Hannah Tutt, marked & artist-signed, ca. 1912 (rim hairlines) **1,150**

Vase, 5 1/4" h., 3 3/4" d., tapering ovoid gourd-form w/a narrow shoulder to a small flat mouth, incised w/four stylized geometric panels in dark green, by Hannah Tutt, marked & artist-signed **19,550**

Vase, 5 1/2" d., a wide bulbous baluster-form body w/the wide shoulder tapering slightly to a wide flat mouth, dark blue matte glaze, impressed mark (nearly invisible hairline at rim) **231**

Marblehead Vase with Grapevine

Vase, 5 1/2" h., a wide flat mouth on a gently tapering ovoid body, decorated w/a band of blue & light green grapevines around the top on a grey ground, chip in base, impressed mark (ILLUS.) **1,380**

Marblehead Vase with Brown Glaze

Vase, 5 1/2" h., ovoid body tapering to a widely flaring rim, brown speckled matte glaze, impressed mark, small bruise on rim (ILLUS.) **575**

Vase, 5 1/2" h., 5" d., short cylindrical bottom below widely flaring flat sides, dark blue matte exterior glaze, lighter blue interior, stamped ship mark & paper label **523**

Small Marblehead Bud Vase

Vase, 6" h., bud-type, wide thick round flaring foot tapering to a tall, slender cylindrical body, overall deep rose glaze (ILLUS.) **345**

Vase, 6" h., wide ovoid body tapering to a short flared rim, matte ochre ground decorated w/five tall panels painted w/blueberries & leaves in matte green & matte blue, each panel framed in dark ochre matte glaze, by Hannah Tutt, marked & artist-signed **12,650**

Unique and Rare Marblehead Vase

Vase, 6 3/4" h., 4" d., simple ovoid form w/a wide, flat mouth, decorated w/triple clusters of tall stylized flowers around the sides w/a lattice-like rim band, in shades of umber, black & cream on a speckled matte green ground, by Hannah Tutt, impressed mark & incised artist mark (ILLUS.) **120,750**

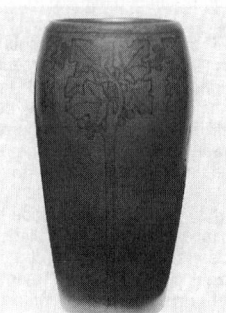

Marblehead Vase with Trees & Berries

Vase, 7" h., gently swelled cylindrical form w/a wide flat rim, painted w/an Arts & Crafts band of tall stylized trees in dark green & brown w/dark red berries against a dark blue ground, impressed mark, original paper label, some minor glaze crawling (ILLUS.) **6,600**

Vase, 7" h., slightly tapering cylindrical form w/a rounded bottom & wide flat rim, decorated around the top w/five delicately painted sea horses & seaweed in shades of blue against a grey ground, by Hanna Tutt, impressed mark (ILLUS. top next page) **11,500**

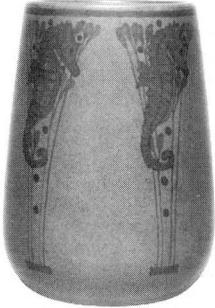

Fine Marblehead Sea Horse Vase

Vase, 7 1/4" h., a wide flat mouth on a tapering swelled cylindrical body, decorated w/repeating stylized fruit trees in matte green & orange on a blue ground, marked, ca. 1915 .... **4,888**

Marblehead Vase with Tall Trees

Vase, 7 1/4" h., gently swelled cylindrical form w/a wide flat rim, decorated w/full-length bluish black stylized trees w/leafy branches w/white berries around the top & the trunks down the sides against a dark blue matte ground, impressed mark, tiny chip on edge of base (ILLUS.) **2,875**

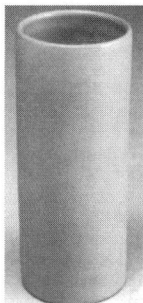

Simple Cylindrical Marblehead Vase

Vase, 7 1/2" h., 3" d., plain cylindrical form, overall pink speckled matte glaze, stamped mark (ILLUS.).................................... **920**

Marblehead Two-color Vase

Vase, 8" h., a wide flat mouth & wide low shoulder on a tapering cylindrical body, incised w/vertical panels of stylized floral & geometric designs in dark olive green on a lighter green ground, by Hannah Tutt, impressed mark & artist-initialed, ca. 1912 (ILLUS.) **13,800**

Rare Marblehead Vase with Ducks

Vase, 8" h., 7" d., wide ovoid form w/a wide flattened shoulder to the closed rim, decorated around the shoulder w/a band of flying mallard ducks in shades of grey on a speckled matte grey ground, stamped & incised marks (ILLUS.) **10,350**
Vase, 8 3/4" h., 3 3/4" d., simple cylindrical form w/rounded edges on the flat base & a narrow rounded shoulder & closed rim, speckled blue matte glaze, ship mark............ **956**
Vase, 8 3/4" h., 4" d., simple cylindrical form w/rounded edges on the flat base & a narrow rounded shoulder & closed rim, greyish mauve speckled matte glaze, ship mark **844**

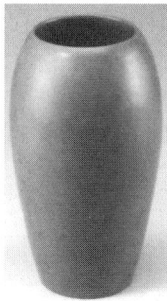

Simple Ovoid Marblehead Vase

Vase, 8 3/4" h., 5" d., simple ovoid body tapering to a wide flat mouth, overall smooth matte green glaze, impressed mark (ILLUS.) **1,150**

Vase, 9" h., tall slender simple waisted form, overall lavender matte glaze, impressed mark (faint hairline in rim) **330**

Marblehead Vase with Quatrefoils

Vase, 9" h.., 3 3/4" d., tall cylindrical form w/rounded base edge & wide closed rim, incised around the rim w/a band of quatrefoils atop long bands down the sides, dark & lighter green mottled matte glaze, impressed & incised marks (ILLUS.) **9,200**

Rare Marblehead Vase with Poppies

Vase, 9" h., 5 1/2" d., cylindrical body rounded at the base & at the closed rim, decorated w/stylized upright poppies around the sides w/the arched leaves forming panels around the body, in three shades of matte olive green, two hairlines from rim, stamped mark (ILLUS.) **10,350**

Marblehead Ringed Wall Pocket

Vase, 9 3/4" h., a rounded base edge on the tall gently tapering cylindrical body w/a flat rim, matte green ground incised & surface-painted w/a tapering stalk of stylized flowers in brown matte glaze, marked & artist-initialed, ca. 1912 .... **21,850**

Wall pocket, tapering conical form w/ringed design, flaring ruffled rim w/hanging hole, dark matte blue glaze, stilt pulls on rim, 4 1/4" w., 8 1/2" h. (ILLUS. previous column) **173**

Wall pocket, widely flaring rounded trumpet form, brown speckled matte exterior glaze, smooth ivory interior glaze, paper label, 7" w., 6" h. (bruise at rim) **450**

Martin Brothers

Martinware, the term used for this pottery, dates from 1873 and is the product of the Martin brothers—Robert, Wallace, Edwin, Walter and Charles—often considered the first British studio potters. From first to final stages, their hand-thrown pottery was completely the work of the team. The early wares may be simple and conventional, but the Martin brothers built up their reputation by producing ornately engraved, incised or carved designs as well as rather bizarre figural wares. The amusing face-jugs are considered some of their finest work. After 1910, the work of the pottery declined and can be considered finished by 1915, though some attempts were made to fire pottery as late as the 1920s.

Bowl-vase, footed wide squatty bulbous form tapering to a flat molded rim, faceted sides, covered in a fine red & green lustered crystalline glaze, incised "4-1900 - Martin Bro. - London and Southall," 1900, 7" d., 5" h. **$523**

Martin Brothers Gargoyle Dish

Dish, figural, the oblong form w/a crouching, grinning gargoyle at one end, the body forming the open dish composed of two tiered dishes, the neck & body w/fine incised lines to resemble hair, tan unglazed clay, very small edge nicks, signed "Martin Bros. - London & Southall - 4-1894," 5 1/2" l., 2 3/4" h. (ILLUS.) **1,870**

Jar, cov., figural, modeled as a large comical bird w/a rounded oversized head w/droopy beak & sleepy eyes, bulbous body & thick legs w/wide webbed feet, on a round platform base, dark brown, black & tan glazing, firing crack in body secured at factory w/beeswax, incised "R.W. Martin - London & Southall," 5 1/2" w., 11 1/2" h. (ILLUS. top next page) **10,450**

Martin Brothers Bird Jar on Base

Jar, cov., modeled as a grotesque bird w/a bulbous oversized head w/large beak & sleepy expression, feathers in green, light blue & black, marked "Martin Bros - London + Southall - 6-1897," oval base mounted on oval ebonized wooden base, 1897, 10" h. **13,500**
Paperweight, figural flying lizard, glazed in black, green & beige, partially obscured mark "Martin Bros - London," 2 1/4 x 4" (restoration to small points)..................... **1,125**

Martin Brothers Decorated Pitcher

Pitcher, 9" h., salt-glazed stoneware, a footed ovoid body tapering to a high widely flaring & pinched neck, D-form strap handle, finely incised & decorated w/birds nestled amid branches, glazed in shades of brown, green & rust against a blue striped ground, marked "6-1-2 - 1-8-50 - Martin Bros London & Southall," 1902 (ILLUS.)................................. **1,500-2,000**
Pitcher, jug-type, 9 3/4" h., ovoid body w/swelled shoulder under D-form handle, short cylindrical neck w/slightly flared rim & small pinched spout, body incised w/sea reptiles in indigo & amber, mark partially obscured by paper label (fleck to rim) **1,800**
Vase, 10 1/4" h., 6" d., wide ovoid body w/a short cylindrical neck, incised overall w/a design of stylized scrolling leafy vines & blossoms in sand, dark & light brown, marked "27.3.84 - R.W. Martin & Bros. - London & Southall," 1884........................... **1,045**

Massier (Clement)

Clement Massier was a French artist potter who worked in the late 19th and early 20th centuries creating exquisite earthenware items with lustre decoration.

Charger, round slightly dished form, overall Mediterranean bay scene w/large pine trees in the right foreground, fine lustred gold on burgundy glazes, impressed "CLEMENT MASSIER - GOLFE JUAN," 13" d. **$1,430**

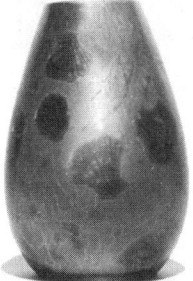

Massier Vase with Unusual Design

Vase, 3 7/8" h., simple ovoid form w/flat rim, clam & seaweed decoration in brilliant metallic glaze, marked "C.M. Golfe Juan A.M." (ILLUS.)... **532**
Vase, 6 3/4" h., 2 1/2" d., bud-type, bottle-shaped, bulbous ovoid body tapering to a very tall slender 'stick' neck, decorated w/a design of mistletoe in a silky red, gold & green iridescent glaze, unmarked.............. **220**
Vase, 8 3/4" h., baluster-shaped w/short flaring neck, glossy ruby glaze w/splotches of leaf-like designs, incised "J. Massier, Vallauris, France - 2008/6" (professional repair to rim) **179**

McCoy

Collectors are now seeking the art wares of two McCoy potteries. One was founded in Roseville, Ohio, in the late 19th century as the J.W. McCoy Pottery, subsequently becoming Brush-McCoy Pottery Co., later Brush Pottery. The other was also founded in Roseville in 1910 as Nelson McCoy Sanitary Stoneware Co., later becoming Nelson McCoy Pottery. In 1967 the pottery was sold to D.T. Chase of the Mount Clemens Pottery Co. who sold his interest to the Lancaster Colony Corp. in 1974. The pottery shop closed in 1985. Cookie jars are especially collectible today.

A helpful reference book is The Collector's Encyclopedia of McCoy Pottery, *by the Huxfords (Collector Books), and* McCoy Cookie Jars From the First to the Latest, *by Harold Nichols (Nichols Publishing, 1987).*

Book ends, decorated w/swallows, ca. 1956, 5 1/2 x 6"................................... **$200-250**
Book ends, model of violin, ca. 1959, 10" h., pr. **100-150**
Cachepot, double w/applied bird, ca. 1949, 10 1/2" l. **35-45**
Cookie jar, Bunch of Bananas, ca. 1948... **125-150**
Cookie jar, Chipmunk, ca. 1960 .... **100-125**

Christmas Tree Cookie Jar

Cookie jar, Christmas Tree, ca. 1959
(ILLUS.)... **800-1,000**
Cookie jar, Corn (ear of corn), ca. 1958 ... **150-175**
Cookie jar, Garbage Can, ca. 1978............... **30-40**
Cookie jar, heart-shaped, Hobnail line, ca.
1940... **400-550**
Cookie jar, Hobby Horse, ca. 1948........... **100-150**

Two Kittens in a Basket Cookie Jar

Cookie jar, Kittens in a Basket, ca. 1950s
(ILLUS.).. **600-700**
Cookie jar, Mr. & Mrs. Owl, ca. 1952 .... **75-95**
Cookie jar, Tomato, ca. 1964 .... **60-70**

Yellow Mouse Cookie Jar

Cookie jar, Yellow Mouse, ca. 1978
(ILLUS.).. **35-45**
Figurine, head of witch, ca. early 1940s,
3" h.. **400-600**
Iced tea server, El Rancho Bar-B-Que
line, ca. 1960, 11 1/2" h. **250-300**
Jardiniere, swallows decoration, ca. late
1930s, 7" h... **90-125**

Jardiniere, fish decoration, ca. 1958,
7 1/2" h... **350-400**

Ring Design Jardiniere & Pedestal

Jardiniere & pedestal base, ring
design, ca. 1930s, overall 29" h., 2 pcs.
(ILLUS.).. **450-550**
Lamp w/original shade, model of pair of
cowboy boots base, original shade, ca.
1956... **150-200**

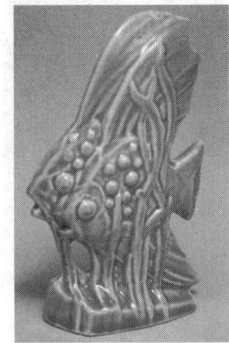

Model of Angelfish

Model of angelfish, aqua, ca. early 1940s,
Cope design, 6" h. (ILLUS.).................... **300-400**
Model of cat, ca. 1940s, 3" h. **300-400**

Large Oil Jar

Oil jar, bulbous ovoid body w/slightly flaring rim, angled shoulder handles, shaded blue, ca. 1930s, 15" h. (ILLUS.) **250-300**

Pitcher, embossed w/parading ducks, ca. 1930s, 4 pt. **90-125**

Pitcher, Donkey, marked "NM," early 1940s, 7" h. **250-300**

Pitcher, 10" h., Butterfly line **150-225**

Pitcher-vase, 7" h., figural parrot, ca. 1952 .... **150-200**

Planter, figural, Madonna, white, , ca. 1960s, rare, 6" h. **200-250**

Planter, model of baby scale, ca. 1954, 5 x 5 1/2" **60-75**

Planter, model of backward bird, ca. early 1940s, 4" h. **60-70**

Planter, model of carriage w/umbrella, ca. 1955, 8 x 9" **150-200**

Planter, model of lemon, ca. 1953, 5 x 6 1/2" **790-110**

Planter, model of Liberty Bell, cold painted black bell, base embossed "4th July 1776," 8 1/4 x 10" **200-350**

Planter, model of pomegranate, ca. 1953, 5 x 6 1/2" **200-250**

Planter, model of rooster on wheel of wheelbarrow, ca. 1955, 10 1/2" l. **100-125**

Planter, model of snowman, ca. 1940s, 4 x 6" **60-75**

Planter, model of stork, ca. 1956, blue & pink, 7 x 7 1/2" **60-75**

Planter, model of "stretch" dachshund, 8 1/4" l. **175-225**

Planter, model of trolley car, ca. 1954, 3 3/4 x 7" **50-60**

Planter, model of wagon wheel, ca. 1954, 8" h. **30-40**

Planter, Plow Boy, ca. 1955, 7 x 8" **100-125**

Planter, rectangular, relief-molded golf scene, ca. 1957, 4 x 6" **150-200**

Planting dish, model of swan, ca. 1955, 10 1/2" l. **350-400**

Planting dish, rectangular, front w/five relief-molded Scottie dog heads, white, brown & green, ca, 1949, 8" l. **50-60**

Platter, 14" l., Butterfly line, ca. 1940s **250-600**

Porch Jar

Porch jar, wide tapering cylindrical body w/ribbed base, embossed leaf & berry decoration below rim, green, marked "NM," ca. 1940s, 9 1/2 x 11" (ILLUS.) .. **200-250**

Spoon rest, Butterfly line, ca. 1953, 4 x 7 1/2" **90-125**

Sprinkler, model of turtle, green w/yellow trim, ca. 1950, 5 1/2 x 10" **80-100**

Tea set: cov. teapot, creamer & open sugar bowl; Pine Cone patt., ca. 1946, 3 pcs. ... **75-100**

Umbrella Stand with Leaf Design

Umbrella stand, cylindrical w/applied handles, ribbed panels alternating w/embossed leaf design panels, glossy brown glaze, ca. 1940s, 19" h. (ILLUS.) **250-350**

Vase, 10" h., 13 1/2" w., Blades of Grass, fan-shaped **250-350**

Vase, 14 1/2" h., Tall Fan, ca. 1954 .... **150-200**

Vase, 14" h., figural seated cat, ca. 1960... **200-250**

Vase, 6" h., footed, heart-shape w/embossed roses, ca. 1940s **60-80**

Vase, 8" h., footed bulbous base w/trumpetform neck & scrolled handles, embossed peacock decoration, ca. 1948 .... **40-60**

Fawn Vase

Vase, 9" h., boot-shaped w/figural fawn & foliage, chartreuse w/green, ca. 1954 (ILLUS.) **100-125**

Vase, 6" h., Hobnail line, Castlegate shape, ca. early 1940s **150-200**

Vase, 6 1/2" h., figural lower tulip, ca. 1953 .... **100-125**

Vase, 8" h., figural chrysanthemum, ca. 1950 .... **100-125**

Vase, 8 1/4" h., figural magnolia, ca. 1953, pink, white, brown & green **150-175**

Vase, 9" h. or 10" h., figural lizard handles **350-500**

Vase, 12" h., strap, double handled, ca. 1947 .... **80-110**

Vase, 14" h., Antique Curio line, ca. 1962 ... **75-100**

Wall pocket, Butterfly line, marked "NM," ca. 1940s, 6 x 7" **250-600**

Wall pocket, figural, clown, white w/red & black trim, ca. 1940s, 8" l. **100-150**

Wall pocket, model of apple, ca. early 1950s, 6 x 7" **60-70**

Wall pocket, model of bellows, ca. mid
1950s, 9 1/2" l. **90-110**
Wall pocket, model of bird bath, late 1940s,
5 x 6 1/2" **90-110**
Wall pocket, model of cuckoo clock, ca.
mid 1950s, 8" l. plus chains & weights.. **125-200**
Wall pocket, model of fan, blue, mid 1950s,
8 x 8 1/2" **75-90**
Wall pocket, model of lovebirds on
trivet, ca. early 1950s, 8 1/2" l. **75-90**
Wall pocket, model of pear, ca. early
1950s, 6 x 7" **70-85**

Merrimac Pottery

*The Merrimac Ceramic Company of Newburyport,
Massachusetts, was initially organized in 1897 by Thomas S. Nickerson for the production of inexpensive garden pottery and decorated tile. Within the year,
production was expanded to include decorative art pottery and this change was reflected in a new name, Merrimac Pottery Company, adopted in 1902. Early glazes
were limited to primarily matte green and yellow but by
1903 a variety of hues, including iridescent and metallic
lustres, were used. Marked only with a paper label until
after 1901, it then bore an impressed mark incorporating
a fish beneath "Merrimac." Fire destroyed the pottery in
1908 and this relatively short span of production makes
the ware scarce and expensive.*

Bowl-vase, wide flat-bottomed form w/low
rounded sides w/a wide shoulder centering a short, wide cylindrical neck, fine
matte green glaze, impressed mark,
9" d., 4" h. (minute fleck on rim) **$1,320**
Jar, cov., tapering cylindrical body w/a wide
rounded shoulder centering a slightly
domed cover w/knob finial, glossy speckled brown glaze, paper label, 3 1/4" d.,
5 1/4" h. (stilt pulls inside rim of cover in
the making) **495**

Large Merrimac Umbrella Stand

Umbrella stand, tall cylindrical form
w/tooled & applied leaves under a leathery matte green glaze, crack to base
crawls along the side, a few small chips
to decoration & some glaze pooling, pa-
per label, 8 1/2" d., 22 3/4" h. (ILLUS.) **4,125**
Vase, miniature, 4" h., 3 1/2" d., squatty bulbous baluster-form w/the wide shoulder
centered by a widely flaring trumpet
neck, feathered matte green & gunmetal
glaze, mark partially obscured by glaze **495**

Vase, 7 1/2" h., 4 1/4" d., slightly swelled
cylindrical form w/a small closed mouth,
tooled & applied w/dogwood blossoms
around the top on tall stems w/leaves
around the base, rich leathery matte
green glaze, impressed mark (opposing
hairlines, one restored) **1,980**

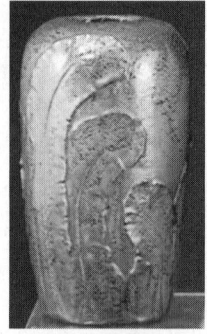

Rare Merrimac Vase with Leaves

Vase, 7 3/4" h., 4 1/2" d., gently swelled cylindrical form w/a rounded shoulder to the
closed rim, tooled & applied w/swirling
leaves, fine feathered matte green glaze,
carved "EB," several nicks to edges of
leaves (ILLUS.) **4,219**

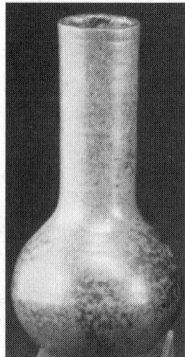

Large Bottle-form Merrimac Vase

Vase, 10" h., 5" d., bulbous nearly spherical
base tapering to a tall cylindrical neck,
fine dark green & mirrored black mottled
glaze, unmarked (ILLUS.) **1,650**

Tall Green Merrimac Vase

Vase, 10 1/2" h., tall ovoid body tapering to a flat molded mouth, overall matte green glaze, stilt pull & small chips on base (ILLUS.) **1,035**

Tall Simple Merrimac Vase

Vase, 11 1/2" h., tall slightly swelled cylindrical body w/a widely flaring rim, overall matte green glaze, impressed chip in rim, small glaze miss at base (ILLUS.) **690**

Vase, 11 1/2" h., 6" d., gently swelled cylindrical body w/a widely flared rim, applied stylized plant sprigs around the rim on tall thin stems w/a band of pointed leaves around the base, leathery semi-matte green glaze, stamped mark (restored chip at rim, hairline down body) **1,980**

Mocha

Mocha decoration is found on basically utilitarian creamware or yellowware articles and is achieved by a simple chemical reaction. A color pigment of brown, blue, green or black is given an acid nature by infusion of tobacco or hops. When this acid nature colorant is applied in blobs to an alkaline ground color, it reacts by spreading in feathery seaweed designs. This type of decoration is usually accompanied by horizontal bands of light color slip. Produced in numerous Staffordshire potteries from the late 18th until the late 19th centuries, its name is derived from the similar markings found on mocha quartz. In addition to the seaweed decoration, mocha wares are also seen with Earthworm and Cat's Eye patterns or a marbleized effect.

Master salt, blue stripes & white band w/green seaweed decoration on yellowware, 2 1/4" h. (short hairlines & interior stain) **$770**

Mug, decorated w/brown stripes w/white band & blue seaweed decoration on yellowware, 3 7/8" h. **358**

Mug, miniature, cylindrical w/arched leaftip handle, narrow brown & light blue stripes flanking a wide grey band w/brown, white & light blue Earthworm patt., 3 1/8" h. (stains, crack) **385**

Pepper pot, cov., baluster-form w/domed top, flared round foot, body decorated w/wide blue band w/black seaweed decoration, tan stripes, 5" h. (slight wear to finial) **770**

Pepper pot, cov., cylindrical body w/short tapered neck w/slightly flared domed top & knob finial, round footed base, wide black band around body w/light blue, orange & white wavy line design, flanked by grey stripes, cobalt feathering on lid, 4 3/4" h. (minor wear, staining, short hairline in top) **1,155**

Pepper pot, cov., cylindrical w/domed top & knob finial, blue & tan bands w/brown check tooled bands, 4 1/4" h. (small flakes on base & lid rim, wear on finial) **1,210**

Pepper pot, cov., squat bulbous yellowware body on short flared round ringed foot, slightly flaring cylindrical neck, body w/white band of pink seaweed decoration, brown & pale blue stripes, 4 1/4" h. (minor flake on base) **1,980**

Pitcher, 5 1/2" h., jug-form w/a wide flat base, narrow blue, white & dark brown bands flanking a wide central tan band w/dark brown Earthworm patt., early 19th c. (damage) **330**

Tureen, cov., round, decorated w/entwined cables & "cat's eyes" on ochre ground, w/green-glazed foliate handles, cover decorated w/two zigzag cables w/green-glazed floral knop, 19th c., 10 3/8" l. across handles (hairlines, minor chips) **5,400**

Moorcroft

William Moorcroft became a designer for James Macintyre & Co. in 1897 and was put in charge of their art pottery production. Moorcroft developed a number of popular designs, including Florian Ware while with Macintyre and continued with that firm until 1913 when they discontinued the production of art pottery.

After leaving Macintyre in 1913, Moorcroft set up his own pottery in Burslem and continued producing the art wares he had designed earlier as well as introducing new patterns. After William's death in 1945, the pottery was operated by his son, Walter.

Large Moorcroft Pomegranate Bowl

Bowl, 8 1/4" d., 4" h., footed wide & deep rounded shape w/flat rim, Pomegranate patt., large red & orange fruits & greenish brown leaves w/purple & red berries in the background, stamped mark (ILLUS.) **$805**

Bowl, 9" d., 4" h., footed wide rounded form w/flat rim, Waving Corn (wheat) patt., decorated in squeezebag w/large curved heads of wheat in green & maroon on a light celadon green ground, stamped Moorcroft & ink mark **715**

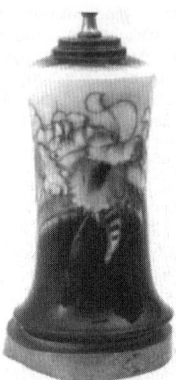

Tall Moorcroft Floral Lamp Base

Lamp base, a metal round base supporting the slightly waisted cylindrical lamp decorated w/bold stylized flowers in red, green & yellow against a cream & cobalt blue ground, signed, replaced socket, minor crazing, 14" h. (ILLUS.)............................ **546**

Perfume bottle w/stopper, figural, round flattened sides molded as a large pansy blossom, painted in lavender & yellow on a cobalt blue ground, hallmarked silver cap, unsigned, 1 3/4" w., 2" h. **660**

Tea set: cov. teapot, open sugar & creamer; Pomegranate patt., large red & yellow fruits w/purple seeds w/yellowish green leaves, green mark, teapot 7 1/2" d., 8" h., the set (small chip & flat hairline in teapot, repair to spout & crack in handle of creamer) **2,860**

Vase, 1 3/4" h., 2" d., miniature, tiny spherical form w/a small flared neck, painted w/stylized roses & blue flowers on a white ground, stamped "MacIntyre Burslem" & script "WM" **935**

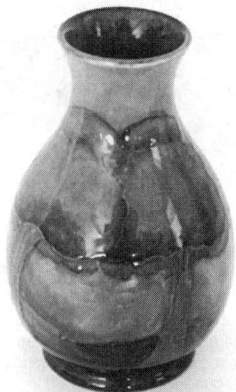

Moorcroft Eventide Pattern Vase

Vase, 5" h., footed baluster-form, Eventide patt., large stylized trees in shades of brown against a light tan & deep rose ground (ILLUS.) **1,265**

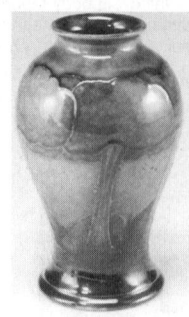

Signed Moorcroft Eventide Vase

Vase, 6 1/2" h., 3 1/2" d., baluster-form w/short flared neck, Eventide patt., squeezebag design of large stylized trees in shades of reddish orange & green flambé glaze, ca. 1925, signed (ILLUS.).. **220**

Vase, 6 3/4" h., 3" d., Florian Ware, slightly waisted cylindrical form w/a rounded base rim & shoulder tapering to a short cylindrical neck, decorated in squeezebag w/blue stylized jonquils & green leaves on a blue ground, ink mark............. **1,980**

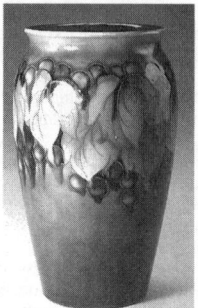

Moorcroft Clematis Pattern Vase

Vase, 7" h., footed ovoid body w/a wide flat mouth, "Clematis" patt., a large blossom & leaves in dark purplish red & orangish red on a reddish orange ground, initials & impressed mark, paper label, mid-20th c., small glaze scratch (ILLUS.) **489**

Moorcroft Vase with Blue Berries

Vase, 9" h., 5 1/4" d., simple ovoid body tapering slightly to a short flaring rim, decorated in squeezebag w/a wide band of large blue berries & pale green leaves around the shoulder against a mottled green & dark blue ground, dark crazing lines around rim, ink signature & stamped mark (ILLUS.) **1,150**

Vase, 9" h., 5 1/2" d., a wide disk foot supporting an ovoid body w/a wide flat mouth, decorated w/large red, garnet & orange fruits & leaves on a dark cobalt blue ground, paper label............................. **2,138**

Vase, 10 1/4" h., bulbous base tapering to a tall neck w/flared rim, decorated w/trailing rose blossoms in cobalt blue & mauve on a sage green lustre ground, signature mark, second quarter 20th c. **2,185**

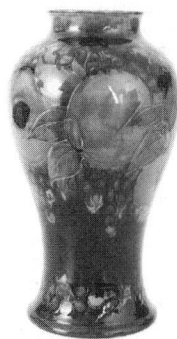

Tall Baluster-form Moorcroft Vase

Vase, 13" h., tall baluster-form body, Pomegranate patt., large deep red fruits w/moss green leaves against a dark blue ground, drill hole for lamp in base, signed (ILLUS.) **690**

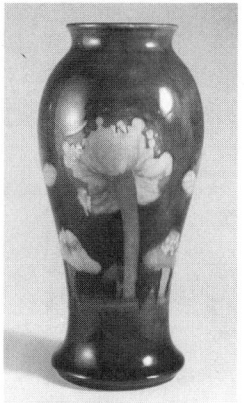

Tall Moorcroft Claremont Vase

Vase, 14" h., tall baluster-form w/a short flared neck, Claremont patt., decorated in red, yellow & purple w/toadstools on a mottled green & blue ground, Moorcroft signature & impressed "Moorcroft - Burslem - England M46," ca. 1916-18 (ILLUS.) **5,100**

Large Moorcroft Spanish Pattern Vase

Vase, 16" h., 10 1/2" d., a round foot below the tall trumpet-form body, Spanish patt., overall bold scrolling blossoms & leaves in reds, pinks, greens & blues, two chips on base, green slip signature mark & stamped "Made for Liberty & Co.," 1903-13 (ILLUS.) **4,312**

Large Moorcroft Vase with Grapes

Vase, 17" h., "Grape and Leaf" patt., wide baluster-form w/a short flaring neck, decorated w/fruit & leaves in shades of orange, red, purple & mauve on a shaded rust & dark blue ground, glossy glaze, impressed mark, ca. 1930 (ILLUS.)................ **4,888**

Newcomb College Pottery

This pottery was established in the art department of Newcomb College, New Orleans, Louisiana, in 1897. Each piece was hand-thrown and bore the potter's mark & decorator's monogram on the base. It was always a studio business and never operated as a factory and its pieces are therefore scarce, with the early wares being eagerly sought. The pottery closed in 1940.

Bowl, 4 1/2" d., 2 1/2" h., footed half-round form w/flat rim, carved around the rim w/a narrow band of pink buds on a green & blue ground, by Sadie Irvine, 1927, marked "NC - IS - PV71" **$1,238**

Bowl-vase, wide spherical form tapering to a wide flat rim, carved w/a continuous landscape of live oaks draped in Spanish moss w/a full moon behind, 1939, marked "NC - Y38 - FHF," 7" d., 5 1/2" h. (very tight short hairline at rim)................... **3,375**

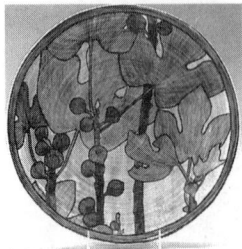

Newcomb Glossy-glazed Charger

Charger, decorated overall w/large fig branches w/leaves & fruit in dark blue & bluish yellow on a pale blue ground, glossy glaze, by Irene Borden Keep, 1902, few tiny clay pimples, marked, 10 3/4" d. (ILLUS.) **10,350**

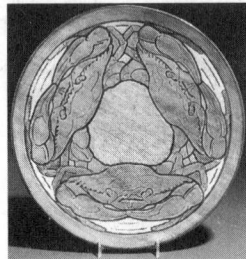

Large Newcomb Charger with Crabs

Charger, incised around the center w/three large blue crabs on a blue ground, by Sabrina Wells, 1904, marked "NC - M - S.E. Wells - YY64," short, tight line on back, 13" d. (ILLUS.) **28,125**

Jar, cov., large bulbous ovoid body w/a fitted domed cover, the upper half of the body carved w/a band of stylized sweet peas, the cover carved w/a central blossom surrounded w/a band reading "Here are sweet peas on tiptoe for a flight," by Mazie T. Ryan, 1903, signed "M.C. - M.T.R. - W - MR - SS - 64," 6" d., 8" h. (ILLUS. top next column) **42,188**

Very Rare Newcomb College Jar

Jardiniere, large bulbous ovoid form w/a wide flat closed rim, decorated w/large white lilies w/yellow centers raised on green stems against a cobalt blue ground, by Harriet Joor, 1903, marked "NC - JM - X97 - HJ," two rim repairs, 10 1/2" d., 8 3/4" h. (ILLUS. right with teapot & vase, below) **13,500**

Teapot, cov., footed conical body w/angled spout & handle, fitted low domed cover w/button finial, carved around the lower body w/a band of wild roses in light pink & yellow on a dark bluish green ground w/dark blue trim, by Alma Mason, 1911, marked "NC - EG44 - A.M. - B.," 5 1/2" d., 4 1/4" h. (ILLUS. front left with jardiniere & vase, below) **3,375**

Newcomb College Tyge with Flowers

Newcomb Jardiniere, Teapot & Vase

Tyge (three-handled mug), wide slightly tapering cylindrical body w/three squared tubular handles from the rim to the base, decorated around the rim w/a band of white flowers against bands of dark blue & white, pale blue lower body & white handles, old tight hairline in one handle, by Marie De Hoa LeBlanc, 1905, 5" d., 3 3/4" h. (ILLUS.) **4,600**

Vase, 3 " h., 3 3/4" d., miniature, bulbous ovoid form tapering to a short flat neck, decorated w/a vertical band of light blue bell-shaped flowers & green leaves around the sides on a cobalt blue ground, by Henrietta Bailey, 1929, marked "NC - HB3359 - JM" **1,463**

Vase, 3 3/4" h., 3 1/4" d., miniature, simple ovoid body w/a flat mouth, painted w/a continuous upright band of strawberries & leaf clusters in dark blue on a pale blue ground, by Ester Elliott, 1902, marked "NC - JM - EHE - R19" (ILLUS. upper left with teapot & jardiniere, previous page)..... **9,000**

Newcomb Vase with Tall Pines

Vase, 5 1/4" h., 3 1/4" d., ovoid body w/a narrow shoulder tapering to a short, wide cylindrical neck, crisply carved w/a landscape of tall pines in bluish green on a washed blue ground, small stilt-pull chips, by Sadie Irvine, 1917, signed (ILLUS.) **3,450**

Newcomb Scenic with Pink Sky

Vase, 5 1/2" h., 3" d., slender ovoid form tapering to a short cylindrical neck, decorated w/a landscape of large oak trees draped w/Spanish moss in shades of light & dark blue & green against a pink sky, by Anna Frances Simpson, 1929 (ILLUS.)... **5,463**

Newcomb Vase with Flower Band

Vase, 5 3/4" h., 3" d., footed cylindrical form w/rounded bottom rim & shoulder centered by a short cylindrical neck, incised around the upper body w/a wide band of stylized flowers in yellow & green on a glossy washed blue ground, opposing hairlines in rim, stilt-pull chip, minute nick on base, by Marie De Hoa LeBlanc, 1903, signed (ILLUS.)................................... **4,600**

Newcomb Vase with Jonquils

Vase, 6 1/2" h., large wide bulbous ovoid form tapering to a thin flat wide rim, carved & painted w/jonquils in white w/yellow centers on green stems w/green leaves against a dark blue ground, by A.F. Simpson, impressed mark (ILLUS.)... **4,400**

Short & Tall Newcomb Vases

Vase, 6 1/2" h., wide squatty bulbous base tapering to cylindrical sides w/a molded rim, decorated w/abstract organic forms up the sides in shades of blue against a green & blue streaky ground, glossy glaze, by Robert Beverly Kennon, impressed mark (ILLUS. left, previous page)... **4,313**

Vase, 7 1/4" h., 3 1/4" d., cylindrical form w/rounded bottom & shoulder tapering to a short flat rim, carved around the upper half w/a wide band of stylized white primrose blossoms on blue leafy stems against a light blue ground over a dark blue lower band, by Mazie Ryan, 1904, marked "NC - SS12 - M. Ryan." **8,438**

Rare Newcomb Vase with Pod Design

Vase, 7 1/4" h., 5 1/4" d., slightly tapering ovoid body w/a wide closed rim, incised around the shoulder w/large stylized seed pods on long stems in shades of blue & greenish blue, interior firing line at rim, by Marie Benson, 1905 (ILLUS.)....... **10,925**

Early Newcomb Vase with Egrets

Vase, 8" h., 6" d., tapering ovoid form w/the shoulder centering a wide low rolled neck flanked by upright angled loop handles, painted w/four different views of large white egrets among sea grass in blue, white & green on a cobalt blue ground, pre-1902, by Marie M. Ross, restoration to one handle, impressed mark (ILLUS.). **25,875**

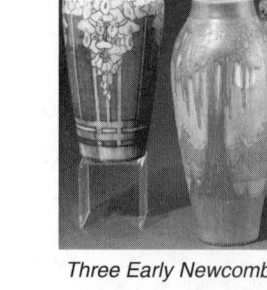

Three Early Newcomb College Vases

Vase, 8 3/4" h., 4 3/4" d., gently tapering cylindrical form w/a rounded shoulder & short cylindrical rim, decorated w/light periwinkle blue wisteria blossoms on a cobalt blue & celadon ground, by Maude Robinson, 1904, restored rim hairline, marked "NC - JM - Maude Robinson - XX41" (ILLUS. left) **13,500**

Rare Newcomb Vase with Flowers

Vase, 9 1/2" h., 4" d., footed cylindrical form w/rounded base & shoulder tapering to a short flat neck, decorated w/stylized yellow flowers & dark blue leaves on a pale denim ground, glossy glaze, four hairlines from rim, unknown artist, dated 1902 (ILLUS.)... **27,600**

Fine Newcomb Landscape Vase

Vase, 10 1/4" h., 6 1/2" d., wide ovoid body tapering to a flat mouth, decorated w/a landscape of live oak trees & Spanish moss w/a full moon in the background, shades of dark & light blue & yellow, by Anna Frances Simpson, marked (ILLUS.) **17,250**

Vase, 10 1/2" h., tall sharply tapering cylindrical form w/small flared mouth, carved & painted eucalyptus leaves & seed pods suspended from the rim, in light pink & green matte on a blue ground, by Sadie Irvine, impressed mark (ILLUS. right with abstract decorated vase)............................ **4,485**

Vase, 11" h., 5" d., tall ovoid form, crisply carved & decorated w/a tall oak tree w/Spanish moss w/a full moon beyond, shades of dark & light blue w/a yellow moon, by A.F. Simpson, 1927, marked "NC - M - AFS - QC35" (ILLUS. center with wisteria vase, previous page) **16,313**

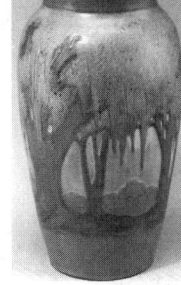

Exceptional Newcomb Landscape

Vase, 11" h., 6" d., slender ovoid form tapering to a short cylindrical neck, decorated w/a continuous landscape of live oak trees draped w/Spanish moss w/a full moon beyond, in shades of dark & light blue, greenish blue & white, exceptional, by Anna Frances Simpson, 1929 (ILLUS.) **17,250**

Tall Newcomb Vase with Trees

Vase, 11 1/4" h., 4 1/2" d., tall slender cylindrical form w/a widely flaring rim, finely carved w/a continuous band of tall cypress & pine trees in medium bluish green on a pale bluish green ground, by Leona Nicholson, 1907, restoration to a hairline, marked "NC - BP46 - M - LN" (ILLUS.) **8,625**

Very Rare Newcomb College Vase

Vase, 12" h., tall gently tapering cylindrical form w/a rounded shoulder centering a short rolled neck, carved & painted bamboo stalks in several tones of green against a blue ground, all covered in a glossy glaze, by Henrietta Bailey, ca. 1909 (ILLUS.) **46,750**

Vase, 12 1/4" h., 7 1/2" d., large tapering ovoid form w/a closed rim, decorated w/tall pine trees in dark blue & green against a background of dark blue & pale & dark yellow, by Harriet Joor, 1902, restoration to line at shoulder, marked "NC - JM - HJ - U87 - Q" (ILLUS. right with wisteria vase, previous page).......................... **21,375**

Rare Newcomb Roadrunner Vase

Vase, 12 1/2" h., 7 3/4" d., wide ovoid body tapering to a short cylindrical neck, decorated around the shoulder w/a wide band of racing roadrunner birds, the birds in bluish white on dark blue, the background in streaky cream & dark blue, glossy glaze, Marie De Hoa LeBlanc, 1902 (ILLUS.)... **43,125**

Very Rare Newcomb Vase with Irises

Vase, 14 1/2" h., 9" d., simple tall ovoid form tapering to a flat mouth, carved overall w/tall blue & yellow irises on tall green leafy stems, glossy glaze, Henrietta Bailey, 1909 (ILLUS.) **46,000**

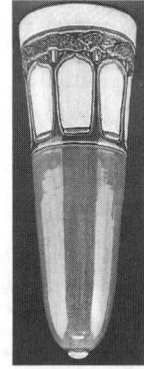

Rare Newcomb College Wall Pocket

Wall pocket, long slender conical form, carved around the upper body w/a band of stylized trees in cobalt blue & green, dark blue lower body, glossy glaze, by Leona Nicholson, ca. 1904, 4" d., 11" l. (ILLUS.) **9,350**

Niloak Pottery

This pottery was made in Benton, Arkansas, and featured hand-thrown varicolored swirled clay decoration in objects of classic forms. Designated Mission Ware, this line is the most desirable of Niloak's production which began early in this century. Less expensive to produce, the cast Hywood Line, finished with either high gloss or semi-matte glazes, was introduced during the economic depression of the 1930s. The pottery ceased operation about 1946.

Bowl, 5" d., Mission Ware, squatty rounded base tapering slightly to the wide, flat rim, swirled red, brown, cream & blue clays, marked **$176**

Bowl, 6 3/4" d., 3" h., Mission Ware, wide deep rounded form w/a flat mouth, swirled dark blue, light blue, dark brown, cream & reddish brown clays, impressed mark, paper label (ILLUS. left) **173**

Box, cov., Mission Ware, squatty bulbous body & high squatty mushroom-shaped cover, swirled dark brown, reddish brown, tan & blue clays, impressed mark, 4" h. **1,035**

Jug, spherical body w/flat bottom, a pointed loop handle on the shoulder opposite a short, round spout, overall mottled golden tan & green matte glaze, ink mark, 6" h. **231**

Lamp base, Mission Ware, tapered ovoid form w/flared round base, swirled marbleized clays in red, blue, cream & taupe, two-socket fixture, early 20th c., 10 1/4" h. **374**

Niloak Mission Ware Covered Jar

Puff box, cov., Mission Ware, footed wide squatty bulbous body w/a low rim & flat inset cover w/pointed finial, swirled dark brown, tan & dark blue clays, 4" h. (ILLUS.) **575**

Vase, 3 1/2" h., miniature, Mission Ware, ovoid form tapering gently to a wide flat

Niloak Bowl and Vases

Large & Small Mission Ware Vases

mouth, swirled light & dark blue, tan & light brown clays, minute flakes (ILLUS. left) 242

Vase, 3 1/2" h., miniature, Mission Ware, wide ovoid form tapering to a heavy molded rim, swirled dark & light brown, dark blue, cream & reddish brown clays, impressed mark (ILLUS. right with bowl, previous page) 150

Vase, 5" h., 6" d., Mission Ware, flat-bottomed wide bulbous form curving to a wide flat rim, swirled dark & light brown, cream, reddish brown & blue clays, impressed mark (ILLUS. right with miniature vase) 265

Niloak Mission Ware Vase

Vase, 6" h., Mission Ware, simple balusterform w/a wide closed rim, swirled red, cream & grey clays, impressed mark (ILLUS.) 209

Vase, 6" h., Mission Ware, wide cylindrical form rounded at the base & top rim, bold swirled bands of dark blue, reddish brown & dark & light brown clays, impressed mark (ILLUS. center with bowl) 403

Two Cylindrical Niloak Vases

Vase, 7 1/4" h., Mission Ware, simple cylindrical form, fine swirls of dark blue, cream & dark brown clays, early impressed mark w/patent pending wording (ILLUS. left) 633

Vase, 8 1/4" h., Mission Ware, tall ovoid form tapering gently to flat rim, unusual decoration of overall incised squiggles in a tan matte glaze over a dark brown base, paper label (ILLUS. top of column) .. 1,150

Unusual Mission Ware Incised Vase

Vase, 8 3/4" h., Mission Ware, large bulbous ovoid body tapering to a short slightly rolled neck, swirled dark & light brown clays, rare ink stamp mark 1,093

Vase, 10" h., Mission Ware, tall simple cylindrical form, bold swirls of medium blue, dark & light brown, cream & reddish brown clays, impressed mark (ILLUS. right with other cylindrical vase) 288

Vase, 11" h., Mission Ware, tall balusterform w/widely flaring flattened neck, bold squiggly swirls of blue, cream, reddish brown, dark & light brown clays, impressed mark (ILLUS. center with miniature vase) 500

Vase, 12 1/4" h., footed bulbous body tapering to a tall flaring trumpet neck, overall dark matte blue glaze, impressed mark 748

Noritake

Noritake china, still in production in Japan, has been exported in large quantities to this country since early in this century. Though the Noritake Company first registered in 1904, it did not use "Noritake" as part of its backstamp until 1918. Interest in Noritake has escalated as collectors now seek out pieces made between the "Nippon" era and World War II (1921-41). The Azalea pattern is also popular with collectors.

Ashtray, horse shoe-shaped $140
Ashtray, round, figural cat on rim...................... 315
Ashtray, round, figural pelican on the rim.......... 195

Ashtray with Figural Bird on Rim

Ashtray, round w/large figural blue, yellow & green bird perched on the rim, pale iridescent orange ground w/black, yellow & brick red top band, 4 3/4" d. (ILLUS.)............. 240

Ashtray, rounded low bowl-form w/incurved rim w/three cigarette notches, shaded dark grey ground decorated w/large stylized green leaves & yellow sunflowers, 4 1/4" d. (ILLUS. top, next page) 45

Noritake Ashtray with Sunflowers

Basket, floral decoration, 4 3/4" h. **75**
Basket, lettuce design, 5 1/4" h. **110**
Bell, blue decoration **200**
Berry set: master bowl & matching sauce
dishes; Art Deco decoration, the set............. **195**

Bowl with Romantic Garden Scene

Bowl, 10 1/2" d., 2" h., rounded gently
lobed rim w/small tab handles, the interi-
or painted w/a garden scene of a Victorian lady in a pink gown holding red flowers w/purple blue bushes behind her & a
slender overhanging tall tree, all on a yel-
low ground (ILLUS.) **235**
Bowl, 6 1/2" d., wide shallow form w/wide
tan outer band & thin black & rust orange
inner bands, raised on three tab feet
(ILLUS. top right column) **120**
Bowl, 6" h., Gemini-type **3,400**
Bowl, Art Deco shape, floral decoration **75**

Banded Noritake Bowl

Bowl, two-handled, peacock feather deco-
ration.. **75**
Box, cov., figural lady seated in a chair.......... **6,700**
Box, cov., geometric Art Deco decoration,
3 1/2" w., 2 1/4" h. **200**

Art Deco Noritake Box

Box, cov., hexagonal, geometric Art Deco
decoration in black, yellow, purple, brown
& green on a pale lavender ground, 4" w.,
3" h. (ILLUS.) **165**
Box base, figural chair, missing seated lady
cover... **750**
Butter tub, tab handles, floral decoration **11**
Cake set: handled cake plate & six match-
ing dessert plates; decoration of a Crino-
line Lady, the set **260**
Calendar holder, narrow rectangular base
w/an upright oblong holder at one end &
a flattened figural rabbit at the other end,
iridized orange & green w/stylized purple
& blue blossoms, 5 1/4" l., 2" h. (ILLUS.
below).. **510**

Calendar Holder with Figural Rabbit

Noritake Condiment Set

Candlesticks, decorated w/an Art Deco la-
dy, 7 1/2" h., pr.. **895**
Charger, round, decorated w/an Oriental
lady & cherry tree... **140**
Cheese dish, cov., floral decoration **70**
Christmas plate, 8 1/2" d., 1998, complete **65**
Cigarette holder, scenic decoration, 3" h......... **110**

Cigarette Holder with Oriental Decor

Cigarette holder, upright vase-form w/ob-
long lobed top over flower-molded ring &
flaring foot, orange ground w/gilt Oriental
landscape, 2 3/4" w., 3" h. (ILLUS.).................. **90**

Compote with Figural Lady Pedestal

Compote, open, 6 3/4" d., 6 3/4" h., wide
shallow bowl w/lightly scalloped rim, decorated w/a lavender blue center dot surrounded by a gold leaf wreath, white center w/swags of gold leaves & blossoms &
lavender blue inside the pale peach border, raised on a pedestal composed of
the standing figures of three Oriental ladies, round base in dark blue & peach
(ILLUS.)... **1,500**

Compote, open, no handles, gold w/white
trim.. **688**
Condiment set: narrow oblong tray w/end
loop handles, holding a small cov. sugar
bowl flanked by pointed salt & pepper
shakers, all w/colorful quaint cottage
landscape, gold trim, tray, 7 3/8" l., over-
all 3 1/4" h., the set (ILLUS., above) **115**
Creamer & open sugar bowl, floral decora-
tion, pr. **95**

Noritake Figural Dresser Jar

Dresser jar, figural cover w/a lady wearing
a dark orange shawl w/black flowers &
holding a yellow & green fan, the cylindrical base in dark lavender forming her
gown, 3 1/4" d., 5 3/4" h. (ILLUS.).................. **790**

Figural Lady Dresser Jar

Dresser jar, figural lady cover decorated
w/gold hair, blue & red bodice & orange,
green & yellow fan, her skirt forming the

cylindrical base decorated w/pale iridescent peach w/large brick red & green
dots, 3 1/4" d., 5 1/4" h. (ILLUS.) **1,075**
Dresser set, floral decoration, 1920s, 6
pieces, the set **115**
Figurine, doe & fawn **57**

Figure of 18th Century Lady

Figurine, standing lady in 18th c. costume,
tall grey hairdo, wearing a dark green &
orange gown, holding pink rose blos-
soms, Chiaramachi mark, 7" h. (ILLUS.) **295**
Honey pot, cov, model of a cottage **195**
Jam jar, cov., Art Deco decoration **220**

Ornate Art Deco Jar

Jar, cov., "Radio City" style, round pedestal
base below tall bell-form jar w/flattened
round cover topped by a small figural
Chinese man holding a gold parasol,
decorated w/wide bands of dark orange
alternating w/dark gold & black bands of
geometric Art Deco designs, 4 1/4" d.,
8 3/4" h. (ILLUS.) **650**
Lemon dish, center handle, Art Deco deco-
ration **95**
Lemon dish, floral decoration **25**
Match holder, figural bear **210**
Mayonnaise set: handled bowl, ladle &
underplate; large stylized white poppy
blossoms & green leaves on a cream
ground, trimmed w/gold & silver,
underplate 6"d., overall 5" h., the set
(ILLUS. top right column) **125**

Mayonnaise Set with Large Florals

Night lady, figural lady, 8 1/4" h. **3,700**
Perfume bottle, scenic decoration **275**

Perfume Bottle with Spanish Lady

**Perfume bottle w/figural flower & leaf
stopper,** upright rectangular bottle
w/short cylindrical neck, base w/an iridescent blue ground decorated w/a
Spanish lady wearing a brightly color se-
rape, 6 1/2" h. (ILLUS.) **1,355**
Place card holders, figural flower bud, set
of 5 .... **130**
Plate, 6" d., butterfly decoration w/irides-
cent finish **42**

Plate with Geisha & Tree Decoration

Plate, 8 1/2" d., white ground painted
around one side w/a back view of a Japanese geisha standing beside a tall flow-
ering prunus tree (ILLUS.) **125**
Powder puff box, cov., figural clam shell
w/an Art Deco decoration **425**
Powder puff box, cov., figural lady **710**

Powder Puff Box with Lady Handle

Powder puff box, cov., round flattened cover centered by a half-lady figural handle, rounded base w/three black scroll feet, decorated in lavender, peach & black, 3 3/4" d., 4 1/4" h. (ILLUS.) **750**

Punch bowl, Art Deco decoration, 16" d., 9" h. **1,500**

Punch snack set, decorated w/an Art Deco lady & exotic bird, the set **270**

Salt & pepper shakers, bulbous bases, decorated w/ladies, pr. **220**

Figural Salt & Pepper Shakers

Salt & pepper shakers, stylized figurals w/domed caps, overall golden iridescent finish, 3 1/2" h., pr. (ILLUS.) **95**

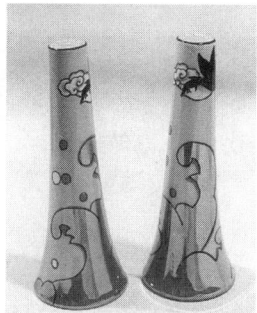

Art Deco Tall Salt & Pepper Shakers

Salt & pepper shakers, tall tapering slender cylindrical form, stylized Art Deco design of iridescent purple waves & caramel sky w/a flying bluebird & white clouds, 6" h., pr. (ILLUS.) **75**

Noritake Shaving Mug with Landscape

Shaving mug, cylindrical w/flared base & rim, h.p. waterside landscape w/cottage in background, decorated tan ring handle, 3 3/4" h. (ILLUS.) **90**

Spooner, scenic decoration **55**

Talcum powder shaker, figural lady **275**

Cup & Saucer with Romantic Scene

Tea cup & saucer, pedestal-base, wide cup decorated on the exterior w/a romantic landscape w/a Victorian lady seated in a garden, in dark shades of green, orange, yellow, blue, white & black, black handle, matching saucer, saucer 5" d., cup 2 1/4" h. (ILLUS.) **350**

Tea set, floral decoration, some wear, 21 pcs. **190**

Tea set, jeweled decoration, 23 pcs. **5,200**

Tea set, child's, 20 pieces including tray, the set **475**

Tea strainer & underplate, floral decoration, 2 pcs. **120**

Vase, 8 1/2" h., decorated w/a nude lady **1,100**

Vase, Art Deco birds & water scene **275**

Vase, decorated w/figure of a masked 1920s vamp lady **1,400**

Wall pocket, decorated w/a lady **810**

Wall pocket, scenic decoration **110**

North Dakota School of Mines

All pottery produced at the University of North Dakota School of Mines was made from North Dakota clay. In 1910, the University hired Margaret Kelly Cable to teach pottery making and she remained at the school until her retirement. Julia Mattson and Margaret Pachl were other instructors between 1923 and 1970. Designs and glazes varied through the years ranging from the Art Nouveau to modern styles. Pieces were marked "University of North Dakota - Grand Forks, N.D. - Made at School of Mines, N.D." within a circle and also signed by the students until 1963. Since that time, the pieces bear only the students' signatures. Items signed "Huck" are by the artist Flora Huckfield and were made between 1923 and 1949.

Small North Dakota Bowl

Bowl, 4 1/2" d., 2" h., low, flat-bottomed cylindrical form, incised continuous scrolling band, green matte glaze, signed (ILLUS.) **201**

Bowl-vase, squatty bulbous body w/a narrow shoulder to a molded rim, carved band decoration of buffalo standing head to head & separated by three wide vertical bands, glossy medium blue carved to rich creamy white, stamped circular mark & incised "JM - 466," 4 1/2" d., 3 3/4" h. (ILLUS. front right, below) **1,913**

Bowl-vase, squatty bulbous body w/short incurved neck & flat mouth, Bentonite clay w/a dark reddish color decorated in the Native American style w/a pattern of birds, stamped circular mark & incised "Armstrong - 1948," 4 3/4" d., 4 1/4" h. (ILLUS. back left, below) **1,013**

Bowl-vase, round straight tapering sides w/a narrow shoulder & molded rim, decorated w/band of carved birds under a matte chartreuse glaze, ink stamp mark & incised "M. Cable - Meadowlark - 155," 5 1/2" d., 3 1/4" h. (ILLUS. front left, below) **675**

Bowl-vase, wide bulbous body, the shoulder tapering to a short cylindrical neck w/flat mouth, embossed w/a band of oxen & covered wagons under a matte brown glaze, stamped circular mark & incised "MC - 186," 7 1/4" d., 6 1/2" h. (ILLUS. far right, below) **1,463**

North Dakota Wheat Bowl-vase

Bowl-vase, squatty bulbous form w/the shoulder tapering up to a flat mouth, carved around the middle w/a wide band showing shocks of wheat, in shades of dark & light brown, by Flora Huckfield, ink stamped "Hoffman - Huck - 1655 - No. Dakota Wheat," 7" d., 4 3/4" h. (ILLUS.).... **1,350**

North Dakota Round Box

Box, cov., low cylindrical form w/low domed fitted cover, the cover embossed w/the head of a Native American chief wearing a headdress, umber ground w/a mocha matte glaze on the cover, by Margaret Cable, stamped mark, incised "M. Cable - 156," 5" d., 2" h. (ILLUS.) **690**

Charger, decorated w/a large stylized five-petal blossom in yellow, white, deep red, blue & black cuerda seca, by Margaret

North Dakota Bowl-vases & Vase

Cable, 1949, ink stamped "M. Cable - 1949 - June Marks," 9 1/2" d. **534**

Vase, 3 1/2" h., 5" d., wide conical form tapering to a small molded mouth, incised w/an overall pointed geometric design, matte green glaze, by M.J. Arnegard, 1932, ink stamped "M.J. Arnegard - 42132" **788**

Vase, 3 3/4" h., 3 1/4" d., miniature, simple ovoid form tapering to a closed rim, incised around the sides w/large upright stylized tulip-like flowers on leafy stems, celadon green semi-matte glaze, ink stamped "53H" **563**

Vase, 3 3/4" h., 4 3/4" d., wide squatty bulbous form tapering to a wide rolled rim, incised around the upper half w/a band of stylized blossoms & leaves, matte green mirocrystalline glaze, by Flora Huckfield, ink stamped "E. Ericson - Huck - 106" **506**

Vase, 4" h., 5 1/2" d., wide flat bottomed ovoid form w/a wide rounded shoulder centered by a short tapering wide mouth, the shoulder decorated w/a wide band of pink prairie roses & green leaves on a cream ground, pink background, by Flora Huckfield, ink stamped "Bridgeman - Huck - 4248" **788**

Vase, 4 3/4" h., 6 1/2" d., wide squatty form w/the flaring lower body below a wide tapering shoulder centered by a short flat mouth, the shoulder carved w/a wide band of stylized flowers, matte caramel glaze, by C.A. Sorbo, ink stamped "C.A. Sorbo - 196" **506**

Vase, 5" h., 4 3/4" d., wide conical body tapering to molded rim, band around & below rim and at base in shades of blue, the center cream ground decorated w/a blue & green scene of a Viking ship sailing on waves & flying birds, stamped circular mark & incised "J. Mattson - 149A - Viking Ship" (ILLUS. w/bowl-vases, bottom, previous page) **1,688**

Vase, 5 1/2" h., simple gently swelled cylindrical form w/a shoulder tapering slightly to a short flaring neck, overall shaded brown & green matte glaze, stamp mark **253**

Vase, 5 3/4" h., 2 3/4" d., gently swelled cylindrical form tapering to a ringed short neck, incised w/a design of a stylized cowboy w/his lariat spelling out "Why not Minot" around the shoulder, light periwinkle blue glaze, by Julia Mattson, ink stamped "JM - 175" **422**

Vase, 9" h., tapering cylindrical body w/a rounded shoulder centering a short slightly flared neck, overall brownish green matte glaze, stamp mark & signed & numbered by J. Mattson (minor flake on bottom rim) **385**

Ohr (George) Pottery

George Ohr, the eccentric potter of Biloxi, Mississippi, worked from about 1883 to 1906. Some think him to be one of the most expert throwers the craft will ever see. The majority of his works were hand-thrown, exceedingly thin-walled items, some of which have a crushed or folded appearance. He considered himself the foremost potter in the world and declined to sell much of his production, instead accumulating a great horde to leave as a legacy to his children. In 1972 this collection was purchased for resale by an antiques dealer.

Ohr Matte Glazed Small Bowl

Bowl, 4 3/4" d., 2 1/2" h., footed squatty bulbous form w/a wide rolled & inwardly folded labial rim w/two pulled-out spouts on the rim, rare green, brown & gunmetal dead-matte glaze, stamped "G.E. Ohr - Biloxi, Miss." (ILLUS.) **$3,335**

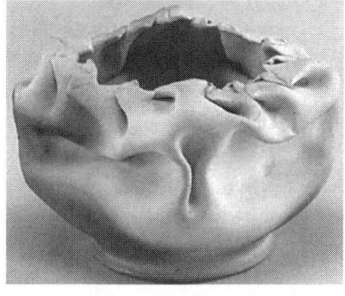

Ohr Bisque Clay Bowl-vase

Bowl-vase, round foot below the compressed four-sided deeply indented & crumpled form w/an incurved pinched & twisted rim, oxidized beige bisque clay, minor kiln kiss, script signature, 5 3/4" w., 3 3/4" h. (ILLUS.) **3,738**

Cup, footed gently flaring rounded form w/dimpled sides & a crenelated rim, hand-built rounded loop handle, exterior w/a mottled mahogany glaze, interior in gunmetal, signed "Geo. E. Ohr - Biloxi Miss.," **1,463**

Unusual George Ohr Cup

Cup, small footring below a large nearly spherical body w/wide flat mouth, looped C-scroll handle, fine dripping gunmetal over mottled & speckled glossy green glaze, stamped mark, 6 3/4" d., 4 1/2" h. (ILLUS.)... **4,313**

Inkstand, a rectangular base w/serpentine front mounted w/a large mule head w/long pointed ears beside a low squatty bowl w/incurved sides, a small tree stump on the other side of the bowl, overall mottled green, brown & gunmetal glaze, stamped "G.E. Ohr - Biloxi," 4 3/4 x 7 1/4", 4" h. (touch-up to both ear tips) **4,500**

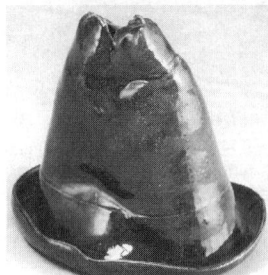

George Ohr Pottery Hat

Model of a hat, tall tapering crown ripped at the top, crumpled sides & upturned brim, red, green & blue glossy glaze, restoration to small rim chip, marked "G.E. Ohr - Biloxi," 4 1/2" l., 4" h. (ILLUS.) **4,313**

Mug, Joe Jefferson-type, double-gourd form w/long pointed strap handle down the side, incised w/"Here's your good health...," overall speckled & mottled dark bluish green glaze, script signature & dated 1896, 5 3/4" d., 6 1/2" h. **2,363**

Ohr Pinch-sided Pitcher

Pitcher, 2 1/2" h., 5" w., four pinched-in sides forming a diamond-shaped top opening, round foot, pointed angled loop handle, light mauve glaze on exterior, chartreuse green interior glaze, signed "Geo. E. Ohr - Biloxi, Miss.," minute rim nick (ILLUS.)... **2,250**

Pitcher, 3" h., 5 1/2" d., footed squatty bulbous body w/a closed rim & small pinched upright rim spout, applied D-form handle, amber, green & gunmetal speckled glaze, signed "G.E. Ohr - Biloxi - Miss." **731**

Pitcher, 3" h., 6" l., footed oblong boat-shape w/widely rolled rim w/pinched spout, ear-shaped loop handle, umber

glaze speckled w/gunmetal, stamped "G.E. Ohr - Biloxi, Miss." **2,185**

Rare George Ohr Teapot

Teapot, cov., footed w/a widely flaring flat-sided lower body below the angled shoulder band & domed top compressed down in the center w/a small cover, snake spout, C-scroll handle, cobalt blue glossy glaze, stamped "G.E. Ohr - Biloxi, Miss.," normal abrasion around rim, small nick on tip of spout, 8 3/4" l., 4" h. (ILLUS.) **11,250**

Ohr Vase with Volcanic Glaze

Vase, 4" h., 3 3/4" d., wide baluster-form w/flattened wide rim, fine cadmium yellow, lavender, green & pink volcanic glaze, stamped "G.E. Ohr - Biloxi, Miss." (ILLUS.)... **3,038**

Vase, 4 1/2" h., 2 1/2" d., footed bulbous spherical lower body tapering to a tall upright twisted, folded & pinched neck, dark speckled olive green glaze, neck in gunmetal glaze, marked "G.E. Ohr - Biloxi, Miss." **2,588**

Vase, 4 1/2" h., 4 1/2" w., a footed wide swelled form w/a deeply folded rim & a collapsed side, overall speckled amber & gunmetal glaze, signed "G.E. OHR - Biloxi, Miss." (ILLUS. second from right, top, next page)... **6,188**

Rare George Ohr Vase

Four George Ohr Vases

Vase, 4 1/2" h., 4 1/2" w., round foot below the squatty bulbous four-sided body w/a deep in-body twist below the pinched, twisted & crumpled ragged rim, glossy indigo glaze w/red, amber & gunmetal, signed "G.E. Ohr - Biloxi, Miss." (ILLUS.).. **16,100**

Vase, 4 1/2" h., 5 1/4" d., footed squatty bulbous body w/large dimples around the middle, tapering to a short, wide cylindrical neck, fine mottled brown & gunmetal glossy glaze, stamped "G.E. Ohr - Biloxi".. **3,150**

Vase, 4 3/4" h., 4 1/4" d., footed cylindrical two-tiered body w/the wide upper tier impressed w/large swirled dimples below the wide short cylindrical neck, overall speckled amber glaze, signed "G.E. Ohr - Biloxi".. **3,656**

Vase, 7" h., 4" d., baluster-form body w/a medial raised band & a deep in-body twist at the neck below the closed rim, unusual green glaze around the lower body w/a drippy red & teal leathery matte glaze on the upper half, script signature (ILLUS. far right with other vases, above).. **8,438**

George Ohr Spotted Vase

Vase, 5" h., 5 1/4" d., bulbous ovoid form w/wide, short cylindrical neck, one side pinched-in, the other side dimpled, large sponged maroon dots, spattered green & red glazes under a sheer semi-matte glaze, clay body showing through, restoration to rim hairline, signed (ILLUS.)......... **8,050**

Vase, 6 1/4" h., 5" d., footed ovoid pillow-style body w/an upright crimped rim folded down across the center, rare pink glaze w/a sponged-on green & gunmetal band, stamped "G.E. OHR - Biloxi, Miss.," small kiln kiss on body, minor glaze nick & a few flakes inside rim (ILLUS. far left with other vases, above) **19,125**

George Ohr Vase with Applied Snake

Vase, 7 1/4" h., 3 3/4" d., flaring foot supporting a tall tapering ovoid body below a cupped neck w/a dimpled band below a plain slightly flared rim band, an applied snake looping around the lower neck & down the body, cobalt blue, amber & raspberry sponged glaze, stamped mark, restoration to base chip, some firing lines on snake, few minute rim nicks (ILLUS.) **10,688**

Vase, 9 1/2" h., 5" d., footed bulbous spherical lower body below a tall neck w/a band of dimples at the bottom below tall flutes to the crimped rim, mirrored cobalt blue & gunmetal glaze, restored rim chip, typical abrasion line in body, script signature & "M" (ILLUS. second from left with other vases, above) **9,563**

Rare George Ohr Whiskey Jug

Whiskey jug, flat-bottomed wide flaring cylindrical lower body below an angled twisted & pinched shoulder centered by a domed upper body w/a short molded spout, an S-scroll snake-like handle from side of neck to shoulder, mottled green & gunmetal lustered glaze, signed, restoration to handle, two minute flecks inside rim, 6" d., 6 1/2" h. (ILLUS.) **4,888**

Overbeck

The four Overbeck sisters, Margaret, Hannah B., Elizabeth G. and Mary F., established their pottery in their old family home in Cambridge City, Indiana in 1911. Different areas of the house and yard were used for the varied production needs.

Their early production consisted mainly of artware before 1937 with most pieces being hand-thrown or hand-built in such forms as vases, bowls, candlesticks, flower frogs, tea sets and tiles. Pieces during this era were decorated generally either with glaze inlay or carving, and several colors of subtle matte glazes were used first with brighter glazes added later.

After the death of Elizabeth G. in 1937 Mary F. became the driving force behind the pottery. The output became less varied, until mainly small molded figures of various sorts of humans, some humorous or grotesque, and animals and birds were the main products. Work was carried on alone by Mary F. until her death in 1955.

Marked pieces of Overbeck usually carry the "OBK" cipher and early wares may carry the initial or initials of the sister(s) who produced it.

Bowl, 5 7/8" d., 2 3/4" h., deep half-round form w/flat rim, red clay w/a glossy glazed interior in rust & maize, matte green drip glazed exterior w/whitish drips from rim, signed "Overbeck - 5 - 3," early 20th c. **$230**

Chalice, round stepped foot & short stem supporting a wide & deep thick rounded bowl, decorated w/a wide band of incised stylized camels & mountains in yellow & gunmetal on a raspberry ground, incised "OBK - E - F.," 5 1/4" d., 6" h. (tight rim crack) **1,688**

Figurines, various comical members of a band, each w/a different musical instrument, decorated in yellow, pink, green & white glazes, incised "OBK," 4 1/2" h., set of 7 (few small chips)............................ **2,363**

Tea set: cov. teapot, cov. sugar bowl, creamer, round trivet & four cups & saucers; all w/simple rounded forms, each decorated w/a panel of stylized white lily-of-the-valley in cuerda seca on a celadon matte ground, marked "OBK - E - H.," teapot 9 1/2" l., 5" h., the set (minor rim nick on creamer, small stilt pull chips on cups)...... **2,475**

Tumblers, cylindrical w/rounded bottom rim, embossed around the upper body w/a band of stylized green crickets on a beige ground, stamped "OBK - E - F.," 3" d., 3 3/4" h., set of 4 .... **1,463**

Vase, 5 3/8" h., tapering cylindrical body, green ground w/three panels decorated w/deeply carved & painted butterflies in green against a chocolate brown ground, by Elizabeth & Hannah Overbeck, marked w/Overbeck logo & initials "E" & "H," together w/copy of "The Chronicle of the Overbeck Pottery" (dark line at rim, not visible on outside) **1,210**

Very Fine Carved Overbeck Vase

Vase, 7 3/8" h., a short cylindrical foot supporting a wide cylindrical body w/a stepped shoulder & short rounded neck, deeply carved & painted w/five sets of stylized lovebirds in rose red & bluish green against an elaborately carved background in red, blue & green, turquoise blue ground, semigloss glaze, Overbeck logo & initials of Elizabeth & Mary Frances (ILLUS.) **8,800**

Owens

Owens pottery was the product of the J.B. Owens Pottery Company, which operated in Ohio from 1890 to 1929. In 1891 it located in Zanesville and produced art pottery from 1896, introducing "Utopian" wares as its first art pottery. The company switched to tile after 1907. Efforts to rebuild after the factory burned in 1928 failed and the company closed in 1929.

Owens Pottery Mark

Jardiniere, footed cylindrical body w/scalloped rim, majolica finish w/embossed scrolled designs in blue, green & white, marked w/raised J.B. Owens shield mark, 8 5/8" h. (minor abrasions)................ **$220**

Jug, Utopian line, ovoid body decorated w/orange carnation by Edith Bell, marked "Utopian Owens 967 AE" w/artist's initials in slip below handle, 5 1/2" h. **248**

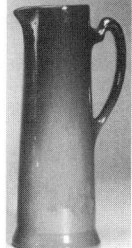

Tall Owens Decorated Pitcher

Pitcher, 12 1/4" h., tankard-form, flaring base below the tall slightly tapering cylindrical body w/a rim spout, arched long handle down the side, underglaze slip decoration of three tulips in yellow, rust & green on a shaded gold to brown ground, impressed mark, minor scratches, early 20th c. (ILLUS.).. **345**

Owens Nursery Rhyme Tile

Tile, square, color scene of "Little Bo Peep" w/rhyme in black & white in upper corner, in wide flat oak frame, minor edge roughness, 12" sq. (ILLUS.).................................. **2,645**

Vase, 4 5/8" h., Metal Deposit line, cylindrical body, flaring slightly at base w/flat flared rim, loop handles, electroplated copper w/embossed repeating geometric patterns, impressed "Owens 2" **440**

Owens Art Vellum Line Vase

Vase, 6" h., Art Vellum line, footed, bulbous shouldered body tapering to flaring rim, h.p. horse head in tan shades on shaded brown matte ground, marked "Owens," shape No. 1114 (ILLUS.) **2,500**

Owens Lotus Line Grey Vase

Vase, 6" h., Lotus line, simple wide ovoid shape tapering slightly to a wide molded rim, a wide shoulder band embossed w/small purple berries & grey leaves on a dark grey ground, a shaded grey to white background, impressed mark, some crazing (ILLUS.).. **287**

Vase, 6 1/2" h., footed spherical form w/incurved flat rim, shaded grey decorated near the rim w/three swimming fish, impressed "L" (minor glaze inconsistencies & discoloration) **280**

Vase, 10 3/4" h., 5 3/4" d., tall ovoid form w/three rings molded around the base, decorated overall in sgraffito w/upright stylized iris-like flowers in orange & blue on a dark brown ground, by Henri Deux, pea-sized burst bubble on shoulder, unmarked **731**

Vase, 11" h., tall ovoid form tapering to a flat mouth, a black ground w/incised tall iris blossoms on leafy stems in shades of dark brown & blue outlined in cream, unsigned... **1,380**

Paul Revere Pottery

This pottery was established in Boston, Massachusetts, in 1906, by a group of philanthropists seeking to establish better conditions for underprivileged young girls of the area. Edith Brown served as supervisor of the small "Saturday Evening Girls Club" pottery operation which was moved, in 1912, to a house close to the Old North Church where Paul Revere's signal lanterns had been placed. The wares were mostly hand decorated in mineral colors and both sgraffito and molded decorations were employed. Although it became popular, it was never a profitable operation and always depended on financial contributions to operate. After the death of Edith Brown in 1932, the pottery foundered and finally closed in 1942.

Bowl, 5 1/4" d., 2" h., wide flat bottom w/low rounded incurved sides, decorated w/a continuous landscape band w/clusters of trees done in cuerda seca, green, grey & blue, 1915, ink mark "4-15 - S.E.G. - A.G." **$935**

Paul Revere/S.E.G. Large Bowl

Bowl, 7 1/4" d., 3 1/4" h., footed deep rounded & gently flaring sides w/rolled rim, decorated in cuerda seca w/an upper wide band w/white trefoil blossoms on a buff & light blue band against the dark blue background, S.E.G. mark (ILLUS.) **1,610**

Bowl, 8 1/4" d., wide flat bottom & low rounded incurved sides, decorated w/a stylized landscape w/clumps of trees in cuerda seca, in green, blue & grey, dark blue interior, ink mark "SEG - 7-20 - bvc" .. **1,650**

Creamer, short wide gently flaring cylindrical form w/a pointed rim spout & D-form handle, plain light blue rim band above alternating dark & light blue stripes, impressed mark, 2 1/4" h................................... **121**

Inkwell, cov., square block-form, the cover decorated w/green trees in a dark blue landscape, base w/dark blue band over lighter blue bottom, inked S.E.G. mark & Bowl Shop paper label, 2 1/2 x 2 3/4", 2" h. **935**

Pitcher, 4 1/2" h., slightly flaring cylindrical body w/a small pinched rim spout & loop handle, decorated on the front under the spout w/an oval reserve showing a reclining white rabbit in green grass w/blue sky beyond, black banding on a light blue background, marked "Jane," impressed mark.. **468**

Plate, 9 3/4" d., dinner, dark blue ground w/a wide white border band decorated in cuerda seca w/black wording "Give Us This Day Our Daily Bread," 1921, ink stamp "S.E.G. 11-21 FL.," bruise to rim (ILLUS. far right, below, top photo) **619**

Plates, 7 1/2" d., round w/wide flanged rim, overall light blue glaze, impressed mark, set of 3 .... **110**

Tea set: cov. teapot, cov. sugar & creamer; each of simple squatty, rounded form, overall greyish blue glaze, one ink-signed, two pieces stamped, 1927, minute glaze burst on rim of creamer, the set (ILLUS, below, bottom photo.)................. **288**

Vase, 4 1/2"h., 2 1/4" d., swelled & gently tapering cylindrical form w/flared rim, decorated in cuerda seca around the rim w/a band of Greek key design in brown & blue on a pale green ground, ink mark "S.E.G. - E.G. - 4-1-?"...................................... **825**

Paul Revere Plate and Vases

Paul Revere Pottery Tea Set

Vase, 4 1/2" h., 3 3/4" d., simple ovoid form w/a closed rim, dark bluish grey ground decorated around the top w/a wide cuerda seca band w/stylized white & blue lotus blossoms, 1914, ink mark "SEG - am - 11-14" (ILLUS. second from right with plate, previous page, top photo) **1,238**

Vase, 5 1/4" h., 4 1/2" d., wide ovoid body w/a closed rim, a continuous abstract landscape of green trees against a frothy white sky & dark blue & grey ground, glossy glaze, 1922, signed "3-22 - S.E.G. - E.G." **1,540**

Vase, 5 3/4" h., 4 1/2" d., simple ovoid body w/a closed rim, matte light green ground decorated around the shoulder w/a wide band of stylized yellow tulips & greenish leaves on white w/black border bands, Paul Revere stamp, illegible date (ILLUS. second from left with plate, previous page, top photo).. **1,238**

Vase, 6 1/2" h., 5" d., ovoid body tapering to a thick, rolled rim, dark blue ground decorated around the shoulder w/a wide cuerda seca band w/yellow stylized tulips & dark blue leaves on a light blue ground, stamped mark (ILLUS. far left with plate, previous page, top photo)............................ **1,463**

Vase, 7" h., wide tapering ovoid body w/a closed rim, mottled multi-toned turquoise blue glaze, ink mark, 1927 .... **231**

Peters & Reed

In 1897 John D. Peters and Adam Reed formed a partnership to produce flowerpots in Zanesville, Ohio. Formally incorporated as Peters and Reed in 1901, this type of production was the mainstay until after 1907 when they gradually expanded into the art pottery field. Frank Ferrell, a former designer at the Weller Pottery, developed the "Moss Aztec" line while associated with Peters and Reed and other art lines followed. Though unmarked, attribution is not difficult once familiar with the various lines. In 1921, Peters and Reed became Zane Pottery which continued in production until 1941.

Moss Aztec Jardiniere

Jardiniere, Moss Aztec line, wide tapering ovoid form w/a wide flat mouth above a molded band of poppy blossoms & four wide buttress panels down the sides, minor chips & nicks, signed, 13" d., 9 3/4" h. (ILLUS.) **$460**

Jardiniere, slightly tapering cylindrical form, molded around the sides w/high-relief rounded blossoms above a beaded base band, matte green glaze w/clay showing through, 5 1/2" d., 4" h. (ILLUS., top right column).. **115**

Peters & Reed Cylindrical Jardiniere

Vase, 12" h., Landsun line, tall slender cylindrical body w/a flared base, streaky pale green, brown & blue banded glaze, ca. 1922, light crazing **115**

Vase, 12" h., Shadow Ware, ovoid body tapering to small molded rim, green & black flambé glossy glaze, stamped "PRP" (few shallow scratches to surface) **303**

Large Peters & Reed Floor Vase

Vase, 18" h., floor-type, tall slightly waisted cylindrical form w/a flaring rim, molded around the top w/large stylized blossoms on slender stems slightly spiraling down the sides, dark green matte glaze w/clay showing through, unsigned (ILLUS.).............. **546**

Pewabic

Mary Chase Perry (Stratton) and Horace J. Caulkins were partners in this Detroit, Michigan pottery. Established in 1903, Pewabic Pottery evolved from their Revelation Pottery, "Pewabic" meaning "clay with copper color" in the language of Michigan's Chippewa Indians. Caulkins attended to the clay formulas and Mary Perry Stratton was artistic creator of forms & glaze formulas, eventually developing a wide range of colors for her finely textured glazes. The pottery's reputation for fine wares and architectural tiles enabled it to survive the depression years of the 1930s. After Caulkins died in 1923, Mrs. Stratton continued to be active in the pottery until her death, at age ninety-four, in 1961. Her contributions to the art pottery field are numerous.

Bowl, 6 3/4" d., 3 3/4" h., hemispherical form w/a slightly flared rim, unusual gunmetal & turquoise dripping lustered glaze, circular stamp mark **$2,025**

Pewabic Footed Bowl

Bowl, 7 1/4" d., 4" h., a small footring below the squatty wide bulbous body tapering to a widely flaring rim, flowing matte brown exterior glaze, lavender & turquoise lustered interior glaze, stamped mark & paper label, small glaze nicks on foot (ILLUS.) **805**

Bowl, 3 3/4" d., 1 3/4" h., spherical w/incurved flat rim, iridescent dove grey lustre w/turquoise interior that flows out onto rim, outlined in brick red, the shoulder decorated w/an impressed pattern of rings, impressed mark..................................... **252**

Miniature Pewabic Bowl-vase

Bowl-vase, miniature, a small footring supporting a wide squatty bulbous body w/a wide short cylindrical neck, mottled teal blue, green & gunmetal glossy glaze, circular mark, 3 3/4" d., 2 3/4" h. (ILLUS.) **460**

Pewabic Volcanic Glazed Bowl-Vase

Bowl-vase, footed wide half-round form w/a wide slightly rounded shoulder to a wide flat mouth, overall lustered volcanic cobalt blue & celadon greyish green glaze, mark covered by glaze, 9 1/4" d., 4 3/4" h. (ILLUS.)... **5,344**

Pewabic Eggplant-shaped Jar

Jar, cov., model of a large eggplant, the top & stem forming the cover, overall dark matte purple flowing glaze, unmarked, 4 1/4" d., 6 3/4" h. (ILLUS.)......................... **2,070**

Jardiniere, footed large, deep bulbous ovoid body w/a wide flat rim band, lustered cobalt blue glaze, stamped "Pewabic - Detroit," 9" d., 8" h. **2,475**

Plate, 10 3/4" d., flattened form w/wide flanged rim, painted w/a radiating design of dragonflies in blue slip on a white

Pewabic Plate and Vases

crackled ground, stamped mark, several glaze flakes & chips to footring, stamped mark (ILLUS. center, bottom previous page)... **1,100**

Miniature Vase with Test Glaze

Vase, 2" h., 2 1/2" d., miniature, test glaze, squatty bulbous body tapering to a short, wide flaring neck, dark Persian blue crackled glaze over a black-glazed lower body, circular stamp & "40B" (ILLUS.) **248**

Pewabic Miniature Vase

Vase, 2 1/4" h., 2 1/4" d., miniature, flat-bottomed ovoid form w/a closed rim, fine celadon green & lavender lustered glaze, no visible mark (ILLUS.) **385**

Vase, 2 1/2" h., 2" d., miniature, cylindrical form slightly tapered at the base, fine turquoise, green & blue lustered dripping glaze, circular stamp mark (ILLUS. third from right with plate, bottom, previous page)... **468**

Two Small Pewabic Vases

Vase, 2 1/2" h., 2" d., miniature, flat-bottomed ovoid form, the rounded shoulder centered by a short cylindrical neck w/slightly flared rim, fine celadon & oxblood lustre glaze, stamped mark (ILLUS. left).. **385**

Vase, 2 1/2" h., 2 1/4" d., miniature ovoid body tapering to a small flat mouth, dripping pink crackled glaze on a blue lustered ground, stamped "PEWABIC - DETROIT" (some deep crazing lines, minute fleck at rim).. **281**

Vase, 2 1/2" h., 2 3/4" d., miniature, simple wide ovoid form w/a closed rim, fine & thick pink, gold & blue lustered dripping glaze, circular stamp mark (ILLUS. second from left with plate, bottom, previous page)... **1,320**

Vase, 2 1/2" h., 3 1/4" d., miniature, sharply tapering cylindrical sides below a wide shoulder tapering to a wide, flat mouth, fine gold, green & ivory lustered glaze, circular stamp mark & paper label (ILLUS. second from right with plate, bottom, previous page)................................... **605**

Vase, 3 1/2" h., 2 1/4" d., miniature footed bottle-form, fine dripping turquoise & gold lustred glaze, hand-incised "PEWABIC" (stilt pull chip on base)................................... **197**

Bulbous Miniature Pewabic Vase

Vase, 3 1/2" h., 3 3/4" d., miniature, footed bulbous body w/an angled shoulder to a low rolled rim, unusual white semi-matte glaze w/a lustered umber rim, stamped mark & paper label (ILLUS.)........................... **575**

Large & Small Pewabic Vases

Vase, 3 3/4" h., 3 3/4" d., bulbous nearly spherical body w/a short cylindrical neck centered on the shoulder, fine thick & leathery cobalt blue & green lustered glaze, circular stamp mark (ILLUS. second from left)... **731**

Vase, 3 3/4" h., 3 3/4" d., miniature, simple ovoid form w/a wide shoulder tapering to a wide, flat mouth, fine dripping turquoise & purple lustered glaze, stamped circular mark.. **660**

Vase, 4 3/4" h., 3 1/2" d., simple ovoid form w/a flat mouth, fine gold & mauve lustered glaze, circular stamp mark (ILLUS. far right with plate, bottom, page 226)........... **715**

Vase, 4 3/4" h., 4" d., bulbous ovoid body w/a short cylindrical neck, fine mirrored gold glaze dripping over a glossy dark blue ground, circular stamp mark, small firing chip at base (ILLUS. far left with plate, bottom, page 226)............................. **1,210**

Vase, 4 3/4" h., 4" d., bulbous wide body w/an angled shoulder tapering to a short flaring neck, lustered celadon green & purple glaze, stamped cylindrical mark, remnant of paper label (ILLUS. right with miniature vase)... **550**

Vase, 5" h., 5" d., footed spherical ringed body tapering to a narrow mouth rim, overall orange matte glaze, circular stamp mark (restoration to small base chip) **450**

Pewabic Baluster-form Vase

Vase, 6" h., wide baluster-form body w/flaring neck, dark greenish blue glaze, impressed mark, some crazing, small firing line in base, small glaze bubbles (ILLUS.)..... **345**

Vase, 6" h., 4 1/4" d., footed wide pear-shaped body tapering to a short flared neck, lustered dripping celadon green & purple glaze, circular stamp & paper label..... **844**

Pewabic Vase with Lustered Glaze

Vase, 7 1/2" h., 4" d., simple ovoid body w/a short, flared neck, lustered copper & gold mottled glaze, stamped mark (ILLUS.) **2,530**

Vase, 7 3/4" h., 5 1/2" d., footed wide bulbous ovoid body tapering to a short flared neck w/flattened rim, fine lustered blue & turquoise mottled glaze, stamped "PEWABIC - DETROIT".. **1,350**

Vase, 8" h., 7" d., the wide squatty base w/a knobby sharply angled shoulder tapering to a wide cylindrical neck molded w/light ribbing & knobby prunts around the wide flattened rim, smooth flowing matte green glaze, unmarked (firing lines around base prunts) **2,530**

Pewabic Vase with Unusual Glaze

Vase, 8 1/4" h., 6" d., flaring & swelled cylindrical sides below a wide angled shoulder centered by a small neck w/molded rim, unusual gunmetal brown, celadon & dripping turquoise mottled glaze, circular paster mark (ILLUS.) **1,610**

Vase, 9 3/4" h., 6 1/2" d., wide baluster-form body w/a short flared neck, brilliant pulled cobalt blue & turquoise lustered glaze, stamped "Pewabic - Detroit" (ILLUS. second from right with other vases).. **5,625**

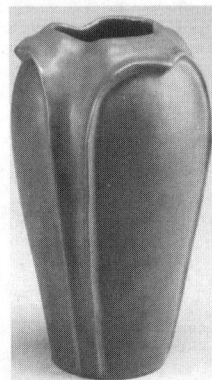

Pewabic Vase with Modeled Leaves

Vase, 10" h., 5 3/4" d., ovoid form w/handmodeled impressed arched leaves alternating w/raised wedged ribs continuing to curved shoulder, smooth matte green glaze, Pewabic stamp w/leaves, small glaze chips around base, T-lines in body (ILLUS.)... **4,600**

Vase, 10 1/2" h., 5" d., squatty bulbous base tapering to a tall ringed body w/a flared mouth, frothy, dripping celadon green & gold lustered glaze, drilled hole in bottom, stamped "PEWABIC - DETROIT" (ILLUS. far right with other vases) **2,363**

Vase, 10 1/2" h., 7" d., wide flaring cylindrical form w/horizontal band, ivory crackle glaze, incised "Pewabic - WBS - 1935"...... **1,125**

Vase, 11" h., 5 3/4" d., bulbous lobed body tapering to a tall slender cylindrical neck & flat rim, covered in a leathery cobalt matte glaze, stamped "Pewabic"................ **2,813**

Vase, 11" h., 8 1/2" d., large wide tapering cylindrical form w/a narrow angled shoulder to a wide flat mouth, embossed w/nubs around the shoulder, rare dripping matte mustard yellow glaze on a caramel ground, stamped "Pewabic" w/leaves (ILLUS. far left with other vases) **11,250**

Pisgah Forest Pottery

Walter Stephen experimented with making pottery shortly after 1900 with his parents in Tennessee. After their deaths in 1910, he eventually moved to the foot of Mt. Pisgah in North Carolina where he became a partner of C.P. Ryman. Together they built a kiln and a shop but this partnership was dissolved in 1916. During 1920 Stephen again began to experiment with pottery and by 1926 had his own pottery and equipment. Pieces are usually marked and may also be signed "W. Stephen" and dated. Walter Stephen died in 1961 but work at the pottery still continues, although on a part-time basis.

Bowl-vase, wide spherical body w/the wide round shoulder centered by a short cylindrical neck, amber glaze w/white & blue crystals, raised Stephen mark, dated 1947, 5 3/4" d., 5" h. **$385**

Bowl-vase, wide spherical form, the rounded shoulder centered by a short wide neck, amber flambé glaze w/celadon crystals, raised Stephen mark & illegible date, 4 1/2" d., 3 3/4" h. **303**

Teapot, cov., spherical form w/inset cover w/button finial, short cylindrical spout & D-form shoulder handle, fine Chinese blue glaze w/red, green & blue highlights, raised mark, 8" w. **231**

Vase, 5" h., 4 3/4" d., wide squatty bulbous lower body tapering to a cylindrical neck w/rolled rim, white & amber glaze w/blue crystals, raised potter mark, dated 1940 ...... **358**

Pisgah Forest Vases

Vase, 6 1/2" h., 4" d., simple baluster-form w/a short, wide flaring neck, fine amber glaze w/tightly packed white & dark blue crystals, raised potter mark, dated 1940 (ILLUS. left) **660**

Vase, 6 1/2" h., 4 1/2" d., tall deeply corseted form w/a wide flaring mouth, amber glaze w/grey crystals, raised potter mark & illegible date.. **413**

Pisgah Forest Vase with Blue Crystals

Vase, 7" h., 4" d., ovoid body tapering to a cylindrical neck, brown & amber flambé glaze w/clusters of large blue crystals, grinding chip at base, embossed mark (ILLUS.).. **605**

Vase, 7 1/2" h., 4 3/4" d., baluster-form tapering to a short, wide rolled neck, amber flambé glaze w/a few blue crystals, raised Pisgah Forest mark & illegible date.. **523**

Vase, 7 3/4" h., 4 3/4" d., wide baluster-form body tapering to a short, wide flaring neck, amber glaze w/white & blue large crystals around the lower half, raised Stephen mark, dated 1949 (ILLUS. right with two other vases) **770**

Vase, 8" h., 5 1/4" d., wide bottle-form w/bulbous tapering body below a tall waisted cylindrical neck, overall white glaze w/white crystals, raised potter mark & dated 1941 (ILLUS. center with two other vases)... **715**

Vase, 12 1/4" h., 8" d., wide bulbous ovoid base centered by a tall cylindrical neck, shaded ivory glaze w/blue & pearl scattered crystals, raised potter's mark & "Stephen - 1946" (firing lines around neck base)... **788**

Purinton

The Purinton Pottery Company was founded in Shippenville, Pennsylvania in 1941 by Bernard S. Purinton. Earlier, beginning in 1936, Mr. Purinton started a smaller pottery operation in Wellsville, Ohio, but by 1941 he wished to expand and chose the site near Shippenville where a large, new plant was constructed.

Most of Purinton's products were cast and then hand-painted with a variety of colorful patterns by local people trained at the factory. One of their best known and most popular designs was Peasant Ware, originally introduced at the Wellsville plant in the 1930s. Until the plant was finally closed in 1959, the company continued to produce a colorful, hand-decorated range of tablewares, kitchenwares, vases and novelty items.

Basket planter, Palm Tree, no cutout, 6 1/4" h. **$299**
Beer mug, Palm Tree, purple intaglio, 16 oz., 4 3/4" h. **380**
Butter dish, tab handle, 6 1/2" l. **80**
Candy dish, w/loop handle **65**
Carafe, Cactus Flower, two-handled, 7 1/2" h. **264**
Children's cereal bowl, w/puppy, 5 1/4" d. **179**
Chop plate, Crescent, footed, 12" d. **249**
Chop plate, Fruits Blessing, signed by Dorothy Purinton, footed, some for meat, 12" d. (one chip)...................................... **501**
Coffee carafe, Autumn Leaves........................... **39**
Coffee mug, 12 oz... **80**
Coffee server, TST shaped, w/lid, 10 1/2" **555**
Coffeepot, cov., eight-cup **75**
Cookie jar, rooster... **335**
Diamond grill platter, oblong, 12" l. **46**
Dinner plate, signed by Dorothy Purinton, w/cabin & trees, 9 3/4" d. **1,031**
Dutch jug, w/ice lip, Cactus, 2 pint **362**
Dutch jug, w/ice lip, Red Ribbon Flower, 2 pint **1,226**
Honey jug, Holly, loop handle, 6 1/4" h. **480**
Honey jug, Palm Tree, loop handle, 6 1/4" h. **130**
Honey jug, Pear, loop handle, 6 1/4" h. **155**
Jam/jelly, tab handle **54**
Oil & vinegar cruet set, tall, 9 1/2" h. **125**
Pig bank, blue.. **19**
Planter, Napco, Yellow Intaglio, rectangular, 6" l. **23**
Rebecca jug, Starflower, 7 1/2" h. **255**
Roll tray, oblong.. **50**
Rum jug planter, 6 1/2" h................................... **61**
Salt & pepper set, Old Salt & wife.................... **85**
Salt & pepper set, shake-n-pour-type, bulbous, 4 1/2" h. **71**
Spaghetti bowl, 14 1/5" d. **205**
Sprinkler, w/red tulips, 5 1/2" h. **114**
Sugar/creamer set, Cactus Flower (sugar some damage)...................................... **238**
Tumblers, 12 oz.. **20**
Winged grease jar **96**

Brown Intaglio
Beanpot, individual.. **46**
Beverage pitcher, 42 oz., 6 1/4" h. **59**
Candleholder, round, 5" d., 2 1/2" h.................. **90**
Candy dish, w/loop handle................................ **37**
Canister set, apartment size............................. **128**
Coffeepot, cov., 8 cup.. **26**
Cookie jar, cov., wide oval, 9 1/2"...................... **50**
Decanter **30**
Dutch jug, w/ice lip, 5 pint, ... **60**
Range grease jar, cov., oval.............................. **47**
Range grease & salt & pepper set **60**
Spaghetti bowl, 14 1/2" d. **72**
Tumbler, 12 oz... **38**

Chartreuse
Cup & saucer **14**
Range salt & pepper shakers, 4" h. **128**
Rum jug, loop handle, cut-outs **136**

Fruit
Cookie jar, cov., wide oval, 9 1/2" **51**
Flour canister, cov., round, wood lid, 8" h. **89**
Oil & vinegar set, conical shaped **77**
Sugar canister, cov., found, wood lid, 8" h. **50**
Tea 'n' toast plate, Wellsville Pear, 8 1/2" d. **18**

Heather
Kent jug, bulbous body, 4 1/2" h........................ **45**
Pickle dish, 6" l. **20**

Maywood
Casserole, cov., 9" l... **30**
Cereal bowl, 5 1/2" d. **13**
Jam/jelly, tab handle.. **53**
Wallpocket, 3 1/2" h. (small hairline)................. **105**

Ming Tree
Cereal bowl, 5 1/4" d. **43**
Chop plate, footed, 12" d. **250**
Fruit bowl, footed, 12" d.................................... **230**

Mountain Rose
Kent jug **32**
Meat platter, oblong, 12" **179**
Sugar/creamer set, 4-petal **74**

Normandy
Candy dish, w/loop handle **52**
Casserole, cov., 9" l... **36**
Fruit bowl, footed, 12" d..................................... **41**
Mini jug salt & pepper set, 2 1/5" h. **18**
Winged vase, bulbous, 6" h. **25**

Other Intaglios
Chop plate, turquoise, footed, 12" d. **125**
Dinner plate, turquoise, 9 3/4" d....................... **24**
Salt & pepper set, turquoise, stacking-type, 2 1/4" h. **43**

Peasant Garden
Grill platter, oblong, 12" l. **257**
Roll tray, oblong **61**
Teapot, cov., 6 cup, domed lid **339**

Pennsylvania Dutch
Chop plate, footed, 12" d. **130**
Dutch jug, 5 pint, ice lip.................................... **511**
Meat platter, oblong, 12"................................... **46**
Mini jug salt & pepper set **108**
Sandwich tray, w/metal handle, 12" d. **180**

Petals
Juice mug, 6 oz.. **53**
Kent jug, bulbous, 4 1/2" h. **164**

Provincial Fruit
Desert bowl, 4" d.. **24**
Meat platter, oblong, 12".................................... **150**

Red Ivy
Mini sugar, 2" h. **31**
Range grease, cov., oval **26**
Range salt & pepper, 4" h. **27**

Saraband
Beanpot, cov., individual, 3 1/4" h. **44**

Dinner plate, 9 1/2" d. **13**
Jam/jelly, tab handle **82**
Kent jug, bulbous body, 4 1/2" h. **108**
Meat platter, oblong, 12" d. **35**
Tea 'n' toast, w/cup **19**

Seaform
Sugar/creamer set, w/tray, 5" h. **123**

Redware

*Red earthenware pottery was made in the American
colonies from the late 1600s. Bowls, crocks and all types
of utilitarian wares were turned out in great abundance
to supplement the pewter and handmade treenware. The
ready availability of the clay, the same used in making
bricks and roof tiles, accounted for the vast production.
The lead-glazed redware retained its reddish color
though a variety of colors could be obtained by adding
various metals to the glaze. Interesting effects occurred
accidentally through unsuspected impurities in the clay
or uneven temperatures in the firing kiln which sometimes resulted in streaks or mottled splotches.*

Redware pottery was seldom marked by the maker.

Bowl, 7 3/4" d., thin, deep bowl w/brown,
green & orange glaze, interior w/orange
splotches over green, incised signature
"Solomon Miller, 18?5" on bottom, 4" h.
(glaze wear, hairlines) **$3,300**
Canning jar, cylindrical body shape, short
shoulder tapers in to outward tapering
neck, incised lines on shoulder, glaze
w/dark brown splotches on neck & shoul-
der, 5 3/4" d., 8 3/4" h. (rim chips) **330**
Cookie mold, Colonial-style man w/deco-
rated coat mounted on horse & blowing
trumpet, attributed to Ephrata, Pennsyl-
vania, 6 1/8" h. (minor edge wear) **990**
Cookie mold, rectangle divided into six
panels w/designs of harp, birds, urn &
deer, 5 1/2 x 8 1/4" (minor damage) **440**
Creamer, ovoid body, flared neck, applied
handle, brown shiny glaze w/stylized floral & fern designs on body and band of
design around neck, New Geneva,
4 3/4" h. (rim flakes) **605**
Creamer, ovoid body w/flared neck, applied
handle, dark brown daubed glaze in zig-
zag design, 4 1/2" h. (rim flakes) **358**
Creamer, paneled w/high curving handle,
applied rose & two doves under spout, a
rosette on handle, attributed to Anthony
Baecher, Strasburg, Virginia, 4 3/4" h.
(pinpoint glaze flakes) **715**
Dish, shallow round form, sgraffito decora-
tion of an incised peacock holding a tulip,
yellow & green slip glaze, Pennsylvania,
early 19th c., 9" d. (glaze chips) **1,610**
Flowerpot, slightly tapering cylindrical
shape w/piecrust rim, two incised lines
below, glaze w/brown running splotches,
no saucer, 5 1/4" d., 4 3/4" h. (minor
edge damage) **138**
Grease lamp, w/saucer base, ovoid front
w/wick holder & applied strap handle,

brownish red glaze w/some roughness,
5 1/4" h. **303**
Jar, cov., conical form w/sloping shoulder &
tapering base, two handles applied at
shoulder, deep green glaze sprinkled
w/brown, incised decoration on the cover, Massachusetts or Rhode Island, late
18th - early 19th c., 9 1/2" h. (chips to
cover edge, glaze loss at rim) **25,300**
Jar, ovoid, decorated w/rows of incised lines
at the shoulder & base, a yellow & green
sponged slip decoration, New England,
early 19th c., 6 1/2" h. (edge roughness) .. **1,840**
Jar, ovoid, w/incised lines under raised lip,
two-tone glaze w/wide, brown vertical
bands, 5 1/4"d., 6 1/4" h. (worn glaze on
rim) **275**
Jar, ovoid w/raised rim, brown daubed
glaze, attributed to Pennsylvania, 4" d.,
4 3/4" h. (small glaze flakes) **193**
Jar, raised bands on the sides w/impressed
geometric & four-pointed star decoration,
running brown glaze w/flakes, Pennsyl-
vania, 8" h. **440**
Jar, slightly concave sides w/reddish glaze
w/yellow splotches, 6" d., 7 1/8" h. (rim
flakes & in-the-making imperfection) **330**
Jug, ovoid shape, applied strap handle,
dark brown brushed decoration & incised
ring detail, 6 3/4" h. (small glued chip on
rim) **385**
Loaf pan, rectangular, w/coggled edge,
decorated w/three sets of yellow wavy
lines, 9 1/2 x 12 3/4", 2" h. (firing imperfections appear as areas of greenish tan,
edge chips) **770**
Milk bowl, deep flared sides, running brown
glaze w/black specks & a pattern similar
to seaweed in mochaware, unglazed exterior, attributed to North Carolina,
9 5/8" d. (minor rim flakes) **193**
Milk pan, circular base w/sides tapering out
to top w/spout, applied handle, three
tooled bands, dark brown sponge design
resembling trees, sponge on rim & handle, 8 1/2" d., 5" h. (minor wear, two old
flakes on rim) **605**
Pie plate, coggled rim, wavy yellow & dark
brown slip lines, 6 1/2" d. (small rim
flake) **275**
Pie plate, w/coggled rim, yellow slip decora-
tion resembling a "V" w/wings or antlers,
6 1/4" d. (rim chip & glaze flake) **440**
Pie plate, w/coggled rim, yellow slip decoration resembling four double flags,
9 1/8" d. (edge damage) **385**
Pitcher, 8" h., ovoid shape w/flared foot &
rim, applied handle, coggled bands
around top, decorated w/orange & brown
spots on a green ground (edge flakes &
glaze scratches) **935**
Pitcher, 6" h., ovoid w/straight neck, no
spout, rolled rim & applied handle, red
clay w/worn glaze & yellow slip design of
leaves under sawtooth arches w/scrolls
on the neck (edge wear) **248**
Pitcher, cov., 6 1/4" h., tankard type, tri-col-
or glaze w/reddish brown ground &

brushed-on streaks in pale yellow & green, applied strap handle & original carved wooden lid w/age crack, attributed to Pennsylvania (flaking) 550

Pitcher, 7 1/4" h., cylindrical, slightly flared rim w/pinch spout, applied strap handle, yellow glaze w/graffito flower & leaves, pinkish red color to clay (hairline & handle has minor wear) 220

Pitcher, 10 1/2" h., bulbous ovoid body tapering to a short cylindrical neck w/pinched spout, applied rim handle, brown & green mottled slip glaze w/incised straight & wavy line decoration at the neck & shoulder, probably Massachusetts or New Hampshire, late 18th - early 19th c. (minor rim nicks, chips at base) 46,000

Plate, 11" d., coggled rim, yellow slip design of three straight lines across center flanked by two groups of three wavy lines on borders opposite each other, green glaze over entire front (small flakes) 385

Preserving jar, cylindrical w/rounded shoulder & wide deep curved mouth band, tooled lines at shoulder, clear glass w/black splotches, 10 5/8" h. (glaze flakes, egde roughness) 385

Vinegar jar, footed squatty bulbous body tapering sharply to a small neck, light green, tan & dark brown mottled glaze, tooled lip & ribbed handle w/thumbprint application, New England, probably Massachusetts, late 18th - early 19th c., 5" h. (minor glaze chips) 9,775

Whistle, figural bird, a large bird on a perch flanked by two smaller birds & two below on a conical-shaped base, decorated w/a brown drip glaze on a yellow ground, England, late 18th - early 19th c., 9 3/8" h. (chips) 403

Robineau (Adelaide)

Adelaide Alsop Robineau began her career as a china painter and teacher. After her marriage to Samuel Robineau in 1899 they founded the magazine Keramic Studio, which was a practical guide to china painting.

After a few years she became frustrated with just simply decorating wares produced by others and she and her husband began production of earthenware and then later, porcelain.

Between 1904 and 1916 Adelaide Robineau produced a limited number of exquisite, detailed works which garnered her several awards at major international expositions.

After World War I their pottery ceased to operate independently and Mrs. Robineau joined the staff of Syracuse University in 1920 and worked there until her retirement in 1928. She died in 1929.

The Robineau Pottery was never a major commercial operation and reportedly sold only about 600 pieces over a twenty-five year period. Many examples were eventually purchased by museums so few examples of her work are offered for sale today.

Jar, cov., footed spherical form covered in mossy green flambé, the cover complete-

ly excised w/a geometric floral design under a bronze glaze, carved "AR - 44 - 1920," 4 1/2 x 4 1/2" (underglaze lines around rim from firing, grinding bruise to edge of base, also in manufacture) **$14,625**

Robineau Rabbit Tile

Tile, square, deeply carved w/the figure of a crouching stylized rabbit w/a matte celadon glaze, carved "AR" mark, several minute edge nicks, very slight surface abrasion, 4 3/4" w. (ILLUS.) **1,238**

Vase, miniature, 2 x 2 1/2", ovoid body w/shoulder tapering to wide cylindrical neck w/closed rim, butterscotch flambé glaze, marked "AR - C - 4 - 11-111.," 1904, minor bruise to rim **2,363**

Vase, miniature, 2 x 2 1/4", ovoid body tapering to short cylindrical neck w/flat rim, green & blue matte crystalline glaze, marked "AR - C - '04 - 11-111.," 1904 .... **1,913**

Vase, 3 3/4" h., 4 1/4" d., spherical form w/molded rim, cobalt blue crystalline glaze, incisedþ"AR" **6,750**

Rockingham Wares

The Marquis of Rockingham first established an earthenware pottery in the Yorkshire district of England around 1745 and it was occupied afterwards by various potters. The well-known mottled brown Rockingham glaze was introduced about 1788 by the Brameld Brothers and became immediately popular. It was during the 1820s that the production of true porcelain began at the factory and continued to be made until the firm closed in 1842. Since that time the so-called Rockingham glaze has been used by various potters in England and the United States, including some famous wares produced in Bennington, Vermont. However, very similar glazes were also used by potteries in other areas of the United States including Ohio and Indiana and only wares specifically attributed to Bennington should use that name. The following listings will include mainly wares featuring the dark brown mottled glaze produced at various sites here and abroad.

Harvest flask, donut shape decorated w/molded fruit vines on either side w/a man holding a tankard on the neck, dark brown glaze, 8 1/2" d. (minor roughness on lip) **$506**

Inkwell, figure of girl w/hat reclining on tree stump, 5" l. 193

Model of a dog, in sitting position, w/head turned to side, on scalloped base, 11" h. (repaired edge chips on base & nose) 358

Model of a dog, in sitting position w/head turned to side, open front legs, molded detail, on oblong base, running brown glaze over yellow, 11 1/2" h. (edge chips on bottom of base) **495**

Model of a lion, reclining, amber-colored running glaze, 4 x 9 1/2", 5 3/4" h. **440**

Storage jar, cov., cylindrical w/stepped base, relief-molded Gothic arched panels & domed lid, 8" d., 9" h. (minor repair to finial) **660**

Toby jug, man in tricorner hat, high, concave base, 5 3/4" h. (glazed-over rim flake) **83**

Rookwood

Considered America's foremost art pottery, the Rook-wood Pottery Company was established in Cincinnati, Ohio in 1880, by Mrs. Maria Nichols Longworth Storer. To accurately record its development, each piece carried the Rookwood insignia, or mark, was dated, and, if individually decorated, was usually signed by the artist. The pottery remained in Cincinnati until 1959 when it was sold to Herschede Hall Clock Company and moved to Starkville, Mississippi, where it continued in operation until 1967.

A private company is now producing a limited variety of pieces using original Rookwood molds.

Bowl, 4" d., slightly tapering upright flattened sides molded w/an Arts & Crafts design, brown & maroon Matte glaze, No. 1674, 1912 .... **$275**

Bowl, 5" d., 4 1/2" h., "50th Anniversary" type, deep flaring rounded sides, the interior decorated w/a wide border band of polychrome blossoms & leaves on a mottled ivory ground, Wax Matte glaze, No. 2253D, 1930, Elizabeth N. Lincoln **422**

Bowl, 6 1/2" d., wide low form w/incurved sides molded w/stylized florals below the closed wide rim, dark blue Matte glaze, No. 1709, 1912 .... **209**

Bowl-vase, wide spherical body w/a wide flat rim, decorated around the rim w/a narrow band of red cherry blossoms on black branches on an ivory ground, the lower body in bluish grey shaded to rose, Vellum glaze, No. 1375, 1920, E.T. Hurley, 9" d., 6 1/4" h. **1,913**

Bowl-vase, molded production piece in a wide low squatty rounded form, the wide top reticulated & molded w/a design of pine cones & needles in light green & pink, No. 1214, Matte glaze, 1909, 7" d., 3" h. **900**

Standard Glaze Cup & Saucer

Cup & saucer, demitasse, the gold ground round saucer w/flared rim, the dark brown cylindrical cup w/D-form handle & gold interior, etched cherry blossom motif w/two blossoms in lighter glaze, the others in silhouette, Standard glaze, No. 208, 1886, Anna Bookprinter, remnants of salesroom label, 3" h., the set (ILLUS.) **476**

Standard Glaze Dresser Tray

Dresser tray, rectangular w/ruffled rim, decorated w/h.p. coral carnations on a shaded dark brown ground, Standard glaze, No. 591, 1894, Elizabeth Lincoln, few nicks & rough areas to edge, 7 x 10 3/4" (ILLUS.) **392**

Ewer, squatty round ribbed melon-form base on small tab feet, the top centered by a tall slender neck w/a wide curled tricorner rim, a slender S-scroll handle from the rim to the shoulder, decorated around the neck w/Black-eyed Susans against a dark brown shaded to pale yellow ground, Standard glaze, No. 571C, 1894, H. Wilcox, 5 1/2" d., 8" h. **731**

Rare Rookwood Jar

Jar, cov., bulbous ovoid body w/reticulated neck & domed cover, white ground decorated around the center w/brightly colored continuous scene depicting seven Chinese figures on horseback riding through rocky terrain w/one rider falling to the ground, by William Hentschel, interior of jar & lid in rich medium blue, artist-initialed, No. 2541, ca. 1921, 9 3/4" h. (ILLUS.) **4,032**

Jug, floor-type, tall ovoid form w/the rounded shoulder centered by a flared molded neck, applied shoulder strap handle, small molded spout at the bottom front, overall glossy brown glaze, stamped "Rookwood - 1884," 16" d., 28" h. **1,069**

Silver-overlaid Rookwood Jug

Jug w/stopper, double-gourd bulbous form w/a short neck & shoulder handle, the handle, neck & round stopper w/silver overlay, the lower body lobe w/a silver overlay grapevine decoration, the upper lobe decorated w/a large ear of corn in yellow & green on a shaded brown ground, Standard glaze, No. S976, ca. 1890, illegible artist, 4 3/4" d., 8 1/2" h. (ILLUS.) **2,300**

Unusual Rookwood Loving Cup

Loving cup, gently flaring cylindrical sides w/a wide flat rim flanked by two D-form angled handles, decorated w/a color bust portrait of a ragged African-American boy against a shaded light green & tan to brown ground, Standard glaze, No. 259, 1895, Bruce Horsfall, 9 1/2" w., 7" h. (ILLUS.) **4,600**

Mug, swelled bottom & tapering cylindrical sides w/a molded rim band, D-form handle, color bust portrait of Native American chief against a shaded deep gold & brown ground, Standard glaze, No. 656, 1896, Matt Daly, 5" w., 5" h. (ILLUS. top, right column) **1,380**

Rookwood Mug with Indian Portrait

Mug, tall tapering cylindrical form w/a large D-form handle, Carved Matt design of stylized oak leaves & acorns in brown & butterfat green, No. 1014D, 1905, 4 1/4" d., 7" h. **478**

Pitcher, 12" h., 5 3/4" d., tall slender ovoid form tapering to a gently flared rim w/pinched spout, applied C-form strap handle on the neck, decorated w/large cluster of gooseberry leaves in yellow, green & brown on a shaded light amber to green ground, Standard glaze, No. 567W, 1891, A.R. Valentien **1,800**

Rare Sea Green Glazed Plaque

Plaque, unusual design of a songbird in flight near leafy stems on a shaded blue ground, unusual Sea Green glaze, A.R. Valentien, framed, 8 x 10" (ILLUS.).......... **19,550**

Rookwood Plaque with Ocean View

Plaque, rectangular, a landscape vista w/a tall lone pine tree in the foreground w/hills & the ocean in the distance, in shades of blue, green, tan & brown, titled "On the Bluffs," mounted in original gilt shadow-box frame, Vellum glaze, 1916, Sara Sax, 8 1/2 x 10 3/4" (ILLUS.) **8,050**

Plaque, rectangular, landscape scene of birch trees on river bank, blue, green & white, Vellum glaze, 1912, E.T. Hurley, wooden frame, plaque 9 x 11" **7,088**

Large Rookwood Vellum Plaque

Plaque, rectangular, a tall unusual mountain & lake vista in shades of blue, green & mauve, mounted in original wide dark coved frame, Vellum glaze, 1912, Ed Diers, 11 1/4 x 16 1/2" (ILLUS.) **6,900**

Plaque with Lake, Trees & Hills

Plaque, a landscape of a meadow leading down to tall slender leafy trees flanking a lake w/mountains in the distance below a pale blue cloudy sky, in shades of purple, blue, dark & light green, tan & brown, Vellum glaze, 1920, Lenore Asbury, framed, 10 x 11 3/4" (ILLUS.) **4,313**

Plaque, foreign landscape w/two distant pointed mountains w/a stream & scrubland in the foreground & tall trees in the front left, titled "Mt. Ararat in Armenia," Vellum glaze, 1914, Sara Sax, framed, framed, 9 x 14 1/4" (ILLUS. below) **5,750**

Scarce Rookwood Tankard with Imp

Tankard, cov., baluster-form w/low domed hinged cover & D-form handle, decorated

Mt. Ararat Vellum Plaque

w/a smiling imp-like character in shaded bright yellow swinging on bare brown branches against a shaded dark to light brown ground, copper overlay on cover, Standard glaze, 1899, Harriet Wilcox, 9" h. (ILLUS.).. **9,200**

Vase, 4" h., 4" d., Jewel Porcelain, bulbous ovoid body tapering to a wide short flat mouth, a pale blue band of stylized cherry blossoms around the shoulder against an oxblood glazed ground, dark blue glazed interior, No. 8903, 1920, Sara Sax.. **1,800**

Blossoms on Yellow Vellum Vase

Vase, 5" h., 3" h., gently tapering ovoid body w/a flat rim, a pale yellow ground decorated around the bottom w/a band of large & small pink blossoms & green leafy branches, Vellum glaze, 1924, Lenore Asbury (ILLUS.) **977**

Vase, 5" h., 3 3/4" d., wide simple ovoid form tapering slightly to a wide, flat mouth, decorated w/a continuous landscape scene w/groups of tall trees in a meadow w/hills in the distance, in shades of dark blue, light blue & cream, Vellum glaze, No. 942E, 1919, Ed Diers................ **1,463**

Vase, 5" h., 7" d., low wide squatty round form w/the wide top tapering up to a short trumpet neck, decorated w/a large cluster of orange & yellow poppies on a dark brown ground, Standard glaze, No. 671B, 1899, E. Lincoln.................................... **450**

Vase, 5 1/2" h., 4" d., wide baluster-form body tapering to a flaring trumpet neck, decorated w/stylized apple blossoms on a pink & ivory butterfat ground, Wax Matte glaze, No. 6148, 1937, Kataro Shirayamadani **1,125**

Rookwood Cherry Blossom Vase

Vase, 5 1/2" h., 5 1/2" d., bulbous footed ovoid body w/a wide, short rolled neck, light pink ground decorated around the

shoulder w/a dark grey branch w/pink cherry blossoms, Vellum glaze, 1925, E.T. Hurley (ILLUS.).. **862**

Vase, 5 1/2" h., 6" d., widely flaring trumpet-form body, decorated w/white dogwood blossoms & dark blue leaves against a sheer olive ground, purple interior, Black Opal glaze, No. 2264E, 1925, Kataro Shirayamadani...................................... **2,925**

Vase, 6" h., a gently tapering cylindrical form topped by a short cylindrical neck, the sides lightly molded w/tapering pointed panels resembling overlapping tall leaves, good green & rose Matte glaze, No. 1824, 1912 .... **495**

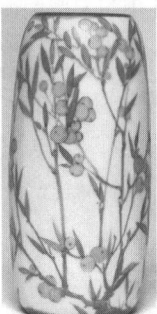

Rookwood Iris Glaze Vases

Vase, 6" h., 3" d., slightly swelled cylindrical body tapering slightly to a flat mouth, decorated w/large pink & white clover blossoms on green arched leafy stems on a shaded creamy yellow to greyish green ground, Iris glaze, No. 951, 1905, Fred Rothenbusch (ILLUS. right)............... **1,380**

Pretty Rookwood Vase with Bayberries

Vase, 6 1/2" h., gently tapering cylindrical form w/a flat rim, decorated w/an elaborate overall design of pink bayberries w/green leaves & brown stems on a pale tan ground, Vellum glaze, No. 2102, 1923, Lorinda Epply (ILLUS.) **4,313**

Vase, 6 1/2" h., 4 1/2" d., tapering bulbous lower body w/a rounded wide shoulder centered by a tall trumpet neck, decorated w/a cluster of white clover blossoms & green leaves on a shaded dark blue to dark grey ground, Iris glaze, No. 754, 1901, Fred Rothenbusch............................. **1,350**

Vase, 6 1/2" h., 5 1/2" d., bulbous ovoid form tapering to a low rolled mouth, decorated in squeezebag w/an abstract triangle & bar geometric design in dark brown on a coffee-colored ground, No. 6201d, 1931, Jens Jensen........................ **1,069**

Vase, 6 3/4" h., 5 1/2" d., Jewel Porcelain, swelled & flaring cylindrical form w/a wide, flat mouth, decorated w/large stylized ivory magnolia blossoms w/ochre trim on a teal blue ground, No. 2189, 1944, Jens Jensen **1,463**

Rookwood Scenic Vellum Vase

Vase, 7" h., wide cylindrical body w/rounded shoulder & short cylindrical neck, landscape scene of tall leafy trees by a lake w/forest in the background, in shades of light & dark green, blue & cream, Vellum glaze, No. 1873, 1922, Fred Rothenbusch (ILLUS.) **1,610**

Vase, 7 1/4" h., 3" d., swelled cylindrical body w/a narrow shoulder tapering to a short rolled neck, decorated w/a continuous marsh landscape in umber & brown surrounded by cobalt blue water, Green Vellum glaze, No. 904E, 1911, Sara Sax .. **5,063**

Vase, 7 1/4" h., 3 1/2" d., gently waisted cylindrical form w/a flat rim, decorated in the Japanese style w/a band of swimming fish around the lower third, shaded from creamy white to medium blue w/dark blue, green & cream fish, Vellum glaze, No. 1358, 1908, E.T. Hurley............. **2,363**

Vase, 7 1/2" h., urn-form, swelled cylindrical lower body below the wide flattened shoulder centered by a wide cylindrical neck w/a wide, flattened rim, molded around the lower body w/a band of large pointed leaves alternating w/stylized blossoms on stems, light brown Matte glaze, No. 2413, 1928.................................... **468**

Vase, 7 1/2" h., 3 1/2" d., gently flaring trumpet-form body on a cushion base, continuous landscape of birch trees & hills in pale blues, green, violet & cream, Vellum glaze, No. 1357E, 1920, Fred Rothenbusch **1,913**

Vase, 7 3/4" h., 4 1/2" d., ovoid body tapering to rolled rim, decorated w/purple columbine on shaded blue to pink ground, No. 913D, 1931, Ed Diers **2,025**

Standard Glaze Vase with Blossoms

Vase, 8" h., footed ovoid body tapering to a short neck w/a widely flaring flattened rim, decorated w/large poppy-like blossoms on slender stems against a dark brown ground, Standard glaze, 1899, light crazing, signed (ILLUS.) **805**

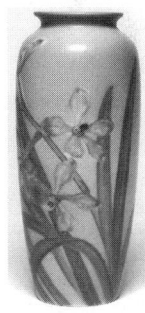

Orchids on Matte Rookwood Vase

Vase, 8" h., gently swelled cylindrical form w/a tapering shoulder to a low, flattened rolled rim, decorated w/large purple orchids & dark green leaves & stems against a shaded lavender to pink ground, Matte glaze, No. 904D, 1942, Kataro Shirayamadani (ILLUS.)................. **4,025**

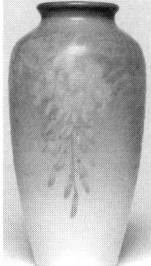

Wisteria Blooms on Rookwood Vase

Vase, 8" h., tall ovoid form w/a rounded shoulder to a short rolled neck, decorated w/large shaded blue wisteria blossoms & green leaves against a dark blue shaded to creamy white ground, Vellum glaze, No. 164E, 1928, E. T. Hurley (ILLUS.) **2,070**

Vase, 8" h., 3 1/2" d., cylindrical form w/a narrow tapering rim band to the wide flat mouth, decorated w/a continuous landscape w/large leafy trees in the foreground & a lake beyond, in shades of light & dark blue & green w/cream & pale yellow, Vellum glaze, No. 952E, 1918, Ed Diers...... **1,800**

Vase, 8" h., 3 1/2" d., tall slender ovoid body tapering slightly to a short neck & flat rim, decorated w/a cluster of tall Shasta daisies on green stems against a shaded dark to light blue ground, Vellum glaze, No. 901, 1913, M.H. McDonald................. **1,350**

Vase, 8" h., 4" d., tapering cylindrical form w/flaring short neck, charcoal ground decorated around the shoulder w/a wide band of stylized pink blossoms & green leaves, Matte glaze, No. 1655E, 1911, O.G. Reed... **1,463**

Shirayamadani Vellum Blossom Vase

Vase, 8 1/4" h., 4" d., low flaring foot below a bulbous flattened lower body below a tall gently flaring trumpet neck, the upper body decorated w/large pink cherry blossoms & green leaves on a pink ground w/violet blue around the lower body & in the interior, Vellum glaze, 1933, K. Shirayamadani (ILLUS.) **1,437**

Vase, 8 1/4" h., 4 1/4" d., baluster-form, decorated in squeezebag w/an overall design of bands of alternating large dark greenish brown triangles & blue circles on a pale blue ground, No. 285, 1928, William Hentschel **1,913**

Vase, 8 1/4" h., 5 1/2" d., six-paneled ovoid body tapering to a cylindrical neck w/flared rim, decorated w/large orange maple leaves against a dark green shaded to mahogany brown ground, Standard glaze, No. 850, 1903, Sallie Coyne **675**

Iris Glaze Vase with Flying Rook

Vase, 8 1/2" h., gently swelled cylindrical form w/a narrow shoulder tapering to a low, flared neck, decorated w/a large black flying rook w/pine boughs & a full moon against a dark blue shaded to creamy white ground, Iris glaze, No. 904, 1908, Clara C. Lindeman (ILLUS.) **8,625**

Vase, 8 1/2" h., 3" d., swelled cylindrical form tapering to a short cylindrical neck, decorated w/white arrowhead blossoms & dark teal blue leaves & grasses on a shaded pink ground, Vellum glaze, No. 932E, 1921, Kataro Shirayamadani **3,375**

Vase, 8 1/2" h., 4" d., gently swelled cylindrical body w/a short tapering neck w/a rolled rim, decorated w/large white Shasta daisies w/yellow centers on tall dark green leafy stems against a shaded pale blue to cream to pink ground, Vellum glaze, No. 614E, 1912, Elizabeth Lincoln.. **1,350**

Vase, 8 1/2" h., 4 1/2" d., ovoid body tapering to a short cylindrical neck, decorated w/long stems of yellow & orange roses against a very dark blue shaded to grey ground, Iris glaze, No. 926C, 1903, Ed Diers **2,138**

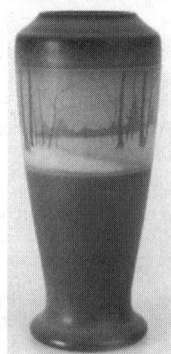

Rookwood Vase with Landscape Band

Vase, 9" h., footed tapering cylindrical form w/a short angled shoulder & flat mouth, decorated around the upper body w/a wide winter landscape scene in white, grey, pink & dark blackish brown, on a dark moss green ground, Vellum glaze, 1912, Shirayamadani (ILLUS.).................. **2,415**

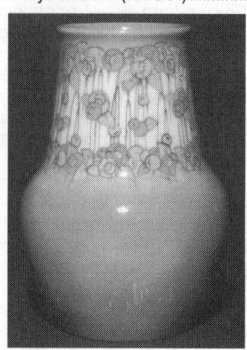

Flower Band on Jewel Porcelain Vase

Vase, 9" h., Jewel Porcelain, bulbous lower body below tall tapering sides w/a rolled rim, painted around the upper body w/a wide band of stylized flowers in rose, blue & green on a yellow ground, lower body in dark greyish blue, turquoise interior, No. 975BT, 1918, Sara Sax (ILLUS.) **4,313**

Vase, 9" h., 4 1/2" d., baluster-form w/a swelled shoulder below the short cylindrical neck, decorated w/large white hydrangea & green leafy stems against a dark green to light grey shaded ground, Iris glaze, No. 909C, 1902, Fred Rothenbusch (ILLUS. left with clover-decorated vase) **2,185**

Vase, 9" h., 5" d., tapering cylindrical body w/a narrow angled shoulder centering a short, wide cylindrical neck, decorated around the shoulder w/a band of stylized white cherry blossoms against a midnight blue ground, Vellum glaze, No. 918V, 1915, C.J. McLaughlin **1,688**

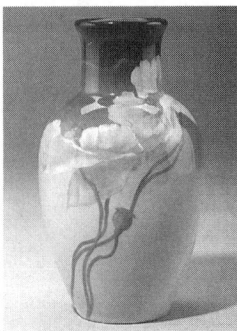

Iris Glaze Vase with Poppies

Vase, 9 1/2" h., 5 1/4" d., large ovoid body tapering to a short cylindrical neck w/flared rim, decorated w/large white poppies on green stems against a shaded dark to light grey ground, Iris glaze, No. 849, 1903, Fred Rothenbusch (ILLUS.) **2,415**

Vase, 10 1/4" h., 7 1/4" d., simple ovoid form w/flat rim, decorated w/a continuous meadow landscape w/oak trees, green, blue & grey against cream ground, Vellum glaze, No. 604C, Ed Diers **4,219**

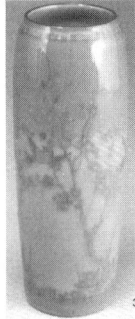

Jewel Porcelain Vase with Blossoms

Vase, 10 1/2" h., 4" d., Jewel Porcelain, slightly swelled cylindrical form, a Japanese style scene of cherry blossoms & flying birds in shades of blue & pink under a glossy pink glaze, No. 951, 1922, Lorinda Epply (ILLUS.) **2,070**

Vase, 10 1/2" h., 5 1/2" d., gently swelled cylindrical form w/a short rolled rim, decorated w/a continuous landscape w/birch trees around a lake, in shades of pale blue, dark blue, greens, purples & cream, Vellum glaze, ungrazed, No. 892B, 1931, Ed Diers **5,063**

Fine Rookwood Jewel Porcelain Vase

Vase, 12" h., 5" d., Jewel Porcelain, footed baluster-form w/a wide short cylindrical neck w/rolled rim, decorated in the Chinese style w/four panels of stylized flying bluebirds above tall stems of hollyhocks in blues & greens on an ivory butterfat ground, No. 2933, 1929, Lorinda Epply (ILLUS.) **4,025**

Vase, 12 1/2" h., 5 1/2" d., slender swelled cylindrical form, decorated w/a continuous sunset landscape w/large tall dark trees in the foreground, in shades of dark blue, black & pale peach pink, Vellum glaze, No. 2032C, 1920, Sara Sax **13,500**

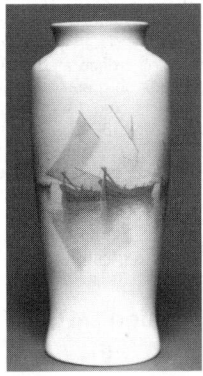

Rookwood Harbor Scene by Schmidt

Vase, 13" h., gently swelling cylindrical form w/an angled shoulder to a short, slightly flared neck, decorated w/a Venetian harbor scene, Glossy glaze, Carl Schmidt (ILLUS.) **13,200**

Tall Scenic Vellum Vase with Trees

Vase, 14" h., baluster-form w/angled shoulder to a short rolled neck, painted w/a landscape w/a large leafy tree across a stream w/hills & mountains in the distance on one side & the stream leading to meadows w/trees on the other, Vellum glaze, No. 2251, 1926, Fred Rothenbusch (ILLUS.) **10,350**

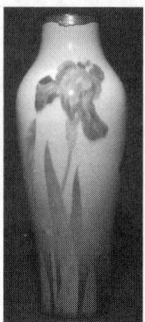

Fine Iris Glaze Vase with Irises

Vase, 14 1/2" h., tall slender ovoid form tapering to a flat rim w/a chased silver overlay narrow band, decorated w/large shaded blue irises on green leafy stems against a shaded blue to dark green ground, Iris glaze, No. 879C, 1904, Albert Valentien (ILLUS.) **12,650**

Vase, 16" h., 6 1/2" d., tall slightly tapering cylindrical form w/a thin flared rim, continuous misty landscape of birch trees around a lake at dusk in shades of pale cream, grey, blue & green, Vellum glaze, No. 1660A, 1912, E.T. Hurley..................... **7,313**

Rose Medallion & Rose Canton

The lovely Chinese ware known as Rose Medallion was made through the past century and into the present one. It features alternating panels of people and flowers or insects with most pieces having four medallions with a central rose or peony medallion. The ware is called Rose Canton if florals and birds or insects fill all the panels. Unless otherwise noted, our listing is for Rose Medallion ware.

Rose Medallion Coffeepot

Coffeepot, cov., flared base on gently tapering body, domed lid w/finial, C-scroll handle, late 19th c., 10" h. (ILLUS.) **$157**

Creamer & cov. sugar, early 20th c., creamer 4 1/2" h., cov. sugar 5" h., pr. **134**

Plates, 9 3/4" d., early 20th c., set of 10 .... **336**

Platter, 11" l., oval form, late 19th c..................... **308**

Platter, 12" l., Rose Mandarin patt., unusual wide rim border decoration w/dragons, goat, horse & Chinese symbols, 19th c. (gilt wear).. **460**

Platter, 13 1/4" l., oval form, late 19th c............. **364**

Rose Medallion Platter

Platter, 13 3/4" l., oval form w/raised rim, late 19th c. (ILLUS.)....................................... **616**

Platter, 15 1/3" l., oval form, late 19th c............ **616**

Porcelain Rose Medallion Platter

Platter, 18 1/2" l., oval, gilt rim on raised border, ca. 1840 (ILLUS.) **1,120**

Soup bowls, late 19th c., 4" h., 10" w., 8" d., set of 7.. **420**

Roseville

Roseville Pottery Company operated in Zanesville, Ohio, from 1898 to 1954 after having been in business for six years prior to that in Muskingum County, Ohio. Art wares similar to those of Owens and Weller Potteries were produced. Items listed here are by patterns or lines.

Apple Blossom (1948)

White apple blossoms in relief on blue, green or pink ground; brown tree branch handles.

Basket, hanging-type, blue ground, 8" **$190**
Console set, 8" l. bowl & pair of 2" h. candleholders, pink ground, No. 328-8" & No. 351-2", 3 pcs. **500**
Cornucopia-vase, pink ground, No. 321-6", 6" h. **120**
Cornucopia-vases, blue ground, No. 321-6", 6" h., pr. **165**
Cornucopia-vases, green ground, No. 321-6", 6" h., pr. **280**
Jardiniere & pedestal base, blue ground, jardiniere, No. 302-8", 8" h., pedestal, No. 305-8", 2 pcs. **880**
Tea set: cov. teapot, creamer & sugar bowl; blue ground, No. 371-P, the set **440**
Tea set: cov. teapot, creamer & sugar bowl; pink ground, No. 371-P, the set **303**
Vase, 6" h., two-handled, squatty base, long cylindrical neck, pink ground, No. 381-6" **155**
Vase, bud, 7" h., base handles, flaring rim, pink ground, No. 379-7" **99**
Vase, bud, 7" h., base handles, flaring rim, green ground, No. 379-7" **88**
Vase, 8 1/4" h., flaring foot w/ovoid body & wide flaring rim, pointed handles from shoulder to middle of neck, green ground, No. 385-8" **185**
Vase, 10" h., swelled cylindrical body w/shaped rim, base handles, blue ground, No. 389-10" **350**
Vase, 15" h., floor-type, double base handles, short globular base, long cylindrical neck, green ground, No. 392-15" **445**

Apple Blossom Floor Vase

Vase, 15" h., floor-type, double base handles, short globular base, long cylindrical neck, blue ground, No. 392-15" (ILLUS.)...... **776**
Vase, 18" h., floor-type, slender ovoid body w/wide cylindrical neck, blue ground, No. 393-18" (two chips & one bruise to base, hairline to rim)... **358**
Window box, end handles, pink ground, No. 368-8", 2 1/2 x 10 1/2" **50**

Aztec (1915)
Muted earthy tones of beige, grey, brown, teal, olive, azure blue or soft white with slip-trailed geometric decoration in contrasting colors.

Vase, 6 3/8" h., tapering cylindrical body w/bulbous top, slip decoration of stylized mushrooms in white & orange w/blue ribbon bands above & below, on a bluish grey ground, artist-initialed "E" & old oval paper label (base & rim chips) **138**

Vase, 8" h., tapering cylinder swelling slightly at top, squeezebag decoration of white trillium on orange stems against a blue/grey ground, unmarked (lentil-size chip to base & 1" hairline to rim) **523**
Vase, 10" h., flared foot w/expanding cylindrical body & flared rim, white & tan decoration against a blue ground, artist-signed **248**

Baneda (1933)
Band of embossed pods, blossoms and leaves on green or raspberry pink ground.

Bowl, 6" d., raspberry pink ground, No. 232-6" **385**
Vase, 5" h., footed, pear-shaped w/small loop handles near rim, raspberry pink ground, No. 601-5" **400**
Vase, 6" h., green ground, No. 605-6", original label **518**
Vase, 7" h., footed wide cylindrical body w/wide collared rim, small loop handles from shoulder to rim, raspberry pink ground, No. 610-7" **500**
Wall pocket, flaring sides, green ground, No. 1269-8", gold foil label, 8" h. (small chip to hole in back) **2,645**

Bittersweet (1940)
Orange bittersweet pods and green leaves on a grey blending to rose, yellow with terra cotta, rose with green or solid green bark-textured ground; brown branch handles.

Basket, low overhead handle, shaped rim, green ground, No. 810-10", 10" h. **193**

Bittersweet Planter

Planter w/undertray, grey ground, No. 856-5", slight interior discoloration from usage & small bruise to one of rim points, 5 1/2" h. (ILLUS.)... **67**
Planter w/undertray, green ground, No. 856-5", 5 1/2" h. (minor crazing) **143**
Vase, 7" h., green ground, No. 879-7"............... **83**
Wall pocket, curving conical form w/overhead handle continuing to one side, grey ground, No. 866-7", 7 1/2" h. **316**

Blackberry (1933)
Band of relief clusters of blackberries with vines and ivory leaves accented in green and terra cotta on a green textured ground.

Basket, hanging-type, 6 1/2" (two flakes to berries).. **633**
Bowl, 6" d., No. 226-6"...................................... **300**
Jardiniere, two-handled, No. 623-6", 6" h. **495**

Jardiniere, two-handled, 8" h............................ **1,045**
Planter, hanging-type, No. 348-5", 5" h. (one rim hanging hole only partially pierced) **800**
Planter, six-sided, gold foil label, 3 3/4 x 10"..... **460**
Vase, 10" h., bulbous base w/wide cylindrical neck, handles at mid-section, No. 577-10 .... **1,648**
Vase, 12 1/2" h., ovoid w/loop handles from shoulder to rim, No. 578-12" (minor chip to bottom)....................................... **1,320**

Bleeding Heart (1938)
Pink blossoms and green leaves on shaded blue, green or pink ground.

Basket, hanging-type, two-handled, blue ground, No. 362-5", 8" d............................... **288**
Basket, hanging-type, two-handled, green ground, No. 362-5", 8" d............................... **242**
Basket, hanging-type, two-handled, pink ground, No. 362-5", 8" w............................. **225**
Basket w/circular handle, brown ground, No. 360-10", 10" h. **403**
Basket w/circular handle, pink ground, 360-10", 10" h., w/gold foil label **331**
Basket w/overhead handle, pink ground, No. 359-8", 7 1/2" h............................... **200**
Basket w/pointed overhead handle, w/flower frog, pink ground, No. 361-12", 12" h., 2 pcs...................................... **300**

Bushberry (1948)
Berries and leaves on blue, green or russet bark-textured ground; brown or green branch handles.

Basket, hanging-type w/original chains, russet ground, No. 465-5", 7" **425**
Basket w/asymmetrical overhead handle, green ground, No. 369-6 1/2", 6 1/2" h. **250**
Basket w/asymmetrical overhead handle, ivory ground, No. 369-6 1/2", 6 1/2" h. **112**
Basket w/asymmetrical overhead handle, green ground, No. 370-8", 8" h.............. **275**
Basket w/asymmetrical overhead handle, blue ground, No. 371-10", 10" h............ **353**

Bushberry Book Ends

Book ends, green ground, No. 9, pr. (ILLUS.)... **300**
Bowl, 3" h., small side handles, globular, green ground, No. 657-3"............................. **120**
Flower frog, blue ground, No. 45...................... **160**
Jardiniere, two-handled, blue ground, No. 657-4", 4" h.................................... **165**
Jardiniere, russet ground, No. 657-5", 5" h..... **170**

Pitcher, 8 3/4" h., russet w/green branch handle, No. 1325 .... **300**
Urn, two-handled, green ground, No. 411-6", 6" h. (couple of very minor nicks to horizontal ridges)............................. **112**
Vase, 3" h., conical w/tiny rim handles, russet ground, No. 283".. **30**
Vase, double bud, 4 1/2" h., gate-form, russet ground, No. 158-4 1/2" **185**
Vase, 6" h., two-handled, russet ground, No. 30-6".. **70**
Vase, 6" h., angular side handles, low foot, globular w/wide neck, green ground, No. 156-6"... **138**
Vase, bud, 7 1/2" h., asymmetrical base handles, cylindrical body, russet ground, No. 152-7"... **145**
Vase, 10" h., two-handled, russet ground, No. 37-10"... **265**
Vase, 12 1/2" h., large asymmetrical side handles, bulging cylinder w/flaring foot, green ground, No. 38-12".......................... **225**
Wall pocket, high-low handles, russet ground, No. 1291-8", 8" h. (glazed over bruise to back) **259**

Carnelian I (1910-15)
Matte glaze with a combination of two colors or two shades of the same color with the darker dripping over the lighter tone or heavy and textured glaze with intermingled colors and some running.

Bowl, 6 1/2" d., 3" h., two-handled, canted sides, pink & grey.............................. **231**
Vase, 5" h., flat pierced handles, rectangular w/slightly bulging sides, rose w/deep purple drip, unmarked, No. 65-2-5.................. **275**
Vase, 5" h., two-handled, squatty bulbous form, shades of green, No. 357-5" **110**
Vase, 5" h., blue & grey ground, No. 642-5"...... **175**
Vase, 7" h., footed bulbous ovoid w/shoulder tapering to wide molded rim, handles from shoulder to rim, green ground, No. 331-7".. **235**
Vase, 7" h., footed bulbous ovoid w/shoulder tapering to wide molded rim, handles from shoulder to rim, rose & grey ground, No. 331-7"... **358**
Wall pocket, conical w/ornate side handles, flaring rim, blue & grey, No. 1251-8" (very minor chips around hanging hole) **242**

Carnelian II (1915)
Intermingled colors, some with a drip effect.

Bowl, 12 1/2" d. footed wide shallow round form, deeply mottled dark rose & tan glaze, foil label... **1,150**
Urn, globular body tapering to flaring rim, scrolled shoulder handles, light & dark blue ground, No. 333-6", 6" h. **413**
Vase, bud, 6" h., footed trumpet-form w/ornate handles from base to mid-section, turquoise ground, No. 341-6"..................... **99**
Vase, 8 1/4" h., squatty bulbous body tapering to flared rim, angled scrolled handles, mottled matte mauve drip glaze, partial paper label **423**
Vase, 10" h., footed tapering cylindrical body w/wide slightly flaring neck, mottled green glaze.. **259**

Wall pocket, slender fanned body flanked by double-scroll handles, intermingled shades of pink & blue, 8" h. 345

Wall pocket, slender fanned body flanked by double-scroll handles, shaded brown ground, 8" h. 460

Cherry Blossom (1933)

Sprigs of cherry blossoms, green leaves and twigs with pink fence against a combed blue-green ground or creamy ivory fence against a terra cotta ground shading to dark brown.

Basket, hanging-type, brown ground, 8" 546

Jardiniere, squatty bulbous body, two-handled, blue-green ground, No. 627-4", 4" h. (overall crazing w/discoloration at base).. 325

Jardiniere, shoulder handles, terra cotta ground, No. 627-7", 7" h. 550

Urn, two-handled, terra cotta ground, No. 350-5", 5" h. 420

Vase, 5" h., two-handled, globular w/wide mouth, terra cotta ground, No. 627-5".......... 275

Vase, 10" h., slender ovoid body w/wide cylindrical neck, loop handles from shoulder to middle of neck, blue-green ground, No. 626-10".. 1,430

Vase, 12" h., tall swelled cylindrical form tapering to a short flaring neck flanked by small loop handles, pink ground, No. 627-12"... 546

Wall pocket, brown ground, No. 1270-8", gold foil label, 8" h. (short tight line to rim)..... 863

Clematis (1944)

Clematis blossoms and heart-shaped green leaves against a vertically textured ground — white blossoms on blue, rose-pink blossoms on green and ivory blossoms on golden brown.

Console bowl, two-handled, green ground, No. 460-12", 12" l. 140

Console bowl, green ground, No. 461-14", 14" l. (fleck to one petal)................................ 110

Vase, 15" h., brown ground, No. 114-15".......... 275

Vase, 15" h., green ground, No. 114-15".......... 765

Columbine (1940s)

Columbine blossoms and foliage on shaded ground — yellow blossoms on blue, pink blossoms on pink shaded to green and blue blossoms on tan shaded to green.

Bowl, 6" d., two-handled, squatty bulbous body w/small angled shoulder handles, tan ground, No. 400-6".................................... 168

Candleholders, tan ground, No. 1145-2 1/2", 2 1/2" h., pr...................................... 60

Candlesticks, flat disk base w/handles rising to nozzle, tan ground, No. 1146-4 1/2", 5" h., pr. 224

Urn-vase, tan ground, No. 150-6", 6" h. 165

Urn-vase, pink ground, No. 151-8", 8" h. 140

Vase, 6" h., tan ground, No. 13-6" 135

Vase, 8" h., handles rising from base, tan ground, No. 19-8" 195

Wall pocket, squared flaring mouth, conical body w/curled tip, brown ground, No. 1290-8" 518

Corinthian (1923)

Deeply fluted ivory and green body below a continuous band of molded grapevine, fruit, foliage and florals in naturalistic colors, narrow ivory and green molded border at the rim.

Bowl, 5" h., No. 121-5".. 60

Candlestick, No. 1048-10", 10" h. 110

Vase, 12" h., cylindrical w/flared rim, No. 235-12" (1/8" glaze flake off one vertical rib)... 110

Wall pocket, No. 1229-12", 12" h. 250

Cosmos (1940)

Embossed blossoms against a wavy horizontal ridged band on a textured ground — ivory band with yellow and orchid blossoms on blue, blue band with white and orchid blossoms on green or tan.

Basket, hanging-type, handles rising from midsection to rim, brown ground, No. 361-5", 7" h.. 230

Basket w/overhead handle, green ground, No. 357-10", 10" h..................................... 250

Bowl, 6" d., two-handled, shaped rim, tan ground, No. 369-6"... 60

Bowl, 6" d., No. 376-6"...................................... 225

Console bowl, blue ground, No. 371-10", 10" l. 160

Console bowl, footed oblong boat-shape w/an undulating & double-notched rim, blue ground, No. 374-14", 15 1/2" l. 193

Jardiniere, two-handled, green ground, No. 649-3" 145

Jardiniere & pedestal base, blue ground, No. 649-10", overall 30" h., 2 pcs. 2,600

Vase, 4" h., double bud, gate-form, tan ground, No. 133-4".. 110

Vase, 4" h., two-handled, globular base & wide neck, green ground, No. 944-4"............ 135

Vase, 4" h., two-handled, globular base & wide neck, tan ground, No. 944-4" 99

Vase, 6" h., green ground, No. 947-6".............. 175

Vase, 9" h., handles rising from midsection of ovoid body to neck, green ground, No. 952-9".. 500

Vase, 12 1/2" h., ovoid w/large loop handles, tan ground, No. 956-12" 300

Wall pocket, fanned conical shape w/high arched handle across the top, tan ground, No. 1285-6", 6 1/2" h......................... 259

Cremona (1927)

Relief-molded floral motifs including a tall stem with small blossoms and arrowhead leaves, wreathed with leaves similar to Velmoss or a web of delicate vines against a background of light green mottled with pale blue or pink with creamy ivory.

Vase, 4" h., squatty w/narrow flared mouth, pink ground, No. 351-4"..................................... 230

Vase, 10" h., footed square tapering body, No. 358-10" 220

Vase, 10" h., baluster-form body w/flaring foot & rim, green ground, No. 350-10" (fleck to tip of one leaf) 193

Vase, 12" h., footed, slender baluster-form body w/narrow shoulder to the cylindrical neck w/flaring rim, green ground, No. 361-12" 385

Della Robbia, Rozane (1906)

Naturalistic or stylized designs executed by hand using the sgraffito method.

Della Robbia Vase with Flower Band

Vase, 9 1/2" h., footed wide ovoid body tapering to a short cylindrical neck, incised decoration of stylized flowers in large teardrops w/bands of spade-shaped leaves around the top & base, in six colors including white, blue, yellow & dark green, signed, minor chip repairs (ILLUS.) **6,325**

Unusual Della Robbia Vase

Vase, 10 1/2" h., flaring foot below compressed round base, tall cylindrical body w/flaring rim, deeply carved & cut-back fish decoration under a multi-tone green glaze, partial wafer mark, restored, minor chip to top (ILLUS.) **2,400**

Vase, 10 1/2" h., large spherical body w/short cylindrical neck, flaring rim, cut-back & incised floral design in shades of blue, aqua & olive green, brown & yellow, restoration to top & bottom **8,800**

Large Della Robbia Vase with Poppies

Vase, 17 1/2" h., 9 1/2" d., tall ovoid body w/the rim reticulated in a Greek key design above five tall rectangular panels decorated in seven colors w/excised poppies in ivory & taupe on a mint green ground, unmarked, discreet restoration around rim & to short hairline (ILLUS.) **18,400**

Rare Della Robbia Floor Vase

Vase, 21" h., 10 1/2" d., floor-type, large ovoid form tapering to a small flattened & flared neck, excised, incised & enameled in seven colors w/yellow daffodils & shiny leaves in shades of green on a mint green & indigo blue ground, probably an exhibition piece, wafer mark & original paper price tag marked $50, signed by H. Smith, professional restoration to rim, several underglaze chips on base, invisible touch-ups to glaze nicks (ILLUS.) **37,375**

Donatello (1915)

Deeply fluted ivory and green body with wide tan band embossed with cherubs at various pursuits in pastoral settings.

Ashtray No. 17-3", 3" h. **100**

Basket, hanging-type, No. 327-6", 7" d., 5" h. **201**

Basket w/tall pointed overhead handle, cylindrical body, No. 304-12", 12" h. **358**

Candlesticks, flaring base & rim w/tall slender cylindrical stem, No. 1022-10", 10" h., pr. **303**

Flower frog, No. 14-2 1/2", 2 1/2" d. **70**

Jardiniere, No. 575-4", 4" h. **95**

Jardiniere, No. 575-6", 7" d., 6" h. **150**

Jardiniere, No. 579-8", 8" h. **250**

Jardiniere, No. 579-10", 10" h. **395**

Jardiniere & pedestal base, 12" h. jardiniere, No. 579-12", overall 34" h., 2 pcs.... **1,300**

Planter, No. 238-7" (pinhead nicks on inside rim) **56**

Powder jar, cov., lid decorated w/scene of cherubs playing musical instruments, 5" d., 2" h. **330**

Umbrella stand, cylindrical, No. 753-10", 10" h. (three glaze nicks to rim, a couple of tight lines to relief band, not through) **413**

Donatello Double Bud Vase

Vase, double bud, gate-form, No. 8 (ILLUS.) **70**
Vase, bud, 10" h., bottle-form, No. 115-10" **255**
Wall pocket, ovoid, No. 1212-9", 9" h. **275-300**
Wall pocket, No. 1202-10", 10" h. **190**
Wall pocket, No. 1219-10", 10" h. **226**
Window box, rectangular, No. 60-12",
6 x 12" l. **295**

Early Embossed Pitchers (pre-1916)
High gloss, utility line of pitchers with various embossed scenes.

Goldenrod, 9 1/2" h., minor bruise to rim &
touch-ups around base **303**
Landscape, 7 1/2" h. **95-100**
The Cow, 7 1/2" h. **413**
Wild Rose, 9 1/2" h., small spout chip **125**

Falline (1933)
Curving panels topped by a semi-scallop separated by vertical peapod decorations; blended backgrounds of tan shading to green and blue or tan shading to darker brown.

Console bowl, shallow w/end loop handles,
tan ground, No. 244-8", 8" l. **394**
Vase, 6" h., footed cylindrical w/large loop
handles from midsection to rim, tan shad-
ing to brown, No. 642-6" **280**
Vase, 6" h., two-handled, ovoid, tan shading
to brown, No. 643-6" **392**
Vase, 8 1/4" h., 6" d., footed trumpet-form
w/a widely flaring rim, low arched handles from under the rim to mid-body, tan
shading to green & blue, 7" l. (Y-shaped
line from rim).. **495**

Florentine (1924-28)
Bark-textured panels alternating with embossed gar-lands of cascading fruit and florals; ivory with tan and green, beige with brown and green or brown with beige and green glaze.

Ashtray, brown ground, No. 17-3", 3" **165**
Bowl, 7" d., No. 125-7" **40**
Candlesticks, flaring base, expanding cy-
lindrical stem, brown, No. 1050-10",
10" h., pr.. **358**
Compote, 4" d., brown ground, No. 6-4" **195**
Jardiniere, brown, No. 130-4", 7" d., 4" h. **165**
Jardiniere, brown, No. 602-8", 8" h. **495**
Sand jar, green ground, 15 x 17" **440**
Wall pocket, conical, No. 1231-12", 12" h. **251**

Foxglove (1940s)
Sprays of pink and white blossoms embossed against a shaded matte-finish ground.

Basket, hanging-type, blue ground, No.
466-5", 10"... **201**
Basket w/circular overhead handle, foot-
ed fan-shape w/shaped rim, green
ground, No. 375-12", 12" h. **275**
Candleholders, pink ground, No. 1150-
4 1/2", 4 1/2" h., pr.. **250**
Console bowl, oval w/cut-out rim & pointed
end handles, blue ground, No. 423-12",
12" l.. **154**
Cornucopia-vase, snail shell-type, blue
ground, No. 166-6" **115**
Cornucopia-vase, green ground, No. 164-
6" **195**

Vase, 6" h., bulbous base tapering to cylindrical neck w/flared rim, angled handles
below rim, blue ground, No. 43-6" **90**
Vase, 8 1/2" h., fan-shaped, handles rising
from disk base to midsection, pink
ground, No. 47-8" **203**
Vase, 8 1/2" h., fan-shaped, handles rising
from disk base to midsection, blue
ground, No. 47-8" **134**
Vase, 14" h., conical w/flaring mouth, four
short handles rising from disk base,
green ground, No. 53-14"................................. **425**
Vase, 16" h., pear-shaped body w/closed
rim, angled handles from lower body to
shoulder, blue ground, No. 55-16".................. **633**
Wall pocket, conical w/flaring rim, loop handles, blue ground, No. 1292-8", 8" h. **335**

Freesia (1945)
Trumpet-shaped blossoms and long slender green leaves against wavy impressed lines — white and laven-der blossoms on blended green; white and yellow blos-soms on shaded blue or terra cotta and brown.

Bowl 6" d., terra cotta ground, No. 464-6"......... **155**
Candleholders, tiny pointed handles,
domed base, blue ground, No. 1160-2",
2" h., pr.. **88**
Console bowl, terra cotta ground, No. 466-
10", 10" l. **143**
Console set: 12" l., 4 1/2" h. console bowl
& pr. of candlesticks; blue ground, No.
468-12", 3 pcs.. **88**
Cookie jar, cov., bulbous ovoid body w/an-
gled shoulder handles, slightly domed lid
w/knob finial, green ground, No. 4-8",
8" h. **350**
Cornucopia-vase, terra cotta ground, No.
198-8", 8" h... **165**
Cornucopia-vases, terra cotta ground, No.
197-6", 6" h., pr.. **121**

Freesia Ewer

Ewer, green ground, No. 19-6", 6" h.
(ILLUS.).. **112**
Lamp, blue ground, No. 145 .... **468**
Urn-vase, two-handled, bulbous body ta-
pering to wide cylindrical neck, terra cotta
ground, No. 196-8", 8" h.................................. **225**
Vase, 6" h., terra cotta ground, No. 117-6"........ **165**
Vase 7" h., two-handled, fan-shaped, terra
cotta, No. 200-7" **165**
Vase, 8" h., footed ovoid body flanked by D-
form handles, blue ground, No. 121-8"......... **149**
Vase, 10 1/2" h., two-handled, trumpet-form
body, blue ground, No. 125-10" **165**
Vase, 15" h., tall slender ovoid body
tapering to narrow cylindrical neck

w/wide flaring rim, pointed shoulder handles, terra cotta ground, No. 128-15"...... **275**

Fuchsia (1939)

Coral pink fuchsia blossoms and green leaves against a background of blue shading to yellow, green shading to terra cotta or terra cotta shading to gold.

Basket, hanging-type, terra cotta ground, No. 359-5", 7" h... **201**

Bowl, 5" d., two-handled, squatty bulbous body w/incurved rim, green ground, No. 348-5" **101**

Cornucopia-vase, blue ground, No. 129-6", 6" h.. **150**

Jardiniere, two-handled, terra cotta ground, No. 645-4", 4" h... **190**

Jardiniere, two-handled, blue ground, No. 645-5", 5" h.. **225**

Pitcher w/ice lip, 8" h., blue ground, No. 1322-8" **420**

Vase, 6" h., ovoid w/handles rising from shoulder to rim, terra cotta ground, No. 892-6" **130**

Vase, 9" h., footed ovoid body w/flared rim & large C-form handles, terra cotta ground, No. 899-9".. **179**

Wall pocket, two-handled, blue ground, No. 1282-8", 8 1/2" h. (minute nick to hanging hole & minor glaze scaling to corner of rim)... **575**

Futura (1928)

Varied line with shapes ranging from Art Deco geometrics to futuristic. Matte glaze is typical although an occasional piece may be high gloss.

Basket, hanging-type, wide sloping shoulders, sharply canted sides, terra cotta & brown w/embossed stylized pastel foliage, No. 344-5", 7 1/2" h. (bruise to rim) **288**

Basket, hanging-type, wide sloping shoulders, sharply canted sides, brown w/embossed stylized pastel foliage, 9" h.............. **230**

Jardiniere, angular handles rising from wide sloping shoulders to rim, sharply canted sides, grey ground, No. 616-8", 8" h.. **495**

Jardiniere, flaring flat sides below the narrow angled shoulder molded w/stylized leaves & a short cylindrical neck, small squared handles, pink & lavender leaves on the grey ground, 9" d., 6" h. **408**

Vase, 6" h., stepped shoulders, square body w/canted sides, grey w/green & blue elongated triangles, No. 380-6" **429**

Vase, 6" h., 3 1/2" d., cylindrical body swelling to wider bands at the top & base, long pierced angled handles down the sides, apricot w/green bands & handles, one w/paper label, No. 381-6"........................ **409**

Vase, 6" h., octagonal cone-shaped body on a conforming low base, bluish green semi-crystalline glaze, No. 397-6" **376**

Vase, bud, 6" h., widely flaring conical foot tapering to a slender tall slightly flaring cylindrical body flanked by slender straight handles from near the rim to the foot, stylized floral design in blue & green on a tan shaded to cream ground, No. 422-6" **413**

Vase, 8" h., 3 3/4" d., star-shaped slender tapering body on stepped circular base, pink & grey ground, No. 385-8", unmarked **392**

Vase, 8" h., 5 3/4" d., a high pyramidal foot w/four straight pierced legs supporting the spherical body w/a small conical mouth, decorated w/white, light blue, green & yellow circles on blue ground, No. 404-8"......................... **1,400-1,500**

Vase, 8" h., 5 3/4" d., a high pyramidal foot w/four straight pierced legs supporting the spherical body w/a small conical mouth, green ground decorated w/purple, yellow & orange circles, No. 404-8" ... **1,054**

Vase, 8 1/4" h., 4 1/4" w., tall triangular body tapering slightly to a stepped triangular foot, the body w/wide light blue triangles flanked by slender dark blue triangles, dark & light blue base, unmarked, No. 383-8"... **935**

Vase, 9 1/2" h., stepped sloping rectangular foot supporting a body w/flat multi-faceted flat sides on lower half & contrasting panels on upper half tapering to small rectangular neck, shaded yellow & green, No. 412-9"................................. **5,060**

Vase, 10" h., squatty bulbous base w/molded ring mid-section, wide cylindrical neck w/flaring rim, No. 435-10" (professional repair of minor rim chips) **715**

Vase, 10" h., 8 1/2" d., narrow base flaring to wide shoulder, graduated ringed neck, orange & green, No. 395-10" **660**

Vase, 10 1/4" h., 5 1/4" d., small buttressed handles at disk base, slightly swollen cylindrical lower portion flaring to a wide mouth, decorated w/blue flowers on green stems against a shaded orange body, No. 431-10", unmarked **1,073**

Vase, 12" h., wide ovoid body on a footring, the neck composed of tapering bands, smooth sides, multi-toned deep green overall glaze, No. 394-12"............................... **920**

Gardenia (1940s)

Large white gardenia blossoms and green leaves over a textured impressed band on a shaded green, grey or tan ground.

Basket w/circular handle, grey ground, No. 609-10", 10" h.. **193**

Basket w/circular handle, green ground, No. 609-10", 10" h.. **180**

Console set: 11" l. footed oblong boat-shaped bowl & a pair of 2" h. candleholders; green ground, No. 374-11 & 651-2, the set.. **165**

Cornucopia-vase, tan ground, No. 621-6", 6" h. **80**

Cornucopia-vase, double, green ground, No. 622-8", 8" h. **70**

Cornucopia-vase, double, grey ground, No. 622-8", 8".. **60**

Ewer, tan ground, No. 618-15", 15" h. (professional repair to base)............................... **225**

Spooner, green ground, No. 656-3", 3" h. **125**

Vase, 8" h., green ground, No. 684-8"............... **195**

Vase, 10" h., green ground, No. 658-10............ **160**

Vase, 10 1/2" h., large handles rising from base to shoulder, ornate rim, tan ground, No. 686-10" **198**

Vase, 12" h., handles rising from low base to midsection, tan ground, No. 687-12" (glaze flakes to bottom) **138**

Wall pocket, large handles, tan ground, No. 666-8", 9 1/2" h. **225**

Imperial II (1924)
Varied line with no common characteristics. Many of the pieces are heavily glazed with colors that run and blend.

Vase, 5 1/2" h., two-handled, bulbous body tapering slightly to short cylindrical neck, blue ground w/glossy mottled ivory glaze on interior which spills over the rim in one area, laced w/tawny yellow, No. 517 .... **150**

Vase, 8 1/4" h., wide ovoid form slightly tapering to a wide, short cylindrical neck, mottled orange & green w/tan glaze w/green, dark brown & blue around the neck **2,415**

Wall pocket, mottled pink & green glaze, No. 1263 .... **403**

Wall pocket, rounded form, relief-molded wavy horizontal lines, red over grey glaze, No. 1262, 6 1/2" h. **575**

Iris (1938)
White or yellow blossoms and green leaves on rose blending with green, light blue deepening to a darker blue or tan shading to green or brown.

Basket, hanging-type, brown ground, 305-5", 8 1/2" h. (glaze flake to all three flowers) **259**

Iris Basket

Basket w/pointed overhead handle, compressed ball form, rose ground, No. 354-8", 8" h. (ILLUS.) **112**

Book ends, rose ground, No. 5, pr. **425**

Bowl, 5" d., two-handled, footed, tan ground, No. 359-5" **165**

Console bowl, pink ground, No. 362-10", 10" l. **80**

Cornucopia-vase, blue ground, No. 132-8", 8" h. **90**

Jardiniere, two-handled, tan ground, No. 647-4", 4" h. **67**

Vase, 4" h., base handles, rose ground, No. 914-4" **99**

Vase, floor-type, 15" h., two large handles rising from shoulder to rim, pink ground, No. 929-15" **475**

Ixia (1930s)
Embossed spray of tiny bell-shaped flowers and slender leaves — white blossoms on pink ground; lavender blossoms on green or yellow ground.

Console bowl, pink ground, No. 331-9", unmarked, 9" l. **80**

Jardiniere, green ground, No. 640-4", 4" h. **60**

Jardiniere, green ground, No. 640-6", 6" h. **80**

Jonquil (1931)
White jonquil blossoms and green leaves in relief against textured tan ground; green lining.

Basket, hanging-type, 7 1/4" **345**

Console bowl, oval, No. 220-10", unmarked, black sticker, 10" l. **225**

Jonquil Crocus Pot

Crocus pot, No. 93-4 1/2", 4 1/2" h. (ILLUS.) **413**

Jonquil Jardiniere

Jardiniere, No. 621-5", 5" h. (ILLUS.) **112**

Vase, 5 1/2" h., No. 542-5 1/2" **150**

Vase, 6 1/2" h., wide bulbous body tapering to flat rim, C-form handles, No. 543-6 1/2" **341**

Vase, 8" h., ovoid body tapering to short cylindrical neck, turned-down shoulder handles, No. 529-8" **325**

Vase, 10" h., compressed bulbous base tapering to wide tapering cylindrical neck w/flat rim, loop handles from mid-section to rim, No. 530-10" **303**

Juvenile (1916 on)
Transfer-printed and painted on creamware with nursery rhyme characters, cute animals and other motifs appealing to children.

Feeding dish w/rolled edge, "Baby's Plate," nursery rhyme, "Higgledy Piggledy..." stamped in red on rolled rim "From G.A. Stower's Furniture Co.," unmarked, 7 1/2" d. **190**

Feeding dish w/rolled edge, nursery rhyme, "Hickory, Dickory Dock," 8" d. **120**

Feeding dish w/rolled edge, nursery rhyme, "Tom, The Piper's Son," 8" d. (slight wear to design) **100**

Juvenile Mugs & Pitchers

Mug, sitting puppy, 2 3/4" h. (ILLUS. far left, above)...................... **213**

Pitcher, 3" h., rabbits (ILLUS. far right, above)...................... **214**

Pitcher, 3 1/2" h., chicks (ILLUS. second from right, above).......................... **233**

Plate, divided, 9 1/2" d., well worn dressed-up pig, duckling wearing high top boots & hat & very worn kitten under an umbrella, chick & running rabbit wearing a jacket, stamped þ"Rv-9" (color worn on border)...... **168**

Magnolia (1943)

Large white blossoms with rose centers and black stems in relief against a blue, green or tan textured ground.

Ashtray, two-handled, low bowl form, green ground, No. 28, 7" d., 2" h. **83**

Basket, hanging-type, green ground, No. 469-5"... **144**

Basket w/ornate overhead handle, footed ovoid body w/long angled overhead handle, green ground, No. 384-8", 8" h............. **173**

Bowl, 14" l., tan ground, No. 452-14"................. **70**

Jardiniere, two-handled, tan ground, No. 665-5", 5" h....................................... **132**

Planter, shell-shaped w/angular base handles, tan ground, No. 183-6", 6" l..................... **60**

Vase, 6" h., angular pointed handles from base to midsection, tan ground, No. 88-6".. **75-150**

Vase, 9" h., green ground, No. 94-9"............. **110**

Vase, 14" h., green ground, No. 97-14", repaired base chip **431**

Wall pocket, overhead handle w/pointed ends, green ground, No. 1294-8 1/2", 8 1/2" h.. **225**

Ming Tree (1949)

High gloss glaze in mint green, turquoise, or white is decorated with ming branch; handles are formed from gnarled branches.

Basket w/overhead branch handle, ruffled rim, blue ground, No. 509-12", 13" h............ **150**

Candleholders, squat melon-ribbed body w/angular branch handles at shoulder, white, No. 551, pr. **50**

Console set: 10" l. bowl, No. 528-10" & pair of candleholders, No. 551; green ground, 3 pcs... **225**

Model of a conch shell, white ground, No. 563-7, minor crazing, 8 1/2" w. **138**

Vase, 8" h., asymmetrical branch handles, blue ground, No. 582-8"................................ **299**

Moderne (1930s)

Art Deco-style rounded and angular shapes trimmed with an embossed panel of vertical lines and modified

swirls and circles, white trimmed with terra cotta, medium blue with white and turquoise with a burnished antique gold.

Bowl, 7 x 11", 4" h., pleated body, white, No. 301-10"... **259**

Bowl-vase, low foot, compressed ball-form, blue ground, No. 299-6", 6 1/2"..................... **173**

Candleholder, triple, turquoise ground, No. 1112-5 1/2", 5 1/2" h. (small nick in base under foot, not visible from side)................... **202**

Candleholder, triple, white, No. 1112-5 1/2", 6" h. **170**

Vase, 6" h., a round foot tapering to a narrow short stem supporting a tall conical body, two small curved handles from foot to lower body, blue ground, No. 788-6" **345**

Vase, triple bud, 7" h., medium blue, No. 792-7" **392**

Vase, bud, 8" h., cone-shaped on low foot, asymmetrical handles rising from base, turquoise, No. 791-8"..................................... **388**

Vase, 9 1/2" h., white ground, No. 799-9" (1/8 x 1" repair on inside edge of rim).......... **225**

Morning Glory (1935)

Delicately colored blossoms and twining vines in white or green with blue.

Basket, w/high pointed overhead handle, globular body, green ground, No. 340-10", restored handle, 10 1/2" h. **385**

Basket, w/high pointed overhead handle, globular body, white ground, No. 340-10", 10 1/2" h. **638**

Bowl, 4" d., squatty bulbous body w/tiny angled shoulder handles, green ground, No. 268-4" (restoration to nick at rim)........... **468**

Console bowl, small pointed end handles, white, 4 1/2 x 11 1/2" **330**

Urn-vase, two-handled, green ground, No. 269-6, 6" h. (glaze nick to rim, light bubbling to glaze on one side)............................. **440**

Urn-vase, two-handled, white ground, No. 269-6, 6" h.. **550**

Vase, 5" h., footed, flaring sides w/small angled handles at midsection, white ground.. **303**

Vase, 7" d., squatty bulbous body w/small angular handles at the shoulder, white ground... **358**

Vase, 7" h., tapering sides, base handles, white ground.. **525**

Vase, 8" h., bulbous ovoid body w/flat mouth, angled shoulder handles, white ground, No. 727-8" (small chip & in-the-making bruise to base) **424**

Vase, 9" h., squatty bulbous ovoid body w/angled handles from mid-section to rim, green ground, No. 729-9" (small chip to handle, three glaze nicks to rim) 523

Vase, 12" h., footed flaring cylindrical body w/a wide closed rim flanked by small pointed loop handles, white ground, No. 731-12", ... 880

Wall pocket, No. 1275-8", 8" h. (tight line to interior) 1,150

Wall pocket, white ground, No. 1275-8", 8" h. (crack to handle & one corner, one small chip) 460

Moss (1930s)
Green moss hanging over brown branch with green leaves; backgrounds are pink, ivory or tan shading to blue.

Basket, hanging-type, blue ground, No. 353-5", unmarked (small abrasion to tip & next to handle) 230

Bowl, 8" d., pink & green, No. 292-8" 170

Wall pocket, bucket-shaped, pink ground, No. 1279-10", 10" h. 431

Mostique (1915)
Indian designs of stylized flowers and arrowhead leaves, slip decorated on bisque, glazed interiors. Occasional bowl glazed on outside as well.

Basket, hanging-type, heart-shaped leaves & geometric designs, grey ground, No. 334-6", 6" h. 450

Basket, hanging-type, heart-shaped leaves & geometric designs, tan ground, 8 1/4" h. (small burst bubbles & nicks to rim) 403

Bowl, 7 1/2" d., floral design, sandy beige ground, No. 73 60

Jardiniere, floral design, tan ground, 8" h. 303

Mostique Jardiniere

Jardiniere, bulbous form w/molded rim, tan ground w/stylized floral design, small chips to rim & enamel, 9" h. (ILLUS.) 397

Jardiniere, grey ground, unmarked, 10" h. (minor chips to rim, chips to base) 330

Mostique Vase

Vase, 10" h., slightly waisted cylinder w/flaring mouth, arrowhead designs, grey ground, No. 164-10" (ILLUS.) 193

Wall pocket, conical, pointed end, floral decoration on grey ground, No. 1224-12", 12" h. (chip to hole) 259

Pauleo (1914)
Prestige line of 222 color combinations and two glaze types, lustre or marbleized.

Lamp, tall ovoid body tapering to a short, wide cylindrical neck w/flared rim, semi-matte blue glaze, original electric lamp fittings, 19" h. 440

Vase, 16" h., footed tall tapering cylindrical body w/wide cylindrical neck, brown, gold & orange glaze, ink mark 1,610

Vase, 16 1/2" h., pearl grey to orange lustre glaze w/yellow & red fruit w/pale green leaves decoration bordered by green bands around shoulder, impressed mark 690

Vase, 18 1/2" h., footed, bulbous base tapering to tall cylindrical neck w/flat rim, shaded red glaze, drilled 403

Vase, floor type, 19" h., footed baluster form w/narrow shoulder tapering to cylindrical neck w/slightly flaring rim, dark brown glaze (chip repair to base, drilled) 322

Peony (1942)
Floral arrangement with green leaves on textured, shaded backgrounds in yellow with brown, pink with blue, and green.

Basket, fan-shaped w/high overhead handle, pink ground, No. 377-8", 8" h. 115

Book ends, pink ground, No. 11, 5 1/2" h., pr. 260

Flower frog, gold ground, No. 47-4", 4" h. 40

Jardiniere, green ground, No. 661-4", 4" h 58

Jardiniere & pedestal base, gold ground, No. 661-8", 8" h., overall, 24 1/2" h., 2 pcs. (two hairlines & small firing fleck to rim, small chip to one leaf of jardiniere & couple of minute flecks to pedestal) 440

Jardiniere & pedestal base, pink ground, No. 661-8", 8" h., 2 pcs. (shallow glaze scaling 1/2" to shoulder, probably from firing) 715

Vase, 7" h., pink ground, No 61-7" 145

Wall pocket, two-handled, brown ground, No. 1293-8", 8" 259

Wall pocket, two-handled, green ground, No. 1293-8", 8" 225

Pine Cone (1931)
Realistic embossed brown pine cones and green pine needles on shaded blue, brown or green ground. (Pink is extremely rare.)

Ashtray, brown ground, No. 499, 4 1/2" l. **200-225**

Book ends, blue ground, No. 1, pr. 288

Bowl, 4" d., brown ground, bulbous w/incurved irregular rim, No. 441-4" 325

Candleholders, flat disk base supporting candle nozzle in the form of a pine cone flanked by needles on one side & branch handle on the other, brown ground, No. 112-3", 3" h., pr. 240

Flowerpot & saucer, blue ground, No. 633-5", 5" h. 288

Match holder, brown ground, No. 498, 3" h. 112
Pitcher w/ice lip, 8" h., footed wide spherical body w/curved rim & squared spout, brown ground, No. 1321 .... **581**
Planter, boat-shaped, blue ground, No. 455-6", 6" l. **234**
Urn-vase, pedestal foot below a tall slightly flaring cylindrical body w/two small twig handles, brown ground, No. 907-7", 7" h. 114
Urn-vase, pedestal foot below a tall slightly flaring cylindrical body w/two small twig handles, blue ground, No. 907-7", 7" h. 230
Vase, 14" h., floor-type, footed tall ovoid form w/small angled twig handles at shoulder, brown ground, No. 850-14", 14" h. **805**

Russco (1930s)
Octagonal rim openings, stacked handles, narrow perpendicular panel front and back. One type glaze is solid matte color; another is matte color with lustrous crystalline over glaze, some of which shows actual grown crystals.

Urn-vase, angular handles, orange, No. 108-6, 7" h. **225**
Vase, 8" h., green w/crystalline overglaze........ **193**
Vase, double bud, 8" h., No. 107-8" **200**
Vase, 8" h., rust ground, No. 696-8"................. **220**

Silhouette (1952)
Recessed area silhouettes nature study or female nudes. Colors are rose, turquoise, tan and white with turquoise.

Bowl, 6", white, No. 726-6"...................................... **70**
Bowl, 8" d., florals, tan ground, No. 727-8".......... **70**
Candleholders, florals, tan ground, No. 751-3", 3" h., pr. **50**
Ewer, bulging base, florals, rose, No. 716-6", 6" h. **80**
Ewer, bulging base, florals, white, No. 716-6", 6" h. **105**
Jardiniere, footed wide nearly spherical body w/an incurved wide irregular rim, small pointed angular shoulder handles, female nudes, blue ground, No. 742-6", 6" h. (tight line to rim, small chip to base, spider lines to base) **303**
Planter, rose ground, No. 768-8", 8" l............... **200**
Rose bowl, female nudes, turquoise blue ground, No. 742-6", 6" h. (repair to base)..... **264**
Urn, four wing-shaped feet on disk base, reclining female nudes, white ground, No. 763-8", 8" h. **358**
Vase, 5" h., florals, turquoise blue ground, No. 779-5".. **135**
Vase, 7" h., florals, double wing-shaped handles above low footed base, cylindrical w/asymmetrical rim, rose, No. 782-7" **78**
Vase, 8" h., urn-form, tapering ovoid body raised on four angled feet on a round disk base, wide slightly flaring mouth, female nude, rose ground, No. 763-8" **374**
Vase, 8" h., rose ground, No. 784-8"................. **245**
Vase, 8" h., white ground, No. 784-8"................. **60**
Vase, 9" h., double, base w/canted sides supporting two square vases w/sloping rims, joined by a stylized branch-form center post, florals, rose ground, No. 757-9" **245**

Wall pocket, bullet-shaped w/angular pierced handles, florals, rose ground, No. 766-8", 8" h....................................... **431**

Snowberry (1946)
Brown branch with small white berries and green leaves embossed over spider-web design in various background colors (blue, green and rose).

Ashtray, round dished form, shaded green ground, 5 1/4" d. **80**
Basket, footed fan-shaped body w/wide looped & pointed handle, shaded green ground, No. 1BK-7", 7" h............................... **193**
Basket, w/asymmetrical overhead handle, shaded blue ground, No. 1BK-8", 8" h.......... **130**
Basket w/curved overhead handle, disk base, shaded green ground, No. 1BK-12", 12" h...................................... **209**

Snowberry Low Bowl

Bowl, 6" d., two-handled, rose ground, small chip at corner of handle, light crazing, No. 1BL1-6" (ILLUS.) **144**
Bowl, 10" d., footed, shaded green ground, No. 1FB-10"....................................... **182**
Console bowl, pointed end handles, shaded green ground, No. 1BL1-10", 10" l. **99**
Console bowl, shaded green ground, No. 1BL-8", 11" l. **88**
Cornucopia-vase, shaded green ground, No. 1CC-8", 8" h. **132**
Jardiniere & pedestal, shaded blue ground, No. 1J-8", 2 pcs. **1,350**
Jardiniere & pedestal base, shaded green ground, No. IJ-8", overall 25" h., 2 pcs. **750**
Pedestal base, rose ground, 16" h. **168**
Rose bowl, two-handled, shaded green, No. 1RB-5", 5" h. **165**
Tray long leaf-shaped, shaded green ground, No. 1BL1-12", 14" l. **200**
Vase, 10" h., shaded green ground, No. 1V2-10" **231**
Vase, 15" h., floor-type, shaded rose ground, 1V1-15".. **750**

Snowberry Wall Pocket

Wall pocket, wide half-round form tapering to a pointed base, low angled handles along the lower sides, shaded green ground, No. 1WP-8", 8" w., 5 1/2" h. (ILLUS.).. **144**
Window box, shaded green ground, No. 1WX-8", 8" l....................................... **289**

Sunflower (1930)

Tall stems support yellow sunflowers whose blooms form a repetitive band. Textured background shades from tan to dark green at base.

Basket, hanging-type,6 3/4" (exterior spider lines & horizontal line to rim)........................ **460**
Jardiniere, No. 619-4", 4" h. **616**
Jardiniere, No. 619-6", 6 1/4" h...................... **1,955**
Planter, wide tapering cylindrical body w/in-curved rim, 5 x 6 1/4" **1,265**
Vase, 5" h., No. 486-5", unmarked **560**
Vase, 6" h., swelled cylindrical body w/short cylindrical neck flanked by small loop handles, No. 485-6" **669**
Vase, 8" h., two-handled, ovoid w/flaring rim, No. 491-8" **1,460**
Vase, 9" h., bulbous base w/wide cylindrical neck, small loop handles, No. 493-9" **1,161**
Wall pocket, No. 1265-7", minute glaze nick to front of pierced back brace, glazed over chip to back corner, 7" h. **1,427**

Thorn Apple (1930s)

White trumpet flower with leaves reverses to thorny pod with leaves. Colors are shaded blue, brown and pink.

Basket, hanging-type, shaded blue ground, No. 355-5", 7" d., 5" h. **288**
Book ends, shaded blue ground, No. 3, pr. **140**

Thorn Apple Centerpiece

Centerpiece, shaded blue ground, No. 313-11", 11" l. (ILLUS.)............................... **134**
Jardiniere, shaded brown ground, No. 638-4", 4" h. **100**
Urn, stepped handles, disk foot, shaded brown ground, No. 304-4" **80**
Urn, stepped handles, disk foot, shaded blue ground, No. 305-6", 6" h. **160**
Vase, bud, 7" h., shaded pink ground, No. 813-7" **145**
Vase, 10 1/2" h., angular handles rising from shoulder to middle of wide neck, footed, shaded brown ground, No. 822-10".. **138**
Vase, 10 1/2" h., angular handles rising from shoulder to middle of wide neck, footed, shaded pink ground, No. 822-10" **225**
Wall pocket, brown ground, No. 356-4", 4" h. (minute nick to back of hole)................. **978**
Wall pocket, triple, shaded brown ground, No. 1280-8", 8" h. (small stilt pull chips) **500**

Topeo (1934)

Simple forms decorated with four vertical evenly spaced cascades of leaves in high relief at their origin, tapering downward to a point. A light green crystalline glaze shades to a mottled medium blue, with cascades in alternating green and pink. A second type is done completely in a high-gloss dark red.

Vase, 6 1/2" h., ovoid w/flaring mouth, shaded blue glaze, No. 656-6" **201**
Vase, 7" h., compressed globular base & flaring mouth, green crystalline glaze shading to blue, No. 658-7 1/4"...................... **403**
Vase, 8" h., blue ground, No. 659-8".................. **633**
Vase, 8 1/4" h., footed ovoid body w/short flaring rim, shaded blue ground, No. 660-8 1/4" **500**
Vase, 12 1/4" h., ovoid tapering sides, green crystalline glaze shading to blue, No. 664-12 1/4"... **863**

Tuscany (1927)

Marble-like finish most often found in a shiny pink, sometimes in matte grey, more rarely in a dull turquoise. Suggestion of leaves and berries, usually at the base of handles, are the only decorations.

Console bowl, rectangular w/rounded ends, mottled pink, unmarked, 11" l. **225**
Console bowl, rectangular w/rounded ends, No. 174-12", 12" l. **250**
Flower frog, mottled pink, small.......................... **65**
Urn-vase, mottled pink, 4" h. **200**
Vase, 5" h., 7" d., mottled turquoise, No. 70-5"... **88**
Vase, 5" h., 7" d., mottled pink, No. 70-5"......... **130**
Vase, 5 1/2" h., fan-shaped, mottled pink ground... **95**
Vase, 7" h., tri-shaped, two-handled, grey, w/original sticker, No. 343-7" **202**
Vase, 8" h., mottled pink ground, No. 344-8"...... **275**
Vase, 10" h., shoulder handles, bulbous body, mottled pink ground, No. 347-10" **395**
Wall pocket, long open handles, rounded rim, grey glaze, No. 1255-8", 8" h.................. **288**

Velmoss (1935)

Characterized by three horizontal wavy lines around the top from which long, blade-like leaves extend downward. Colors are green, blue, tan and pink.

Jardiniere, footed spherical body w/short wide neck & pointed shoulder handles, mottled blue glaze, No. 264-5", 5" h.............. **207**
Urn-vase, angular pointed side handles, mottled pink, No. 265-6", 6" h. **132**
Vase, 6" h., swelled cylindrical body w/pointed shoulder handles, mottled raspberry red glaze, No. 714-6", gold foil label **255**
Vase, 14 1/2" h., tall trumpet-form body w/low foot, angular pointed handles, mottled rose glaze, No. 722-14" **616**

Water Lily (1940s)

Water lily and pad in various color combinations: tan to brown with yellow lily, blue with white lily, pink to green with pink lily.

Basket, hanging-type, shaded blue ground, No. 468-5", 9" h. **110**
Basket, w/asymmetrical overhead handle, curved & sharply scalloped rim, shaded blue ground, No. 382-12", 12" h. **160**
Basket w/pointed asymmetrical overhead handle & pleated rim, pink shading to green ground, No. 381-10", 10" h. **100**
Basket w/pointed overhead handle, cylindrical w/flaring rim, shaded blue ground, No. 380-8", 8" h. **140**

Ewer, flared bottom, blended blue ground,
No. 10-6", 6" h.. 70
Flower holder, two-handled, fan-shaped
body, gold shading to brown ground, No.
48, 4 1/2" h. 90

Water Lily Flowerpot

Flowerpot w/saucer, gold shading to
brown ground, No. 664-5, clay fold on in-
ner rim of pot, 5" h. (ILLUS.)......................... 101
Jardiniere & pedestal base, blended blue
ground, overall 24" h., 2 pcs. 448
Vase, 9" h., footed bulbous ovoid body w/a
large trumpet neck flanked by angled
handles, gold shading to brown ground,
No. 79-9".. 160
Vase, 9" h., footed bulbous ovoid body w/a
large trumpet neck flanked by angled
handles, pink shaded to green ground,
No. 79-9".. 207
Vase, 18" h., floor-type, tall baluster-form
w/pointed shoulder handles, gold shad-
ing to brown ground, No. 85-18" 425

White Rose (1940s)
*White roses and green leaves against a vertically
combed ground of blended blue, brown shading to green
or pink shading to green.*

Basket, hanging-type, pink shading to
green ground, No. 463-5", 5" h..................... 325
Basket w/pointed circular handle, pink
shading to green ground, No. 363-10",
10" h.. 303
Cornucopia-vase, brown shading to green
ground, No. 144-8", 8" h. 190
Jardiniere & pedestal base, blended blue
ground, No. 653-8", 8" h., 2 pcs. 770
Tea set: cov. teapot, sugar bowl & creamer;
brown shading to green ground, Nos. 1T,
1S, 1C, 3 pcs.. 385
Urn-vase, handles rising from base to rim,
footed, pink shading to green ground, No.
146-6", 6" h... 150
Vase, double bud, 4 1/2" h., two cylinders
joined by an arched bridge, brown shad-
ing to green ground, No. 148........................ 160
Vase, 5" h., footed trumpet-form body
w/notched rim & asymmetrical base loop
handles, brown shading to green ground,
980-6" 120
Vase, 7" h., pink shading to green ground,
No. 983-7".. 165
Vase, 8" h., flattened ovoid body on a rect-
angular foot, small pointed shoulder handles, blended blue ground, No. 984-8"......... 265
Vase, 9" h., footed, wide tapering cylindrical
body w/large handles from foot to

shoulder, notched rim, pink shading to
green ground, No. 986-9"............................... 300
Wall pocket, swirled handle, flaring rim,
pink shading to blue ground, No. 1288-
6", 6 1/2" h... 345
Wall pocket, conical w/flaring rim w/over-
head handle continuing to one side, pink
shading to green ground, No. 1289-8",
8 1/2" h.. 345

Wincraft (1948)
*Revived shapes from older lines such as Pine Cone,
Bushberry, Cremona, Primrose and others. Vases with
animal motifs, contemporary shapes in high gloss of
blue, tan, lime and green.*

Ashtray, glossy turquoise blue ground, No.
240-T... 60
Bowl, 8" d., glossy blue ground, No. 226-8"...... 132
Coffeepot, cov., glossy tan, No. 250-P,
9 1/2" h... 140
Console bowl, brown ground, No. 233-14",
14" l. (small glaze chip to interior, colored-in chip to both rim & base)................... 173
Planter, blue, No. 256-5", 5" h........................... 80
Vase, 6" h., blue ground, No. 241-6"................ 154
Vase, 8" h., flowing lily form w/asymmetrical
side handles, tulip & foliage in relief on
shaded blue ground, No. 282-8" 121

Wisteria (1933)
*Lavender wisteria blossoms and green vines against
a roughly textured brown shading to deep blue ground,
rarely found in only brown.*

Basket, hanging-type, brown ground,
7 1/2" h.. 633
Urn, blue ground, No. 632-5", 5" h.................... 683

Wisteria Urn

Urn, bulbous body w/wide flat mouth, small
loop shoulder handles, brown ground,
6" h. (ILLUS.) 518
Vase, 6" h., ovoid body tapering to short cylindrical neck flanked by small loop handles, brown ground, No. 631-6".................... 480
Vase, 6 1/2" h., globular w/angular rim handles, blue ground, No. 637-6 1/2"................ 650
Vase, 6 1/2" h., globular w/angular rim handles, brown ground, No. 637-6 1/2".............. 768

Zephyr Lily (1946)
*Tall lilies and slender leaves adorn swirl-textured
backgrounds of Bermuda Blue, Evergreen and Sienna
Tan.*

Basket, hanging-type, green ground, No.
472-5", 7 1/2" w. 188

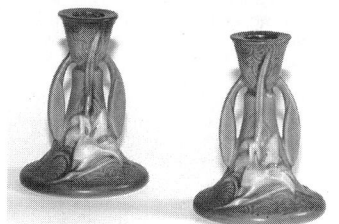

Zephyr Lily Candlesticks

Candlesticks, blue ground, No. 1163-
4 1/2", pr. (ILLUS.).. **225**

Console bowl, low oblong form w/curved
end tab handles, blue ground, No. 474-
8", 8" l. **110**

Cornucopia-vase, terra cotta ground, No.
203-6", 6" h. **135**

Ewer, blue ground, No. 22-6", 6" h. **120**

Ewer, footed flaring lower body w/angled
shoulder tapering to a tall forked neck
w/upright tall spout, long low arched han-
dle, green ground, No. 23-10", 10" h. **135**

Rose bowl, terra cotta ground, No. 471-6",
6" h. **180**

Vase, 6" h., two-handled, terra cotta, No.
130-6" **165**

Royal Copenhagen

Although The Royal Copenhagen factory in Denmark has been in business for over 200 years, very little has been written about it. That is not to say the very beautiful porcelain it produces is not easily recognizable. Besides the gorgeous dinnerware, such as "Blue Fluted" and "Flora Danica," it produced, and still produces, wonderful figurines depicting animals and people. The company employs talented artists as both modelers and painters. Once you become familiar with the colors, glazes and beauty of these figurines, you will have no trouble in recognizing them at a glance.

Collecting these magnificent figurines seems as popular now as in the past. As with most objects, and certainly true of these figurines, value will depend on the complexity, size, age and rarity of the piece. There is other Danish porcelain on the market today, but the Royal Copenhagen figurines can readily be recognized by the mark on the bottom with the dark blue, three wavy lines. Accept no imitations!

Figure of boy, Sandman (Wee-Willie-Wink-
ie), standing on white square stepped
base & leaning on an umbrella, holding
another, dressed in grey, No. 1145, 6" h. **$100**

Figure of boy on gourd, young barefoot
boy wearing white shirt & blue overalls
seated astride a large green gourd, No.
4539, 4 1/4 x 4 1/2" **100**

Model of bird, Budgie on Gourd, white bird
w/blue trim on dark blue gourd, No. 4682,
4 x 5 1/2" **165**

Model of cow & calf, Mother cow licking
calf nestled against her, white w/shaded
grey & black spots, No. 800, 5 x 11" **35**

Model of dog, Male Boxer, standing, white
& shaded tan & grey w/black face, No.
3634, 5 1/2 x 7" **150**

Model of elk (moose), reclining position,
shaded grey & white w/white antlers, No.
2813, 9 x 10" **450**

Model of mink, white w/black eyes & brown
nose, No. 4654, 3 3/4 x 7" **180**

Model of piglets, pair of piglets fused together, white w/grey spots, pink snout,
No. 683, 2 1/2 x 4 1/2" **100**

Model of sea lion, head raised, shades of
tan & grey, No. 265, 7 x 12" **350**

Royal Dux

This factory in Bohemia was noted for the figural porcelain wares in the Art Nouveau style which were exported around the turn of the 20th century. Other notable figural pieces were produced through the 1930s and the factory was nationalized after World War II.

Two Royal Dux Female Busts

Bust of lady, ornately dressed in late Victorian costume, a large pierced lacy hat
w/ribbons & a high & widely flaring ruffled
lacy collar w/ribbons, decorated in pale
pink, green & yellow w/the hat in pink,
molded rectangular pad mark impressed
"452 - A," applied pink triangle impressed
"Royal Dux Bohemia," early 20th c.,
some restoration, 21 3/4" h. (ILLUS. left) **$1,800**

Bust of water nymph, shown emerging
from foaming blue waves amid pink orchids & green leaves, her skin & face
w/naturalistic coloring, molded rectangular pad mark w/"507," applied pink triangle mark w/"Royal Dux Bohemia," early
20th c., part of one orchid petal missing,
small chips to leaves & other petals,
21 1/4" h. (ILLUS. right with bust of lady).. **4,800**

Ornate Royal Dux Figural Centerpiece

Centerpiece, figural, a large shaped ornately scalloped & pierced bowl atop a
pierced curved flowering vine pedestal
w/a full-length Art Nouveau maiden in a

swirled gown also supporting the bowl, on a scalloped & swirled rounded base, natural colors, ca. 1900, 16" h. (ILLUS.)....... **900**

Large Figural Royal Dux Vase

Vases, 37 1/4" h., figural, a tall flaring cluster of banana tree leaves & fruit behind the standing figure of an Arab girl leaning on a tall jug, other one w/man beneath the tree playing a lute, heavy gold trim on white w/pink trim, marked "Royal Dux - Made in Czechoslovakia," ca. 1920s, pr. (ILLUS. of one)... **1,210**

Royal Worcester

This porcelain has been made by the Royal Worcester Porcelain Co. at Worcester, England, from 1862 to the present. Royal Worcester is distinguished from wares made at Worcester between 1751 and 1862 that are referred to as only Worcester by collectors.

Compote, 7 3/4" d., flower petal shape on poppy pod-form base, decorated in floral design w/gilt decoration **$616**

Ewer, copper-colored glaze w/raised gold decoration including flying birds & molded floral decoration on the handle, ending w/a dragon head finial at the top, green crown mark, also "Patented Metallic" w/an additional impressed crown mark, 11 3/4" h. **220**

Ewer, flared extended rim & gilt handle, ovoid body raised on pedestal base, decorated w/floral design & gilt decoration, 7 3/4" h., ca. 1893 .... **224**

Pitcher, 5 1/2" h., bulbous body w/floral decoration, gilt twig handle, ca. 1890........... **224**

Royal Worcester Pitcher & Vase

Pitcher, 6" h., flared scalloped rim, leaf spout & twig handle on bulbous body, decorated in floral design w/gilt decoration, ca. 1889 (ILLUS. left).................. **476**

Royal Worcester Beverage Pitcher

Pitcher, 7 3/4" h., gilt rim w/lion head spout & lion paw handle, cylindrical body, decorated in floral design w/gilt decoration, ca. 1889 (ILLUS.) **896**

Pitcher, 8 7/8" h., gilt rim w/lion head spout, cylindrical body w/lion paw handle, decorated in floral design w/gilt decoration, ca. 1889 .... **952**

One Plate of Royal Worcester Set

Plates, quatrefoil shape, each h.p. w/a different fish, gilt rims w/shells at corners, marked "Manufactured by the Worcester Royal Porcelain Co. for Richard Briggs Boston" w/the circle mark (no crown), 8 3/4" sq., minor wear, the set of 4 (ILLUS. of one) **413**

Plates, all decorated w/different polychrome flowers, gilt rims, "Designed by A.H. Williamson," mid-20th-c., 9 1/4" d., set of 12 .... **330**

Service plates, decorated w/a band of Neoclassical gilt enamel, border w/raised gilt enamel w/scrolls & urns, on a lapis blue ground, ca. 1920, 10 3/8" d., set of 18...... **2,185**

Tea set: 6 1/2" h. teapot, 3" h. creamer & 3 1/2" h. open sugar; melon ribbed bodies w/applied water lily pad decoration in gilt w/red veins, teapot w/lily pad lid, marked for 1888 & 1889, the set (repaired, minor wear) **220**

Vase, 10 3/4" h., narrow flared rim over bulbous body raised on scalloped pedestal base, decorated w/floral design & gilt decoration, ca. 1891 (ILLUS. right) **1,568**

Satsuma

These decorated wares have been produced in Japan since the end of the 18th century. The early pieces are scarce and high-priced. Later Satsuma wares are plentiful and, with prices rising, as highly collectible as earlier pieces.

Satsuma Bowl Decorated in Relief

Bowl, 9 5/8" d., round, decorated w/figures of man & woman w/haloes in relief sitting among other painted figures, in gold on white ground, signed "Hododa, Shimazu Mon," ca. 1868-1912 (ILLUS.).................. **$2,240**

Satsuma Covered Jar

Jar, cov., ovoid body, lid w/foo-lion finial, all decorated w/interior scenes of people, in iron reds, blues & black w/heavy gilding, Meiji period, 10" h. (ILLUS.).......................... **560**

One of Set of Satsuma Cabinet Plates

Plates, 8 1/2" d., set of 12 cabinet plates signed "Kinkozan zo," each decorated w/gilt border, painted flowers w/gilt scrollwork on dark blue ground, centering cartouches of various birds in wooded landscapes, each different, each marked w/impressed & painted mark on underside, extremely rare, the set (ILLUS. of one)............ **25,760**

Satsuma Miniature Vase

Vase, 2 1/2" h., miniature vase w/classical form w/flaring rim & decorated w/wisteria on cream ground, signed "Kinkozan," ca. 1868-1912 (ILLUS.)........................ **560**

Satsuma Signed Vase

Vase, cov., baluster form w/flaring rim, lid w/finial, ringed base, decorated w/haloed Arhats on gold ground, signed "Hododa, Shimazu Mon," ca. 1868-1912, drilled for lamp (ILLUS.)................................. **504**

One of a Pair of Satsuma Vases

Vases, 19 1/4" h., bulbous form w/ring rim, each decorated in fanciful manner w/figures in a garden scene, ca. 1880, pr. (ILLUS. of one)................................. **672**

Shawnee

The Shawnee Pottery Company of Zanesville, Ohio opened its doors for operation in 1936 and, sadly, closed in 1961. The pottery was inexpensive for its quality and was readily purchased at dimestores as well as department stores. Sears-Roebuck, Butler Bros., Woolworths and S. Kresge were just a few of the companies that were long-time retailers of this fine pottery.

Shawnee Pottery Company had a wide array of merchandise to offer from knick-knacks to dinnerware, though Shawnee is quite often associated with colorful pig cookie jars and dazzling "Corn King" line dinnerware. Planters, miniatures, cookie jars & corn line are much in demand by today's avid collectors. Factory seconds were purchased by outside decorators and trimmed with gold, decals and unusual hand painting which made those pieces extremely desirable in today's market and also enhances the value considerably.

Shawnee Pottery has become the most sought-after pottery in today's collectible market.

Reference books available are Mark E. Supnick's book Collecting Shawnee Pottery, The Collector's Guide to Shawnee Pottery by Duane and Janice Vanderbilt or Shawnee Pottery - An Identification & Value Guide by Jim and Bev Mangus.

Figural Howdy Doody Bank

Bank, figural, Howdy Doody riding a pig, marked "Bob Smith U.S.A.," 6 3/4" h. (ILLUS.) **$500-550**

Book ends, figural dog head, setter, marked "U.S.A.," 3 3/4" h., pr. **65-75**

Casserole, cov., Corn King patt., No. 74 .... **85**

Cigarette box, cov., embossed Indian arrowhead on lid, brown, marked "Shawnee," 3 1/4 x 4 1/2" **400-500**

Valencia Line Coffeepot

Coffeepot, cov., Valencia line, tangerine glaze, 7 1/2" h. (ILLUS.) **95-125**

Cookie jar, figural Cinderella, unmarked **125**

Cookie jar, figural Dutch Boy (Jack), paint under glaze, striped pants, marked "U.S.A.," 11" h. **125-150**

Cookie jar, figural Dutch Girl (Jill), paint under glaze, marked "U.S.A.," 11 1/2" h. **125-150**

Cookie jar, figural Great Northern Girl, marked "Great Northern U.S.A. 1026," 10" h. **375-425**

Cookie jar, figural Owl, gold trim & hand-decoration **150**

Dutch Style Red Feather Creamer

Creamer, ball-type, Dutch Style, decorated w/red feather, marked "U.S.A. 12," 4 1/2" h. (ILLUS.) **95-125**

Creamer, figural Puss 'n Boots, marked "Patented Puss N Boots U.S.A.," 4 1/2" h. **45-65**

Valencia Line Dealer's Display Sign

Dealer's display sign, figural Spanish dancers, "Valencia" embossed across base, tangerine glaze, 11 1/4" h. (ILLUS.) **400-450**

Head vase Polynesian woman, marked "Shawnee U.S.A. 896," 5 3/4" h. **75-95**

Lamp base, figural Rabbit eating ear of corn, unmarked, 6 1/2" h. **75-85**

Mixing bowl, Corn King line, marked "Shawnee 6," 6" d. **50**

Pitcher, ball-type, 7 1/4" h., Pennsylvania Dutch patt., marked "U.S.A." **95-125**

Pitcher, 7 1/2" h., figural Chanticleer Rooster, marked "Patented Chanticleer U.S.A." .. **75-85**

Planter, model of a canopy bed, marked "Shawnee U.S.A. 734," 7 3/4" h. **75-95**

Planter, model of a highchair & kitten, pink or blue, marked "U.S.A. 727," each........... **75-85**

Flower & Fern Salt Box

Salt box, cov., Flower & Fern patt., yellow, marked "U.S.A.," 4 3/4" h. (ILLUS.) **95-125**
Salt & pepper shakers, figural Corn King, No. 77, pr. **37**
Salt & pepper shakers, figural cottage, pr. **275-325**
Snack jar/bean pot, cov., tab-handled, Lobster Ware, figural lobster finial on lid, marked "Kenwood U.S.A. 925." 8" h. **375-400**
Sugar bowl, cov., Corn King line, No. 78, 5 1/4" h. **55-65**
Sugar bowl, cov., figural cottage, marked "U.S.A. 8," 4 1/2" h. **375-425**
Teapot, cov., figural Granny Ann, peach & blue, marked "Patented Granny Ann, U.S.A.," 8" h. **100-125**
Teapot, cov., figural Piper's Son, marked "Tom the Piper's Son patented U.S.A. 44," 7" h. **100-125**
Wall pocket, model of a birdhouse, No. 830, brown & tan w/gold trim **30**

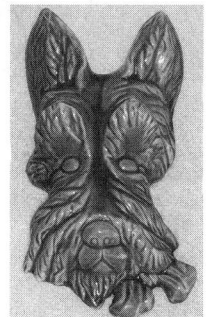

Scotty Dog Wall Pocket

Wall pocket, Scotty Dog head, unmarked, 9 1/2" h. (ILLUS.) **65-95**
Wall pocket, Sunflower patt., marked "U.S.A.," 6 3/4" h.. **35-45**

Shelley China

Members of the Shelley family were in the pottery business in England as early as the 18th century. In 1872 Joseph Shelley formed a partnership with James Wileman of Wileman & Co. who operated the Foley China Works. The Wileman & Co. name was used for the firm for the next fifty years, and between 1890 and 1910 the words "The Foley" appeared above conjoined "WC" initials.

Beginning in 1910 the Shelley family name in a shield appeared on wares, although the firm's official name

was still Wileman & Co. The company's name was finally changed to Shelley in 1925 and then Shelley China Ltd. after 1965. The firm changed hands in the 1960s and became part of the Doulton Group in 1971.

At first only average quality earthenwares were produced but in the late 1890s new shapes and better quality decorations were used.

Bone china was introduced at Shelley before World War I and these fine dinnerwares became very popular in the United States and are increasingly popular today with collectors. Thin "eggshell china" teawares, miniatures and souvenir items were widely marketed during the 1920s and 1930s and are sought-after today.

Ashtray, advertising-type, "Greer's O.V.H." ... **$100**
Backbar water pitcher, "White Horse" **500**
Bowl, berry, Blue Rock patt. **40**
Breakfast set: two-cup cov. coffeepot, creamer, open sugar bowl, two 8" d. plates, two 6" d. plates, two 5 1/2" d. bowls & one cov. pancake dish; Stocks patt., Dainty shape, the set **1,000**
Butter dish, cov., Dainty White patt. **100**
Butter pat, Primrose patt. **95**
Cake set: 10" handled cake plate & six 6" d. plates; Wild Flower patt., the set **250**
Candlestick, Art Deco-style, orange glaze, 2 1/2" h. **150**

Cloisonné Pattern Candlestick

Candlestick, flaring round base below the tapering shaft & bulbed candle socket, down-curved handle from socket to base, Cloisonné patt., 6 1/2" h. (ILLUS.) **250**
Candy dish, Dainty Pink patt., 4 1/2" l. **65**
Coffeepot, cov., Bluebells patt., Vincent shape.. **350**
Coffeepot, cov., Campanula patt., tall tapering ovoid body w/domed cover, 7" h. **300**

Dainty Blue Coffee, Tea & Water Pots

Coffeepot, cov., Dainty Blue patt., Dainty shape (ILLUS. right, bottom, previous page)............... 600
Coffeepot, cov., Violets patt., Mayfair shape............. 400

Dainty Floral Creamer & Sugar Bowl

Creamer & open sugar bowl, Floral patt., Dainty shape w/floral-molded handle, pr. (ILLUS.)............. 300
Creamer & open sugar bowl, Wileman & Co., pr............. 100
Creamer, open sugar bowl & tray, Blue Rock patt., 3 pcs............. 165
Creamer & sugar bowl, Harebell patt., pr............. 90
Cup & saucer, Begonia patt., six-flute shape............. 78
Cup & saucer, Black Dainty patt., Dainty shape, rare 1,200

Chinoiserie Pattern Cup & Saucer

Cup & saucer, Chinoiserie patt., Ripon shape (ILLUS.)............. 200
Cup & saucer, Countryside (Chintz style) patt., gold foot & scroll handle 204

Dainty Cup & Saucer w/Floral Handle

Cup & saucer, Dainty shape, lavender & cream w/floral-molded handle (ILLUS.) 200
Cup & saucer, Dainty shape, solid color 50
Cup & saucer, demitasse, Acacia patt., Regent shape 100

Floral-Handled Cup & Saucer

Cup & saucer, Floral patt., Queen Anne shape w/floral-molded handle (ILLUS.)......... 400

Cup & saucer, Floral patt., Vogue (Art Deco style) shape............. 300
Cup & saucer, Japan patt., Alexandra shape, Wileman & Co............. 100
Cup & saucer, miniature, Lily of the Valley patt., Westminster shape 325
Cup & saucer, Polka Dot patt. 100
Cup & saucer, Regency patt., Dainty shape........ 60
Cup & saucer, Rock Garden patt., footed Oleander shape............. 170
Cup & saucer, Stocks patt., Stratford shape........ 60
Cup & saucer, demitasse, Forget-Me-Not patt............. 48
Cups & saucers, demitasse, footed, pink w/aqua dots, gold lined, 6 each, 12 pcs. 350
Demitasse pot, cov., Wildflowers patt., Dainty shape............. 300
Dessert set: cup & saucer & dessert plate; Campanula patt., 3 pcs. 130
Dessert set: cup & saucer & dessert plate; Rosebud patt............. 110
Dessert set: cup & saucer & dessert plate; Rock Garden patt., 3 pcs. 125
Egg cup, Dainty Shamrock patt. 55
Hot water pot, cov., Dainty Blue patt., Dainty shape (ILLUS. center with coffeepot) 600
Hot water pot, cov., Dainty patt. 500

Shelley Floral Pattern Invalid Feeder

Invalid feeder, Floral patt. (ILLUS.)............. 250
Jam pot w/metal cover & holder, Bridal Rose patt., the set............. 175
Jelly mold, model of a large white chicken 200
Loving cup, Bermuda commemorative, "1609-1959," 4 1/2 x 7"............. 100
Luncheon set: 8" plate, cup & saucer; Harebell patt., 3 pcs............. 100
Luncheon set: 8" plate, cup & saucer; Stocks patt., 3 pcs............. 90

Blue Iris Luncheon Set

Luncheon set (trio): cup, saucer & plate; Blue Iris patt., Queen Anne shape, the set (ILLUS.) 200

Gladiolus Luncheon Set

Luncheon set (trio): cup, saucer & plate; Gladiolus patt., Eve (Art Deco style) shape, the set (ILLUS.)................................ 250

Japan Pattern Luncheon Set

Luncheon set (trio): cup, saucer & plate; Japan patt., Fairy shape, Wileman & Co., the set (ILLUS.)... 200

Thistle Pattern Luncheon Set

Luncheon set (trio): cup, saucer & plate; Thistle patt., Alexandra shape, Wileman & Co., the set (ILLUS.)................................... 125
Mint dish, Dainty Blue patt. 72

Shelley Model of a Drake

Model of a drake duck, brown head, grey & black body, Bird Series #12, 4 1/2" h. (ILLUS.)... 500
Mug, decorated w/the coat-of-arms of Wales, 3" h. 100
Napkin ring, Harmony patt................................ 100
Nut dish, Old England patt., signed by Eric Slater 75

Pitcher, water, jug-form, Blue Dragon patt. 500
Plate, dinner, Harebell patt..................................... 75

Festoons & Fruit Pattern Plate

Plate, Festoons & Fruit patt., Roseberry shape (ILLUS.).. 50-100
Plate, 6" d., Rock Garden patt. 40
Plate, 8" d., luncheon, Blue Rock patt. 56

Jacobean Pattern Plate

Plate, 8 3/4" d., Jacobean patt. (ILLUS.)........ 50-60
Platter, 10 x 13", meat, Blue Rock patt. 140

Harmony Pattern Two-Piece Reamer

Reamer & base, Harmony patt., streaky mottled pink & green glaze, 2 pc. (ILLUS.)... 350
Shaving mug, Harmony patt. 175

Blue Gladiolus Art Deco Tea Set

Tea set, Blue Gladiolus patt., Eve (Art Deco style) shape, 21 pcs. (ILLUS. of part) 3,000

Tea set, Green Lines & Bands patt., Eve (Art Deco style) shape, 21 pcs. **2,500**

Red Blocks Art Deco Tea Set

Tea set, Red Blocks patt., Mode (Art Deco style) shape, teapot & 22 pcs. (ILLUS. of part)... **3,500**

Sun-Ray Art Deco Tea Set

Tea set, Sun-Ray patt., Vogue (Art Deco style) shape, 21 pcs. (ILLUS. of part)......... **3,000**
Tea set, Yellow Phlox patt., Regent shape, teapot & 37 pcs. **2,000**
Teapot, cov., Begonia patt................................. **400**
Teapot, cov., Dainty Blue patt., Dainty shape (ILLUS. left with coffeepot)................. **650**
Teapot, cov., Dainty Blue patt., large................ **650**
Teapot, cov., Harebell patt. **400**

Harmony Drip-Ware Teapot

Teapot, cov., Harmony Drip-Ware, Cambridge shape (ILLUS.)..................................... **600**
Teapot, cov., Hollyhocks patt., Regent shape.. **400**

Rare Laburnum Pattern Teapot

Teapot, cov., Laburnum patt., Eve (Art Deco style) shape (ILLUS.)............................ **800**
Toast rack, Harmony Ware patt. **150**

Rare Shelley Umbrella Stand

Umbrella stand, advertising-type, columnar form w/molded pilasters flanking arched niches around the side, dark blue ground printed in white w/"Shelley China - Potters to The World," 27" h. (ILLUS.)..... **3,500**
Vase, 5" h., Balloons & Flashes patt.................. **125**
Vase, 5" h., Cloisonné patt. **200**

Harmony Ware Moresque Vase

Vase, 6" h., tall waisted shape, Harmony Ware, Moresque patt., stylized blossoms in orange, pale & dark blue & brown (ILLUS.).. **150**
Vegetable bowl, open, oval, Harebell patt., 9 1/2" l. **160**

Nursery Ware by Mabel Lucie Attwell
Baby feeding plate, color scene inscribed "Fairy Folk with Tiny Wings..."......................... **350**

Boo-Boo Cruet Set

Cruet set: three mushroom-shaped covered pots & figural shaker on four-lobed tray; Boo-Boo set (ILLUS.).......................... **1,000**
Figurine, Boo-Boo with knapsack.................. **1,000**
Figurine, Boo-Boo with mushroom................ **1,000**
Figurine, Golfer... **2,200**

Child's Mug and Saucer Set

Mug & saucer, color scene of Mother Rabbit & baby Rabbity, inscribed "When Rabbity fell...," the set (ILLUS.).............................. **375**

Child's Platter with Duck Scene

Platter, 8" l., squared shape w/molded handles, color scene of mother duck & children, inscribed "Will Somebody Kindly Tell..." (ILLUS.).. **300**

Boo-Boo Figural Tea Set

Tea set: cov. teapot, creamer & open sugar; Boo-Boo set w/mushroom-shaped open sugar & mushroom house-shaped teapot w/figural Boo-Boo creamer, the set (ILLUS.).. **2,500**

Intarsio Art Pottery (1997-99)

Intarsio Art Pottery Clock

Clock, table model, Art Nouveau-style upright case w/a brown border around a colored central panel w/a dial above a scene of a Medieval couple by a sundial above the inscription "The Days May Come - The Days May Go..."(ILLUS.)...................... **1,800**

Intarsio Art Pottery Cracker Jar

Cracker jar, cov., footed bulbous body w/silver plate rim, cover & bail handle, wide color band decorated w/scenes from Shakespeare plays, 6" h. (ILLUS.).... **1,000**

Caricature Teapot of Lord Salisbury

Teapot, cov., caricature of Lord Salisbury, dark green, black, tan & brown (ILLUS.) ... **1,100**
Toby mug, "The Irishman," 7 1/2" h. **900**
Vase, 8 1/2" h., bulbous body centered by a wide cylindrical neck w/four curved handles from neck to shoulder, decorated w/a central band of brown & white chickens on a blue & green ground, bands of brown scrolls on a green ground above & below & a dark blue neck w/white & yellow flowers & green leaves, green handles **2,000**

Intarsio Art Nouveau-style Wash Set

Wash bowl & pitcher set, Art Nouveau design w/large stylized flowers in yellow & shaded blue to white on green swirled leafy stems on a dark green & black ground, bowl 18" d., the set (ILLUS.)......... **2,500**

Spatterware

This ceramic ware takes its name from the "spattered" decoration, in various colors, generally used to trim pieces hand-painted with rustic center designs of flowers, birds, houses, etc. Popular in the early 19th century, most was imported from England.

Related wares, called "stick spatter," had free-hand designs applied with pieces of cut sponge attached to sticks, hence the name. Examples date from the 19th and early 20th century and were produced in England, Europe and America.

Some early spatter-decorated wares were marked by the manufacturers, but not many. Twentieth century reproductions are also sometimes marked, including those produced by Boleslaw Cybis.

Creamer, blue spatter, Fort patt. in grey & brown w/green spatter trees, 4" h. (stains).. **$248**

Creamer, yellow spatter, w/peafowl in red, yellow & slate blue on a green spatter branch, molded leaf handle, chip & darkened crazing, 3 1/2" h. (ILLUS. third from right w/assorted spatterware, below).......... **4,125**

Cup, handleless, free-hand Rooster patt. in yellow, blue & red w/a blue spatter border.. **1,100**

Cup & saucer, green spatter, handleless, w/schoolhouse design in red & dark brown, staining, colors differ slightly (ILLUS. center w/assorted spatterware, below).. **1,870**

Cup & saucer, handleless, blue spatter, Dahlia patt. in red, blue & green (short hairlines, some areas where enamel didn't adhere) **220**

Cup & saucer, handleless, green w/brown spatter, picture of red schoolhouse in center, minor stains (ILLUS. front center w/group of spatterware, top, next page) **2,750**

Cup & saucer, handleless, Rainbow spatter, slightly oversize w/red, green & blue decoration w/blue on inside cup rim (tiny pinpoint flake on rim of saucer)................... **1,100**

Cup & saucer, handleless, red spatter, light sponging w/an open-bodied peafowl design in green, light blue & yellow wavy lines (ILLUS. far right w/assorted spatterware, below)...................................... **413**

Cup & saucer, handleless, yellow spatter, blue, black & green morning glory design, deep yellow (minor wear, blue has flakes & stains, & saucer has hairline) **990**

Cup & saucer, handleless, yellow spatter, design of red tulip w/green leaves, strong yellow **3,190**

Cup & saucer, handleless, yellow spatterware, red & green cockscomb center design, cup has minor stain (ILLUS. of cup & saucer far left w/assorted spatterware, below).. **2,640**

Cups & saucers, two cups, two saucers, handleless, blue spatter rims w/red & green roses, pr. **385**

Mug, Rainbow spatter, purple & blue vertical stripes w/leaf molded handle ends, 2 3/4" h. (ILLUS. third from left w/assorted spatterware, below) **935**

Pitcher, 6 3/8" h., yellow spatter, red & green tulip on both sides, paneled w/a molded fan under spout (some flakes, interior stains & restored spout) **4,675**

Pitcher, 6 5/8" h., slightly bulbous form, blue spatter, red & green parrot design on side, crow's feet, stains (ILLUS. back row, right w/group of spatterware, top next page).. **3,410**

Pitcher, 7 3/8" h., Rainbow spatter in blue, red, yellow, green & black swirled stripes w/red on inside rim & handle, molded shoulder, scroll handle & spout, rim flake,

Assorted Spatterware

Spatterware Group

Spatterware Group

short hairline (ILLUS. far left w/spatterware group, bottom previous page)........... **7,150**

Plate, 8 1/2" d., blue spatter, molded feather edge w/red, yellow & blue peafowl center, old paper labels on back w/some history..................... **688**

Plate, 8 1/2" d., Rainbow spatter, light red, blue & yellow stripes on paneled border, minor knife scratches (ILLUS. far right w/spatterware group, bottom previous page)..................... **2,640**

Plate, 8 1/4" d., Rainbow spatter, red & blue rainbow border w/bull's-eye center, hairline, minor surface flake (ILLUS. second from left w/group of spatterware, above)..................... **935**

Plate, 8 3/4" d., Rainbow spatter, red, blue & yellow border (rim chip)..................... **1,320**

Plate, 8 3/8" d., deep yellow w/red & green thistle center (chip & light staining)............. **1,540**

Plate, 9 1/4" d., blue spatter, paneled border, red & green Adam's rose in center (minor stains)..................... **303**

Plate, 9 3/4" d., strong yellow paneled rim w/red & green thistle center, light crazing & staining (ILLUS. second from left w/spatterware group, bottom previous page)..................... **3,960**

Plate, 8 1/2" d., Rainbow spatter w/paneled border of red, yellow & blue stripes **2,860**

Plate, 8 3/4" d., free-hand Peafowl patt. in red, blue & green, blue spatter overall background (stains)..................... **770**

Platter, 12 1/2" l., Rainbow spatter, octagonal shape w/red & green border, center w/a large red & blue tulip w/green leaves, hairline, stains, flaking (ILLUS. far left w/group of spatterware, above).................. **4,620**

Platter, 15 3/4" l., octagonal oblong shape, decorated w/cluster of buds pattern in burgundy & green on white central ground, blue spatter outer rim has been reglazed (in-the-making hairline at one end of the well)..................... **1,045**

Soup bowl, blue spatter, paneled rim w/green, yellow & red peafowl in center, 10 1/2" d. (rim flakes)..................... **880**

Sugar bowl, cov., Rainbow spatter, ovoid shape w/yellow & blue stripes & red & green thistle design, 5 1/4" h. (hairline & repair) **3,740**

Teapot, cov., blue spatter, baluster shape, paneled w/molded arches on shoulder,

Peafowl in green, ochre & pink, 8 5/8" h. (some flakes & restored finial)....................... **990**

Teapot, cov., green thumbprint spatter design of leaves w/red, yellow & blue peafowl on a branch, 6 1/2" h. (slightly ground spout, fading to green on lid) **1,870**

Teapot, cov., Rainbow spatter, paneled baluster form w/molded arch designs on shoulder & spout, red & blue, 9 1/4" h. (flakes, hairline & glued finial) **550**

Teapot, cov., tapering octagonal body w/flared rim, swan's-neck spout & high angled handle, fitted high domed cover w/knop finial, over blue spatter decoration, 9" h. (minor hairline, flakes on spout & finial wear) **330**

Vegetable bowl, cov., Rainbow spatter, octagonal shape w/footed base & shell-shaped finial, blue & purple w/brighter colors inside base, impressed "Porcelaine Opaque - & G. Alcock," stains, 7 3/4" h, 10 1/4" l. (ILLUS. far right w/group of spatterware, above) **2,200**

Vegetable bowl, open, octagonal, w/red & green stripes, red & blue tulip center, 2 x 6", 8 1/2" l., hairlines (ILLUS. second from right w/spatterware group, previous page) **2,530**

Wash bowl, blue spatter, round paneled bowl, interior w/design of blue & yellow tulip & red blossoms, 14" d., 14 1/2" h. (stains, hairline & spider)..................... **1,210**

Waste bowl, flared sides on footed ring base, green w/one peafowl in black, ochre & blue, repair, 5 1/2" d. (ILLUS. center w/spatterware group, bottom, previous page) **220**

Staffordshire Figures

Small figures and groups made of pottery were produced by the majority of the Staffordshire, England potters in the 19th century and were used as mantel decorations or "chimney ornaments," as they were sometimes called. Pairs of dogs were favorites and were turned out by the carload, and 19th century pieces are still available. Well-painted reproductions also abound and collectors are urged to exercise caution before investing.

Benjamin Franklin, standing figure of Franklin holds a document in one hand & his tricornered hat in the other, cobalt coat w/purple, green & red vest & striped pants, gold trim, 14 1/2" h. **$853**

Benjamin Franklin, standing figure wears dark blue coat & vest w/burgundy & green-on-white pattern, gold lettering on square base spells "Franklin," 14 1/2" h. (crazing, w/areas of blue "pooling" in the glaze) 990

Dogs, seated dogs looking right & left, hollow body molding w/black & grey decoration, early, 11 1/4" h., pr. (hairlines) 550

Figure group, a standing man & woman in Scottish dress, polychrome decoration, ca. 1850, 14 1/4" h. 448

Figure group, figure of a Scotsman in kilt w/a dog, ca. 1865, 14 1/2" h. 420

Figure group, standing figures of man & woman in colorful clothing w/sheep on either side at their feet, raised lettering on base spells "Welsh Shepherds," 14" h. (restoration) 385

Zebra, black & white zebra stands pawing grassy ground that makes up green & yellow base, 19th c., 5" h. 224

Staffordshire Transfer Wares

The process of transfer-printing designs on earthenwares developed in England in the late 18th century and by the mid-19th century most common ceramic wares were decorated in this manner, most often with romantic European or Oriental landscape scenes, animals or flowers. The earliest such wares were printed in dark blue but a little later light blue, pink, purple, red, black, green and brown were used. A majority of these wares were produced at various English potteries right up until the turn of the 20th century but French and other European firms also made similar pieces and all are quite collectible. The best reference on this area is Petra Williams' book Staffordshire Romantic Transfer Patterns - Cup Plates and Early Victorian China *(Fountain House East, 1978).*

Bowl, 9" d., 4 1/8" h., reticulated, footed bowl w/scalloped edge & molded handles, light blue romantic transfer scene of boatmen on a lake, "Interlachen," marked "Late Spode, Copeland and Garrett" (minor edge wear) $495

Cup & saucer, handleless, blue transfer of sparrows near an urn of flowers (minor wear) 248

Pitcher, 5 1/2" h., ovoid body, short, slightly tapered neck, applied handle, blue transfer of girl picking flowers & boy robbing a bird's nest, floral border (flake on base, spout has roughness) 495

Pitcher, 8 1/2" h., "Abbey Ruins" patt., bulbous body w/short tapered foot & flared neck, molded floral C-scroll handle, light blue romantic transfer scene w/deer & ruins, transfer label "T. Mayer, Longport" (firing separations in handle, minor wear w/crow's feet) 275

Plate, 10 1/4" d., blue transfer from the Quadruped series of a lion surrounded by deer, goats, zebras & horses 385

Platter, 15 1/21" l., "Canova" patt., scalloped edge, red transfer scene of canal & gondola, by T. Mayer Stoke Upon Trent 330

Platter, 14 3/4 x 18 7/8", wide oval form, a central oval reserve filled w/large fruits including melon, peaches, pears & leaves,

the wide flanged rim w/flowers & leaves, dark blue, ca. 1830 (wear) 770

Platter, 14 1/2 x 19", "Sheltered Peasants" patt., blue transfer w/depiction of man, woman & child w/sheep beneath trees, cathedral in background, fruit & flower border (glaze flaking on rim) 770

Teapot, cov., bulbous body w/scalloped rim, flared neck & base, applied handle, dark blue transfer of flowers & an urn w/American eagle w/shield, unmarked Clews, 6 1/2" h. (lid has chips) 660

Teapot, cov., dark blue central transfer of a man fishing w/a manor house in background, surrounded by floral rosette design, molded flower finial, 7 1/2" h. 468

Vegetable dish, open, oblong, "Arctic Scenery" patt., black transfer of scene of explorer w/Eskimos building igloo, border w/flowers & animals including leopards & buffalo, first half 19th c., 11" l. 935

Vegetable dish & underplate, open, oblong, open looped rims w/rope twist handles, medium blue transfer of scene of shepherds near waterfall, impressed & transfer label "Riley's Semi-China," 11" l., 2 pcs. 468

Waste bowl, footed w/deep, flat & flared sides, large florals & urns w/eagles & shields, interior w/an Oriental building, dark blue, ca. 1830, 5 1/2" d., 3 1/16" h. (minor roughness) 385

Stoneware

Stoneware is essentially a vitreous pottery, impervious to water even in its unglazed state, that has been produced by potteries all over the world for centuries. Utilitarian wares such as crocks, jugs, churns and the like, were the most common productions in the numerous potteries that sprang into existence in the United States during the 19th century. These items were often enhanced by the application of a cobalt blue oxide decoration. In addition to the coarse, primarily salt-glazed stonewares, there are other categories of stoneware known by such special names as basalt, jasper and others.

Batter jug, cov., ovoid shape w/bale handle & old tin lid, angled straight spout w/tin collar, 11" h. $468

Crock, cylindrical, w/cobalt decoration of long-beaked bird on a cherry branch, impressed "6," 10" h. 495

Pitcher, 10 5/8" h., ovoid body w/raised ring base w/slightly flared rim, short cylindrical neck, applied handle, cobalt floral decoration & line detail around spout & handle (some pot stones) 880

Stoneware Pitcher

Pitcher, 10" h., bulbous body w/slightly flared base & slightly tapered neck, applied strap handle, freehand cobalt foliage decoration starts at bottom below spout & extends back almost to handle, small fan or leaf designs near the top, wavy lines below the neck rim, incised line detail around the body, firing separations in side & bottom (ILLUS.) **3,410**

Pitcher, 9" h., blue & white, molded rings top & bottom w/bright blue sponging **385**

Water cooler, tall domed beehive form w/short neck, applied shoulder handles, w/cobalt decoration of chicken pecking at an ear of corn, unusual orange peel glaze, impressed "6" & "New York Stoneware Co. Fort Edward...," 19 1/2" h. (two daubs of translucent glaze & short hairlines at base, made into a lamp but not drilled) **2,750**

Teco Pottery

Teco Pottery was actually the line of art pottery introduced by the American Terra Cotta and Ceramic Company of Terra Cotta (Crystal Lake), Illinois in 1902. Founded by William D. Gates in 1881, American Terra Cotta originally produced only bricks and drain tile. Because of superior facilities for experimentation, including a chemical laboratory, the company was able to develop an art pottery line, favoring a matte green glaze in the earlier years but eventually achieving a wide range of colors including a metallic lustre glaze and a crystalline glaze. Though some hand-thrown pottery was made, Gates favored a molded ware because it was less expensive to produce. By 1923, Teco Pottery was no longer being made and in 1930 American Terra Cotta and Ceramic Company was sold. A book on the topic is Teco: Art Pottery of the Prairie School, *by Sharon S. Darling (Erie Art Museum, 1990).*

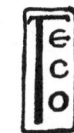

Teco Mark

Bowl, 4 1/2" d., wide flat bottom w/low incurved sides, green matte glaze, impressed marks, No. 350 .... **$286**

Fine Teco Bowl-vase

Bowl-vase, wide sharply tapering round bowl supported by four heavy squared pierced buttress legs around the rim, design by Holmes Smith, fine green matte glaze w/charcoal highlights, impressed marks, minor crazing on interior, 12" d. (ILLUS.) **5,500**

Box, cov., squatty rounded rectangular form sharply incurved to the rectangular base, w/a flat fitted rectangular cover, smooth

matte green glaze w/charcoaling, stamped mark, 2 1/2 x 3 1/2", 2 1/4" h. (bruise on base) **788**

Chamberstick, a wide round dished base w/a tapering short center shaft w/a thick molded socket rim & an open squared handle from the rim to the base rim, good ivory matte glaze, impressed marks, paper label, 5" d. (flaw in glaze on handle in making) **523**

Chamberstick, a wide round dished base w/a tapering short center shaft w/a thick molded socket rim & an open squared handle from the rim to the base rim, good green matte glaze, impressed marks, paper label, 5" d. **605**

Chamberstick, wide cushion foot centered by a tall slender waisted cylindrical shaft molded w/stylized leaves & flowers, a long loop handle from the upper side to the base of the shaft, smooth matte green glaze, paper label, 5" d., 10 3/4" h. **900**

Pitcher, 8 1/2" h., 5" d., tall slender waisted body w/a wide rim w/pinched spout & integral pinched & forked loop handle reaching down nearly to the bottom, mottled matte green & charcoal glaze, stamped mark **844**

Vase, 3" h., 1 1/4" d., miniature, simple ovoid form w/two tiny buttress handles at the rim, smooth matte green glaze, original paper label **956**

Vase, 4" h., bulbous nearly spherical form tapering slightly to a wide short flared neck, dark matte green glaze, impressed mark & incised number **440**

Vase, 4" h., slightly tapering cylindrical form w/four deep oval indentations up the sides below the short flared neck, green matte glaze, No. 356 .... **605**

Vase, 4 1/2" h., bulbous rounded base w/a deep indentation on each side & tapering to a wide squared neck, good matte green glaze, impressed mark **660**

Vase, 4 1/2" h., gently flaring wide cylindrical body w/an angled shoulder tapering to a flat mouth, green matte glaze, impressed marks, paper label **770**

Vase, 4 3/4" h., gently tapering cylindrical body w/slightly flared flat rim, molded w/thin rings up the sides, green matte glaze, impressed mark **495**

Vase, 5" h., footed squatty bulbous lower body tapering to a waisted neck w/a four-ruffle flared rim, good green matte glaze, impressed marks **715**

Vase, 6 1/4" h., 6 1/2" d., a wide cylindrical finely ringed body w/three long squared handles from the rim to the base, each handle w/ribbing down the front, smooth matte green glaze, fine charcoaling, stamped mark (bruise to rim) **1,238**

Vase, 6 1/2" h., bulbous ovoid four-sided form tapering to four short pierced buttress shoulder handles attaching to the flattened pierced rim & mouth, molded leaf design at the bottom center of each side, green matte glaze w/light charcoaling, designed by Fritz Albert, impressed marks (ILLUS. top next page) **3,850**

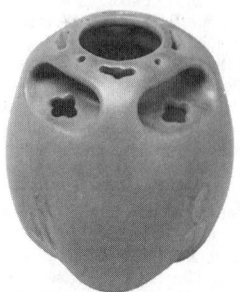

Unusual Pierced Teco Vase

Vase, 6 1/2" h., large mug-form, the wide cylindrical body w/thin narrow rings & molded looped scrolls at the front, a long low angled open handle down the side, dark matte green glaze, impressed mark **550**

Vase, 6 3/4" h., simple ovoid body tapering to a short flared neck, green matte glaze, impressed marks **523**

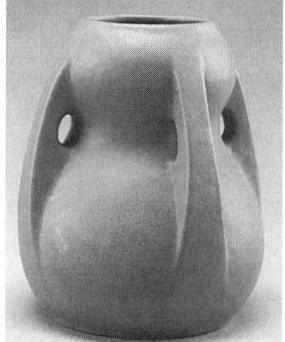

Double-gourd Teco Handled Vase

Vase, 7" h., 6" d., bulbous double-gourd form body w/four heavy curved buttress handles from the rim to the base, fine leathery matte green glaze, small long bruise at rim, stamped mark (ILLUS.) **2,990**

Three Teco Buttress-handled Vases

Vase, 7 1/4" h., 4 1/4" d., conical body tapering to a flared neck w/a thick rim band issuing four heavy squared buttress handles from the rim to the base, smooth medium green matte glaze, short abrasion to rim, stamped mark (ILLUS. left with buttress-handled vases) **4,025**

Vase, 7 1/4" h., 4 1/4" d., ovoid body tapering to a flaring cylindrical neck flanked by heavy square buttress handles going down the sides, mottled matte green glaze, some glaze curdling to base, No. 435, stamped mark (ILLUS. center, bottom left column) **3,220**

Vase, 7 1/2" h., a bulbous spherical base tapering to a tall slender tapering neck topped by a squatty cupped & closed rim, green matte glaze, impressed mark **715**

Vase, 7 1/2" h., 4 1/4" d., conical body tapering to a flared neck w/a thick rim band issuing four heavy squared buttress handles from the rim to the base, smooth matte brown glaze, mark obscured by glaze (ILLUS. right with buttress-handled vases, bottom left column) **3,450**

Tall Teco Vase with Buttresses

Vase, 10 1/4" h., 5 3/4" d., tapering cylindrical body w/a wide flattened rim, four low square buttress handles down the sides, green & charcoal mottled glaze w/a splotch of yellow under the rim, marked, invisible restoration to a few chips, base & mark (ILLUS.) **2,185**

Tall Buttress-handled Teco Vase

Vase, 11 1/4" h., 3 3/4" d., tall slender swelled cylindrical body tapering to a slightly flaring neck flanked by squared short buttress handles continuing down the sides to the base, smooth matte green glaze, stamped mark (ILLUS.) **5,175**

Teco Vase with Entwined Handles

Vase, 11 1/2" h., 9" d., large ovoid body w/a narrow shoulder tapering to a wide short cylindrical neck w/a thick flattened rim, pairs of entwined loop handles on each side from rim to shoulder, smooth matte green glaze, stamped mark & remnant of paper label (ILLUS.) **5,175**

Unusual Tall Teco Bud Vase

Vase, 12 1/2" h., 5 1/2" d., bud-type, an unusual organic form w/two upturned & two downturned handles projecting from the rim above the slender two-lobed stem above forked short leaves above the multi-petaled foot, heavily charcoaled matte green glaze, No. 153, stamped mark, three tiny chips to base (ILLUS.)...... **2,415**

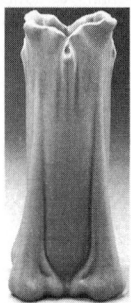

Tall Organic-form Teco Vase

Vase, 13 3/4" h., 8 1/4" d., tall cylindrical organic form w/pinched four-petaled scalloped & gently flared rim, long bulbed buttresses down the sides forming feet, smooth green matte glaze, stamped mark, flat chip to one rim petal, bruise to another (ILLUS.) **2,300**

Rare Tall Paneled Teco Vase

Vase, 14 3/4" h., tall tapering four-sided form w/long panels to small open buttresses around the small flat mouth, fine green matte charcoaled glaze, designed by Fritz Albert, No. 181A, marked (ILLUS.) **33,350**
Vase, 16 1/2" h., 8" d., footed wide squatty bulbous lower body w/a wide shoulder tapering to a very tall slender lobed neck w/flared rim, smooth matte green glaze, stamped mark (restored rim section) **1,688**

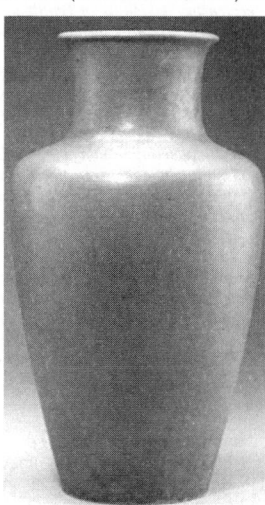

Large Plain Teco Floor Vase

Vase, 20 1/4" h., 10 3/4" d., floor-type, tapering cylindrical body below a wide shoulder tapering to a wide cylindrical neck w/rolled rim, leathery matte green glaze, stamped mark, several small base chips (ILLUS.).. **4,313**

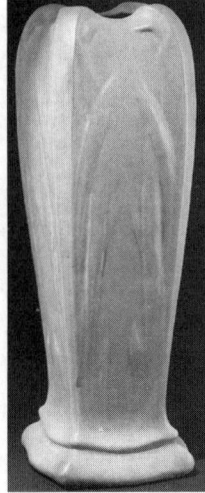

Large Teco Floor Vase

Vase, 22" h., 8 1/2" w., floor-type, a flared stepped foot on the swelled squared body w/molded buttress corners at the closed mouth, molded on each side w/tall slender leaves, microcrystalline matte green glaze, stamped "Teco 343," restoration to base chip, four hairlines at rim (ILLUS.).. **6,188**

Teplitz - Amphora

In the late 19th and early 20th centuries numerous potteries operated in the vicinity of Teplitz in the Bohemian region of what was Austria but is now the Czech Republic. They included Amphora, RStK, Stellmacher, Ernst Wahliss, Paul Dachsel, Imperial and lesser-known potteries such as Johanne Maresh, Julius Dressler, Bernard Bloch and Heliosine.

The number of collectors in this category is growing while availability of better or rarer pieces is shrinking. Consequently, prices for all pieces are appreciating, while those for better and/or rarer pieces, including restored rare pieces, are soaring.

The price ranges presented here are retail. They presume mint or near mint condition or, in the case of very rare damaged pieces, proper restoration. They reflect such variables as rarity, design, quality of glaze, size and the intangible "in-vogue factor." They are the prices that knowledgeable sellers will charge and knowledgeable collectors will pay.

Bust of a woman, wearing elaborate dress w/applied floral detail on front & headband, light green, purple, red & tan tinting on white background, very faint mark "R St K, Turn, Teplitz, Bohemia," 19 1/2" h. (edge chips).. **$935**

Elephant & Tigers Amphora Group

Figure group, model of a bull elephant being attacked by two male tigers, natural tones of browns, cream, tan & green w/gilt trim on rockwork base, printed & impressed Amphora marks, ca. 1920, 26" h. (ILLUS.) **920**

Ornate Amphora Jardiniere

Jardiniere, bulbous squatty form w/wide flat mouth, molded around the lower body w/large horse chestnut leaf clusters & nuts, the wide shoulder molded w/threaded rings centered by jewels, shades of light & dark brown & dark green & greenish gold w/gilt highlights, impressed "Amphora - 02050 - D.," ca. 1900, 19" d., 14 3/4" h. (ILLUS.)...................................... **4,025**

Vase, 11" h., mermaid perches on side w/net of fish, another swims alongside crab, lobster & shells in ocean surf, ivory w/shades of green, brown & pink, gilt accents, marked "Turn-Teplitz, Bohemia" (minor edge damage) **743**

Vase, 5 1/2" h., 3 3/4" d., bottle-form w/a footed squatty wide ovoid body tapering sharply to a slender cylindrical neck w/a wide bulbed rim, painted w/a bust portrait of an Art Nouveau maiden w/long hair trimmed w/blue enameled flowers, cream background, impressed "Amphora 492"........ **440**

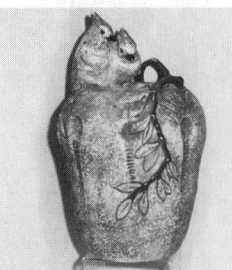

Amphora Vase with Birds & Branch

Vase, 10" h., tapering ovoid form w/indent-
ed teardrops around the sides, molded &
applied w/a pair of bluebirds at the top
w/a twig & leaf handle from the rim down
the front, green mottled ground, blue, rust
& brown trim, Riessner - Amphora
mark, ca. 1930 (ILLUS.) **220**

Vase, 10 1/2" h., Imperial Ware, wide semi-
ovoid form w/flat rim, decorated w/two
exotic birds in bright blues, pink, green &
brown enamels on a soft brown matte
ground, dark blue loop handles & rim
w/lighter blue dots around rim & stylized
reddish brown leaves & green flowers in
a continuous band around the base, impressed marks & "Amphora" & "Austria"
in ovals w/"Campina" inside a rectangle &
the numbers "11614" & "64"........................... **275**

Vase, 10 1/2" h., wonderful Teplitz Art Nouveau form by Bernard Bloch featuring a
large ocean wave finished in sea green
tossing a scantily clad finely detailed
flesh-toned mermaid w/two finned legs
instead of a tail & a large brown-shelled
sea turtle, designed by Schwarz, increasingly sought by Amphora collectors who
consider it an early form of Amphora-
Teplitz, value increasing, impressed
"Schwarz - BB" & dot in a half-circle & "M
- 7099".. **1,500-2,000**

Vase, 10 3/4" h., exquisitely executed form
consisting of several variously colored
thistles in high-relief, realistic detail w/the
body in a soft mottled blue w/tinges of
soft greens, yellow, pinks & washed
w/gold overtones, two gold handles, impressed "Amphora" & "Austria" in ovals, a
crown & "2213 - 64 - G" **2,000-2,500**

Amphora Vase with Goat in Landscape

Vase, 10 3/4" h., simple ovoid form tapering
to a low flat neck, the upper portion decorated w/a painted pastoral scene w/a
goat reclining by trees in a field in blue
tones on a cream ground, the lower portion w/raised repeating scallops, circle &
columns in glossy glazed black, the columns in mottled iridescent colors, gilt
trim, impressed Amphora lozenge mark
& "32 59," early 20th c. (ILLUS.) **920**

Vase, 11 1/8" h., large pear-shaped body
tapering to a short cylindrical neck, wide
curved integral side handles pierced
w/three openings, mottled matte green &
brown glaze, inscribed cipher & mark of
Riessner & Kessel (crazing, base chip) **1,035**

Vase, 14" h., figural, three curious mice, two
at the top & one at the bottom, mischie-
vously explore a forbidden environment,
bluish green w/splotches of red & goldish
leaves, iridescent glaze, a rare design,
impressed "Amphora" & "Austria" in
ovals, a crown & "4522-52".............. **3,000-3,500**

Vase, 14 1/4" h., elegant center-pillared
piece surrounded by four supporting
arms extending from the underside of the
bowl-form top to the bottom, a flowing design decorated w/block-outlined painted
floral designs, mottled green & tan w/gold
luster, similar pieces designed by Paul
Dachsel in his own factory so may have
designed this piece, impressed "Amphora" & "Austria" in ovals, a crown & "3899
- 42" **1,200-1,500**

Vase, 14 5/8" h., a figural fantasy piece, a
different variety of dragon vase but not
highly glazed, the dragon is mostly brown
but it features a well-defined head, body,
clawed feet & tail, a snake tongue drapes
from the mouth, hideously beautiful, the
body contrasts nicely w/the metallic
greenish blue iridescence of the mottled
background, found in various glazes, impressed "Amphora" & "Austria" in oval, a
crown & "C 4543" **3,000-4,000**

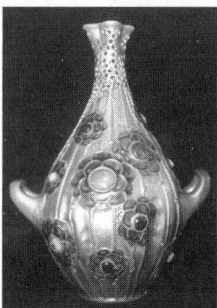

Rare Jeweled Amphora Vase

Vase, 16" h., bulbous ovoid body tapering to
a slender flaring lobed reticulated neck,
outswept loop handles at the lower sides,
shimmering burnished gold ground w/red
touches, adorned randomly w/twenty
large variously colored 'jewels,' one handle in red, the other in gold, overall molded vertical ribbing, rare form, impressed
"Amphora" in an oval, crown, old "RStK"
mark & "3349" (ILLUS.) **7,500-8,000**

Amphora Vase with Judaica Decor

Vase, 16" h., Judaica decoration, double cylindrical necks w/gently scalloped rims continuing into a tubular oval body raised on a flaring oblong foot, decorated around the necks & body w/raised Star-of-David designs & applied domed 'jewels,' glossy teal blue & brown glazes & opalescent glazed 'jewels,' textured gilt ground, impressed Amphora marks, early 20th c. (ILLUS.).. **690**

Amphora Sea Serpent & Crab Vase

Vase, 22 1/4" h., figural, a bulbous base tapering to a tall slender cylindrical body, a large relief-molded sea serpent wrapped down the sides w/a molded crab grasping the lower body, shaded ivory & brown glaze on an iridescent blue, green & gilt ground, impressed Amphora, Austria mark w/crown, early 20th c., minor gilt wear at rim (ILLUS.) **5,750**

Tiffany Pottery

In 1902 Louis C. Tiffany expanded Tiffany Studios to include ceramics, enamels, gold, silver and gemstones. Tiffany pottery was usually molded rather than wheel-thrown, but it was carefully finished by hand. A limited amount was produced until about 1914. It is scarce.

Tiffany Pottery Mark

Tiffany Pottery Square Bottle

Bottle, square upright form w/a small round neck centered on the flat top, incised abstract design around the sides, textured

cobalt blue & turquoise matte glaze, incised "LCT," 4" w., 6 1/2" h. (ILLUS.)....... **$1,380**

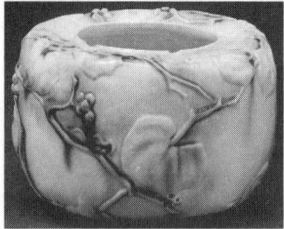

Tiffany Pottery Vase with Vines

Bowl-vase, wide short cylindrical form w/flattened rounded base & top rim w/closed mouth, molded w/a bold design of vines, leaves & berries under an Old Ivory glaze, incised "LCT" & etched "Favrile Pottery - P22Y Tiffany," three chips, tight line at rim, nick on branch on top, 7 1/2" d., 5" h. (ILLUS.)....................... **4,500**

Rare Tiffany Pottery Box and Ewer

Box, cov., flat-bottomed w/deep gently rounded flaring sides molded w/a berry & twig design, the domed cover w/a matching design, deep yellow & orange berries on a dark green ground, marked "LCT - 7," 5 1/2" d., 4" h. (ILLUS. right)................. **9,600**

Ewer, flat-bottomed conical form w/a deep cupped neck w/long pinched spout, long tapering handle from edge of neck to base, lightly molded overall w/a design of a stylized parrot, mottled light green & black glaze, marked "L.C.T. - P 159," 8 3/4" h. (ILLUS. left with box)................... **5,100**

Tiffany Vase with Reticulated Shoulder

Vase, 5 1/2" h., wide baluster-form body w/the shoulder reticulated w/a wide band of cherry blossoms on stems, tan bisque finish (ILLUS.) **1,725**

Vase, 6 5/8" h., wide gently waisted cylindrical form, molded up the sides w/long pointed leaves w/three leaf stems forming arched loop handles down the sides, streaky light & dark blue glaze, signed "LCT - Tiffany Favrile Pottery - P 412" (chip to rim).. **4,800**

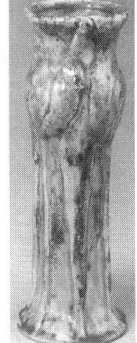

Tiffany Pottery Bud Vase

Vase, 7" h., bud-type, slender cylindrical form w/ribbed stems up the sides to swelled molded blossoms at the top just below the flaring rim, rare mottled bluish green glaze w/brown showing through, incised "LCT - 65D - EL," repaired chip on base (ILLUS.)... **2,300**

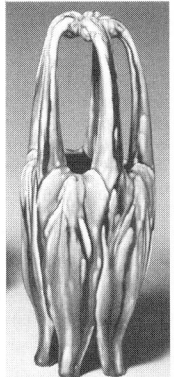

Very Rare Tiffany Pottery Fern Vase

Vase, 11 1/8" h., molded stylized fern design, the body formed by a cluster of molded fern fronds which extend down to form short legs, a cluster of tall slender fronds extend up from the rim & arch together to form open handles, streaky green & dark gold glaze on a creamy body, signed "Tiffany - Pottery - H 9 A - Coll - 49B," firing crack around base (ILLUS.)... **21,450**

Tiles

Tiles have been made by potteries in the United States and abroad for many years. Apart from small tea tiles used on tables, there are also decorative tiles for fireplaces, floors and walls and this is where present collector interest lies, especially in the late 19th century American-made art pottery tiles.

American Encaustic Tiles

American Encaustic Tiling Company, Zanesville, Ohio, rectangular, molded figure of a Colonial gentleman holding a cane & gloves under a glossy brown glaze, impressed "American Encaustic Tiling Co. Limited New York Works Zanesville, O.," minor flaws, 5 7/8 x 18" (ILLUS. right)... **$330**

American Encaustic Tiling Company, Zanesville, Ohio, rectangular, molded figure of a young Colonial woman holding a fan under a glossy brown glaze, impressed "American Encaustic Tiling Co. Limited New York Works Zanesville, O.," minor flaws, 5 7/8 x 18" (ILLUS. left)............. **330**

American Encaustic Stove Tile

American Encaustic Tiling Company, Zanesville, Ohio, rectangular stove tile depicting a seated Roman soldier w/one arm resting across the shoulder of a bear standing beside him, blue high glaze, unmarked, small glaze nicks to edges, 4 1/4 x 7 3/8" (ILLUS.) **280**

Franklin Pottery Faience Tile

Franklin Pottery, Lansdale, Pennsylvania, rectangular, faience tile w/colorful parrot perched on a branch, gloss & matte glazes of blues, green, pink, black & yellow, back die-impressed "Franklin Pottery Faience," ca. 1936, accompanied by photocopy of Franklin Tile catalog, very minor chips to back edges, tile 8 7/8 x 8 3/4" (ILLUS.) **605**

Grueby Faience & Tile Company, Boston, Massachusetts, square, decorated in cuenca w/a stylized yellow stag w/brown antlers under a green leafy tree w/green grass & pale blue sky, in a new wide flat oak Arts & Crafts frame, unmarked, tile 4" w. **1,069**

Grueby Faience & Tile Company, Boston, Massachusetts, decorated in cuenca w/a large pale yellow seated rabbit in a cabbage patch w/light bluish green foliage against a dark green ground, artist-initialed, in a new wide flat oak Arts & Crafts frame, tile 6" w. (some surface abrasion) .. **3,375**

Rare Grueby Turtle Tile

Grueby Faience & Tile Company, Boston, Massachusetts, square, decorated in cuenca w/a turtle in shades of brown & ivory below a bough of green leaves all on an ochre matte ground, stamped mark & paper label, 6" w. (ILLUS.) **7,450**

Grueby Faience & Tile Company, Boston, Massachusetts, rectangular, decorated in cuenca w/a yellow chamberstick & candle against a green ground below molded wording "Grueby Tile," artist-initialed, in a new wide flat Arts & Crafts oak frame, tile 4 1/2 x 6" **4,500**

Grueby Tile with Horses

Grueby Faience & Tile Company, Boston, Massachusetts, square, decorated w/a row of prancing white horses in cuenca on a blue & green ground, unmarked, restoration to edge chip, 6 1/4" w. (ILLUS.) **3,450**

Grueby Tile in Tiffany Brass Frame

Grueby Faience & Tile Company, Boston, Massachusetts, square, decorated in cuenca w/a yellow tulip blossom flanked by pairs of large arched leaves on a green ground, mounted in a brass Tiffany Studios frame w/squared floral-form feet, 7" w. (ILLUS.) **5,750**

Grueby Tile with Sailing Galleon

Grueby Faience & Tile Company, Boston, Massachusetts, square, a galleon under full sail, in cream & brown on a dark green ground, unsigned, 8" w. (ILLUS.) **2,013**

Grueby Faience & Tile Company, Boston, Massachusetts, seven-tile frieze designed by Addison Le Boutillier, titled "The Pines," decorated in cuenca w/pine trees in a valley, green, blue, brown & cobalt matte oatmealy glazes, ca. 1902, small chip to corner of one tile, 6 x 42" ... **42,188**

Kensington Art Tile Company, square, embossed image of a greyhound, shaded tan & brown high glaze, marked w/Kensington logo, minor edge & surface chips, 6" sq. **275**

Marblehead Pottery, Marblehead, Massachusetts, square, a matte-painted stylized landscape silhouetted against an evening sky, in shades of blues & yellows, ship mark, 5 3/4" sq. (several small edge nicks) **1,913**

Fine Marblehead Framed Tile

Marblehead Pottery, Marblehead, Massachusetts, square, painted w/a stylized floral design of blue delphiniums & green leaves on a white ground, in a wide flat oak frame, paper label, 6" w. (ILLUS.) **1,100**

Marblehead Pottery, Marblehead, Massachusetts, square, decorated w/a scene of a house in a landscape, the house in colors of transparent rust & blue bordered by green grass, flanked by trees in matte blue & brown, the whole on a matte grey ground, marked, ca. 1908, 6 1/4" w. (few minor edge chips) **1,150**

Marblehead Pottery, Marblehead, Massachusetts, square, embossed w/a large stylized spreading oak tree in a forest, fine dark green crystalline matte glaze, mounted in a fine flat wide oak frame w/rounded corners in the style of Greene & Greene, tile w/stamped ship mark & paper label, 6 1/4" sq. **3,656**

Unusual Muresque Pottery Tile

Muresque Pottery, Oakland, California, square, a molded Southwestern landscape w/palm tree & adobe home, in cream, tan, green & blue, impressed "Muresque - Oakland," early 20th c., framed, 6" sq. (ILLUS.) **460**

Newcomb College Tile with Galleon

Newcomb College Pottery, New Orleans, Louisiana, square, molded design depicting a galleon under full sail w/dolphins alongside, Persian blue crackled glaze, by Leona Nicholson, marked, 5 1/4" sq. (ILLUS.) **805**

Norweta Tile with Minstrels

Norweta (Northwestern Terra Cotta Company), Chicago, Illinois, rectangular, colorful scene of six performing minstrels dancing & playing musical instruments against a cream matte glaze, surface embossed "Norweta," two cast holes in top edge for hanging, professional repair of vertical crack across center, 4 1/2 x 14 1/2" (ILLUS.).................................. **935**

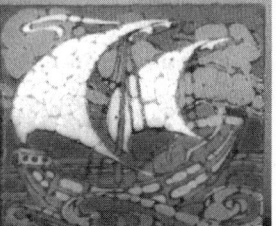

Large Owens Framed Tile

Owens Floor & Wall Tile Company (Empire), Zanesville, Ohio, rectangular, decorated in cuenca w/a landscape of large trees in green, brown & blue, mounted in a narrow wood frame, no visible mark, small chips in two corners, firing bubbles, 8 1/2 x 11 1/2" (ILLUS.).............................. **1,320**

Pardee Tile with Sailing Ship

Pardee, C. Works, Perth Amboy, New Jersey, square, depicts a large brown & white sailing ship at sea, shaded blue sky & shaded green sea, rich matte glaze, embossed on back "The C. Pardee Works" & "- O," two small nicks on edges, 4 1/4" sq. (ILLUS.).. **330**

Pardee, C. Works, Perth Amboy, New Jersey, square, yellow & green tulip on pale blue matte glaze ground, artist-initialed in blue slip "PS," the back embossed "The C. Pardee Work," 4 1/4" sq............................. **220**

Rookwood Pottery, Cincinnati, Ohio, four-tile frieze, decorated in cuenca & forming a continuous landscape w/large green & brown trees & green grass & bushes in the foreground, a long blue lake in the center ground & a series of mountains in green in the background, impressed mark, previously mounted w/remnants of

Rare Rookwood Tile Frieze

mounting mortar, one reglued corner, minor corner chips, 12 x 48" (ILLUS.) **23,000**

Rare Framed Van Briggle Tile

Van Briggle Pottery, Colorado Springs, Colorado, square, a kingfisher perched on a branch, in polychrome glazes including brown, white, green & blue, unmarked, in wide flat oak period frame, minute glaze flecks, 6" w. (ILLUS.)............. **4,600**

Torquay Pottery

In the second half of the 19th century several art potteries were established in the South Devon region of England to take advantage of a belt of fine red clay. The coastal town of Torquay gives its name to this range of wares which often featured incised sgraffito decoration or colorful country-style decoration with mottos.

The most notable potteries operating in the Torquay area were the Watcombe Pottery, The Torquay Terracotta Company and the Aller Vale Art Pottery, which merged with Watcombe Pottery in 1901 and continued production until 1962. Other firms whose wares are collectible include Longpark Pottery and The Devonmoor Art Pottery.

Early wares feature unglazed terra cotta items in the Victorian taste including classical busts, statuary and vases and some painted and glazed wares including examples with a celeste blue interior or highlights. In addition to sgraffito designs other decorations included flowers, Barbotine glazes, Devon pixies framed in leafy scrolls and grotesque figures of cats, dogs and other fanciful animals produced in the 1890s.

The dozen or so potteries flourishing in the region at the turn of the 20th century introduced their most popular product, motto wares, which became the bread and butter line of the local industry. The most popular patterns in this line included Cottage, Black and Colored Cockerels and Scandy, based on Scandinavian rosemaling designs. Most of the mottoes were written in English

with a few in Welsh. On early examples the sayings were often in Devonian dialect. These motto wares were sold for years at area seaside resorts and other tourist areas with some pieces exported to Australia, Canada and, to a lesser extent, the U.S.A. In addition to standard size teawares and novelties some miniatures and even oversized pieces were offered.

Production at the potteries stopped during World War II and some of the plants were destroyed in enemy raids. The Watcombe Pottery became Royal Watcombe after the war and Longpark also started up again, but produced simpler patterns. The Dartmouth Pottery started in 1947 and produced cottages similar to those made at Watcombe and also developed a line of figural animals, banks and novelty jugs. The Babbacombe Pottery (1950-59) and St. Marychurch Pottery (ca. 1962-69) were the last two firms to turn out motto wares but these later designs were painted on and the pieces were lighter in color with less detailing.

Many books on the various potteries are available and information can be obtained from the products manager of the North American Torquay Society.

Torquay Motto Ware Ashtray

Ashtray, rectangular, Motto Ware, Cottage patt., "Better to Smoke Here Than Hereafter - Paignton," 3 1/4 x 5 1/4" (ILLUS.) **$45**

Torquay Pottery Chamberstick

Chamberstick, Motto Ware, Sailboat patt., round dished base w/a cylindrical standard w/side handle below the wide cupped socket, "Guid Nicht an Joy Be Wi Ye," 3 1/2" d., 4 1/4" h. (ILLUS.)........................ **85**

Isle of Wight Torquay Souvenir Cream

Creamer, Motto Ware, Cottage patt., bulbous base tapering slightly to wide cylindrical sides w/slightly flared rim & pinched spout, C-scroll handle, "Help yourself to Milk - Isle of Wight," 3 1/2" d., 3 3/4" h. (ILLUS.) **65**

Torquay Bulbous Creamer with Motto

Creamer, Motto Ware, Cottage patt., bulbous ovoid body w/a wide flat rim & pinched spout, C-scroll handle, "Take A Little Milk - Mevrgissey," 3 1/4" d., 3" h. (ILLUS.) **55**

Torquay Motto Ware Jam Jar

Jam jar, cov., Motto Ware, Cottage patt., cylindrical w/a low pyramidal cover w/knob finial & spoon notch at rim, "Go Asy Wi It Now," 3 1/4" d., 4 1/4" h. (ILLUS.) **65**

Van Briggle

The Van Briggle Pottery was established by Artus Van Briggle, who formerly worked for Rookwood Pottery, in Colorado Springs, Colorado at the turn of the century. He died in 1904 but the pottery was carried on by his widow and others. From 1900 until 1920, the pieces were dated. It remains in production today, specializing in Art Pottery.

Bowl, 6" d., 3" h., wide flat-bottomed squatty bulbous form w/the sharply tapering top centered w/a wide, flat molded mouth, light turquoise matte glaze, Shape No. 50B, 1905 .... **$900**

Fine Early Van Briggle Bowl-Vase

Bowl-vase, a wide squatty bulbous form tapering to a wide, flat mouth, molded around the sides w/stylized undulating & looping floral designs, dark brown clay shows through the fine suspended blue matte glaze, dated 1907, 5" d. (ILLUS.) **4,675**

Van Briggle Bowl-Vase with Leaves

Bowl-vase, large squatty bulbous ovoid form tapering to a wide flat mouth, molded around the shoulder w/a band on pointed leaves atop long curved stems, matte brown glaze, 1916, 7" d., 4 3/4" h. (ILLUS.) **920**

Bowl-vase, squatty bulbous deep vessel w/a wide shoulder & molded flat mouth, good matte green glaze, ca. 1905, 5 1/2" h. **880**

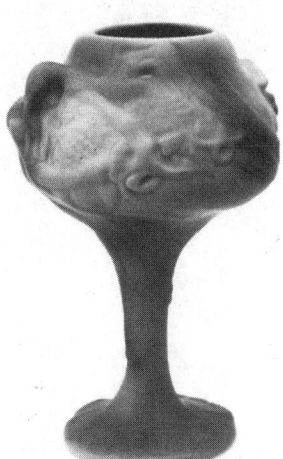

Van Briggle Mermaid Chalice

Chalice, a round foot & slender stem supporting a squatty bulbous cup tapering to a flat rim, molded around the cup w/the figure of a mermaid, swirled light green & dark blue matte glaze, signed, small glaze miss, paint flecks, 10 1/2" h. (ILLUS.)...................................... **6,325**

Vase, 3 3/4" h., 4 1/2" h., flat-bottomed spherical form w/a flat molded mouth, pale turquoise matte glaze, dated 1903 (ILLUS. bottom row, center, with group, below)... **900**

Vase, 3 3/4" h., 5" d., flat-bottomed squatty bulbous tapering body w/the wide shoulder centered by a short, wide cylindrical neck, embossed around the sides w/butterflies, green & pale red matte glaze, Shape No. 626, 1908-11 (overfired, restoration to rim chip).................................... **506**

Vase, 4" h., a small footring supporting a bulbous nearly spherical body tapering slightly to a wide, flat molded rim, molded down the sides w/swirled florals, unusual purple, grey & green matte glaze, ca. 1907-12 .... **715**

Vase, 4 3/4" h., 3 3/4" d., squatty bulbous lower body tapering to a tall cylindrical neck w/a molded rim, the lower body molded w/swirled pointed leaves, bluish green matte glaze, Shape No. 730, 1908-11 .... **534**

Vase, 5 1/4" h., 3 1/2" d., simple ovoid form w/small molded mouth, embossed w/large stylized crocus blossoms around the shoulder w/stems down the sides, green & pink matte glaze, Shape No. 823, ca. 1910 (ILLUS. front row, second from left, below) **506**

Vase, 5 3/4" h., 3 3/4" d., wide low rounded base below a sharply tapering cylindrical body w/flat rim, matte mustard yellow glaze, Shape No. 825, 1908-11 (ILLUS. front row, second from right, below) **534**

Vase, 6" h., slightly tapering swelled cylindrical body w/a tiny flat neck, molded w/small stylized upright buds on stems spaced around the sides, dark brown matte glaze, incised mark, ca. 1915.............. **440**

Vase, 6" h., 4" d., wide low rounded base below a sharply tapering cylindrical body w/flat rim, embossed around the lower body & up the sides w/medallions of wheat sheaves, fine leathery matte green glaze, Shape No. 347, 1905 (ILLUS. front row, far left, with group, below) **2,138**

Small Van Briggle Vase with Flowers

Vase, 6" h., 4 1/4" d., wide squatty bulbous base tapering sharply to a cylindrical neck, molded around the lower body w/five-petal blossoms & leaves w/stems & leaves up the sides, chartreuse matte mottled glaze, Shape No. 188, 1903 (ILLUS.)... **2,415**

Vase, 6 1/2" h., 3 3/4" d., footed bulbous bottle-form body tapering to a thick closed rim, embossed down the sides w/stylized flowers & long tiered rows of leaves, feathered dark matte green glaze, 1908-11 (ILLUS. top next page)...... **1,035**

Large Group of Van Briggle Vases

Bottle-form Van Briggle Vase

Vase, 7" h., slender cylindrical lower body w/a swelled shoulder tapering slightly to a flat mouth, molded around the shoulder w/dragonflies extending down the sides, dark blue to deep red matte glaze, post-1920s **319**

Vase, 7" h., 6 1/2" d., wide bulbous ovoid body w/a wide short rolled rim, embossed around the sides w/large butterflies, cobalt & turquoise matte glaze, 1916 .... **513**

Van Briggle Vase with Pointed Leaves

Vase, 7 1/4" h., 3 1/4" d., slightly swelled cylindrical form w/a wide, flat mouth, molded around the body w/long downward-pointing spearpoint leaves, frothy & oatmealy green matte glaze w/brown clay showing through, 1905 (ILLUS.) **2,875**

Vase, 7 1/4" h., 3 1/2" d., swelled cylindrical form w/a narrow shoulder centered by a short cylindrical neck, embossed around the neck w/poppy pods w/the slender vines curving down the sides, purple matte glaze, Shape No. 830, 1915 (ILLUS. back row, far left, with group, bottom previous page) **1,125**

Vase, 7 1/4" h., 4" d., gently swelled ovoid body tapering to a short neck w/thick molded rim, embossed around the neck w/stylized flower blossoms on slender stems down the sides, fine leathery dark blue glaze, Shape No. 287, 1905 (ILLUS. back row, far right, with group, bottom previous page) **3,150**

Vase, 7 1/2" h., slender swelled cylindrical body tapering to a small, flat molded mouth, molded around the shoulder w/large tulip blossoms atop long leafy stems, multi-toned blue matte glaze, ca. 1915-20 .... **523**

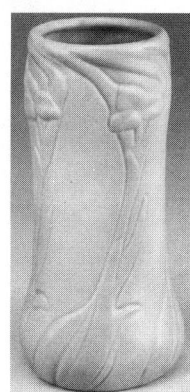

Van Briggle Vase with Trilliums

Vase, 7 1/2" h., 3 1/2" d., slightly waisted cylindrical form, molded w/crisp trillium leaves & blossoms swirling up around the sides & rim, leathery light blue matte glaze, 1905, Shape No. 296 (ILLUS.) **2,090**

Rare Van Briggle "Dos Cebezos" Vase

Vase, 7 3/4" h., 4 3/4" d., "Dos Cebezos," ovoid body tapering to a cylindrical neck, closed shoulder handles molded as two women in flowing garments, unusual mottled charcoal & greyish blue matte flambé glaze, 1902 (ILLUS.) **20,750**

Vase, 7 3/4" h., 5" d., slightly lobed gourd-form body w/a flat mouth, embossed w/stylized flowers around the top, fine teal blue glaze, Shape No. 864, 1912 (tight hairline in rim) **731**

Vase, 8" h., 5 1/2" d., wide simple ovoid body tapering to a short cylindrical neck, overall turquoise matte glaze, Shape No. 269, 1906 (ILLUS. front row, far right, with group, bottom previous page) **1,069**

Baluster-form Van Briggle Blue Vase

Vase, 8 1/4" h., 4 1/2" d., baluster-form w/a rounded shoulder to a short cylindrical neck, embossed around the shoulder w/stylized blossoms, the stems down the sides, sheer robin's-egg blue glaze w/clay showing through, 1906 (ILLUS.) **1,840**

Vase, 8 1/2" h., 3 1/2" d., slender baluster-form w/a short neck, lavender matte glaze, Shape No. 343C, 1905 .... **1,013**

Vase, 9" h., 4" d., tall waisted form w/the swelled top below a wide molded rim, embossed around the shoulder w/large daffodil blossoms on tall leafy stems swirled down the sides, bluish green matte glaze, Shape No. 120, 1920s, two small flat base chips, small bruise on rim, bottom dirty (ILLUS. back row, center, with group, page 276) **619**

Vase, 10 1/2" h., "Lorelei," figural mermaid wrapped around the tall swelled body, black matte glaze, post-1930s **825**

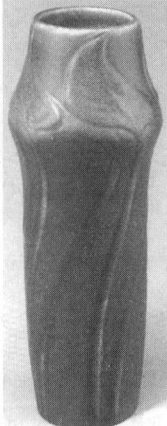

Van Briggle Vase with Leaves & Stems

Vase, 10 1/2" h., 4" d., tall cylindrical form w/swelled shoulder & tapering neck, embossed around the neck w/large curled leaves on long stems swirled down the sides, matte green & tobacco brown feathered glaze, 1906, Shape No. 289 (ILLUS.) **4,888**

Vase, 11" h., 9 1/2" w., "Lady of the Lily" figural design, a large nude Art Nouveau maiden w/arched back & leaning against the side of a large, widely flaring lily-form vase, brown & green mottled matte glaze, 1930s (dirty bottom, few deep crazing lines in base) **2,138**

Lady of the Lily Van Briggle Vase

Vase, 11 1/2" h., 9 1/2" w., "Lady of the Lily," figural w/nude maiden rising from waves & curving back to lean against a large lily-form vase, Persian Rose matte glaze, 1920s, dirt on base (ILLUS.) **1,955**

Van Briggle Peacock Feather Vase

Vase, 16 1/2" h., 8 1/2" d., tapering cylindrical form w/a bulbed shoulder & flat rim, embossed up & around the sides w/large peacock feathers under a frothy turquoise matte glaze on a red clay body, ca. 1910, Shape No. 07, remnant of paper price tag (ILLUS.) **7,475**

Warwick

Numerous collectors have turned their attention to the productions of the Warwick China Manufacturing Company that operated in Wheeling, West Virginia, from 1887 until 1951. Prime interest would seem to lie in items produced before 1914 that were decorated with decal portraits of beautiful women, monks and Indians. Fraternal Order items, as well as floral and fruit decorated items, are also popular with collectors.

Vase, 8 1/2" h., Dahlia shape, tan shading to tan ground, color beechnut decoration, matte finish, M-2 .... **$260**

Vase, 9" h., Carnation shape, brown shading to brown ground, color floral decoration, A-40 145

Vase, 9" h., Carnation shape, overall red ground w/color poinsettia decoration, E-2 175

Vase, 9 1/2" h., Lily shape, brown shading to brown ground, color floral decoration, A-25 200

Vase, 9 1/2" h., Louise shape, brown shading to brown ground, color rose decoration, Secret Red No. 250

Vase, 9 1/2" h., Peerless shape, brown shading to brown ground, color floral decoration, A-40 225

Vase, 9 1/2" h., Rosalie shape, green shading to green ground, color decoration w/roses, F-2 245

Vase, 10" h., Warwick shape, turquoise shading to pink shading to turquoise, color portrait, "Aunt Hilda" type decoration, woman w/shawl over head, H-1 400

Vase, 10 1/4" h., Bonnie shape, brown shading to brown ground, color floral decoration, A-40 290

Vase, 10 1/2" h., Cloverleaf shape, brown shading to brown ground, color floral decoration, A-16 275

Vase, 10 1/2" h., Favorite shape, tan shading to tan ground, color portrait of woman in green dress, matte finish, M-1 290

Vase, 10 1/2" h., Maria shape, overall charcoal ground, color nude portrait, signed "Carreno," C-1 265

Vase, 10 1/2" h., Poppy shape, brown shading to brown ground, color floral decoration, A-27 265

Vase, 10 1/2" h., Poppy shape, overall charcoal ground, color floral decoration, C-6 290

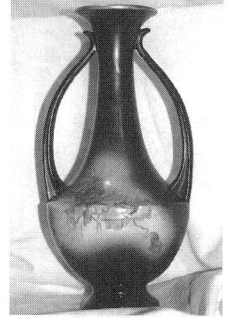

Geran-shape Warwick Vase

Vase, 11" h., Geran shape, overall charcoal ground w/red floral cluster, No. C-6 (ILLUS.) 250

Vase, 11" h., Hyacinth shape, brown shading to brown ground, color floral decoration, A-16 240

Weller

This pottery was made from 1872 to 1945 at a pottery established originally by Samuel A. Weller at Fultonham, Ohio, and moved in 1882 to Zanesville. Numerous

lines were produced and listings below are by the pattern or lines.

Reference books on Weller include The Collectors Encyclopedia of Weller Pottery *by Sharon & Bob Huxford (Collector Books, 1979) and* All About Weller *by Ann Gilbert McDonald (Antique Publications, 1989). ALSO SEE* Antique Trader Books Pottery and Porcelain - Ceramics Price Guide, 3rd Edition.

BLUE & DECORATED HUDSON (1919)
Hand-painted lifelike sprays of fruit blossoms and flowers in shades of pink and blue on a rich dark blue ground.

Six-sided Blue & Decorated Vase

Vase, 11 7/8" h., hexagonal, decorated w/yellow & pink nasturtiums, unmarked (ILLUS.) **$504**

BLUE LOUWELSA (ca. 1905)

Tall Louwelsa Blue Vase with Berries

Vase, 10 7/8" h., tall slender ovoid body tapering to a very slender neck w/flared rim, decorated w/dark & light blue blackberries & vines under a shaded light to dark blue overall glaze, incised "X 431" & "A 59," very minor glaze scratch (ILLUS.).. **1,760**

COPPERTONE (late 1920s)
Various shapes with an overall mottled bright green glaze on a "copper" glaze base. Some pieces with figural frog or fish handles. Models of frogs also included.

Bowl w/original flower holder, 11" d., low form w/flaring sides & down-curved rim, incised "Weller Hand Made" (ILLUS. bottom row, second from right, below)......... **173**

Coppertone Center Bowl & Frog

Center bowl & flower frog, shallow form w/flaring sides, embossed w/lily pads & buds, flower frog in the form of a cluster of leaves centered by an upright water lily blossom, bowl 12" d., 3" h., 2 pcs. (ILLUS.)..................................... **650-850**

Console bowl, shallow oblong form w/frog seated near water lily on one end, 11" l. (ILLUS. bottom row, left, below).................... **805**

Model of a frog, green, tan, brown & black matte glaze, 2 1/2" h. (ILLUS. bottom row, third from left, below)........................... **322**

Vase, 6" h., tapering ovoid body w/a wide closed flat rim, overall vivid mottled green over dark brown glaze, unmarked (ILLUS. bottom row, far right, with bowl & flower holder, below)....................................... **633**

Vase, 6" h., wide tapering cylindrical form (ILLUS. top row, far right, with bowl and flower holder, below)...................................... **334**

Vase, 6" h., wide tapering cylindrical form w/molded rim (ILLUS. top row, far left, with bowl and flower holder, below).............. **161**

Vase, 6 1/2" h., footed slender gently flaring cylindrical body, mottled heavy green over a blackish brown ground, incised mark (ILLUS. top row, fourth from right, with bowl & flower holder, below)............ **297**

Vase, 6 1/2" h., footed tapering cylindrical form, incised "Weller Hand Made" (ILLUS. top row, third from right, with bowl and flower holder, below)...................... **115**

Weller Coppertone Spherical Vase

Vase, 7" h., large spherical form tapering to a wide flaring neck flanked by heavy D-form handles, signed (ILLUS.)....................... **374**

Vase, 8" h., footed, two-handled base w/wide flaring rim (ILLUS. top row, third from left, with bowl and flower holder, below)... **265**

Vase, 8 1/2" h., footed wide trumpet form (ILLUS. bottom row, third from right, with bowl & flower holder, below)........................... **403**

Vase, 9 1/8" h., round foot & trumpet-shaped body molded around the scalloped rim w/lily pads & buds, matte olive green shading to tan, black round stamp...... **374**

Vase, 11" h., footed bulbous base w/wide cylindrical neck w/slightly flared rim, large loop handles from shoulder to rim (ILLUS. top row, second from left, with bowl & flower holder, below)........................... **431**

Vase, 11" h., footed bulbous base w/wide trumpet-form neck, heavy strap handles, incised "Weller Hand Made" (ILLUS. top row, second from right, with bowl & flower holder, below) **575**

Vase, 15 1/4" h., footed trumpet-form body" (ILLUS. bottom row, second from left, with bowl & flower holder, below) **1,144**

DICKENSWARE 2ND LINE(early 1900s)

Various incised "sgraffito" designs usually with a matte glaze. Quality of the artwork greatly affects price.

Ewer, tall slender cylindrical body w/flaring ringed foot, C-form handle, decorated

A Variety of Coppertone Items

w/a bust profile portrait of "Chief Hollowhorn Bear," shaded tan to dark green ground, 16" **750-1,250**
Mug, depicts detailed image of deer **175-250**
Mug, decorated w/scene of monk drinking from mug, green ground, 5 1/2" h. **385**
Mug, bust portrait of American Indian "Tame Wolf," artist-signed, 6 1/4" h **625-750**
Pitcher, 10 1/2" h., portrait of monk, blue & white, marked "X"..................................... **625-750**
Vase, 5 1/4" h., 5 1/4" w., pocket-form, flattened bulbous ovoid sides tapering to a short flaring rim pinched together at the center, sgraffito marsh scene w/a duck & reeds by a lake in shades of brown & green, die-stamped "Dickensware - Weller - X352"..................................... **220-250**
Vase, 8 7/8" h., ovoid body w/short wide flaring neck, shows scene of a young woman wearing blue gown, sitting in a crescent moon playing a long-necked mandolin, green & yellow, decorated by Anthony Dunlavy, impressed "Dickensware - Weller" & "X31" w/"M" incised on base, artist-initialed (glaze nicks on rim)....... **385**
Vase, 9 1/4" h., slightly expanding cylindrical body w/wide flaring rim, golfing scene featuring a golfer & caddy, trees & a fence, brown, gold & blue, marked "Dickensware - Weller" & impressed "X 169," "12" & "KVV".. **2,200**
Vase, 11 7/8" h., tall waisted cylindrical body w/narrow shoulder & short flaring neck, depicts an intricately carved & colorfully painted scene of Colonial life w/seven people, three horses & two statues in a densely wooded area, all in 18th c. costume, brown, green, grey & black glossy glaze, impressed marks "Dickensware - Weller" & "X 48," "8" & "W" (rim chip has been professionally repaired) **1,540**
Vase, 12 3/8" h., slender waisted cylindrical form w/short cylindrical neck & flaring rim, decorated w/scene of a nude woman & an angel w/flowers & flowering trees, impressed "Dickens Ware Weller" (profession repair of rim chip) **896**
Vase, 12 1/2" h., tall cylindrical body w/a narrow shoulder to the short rolled rim, continuous landscape scene of white mounted knights in deep woods, blue sky above, glossy glaze.......................... **3,100-3,750**
Vase, 14" h., tall slender ovoid body w/short narrow flared neck, decorated w/an outdoor scene showing a young mother walking through a wooded area w/her two daughters, all dressed in white, shaded brown ground w/green trees in background, artist-initialed, small chip on rim, die-stamped "Dickensware - Weller X 290 0".. **990**
Vase, 16" h., etched scene w/hunting dogs.. **1,400-2,500**
Vase, 17" h., slender cylindrical form w/incised Venetian scene by C.A. Dusenbery, impressed mark (ILLUS. right, top right column)... **1,150**
Vase, 17 7/8" h., very tall slender cylindrical body w/a narrow rounded shoulder to the short rolled neck, decorated w/a standing monk tasting wine, in browns & yellow

against a shaded brown to gold ground, glossy glaze, decorated by Mary Gellier, ca. 1900, marked & artist-signed .. **1,650**

Two Scenic Dickensware Vases

Vase, 20" h., baluster-form w/wide cylindrical neck w/flared rim, decorated w/incised & painted scene of marching soldiers, impressed mark, restoration (ILLUS. left) **575**

EOCEAN AND EOCEAN ROSE (1898-1925)
Early art line with various hand-painted flowers on shaded grounds, usually with a clear glossy glaze. Quality of artwork varies greatly.

Vase, 5 1/8" h., squared shape, pink, white & blue flowers on slate blue ground, ca. 1910.. **165**
Vase, 5 1/8" h., squatty bulbous body on a narrow footring, tapering to a cylindrical neck w/rolled rim, decorated around the shoulder w/large maroon & grey Virginia creeper leaves & berries, against a grey/green to pale green ground, decorated by Claude Leffler, incised "Eocean Rose Weller" & stamped "9056," artist-initialed (professionally repaired small glaze nicks on rim & foot)................................ **303**
Vase, bud, 5 1/2" h., slip-painted florals on shaded pale blue to grey ground **75**
Vase, 6" h., 5" d., swelled cylindrical body w/a wide flat shoulder to the short cylindrical neck, decorated w/dogwood branches in white & purple against a shaded dark blue to ivory ground, glossy glaze, marked, Eocean Rose **330**
Vase, 6 1/2" h., 3" d., simple cylindrical body, decorated w/a large polychrome stork standing on one leg against a shaded dark grey to white ground, incised "Eocean - Weller" (crazed).................. **900-1,100**
Vase, 8" h., 2 1/2" d., slender cylindrical body w/a narrow round shoulder & short rolled neck, decorated w/purple & green lily-of-the-valley against a shaded black to light green ground, die-stamped circle mark... **400-425**
Vase, 10 3/8" h., gently tapering cylindrical body w/a swelled shoulder tapering to a short cylindrical rim, decorated w/pink wild roses on shaded green glossy ground, decorated by Levi J. Burgess, artist-signed, stamped "Weller" & incised "Eocean," "X" & "50"....................................... **935**
Vase, 10 5/8" h., wide slightly tapering cylindrical body w/a wide shoulder to the compressed incurved short neck, decorated w/a band of swimming green fish against

a shaded dark green to cream ground, signed, ca. 1905, Eocean Rose **2,500-2,800**

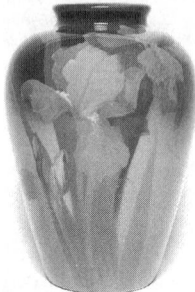

Eocean Vase with Iris Decoration

Vase, 11" h., bulbous ovoid form, painted iris decoration on shaded tan & brown ground, impressed mark, artist-signed (ILLUS.)... **3,163**

Vase, 12 3/4" h., tall ovoid form w/wide rolled rim, decorated w/red & white tulips & green leaves on glossy white ground, incised "Eocean - Weller," "F" & impressed "X 467," artist-signed **1,320**

Vase, 12 3/4" h., 4 3/4" d., slender tapering body w/six open handles rising from narrow shoulder to flared rim, decorated w/large green & violet leaves against a shaded pale pink & dark green ground **900-1,400**

Vase, 12 7/8" h., slender ovoid body w/wide flat mouth, wisteria decoration on shaded brown to yellow ground, glossy glaze, marked & incised "X," artist-initialed (tight 2" hairline from rim) **468**

Vase, 14 1/8" h., tall cylindrical body w/the narrow flat shoulder tapering to a short rolled neck, decorated w/two finely detailed fish swimming among lily pads & flowers, dark greyish green to pale green ground, decorated by Eugene Roberts, incised "Eocean Rose Weller" & impressed with shape number 579, artist-signed **3,850**

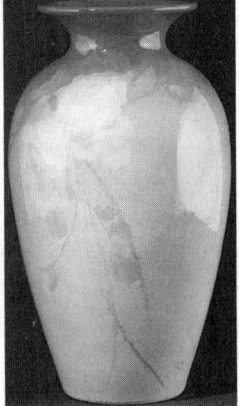

Rare Large Weller Eocean Vase

Vase, 24" h., 12" d., large ovoid body tapering to a short widely flaring neck, decorated w/large white tea roses & pale green leafy stems on a dark blue shaded to creamy white ground, by Mae Timberlake, incised mark & artist-signed, couple of minor flakes on base (ILLUS.) **7,313**

ETNA (1906)
Colors similar to Early Eocean line but designs are molded in low relief and colored.

Lemonade set: a 14" h. tankard pitcher & two cylindrical mugs; each w/an angled handle decorated w/a large cluster of deep reddish purple grapes & green leaves at the top against a shaded grey to pink ground, signed, 3 pcs. (hairline in one mug)... **400-450**

Etna Vase

Vase, 5" h., footed squatty bulbous body tapering to wide cylindrical neck w/molded rim, decorated w/purple & mauve nasturtiums, impressed "Etna" on bottom & "Weller" on side & bottom (ILLUS.) **168**

Vase, 6 1/2" h., footed angular bulbous body tapering to a wide cylindrical neck w/slightly flaring rim, slip-painted floral design.. **125**

Vase, 7" h., cylindrical, decorated w/yellow dandelions on grey ground **165**

Vase, 8 3/8" h., gently flaring cylindrical body tapering to a short wide neck, decorated w/embossed flowers in pink & yellow on a shaded grey to pink ground **220**

Vase, 8 1/2" h., cylindrical body tapering to short slightly flared rim, decorated w/embossed pink thistles & green leaves on grey shaded to cream ground, marked "Weller" on side & on bottom in small block letters **248**

Vase, 10 1/2" h., tapering cylindrical body w/flat rim, dark charcoal shaded to grey, decorated at the neck & base w/lavender nasturtium blooms, base impressed "Weller" & "Etna," body incised "Weller" in body near lower blooms (moderate crazing) **190**

Vase, 10 7/8" h., tall gently flaring cylindrical body w/flat shoulder tapering to a short rolled rim, embossed pink carnation decoration on dark blue shaded to pink ground.. **220**

Vase, 11" h., tall ovoid body w/bulbous short neck w/closed rim flanked by short twisted strap handles, low-relief floral

bouquet in rosy red & pale green leafy
stems against a shaded grey ground **300**
Vase, 13 3/8" h., gently swelled cylindrical
body tapering to a short cylindrical neck,
decorated w/embossed pink roses, grey
to ivory ground **550**
Vase, 15" h., baluster-form body w/shoulder
tapering to closed mouth, decorated
w/embossed grape vines in blues & reds
on a shaded green to grey ground,
stamped "Weller" **605**

FLEMISH (mid-teens to 1928)
*Clusters of pink roses and green leaves, often against
a molded light brown basketweave ground. Some pieces
molded with fruit or small figural birds. Matte glaze.*

Basket, hanging-type w/chains, 7" h................. **125**
Jardiniere, birds on wire scene, 7 1/2" h. **250**
Jardiniere, wide slightly swelled cylindrical
body, pink floral decoration on cream
ground, 8 1/2" h. **175**
Jardiniere, decorated w/four lion heads &
garlands, 13" d., 10" h. **250**
Pedestal base, decorated w/bright blue
cockatoo, 21 5/8" h. (5 1/2" portion of up-
per rim chipped off & reglued) **336**
Planter, figural log, 4 1/2" h. **35**
Tub, basket-shaped w/rim handles, rose
swag on front, 8 1/2" d., 5 1/2" h. **165**
Vase, 8 1/2" h., footed cylindrical body
w/embossed rose tied w/yellow bow, im-
pressed "Weller" in large block letters **193**

Flemish Ovoid Vase

Vase, 12 1/4" h., ovoid form w/flaring cylindrical neck, decorated w/red flowers on
green vines, brown matte glaze, minor
chip, impressed mark (ILLUS.)...................... **748**

GLENDALE (early to late 1920s)
*Various relief-molded birds in their natural habi-
tats, lifelike coloring.*

Vase, 6" h., cylindrical, large standing
marsh bird... **400**
Vase, 6 1/2" h., ovoid body w/slightly taper-
ing neck & a flat rim, decorated w/outdoor
scene of a bird in flight.................................. **365**
Vase, 7" h., baluster-form body w/gently
flaring rim, decorated w/a brown bird
standing beside its ground nest w/eggs,

green grass & white & yellow daisies un-
der a blue sky in background **450**
Vase, double-bud, 7" h., gate-form, tree
trunk-form vases flank a panel embossed
w/a bird & nest w/four eggs, original label...... **326**

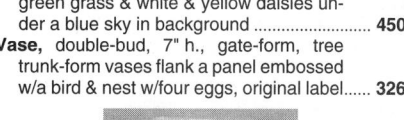

Glendale Vase

Vase, 11 3/8" h., bulbous base tapering to
cylindrical neck & flat rim, decorated
w/long-legged plover guarding a nest of
speckled eggs surrounded by cattails & a
patch of wild berries in red & deep blue,
ink stamped "Weller Ware" (ILLUS.) **1,568**
Vase, 11 7/8" h., baluster-form tapering to
flaring rim, decorated scene of a gold-
finch on a nest, yellow & orange butterflies, thistles & daisies, ink stamped
"Weller Ware," no artist signature **1,904**

HUDSON (1917-34)
*Underglaze slip-painted decoration, "parchment-vel-
lum" transparent glaze.*

Vase, 7" h., swelled cylindrical body w/a
flaring base & widely flaring rim, decorated around the top w/a pink, yellow & blue
blossom against a group of pale green
leaves all against a shaded white to pale
green ground, decorated by Sara
Timberlake, ca. 1920, marked............... **250-275**
Vase, 7" h., 3 1/2" d., ovoid, decorated
w/white & pink dogwood blossoms
against a blue shading to cream to pink
ground, artist-signed **300-350**
Vase, 7 7/8" h., ovoid body w/flat rim, decorated w/white & yellow wild roses, artist-
signed, silver foil half kiln label over a half
kiln ink stamp logo.. **448**
Vase, 8 1/4" h., 3 1/2" d., baluster-form,
decorated w/slip-painted trefoil blossoms
in dark & light blue w/green leaves on a
blue to cream ground, die-stamped
"WELLER" **350-400**
Vase, 8 5/8" h., decorated w/a Spanish car-
avel under full sail moving over blue sea
w/white-capped waves, two other crafts
behind, flying sea gulls accompany the
boats, shaded blue to pink ground w/red
& yellow designs on sails, decorated by
Hester Pillsbury, artist-signed on side,
the base marked w/the letter "A" in black
slip.. **4,510**

Vase, 8 7/8" h., swelled cylindrical body w/a short molded mouth, decorated w/large white jonquils on pale green leafy stems against a green to pale cream ground, stamped "Weller" in block letters............ **450-500**

Vase, 9 3/8" h., swelled cylindrical shouldered body w/a short rounded neck w/flat rim, decorated around the top half w/large creamy white nasturtium blossoms & green leaves & vines against a shaded blue to pale green ground, decorated by Sarah McLaughlin, ca. 1920, artist-signed & marked............................ **500-550**

Vase, 9 1/2" h., 5" d., swelling cylindrical body w/a wide shoulder tapering to a short wide mouth, decorated around the upper half w/large white & blue morning glories & green leaves against a shaded blue to green ground, decorated by Hester Pillsbury, artist's initials on side, black kiln mark on base.................................... **600-650**

Floral Decorated Hudson Vase

Vase, 12" h., ovoid body tapering to flaring rim, pink & blue floral decoration on a shaded green & blue ground, decorated by Sarah McLaughlin, impressed mark (ILLUS.).. **2,530**

Large Hudson Vase with Roses

Vase, 12" h., ovoid body w/cylindrical neck & slightly flaring rim, front decorated w/large rose blossoms w/a bee & roses on the obverse, by Hester Pillsbury, incised mark, minor flake to base (ILLUS.)... **2,530**

Vase, 12 1/4" h., bulbous ovoid body tapering to a cylindrical neck w/flaring rim, decorated w/a scene depicting a distant city across a bay, tall bamboo shoots & leaves tower over sea gulls flying toward wood pilings in the bay, impressed "Weller" (a 1/2" drill hole in bottom professionally repaired).................................... **2,200**

Vase, 13 1/2" h., urn-form, the wide ovoid body tapering to a short cylindrical neck w/rolled rim, wide strap handles from neck to shoulder, decorated w/a scenic design of a large peacock resting near a large wrought-iron gate & stone fence in shades of blue, white, yellow, green & black against a mottled blue-green to tan ground, attributed to Mae Timberlake, the base marked w/a letter "A" in black slip...... **4,500-6,000**

JAP BIRDIMAL (1904)

Stylized Japanese-inspired figural bird or animal designs on various solid colored grounds.

Jap Birdimal Umbrella Stand

Umbrella stand, wide cylindrical form w/narrow shoulder & slightly flaring rim, landscape decoration w/large blue trees, impressed mark, minor chips, 20" h. (ILLUS.).. **1,035**

Vase, 4 1/2" h., spherical body on three outswept knob feet, tricorner rounded rim, bluish grey ground decorated w/two white geese in flight **265**

Rare Jap Birdimal Weller Vase

Vase, 12 7/8" h., very tall slender & slightly waisted cylindrical form w/an angled shoulder tapering to a short wide trumpet neck, decorated w/a full-length geisha girl & stylized trees in slip-trail outline, glossy glazed in shades of olive green, yellow, rust, brown & blue on a black ground, incised "Weller Faience - Rhead," ca. 1904 (ILLUS.) **1,955**

SICARDO (1902-07)

Various shapes with iridescent glaze of metallic shadings in greens, blues, crimson, purple or coppertone decorated with vines, flowers, stars or free-form geometric lines.

Jardiniere, very wide bulbous body raised on short arcaded feet, the sides boldly embossed w/large Moorish arabesques, tapering to a wide short flaring scalloped neck, iridescent purple, gold & green glaze, painted "Weller SICARD" on the side, 14 1/2" d., 12 1/2" h. **1,500-2,000**

Vase, 3 1/4" h., 5 3/4" d., footed wide & low cushion-form body centered by a short widely flaring trefoil neck, bright satiny decoration of gold arabesques against a lustred green & burgundy ground, signed on the side **700-800**

Vase, 5" h., baluster-form, a multicolored iridescent glaze decorated w/mistletoe branches, signed **400-450**

Vase, 6 1/2" h., 4 1/4" d., tapering ovoid body w/a bulbous compressed & closed neck flanked by small loop handles, iridescent gold flowers on a deep purple ground, unmarked **850-1,100**

Vase, 7" h., tall tri-lobed upright undulating body, floral designs on sides, covered in iridescent glaze in shades of green & gold **1,150-1,300**

Vase, 8 1/2" h., 5 3/4" d., ovoid gourd-form w/wide shoulder & bulbed tapering neck, decorated w/swirling poppies & leaves w/a lustrous gold, blue, green & purple glaze, signed **2,925**

Vase, 8 5/8" h., wide bulbous ovoid body tapering sharply to a molded flat mouth, incurved loop handles on the sides, decorated w/several snails amid leafy vegetation, base cut "36," signed "Weller Sicard," ca. 1905 (glaze flaw from bottom up side 1/2") **950-1,100**

Vase, 9" h., wide ovoid shouldered body tapering to a short rounded neck w/flat rim, decorated w/flowing chrysanthemums & buds against a background of scattered dots, ca. 1904 .... **2,200-2,600**

Vase, 13" h., 5 3/4" d., bulbous top w/closed small mouth above tapering cylindrical sides, embossed w/large, tall irises, rich burgundy & gold lustre glaze, unmarked **7,700-8,500**

Vase, 14 1/2" h., 7" d., tall ovoid form w/a rounded shoulder centering a short rolled neck, decorated overall w/poppies & vining leaves in celadon & gold on a purple iridescent ground, marked (restored drill hole in base) **2,925**

Vase, 19 1/2" h., 13" d., Art Nouveau style, ovoid body on scroll-molded feet, the sides tapering to a bulbous, pierced rim molded w/whiplash swirls above large pendent blossoms above the relief-molded figures of two swirling Art Nouveau maidens flanked by long scrolls, the body flanked by large, long pierced scrolling handles continuing down to the scrolled feet, gold, green, blue & purple iridescent glaze, signed "Weller - Sicard" **7,700-9,500**

Vase, floor-type, 21 3/4" h., wide ovoid body w/a molded mouth, decorated w/large Art Nouveau stylized poppies against a streaked ground, ca. 1905, signed **12,100**

WOODCRAFT (1917)

Rustic designs simulating the appearance of stumps, logs and tree trunks. Some pieces are adorned with owls, squirrels, dogs and other animals. Matte finish.

Bowl, 6 1/4" d., 3" h., footed, deep gently flaring form w/scalloped rim, relief-molded squirrel decoration, marked in black slip "29" **101**

Candlestick, double, modeled as an owl perched at the top of an apple tree between candle nozzles, 8" w., 13 1/2" h. **325-350**

Flower frog, figural lobster **120-170**

Lawn ornament, figural, model of a large squirrel seated & holding an acorn, mottled brown & green, stamped "WELLER POTTERY," 11 1/2" w., 11 3/4" h. (restoration to ears, tight hairline in tail) **2,000-2,500**

Planter, log-form w/molded leaf & narrow strap handle at top center, 11" l., 4 1/4" h. **75-100**

Vase, 12" h., smooth tree trunk form w/molded leafy branch around rim & down sides w/hanging purple plums **175-225**

Vase, 13" h., waisted cylindrical tree trunk form w/relief-molded branch, apple & leaves down the front **250-300**

Wall hanging, model of a large climbing squirrel, matte brown & green glaze, black ink kiln mark, 4 3/4" w., 13 1/2" h. **1,200-1,500**

Wall pocket, conical w/applied figural squirrel, 9 1/2" h. **316**

Wheatley Pottery

Thomas J. Wheatley was one of the original founders of the art pottery movement in Cincinnati, Ohio in the early 1880s. In 1879 the Cincinnati Art Pottery was formed and after some legal problems it operated under the name T.J. Wheatley & Company. Its production featured Limoges-style hand-painted decorations and most pieces were carefully marked and often dated.

In 1882 Wheatley disassociated himself from the Cincinnati Art Pottery and opened another pottery which was destroyed by fire in 1884. Around 1900 Wheatley finally resumed making art pottery in Cincinnati and in 1903 he founded the Wheatley Pottery Company with a new partner, Isaac Kahn.

The new pottery from this company featured colored matte glazes over relief work designs and green, yellow and blue were the most often used colors. There were imitations of the well-known Grueby Pottery wares as well as artware, garden pottery and architectural pieces. Artwork was apparently not made much after 1907. This plant was destroyed by fire in 1910 but was rebuilt and run by Wheatley until his death in 1917. Wheatley artware was generally unmarked except for a paper label.

Teco-style Wheatley Jardiniere

Jardiniere, wide thick ovoid body w/a thick squared rim band joining four heavy squared buttresses down the sides, feathered matte green glaze, in the style of Teco, small chip on edge of foot, 9" d., 7" h. (ILLUS.) **$920**

Wheatley Lamp with Buttresses

Lamp base, thick slightly tapering cylindrical body w/a wide squared rim band issuing four thick squared buttresses down the side, a copper tube running through the lower buttresses, fine feathered matte green glaze, unmarked, 8 1/2" d., 11" h. (ILLUS.) **575**

Wheatley Lamp Base and Vases

Lamp base, wide tapering double gourd-form body w/four heavy squared buttress handles from the top rim to the base, leathery matte green glaze, w/original oil font insert, several burst bubbles, incised "WP - 672," 10 1/2" d., 11 1/2" h. (ILLUS. back left) **2,813**

Lamp base, wide round flaring base tapering to a slender baluster-form standard, embossed oblong leaves around the foot w/the stems continuing up the standard, fine leathery matte green glaze, unmarked, 10" d., 16 1/4" h. **1,575**

Vase, 6" h., 5" d., wide ovoid body tapering slightly to a wide flat mouth, embossed w/large upright arrowhead leaves around the sides, matte green glaze, incised "WP," several burst bubbles (ILLUS. front left with lamp base, above) **788**

Large & Small Wheatley Vases

Vase, 6 3/4" h., 5" d., ovoid shouldered form w/a short, wide neck & flat rim, molded w/a continuous vertical band of wide tapering ribbed leaves, mottled matte green glaze, several clay pimples, mark partially obscured (ILLUS. center) **956**

Vase, 7 1/4" h., 7 1/4" d., squatty bulbous body molded around the lower half w/a band of overlapping rounded, pointed leaves, the sides tapering to a cylindrical neck w/narrow molded rings, frothy light green & amber glaze, signed "WP" (several burst glaze bubbles) **900**

Vase, 7 1/4" h., 9" d., a deep thick rounded form w/a thick squared flat rim band issuing four heavy squared buttresses down the sides, flower dead-matte green glaze, marked "61" (ILLUS. front right with lamp base, top, previous page) **1,800**

Wheatley Vase with Buttress Feet

Vase, 10 1/2" h., four heavy square buttress feet tapering up the wide slightly tapering cylindrical sides, wide molded mouth, overall matte green glaze, illegible mark, several small glaze chips on feet (ILLUS.) **1,438**

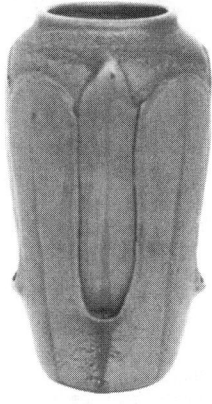

Wheatley Vase with Upright Leaves

Vase, 8 1/2" h., slightly ovoid body tapering to a wide flat mouth, the sides molded w/alternating upright pointed & rounded leaves, matte green glaze, several small chips on leaf edges (ILLUS.) **978**

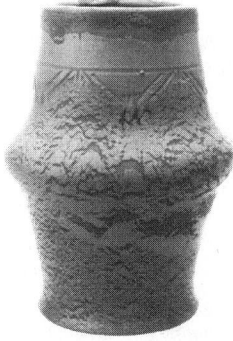

Wheatley Vase with Incised Design

Vase, 11 1/2" h., slightly swelled cylindrical form w/a wide bulbed ring around the middle, wide flat rim, mottled matte green glaze w/incised geometric design, unmarked (ILLUS.) **978**

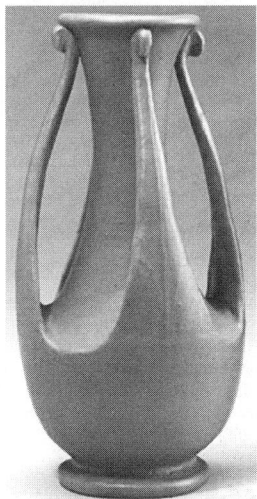

Wheatley Vase with Tendril Handles

Vase, 10 1/4" h., 5" d., footed baluster-form body w/the shoulder issuing four long scrolled tendril-like handles to the rim, matte green glaze, marked (ILLUS.) **1,035**

Large Tapering Wheatley Vase

Vase, 11 1/2" h., 9 1/4" d., small rectangular feet supporting the wide tapering cylindrical body w/a wide, thick molded rim w/four projecting blocks above buttresses, pulled matte green glaze, base pierced w/five drainage holes in the making, signed, some minor glaze flecks, chips to feet (ILLUS.) **2,070**

Vase, 12" h., 7 1/2" d., large slightly tapering cylindrical form w/a thick rolled rim above a recessed neck band w/four small buttress handles, embossed around the sides w/large, rounded veined leaves alternating w/buds on the rim, curdled medium matte green glaze, marked "WP - C13," couple of burst bubbles (ILLUS. back right with lamp base) **2,700**

Vase, 12 1/2" h., 6" d., simple ovoid body tapering to a short cylindrical neck, the sides molded w/tall arrowroot leaves, medium matte green glaze, mark obscured (several clay pimples & burst bubbles).. **1,800**

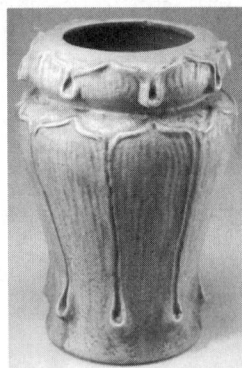

Wheatley Grueby-style Vase

Vase, 12 1/2" h., 9" d., wide baluster-form w/wide cushion neck, in the style of Grueby's Kendrick vase, molded around the sides & neck w/wide leaves, fine frothy matte light brown glaze, small chip to edge of neck, remnants of paint (ILLUS.).. **3,450**

"Kendrick" Vase

Vase, 13" h., 9" d., large ovoid body w/a wide squatty bulbed neck w/incurved rim, molded around the sides w/wide tapering ribbed leaves w/matching shorter leaves around the neck, leathery green matte glaze, two small chips on side decoration, marked, after a model by G.P. Kendrick (ILLUS.) **3,938**

Teco-form Wheatley Vase

Vase, 14 1/4" h., 8" d., based on a Teco form, a bulbous bottom tapering slightly to wide cylindrical body w/a four-scallop ring issuing four vine-like handles down the sides, frothy matte green glaze, incised "WP - 615" (ILLUS.)........................... **2,875**

Vase, 14 1/4" h., 8" d., footed bulbous base narrowing slightly to a tall, wide cylindrical neck flanked by four arched & webbed handles from the rim to the shoulder, leathery matte green glaze, incised "WP" (several burst bubbles, few glaze chips at rim, grinding chips to base).. **3,150**

Large Wheatley Vase with Cubes

Vase, 14 1/2" h., 9 1/4" h., footed tapering slightly ovoid body molded w/tall ribbed & pointed leaves up the sides alternating w/shorter leaves topped by projecting blocks embossed on the front w/small swastikas, frothy matte green glaze, no visible mark, several burst bubbles, touch-ups to two corners of cubes & tip of one leaf (ILLUS.) **1,610**

Vase, 18 1/2" h., 10 1/2" d., tall paneled ovoid form w/a short rolled neck, each panel molded w/a tall serrated & veined leaf alternating w/a stem topped by a three-petal blossom, leathery matte green glaze, two glaze chips on ribs, incised "WP" (ILLUS. right with small vase).. **3,938**

Vase, 20" h., 10" d., the tall swelled cylindrical body tapering to a slightly bulbed cylindrical neck flanked by pointed tall buttress handles down the side, each w/a half-round cut-out, the body molded w/tall ribbed & pointed leaves alternating w/stylized blossom buds around the neck, dark leathery matte green glaze, mark obscured, long grinding chip on base (ILLUS. left with small vase).............. **4,500**

Wall pocket, half-round body composed of three wide, tapering leaf-form panels curled in at the top & alternating w/buds, a low arched backplate w/hanging hole, curdled medium matte green glaze, unmarked, 9 1/4" w., 8" h.................................. **675**

Willow Wares

This pseudo-Chinese pattern has been used by numerous firms throughout the years. The original design is attributed to Thomas Minton about 1780 and Thomas Turner is believed to have first produced the ware during his tenure at the Caughley works. The blue underglaze transfer print pattern has never been out of production since that time. An Oriental landscape incorporating a bridge, pagoda, trees, figures and birds supposedly tells the story of lovers fleeing a cruel father who wished to prevent their marriage. The gods, having pity on them, changed them into birds, enabling them to fly away and seek their happiness together.

Blue

Ashtray, figural whale, ca. 1960, Japan....... **$50-55**
Ashtray, unmarked, American............................. 15
Bank, figural, stacked pigs, ca. 1960, Japan, 7" h.. **50-55**
Batter jug, frosted, Hazel Atlas Glass, 9" h.. **100-125**
Batter jug, Moriyama, Japan, 9 1/2" h. **125-150**
Bell, modern, Enesco, Japan 15
Bone dish, ca. 1890, unmarked, England **40-50**

Blue Willow Bone Dish

Bone dish, Buffalo Pottery, 6 1/2" l. (ILLUS.).. **75-80**
Bowl, berry, Allertons, England **12-15**
Bowl, berry, Japan.. 8
Bowl, berry, milk glass, Hazel Atlas...................... 15
Bowl, individual, 5 1/4" oval, J. Maddock............. 20
Bowl, soup, 8" d., Japan 18-20
Bowl, 6 1/2 x 8 1/4", Ridgways, England 50-55
Bowl, salad, 10" d., Japan.................................... 75
Butter dish, cov., Ridgways, England....... **175-185**
Butter dish, in wood holder, 6" d. **50-75**
Butter dish, cov., for stick, Japan, rectangular, 7" l.. **60-70**
Butter dish, cov., 8" d., England...................... 100
Butter pat, Buffalo Pottery...................................... 25
Butter pat, Wood & Sons 25
Cake plate, Green & Co., 8" sq. 40-45
Canister, cov., round, tin, 5 3/4" h. 20-25

Blue Willow Coffee Canister

Canister, labeled "Coffee," marked "Willow," Australia, ca. 1920s, 5 3/4" h. (ILLUS.).. **45-50**
Canister set: cov., "Coffee," "Flour," "Sugar," "Tea," barrel-shaped, ca. 1960s, Japan, the set... **350-400**
Chamber pot, Wedgwood, 9" d................. **175-200**
Cheese dish, cov., rectangular, unmarked, England.. **175**

Blue Willow Cheese Stand

Cheese stand, J. Meir & Sons, England, 8 1/2" d. (ILLUS.)..................................... **195-225**
Condiment cruet set: cov. oil & vinegar & mustard cruet, salt & pepper; carousel-type base w/wooden handle, Japan, 7 1/2" h., the set...................................... **175-200**

Blue Willow Cracker Jar

Cracker jar, cov., silver lid & handle, Minton, England, 5" h. (ILLUS.)............................. **175**
Creamer, Allerton, England.................................. 60

Blue Willow Cow-shaped Creamer

Creamer, cow-shaped, W. Kent, England, 1920s-50s (ILLUS.) **300-400**
Creamer, individual, Shenango China Co...... **25-30**
Creamer, John Steventon **40**

Blue Willow Figural Cow Creamer

Creamer w/original stopper, figural cow standing on oval base, mouth forms spout & tail forms handle, ca. 1850, unmarked, England, 7" l., 5" h. (ILLUS.) ... **700-800**
Cruets w/original stoppers, oil & vinegar, Japan, 6" h., the set **65**
Cup & saucer, Booth **40-45**
Cup & saucer, Buffalo Pottery **40-45**
Cup & saucer, child's, ca. 1900, unmarked, England **50**
Cup & saucer, demitasse, Copeland, England **40**
Cup & saucer, "For Auld Lang Syne," W. Adams, England, oversized **100-125**
Cup & saucer, Japan **10-15**
Drainer, butter, ca. 1890, England, 6" sq. **75**
Egg cup, Booths, England, 4" h. **45-50**
Egg cup, Japan, 4" h. **20-25**
Egg cup, Allerton, England, 4 1/2" h. **40-45**
Ginger jar, cov., Japan, 5" h. **30**
Ginger jar, cov., Mason's, 9" h. **60-75**
Gravy boat, Buffalo Pottery **75-85**

Blue Willow Gravy Boat

Gravy boat, ca. 1890, unmarked, England, 7" l. (ILLUS.) **60-65**
Gravy boat w/attached underplate, double-spouted, Ridgways, England **75-85**

Hot pot, electric, Japan, 6" h. **75**
Invalid feeder, ca. 1860, unmarked, England **175-200**
Knife rest, ca. 1860, unmarked, England **85-95**
Ladle, pattern in bowl, unmarked, England, 6" l. **125-135**
Ladle, pattern in bowl, floral handle, unmarked, England, 12" l. **185-200**
Lamp, w/ceramic shade, Japan, 8" h. **75**
Lamp, w/reflector plate, Japan, 8" h. **85-95**
Lamp, Wedgwood, England, 10" h. **200-225**
Lighter, teacup-shaped, Japan **45-50**
Mug, "Farmer's," Japan, 4" h. **18-20**

Blue Willow Mug

Mug, barrel-shaped mold, Granger & Worcester, England, ca. 1850, 4 1/4" h. (ILLUS.) **250-275**

Willow Ware Mug

Mug, Maling, England, 4 1/2" h. (ILLUS.) **85-95**
Mustache cup & saucer, Hammersley & Co. **150-175**

Blue Willow Mustard Pot

Mustard pot, cov., ca. 1870, unmarked, England, 3" h. (ILLUS.) **100-125**
Napkin holder, Japan **50-65**

Blue Willow Nut Dish

Nut dish, scalloped shape, ca. 1900, 7" l.
(ILLUS.) **75-85**
Pastry stand, three-tiered plates, Royal
China Co., Sebring, Ohio, 13" h. **40-50**
Pepper pot, ca. 1870, England, 4" h. **100-125**

Willow Ware Pepper Shaker

Pepper shaker, "Prestopan," unmarked,
Scotland, 5 1/4" h. (ILLUS.) **250-275**

Blue Willow Pitcher

Pitcher, 5 1/2" h., Ridgway, England
(ILLUS.) **85-95**

Buffalo Pottery Blue Willow Pitcher

Pitcher, cov., 5 1/2" h., Buffalo Pottery
(ILLUS.) **200-225**
Pitcher, 6" h., scalloped rim, Allerton, En-
gland **125-150**

Blue Willow "Chicago Jug"

Pitcher, 7" h., "Chicago Jug," ca. 1907, Buffalo Pottery, 3 pt. (ILLUS.) **200-225**
Pitcher, 8" h., glass, Johnson Bros., En-
gland **35-40**
Pitcher w/ice lip, 10" h., Japan **100**

Blue Willow Placecard Holder

Placecard holder, unmarked, England, ca.
1870s, 2 1/2" d. (ILLUS.) **85-100**
Placemat, cloth, 16 x 12" **18-20**
Plate, 10 1/4" d., paper, Fonda **1-2**
Plate, 10" d., tin, ca. 1988, Robert Steffy **10-12**
Plate, 7 1/2" d., Arklow, Ireland **20**
Plate, bread & butter, Allerton, England **12-15**
Plate, bread & butter, Japan **5-7**
Plate, charger, 11 3/4" d., Moriyama, Made
in Japan **75-95**
Plate, charger, 12" d., Buffalo Pottery **75-95**
Plate, child's, 4 1/2" d., Japan **10-15**
Plate, "Child's Day 1971," sandman w/wil-
low umbrella, Wedgwood **65-75**
Plate, dinner, Booth's, England **40-45**

Buffalo Blue Willow Dinner Plate

Plate, dinner, Buffalo Pottery, 1911 (ILLUS.).. **30-35**
Plate, dinner, ca. 1870, unmarked, England .. **40-50**
Plate, dinner, Cambridge, blue patt. on clear
 glass.. **40-50**
Plate, dinner, flow blue, Royal Doulton........... **75-85**
Plate, dinner, Holland **18-20**
Plate, dinner, Japan **10-15**
Plate, dinner, Mandarin patt., Copeland,
 England **40-50**
Plate, dinner, modern, Royal Wessex................ **6-8**
Plate, dinner, Paden City Pottery.................... **30-35**
Plate, dinner, restaurant ware, Jackson **15-20**
Plate, dinner, Royal China Co......................... **10-15**
Plate, dinner, scalloped rim, Allerton,
 England **30-35**
Plate, grill, 10 1/2" d., Holland **18-20**
Plate, grill, 10" d., Japan **18-20**
Plate, grill, Allerton, England **45-50**
Plate, luncheon, Wedgwood, England............ **20-25**
Plate, luncheon, Worcester patt...................... **35-40**

Blue Willow Wedgwood Platter

Platter, 9 x 11" l., rectangular, Wedgwood
 & Co., England (ILLUS.) **100-125**
Platter, 8 1/2 x 11 1/2" l., oval, scalloped
 rim, Buffalo Pottery.................................. **100-125**
Platter, 9 x 12" l., oval, American **15-18**
Platter, 9 x 12" l., oval, Japan **20-25**
Platter, 9 x 12" l., rectangular, Allerton,
 England **150-175**
Platter, 11 x 14" l., oval, Johnson Bros.,
 England **65-75**
Platter, 11 x 14" l., rectangular, Buffalo Pot-
 tery **150-175**
Platter, 11 x 14" l., rectangular, ca. 1880s,
 unmarked, England **150-175**
Platter, 15 x 19" l., rectangular, well &
 tree, ca. 1890, unmarked, England........ **350-375**
Pudding mold, England, 4 1/2" h. **40-45**

Willow Ware Punch Cup

Punch cup, pedestal foot, unmarked,
 England, ca. 1900, 3 1/2" h. (ILLUS.)......... **50-75**
Relish dish, leaf-shaped, ca. 1870,
 England **100-125**

Blue Willow Salt Box

Salt box, cov., ca. 1960, wooden lid, Japan,
 5 x 5" (ILLUS.) **195-225**
Salt dip, master, pedestal base, unmarked,
 England, 2" h.. **100-125**
Salt & pepper shakers, Japan, pr................. **35-40**

Blue Willow Sauce Tureen

Sauce tureen, cov., England, ca. 1880s,
 5" h. (ILLUS.) **125-150**
Soup tureen, cov., ca. 1880, unmarked,
 England.. **400-450**
Spoon rest, Japan.. **35-40**

Blue Willow Sugar Barrel

Sugar Barrel, cov., silver lid & handle,
 unmarked, England, ca. 1880s, 5" h.
 (ILLUS.).. **175-200**
Sugar bowl, cov., Japan **20-25**
Sugar bowl, cov., Ridgway, England **50-60**
Tablecloth, Simtex **45-55**
Tea set, child's, Japan, service for six in box
 .... **250-300**
Tea set, child's, tin, Ohio Art Co., Bryan,
 Ohio, service for four **125-150**
Tea tile, ca. 1900, unmarked, England, 6"
 sq. **75**
Tea tile, Minton, England, 6" sq. **75**
Teapot, child's, Made in Occupied Japan...... **40-45**
Teapot, cov., ca. 1890, Royal Doulton **300-350**
Teapot, cov., child's, Japan............................. **35-40**

Teapot, cov., Homer Laughlin **75-85**
Teapot, cov., round, Allerton, England **250-275**

Miniature Teapot

Teapot, cov., miniature, modern, Windsor,
3 3/4" h. (ILLUS.) **15-20**
Teapot, individual, Moriyama, Japan,
4 1/2" h. **75-100**
Teapot, cov., Sadler, 4 3/4" h. **40-45**

Blue Willow Enamel Teapot

Teapot, cov., enamel, unmarked, 7" h.
(ILLUS.) **75-85**
Teapot cozy, modern, willow fabric **40-45**

Teapot & Trivet

Teapot w/trivet, cov., Grimwades, 6" h., 2
pcs. (ILLUS.) **250-275**

"Yorkshire Relish" Tip Tray

Tip tray, "Yorkshire Relish," England, 4" d.
(ILLUS.) **50-60**

Blue Willow Tip Tray

Tip tray, "Schweppes Lemon Squash," England, 4 1/2" d. (ILLUS.) **85-95**

Blue Willow Toby Jug

Toby jug, w/Blue Willow jacket, unmarked,
England, 6" h. (ILLUS.) **500-600**
Toby jug, w/Blue Willow jacket, W. Kent,
England, 6" h. **500-600**
Toothbrush holder, Wedgwood, England,
5 1/4" h. **95**
Tray, round, brass, 6" d. **50**
Vegetable bowl, open, Japan, 10 1/2" oval **35**
Wash pitcher & bowl, ca. 1890, unmarked,
England, the set **500-600**

Blue Willow Wash Bowl & Pitcher

Wash pitcher & bowl, Royal Doulton, the
set (ILLUS.) **700-900**

Other Colors
Butter dish, 7" rectangular for stick, red, Japan **65-75**
Butter pat, red, Japan **20**
Charger, brown, Buffalo China, 11" d. **60-70**
Coffeepot, cov., ca. 1890, brown, unmarked, England, 8 3/4" h. **200-225**

Purple Willow Ware Cup

Cup, purple, handleless, unmarked, England (ILLUS.) **75-85**
Cup & saucer, red, ca. 1930, Buffalo China.. **30-35**
Egg cup, red, England, 4 1/2" h. **35-40**

Red Willow Ware Pitcher

Pitcher, 5" h., red, "Old Gustavsberg," Sweden (ILLUS.) **65-75**
Plate, 2 3/4" d., green, miniature, modern, Coalport, England.. **20-25**

Brown Willow Ware Child's Plate

Plate, 4 3/4" d., brown, child's, E.M. & Co. (ILLUS.) **50-60**
Plate, 6" d., restaurant ware, brown, Buffalo China **15**
Plate, 9" d., ca. 1890, brown, John Meir & Son... **20-25**
Plate, 9" d., Mandarin patt., red, Copeland.... **35-40**
Plate, 9" d., purple, Britannia Pottery **35-40**
Plate, bread & butter, 6" d., green, Japan **18-20**
Plate, dinner, red, Japan **15-20**
Plate, grill, 11 1/4" d., green, Royal Willow China **30-35**
Platter, 9", brown, early, unmarked, England **90-100**
Platter, cov., 9", red, Petrus Regout, Holland **35-45**
Platter, 9 1/4 x 11 1/4", rectangular, red, Allerton, England.. **175-200**
Platter, 11 x 19" l., rectangular, green, John Steventon & Sons.................................... **125-150**
Sugar bowl, red, Japan **25-35**

Teapot, cov., purple, Britannia Pottery **200-225**
Teapot, cov., red, child's, E.M. & Co., England.. **140-150**
Teapot, cov., red, restaurant ware, Sterling China.. **75-85**
Vegetable bowl, cov., round, green, Victoria Porcelain **100-125**
Vegetable bowl, red, Allertons, 7" d. **50-60**
Vegetable bowl, red, cov., Japan, 10" d. **30**

Yellow-Glazed Earthenware

In the past this early English ware was often referred to as "Canary Lustre," but recently a more accurate title has come into use.

Produced in the late 18th and early 19th centuries, pieces featured an overall yellow glaze, often decorated with silver or copper lustre designs or black, brown or red transfer-printed scenes.

Most pieces are not marked and today the scarcity of examples in good condition keeps market prices high.

Creamer, urn shape w/molded ring handle, decorated w/black stripes & transfer of fishermen in front of gate house, 5 1/2" h. (colored-in rim flake) **$385**
Mustard pot, cov., painted w/alternating zigzag bands of brown & red, ca. 1820-30, 2 7/8" h. **2,520**
Pitcher, 7 1/2" h., transfer-printed on each side w/octagonal panel of fruit & birds, inscribed & dated beneath spout in blue enamel "S.Gray:Hodnet, 1810" (rim chip).. **1,080**

Yellow-Glazed Earthenware Plate

Plate, 8 3/8" d., modeled as a leafy bunch of grapes resting in a basket, bright yellow, gold & green, ca. 1820-30 (ILLUS.)............ **1,920**
Teapot, cov., ovoid body w/flared rim, black transfer of a woman playing piano or harpsichord accompanied by two children playing triangle & tambourine, black stripes, 5 1/8" h. (short rim hairline & lid repairs) **495**

Zsolnay

This pottery was made in Pecs, Hungary, in a factory founded in 1862 by Vilmos Zsolnay. Utilitarian earthenware was originally produced but by the turn of the 20th century ornamental Art Nouveau style wares with bright colors and lustre decoration were produced and these wares are especially sought today. Currently Zsolnay pieces are being made in a new factory.

Zsolnay Center Bowl with Polar Bear

Center bowl, long oblong boat-shaped form, the top of one end w/a standing figural polar bear peering into water that forms the walls of the piece, waves & fish in relief, iridescent purple, blue & amber glaze w/matte lustre, convex round trademark stamp, early 20th c., chips on base, minor wear, 6 1/2 x 19", 9" h. (ILLUS.)........ **$690**

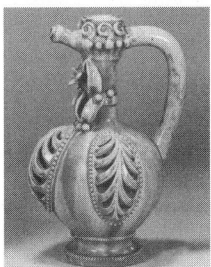

Zsolnay Ewer

Ewer, spherical body and elongated neck fitted w/spout & handle, raised on pedestal base, all-over applied decoration, underside marked "Zsolnay 7," ca. 1830, 12" h. (ILLUS.)... **420**

Rare Zsolnay Umbrella Stand

Umbrella stand, tall slightly waisted cylindrical form w/rolled rim, the sides decorated w/dark golden iridescent fish swimming in iridescent swirls of dark blue, purple & gold, impressed "Zsolnay - Pecs - 4036 - 21," ca. 1900, 26 3/4" h. (ILLUS.).............. **14,400**
Vase, 10" h., 5" d., tall slender ovoid body tapering to a flat rim, decorated w/ruby red pomegranate design against a nacreous "Eocin" ground, die-stamped & wax-resist mark **1,760**

CHARACTER COLLECTIBLES

Numerous objects made in the likeness of or named after comic strip and comic book personalities or characters

abounded from the 1920s to the present. Scores of these are now being eagerly collected and prices still vary widely. Also see POP CULTURE COLLECTIBLES, RADIO & TELEVISION MEMORABILIA, WESTERN CHARACTER COLLECTIBLES, SPACE AGE COLLECTIBLES and TOYS and "ANTIQUE TRADER TOY PRICE GUIDE."

Archie puzzle, jigsaw-type, Archie slips on banana peel, frame tray-type, Whitman, 1972.. **$10-25**

Aurora Robin the Boy Wonder Kit

Batman model kit, Robin the Boy Wonder, 1/12 scale, Aurora, 1966 (ILLUS.)............. **45-85**

Aurora Bride of Frankenstein Kit

Bride of Frankenstein model kit, Aurora, 1965 (ILLUS.).. **300-850**
Bride of Frankenstein model kit, Polar Lights, Aurora reissue, 1997 .... **20-35**

Bride of Frankenstein & Frankenstein

Bride of Frankenstein model kit, "Tiny Terrors," painted by Joe Fex, Mad Lab, resin kits sculpted by Michael Parks, 1990s-present, 4 1/2" h. (ILLUS.).............. **15-30**

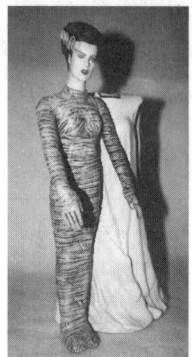

Horizon Bride of Frankenstein Kit

Bride of Frankenstein model kit, w/optional gown, Sci-Fi Art Kits, painted by Joe Fex, Horizon, vinyl kits, 1988 (ILLUS.)....... **25-40**

Aurora Captain America Kit

Captain America model kit, 1/12 scale, Aurora, 1966 (ILLUS.).................................. **75-250**

Casper the Friendly Ghost puzzle, jigsaw-type, four designs, Ja-Ru, 1988, each **5-10**

Christopher Robin & Winnie-the-Pooh dolls, Christopher Robin w/pressed felt swivel head, painted brown eyes, single-stroke brows, accented nostrils, closed mouth, mohair wig, pressed felt body, wearing blue smock, brown shorts w/suspenders, white hat, white knit underclothing, brown leather sandals, 11" h., animal characters include 5" h. Pooh bear, 6" l. Eeyore, 4 1/2" l. Tigger & 3" h. Piglet, Pooh, Eeyore & Tigger w/swivel heads & jointed shoulders & hips, Piglet w/jointed shoulders, all but Piglet have authentic R. John Wright Winnie-the-Pooh label & all have RJW gold button w/tag No. 1117, all items contained in individual boxes w/labels numbered 1117/3500, certificates & registration cards, mint, the set **1,300**

Creature from the Black Lagoon puzzle, jigsaw-type, 300 pieces, glow-type, cover of famous monsters, APC, 1975 .... **50-75**

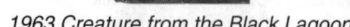

Creature from the Black Lagoon Kit

Creature from the Black Lagoon model kit, 1/8 scale, Dark Horse, cold-cast porcelain kits, 1991 (ILLUS.)........................ **125-150**

1963 Creature from the Black Lagoon

Creature from the Black Lagoon model kit, Aurora, 1963, 8 1/2" h. (ILLUS.)....... **125-400**

Creature from the Black Lagoon model kit, Billiken, 1991 .... **50-100**

Creature from the Black Lagoon model kit, Frightening Lightning, glow version, Aurora, 1969 .... **55-200**

Creature from the Black Lagoon model kit, Gillman, 1/5 scale, Tsukuda, vinyl kits (Japanese), 1981 .... **150-200**

Creature from the Black Lagoon model kit, glow version, Aurora, 1972 .... **55-125**

Creature from the Black Lagoon model kit, Horizon, vinyl kits, 1993, built-up 12" .. **40-65**

Creature from the Black Lagoon model kit, Monogram (most re-issued Aurora), 1994 .... **15-20**

1975 Aurora Creature Kit

Creature from the Black Lagoon model kit, Monsters of the Movies series, painted by Dennis Grimm, Aurora, 1975, 7 1/4" h. (ILLUS.) **75-225**

Creature from the Black Lagoon model kit, "Tiny Terrors," Mad Lab, resin kits sculpted by Michael Parks, 1991, 4 1/4" h. **15-30**

Dick Tracy Detective Club Badge

Dick Tracy badge, stamped brass, spread-winged eagle over bust of Dick Tracy & "Dick Tracy Detective Club," leather back & snap fastener, 2 1/2 x 2 3/4" (ILLUS.) **85**

Dick Tracy Squad Car No. 1

Dick Tracy toy, key-wind tin "Dick Tracy Squad Car No. 1," dark green body w/yellow wording, red plastic working siren light on roof, rubber wheels, Marx, ca. 1950s, 11" l. (ILLUS.) **165**

Doctor Dolittle model kit, Good Ship Flounder, Aurora, 1968 .... **30-75**

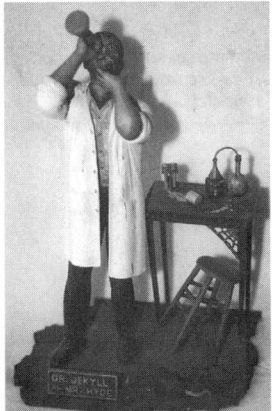

Aurora Dr. Jekyll as Mr. Hyde Kit

Dr. Jekyll model kit, Dr. Jekyll as Mr. Hyde, painted by Evan Stuart, Aurora, 1964 (ILLUS.) **200-300**

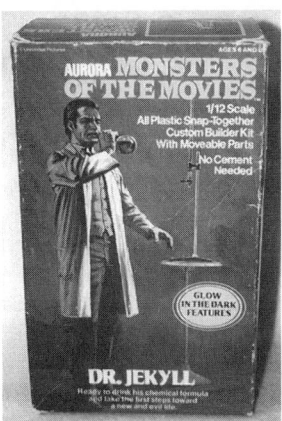

Aurora Dr. Jekyll Kit

Dr. Jekyll model kit, Dr. Jekyll, Monsters of the Movies series, glow pieces, Aurora, 1975 (ILLUS.) **50-125**

Monogram Dracula Kit

Dracula model kit, 1991, Monogram, most re-issued Aurora (ILLUS.) **20-45**

Aurora Dracula Kit

Dracula model kit, Aurora, 1962 (ILLUS.) .. **25-300**

Dracula model kit, Billiken, vinyl & resin, 1980s-present **130-200**

Horizon Bram Stoker's Dracula Bat Kit

Dracula model kit, Bram Stoker's Dracula, Dracula Bat version, Horizon, vinyl kits, 1990s (ILLUS.) **35-65**

Horizon Bram Stoker's Dracula Wolf Kit

Dracula model kit, Bram Stoker's Dracula, Dracula Wolf version, Horizon, vinyl kits, 1990s (ILLUS.) **35-65**

Dracula model kit, Dracula's Dragster, Aurora, 1965.. **250-400**

Dracula model kit, Frightening Lightning, glow version, Aurora, 1969 .... **150-325**

Dracula model kit, glow version, Aurora, 1972 .... **25-75**

Dracula model kit, Luminators, glows in dark, Monogram (most re-issued Aurora), 1991 .... **15-25**

Dracula model kit, Monsters of the Movies series, Aurora reissue, Revell, plastic kits, 1999 .... **8-15**

Mad Lab Dracula Kit

Dracula model kit, "Tiny Terrors," Mad Lab, resin kits sculpted by Michael Parks, 1990s-present (ILLUS.) **20-30**

Dracula puzzle, jigsaw-type, 200 pieces in canister, APC, 1974 .... **15-30**

Dracula puzzle, jigsaw-type, 200 pieces, Western, 1991 .... **8-12**

Dracula puzzle, jigsaw-type, frame tray-type, 11 pieces **8-10**

Dracula puzzle, jigsaw-type, frame tray-type, Jaymar, 1963 .... **40-60**

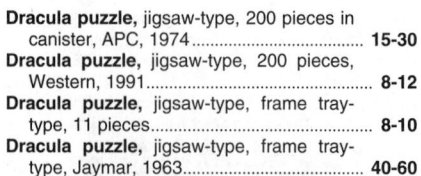

E.T. Jigsaw Puzzle

E.T., The Extra-Terrestrial puzzle, jigsaw-type, 15 pieces, frame tray-type, various designs, Craftmaster, 1982, each (ILLUS. of one) **10-18**

Tsukuda Frankenstein Kit

Frankenstein model kit, 1/5 scale, painted by Joe Fex, Tsukuda, vinyl kits (Japanese), 1986 (ILLUS.) **85-125**

Aurora Frankenstein Model Kit

Frankenstein model kit, Aurora, 1961 (ILLUS.)... **25-250**

Frankenstein model kit, Billiken, vinyl & resin,1991 .... **75-125**

Frankenstein model kit, Frankenstein bust, Boris Karloff likeness, by Miles Teves, life-size, resin, Ciné Art, 1990s.. **595-650**

Frankenstein model kit, Frankenstein, "Tiny Terrors," wearing boxer shorts, Mad Lab, resin kits sculpted by Michael Parks, 1992, 4 1/4" h. **15-25**

Frankenstein model kit, Frankenstein's Daughter, "Tiny Terrors," Mad Lab, resin kits sculpted by Michael Parks, 1990s-present, 4 1/2" h. **20-30**

Frankenstein model kit, Frankenstein's Flivver, Aurora, 1965 .... **300-400**

Frankenstein model kit, Frightening Lightning, glow version, Aurora, 1969 .... **25-150**

Aurora "Big Frankie" Kit

Frankenstein model kit, Gigantic Frankenstein, "Big Frankie," painted by Evan Stuart, Aurora, 1964 (ILLUS.) **700-1,200**

Aurora Frankenstein Glow Kit

Frankenstein model kit, glow version, Aurora, 1972 (ILLUS.) **25-75**

Frankenstein model kit, Luminators, glows in dark, Monogram (most re-issued Aurora), 1991 .... **15-25**

Frankenstein model kit, Monster Scenes, Aurora, 1971 .... **50-100**

Frankenstein model kit, Monsters of the Movies series, Aurora, 1974 .... **150-250**

Revell Frankenstein Kit

Frankenstein model kit, Monsters of the Movies series, Aurora reissue, Revell, plastic kits, 1999 (ILLUS.) **8-15**

Horizon Frankenstein Kit

Frankenstein model kit, painted by Joe Fex, Horizon, vinyl kits, 1993 (ILLUS.) **40-65**

Frankenstein model kit, Teenage Frankenstein, "Tiny Terrors," Mad Lab, resin kits sculpted by Michael Parks, 1990s-present **15-25**

Mad Lab Frankenstein Kit

Frankenstein model kit, "Tiny Terrors," holding a bottle marked "Hootch," painted by Joe Fex, Mad Lab, resin kits sculpted by Michael Parks, 1991, 4" h. (ILLUS.).. **15-25**

Frankenstein model kit, "Tiny Terrors," painted by Joe Fex, Mad Lab, resin kits sculpted by Michael Parks, 1990s-present, 4 1/4" h. (ILLUS. w/Bride of Frankenstein) **15-25**

Dark Horse Frankenstein Kit

Frankenstein model kit, w/metal chains, Dark Horse, cold-cast porcelain kits, 1991, 10 1/2" h. (ILLUS.)....................... **110-140**

Frankenstein puzzle, jigsaw-type, 200 pieces in canister, APC, 1974 .... **15-35**

Frankenstein puzzle, jigsaw-type, "Frankenstein vs. Wolfman," Jaymar, 1963, 7 x 10" box **65-90**

Frankenstein puzzle, jigsaw-type, "Frankenstein Vs. Wolfman," Jaymar, 1963, 8 x 12" box.. **150-180**

Frankenstein puzzle, slide-type, Roalex, 1960s.. **35-45**

Frankenstein toy, windup tin, Marx, 1960, 6" h... **150-350**

Frankenstein toy, windup tin, Robot House, 1991, 9" h..................................... **85-115**

Ghidrah model kit, Monsters of the Movies series, Aurora, 1975............................... **150-500**

Ghostbusters model kit, Ghostbusters Terror Dog, 1/6 scale, Tsukuda, vinyl kits (Japanese), 1980s-present **75-100**

Godzilla model kit, 1/160 scale, Tsukuda, vinyl kits (Japanese), 1964..................... **125-150**

Godzilla model kit, glow version, Aurora, 1969 .... **75-300**

Aurora Godzilla Glow Kit

Godzilla model kit, glow version, Aurora, 1972 (ILLUS.)... **75-175**

Godzilla model kit, Godzilla's Go-Cart, Aurora, 1966.. **650-3,000**

Aurora Godzilla Kit

Godzilla model kit, painted by Evan Stuart, Aurora, 1964 (ILLUS.) **85-500**

Lindberg Godzilla Kit

Godzilla model kit, super detailed, snap-fit, painted by Joe Fex, Lindberg, plastic kits, 1995, 7 1/2" h. (ILLUS.)............................... **10-15**

Mad Lab Godzilla Kit

Godzilla model kit, "Tiny Terrors," stomping Godzilla, Mad Lab, resin kits sculpted by Michael Parks, 1991, 3 1/2" h. (ILLUS.)... **20-40**

Godzilla model kit, vinyl, Billiken, 1954 style **65-95**

Godzilla model kit, vinyl, Billiken, 1962 style **50-90**

Godzilla model kit, vinyl, Billiken, 1964 style **65-95**

Godzilla model kit, vinyl, Billiken, 1992 style **85-110**

Monogram Godzilla Kit

Godzilla model kit, w/glow pieces, discontinued, Monogram (most re-issued Aurora), 1978 (ILLUS.) **60-120**
Godzilla puzzle, jigsaw-type, 150 pieces, HG Toys, 1975, 10 x 14" **25-45**
Godzilla puzzle, jigsaw-type, "Godzilla - King of the Creatures," APC, 1978 .... **20-30**
Gremlins automobile, die-cast, Gizmo in pink Corvette, small version, 1984 .... **125-275**
Gremlins automobile, plastic & metal, Gizmo in pink Corvette, Ertl, 1984, 5 1/2 x 12 1/2" **125-275**
Happy Hooligan toy, roly-poly, papiermaché w/black & white painted outfit, red buttons, fabric ruff around neck, ca. 1910, 9 1/2" h. (light splitting,wear) **546**
Hunchback of Notre Dame model kit, Aurora, 1964 .... **85-300**
Hunchback of Notre Dame model kit, Frightening Lightning, glow version, Aurora, 1969 .... **25-150**

Hunchback of Notre Dame Glow Kit

Hunchback of Notre Dame model kit, glow version, Aurora, 1972 (ILLUS.) **25-75**

Jack Armstrong Hike-o-meter

Jack Armstrong Hike-o-meter, steel, round blue pedometer w/belt ring, 2 3/4" d. (ILLUS.) **28**

Aurora King Kong Kit

King Kong model kit, Aurora, 1964, 10" h. (ILLUS.) **75-400**
King Kong model kit, Dark Horse, coldcast porcelain kits, sculpted by Ray Harryhausen **115-155**
King Kong model kit, Frightening Lightning, glow version, Aurora, 1969, 10" h... **75-250**

Aurora King Kong Glow Kit

King Kong model kit, glow version, painted by Evan Stuart, Aurora, 1972 (ILLUS.) **75-175**
King Kong model kit, King Kong bust, Dark Horse, cold-cast porcelain kits **75-95**
King Kong model kit, King Kong's Thronester, Aurora, 1966 .... **350-1,000**

Luminators King Kong Kit

King Kong model kit, Luminators, glows in dark, Monogram (most re-issued Aurora), 1991 .... **25-75**
King Kong model kit, "Stranglehold," Kong w/snake, Mad Lab, resin kits sculpted by Michael Parks, 1990s-present, 13" h. **100-130**

Mad Lab King Kong Kit

King Kong model kit, "Tiny Terrors," including dead T-Rex (not shown), Mad Lab, resin kits sculpted by Michael Parks, 1990s-present, 3 1/2" h. (ILLUS.) **20-30**

Tsukuda King Kong Kit

King Kong model kit, Tsukuda, 1/5 scale, vinyl kits (Japanese), 1986 (ILLUS.)......... **85-125**

King Kong Jigsaw Puzzle

King Kong puzzle, jigsaw-type, Dino's King Kong, 81 pieces in canister box, American Publishing, 1976, 5 1/2" h. (ILLUS.).... **20-30**

Li'l Abner Tray

Li'l Abner tray, spelter w/copper flash finish, w/embossed characters from the Li'l Abner comic strip, marked "1968 - Capp Enterprises Inc. - made in Japan," 5 1/2 x 6 1/2" (ILLUS.) **24**

Aurora Mr. Hyde Kit

Mr. Hyde model kit, Monsters of the Movies series, glow pieces, Aurora, 1975 (ILLUS.)... **50-125**

Aurora Mummy Kit

Mummy (The) model kit, Aurora, 1963 (ILLUS.)... **25-300**
Mummy (The) model kit, Billiken, 1990 .... **100-150**

Aurora Mummy Glow Kit

Mummy (The) model kit, Frightening Lightning, glow version, Aurora, 1969 (ILLUS.) **25-150**
Mummy (The) model kit, glow version, Aurora, 1972 .... **25-60**

Monogram Luminators Mummy Kit

Mummy (The) model kit, Luminators,
glows in dark, Monogram (most re-issued
Aurora), 1991 (ILLUS.) **15-25**
Mummy (The) model kit, Monogram (most
re-issued Aurora) 1983.............................. **20-35**
Mummy (The) model kit, Mummy's (The)
Chariot, Aurora, 1965............................ **250-450**

Polar Lights Mummy's Chariot Kit

Mummy (The) model kit, Mummy's (The)
Chariot, Polar Lights,   Aurora reissue,
glow version, Frightening Lightning, 1995
(ILLUS.)... **15-25**
Mummy (The) model kit, No. 39, "Mummy
Man," 1/5 scale, Tsukuda, vinyl kits (Jap-
anese), 1986.. **80-120**
Mummy (The) model kit, "Tiny Terrors,"
Mad Lab, resin kits sculpted by Michael
Parks, 1992, 4 1/2" h................................... **15-25**

Horizon Mummy Kit

Mummy (The) model kit, Tom Tyler as the
Mummy, painted by Joe Fex, Horizon, vi-
nyl kits, 1993 (ILLUS.).................................. **40-65**
Mummy (The) puzzle, jigsaw-type, Jaymar,
1963, 7 x 10" box...................................... **75-130**
Mummy (The) puzzle, jigsaw-type, Jaymar,
1963, 8 x 12" box...................................... **100-180**
Mummy toy, windup tin, Robot House,
1992, 9" h.. **85-115**
Phantom of the Opera model kit, Billiken,
1980s (ILLUS. top of next column) **200-250**
Phantom of the Opera model kit, Frightening Lightning series, Aurora, 1969 .... **250-350**
Phantom of the Opera model kit, glow ver-
sion, Aurora, 1969 .... **25-150**

Billiken Phantom of the Opera Kit

Phantom of the Opera model kit, glow ver-
sion, Aurora, 1972...................................... **25-80**
Phantom of the Opera model kit, Lumina-
tors, glows in dark, Monogram (most re-
issued Aurora), 1992 .... **15-25**

Aurora Phantom of the Opera Kit

Phantom of the Opera model kit, painted
by Joe Fex, Aurora, 1963 (ILLUS.).......... **25-300**
Phantom of the Opera model kit, Sci-Fi
Art Kits, Horizon, vinyl kits, 1988 .... **25-40**
Planet of the Apes model kit, Caesar, Ad-
dar - Plastic Kits, 1/11 scale, 1974 .... **30-60**

Addar Cornelius Kit

Planet of the Apes model kit, Cornelius,
Addar, plastic kits, 1/11 scale, 1973
(ILLUS.).. **20-45**
Planet of the Apes model kit, Dr. Zaius,
Addar, plastic kits, 1/11 scale, 1973.......... **25-50**
Planet of the Apes model kit, Dr. Zira, Ad-
dar, plastic kits, 1/11 scale, 1974............... **20-40**

Addar General Aldo Kit

Planet of the Apes model kit, General Aldo, Addar, plastic kits, 1/11 scale, 1973 (ILLUS.)... **20-40**

Addar General Ursus Kit

Planet of the Apes model kit, General Ursus, Planet of the Apes, Addar - Plastic Kits, 1/11 scale, painted by Joe Fex, 1973 (ILLUS.)... **30-60**
Planet of the Apes model kit, stallion & soldier, Addar, plastic kits, 1/11 scale, 1974.. **40-80**
Popeye vehicle, die-cast metal, Popeye's Paddle Wagon Jr., Corgi **100-200**
Popeye vehicle, die-cast metal, Popeye's Paddle Wagon, w/Swee' Pea in lifeboat, Corgi, 5" l. **250-500**

Rare Popeye & Olive Oyl Windup Toy

Popeye & Olive Oyl toy, windup tin, Popeye dances on roof next to Olive Oyl seated on spinach crate playing the accordion, other comic strip characters around the sides of the base, Marx, near mint, 8 1/2" h. (ILLUS.)................................. **2,650**
Road Runner model kit, Beep Beep Road Runner, MPC, plastic kits, 1960s-present.. **45-75**

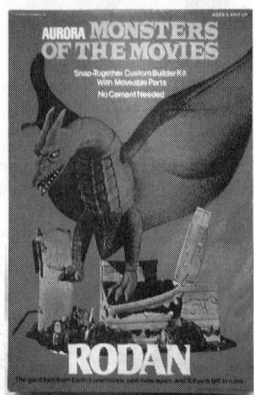

Aurora Rodan Kit

Rodan model kit, Monsters of the Movies series, Aurora, 1975 (ILLUS.).................. **150-500**
Rodan model kit, Tsukuda, 1/160 scale, vinyl kits (Japanese), 1994 .... **80-120**
Smurf automobile, die-cast metal, Smurf in log car, "Smurf #3," Ertl, 1982, 1 1/2" l. **10-20**

Smurfette in Car Toy

Smurf automobile, die-cast metal, Smurfette in car, "Smurf #1," Ertl, 1982, 1 1/2" l. (ILLUS.) **10-20**
Smurfs automobile, die-cast metal, Smurf in car, "Smurf #2," Ertl, 1982 .... **10-20**

Aurora Superboy Kit

Superboy model kit, w/eight page comic book, 1/8 scale, Aurora, 1974 reissue (ILLUS.) **20-50**

Monogram Superman Kit

Superman model kit, blue, Monogram (most re-issued Aurora), 1978 (ILLUS.) **20-50**

Superman Aurora Model Kit

Superman model kit, plastic, 1/8 scale, painting-style box cover art, Aurora, 1963, 4 x 13" box (ILLUS.) **50-300**
Tarzan model kit, 1/11 scale, in original long box, Aurora, 1967 .... **45-200**
Tarzan model kit, 1/11 scale, w/eight page comic book, Aurora, 1974 .... **20-50**
Wile E. Coyote model kit, MPC, plastic kits, 1960s-present **45-75**

Aurora Wolfman Kit

Wolf Man (The) model kit, Aurora, 1962 (ILLUS.) **25-300**
Wolf Man (The) model kit, Frightening Lightning, glow version, Aurora, 1969 ...... **25-150**
Wolf Man (The) model kit, glow version, Aurora, 1972 .... **25-75**
Wolf Man (The) model kit, Monsters of the Movies series, Aurora, 1974 .... **175-250**

Polar Lights Wolf Man Kit

Wolf Man (The) model kit, original model design, Aurora, 1998 (ILLUS.) **15-25**
Wolf Man (The) model kit, Tsukuda, 1/6 scale, vinyl kits (Japanese), 1986.............. **40-80**

Monogram Wolf Man Kit

Wolf Man (The) model kit, w/optional glow pieces, Monogram (most re-issued Aurora), painted by Joe Fex,1983 (ILLUS.)....... **20-45**
Wolf Man (The) model kit, Wolfman, "Tiny Terrors," marked "ML MP," Mad Lab, resin kits sculpted by Michael Parks, 1990s-present, 4" h. **15-25**
Wolf Man (The) model kit, Wolfman's Wagon, Aurora,1965................................. **300-400**
Wolf Man (The) model kit, Wolfman's Wagon, Aurora, reproduction, unmarked, 1990s... **40-95**
Wolfman puzzle, jigsaw-type, 200 pieces in canister, APC, 1974 .... **15-30**
Wolfman puzzle, jigsaw-type, 200 pieces, Western (Golden), 1991 .... **10-15**
Wolfman puzzle, jigsaw-type, Jaymar, 1963, 7 x 10" box.................................... **75-130**
Wolfman puzzle, jigsaw-type, Jaymar, 1963, 8 x 12" box.................................... **100-180**

Aurora Wonder Woman Kit

Wonder Woman model kit, 1/12 scale, Aurora, 1965 (ILLUS.)............................ **150-400**

CHESS COLLECTIBLES

Antique Boards & Chess Collectibles

Chess board, boxwood & mahogany, English, 19th c................................. **$242**
Chess board, folding, Leuchars Cartonpierre, signed "Leuchars...Picadilly" in Gothic script, 19th c. (some cracks & wear)... **427**
Chess board, rosewood & boxwood, English, 19th c................................. **384**
Chess board, rosewood & boxwood w/mahogany border inset w/ivory peg holes, English, mid 19th c. **569**
Chess box, rosewood & metal, mounted, box of rectangular form w/strapwork decoration, two rooks depicted in metal inlay to the lid, ca. 1830 .... **128**

King Chess Piece

Chess piece, King, ivory, in the form of an elephant w/howdah on its back & raised on a carved oval base, East Indian, "John Company," Berhempore, early to mid 19th c., slight chipping & splits (ILLUS.) **683**

"European vs. Moors" Chess Set

Chess set, ivory, "European vs. Moors," Moorish side stained green, European side left natural, comprising: a white bishop as "Fou" w/clerical headdress & hooked nose, four white pawns as Europeans in bust form, a green bishop, two green knights as horsemen, & two green pawns as Moors in bust form, two ivory rooks stained green & left natural as turrets, French, Dieppe, bust part set, late 18th - early 19th c., three pieces missing bases & one piece has loose base (ILLUS.)..................................... **399**
Games compendium, mahogany & brass mounted, hinged lid enclosing fitted interior for various games including chess, draughts, backgammon, bezique, dominoes, table croquet, whist, cribbage, race games, w/drawer under & original guide, English, late 19th - early 20th c. (some pieces missing or damaged).......................... **455**
Games compendium, mahogany, hinged lid opening to reveal an interior fitted w/an Old English style boxwood & ebony chess set, a leather chess board, a pack of Christchurch Oxford playing cards, a cribbage board, dominoes, boxwood and ebonized counters & lead race horses, English, ca. 1920... **285**

English Games Compendium

Games compendium, oak, hinged lid above two hinged doors, opening to reveal a Staunton style boxwood & ebonized chess set, fitted interior including a cribbage board, set of boxwood & ebonized counters, lead race horses, draughts, bone dominoes, bone gaming counters, bezique & whist, English, late 19th - early 20th c. (ILLUS.) **1,252**

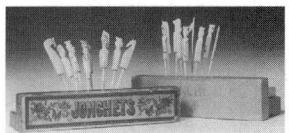

French Jonchets Set

Jonchets set, bone, in original box w/retailers label, together w/similar part Jonchets set, in original box w/retailers label, French (ILLUS.).. **128**

Mah-Jong set, bone & bamboo mounted tiles within five drawer hardwood box, w/leather-cased set for Bezique, Chinese..... **356**

Chess Tournament Clock

Tournament clock, chess, dials marked "The Reliable Chess Timer," and "Wm E. Tanner Assembd by Redhill. Surrey," "Made in Germany," in a stained wooden case, case chipped (ILLUS.).......................... **384**

English Playing Sets

Chess set, bone, barley corn set, English, 19th c. (w/replacement parts, some chipping & splints).. **171**

Chess set, bone, barley corn set, one side stained red, the other side left natural, kings w/"cogged" finials, queens w/reeded ball knops, knights as horse heads, rooks as squat turrets, in a pine box w/hinged lid, English, 19th c. **93**

Chess set, bone, barley corn set, one side stained red, the other side left natural, kings w/pointed finials, queens w/reeded ball knop finials, knights as horse heads, rooks as turrets w/flags, English, 19th c. **135**

Chess set, bone, barley corn set, one side stained red, the other side left natural, w/leather covered board/box in the form of a book, English, 19th c. (five associated red pawns & two associated white pawns).. **171**

Chess set, boxwood, "Blindman's" playing set, together w/associated folding board, English, late 19th c. **171**

Edinburgh Upright Chess Set

Chess set, boxwood & ebony, Edinburgh upright set, boxwood side w/toffee-colored patination, in an oak box w/crest carved in lid, late 19th c., one replacement black pawn & some chipping (ILLUS.).. **427**

Chess set, boxwood & ebony, Edinburgh upright set, late 19th c. (missing one ebony knight & some pieces chipped)............... **128**

English Boxwood & Ebony Chess Set

Chess set, boxwood & ebony, in a rectangular & stained wooden box, English, 19th c., minor chipping (ILLUS.) **171**

Boxed English Chess Set

Chess set, boxwood & ebony, kings w/crosses, knights w/carved horses' heads, rooks as towers, in a wooden box w/sliding lid, English, 19th c. (ILLUS.)` **370**

English Ivory Barley Corn Chess Set

Chess set, ivory, barley corn set, one side stained black, the other side left natural, kings w/petaled finials, queens w/ball knops, rooks as turrets, w/rosewood & satinwood board, English, 19th c. (ILLUS.).. **1,210**

Chess set, ivory, barley corn set, one side stained red, the other side left natural, the pieces of slender tapering shape, kings surmounted w/Maltese cross finials, queens w/reeded ball finials, bishops w/split & open mitres, knights as carved horse heads, rooks as turrets w/reeded ball finial mounts, pawns w/baluster knops, in a wooden box w/sliding lid, English, 19th c. **256**

Chess set, ivory, Calvert style playing set, one side stained red, the other side left natural, kings & queens w/multi-knops to the center sections, knights as horse heads, rooks as turrets on raised stems, in wooden box w/sliding lid, English, ca. 1850... **214**

Calvert Style Playing Chess Set

Chess set, ivory, Calvert style playing set, one side stained red, the other side left natural, kings w/two tiered pierced galleries, queens w/single pierced galleries, bishops w/split mitres, knights as horse heads, rooks as raised and stepped turrets, pawns w/baluster stems, w/an early 19th c. mahogany tea caddy in use as a chess box, English, 19th c., one knight & one white pawn w/repair (ILLUS.) **783**

Chess set, pewter, Waterloo Museum, Battle of Waterloo set, the Allied side w/red enameled bases, the French side w/blue enameled bases, each piece individually cast, the red king & queen as Wellington & the Duchess of Wellington, the blue king & queen as Napoleon & Marie-Louise, blue bishop as Grouchy, blue knight as Ney, the pawns representing various regiments, together w/a fitted presentation board/box, by the Franklin Mint, 20th c. **142**

Rosewood & Boxwood Chess Set

Chess set, rosewood & boxwood, kings surmounted w/Maltese crosses, queens w/feather finials, bishops w/open mitres, knights as carved horse heads, rooks as turrets w/flags, in an oak box, revarnished & minor chipping (ILLUS.) **299**

Chess set, rosewood & boxwood, Lund style playing set, w/concentrically turned stems, kings w/Maltese crosses, queens w/feather finials, bishops w/split open mitres, knights carved as horse heads, rooks as castellated towers, pawns w/crescent gadrooned knops, English, 19th c. **2,989**

Chess set, rosewood & boxwood set, old English pattern, kings w/Maltese crosses, queens w/feather finials, bishops w/split open mitres, knights carved as horse heads, rooks as turrets, in a mahogany box, English, 19th c. (some chipping) **171**

Chess set, silver & silver gilt, the pawns similar to a design by Charles Perry, the maker's mark: C.E. London, 1972, the stylized geometric pieces interlocking to form two cylinders, w/a leather & silver interlocking board in a fitted black leather case, together with a certificate of authenticity, to commemorate the Fischer-Spassky match at Reykjavik in 1972, Limited Edition of 650 sets, designed & made by Cy Endfield **783**

Chess set, "Wedgwood" style jasper figural set, after a design by Flaxman, the opposing sides in blue & white, the pieces modeled from Macbeth, the pawns individually modeled as soldiers (two possible replacement pawns & one pawn restored) **1,025**

European Sets

Bone "Lyon" Chess Set

Chess set, bone, "Lyon" set, one side stained red, the other left natural, kings & queens w/urn-shaped stems & finials, pierced to the waist, the other pieces w/bulbous bases, French, 19th c. (ILLUS.) **1,309**

Early "Lyon" Chess Set

Chess set, bone mounted ebony & boxwood, "Lyon" set, the pieces are of bulbous knop form, kings & queens terminating in crowns, bishops w/peg finials, knights carved as horse heads, rooks as towers, French, late 18th - early 19th c., minor chipping & signs of restoration (ILLUS.) **1,565**

Chess set, bone, playing set, kings & queens of slender form, kings w/double galleries, bishops w/squat mitres, knights w/arched horse heads, rooks as towers in monobloc form, German, 19th c. (some cracks & chipping, & replaced pawn) **157**

Danish Selenus Chess Set

Chess set, bone, Selenus set, one side stained brown w/contrasting finials, the other side left natural w/brown stained finials, kings w/two galleries, queens w/one gallery, bishops w/slant-cut upper finials, knights as horse heads, rooks as turrets w/tapering finials, pawns w/baluster knops, Danish, 19th c., slight chipping (ILLUS.) **555**

German Selenus Chess Set

Chess set, bone, Selenus set, one side stained red, the other left natural, kings, queens & bishops w/finials in alternate color, kings & queens w/pierced crown knop stems, bishops w/petaled knops, rooks as turrets w/knopped finials, German, 19th c. (ILLUS.) **826**

Chess set, bone, Selenus set, one side stained red, the other side left natural, kings w/double pierced galleries & reeded cone finials, queens w/one gallery & reeded cone finials, bishops w/petaled crowns, knights as horse heads, rooks as elongated towers, German, 19th c. (some chipping) **157**

"Morphy" Style Chess Set

Chess set, cast brass, "Morphy" style set, after the Zimmerman foundry, the Romans against the Barbarians, one side plated - Romans, kings & queens wearing robes, Barbarian bishops w/winged helmets, Roman bishops w/raised swords, knights as rearing horses, rooks as elephants w/howdahs, Barbarian pawns w/clubs, Roman pawns w/swords & shields, in a wooden box (ILLUS.) **854**

"American Civil War" Chess Set

Chess set, ceramic, "American Civil War" figural set, the set depicting the armies of the North & South, the North glazed in blue, the South glazed in white, the kings as Lincoln for the North & Lee for the South, the queens as Grant & Davis, the bishops as Butler, Sherman, Pemberton & Beauregard, the knights as horse heads, the rooks as columns, the pawns as individual generals, late 20th c. (ILLUS.) **1,252**

Russian "Baltic Sea War" Chess Set

Chess set, ceramic, "Baltic Sea War" figural set, the set depicting historical personalities of the Peter I epoch, kings as Peter I of Russia, 1672-1715, & Karl XII of Sweden, 1682-1718, queens as Katherine I,

1684-1727, & Sonja Alexeevna, 1657-1704, bishops as Menshikov, 1670-1729, & Alexi Petrovich, 1690-1718, knights as horse heads, rooks as warships, pawns as Russian & Swedish soldiers, Russian, late 20th c. (ILLUS.) **1,167**

"Catherine the Great" Chess Set

Chess set, ceramic, "Catherine the Great" figural set, of bust form, one side painted w/polychrome detail, the other side painted white w/gilt decoration, the kings as Catherine II, 1729-1796, the queens as Potemkin-Tavricheski G.A., bishops as Suvorow A.V. & Lomonosox M.V., knights as private monogram of Catherine II, rooks as eagles, pawns as contemporary Russian figures, Russian, 20th c. (ILLUS.) **683**

Continental Space "Quasar" Chess Set

Chess set, ceramic, Continental Space "Quasar" set, w/incised & gilt decoration, stylized form, one side white, the other side black, late 20th c. (ILLUS.) **342**

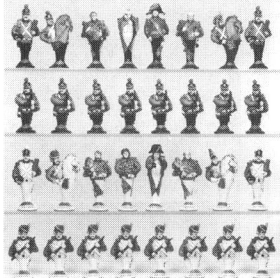

Russian Napoleonic Chess Set

Chess set, ceramic, Napoleonic figural set, the set depicting historical personalities of the Russian & French armies, the French decorated in a blue glaze, the Russian in a green glaze, kings as Alexander I of Russia, 1777-1825, & Napoleon I of France, 1769-1821, queens as Mikhail Kutuzo, general field marshal commander-in-chief of Russian army, Joachim Murat, marshal of France, knights as Mikhail Barclay de Tolly-Count & Piotr Bagration for Russia, Louis Nicolas Davout & Eugene Beuharnais for France, rooks as cossacks & dragoons, bishops as canoneers, pawns as infantry, Russian, late 20th c., minor restoration (ILLUS.)....................................... **996**

Chess set, glazed earthenware, figural "wine bottle" set, of bust type raised on socles, one side glazed brown, the other side white, the king & queen modeled as crowned monarchs, pawns as soldiers, all pieces w/labels for "Red Wine Cala-massi..." and "Imported by...Boston, Mas. USA," Italian... **185**

"Archangel" Pattern Chess Set

Chess set, ivory, "Archangel" pattern set, one side stained a chestnut brown color, the other side left natural, the kings, queens, bishops & pawns w/finials carved as faces, knights carved as horse heads, rooks as small squat turrets, Russian (ILLUS.)... **1,167**

Chess set, ivory & bone, Selenus set, one side stained brown, the other side left natural, kings & queens w/pierced knops, knights as horse heads, pawns w/baluster knopped stems, German, 19th c., (some chipping & restoration, the brown king, rook & white knights damaged) **171**

German Playing Chess Set

Chess set, ivory playing set, one side stained red, the other side natural, kings & queens w/"spiked" finials, bishops as open mitres above baluster stems, rooks as turrets w/spires, in an early 19th c. mahogany box, German, late 18th - early 19th c. , minor chipping (ILLUS.)................ **1,067**

Murano Glass Chest Set

Chess set, Murano glass, one side black, the other side clear, the set of stylized form, kings w/faceted ball finials, knights as raised crescents, each piece signed "Murano, 94," together w/associated board w/black & grey alternating squares raised on blue faceted glass ball feet, signed "Murano, 94" (ILLUS.)........................ **712**

South German Figural Part Chess Set

Chess set, pearwood, carved figural part set, the opposing sides in lighter & darker hues, all pieces on reel shaped bases, kings & queens in medieval dress, bishops wearing tasseled caps & holding staffs, knights as rearing horses, rooks as gothic towers, pawns individually carved as South German villagers in tail coats, breeches & tricorn hats, South German, 19th c., missing bishop & a pawn, some pieces chipped and parts missing (ILLUS.)... **2,277**

Chess set, porcelain, Continental figural set, one side blue, the other side red, kings & queens in medieval dress, knights as horse heads, rooks as castellated towers, pawns as henchmen, late 20th c.. **356**

Russian Figural Chess Set

Chess set, porcelain, figural set, one side predominantly in yellow, the other side predominantly black, kings in uniform w/greyhounds, queens wearing crowns, holding fans, & w/cats at their side, bishops in uniform, w/dogs at their sides, knights as horses, rooks as longboats, Russian, late 20th c. (ILLUS.) **114**

Silver-Colored Metal Bust Chess Set

Chess set, "silver-colored metal" bust set, the pieces of bust form & raised on tapering socles, one side a "silver colour," the other side w/an oxidized finish, kings as men's heads w/beards, queens w/hair tied back, bishops wearing hats, knights as horse heads, rooks as windmills, pawns as men's heads, French, postwar, the pieces w/marks to the underside (ILLUS.) **455**

Italian Chess Set

Chess set, silvered & gilded metal, figural set, each piece signed, depicting Napoleonic armies, kings & queens as monarchs, bishops as guards, knights as horsemen, rooks as towers, pawns as foot soldiers, on the companion board, the square in white & green onyx on a silvered metal plinth cast w/relief scrolls & foliage on rearing horse supports, by Giuseppe Vasari, Italian, 20th c. (ILLUS.) **541**

Indian, Far Eastern & South American Sets

Chess set, bone, "Sikh" set, of bust form, one side w/black stained bases, the other side left natural, kings, queens & pawns wearing turbans, knights as Pegasus, rooks as elephants, Indian, late 20th c. **157**

"Burmese" Style Chess Set

Chess set, ivory, "Burmese" style set, one side stained red, the other side left natural, the pieces w/elaborate carved detail, kings & queens w/pierced crowns, bishops w/mitres, knights as horse heads, rooks as turrets flying flags, Cantonese export, 19th c., slight splitting to pieces (ILLUS.) **2,420**

Chinese Export Figural Chess Set

Chess set, ivory, figural set, Canton, one side stained red, the other side left natural, the pieces in traditional Chinese dress & raised on puzzleball bases, kings & queens as the Emperor & Empress, bishops as mandarins, knights as horsemen, rooks as elephants, pawns as foot soldiers, together w/thirty-two ivory gaming counters carved w/various figural scenes, an ivory shaker, & a Chinese black lacquered & gilt wooden game board w/chinoiserie decoration, Chinese export, 19th c. (ILLUS.) **1,352**

Chess set, ivory, figural set, one side stained green w/black stripe to base, the other side left natural, kings as elephants w/howdahs, queens as elephants, bishops as camels, knights as horses, rooks as elephants, pawns as foot soldiers, Indian, early 20th c. (three pawns w/chips) **256**

Chess set, ivory, figural set, one side stained red, the other side left natural, the pieces in traditional dress, Cantonese export, late 19th c. (some chipping & damage to pieces) **213**

Chess set, ivory, figural set, one side stained red, the other side left natural, the pieces in traditional dress, Cantonese export, late 19th c. (some chipping & damage to pieces) **213**

Chinese Export Chess Set

Chess set, ivory, figural set, one side stained red, the other side left natural & raised on puzzleball bases, the white king & queen as George III & Queen Charlotte, the remaining pieces in traditional Chinese dress, together w/a black lacquered and gilded wooden board w/chinoiserie decoration, Chinese export, 19th c. (ILLUS.) **541**

Ivory Indian Chess Set

Chess set, ivory, figural set, Rajhastan, one side w/ovoid bases w/black stripe, the other side left natural, kings as elephants w/howdahs, queens as elephants, bishops as camels, knights as horses, rooks as elephants, Indian, 20th c. (ILLUS.)............ **569**

Chess set, ivory, figural set, the bases on one side painted gold & detail picked out in gold, the other side natural, kings & queens w/howdahs, bishops as camels, knights as horses, rooks as elephants, pawns as foot soldiers, Indian, 20th c........... **242**

Ivory & Horn Indian Chess Set

Chess set, ivory & horn, playing set, kings & queens w/pierced crowns & baluster knops, bishops w/mitres, knights as carved horse heads, rooks as dense towers w/inverted umbrella finials, Indian export, mid-19th c. (ILLUS.) **712**

Chess set, ivory, one side stained red, the other side left natural, the figures in traditional dress & raised on puzzleball bases, kings & queens as Emperor & Empress, bishops as mandarins, knights as horses, rooks as elephants, Cantonese export, 19th c. (one red rook w/associated base, some chipping & damage) **455**

Ivory Chess Set

Chess set, ivory, one side stained red, the other side left natural, the pieces w/bulbous knops, the kings w/crosses, the knights as carved horse heads, the rooks as turrets, Indian, 19th c., w/replacement parts, the pawns w/slight variation in shape & size (ILLUS.) **455**

Indian Chess Set

Chess set, ivory, Vizgapatam, one side stained green, the other side left natural, the pieces w/elaborate carved decoration, kings & queens w/petaled knops & pierced galleries, bishops w/pierced flame mitres, knights as horse "John Company" heads, rooks as turrets, Indian, 19th c., rooks missing flags & some chipping (ILLUS.) **1,566**

Red & Natural Indian Chess Set

Chess set, ivory, Vizgapatam, one side stained red, the other side left natural, kings & queens w/pierced tops & splayed finials, one side carved w/monarch faces, bishops w/mitres & carved w/face to one side, knights as horse heads, rooks as turrets w/flags, Indian, 19th c., chip to red king (ILLUS.) **1,067**

Indian Vizgapatam Chess Set

Chess set, ivory, Vizgapatam, one side stained red, the other side left natural, extensively carved, the king & queen w/petaled knops & pierced galleries, the bishop w/arrowhead finials, the knights w/carved horse heads, the rooks as pierced turrets w/flags, Indian, 19th c., minor chipping, one red pawn missing finial & slight variation in size & shape of pawns (ILLUS.) **4,270**

Chess set, ivory, w/bone additions, one side stained red & lacquered, the other left natural, on puzzle ball bases, carved as members of the court, mounted knights, rooks as castellated elephants & pawns as mounted soldiers, in a walnut box, Cantonese export, 19th c. (signs of restoration, chipping & cracks) **455**

Indian Export Chess/Backgammon Set

Chess/Backgammon set, ivory & horn, playing set, Vizgapatam, kings & queens w/pierced crowns & baluster knops, bishops w/mitres, knights as horse heads, rooks as turrets w/flags, together w/Vizgapatam ivory, sandalwood & horn inlaid chess/backgammon board/box, with penwork decorated borders, three matching ivory & penwork decorated counter boxes, a pair of ivory & horn shakers, & thirty-two ivory & horn gaming counters, Indian export, early 19th c. (ILLUS.) **3,131**

Sandalwood & Ivory Chess Set

Chess/Backgammon set, sandalwood & ivory, inlaid, the board w/alternating squares inlaid w/sedlei work & left natural w/carved hardwood floriate border, together with thirty-two ivory gaming counters, sixteen stained red & sixteen left natural, two ivory shakers stained red & two dice, Indian, ca. 1900, slight chipping (ILLUS.) **598**

Jaques Staunton & Staunton Style Sets

Chess board, Jaques "In Statu Quo" traveling board, mahogany board w/locking mechanism & stamped "Jaques. & Son ... Patentees ... London ... In Statu Quo ... Chess Board" (missing chess pieces).............. **85**

Chess set, bone pieces, Jaques "In Statu Quo" traveling set, pieces stained red & left natural, mahogany board w/locking mechanism & stamped "Jaques ... Patentees ... London ... In Statu Quo ... Chess Board" **299**

Chess set, bone pieces, Jaques "In Statu Quo" traveling set, pieces stained red & left natural, mahogany board w/locking mechanism, the inset brass plaque marked "J. Jaques. & Son, Makers, London," the board stamped "In Statu Quo ... Patent ... London," in a black leather slipcase stamped w/the Jaques mark in gilt (w/minor chipping & slipcase as found) **413**

Chess set, bone pieces, Jaques "In Statu Quo" traveling set, pieces stained red & left natural, mahogany board w/locking mechanism & stamped "Jaques ... patentees ... London ... In Statu Quo ... Chess Board," in a black leather slipcase stamped w/the Jaques mark in gilt **598**

"In Statu Quo" Traveling Chess Set

Chess set, bone pieces, Jaques "In Statu Quo" traveling set, pieces stained red & left natural, mahogany board w/locking mechanism & appropriate spaces for captured pieces, the insert brass plaque inscribed "J. Jaques & Son Makers London," the board stamped "In Statu Quo Patent Chess Board," in a leather carrying case (ILLUS.) **740**

Staunton Chess Set

Chess set, boxwood & ebonized set, Staunton pattern, in a wooden box w/white label marked "Staunton Chessmen ... The British Chess Company" (ILLUS.)................. **455**

Chess set, boxwood & ebony, both kings stamped "Jaques London," in a mahogany stained box w/brass plaque to lid, inscribed "Shell-Mex Chess Club ...," w/rosewood & satinwood chess board, stamped "J. Jaques" **399**

Chess set, boxwood & ebony, both kings stamped "Jaques London," in a wooden box w/green label marked "Jaques and Son, London" (both kings missing crosses & chips to pawns)........................ **256**

Weighted Club Chess Set

Chess set, boxwood & ebony, weighted club set, boxwood side w/a toffee patination, both kings stamped "Jaques London," in a mahogany box lined inside w/green baize & a green label marked "J. Jaques & Son Ltd, London, England," one black knight missing finial, minor chipping & splits (ILLUS.)........................... **1,025**

Chess set, boxwood & ebony, weighted set, both kings stamped "Jaques London," in a wooden box w/green label marked "Jaques & Son, London" **512**

Chess set, boxwood & ebony, weighted set, Staunton pattern, in a mahogany box lined inside w/green baize, w/a satinwood & rosewood inlaid chess board (some splits & two replacement pawns)........ **213**

Chess set, boxwood & ebony, weighted set, Staunton pattern, in a wooden box w/a white label marked "No. 3C Loaded," by the British Chess Co. **442**

Staunton Pattern Chess Set

Chess set, boxwood & ebony, weighted set, Staunton pattern, the boxwood side w/a toffee patination, late 19th c., some chipping & splits to pieces (ILLUS.)..................... **213**

Weighted Boxwood & Ebony Chess Set

Chess set, boxwood & ebony, weighted set, Staunton pattern, the white king stamped "J. Jaques London," one black & one white knight & rook stamped "B & Co," the knights as horse heads w/glass eyes, in a mahogany box w/brass corners & an oval gilt label to inside marked "The Regulation Chessmen B & Co London" (ILLUS.)... **925**

Chess set, boxwood & ebony, weighted set, white king stamped "Jaques London," in a mahogany box w/a green label marked "J. Jaques & Son, London" **712**

Celluloid Chess Set

Chess set, celluloid, one side red, the other white, both kings stamped "Jaques London," in a wooden box w/sliding lid & a green label marked "J. Jaques & Sons, Ltd, London, England," one white bishop w/repair (ILLUS.).. **427**

Jaques Ivory Chess Set

Chess set, ivory, one side stained red, the other left natural, the white king signed "Jaques London" on the underside, the set in a fitted mahogany presentation box w/two blue velvet lined trays, the lid w/a metal plaque inscribed "Presented to Edmund Thorold, M.A. by the members of the Athenaeum Chess Club, Sheffield 1864," the box w/a red label marked "Jaques London," 19th c. (ILLUS.)............ **11,102**

Staunton Pattern Ivory Chess Set

Chess set, ivory, Staunton pattern in Jaques manner, one side stained red, the other side left natural, in red leather covered casket, stamped "Staunton Chessmen" on the lid in gilt, facsimile signature of Howard Staunton in gilt on the front, red stain faded (ILLUS.) **925**

Traveling Chess Set

Chess set, pegged bone pieces, Jaques "In Statu Quo" traveling set, pieces stained red & left natural, mahogany board

w/locking mechanism stamped "In Statu Quo ... Chess Board ... Jaques Petentees London," in a black leather slipcase, slipcase as found (ILLUS.).............................. **384**
Chess set, pegged bone pieces, stained red & left natural, in a mahogany board, English **285**

CHILDREN'S BOOKS

Exactly what is a classic? What makes one book fall into this category while another one doesn't? Classics are considered by most to be those volumes of work that have stood the test of time. They are as treasured today as they were when first penned by their authors and illustrated by their illustrators. They are easy to collect for most "classics" have been published many times. Some have so many editions that a total collection could be amassed consisting of one single title. Illustrations are a major factor in determining prices, and book jackets can double the value.

A Child's Garden of Verses

A Child's Garden of Verses, R.L. Stevenson, 1930 edition, Saalfield, oversized w/illustrations by Clara Burd (ILLUS.) **$85**
A Child's Garden of Verses, R. L. Stevenson, 1940 Saalfield edition w/illustrations by Peat.. **60**
A Child's Garden of Verses, R.L. Stevenson, 1940 Saalfield edition w/illustrations by Peat, w/dust jacket...................................... **120**
A Christmas Carol, C. Dickens, 1911 edition, London, illustrated by A.C. Michael **60**

A Christmas Carol

A Christmas Carol, C. Dickens, 1929, Saalfield, illustrations by Pear (ILLUS.) 30

Adventures of Huckleberry Finn, M. Twain, 1940 edition, illustrations by Norman Rockwell.. 40

Adventures of Huckleberry Finn

Adventures of Huckleberry Finn, M. Twain, Whitman edition, 1955 (ILLUS.) 15

Adventures of Pinocchio, C. Collodi, 1916, Whitman, color illustration by Alice Carsey 35

Adventures of Tom Sawyer, M. Twain, 1936 edition, illustrations by Norman Rockwell... 45

Adventures of Tom Sawyer

Adventures of Tom Sawyer, M. Twain, Whitman edition, 1955 (ILLUS.) 20

Aesop's Fables, 1848 edition, Coates, illustrations by John Tenniel........................... 150

Aesop's Fables, 1913 edition, Platt & Peck, color plate illustrations by Conde 45

Ali Baba and the Forty Thieves, A. Mansbridge, ca. 1920s, London, illustrated by author 15

Alice's Adventures in Wonderland

Alice's Adventures in Wonderland, Lewis Carroll, 1897 edition, Altemus, paste-on cover illustration (ILLUS.)................................... 85

Alice's Adventures in Wonderland, Lewis Carroll, 1907, color plate illustrations by Bessie Pease Gutmann................................... 225

Alice's Adventures in Wonderland, Lewis Carroll, 1947, Grosset & Dunlap 20

Alice's Adventures in Wonderland, Lewis Carroll, undated, Donahue, illustrations by John Tenniel 75

Bambi, F.Salten, 1929 edition, Grosset, illustrations by Wiese 25

Charlotte's Web

Charlotte's Web, E.B. White, Harper, 1952, illustrations by Williams, first American edition with dust jacket (ILLUS.) 450

Daddy Long Legs

Daddy Long Legs, Jean Webster, Grosset & Dunlap, 1940 (ILLUS.).................................. 30

Dog of Flanders

Dog of Flanders, Louise De La Rame, 1926 edition, Saalfield, illustrated by Frances Brundage (ILLUS.).............................. 15

Emerald City of Oz, L. Frank Baum, 1910, Reilly & Britton, illustrated by Neill **300**
Gulliver's Travels, Jonathon Swift, 1917, illustrations by Pogany **50**

Gulliver's Travels

Gulliver's Travels, Jonathon Swift, Garden City Publishers, illustrations by Mossa, ca. 1930s (ILLUS.) **35**
Hans Brinker, Mary Mapes Dodge, 1915, Scribner, illustrated by George Edwards **50**

Hans Brinker

Hans Brinker, Mary Mapes Dodge, 1925 edition, Winston, illustration by Clara Burd (ILLUS.) **40**
Hans Brinker, Mary Mapes Dodge, 1947 edition, Grosset Dunlap, illustrations by C.L. Baldridge **20**
Heidi, Johanna Spyri, 1919 edition, Lippincott, illustrations by Kirk **65**
Heidi, Johanna Spyri, 1922 edition, Philadelphia, illustrations by Jessie Wilcox Smith **200**

Heidi

Heidi, Johanna Spyri, Grosset & Dunlap, 1945, illustrated by Sharp (ILLUS.) **20**
Jungle Book, R. Kipling, 1908, London, illustrations by Detmold **120**
Jungle Book, R. Kipling, 1932 edition, Doubleday, illustrations by Wiese **40**

Just So Stories for Little Children, R. Kipling, 1902, Macmillan, Illustrated by Eichenberg **200**

King Arthur and His Knights

King Arthur and His Knights, E.L. Merchant, 1927, Winston, illustrations by Frank Godwin (ILLUS.) **30**
Legend of Sleepy Hollow, W. Irving, 1926 edition, Saalfield, illustrations by Frances Brundage **20**
Little Engine That Could, W. Piper, 1930 Platt & Munk, small w/paper over board cover, illustrations by Lenski............................ **45**
Little Lord Fauntleroy, Frances H. Burnett, 1888 edition, Warne, illustrated by Birch **100**
Little Lord Fauntleroy, Frances H. Burnett, 1906 edition, small size **20**
Little Men, by Louisa May Alcott, 1901, Little Brown, illustrated by Birch **75**
Little Men, Louisa May Alcott, 1933 edition, Blue Ribbon, illustrated by Erick Berry **25**

Little Men

Little Men, Louisa May Alcott, Garden City Publishers, 1933, illustrated by Harve Stein (ILLUS.) **35**
Little Women, Louisa May Alcott, 1925 edition, Little Brown, illustrated by Jessie Wilcox Smith **75**
Little Women, Louisa May Alcott, undated 1930 edition, Donohue, oversized, color cover **30**
Mary Poppins, P. L. Travers, 1934, Reynal, 1st American edition, illustrations by Mary Shepard **100**

Moby Dick, The White Whale

Moby Dick, The White Whale, H. Melville, Winston edition, 1931 (ILLUS.) **35**

Penrod

Penrod, Booth Tarkington, Grosset & Dunlap, 1940 (ILLUS.) **15**
Peter and Wendy, J.M. Barrie, 1911, Scribner, First American Edition **60**
Peter Pan in Kensington Gardens, J. M. Barrie, 1906, London, 50 color plates by Arthur Rackham **300**

Pilgrim's Progress

Pilgrim's Progress, John Bunyun, early Donohue edition, ca. 1890s (ILLUS.) **50**
Pinocchio, C. Collodi, 1920 edition, illustrations by Maria Kirk **50**
Pollyanna, 1913, Eleanor Porter, Page, illustrations by Mulford **100**
Rip Van Winkle, W. Irving, 1897 edition, Russell, illustrations by Will Bradley **100**
Rip Van Winkle, W. Irving, 1921 edition, McKay, illustrations by N.C. Wyeth **65**

Rip Van Winkle

Rip Van Winkle, W. Irving, 1939 edition, Garden City Publishers, illustrations by Everett Shinn (ILLUS.) **50**
Robin Hood, World Syndicate edition, ca. 1920s **25**

Robin Hood

Robin Hood (The Merry Adventures of), H. Pyle, 1883, stamped leather cover (ILLUS.) **400**

Robinson Crusoe

Robinson Crusoe, Daniel Defoe, M.A. Donahue edition, 1922 (ILLUS.) **30**
Robinson Crusoe, Daniel Defoe, oversized 1920 edition, Defoe, Cosmopolitan, illustrations by N.C. Wyeth.................................... **100**
Second Jungle Book, R. Kipling, 1895 edition, Century Co., illustrations by John Lockwood, first American edition **65**
Secret Garden, F.H. Burnett, 1911, Stokes, pictorial cover, color plate illustrations by Maria Kirk.. **100**

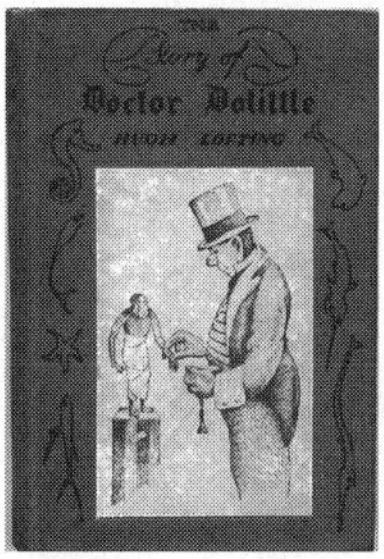

Story of Dr. Dolittle

Story of Dr. Dolittle, Hugh Lofting, Stokes, 1920 (ILLUS.)... **175**
Story of Dr. Dolittle, Hugh Lofting, Stokes, 34th printing, 1943 .... **30**
Story of Ferdinand, 1936, by Munro Leaf, illustrated by Robert Lawson, first edition...... **150**
Story of Ferdinand, 1936, by Munro Leaf, illustrated by Robert Lawson, later editions **35**
Swiss Family Robinson, J.R. Wyss, 1853 edition, illustrated by Willis Hazard............... **125**

Swiss Family Robinson

Swiss Family Robinson, J.R. Wyss, McLoughlin Brothers edition, no date (ILLUS.) **50**

Tales from Shakespeare

Tales from Shakespeare, Charles & Mary Lamb, 1924 edition, Winston, illustrated by Frank Godwin (ILLUS.) **20**

The Aesop for Children, 1919, Chicago, illustrated by Milo Winter **40**

The Little Lame Prince and The Adventures of a Brownie, D.M. Mulock, ca. 1920s, Winston, illustrations by Prittle & Fitz **30**

The Little Lame Prince and The Adventures of a Brownie

The Little Lame Prince and The Adventures of a Brownie, D.M. Mulock, early McLoughlin edition (ILLUS.) **45**

The Little White Bird

The Little White Bird, J. M. Barrie, 1902, Charles Scribner (ILLUS.) **150**

The Prince and The Pauper

The Prince and The Pauper, M. Twain, Winston, 1937, 1st illustrated edition (ILLUS.) **40**

The Red Pony

The Red Pony, J. Steinbeck, 1945, Viking Press, illustrations by Wesley Dennis (ILLUS.) **50**

The Wizard of Oz, L. Frank Baum, 1944 edition, Bobbs Merrill, illustrations by Copeland **25**

The Woodman of Oz, L. Frank Baum, 1918, Reilly & Britton, 12 color plates by Neill **100**

The Yearling, Marjorie K. Rawlings, 1939, Scribner (Pulitzer Prize), 1st trade edition, illustrations by N.C. Wyeth **65**

Toby Tyler, James Otis, 1881, Harper, 1st edition, illustrated by R.H. Rodgers **350**

Toby Tyler

Toby Tyler, James Otis, Winston edition, 1937, illustrated by Everett Shinn (ILLUS.) **30**

20,000 Leagues Under the Sea

Twenty Thousand Leagues Under the Sea, Jules Verne, Winston edition, 1932 (ILLUS.) **35**

Water Babies, Charles Kingsley, 1915 edition, Houghton, illustrations by Robinson **200**

Water Babies, James Kingsley, 1916 edition, Dodd Mead, illustrations by Jessie Wilcox Smith **200**

Picture

Anyone interested in great graphics and availability will find the area of picture books to be a good choice. Easy to find, picture books have been accessible to all children, whether personally or through the many libraries across the land. Most people have a special favorite - the one they remember best from their childhood. Some people collect by title, author or illustrator. But the rule of thumb is, "What you see and like is what you get." In other words, it's usually the cover that counts!

Illustration & Title Page from "A Child's Garden of Verses"

"A Child's Garden of Verses," by Robert Louis Stevenson, Platt & Munk, illustrated by Eulalie, 1932 (ILLUS.) **25**

"A Child's Garden of Verses," by Robert Louis Stevenson, Saalfield, illustrations by Clara Burd, 1930 edition **85**

"ABC Bunny," by Wanda Gag, McCann, oversized w/color illustration on paper-over-board cover, black & white illustrations, 1933 .... **65**

"Adventures for Beginners," by Margaret Friskey, Follett, an ABC, oversized, 28 pg., illustrated by Katherine Evans, 1944 .... **25**

"Aesop for Children," Chicago, 1919 .... **75**

"Aesop's Fables," Platt & Peck, color plate illustrations by J.M. Conde, 1913 edition **45**

"Ali Baba"

"Ali Baba," by Arthur Mansbridge, M.A. Donahue, no illustrator given but profusely illustrated in black & white, no date, ca. 1910 (ILLUS.) **22**

"American Alphabet," by Maude & Miska Petersham, MacMillan, illustrated by authors, 1941 .... **45**

"And to Think That I Saw it on Mulberry Street," by Dr. Seuss, Vanguard, oversized, illustrations by author, 1937 .... **125**

"Angora Twinnies," by Margaret Evans Price, illustrations by author, New York, 1917 .... **35**

"Angus and the Ducks," by Marjorie Flack, Doubleday, illustrations by author, 1930 .... **45**

"Animal ABC" Picture Book

"Animal ABC," by Milo Winter, Merrill, oversized on linen, 1935 (ILLUS.) **25**

"Animal Fun ABC," Charles Graham & Co., illustrated by Harry Roundtree, New York ....

"Anne Anderson's Fairy Book"

"Anne Anderson's Fairy Book," London, 1928 (ILLUS.)... **70**

Illustration from "Baby's Opera"

"Baby's Opera," Warne & McLoughlin, main difference in publishers is that McLoughlin's colors are more vibrant, illustrations by Walter Crane, 1877 (ILLUS.)... **160**

"Banana Tree House," by Phillis Garrard, Coward McCann, watercolor illustrations by Berta & Elmer Hader, 1938...................... **45**

"Belinda Balloon and the Big Wind," by Elisabeth Honness, Grosset, hardcover w/illustrations by Pelagie Doane, 1940 .... **15**

"Billy, Boy Scout" Picture Book

"Billy, Boy Scout," Sam'l Gabriel & Sons, hard board cover, 1916 (ILLUS.)....................... **70**

"Bobby and the Big Road," by Maud Lindsay, Lothrop, color illustrations, no date **45**

"Brownies at Home," Century, illustrations & story by Palmer Cox, 1893........................ **150**

"Bunny's Easter Gift"

"Bunny's Easter Gift," by Bill & Bernard Martin, The Tell-Well Press, bunny is flocked on the cover, illustrated by authors, 1948 (ILLUS.)... **15**

"Calico Pets," by Fern Bisel Peat, Saalfield, oversized, illustrations by author, 1931 .... **45**

"Children's Book of Animal Pictures," by Lorinda Bryant, Century, oversized, black & white photo illustrations, 1931............ **30**

"Children's Mother Goose," Reilly & Lee, oversized, illustrations by William Donahey, 1921 .... **125**

"Cock and the Hen," by Rudolph Mates, Harper, illustrations by author, 1925 .... **35**

"Cubby Bear," by Katherine Hawley, Whitman, a Stand-out Book with cut-out shape of bear glued to cover, illustrated by Juanita Bennett, 1936 .... **25**

"Curious George," by H.A. Rey, Houghton, illustrations by author, 1941............................ **55**

"Curly Haired Hen," by Vimar, Fitzgerald, oversized, black & white illustrations by Nora Hills, 1914.. **45**

"Denslow's Animal Fair," all color illustrations, illustrations by W.W. Denslow, NY, 1904... **200**

"Dolly Dimples and Billy Bounce," by Grace Drayton, Cupples & Leon, illustrated by author, 1931 .... **200**

"Dorothy's Dolls," by Milton Goldsmith, Cupples & Leon, small size, color plates by H. Harmony, 1908.................................... **35**

"Duck and the Kangaroo and Other Nonsense Rhymes," by Edward Lear, Whitman, illustrations by Keith Ward, 1932 .... **35**

"Eddie and the Fire Engine," by Carolyn Haywood, Morrow, cloth over board cover, illustrated by author, 1949.......................... **20**

"Five Little Bears," by Sterling North, Rand McNally, illustrations by Clarence Biers & Hazel Frazee, 1935..................................... **20**

"Fraidy Cat," a Glowing-Eye book by Marjorie Barrows, Rand McNally, illustrated paper-over-board book w/holes throughout for mounted glow-in-the-dark eyes, illustrations by Barbara Maynard, 1942............ **50**

"Golden Goose Book," Warne, illustrations by Leslie Brooke, 1906 .... **55**

"Golliwogg's Circus," by Bertha Upton, Longmans, oblong oversized, illustrations by author, 1903 .... **150**

"Goody-Naughty Book," by Sarah Cory Rippey, Rand McNally, illustrations by Blanche Fisher Wright, 1913 .... **45**

"Grasshopper Green," by John Rae, Volland, illustrations by author, no date **35**

"Grimm's Fairy Tales"

"Grimm's Fairy Tales," Whitman, black & white illustrations, 1941 (ILLUS.)..................... **15**

"Hansel and Gretel"

"Hansel and Gretel," Donahue, black & white illustration, Classic Fairy Tales have been published in many versions, no illustrator names, ca. 1900 (ILLUS.) **22**

"Hansel and Gretel" Picture Book

"Hansel and Gretel," first edition, Little Golden Book, illustrated by Erika Weihs, 1943 (ILLUS.) **20**

"Happy Day," by Ruth Krauss, Harper, oversized, black & white illustrations by Marc Simont, 1949 .... **20**

"Happy Hours," by Elizabeth Daniels, Rand McNally, black & white photo illustrations, 1934 .... **15**

"Herman the Brave Pig," by Miriam Mason, McMillan, illustrations by George & Doris Hauman, 1949 .... **15**

"Horton Hatches the Egg"

"Horton Hatches the Egg," by Dr. Seuss, Random House, oversized, illustrations by author, 1940 (ILLUS.) **45**

"House that Jack Built," Warne, illustrated by Randolph Caldecott, 1879 .... **75**

"How Do You Get There?" by H.A. & Margret Rey, Houghton, illustrations by author, 1941 .... **40**

"How the Camel Got His Hump," by Rudyard Kipling, 1940s, Garden City Books, color illustrations **15**

"Jack and the Beanstalk," Rand McNally, small size, illustrations by Margaret Evans Price, 1927 .... **30**

"Jack o' Lantern Twins," by Anne McCauley, Lyons, illustrations by Vera Stone Norman, 1941 .... **20**

"Jessie Wilcox Smith's Mother Goose," oversized, illustrated by author, New York, 1914 .... **250**

"Jolly Jump-Ups on Vacation," McLoughlin Brothers, illustrated pop-ups by Geraldine Clyne, 1942 .... **60**

"Kewpies, Their Book," by Rose O'Neill, Stokes, illustrations by author, 1913 .... **100**

"Kiddie Rhymes," by Margaret Hays, Jacobs, oversized, 29 pg., color plates & black & white illustrations by Grace Wiederseim (Grace Drayton), 1911 .... **75**

"Let's Play Fireman," by Edith Lowe, Whitman, illustrated by Ruth Newton, small version, 1939 .... **25**

"Let's Play Store," by Edith Lowe, Whitman, illustrated by Ruth Newton, small version, 1939 .... **25**

"Let's Pretend," by William Mac Harg, 1914, Volland, color illustrations by Bonnibel Butler **55**

"Little Black Sambo," by Helen Bannerman, Platt & Munk, color illustrations by Eulalie, 1925 .... **75**

"Little Black Sambo" Picture Book

"Little Black Sambo," by Helen Bannerman, Saalfield, illustrated by Ethel Hays, 1942 (ILLUS.) **55**

"Little Black Sambo," by Helen Bannerman, Stokes, author illustrated, 1901 .... **350**

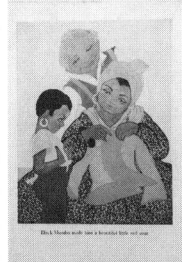

Illustration from "Little Black Sambo"

"Little Black Sambo," by Helen Bannerman, The Harter Publishing Co., illustrated by Fern Bisel Peat, 1931 (ILLUS.) **150**

"Little Brown Bruno," by Alice Radford, Rand McNally, black & white illustrations by Clayton Rawson, 1931 .... **15**

"Little Fire Engine," by Lois Lenski, illustrated by author, NY, 1946 .... **45**

"Little Lulu," Curtis, collection of previously published cartoons by Marge, 1935 .... **50**

"Little Miss Ducky Daddles," by Edward McCandlish, Stoll & Edwards, illustrations by author, 1926 .... **25**

"Little Toot," by Hardie Gramatky, Putnam, author illustrated, 1939 .... **50**

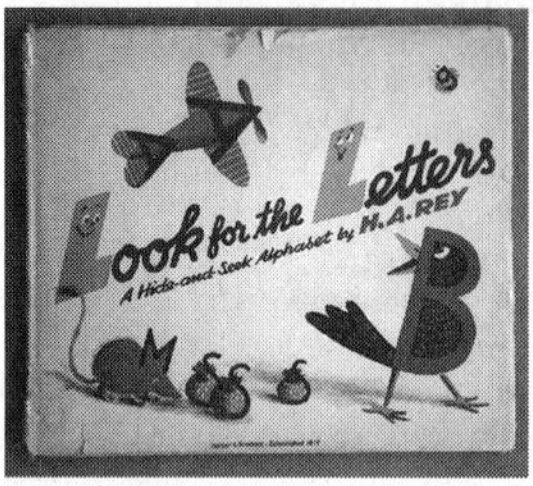

"Look for the Letters"

"Look for the Letters," by H.A. Rey, Harper Brothers, illustrations by author, 1945 (ILLUS.) **30**

"Make Way for Ducklings," by Robert McCloskey, Viking, first edition, black & white illustrations by author, 1941 .... **50**

"Maud Humphrey's Book of Fairy Tales," Stokes, color illustrations by author, 1892 ..... **240**

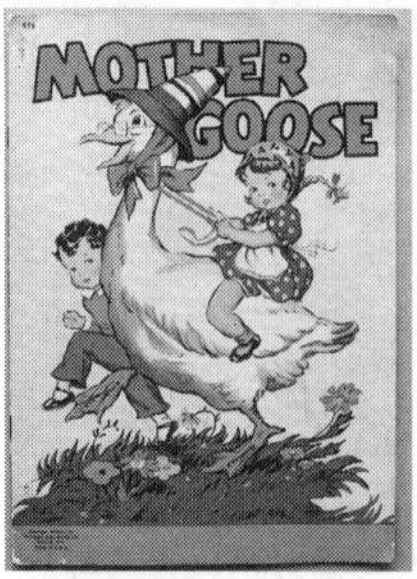

"Mother Goose"

"Mother Goose," Whitman, no illustrator given, 1941 (ILLUS.) **12**

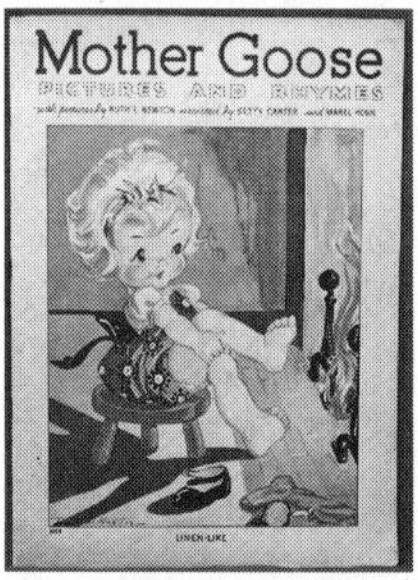

"Mother Goose Pictures and Rhymes"

"Mother Goose Pictures and Rhymes," by Ruth Newton assisted by Betty Carter & Mabel Horn, Whitman, illustrated by Newton, 1934 (ILLUS.) **30**

"Muggins Mouse," by Marjorie Barrows, Reilly, illustrated by Keith Ward, 1932 .... **50**

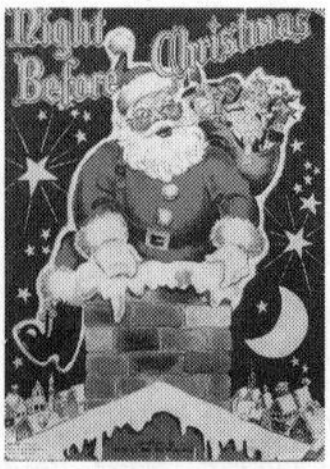

"Night Before Christmas"

"Night Before Christmas," by Clement Clarke Moore, Whitman, illustrated by Hilda Miloche & Wilma Kane, 1947 (ILLUS.) **20**

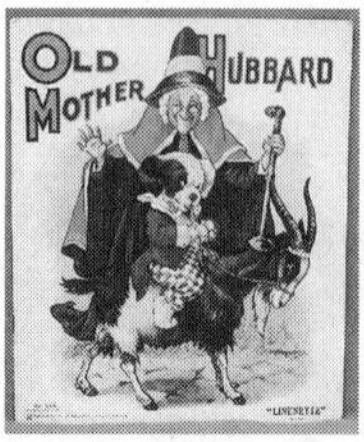

"Old Mother Hubbard"

"Old Mother Hubbard," Sam'l Gabriel & Sons, "Linenette" illustrations are signed AEK, 1921 (ILLUS.) **37**

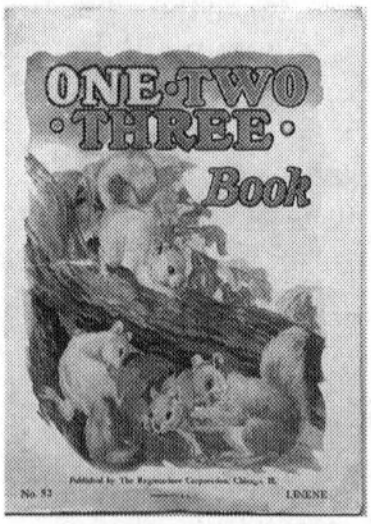

"One. Two. Three. Book"

"One. Two. Three. Book," no author or illustrator given, Linene, Regensteiner Corp., 1925 (ILLUS.) **25**

"Pat the Bunny," by Dorothy Kunhardt, Whitman, small spiral-bound "touch" picture book, illustrated by author, undated, ca. 1940 .... **35**

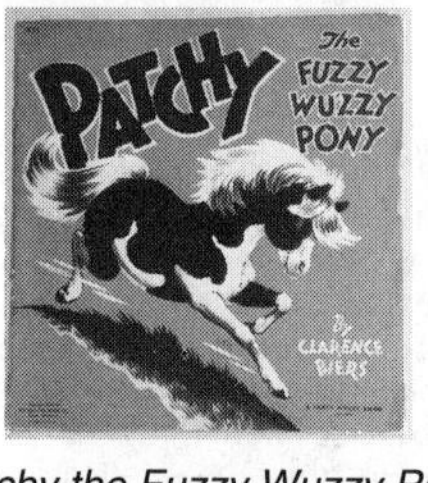

"Patchy the Fuzzy Wuzzy Pony"

"Patchy the Fuzzy Wuzzy Pony," by Clarence Biers, Whitman, illustrations by author, 1946 (ILLUS.) **25**

"Raggedy Ann's Wishing Pebble"

"Raven Wing"

"Sailor Tommy"

"Santa Claus and the Little Lost Kitten"

"The Story Book of Transportation"

"Hot Cross Buns" & "Handy Pandy" from the Bye-Lo Series

"The Children's Picture Book"

"The Children's Picture Book," by Hazel Frazee, Whitman, illustrated by author, 1929 (ILLUS.) 30

"The Cold Blooded Penguin"

"The Cold Blooded Penguin," by Robert Edmonds, from the Walt Disney Little Library, illustrations Walt Disney Studios, 1944 (ILLUS.) 35

"The Flying Scotsman," by Doris Crockford, Oxford University Press, oblong picture book, color illustrations by Rachel Boger & Henry Cartwright, undated, ca. 1937 35

"The Gateway to Storyland," edited by Watty Piper, Platt & Munk, oversized, illustrations by Eulalie, 1925 65

"The Jolly Jingle Picture Book," by Leroy Jackson, Rand McNally, illustrated by Ruth Eger, 1937 65

"The Little Engine That Could"

"The Little Engine That Could," by Lois Lenski & edited by Watty Piper, Platt & Munk, original copyright 1930, 1954 version (ILLUS.) 20

"The Little King," by Otto Soglow, John Martin's House, oversized, cartoon illustrations by author, 1945 40

"The Little Red Hen"

"The Little Red Hen," Merrill, illustrations by Milo Winter, 1937 (ILLUS.) 32

"The New House in the Forest"

"The New House in the Forest," by Lucy Sprague Mitchell, first edition, Little Golden Book, illustrations by Eloise Wilkin, 1946 (ILLUS.) 25

"The Night Before Christmas"

"The Night Before Christmas," Saalfield, illustrated by Frances Brundage, no date (ILLUS.) 60

"The Otherside Book," by Edith Mitchell, Reilly Britton, oversized, illustrations by author, 1915 45

Picture from "The Tale of Peter Rabbit"

"The Tale of Peter Rabbit," animated by Julian Wehr, Grosset & Dunlap, 1943 (ILLUS.) 50

"The Teddy Bears Go Fishing"

"The Teddy Bears Go Fishing," by Bray, Reilly & Britton, illustrations by author, 1907 (ILLUS.) **45**

"The Three Bears"

"The Three Bears," Whitman, illustrations by Charlotte Stone, 1933 (ILLUS.) **35**

"The Three Little Pigs"

"The Three Little Pigs," Whitman, no author or illustrator given, 1942 (ILLUS.) **12**

"The Town Mouse and The Country Mouse," Saalfield, linen-like paper, illustration by Ethel Hays, 1942 .... **30**

"Thornton Burgess Animal Stories," Platt & Munk, color & black & white illustrations throughout by Harrison Cady, 1942 .... **25**

"Three Little Indians," by Ann Leavitt, Rand McNally, illustrations by H.C. & Lucille Holling, 1937 .... **35**

"Three Little Pigs," by John Rea Neill, McKay, small size, illustrated by author, 1940 .... **30**

"Tiny Tots, Simple Objects," by Corrine Malvern, Whitman, oversized, illustrations by author, 1948 .... **20**

"Tony Sarg's Book for Children," Greenberg, oversized, w/cut-out theater, lifting curtain & turning wheel mounted on inside of front cover that shows scenes from "Little Red Riding Hood," 1924 .... **90**

Two Titles From "Uncle Wiggly" Series

"Uncle Wiggly," books by Howard Garis, small size, Whitman series w/illustrations by Lang Campbell, ca. 1930s-1940s, each (ILLUS.) **20**

"Us Kids and the Circus," by Gertrude Kay, Volland, illustrations by author, 1927 .... **55**

"Walt Disney's Pinocchio"

"Walt Disney's Pinocchio," from the Walt Disney Children's Library, Whitman, story & illustrations from the motion picture, 1940 (ILLUS.) **35**

Picture in "Walt Disney's Uncle Remus"

"Walt Disney's Uncle Remus," by Joel Chandler Harris, first edition, Little Golden Book, illustrated by Bob Grant & Marion Palmer, 1947 (ILLUS.) **18**

"I Want to be a Circus Man"

"I Want to be a Circus Man," by Marion McNeil, Saalfield, illustrated by Corrine Bailey, 1934 (ILLUS.) **15**

"What Happened to Tommy," illustrated by Frances Brundage, NY, ca. 1920s **40**

"When Our Ship Comes In," by Dorothy Foley, Saalfield, oversized, color & Black & white illustrations by Forrest Orr, 1938........ **20**

"Wooden Willie" Picture Book

"Wooden Willie," by Johnny Gruelle, Donahue, 1927 (ILLUS.)..................................... **50**

CHILDREN'S DISHES

Children's Feeding Dishes

Getting toddlers to eat has always been a struggle for many mothers. In 1948 E. Nudelman received a patent for an amusement device designed to help moms. This was a pig that hung on the side of a bowl; the mouth was hinged, creating the effect of feeding the pig while also feeding the baby. The food actually traveled through the pig's mouth and back into the bowl. Produced by Topic Toys in 1949, it was marketed as Hungry Piggy. This opened the door for other designs and other dishes. Some were designed so a separate feeder sat on the side of the dish and others so the feeder was actually attached to the dish, usually in the form of a head.

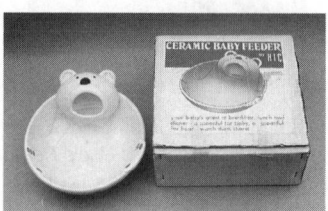

Bear Feeder with Box

Bear, bowl 6" d., marked "HIC Japan," 1985, found in several colors; matching cup, $5-8 (ILLUS. of bowl w/box) **$35-45**

Bear Head Feeder with Box

Bear head on bowl, made in Taiwan, probably 1980s, bear holds spoon & fork in its paws, 6" d. (ILLUS.) **35-45**

Rare Cleminsons Clown Feeder

Clown, by California Cleminsons, ca. 1955, rare **125-175**

"All Gone" Clown Head Feeder

Clown head, attaches to similarly decorated bowl that reads "All Gone" inside, no markings, probably Japanese, found in different colors; feeder only, $45-55; bowl only, $30-40; set (ILLUS.) **75-95**

Clown Head Feeder

Clown head, pink, attached to bowl with black buttons showing in bottom of bowl, 6" d. **65-85**

Ross Products Duck Feeder

Duck feeder, marked "Ross Products - Hand Decorated," bowl reads "One for Baby, One for The Duck," 5" duck, feeder only, $65-75; bowl only, $40-50; the set (ILLUS).. **100-125**

Hungry Piggy

Hungry Piggy, 3" pink plastic pig hooks onto blue plastic bowl, pig in bottom of bowl reads "All Gone," some sets found w/utensils held by pigs or bunnies; add $15-25 for original box (ILLUS.)................. **55-75**
"One for the Baby One for the Clown" bowl w/writing similar to Ross Products duck dish (ILLUS. left, below)................ **100-125**

Puppy Tu Feeder

Puppy Tu, made by Crest Specialties Products, similar in design to Hungry Piggy, comes w/utensils w/puppy heads on end of fork & spoon, pink or blue sets; add $15-25 for original box (ILLUS.)................. **55-75**

Two Novelty Feeders

"This Little Pig Went to Market" bowl w/attached pig head (ILLUS. right w/clown dish)... **100-125**

Wunfer Bird Feeder Set & Box

Wunfer Bird, by Cardinal China, dates to 1954, sold as a set w/white bowl; feeder only, $60-80; bowl only, $20-30, the set (ILLUS.).. **80-100**

Novelty & Whistle Cups

Ceramic

In the early 1950s ceramic cups from Japan were a popular import item sold in the local 5 & 10 cent stores. Many of these had figural handles or attached whistles, the intent being to make mealtime fun and encourage children to drink their milk or juice. All cups listed are approximately 3 1/2" unless otherwise noted. Many of these cups are found in both pink and blue colors.

"Always Drink Milk" Whimsical Cup

"Always Drink Milk," common, w/Bambi-type deer on front & deer handle (ILLUS.).. **15-20**

Dutch Character Novelty Cups

"Always Drink Milk," Dutch couple on front & boy-shaped handle, common (ILLUS.).. **30-40**

Lamb Whimsical Cup

"Always Drink Milk," lamb & sheep on front & lamb-shaped handle (ILLUS.)........ **30-40**

Little Boy Blue Novelty Cups

"Always Drink Milk," Little Boy Blue on front & Little Boy Blue-shaped handle (ILLUS.).. **35-45**

Rabbit Whimsical Cup

"Always Drink Milk," rabbit on front & floppy-eared rabbit handle (ILLUS.)................. **30-40**

"Count Down, Blast Off" Whistle Mug

"Count Down, Blast Off," space mug, rocket ship on handle is whistle, bottom says "Personal Property of [space for child's name]" (ILLUS.) **25-35**

Bear "Drink Milk and Whistle" Cup

"Drink Milk and Whistle," three small bears play on front while little bear sits on handle w/separate whistle (ILLUS.)............ **45-55**

Train Whistle Cup

"Drink Milk and Whistle," train on front & little train w/attached whistle on handle (ILLUS.).. **50-60**
"Drink Milk and Whistle," tugboat on front & little tugboat w/attached whistle on handle.. **50-60**
"Drink More Juice," leaping deer on front & deer handle, matches some milk cups, 2 1/2" (ILLUS. right w/"Juice for Good Teeth" cup) **25-35**

"Drink Orange Juice" Novelty Cups

"Drink Orange Juice," oranges on front, one w/smiley face (ILLUS. two sides) **10-20**
"Drink Orange Juice Every Day," clown w/elephants on front (ILLUS. right w/sheep cup, below) **40-50**
"Drink Orange Juice Every Day," sheep on front w/lamb handle (ILLUS. left w/clown & elephant cup, below)................. **40-50**

Piper Whistle Cup

Animal Novelty Juice Cups

"Drink Your Juice & Whistle A Merry Tune," orange on front, piper on back, whistle in handle (ILLUS.) **25-35**

Cowboy Whimsical Cups

"I Like Milk," horse head inside horseshoe on front & cowboy-shaped handle (ILLUS.) **35-45**

Juice Novelty Cups

"Juice for Good Teeth," rabbit on front & rabbit handle, matches some milk cups, 2 1/2" (ILLUS. left w/"Drink More Juice" cup) **25-35**

"Let's All Sing ..." Whistle Cup

"Let's All Sing Like The Birdies Sing For Milk," mother bird w/songbook teaching babies to sing, bird w/whistle tail on handle (ILLUS.) **30-40**

New Hampshire Souvenir Whistle Cup

"Old Man Of The Mountain, Franconia Notch, NH," souvenir whistle cup, bird tail is the whistle (ILLUS.) **45-55**

"Sing a Song of Sixpence" Whistle Cup

"Sing a Song of Sixpence," marked "Genuine Staffordshire Hand Painted Shorter & Son Ltd., England," birds coming out of pie on front, bird's tail is whistle (ILLUS.) .. **40-50**

"Sing For Your Milk" Whistle Cup

"Sing For Your Milk," two chickens on front, chicken w/whistle tail on handle (ILLUS.) **30-40**

Florida Souvenir Whistle Cup

"Sip N' Whistle Milk Mug For A Little Dear," similar to other Sip & Whistle Mugs, but this is a Florida souvenir, poem on the back reads "Whistle Whistle On My Cup, When I Blow, Mom Fills It Up" (ILLUS.) **45-55**

"Sip N' Whistle" Milk Mug

"Sip N' Whistle Milk Mug For A Little Dear," whistle cup & straw, bird tail is whistle & stem is straw, poem on back reads, "Whistle Whistle On My Cup, When I Blow, Mom Fills It Up" (ILLUS.) **45-55**

"Today I Am a Little Dear" Whistle Cup

"Today I Am a Little Dear" on front w/deer & "Today I Am a Little Stinker" w/skunk on back, bird w/whistle tail on handle (ILLUS.) **45-55**

Tomato Whimsical Cup

"Tomato Juice Is Good," tomato hanging from vine on front (ILLUS.) **10-15**

"Tweet Like a Birdie ..." Whistle Cup

"Tweet Like a Birdie For Your Milk," three baby birds on front, mother bird w/whistle tail protruding from side of cup (ILLUS.) **30-40**

Common Whistle Cup

"Whistle For Milk," common cup, but smaller in height, two birds face each other on front (ILLUS.) **20-25**

Puppy & Frog Whistle Cup

"Whistle For Milk," puppy & frog on front, puppy w/whistle in bow on handle & frog in bottom of cup (ILLUS.) **45-55**

Bird in Cage Whistle Cup

"Whistle For Your Milk," bird in cage on front w/bird on handle w/whistle in tail (ILLUS.) **30-40**

Clown "Whistle For Your Milk" Cup

"Whistle For Your Milk," clown w/balloons, Spencer Gifts, 1976 (ILLUS.) **15-25**

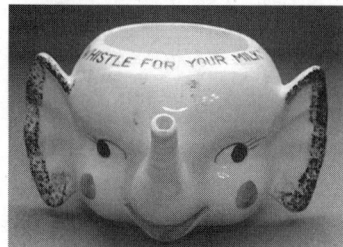

Elephant Head Whistle Cup

"Whistle For Your Milk," elephant head, trunk is whistle & ears are handles (ILLUS.) **35-40**

"Whistle For Your Milk" Whistle Cup

"Whistle For Your Milk," most common whistle cup found, two birds facing away from handle, bird on handle, tail is whistle, "Ross Products - Hand Decorated Japan" (ILLUS.) **15-25**

Owl "Whistle For Your Milk" Whistle Cup

"Whistle For Your Milk," owl w/plastic roly-poly eyes, ceramic whistle is separate piece (ILLUS.) **45-55**

Puppy Whistle Cup Variations

"Whistle For Your Milk," w/little dog on front & another sitting on handle w/separate whistle, found w/painted & plastic wiggly eyes, each (ILLUS.) **45-55**

CHILDREN'S FIGURAL TOOTHBRUSH HOLDERS

Convincing children to brush their teeth is always a challenge. Figural toothbrush holders made this chore a bit easier because children had something fun and cute to hold their toothbrush and oftentimes toothpaste. Toothbrushes have been found in the ancient pyramids, but the cute and comical devices to hold them have only been found as early as the late 1920s or early 1930s, and most are from the 1940s and 1950s. Nursery rhyme characters, children , cartoon characters, cowboys, soldiers and animals were popular themes. Whimsical holders are still produced, but the pieces today tend towards cartoon characters and are much larger in size than the older models. Some of the early toothbrush holders were tin lithographs, wooden, or bisque, while later ones were produced in ceramic and chalkware. Many early pieces were made in the United States, and later pieces came from both Japan and Germany; those made in Germany command higher prices.

—D. Gillham

Angel Toothbrush Holder

Angel, front reads "Be an angel put your brush here," holds four toothbrushes, 6 1/4" h. (ILLUS.) **$75-100**

Spotted Cow Toothbrush Holder

Animal: Cow, spotted, w/bell, made in Japan, contains two holes & tray, 3 1/4" h. . **95-125**
Animal: Cow, three holders w/tray **95-125**

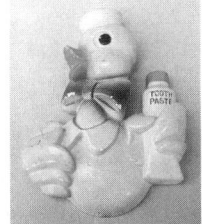

Chalkware Duck Toothbrush Holder

Animal: Duck, chalkware, Miller Studio, sailor duck holds tube of toothpaste, one wing holds toothbrush, 1968, 7" h. (ILLUS.) **20-30**

Chalkware Fish Toothbrush Holder

Animal: Fish, chalkware, Miller Studio, toothbrushes go in each fin, ca. 1965, 7" h. (ILLUS.) **20-30**

Pink Elephant Toothbrush Holder

Animal: Pink Elephant, sitting, three holes w/tray, made in Japan, 5" h. (ILLUS.) **85-95**

Plaid Horse Toothbrush Holder

Animal: Plaid Horse, marked "Made in Japan," three holders w/tray, can stand or hang on wall (ILLUS.) **85-95**

Rabbit Toothbrush Holder

Animal: Rabbit, holds hat, reads "Brush and be bright" on front of tray, 4 1/2" h. (ILLUS.) **95-125**

Tin Lithograph Toothbrush Holder

Animal: Rabbit, tin lithograph, made in USA, possibly Ohio Art, holder is combined w/timer for child to time how long to brush teeth (ILLUS.) **175-225**

Baker (The), figural, man wearing white hat, w/red shirt w/blue tie, white pants & white apron, three holders by arms, w/front tray, can stand or hang, marked "Made in Japan," 5" h. (ILLUS. center w/Butcher & Candlestick Maker) **55-75**

Boy, w/cap & bulldog, two holders & tray, appears to be companion to little girl holder, 6" h. (ILLUS. right w/girl, next page) **95-125**

Butcher, Baker & Candlestick Maker Toothbrush Holders

Butcher (The), figural, man wearing red hat, w/blue striped shirt, red checked pants & white apron, three holders by arms, w/front tray, marked "Made in Japan," 5" h. (ILLUS. left w/Baker & Candlestick Maker).............................. **55-75**

Candlestick Maker (The), figural, bald man w/glasses wearing blue shirt w/red tie, red & white striped apron & black pants, three holders in pockets of apron, w/front tray, can stand or hang, marked "Made in Japan," 5" h. (ILLUS. right w/Butcher & Baker)... **55-75**

Little Orphan Annie Toothbrush Holder

Cartoon characters, Little Orphan Annie & Sandy, marked "©Famous Artists Syndicate S631, made in Japan," two holders in back, drain hole in bottom, 3" w., 3 1/2" h. (ILLUS.)....................................... **95-125**

Cartoon Toothbrush Holders

Cartoon characters, Moon Mullins & Kayo, bisque, w/one holder (ILLUS. left w/Popeye).. **95**

Cartoon characters, Orphan Annie & Sandy, bisque, w/two holders (ILLUS. right w/Popeye & Moon Mullins) **95**

Cartoon characters, Popeye, bisque, toothbrush goes through arm & rests on pant leg, drainage hole in bottom, marked "Made in Japan," very rare, 4 1/2" h. (ILLUS. center w/Little Orphan Annie & Moon Mullins)................................. **550+**

Cowboy Toothbrush Holder

Cowboy w/holsters, has holders for toothbrush & toothpaste (ILLUS.) **75-95**

Disney characters, Mickey & Minnie w/Pluto, bisque, two holders in back, marked "Made in Japan, Walt Disney," 4" w., 3 1/2" h. (ILLUS. center w/Disney characters).. **200-300**

Disney characters, pig playing the flute, ceramic, Maws (marked Foreign), w/one holder in back (ILLUS. right w/Disney characters).. **150**

Disney Toothbrush Holders

Disney characters, Three Pigs, bisque, two holders in back (ILLUS. left w/Disney characters).. **100**

Black & White Dog Toothbrush Holder

Dog, black & white, toothbrush fits in slot in mouth, 3 1/2" h. (ILLUS.)........................... **85-110**

Toothache Dog Toothbrush Holder

Dog w/toothache, towel around head, paw holds toothbrush, front reads "Don't forget the teeth," 3 1/4" h. (ILLUS.).............. **85-110**

Dutch Boy Toothbrush Holder

Dutch boy, wooden, in original box w/poem about its use, 4 1/2" h. (ILLUS.)................. **65-85**

Children & Dogs Toothbrush Holders

Girl, in hat w/dog, two holders & tray, 6" h. (ILLUS. left w/boy).................................... **95-125**

Lone Ranger Toothbrush Holder

Lone Ranger (The), composite, figure on rearing Silver, wire holder near Silver's front leg (ILLUS.) **80-100**

Nursery rhyme characters, Little Red Riding Hood, one holder, feet form tray, marked "Made in Japan," 5" h. **55-75**

Nursery rhyme characters, Old King Cole, one holder, free form tray, marked "Made in Japan," 5" h. **55-75**

Nursery rhyme characters, Three Bears, two holders w/tray, marked "Made in Japan," 5" h.)... **55-75**

Pierrot Toothbrush Holder

Pierrot, holds mask, made in Japan, 5 1/2" h. (ILLUS.) **95-125**

Pinocchio Toothbrush Holder

Pinocchio, California Cleminson's, flat holder hangs on wall, toothbrush hangs on nose, original box features poem confirming that this is a toothbrush holder (ILLUS.) **95-110**

Pirate Toothbrush Holder

Pirate, arms hold toothbrushes & sit in boots, w/tray, stands or hangs, 5" h. (ILLUS.) **95-125**

Soldier Toothbrush Holders

Soldier, man w/red pill box hat, red shirt & blue pants, w/holders through arms into big brown boots (ILLUS. left) **55**
Soldier, marked "Made in Japan," holders in boots, 4 3/4" h. **45**
Soldier, w/red shirt & black pants & hat, w/sash across front, holders through arms into boots, feet create tray, no markings, stands or hangs (ILLUS. right) **55**
Soldier, w/uniform of blue & red, one holder by left arm for brush, w/tray in front, stands or hangs, marked "Made in Japan," 6 1/2" h. (ILLUS. center) **45**

"Dearie is Weary" Holder

Woman in apron, apron reads "Dearie is Weary," base reads "Please Put Them Away," holds six toothbrushes, 6" (ILLUS.) **95-125**

CHRISTMAS COLLECTIBLES

Miscellaneous

Christmas tree fence, cast-iron, eight sections topped w/fleur-de-lys, green paint, illegible cast label, 11 3/4" l. (minor wear to paint) **$165**

Folk Art Santa Pull Toy

Folk art carving, Santa on reindeer pull toy, made by members of the Schifferl family of Wisconsin (ILLUS.) **3,080**

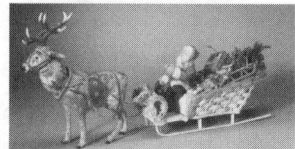

Nodding Reindeer with Santa's Sleigh

Nodder display piece, nodding reindeer w/Santa in sleigh, crushed plush reindeer, Santa driving white sleigh full of toys (not original to piece), balance mechanism provides eight hours of nodding, hard rubber antlers provide balance, F.A.O. Schwarz exclusive, comes w/copy of ad from Schwarz' Toy Bazaar Centennial Christmas Catalog showing this display piece, 17" h. to tip of antlers, 37" l. (ILLUS.) **3,450**

German Wax Tree Topper Angel

Tree topper Christmas angel, poured wax head & hands, painted features, open-closed mouth, cone-shaped body, paper wings, flowing costume of maroon velvet w/gold trim, gold halo, German, ca. 1920, 15" h. (ILLUS.)..................................... **86**

Santa Claus Collectibles

No other character is better known than Santa Claus, the jolly old elf who works all year making those wonderful toys that he delivers on Christmas Eve to good girls and boys. If we live in America, we've all been a part of his magic, whether as children with high hopes and sparkling dreams or adults who love those children. For Santa Claus collectors, the mystical magic is always present, for no matter your collecting budget there is a Santa in some form ready and waiting for purchase.

A-B-C blocks, Mr. Kris Kringle, McLoughlin Bros., 1890s **225**

Ad Featuring Santa

Ad, featuring Santa, full page, Gold Medal Flour, black & white, Ladies' Home Journal, December 1916 (ILLUS.)........................... **15**
Beverage set, ceramic, winking Santa, pitcher & 6 cups, by Holt Howard, 1960.......... **60**

Book, Santa Claus, a Fuzzy Wuzzy book, by Eileen Vaughan, Whitman, 1947................ **15**

Santa Claus and the Little Lost Kitten

Book, Santa Claus and the Little Lost Kitten, a Fuzzy Wuzzy book, Whitman, 1952 (ILLUS.)... **25-30**
Book, Talking to Santa Claus, W.B. Conkey Co., hardback, 1898... **30**

The Night Before Christmas Book

Book, The Night Before Christmas, Whitman, 1940 (ILLUS.).................................... **18**
Cake mold, cast iron, Santa Claus, "Hello Kiddies" on front, Griswold, 12" h. **300**
Candleholder, totem pole Santa, Holt Howard, 1958, stacked up to 8 1/2" **22**
Candleholders, ceramic, Santa driving car, 1958.. **35**
Candy container, hard cardboard, w/spring neck, rabbit fur beard, German, ca. 1940s.. **75**
Candy container, plastic, Santa on skies, marked Rosbro Plastic, 4 1/2"......................... **18**
Chocolate mold, metal, antique, marked w/the number 5934 & 59, 4 1/2" w., 9 1/2" h... **325**

Christmas Cards

Christmas cards, to be cut out & sent, by Saalfield, 1946 (ILLUS.)..................................... **15**
Clicker, lithographed tin, w/image of Santa at base of chimney w/sack of toys, ca. 1930s, 1 3/4" **75**

Coloring book, Hi! Santa, uncolored, large format, by Merrill Publisher, 1954 .... **8**

Cubes, Jolly Santa Claus, depicting six different Santa scenes, very hard to find, McLoughlin Bros., 1890s **1,000**

Doll, composition face & black boots, cloth clothes, carries tree & has burlap bag, ca. 1930s, 7 1/2" **80**

Doll, composition head & hands, w/cloth suit, ca. 1930s, 19" **75**

Doll, molded cloth face w/painted features, blue eyes & red cheeks w/a white mohair beard, the body formed by a red flannel suit w/white mohair trim, black fabric boots, black belt, encloses a turnkey music box playing Silent Night, ca. 1930s, 28" h. (overall light fading & soiling) **230**

Stuffed Cloth Santa Doll

Doll, stuffed cloth, by Edward Peck, ca. 1880s (ILLUS.) **150**

Vinyl Santa Doll

Doll, vinyl & plush, Santa, 12" (ILLUS.) **30**

Figure, celluloid, one piece, made in Occupied Japan, ca. 1940s, 4" **45**

Figure, celluloid, Santa in truck w/house & tree in back, Japan, 4" **75**

Figure, ceramic, Santa family on sled w/ceramic candy cane runners, red flocked clothing, Napco, Japan, 9" l., 4" h. **25**

Ceramic Sitting Santa

Figure, ceramic, sitting Santa, spaghetti trim, marked Japan, 3 1/2" h. (ILLUS.) **15**

Early Chalkware Santa

Figure, chalkware, early, 20" (ILLUS.) **100**

Figure, clay faced Santa, dressed w/foil wrapped package on back, soft cotton beard, holding two ski poles & standing on heavy cardboard skies, made in Occupied Japan, 6" **95**

Hallmark Handcrafted Santa

Figure, handcrafted Santa, Hallmark, 1975, no box (ILLUS.) **125**

Figure, papier-maché, dressed, German, early **275**

Figure, spun cotton, w/Dresden trim, Germany, 3" **175**

Figure, wax, Fannie Farmer, ca. 1950s **45**

Santa Claus Game

Game, Santa Claus, by Parker Brothers, early (ILLUS.) **375**

Santa Claus Gift Book

Gift book, Santa Claus, Hurt & Co., ca. 1890s (ILLUS.) **30**

Paper Gift Tags

Gift tags, paper, ca. 1940s **1**

Greeting Card Booklet

Greeting card booklet, embossed, ca. 1930s (ILLUS.) **12**
Handkerchief, linen w/embroidered Santas, ca. 1940s, 2 1/2" sq. **12**
Mask, papier-maché, w/streamer trim & cotton bears, early 1900s **65**
Nodder, celluloid, Santa w/lantern, 7" **400**
Nodder candy box, heavy paper w/composition head & fur beard, flocked clothes, w/"spring" neck, made in West Germany, 9" h. **90**
Ornament, Santa at chimney, mold-blown glass, Germany, 3" **150**
Ornament, Santa in airplane, tinsel wire wings, mold-blown glass, Germany, ca. 1950s **25**
Ornament, Santa w/bag & toys, mold-blown glass, ca. 1940s, 3" **45**
Ornament, Santa's Motorcar, Hallmark, from the Here Comes Santa Series, 1st in series, 1979, MIB **690**

Early Christmas Party Paper Dolls

Paper doll, Betty Bonnet's Christmas Party, sheet w/Santa outfit, Ladies' Home Journal, December 1916 (ILLUS.) **22**
Pez dispenser, Santa, full body, no feet **125**

Santa & Child Photograph

Photograph, Santa & child, 1951 (ILLUS.) **10**
Planter, ceramic, singing girl holding Santa head, spaghetti trim, Lefton, Japan, 4 1/2" h. **18**
Planter, Santa's sleigh w/Santa driver & celluloid reindeer, 1940, 12" l. **125**
Postcard, girl whispering to Santa, dated 1909 .... **6**

Santa Postcard

Postcard, Santa & elf-like brownie, used, postmarked 1916, Stecher Litho (ILLUS.) **10**
Puzzle, inlaid heavy cardboard, Santa's Workshop, by Lowe, late 1940s **7**

"I Saw Mommy Kissing Santa Claus"

Record, Peter Pan, "I Saw Mommy Kissing
Santa Claus," ca. 1950s (ILLUS.) **12**
Roly poly, celluloid, Irwin, 1930s, 3 1/4" **65**
Roly poly, papier-maché, Schoenhut, 14" **1,750**

Plastic Roly Poly

Roly poly, plastic, late 1950s-early 1960s
(ILLUS.) **12**
Salt & pepper shakers, ceramic, Mr. & Mrs.
Santa, marked Napco, Japan, spaghetti
trim, ca. 1950s, 4" h. **20**

The Night Before Christmas

Shape book, The Night Before Christmas,
by M.A. Donohue & Co., paperback,
early (ILLUS.) **18**

"Santa Claus is Coming to Town"

Sheet music, "Santa Claus is Coming to
Town," 1934 (ILLUS.).. **4**
Spoon, sterling, full figural Santa, very de-
tailed, marked for the Mayer Bros., 5"........... **115**
Toy, Happy Santa, battery-operated, rolls
along while head turns w/one arm playing
drum, the other ringing a bell, hat lights
up, original box, by Cragstan Corp.,
made in Japan, 12" h. **105**
Toy, lithographed tin, Santa Claus walker,
by Chein, 5 1/4"... **600**

Santa Squeaky Toy

Toy, squeaky, by the Edward Mobley Co.,
late 1940s-early 1950s, 12" (ILLUS.).............. **30**

Coca-Cola Vinyl Santa Toy

Toy, vinyl, plush, Coca-Cola, by
Rushton, ca. 1950s, 18" (ILLUS.).................... **55**
Toy, windup tin, w/celluloid head & bell,
rocks back & forth ringing bell, original
key, Japan, 6" h.. **145**

Wooden Jointed Santa Toy

Toy, wooden, jointed Santa, w/flexible vinyl
beard, jumps when string is pulled, ca.
1950s (ILLUS.).. **10**

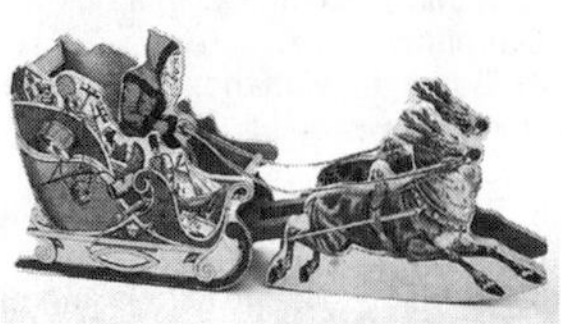

Santa Claus Sleigh

Toy, wooden lithograph, Santa Claus sleigh pulled by reindeer, 1891 (ILLUS.)................. **495**

Advertising Santa Claus Trade Card

Trade card, advertising Santa Claus card, 1890s (ILLUS.)... **30**

Father Christmas Trade Card

Trade card, Father Christmas holding tree, Bee-Hive, by Mayer, Merkel & Ottmann Lith., NY, ca. 1870s, 2 1/2" x 4" (ILLUS.)......... **25**

CIRCUS COLLECTIBLES

The romance of the "Big Top," stirred by memories of sawdust, spangles, thrills and chills, has captured the imagination of the American public for over 100 years. Though the heyday of the traveling circus is now past, dedicated collectors and fans of all ages eagerly seek out choice memorabilia from the late 19th and early 20th centuries, the "golden age" of circuses.

Bank, cast iron, mechanical type, "Circus Bank," pony circles ring w/clown, Shepard Hardware Company, ca. 1888, very rare, top condition..................................... **$45,000**

Chein Tin Clown Bank

Bank, tin, semi-mechanical, color clown head w/opening in mouth, press button & tongue comes out for the coin, Chein, 1939, paint wear, 5 1/4" h. (ILLUS.) **200**

Howdy Doody's Circus Golden Book

Book, "Howdy Doody's Circus," Little Golden Book, 1950 (ILLUS.) **25**

Tom and Jerry Circus Book

Book, "M-G-M's Tom and Jerry and The Toy Circus," Whitman, 1953 (ILLUS.)............. **12**

The Circus by Ideals Publishing

Book, "The Circus - an Ideals publication," large color photo cover of a group of clowns, including Emmett Kelly, book features a history of the circus, posters, advertising, acts & stories, 1961 (ILLUS.)........ **25**

Disney's Toby Tyler Book

Book, "Walt Disney's Toby Tyler," cover color picture of Toby carrying tray of candy apples, Whitman Publishing, 1960 (ILLUS.)... 10

Cardboard cut-outs, Coca-Cola premium, light cardboard w/printed design of a clown holding a glass of Coca-Cola, box side shows various circus cut-outs for children, 1932, box 10 x 15" 85

Cardboard cut-outs, Coca-Cola premium, light cardboard w/printed design of a clown holding a bottle of Coca-Cola, box side shows various circus cut-outs for children, 1932, box 10 x 15" 200

Cereal box, Kellogg's Sugar Smacks, features Paul Jung or Lou Jacobs, famous Ringling clowns in full makeup, 1953, each box... 200-300

Cereal premium, Post Toasties Corn Flakes, a different circus figure in each box, included a ringmaster, monkey, elephant, weightlifter or Emmett Kelley clown, all associated w/the Ringling Bros. - Barnum & Bailey Circus, 17 different, 1956, each 5" h., each...................................... 15

Christmas greeting cards, from Ringling Bros. and Barnum & Bailey Circus, 1920s, each 20

The Shadow 1970s Comic Book

Comic book, "The Shadow - Who is ...The Freak Show Killer? - The Shadow Knows," DC Comics, Volume 1, No. 2, 1973-74 (ILLUS.)... 15

Cracker Jack prize, tin circus wagon, five different ones available, 1947, very rare, each.. 110

Display figures, Coca-Cola premiums, 3-D pieces featuring circus clowns, one shown carrying popcorn & a Coke, the other driving a train w/a cup of Coke shown & candy in the back, 1960s, each figure.. 50

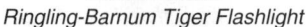

Ringling-Barnum Tiger Flashlight

Flashlight, Ringling Bros. and Barnum & Bailey, features a large tiger head at the end, when light is turned on, the reflector twirls, creating special effects, made in various years in different styles, 9 1/2" l. (ILLUS.).. 5

Game, board-type, "Game of the Day at the Circus," McLoughlin Bros., 1898, fine condition in original box.................................... 900

Magazine & program, Ringling Brothers and Barnum & Bailey Circus, cover w/black background & picture of a clown, interior photos, features & comics, 1948 40

Carnival-Fun Fair Poster

Menu, Ringling Brothers and Barnum & Bailey Combined Circus - 4th of July - The World's Largest Amusement Institution at Home on the Nation's Birthday, Bridgeport, Connecticut, 1920, 6 1/4 x 9 1/2" 30

Movie poster, "Charlie Chan at the Circus," starring Warner Oland, 20th Century, 1936, features a murder scene under the Big Top, one sheet, 27 x 41" 2,500

Movie poster, "The Circus," starring Charlie Chaplin, United Artists, 1928, one-sheet, Chaplin as the Little Tramp in front of circus tents, 27 x 41" 14,000

Pennant, felt, Hopalong Cassidy, navy blue w/white illustrations of Hoppy on his horse, his name in rope script & the name of the Cole Brothers Circus where he was appearing, very rare 150

Pennant, felt, "Roy Rogers Thrill Circus," shows Roy on a bucking bronco, late 1940s, l.. 110

Pinback button, "I Am A Lion Tamer in Mandel Brothers Circus," black, white, red & yellow, ca. 1930-40.................................. 20

Postcard, promoting the early TV show "Super Circus," shows six cast members including Claude Kirchner, Mary Hartline & clowns Cliffy, Nicky & Scampy, show ran 1949-1956, mid-1950s 50

Poster, amusement park, "Carnival and Fun Fair - 1,000 Smiles an Hour," various colorful action scenes including The Death Riders & The Ghost Train, 1930s, framed (ILLUS. bottom previous page) 300

Poster, "Clyde Beatty - Cole Circus," featuring scenes of the combined circus w/a large clown covering half the poster, 1950s, 14 x 21" 60

Poster, "Christianai-Wallace Brothers Circus," noted as the world's largest w/shows twice daily, features a bareback rider & clown, 1950, 36 x 40" 80

Poster, "Famous Cole 3 Ring Circus," four-color image featuring Captain Robert Grubb & his Kentucky horses, 1958, 28 x 44" 110

Poster, "Famous Cole 3 Ring Circus," four-color image featuring Miss Patti foot juggling giant dominos, 1958, 28 x 44"............. 100

Poster, "Famous Cole 3 Ring Circus," four-color images featuring the Ferrieras w/a handstand at the top of a perch pole, 28 x 44" 100

Canadian International Circus Poster

Poster, "George Carden Presents The Great Canadian International Circus," colorful vignettes of a clown & performing animals, schedule & charges at the bottom, 1995, 17 1/2 x 23 1/4" (ILLUS.)............... 15

Poster, "Gilmore Traveling Circus," a show sponsored by Gilmore Oil Company of California that left Los Angeles each spring & visited Gilmore gas stations, traveled in California, Oregon & Washington, scene of clowns & caged lions, 1930s.. 900

Poster, "Pinder Circus of Europe," featuring a clown in each corner w/a large tent in the center, 1950, 46 1/2 x 63 1/2"................. 800

Poster, "Ringling Brothers and Barnum & Bailey Circus," promoting 108th year w/color scenes of elephants, tigers, horses, etc., 28 x 40"... 125

Poster, "Ringling Brothers and Barnum & Bailey Circus," promoting 200 Years of Circus in America, color scene of elephant w/waving clown, 1975, 28 x 40".......... 125

Poster, "Robbins Brothers Circus," color scene of equestrienne flying threw a hoop on horseback, late 1940s-early 1950s, 28 x 44" 160

Poster, "Robbins Brothers Circus," four-color scene w/nine elephants in a pyramid in the foreground, London Bridge in the background, 28 x 44" 125

Poster, "Sells-Floto Circus featuring Tom Mix in Person and Tony - His Wonder Horse," scene of Tom & Tony w/mountains in the background, late 1930s............... 500

Poster, "Tom Mix Circus and Wild West Show," features Tom Mix & Tony & bucking broncos, a clown in the right corner holding a sign promoting the show, 1938...... 800

Poster, "Tom Mix Circus - Lions Field Tomorrow - Tom Mix and Tony in Person," black & white w/a description of the major attractions, 1938... 450

Program, Christiani Brothers Circus, 12 pp., 1960... 15

Garden Bros. Circus Program

Program, Garden Bros. Circus, color front cover art features Alvin & the Chipmunks in one corner w/clown, horse & ladies on an elephant, 58th Annual Edition, 10 x 13" (ILLUS.)... 20

Ringling Bros. 1974 Program

Program, Ringling Bros. and Barnum & Bailey Circus, colorful cover w/color photo of Gunther Gerbel-Williams in the center surrounded by colorful sunburst & other acts around the sides, 103rd Edition, 1974, 10 x 13" (ILLUS.) **40**

Shrine Circus Program for 1987

Program, Shrine Circus 1987 - Stoneroad Mall - Guelph (Ontario), large color comical clown juggling on the cover, Pepsi ad on the back, 44 pp. (ILLUS.) **10**

Program, Shrine Circus - Boston Gardens, cover scene of lady on camel, a band & two Shriners, 1956... **22**

The Moscow Circus-Canada Program

Program, The Moscow Circus - Canada - '87, large brown Russian bear in front of red star & tan & yellow stripes, Coca-Cola ad on the back cover, 8 1/2 x 11" (ILLUS.) **15**

Rattle, tin, flattened round top w/a colorful clown face, in yellow, red, blue & white, used to make noise during the circus show, 1940s (ILLUS. top right column)............ **10**

(Three) 3-D viewing glasses, to accompany the 3-D Polack Brothers Circus 3-D card set issued by Quaker Muffets cereal in 1953................. **10**

Tin Circus Noisemaker Rattle

Tom Mix circus ring, sold through his show, 1930s, rare... **150**

Toy, Kellogg's Sugar Smacks cereal premium, Paul Jung - Lou Jacobs cardboard shuttle toy, each clown displayed w/moveable hands, ca. 1953, each................. **50**

Magnetic Circus Toy

Toy, "Magnetic Circus," red & yellow metal board w/various metal figures including Stupo the Clown, Ringo the Hoop, Pinto the Pony, etc., package shows various animal acts, Smethport Specialty Company, Smethport, Pennsylvania, ca. 1920s, board 4 3/4 x 7 1/4", boxed set (ILLUS.)... **100**

Toy set, Britain's Circus, cast metal set including spectator stands, wooden circus ring, performers, ringmaster, etc., backdrop of a tent interior, limited edition of 3,000, the boxed set **600**

Toy set, Chipperfields Circus vehicles manufactured by Corgi of England, Booking Office Set No. 426, 1963-65, complete......... **950**

Toy set, Chipperfields Circus vehicles manufactured by Corgi of England,Giraffe Truck Set No. 503, 1966, complete **950**

Toy set, "Ringling Brothers and Barnum & Bailey Circus - Toy Circus," includes various circus acts including trapeze, high wire, wild animal & more, four acts per box, various sets, sealed in box , box 12 x 17" **100**

Toy set, "Ringling Brothers and Barnum & Bailey Circus - Toy Circus," includes various circus acts including trapeze, high wire, wild animal & more, four acts per box, various sets, sealed in rare tote box...... **400**

Toy set, "Super Circus Punchout Toys," Canada Dry Soda premium, included 10 sheets each w/an act or one of the main characters in the TV show, 1950, the mint set **200**

Toy vehicle, circus crane truck, from Chipperfields Circus sets by Corgi of England,
1960s... **225**

Toy vehicle, circus crane w/cage wagon,
from Chipperfields Circus sets by Corgi
of England, 1960s.. **400**

Toy vehicle, circus human cannonball
truck, from Chipperfields Circus sets by
Corgi of England, 1960s.............................. **100**

Toy vehicle, circus landrover & elephant
cage, from Chipperfields Circus sets by
Corgi of England, 1960s.............................. **275**

3-D Polack Circus Trading Cards

Trading cards, 3-D images from the Polack
Brothers Circus, issued by Quaker Muffets cereal, set of 16 cards & also separate 3-D viewing glasses, each card of
rust or blue color, a second set of 20
cards issued later the same year, 1953,
each card (ILLUS. of two)................................. **10**

CLOCKS

New Haven Clock Co. Banjo Clock

Banjo clock, New Haven Clock Company,
wood & brass, the round dial at the top
w/Arabic numerals & surmounted by a
spread-winged eagle finial, the narrow tapering tall throat flanked by long brass C-
scrolls & inset w/a reverse-painted glass
panel w/gilt scrolls over an eagle & American shield, the rectangular wood base
enclosing a reverse-painted glass panel
decorated in color w/two sailing ships
flanking an American eagle & shield, tapering base drop, late 19th - early 20th c.,
6 x 12", 40" h. (ILLUS.).............................. **$2,400**

English Victorian Bracket Clock

Bracket clock, Smith & Sons, Clerkenwell,
England, ebonized & bronze-mounted
case, an arched top pierced w/square
pediment surmounted by a flame finial &
small corner finials, over an arched
glazed panel door w/pierced bronzed
spandrels & opening to an arched silver
gilt dial w/Roman numerals, on a platform
molded base raised on scroll bronze feet,
fitted w/Whittington & Westminster
chimes, pendulum needs repair, ca.
1850, 9 x 14", 26" h. (ILLUS.)..................... **2,800**

Colonial Clock Grandfather Clock

Grandfather, Colonial Clock Company,
Neoclassical-style mahogany case, the
rectangular top w/a flaring cornice over a
carved dentil band above roundels &
reeded panels over carved bellflower
drops flanking the tall glazed door w/an
upper small panel over the white & brass
dial w/Arabic numerals & the lower panel
w/Gothic arch lattice, a bottom panel w/a
carved swag above small block feet,
original finish, ca. 1920s, 10 x 14", 64" h.
(ILLUS.).. **1,000**

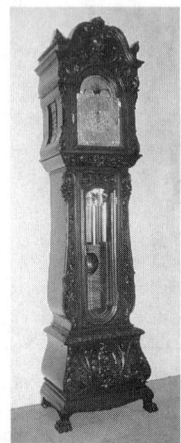

Exceptional Carved Oak Grandfather

Grandfather, Colonial Revival, carved oak, the very high broken-scroll pediment over a wide frieze boldly carved w/scrolls centering a lion mask above scrolled sides flanking the arched glazed door opening to a steel & brass dial w/moon phase & Arabic numerals, the tall body topped by a carved flaring cornice above an oblong door w/beveled glass flanked by serpentine sides w/front scroll carving, the stepped-out lower case w/a wide carved flaring band over a bombé section boldly carved on the front w/leafy scrolls, serpentine apron & bold front paw feet, original finish, Europe, ca. 1890, 16 x 22", 108" h. (ILLUS.) **20,000**

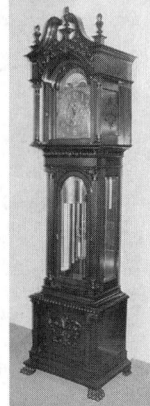

Beautiful Colonial Revival Grandfather

Grandfather, Colonial Revival, mahogany, the high broken-scroll pediment w/a raised central flame-turned finial w/matching corner finials above the ornate scroll-carved frieze above reeded columns flanking the set-back arched glazed door opening to a steel & brass dial w/ moon phase & Arabic numerals, pierced brass sides, the tall body topped

by a carved egg-and-dart band above the arched door w/beveled glass flanked by reeded columns, beveled glass side panels, the stepped-out lower case w/a gadrooned band above pilasters flanking an ornate scroll-carved panel, molded base on heavy paw front feet, nine-tube chiming movement, signed "Elite Germany," original finish, ca. 1885, 16 x 20", 100" h. (ILLUS.) **12,000**

Cherry Federal Grandfather Clock

Grandfather, Federal style, cherry case, arched scroll-carved crest on conforming molded cornice above the matching glazed door flanked by free-standing colonettes, opening to a white-painted dial w/Roman numerals & a painted moon phase, the narrow body of the case w/quarter-round columns at the sides flanking the narrow line-inlaid door, stepped-out lower case w/band inlay & a shaped apron & short French feet, old refinish, ca. 1810, 12 x 15", 86" h. (ILLUS.) **3,500**

English Inlaid Oak Grandfather Clock

Grandfather, Georgian, oak case w/banded inlay, the broken-scroll pediment centering a brass ball & eagle finial w/matching corner finials, a wide frieze above the arched glazed door opening to a painted dial w/moon phase, Roman numerals & painted figurals in corner, the door flanked by slender squared columns, the waisted body w/reeded pilasters flanking the cross-banded door, the stepped-out lower case w/banded inlay & raised on small bracket feet, wooden works, England, ca. 1800, refinished, 12 x 18", 84" h. (ILLUS.) **2,600**

Boldly Carved Oak Grandfather Clock

Grandfather, Georgian, oak, the broken-scroll pediment centered by a brass ball & eagle finials above a frieze band carved w/bold stylized leaves over the arched glazed door opening to the brass & filigree dial w/moon phase & Roman numerals all surrounded by a narrow carved gadrooned band flanked by slender colonettes & serpentined back side rails, the tall body w/quarter-round columns flanking the tall door w/carved gadroon bands enclosing a large stylized carving of a pot issuing a long flowering leafy vine, the stepped-out lower case carved at the front w/bold stylized leaves & flowers, short serpentine apron & tiny ogee feet, probably English, ca. 1830s, refinished, 12 x 16", 88" h. (ILLUS.) **3,300**

Oak English Grandfather Clock

Grandfather, Georgian, oak, broken-scroll pediment above a square glazed door opening to the white dial w/Roman numerals & painted spandrels, flanked by free-standing colonettes, the tall body w/a long solid door, tall stepped out lower section missing the footed base, old refinish, England, ca. 1820, 12 x 15", 80" h. (ILLUS.) **900**

Rare Joseph Taylor Grandfather Clock

Grandfather, Joseph Taylor, York, Pennsylvania, Chippendale style tiger stripe maple case, broken-scroll pediment w/an urn-form central urn & matching corner finials above an arched recess & glazed door flanked by slender colonettes, opening to a painted dial w/upper moon phrase in color, floral-painted spandrels & Arabic numerals, tall narrow body w/narrow paneled door, stepped-out base w/paneled front on small French feet, early 19th c. (ILLUS.) **30,250**

English Grandfather Clock

Grandfather, Marmaduke Storr, London, England, Georgian, figured mahogany case w/an arched & molded crest & frieze band over the conforming door opening to a painted dial w/Roman numerals, an upper moon dial w/engraved sun & globe

& applied castings in the spandrels painted grey, door flanked by small reeded quarter-round columns w/brass caps & bottom applied w/brass wire decoration a quarter of the way up from bottom, the tall narrow body w/a tall arched-top door flanked by similar columns, stepped-out base w/base molding & serpentine apron, 18th c., pieced restorations on hood & base ended out, pendulum needs repair & weights, missing winding key, 90" h. (ILLUS.).. **3,850**

Victorian English Grandfather Clock

Grandfather, Victorian Baroque-style, carved oak case w/a scrolled pediment centered by a turned knob finial above a leaf-carved frieze over an arched molding & conforming glass door flanked by colonettes, opening to the brass & silver dial w/scrolls & round plaque above dial w/Roman numerals & ornate scrolled spandrels, the tall body topped by a carved band of acanthus leaves over a tall narrow paneled door carved w/a lion mask at the top & bottom & swags & scrolls down the middle, leafy scroll vines down the sides, the stepped-out base w/a raised square panel carved w/leafy scrolls framing a small classical head, leafy scrolls around the edges, the molded base over a scalloped apron centered by a carved shell, England, ca. 1890, 14 1/2 x 23 1/2", 91" h. (ILLUS.) **1,792**

Fine French Bronze & Porcelain Set

Mantel garniture set, Louis XV Revival, gilt-bronze & porcelain, the tall upright gilt-bronze clock case cast w/ornate scrolls & swags & topped by a porcelain & bronze urn finial, the round porcelain dial w/Roman numerals centered by painted cupids above a lower porcelain plaque also painted w/cupids, on a pierced swag-footed base, w/a pair of five-light candelabra w/four upturned arms & a taller central shaft each ending in a candle socket above an urn-shaped porcelain & bronze shaft raised on an ornate scroll-cast footed base w/insert porcelain plaque, France, late 19th c., the set (ILLUS.) **1,500**

Shelf or mantel, Bishop & Bradley, Watertown, Connecticut, Federal, figured mahogany & églomisé pillar & scroll mantel clock w/three gold-tone urn finials, black Roman numerals on white face w/gold decoration in corners of dial, reverse-painted scene below dial of large & small buildings in wooded setting w/oversized sun, labeled, ca. 1810, 5 x 17", 32" h. **1,800**

Unique Sailor & Griffin Clock

Shelf or mantel, cast metal, figural, a standing sailor at a large ship's wheel enclosing the clock w/a copper bezel w/Arabic numerals around a domed glass dial, a large winged griffin on a scrolled banner below the sailor & wheel, gold finish, early 20th c., 10" w., 11" h. (ILLUS.)....... **159**

American Classical Double-decker

Shelf or mantel, Classical double-decker-style, mahogany, the high front cornice deeply carved w/acanthus leaves flanking a gilt S-scroll design flanked by carved gilt pineapple corner finials, the two-part case w/a square glazed upper door flanked by turned reeded & leaf-carved pilasters & opening to a white dial w/Roman numerals & gilt painted spandrels, the lower case w/a taller reverse-painted glazed door featuring an oval reserve w/a color bust portrait of George Washington surrounded by black & flanked by carved pilasters matching upper ones, flat base on carved paw feet, original finish, ca. 1830-40, 7 x 16", 36" h. (ILLUS.)... 900

Shelf or mantel, Classical style triple-decker, mahogany & mahogany veneer, the wide ogee cornice above a two-part glazed door opening to a painted dial w/Roman numerals above a lower reverse-painted glass pane decorated w/a white circle centering flowers & framed by black, the door flanked by bold half-round turned columns, the lower case w/a small glazed door flanked by ogee sides, refinished, ca. 1830, 8 x 18", 30" h. (ILLUS. center, below)......................... 450

Shelf or mantel, Eli Terry & Sons, Federal, pillar & scroll clock, mahogany veneer over pine, tapered legs & scalloped aprons w/freestanding pilasters, gold & black fan spandrels, wooden face w/gold scrolling & black numbers (repainted), lower part of door w/reverse-painted scene of white house w/five chimneys & blue roof, a river & sailboat at the right, brass finials are early two-piece castings, wooden works include weights & pendulum, early 19th c., 4 1/2 x 17 1/4", 29 1/4" h. (restorations, replacements)...... **1,650**

French Empire Rosewood Clock

Shelf or mantel, Empire style, rosewood upright case w/molded crown supported by four columns w/gilt-bronze bases & capitals, on a deep molded rectangular plinth on bun feet, large round brass dial w/scroll-stamped border & Roman numerals, large leaf-stamped pendulum bob, time & strike movement, France, ca. 1840, 7 x 11 1/2", 22" h. (ILLUS.).............. **1,120**

Shelf or mantel, Federal Revival style, inlaid mahogany case, the pointed arched case w/line inlay above the round glass door opening to the steel dial w/Arabic numerals above a lower line-inlaid panel centered by an inlaid classical paterae, deep molded base w/line inlay, original finish, ca. 1910, sold by Bailey, Banks & Biddle, Philadelphia, 7 x 11', 15" h. (ILLUS. right w/triple-decker clock, below) 400

Three Varied Mantel Clocks

Bronzed Metal Figural Lion Clock

Shelf or mantel, figural, bronzed metal, a large figural female lion w/a gilt-metal finish resting above a rockwork base inset w/a round clock w/an enameled porcelain dial w/Arabic numerals, all on a red marble rectangular platform w/small brass feet, France, late 19th c. (ILLUS.)................. 360

Shelf or mantel, French, green marble base w/white & red striations, ormolu paw feet & trim w/beveled glass door & enameled face, cast spelter cherub holds basket of fruit, includes key & pendulum, 18" h. (staff has broken tip) 275

Ornate Gilt-bronze & Enamel Clock

Shelf or mantel, gilt-bronze & enamel, an ornate rococo design w/a scrolling easel-form frame enclosing two porcelain panels h.p. w/18th c. courting scenes, the large lower panel centered by a small clock dial w/Roman numerals, France, late 19th - early 20th c., 4" w., 7 1/2" h. (ILLUS.).. **2,450**

Figural Gilt-bronze & Enamel Clock

Shelf or mantel, gilt-bronze & enamel, an ornate scrolled lower case on scroll feet enclosing an enameled panel showing a classical maiden & topped by a full-figure seated Victorian lady at the top right, a smaller scrolled case projecting from the top left & enclosing a smaller enameled panel centered by a small clock dial w/Roman numerals, France, late 19th - early 20th c., 3 1/2" w., 5 3/4" h. (ILLUS.).. **2,295**

Fine French Rococo-style Clock

Shelf or mantel, Japy Freres, France, Rococo-style, tortoiseshell & bronze doré case, flattened shield-shaped body w/shaped molded pediment & long bronze leafy scrolls down the sides & across the base, round brass & enameled dial w/Roman numerals, time & strike movement, on small scroll feet, late 19th c., 7 x 14", 23 1/2" h. (ILLUS.)............ **2,688**

French Rococo Gilt-metal Clock

Shelf or mantel, Rococo-style, gilded cast-metal case, upright rounded case w/a figural putto w/flowers at the top above a cartouche & slender scrolls down the sides framing the round porcelain dial w/Roman numerals, a porcelain panel in the lower case w/h.p. figural scenes, cast cartouche at apron continuing to incurved scroll feet, France, late 19th - early 20th c., 5 x 8", 16" h. (ILLUS.)..................... 450

L. & J.G. Stickley Mission Oak Clock

Shelf or mantel, Stickley (L. & J.G.) Mission Oak rectangular case, the front w/a paneled opening for the copper dial w/Arabic numerals above a small six-pane glazed panel & a simple knob, early 20th c. (ILLUS.) **9,200**

Shelf or mantel, Victorian temple-style, black marble case w/peaked pediment line-incised decor & mother-of-pearl inlay above a round dial w/open escapement & Roman numerals flanked by further inlay, wider platform base w/line-incised decor & central roundel, ca. 1880, 6 x 8", 10" h. (ILLUS. left with triple-decker clock) **400**

Rare Victorian Skeleton Clock

Skeleton clock, Blackhurst, England, brass, the round pierced dial w/flanges marked w/Roman numerals mounted in front of the open works framed by pierced scrolls & raised on tall flat scrolls above the stepped oval white marble base w/bun feet, ca. 1855 (ILLUS.) **3,740**

Rare Monumental Store Clock

Store floor clock, Victorian Renaissance style, walnut & burl walnut, the top stepped breakfront pediment above a conforming case, the central stepped-out section w/carved columns flanking a tall arched door glazed at the top over the round dial w/Roman numerals & w/four long raised burl panels below centering a roundel, the narrow setback side sections fitted w/long glass doors, one enclosing a thermometer measured in centigrade, the other w/a thermometer measured in fahrenheit, all on a conforming base w/a heavy molded band supported by four large carved seated winged lions on the deep platform base on compressed bun feet, possibly French, ca. 1880, original finish, 20 x 44", 99" h. (ILLUS.) **35,000**

Sessions Advertising Wall Clock

Wall clock, Sessions advertising-type, tall simple oak case w/flat cornice above a two-part glazed door framed w/reeded molding, the upper door opening to a white dial w/Roman numerals framed w/month numerals, the lower door w/gold reverse-painted advertising reading "Time To Buy - Calumet - Baking Powder - 'Best by Test,'" late 19th-early 20th c., 34" h. (ILLUS.) **690**

Frick Clock Co. Wall Regulator

Wall regulator, Fred. Frick Clock Co., Waynesboro, Pennsylvania, oak case, flat flaring stepped cornice above a long door w/arched glass panel opening to a round dial w/Roman numerals & seconds dial, stepped-out shelf support w/rounded & paneled front, late 19th - early 20th c. (ILLUS.)...................... **185**

Wall regulator, Jos. Stand, Zwittan, Switzerland, walnut case w/shell-carved pediment flanked by finials over stepped cornice, central glass door flanked by reeded engaged columns, tapered base flanked by drop finials & ending in a carved shell, three-train weight-driven chiming movement, enameled dial w/Roman numerals & signed by the maker, late 19th c., 52" h.......................... **1,265**

Victorian Eastlake Wall Regulator

Wall regulator, Victorian Eastlake style case, walnut, molded flat top w/blocked ears above molded sides w/slender colonettes flanking a tall arched glazed door opening to the round dial w/Roman numerals above the brass pendulum, line-incised & stepped-back bottom apron w/a row of knobs & scallop-cut rim, time & strike movement, original finish, ca. 1880, 8 x 15", 40" h. (ILLUS.)......................... **650**

CLOISONNÉ & RELATED WARES

Cloisonné comes from the French term cloison (cell). Standard cloisonné has a metal body covered with motifs made of wire cells filled with enamels.Standard Cloisonné: A sheet of metal is bent and hammered into the desired shape. An artist paints the design onto the metal. The wires are bent into shapes and placed on their edges to form partitions (cells) or cloisons. A layer of enamel (powdered glass) is sifted over the wires and gently fired to secure them in place. The cells are packed with enamel in powdered form. The colors of the fused enamel depends upon the mixture of natural minerals with the crushed glass. The cells are packed again and refired until the cells are filled to the top or reach the height of the wires. The piece is polished with stones of various coarseness and then with charcoal and finally powdered horn mixed with oil until the proper finish is obtained.

Chinese Cloisonné: Chinese cloisonne is termed Ching tai lan after the period in the Ming Dynasty in which it was developed. Pieces can have a gold, bronze, copper or brass body. There can be the presence of pitting. Ground coloring includes rust, black, ox blood, white, turquoise, green, etc. In addition to the prime motif there can be background designs of diapers (repetitive patterns). Objects include animals, figures, water pipes and snuff bottles as well as ornamental, occasional and functional wares. Chinese cloisonne can be marked with Reign Marks (period markings).

Japanese Cloisonné: The body of an object can be silver, brass, ceramic (pottery or porcelain), bronze, copper, papier-maché or lacquer. Japanese cloisonné can have fancy marks, artists signatures or seals. Enamels can be opaque, transparent or translucent. Designs are naturalistic and do not have to cover the entire piece. Objects include netsuke, belt buckles, tsuba, pins and inro as well as ornamental and functional wares. Japanese cloisonné, also termed Shippo Yaki, includes the following techniques: Yusen - wires; Musen - wireless; Yu Musen - wire and wireless; Shotai (plique-à-jour) - transparent enamels with the body etched away; Moriage (cameo) - a motif in relief; Totai - ceramic bodies; Ginbari - silver coin wrapped around a metal body having translucent or transparent enamel; Akasuk (Pigeon Blood) red. Saiyu: The design is embossed by pressing and hammering, and the enamel is applied on the raised parts.The term goldstone applies to the enamel, which has iron pyrite and/or copper filings added to it so that it glitters like gold. Fishscale simply refers to a repetitive motif that resembles the scales of a fish.Counter enameling is found on both Japanese and Chinese cloisonné. Usually used inside and/or on bases to counteract the expansion and contraction of the enamel and metal, it strengthens the body.Repoussé is relief formed by pressing or hammering a motif from the back.Basse Taille: A translucent enamel over metal, the metal having motifs in various heights of relief. This is produced by the Chinese and usually machine made.Champlevé: A technique in which the metal body is engraved, etched, stamped or chiseled with sunken designs, with enamels used to fill the depressions, leaving divisions in relief. It is void of wires.

Chinese

Basin, cloisonné, shallow, decorated w/red & yellow lotus blossoms & scrolls on a turquoise ground, late Ming dynasty, 9" d. **$3,000-5,000**

Bowl, enamel on copper, w/matching cover & underplate, dragons & flames on a blue ground, the interior of bowl & lid & underside of underplate pale green, Canton, 19th c., 4" d. **600-800**

Candlestick holder, cloisonné, a white enameled goose standing on a dish, the rim w/dragon scrolls, the underside w/petal forms & lappets, 20th c. in 18th c. style, 8" h. **800-1,200**

Clock, cloisonné & gilt metal, rectangular section, set between a domed top, tiered base, the cloisonné w/panels of flowers on a bright blue ground w/keyfret diaper, 19th c., 19" h. **2,500-4,500**

Dish, enamel on copper, Famille Rose, the center w/European subject of gentleman standing beside a seated lady in landscape within a border filled w/small repetitive diapers & reserves filled w/scenic vignettes, Canton, Qianlong, 10" d. **3,500-4,500**

Dish, enamel on copper, the interior w/scenic motif of figures in a garden, Famille Rose, the underside w/flowers & fruit, Canton, 18th c., 6" d. (chipping & scratches) **500-700**

Figure of Buddha, champlevé, seated in dhyanasana on double lotus throne, both hands in dhyanamudra, champlevé decorated robe, downcast face, elongated ears, hair in a usnisa, late 18th-early 19th c., 7" h. **1,200-1,800**

Jar, w/domed lid, cloisonné, decorated overall w/chrysanthemums & leaves on diapered ground of T pattern, 6" h. **150-200**

Jar, cov., cloisonné, dark green ground w/flowerheads in colors, marked "China," ca. 1935, 6 1/4" h. **100-150**

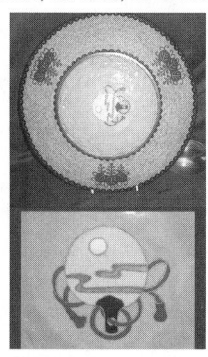

One of a Pair of Cloisonné Jars

Jars, cov., footed ball form, brown mica ground w/reserves in blue, decorated w/butterflies, phoenix & flowers, late 19th c., 4 1/2" d., 5" h., pr. (ILLUS. of one) **248**

Models of quails, cloisonné, each standing w/heads turned sideways, yellow enamel w/gilt wires, black markings, the back as detachable covers, the feet & beaks gilded, 18th c., 5" h., pr. **2,500-3,500**

Plaque, cloisonné, circular w/design of birds perched in blossoming prunus branches, framed, 19th c., frame size 28" x 28" **4,500-6,500**

Plaque, cloisonné, rectangular, scenic motif w/pagoda & boat, framed, frame size 14" x 10" **700-900**

Smoking set: ashtray, matchbox holder, cylindrical cigarette jar; cloisonné, diaper pattern on a black ground, ca. 1930, the set **150-200**

Vase, cloisonné, Meiping form, lotus & scrolls in red, green, white & yellow on a turquoise ground, dents, enamel missing, Ming dynasty, 11" h. **2,000-3,000**

Vase, cloisonné, Gu form, green lappets, white lotus on a blue ground, the foot w/lotus & scroll, 19th c., 12" h. **700-900**

Vase, cloisonné, Qianlong mark of the period, the body decorated w/wide bands of alternating phoenix, archaistic motif, turquoise ground & primary hues, the handles Taotie form, the tall waisted neck w/further bands, 25" h. **25,000-45,000**

Vases, tapered bulbous bodies, each decorated w/scenes of cranes & lotus flowers in vivid colors on blue ground, early 20th c., 10" d., 6" h., pr. **252**

Bowl, cloisonné, Japanese plique-a-jour, translucent enamels within silver wires w/flowers, chrome rim & foot, unsigned, 20th c., 4" d. **800-1,200**

Box, cov., cloisonné, hammered copper w/moriage peony blossoms, impressed Ando mark, early 20th c., 4" w. **2,000-3,000**

Japanese Box

Box, cov., interior gilding, signed "Inaba," early 20th c., slightly discolored, 3 1/2" (ILLUS.) **750-950**

Box, cover & tray, cloisonné, hammered copper w/moriage motifs of pomegranates & foliage, impressed Ando mark, early 20th c., 6" w. **2,500-3,800**

Censer, cov., cloisonné, midnight blue ground, spherical form decorated overall w/cranes in flight, the lid w/lappet border, bud form finial, ca. 1900, 6" h. **400-650**

Censer, cov., cloisonné, tripod form, black ground, extended handles, alternating shields of phoenix & dragon, w/floral borders above & below, on three straight legs, ca. 1910, 4 3/4" h. **800-1,200**

Charger, cloisonné, bird & flowers on a turquoise ground, ca. 1900, 12" d. **200-300**

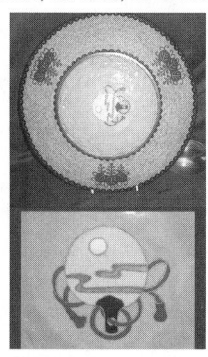

Japanese Charger with Mallet

Charger, cloisonné, light background w/groups of stylized florals, the center of the bottom decorated w/an interesting large "Daikoku's mallet" design, Meiji period (1868-1912), 12" d. (ILLUS. of bottom) **1,000-1,500**

Japanese Lobed Charger

Charger, the interior w/three scrolled & shaped reserves each decorated w/scenes of birds or flowers, diapered & blossom ground w/a dark border band of scalloped lobed designs, fair amount of wear & some wire corrosion where the gilt is worn off, late 19th c., 12 d. (ILLUS.).. **400-500**

Charger, cloisonné, three birds in flight above flowering branches, black ground, ca. 1910, 12 1/2" d.................... **250-375**

Japanese Four-lobed Charger

Charger, cloisonné, wide four-lobed form, the whole interior decorated w/a large flowering bush & small flying birds, narrow border band, bit of enamel missing inside foot rim, probably fired that way, Meiji period, 12 x 16" (ILLUS.).......... **1,200-1,800**

Japanese Charger with Cranes

Charger, cloisonné, flying cranes motif, gilt wires, fine condition, Meiji period, 17" d., minor pitting & color flaws (ILLUS.). **1,500-1,800**

Jar, cloisonné, in the style of Namikawa Yasuyuki, copper & silver wires, two cream colored panels filled w/insects & foliated branches, the shoulder & sides w/floral bands, early 20th c., 6" h. (cover missing) **1,500-2,500**

Table lamp, cloisonné, tall, vase form w/deep blue, green, burgundy, black & mauve design of birds & flowers, goldstone, 34" h. to harp finial **248**

Table Screen with Garden Design

Table screen, cloisonné, four-panel w/a continuous garden design of large flowering shrubs & small flying birds against a dark background, silver wires, impressed Inaba mark on back, 20th c., 8" h. (ILLUS.) **3,000-4,500**

Vase, cloisonné, beaker form, green w/narcissus, the interior green, Ando mark on foot rim, post- WWII (noted damage dings).. **250-500**

Vase, cloisonné, beaker form, red, white & pink orchids, the interior red, the foot rim marked "Ando," post-WWII **500-750**

Japanese Flying Cranes Vase

Vase, cloisonné, blue ground w/flying cranes, the wires w/five different thicknesses, some tapered, brass mounts, early 20th c., some pitting, minor chip, 4 1/2" (ILLUS.) **700-950**

Vase, cloisonné, ovoid form, copper wires, the ground alternating from oxblood to pale brown in vertical bands filled w/insects, early 20th c., 4 3/4"...................... **600-900**

Vase, cloisonné, Yu Musen, pink ground, the base surrounded w/white heron, early 20th c., 5" h. (damaged)...................... **400-600**

Vase, cloisonné, Akasuke (red) on silver foil stippled w/motif of bird & branch, silver wires w/motifs of white roses & green foliage, the rim marked "Ando," post-WWII, 6" h. **300-500**

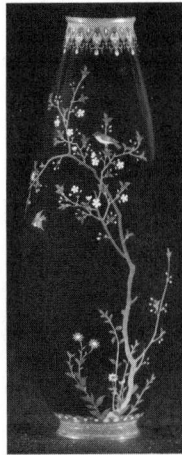

Japanese Floral & Bird Vase

Vase, cloisonné, brass rims, silver wires, deep blue ground w/motif of birds & flowers in the manner of Hayashi, late Meiji period, 6 h. (ILLUS.) **1,000-1,500**

Vase, cloisonné, gilt wires, very fine motif of polychrome hydrangea & foliage, signed "Adachi," some pitting, brass mounts, early 20th c., 6" h. **750-1,000**

Vase, cloisonné, ginbari, silver mounts, short neck, ovoid body decorated w/gold fish, base signed "Kawaguchi," late Meiji period, 6" h. (cracks & oxidation to silver).. **300-450**

Vase, cloisonné, ovoid form w/waisted neck & everted rim, opaque & translucent enamels w/archaistically shaped panels filled w/birds above lappets, signed "Ando," early 20th c., 6 3/4" h. **1,800-2,500**

Vase, cloisonné, ovoid form w/blossoming flowers & birds on branches, silver wires, black ground, unsigned, ca. 1900, 8" h.. **1,500-2,200**

Vase, cloisonné, style of Ando, shouldered ovoid form, green ground decorated w/three carp, wire & wireless, silver mounts, early 20th c., 8 3/4" h......... **1,000-1,500**

Japanese Vase with Flowers

Vase, cloisonné, the motif w/gilt wires of various thickness, copper rings for flowers, marked "Ando" & "Jungin" ("silver" in Japanese), 9 1/2" h. (ILLUS.) **2,000-3,000**

Vase, champlevé, motif of blossoms & foliage in band around the center, base marked, ca. 1930, 10" h. **75-125**

Vase, cloisonné, ovoid form tapering toward the base, pale muted shaded blue ground decorated w/sparrow & paper whites w/long leaves, wire & wireless, the rim & base silver, signed "Namikawa Sosuke," Meiji period, 10 1/2" h. (minor star crack)... **15,000-25,000**

Vase, cloisonné, ovoid form w/flared rim, the body w/color enamels on a pale blue ground, birds flying above a lakescape, silver rims, signed "Ota," early 20th c., 10 3/4".. **3,000-5,000**

Vase, champlevé, three bands of flowers & scrolls in red, blue & green, mounted as a lamp, 14" h. **100-175**

Vases, cloisonné, gilt, silver & brass wires, wide footed ovoid form w/a wide shoulder & rolled neck, decorated overall w/delicate flowering prunus blossoms & limbs on a dark ground, the foot rim stamped "Jungin" ("silver") & a Hayashi silver wire mark in base, Hayashi Kodenji mark in silver wires, impressed gin mark on foot rim, late Meiji period, mirror images, 3 1/2 h., pr. **4,500-6,500**

CLOTHING

Sleeveless Evening Dress

Evening dress, pale pink satin sleeveless dress, bloused bodice w/metallic lace underbodice, dropped waistline w/sash that falls to back, diamantes in starburst pattern on sides of bodice, flying panel back, labeled "F Worth" at waistband, House of Worth, 1924 (ILLUS.) **$1,265**

Bes Ben Flower Hat

Hat, fitted hat composed of green plastic leaves & white flowers, labeled "Bes Ben - Made in Chicago" & "208" on underside, 1940s (ILLUS.) **230**

Orange Beaded Mini-dress

Mini-dress, orange silk Charmeuse A-line sleeveless dress w/round neckline, Native American-inspired multi-colored embroidery at neckline, armholes & hem, beading of faux blue & green gems, gold bugle beads, faux pearls & silver, blue, gold & turquoise appliqué, labeled "Sara Fredericks" at neckline, 1960s (ILLUS.) **230**

Rare Silk Mandarin Imperial Robe

Robe, embroidered silk Mandarin imperial court robe, w/five claw dragons in gold & silver thread, clouds & bats on a bronze ground, sleeves dark blue w/smaller matching dragons, rare, 46 3/4" l. (ILLUS.) **2,750**

House of Worth Pale Pink Tea Gown

Tea gown, pink satin floor-length gown w/pink net, faux pearl & diamante embellishment, empire-waist bodice w/flesh-colored net at bust & shoulders, pink net hanging sleeves weighted w/three crystal seed bead tassels, skirt w/falling train at back hem, off center, terminating in large seed bead tassel, House of Worth, 1914 (ILLUS.) **978**

COCA-COLA ITEMS

Coca-Cola promotion has been achieved through the issuance of scores of small objects through the years. These, together with trays, signs and other articles bearing the name of this soft drink, are now sought by many collectors. The major reference in this field is Petretti's Coca-Cola Collectibles Price Guide, 10th Edition, by Allan Petretti (Antique Trader Books). An asterisk (*) indicates a piece which has been reproduced.

Coca-Cola Backbar Display

Backbar display, banner-type, w/five connected pictures of women drinking Coke, each in an ornate white/grey border, w/Coca-Cola logo on top & "... add Zest to the hour" in banner at bottom (ILLUS.) **$1,850**

Barrel-shaped Coca-Cola Pottery Bank

Bank, pottery, barrel-shaped, red w/white embossed wording, Haeger Pottery (ILLUS.) **225**

Vintage Coca-Cola Six-pack Carrier

Bottle carrier, "Season's Greetings - Drink Coca-Cola," cardboard six-pack carrier, red bands w/white wording alternating w/white bands of holly sprigs against white, ca. 1930s, unused, 7 1/4 x 13" (ILLUS.) **121**

Coca-Cola Bottle-shaped Opener

Bottle opener, bottle-shaped metal w/ribbing & name on one side & a red fired-on round logo on the other side, some scratches & soiling, 8" l. (ILLUS. of two sides) **61**

Carton insert, "Serve Coca-Cola - Stock up for the Holidays," die-cut cardboard w/a colorful image of Santa Claus holding a bottle of Coke in front of the round logo & above a white card & a six-pack of Coca-Cola, dated 1952, unused, 12 1/2 x 21 1/2" **55**

Coca-Cola Cooler

Cooler, ice-chest type, w/"Drink Coca-Cola" on side, 1939 salesman sample (ILLUS.).. **4,400**

Coca-Cola Buddy Lee Doll

Doll, hard plastic head w/stiff neck, painted eyes to side, single-stroke brows, painted upper lashes, closed smiling mouth, molded & painted hair, body jointed at shoulders only, molded & painted black boots, dressed in original Coca-Cola uniform w/hat, "Buddy Lee" on back, "Union Made - Lee - Sanforized" on tag on pants, 12" h., light rub, some deterioration to fabric (ILLUS.) **650**

Coca-Cola Verbena Festoon

Festoon, yellow verbena garlands surround picture of woman drinking Coke in center & "Drink Coca-Cola - Delicious and Refreshing" in white on green-bordered red boxes at center & each end (ILLUS.) **3,250**

Coca-Cola Attendant's Hat

Hat, "Coca-Cola," cloth attendant's hat, green w/red stripe & logo on both sides, minor wear & soiling, tag inside reads "Made by Bone-Crow Co., Waco, Texas" (ILLUS.) **61**

Coca-Cola Menu Board

Menu board, rectangular, black w/white border, "Drink Coca-Cola" in red panel at top, "Delicious and Refreshing" in yellow at bottom w/silhouette of woman drinking from bottle of Coke in yellow circle at bottom right & "5¢" in yellow circle at right just under top panel (ILLUS.) **300**

Coca-Cola Santa Display Insert Sign

Sign, cardboard display insert-type, full-figure color image of a smiling Santa Claus against a gold background, w/hanging tree ornaments, one in red printed in white "Serve Coca-Cola in Bottles," dark blue wording reads "Good taste for all - Take enough home," figure of Santa continues into bottom tabs, dated 1954, new unused condition, colorful, 12 x 20" (ILLUS.) **44**

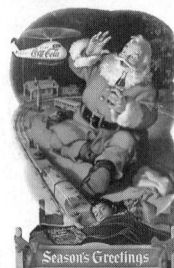

Classic Coca-Cola Santa Sign

Sign, die-cut cardboard, a tall colorful scene of Santa Claus seated among toys above the head of a sleeping boy in bed, "Season's Greetings" in red & white across the end of the bed, dated 1962, light overall edge wear, light crease at left edge, minor wear w/scattered spotting, 31 1/2 x 49" (ILLUS.) **440**

Coca-Cola Santa Die-cut Sign

Sign, die-cut counter-top cardboard style, a standing figure of Santa Claus holding a bottle of Coke in one hand & reading a letter, a big sack of letters in front w/a large red dot Coca-Cola logo button over a gold banner reading "Greetings," dated 1945, few scuffs, 8 1/2 x 14" (ILLUS.) **413**

Scarce Coca-Cola Arrow Sign

Sign, die-cut double-sided tin arrow, shaft in white w/large Coca-Cola logo in white, black tail & tip w/white wording reading "Ice Cold - Sold Here," dated 1929, nicks, scratches & overall flecks, 7 11/16 x 29 7/8" (ILLUS.) **1,045**

Large Framed Coca-Cola Sign

Sign, double-sided porcelain in original iron frame w/hooks, rectangular, w/a green band w/gold wording at top reading "Fountain Service" above red ground section w/white wording reading "Drink Coca-Cola - Delicious and Refreshing," ca. 1930s, some light scratches & small chips, one hanger pulled away, 42 x 60 1/4" (ILLUS.) **2,530**

Hanging Coca-Cola Two-sided Sign

Sign, double-sided porcelain, square w/rounded corners & original factory hanging hooks at the top, color image of a large red, white & steel grey stairstep-shaped soda dispenser, dated 1939, minor edge chips, small hole at bottom center, few tiny edge chips & scattered scratches, 25 1/4 x 26 1/4" (ILLUS.) **1,430**

Embossed Tin Coca-Cola Script Sign

Sign, embossed tin, narrow rectangular form, a dark green border band & thin yellow band around a dark red ground w/white wording reading "Drink Coca-Cola," very minor scattered nicks & scratches, few bends at top, 5 3/4 x 17 3/4" (ILLUS.) **358**

Sign, round embossed tin, narrow green & yellow border bands around the red ground printed in large yellow & white wording "Ice Cold - Coca-Cola - Sold Here," dated 1933, 19 5/8" d. (two light creases at bottom, small chip & few tiny nicks) **440**

Sign, "the gift for thirst," a color poster w/a large bust portrait of Santa Claus at the left holding a bottle of Coke, children w/Christmas gifts on the right below the Coca-Cola logo, all on a dark background, dated 1952, 10 1/2 x 23" **44**

Authorized Repro Syrup Dispenser

Syrup dispenser, authorized 1970s reproduction of soda fountain syrup dispenser in cream w/gold detail & "Coca-Cola" in red on front (ILLUS.) **1,000**

1935 Coke Tray

Tray, rectangular w/raised rim w/rolled edge, "Drink Coca-Cola" in top & bottom borders, center w/picture of woman in evening dress holding glass of Coca-Cola, 1935 (ILLUS.) **440**

Coca-Cola Vending Machine

Vending machine, 10-cent Coca-Cola vending machine in red w/ "Drink Coca-Cola" & "Ice Cold" in white lettering, 1945 (ILLUS.) **1,125**

Restored Model 72 Vending Machine

Vending machine, Model 72 upright machine, tall w/rounded top corners, dark red w/white wording across the top & colored pictures of a hand holding a bottle on each side, double-chute type, dime operation, meticulously restored, 16 x 25", 58" h. (ILLUS.) **1,045**

Model 81A Coke Vending Machine

Vending machine, Model 81A machine, tall upright form w/rounded top, dark red w/small white wording across the top, long narrow dispensing door on the left side, dime operation, slot mechanism on the right, professionally restored, works, 18 x 27 1/4", 58 1/2" h. (ILLUS.) **3,471**

COLD WAR COLLECTIBLES

Many Americans came of age during the years of the Cold War which started shortly after World War II and suddenly came to an end in the late 1980s. The fall of the Iron Curtain in Eastern Europe and the breakup of the Soviet Union ushered in a new era in world history. Now mementos from the troubled period in the 20th century will become increasingly collectible.

Advertisement, Bell Telephone System, "Defense is on the Lines," full-page black & white ad that ran in the March 22, 1952 issue of Collier's, features Civil Defense members in action **$25**

Advertisement, U.S. Steel, "Building Bridges More Quickly for the Army in These Times," black & white ad covering continued preparations during the Korean War, ran in March 22, 1952 issue of Collier's **25**

Aircraft model, "Famous Jets" series, cardboard cut-outs from Kellogg's Rice Krispies boxes, assembled into various planes, 1955, each model **15**

"Your Basement Fallout Shelter" Book

Book, "Your Basement Fallout Shelter," part of the Civil Defense Books series, detailed construction diagram & information on filling the shelter, 1955, 36 pp., 5 1/4 x 8" (ILLUS.) **20**

Card set, "Freedom's War," color scenes from World War II & the Korean War, Topps, early 1950s, 203 cards in the set, each card 2 1/16 x 2 5/8", the set **450**

Civil Defense helmet, rounded brim, off-white w/CD insignia on front, 1950s, 10 1/2 x 12 1/2" **25**

Comic book, "All Capp's Li'l Abner Joins the Navy," color w/Li'l Abner & Daisy Mae on the cover, recruitment book for the U.S. Navy during the Korean War, Toby Press, 1951 .... **125**

Commander Battle Comic Book

Comic book, "Commander Battle Atomic Sub," American Comics Group #2, action color cover scene, 1954 (ILLUS.) **80**

Design for Survival Comic Book

Comic book, "Design for Survival (General Thomas S. Power's)," color cover art of B-58 carrying a nuclear bomb w/jet fighter support, American Security Press Council, only one edition issued, 1968 (ILLUS.) **25**

Comic book, "The Truth Behind the Trial," by Cardinal Mindszenty, fact-based account of the trial & imprisonment of the Cardinal in Hungary by the Communists, later made into a movie, 1949, Catechetical Guild Education Society **35**

Toy Dollhouse with Bomb Shelter

Dollhouse, part of a Marx Playset, printed tin house w/a bomb shelter replacing the garage, 1960 (ILLUS.) **200**

Popular Science with Polar Cars

Magazine, "Popular Science," August 1947, cover story "Polar Prowl Cars," feature on these vehicles as well as a story on germ warfare & one on a new medium range bomber (ILLUS.) **10**

Popular Science Uranium Issue

Magazine, "Popular Science," August 1954, cover story "Finding Fortunes in Uranium," cover features a miner on a small mine train w/cars in a uranium mine (ILLUS.) **10**

Model, "Atomic Submarine," cardboard cut-out from Cheerios cereal boxes, fires torpedo at enemy ships, box art features boy playing in water w/a torpedo being fired from the submarine, 1958, 12" l. **60**

Model kit, "Air Force Patrol," Monogram Model Company, kit No. MGP 7, includes B-66 dropping nuclear weapon, colorful artwork on box, 1960, mint **150**

Model kit, "Strategic Air Command," Revell, features various aircraft, mint in unopened box **200**

Model set, "Military Airbase," cardboard cut-outs from Cheerios cereal boxes, included various buildings, a missile defense station w/small spring-firing missiles & a radar building, overall 30" l., 1958, complete set **175**

Movie poster, "Failsafe," starring Henry Fonda, Columbia, 1964, one-sheet, 27 x 41" **35**

Movie poster, "Hell and High Water," starring Richard Widmark, 20th Century, 1954, one-sheet, 24 x 41" **30**

Movie poster, "I Married a Communist," starring Robert Ryan & Lorraine Day, RKO, 1949, one-sheet, 27 x 41" **85**

Movie poster, "Invasion USA," starring Gerald Mohr & Peggie Castle, Columbia, 1952, one-sheet, 27 x 41" **80**

Movie poster, "Panic in the Year Zero," starring Ray Milland & Frankie Avalon, AIP, 1962, one-sheet, 27 x 41" **45**

Movie poster, "Strategic Air Command," Paramount, 1954, starring Jimmy Stewart & June Allyson, one-sheet, 27 x 41" **100**

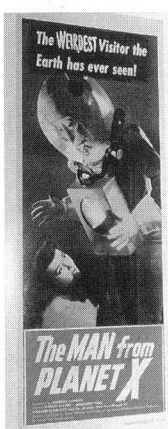

"The Man From Planet X" Poster

Movie poster, "The Man From Planet X," United Artists, 1951, starring Robert Clarke & Raymond Bond, one-sheet, 27 x 41" (ILLUS.) **3,000**

Movie shorts, color or black & white, includes "American Cities Atomic Fallout Strategy," "You Can Beat the Atomic Bomb," "The Medical Effects of Radiation," "A New Look at the H-Bomb," & "Your U.S. Civil Defense in Action," each....... **30**

Phonograph record, "If the Bomb Falls," Tops Records, side one "What to do in Case of a Nuclear Attack," side two "Supplies Needed for Several People," rare, 1962... **125**

Phonograph record, "Inside a Communist Cell," Karl Prussion, Key Records, Los Angeles, contains stories & songs such as "Is Communism Political?" & "The Soup of Subversion," 33 1/3 rpm, 1961........ **100**

Phonograph record, "The Complacent Americans," CEE-DEE Records, Los Angeles, includes 38 authentic sound effects including a H-bomb blast, 33 1/3 rpm, rare, 1961 .... **100**

Pinback button, "Retire J. Edgar Hoover," metal, orange & yellow w/picture of Hoover, late 1960s... **12**

Pinback button, "Vietnam - March 26 Mass Protest 1966," lime green & dark blue, issued by the Vietnam Peace Parade Committee **8**

Playset, Marx No. 4802, "The Distant Early Warning System and Satellite Base (Dew Line)," one of several sets from Marx that featured buildings, furniture, figures, this one w/a bookcase labeled "Store Atomic Bombs Here," rare, the complete set **650**

Playset, Marx No. 6013, "Strategic Air Command," includes buildings, furniture, radar trailers, anti-aircraft guns & various planes, late 1950s, rare, the set **800**

Political button, "Goldwater for President," metal, photo in center, 1964 campaign, 6" d. **30**

Political button, "LSD - Not LBJ," metal, lime green on dark green, 1968 presidential campaign **20**

Postcard Folder of Oak Ridge

Postcard folder, "Oak Ridge, Tennessee - Home of the Atomic Bomb," printed in color w/all the major buildings shown, cover features a nuclear mushroom cloud in the background, 1950 (ILLUS.) **100**

Poster, "Radioactive Fallout - You Can Protect Yourself - Get the Facts from your Civil Defense Director," shows a city attacked by a nuclear bomb, Civil Defense logo in the corner **45**

Puzzle, skill-type, tin box-form, "Drop the Atomic Bomb on Japan," printed in black & orange w/bomb heading towards Japan, small metal balls fit into holes representing Japanese cities, A.C. Gilbert Company, 1946 .... **400**

Sign, Civil Defense, either "Attack Warning - What to Do" or "Attention - Alert Signal -

What to Do," each large colorful sign shows sound waves to indicate an air raid siren going off, 1950s-60s, each **40**

Sign, "Sign of Protection - Your Community in Action - Moving water, food, medicines into shelters," shows people moving supplies into public shelters, large size for posting in public buildings & workplaces, 1950s **75**

Sign, "Support the National Fallout Shelter Program - Your Sign of Community Protection," shows various city scenes including homes & schools, large size, 1960 .... **30**

Defenders of America Cards

Trading cards, "Defenders of America," set featuring missiles & aircraft of the Cold War era, issued by Popsicle Ice Cream, 1959, each card (ILLUS. of two) **10**

Trading cards, "Fight the Red Menace or Children's Crusade Against Communism," color images of attacking Communists & atomic war scenes, Bowman, 1951, set of 48, each card 2 1/2 x 3 1/8", each card **25**

Atomic Train Set Advertisement

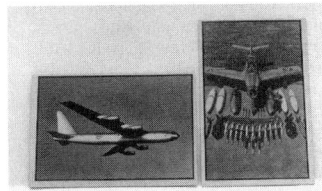

Power for Peace Trading Cards

Trading cards, "Power for Peace," color images of various military weapons, aircrafts & soldiers w/some showing atomic bomb blasts, each card 2 1/2 x 3 1/4", 96 in the set, complete set (ILLUS. of part) **300**

Wings Trading Card of Russian MIG

Trading cards, "Wings," color images of military & civilian planes of the 1950s, Topps, each card 2 1/2 x 3 3/4", the set (ILLUS. of one)... **550**

Train set, "Atomic Train," includes engine, three cars including an atomic cannon car, & caboose, by Kusan-Auburn Company, Nashville, Tennessee, 1950s, complete mint set (ILLUS. of advertisement previous page) **500**

Video cassette, "Duck and Cover," shows actions to take during atomic attack, also includes other propaganda material of the 1950s **25**

COMPACTS & VANITY CASES

A lady's powder compact is a small portable cosmetic make-up box that contains powder, a mirror and puff. Eventually, the more elaborate compact, the "vanity case," evolved, containing a mirror, puffs and compartments for powder, rouge and/or lipstick. Compacts made prior to the 1960s when women opted for the "au natural" look are considered vintage. These vintage compacts were made in a variety of shapes, sizes, combinations, styles and in every conceivable natural or man-made material. Figural, enamel, premium, commemorative, patriotic, Art Deco and souvenir compacts were designed as a reflection of the times and are very desirable. The vintage compacts that are multipurpose, combined with another accessory—the compact/watch, compact/music box, compact/fan, compact/purse, compact/perfumer, compact/lighter, compact/cane, compact/hatpin—are but a few of the combination compacts that are not only sought after by the compact collector but also appeal to collectors of the secondary accessory.

Today vintage compacts and vanity cases are very desirable collectibles. There are compacts and vanities

to suit every taste and purse. The "old" compacts are the "new" collectibles. Compacts have come into their own as collectibles. They are listed as a separate category in price guides, sold in prestigious auction houses, displayed in museums, and several books and many articles on the collectible compact have been written. There is also a newsletter, Powder Puff, written by and for compact collectors. The beauty and intricate workmanship of the vintage compacts make them works of fantasy and art in miniature.

For additional information on the history and values of compacts and vanity cases, readers should consult Vintage and Vogue Ladies' Compacts *by Roselyn Gerson, Collector Books, KY.*

Black compact, round, designed to resemble a record, complete w/grooves & red center label which reads "Melody, J.D. Creation," interior reveals beveled mirror, puff & powder well. Also available w/blue, green or cream-colored center labels. Made for the international market. Available in the U.S. under the Columbia Records name label **$225**

Brushed goldtone, miniature, unusual bolster-shaped compact set on two moving wheels, rhinestones centered on wheels, complete w/steering post, interior reveals beveled mirror, sifter & puff............................. **250**

Goldtone Compact with Wrist Cuff

Brushed goldtone, round compact, lid decorated w/polished goldtone stars, black silk carrying wrist cuff, reverse side of cuff has snap-shut miniature pocket for money, complete w/black tassel, interior reveals mirror & powder well (ILLUS.) **225**

Brushed goldtone, round, jeweled powder compact, lid set w/round mobe pearl framed by pronged, faceted turquoise stones, twist closure, Germaine Monteil......... **45**

Volupte Compact

Brushed goldtone, square compact w/penny centered on lid, Volupte (ILLUS.) **60**

"Tennis Ball" Compact

Brushed goldtone, "Tennis Ball" compact, lid decorated w/crystal seams & tennis racket charm, Estee Lauder (ILLUS.)............ **125**

Brushed silvertone, round, "Odyssey" compact, lid beautifully decorated w/pastel-colored crystals, interior reveals mirror, puff & pressed powder well, Nieman Marcus exclusive, Debbie J. Palmer................ **60**

Celluloid, round, black, compact lid decorated w/a beautiful Art Deco woman's face, hand-engraved & hand-painted, Antonin of France **150**

Crystal-studded, round, "Stained Glass Window," lid beautifully decorated w/red, pink, white, blue, green & light blue crystal design, interior reveals framed mirror, powder compartment & puff, marked "Stratton England" for Katherine Baumann **325**

Enameled, oblong, blue enamel Bicycle design compact made to resemble a deck of cards, reverse side shows an Ace of Hearts, interior contains framed mirror, puff & powder well **175**

Baseball-shaped Compact

Enameled, round, white enameled powder compact designed to resemble a baseball complete w/red enamel stitching (ILLUS.).. **275**

Enameled compact/bracelet cuff, round, red enamel "A Century of Progress, 1934," silvertone disc centered on lid, silvertone cuff bracelet, interior reveals metal mirror, puff & swivel powder well......... **175**

Enameled compact/perfume combination, oval, black enamel compact suspended by two ornate filigree chains from a finger ring, lid centered w/oval floral silver disc, silver perfume screw-top, gilt interior w/powder compartment, mirror framed in gilt braid, Austria **375**

Goldtone, miniature compact/chair, coin decorates top lid, cabriole legs, interior reveals beveled mirror, puff & sifter, signed "Robert Original" **450**

Goldtone, oblong, ribbed "Golden Envelope" compact, interior contains framed mirror, powder well & puff, Estee Lauder **55**

Goldtone, petit point crescent-shaped vanity case w/powder & rouge compartments & sliding lipstick **150**

Antique Compact/Pendant

Goldtone, round, antique compact/pendant decorated w/scrollwork, turquoise stones & pearls, complete w/matching chain, France (ILLUS.)... **275**

Goldtone, round compact, blue iridescent enamel lid decorated w/two white swans, interior reveals framed mirror, powder well, sifter & puff. Label on mirror reads "To open inner door, press mirror lid gently back, door swings open. To shut, bring mirror lid forward and press door down," Stratton... **65**

Watch Fob Style Compact

Goldtone, round, watch fob style powder compact, lid & fob imprinted w/red & black enamel "I love you" sentiments in English, French & Spanish, enameled angels w/bow & arrow, red band connects fob & compact (ILLUS.) **175**

Goldtone, shaped as hand mirror w/green enamel decorated lid, interior & exterior mirrors, France **125**

Goldtone, square compact & matching lipstick in slipcase, lid of compact & top of lipstick decorated w/little birds & pearls, Flato **110**

Simplicity Pattern Book Cover Compact

Goldtone, square "Simplicity Pattern" powder compact, "Simplicity" printed in goldtone on powder puff, lid decorated w/colorful replica of a Simplicity pattern book cover, Wadsworth (ILLUS.) **275**

"Grand Piano" Compact

Goldtone & black enamel, "Grand Piano" compact, highlighted w/crystals, Estee Lauder (ILLUS.) **150**

Goldtone & black matte enamel, compact/music box, slide-out lipstick, lid designed as piano keyboard **150**

Goldtone & blue enamel compact, lid w/heart-shaped enamel flower, Kigu, England **75**

Goldtone compact/bracelet, square compact centered on a flexible mesh bracelet, lid of compact decorated w/a filigree flower **250**

Goldtone Trinity Plate, two-sided vanity, lids & rim decorated w/filigree overlay enhanced w/cabochon & faceted blue & green colored stones, one side opens to reveal mirror & powder well, other side reveals pocket w/pull string powder puff, black tassel & carrying cord **500**

Green enameled vanity, lid decorated w/enameled basket of flowers, interior reveals beveled mirror, powder compartment & two coin holders, complete w/goldtone carrying chain **350**

Marbleized composition compact/bracelet, round, white, lid decorated w/circle of red faceted stones, adjustable black grosgrain band **175**

Mother-of-pearl, stylized checkerboard compact designed to resemble a book **75**

Plastic composition, brown, compact lids decorated w/embossed textured cranes, interior reveals mirror & powder well, carrying cord, tassel **325**

Estee Lauder Compact

Polished goldtone, round, compact lid centered w/a silvertone disc w/a raised Roman profile, replica of an ancient Roman coin, Estee Lauder (ILLUS.) **175**

Polished goldtone compact, earrings & pin set, stylized heart-shaped compact, lid centered w/applied heart enhanced w/red stones, matching earrings & pin, Elgin American **175**

Silvertone, heart-shaped compact, souvenir of Washington, DC, polished goldtone DC attractions on lid **40**

Silvertone, oblong, compact/pendant, cutoff corners, white enamel lid decorated w/black silhouette of a period lady, back opens to reveal metal mirror & powder well, complete w/chain **125**

Silvertone, round, centered w/head of Medusa surrounded by an engraved Greek key design, interior reveals metal mirror, signed puff & powder impressed w/head of Medusa, Versace **50**

Silvertone & black enamel, metal compact/lighter/cigarette case combination, lid centered w/silvertone cartouche, Marathon **175**

Dress Clip/Compact Combination

Silvertone dress clip/compact combination, round black lid centered w/white profile silhouette of a woman's face, interior reveals metal mirror & perforated rotating powder well (ILLUS.) **125**

Silvertone "Petite Boudoir" compact, designed to resemble vanity table, collapsible cabriole legs, exterior & interior metal mirrors, presentation box reads "Miniature replica of Marie Antoinette's carved golden dressing table," Volupte **275**

Sterling & black enamel, round compact w/small plastic dome centered on lid enclosing a three-dimensional head of a Scottie dog, Germany 150

Sterling compact/cane combination, cane handle is the compact, gilded interior contains framed mirror & powder compartment, lid decorated w/black Siamese scene, mahogany wood shaft, metal ferrule protector at end of stick, hallmarked 425

Vanity ring, oblong, rounded corners, lid centered w/a crystal, double shank opens for use as a bracelet or pendant, gift w/purchase of two-year subscription ($1.00) to Woman's World magazine, 1925 225

CURRIER & IVES PRINTS

This lithographic firm was founded in 1835 by Nathaniel Currier with James M. Ives becoming a partner in 1857. Current events of the day were portrayed in the early days and the prints were hand-colored. Landscapes, vessels, sport and hunting scenes of the West all became popular subjects. The firm was in existence until 1906. All prints listed are hand-colored unless otherwise noted. Numbers at the end of the listings refer to those used in Currier & Ives Prints-An Illustrated Checklist, *by Frederick A. Conningham (Crown Publishers).*

American Clipper Ship "Witch of the Wave (The)," medium folio, undated, N. Currier, framed, 115 (overall toning, scattered staining, fox marks, creases throughout sheet, deformations to paper throughout image) **$863**

American Farm Scenes - No. 2 (Summer), large folio, 1853, N. Currier, unframed, 135 (toning)... **2,990**

American Farm Scenes - No. 3 (Autumn), large folio, N. Currier, 1853, unframed, 133 (mat & other staining, toning)......... **2,415**

American Frontier Life - The Hunter's Stratagem, large folio, 1862, framed, 158 (staining & foxing to margins & reverse).. **4,313**

American Homestead - Summer, small folio, 1868, framed, 171 (margins trimmed, light stains)....................................... 220

American Winter Scenes - Evening, large folio, N. Currier, 1854, unframed, 207, slight foxing (slight toning at right edge) .. **19,550**

American Winter Scenes - Morning, large folio, 1854, N. Currier, framed, 208 (toning, staining to reverse, scattered fox marks)... **19,550**

American Winter Sports - Trout Fishing "On Chateaugay Lake," large folio, 1856, N. Currier, framed, 210 (staining, minor nicks & tears to edges) **4,888**

Battle of the Wilderness (The) - undated, framed, (some staining & foxing, small restored hole, wear on frame) 220

Battle of the Wilderness, Va., May 5th & 6th, 1864 (The), small folio, undated, framed, 436 (slight overall discoloration, minor defects)....................................... 173

Bombardment of Fort Pulaski, Cockspur Island, Geo. 10th/11th of April 1862, medium folio, contemporary frame, 595,

11 13/16 x 15, frame 13 1/2 x 17 5/8" (small line of stain along bottom margin)....... 220

Celebrated Horse DEXTER (The) - "The King of the Turf," large folio, 1865, unframed, 883 (staining, soiling, annotations to reverse)............................... **1,840**

Celebrated Horse George M. Patchen (The) - "The champion of the Turf," large folio, 1860, unframed, 885 (toning) .. **3,220**

Celebrated Mare Flora Temple - "The Queen of the Turf," large folio, 1860, unframed, 892 (toning, staining, some possibly retouched)............................... **1,265**

Central Park, The Drive, medium folio, 1862, framed, 951 (minor light & mat stain, few short nicks & tear at edges)....... **1,725**

Champion Pacer Johnston (The), large folio, 1884, framed, 968, (toning, staining, scattered foxing).................................. 345

Champion Trotting Stallion SMUGGLER (The), large folio, 1875, unframed, 983 (staining, fox marks, rubs to image, annotations on reverse, tears & losses to edges).. **3,450**

Clipper Ship "Dreadnought," large folio, 1854, N. Currier, framed, 1143 (staining, toning & foxing, ink annotations partially removed).. **1,955**

Clipper Ship "Great Republic," large folio, 1853, N. Currier, framed, 1146 (abrasions to image, toning, staining, scattered fox marks, pinholes at edge of image) **4,025**

Clipper Ship "Sovereign of the Seas," large folio, 1852, N. Currier, framed, 1167 (some retouched abrasions within image, toning)...................................... **2,415**

Darktown Fire Brigade (The) - The Last Shake, small folio, 1885, matted & framed, 1395 (stains, minor edge damage).. 248

Deer Shooting - In the Northern Woods, medium folio, undated, framed, 1539 690

Eventide - October - The Village Inn, large folio, 1867, framed, 1780 (faint water stains, a few skinned areas on verso, mat stain)... **1,093**

Farm-Yard in Winter (The), large folio, 1861, framed, 1881 (mat stain, fox marks, repaired tears & losses top of sheet edge) **6,038**

Farmer's Home (The) - Autumn, large folio, 1864, framed, 1889 (overall staining & toning, scattered fox marks, some abrasions within image)...................... **2,760**

Fording the River, large folio, undated, unframed, 2082 (toning, stains, fox marks, repaired tear in upper right corner).............. 374

Four-in-Hand, large folio, 1861, unframed, 2092 (toning, scattered fox marks, repair/retouch to sky)................................ **1,955**

Fox-Hunting, The Death, handcolored lithograph, medium folio, molded frame, 18 x 21 1/2" w/frame (minor fading & edge damage, stains) 440

Frozen Up, medium folio, 1872, framed, 2155 (staining & toning, scattered fox marks, vertical crease through right edge of image)... **1,610**

DECOYS

Rare Black Duck Decoy

Black duck, by Ben Pease, carved wood, very rare (ILLUS.) **$17,000**

Brant Goose Decoy

Brant goose, by Joseph Lincoln, carved wood, black & greys (ILLUS.) **19,800**

Nathan Cobb Jr. Brant Decoy

Brant goose, by Nathan Cobb Jr., carved wood, black head, neck & wings, dappled grey body (ILLUS.) **60,500**

Eider Drake Decoy

Eider drake w/mussel in mouth, by Gus Wilson, Monhegan Island & South Portland, Maine, his earlier "Monhegan Island" style, oversided wood decoy w/inlet head, carved eyes & bill, relief wing carving, second quarter 20th c., minor wear, chipping, cracks (ILLUS.) **82,250**
Goose, carved wood, swimmer w/brown & white paint on body, black neck & bill, glass eyes, initialed "R" on base, 22" l. (wear & a few splits in base) **1,815**

Greenwing Teal Drake

Greenwing teal drake, by the Ward Brothers, carved wood, speckled breast in earthtones & black, 1936 (ILLUS.) **16,000**

Greenwing Teal Hen Decoy

Greenwing teal hen, Amiel Garibaldi, Sacramento, California, carved wood, slight relief wing carving & glass eyes, head turned slightly to side, second quarter 20th c., minor wear, reglued crack (ILLUS.) **1,265**

Heron Decoy

Heron, carved wood, grey/beige colors, standing on rounded base, Massachusetts, ca. 1890 (ILLUS.) **57,750**

Illinois River Mallard Hen

Mallard hen, by Bert Graves, carved wood, hen looks over should, in browns & beiges, Illinois River decoy (ILLUS.) **24,750**

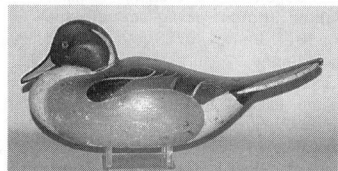

"Lowhead" Pintail Drake

Pintail drake, by the Ward Brothers, carved wood, "lowhead" style, black, brown, tan, taupe, beige & teal (ILLUS.) **74,500**

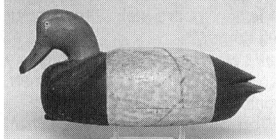

Very Rare Red-head Drake

Red-head drake, by Elkanah Cobb, carved wood, black breast & tail, middle body of dappled grey, deep reddish head & neck, black beak, yellow eyes, very rare (ILLUS.) **56,100**

Swan Decoy

Swan, two-piece hollow-form body, solid neck & head, carved & painted white, American, late 19th c., wood & paint loss, early repair, (ILLUS.) **4,888**

Wood Duck Drake Decoy

Wood duck drake, by Elmer Crowell, carved wood, sitting duck in black, browns, gold, gray & white (ILLUS.) **24,750**

DISNEY COLLECTIBLES

Scores of objects ranging from watches to dolls have been created showing Walt Disney's copyrighted animated cartoon characters, and an increasing number of collectors now are seeking these, made primarily by licensed manufacturers.

ALSO SEE Antique Trader Toy Price Guide.

Big Bad Wolf Windup Tin Toy

Big Bad Wolf (from "Three Little Pigs") **toy,** windup tin, hopping Big Bad Wolf figure, Japan, Walt Disney Productions, 4 3/4" h. (ILLUS.) **$550**
Black Hole model kit, Maximilian robot, from Disney film, MPC, plastic kits, 1979, 11" h. **15-35**

Black Hole model kit, V.I.N. Cent. robot, from Disney film, MPC, plastic kits, 1979, 8 1/2" h. **20-40**
Clarabelle Cow tumbler, clear glass, w/drawing of Clarabelle Cow in red on front next to vertical "Clarabelle Cow," 1936 (ILLUS. right with Mickey Mouse tumblers) **30**
Davy Crockett at the Alamo playset based on the Disney TV show, Marx, No. 3530, 1955 .... **125-450**
Disney characters certificate, WW II war bond, 22 Disney characters illustrated, unused **65**
Disney characters cookie jar, school bus-shaped, 1961 .... **800**
Disney characters model kit, brightly colored, paintable plastic figures, 1960s-70s, Marx, about 6" h., each **2-6**
Disney characters paint set, illustration on box cover shows several Disney characters, Walt Disney Enterprises, 1939 .... **120**
Disney characters phonograph records, three Victor picture records with jackets, beautiful Disney cartoons, full sides of records, songs include Big Bad Wolf, Mickey, Minnie's in Town, Lullaby Land of Nowhere, Bogeyman and other Silly Symphony Songs, records 7" d., set of 3 ...... **305**
Disney characters puzzle blocks, set of forty 1 1/4" square blocks form six puzzles w/Mickey Mouse, Donald Duck, etc., all in original wooden hinged box w/clasps & signed on front "Garnier Made in France - Copyright Walt Disney Productions," 9 1/2 x 14 1/2", the set **205**
Disney characters rug, Mickey & Minnie on train, Pluto, Bambi & others, 1960 copyright, 4' x 5 1/2' **350**
Disney characters sand sifter, tin, Horace, Clarabelle, Mickey & Pluto at beach, Ohio Art, 1938 .... **225**
Disney characters toy, tin top, featuring Mickey, Donald & Pluto, good w/very good box, Chein **190**
Disney characters tray, lithographed tin, pictures Mickey, Pluto, Donald, Dewey, Louie, Huey, & Professor Von Drake, Wonderful World of Color, RCA Victor premium, 1961, 8 x 12" **60**
Disneyland game, board-type, "Frontierland," Parker Bros., 1955 .... **48**
Disneyland game, "Walt Disney's Tomorrowland Rocket to the Moon," 1956 .... **95**
Disneyland matchbook, the front states "Meet me at Disneyland" w/the "Frito" kid on the jacket, the back states "Visit casa de Fritos" & "Authentic Mexican Food - In Frontierland - Disneyland," never used, mint condition, copyright 1960, fine graphics, 2" x 2" **37**
Disneyland toy, "Disneyland Rocketship Control Board," in original box **600**
Disneyland toy, Happy Birthday Carousel, tin, 1960s, in original box **350**
Donald Duck book, "Donald Duck & His Friends," Walt Disney Productions, 1939 .... **55**
Donald Duck book, "Donald Duck & His Misadventures," 1937 .... **18**

Early Donald Duck Hard Cover Book

Donald Duck book, "Donald Duck - Illustrated by the Staff of the Walt Disney Studios," first hard cover book appearance of Donald, large long-billed Donald on the cover against a pale yellow ground, w/dust jacket, 36 pp., 9 1/2 x 10 1/2" (ILLUS.) **1,761**

Donald Duck book, "Walt Disney Story of Donald Duck," 1938.................... **160**

Donald Duck bottle cap, "Donald Duck Cola" **8**

Donald Duck bowl, Beetleware, yellow w/raised ABCs.................................... **26**

Donald Duck Bread bank, flat, cardboard, mint condition **65**

Donald Duck candy bar wrapper, "Donald Duck Milk Chocolate," by Comic Candies, Brooklyn, NY, 1940s.................. **50**

Donald Duck card game, 1949 .... **105**

Donald Duck cookie jar, cov., barrel-shaped, embossed figure of Donald in a chef's outfit w/bowl & spoon on the side, marked "Donald Duck Walt Disney Productions".. **75**

Donald Duck cookie jar, cov., ceramic, head-shaped, marked "Walt Disney Productions WD5" & paper label "Original Dan Brechner Exclusive Japan".................. **700**

Donald Duck cookie jar, cov., Donald standing, "Copyright Walt Disney USA"........ **425**

Donald Duck cookie jar, cov., seated Donald, Abingdon, small............................ **150**

Donald Duck doll, composition & cloth, Donald in Russian costume w/cape & tall hat, w/original tag, 9" h. **1,700**

Donald Duck doll, composition, long-billed Donald w/socket head, black-painted side-glancing eyes, molded & painted blue sailor hat, accented nostrils, one-piece body w/sailor shirt, wearing original black plush hat & velvet cape, marked "Walt Disney, Knickerbocker Toy Co." on back, 9" h. (general crazing & fine cracks in finish of composition under cape)............. **925**

Donald Duck doll, stuffed cloth, Donald w/a long bill, sailor suit, tie & collar, Knickerbocker, 1930s, 18" h. **550**

Donald Duck doll, stuffed cloth, long-billed Donald fitted w/music box (overwound) & swivel neck, dressed as a band leader w/a red jacket trimmed in gold piping w/brass buttons & a "bearskin" hat, Knickerbocker, 16" h. **1,760**

Donald Duck doorstop, cast metal, Donald holds stop sign, 1971, 8 3/8" h........................ **225**

Donald Duck feeding dish, three-compartment, blue, Patriot China, ca. 1940, 8" d. **125-150**

Donald Duck figure, bisque, long-billed, 1930s, 4 1/2" h.................................... **350**

Donald Duck figure, bisque, playing accordion, yellow bill, blue sailor hat, original paint, 3" h... **85**

Donald Duck figure, bisque, w/sword in right hand, 3 1/2" h............................... **130-135**

Donald Duck figure, rubber, movable head, Sun Rubber Co., 8" h................... **150-175**

Donald Duck figure, rubber, w/long beak, Bendey W. D. Toy, 8 1/2" h. **50-75**

Donald Duck game, "Ring Toss," wood & rubber, 1950s, 12" h. Donald figure **100-125**

Donald Duck lamp, ceramic, figure of Donald holding candlestick, ca. 1950s .. **150-200**

Donald Duck letter opener, celluloid, 1936...... **135**

Donald Duck Magic Slate, Donald on cardboard slate, with stylus, Strathmore Company, 1953, 8 x 13".. **30**

Donald Duck night light, General Electric Co., 1965, on original card............................ **55**

Donald Duck pin, figural, cloisonné, 1930s...... **225**

Donald Duck planter, pottery, Donald in cowboy suit... **75-100**

Donald Duck ring, sterling silver, Osbee, 1947.. **70-90**

Donald Duck rocker, wooden, Mengel, fair to good condition **225**

Donald Duck rug, Donald fishing, a small seal in the background, 26 x 54" **150-175**

Donald Duck rug, shows Donald carrying Chip 'n' Dale in buckets (one in each hand), 21" w., 3' l.................................... **125-150**

Donald Duck sand pail, lithographed tin, slightly tapering cylindrical shade w/slender tube bail handle, illustrated w/Donald in an old-fashioned swimsuit flexing his muscles, very good condition................. **175-200**

Donald Duck sheet music, "Three Caballeros".. **48**

Box of Donald Duck Soda Straws

Donald Duck soda straws, multicolor box of 100, Herz Mfg. Co., New York, New York, 1940s, 3/4 x 3 3/4 x 8 3/4" box (ILLUS.).. **35**

Donald Duck tea set: cov. teapot, creamer, sugar bowl, tray & six cups, saucers & plates; tin, Ohio Art Co., Bryan, Ohio, marked "Walt Disney Productions," 1939, the set.. **400**

Line Mar Disney Dipsy Car Toy

Donald Duck Acrobat Toy

Donald Duck toy, acrobat toy w/celluloid figure in wire frame w/Disneyland pennant attached, clockwork motor, Line Mar, in box (ILLUS.) **546**

Donald Duck toy, balancing-type, a celluloid long-billed Donald w/jointed arms standing atop an orange & white weighted base, Japan, ca. 1930s, 7" h. (small split at back of neck, arms detached but present) **600**

Donald Duck toy, battery-operated, locomotive w/Donald as engineer **445**

Donald Duck toy, pull-type, "Dogcart Donald," Fisher-Price No. 149, Donald Duck in cart w/Pluto in the lead, 1936 .... **700**

Donald Duck toy, pull-type, "Donald Duck Cart," Fisher-Price No. 605, Donald pulls cart, 1954 .... **300**

Donald Duck toy, pull-type, "Donald Duck Chick Cart," Fisher-Price No. 469, Donald on platform w/round container decorated w/chicks, 1938 .... **550**

Donald Duck toy, pull-type, "Donald Duck Drum Major," Fisher-Price No. 400, 1946 ..... **255**

Donald Duck toy, pull-type, "Donald Duck Drum Major," Fisher-Price No. 463, 1939 ..... **500**

Donald Duck toy, pull-type, "Donald Duck Xylophone," Fisher-Price No. 185, Donald plays xylophone, 1938 .... **800**

Donald Duck toy, pull-type, "Doughboy Donald," Fisher-Price No. 744, Donald Duck as a soldier, 1942 .... **600**

Donald Duck toy, pull-type, "Talking Donald," Fisher-Price No. 765, 1955 .... **225**

Donald Duck toy, roly-poly, celluloid, Donald in an orange shirt & cap, paper label on base, Japan, ca. 1935, 6 1/2" h. (beak paint faded, light paint wear to hands) **650**

Donald Duck toy, windup celluloid, Donald Duck carousel, figure of Donald under umbrella suspended w/jointed knobbed bars, on a wheeled base w/the mechanism, rolls forward & revolves carousel when wound, Japan, ca. 1930s, 6 1/2" h....... **980**

Donald Duck toy, windup tin, convertible vehicle w/celluloid Donald as the driver, in carton **425-450**

Donald Duck toy, windup tin, "Disney Dipsy Car," Donald w/plastic head behind the wheel of a tractor-like vehicle, Line Mar, Japan, w/original box, 6" (ILLUS. above) **825-875**

Donald Duck toy, windup tin, "Fire Chief Crazy Car," lithographed tin, Donald driving & spinning head, car body w/various Disney characters, Line Mar, Japan, 5 1/4" l. (some scrapes) **225-250**

Donald Duck toy, windup tin, "Gym Toy" acrobat, Donald performing on a keywind wire bar, Line Mar, Japan, w/original box, 9" h. **750**

Donald Duck toy, windup-type, "Donald Duck Back-Up," Fisher-Price No. 358, 1936 .... **800**

Donald Duck & Donna Duck toy, pull-type, "Donald and Donna Duck," Fisher-Price, No. 160, one of the most unusual & rarest Disney toys because Donna became Daisy, Donald plays a xylophone & serenades "Donna," 1937 .... **1,500**

Donald Duck & nephews toy, pull-type, "Donald Duck & Nephews," Fisher-Price No. 479, Donald w/Huey & Louie trailing behind, 1941 .... **450**

Dumbo song book, 1941 .... **80**

Dumbo toy, pull-type, "Dumbo Circus Racer," Fisher-Price No. 738, Dumbo w/rubber arms drives race car, 1941...................... **775**

Dwarf Bashful doll, molded mask character face, oilcloth body, painted features, plush beard, blue felt hat marked "Bashful," red coat & brown pants, ca. 1930s, 12" h. (line of paint cracking through bridge of nose) **201**

Dwarf Dopey figure, ceramic, marked "Leeds".. **50**

Dwarf Dopey glass, dairy promotion, 1938 .... **28**

Dwarf Dopey toy, pull-type, "Dopey Dwarf," Fisher-Price No. 770, Dopey beats drum, 1939.. **600**

Dwarf Grumpy figure, bisque, 4" h. **85**

Dwarfs Bashful, Doc, Dopey, Grumpy, Sleepy, Sneezy & Happy figures, composition, each w/jointed arms & dressed in velveteen jackets, pants & hats marked w/their names, Knickerbocker, ca. 1930s, average 8 1/2" h. (two w/repaired feet), the set of 7.. **2,700**

Elmer Elephant toy, pull-type, "Elmer Elephant," Fisher-Price No. 206A **325**

Fantasia bowl, ceramic, Goldfish Bowl #121, round, white w/h.p. decoration of three goldfish w/flowing tails in purple, yellow, orange & green, Vernon Kilns, 1940-41, 8" d., 6" h. **622**

Fantasia bowl, ceramic, Sprite Bowl #125, round shallow shape, white decorated w/h.p. designs of sprites in blue & yellow, Vernon Kilns, 1940-41, 10" d., 3" h. (ILLUS.).. **1,742**

Fantasia drawing, original storyboard drawing from "The Sorcerer's Apprentice" segment, color scene of Mickey Mouse asleep in the wizard's chair wearing the wizard's hat, 7 x 8 3/4" (ILLUS. below).. **4,767**

Two Fantasia Blonde Centaurettes

Fantasia figures, china, Centaurettes, blonde, Vernon Kilns, 1940-41, Nos. 17 & 18, 8" h., pr. (ILLUS.)................................. **1,648**

Vernon Kilns Fantasia "Sprite" Bowl

Vernon Kilns Fantasia Centaur

Original Fantasia Storyboard Drawing

Set of Baby Satyrs from Fantasia

Fantasia figurine, ceramic, Centaur #31, Vernon Kilns,1940-41, 10" h. (ILLUS.)....... **1,995**

Bowing Ostrich Figurine from Fantasia

Fantasia figurine, ceramic, Ostrich bowing, Vernon Kilns, 6 1/2" h. (ILLUS.) **1,021**
Fantasia figurine, ceramic, Ostrich standing w/wings spread, Vernon Kilns, 1940-41, 9" h. **1,360**
Fantasia figurines, ceramic, baby Pegasus, #19 (Black), #19 (Gray) & #21, Vernon Kilns, 1940-41, 5-6" h., the set **633**
Fantasia figurines, ceramic, baby Satyrs, various poses, Vernon Kilns,1940-41, 4" h., complete set of 6 (ILLUS.) **1,021**
Fantasia figurines, ceramic, baby Sprites, various poses, Vernon Kilns, 1940-41, 4" h., complete set of 6 .... **1,497**

Three Hippos from Fantasia

Fantasia figurines, ceramic, Hippos in tutus, various poses, pink & grey, Vernon Kilns, 1940-41, 5" h., set of 3 (ILLUS.)....... **2,132**

Rare Fantasia Movie Window Card

Fantasia movie window card, color-printed cardboard, large color center scene of various characters from the movie dancing around the title, the name of the theater & dates of the showing in large type across the top, jumbo size, minor professional restoration, 22 x 28" (ILLUS.) **675**

Vernon Kilns Winged Pegasus Vase

Fantasia vase, ceramic, Winged Pegasus Vase #27, oblong bulbous shape w/flat sides tapering to rectangular base & opening, white w/molded decoration of sleeping Pegasus perched on a branch on the sides & outlined in colors, Vernon Kilns, 1940-41, 8" h., 11 1/2" l. (ILLUS.).... **1,631**
Fantasyland tie tack, sterling silver **30-40**
Ferdinand the Bull bank, chalkware, early Carnival-type, 9" h.. **50**
Ferdinand the Bull mask, Halloween-type, canvas... **125**

Key-wind Ferdinand Toy

Ferdinand the Bull toy, key-wind tin, walking Ferdinand w/fabric flowers in his mouth, marked "Japan - Walt Disney Productions," 5 1/2" l., 4" h. (ILLUS.).................. **295**

Ferdinand the Bull toy, pull-type, lithographed paper on wood, seated cut-out of Ferdinand on a green wood platform w/red metal wheels, Fisher-Price No. 434, 1939 .... **715**

Flower the Skunk (Bambi) figure, ceramic, miniature, Hagen-Reneker...................... **105**

Hercules movie cel, Phil, Hercules & Pegasus practice balancing on one leg in training, against a large sunset background, six cel set-up, three are production underlays, one a production overlay/underlay, 1972, 12 1/2 x 17"................ **3,450**

Horace Horsecollar figure, bisque, 1930s...... **150**

Horace Horsecollar tumbler, clear cylindrical glass w/red & blue enamel decoration of Horace playing a flute **151**

"Lady and the Tramp" Movie Cel

Lady and the Tramp movie cel, scene of Lady & Tramp w/puppies & child sitting near Christmas tree, 300 of limited edition of 500, framed & matted under glass, in modern beveled wood frame, 9 x 11 1/2" image size (ILLUS.)...................... **375**

Lady & The Tramp playset, based on the Disney movie, Marx, 1961...................... **125-400**

Ludwig Von Drake toy, plastic figure w/cloth jacket, "Twistable," Marx, mint in box **125**

Mary Poppins medicine spoonholder, ceramic, 1964.. **60**

Mary Poppins sugar shell, silver plate, 1964 .... **60**

Mickey Mouse Advent calendar, 1970, mint in package **70**

Mickey Mouse bank, aluminum, figure of Mickey w/hands on hips, France, early 1930s, Moore No. 201, 8" h. **2,800**

Mickey Mouse bank, ceramic, shaped like a television, picture of Mickey & Pluto on "screen".. **95**

Mickey Mouse bank, composition & tin, the still bank in the form of Mickey standing & wearing short pants & oversized shoes & resting against a large tree trunk w/curved lid & embossed studs & handles, painted trim, embossed across front of base "Walt Disney Crown," ca. 1940s, 6 1/4" h... **275**

Mickey Mouse bank, treasure chest shape, souvenir of 1933 Chicago World's Fair, Zell Products Co., Moore No. 204 .... **125-150**

Mickey Mouse book, "Mickey Mouse & Boy Thursday," Whitman, 1948 .... **60**

Mickey Mouse book, "Mickey Mouse Circus," pop-up type, 1933................................ **505**

Mickey Mouse book, "Mickey Mouse Fire Brigade," 1936, published by Whitman, hard cover w/original dust jacket, 10 x 7 x 3/4" **80-100**

Mickey Mouse book, "Mickey Mouse in Pygmy Land," 1936, Walt Disney Enterprises, 7 1/8 x 9 1/2", 70 pp. **125-150**

Mickey Mouse book, "Mickey Mouse Stories," Book No. 2, Mickey & Pluto on soft cover, Dave McKay Publications, 1934, unused, 3/8 x 6 1/4 x 8 1/2" **100-150**

Mickey Mouse book, "Mickey Mouse The Mail Pilot," Big Little Book, Whitman Pub. Co., 1933 .... **100-125**

Mickey Mouse boots, child's, rubber, 1930s **400**

Mickey Mouse Comic Book

Mickey Mouse comic book, "Mickey Mouse Outwits the Phantom Blot," first Mickey Mouse comic book, four-color #16, 1941 (ILLUS.)...................................... **1,234**

Mickey Mouse marionette, painted wood, cloth outfit, made by Pelham, 24" h........ **700-750**

Mickey Mouse mask, rubber, ca. 1940s............. **90**

Mickey Mouse mug, ceramic, marked "Patriot China" & "W. D. E." (Walt Disney Enterprises).. **80-90**

Mickey Mouse necklace, enameled figure of Mickey & two Minnie figures on silver chain.. **125-150**

Mickey Mouse pail, lithographed tin, "Happynak," England, 1939............................ **225-250**

Mickey Mouse pinback button, celluloid, "Good Teeth," 1930s.................................... **145**

Mickey Mouse plate, three-section feeding dish, Patriotic China, 7" d....................... **200-250**

Mickey Mouse pocket watch, Bicentennial edition, Bradley, 1976, w/box **200-250**

Mickey Mouse rug, pictures Mickey playing the accordion & Donald Duck & Pluto dancing, 20 x 35".................................. **325-350**

Mickey Mouse snow shovel, child's, litho tin, Mickey, Pluto & snowmen, Ohio Art Co., 1930s.. **175-200**

Mickey Mouse teaspoon, silver plate, Branford, 1930s **30-50**

Mickey Mouse toy, battery-operated, remote control, "Drumming Mickey Mouse," featuring lithographed tin Mickey in cloth outfit, he drums, walks & nods his head as his eyes light up, Line Mar, ca. 1955, w/original box, 11" h. **1,200**

Mickey Mouse toy, bicycle clip-on type, battery-operated, "Mickey Mouse Talking Cycle Buddy," by Stelber, mint in box **260**

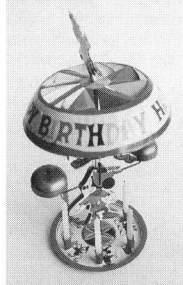

Mickey Mouse Candle Toy

Mickey Mouse toy, candle-powered spinning-type, lithographed tin, a carousel-style top centered w/a flat figure of Mickey, raised on a center post & suspending figures of Pluto, Bambi & Dumbo forming chimes above a cross-wire topped at each end by a small dome bell, all above a standing figure of Mickey wearing Robin Hood garb in the center of a disk base w/small sockets for birthday candles, "Happy Birthday" printed around the top, Japan, w/original box, 5" d., 8 1/4" h. (ILLUS.) **325**

Mickey Mouse Motorized Toy

Mickey Mouse toy, celluloid Mickey Mouse figure w/parasol of dangling balls, wheeled base, clockwork motor, Japanese, 8" h. (ILLUS.) **1,438**

Mickey Mouse toy, pull-type, "Mickey Mouse Band," Fisher-Price No. 530, Pluto w/cymbal tail & Mickey beating drum w/"pushy" stick, 1935 .... **900**

Mickey Mouse toy, pull-type, "Mickey Mouse Choo-Choo," Fisher-Price No. 432, Mickey driving engine, ringing bell, 1938.. **600**

Mickey Mouse toy, pull-type,"Mickey Mouse Puddle Jumper," Fisher-Price No. 310, Mickey drives two part car w/back end that sways & bounces him from side to side, 1953.. **160**

Mickey Mouse toy, top, tin spinning-type, Walt Disney Enterprises, 1930s............. **425-450**

Mickey Mouse Wind-up Toy

Mickey Mouse toy, wind-up Mickey plays xylophone, Marx, in box (ILLUS.) **660**

Disney Tumblers

Mickey Mouse tumbler, clear glass, w/drawing of Mickey Mouse in black over "Mickey Mouse," 1936 (ILLUS. center)............ **40**

Mickey Mouse tumbler, milk glass, w/black picture of vintage Mickey over "Mickey Mouse - (c)Walt E Disney," black line just below lip, 1931 (ILLUS. left) **130**

Mickey Mouse wall pocket, china, lustre glaze, 1930s... **225-250**

Mickey Mouse Porcelain Wash Basin

Mickey Mouse wash set: pitcher, wash basin & soap holder; porcelain, decorated w/full-color images of Mickey & silver accent lines, made in France by Faiencerie D'Onnaing, 1930s, pitcher 9 3/4" h., basin 13" d., soap holder 4 x 9 1/4", the set (ILLUS. of wash basin) **2,527**

Mickey Mouse Club barrette **25**

Mickey Mouse Club 1950s Costume

Mickey Mouse Club costume, Mouseke-teer, Mickey Mouse mask & cap w/ears, 1950s, mint in box (ILLUS.) **282**

Mickey Mouse Club newsreel w/sound, includes camera, screen & records, in original box, Mattel **200-225**

Mickey Mouse Club roller skates, mint in box **125-150**

Mickey Mouse Club yo-yo, 1950s, on orig-inal card.. **30-40**

Mickey & Minnie Mouse cookie jar, cov., pottery, "turnabout," Leeds China Co.... **450-550**

Mickey & Minnie Mouse figures, celluloid, jointed, w/label on foot "M. M. Copr. 1928-30 by Walter E. Disney," 5" h., pr. **575-600**

Mickey & Minnie Mouse figures, ceramic, Mickey holding flowers to give to Minnie, decorated in light blue, white & yellow, American Pottery Co., 6" h., pr........ **1,000-1,200**

Mickey & Minnie Mouse paper doll set, four outfits for each including cowboy, drum major & swimming, Saalfield, 1933, 10 1/2" h... **235**

Mickey & Minnie Mouse platter, china, lus-tre glaze, pictures Mickey & Minnie din-ing, 5" l... **75-95**

Mickey & Minnie Mouse toy, windup tin, Mickey & Minnie Mouse handcar, compo-sition figures on each end of the center handlebar, red car, w/original box, Lionel, 1930s, rubber legs replaced **2,195**

Minnie & Mickey Mouse Chair

Mickey & Minnie Mouse chair, die-cut wood chair by Kroehler, Mickey & Minnie sit on either side in full-color cut-out stan-chions, seat is red, 1930s, 24" h., some paint wear (ILLUS.) **1,516**

Mickey, Minnie & Pluto vase, tall cylindrical metal vase on oblong base also fitted w/Fun-E-Flex wooden figures of Mickey, Minnie & Pluto, ca. 1934, overall 8" h... **900-1,000**

Mickey Mouse & Pluto ashtray, china, lus-tre glaze, figure of Mickey seated playing banjo & Pluto listening on the back rim, Japan, 1930s, 3" w., 3" h. **235-265**

Mickey Mouse & Pluto figure, plastic & rubber, featuring a pie-cut eyed Mickey astride a yellow Pluto, all hand-painted, Japan, 3" h. **550-600**

Minnie Mouse book, "Minnie Mouse & The Antique Chair," 1948 .... **25-50**

Minnie Mouse costume, Halloween-type, 1950s, w/original box **200-250**

Minnie Mouse figure, bisque, Minnie play-ing concertina, Japan, 1930s, 3 1/2" h.... **150-175**

Minnie Mouse figure, bisque, Minnie play-ing mandolin, Japan, 1930s, 3 1/2" h............ **400**

Minnie Mouse figure, celluloid, wearing a black & blue short dress, yellow gloves & red shoes & hat, Japan, ca. 1930s, 6" h.. **575-600**

Minnie Mouse fork & spoon, sterling sil-ver, pie-eyed style Minnie, cut-out han-dles, International Sterling, pr. **200-250**

Nightmare Before Christmas game, vid-eo-type, hand-held, Tiger Electronics, 1993... **25-50**

Nightmare Before Christmas action fig-ure, Behemoth, Hasbro, 1993, 5 1/2" h..... **30-65**

Dr. Finklestein Action Figure

Nightmare Before Christmas action fig-ure, Dr. Finklestein, Hasbro, 1993, 5 1/2" h. (ILLUS.)..................................... **70-140**

Nightmare Before Christmas action fig-ure, Jack as Santa, Hasbro, 1993, 9" h. ... **30-65**

Nightmare Before Christmas action fig-ure, Lock, Shock & Barrel in walking tub, Applause, 1993, 4 x 5" **15-35**

Nightmare Before Christmas action fig-ure, Mayor, Hasbro, 1993, 7 1/2" h......... **70-140**

Oogie Boogie Action Figure

Nightmare Before Christmas action figure, Oogie Boogie w/bugs inside, Hasbro, 1993, 7" h. (ILLUS.) **100-300**
Nightmare Before Christmas action figure, Sally, Hasbro, 1993, 7" h. **40-100**
Nightmare Before Christmas action figure, Santa, Hasbro, 1993, 6" h. **100-300**
Nightmare Before Christmas action figure, Wolf, Hasbro, 1993, 5" h. **45-120**
Nightmare Before Christmas action figure, Zero, Applause, 1993, 3 1/2" h. **10-15**
Nightmare Before Christmas activity book, Golden, 1993, 5 x 7 3/4" **8-15**
Nightmare Before Christmas bank, Mayor, ceramic, Schmid, 1993, 8" h. **100-150**
Nightmare Before Christmas bubble bath bottle, Jack, figural, Centura Brand, Disney, 1993, 9 1/2" h. **20-40**
Nightmare Before Christmas doll, Oogie Boogie, boxed, Hasbro, 1993, 13" h........ **50-140**

Hasbro Cloth Sally Doll

Nightmare Before Christmas doll, Sally, cloth, removable limbs, boxed, Hasbro, 1993, 14" h. (ILLUS.) **200-450**
Nightmare Before Christmas doll/puppet, Santa, plush, boxed, Hasbro, 1993, 12" h.. **25-100**
Nightmare Before Christmas dolls, Lock, Shock & Barrel, boxed, Hasbro, 1993, 4 1/2" h., set of 3........................... **100-250**
Nightmare Before Christmas figure, Dr. Finklestein, plastic PVC, Applause, 1993, 4" h.. **20-30**
Nightmare Before Christmas figure, Jack, bend-em, Applause, 1993, 9 1/2" h. **12-35**
Nightmare Before Christmas figure, Jack & Sally w/moon, plastic PVC, Applause, video promotion figure, 6" h. **15-20**
Nightmare Before Christmas figure, Jack & Zero, plastic PVC, Applause, 3 1/2" h. **12-20**
Nightmare Before Christmas figure, Lock, Shock or Barrel, Applause, 1993, 2 1/2" h., sold separately, each **6-10**
Nightmare Before Christmas figure, Oogie Boogie, Applause, 1993, 3 1/2" h. **15-25**
Nightmare Before Christmas kite, pictures Jack on hill **15-20**
Nightmare Before Christmas puppet, plush, Applause, 1993, 9" h. **25-60**

Talking Jack Doll with Zero

Nightmare Before Christmas talking doll, Jack w/Zero, Hasbro, 1993, 15" h. (ILLUS.).. **100-250**

Revell Perri Squirrel Kit

Perri Squirrel model kit, from Disney film, life-size w/sprinkle-on fur, Revell, plastic kits, 1958 (ILLUS.) **25-85**
Peter Pan movie poster, one-sheet, color print showing a large Peter standing to one side w/a band of small characters above & below him, title to the left, linen-backed, 1953, 27 x 41" **500-550**
Pinocchio charm, plastic, 1" h............................ **25**
Pinocchio doll, composition, jointed body, Walt Disney Productions, Crown Toy Co., 9" h... **200-250**
Pinocchio doll, stuffed cloth & wood, a cloth head w/painted features & a jointed wooden body, wearing a blue shirt & bow tie & red shorts, Richard G. Krueger, 16 1/2" h.. **375-425**
Pinocchio figure, pressed wood, Multi-Wood Products, Chicago, 1940s, 5" h..... **95-100**
Pinocchio figure, rubber, red & yellow outfit w/blue tie, Dakin, 8" h............................. **35-45**
Pinocchio mask, paper, Gillette Blue Blades advertising premium, uncut, 1939........ **35**
Pinocchio pinback button, celluloid, "Good Teeth," 1940s....................................... **135**
Pinocchio postcard, original wrapper, France **225**
Pinocchio toy, pull-type, "Pinocchio Express," Fisher-Price No. 720, Pinocchio riding one-wheeled bike, 1939 .... **500**
Pinocchio toy, windup tin, acrobat Pinocchio somersaults above a swaying base, Marx, ca. 1939, 14 3/4" h. **475-525**
Pinocchio toy, windup tin, delivery wagon, Pinocchio pedaling a three-wheeled vehicle, the front-mounted box lithographed

w/Jiminy, Figaro & other characters, Marx, 9" l.. **525**

Pinocchio & Foulfellow figure group, bisque, United China & Glass, 7" h. **125-150**

Pluto child's desk-table, wooden, a sawhorse-form base w/a cut-out head of Pluto, mounted w/a slightly slanted desk unit w/a Masonite lifting chalkboard top, some water stains on head, marked "Copyright - Walt Disney Productions," 35" l, 26" h. **400-450**

Pluto salt & pepper shakers w/original tops, ceramic, Leeds, pr. **40-50**

Pluto toy, windup tin & celluloid, "Gym-Toys Acrobat," featuring a celluloid Pluto on a trapeze, Line Mar, Japan, in original box, 9" h... **325-425**

Pluto toy, windup tin, "Rollover," plush-covered Pluto runs forward, rolls over & raises up on his feet to beg, "Watch Me Roll Over" on side, Line Mar, in original box, 6 1/2" l. **275-325**

Silly Symphony Promotional Calendar

Silly Symphony calendar, full-color promotional calendar, 12 pages spiral bound, each w/different image of characters from Disney's Silly Symphony cartoon series, 1938, 9 x 16 1/2" unopened (ILLUS. of part) **1,021**

Snow White kitchen appliances, refrigerator, sink & stove, lithographed tin, Wolverine, mint in original box, the set........ **250-300**

Snow White postcard, Valentine & Sons **35**

Snow White serving tray, lithographed tin, Disney Enterprises **50-75**

Snow White & the Seven Dwarfs display banner, rectangular "Jingle Club" banner, lithographically printed directly on linen in dark teal w/picture of Snow White & the Seven Dwarfs and the Jingle Book of Snow White and the Seven Dwarfs in primary colors & "Boys and Girls - Join Walt Disney's Snow White and the Seven Dwarfs Jingle Club - Get your official membership button and Walt Disney's Snow White and the Seven Dwarfs jingle book," w/an original Jingle Club pinback button & booklet, banner 35 x 59", the group (ILLUS. of banner, below) **6,568**

Rare Snow White Biscuit Tin

Snow White & the Seven Dwarfs biscuit tin, rectangular lunchbox-style w/rounded corners & double swing handles, the top printed in color w/a scene of Snow White dancing w/the Dwarfs, made in Switzerland, 1939, excellent condition, 4 1/2 x 7 3/4", 3 3/4" h. (ILLUS.) **1,583**

Snow White Jingle Club Display Banner

Snow White & the Seven Dwarfs blocks, "Safety Blocks," painted wood, a different character on each block, Halsam, 1938, in original box, the set **275-325**

Early Snow White & Dwarfs Dolls

Snow White & the Seven Dwarfs dolls, velvet cloth bodies jointed at shoulders & hips, cloth mask faces w/painted features, Snow White w/yarn wig, Dwarfs w/white plush beards, Snow White wearing original yellow organdy dress w/pale blue velvet bodice & original underclothing, Dwarfs clothing part of the body w/separate velvet hats, unmarked, late 1930s, Dwarfs 12" h., Snow White 19" h., the set (ILLUS.) **2,200**

Snow White & the Seven Dwarfs radio, painted pressed Syroco wood upright case, molded w/a scene of Snow White dancing w/four Dwarfs before an open window flanked by shutters, Dwarfs Doc & Grumpy look out from the window while Dopey peers from behind the top of one shutter, stamped "Emerson" above the window, maker's plate on the back, turning knob in center of window w/selection numbers notched around the window edges, 1937, works perfectly, 5 1/2 x 7 1/4 x 7 1/2" **2,220**

Snow White & the Seven Dwarfs rug, ca. 1949, 21 x 39" **125-150**

Snow White & the Seven Dwarfs sheet music, "Some Day My Prince Will Come" .. **40-50**

Snow White & the Seven Dwarfs tea set, lithographed tin, ca. 1940, 12 pcs. **275-300**

Snow White & The Seven Dwarfs window card, color-printed cardboard, showing the Dwarfs' heads around a black center block w/the film title, the name of the movie theater & dates of showing across the top in black, 1937, excellent condition, 22 x 30"... **2,218**

Three Little Pigs figure, bisque, pig playing violin, 1930s, 4 1/2" h. **60-70**

Thumper (from Bambi) figure, ceramic, No. 36, Goebel, Germany **200-250**

Thumper (from Bambi) toy, pull-type, "Thumper Bunny," Fisher-Price No. 533, Thumper riding platform in front of cart, 1942 .... **500**

Uncle Scrooge bank, ceramic, shown seated in bed, Japan, 1961 .... **175-200**

Rare Signed Walt Disney Photograph

Walt Disney photograph, black & white studio portrait of Walt Disney w/a personal inscription (ILLUS.) **2,839**

Zorro Playset in Box

Zorro playset, based on Disney TV series, Marx, No. 3754, 1958 (ILLUS.) **300-1,450**

DOLL FURNITURE & ACCESSORIES

Early Toy Doll Bath

Doll bath, painted & lithographed tin, two-piece, a deep oblong bathtub w/spigot at the foot set on a conforming base raised on four legs joined by a medial shelf, worn pink paint decorated around the sides w/black transfer-printed scenes of toddlers, 3 x 7 1/4" l., 5 1/2" h. (ILLUS.) **$185**

Doll Boots

Doll boots, high-button heeled lady doll boots, dark brown-bronze leather piped w/brown silk, four silver metal buttons on each boot, leather sole stamped "HURET A PARIS," French, ca. 1870, 2 1/2" l. (ILLUS.) **1,265**

Pine Dollhouse

Dollhouse, pine, story-and-a-half, old worn red paint & white trim (ILLUS.) **660**

Three-story Dollhouse

Dollhouse, three-story w/two rooms on each floor, glass windows, paneled interior doors, side porch & chimney, yellow w/white trim, ca. 1900, 23 x 51", 60" h. (ILLUS.) **1,610**

Schoenhut Dollhouse

Dollhouse, wood & fiberboard, No. 5/50 two-story model, embossed faux grey stone siding & green tile roof, off-white window & door trim, wooden front steps & chimney, eight rooms plus attic, finished in lithographed paper to represent woodwork, doors & wallpaper, contains Tootsietoy furniture sets, Schoenhut, 1923, 23 5/8 x 25 1/2", 27 5/8" h., some damage (ILLUS.) **2,415**

Dollhouse with Gambrel Roof

Dollhouse, wood painted white w/gambrel roof, red pasteboard scalloped shingles, front-opening half doors, six rooms, original paper wall & floor coverings, hinged door in rear roof, front steps, w/furniture, bisque dolls, accessories & rugs, 17 1/4 x 28 1/4 x 32 1/2" (ILLUS.) **920**

Parasol, French Fashion-type, turned ivory handle, eight-pronged brass frame, opens & closes, original pink silk cover w/matching applied pinked pink ribbon trim, topped w/pierced ivory ferrule w/brass ring, original box of embossed watered silk paper w/gold edging on lid, France, ca. 1870, overall 8" l. **633**

Cast-iron Dollhouse Potty Chair

Potty chair, cast iron, dollhouse-size, arched back continuing to form arms, serving tray at front, hole in seat, original red paint, early 20th c., 2 1/2" h. (ILLUS.) **49**

DOLLS

Also see: STEIFF TOYS & DOLLS.

A.M. bisque socket head baby, marked "Germany - G 327 B DRGM 259 A 12 M," blue glass rocker eyes set stationary, open mouth w/two upper teeth, blonde mohair wig, bent-limb composition baby body, wearing fine period white batiste & lacy baby gown & bonnet, 14 3/4" (white area at rim on back of head) **$403**

A.M. bisque socket head black character baby, marked "AM Germany 362/4. K," brown sleep eyes, molded black curly hair, open mouth w/four upper teeth, red lips, nostril & eye dots, pierced ears, one earring, bent-limb composition baby body w/clenched fists, original finish matches head, wearing a yellow floral print organdy dress & underwear, 15 1/2" (some wear on back of head) **489**

Alexander Bridesmaid & Wendy Dolls

Alexander (Madame) "Bridesmaid," marked, vinyl head w/blonde hair & sleep eyes, vinyl jointed body, wearing original long pink gown & straw bonnet w/net ties, carrying original floral bouquet, 8" (ILLUS. left).. **750**

Alexander (Madame) "Cissy," marked on dress tag "'Cissy' by Madame Alexander," hard plastic head, blue sleep eyes w/real lashes, closed mouth, original blonde wig in original set, vinyl body & limbs, wearing original queen outfit w/white damask gown, jeweled bracelets, blue diagonal sash, stockings, high heeled shoes, original box, ca. 1955, 21" (some box damage) **1,495**

Alexander (Madame) "Marme," hard plastic head & body, grey sleep eyes, closed mouth, dark brown wig in snood, wearing a grey & pink print dress w/original tags, organdy shawl, shoes & socks, ca. 1955, 14" (mark at left temple, toning to clothes) **201**

Alexander (Madame) "Wendy," marked, #580, vinyl head w/auburn hair & sleep eyes, jointed vinyl body, wearing original peach coat w/black buttons & matching bonnet over a pale blue dress w/lace collar, original shoes & socks, w/box (ILLUS. right with bridesmaid) **575**

Violin Player Automaton

Automaton, Violin Player, man w/bisque head w/blue glass eyes, blond human hair wig, open mouth w/teeth, jointed composition body, wearing original 18th c. court dress & holding a violin in one hand & movable bow in the other, original interior music box, 15" (ILLUS.) **950**

Bahr & Proschild bisque socket head girl, marked "252 dep," brown stationary eyes, open mouth, pierced ears, blonde h.h. wig, wood & composition straight-wrist body, wearing a white dotted Swiss dress & underwear, 11 1/2" **288**

#1 Blonde Ponytail Barbie

Barbie, #1 Barbie, blonde ponytail, earrings, black & white striped swimsuit, on plastic stand w/box (ILLUS.) **4,700**

American Girl Barbie in Box

Barbie, American Girl Barbie, short blonde hair, striped blouse & blue shorts, original plastic around head, mounted in original box (ILLUS.) **950**

Barbie Theatre Date Japanese Version

Barbie, "Barbie's Theatre Date" fashion doll, auburn hair in ponytail, white & gold brocade outfit w/pink blouse & brown shoes, made for the Japanese market (ILLUS.).. **1,600**

German American Girl Barbie in Box

Barbie, German American Girl Barbie, long brown hair, blue eyes, striped blouse, blue shorts, in original box (ILLUS.) **1,900**

Boxed Twist 'n Turn Barbie

Barbie, "Twist 'n Turn Barbie," wearing colored red, yellow, pink & orange mod-design swimsuit, near mint in box, 1960s (ILLUS.).. **425**

Bruckner cloth "topsy-turvy" girl, original sewn-on label reads "Bruckner Doll," crisp printed features, brown face w/black mohair framing face, red cap & blouse, red & white gingham skirt & white apron & a white face w/blonde printed hair, gingham outfit, American, early 20th c., 12" **633**

Century Doll Co. - Kestner bisque socket head character baby, marked "Century Doll Co. Kestner Germany," brown sleep eyes, open-closed smiling mouth w/two upper molded teeth & tongue, deep modeling across bridge of nose, light dimples, flange neck on cloth body w/side-swivel cloth legs, squeaker mechanism in body waves composition hands, wearing long white lawn baby gown, ca. 1920s, 17" (squeaker not working)..................................... **546**

Cloth "Philadelphia Baby," molded painted head & shoulders, heavily lidded brown-painted eyes, deeply modeled mouth, painted brown hair, cloth body w/painted lower limbs, wearing white undergarments, green & white striped cotton shift, ca. 1900, 21" (overall wear & paint rubs & loss to hair & on limbs).......... **1,093**

Heubach (Gebruder) bisque character head baby, marked "7684" w/sunburst mark, painted hair, painted blue intaglio eyes, open-closed screaming mouth, furrowed brow, straight-limb composition toddler body, wearing maroon shot overalls & white shirt, 10 1/2" (tiny scratch on left cheek) **690**

Ideal "Daddy's Girl" Standing Doll

Ideal "Daddy's Girl" vinyl girl, marked, tall standing girl w/smiling vinyl head w/blue eyes & long dark brown hair, wearing original plaid dress & straw hat, black shoes, 42" (ILLUS.) **735**

Ideal "Miss Curity" composition lady, un-marked, composition head w/blue sleep eyes w/lashes, closed mouth w/bright red lips, color blush on cheeks & knees, orig-inal set blonde mohair wig, jointed com-position body, wearing original nurse's white outfit w/name on the cap, ca. 1945, 21" (pinpoint black spot on cheek, lower leg broken & reglued) **288**

Jumeau Girl with Striped Dress

Jumeau (E.) bisque head girl, marked, brown paperweight eyes, closed mouth, brown wig, pierced eyes, jointed compo-sition body, wearing old dress of pale blue, pink & white striped material, old leather shoes, 17" (ILLUS.) **9,000**

Jumeau (E.) bisque head girl, marked "Depose E 7 J," brown paperweight eyes in hand-cut openings, closed mouth, pierced ears, brown synthetic wig over bare original skin wig, eight-ball composi-tion body w/jointed straight wrists, Jumeau label on body, wearing cotton undergarments, brown tweedy dress & hat w/maroon satin trim, brown leather keystone shoes, 16 1/2" (uneven black edge lines at eye openings) **4,025**

Large Jumeau Girl Doll

Jumeau (E.) bisque head girl, marked "Deposé Jumeau 12," blue paperweight eyes, closed mouth, pierced applied ears, cork pate w/original blonde mohair wig, straight-wrist composition body, wearing a white lawn dress w/blue ribbon trim & blue leather shoes, small chip on lower eyelid, ca. 1885, 26" (ILLUS.) **6,325**

Fine Jumeau in Early Satin-Silk Dress

Jumeau (E.) bisque head girl, marked "E.J. - France," brown paperweight eyes, mauve eye shadow, closed mouth, pierced applied ears, cork pate & original blonde mohair wig, jointed straight-wrist eight-ball composition marked body, original red Jumeau earrings, commer-cial aqua satin & ecru silk faille dress, brown leather shoes, ca. 1885, tiny red age line side of nose, some wig wear, dress fragile, 20" (ILLUS.) **5,463**

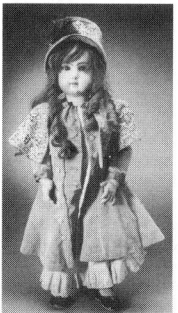

Large Jumeau with Coat & Bonnet

Jumeau (E.) bisque head girl, red-stamped "Tete Jumeau" mark, blue pa-perweight eyes, open/closed mouth, pierced ears, dark blonde Chereox natu-ral hair wig, straight-wrist composition marked body, wearing a lace-trimmed slip & long jacket w/lace trim & matching bonnet, tiny flakes at ears, damage & restoration to body, 28" (ILLUS.) **3,450**

Jumeau (E.) bisque socket head "Alice" girl, marked "Depose Tete Jumeau 6," brown paperweight eyes, open mouth w/upper teeth, cork pate w/original light brown mohair wig, fully articulated com-position body, commercial pale green silk taffeta dress & brimmed bonnet w/purple trim, 16 1/2" **2,070**

Jumeau (E.) bisque swivel head lady, unmarked, cobalt blue eyes w/mauve shadowing above, lightly feathered brows, closed mouth, pierced ears, light brown h.h. wig, cloth body w/kid arms & legs w/blue leather high button boots, wearing a period dark green silk taffeta dress, black lace trim, straw hat, additional brown crepe wrapper & lace hat, ca. 1870s, 17 1/2" (shoulder plate w/discolored line in making, break at wrist, lace sleeve trim detached)................................. **2,070**

K*R Character Head Girl

K(star)R bisque character head girl, marked "K*R - Simon Halbig - 126-46," blue flirty sleep eyes w/metal lids, open mouth w/two upper teeth & tongue, brown mohair wig w/pulls, fully-articulated slant-hip composition & wood toddler body, wearing a white & red dotted Swiss dress, shoes & socks, splits to wood in body, 20" (ILLUS.)... **633**

K (star) R bisque head character boy, marked "K*R Simon & Halbig 115/A 48," brown sleep eyes, closed pouty mouth, reddish blond caracal wig, side-jointed composition toddler body, wearing a red & green plush jester's costume, retains original pink gingham outfit, 19" (wig pulls, small red spot on cheek)................... **4,313**

K (star) R bisque socket head character girl, marked "K*R Simon Halbig 122," blue sleep eyes, open mouth w/two upper teeth, blonde mohair wig, fully articulated composition toddler body, side-slant legs, wearing a green cotton dress, 12" (some paint scuffs)................................. **920**

Kathe Kruse Boy Doll

Kathe Kruse boy, marked w/partial paper label, cloth w/blond wig, swivel head w/painted face, slight blush to cheeks, on a muslin body w/jointed hips, wearing a white cotton sailor suit, missing hat, shoes & socks, ca. 1930, 20" (ILLUS.)...... **1,725**

Rare Kruse "Schlenkerchen" Doll

Kathe Kruse character toddler, "Schlenkerchen," soles stamped "Kathe Kruse - Germany," all-stockinette, pressed & oil-painted double-seam head, painted features, brown hair, shaded brown painted eyes w/eyeliner, light upper lashes, closed smiling mouth, cloth neck ring, stockinette covered, padded armature frame body, mitten hands, rounded feet, unlaundered off-white undergarments only, ca. 1922, 13" (ILLUS.)........................ **5,463**

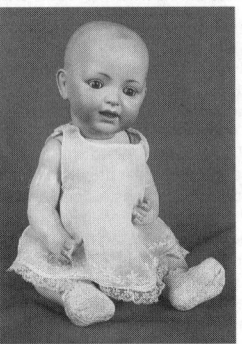

Kestner Solid Dome Head Baby

Kestner (J.D.) bisque socket head baby, marked, solid dome head w/light painted hair, blue sleep eyes, open mouth w/tongue, jointed composition baby body, w/light lace-trimmed nightshirt & knitted booties, 15" (ILLUS.)........................... **450**

Kestner (J.D.) bisque socket head character baby, marked "K Made in Germany - 14. JDK 211," blue glass sleep eyes, open-closed mouth, original blonde mohair wig & plaster pate, bent-limb composition baby body, wearing a finely knit cream-colored outfit including cap & booties, remnants of paper crown sticker on neck, ca. 1920, 13 1/2"..................................... **489**

Kestner (J.D.) bisque socket head girl, marked "129," brown sleep eyes, open

mouth w/inset teeth, original blonde mohair wig, full jointed composition body,
wearing a pale pink & net lace dress &
matching shoes, 16" (tiny white spot on
cheek) 805

Kestner Mold 143 Girl

Kestner (J.D.) bisque socket head girl,
marked, mold No.143, blue glass eyes
w/painted brows, open mouth, brown
hair, jointed composition body, wearing a
white lace-trimmed dress, socks &
shoes, 12" (ILLUS.) 750

Kley & Hahn Character Girl

Kley & Hahn bisque head character girl,
marked, Mold 546, blue sleep eyes,
closed mouth, dark blonde wig, jointed
composition body, wearing white lace-
trimmed blouse & dark skirt, floral wreath
in her hair, small 1/2" hairline, 20"
(ILLUS.) 2,100
**Konig & Wernicke bisque socket head
character baby,** marked "K + W" in red
circle, blue sleep eyes, open mouth
w/two upper teeth & wobble tongue,
"breather" w/pierced nostrils, original
brown mohair wig, bent-limb composition
baby body, wearing later nightshirt, 27"
(dark painted tongue, tiny white spot &
line on cheeks) 805

Lenci girl, all-felt, painted blue side-glancing eyes, blonde mohair wig, swivel
head, jointed limbs, wearing a blue felt &
organdy dress & shoes, organdy
underwear, ca. 1930, 21" 575
Lenci girl, miniature, pressed felt, brown-
painted eyes, closed serious mouth,
blonde mohair wig, jointed limbs, white
organdy sleeveless dress, blue felt trim,
pink & blue applied felt flowers, woven
faux straw bonnet, matching trim, matching felt shoes, ca. 1930, 8" (toning & soil-
ing to flowers) 316
Lenci "Mary Pickford" lady, long-limbed
style, felt, a felt face w/light greyish blue
painted eyes to right, long nose, closed
mouth, long bare felt arms, classic Lenci
fingers, white & green organdy summer
frock, felt wide-brimmed bonnet, all
trimmed w/felt flowers & ruffles, silk
stockings, pale green felt shoes w/felt
flowers, original Lenci tag sewn on
dress, ca. 1930, 28" (small stain on back
of skirt) 1,840
Papier-maché shoulder head lady, black-
painted head & features, short curly hair,
red lips, painted-on gold-toned necklace,
milliner's model-style body of brown cloth
w/wood lower limbs, pink cotton dress
overlaid w/tiers of lace, mid-19th c.,
8 3/4" (fine crack on shoulder mold line &
right side of head) 748
S.F.B.J. bisque head boy, marked
"S.F.B.J. 60 Paris 3," dark pupil-less
sleeping eyes, open mouth w/four upper
teeth, dark blond h.h. wig, jointed composition body, wearing olive green wool suit
& hat, brown shoes, early 20th c., 20"
(surface scratch line back of head, two
broken fingers, paint loss, wear) 460
Schmidt (Franz) bisque socket head girl,
marked "S + C 7 1/2 85," stationary
brown glass eyes, open mouth w/upper
teeth, pierced ears, replaced long
blonde h.h. wig, chunky fully-jointed
composition body, wearing period undergarments & a dark blue silk twill dress,
33 1/2" (repairs & some repaint to body)... 1,035

Schoenhut Character Head Boy

Schoenhut character head walking boy,
marked, carved sober face w/molded &
painted features & painted hair, jointed

shoulders & hips, original decals on back of head & back, wearing a cotton Russian-style romper suit, some paint wear, 17 1/4" (ILLUS.) **518**

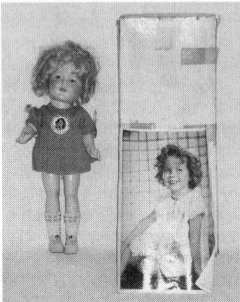

Shirley Temple Doll & Signed Photo

Shirley Temple composition doll, marked, composition head w/sleep eyes & blonde wig, jointed composition body, wearing short dark blue dress w/original pin, tan shoes & socks, w/box & autographed photo, 13" (ILLUS.) **1,018**

Fine Simon & Halbig Character Girl

Simon & Halbig bisque socket head character girl, marked "S & H - 1279 - DEP - Germany - 3," blue sleep eyes, pierced ears, open mouth w/dimples, raised molded fly-away eyebrows, original dark brown mohair wig, fully articulated composition & wood body w/some wear & scuffing, wearing period white cotton dress, patterned black cape & high-brim black velvet hat, early 20th c., 28" h. (ILLUS.) **4,313**

Simon & Halbig No. 949 Girl

Simon & Halbig bisque socket head girl, marked "949," brown stationary eyes, closed mouth, pierced ears, blonde mohair wig, fully articulated composition marked body, wearing a yellow cotton faille dress, tiny rub on side of cheek, 28" (ILLUS.) **2,530**

Simon & Halbig bisque socket head girl, marked "SH 949," blue lined paperweight eyes, closed mouth, pierced ears, new auburn h.h. wig on flat solid dome head w/three holes, straight-wrist jointed composition body, wearing a pink flowered print cotton dress, 12" (nose rub) **1,150**

Steiner (Jules) bisque socket head girl, marked "J. Steiner Bte SGDG Paris Fire A 6," stamped in red "Le Parisien," blue paperweight eyes, closed mouth, pierced ears, new long auburn wig, straight-limb Steiner composition body w/slender fingers, wearing a period-style blue dress & shoes, 14" **2,185**

Stuffed Vinyl Davy Crockett Doll

Stuffed vinyl, "Davy Crockett," sewn flattened vinyl body in brown & cream printed w/name & gun designs, molded plastic mask face & mohair brown wig, ca. 1955, 10" (ILLUS.) **66**

Vogue "Ginny," marked "Ginny - Vogue Dolls - Inc. - Pat. No. 2887954 - Made in U.S.A.," Vogue tag on dress, hard plastic head, blue sleep eyes w/molded lashes, single-stroke brows, closed mouth, strong cheek color, original blonde side-part hair, dressed as Little Red Riding Hood in a red polka dot dress, red suede-like cape & hat, red straw basket, red shoes, white socks, original hinged lid pink box #52, Gilchrest's illegible price guide, ca. 1952 (eyes stuck in downcast position) **489**

Wax over papier-maché shoulder head lady, unmarked, cornflower blue stationary eyes, closed pink-painted mouth, pierced ears, original blonde mohair wig pulled back into snood, cloth body, wooden lower limbs, blue-painted boots, period ecru silk dress, lavender straw hat, news pink hat box w/new purple hat, ca. 1870s, 24" (possible mouth retouch, light cracking & mottling to shoulder plate & by eye, some scoring to wood)............................ **288**

DOORSTOPS

All doorstops listed are flat-back cast iron unless otherwise noted. Most names are taken from Doorstops—Identification & Values, *by Jeanne Bertoia (Collector Books, 1985).*

Aunt Jemima, full-figured black Mammy w/hands on hips, wearing white kerchief, large dark blue crossed shawl over a red blouse, wide white apron over long red dress, 8 x 13 1/4" **$264**

Lily Flowers in Basket Doorstop

Basket of Flowers, large creamy yellow lily blossoms & thick green leaves in a creamy yellow basket w/a criss-cross design & upright arched handle, slight paint wear (ILLUS.) **138**

Colonial Lawyer, standing man in front of square pedestal, white wig, red long coat w/black trim, black kneebreeches, holding a gold-trimmed black tricorn hat in one hand, rounded base, marked "Trade (triangle - WS) Mark," 9 5/8" h. (some wear) **176**

Court lady w/open fan, elegantly dressed 18th c. lady in a low-cut, wide tiered deep red gown w/gold swag trim, white bouffant hair w/red bow, gold necklace, large open yellow fan in one hand **154**

Daisy Bowl, high mound of bright Shasta daisies, dark blue mums & small yellow blossoms in a white ribbed rounded bowl w/a flaring ringed base, Hubley No. 452, 5 1/8 x 7 1/2" (slight wear)............................. **171**

 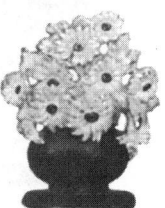

Daisy Bowl & Flower Basket

Daisy Bowl, large, high bouquet of dark yellow black-eyed Susans in a squatty bulbous footed black bowl, Hubley, 6 x 7" (ILLUS. right) **198**

Flat-backed Boston Terrier

Dog, Boston Terrier, flat-backed style, black & white dog facing left, standing on an oblong grassy base painted black, 9 5/8 x 11 3/4" (ILLUS.)................................... **396**

Dog, German Shepherd, flat-backed style, raised on a narrow trestle bar-style base (worn brown paint) **132**

Dog, Greyhound, tall slender dog in white w/black spots standing on a narrow oblong green base (some paint wear)............... **198**

Dog, Terrier, free-standing full-bodied dog w/head turned toward viewer, short tail erect, white w/brown patches (slight wear)... **83**

Dog, Whippet, standing black dog w/white spots, on thin rectangular base, 6 3/4 x 7 1/2" (slight paint wear) **160**

Drum Major, standing figure carrying long yellow baton, tall plumed red hat, red jacket & white pants, on small pale green square base, 13 1/2" h. (slight wear) **264**

Duck w/Top Hat, walking comical bird in green & yellow wearing dark red hat & pants, rectangular black base, 7 1/2" h. (some paint wear)... **176**

Flower Basket, low wide dark green latticework basket w/short pointed & ringed center handle, filled w/a wide, low bouquet of mixed flowers in shades of pale blue, lavender & purple, 10 7/8 x 11" **149**

Flower Basket, small wicker basket w/wide flaring rim & wide arched handle centered by a blue ribbon above mixed roses & flowers in red, yellow & blue, black beveled base, 8 1/4" h. (light paint wear)............ **143**

Flower Basket, tall widely flaring tan wicker basket w/a narrow center handle tied w/a large yellow ribbon above a mixed bouquet of yellow blossoms & green leaves, stepped pale green & black base, some paint wear (ILLUS. left with Daisy Bowl)....... **242**

Flowerpot Doorstop

Flowerpot, flowerpot on semi-circular base in brown paint, filled w/yellow & orange/red flowers & green leaves, marked on the back "Hubley 330," 7 1/4" h. (ILLUS.) **55**

French Basket, tall yellow wicker basket w/high arched handle w/ribbon, pink, blue, yellow & purple flowers, Hubley No. 69, 11" h. (some light paint wear) **232**

Fruit Basket, tall wicker basket w/high rounded rim & arched entwined handle, filled w/a low mound of mixed fruits including grapes, banana & oranges, on a black rectangular base (some paint wear) **149**

Galleon Doorstop

Galleon, cast aluminum, three-masted ship under full sail w/long banners atop each mast, raised star & cross on center sail, original painted surface, by O.B. Campbell, St. Johns, Michigan, 11 3/4 x 13" **30**

Geisha, Japanese lady kneeling on rectangular base & playing stringed instrument, pale yellow floral-painted kimono, deep red base, Hubley, 6 x 7" (slight wear) **231**

Girl Holding Flowers Doorstop

Girl Holding Flowers, full-figured mid-Victorian girl wearing a blue & white bonnet, white shawl & long, full, blue dress, holding a bouquet of colored flowers in her hands, some paint wear, pot metal, 7 1/2" h. (ILLUS.) **220**

Gladiolus, yellow flowers in a white urn-form vase, Hubley, 10" h. **160**

Prancing Horse Doorstop

Horse, in the form of a prancing circus horse in dappled bronze color, w/long black tail & mane, red & white striped band around horse's mid-section, on painted wooden stand, original painted surface, base probably an old replacement, 4 3/4 x 9 1/4 x 11" (ILLUS.) **200**

Lil Red Riding Hood Doorstop

Lil Red Riding Hood, short stocky girl in red hood & cape w/green bow at neck, holding basket of goodies in one arm, on oblong worn green mound base, Hubley No. 95, 9 1/2" h. (ILLUS.) **396**

Maid, curtsying, white cap & long apron over long black dress, green base, cJo No. 1242, 8 7/8" h. (slight wear) **253**

Marigolds in Ringed Vase

Marigolds, large yellow marigolds w/smaller dark blue, red & pale blue flowers in a ringed inverted beehive-form vase on a black rectangular base, Hubley No. 315, some paint wear, 7 1/2 x 8" (ILLUS.) **154**

Minuteman, standing man in Colonial dress resting his hands on a standing rifle at front, black tricorn hat & long coat, white & yellow kneebreeches, square black base (some paint wear) **209**

Parrot, large full-bodied yellow & green parrot w/topknot perched on a dark brown stump base, Albany Foundry, 12 1/2" h. (some paint wear) **165**

Parrot in Ring (small), round gold ring w/a small perched green, red & yellow parrot, on a dark green rectangular base, 7 x 8" (some paint wear) **127**

Petunias & Asters, yellow & blue flowers in a short wicker basket, Hubley No. 470, 9 1/2" h. (some paint wear) **154**

Rose Basket, yellow roses & blue, pink & red blossoms in a yellow wicker basket, Hubley No. 121, 11" h. **132**

Rose Vase, pink roses & green leaves in a white cornucopia-form vase on rectangular base, Hubley, 10 1/8" h. **165**

Scottie Dogs Doorstop

Scottie Dogs, two Scotties w/perked ears sit on base, original black paint, 8 1/2" l. (ILLUS.) **100**

Squirrel, figure of squirrel sitting on a log & holding nut to mouth w/front paws, oval-shaped base, old black paint, unmarked Bradley and Hubbard, 10 3/4" h. **495**

Squirrel, figure of squirrel sitting on hind legs & holding nut to mouth w/front paws, half-round base, 6 3/4" h. **330**

Squirrel, figure of squirrel sitting on log eating a nut w/front paws, on oval-shaped base, old white, brown & green paint, unmarked Bradley & Hubbard, 11 1/8" h. (minor wear) **550**

Woman Holding Flower Basket, standing lady in Colonial dress & bonnet, her arms at her sides w/each hand holding a basket of flowers, blue dress w/blue band, cJo No. 1270, 8" h. (some paint wear) **220**

ENAMELS

Enamels have been used to decorate a variety of substances, particularly metals. The best-known small enameled wares such as patch and other small boxes and napkin rings, are the Battersea Enamels made by the Battersea Enamel Works in the last half of the 18th century. However, the term is often loosely applied to other English enamels. Russian enamels, usually on a silver or gold base, are famous and expensive. Early 20th century French enamel on copper wares and those items produced in China at the turn of the 20th century in imitation of the early Russian style are also drawing dealer and collector attention.

Bodkin holder, robin's egg-blue ground w/scrolled cartouches of figural landscape scenes, South Staffordshire, England, late 18th c., 5 " l. **$978**

Bonbonniere, model of a boar head, the cover decorated w/scene of boar hunting, South Staffordshire, England, late 18th c., 2 3/4" l. **2,530**

Box, cov., enamel & sterling silver, ovoid, base w/ropetwist banding, top w/gold-washed rim, reversible lid w/blue enamel centered by gold-washed bead on one side, other side w/a late 19th c. tintype under glass, early 20th c., maker's mark "Potter Mellen," possibly American, 2" l., 1 1/4" h. **431**

Box, cov., oval, the flat lid w/metal loop border band around the white ground painted in jewel-like colors of blue & green w/tiny red flowers around a central oval w/a tiny polychrome floral bouquet, England, late 18th - early 19th c., 1 7/8" l. **275**

Box, cov., oval, the top in white w/polychrome decoration of a tulip & cluster of other flowers, England, late 18th - early 19th c., 2 3/8" l. (wear, hairlines) **330**

Box, cov., rectangular box enameled w/couples in landscapes, top w/hinged oval cover opening to reveal a hinged singing bird, fitted box w/key, Swiss, early 20th c., 4" l. **3,162**

Box, cov., rectangular, the flat cover w/a white ground decorated around the border w/raised foliage scrolls enclosing a transfer-printed landscape scene of a river w/bridge, farmer, etc., highlighted in gilt & purple, gilt-metal fittings, England, late 18th c., 2 7/8" l. (some wear & edge damage) **495**

Box, cov., miniature, Battersea-type, scene of couple on cover & reading "I Love Well to Kiss and Tell," mirror in cover, 1 1/2" l. (some damage) **77**

Box, cov., miniature, Battersea-type, scene of couple on cover & reading "May Thy Hand and Mine Forever Entwine," mirror in cover, 1 3/4" l. **77**

Candlesticks, domed & scalloped base centering a double-knop lower stem below a tapering columnar section below the tall cylindrical socket w/a wide flared rim, deep blue ground w/white dots, gilt foliage & scrolled cartouches w/polychrome pastoral scenes of figures in landscapes, South Staffordshire, England, late 18th c., restorations, 14 1/4" h., pr. **2,300**

Casket, cov., enamel on gilt-bronze, the rectangular case on four small knob feet, the sides w/central oblong reserves w/a blue ground & overall ornate yellow, brown & red leafy scrolls & a black-trimmed pointed center reserve on the front, the hinged domed cover w/a pointed hasp & an arched scroll-ended swing handle w/blue trim, the cover w/a series of overlapping circles against a blue ground trimmed w/yellow, red & gold, black & gold leafy scroll border bands, France, ca. 1900, 4 x 7", 6" h. **3,024**

Jewelry box, casket-form, enamel & ebony, the four-sided domed top surmounted by a rectangular platform w/a rearing equestrian figure, the stepped wide top cornice over a rectangular case fitted around the sides w/enameled figural & landscape plaques, the front w/two hinged doors w/oval plaques opening to two drawers w/matching plaques & further plaques on the door interiors, flaring ogee platform w/gilt-metal mounts raised on four knob feet on platforms, Vienna, Austria, late 19th c., 6 1/4" h.. **2,415**

Kovsh, enamel on silver, squatty boat-shaped bowl w/a flattened hook end handle, overall floral scrolls in blues, whites & rose pink, blue dot band borders, by Gustav Klingert, Russia, ca. 1900, 8" l. **4,480**

Enameled Miniature Harp

Model of a harp, the gilt-metal framework decorated along the sides w/enameled panels showing 18th c. courting scenes & cupids, France, late 19th - early 20th c., 5" h. (ILLUS.).. **1,595**

Fine Enameled Mini Screen with Clock

Model of a screen, gilt-metal & guilloche enamel, a two-fold screen w/scroll-cast frame & feet enclosing red enameled panels h.p. w/white enamel landscape scenes, the left panel inset w/a tiny clock dial, France, open 2 3/4 x 3 1/4" (ILLUS.)..... **795**

Salt cellar, oval form, white ground w/gilt scrolled cartouches, polychrome decorated w/figural landscapes, South Staffordshire, England, late 18th c., 2 1/2" l. **288**

Salt dips, low wide rounded body on three spade feet, gilded metal rim above the sides w/a pink ground decorated w/white dotted trelliswork & three white scroll-edged reserves w/polychrome flowers, attributed to Bilston, England, 18th c., 2 1/2" d., pr. (wear, one w/damage to feet)... **440**

Spoons, enameled bronze, herm-form handles, the bowls enameled on both sides w/figural scenes, Vienna, Austria, late 19th c., 5" l., set of 6 .... **633**

Teaspoons, enameled silver, slender tapering enameled & ring-turned handle to a deep teardrop-form bowl enameled on the back w/ornate scrolling stylized florals in shades of blue, rose, red & black, Russia, ca. 1900, the set **1,900**

Vase, Art Deco-style, enamel-on-copper, bulbous body tapering to a tiny flared mouth, exterior enameled w/stylized drapery fabric in shades of pale green & white decorated w/various blossoms in shades of crimson, rose & green, signed in gilt "Fauré-Limoges/France," ca. 1925, 11 1/2" h. **6,325**

Vase, Art Deco-style, enamel-on-copper, ovoid body tapering to a tiny flared mouth, cobalt interior, exterior enameled in high relief w/geometric devices & entrelacs in shades of white, aquamarine, teal, sky & cobalt blue over a silvered ground, signed in gilt "C. Fauré - Limoges - Made in France," ca. 1925, 10" h............. **6,900**

Vase, Art Deco-style, enamel-on-copper, the ovoid body tapering to a tiny round mouth, decorated w/an overall banded geometric design w/light & dark patterned bands in ruby red, pink, black, white & silver, signed in gilt "C. FAURÉ - Limoges," France, ca. 1925, 11 3/8" h....... **2,875**

Vase, cov., Art Deco-style, enamel-on-copper, ovoid body, clear-enameled interior, exterior enameled w/panels of overlapping lozenges, in shades of white, black, sky & cobalt blue, over silvered background, cap lid, signed in gilt "Fauré - Limoges - France," ca. 1925, 16 3/8" h. **7,475**

Vase, enamel on copper, footed tapering ovoid form w/small flared rim, decorated w/stylized tropical leaves in green against a landscape of geometric designs in lavender, white & deep blue, painted "C. Fauré - Limoges - France," ca. 1920s, 11 1/2" h. **2,185**

EPERGNES

Epergnes were popular as centerpieces on tables of the 19th century. Many have receptacles of colored glass for holding sweetmeats, fruit or flowers. Early epergnes were made entirely of metal, including silver.

One-piece Epergne

Amber glass, one-piece, squat bulbous bowl on blue applied feet, teardrop-shaped vase, sapphire blue glass applied trim, dainty colored enammeled flowers & leaves, teardrops & rigaree trim, 14 3/8" h. (ILLUS.) **$395**

Cranberry Opalescent Epergne

Cranberry opalescent, round pink/cranberry base w/fluted vaseline edge, four jack-in-the-pulpit-form vases in pink/cranberry w/vaseline rims & rigaree trim (ILLUS.) **1,500**

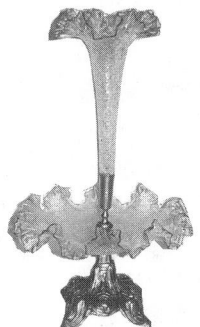

Green Overshot Glass Epergne

Green overshot glass, ruffle-edged bowl w/trumpet-form vase, also w/ruffled edge, footed ormolu base & vase holder, 16 1/2" h. (ILLUS.) **325**

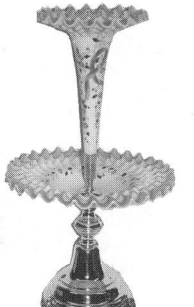

Peach Satin Glass Epergne

Satin glass, closely ruffled shallow bowl, trumpet form vase w/ruffled rim, shading from deeper peach to lighter, w/allover enameled decoration of blue flowers, green & brown leaves, purple banner on vase, resilvered foot base (ILLUS.) **795**

Satin Glass Epergne

Satin glass, shallow scalloped bowl & lily-form vase w/fluted edges, pink & white w/hobnail effect, resilvered base & vase holder, 13 3/4" h. (ILLUS.) **365**

FIREARMS

Carbine, British constabulary 76-caliber carbine, ca. 1856, 40" l. **$448**

Fowling gun, Edmunds, eight-gage percussion fowling gun, marked "Edmunds, Birmingham," 18th c., in the 1800s the barrel was converted to the percussion ignition system as indicated by the 1813 Birmingham mark, 64" l. **476**

Long rifle, percussion model, curly maple stock, engraved brass patchbox w/acorn top, small oval cap box beneath cheek piece, brass hardware w/forged iron trigger guard & nickel silver inlays, octagonal 41" barrel signed "N. Oates," 57" l. (restored forearm split, small hairline near side plate) **825**

Long rifle, percussion-type, curly maple stock w/old dark finish & checkering at the wrist, brass hardware includes engraved four-part patchbox & small side plate, nickel silver thumb piece, stamped signature for J. Fordney, Lancaster, Pa., engraved lock is marked "Warranted," 43 1/4" l. barrel... **1,375**

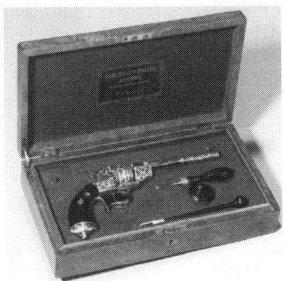

French Pin-fire Revolver in Case

Revolver, pin-fire model, w/gold & silver damascene engraving, w/original fitted case w/cleaning tools, made for Oberea de Hermanos Eibar & retailed by Barcenas Y Posada Amneria, Habana Cuba, French, 19th c. (ILLUS.) **4,032**

Rifle, half stock model, curly maple stock w/"fish belly" configuration, 33 3/4" octagonal barrel, brass hardware w/back action lock signed "Golcher," small brass cap box, 50 1/4" l. (stock restoration near tang) **715**

Rifle, half stock percussion type, curly maple stock w/original dark finish & appropriate wear, well-shaped lock mortise w/stamped signature for "Manton" on the lock plate, half moon-shaped cheek piece, brass hardware including small cap box, 34 1/4" octagon barrel has browned finish & turned muzzle, unsigned but probably Ohio, 50 1/2" l. **605**

FIREPLACE & HEARTH ITEMS

Andirons, cast iron, Arts & Crafts style, w/applied diamond designs & simulated hammered surface, "B.&H." mark for Bradley & Hubbard, Meridian, Connecticut, 20 3/4" h. **$440**

Bellows, decorated w/original rosemaling including green-yellow, black & dark red on lighter red ground, green edging, worn leather, 18 3/8" l. **578**

Bellows, leather w/brass nozzle, original dark mustard ground w/stenciled fruit in copper, black, green & red, 18" l. (releathered, some edge damage & wear) **110**

Bellows, maple, Federal style, painted yellow and stencil decorated w/depiction of Massachusetts State House, New England, early 19th c., 18 1/2" l., pr. **2,400**

Bellows, turtle-back type, leather w/brass nozzle, original mustard ground w/green edging, stenciled tulips in red & gold w/h.p. green & black leaves, 17 1/4" l. (releathered, nozzle is loose) **220**

Bellows, turtle-back type, original yellow w/freehand & stenciled flowers in red, green & gold, green border, brass nozzle w/original worn leather, 17" l. (some wear) **275**

Fender, brass, wrought-iron framework, molded base & two bands of finely detailed piercings, cast paw feet, early 20th c., 15 x 46 1/2", 11 1/2" h. **275**

Federal-style Fire Grate

Fire grate, cast iron, Federal style, framework has molded trim along back & sides w/cement lining, serpentine front w/beaded trim, engraved foliage & piercings w/applied rosettes, tapered front legs & urn finials, 38 1/8" l. (ILLUS.) **523**

FISHING COLLECTIBLES
Books & Paper Items

Fishing Tackle Catalog, 1847

Catalog, for "Martin L. Bradford, Importer, And Wholesale and Retail Dealer in Fishing Tackle," Boston, 1847 (ILLUS.) **$2,475**

Lures

Tiny Harkauf Fly Rod Lure

Harkauf, wood fly rod lure, in blue/green w/white belly, three red stripes & yellow eyes, 1 1/8" l. (ILLUS.) **550**

Heddon Model 150 Minnow Lure

Heddon Underwater Minnow, wood, model 150, in original box w/"Genuine Heddon Dowagiac Minnow" on lid w/picture of fish taking the bait (ILLUS.) **935**

South Bend Fishing Tackle Lure

South Bend Fishing Tackle Company, wooden Truck-Oreno in red & white w/long red & white feathers at end, yellow eyes (ILLUS.) **2,970**

Reels

Blue Grass Model No. 7 Casting Reel

Horton Mfg., Blue Grass model No. 7 bait casting reel, Bristol, Connecticut (ILLUS.) **880**

Model 44A Trout Fly Reel

Leonard, H.L., model 44A trout fly reel, New York (ILLUS.)....................................... **2,970**

Blue Grass Model No. 4 Casting Reel

Meek, B.F. & Sons, Blue Grass model No. 4 bait casting reel, Louisville, Kentucky (ILLUS.)... **660**

Prototype Trout Fly Reel

Orvis, C.F., prototype of the 1874 patent trout fly reel, in original hinged walnut box, Manchester, Vermont (ILLUS.)........... **1,870**

Rods

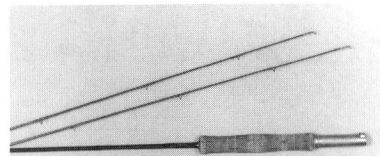

Rare 7' Aristocrat Fishing Rod

Goodwin Granger, Aristocrat model, Denver, Colorado, rare, 7' l. (ILLUS.)............... **1,100**

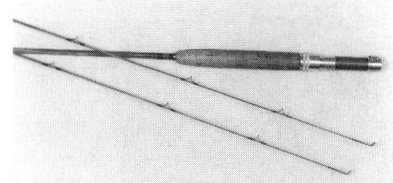

Split Bamboo Fly Rod

Halstead, George H., split bamboo fly rod, Danbury, Connecticut, ca. 1940, 7 1/2' l., restored (ILLUS.)... **3,410**

Miscellaneous

Howe's Vacuum Bass Bait Box

Bait box, tin, rectangular, deep blue, empty, w/"Howe's Vacuum Bass Bait - Price 75 cts. - Vacuum Bait Co. - Patented - North Manchester, Ind." on lid (ILLUS.)................... **880**

Rattan Creel

Creel, rattan, leather-trimmed, "Turtle Trade Mark" (ILLUS.) **2,640**

Leather-trimmed Split Willow Creel

Creel, split willow, leather-trimmed, size 15, by George Lawrence of Portland, Oregon, 1950, unused (ILLUS.)........................ **9,020**

Wood Tackle Box

Tackle box, leather-covered wood, w/hinged lid, inside divided into compartments, another shallow section divided into four parts can be taken out, American (ILLUS.) **1,100**

FRAKTUR

Fraktur paintings are decorative birth and marriage certificates of the 18th and 19th centuries and also include family registers and similar documents. Illuminated family documents, birth and baptismal certificates, religious texts and rewards of merit, in a particular style, are known as "fraktur" because of the similarity to the 16th century type-face of that name. Gay watercolor borders, frequently incorporating stylized birds, often frame the hand-lettered documents, which were executed by local ministers, schoolmasters or itinerant penman. Most are of Pennsylvania Dutch origin.

Birth & baptism record, rectangular, w/images of flowering plants on either side in yellow, red, black & green, w/birds perched at tops, two large flowers at center between the birds, for "Magelsi Preiss, Sept 27, 1798," Northumberland County, Pennsylvania, curly maple frame, 14 3/4 x 18" (glued to backing w/restorations & damage) **$660**
Certificate of Birth and Baptism, titled "Welentines," pen & ink w/verses in boxes topped by naive black & yellow watercolor parrots on red, yellow & green flowers, center records birth of "John David Myers" in 1828 in "Stark County, Tuskarawas (sic) Township," "Was printed in the year 1831," old frame w/red paint, Ohio, 11 1/8 x 13 5/8" w/frame (stains w/some damage & fold lines)......... **1,980**

Henry Young Fraktur

Drawing, dated 1838 from "Centre County in Staate Pennsylvanien," features a mantel inscribed "Geburts und Tauf Schein," w/blue, yellow & red pillars & large urns at the top, two women, one wearing a yellow dress, the other a white dress w/yellow sash, flanking the message, handcolored, attributed to Henry Young, in yellow & blue frame (ILLUS.)..... **2,750**
Drawing, rectangular, w/image of large heart in center flanked by two smaller hearts, parrots in upper corners & large tulip at center, other flowers & smaller tulips surrounding hearts, "Friederick Krebs" at bottom & printed "Reading 1791," laid down on paper backing, in reeded frame w/dry green paint, 15 3/4 x 19 1/4 (old fold lines in center, some holes).. **1,595**
Drawing, watercolor, decorated w/Valentine hearts & two cherubs, tulips & star flowers, all in shades of pink, blue, yellow, green, red & brown, hearts have verses in German, frame w/dark aligatored red, 14 1/2 x 17 7/8" (crease lines & some edge damage)................................ **1,980**
Drawing w/verse, image of large stepped urn on plinth on which is verse in German that includes "Carolina Bortz, Hempfield Taunschip, Westmoreland Kounty, Pennsylvanien, 1840," all bordered in blue & yellow w/black on white foliage design, rose vining on either side, molded frame has late green & red paint, 15 x 18" w/frame (glued to backing w/fold lines & small holes, light stains) **3,190**

FRAMES

Pine Needle Bronze Over Glass Frame

Bronze & glass, rectangular w/wide panels, Pine Needle patt. in bronze w/caramel slag glass backing, Tiffany Studios, New York, 6 1/2 x 7 1/2", one panel of glass cracked (ILLUS.) **$375**

Pierced-design Picture Frame

Cast brass, beaded-rim rectangular form w/pierced decoration of heavy stylized leaves & scrolls & overhanging wave design on top, marked on reverse "2140 - NB & IW," gold tone, 9 x 12 1/4" (ILLUS.) **85**

Quatrefoil Frame

Cast brass, quatrefoil, footed frame w/ornate pierced decoration of cherubs, C-scrolls & roses, style number "670," 6 1/4 x 10" (ILLUS.) **165**

Rose Motif Frame

Cast brass, rectangular frame in rose motif, w/scroll feet, elaborate C-scroll decoration on back brace, marked "896," 6 1/4 x 9" (ILLUS.) **85**

Polychrome Frame

Cast iron, decorated along corners w/roses, polychrome paint, 5 1/4 x 7", some rust (ILLUS.) **60**

Cast-Iron Frame with Oval Opening

Cast iron, ornate pierced scroll design w/scrolled legs at base & scrolled ears at top flanking the top flower & scroll cartouche, oval center opening, bronzed finish, marked w/number 541, late 19th - early 20th c., 8 7/8 x 13" (ILLUS.) **165**

Gold-tone Iron Frame

Cast iron, rectangular gold-tone frame w/elaborate pierced decoration of stylized leaves & scrolls, marked on reverse w/style number "08576," 8 3/4 x 10" (ILLUS.) **68**

Jack-in-the-Pulpit Frame

Cast iron, rectangular, w/pierced decoration in jack-in-the-pulpit motif, dull bronze finish, 7 x 10 1/4" (ILLUS.) **300**

Large Pierced Oval Frame & Mirror

Cast iron, tall upright oval form w/a repeating border of pierced trefoils & leaves, an arched leafy scroll crest & a pierced scroll support at the bottom, gilt finish, enclosing an oval beveled mirror, late 19th - early 20th c., 13 x 18 3/4" (ILLUS.)............... **189**

Ornate Frame with Candlearms

Cast iron, very ornate pierced scroll-cast frame w/the arched top centered by a mask of Bacchus, two scrolled

candlearms at the base, enclosing a rectangular beveled mirror w/arched top, gilt finish, late 19th - early 20th c., 10 x 16 1/2" (ILLUS.) **195**

Pierced Design Frame

Spelter, delicate pierced design of stylized C-scrolls & leaves applied to oval frame w/bronze finish, 5 1/2 x 6 5/8" (ILLUS.) **75**

FRATERNAL ORDER COLLECTIBLES

What do George Washington, Oliver Hardy and Gene Autry all have in common? They share a bond that traverses all walks of life—membership in the world's oldest fraternal organization, the Free & Accepted Masons (F&AM). Dating back to 14th century England, this organization's roots are steeped in the architectural craft guilds and operative lodges—builders, stone masons and the like. From these early members come the elements of the Masonic emblem...a level, plumb and square, and the "G" to signify their belief in God.

Masonic ephemera, bric-a-brac and sacred books are abundant. In addition to the Masons, collectibles from sub-groups like the Order of the Eastern Star (OES), Shriners (32nd degree Masons), Scottish Rite, Knights Templar, etc. create a wide range of memorabilia that is prized by today's collectors.

Masonic ashtray, bronze, raised Masonic emblem in center, marked "AZTEC" on back, 5 1/4" d. **$10-15**

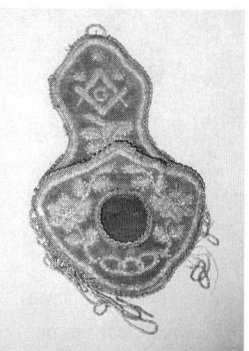

Masonic Ceremonial Shoe

Masonic ceremonial shoe, gold velvet w/beading, 8 1/4" l. (ILLUS.)....................... **25-35**

Various Masonic Molds

Masonic chocolate mold, pewter, Masonic symbol (ILLUS. left w/Scottish Rite chocolate mold) **30-40**

Masonic clock, brass, clock framed by Masonic emblem, 6 1/2" h. **35-40**

Masonic fabric, toile, red on natural white, w/design of arch in center surrounded by assorted Masonic symbols, 20 5/8 x 23 1/4" (stains, frame has worn gold liner) **303**

Masonic Match Holder

Masonic match holder, hanging-type, wood, two conical holders on shield form w/compass & ruler design above, 9 1/4" h. (ILLUS.) **30-35**

Masonic match holder, wooden w/Masonic symbol, 9" h. **35-40**

Masonic motto, "What is a Mason?" marked "Copr. 1923, The House of Art, NY, No. 238," framed, 7 3/4 x 10 3/4" **12-15**

Masonic Mug

Masonic mug, ceramic, cylindrical body w/D-form handle, cream w/blue & gold Masonic emblem, 4 3/4" h. (ILLUS.)............. **8-10**

Masonic mug, white milk glass w/blue Masonic emblem, marked "Masonic Lamp Golden Jubilee, 1919-1969," 5 3/8" h. **10**

Masonic panel, white lace in metal frame, 14 x 20" **45-55**

Masonic picture, gold foil images of Masonic emblem w/tools, framed in oval Victorian frame **75**

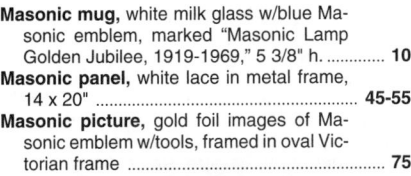

Masonic Pitcher

Masonic pitcher, ceramic, cylindrical body w/flared base, pinched rim spout & large C-form handle, blue & white w/black Masonic symbol, 16" h. (ILLUS.)..................... **50-60**

Masonic Plaque

Masonic plaque, wood w/Masonic emblem mounted on brown velvet backing, 8 1/2 x 13 1/2" (ILLUS.).............................. **15-20**

Masonic plate, ceramic, white w/medium blue highlights & gold trim, reading "175th Anniversary - Grand Lodge Free & Accepted Masons of the State of New York," image of lodge building in center above the dates 1781-1956, 8" d. **30-40**

Masonic Sash Pin

Masonic sash pin, round, blue & gold w/Masonic emblem in center, marked "The Caledonians Continental Lodge 76,

Waterbury, Connecticut," 4 1/2" d.
(ILLUS.)... **35-45**

Masonic shelf, mahogany, fretwork design
centered by Masonic emblem,
3 1/2 x 9 7/8 x 22" **35-45**

Masonic thermometer, metal, scrolled border w/square & compass frame, 7 1/2" h. **35**

OES (Order of the Eastern Star) ashtray,
ceramic, white w/OES emblem in center,
6" sq. **6-8**

Order of the Eastern Star ashtray, tin, embossed w/OES LOGO, 4 1/2" d..................... **8-10**

Order of the Eastern Star book, "The Eastern Star - The Evolution from a Rite to an Order" by Harold Van Buren Voorhis, Macory Publishing & Masonic Supply Company, Inc., New York, copyright 1938, 1954 .... **15**

Order of the Eastern Star coffeepot, cov., ceramic, bulbous body w/swan's neck spout & C-form handle w/thumbrest, white w/four-color OES emblem & gold trim, 7 1/2" h. **20-30**

OES Creamer & Sugar Bowl

Order of the Eastern Star creamer & cov. sugar bowl, ceramic, white w/four-color OES emblems & gold trim, marked "Lefton China, Hand Painted, Reg. U.S. Pat. Off., 2789," (ILLUS.).................... **15-20**

Order of the Eastern Star doily, hand-crocheted, white star form centered by OES emblem, 7 1/2" w. **3-5**

Order of the Eastern Star vase, ceramic, book-form, white w/gold trim, one side w/The Lord's Prayer in gold, OES emblem on other, marked "24 KT. Gold, Made in U.S.A.," 3 1/2 x 4 1/2" **15**

Order of the Eastern Star whimsey, ceramic, model of Victorian lady's shoe, white w/OES emblem & gold trim, 4" h. **8-10**

Scottish Rite chocolate mold, pewter, Scottish Rite symbol (ILLUS. right w/Masonic Mold) **50-60**

Scottish Rite Sword

Scottish Rite sword, 36" l. (ILLUS.) **50-60**

Shriner chocolate mold, pewter, Shriner symbol (ILLUS. center w/Masonic mold) ... **50-60**

Shriner doll, bobble head-type, image of Shriner wearing a fez, 7 1/2" h......................... **25**

Shriner paperweight, brass, w/Shrine emblem, marked on base "The Henderson Ames Co., Kalamazoo, Mich., Masonic and Shrine Supplies," 4 1/2" h. **25-35**

FRUIT JARS

Acme (LG Co. around 5-pointed star) Trademark 1893 - Mason's Patent Nov. 30th 1858 (on reverse), cylindrical w/ground mouth & zinc lid, smooth base, 1890-1900, aqua, pt..................................... **$235**

Adams & Co. - Manufacturers - Pittsburgh, Pa, cylindrical, applied collared mouth w/embossed clear glass lid, smooth base, 1865-1880, aqua, qt............... **476**

American (The) - NAG Co. (monogram) - Porcelain Lined, cylindrical, ground mouth w/zinc lid, smooth base, Canada, 1870-90, midget pt..................................... **134**

Two Atlas E-Z Seal Fruit Jars

Atlas E-Z Seal, "Atlas E-Z Seal Trademark Reg." on base, original glass lid w/wire bail, light blue, qt. (ILLUS. left)....................... **22**

Atlas E-Z Seal, "Atlas E-Z Seal Trademark Reg." on base, original glass lid w/wire bail, reddish amber, qt. (ILLUS. right)............. **44**

Half-gallon Ball Perfect Mason

Ball Perfect Mason, cylindrical, machined mouth w/zinc lid, smooth base, 1900-30, olive amber, 1/2 gal. (ILLUS.)......................... **246**

Ball Standard Quart Fruit Jar

Ball Standard, ABM groove ring wax sealer, smooth base, rich yellow olive, qt., some chipping around edge of lip, ca. 1915-25 (ILLUS.) **275**

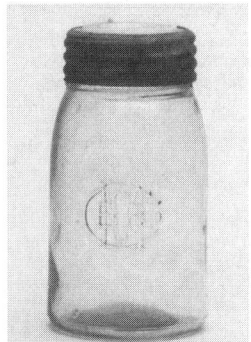

BBGM Co. Midget Pint Fruit Jar

BBGM Co. (monogram), cylindrical, ground mouth w/zinc band & glass lid, smooth base, aqua, midget pt. (ILLUS.) **672**

Beck, Phillips & Co. Pitts. Pa (on base), cylindrical, applied collared mouth w/original Willoughby stopple, smooth base, 1860-80, aqua, 1/2 gal. **336**

Bee Hive (below molded beehive & Trade Mark at top), cylindrical, machined mouth w/glass lid & zinc band, smooth base, 1880-1900, clear, midget pt. **616**

Cunningham & Co. Pittsburgh, PA (on base), tooled mouth w/outward rolled lip, smooth base, deep bluish aqua, 1/2 gal. **83**

Cunningham & Co. Pittsburgh, PA (on base), tooled mouth w/outward rolled lip, smooth base, light to medium kelly green, qt. **440**

Daisy (The) Jar, cylindrical, ground mouth w/glass lid & iron & steel yoke clamp, smooth base, 1880-1900, clear, qt. (some interior haze, weak embossing) **90**

Dakin & Compy - Tea & Coffee Merchants - Number One - Saint Paul's - Churchyard - London, tall cylindrical form w/applied round collared mouth, smooth base, England, 1860-80, bright yellowish olive green, 3 3/8" d., 3 3/4" h. **392**

Dayton, Prentiss & Borden. New York., cylindrical, outward rolled collared

mouth, pontil, 1845-60, aqua, qt. (some light interior haze) **476**

Dexter (encircled by fruits & vegetables), cylindrical, ground mouth w/glass lid & zinc band, smooth base, 1870-90, aqua, midget pt. (two small chips in lid) **896**

Eagle, cylindrical, applied collared mouth w/glass lid & iron yoke clamp, smooth base, 1860-80, aqua, pt. **256**

Earl's Patent (circle of stars around larger star) Feb. 2d. 1864 - American Improved Preserve Can, cylindrical, ground mouth w/glass lid & iron yoke clamp, smooth base, aqua, qt. (small flat chip on top of lid, reproduction metal clamp) **1,120**

Rare Excelsior Midget Pint Jar

Excelsior, cylindrical, ground mouth w/glass lid & zinc band, smooth base, 1860-80, some metal loss on metal band, aqua, midget pt. (ILLUS.) **1,008**

Excelsior, tapering cylindrical form, ground mouth w/glass lid & zinc band, smooth base, 1870-90, aqua, qt. **308**

F.B. Co. - 2 (on base), applied groove ring wax sealer, smooth base, tin lid, ca. 1880-90, amber, qt. **198**

F.C.G. Co. (on base), cylindrical, applied wax sealer mouth, smooth base, 1860-80, bright medium citron, 1/2 gal. **532**

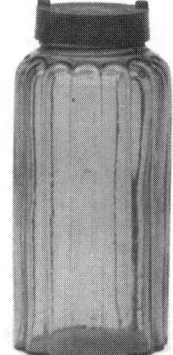

Rare Fruit Jar with Marked Lid

Gray, Hemingray & Bros. - Cincinnati, Ohio (on lid), cylindrical w/fifteen wide vertical flutes, ground mouth w/zinc lid,

smooth base, 1860-70, medium teal
green, qt. (ILLUS.).. **3,640**

Very Rare Small Haines Improved Jar

Haines's Improved, short domed
cylindrical form, applied collared mouth
w/glass lid, smooth base, epoxy-filled
hole near base, 1870-90, greenish aqua,
10 oz. (ILLUS.)... **784**
Hero (The), cylindrical, ground mouth
w/embossed zinc lid, glass insert & zinc
screw band, smooth base, 1865-80, light
sea green, pt. **364**
Hero (The), cylindrical, ground mouth
w/embossed zinc lid & zinc screw band,
smooth base, 1865-80, sea green, 1/2
gal. **146**
K.Y.G.W. (on base), applied groove ring
wax sealer, smooth base, medium yellow
green, ca. 1890, qt. **358**
**Kerr - Self Sealing - United States - Bi-
centennial - 1776-1976,** figural Liberty
Bell, ground mouth w/metal lid, smooth
base, ca. 1976, yellowish green, qt. **616**
**Kerr - Self Sealing - United States - Bi-
centennial - 1776-1976,** figural Liberty
Bell, ground mouth w/metal lid, smooth
base, ca. 1976, clear, qt. **2,016**

Rare Bicentennial Kerr Fruit Jar

**Kerr - Self Sealing - United States - Bi-
centennial - 1776-1976,** figural Liberty
Bell, ground mouth w/metal lid, smooth
base, ca. 1976, amber, qt. (ILLUS.) **2,688**
**Ludlow's Patent June 28 1859 & August
6 1861 (on lid),** ground lip, smooth base,
original glass lid & metal cage-like
yoke, ca. 1865, bluish green, pt. (reproduction closure, potstone bruise w/two
small legs)... **280**
M.G. Co. A (on base), applied groove ring
wax sealer, smooth base, ca. 1880-90,
medium yellowish green, qt. **330**

M.G. Co. (on base), applied groove ring
wax sealer, smooth base, ca. 1880-90,
deep amber, qt................................. **253**
Mason's C.B. Co. (monogram) Improved,
original zinc lid w/glass insert, bright reddish amber, 1/2 gal. (minor interior stain)...... **121**

Rare Mason's - CFJ Co. Fruit Jar

**Mason's C.F.J. Co. (monogram) Patent
Nov 30th 1858,** ground lip, "G224" on
smooth base, zinc screw lid, ca. 1865-
1885, medium yellowish green, 1/2 gal.
(ILLUS.).. **825**

Rare Mason's CFJ Co. Midget Pint

**Mason's C.F.J. Co. (monogram) Patent
Nov 30th 1858,** ground lip, smooth base,
zinc screw lid, ca. 1865-1885, light to
medium yellowish green, midget pt.
(ILLUS.)' **616**

Mason's Patent Jar with Cross

Mason's (cross) Patent Nov 30th 1858,
ground lip, smooth base marked "Pat
Nov 26 67," zinc screw lid, ca. 1865-
1885, light green, tiny nick on front panel,
qt. (ILLUS.) **99**

Mason's (cross) Patent Nov 30th 1858, ground lip, smooth base marked "Pat Nov 26 67," zinc screw lid, ca. 1865-1885, amber, 1/2 gal. **154**

Mason's (cross) Patent Nov 30th 1858, ground lip, smooth base marked "Pat Nov 26 67," zinc screw lid, ca. 1865-1885, bright yellowish amber, qt. (slightly weak lettering) **168**

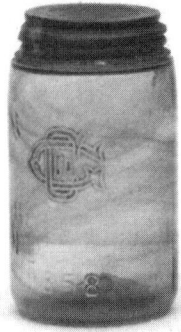

Rare Mason's GC Co. Fruit Jar

Mason's GC Co. (monogram) Patent Nov 30th 1858, cylindrical, ground mouth w/zinc lid, smooth base, 1870-1890, aqua w/profuse yellowish amber striations, pt. (ILLUS.) **1,792**

Amethyst Mason's Patent Fruit Jar

Mason's Patent Nov 30th 1858, ABM, original zinc lid, amethyst, minor interior stain, 1/2 gal. (ILLUS.) **132**

Rare Mason's Half-Pint Midget Jar

Mason's Patent - Nov 30th 1858, ground lip, matching color glass insert embossed "Mason's Improved - Patd May 10, 1870," smooth base, zinc screw band, highly whittled, pale citron or apple green, 1/2 pt. midget (ILLUS.) **413**

Mason's Patent Nov 30th 1858 - (cross on reverse), ground lip, smooth base, zinc screw lid, ca. 1865-1885, bright canary yellow, 1/2 gal. **132**

Mason's Patent Nov 30th 1858 - (cross on reverse), ground lip, smooth base, zinc screw lid, ca. 1865-1885, medium to light amber, weak strike, qt. **88**

Mason's Patent - Nov 30th 1858 - Dupont (in circle) smooth base, ground lip, zinc screw-on lid, bluish aqua, 1/2 gal. **330**

Mason's Patent - Nov 30th 1858 - HG Co. (monogram on reverse), cylindrical w/ground mouth & zinc lid, smooth base, 1860-80, deep aqua, midget pt. **728**

Millville Atmospheric Fruit Jar - Whitall's Patent June 18th 1861, applied groove ring wax sealer, original glass lid & metal yoke, smooth base, ca. 1865-1870, bluish aqua, qt. **55**

Millville - (W)Hitall's Paten(t), applied mouth w/glass lid & iron yoke clamp, smooth base, aqua, 1/2 pt. **476**

Myer (Made By The) Fruit Jar Co. - Detroit, Mich., cylindrical w/ground mouth, smooth base, 1870-90, aqua., qt. (no closure, weak embossing) **476**

No. 1, cylindrical, applied square collared mouth w/"JD Willoughby" stopper, smooth base, 1860-70, qt. (large exterior bubble w/some residue) **392**

Pansy, cylindrical, ground mouth & glass lid w/zinc band, smooth base, ca. 1880-1900, aqua, 1/2 gal. **101**

Patent - June 9, 1863 - Cin. O (on lid), cylindrical, ground mouth w/tin lid, smooth base, 1860-80, qt. (small fissure in body) **213**

Rare Labeled Fruit Jar

Patented - Oct. 19, 1858 (on glass lid), ground mouth w/glass lid, smooth base, applied gold & black label reading "Gambogia," ca. 1858-70, qt. (ILLUS.) **1,792**

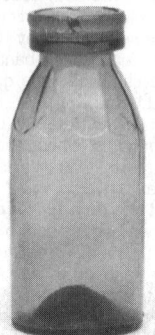

Very Rare Early Petal-style Fruit Jar

Petal-style, mold-blown, cylindrical w/petaled shoulders, applied heavy collared mouth, red iron deep pontil mark, sapphire to powdery blue, no wording, ca. 1845-60, qt. (ILLUS.)..................................... **6,750**

Scarce Protector Fruit Jar

Protector, cylindrical, ground mouth w/original tin lid, smooth base, aqua, long shallow bruise on mouth probably from manufacture, pt. (ILLUS.)...................................... **728**

Puritan (The) - Trademark (sailing ship) - Fruit Jar, ground mouth w/glass lid & iron ring & clamp, smooth base, aqua, 1/2 gal. (some minor mouth roughness & chipping, some roughness on lid)..... **476**

San Francisco Glass Works, applied groove ring wax sealer, tin lid, smooth base, ca. 1875-1895, aqua, qt. (chip on outer ring of mouth w/a shallow sliver at side of mouth)... **476**

Scarce Schaffer Pint Jar

Schaffer (The) Jar - Rochester N.Y., ground mouth w/glass lid & wire bail, smooth base, 1870-90, mouth roughness, some inside haze, pt. (ILLUS.)............ **672**

Rare Seller & Co. Fruit Jar.

Seller (M.) & Co. - Portland, O., applied wax sealer mouth w/tin lid, smooth base, light bluish green, qt. (ILLUS.)....................... **896**

Star Flask Co. - New Albany, Ind., crude wax sealer top, very crude, bluish aqua, qt. (hint of interior stain).................................... **66**

Star (over five-pointed star), cylindrical, ground mouth w/marked zinc cap & zinc band, smooth base, 1860-80, aqua, qt. (tiny pinhole in tin lid)..................................... **112**

Swayzee's Improved Mason, smooth lip, original zinc lid, bright green, qt. **231**

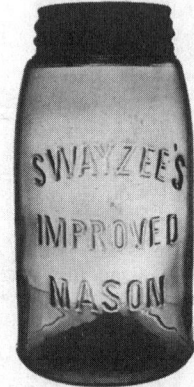

Swayzee's Improved Mason Jar

Swayzee's Improved Mason, smooth lip, original zinc lid, medium green, a few scratches, qt. (ILLUS.)..................................... **88**

Triumph No. 1, ground lip, smooth base, ca. 1860-70, bluish aqua, qt. (some overall inside light milky stain) **358**

Victory 1 (encircled by) Patd Feby 9th 1864 Reisd June 22nd 1867, reverse w/"Pacific Glass Work San Francisco," original glass & metal closure, medium green, qt... **1,210**

FURNITURE

Furniture made in the United States during the 18th and 19th centuries is coveted by collectors. American antique furniture has a European background, primarily English, since the influence of the Continent usually found its way to America by way of England. If the style did not originate in England, it came to America by way of England. For this reason, some American furniture styles carry the name of an English monarch or an English designer. However, we must realize that, until recently, little research has been conducted and even less published on the Spanish and French influences in the area of the California missions and New Orleans.

After the American revolution, cabinetmakers in the United States shunned the prevailing styles in England and chose to bring the French styles of Napoleon's Empire to the United States and we have the uniquely named "American Empire" (Classical) style of furniture in a country that never had an emperor.

During the Victorian period, quality furniture began to be mass-produced in this country with its rapidly growing population. So much walnut furniture was manufactured, the vast supply of walnut was virtually depleted and it was of necessity that oak furniture became fashionable as the 19th century drew to a close.

For our purposes, the general guidelines for dating will be: Pilgrim Century - 1620-85 William & Mary - 1685-1720 Queen Anne - 1720-50 Chippendale - 1750-85 Federal - 1785-1820 Hepplewhite - 1785-1820 Sheraton - 1800-20 American Empire (Classical) - 1815-40 Victorian - 1840-1900 Early Victorian - 1840-50 Gothic Revival - 1840-90 Rococo (Louis XV) - 1845-70 Renaissance - 1860-85 Louis XVI - 1865-75 Eastlake - 1870-95 Jacobean & Turkish Revival - 1870-95 Aesthetic Movement - 1880-1900 Art Nouveau - 1890-1918 Turn-of-the-Century - 1895-1910 Mission (Arts & Crafts movement) - 1900-15 Art Deco - 1925-40

All furniture included in this listing is American unless otherwise noted.

Bedroom Suites

Arts & Crafts style: double bed, tall chest of drawers, wardrobe, nightstand, dressing table & bench & free-standing mirror; oak, each piece w/the main panels decorated w/a rectangular reserve enclosed by an arch & leaftip design, cabinet pieces w/vertical panels doors w/long flat wrought-iron strap hinges & ring pulls in the shape of inverted hearts, original finish, ca. 1915, England, wardrobe 16 x 48", 78" h. (ILLUS. of part, below) ... **$2,000**

Colonial Revival style: double bed, princess-style chest of drawers w/mirror, washstand; oak & oak veneer, the highback bed w/a plain round headboard w/a small scroll-carved crest & matching lower footboard, both chest of drawers & washstand w/rectangular tops w/serpentine edges above a serpentine case, w/a pair of drawers over a single long, deep drawer, the washstand w/a towel bar between S-scroll uprights & a long drawer over two small drawers & a door in base, all on short cabriole legs on casters, ca. 1900, refinished, chest of drawers 78" h., the set (ILLUS. top of next page) **2,800**

English Arts & Crafts Bedroom Suite

Colonial Revival Oak Bedroom Suite

Louis XV-Style Marquetry Bed

Louis XV-Style: double bed & two-door armoire; mahogany marquetry, each of undulating outline, the bed w/the head- and footboard ornately decorated w/leafy scrolls, urns & other classical designs in light inlay all bordered by brass bands w/gilt-brass mounts on the top rails & on the legs, serpentine siderails, the armoire w/an arched crest w/gilt-brass scroll mount above a pair of tall cupboard doors w/tall beveled mirrors, delicate marquetry band above the doors & on the drawer across the bottom, demountable, original finish, France, ca. 1890, armoire 20 x 50", 96" h., the set (ILLUS. of bed) .. **15,000**

Victorian Eastlake substyle: a high-back half-tester bed & tall chest of drawers; walnut & burl walnut, the bed w/a rectangular half-tester canopy w/flaring molded cornice above a scallop-cut & scroll-cut front, raised on curved & pierced spindled brackets on the side stiles of the headboard, headboard w/a scroll-carved crown crest above a scroll-carved band & burl panel over narrow burl panel & an arch-topped wide lower burl panel, spiral-turned side stiles, the lower footboard w/a gently arched

Fine Eastlake Half-tester Bed

crestrail over scroll carving & a wide burl panel, scroll-cut top corner ears & spiral-turned side stiles, original side rails, refinished, ca. 1880, w/a matching marble-topped chest of drawers, bed 60" w., 10' h., 2 pcs. (ILLUS. of bed)........ **10,500**

Victorian Eastlake Fancy Suite

Victorian Eastlake substyle: highback double bed & chest of drawers w/tall mirror; walnut & burl walnut, the bed & chest w/matching ornate crestrails w/a central raised shell- and scroll-carved crest over a low stick-and-ball gallery above freestanding colonettes flanked by angled cornice corners, the bed w/a wide burl panel over lower horizontal panels, the top w/raised burl panels, a matching lower footboard, the crest & colonettes on side stiles fitted w/small candle shelves flanking the tall rectangular swivel mirror above the rectangular white marble top on a case w/three long drawers w/pear-shaped drop pulls & raised burl panels, original finish, ca. 1875-85, chest 20 x 42", 90" h. (ILLUS.)............................. **3,000**

Victorian Golden Oak style: double bed, chest of drawers w/mirror & washstand; oak, the highback bed & chest w/a fan- and scroll-carved wide crest over incised leaf sprigs, the lower bed footboard w/further incised leafy & blossom sprigs, the washstand w/a tall towel bar above a carved backsplash & a case w/two long drawers over a pair of paneled cupboard doors, original stamped brass pulls, original finish, ca. 1890-1900, chest of drawers 78" h., the set (ILLUS. below).............. **3,000**

Victorian Renaissance Revival: walnut & burl walnut, each piece w/a high arched pedimented top centered by a large arched scroll-carved cartouche above a frieze band w/raised burl panels, the chest of drawers w/a tall rectangular round-topped mirror flanked by shaped sides fitted w/two small candleshelves & trimmed w/burl panels & side scrolls, a stepped top w/a square white marble top

Tall Chest from Renaissance Suite

w/molded edges above two small drawers flanking the central well w/a white marble top, two long bottom drawers w/pairs of raised burl panels, deep molded base, brass & black teardrop pulls, ca. 1875, bed 54" w., 7' 8" h., four pieces (ILLUS. of chest of drawers).. **11,200**

Victorian Renaissance Revival substyle: double bed & chest of drawers w/mirror; walnut & burl walnut; the bed w/a high headboard w/an ornately scroll- and pierce-carved crest & gallery over a large

Fine Golden Oak Bedroom Suite

Renaissance Walnut & Burl Set

central roundel framed by leafy scrolls all above a wide burl panel, a matching lower footboard, the chest of drawers w/a matching crest above the large swiveling rectangular beveled mirror, a red marble top on the case w/a pair of drawers over two long drawers, all w/fine burl veneer, original cast-brass hardware, original finish., ca. 1880, chest 21 x 42", 84" h., the set (ILLUS.)... **6,500**

Victorian Renaissance Revival substyle: double highback bed, tall chest of drawers w/mirror & nightstand; walnut & burl walnut, the bed & chest w/very high arched crestrails centered by a floral-carved crest over a panel w/ornate scroll & pendant carving & raised burl panels, the bed headboard w/a large rectangular burl panel flanked by spearpoint finials over the lower back panels, the lower footboard w/gently arched crest, the chest w/tall paneled stiles flanking a tall rectangular mirror flanked by spearpoint finials & small candle shelves above two white marble tops each over two small drawers flanking a drop well w/a white

marble top, a long raised panel drawer across the bottom, washstand w/white marble top over a drawer & single paneled door, angled front corners on all pieces, refinished, ca. 1870-75, bed 58 x 78", 96" h., the set (ILLUS. bottom of page).. **10,000**

French Renaissance Revival Suite

Victorian Renaissance Revival substyle: highback double bed, chest of drawers w/mirror & two nightstands; mahogany & satinwood inlays; the bed headboard & chest crestrail w/central carved palmette flanked by carved leaf bands & turned corner finials, the bed w/a wide banded burl panel flanked by free-standing colonettes at the sides, a matching lower footboard, the chest crest over slender turned stiles flanking a tall arched mirror above a white marble top fitted w/two small marble-topped hanky drawers over a case w/a pair of drawers over three long graduated drawers all w/narrow mahogany burl panels, each nightstand w/a white marble top over a small drawer over a small door raised on turned sup-

Fine Renaissance Revival Suite

ports to a medial shelf on knob-and-peg feet on casters, France, ca. 1875, original finish, chest 84" h., the set (ILLUS.)..... **4,500**

Ornate Victorian Rococo Highback Bed

Victorian Rococo substyle: highback double bed & chest of drawers w/mirror; carved walnut, the very tall bed headboard w/an arched scroll-bordered crestrail topped by ornate pierced carved scrolls centering a cartouche above a curved burl panel & a pair of carved urn finials flanking a very large round veneer panel & serpentine sides, the lower footboard w/an arched crest w/scrolls over raised banded panels & scrolls between quarter-round corners, the chest w/an arched crestrail w/cartouche over the tall arched mirror flanked by shaped sides w/small candle shelves above the rectangular white marble top w/a bowed front over a conforming case w/three long veneered drawers w/burl veneering & leaf-carved pulls, rounded front corners, original finish, ca. 1860, bed 64 x 83", 100" h., the set (ILLUS. of bed)................ **12,000**

Beds

Fine Anglo-Indian Carved Tester Bed

Anglo-Indian tall-poster tester bed, rosewood-like wood, the rectangular deep

ogee & serpentine tester frame raised on ring-, knob- and paneled-rod-turned posts, the headboard w/an ornately pierced & scroll-carved design, caned mattress support, three-quarter size, ca. 1835, 90" h. (ILLUS.) **950**

Chippendale Revival Twin Bed

Chippendale Revival style twin beds, mahogany & mahogany veneer, the high headboard w/a broken scroll crest w/carved florettes flanking a central urn & flame finial, tall reeded turned & tapering headposts w/acorn finials, the footboard w/lower matching posts & a serpentined arch top w/gadrooned edging, gadrooned band on footboard rail, headboard w/turned tapering legs w/knob feet, footboard w/claw-and-ball feet, refinished, ca. 1920s, 48" w., 56" h. headboard, pr. (ILLUS. of one) **1,400**

Classical Country-style Painted Bed

Classical country-style bed, painted & decorated, the scrolling headboard w/central integrated plinth flanked by ball-topped boldly turned headposts continuing to baluster-form legs, joined by square rails fitted for roping to similar turned footposts joined by a baluster-, knob- and ring-turned rail above the turned legs, original wood grained paint simulating rosewood, Vermont, ca. 1830s, minor surface imperfections, 56 1/4 x 80 1/2", 48 1/2" h. (ILLUS.) **978**

Classical Revival Poster Bed

Classical Revival four-poster bed, mahogany & mahogany veneer, each square corner post topped by ring-turned & leaf-carved sections w/pineapple finials, wide veneered head- and footboard w/round crestrails w/pointed, reeded end finials, short turned tapering legs, original finish & wood casters, three-quarter size, late 19th c., 50" w., 5' 6" h. (ILLUS.)........... **1,000**

Classical Revival Tall-poster Bed

Classical Revival tall-poster bed, mahogany & mahogany veneer, the headboard w/a high scroll-carved crest & bold mahogany veneer between ring- and ball-turned headposts w/spiraled leaf carving & reeded urn-form finials, the lower arched & shaped footboard w/matching posts, raised on turned tapering legs w/carved paw feet, original finish, ca. 1900-10, 58 x 80", 80" h. (ILLUS.).............. **3,000**

Classical tall-poster bed, cherry, the four slender baluster- and ring-turned posts w/baluster-form finials joined by original rails, a simple headboard w/rounded sides, rails fitted for roping, New England, 1830s, 54 x 72", 93" h. (old refinish, imperfections) **3,220**

Classical Tall-poster Bed

Classical tall-poster bed, stained poplar, the flat-topped scroll-cut headboard flanked by tall hexagonal posts tapering to a paneled pointed top w/mushroom finial, original siderails w/knobs for ropes, footboard w/matching posts & a low shaped upper rail, turned tapering legs w/bun feet, original dark finish, ca. 1830, 58" w., 7' 6" h. (ILLUS.) **1,600**

Ornate Classical Tester Bed

Classical tall-poster tester bed, mahogany, the wide flaring tester frame raised on slender spiral-turned tall posts, the headposts flanking a high arched & scroll-carved headboard, the footboard w/a low spindle cross rail, on ring- and baluster-turned legs, old refinish, ca. 1830s, 60 x 80", 96" h. (ILLUS.) **7,500**

Early American rope bed, country-style low-poster, painted poplar, the headboard w/a wide peaked board flanked by simple turned posts w/ball finials & baluster-turned legs w/peg feet, slightly lower matching footboard, old red paint, pegged construction, old siderails, early 19th c., 35 1/2" x 65 1/2", 32 1/2" h. (split on one return) **523**

Federal country-style tall-poster bed, maple, the four octagonal tapering posts joined by the shaped headboard w/arched tester, on octagonal legs, old refinish, New England, early 19th c., 72 1/2" l., tester 76" h. **920**

Federal Revival Tall Poster Twin Bed

Federal Revival tall-poster twin beds, mahogany, the shaped & arched headboard flanked by tall slender baluster-turned & reeded posts topped by urn-form finials, matching footposts w/a fabric-draped cross rail, to hold box spring, refinished, ca. 1920s, 45 x 76", 72" h., pr. (ILLUS. of one) **850**

Federal-Style Child's Bed

Federal-Style child's tall-poster tester bed, maple, the arched canopy frame w/small center urn finial raised on a tester frame on tall slender tapering corner posts of the high spindle-sided rails, raised on baluster- and ring-turned tapering legs on casters, original finish, ca. 1920s, 24 x 48", 5' h. (ILLUS.)........................ **800**

High-quality Victorian Child's Bed

Late Victorian child's bed, carved mahogany, the paneled headboard w/a high scalloped & swag-carved crestrail flanked by turned corner finials flanked by gently curved siderails over bands of tall slender turned spindles above a lower swag-carved panel, spindles in the footboard above a swag-carved panel, on slender turned legs on casters, ca. 1890s, 36 x 72", 4' h. (ILLUS.) **6,600**

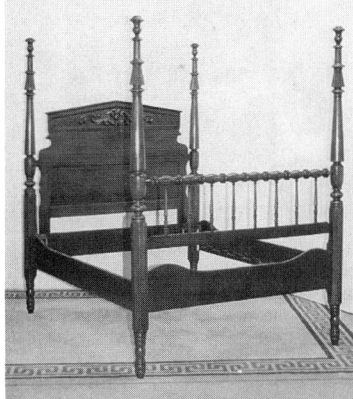

Victorian Colonial Revival Poster Bed

Victorian Colonial Revival tall-poster bed, walnut, the high peaked headboard w/applied scroll carving flanked by slender ring- and rod-turned tapering posts & ring-turned legs, the footboard w/a baluster- and ring-turned rail over eight slender turned spindles to a lower rail, all between matching posts, last quarter 19th c., 56 x 76", 68" h. (ILLUS.) **800**

Victorian Golden Oak Double Bed

Victorian Golden Oak bed, the high headboard w/a scroll- and shell-carved center crest above a leaf-carved frieze band flanked by carved ears over rectangular panels, the lower footboard w/a heavy rounded crestrail over a wide panel, refinished, ca. 1910, full size, headboard 72" h. (ILLUS.) **800**

Tall Golden Oak Double Bed

Victorian Golden Oak bed, the high squared headboard w/a heavy rounded crestrail centered by a pointed & scroll-carved crest over a wide section w/a delicate large panel of applied leafy scrolls flanked by squared stiles w/simple scroll carving, the low footboard w/a heavy rounded crestrail over delicate scrolling, original dark finish, ca. 1900, 58 x 78", 80" h. (ILLUS.).. **1,400**

Simple Golden Oak Double Bed

Victorian Golden Oak bed, the medium-height headboard w/an arched crestrail above a delicate carved scroll design, the footboard w/a flat crestrail over simple panels, refinished, ca. 1900, 58 x 78", 72" h. (ILLUS.).. **650**

Late Victorian Fold-down Murphy Bed

Victorian "Murphy" bed, maple or birch stained to resemble mahogany, the upright case resembling a tall chest of drawers w/a high crestrail w/simple carved scrolls over a rectangular top above a false front of two drawers over three drawers w/some scroll trim, real cast-brass hardware, front folds down to reveal a three-quarters bed, refinished, ca. 1900, 24 deep, 48" w., 60" h. (ILLUS.) **500**

Tall Renaissance Revival Bed

Victorian Renaissance Revival bed, walnut & burl walnut, tall-back style, the very tall headboard w/an arched & molded pediment crest centered by a tall leaf- and scroll-carved finial & scroll & burl panel trim above projecting blocks over slender turned columns & shaped sides flanking a tall raised panel flanked by shorter side panels w/corner blocks w/turned finials, the lower footboard w/a flat top rail over rectangular, round & arched raised burl panels, canted blocked corners w/turned columns, old refinish, ca. 1875, 58" w., 8' h. (ILLUS.) **3,500**

Very Fine Renaissance Revival Bed

Victorian Renaissance Revival bed, walnut & rosewood burl veneer, the very high headboard w/an ornate arched & rounded crestrail centered by a large carved cartouche finial over grape cluster carving flanked by scrolls at the sides & above a row of three arched panels w/raised burl reserves all flanked by block- and scroll-turned stiles w/turned urn-form finials, a matching arched footboard w/similar arched panels & burl trim flanked by curved corner posts, refinished, ca. 1865, 58 x 78", 96" h. (ILLUS.) **5,500**

Well-carved Victorian Rococo Bed

Victorian Rococo bed, walnut, the medium-height headboard w/an arched & stepped crestrail topped by an ornate scroll-carved crest over another raised molding matching crestrail form, tapering rounded corner posts, matching lower footboard w/ornate ribbon-tied flower & scroll panel over a lower narrow oval panel centered by further scroll carving & flanked by rounded corners, possibly Philadelphia, ca. 1860, refinished, 58 x 78", 58" h. (ILLUS.) **5,500**

Victorian Rococo Child's Bed

Victorian Rococo child's bed, walnut, crib-style, the headboard w/an arched & scroll-carved crestrail over two Gothic arch panels flanked by paneled side posts w/turned finials, deep solid two-panel sides, the footboard composed of a row of flat vasiform splats between the paneled side posts w/turned finial, simple baluster- and ring-turned legs, worn original finish, ca. 1860s, 30 x 48", 32" h. (ILLUS.) **600**

Victorian Rococo half-tester bed, mahogany & mahogany veneer, the large rectangular cloth-lined half-tester w/serpentine edges & an ornate scroll-carved crest flanked by heavy turned & reeded finials, a beaded band around the edges, raised on tall round tapering posts flanking a high arched & stepped headboard w/ornate scroll & scroll carving above a

Rare Mallard Half-tester Bed

large rectangular burl panel w/notched corners w/roundels, wide side rails w/raised oval banding & roundels & the low footboard w/small arched crest & scalloped corner brackets above raised oval banding & a roundel, heavy, turned, tapering footposts w/ring- and bead-carved finials, attributed to Prudent Mallard, New Orleans, Louisiana, ca. 1855, refinished, queen size, 126" h. (ILLUS.) .. **30,000**

Victorian Rococo Half-tester Bed

Victorian Rococo half-tester bed, mahogany & mahogany veneer, the large rectangular half-tester w/serpentine sides & a scroll-carved crest & corner finials supported by pierced scroll-carved braces to the slender ring- and rod-turned headposts flanking the arched & scroll-carved headboard centered by a large oval burl panel, the lower footboard w/low arched & scroll-carved crest flanked by heavy, short footposts w/turned finials & legs, refinished, ca. 1855-60, 60 x 80", 118" h. (ILLUS.) **4,000**

Benches

Bucket (or water) bench, painted pine, a wide flat crestrail joining the high ends w/downswept tapering sides flanking a wide open shelf, low bootjack ends joined by a narrow flat front & back rail, original bluish grey putty paint, New England, late 18th c., 9 1/2 x 31", 24" h. (minor paint wear & loss) **2,185**

Country-style Bucket Bench

Bucket (or water) bench, pine & poplar, a low narrow shelf raised on stepped-back sides above two lower open shelves all joined by a vertical back brace & board ends w/bootjack legs, refinished, mixture of square & round nails w/some alterations, 19th c., 14 3/4 x 41", 40 1/2" h. (ILLUS.) **880**

Country-style bench, painted pine, a long narrow rectangular top flanked by wide side braces joined to the wide end bootjack legs, blue paint, New England, early 19th c., 11 1/4 x 60 1/2", 19" h. (minor surface imperfections) **403**

Country-style bench, painted, the rectangular plank seat w/canted corners & a scrubbed finish, side aprons w/rounded ends, board ends w/bootjack feet, worn green paint, legs mortised through the top, 14 x 55 1/2", 18 1/4" h. (paper & cardboard stuck to top in some places) **110**

Foot bench, Classical, mahogany & mahogany veneer, the gold velvet slip seat above the pierced & scrolling sides on casters, old surface, England, 1860-80, 19 3/4 x 23 3/4", 17" h. (minor imperfections) **345**

Golden Oak Hall Bench

Hall bench, Victorian Golden Oak substyle, a wide crestrail w/a serpentine top edge above long carved scrolls over a row of five slender turned spindles, flat back stiles w/curved ears above the shaped open arms on incurved arm supports flanking the rectangular lift-lid seat over a deep well, simple cabriole legs, refinished, ca. 1900, 16 x 30", 32" h. (ILLUS.) **450**

Jacobean Revival Oak Hall Bench

Jacobean Revival hall bench, carved oak, the high, long rectangular back w/a flat crestrail over the carved words "Begin Well and End Well" over the large rectangular raised panels, the center panel w/winged griffins flanking a shield carved "1671," the side panels carved w/large urns overflowing w/flowers & leaves, flat shaped open arms w/lion head hand grips, short knob-turned arm supports over the long plank seat w/a scallop-carved seatrail, on baluster- and block-turned front legs joined by flat stretchers to the flat rear legs, original fumed finish, may be missing a stretcher, ca. 1890s, 24 x 64", 40" h. (ILLUS.) **1,500**

Unique Carved Oak Hall Bench

Victorian Baroque-style hall bench, carved oak, the very high back w/a wide flat & flaring crestrail w/a carved cornice over a long narrow panel carved in relief w/an ocean scene of Columbus arriving in the New World centered by the Statue of Liberty in New York Harbor all flanked by large carved cartouches & above another wide three-panel frieze carved in relief w/allegorical religious scenes all above a high upholstered back flanked by free-standing carved figures, one probably representing Columbus & the other a knight, the heavy flat molded arms above upholstered sides, the front arm supports carved w/lion masks & baroque designs flanking the three-panel seatrail carved w/scrolls & rosettes, flat molded base on bun feet, possibly made for the 1893 Chicago Columbian Exposition, 24 x 60", 72" h. (ILLUS.) **3,500**

Ornate Horner Oak Hall Bench

Victorian Baroque-style hall bench, carved quarter-sawn oak, a massive design w/a high flat molded crestrail over a wide frieze band carved w/ornate flowering & leafy scrolls above a simple lower panel centered by a small rectangular raised panel all flanked by large figural dolphin-carved arms above a deep bombé apron w/the front carved w/further flowering leafy scrolls, lift-seat, molded base w/front paw feet, Horner Company, New York, New York, ca. 1890, 24 x 54", 38" h. (ILLUS.) **4,000**

Bookcases

Arts & Crafts Oak Bookcase

Arts & Crafts bookcase, quarter-sawn oak, the rectangular top w/rounded cornice above a pair of tall doors w/oblong geometrically-glazed upper panels over tall

plain glass panels opening to three shelves, flat base raised on front paw feet on casters, refinished, ca. 1900, 15 x 40", 5' 2" h. (ILLUS.) **1,400**

Fine Classical Mahogany Bookcase

Classical bookcase, parcel-gilt mahogany & mahogany veneer, two-part construction: the upper section w/a rectangular top over a wide flattened flaring cornice over a deep veneered frieze band above a pair of glazed cupboard doors flanked by large carved parcel-gilt scrolls at the top & base sides above a row of three small round-fronted drawers; the lower section w/a projecting rectangular top above a long arched frieze drawer, raised on heavy scrolled legs carved at the front w/acanthus leaf, the sides w/grapevines & ending in large paw feet, above an incurved lower shelf raised on foliate-carved toupie feet, possibly Philadelphia, ca. 1830, 22 1/2 x 43", 5' 11 1/2" h. (ILLUS.) **9,200**

Classical Revival Mahogany Bookcase

Classical Revival bookcase, mahogany & mahogany veneer, the long rectangular top w/flat ogee cornice end sections flanking a central scroll-carved cornice section carved w/a baby's face, above a three-door case w/tall glazed doors opening to wooden shelves, molded base raised on carved paw feet on casters, refinished, ca. 1900, 18 x 54", 5' 10" h. (ILLUS.) **2,600**

Early Oak Stacking Bookcase

Early 20th century bookcase, oak, three-section stacking lawyer's-type, a rectangular top w/rounded front corners & a dentil molding above a long lift-front glass door flanked by reeded columns stacking on two lower matching sections, deep molded base w/a long drawer w/brass bail pulls flanked by shaped sides & a molded flat bottom, original dark finish, possibly by Globe Wernecke, ca. 1900, 12 x 34", 42" h. (ILLUS.)............................ **1,200**

Unusual Oak Stacking Bookcase

Early 20th century bookcase, quarter-sawn oak, four-section stacking lawyer's-type, the rectangular top w/a flared rounded cornice above the top section w/a leaded glass lift-front door above two matching sections w/plain glass lift-front doors set on the stepped-out bottom section w/a large glass lift-front door on a flat rounded base rail, refinished, ca. 1910, 18 x 32", 4' 10" h. (ILLUS.).......................... **1,200**

Quarter-sawn Oak Stacking Bookcase

Early 20th century bookcase, quarter-sawn oak, four-section stacking lawyer's-type, the rectangular top w/a flared rounded cornice above a two-pane glazed lift-front door over three lower stacked sections on a flat flared base, brass knobs, original dark finish, ca. 1910, 16 x 44", 4' 2" h. (ILLUS.) **1,400**

Three-stack Lawyer's Bookcase

Early 20th century bookcase, quarter-sawn oak, three-section stacking lawyer's-type, the top section w/a rounded cornice over a lift-front door w/geometrically-leaded clear glass, the two lower sections w/lift-front glazed doors, base section w/a narrow ogee-front long drawer, labeled by the Macey Stacking Bookcase Co., refinished, ca. 1910, 13 x 36", 42" h. (ILLUS.) **950**

Federal Revival Stacking Bookcase

Federal Revival bookcase, mahogany & mahogany veneer, two-part, each half composed of four rectangular stacking sections w/glazed lift-front doors, raised on five slender square tapering legs, made by Macey's Stacking Bookcase Company, original finish, ca. 1910, 14 x 50", 4' 6" h. (ILLUS.) **1,200**

Georgian-Style Mahogany Bookcase

Georgian-Style bookcase, mahogany, three-door design, a rectangular top above a Chinese trellis-carved frieze band above the three tall glazed doors w/serpentine edged glazed panels over short matching blind panels, flanked by canted front corners w/garland-carved bands above reeded bands, molded base on scroll-cut bracket feet, England, ca. 1920, 18 x 72", 5' 4" h. (ILLUS.) **2,000**

Late Victorian Bookcase-Curio Cabinet

Late Victorian bookcase, stained maple, the serpentine scroll-carved crestrail above the rectangular top w/a bowed central section above a conforming case w/a pair of frosted glass small cupboard doors w/oval molding flanking a central bowed glazed cupboard door, all above a tall, wide glazed cupboard door w/a scroll-

carved serpentine top opening to three adjustable wood shelves, shaped apron & simple bracket feet, original finish, ca. 1890s, 16 x 38", 5' 10" h. (ILLUS.) **2,000**

Mission-style (Arts & Crafts movement) bookcase, oak, a rectangular top w/a short three-quarters gallery above a tall single door w/ten small panes of glass in two rows above a single large pane, opening to wooden shelves, flat front apron w/bracket feet, on casters, Lifetime Furniture Co., 13 1/2 x 28", 56 1/2" h. **1,035**

Mission-Style One-door Bookcase

Mission-style (Arts & Crafts movement) bookcase, oak, quarter-sawn oak w/mortise-and-tenon construction, the rectangular top above a single tall 12-pane glazed cupboard door opening to three shelves, square stile legs on wooden casters, original finish, ca. 1910, 16 x 28", 56" h. (ILLUS.) **1,100**

Liberty & Company Oak Bookcase

Mission-style (Arts & Crafts movement) bookcase, oak, the narrow rectangular top w/a high three-quarters gallery above a molded cornice over two open small shelves flanking a small 8-pane glazed cupboard door over two long lower shelves, original finish, Liberty & Company, England, ca. 1900, 10 1/4 x 37", 47" h. (ILLUS.) **3,105**

Mission-style (Arts & Crafts movement) bookcase, oak, the rectangular top w/a low three-quarters gallery w/keyed through-tenons above a single tall 16-pane glazed door opening to shelves, flat apron & keyed through-tenons at the base, "Handcraft" mark of L. & J.G. Stickley, 12 x 29 3/4", 55 1/4" h. (refinished, hardware replaced, non-original latch removed leaving screw holes near lock) **3,738**

Gustav Stickley Two-door Bookcase

Mission-style (Arts & Crafts movement) bookcase, oak, the rectangular top w/a lower three-quarters gallery & through-tenon construction above a pair of tall 8-pane glazed doors opening to three wooden shelves, 8-pane glazed sides, flat apron, hammered copper V-pulls, excellent new finish, branded mark & remnants of paper label of Gustav Stickley, Model No. 815, 15 x 41 1/4", 64" h. (ILLUS.) **6,900**

Rococo Revival Carved Bookcase

Rococo Revival style bookcase, walnut & walnut veneer, the rectangular top w/molded edges above a frieze band carved w/a row of rosettes above a pair of tall glazed cupboard doors w/applied leafy scroll & geometric wooden grillwork,

scroll-carved apron & short scroll-carved cabriole front legs, refinished, ca. 1920s, 16 x 34", 48" h. (ILLUS.) **1,000**

Aesthetic Movement Oak Bookcase

Victorian Aesthetic Movement bookcase, quarter-sawn oak, the rectangular top w/a low three-quarters gallery centered by a low arched crest carved w/acorns & oak leaves above a square central paneled door carved w/a spray of oak leaves & acorns flanked by open side compartments backed by rectangular beveled mirrors & arched framing w/ring- and baluster-turned corner supports above a case w/three tall glazed cupboard doors opening to three shelves, a row of three drawers w/stamped brass pulls across the bottom, molded base on casters, refinished, ca. 1895, 18 x 60", 6' h. (ILLUS.) **3,500**

Aesthetic Carved Breakfront Bookcase

Victorian Aesthetic Movement substyle "breakfront" bookcase, walnut & burl walnut, the taller central projecting section w/a rectangular top & arched crestrail w/a scroll-carved crest & a band of carved scrolls above a dentil-carved cornice over a tall beveled glass door topped by a narrow rectangular panel carved w/a globe map flanked by olive branches opening to four wood shelves above the stepped-out base w/a burl-veneered drawer, the lower side cases w/a rectangular top w/a pierced-carved gallery composed of stylized leafy blossoms raised on a turned corner spindle over an open shelf w/a burled back panel over a scallop-cut & zigzag-incised frieze opening to three shelves above a projecting base & a veneered drawer, brass ring pulls on drawers, molded base, refinished, ca. 1880s, 18 3/4 x 68", 6' 2" h. (ILLUS.) **9,500**

Fine Baroque Revival Bookcase

Victorian Baroque Revival bookcase, mahogany & mahogany veneer, the rectangular top w/a narrow beaded flared cornice above a wide frieze band ornately carved w/leafy scrolls above a pair of wide single pane glazed doors flanked by reeded slender pilasters, two ornately scroll-carved drawers at the bottom w/lion head pulls, molded base raised on large paw feet on casters, refinished, ca. 1890, 18 x 50", 5' h. (ILLUS.) **2,800**

Victorian Classical Double Bookcase

Victorian Classical bookcase, walnut, the rectangular top w/a deep coved cornice above a pair of tall 4-pane glazed doors w/pierced scroll-carved top corner brackets opening to adjustable shelves over the stepped-out base w/a pair of drawers w/black pear-shaped drop pulls, deep flat molded base, refinished, ca. 1850-70, 20 x 48", 6' 8" h. (ILLUS.) **1,800**

Victorian Country-style Tall Bookcase

Victorian country-style bookcase, walnut, the rectangular top w/a deep stepped & flaring cornice above a pair of 4-pane arch-topped doors w/solid lower panels opening to five adjustable shelves, the stepped-out lower section w/a single long paneled drawer w/wood knob pulls, slightly scalloped apron & simple bracket feet, demountable, refinished, ca. 1850, 18 x 45", 7' h. (ILLUS.) **2,500**

Fine Golden Oak Double Bookcase

Victorian Golden Oak bookcase, quartersawn oak, a long low crestrail w/rounded ends above the rectangular top w/narrow carved frieze band above a long open compartment w/spindled end panels & two long narrow beveled mirrors above a scroll-carved band over a pair of tall glazed cupboard doors opening to two adjustable shelves, deep molded base on thin square feet, refinished, ca. 1900, 18 x 60", 68" h. (ILLUS.) **3,300**

Golden Oak Bookcase with Top Shelf

Victorian Golden Oak bookcase, quarter-sawn oak, the superstructure w/a low crestrail w/a small center swag carving above a narrow rectangular shelf raised on pierced & leaf-carved front supports & backed by a rectangular beveled mirror, the rectangular top above an incised band of wavy carving centered above the pair of tall glazed cupboard doors opening to four wooden shelves, gently carved apron on original porcelain casters, refinished, ca. 1905, 18 x 40", 5' 10" h. (ILLUS.).. **950**

Large Oak Breakfront Bookcase

Victorian Renaissance Revival book-case, oak, breakfront-style, the high central section w/a rectangular top & deep widely flaring cornice supported on carved brackets & half-round spindles over a tall arched & glazed cupboard door w/raised panels at the top corners & at the bottom opening to shelves, the stepped-back side sections each w/a rectangular top w/a deep widely flaring cornice above a plain frieze band over a tall narrow three-paneled door, the stepped-out base w/a group of four drawers w/metal pulls, a heavy flaring base molding on compressed bun feet, original finish, late quarter 19th c., 24 x 64", 7' 4" h. (ILLUS.) **3,000**

Breakfront Renaissance Bookcase

Victorian Renaissance Revival book-case, walnut & burl walnut, breakfront style, the tall central projecting section w/a high crest topped by a broken-scroll crestrail centered by a high carved flame-form finial above deep molding over an arched panel centered by a large relief-carved bust of a woman w/a floral wreath in her hair all above a tall arched glazed door opening to adjustable shelves, the lower side cabinets w/broken-scroll crests on molded flaring cornices above burl frieze panels over the arched glazed cupboard doors opening to adjustable shelves, three drawers across the base each w/a raised burl panel & pairs of brass loop & bar pulls, deep molded flat base, refinished, ca. 1870, 22 x 72", 8' 5" h. (ILLUS.) **9,000**

Renaissance Revival Bookcase

**Victorian Renaissance Revival book-
case,** walnut & burl walnut, two-part construction: the top section w/a rectangular
top w/a flaring stepped cornice above a
paneled frieze band w/burl panels & a
center roundel above a pair of tall arched
glazed doors w/triangular burl panels at
the top corners & flanked by leaf-carved
drops & raised burl panels down the
sides, opening to three shelves; the lower
stepped-out section w/a pair of deep
drawers w/long shaped raised burl panels & black pear-shaped pulls flanked by
burl panels, deep molded plinth base, ca.
1875, 20 x 42", 64" h. (ILLUS.).................. **2,000**

Walnut Renaissance Revival Bookcase

**Victorian Renaissance Revival book-
case,** walnut, the rectangular top w/a flaring reeded cornice above a scroll-carved
frieze band over a pair of tall arched &
glazed cupboard doors w/scroll carving in
the upper corners & opening to three
wooden shelves, reeded & leaf-carved
quarter-columns at the front sides, a lower molding above a pair of paneled drawers above the flat molded base, original
hardware, original finish, ca. 1880,
19 x 44", 54" h. (ILLUS.).............................. **2,400**
Victorian Renaissance-Style bookcase,
carved oak, a rectangular top w/a deep
flaring carved cornice above a wide frieze
band w/ornate scroll carving centered by
a cartouche above a molded rail over a
pair of tall glazed cupboard doors
w/arched panes enclosed w/narrow gadrooned molding & flanked by carved
fruiting vines down the sides, a wide flaring mid-molding above a pair of paneled
cupboard doors w/square beaded molding enclosing carved scrolled grape clusters flanked by further fruiting vines at the
sides, deep flaring carved base molding,
original finish, Europe, last quarter
19th c., 22 x 40", 6' 2" h. **2,500**

Cabinets

Chippendale Revival China Cabinet

China cabinet, corner-style, Chippendale
Revival style, mahogany & mahogany
veneer, the broken-scroll crest w/center
ring-turned finial over leafy scroll carving
above a gadrooned band over a pair of
tall curved-front glazed doors opening to
glass shelves & a mirrored interior, a gadrooned base band above the leaf-
carved front cabriole legs ending in claw-
and-ball feet, square tapering rear leg,
original dark finish, last quarter 19th c.,
22 x 36", 80" h. (ILLUS.) **2,200**

Inlaid Federal Revival China Cabinet

China cabinet, Federal Revival style, mahogany & inlaid mahogany veneer, the
half-round top w/a flat front above a conforming case above a frieze band inlaid
w/a scalloped band of bellflowers over a
tall geometrically-glazed door w/a lower
panel inlaid w/an almond-shaped reserve, curved sides above plain recessed
panels, raised on four slender square tapering legs ending in spade feet, original
finish, ca. 1930, 18 x 44", 60" h. (ILLUS.)...... **900**

China cabinet, Mission-style (Arts & Crafts movement), oak, a gently arched crestrail w/a plate rail on the rectangular top overhanging the case & supported by corbels, the case w/a pair of tall glazed cupboard doors over a long drawer across the bottom, glazed sides, strap hinges & hammered copper pulls, good original finish & condition, branded Limbert mark & retail label, 17 x 46", 61 3/4" h. (missing door pull) **5,175**

Victorian Aesthetic China Cabinet

China cabinet, Victorian Aesthetic substyle, walnut, the rectangular top w/a high ornate crest centered by a large notched roundel above line-incised panels & small corner roundels above a flared, molded cornice over a sawtooth-cut frieze band above a pair of tall glazed cupboard doors opening to shelves, the stepped-out lower case w/four long graduated drawers w/line-incised bands & simple rectangular brass pulls, sawtooth-incised arched apron, refinished, ca. 1880, 21 x 36", 90" h. (ILLUS.).................... **1,500**

Oak Side-by-Side China Cabinet

China cabinet, Victorian Golden Oak period, side-by-side design, a long crestrail w/a small carved & pointed center crest above a long narrow shelf w/a round bar along the front edge & supported on C-scroll carved uprights on the long top backed by a narrow beveled mirror w/rounded ends, one side of the case w/a tall curved glass door opening to four shelves beside the half w/a pair of small cupboard doors w/asymmetrical leaded glass panels above a wide hinged slant front a scroll-carved design opening to a fitted desk interior above a stack of three curve-fronted drawers w/brass bail pulls, double-lobed base molding raised on short cabriole front legs ending in claw-and-ball feet, refinished, ca. 1900, 20 x 40", 6' 10" h. (ILLUS.) **1,750**

Ornate Golden Oak China Cabinet

China cabinet, Victorian Golden Oak style, the high crestrail centered by a pointed scroll-carved crest over leafy scrolls & rounded carved corners over the half-round top w/blocked projections at the front & a deep cornice above slender tall turned & leaf-carved columns flanking the wide curved glass center door, curved glass sides, four interior wooden shelves against a mirror back, molded conforming apron raised on four short cabriole legs w/paw feet, refinished, ca. 1895, 20 x 48", 5' 10" h. (ILLUS.) **3,000**

Decorative Oak China Cabinet

China cabinet, Victorian Golden Oak style, the high top crestrail w/a stepped, scroll-cut outline & a shell-and-scroll carved crest above the oblong beveled mirror, the half-round top w/a flat front above a conforming bead-carved cornice over a large flat glazed door w/rounded corners & scroll-carved borders, curved glass sides, opening to four wooden shelves, scalloped apron on short blocked cabriole legs, refinished, ca. 1895, 18 x 50", 72" h. (ILLUS.).. **1,750**

Fine Golden Oak China Cabinet

China cabinet, Victorian Golden Oak, the half-round top w/a high pointed & ornately scroll-carved crest above a pair of projecting tall reeded columns dividing the curved front glass door from the curved glass sides, molded conforming base raised on front paw feet on casters, encloses four wooden shelves w/a mirrored back at the top shelf, refinished, ca. 1895, 20 x 44", 70" h. (ILLUS.).................... **3,400**

Chippendale Revival Curio Cabinet

Curio cabinet, Chippendale Revival style, mahogany, two-part construction: the very tall upper section w/a broken-scroll pediment w/pierced lattice carving & a small

central platform finial above a cornice w/a dentil molding over a lattice-carved frieze band above the very tall geometrically-glazed cupboard doors opening to shelves; the stepped-out lower section w/a rectangular top w/molded edge above a long deep drawer w/lattice-carved border banding flanked by lattice-carved side stiles, narrow serpentine apron raised on slender carved cabriole legs ending in scroll feet on pegs, original finish, ca. 1890s, 20 x 34", 7' 6" h. (ILLUS.)................. **1,800**

Louis-XV Style Giltwood Curio Cabinet

Curio cabinet, Louis XV-Style, giltwood, a tan marble rectangular top w/rounded corners above a conforming case w/a wide frieze band of ornate leafy scrolls above a wide single-pane glazed door flanked by half-nude caryatids & scrolls at the front corners & glass side panels, the deep apron w/a center scroll drop, short demi-cabriole legs w/scroll-carved knees, two interior shelves, Europe, ca. 1900, 16 x 28", 42" h. (ILLUS.) **1,800**

Louis XVI-Style Giltwood Curio Cabinet

Curio cabinet, Louis XVI-Style, carved gilt-wood, the flat top inlaid w/marble above an ornate molded cornice above a tall glazed door trimmed w/elaborate molded floral swags & oblong edges flanked by canted front corners w/further scroll & rosette decoration, molded & pierced apron raised on short turned, tapering legs, cloth-lined, France, ca. 1890, 20 x 36", 70" h. (ILLUS.)... **3,000**

Elaborate Victorian Dental Cabinet

Dental cabinet, Victorian Golden Oak style, quarter-sawn oak, "Harvard" model, the top superstructure w/an arched & scalloped crestrail centered by a scrolled cartouche above two S-form narrow shelves supported by slender turned spindles above a rectangular top backed by a narrow rectangular beveled mirror, the case w/a tall stack of narrow swing-out drawers on the left & another small swing-out stack on the left above a small slant front writing surface opening to a fitted interior, the lower case w/six small molded drawers on the left side & a large tambour-door compartment over a narrow & deep drawer on the right, original simple brass bail pulls, refinished, ca. 1890-1900, closed 18 x 34", 78" h. (ILLUS.) **5,500**

Arts & Crafts Medicine Cabinet

Medicine cabinet, Arts & Crafts movement, oak, the high three-quarters gallery w/the taller arched sides w/pierced thin slits above a single square mirrored door, gently arched apron, good refinished condition, early 20th c., 7 x 18", 29" h. (ILLUS.)... **633**

Simple Arts & Crafts Music Cabinet

Music cabinet, Arts & Crafts style, quarter-sawn oak, a rectangular top above a tall flat door w/wide flat brass hinges & flanked by side stiles gently flaring at the top & feet, opens to shelves & dividers, original dark finish & wooden casters, ca. 1910, 9 x 12", 32" h. (ILLUS.)......................... **250**

Classical Revival Music Cabinet

Music cabinet, Classical Revival style, mahogany veneer, a rounded crestrail w/a scroll-carved center finial above the rectangular top over a case w/a round-fronted veneered drawer w/round brass pulls & a brass keyhole escutcheon above a flat paneled door w/fine crotch-grained veneering & a brass knob, gadrooned base band, raised on short cabriole legs ending in carved paw feet, refinished, ca. 1910, 14 x 22", 42" h. (ILLUS.) **650**

Classical Revival Music Cabinet

Music cabinet, Victorian Classical Revival substyle, mahogany, a high top crest w/a flat crestrail w/delicate center carving & curved scroll-carved ends enclosing an oblong beveled mirror, the rectangular top over a scroll-carved frieze band above a pair of tall cupboard doors w/rectangular beveled mirrors w/notched corners & ormolu sunburst mounts at each corner, quarter-round reeded columns at side, sides w/ormolu capitals & bases, narrow apron w/small carved center drop, raised on ring-turned & tapering feet w/ormolu tips, ca. 1890, 16 x 28", 4' h. (ILLUS.) **1,900**

Victorian Folk Art Music Cabinet

Music cabinet, Victorian whimsical folk art-style, walnut & rosewood, a high broken-scroll crestrail above a narrow shelf over the rectangular top w/an egg-and-dart cornice over a divided lower cabinet, on the left side are three shelves enclosed by fancy cut-out galleries including a lyre form & a harp & violin form, on the right side is a drawer w/a dark central band over a tall cabinet door w/three angular panels, the center panel carved w/the word "Musica," scallop-cut left side &

apron, on flat shaped legs, last quarter 19th c., original finish, 16 x 24", 42" h. (ILLUS.).. **1,400**

Louis XV-Style Curio-Music Cabinet

Music & curio cabinet, Louis XV-Style, Vernis Martin finish, a rectangular glass top w/serpentine front banded w/brass above a conforming case, a low mirror-backed curio display section w/glass on three sides & trimmed w/brass banding above a medial brass band above a single wide door centered by a rectangular allegorical painted panel w/brass banding & a scalloped apron, brass-banded side panels, raised on simple cabriole legs w/brass mounts, early 20th c., 15 x 20", 36" h. (ILLUS.) **750**

Fine Baroque Revival Silver Cabinet

Silver cabinet, Baroque Revival style, figured walnut veneer, the arched top w/a small medallion crest over the molded crestrail above the case w/a wide center door w/an upper arched & glazed panel w/scrolling grillwork over a veneered panel flanked by narrow side panels inset w/oval glass panes w/cut starburst designs, the lower section w/a deep mid-molding over a case w/a single wide, deep drawer w/three arched panels in the front trimmed w/burl, burl banding & scrolls & w/brass teardrop pulls, raised & carved vertical dividers, a molded carved bottom molding w/a carved center drop raised on four legs w/bulbous reeded & gadrooned turnings above an incurved medial shelf on bun feet, original dark finish, ca. 1930, 20 x 42", 6' 4" h. (ILLUS.) 950

Colonial Revival Silver Cabinet

Silver cabinet, Colonial Revival style, walnut & walnut veneer, two-part construction: the upper section w/a rectangular top over a pair of large arch-topped molding-trimmed doors centered by a scroll-carved panel & fitted w/a large scrolled brass keyplate; the lower section w/a mid-molding above a narrow block-veneered band & a pierced & scroll-carved apron, raised on cabriole legs w/scroll-carved returns & ending in Spanish feet, joined by a serpentine scrolled stretcher, original finish, ca. 1920s, 19 x 44", 5' 6" h. (ILLUS.) 800

Unusual Victorian Spool Cabinet

Spool cabinet, late Victorian, walnut, the rectangular top w/a deep molded cornice above a gently slanting front w/seven narrow glass-fronted drawers w/metal pulls above three long narrow bottom drawers w/wooden pulls & traces of original advertising, paneled sides, deep molded base, original finish, ca. 1880-90, 16 x 20", 24" h. (ILLUS.) 950

Clark's Walnut Spool Cabinet

Spool cabinet, Victorian Eastlake substyle, walnut, the rectangular top w/molded edge above a case w/six long shallow drawers each w/an inset panel w/black wording, carved & molded front side stiles, molded flat base, cast-brass hinged pulls, reads "Clark's - White - O.N.T. - Sole Agent - George A. Clark - Fast Black," some wear to glass panels, wood refinished, ca. 1880s, 18 x 22", 22" h. (ILLUS.) 1,200

Fine Clark's Walnut Spool Cabinet

Spool cabinet, walnut, rectangular top w/molded edges above a case w/six long narrow drawers w/teardrop pulls, each w/a red etched-glass panel w/wording, flat molded base, panels read "Clark's - Spool Cotton - O.N.T. - Sole Agent - George A. Clark - On White Spools," refinished, late 19th c., 16 x 22", 20" h. (ILLUS.) 2,200

Massive Baroque Revival China Cabinet

Step-back wall china cabinet, Victorian Baroque Revival substyle, carved oak, two-part construction: the upper section w/a rectangular top w/blocked ends centered by an arched & scroll-carved crest centered by a carved finial over an oval button & flanked by urn-form corner finials above the stepped & carved cornice over a wide frieze band w/ornate carved scrolls over a pair of glazed cupboard doors w/beaded edging flanked by slender reeded & carved colonettes above a beaded base band all raised on figural lion-carved supports flanking a recessed panel-carved back; the projecting lower section w/a carved border above a pair of gadroon-carved drawers w/brass ring pulls above a pair of cupboard doors w/raised beaded border bands enclosing oval raised panels enclosing finely carved trophy designs & surrounded by a leaf sprig at each corner, slender turned colonettes down the sides, on a flaring carved & blocked base on bun feet, original finish, Europe, ca. 1880, 22 x 50", 8' h. (ILLUS.)... **3,000**

French Louis XV-Style Inlaid Vitrine

Vitrine cabinet, Louis XV-Style, marquetry inlay in mahogany, the flat lobed top over a coved, inlaid cornice above a conforming case w/a tall bowed & glazed center door opening to glass shelves & a mirrored back, bowed glazed sides, each section w/gilt-brass mounts & trim & w/ornate floral & urn inlays in the lower sections, raised on four simple cabriole legs w/gilt-brass mounts, original finish, France, ca. 1900, 20 x 30", 66" h. (ILLUS.) **2,400**

Vitrine cabinet, Louis XVI-Style, Vernis Martin finish, the oblong marble top w/serpentine edges mounted w/a pierced brass gallery above a frieze band of looping scrolls above a serpentine-fronted door w/a large glass panel above a lower Vernis Martin panel painted w/a romantic scene of an 18th c. couple in a landscape, the bowed glass sides above similar painted panels, raised on simple squared cabriole legs w/gilt-brass mounts, original finish, ca. 1920s, 18 x 30", 5' 4" h. (ILLUS. top of column).... **1,500**

Louis XVI-Style Vitrine Cabinet

Chairs

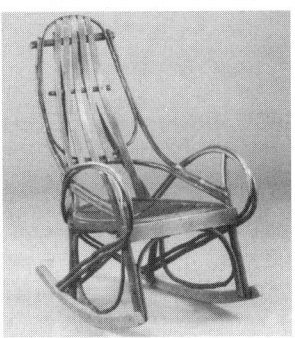

Adirondack Rustic Bentwood Rocker

Adirondack rustic bentwood rocker, the tall rounded back & arms composed of long bentwood branches forming loops, the back w/five tall slender slats, the seat composed of narrow slats, on rockers, unmarked, late 19th - early 20th c., 38 1/2" h. (ILLUS.).. **201**

Arts & Crafts Oak Dining Chairs

Arts & Crafts dining chairs, oak, the tall back w/a wide slightly incurved flat crestrail w/scroll carving above a central section of slender square spindles, the square stiles w/pointed tops, leather-up-holstered seats w/tack trim, flat apron carved detail on simple turned front legs, original dark finish, ca. 1900, 42" h., set of six (ILLUS.)... **1,200**

Bentwood armchair, a wide arched crest on the U-form bentwood crestrail forming short arms over U-form bentwood arm supports, wide shaped seat on squared & shaped legs joined by high bentwood stretchers, designed by Josef Hoffman, J.& J. Kohn, Vienna, Austria, early 20th c., 32 1/2" h. **633**

Pair of Early Chinese Armchairs

Chinese armchairs, elm-like hardwood, a wide U-shaped crestrail above a flat splat & two spindles on each side, paneled square seat raised on flat legs joined by worn stretchers, pegged & mortise & tenon construction, original finish, Ming Dynasty, China, 32" h., pr. (ILLUS.) **800**

Chippendale armchair, walnut, the scratch-carved & scrolled serpentine crestrail ending in reeded ears above the stiles flanking a scroll-pierced splat centered by a diamond design, serpentine open arms w/curled hand grips on incurved arm supports over the replaced upholstered slip seat, square front legs & canted back legs joined by flat box stretchers, old refinished, late 18th c., 38" h. **5,175**

Walnut Chippendale Side Chair

Chippendale country-style side chairs, walnut, the oxbow crestrail above a scroll-carved solid back splat flanked by slightly curved stiles above the upholstered slip seat, square legs joined by flat box stretchers, Pennsylvania, late 18th c., set of 4 (ILLUS. of one)........................ **9,900**

Chippendale "lolling" armchair, cherry, the tall rectangular upholstered back w/a serpentine crest above padded open arms on incurved arm supports above the wide upholstered seat raised on square molded front legs joined by square stretchers to the square raking rear legs, old refinish, Connecticut, 1765-75, 41" h. (minor repairs) **20,700**

Irish Chippendale Revival Armchair

Chippendale Revival armchair, carved mahogany, the scroll-carved serpentine crestrail centered by a shell carving above the ornate pierced & scroll-carved splat, shaped open arms ending in curled hand grips above the scroll-carved incurved supports, wide overupholstered seat w/a serpentine seatrail carved w/gadrooning, cabriole front legs w/shell- and scroll-carved knees & ending in raised scroll feet, original finish, Irish, ca. 1910, 39" h. (ILLUS.) **1,000**

Chippendale Revival Dining Chairs

Chippendale Revival dining chairs, mahogany, the yoked crestrail above a pierced vasiform splat flanked by stiles above the upholstered slip seat, cabriole front legs w/shell-carved knees & claw-and-ball feet, original finish, old upholstery, ca. 1890, four side chairs & one armchair, 36" h., the set (ILLUS.)........ **1,500**

Fine Chippendale Revival Side Chair

Chippendale Revival side chairs, mahogany, the yoked crestrail centered by a carved pointed leaf reserve & further scrolls at the ears above the pierced scroll-carved vasiform splat, wide trapezoidal over-upholstered seat, cabriole front legs w/leaf-carved knees & claw-and-ball feet, old upholstery, original finish, late 19th - early 20th c., 38" h., pr. (ILLUS. of one).. **600**

Chippendale Revival Wing Chair

Chippendale Revival wing- armchair, walnut, the high upholstered back w/an arched crestrail above deep, wide serpentine wings over outscrolled arms, wide cushion seat, serpentine seatrail & short cabriole front legs w/carved knees & ending in pad feet, original black leather upholstery, ca. 1920s, 48" h. (ILLUS.)... **1,200**

Chippendale side chair, stained birch & maple, the serpentine crestrail centered by a carved shell & ending in carved ears above a pierced scroll-carved splat on a molded shoe flanked by raked molded stiles, a trapezoidal slip seat in a flat beaded frame, raised on molded Marlborough front legs joined to the square raked rear legs by molded box stretchers, old refinish, Massachusetts, 1780-90, 38" h.. **2,530**

Chippendale side chair, walnut, transitional-style, the serpentine crestrail centered by a fluted shell & terminating in flattened upturned ears over a solid scroll-carved

vasiform splat flanked by square tapering stiles w/rounded back, trapezoidal molded & upholstered slip seat over a cyma-curved seatrail, on front cabriole legs ending in trifid feet, rear rounded racked legs, old surface, 20th c. blue silk damask upholstery, Philadelphia, ca. 1740-85, 41" h. (minor imperfections)................. **9,775**

Fine Chippendale Side Chair

Chippendale side chairs, mahogany, the serpentine crestrail w/ears centered by a simple shell-carved crest above the ornate pierced & scroll-carved vasiform splat, trapezoidal upholstered slip seat, flat seatrail on cabriole front legs ending in claw-and-ball feet, second half 18th c., pr. (ILLUS. of one)..................................... **13,200**

Chippendale wing- armchair, mahogany, the tall upholstered back w/a serpentined crest flanked by wide outswept & rounded tapering wings above the low outswept scrolled upholstered arms, wide cushion seat, on square legs joined by rectangular box stretchers, New England, old refinish, ca. 1760-80, 46" h. (minor imperfections) **6,325**

Chippendale-Style Child's Armchair

Chippendale-Style child's armchair, mahogany, the arched crestrail over a slender pierced vase-form splat & gently flared stiles, shaped open arms on incurved arm supports above the seat frame, raised on cabriole front legs w/claw-and-ball feet, original finish, ca. 1920, no seat, 14 x 16", 30" h. (ILLUS.)........ **150**

Fine Classical Mahogany Armchair

Classical armchair, mahogany & mahogany veneer, the wide rounded crestrail above a wide urn-form splat flanked by stiles joined to the open scroll-carved arms above the upholstered seat, veneered seatrail above the modified cabriole front legs & square stile rear legs, refinished, ca. 1840, 35" h. (ILLUS.) **250**

Carved Classical Dining Chair

Classical dining chairs, mahogany & mahogany veneer, the wide gently arched crestrail w/rounded ends carved w/palmettes raised on molded stiles above a scroll- and palmette-carved medial rail, trapezoidal over-upholstered seat on reeded square front sabre legs, original finish, original horsehair upholstery, ca. 1830s, 30" h., set of eight (ILLUS. of one).. **4,000**

Large Classical Revival Armchair

Classical Revival armchair, carved oak, the wide square upholstered back flanked by large boldly carved seated winged lions forming the arms, a wide spring-upholstered seat above a leaf-carved seat frame raised on canted front legs ending in large paw feet, square tapering rear legs, leather upholstery, refinished, American-made, ca. 1880-90, 40" h. (ILLUS.) **5,500**

Simple Classical Side Chairs

Classical side chairs, mahogany, the flat crestrail w/an incised rectangular panel above a ring- and fan-carved lower rail above the upholstered slip seat, flat seatrail on simple turned & tapering front legs, old finish, modern upholstery, ca. 1830, 32" h., set of four (ILLUS. of two) **800**

Unique Colonial Revival Corner Chair

Colonial Revival corner armchair, oak, the thick U-form backrail centered by a wide flaring & curved crest w/incised leaf & loop design, the top of the arms w/further designs, raised on three ring- and baluster-turned spindles alternating w/two slightly tapering pierced splats w/carved designs, upholstered seat w/a flat seatrail carved w/a band of looping arches, ring- and baluster-turned legs ending in peg feet, dark fumed finish, replaced upholstery, late 19th c., 32" h. (ILLUS.) **400**

Country-style Child's Rocking Chair

Country-style child's rocking chair w/arms, painted & decorated, a flat crestrail above five plain spindles flanked by simple turned stiles over the turned open arms, original woven splint seat, plain turned legs & double turned stretchers at the front & sides, original red paint w/black striping, mid-19th c., 15 x 16", 27" h. (ILLUS.).................................. **200**

Early 20th century dining chairs, mahogany, each w/a wide serpentine crestrail above a flat tapering center slat above a squared seat w/later needlework seats, square tapering & gently flared front legs,

original dark finish, ca. 1910, 40" h., set of six (ILLUS. at bottom of page)................... **750**

Early Carved Roman Chair

Early 20th century Roman chair, carved mahogany, the wide back carved ornately w/an infant's head at the top center enclosed by scrolls above overall large scrolls & a cartouche within the scalloped edges, the U-form back stiles w/ball finials, downswept open arms above the solid curved seat raised on inverted U-form legs ending in paw feet & joined by pierced side stretchers, original dark finish, ca. 1910, 36" h. (ILLUS.)............ **450**

Early American "banister-back" side chair, painted, a high arched & scalloped crestrail above three half-round split banisters flanked by tall rod- and knob-turned stiles w/double-knop finials & w/a lower rail, above a replaced woven rush seat, block-, knob- and baluster-turned front legs ending in Spanish feet & joined by a double-knob turned front stretcher, plain double side stretchers & a single rear

Early 20th Century Dining Chairs

stretcher, old black paint, New England, late 18th c., 45" h. (repairs).............................. **748**

Painted Banister-back Side Chair

Early American "banister-back" side chair, painted, the double-arch wide crestrail above three half balusters joined to a shaped lower rail all between the tall baluster-, ring- and rod-turned stiles w/ring-turned finials, woven rush seat, ring- and rod-turned front legs joined by double knob-turned front stretchers & plain turned side & back stretchers, old black paint w/gilt designs, possibly Connecticut, last half 18th c., 41 3/4" h. (ILLUS.) **1,093**

Early American country-style child's "ladder-back" highchair, painted, the back w/three arched slats flanked by tall simple turned stiles w/tall finials above simple open arms joined to turned arm supports forming front legs w/turned button finials, low replaced woven rush seat, simple turned stretchers, yellow paint over earlier red, New England, late 18th c., 25" h. **345**

Early American country-style child's "ladder-back" highchair, painted, the tall rear stiles slightly canted inward forming rear legs & back stiles w/ring-turned knob finials above two narrow arched back slats, simple spindle open arms joined to the tall front legs continuing to form arm supports, woven rush seat, double stretchers at the front & sides, single at the rear, original dark brown paint, New England, mid-18th c., 37 1/2" h. **2,185**

Early "Ladder-back" Armchair

Early American country-style "ladder-back" armchair, probably maple, the tall back w/five arched slats between turned stiles w/oblong finials, the shaped open arms w/baluster-turned arm supports continuing to the front legs & flanking the replaced woven rush seat, double knob- and baluster-turned stretchers in the front & simple turned stretchers at the sides & back, original dark finish, ca. 1820, 46" h. (ILLUS.) **350**

Early American "ladder-back" armchair, painted, the tall back w/five high arched reverse-graduated slats between slender stiles w/button finials, shaped open arms on baluster-turned arm supports above the replaced woven rush seat, knob- and rod-turned front legs continuing from arm supports & ending in knob- and peg front feet, double-knob turned front stretcher, plain double side & single rear stretchers, old black paint, Delaware River Valley, last half 18th c., 46 3/4" h. (minor imperfections) **2,990**

Early Painted Boston Rocker

Federal country-style "Boston" rocker, painted & decorated, the high back w/a curved crestrail centered by a rectangular plaque decorated w/stenciled grapes & vines, raised on simple stiles flanking the seven slender back spindles, shaped open arms on a bamboo-turned spindle & arm support, wide S-scroll seat raised on canted knob- and ring-turned front legs joined by a turned front stretcher & bamboo-turned side & back stretchers & legs on rockers, original mustard yellow paint & decoration, ca. 1830, 46" h. (ILLUS.) **375**

Federal country-style "Boston" rocker, painted & decorated, the tall back w/a down-curved wide crestrail centered by a rectangular panel above seven slender curved spindles & shaped arms on turned spindles, wide S-shaped seat on turned legs on rockers joined by turned box stretchers, old white background paint w/colorful flowers outlined in gold on the crestrail & further painted flowers & medallions on the seat, carpet-cutter

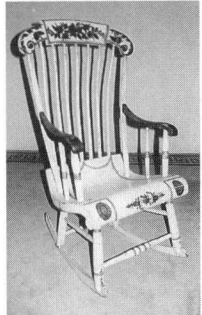

Decorated Early Boston Rocker

curved crestrail above a three-bar & ball medial rail & lower rail over four short turned spindles all between the tapering & backswept stiles, shaped plank seat on slightly canted bamboo-turned legs joined by turned stretchers, the crestrail w/free-hand painted fruit & foliate designs w/further stenciled designs on the back & seat, New England, ca. 1825-30, minor imperfections, 33" h. (ILLUS.) **345**

Federal Revival Dining Chairs

rockers, original surface, ca. 1830, 42" h. (ILLUS.) **400**

Federal Arrow-back Fancy Chairs

Federal country-style "fancy" chairs, painted & decorated, the crestrail w/a pillow rest above two gently curved rails w/four arrow slats all flanked by tapering canted stiles, wide rounded plank seat on ring- and rod-turned canted legs joined by turned stretchers, original yellow painted w/green trim & color stenciled florals on back & apron, ca. 1830-50, 34" h., set of six (ILLUS.) **1,200**

Federal Country-style "Fancy" Chair

Federal country-style "fancy" side chair, painted & decorated, the wide slightly

Federal Revival dining chairs, inlaid mahogany, the squared back w/banded inlay enclosing a vasi-form splat w/line inlay, upholstered seat, flat seatrail w/banded inlay & square tapering front legs w/banded inlay, original finish, early 20th c., 40" h., four side & two armchairs, the set (ILLUS.) **1,200**

Federal wing- armchair, mahogany, the high upholstered back w/a serpentine crest flanked by wide outswept, rounded & tapering upholstered wings above low upholstered rolled arms, wide cushion seat, on square tapering reeded front legs & canted square rear legs joined by flat box stretchers, New England, ca. 1790, old refinish, 46" h. (imperfections) ... **6,325**

French Rococo-Style Armchair

French Rococo-style armchair, mahogany, the narrow floral-carved crestrail above the upholstered back separated by carved stiles from the high upholstered arms w/curved rails continuing to form the arm supports flanking the cushion seat, deep apron above a floral swag-carved seatrail & short scroll-carved front legs, original finish & pale green brocade upholstery, ca. 1920s, 38" h. (ILLUS.) **400**

Herman Miller rocker, designed by Charles Eames, yellow molded fiberglass seat mounted on steel rod base w/birch runners, overall 26 1/2" h. (some discoloration) **440**

Herman Miller side chairs, Eiffel Tower design by Charles Eames, black enameled wire grid frames w/original brown leather coverings, overall 32" h., set of four **660**

Louis XV Revival Upholstered Armchair

Louis XV Revival armchair, mahogany, the oval medallion back w/figural needlepoint upholstery w/brass tack trim, arched & shaped padded open arms on carved incurved arms over the wide needlepoint-upholstered spring seat w/brass tack trim, serpentine seatrail w/shell and scroll carving, carved cabriole front legs ending in scroll feet on pegs, original finish, ca. 1920s, 38" h. (ILLUS.) **650**

French Louis XV-Style Armchairs

Louis XV-Style armchairs, fruitwood, the squared serpentine backrail w/floral-carved crest enclosing the original needlepoint upholstery, padded & shaped open arms above the wide over-upholstered needlepoint seat, serpentine scroll-carved seatrail on carved cabriole legs, original finish, France, ca. 1920s, 34" h., pr. (ILLUS.) **900**

Unusual Louis XV-Style Hooded Chair

Louis XV-Style hooded armchair, white gesso on wood frame, the arched shell-form paneled & upholstered top above a tall upholstered back & side wings over low padded closed arms, cushion seat above serpentine seatrail continuing to demi-cabriole front legs, original paint & gilt highlights, ca. 1920s, 32" w., 4' 6" h. (ILLUS.) **800**

Mission-style (Arts & Crafts movement) armchair, oak, fixed-back drop-arm style, the upright back w/five horizontal slats between square stiles above wide flat & gently sloped arms over further slats, wide gently arched front seatrail, fine condition w/waxed finish, "Handcraft" label of L. & J.G. Stickley, 41" h. (replaced drop-in leather spring seat & back cushion) **5,750**

Mission-style (Arts & Crafts movement) dining chairs, oak, a wide gently arched crestrail over three vertical slats flanked by square stiles, upholstered overhanging seats, square legs w/flat high stretcher in the front & double stretchers at the sides, cleaned original finish, branded Limbert mark & original retail labels, 36" h., five side chairs & one armchair, the set of six **2,530**

Set of Mission Oak Dining Chairs

Mission-style (Arts & Crafts movement) dining chairs, oak, each w/a gently curved top rail over a narrower lower rail between the square stiles, square seatrail on square legs joined by flat stretchers, no seats, L. & J.G. Stickley, refinished, ca. 1920, 36" h., set of 4 (ILLUS.) **2,000**

Unmarked Stickley Sewing Rocker

Mission-style (Arts & Crafts movement) sewing rocker, mahogany, the tall back w/square stiles flanking flat rails above & below a cluster of eight slender square spindles, new inset leather-covered seat, original finish, unmarked L. & J. G. Stickley, early 20th c., 36" h. (ILLUS.) **316**

Mission Oak Sewing Rocker

Mission-style (Arts & Crafts movement) sewing rocker, oak, the back w/three wide slates between square stiles, replaced woven rush seat, flat front & rear stretchers & flat double side stretchers, original finish, ca. 1910, 32" h. (ILLUS.) **350**

Simple Mission Oak Sewing Rocker

Mission-style (Arts & Crafts movement) sewing rocker, oak, the upright rectangular back w/a single flat splat above the seat w/original leather inset trimmed w/brass tacks, square legs joined by flat stretchers, mortise-and-tenon construction, ca. 1910, 34" h. (ILLUS.) **250**

Mission-style (Arts & Crafts movement) slipper chair, oak, the wide squared back w/numerous slender square spindles above the drop-in upholstered seat, deep seatrails & square legs joined by side stretchers, original finish, unmarked Gustav Stickley, 32 1/2" h. (new green leather seat) **978**

Neoclassical Revival Painted Armchair

Neoclassical Revival armchair, painted & decorated, a gently rolled needlepoint-upholstered back flanked by wing-carved stiles continuing into leafy scroll arms terminating in large blossom medallions flanking the wide upholstered seat w/an incurved seatrail, ring-turned & reeded tapering front legs, reeded tapering rear legs, painted white & gold, original surface, ca. 1920s, 36" h. (ILLUS.) **800**

Ornately Carved Chinese Armchairs

Oriental armchairs, carved dark hardwood, one w/a cartouche-form back panel ornately carved w/scrolls w/the heavy curved open arms w/figural handgrips, the wide seat w/deep scroll-carved apron raised on heavy dot-incised cabriole legs w/scroll feet, the other w/the pierced back panel carved w/entwined dragons w/the arms formed by their necks & the heads forming the handgrips, the wide seat above a deep scroll-carved apron & heavy cabriole legs w/dot-incised bands & scroll feet, China, last quarter 19th c., each 34" h., group of two, each (ILLUS.) **800**

Ornately Carved Chinese Side Chair

Oriental side chair, ebonized carved hardwood, the tall solid wood balloon back ornately pierce-carved w/a design of a large looping dragon among clouds & scrolls, the serpentine plank seat w/carved band at front above a pierced & scroll-carved apron above front cabriole legs w/animal masks at knees & ending in paw feet, original dark finish, China, ca. 1910, 38" h. (ILLUS.) **450**

Rare Prairie Style Oak Armchair

Prairie Style - Arts & Crafts armchairs, oak, original green leather upholstered back panel & deep seat within a cube-form framework composed of multiple slender square slats, ball feet, architect-designed for the boardroom of the Merchants National Bank of Winona, Minnesota, made by Purcell, Feick & Elmslie, ca. 1905, original finish, 37" h., pr. (ILLUS. of one) **25,000**

Rare Queen Anne Ladder-back Chair

Queen Anne country-style "ladder-back" armchair, maple, the tall back w/six arched graduated slats flanked by turned stiles, shaped arms w/scrolled terminals on baluster-turned arm supports, woven rush seat, cabriole front legs joined by a double-knob turned stretcher & ending in crooked pad feet, plain side & back stretchers, old refinish, finial & height loss, attributed to Solomon Fussell, Philadelphia, 1740s, 43 3/4" h. (ILLUS.) **20,700**

Maple Country Queen Anne Side Chair

Queen Anne country-style side chair, maple, the serpentine crestrail w/raked, molded ears above a vasiform splat, a trapezoidal seat on block-, baluster- and ring-turned legs ending in Spanish front feet, double-knob turned front stretcher & simple turned side & back stretchers, 20th c. needlepoint seat upholstery, old surface, Massachusetts, mid-18th c., minor imperfections, 40" h. (ILLUS.) **3,105**

Country Queen Anne Side Chair

Queen Anne country-style side chair, painted hardwood, the oxbow crestrail above a vase-form splat flanked by baluster- and ring-turned stiles over the replaced woven seat, simple turned front legs joined by a worn baluster-turned front stretcher & plain side & rear stretchers, old finish, possibly original black paint, 1750-80, 40" h. (ILLUS.) **200-400**

Queen Anne country-style side chairs, stained maple, a simple ox-yoke crestrail on tapering outswept stiles flanking a plain vasiform splat above a woven rush seat, baluster-, block- and ring-turned front legs joined by a ball-turned stretcher & ending in simple Spanish feet, square canted rear legs & three flat stretchers, reddish brown stain, old surface, New England, late 18th c., 39 1/4" h., pr. **3,105**

Queen Anne Revival Dining Chair

Queen Anne Revival dining chairs, mahogany, the gently arched crestrail centered by wheat & leaf carving above the vasiform splat w/spooned carving & the molded shaped stiles, original needlepoint seat w/unicorn design, simple cabriole front legs ending in pad feet, old refinish, late 19th - early 20th c., 38" h., pr. (ILLUS. of one).. **800**

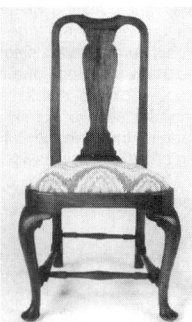

Boston Queen Anne Side Chair

Queen Anne side chair, black walnut, the yoked crestrail continues to reverse-curved tapering stiles rounded in the back, flanking a similarly reverse-curved vasiform splat above a compass slip seat w/front & side shaping above the front cabriole legs ending in pad feet & joined by turned stretchers to the square raking rear legs, early dark surface, Boston, 1730-60, 20th c. upholstery, minor imperfections, 40" h. (ILLUS.)................................ **9,775**

Queen Anne side chair, maple, the yoked crest above a vasiform splat ending in a molded shoe flanked by raked, chamfered stiles, the trapezoidal slip seat w/a scalloped front apron, on cabriole front legs ending in raised pad feet, baluster-

and block-turned stretchers, refinished, Massachusetts, 1740-60, 40" h. (minor imperfections) **4,025**

Queen Anne side chair, walnut, the yoked crestrail continuing to square tapering reverse-curved stiles flanking a vasiform splat above a compass-shaped slip-seat & front cabriole legs ending in pad feet, swelled box stretchers, old refinish, Boston, 1740-60, 20th c. embroidered seat cover, 39 1/2" h. (imperfections)................ **9,200**

Queen Anne-Style lolling armchairs, mahogany, w/cabriole legs & scrolled returns w/pad feet, bowed seat w/shaped arms, bright multicolored floral upholstery, overall 42 1/2" h., pr. **990**

Queen Anne-Style Rocking Chair

Queen Anne-Style rocking chair w/arms, mahogany & mahogany veneer, the rounded back w/a looping pierced vase-form splat w/carved leaf trim, shaped & curved open arms above the upholstered spring seat, curved seatrail raised on cabriole front legs w/scroll feet & square rear legs on rockers, reupholstered, original finish, early 20th c., 38" h. (ILLUS.) **450**

Queen Anne-Style wing- armchair, mahogany, the tall upholstered back w/a serpentine crest above the flared shallow rounded wings continuing into out-scrolled upholstered arms, wide cushion seat, cabriole front legs ending in pad feet joined to square canted rear legs by turned H-stretcher, labeled by the Hickory Chair Co., 20th c., 46" h. (areas of edge wear).. **385**

Ornate Rococo Revival Corner Chair

Rococo Revival corner chair, carved gilt-wood, the U-form crestrail ornately carved w/a full-relief reclining classical woman beside a shield & scrolls, the drapery-wrapped rail continuing to full figure arm supports carved as classical women, a central back splat flanked by relief-carved serpents, deep round upholstered spring seat, round carved seatrail w/a large scroll-carved central drop, on gently curved front legs trimmed w/beading & raised on peg feet, remnant of original upholstery, probably French, ca. 1890, 32" h. (ILLUS.) **1,800**

Pretty Aesthetic Movement Armchair

Victorian Aesthetic Movement armchair, walnut, a wide rectangular upholstered back panel flanked by simple stiles & raised on a pierced rail w/repeating quatrefoil design, upholstered outswept arms continuing to form the seat & w/conforming arm supports carved w/scrolls & loop bands above a panel of carved florettes & leaves & a dentil apron, canted angular legs on porcelain casters, new upholstery, refinished, ca. 1885, 30" h. (ILLUS.) **400**

Baroque Revival Armchair

Victorian Baroque Revival armchair, carved mahogany, a flat pierce-carved crestrail flanked by squared, pointed finials above the wide upholstered back, scrolled open arms ending in carved faces above the carved square tapering armrests above the wide upholstered seat, ring-, ball- and block-turned legs on low blocked feet, legs joined by a turned

H-stretcher, original finish, late 19th c., 42" h. (ILLUS.) **650**

Victorian Baroque Revival dining chairs, carved oak, the arched crestrail carved w/fruit & flowers & centered by a cut-out handhold above a square upholstered back panel raised above the square seat w/inset upholstered panel within a carved seat frame, carved apron, raised on block- and knob-turned front legs joined by a spiral-twist stretcher w/spiral-turned rear legs & turned H-stretcher, original dark finish, late 19th c., 18" h., 34" h., set of 8 (back & seat panels probably originally caned) **800**

Unique Ornate Baroque-Style Rocker

Victorian Baroque Revival rocking chair w/arms, carved fruitwood, unique highly carved design, the back w/a diamond-shaped panel topped by a high pierced scroll-carved crest w/a figural putto at one side flanked by heavy curved arms w/scroll-carved grips resting on pierce-carved sides composed of large leafy scrolls w/large figural caryatids forming the arm supports & front legs, the heavy curved rockers w/carved scrolls at the rear tips & figural busts over scrolls at the front tips, made for the Chicago Columbian Exposition of 1893, deaccessioned by the Chicago Museum of Science and Industry, probably Italian, 36 x 52", 4' h. (ILLUS.) **10,000**

Baroque-style Armchair and Rocker

Victorian Baroque-style armchair & rocker, carved mahogany, each w/a deep barrel-back w/the heavy crestrail centered by a carved lion mask & continuing down to form the arms carved w/large winged griffin heads & scrolled front stiles ending in large paw feet, original dark finish, ca. 1890, newer upholstery, 40" h., the pair (ILLUS.) **3,800**

Victorian Baroque-style Dining Chairs

Victorian Baroque-style dining chairs,
mahogany, the tall back w/an arched crestrail carved w/scrolls & dolphins above
the upholstered back panel flanked by
herringbone-carved stiles, wide over-upholstered seat w/a flat seatrail on square
tapering herringbone-carved front legs
on casters, original finish, new
upholstery, ca. 1880-1900, 38" h., set of
six (ILLUS.) **2,000**

Morris Chair with Dolphin Stretcher

Victorian Baroque-style Morris armchair,
quarter-sawn oak, the tall upholstered
back pad resting on an adjustable reclining back frame flanked by wide arched
arms over turned spindles & reeded urn-
form arm supports flanking the wide
cushion seat, seatrail w/heavy paneled
corner blocks over legs w/reeded knobs
connected by long slender dolphin-forms
carved as the stretcher, original finish,
old upholstery, ca. 1900, 44" h. (ILLUS.) **850**

Victorian Classical Revival armchair, oak
& walnut, the tall back w/a fan-carved
rounded crestrail above a pierce-carved
back w/a lyre-form splat carved w/bold
scrolls, the back stiles w/square knob finials above narrow shaped side wings

Unique Classical Revival Armchair

above the wide flat arms w/scrolled hand
grips raised on a flat armrest, the long
caned trapezoidal seat lifting to expose a
hole for a chamber pot, deep apron, simple turned front legs on casters, original
finish, last quarter 19th c., 40" h.
(ILLUS.) **250**

Victorian Eastlake Office Chair

Victorian Eastlake office chair, walnut, the squared back w/simple molding centered by an upholstered panel over a stick-and-ball base band, padded straight arms over stick-and-ball bands & carved rosettes, revolving on a metal post on a cross-form base w/incised decoration, on casters, from the Minnesota House of Representatives, ca. 1885, new Naugahyde upholstery, 42" h. (ILLUS.) **650**

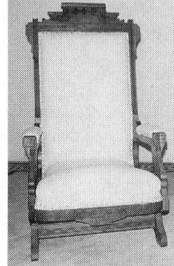

Victorian Eastlake Platform Rocker

Victorian Eastlake platform rocker, walnut, the angular crestrail w/carved stylized flowers above a narrow frieze band flanked by blocked ears above the tall upholstered back, padded open arms w/angular arm supports over the upholstered spring seat, burled seatrail w/central drop, on a platform rocker base, refinished, new upholstery, ca. 1885, 44" h. (ILLUS.) **300**

Elizabethan Revival Slipper Chair

Victorian Elizabethan Revival slipper chair, walnut, the tall narrow back ornately pierce-carved w/an arched crest & cartouche over leaf scrolls flanked by spiral-turned stiles above the early needlepoint spring seat, short knob- and block-turned front legs joined by block- and ring-turned H-stretcher, on casters, original finish, ca. 1870, 34" h. (ILLUS.) **500**

Victorian Golden Oak child's highchair, convertible-type, a wide rounded crestrail w/a lower pressed arched design over six slender turned spindles & baluster-turned stiles flanked by arms on turned spindles & arm supports & a swing-up rectangular feeding tray, square seat w/padded center fitted at the front w/a footrest & raised on

Oak Highchair/Stroller Combination

tall flattened cross-form hinged legs on iron wheels which lower the seat to form a stroller, refinished, ca. 1900, highchair 40" h. (ILLUS.) **500**

Fancy Oak Pressed-back Side Chairs

Victorian Golden Oak pressed-back kitchen chairs, the wide crest w/scalloped & rounded edges decorated w/a stamped design of undulating leaves & water lilies & long facing fish above ring-turned stiles flanking seven slender knob-turned spindles above a shaped matching lower back rail, squared cane seat on ring- and rod-turned front legs joined by double turned stretchers, refinished, ca. 1900, 38" h., set of four (ILLUS. of two) **1,000**

Ornate Golden Oak Rocking Chair

Victorian Golden Oak rocking chair w/arms, quarter-sawn oak, the tall back w/two scalloped crestrails joined by a central roundel & a row of tiny spindles, the upper rail w/stylized lion-carved ears, over a slender center carved vase-form splat flanked by slender bead-turned spindles all flanked by knob- and rod-turned stiles, shaped flat arms over knob-turned spindles & arm rests above a shaped round pressed composition seat (not shown), ring- and knob-turned front legs joined by double turned stretchers, refinished, ca. 1890s, 45" h. (ILLUS.) **350**

Victorian Gothic Revival Slipper Chair

Victorian Gothic Revival slipper chair, walnut, the tall pierced back w/a Gothic arch crest w/small spindle finials & pierced arches, trefoils & other designs above bobbin-turned stiles w/finials & bobbin-turned back rails & spindles centered by a pierced Gothic design splat, over-upholstered spring seat, short bobbin-turned front legs on casters, old possibly original fabric, original finish, ca. 1855, 40" h. (ILLUS.) **350**

Late Victorian Novelty-type Rocker

Victorian novelty rocking chair w/arms, stained hardwood, the flared flat crestrail centered by a carved grotesque mask above a tall vasiform splat flanked by slender baluster-turned spindles & heavy baluster- and ring-turned stiles, shaped arms over pairs of baluster- and ring-turned spindles & canted arm supports, wide shaped seat on baluster- and ring-turned legs joined by a turned H-stretcher, old mahogany finish, ca. 1900, 42" h. (ILLUS.) **375**

Hunzinger Patent Side Chair

Victorian "patent" side chair, walnut, a novelty design w/the back frame composed of bold bobbin-turned rails enclosing an oval upholstered panel, the side stiles continuing down to form the front legs which flank the round upholstered seat & front seat supports on a turned cross stretcher, George Hunzinger, ca. 1880, original finish, reupholstered, 32" h. (ILLUS.) **650**

John Jelliff Renaissance Armchairs

Victorian Renaissance Revival armchairs, walnut & burl walnut, the arched back panel w/a carved crestrail composed of turned rods flanking a central roundel & w/projecting turned corner ears, a tufted upholstered panel above the lower back rail centered by another roundel, open padded arms w/the arm supports carved as ladies' heads, the wide upholstered seat w/a bowed seatrail above a conforming apron w/burl trim, knob- and ring-turned tapering front legs on casters, by John Jelliff, Newark, New Jersey, new upholstery, original finish, ca. 1875, 38" h., pr. (ILLUS.) **3,000**

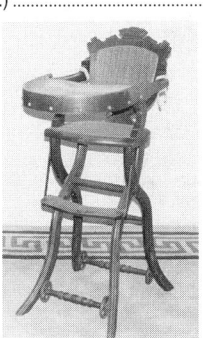

Victorian Convertible Highchair/Rocker

Victorian Renaissance Revival convertible highchair/rocker/stroller, walnut, the caned shield-shaped back w/a scallop-cut arched crest above a swing-up serving tray over the caned seat, raised on tall serpentine crossed legs hinged to lower the seat & convert it to either a rocking chair or stroller w/small metal wheels, original finish, ca. 1880, upright 40" h. (ILLUS.)... 450

Rare Branch-carved Hall Chair

Victorian Renaissance Revival hall chair, carved walnut, the tall pierced back ornately carved w/a pointed palmette crest above entwined leafy oak branches w/large acorns, above the flat trapezoidal seat w/molded edges above a curved apron carved w/crossed oak leaves & acorns, raised on ring- and rod-turned reeded legs w/knob feet, by Mitchell and Rammelsberg of Cincinnati, Ohio, 18 x 20", 4' h. (ILLUS.)................................ 5,000

Fine Renaissance Revival Chair

Victorian Renaissance Revival lady's chair, walnut, the tall back w/a finely carved peaked crestrail enclosing an oval medallion w/a lady's bust, carved corner finials & drops above the large oval upholstered back panel over a molded & carved lower rail, downswept skirt guards on the wide rounded seat w/a carved seatrail, on trumpet-turned front legs, attributed to John Jelliff, newer upholstery, original finish, ca. 1875, 36" h. (ILLUS.) 400

Fine Renaissance Revival Side Chair

Victorian Renaissance Revival side chairs, walnut & burl walnut, the corseted upholstered back w/a wide curved crestrail w/burl panels & scrolls, scroll trim above angular carved skirt guards above the deep round upholstered spring seat, burled seatrail w/center shield reserve raised on trumpet-turned front legs on original metal casters, original finish, early upholstery, ca. 1875, 32" h., pr. (ILLUS. of one).. 800

Renaissance Revival Slipper Chair

Victorian Renaissance Revival slipper chair, walnut & burl walnut, the scroll- and pierce-carved crestrail centered by a fruit-carved crest above the oblong upholstered back panel on a scroll-carved lower rail & flanked by ring-, knob- and baluster-turned stiles, double C-scroll skirt guards flank the oblong upholstered seat, leaf- and scroll-carved mount on front apron, raised on ring-turned front legs on casters, old refinish, ca. 1870, 36" h. (ILLUS.).................. 450

Victorian Renaissance Revival youth chair, walnut, the squared upholstered back w/a gently arched crestrail centered by a scroll crest & w/scrolled ears, padded open arms w/outscrolled arm supports above the wide upholstered seat, ring- and rod-turned & tapering front legs joined by a wide, shaped foot rest, square tapering & gently raked rear legs,

Fine Renaissance Revival Youth Chair

ring-turned side & back stretchers, new upholstery, original finish, ca. 1875, 40" h. (ILLUS.).. **1,200**

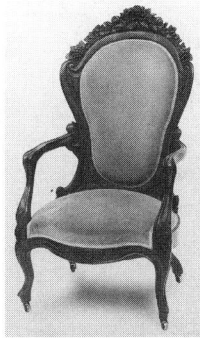

"Rosalie with Grapes" Pattern Armchair

Victorian Rococo armchair, carved & laminated rosewood, the tall balloon back w/a tapering oval upholstered panel framed w/a wide arched crest of ornate floral & grape carving & long scroll-carved sides above the curved & molded open arms on incurved arm supports above the wide upholstered seat w/a serpentine seatrail, raised on demi-cabriole front legs w/floral-carved knees & raised on casters, canted square rear legs on casters, by John H. Belter, New York City, "Rosalie with Grapes" patt., ca. 1855 (ILLUS.)... **4,480**

Ornate Rosewood Rococo Armchair

Victorian Rococo armchair, carved rosewood, the massive balloon back w/a very wide frame carved w/large floral clusters & scrolls & enclosing the tufted upholstered back, scroll-carved padded open arms above the wide serpentine over-upholstered seat w/a floral- and scroll-carved seatrail, demi-cabriole front legs ending in scroll feet on casters, attributed to George Henkels, Philadelphia, ca. 1855, new upholstery, 46" h. (ILLUS.)....... **3,500**

Victorian Rococo Rosewood Armchair

Victorian Rococo armchair, carved rosewood, the tall shaped & upholstered balloon back w/a high pierced & scroll-carved crest joined to pierce-carved scrolls down the sides above the padded open arms w/incurved & leaf-carved arm supports, wide upholstered spring seat w/a serpentine seatrail w/a scroll-carved apron, raised on demi-cabriole front legs & canted square rear legs all on porcelain casters, original finish, ca. 1850-60, 44" h. (ILLUS.) **1,600**

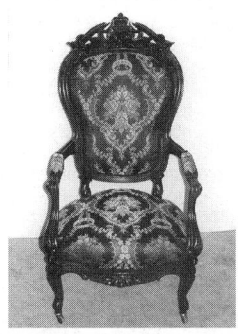

Rococo Carved Rosewood Armchair

Victorian Rococo armchair, carved rosewood, the tall upholstered balloon back w/a high arched & pierce-carved crest w/bold fruit & floral carving on the molded frame raised above the upholstered spring seat flanked by padded shaped open arms w/incurved supports, serpentine seatrail w/nut-carved center, on demi-cabriole front legs on original casters, refinished, new upholstery, ca. 1860, 44" h. (ILLUS.) **1,200**

Victorian Rococo Open-arm Armchair

Victorian Rococo armchair, mahogany, the tall upholstered balloon back w/a molded frame & pierced scroll-carved crest, shaped & padded open arms on incurved arm supports flanking the wide upholstered seat w/a serpentine molded seatrail continuing to the demi-cabriole front legs on casters, old refinish, newer upholstery, ca. 1870, 44" h. (ILLUS.) **650**

Belter "Rosalie" Pattern Armchairs

Victorian Rococo armchairs, carved & laminated rosewood, a tall shaped upholstered balloon back w/an ornately floral-carved crest, base of back also scroll-carved, shaped & molded open arms above the upholstered spring seat w/a serpentine seatrail w/floral carving, on demi-cabriole front legs on casters,"Rosalie" patt., John Henry Belter, New York, ca. 1855, old, possibly original upholstery, original finish, 47" h., pr. (ILLUS.).. **9,500**

Rococo Gentleman's & Lady's Chairs

Victorian Rococo gentleman's & lady's chairs, ebonized & natural walnut, the gentleman's armchair w/a high waisted balloon back w/a large arched loop at the crest continuing to floral- & leaf- pierce-carved sides flanking the upholstered panel, open padded arms on incurved arm supports over the wide spring seat w/serpentine seatrail pierced-carved decoration, on demi-cabriole legs on casters, the matching lady's chair w/a small balloon back & S-scrolled skirt guards, original finish, later upholstery, gentleman's chair 48" h., pr. (ILLUS.)........ **1,500**

Unusual Iron-framed Victorian Rocker

Victorian Rococo platform rocking chair, upholstered iron & wood, the openwork scrolling iron framework w/a high padded headrest above the tall shaped upholstered back flanked by serpentine padded arms rests on iron scroll supports, a squared upholstered seat raised on high curved iron spring supports raised on long slender wooden rails, old reupholstery, original painted surface, repaired headrest, ca. 1850-60, 46" h. (ILLUS.) **550**

Victorian Rococo "Lincoln" Rocker

Victorian Rococo rocking chair w/arms, carved walnut, so-called "Lincoln" or "Grecian" style, tall upholstered balloon back w/a rounded crestrail carved w/a fruit- and nut-carved crest above the molded waisted frame over the padded ornately scroll-carved open arms above the upholstered spring seat, scroll-carved serpentine seatrail on short tapering legs on rockers, refinished, ca. 1860, 46" h. (ILLUS.) **650**

Victorian Rococo Rocking Chair

Victorian Rococo rocking chair w/arms, the large shaped balloon-back w/a fruit-carved crest enclosing a needlepoint upholstery panel above curved padded open arms on incurved molded arm supports, wide needlepoint upholstered seat w/a serpentine seatrail & demi-cabriole front legs, on rockers, ca. 1860s, 38" h. (ILLUS.) **650**

Unique Rococo "Grecian" Rocker

Victorian Rococo rocking chair w/arms, walnut, so-called "Grecian" or "Lincoln" style, the tall upholstered & shaped back w/a curved crestrail carved w/fruits & flowers & continuing to form sides of back & the padded scrolled arms on S-scroll arm supports, wide upholstered rolled seat raised on long double-S scrolls resting on the long serpentine rockers, refinished, old velvet upholstery, ca. 1850-70, 42" h. (ILLUS.).. **450**

Victorian Rococo side chair, carved & laminated rosewood, an oblong tufted upholstered back panel framed w/an elaborately pierce-carved arched framewood tapering down to arched skirt guards on the high upholstered spring seat w/a serpentine seatrail decorated w/a center shell carving, raised on cabriole front legs w/shell-carved knees & ending in scroll feet on casters, original finish, upholstery, attributed to Charles A.

Baudouine-style Rococo Side Chair

Baudouine, New York City, 40" h. (ILLUS.).. **2,400**

Belter Carved Rosewood Side Chair

Victorian Rococo side chair, carved & laminated rosewood, the tall back framework composed of large carved C-scrolls enclosing pierce-carved grapevines & w/a carved floral crest all centered by a small round upholstered panel, the deep over-upholstered spring seat on a serpentine seatrail w/floral carving & cabriole front legs w/floral-carved knees, on casters, original finish, reupholstered, John Henry Belter, ca. 1855, 40" h. (ILLUS.) **3,800**

Belter "Rosalie" Pattern Side Chair

Victorian Rococo side chair, carved & laminated rosewood, the tall balloon back w/a tufted upholstered panel within a scroll-carved frame topped by an arched fruit & blossom-carved crest, the wide upholstered spring seat w/a serpentine seatrail carved w/a central floral cluster, raised on demi-cabriole front legs w/carved knees & casters, "Rosalie" patt. by J.H. Belter, New York City, ca. 1855, original finish, old reupholstery, 40" h. (ILLUS.)... **2,400**

Set of Meeks Rosewood Side Chairs

Victorian Rococo side chairs, carved & laminated rosewood, a balloon-form tufted upholstered back panel framed by an ornate pierce-carved frame w/a peaked crestrail w/a center cartouche flanked by ropetwist-carved scroll bands continuing to further scroll carving down the sides to the lower rail & skirt guards, wide rounded upholstered spring seat, serpentine seatrail w/central carved cartouche, raised on demi-cabriole front legs, Stanton Hall patt. by J. & J.W. Meeks, New York City, ca. 1855, original finish, old but not original upholstery, 40" h., set of 3 (ILLUS.)... **4,500**

Meeks Stanton Hall Pattern Side Chair

Victorian Rococo side chairs, carved & laminated rosewood, the arched & peaked crestrail w/a central floral-carved cartouche flanked by bead-carved bands over pierced scrolls, the serpentine sides w/further scroll carving enclosing the tufted upholstered back, raised above the rounded serpentine seat w/a carved seatrail & demi-cabriole front legs, Stanton

Hall patt., J. & J. W. Meeks, New York, ca. 1855, old replaced upholstery, 40" h., pr. (ILLUS. of one) **3,200**

Meeks-style Rosewood Slipper Chair

Victorian Rococo slipper chair, carved & laminated rosewood, the tall balloon-form wood back ornately pierce-carved w/tight scrolls & grape clusters below a high arched & rope twist-carved crest, the deep upholstered spring seat on a narrow seatrail w/a carved front medallion between the short carved & shaped front legs, attributed to J. & J.W. Meeks, New York City, ca. 1855, old reupholstery, original finish, ca. 1855, 42" h. (ILLUS.) **1,600**

Ornate Victorian Rococo Slipper Chair

Victorian Rococo slipper chair, carved walnut, the tall pierce-carved back w/an arched crestrail carved w/scrolls & a central fruit cluster above a hairpin-shaped molding enclosing a large pierced leafy scroll design, slender ring-turned back stiles above low scrolled skirt guards flanking the balloon-form upholstered seat, ring- and knob-turned front legs on casters, refinished, ca. 1850-60, 38" h. (ILLUS.).. **450**

Fine Rococo Slipper Chair

Victorian Rococo slipper chair, pierce-carved laminated rosewood, the tall serpentine-framed back w/a floral-carved crest above ornate looping vines & a central grape cluster, rounded upholstered spring seat on a conforming seatrail w/a carved front border, raised on slender tapering squared legs w/carved knees, attributed to Meeks of New York, ca. 1850-60, refinished, 40" h. (ILLUS.) **1,200**

Victorian Rococo Side Chair

Victorian Rococo side chairs, carved rosewood, an oval back w/a finger-carved frame w/a carved floral crest enclosing the upholstered panel, raised above the over-upholstered spring demi-seat w/a serpentine seatrail w/finger-carving continuing into demi-cabriole front legs on casters, reupholstered in red floral damask, ca. 1860, 39" h., repairs, set of 4 (ILLUS. of one)......................... **528**

Victorian Rococo Side Chairs

Victorian Rococo side chairs, rosewood, the balloon back w/an arched & scroll-carved crestrail w/small panels above a scroll-carved lower rail, the upholstered spring seat w/a carved curved seatrail & simple cabriole front legs, original finish, later upholstery, ca. 1865, 34" h., set of four (ILLUS. of two) **800**

Arts & Crafts Painted Wicker Armchair

Wicker armchair, Arts & Crafts style, the tall wide squared back composed of tightly woven borders around a tightly woven back panel w/a cross-form pierced design, wide flat arms above loose lattice-work sides, woven seat above a lattice-work apron w/curved border, worn dark green paint, early 20th c., 37" h. (ILLUS.)...... **172**

Wicker Rocker and Side Chair

Wicker rocking chair, the wide rolled & tightly woven crestrail curves down to form a continuous band w/wide arms & seatrail, the back w/a decorative finely woven central square framed by diamond lattice weaving, tightly woven seat, scroll band under seatrail, wrapped legs on rockers, original dark green paint, ca. 1900, 36" h. (ILLUS. left with side chair) **250**

Wicker side chair, the tall ornate back w/a long, upturned C-scroll crestrail centered by a half-round crest enclosing wicker oval loops & topped by small ball finials, the back composed of a decorative fanned woven design trimmed w/small balls & tight scrolls at the base, caned seat over an ornate scrolled seatrail & wrapped legs w/decorative wicker trim, original varnished surface, ca. 1890, 36" h. (ILLUS. right with wicker rocker)........ **300**

William & Mary child's "ladder-back" highchair, turned & painted maple, the tall inwardly-canted rear stiles form back legs & ring- and rod-turned backed stiles w/knob finials flanking three graduated arched slats, shaped open arms on front baluster-, rod- and ring-turned arm supports continuing to form the legs, woven rush seat, double stretchers at the front & sides & single at the rear, original dark brown paint, New England, early 18th c., 37" h.. **12,650**

William & Mary Revival Armchair

William & Mary Revival armchair, walnut, the tall squared & upholstered back w/an arched & scroll-cut crestrail, the long shaped open arms w/scroll ends raised on incurved arm supports over the wide, deep upholstered seat, scroll-carved legs joined by a wide arched front stretcher, original finish & needlepoint upholstery, late 19th - early 20th c., 45" h. (ILLUS.)........ **500**

William & Mary Revival Wing Chair

William & Mary Revival wing- armchair, mahogany, the tall upholstered back w/an arched crest flanked by rounded

tapering side wings over outscrolled upholstered arms, cushion seat on deep upholstered seatrail, scroll-carved cabriole front legs ending in hoof feet joined by an S-scroll carved front stretcher & serpentine side stretchers, reupholstered w/brass tack trim, early 20th c., 48" h. (ILLUS.)............................... **1,200**

Windsor "braced bow-back" armchair, the arched crestrail over seven slender finely turned spindles & a pair of forked back braces, serpentine arms over a baluster-turned spindle & canted baluster-turned arm support, slightly shaped saddle seat, canted baluster- and ring-turned legs joined by a swelled H-stretcher, dark blue over old black repaint, underside of seat initialed in chalk "A.K.," Rhode Island, late 18th c., 36" h. (iron brace on one arm, tail piece expertly repaired)......... **1,430**

Windsor Comb-back Armchair

Windsor "comb-back" armchair, painted, the tall comb w/four slender bamboo-turned spindles & stiles above a birdcage crestrail over seven bamboo-turned spindles between raked bamboo-turned stiles, shaped arms over a turned spindle & canted turned arm support, wide shaped & incised seat on canted bamboo-turned legs joined by turned box stretchers, old green paint, New England, ca. 1810, 48" h. (ILLUS.)............. **1,725**

Painted Windsor Comb-back Rocker

Windsor "comb-back" rocking chair w/arms, painted & decorated pine & maple, the tall comb w/a rectangular crestrail over five slender spindles above the shaped back crestrail flanked by rabbit-ear curved stiles flanking five tall slender spindles, S-scroll arms on a spindle & canted arm support over the wide dished plank seat, simple turned canted legs on inset rockers, original painted & stenciled decoration w/blossoms & leaves on the crestrails against a dark brown ground, ca. 1830, 46" h. (ILLUS.) **450**

Windsor Fan-back Side Chair

Windsor "fan-back" side chair, maple & ash, the serpentine crestrail above six turned spindles between slender baluster- and ring-turned canted stiles, the shaped saddle seat on splayed baluster- and ring-turned legs joined by a swelled H-stretcher, old dark surface, New England, ca. 1780-90, 37" h. (ILLUS.) **863**

Windsor "fan-back" side chair, painted, the serpentine crestrail w/scrolled ears above seven slender spindles flanked by canted slender baluster- and rod-turned stiles, shaped saddle seat, canted baluster-, ring- and rod-turned legs joined by a swelled H-stretcher, retains some old green paint, New England, ca. 1780, 35 1/4" h. (minor imperfections) **1,265**

Fan-back Writing-arm Windsor

Windsor "fan-back" writing-arm armchair, the serpentine crestrail over seven slender spindles above the heavy U-form medial rail ending in a carved hand grip at one side & an oblong writing surface

over a small drawer on the other side, spindles below medial rail & arms w/baluster- and ring-turned arm supports & a brace for the writing surface, wide shaped saddle seat, canted baluster- and ring-turned legs joined by a swelled H-stretcher, old refinish, traces of original color, Connecticut, ca. 1780, imperfections, repairs, 38 1/2" h. (ILLUS.) **2,070**

Windsor Revival Oak Armchair

Windsor Revival armchair, oak, the high bowed backrail w/scroll-carved trim above seven slender bobbin-turned spindles, shaped arms ending in carved lions' heads above three bobbin-turned spindles & a canted, bobbin-turned arm support, shaped saddle seat on ring-, rod- and baluster-turned front legs ending in paw feet & ring- and baluster-turned rear legs all joined by turned double stretchers, ca. 1895, refinished, 42" h. (ILLUS.)... **450**

Rod-back Windsor Side Chair

Windsor "rod-back" side chairs, painted, the narrow slightly arched crestrail over seven bamboo-turned spindles & canted stiles above the incised saddle seat on slightly splayed bamboo-turned legs joined by turned stretchers, old black paint w/vestiges of floral & other yellow accents, New England, early 19th c., surface imperfections, 34 1/2" h., pr. (ILLUS. of one) **1,265**

Windsor "sack-back" armchair, painted, a high arched crestrail over seven slender spindles continuing through the narrow center rails which extend to form curved arms raised on another spindle &

a canted ring- and baluster-turned arm support, wide oblong shaped saddle seat raised on canted baluster-, ring- and rod-turned legs joined by an H-stretcher, old worn green paint, probably Connecticut, ca. 1780-90, 35 1/2" h. (minor imperfections) **3,738**

Windsor "sack-back" armchair, painted, a high bowed crestrail above seven slender spindles continuing through a narrow U-form center rail continuing to form arms w/shaped ends, two spindles & a canted baluster- and ring-turned arm support under each arm & above the oblong shaped seat, on canted ring-, baluster- and rod-turned legs joined by a swelled H-stretcher, old red paint, New England, ca. 1780-90, 38" h. (repairs) **2,530**

Child's Step-down Windsor Side Chair

Windsor "step-down" child's side chair, painted & decorated, the stepped crestrail above seven slender spindles between curved stiles over the shaped saddle seat, slightly canted bamboo-turned legs joined by turned box stretchers, probably old black repaint w/gold floral stencil on crestrail & gold trim on legs,ca. 1820, 30" h. (ILLUS.) **250**

Windsor-Style Rocking Chair

Windsor-Style rocking chair w/arms, oak, a narrow serpentine scroll-carved crestrail above a back w/eight tall baluster-turned spindles & stiles backed by turned brace spindles, shaped arms on baluster-turned spindles & canted arm supports,

wide shaped seat, slightly canted baluster- and knob-turned legs joined by a turned H-stretcher, refinished, ca. 1900, 44" h. (ILLUS.) **450**

Chests & Chests of Drawers

Victorian Oak Apothecary Chest

Apothecary chest, oak, a long rectangular top w/a molded edge over a case of drawers w/four small graduated drawers arranged in eight rows, each drawer w/cast-metal pulls, deep molded base, paneled ends, original finish, late 19th c., 22 x 76", 36" h. (ILLUS.) **2,400**

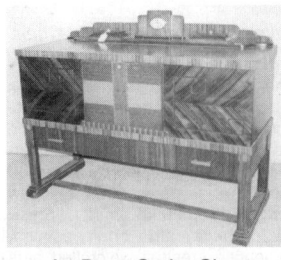

Art Deco Cedar Chest

Art Deco cedar chest, red cedar-lined w/mixed rosewood & mahogany exterior veneering, a low stepped crestrail centered by a built-in electric clock & w/small hanky drawers over the rectangular top lifting above a deep well, the front w/elaborate light & dark veneering w/incised angular line detail above a pair of long bottom drawers w/yellow Bakelite pulls, on square legs on a trestle base, refinished, ca. 1930s, 20 x 44", 30" h. (ILLUS.)... **400**

Arts & Crafts Oak Blanket Chest

Arts & Crafts blanket chest, oak, the rectangular top opening to a deep well, the front divided into two panels each w/applied cross braces, paneled ends w/further braces, on casters, label of the Brooks Company, new finish, early 20th c., 19 3/4 x 48 3/4", 18 1/2" h. (ILLUS.) **1,725**

Ornate Baroque Coffer Chest

Baroque style coffer chest, carved oak, long hinged plank top opening to a deep well, a gadrooned edge molding above a long rectangular carved panel w/raised edge molding enclosing ornately carved leafy vines, flowers & fruits, front corners w/relief-carved caryatids, wide rounded gadrooned base molding above heavy paw front feet, paneled ends w/heavy iron bail handles, probably original finish, Europe, probably 17th c., 21 x 55", 20" h. (ILLUS.) **3,000**

Blanket chest, country-style, painted & decorated pine, a rectangular top w/molded edges opening to a well w/till, wrought-iron hinges, base molding in front, bootjack end cut-outs, original yellow, red & black grained decoration, Rhode Island, late 18th - early 19th c., 19 1/4 x 45", 24 1/2" h. **2,200**

Blanket chest, early American country-style, painted & decorated, six-board construction, the rectangular top w/molded edges opening to a well w/a scratch-beaded lidded till labeled "dry goods" above a drawer titled "A. Perkins," smoke-grained interior w/greenish grey paint, the exterior w/bootjack ends, decorated w/overall wood graining simulating mahogany, the top outlined in yellow & green striping w/floral corners, original paint & decoration, Massachusetts, late 18th c., 18 1/4 x 46 1/2", 25" h. (minor surface imperfections)................................ **2,300**

Early Painted Pine Blanket Chest

Blanket chest, early American country-style, painted pine, the rectangular top w/molded edges opening to a deep well,

a mid-molding above the lower case w/two long drawers w/replaced metal bin handles, paneled ends, modern blue paint, New England, ca. 1830, 18 x 44", 40" h. (ILLUS.) **600**

Fancy Paint-decorated Blanket Chest

Blanket chest, painted & decorated pine, a rectangular hinged top w/original geometric patterned sponged painting to resemble inlay, the front w/similar sponging w/a large diamond panel within a rectangular panel, bail end handles, flat molded base, mid-19th c., 18 x 40", 20" h. (ILLUS.) **400**

Blanket chest, painted & decorated pine, six-board construction, the hinged rectangular top w/molded edges opening to a well w/a beaded lidded till, the base w/a straight skirt & arched feet & sides, red & gold wood graining imitating mahogany, old surface, probably Maine, 1820-30, 15 7/8 x 43 1/3", 21 1/2" h. (repair to a foot, minor losses to two rear feet) **2,760**

Blanket chest, painted pine, six-board construction, the rectangular top w/molded edges opening to a well w/a lidded till over drawers, the front w/thin rope-twist insets near the top & bottom edges, an oval brass keyhole escutcheon, deep molded base, original blue paint, New England, last quarter 18th c., 17 3/4 x 44 1/4", 17 1/3" h. (molding loss) **3,565**

English Chippendale Chest

Chippendale chest of drawers, mahogany, rectangular top w/deep molded cornice above a case w/a pair of thumb-molded drawers over three long graduated drawers all w/brass butterfly pulls, molded case & scrolled bracket feet, probably English, ca. 1780, old refinish, probably replaced brasses, 20 x 40", 42" h. (ILLUS.) **1,000**

Chippendale chest of drawers, painted & decorated cherry, the rectangular top w/molded edges above four long graduated cockbeaded drawers w/butterfly pulls on a molded base w/ogee bracket feet, overall simulated mahogany wood graining in dark reddish brown, drawers outlined in black paint, Connecticut, 18th c., 29 1/4 x 39 1/4", 36 1/2" h. (replaced brasses, minor foot repair) **1,438**

Chippendale Chest-on-Chest

Chippendale chest-on-chest, mahogany, two-part construction: the upper section w/a rectangular top w/a wide coved cornice above a dentil-carved frieze band over a row of three drawers over two drawers over three long drawers all w/brass butterfly pulls; the lower section w/a mid-molding over a case w/three long drawers, molded base on large ogee bracket feet, inlaid keyhole escutcheons, replaced brasses, ca. 1780, early 20th c. refinish, 23 x 42", 80" h. (ILLUS.) **3,000**

Chippendale country-style blanket chest, inlaid walnut, a rectangular top w/molded edges opening to a well w/a lidded till over a concealed drawer, the dovetailed cast w/two drawers at the bottom w/simple bail pulls, molded base on molded bracket feet, probably Roanoke River Basin, North Carolina, late 18th c., 25" h. (refinished, replaced pulls, minor imperfections) **4,888**

Country Chippendale Blanket Chest

Chippendale country-style blanket chest, pine, a rectangular hinged top w/molded edges opening to a deep well w/a lidded till above the dovetailed case,

two cockbeaded drawers at the bottom above a base molded & scroll-cut bracket feet, original brass pulls, old refinish, ca. 1775, 21 x 46", 24" h. (ILLUS.) **1,500**

Chippendale country-style chest of drawers, pine, a rectangular top w/a molded cornice above a case of five long graduated thumb-molded drawers w/butterfly pulls & keyhole escutcheons, molded base on scrolled bracket feet, original pulls, two original escutcheons, old refinish, New England, 18th c., 17 1/2 x 37 1/2", 42 1/4" h. (imperfections) **1,610**

Chippendale Revival Cedar Chest

Chippendale Revival cedar chest, mahogany, the rectangular top w/molded edges opening to a deep well above a case w/false drawers, a long drawer over a pair of small, deep drawers flanking a larger deep central panel w/fine shell & scroll carving, serpentine apron w/central shell carving, cabriole legs ending in claw-and ball feet, original finish, made by Lane, early 20th c., 20 x 40", 30" h. (ILLUS.) **650**

Chippendale "serpentine-front" chest of drawers, mahogany & mahogany veneer, the rectangular top w/molded edges & serpentine front above a conforming case w/canted front corners & four long graduated cockbeaded drawers w/figured veneers, molded base on C-shaped bracket feet w/a cusp, original round brasses, old surface, Portsmouth, New Hampshire, 1795-1810, 25 x 40 1/2", 36 1/2" h. (imperfections) **13,800**

Rhode Island Chippendale Tall Chest

Chippendale tall chest of drawers, tiger stripe maple, the rectangular top w/a deep flaring cornice over a row of three small drawers, the center one w/fan carving, above five long, graduated thumb-molded drawers all w/brass butterfly pulls & keyhole escutcheons, molded base w/a center drop pendant & tall scroll-cut bracket feet, mostly original brasses, early surface, Rhode Island, 1770-90, imperfections, 17 1/4 x 40 1/4", 58 1/4" h. (ILLUS.) **11,500**

Chippendale tall chest of drawers, walnut, a rectangular top w/a flaring deep coved cornice above a case w/a row of three small drawers over a pair of drawers above a stack of five long graduated thumb-molded drawers all w/large butterfly brasses & keyhole escutcheons, drawers flanked by quarter-round engaged fluted columns, a heavy molded base raised on tall ogee bracket feet w/scrolled spurs on platforms, original escutcheons, Chester County, Pennsylvania, dated "1784," 22 1/4 x 40 1/4", 64" h. (replaced brasses, refinished, minor repairs) **13,800**

Pennsylvania Tall Chest of Drawers

Chippendale tall chest of drawers, walnut, the rectangular top w/a deep stepped cornice above a row of three thumb-molded drawers over four long graduated thumb-molded drawers all w/brass butterfly pulls & keyhole escutcheons, molded base on scroll-cut bracket feet, Pennsylvania, 1760-80, original pulls, old refinish, restoration, 23 x 43", 49 1/2" h. (ILLUS.) **1,725**

Chippendale-Style Blanket Chest

Chippendale-Style blanket chest, pine, rectangular hinged top opening to a deep well over a single long drawer w/turned wood knobs, the front centered by a carved fan, dovetail & square nail construction, single-board sides, bracket feet, refinished, ca. 1900, 17 x 40", 28" h. (ILLUS.) **450**

Classical Mahogany Butler's Chest

Classical butler's chest, mahogany & mahogany veneer, a rectangular black marble top w/rounded front corners above an ogee-fronted false drawer folding down to form a writing surface & enclosing a fitted interior above three long working drawers w/original panel-cut glass pulls, deep molded base on corner block feet, French polish finish, ca. 1840, 18 x 42", 38" h. (ILLUS.) **1,800**

Classical chest of drawers, cherry & cherry veneer, the scrolling backsplash w/brass mounts above a pair of cockbeaded drawers flanked by crosshatched panels resting on the stepped-out rectangular top over a single long projecting drawer flanked by further crosshatched panels above three long stepped-back long drawers flanked by spiral-turned columns w/black-painted capitals & bases, round brasses w/ring pulls, on ring- and baluster-turned legs ending in peg feet, Vermont or New York State, 1825-35, 23 x 42 1/2", 54 1/4" h. (replaced brasses, refinished, minor imperfections) **1,840**

Mahogany & Birch Classical Chest

Classical chest of drawers, mahogany & birch, the high rounded splashback w/scroll-cut ends above a pair of small hanky drawers on the rectangular top above a long stepped-out drawer flanked by acanthus leaf-carved panels over three long stepped-back drawers flanked by thistle, leaf & reeded baluster half-round columns, on short ovoid feet on casters, replaced round brass pulls, possibly original finish, ca. 1830, 22 x 42", 44" h. (ILLUS.) **800**

Simple Classical Chest of Drawers

Classical chest of drawers, mahogany & crotch-grain mahogany veneer, a rectangular top above a case w/a long deep top drawer over three long graduated drawers all w/replaced round pulls & original oval keyhole escutcheons, flat apron & carved paw front feet, original finish, ca. 1840, 20 x 44", 42" h. (ILLUS.) **1,400**

Classical country-style chest of drawers, cherry & bird's-eye maple veneer, the high crestboard w/long delicately scrolled top above the rectangular top over a case w/a slightly projecting long, deep rectangular drawer w/maple veneer front & round brass pulls above three shorter long graduated matching drawers flanked by knob- and rod-turned pilasters, on knob- and rod-turned legs on casters, old replaced pulls, early 19th c., 21 x 42", 52 1/2" h. (old splits in edges & one beading of lower drawer) **1,155**

Classical Country-style Chest

Classical country-style chest of drawers, figured maple & walnut, a low scroll-ended backsplash on the rectangular top overhanging a pair of narrow drawers flanked by projecting blocks above a stack of three reverse-graduated long drawers w/Rockingham glazed pottery knobs, scalloped corner brackets on base, refinished, ca. 1840-50, 18 x 38", 45" h. (ILLUS.) **450**

Classical country-style child's chest of drawers, painted maple, the elevated backboard w/scrolled terminals above two small drawers on a stepped-out case of four long drawers flanked by colonette columns ending in bulbous turned feet, original red paint & hardware, New England, 1825-35, 11 x 17 3/8", 21 3/4" h. (very minor surface imperfections) **1,840**

Classical Revival Mirrored Chest

Classical Revival chest of drawers, mahogany & mahogany veneer, princess-style, the tall mirrored back composed of an oblong central beveled mirror w/a palmette-carved finial & scroll-topped support posts flanked by shorter hinged oblong beveled mirrors w/scroll-carved outer ears over scroll-carved bands on the drop-well base w/a curve-fronted small drawer on each side of the well over two long serpentine-front drawers, all w/simple brass bail pulls, serpentine apron w/a small scroll-carved center drop raised on short cabriole front legs on casters, refinished, ca. 1910, 20 x 42", 6' 4" h. (ILLUS.) **1,200**

Fine Classical Revival Chest

Classical Revival chest of drawers, walnut & figured walnut veneer, the rectangular top w/ovolo front corners above a pair of drawers centered by an acanthus-carved panel & flanked by the leaf-carved top of quarter-round columns down the sides flanking the lower four long drawers w/large stamped brass pulls, scroll-carved serpentine apron, on casters, original finish & hardware, ca. 1890, 21 x 40", 52" h. (ILLUS.).............................. **1,000**

Tall Oak Classical Revival Chest

Classical Revival tall chest of drawers, quarter-sawn oak, a rectangular framed mirror w/a scroll-carved crest tilting between two scrolled uprights over the rectangular top w/molded edges over a tall case w/a pair of round-fronted drawers over four long flat drawers all w/pierced brass pulls, short front legs w/paw feet, refinished, ca. 1900, 18 x 34", 70" h. (ILLUS.)................................. **800**

Classical Transitional Chest

Classical Transitional chest of drawers, mahogany & crotch-grain mahogany veneer, a tall waisted oval mirror w/scroll-carved trim swiveling between tall carved wishbone supports above a pair of small hanky drawers on the white marble top over a case w/a long ogee-front drawer over a stack of three long drawers w/simple wooden knobs, beaded band above scalloped apron, on casters,

original finish, some veneer chipping, ca. 1850, 20 x 38", overall 72" h. (ILLUS.) **800**

Colonial Revival Tall Mahogany Chest

Colonial Revival serpentine-front tall chest of drawers, mahogany veneer, a large rectangular mirror w/a scalloped & leaf-carved crest swiveling between leaf-carved uprights on the rectangular top w/molded edges & a serpentine front above a tall case w/serpentine drawers, a pair of drawers over a stack of four long drawers, all w/pierced brass pulls, serpentine apron w/scroll carving, short cabriole front legs on casters, refinished, original brasses, ca. 1910, 19 x 38", overall 74" h. (ILLUS.) **600**

Tall Bird's-eye Maple Lingerie Chest

Colonial Revival tall lingerie chest of drawers, bird's-eye maple veneer, a large arched crescent-form mirror swiveling between slender columnar supports w/urn finials above the rectangular top w/serpentine edges over a conforming serpentine case w/two small drawers beside a small cupboard door above four long graduated drawers all w/pierced brass pulls, serpentine apron & simple short cabriole front legs, early 20th c., 27" w., 5' 9" h. (ILLUS.) **1,400**

Early American country-style chest of drawers, painted pine, a rectangular top w/molded edges above a case w/three long, deep drawers w/replaced brass teardrop pulls w/a heavy molding between each drawer, a deep double-arch scrolled front apron, wide arched boot-jack sides, old black paint, Brandford, Connecticut area, 18th c., 14 1/2 x 27 1/2", 34 1/2" h. (repairs)........... **5,463**

Federal "bow-front" chest of drawers, birch w/bird's-eye maple & cross-grained mahogany veneer, a rectangular top w/ovolo corners & curved front above a conforming case of four long reverse-graduated drawers w/bird's-eye maple banded w/mahogany above an ornately scalloped bird's-eye maple apron, raised on slender baluster-turned legs w/knob feet, old round refinished brasses, Massachusetts, ca. 1810, 21 x 46 1/2", 40 1/2" h. (minor imperfections) **8,625**

Federal Bow-front Chest of Drawers

Federal "bow-front" chest of drawers, mahogany veneer & cherry, the rectangular top w/a bowed front veneered along the edge above a conforming case of four long graduated drawers each w/light & dark figured veneers in outline, scalloped apron, ring- and baluster-turned legs w/peg feet, original oval brasses & keyhole escutcheons, old refinish, probably Providence, Rhode Island, ca. 1810, minor repairs, 21 x 40 1/4", 41" h. (ILLUS.)... **3,220**

Federal "bowfront" chest of drawers, cherry & mahogany veneer, rectangular top w/bowed front w/ovolo corners above a conforming case of four long cockbeaded graduated mahogany veneered drawers w/stringing in ovolo outline flanked by ring-turned & spiral-carved quarter engaged columns over the short tightly scalloped apron, raised on tapering turned & reeded legs ending in button feet, original oval brasses & keyhole escutcheons, New Hampshire or Vermont, 1815-25, 21 5/8 x 40", 43 1/4" h. (refinished, minor imperfections)........................ **4,025**

Federal chest of drawers, cherry & bird's-eye maple inlaid, rectangular two-board top w/an inlaid edge above a case of four reverse-graduated cockbeaded drawers veneered in bird's-eye maple surrounded by cross-banded mahogany veneer, a cyma-curved skirt w/spurs centered by a figured maple diamond outlined in pat-

terned inlay, on turned swelled legs ending in small ball feet, original oval brasses & keyhole escutcheons, old refinish, attributed to Spooner and Fitts, Athol, Massachusetts, 1808-13, 18 1/4 x 39 1/2", 38 1/2" h. (minor imperfections)............... **17,250**

Federal chest of drawers, inlaid cherry, a rectangular top w/string-inlaid edges above a case of four graduated scratch-beaded drawers w/stringing in an ovolo outline, a serpentine skirt w/a circular cut-out flanked by tall shaped French feet, original oval brasses, early surface, Massachusetts or Rhode Island, ca. 1806, 19 x 37 1/2", 39" h. (minor imperfections).. **4,888**

Federal chest of drawers, inlaid cherry, rectangular top w/inlaid edges above a case of four long graduated cockbeaded drawers w/stringing in outline, scalloped apron w/central cut-out raised on French feet, original oval brasses & surface, Massachusetts or New Hampshire, ca. 1815-20, 19 3/4 x 39 1/2", 40 1/4" h. (imperfections)... **1,840**

Inlaid Cherry Federal Chest of Drawers

Federal chest of drawers, inlaid cherry, the rectangular top w/a dash-inlaid edge above a case of four long drawers w/original round brass pulls, an inlaid dash band at the bottom above the scallop-cut apron centered by an oval inlay, tall French feet, old finish, ca. 1810, 20 x 40", 42" h. (ILLUS.) **2,000**

Federal Country-style Cherry Chest

Federal country-style chest of drawers, cherry, a rectangular top above a case w/four long graduated drawers w/old replaced oval brasses, scalloped apron & tall French feet, old refinish, Connecticut, early 19th c., 18 x 40", 42" h. (ILLUS.)....... **1,100**

Federal country-style chest of drawers, painted & decorated, a rectangular top overhanging a case w/four long graduated drawers w/oval brasses & keyhole escutcheons above a serpentine apron & tall French feet, decorated overall w/red & gold grained paint w/drawers outlined in gold paint imitating stringing, old surface, replaced brasses, Middlebury, Vermont area, ca. 1814, 17 3/4 x 40 1/2", 39 1/2" h. (replaced brasses, minor repairs).. **2,300**

Federal Country-style Chest

Federal country-style chest of drawers, painted hardwood, the rectangular top over a case of four long, graduated drawers w/simple turned wood knobs, double-arched apron, on heavy baluster- and ring-turned legs, scraped down to original blue paint, ca. 1830, 20 x 40", 44 " h. (ILLUS.) **900**

Federal country-style chest of drawers, tiger stripe & bird's-eye maple, a rectangular top w/ovolo corners above a case w/four graduated long bird's-eye maple drawers flanked by reeded columns w/rows of carved three-dimensional rectangles repeated on the reeding, ring- and baluster-turned legs w/small ball feet, old refinish, old replaced round brasses, probably Vermont, ca. 1820-25, 19 x 42", 41 1/2" h. (imperfections) **4,025**

Federal Country-style Sugar Chest

Federal country-style sugar chest, walnut, rectangular hinged top opening to a storage compartment, the top widely overhanging the case w/a top false drawer front over two working drawers all w/turned wood pulls, ring- and rod-turned legs w/peg feet, original finish, ca. 1820s, 18 x 22", 32" h. (ILLUS.) **1,200**

Federal tall chest of drawers, inlaid mahogany, the rectangular top w/a coved cornice above an inlaid band over a row of three small drawers w/oval band inlay above a stack of five long graduated drawers w/oval band inlay & flanked by long inlay bands down the front edges, an inlaid diamond band at the base, scroll-cut French feet, original oval brasses & inlaid keyhole escutcheons, Lancaster County, Pennsylvania, early 19th c. **9,350**

Federal Tall Chest of Drawers

Federal tall chest of drawers, walnut, the rectangular top w/a wide coved cornice above a case w/a row of three drawers above another row of three drawers w/two wide drawers flanking a small central drawer all above five long graduated drawers all w/turned wood pulls, scalloped apron & tall French feet, refinished, early 19th c. (ILLUS.).................................. **7,280**

French Provincial-Style Tall Chest

French Provincial-Style tall chest of drawers, inlaid walnut, a rectangular top w/serpentine ends above a tall case w/six long graduated drawers w/oblong panels centered by light wood leafy scroll inlays, paneled sides, serpentine apron, simple cabriole legs ending in scroll feet, keys used to pull open each drawer, original finish, ca. 1920s, 18 x 36", 5' h. (ILLUS.)...... **600**

Jacobean Revival Coffer Chest

Jacobean Revival coffer chest, carved oak, the rectangular top w/three recessed panels opening to a deep well, the front w/three framed & recessed panels w/diamond & florette or arched palmette chip-carved designs, front stile legs w/chip-carved bands, old fumed finish, Europe, late 19th c., 20 x 48", 22" h. (ILLUS.) **500**

Late Victorian Marble-topped Chest

Late Victorian chest of drawers, walnut & walnut veneer, the tall superstructure w/a serpentine scallop-carved crestrail above a burl band flanked by large rounded leafy scrolls at the corners above a molded rail over a veneer band & scroll trim above line-incised supports flanking the swiveling rectangular beveled mirror w/a serpentine top, all resting on the rectangular rouge marble top overhanging a slightly bowed case w/a row of three drawers over two long drawers all w/stamped brass pulls, scroll-carved curved apron on carved feet, ca. 1890s, original hardware & finish, 22 x 42", 6' 2" h. (ILLUS.)...................................... **850**

Oak Michigan Chair Company Chest

Mission-style (Arts & Crafts movement) chest of drawers, oak, a rectangular top over a pair of wide flush doors opening to interior drawers over three long graduated drawers below, simple brass bail pulls, red decal mark of the Michigan Chair Company, early 20th c., 24 x 32", 49" h. (ILLUS.) **1,840**

Gustav Stickley Mission Oak Chest

Mission-style (Arts & Crafts movement) chest of drawers, oak, a rectangular top w/a low splashback overhanging the case w/a pair of drawers over three long drawers all w/hammered copper pulls, paneled sides, original finish, bails slightly bent, branded mark of Gustav Stickley, 20 x 36", 42 1/2" h. (ILLUS.)....................... **5,750**

Early Painted Mule Chest

Mule chest, (box chest w/one or more drawers below a storage compartment), painted pine & poplar, the rectangular hinged top w/molded edges opening above a deep well, the front w/two false-front drawers w/round brass knobs above two long working drawers, on simple bracket feet, old mustard yellow paint over original red, replaced pulls, New England, early 19th c., 18 x 38", 42" h. (ILLUS.) **650**

Country Chippendale Mule Chest

Mule chest (box chest w/one or more drawers below a storage compartment), Chippendale country-style, pine & poplar, the hinged cotter-pin rectangular top opening to a deep well above two long base drawers w/batwing pulls & keyhole escutcheons, molded base w/bracket feet, old refinish, late 18th c., 18 x 48", 42" h. (ILLUS.) **650**

Mule chest (box chest w/one or more drawers below a storage compartment), Federal country-style, painted, a rectangular top opening to a deep well, two drawers at the bottom, molded base on tall bracket feet, old red paint, New England, 1800-10, 20 x 41", 43" h. (imperfections, restoration) **1,380**

Very Rare Early Pilgrim Chest

Pilgrim Century chest of drawers, oak & white pine, paneled & joined construction, the oak top w/molding below, above the case of four long drawers w/applied moldings in geometric shapes & hung w/channeled drawer sides flanked by rectangular shapes of applied moldings above a molded base w/frontal ball feet & rear stile legs, replaced turned wood pulls, old refinished dark reddish brown surface, the oak paneled sides w/old refinish & dark painted moldings, restored, Salem, Massachusetts, 1660-90, 21 3/4 x 42", 39 3/4" h. (ILLUS.) **189,500**

Rare Queen Anne Chest-on-Frame

Queen Anne chest-on-frame, tiger stripe maple, white pine & beech, two-part construction: the upper section w/a rectangular top w/a coved cornice above a pair of drawers over four long graduated drawers w/butterfly brasses & keyhole escutcheons; the lower case w/a wide stepped-out mid-molding over an apron w/two deep scallops w/pendent drops, cabriole legs ending in raised pad feet, original brasses & escutcheons, New Hampshire, 1730-40, imperfections, 17 3/4 x 36 1/2", 57" h. (ILLUS.) **25,300**

Fine Aesthetic Movement Tall Chest

Victorian Aesthetic Movement tall chest of drawers, walnut & burl walnut, the rectangular top w/a low splashboard centered by a pierce-carved palmette & knob finial over a panel above a stepped-back section w/a pair of long paneled doors carved w/flowering leafy branches above a stepped-out lower case w/a long drawer divided into two floral- and branch-carved panels centered by a round brass pull, over five long graduated drawers w/fancy burl panels & angular brass bail pulls, reeded side stiles, wainscoted side panels, refinished, ca. 1880, 19 x 36", 68" h. (ILLUS.) **2,500**

Victorian Cottage-style Chest

Victorian cottage-style chest of drawers, chestnut & walnut, a splashback centered by a walnut arch & roundel flanked by two handkerchief drawers w/walnut quarter-round corner posts resting on the rectangular top w/molded edges above the case w/a stepped-out long drawer w/walnut banding & carved leaf pulls flanked by bobbin-turned side spindles above three more long reverse-graduated drawers w/similar decoration & further half-round turnings, refinished, ca. 1875, 18 x 40", 48" h. (ILLUS.) **600**

Country Eastlake Chest of Drawers

Victorian country-style Eastlake chest of drawers, pine, a tall rectangular upright mirror within a wide, flat scallop-cut frame flanked by ornate scroll-cut supports above a pair of small hanky drawers on the rectangular top, a narrow scallop-cut

frieze under the top & above a case of four long, graduated drawers, paneled sides w/diamond-form moldings, scalloped bracket feet, porcelain knobs on hanky drawers & carved wood pulls on the other drawers, refinished, ca. 1880, 18 x 40", overall 72" h. (ILLUS.) **650**

Decorated Eastlake Birch Chest

Victorian Eastlake chest of drawers, birch, the splashback w/an angular leaf-incised band flanked by small line-incised hanky drawers on the rectangular top, the case w/four long, graduated drawers w/incised bands flanking angular leaf-incised bands, angular brass pulls, deep molded base, original hardware, refinished, ca. 1885, 20 x 36", 48" h. (ILLUS.) **500**

Decorative Eastlake Chest of Drawers

Victorian Eastlake chest of drawers, walnut & burl walnut, the superstructure w/a crestrail composed of small carved open arches above a narrow panel w/line-incised scrolls flanked by reeded corner blocks above reeded supports flanking the large rectangular swiveling mirror w/a notch-cut framework above a lower panel carved w/stylized blossoms, the rectangular top w/molded edge above a case of three long line-incised & blossom-carved drawers w/brass pulls, blocks & reeded base side stiles, on casters, some original hardware, refinished, ca. 1885, 20 x 40", 6' 4" h. (ILLUS.) **650**

Nice Eastlake Child's Chest & Mirror

Victorian Eastlake child's chest of drawers, walnut & burl walnut, the superstructure w/an arched crest flanked by spearpoint finials above a band of pierce-cut leaves over the flat supports flanking the long rectangular swivel mirror, candle shelves & burl panels on lower sides above the rectangular white marble top, the case w/three long, graduated drawers w/rectangular burl panels & black pear-shaped drop pulls, refinished, ca. 1885, 14 x 22", 50" h. (ILLUS.) **500**

Tall Eastlake Gentleman's Chest

Victorian Eastlake gentleman's tall chest of drawers, walnut & burl walnut, the

high crest centered by arched scrolls over a molding w/arched ends over tightly carved leafy scrolls flanking a long burl panel all flanked by tapering end brackets on the rectangular top, the case w/two stacks of three small line-incised drawers flanking a pair of flat scroll-trimmed doors over a long gadrooned panel over three long burl-fronted drawers w/large stamped brass pulls, molded base, original hardware, original finish, ca. 1880, 21 x 38", 60" h. (ILLUS.).. **1,800**

Fine Eastlake Lock-side Chest

Victorian Eastlake tall chest of drawers, walnut & burl walnut, lock-side type, the crestrail arched & scroll-carved in the center over a raised molding over a burl band flanked by stepped side brackets on the rectangular top w/molded edges, the case w/one long slightly stepped-out drawer over a stack of five additional long drawers accessed through a hinged side column, original stamped brass hardware, molded base, original finish, ca. 1885, 20 x 42", 64" h. (ILLUS.) **1,800**

Golden Oak Chest with Large Mirror

Victorian Golden Oak chest of drawers, oak, a large squared beveled mirror w/rounded corners in a framework w/a scroll-carved crestrail, swiveling between tall slender S-scroll uprights above a backboard w/center scrolls above the rectangular top w/serpentine front overhanging a case w/a pair of deep drawers w/serpentine fronts over two long plain drawers all w/pierced brass pulls, narrow shaped apron, short squared & shaped legs on casters, ca. 1900, refinished, 22 x 38", overall 72" h. (ILLUS.) **500**

Golden Oak Chest with Tall Mirror

Victorian Golden Oak chest of drawers, the left side w/a tall rectangular beveled mirror swiveling within a simple rectangular framework w/a scroll-carved crestrail, the top right side w/a low carved arched crestrail above a square shelf over a raised panel square door above a stack of two small drawers all above two long bottom drawers w/stamped brass pulls, serpentine apron, on casters, refinished, ca. 1900-10, 20 x 40", 6' 4" h. (ILLUS.) **750**

Child's Miniature Oak Chest

Victorian Golden Oak child's miniature chest of drawers, oak, rectangular top over a band of beaded carving over three long drawers w/wooden knobs, scalloped apron, three-panel sides, original finish, ca. 1910, 8 x 22", 20" h. (ILLUS.) **250**

Golden Oak Tall Chest of Drawers

Victorian Golden Oak tall chest of drawers, oak, a high serpentine crestrail w/scroll-carved trim above the rectangular top w/molded serpentine front edge overhanging the case w/a pair of deep serpentine-front drawers projecting above four flat long drawers all w/simple brass bail pulls, serpentine apron, short stile legs, replaced hardware, refinished, ca. 1900, 20 x 38", 56" h. (ILLUS.) **500**

Golden Oak Tall Lingerie Chest

Victorian Golden Oak tall lingerie chest of drawers, oak, a round beveled mirror w/arched bottom in a conforming flat frame swiveling between slender outswept uprights over a scroll-carved crestrail on the rectangular top, a simple case of four deep drawers w/pierced brass pulls & keyhole escutcheons, serpentine apron & short shaped front legs, paneled sides, on replaced casters, refinished, ca. 1915-20, 18 x 24", overall 72" h. (ILLUS.).. **900**

Marble-topped Renaissance Chest

Victorian Renaissance Revival chest of drawers, carved walnut, the tall superstructure w/a tall arched beveled mirror frame w/a tall leaf-carved finial flanked by scrolls, the whole swiveling between slender uprights w/two small graduated open shelves at each side above narrow open panels & side finials, the rectangular white marble top w/molded edge set w/two narrow stepped hanky boxes w/hinged lift lids, the case w/a long drawer w/a raised oval molding & leaf-carved pulls flanked by rounded front corners projecting slightly over two lower matching long drawers, deep molded flat base, original finish, ca. 1860, 20 x 40", 6' 8" h. (ILLUS.)... **2,500**

Burled Renaissance Revival Chest

Victorian Renaissance Revival chest of drawers, walnut & burl walnut, an arched central crestrail flanked by two small handkerchief drawers w/raised burl panels on the rectangular top w/molded edges above a long projecting drawer w/a pair of raised & pointed burl panels flanking a central shield-shaped burl panel w/further raised burl panels at the outside edge, above two matching recessed long drawers flanked by turned columns over a fourth projecting bottom drawer matching the top drawer, all w/black pear-shaped drop pulls, molded base w/scalloped apron on porcelain casters, refinished, ca. 1875, 22 x 40", 48" h. (ILLUS.) **600**

Fine Renaissance Revival Chest

Victorian Renaissance Revival chest of drawers, walnut & burl walnut, drop-well style, the tall superstructure w/a tall pedimented crest w/carved palmette & scrolls above an arched molded crestrail over a frieze band w/two raised burl panels flanked by scroll-carved brackets on the side panels w/narrow raised burl panels above small candle shelves & tall S-scroll carved brackets all centering a tall mirror, raised side sections w/rectangular white marble tops w/molded edges above stacks of two small drawers flanking the white marble-topped drop well above two long lower drawers w/double raised burl panels centered by cartouche-form carvings & fitted w/brass & wood pulls, canted front corners on base, deep molded flat apron, old refinish, ca. 1870s, 22 x 44", 7' 6" h. (ILLUS.) **1,800**

Victorian Rococo "bow-front" chest of drawers, carved rosewood, the superstructure w/a tall arched mirror in a wide molded frame supported within a framework w/a high arched & scroll-cut cornice

Rococo "Bow-front" Chest of Drawers

w/a central cartouche above shaped & molded sides above small hanky drawers on the rectangular white marble top w/a bowed center above a case of three conforming long drawers w/raised oval molding, scroll-carved escutcheons & turned round wood pulls, chamfered front corners w/scroll trim, deep molded base, ca. 1855-60, refinished, 22 x 42", overall 90" h. (ILLUS.).. **2,400**

Rococo Chest with Curio Shelves

Victorian Rococo chest of drawers, rosewood, the superstructure w/a tall arched mirror in a deep molded frame topped w/an ornate scroll-carved crest w/a central cartouche above two mirror-backed curio shelves on each side over small hanky drawers, all above the rectangular white marble top w/rounded front corners, the case w/four long graduated drawers w/raised oval molding & a single round center pull flanked by scroll-trimmed chamfered front corners,

deep molded base, original finish, ca. 1855-60, 20 x 42", overall 80" h. (ILLUS.).. **2,400**

Rococo Double Serpentine Chest

Victorian Rococo "double serpentine-front" chest of drawers, mahogany & mahogany veneer, a tall oblong mirror enclosed by a serpentine frame w/a shell- and scroll-carved crest & supported between ornately carved tall S-scroll uprights on the rectangular white marble top w/a double serpentine shaped front above a conforming case of four long drawers w/scroll-carved keyhole escutcheons flanked by carved serpentine angled front corner stiles, a deep scroll-carved & scalloped apron on bracket feet on casters, brass butterfly brasses added ca. 1890, ca. 1855-60, original finish, 22 x 42", overall 84" h. (ILLUS.) **2,800**

William & Mary country-style chest of drawers, painted poplar, a rectangular top w/molded edges & braces under ends above a case of four long beaded drawers w/replaced brass teardrop pulls, a heavy base molding, raised on short turned legs w/heavy ball feet, later black paint over earlier black, Connecticut, early 18th c., 17 1/2 x 37", 41" h. (restored)... **3,220**

Cradles

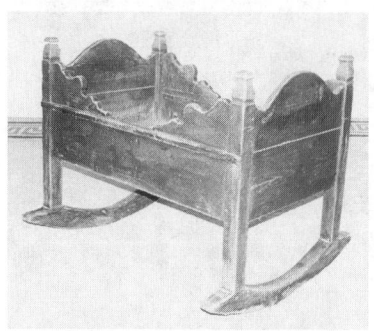

Wisconsin Country-style Cradle

Low cradle on rockers, butternut, a rectangular frame w/arched foot- and headboards & scallop-cut brackets at each corner of the sides, heavy square stiles w/tapering finials continuing to form tall legs on rockers, original dark finish, found in Wisconsin, ca. 1850s, 20 x 36", 26" h. (ILLUS.).. 300

Victorian Eastlake Cradle

Victorian Eastlake, walnut, the head- and footboards w/openwork panels at the top w/a flat crestrail flanked by block- and knob-turned stiles w/knob finials above a central pierce-carved wheel device & slender spokes, flat siderails above numerous simple turned spindles, on curved supports rocking on the platform base w/outswept legs on casters, original finish, ca. 1885, 20 x 38", 36" h. (ILLUS.)..... 450

Renaissance Revival Walnut Cradle

Victorian Renaissance Revival "platform" cradle, walnut, the tall headboard w/a high scallop-cut crest over carved scrolls flanking a block-framed panel over a long rectangular panel w/a raised burl panel flanked by flat rounded finials, the low footboard w/simple arched crestrail, the sides composed of ring- and rod-turned spindles, rocking on a platform base raised on ring- and rod-turned tapering legs on casters, refinished, ca. 1875, 24 x 44", 40" h. (ILLUS.)....................... 550

Cupboards

China Cupboard with Upper Door

China cupboard, Victorian Golden Oak, quarter-sawn oak, a half-round top w/a small scroll-carved crest above a short rectangular bowed glazed door flanked by open shelves backed by small squared beveled mirrors above the half-round case w/a tall glazed bowed center door flanked by curved sides, four wooden shelves & a mirrored back in the upper half, narrow molded base on two short cabriole front legs w/paw feet & shaped rear legs, refinished, ca. 1900, 18 x 48", 6' 4" h. (ILLUS.) **2,500**

Corner cupboard, Chippendale country-style, painted poplar, one-piece construction, the flat top w/a deep molded cornice centered by a blocked keystone above a rounded molding flanking the conforming 8-pane glazed door, a lower paneled door below opening to a single shelf, old green paint, Connecticut, 18th c., 14 3/4 x 34", 85" h. (restoration)......... **10,925**

Quality Chippendale Revival Cupboard

Corner cupboard, Chippendale Revival, mahogany, the top w/an ornate broken-scroll cornice w/heavy molding & florettes above a shell- and scroll-carved panel & mounted w/three urn-and-plume carved finials above a pair of 4-pane arched cupboard doors opening to shelves & flanked by slender colonettes, a mid-molding above the lower case w/a long drawer w/butterfly brasses above a pair of short raised panel cupboard doors each carved w/large oblong shell designs & flanked by small corner colonettes, the gadrooned base band above short cabriole legs w/shell-carved knees above the large ball-and-claw feet, original finish, late 19th c., 24 x 36", 102" h. (ILLUS.)....... **5,000**

Fine Chippendale Revival Cupboard

Corner cupboard, Chippendale Revival style, mahogany, two-part construction: the tall upper section w/a broken-scroll crestrail w/leaf-carved detail & brass mounts above a flared cornice over a pair of tall glazed doors flanked by reeded pilasters w/brass capitals & bases; the lower section w/a mid-molding over a single long, deep drawer w/ornate carved leafy scrolls & oval brasses, carved dentil, scalloped apron above tall cabriole front legs w/shell-carved knees & ending in claw-and-ball feet, original finish & hardware, late 19th c., 20 x 38", 86" h. (ILLUS.)... **2,000**

Exceptional Country Corner Cupboard

Corner cupboard, country-style, painted pine, two-part construction: the upper section w/a deep coved cornice above a tall 12-pane glazed cupboard door opening to shelves; the lower section w/a mid-molding over a pair of overlapping drawers above a pair of paneled cupboard doors, serpentine apron & high bracket feet, worn original white paint w/vinegar graining in red & yellow ochre, dark grey on apron & feet, one pane replaced, some edge damage & replaced brass knobs, 48 1/2" w., 7' 8 1/2" h. (ILLUS.).... **19,250**

Early Country Pine Corner Cupboard

Corner cupboard, country-style, pine, one piece construction, the flat top w/a narrow cornice over a long cupboard door w/two raised panels above a mid-molding & a small lower raised panel door, flat base, four interior shelves w/old repaint, old refinish, late 18th c., 20 x 30", 80" h. (ILLUS.)... **2,000**

Large English Pine Corner Cupboard

Corner cupboard, country-style, pine, one-piece construction, the top w/a deep flaring & dentil-carved cornice above a pair of tall arched & paneled cupboard doors opening to three shaped shelves, a mid-molding over a pair of shorter paneled lower doors, deep flat molded base, scrubbed waxed finish, England, mid-19th c., 24 x 40", 84" h. (ILLUS.)................. **2,000**

Federal Country Corner Cupboard

Corner cupboard, Federal country-style, cherry, maple & tiger stripe maple, two-part construction: the upper section w/a deep molded cornice over a single large 12-pane glazed cupboard door opening to three shelves w/plate rails & beaded edges, the door flanked by narrow bands of beading & canted corners; the stepped-out lower section w/three small drawers over two paneled doors opening to a shelf, wide canted front corners, narrow molded base w/worn bracket feet, probably New Jersey, ca. 1820, replaced hardware, old refinish, repairs, height loss, 27 x 52", 84 1/2" h. (ILLUS.).............. **3,220**

Fine Federal Style Corner Cupboard

Corner cupboard, Federal Revival style, mahogany, two-part construction: the upper section w/a broken-arch crest w/molded edges above a pair of tall glazed cupboard doors w/detailed serpentine applied grillwork flanked by slender colonettes & chamfered front corners; the lower section w/a mid-molding over a pair of paneled cupboard doors, molded base on front paw feet, original dark finish, late 19th - early 20th c., 24 x 38", 96" h. (ILLUS.) **2,800**

English Georgian Corner Cupboard

Corner cupboard, Georgian style, mahogany, two-piece construction: the upper section w/a flat top & deep flared cornice over a pair of tall geometrically-glazed cupboard doors opening to three shelves; the lower section w/a mid-molding over a pair of paneled cupboard doors, serpentine apron & heavy bracket feet, England, ca. 1820, 24 x 38", 86" h. (ILLUS.).. **2,000**

French Neoclassical Corner Cupboard

Corner cupboard, Neoclassical style, barrel-front hanging-type, mahogany & satinwood inlay, the quarter-round top w/a molded cornice above a pair of tall curved cupboard doors w/a center almond-shaped pinwheel inlay & banded border inlay, on a narrow flat base molding, French polished finish not original, France, ca. 1830, 20 x 26", 44" h. (ILLUS.).. **850**

Nice Golden Oak Corner Cupboard

Corner cupboard, Victorian Golden Oak style, the triangular top w/two crestrails arching together at the back & decorated incused scrolls, the case w/a single tall glazed door w/the down-curved top rail boldly incised & carved w/tight leafy scrolls, opening to four wooden shelves, scalloped apron, on casters, original hardware, refinished, ca. 1900, 18 x 26", 64" h. (ILLUS.).. **1,100**

Great Folky Hanging Corner Cupboard

Hanging corner cupboard, Victorian country-style, walnut, the high pointed top crest composed of large pierce-carved scrolling grapevines w/leaves & fruit above the flat top w/deep angled sides, the case w/a wide flat door decorated w/carved & incised folk art designs of leaf sprigs around a heart-like design w/a florette trimmed w/green & black highlights, the wide angled sides w/shallow carved long flowering leafy vines, molded base & narrow scalloped sides, turned door pulls, single inside shelf, original cleaned finish, ca. 1880, 15 x 20", 36" h. (ILLUS.)...... **850**

Fine Victorian Hanging Cupboard

Hanging corner cupboard, Victorian Renaissance Revival style, cherry, the quarter-round top w/a coved cornice over a frieze band cut w/a row of roundels above to tall paneled cupboard doors each w/an arrangement of large & small raised panels flanked by pairs of long, narrow side panels centering a roundel & topped by a carved capital, three interior shelves, molded base above a scalloped base band of short bobbin spindles, original finish, ca. 1880, 24 x 40", 72" h. (ILLUS.).. **2,500**

Country Pine Hanging Cupboard

Hanging cupboard, pine, a rectangular top w/a wide flaring & stepped cornice above a single wide paneled door centered by a raised diamond device & metal latch above a narrow base drawer w/simple wood knob, refinished w/traces of old green paint, early 20th c., 10 x 20", 24" h. (ILLUS.)... **200**

Country Pine Hanging Wall Cupboard

Hanging wall cupboard, pine, an arched scroll-cut crestrail w/applied scroll panel over a narrow molded cornice over scroll-cut brackets above a pair of tall, narrow raised-panel doors w/a cast-iron latch above a single drawer below, deep molded base, square nail & dovetailed construction, last quarter 19th c., refinished, 12 x 19", 28" h. (ILLUS.)................................ **500**

Hutch cupboard, country-style, painted & decorated, one-piece construction, the wide rectangular top supported at the front w/wide rounded brackets above a tall back w/two narrow open shelves above the stepped-out lower case w/a molded serpentine front over a single long drawer over a pair of paneled cupboard doors, a serpentine apron & short square legs, decorated overall w/bright folk art painted in red, pink, yellow & green on a creamy white ground, the upper section w/large red hearts & florals w/a large heart flanked by pineapples between the upper shelves, the lower back w/two facing stylized colonial figures holding a long swag supporting the words "Eat - drink - be merry," also signed "anno 53," by Peter Hunt, Cape Cod, Massachusetts, 1953, 17 3/4 x 36", 62 1/2" h. (minor surface wear) **1,093**

Country Pine Jelly Cupboard

Jelly cupboard, country-style, pine, a rectangular top above a pair of flat drawers cut into the raised molding around the edges of the front & over a pair of tall raised-panel cupboard doors, square nail construction, porcelain pulls on the drawers, refinished, ca. 1870, 18 x 42", 54" h. (ILLUS.)... **450**

Country-style Jelly Cupboard

Jelly cupboard, country-style, poplar, the rectangular top w/a high three-quarters gallery above a pair of drawers w/simple wood pulls above a pair of tall paneled cupboard doors w/a cast-iron latch w/porcelain knob, scalloped apron, square nail construction, original finish, ca. 1870, 20 x 42", 4' 10" h. (ILLUS.) **600**

Jelly cupboard, poplar w/old red paint, shaped bracket feet & cyma curved cutouts on the one-board ends, two paneled doors in the base & two dovetailed drawers above, one-board top w/short back splash w/cutouts on corners, square nail construction, 19 x 44 1/2", 50 1/2" h. **1,870**

Country-style Victorian Jelly Cupboard

Jelly cupboard, Victorian country-style, butternut & walnut, a serpentine crestrail on the rectangular top above a pair of drawers over a pair of tall doors w/oblong panels w/pointed ends, a low double-arch apron & bracket feet, pegged construction, refinished, mid-19th c., 18 x 42", 4' 6" h. (ILLUS.)................................ **750**

Hoosier-style Kitchen Cupboard

Kitchen cupboard, Hoosier-style, oak, the central projecting cupboard section w/a rectangular top above a pair of paneled & geometrically-glazed cupboard doors above a pull-down door opening to fitted kitchen accessories over a projecting white porcelain work surface above a pair of drawers over a pair of cupboard doors, flanked by tall three-panel set-back cupboard doors, original finish, ca. 1930, 28 x 84", 6' h. (ILLUS.).................................. **1,200**

Late Victorian Kitchen Cupboard

Kitchen cupboard, late Victorian, ash, two-part construction: the upper section w/a rectangular top & high arched, shaped & scroll-carved front crest above a pair of rectangular glazed cupboard doors w/serpentine top molding opening to two shelves & above a narrow scalloped border band & shaped sides flanking an open pie shelf; the lower section w/a rectangular top w/molded edge over a pair of drawers w/stamped brass pulls over a pair of double-paneled doors, simple apron & bracket feet, carved wood keyhole escutcheons, refinished, ca. 1900, 20 x 42", 7' 2" h. (ILLUS.)............................. **1,600**

Late Victorian Ash Kitchen Cupboard

Kitchen cupboard, late Victorian, ash, two-part construction: the upper section w/a high scallop-cut crest w/a row of roundels above a deep stepped cornice over a pair of tall 2-pane glazed cupboard doors w/arched tops opening to shelves above a high pie shelf opening; the stepped-out lower section w/a rectangular top over a pair of drawers decorated w/incised leaf bands & stamped brass pulls over a pair of paneled cupboard doors, scroll-cut brackets at front stile legs, original hardware, refinished, ca. 1890-1900, 20 x 40", 90" h. (ILLUS.) **1,800**

Tall Golden Oak Kitchen Cupboard

Kitchen cupboard, late Victorian Golden Oak style, two-part construction: the upper section w/a very high serpentine & scroll-carved crest w/flared ends above an egg-and-dart carved cornice over a scalloped frieze band above a pair of tall glazed cupboard doors w/serpentine tops trimmed w/long scrolls, opening to wooden shelves; the stepped-out lower section w/a rectangular top over a pair of drawers over a single long drawer over a pair of paneled cupboard doors, slightly serpentine apron on casters, original stamped brass hardware, refinished, ca. 1900, 21 x 46", overall 92" h. (ILLUS.) **2,200**

Linen press, Federal country-style, cherry, two-part construction: the upper section w/a rectangular top w/a flaring molded cornice over a molded frieze band above a pair of tall paneled cupboard doors opening to four shelves; the lower section w/a mid-molding over a case w/three long graduated thumb-molded drawers w/bail pulls, molded base on ogee bracket feet, New York State, early 19th c., 22 1/2 x 50", 86 1/2" h. (refinished, restored) **4,600**

Georgian English Linen Press

Linen press, George III style, mahogany, the rectangular top w/a wide flaring cornice carved w/dentil molding above a pair of wide & tall paneled cupboard doors each above a stack of three cockbeaded drawers, scrolled brass keyhole escutcheons on the doors, simple brass bail pulls on drawers, molded base on bracket feet, original finish, England, ca. 1800, 22 x 52", 84" h. (ILLUS.) **2,200**

Pewter cupboard, early American country-style, painted poplar, two-part construction: the upper section w/a rectangular top w/cornice above stepped-back sides flanking two shelves w/heavy molded edges; the stepped-out lower section w/a single scratch-beaded door opening to a single shelf, base molding & shaped feet, early red paint, Connecticut, late 18th c., 15 x 56 3/4', 81 1/2" h. (hinge changed, restoration) **10,350**

Early Painted Pewter Cupboard

Pewter cupboard, painted hardwood, the rectangular top w/a deep stepped & flaring cornice above a hutch top w/two long shelves flanked by deeply scalloped sides above the stepped-out lower section w/a molded edge over a pair of drawers over a pair of paneled cupboard doors, molded base w/bracket feet, original wood knobs, original worn red paint, Pennsylvania, early 19th c., originally one-piece later cut at the waist (ILLUS.) **5,720**

Early Pine Pewter Cupboard

Pewter cupboard, pine, rectangular top over a narrow scalloped apron over a tall two-shelf open section w/two wide backboards & one-board sides w/upper scallops, the lower projecting section w/a pair of plain flat doors w/replaced hardware, flat apron w/simple bracket feet, refinished, ca. 1830, 21 x 42", 6' 8" h. (ILLUS.) **1,200**

Unusual Victorian Pewter Cupboard

Pewter cupboard, Victorian Aesthetic Movement country-style, pine, the tall back w/a narrow rectangular top w/a scallop-cut gallery & an undulating front rail above a frieze band cut w/a row of quatrefoils over the opening compartment of three long graduated shelves between tapering sides, each shelf w/through keyed-tenon construction, the rectangular top also w/through keyed-tenons above a pair of flat drawers w/brass butterfly pulls over a pair of paneled cupboard doors w/stamped brass lion mask & ring pulls, base w/further through keyed-tenons & raised on flat bracket feet, Pennsylvania, ca.1870, original worn finish, 22 x 58", 90" h. (ILLUS.) **2,000**

Tall Pie Safe with Punched Tin Panels

Pie safe, country-style, pine, the rectangular top over a pair of tall four-panel doors each set w/a simple punched tin panel above a flat apron, four further punched tin panels at each side, tall square stile legs on casters, refinished, last quarter 19th c., 17 x 42", 64" h. (ILLUS.)................. **1,100**

Early Walnut Pie Safe

Pie safe, country-style, walnut, the rectangular top above a pair of tall four-panel cupboard doors w/each panel inset w/a pierced tin panel decorated w/a large central round petaled florette & a quarter-round design in each corner, the doors above a single long narrow drawer at the base w/turned wood knobs, four matching tin panels on each side, raised on tall flat scalloped front legs, refinished, 1860-80, 16 x 48", 75" h. (ILLUS.)....................... **1,500**

Stained Cherry Step-back Cupboard

Step-back wall cupboard, cherry-stained poplar, two-part construction: the upper section w/a rectangular top & deep coved cornice above a pair of tall glazed cupboard doors w/beveled inner edges, opening to two wooden shelves; the stepped-out lower section w/a pair of narrow line-incised drawers over a pair of line-incised paneled cupboard doors, simple shaped apron, paneled sides, ca. 1890s, 20 x 42", 82" h. (ILLUS.) **1,000**

One-piece Pine Step-back Cupboard

Step-back wall cupboard, country-style, pine, one-piece construction, the rectangular top w/a simple cornice above a pair of tall paneled doors w/the panels decorated w/scalloped inner edges over a pair of narrow drawers, the stepped-out lower case w/a long deep drawer above a stack of three deep drawers beside a deep pull-out potato bin w/a decorative paneled front, simple notch-cut feet, simple hand-grip wooden pulls on the drawers & metal pull on bin, Norwegian-American, Midwest, ca. 1870-80, refinished, 21 x 42", 84" h. (ILLUS.).................. **950**

Painted Step-back Wall Cupboard

Step-back wall cupboard, Chippendale country style, painted & decorated, two-part construction: the upper section w/a rectangular top w/a wide, shallow dentil-carved cornice above a pair of wide 6-pane glazed cupboard doors flanking three fixed central panes above an open pie shelf; the stepped-out lower section w/a rectangular top over a row of three drawers over two paneled doors elaborately painted w/vases of flowers on a white ground, overall blue paint w/red

highlights, molded base on bracket free, 1920s repaint, Pennsylvania, ca. 1790, 22 x 56", 86" h. (ILLUS.) **4,400**

French Canadian Wall Cupboard

Step-back wall cupboard, country-style, painted, two-part construction: the upper section w/a long rectangular top w/a widely flaring flat cornice over a row of three paneled cupboard doors w/turned wood knobs opening to shelves; the stepped-out lower section w/three more paneled cupboard doors above a scroll-cut apron, early finish, French Canadian, ca. 1820 (ILLUS.)...................... **3,300**

Primitive Pine Step-back Cupboard

Step-back wall cupboard, country-style, poplar, one piece construction, the rectangular top w/a heavy stepped cornice above a pair of 2-pane glazed cupboard doors flanked by wide side boards above a deep recess flanked by incurved sides on the rectangular top, the lower case w/a pair of drawers over a pair of paneled cupboard doors, slightly serpentine apron, pegged construction, inlaid bone keyhole escutcheons, refinished, ca. 1850s, 23 x 48", 84" h. (ILLUS.) **1,500**

Ohio River Step-back Wall Cupboard

Step-back wall cupboard, country-style, walnut, two-piece construction: the upper section w/a rectangular top w/a deep coved corner w/beveled corners above a pair of tall 3-pane glazed cupboard doors opening to shelves & flanked by narrow beveled front corners; the stepped-out lower section w/rectangular top w/beveled corners over a pair of shallow drawers w/wooden knobs over a pair of paneled cupboard doors w/large oblong recessed panels, scallop-cut apron on bracket feet, refinished, Ohio River Valley region, mid-19th c., 19 x 46", 87" h. (ILLUS.).. **2,500**

Step-back wall cupboard, painted pine, one-piece construction, the rectangular top w/the front slightly projecting above a slighted canted case w/a pair of tall narrow plain doors flanked by wide side stiles, a narrow stepped out shelf above the lower case w/a single plain door, old red wash, three shelves in lower section, square nail construction, New England, 19th c., 15 1/2 x 36", 70" h. (age splits, wear w/later boards added on bottom)....... **1,540**

European Pine Step-back Cupboard

Step-back wall cupboard, painted pine, two-part construction: the upper section w/a rectangular top & coved cornice over a pair of 2-pane glazed cupboard doors over two drawers raised above the rectangular lower top by short baluster-turned posts; the lower section w/an overhanging top above three long drawers w/porcelain knobs, molded base & turnip-form feet, original paint decoration, Europe, ca. 1870, 22 x 42", 86" h. (ILLUS.) **1,500**

Ornately Carved Baroque Cupboard

Step-back wall cupboard, Victorian Baroque Revival substyle, carved oak, two-part construction: the upper section w/a rectangular top w/a high ornately-cut crestrail centered by a carved grotesque mask of Bacchus clenching grapevines, which scroll across the front of the crestrail, in his teeth above a deep stepped & flaring cornice above a frieze band carved w/grapevine & centered by a scroll-carved mount, all above a pair of tall glazed cupboard doors w/narrow beaded molding flanked by fruit- and leaf-carved side rails, the stepped-out lower section w/a molded edge above a pair of drawers carved w/scrolling grapevines over a pair of paneled cupboard doors bordered by beaded molding & carved in bold relief w/figural tavern scenes, further fruit & leaf carving down the sides, carved flaring flat base molding on bun feet, refinished, Europe, late 19th c., 22 x 44", 8' 4" h. (ILLUS.)............................ **3,400**

Step-back wall cupboard, Victorian Baroque style, oak, two-part construction: the upper section w/a rectangular top over a deep gadrooned cornice over a scroll-carved frieze band over a pair of tall geometrically-glazed cupboard doors w/beveled glass & a central beaded band & flanked by slender reeded panels at the sides; the stepped-out lower section w/a long, deep drawer w/a rectangular molded panel enclosing ornate scroll carving & metal bail pulls above a beaded band &

Elaborate Baroque-style Cupboard

a pair of slightly recessed cupboard doors w/raised geometric panels flanked by heavy spiral-carved columns & paw feet, deep flaring, molded base band, Europe, ca. 1880, old refinish, 21 x 42", 84" h. (ILLUS.)... **1,800**

Victorian Country Step-back Cupboard

Step-back wall cupboard, Victorian country-style, pine, two-piece construction: the upper section w/a rectangular top w/angled front corners over a deep stepped & flaring cornice over a frieze band of carved arrowhead devices separated by three half-round drop spindles over a pair of 4-pane glazed cupboard doors w/thumb latches & small half-round spindles applied to dividing rails above a pair of small drawers w/raised panels separated w/applied low pyramidal blocks; the stepped-out lower section w/a pair of double-paneled cupboard doors w/a small button in the center of each panel & cast-iron latches, flanked at the sides by chamfered corners w/half-round applied spindles, flat molded apron on bracket feet, refinished, ca. 1860, 23 x 58", 7' 1" h. (ILLUS.) **4,500**

Late Victorian Step-back Cupboard

Step-back wall cupboard, Victorian country-style, stained maple, two-part construction: the upper section w/a rectangular top w/a flared cornice above a pair of tall 3-pane glazed cupboard doors opening to two shelves; the stepped-out lower section w/a pair of narrow drawers over a pair of paneled doors, apron w/small center drop, simple bracket feet, cleaned down to original stain, second half 19th c., 20 x 42", 6' 10" h. (ILLUS.)..... **1,000**

Victorian Country Step-back Cupboard

Step-back wall cupboard, Victorian country-style, walnut, two-part construction: the upper section w/a rectangular top over a deep flat & flaring cornice over a pair of 3-pane tall glazed cupboard doors w/edge molding & opening to shelves, flanked by quarter-round bobbin turning at the front corners above two long shallow drawers; the stepped-out lower section w/four long graduated drawers w/raised oval banding & leaf-carved drawer pulls, molded flat base, refinished, ca. 1870, 22 x 40", 84" h. (ILLUS.)................... **1,800**

Fancy Oak Step-back Wall Cupboard

Step-back wall cupboard, Victorian Golden Oak substyle, two-part construction: the upper section w/a high serpentine & scroll-carved front crestrail above an egg-and-dart molding above a pair of glazed cupboard doors w/shaped tops trimmed w/carved scrolls & opening to two shelves; the lower section w/a rectangular support shelf raised on S-scroll brackets & a paneled back on the rectangular top w/molded edges above a pair of drawers w/stamped brass pulls over a single long drawer all flanked by sunbursts & diamond carving above a pair of large paneled cupboard doors w/bold scroll-carved designs, serpentine apron & bracket feet, refinished, ca. 1900, 18 x 42", 7' 8" h. (ILLUS.)........................... **3,600**

Fine Pennsylvania Wall Cupboard

Step-back wall cupboard, walnut, two-part construction: the upper section w/a rectangular top w/a very widely flaring deep stepped cornice over a frieze band

w/three large blocks above a pair of 9-pane glazed cupboard doors opening to shelves & flanked by reeded pilasters, an arched open pie shelf flanked by a small drawer on each side; the stepped-out lower section w/a rectangular top over a row of three drawers w/simple bail pulls over two double-panel cupboard doors, molded base on tall ogee bracket feet, Pennsylvania, early 19th c. (ILLUS.)........ **26,400**

Gothic Revival Oak Wall Cupboard

Wall cupboard, late Victorian Gothic Revival, quarter-sawn oak, a high ornately pierce-carved crest centered by a chalice overflowing w/grapevines continuing down the side of the crest, the flaring crestrail w/sawtooth carving above a single glazed door w/carved trefoils in the upper corners above a glazed arched panel w/Gothic arch muntins centered by a carved rose wreath, sawtooth bands down the sides & at the base above a single drawer w/a wooden knob, simple molded base, probably used for storing wine & hosts in a Roman Catholic church, original finish, ca. 1900, 12 x 21", 34" h. (ILLUS.)... **950**

Large Baroque-Style Wall Cupboard

Wall cupboard, Victorian Baroque Style, mahogany, two-part construction: the upper tall section w/a rectangular top over a flared stepped cornice over a frieze band w/three narrow carved panels over two tall narrow doors flanking a wide central door, each door w/raised rectangular molding enclosing scroll carving & a long cornucopia in the center door, all flanked by pairs of slender free-standing colonettes, supported at the front by large baluster- and ring-turned posts & the solid back panel decorated w/a narrow spindled gallery shelf; the stepped-out lower section w/a pair of drawers over a pair of paneled doors w/a rectangular design composed of raised blocks & panels, reeded ring- and knob-turned colonettes at the front corners above the wide molded base on bun feet, Europe, original finish, ca. 1880, 20 x 44", 90" h. (ILLUS.).. **1,800**

Simple Walnut Wall Cupboard

Wall cupboard, Victorian country-style, walnut, one piece construction, a rectangular top w/no cornice above a pair of 6-pane glazed cupboard doors opening to shelves above a pair of drawers w/wooden knobs over a pair of paneled doors w/a cast-iron latch w/porcelain knob, scalloped apron, original finish & hardware, second half 19th c., 18 x 38", 78" h. (ILLUS.).. **1,000**

Welsh cupboard, pine & poplar, two-part construction: the upper section w/a rectangular top w/a deep flared cornice above a large three-shelved open compartment w/a scalloped top rail & sides; the stepped-out lower section w/a fold-out work surface above a case w/a row of three drawers over a square cupboard door beside two long drawers all w/turned wood knobs, flat base w/narrow

Late European Welsh Cupboard

molding, raised on bun feet on pegs, waxed finish, Europe, ca. 1910, 24 x 60", 6' 10" h. (ILLUS.) **1,400**

Desks

Chippendale "oxbow-front" slant-front desk, birch, a narrow rectangular top over a wide hinged slant front opening to an interior fitted w/small drawers & open valanced compartments, the double-bowed case w/four long graduated cockbeaded drawers, molded base w/central drop & ogee bracket feet, simple bail pulls, Ipswich or Newburyport, Massachusetts, ca. 1780, 20 1/2 x 42 1/4", 43 1/8" h. (old refinish, replaced brasses, imperfections) **4,600**

Chippendale Revival Slant-front Desk

Chippendale Revival slant-front desk, quarter-sawn oak, the narrow rectangular top w/a low wood & brass beaded gallery over the wide hinged slant front w/a large shell-carved center design & scroll-carved corners opening to a fitted interior above a case w/pull-out slide supports flanking a long drawer over three long drawers all w/stamped brass pulls & keyhole escutcheons, quarter-round spiral-turned columns at the sides, gadrooned base band on scroll-carved claw-and-ball feet, original hardware & finish, late 19th - early 20th c., 20 x 34", 40" h. (ILLUS.).... **2,500**

Chippendale Revival Oak Writing Desk

Chippendale Revival writing desk, oak, the rectangular top w/rounded corners above an ogee case w/a pair of long drawers at the front above a small drawer on each side of the kneehole opening, scalloped & scroll-carved apron, raised on bold cabriole legs ending in large paw feet, refinished, late 19th c., 26 x 52", 30" h. (ILLUS.) **2,000**

Chippendale slant-front desk, cherry, a narrow rectangular top over a wide hinged slant lid opening to a two-stepped interior of valanced compartments flanking a central valanced drawer over small drawers, the lower case w/four long graduated thumb-molded drawers w/butterfly brasses & keyhole escutcheons, molded base on ogee bracket feet w/scrolls on platforms, brasses appear original, old refinish, New London County, Connecticut, 1760-80, 22 x 38 3/4", 43 3/4" h. (some repairs) **10,925**

Chippendale Slant-front Desk

Chippendale slant-front desk, figured mahogany, a narrow top above a wide hinged slant front opening to an interior fitted w/six slots over four small drawers centered by a bowed center prospect door, the case w/pull-out slide supports flanking a long drawer over three long graduated drawers w/simple bail pulls, molded base on high bracket feet, replaced hardware, refinished, late 18th c., 18 x 38", 38" h. (ILLUS.) **2,000**

Chippendale-Style Block-front Desk

Chippendale-Style block-front desk, mahogany, rectangular top w/molded edge above a case w/a long blocked top drawer over two racks of three blocked drawers on each side of the kneehole w/a scalloped top & a recessed cupboard door, molded base raised on claw-and-ball feet, Centennial-type, late 19th c., 20 x 36", 30" h. (ILLUS.) **1,500**

Fine Classical Revival Desk

Classical Revival desk, mahogany & mahogany veneer, a superstructure w/a center raised rectangular two-door compartment flanked by leaf-carved pilasters further flanked by stacks of three convex drawers, all on the rectangular top w/a pull-out writing surface above a long narrow round-fronted drawer over two smaller round-fronted drawers flanking the kneehole, carved acanthus leaf carving at the sides, raised on four turned & leaf-carved supports on blocks joined by a turned & carved H-stretcher, on large paw feet, late 19th c., 22 x 44", 45" h. (ILLUS.) **1,950**

Classical slant-front desk, mahogany & mahogany veneer, the narrow rectangular top above the wide hinged fall-front w/ornate crotch grain veneering opening

Classical Mahogany Slant-front Desk

to an interior fitted w/pigeonholes & small drawers, the case w/a long round-front drawer projecting above three long graduated flat drawers flanked by free-standing columns w/carved capitals, all drawers w/fine veneering, plinth base raised on double-knob turned feet, original round brass pulls, old refinish, ca. 1840, 22 x 40", 45" h. (ILLUS.)............................... **1,700**

Colonial Revival Lady's Desk

Colonial Revival lady's writing desk, quarter-sawn oak, the scalloped & scroll-carved crestrail over a narrow shelf above the wide hinged slant front decorated w/applied delicate scrolling & opening to a fitted interior w/pigeonholes, small drawers & the fold-down writing surface, the serpentine lower case w/a long conforming top drawer over a pair of small drawers flanking the bracket-trimmed kneehole opening, raised on slender simple cabriole front legs, original pierced brass hardware, refinished, ca. 1910, 18 x 32", 44" h. (ILLUS.)... **1,200**

Country-style Plantation Desk

Country-style "plantation" desk, butternut, two-part construction: the tall upper section w/a rectangular top w/deep stepped & flaring cornice above an open-fronted case w/32 pigeonholes above vertical slots flanking a galleried central compartment over a pair of drawers; the stepped-out lower section w/a rectangular top over a single long drawer w/carved pulls, on ring-, knob- and baluster-turned legs w/knob feet, long oval raised molding at the sides of the upper case, ca. 1860-70, 26 x 38", 6' 8" h. (ILLUS.) **750**

Early 20th century "roll-top" desk, oak, the S-scroll top w/a sliding tambour top opening to an interior fitted w/numerous pigeonholes & small drawers over the writing surface, the lower case w/a pull-out slide on each side above a stack of three small & one deep drawer flanking the kneehole opening, paneled sides, original finish, ca. 1910, 30 x 60", 48" h. .. **1,800**

Early Country Pine Stand-up Desk

Early American country-style stand-up desk, pine, a narrow top above a wide hinged slant lid w/molded lip opening to an interior of eight valanced compartments separated by scrolling dividers above four small drawers & an open well over a molded strip, the case w/a single long shallow drawer over a pair of raised panel doors opening to a single shelf, flat apron, bootjack cut-out sides, old refinish, late 19th c. grain painting on one side, New England, late 18th - early 19th c., some hardware changes, losses, 20 3/4 x 38 1/2", 48" h. (ILLUS.) **2,070**

Early American desk-on-frame, pine, two-part construction: the top desk section w/a narrow rectangular top above the wide hinged slant form opening to a fitted interior & over a single long drawer w/simple brass bail pulls & a keyhole escutcheon & flanked by slide supports; the lower section w/a molded rail above a deep apron raised on four baluster- and ring-turned legs joined by box stretchers & on small knob feet, old refinish w/brown stain, New England, second half 18th c., 19 x 29 3/4", 42 1/2" h. (imperfections)...... **2,415**

Federal country-style school master's desk, painted & decorated pine, the top w/a low three-quarters gallery above a hinged slant top opening to an interior fitted w/three small drawers above the apron w/another long drawer, raised on tall square tapering legs, original red & gold fancy swirled grain painting, some hardware changes, Rhode Island, early 19th c., 20 3/4 x 24 3/8", 36 1/4" h. **4,888**

Fine Country Federal Slant-front Desk

Federal country-style slant-front desk, stained birch, a narrow rectangular top above the wide hinged slant front opening to an interior fitted w/a two-stepped interior of valanced compartments, separated by scrolled dividers flanking a central drawer & small drawers, the case w/four long graduated cockbeaded drawers w/butterfly brasses & keyhole escutcheons, molded base w/central drop pendant, on arched bracket feet, original brasses & red surface, old replaced feet, Boston, early 19th c., attributed to cabinetmaker Samuel Drew, 20 1/4 x 41", 42" h. (ILLUS.)... **6,325**

Nice Federal Cherry Slant-front Desk

Federal slant-front desk, cherry, a narrow rectangular top above a wide hinged fall front opening to a fitted interior, above pull-out supports flanking a long drawer over three additional long drawers each w/oval brasses & keyhole escutcheons, scalloped apron & tall French feet, old refinish, ca. 1810, 21 x 38", 40" h. (ILLUS.)... **2,400**

Federal Slant-front Walnut Desk

Federal slant-front desk, walnut, a narrow rectangular top above a wide hinged slant front opening to a fitted interior, the case w/slide supports flanking a long top drawer over three long drawers all w/old replaced butterfly brasses, gently arched narrow apron on short French feet, old refinish, late 18th - early 19th c., 19 x 40", 40" h. (ILLUS.) **1,800**

Victorian Butternut Roll-top Desk

Late Victorian "roll-top" desk, butternut, a narrow rectangular top over unique S-scroll sides flanking the tambour cover opening to pigeonholes & small drawers over the writing surface, the base w/molded edges over two stacks of four graduated drawers flanking the kneehole opening w/scalloped top corner brackets, heavy molded base, paneled sides, refinished, ca. 1890-1900, 32 x 54", 42" h. (ILLUS.) **1,200**

Walnut Roll-top Desk

Late Victorian "roll-top" desk, walnut, a narrow rectangular top over the S-scroll opening to an interior fitted w/pigeonholes & small drawers above the writing surface, an edge molding over the kneehole opening beside a band of five small drawers w/leaf-carved pulls, paneled sides at top & bottom sides, molded base, refinished, last quarter 19th c., 30 x 48", 48" h. (ILLUS.).............................. **2,400**

Louis XVI-Style Inlaid Fall-front Desk

Louis XVI-Style "fall-front" desk, inlaid mahogany, the rectangular top w/a thin pierced brass gallery above the wide hinged slat front w/a recessed panel inlaid w/a delicate classical urn & scrolls opening to a fitted interior, the apron w/a single long drawer w/cast brass pulls & scrolling inlay, on simple cabriole legs w/brass mounts at the knees & feet, possibly original finish, France, early 20th c., 17 x 28", 40" h. (ILLUS.)................................. **800**
Mission-style (Arts & Crafts movement) desk, oak, upright fall-front style, a narrow top w/a high three-quarters gallery w/through-mortise sides above a wide paneled fall front w/long hammered copper strap hinges opening to a fitted interior above two open shelves below, short square stile legs, original dark finish, Gustav Stickley mark, retail label, ca. 1903, 10 3/4 x 25 3/4", 51" h. (edge chip to center of one leg) **7,475**

Stickley Brothers Fall-front Desk

Mission-style (Arts & Crafts movement) "fall-front" desk, oak, the narrow top w/a low three-quarters gallery w/rounded ends & through-tenon construction above the wide slant front w/long stylized patinated metal strap hinges & opening to a fitted interior, the case w/a pair of drawers over a single long drawer each w/round metal pulls, a lower medial shelf flanked by pairs of arched side cut-outs, original finish, unmarked Stickley Brothers, 13 x 32", 47 1/4" h. (ILLUS.) **2,530**

Gustav Stickley Postcard Desk

Mission-style (Arts & Crafts movement) postcard desk, oak, the boxed gallery on the top composed of a small paneled square door at each end flanking letter slots & shelves over a low compartment, the rectangular top over an apron w/a pair of drawers w/hammered copper pulls, heavy square legs, good new finish, red decal mark of Gustav Stickley, 26 x 41 1/2", 40" h. (ILLUS.)........................ **2,645**
Plantation desk, chestnut & walnut, two-part construction: the upper section w/a rectangular top over a deep coved cornice over a pair of tall raised panel doors opening to an interior fitted w/rows of pigeonholes over vertical letter slots above

Chestnut & Walnut Plantation Desk

Aesthetic Movement Captain's Desk

a pair of shallow drawers; the stepped-out lower section w/a single long drawer w/turned wood knobs, ring-, rod- and knob-turned legs, refinished, second half 19th c., 24 x 38", 76" h. (ILLUS.).................... **850**

Victorian Aesthetic Movement captain's desk, walnut & burl walnut, the superstructure w/a high peaked center crest topped by a short spindled gallery over a sloped shingle-like "roof" projecting above a band of ebonized scallops & flanked by small open shelves w/scallop-cut aprons raised on block- and ring-turned columnar supports flanking a projecting small central compartment w/a beveled mirror in the door flanked by side panels decorated w/incised & ebonized geometric incised lines, a wide hinged slope-front writing surface opening to a fitted well above a line-incised & ebonized front apron projecting above the lower case & supported by ring-, knob- and rod-turned slender spindles flanking a pair of paneled doors decorated w/burl & gilt-incised line decoration, original finish, ca. 1880, 22 x 30", 4' 2" h. (ILLUS.) **2,000**

Victorian Aesthetic Movement partner's desk, cherry, the rectangular top w/molded edges inset w/leather w/a brass beaded border, the case fitted on each side w/a long shallow center drawer over the kneehole opening flanked by top drawers w/bold fan carving above cupboard doors opening to reveal either

Fine Victorian Cherry Partner's Desk

upright letter slots or a stack of smaller drawers, spiral- and ring-turned columns flanking the kneehole opening, each half w/a beaded open gallery border, a center flat footrest, original metal casters & hardware, refinished, ca. 1880, 30 x 60", 30" h. (ILLUS. bottom previous page) **2,500**

Baroque Desk on Griffin Supports

Victorian Baroque Revival partner's desk, mahogany, the rectangular top w/molded edges & rounded corners above a case w/an upper rounded border w/three drawers on each side & carved overall w/ornate baroque scrolls, a lower pair of matched end drawers on each side flanking the arched kneehole openings, raised at each corner on large carved figural winged griffins on a long cross-form stretcher w/egg-and-dart-carved incurved sides, on gadroon-carved block feet, original finish, attributed to J. R. Horner, New York City, ca. 1880, 30 x 60", 30" h. (ILLUS.) **12,500**

Country Eastlake Captain's Desk

Victorian Eastlake country-style captain's desk, walnut, the superstructure w/an arched, pierced & scroll-cut crestrail flanked by pointed side rails over the narrow shelf above a lower open shelf flanked by pierced, arched sides above a small line-inlaid drawer flanking an open compartment, the slant-front case w/a wide lid opening to a well & w/a small candle shelf to one side, raised on pierce-carved cross-form supports joined by a ring- and baluster-turned cross stretcher w/a small turned finial, original finish, ca. 1875-85, 24 x 30", 42" h. (ILLUS.) **650**

Golden Oak Cylinder-front Desk

Victorian Golden Oak "cylinder-front" desk, a high serpentine crestrail w/ornate stamped scrolls above rounded scroll-stamped sides flanking the rectangular top above the paneled cylinder-front opening to an interior of pigeon-holes, a drawer & pull-out writing surface, the lower case w/a long scroll-stamped drawer projecting above a stack of two smaller drawers w/stamped scrolls beside shell-stamped paneled cupboard doors, heavy molded base, paneled sides, original iron hardware, original finish, ca. 1895, 22 x 40", 50" h. (ILLUS.) .. **1,800**

Fine Victorian Fall-front Writing Desk

Victorian Renaissance Revival "fall-front" writing desk, walnut & burl walnut, the peaked crestrail centered by a palmette finial above two tapering raised burl panels over a narrow top shelf supported by pierced scroll-cut brackets flanking another shelf w/a paneled back w/a long raised burl panel, all above the wide hinged fall front opening to an interior fitted w/pigeonholes, paper slots & small drawers above the felt-lined writing surface, the lower case w/a long drawer w/a raised burl panel & brass ring pulls over a band of molding above a stack of three matching, slighting inset drawers flanked by blocked sides, deep molded flat base, original hardware, refinished, ca. 1875, 20 x 30", 60" h. (ILLUS.) **2,400**

Wooton Patent Secretary/Desk

Victorian Renaissance Revival "patent" desk, walnut, burl walnut & burl bird's-eye maple, a rectangular top w/a high blocked & pierced carved gallery above a pair of rounded wide swing-out doors fitted w/either pigeonholes or paper slots flanking the central case w/a fold-down writing surface & numerous veneered small drawers & slots, deep molded base w/long molded shoe feet on casters, Wooton Patent Secretary, Standard grade, ca. 1876 (ILLUS. open) **15,000-20,000**

Pretty Victorian Rococo Lady's Desk

Victorian Rococo lady's writing desk, carved rosewood, the top w/a raised superstructure w/a delicate pierced scroll-carved rail above a narrow shelf supported by scroll-carved brackets above a stepped-back compartment w/a serpentine front above a group of four conforming shallow drawers, the stepped-out writing surface top w/serpentine molded edges above a serpentine apron carved at the center w/leafy scrolls & a cartouche, on slender cabriole legs w/scroll-carved needs & small peg feet, probably New York City, ca. 1850s, refinished, 21 x 36", 50" h. (ILLUS.).............................. **1,800**

Dining Room Suites

Fine Horner Baroque-Style Table

Victorian Baroque-Style: round dining table w/eight leaves, eight dining chairs, a server, a sideboard & a china cabinet; oak, the expandable table w/a round top over a wide curved apron carved w/ornate scrolls, raised on a heavy central column w/a reeded base band flanked by four full-relief carved seated griffins w/the heads supporting large brackets, seated on a cross-form plinth base, the chairs w/high serpentine crestrails w/scrolls centered by a carved lion face mask, square upholstered back panel, over-upholstered seat, simple cabriole front legs w/paw feet, sideboard w/a wide rectangular top w/a curved scroll-carved cornice raised on frontal support columns carved as seated winged griffins, the back w/a large rectangular beveled mirror, the rectangular top w/a bowed central section above a conforming case w/three scroll-carved drawers above a pair of paneled & scroll-carved cabinet doors flanking two bow-front scroll-carved drawers over a long scroll-carved drawer at the bottom above the heavy molded base, by R. J. Horner Company, New York, New York, ca. 1885, original finish, table 60" d., the set (ILLUS. of table) **19,500**

Baroque-Style China Cabinet from Set

William & Mary Revival Dining Suite

Victorian Baroque-Style: round table w/six leaves, twelve chairs, tall china cabinet, sideboard & server; oak, each piece with elaborate carving, the rounded expandable dining table w/carved apron above a heavy turned round leaf-carved center post flanked by four ornately carved winged griffins below spiral-turned support legs, each chair w/a high arched carved crest & spiral-turned stiles flanking an oval caned back panel over the caned seat on turned legs & stretchers, the china cabinet w/a high crest carved w/pierced scrolls & a center cartouche above a leaf-carved corner & scroll-carved frieze band centered by a mask carving over two tall glazed cupboard doors flanked by spiral-turned side stiles, deep molded & carved base, dark original finish, ca. 1880s, the set (ILLUS. of china cabinet, previous page)................... **25,000**

William & Mary Revival: oval table, five side chairs & one armchair; oak, each chair w/a tall back w/a yoked crest centered by a pierced scroll crest above a large pierce-carved splat enclosing an oval upholstered panel, upholstered slip seat on a carved seatrail & S-scroll front legs joined by a curved H-stretcher to the rear legs, the oval table w/a scroll-carved apron, raised on four large flat leg panels w/shell, floral & scroll carving centered by a caned oval panel & drop-down supports at each end, w/six leaves, original finish, late 19th c., table 54" l., 30" h., armchair 46" h., the set (ILLUS. above)..... **3,500**

Dry Sinks

Cherry & maple, an arched backrail above the long rectangular well w/molded edges above a pair of mortised light wood-framed doors w/raised poplar panels, simple bracket feet, two-board ends, old mellow refinish, found in Ohio, arched backrail replacement, second half 19th c.)... **935**

Early Pine Dry Sink

Pine & tiger stripe maple, a long, deep rectangular well above a case w/a pair of drawers w/wooden knobs over a pair of paneled cupboard doors w/original butt hinges & a cast-iron latch, bracket feet, old refinish, second half 19th c., 19 x 52", 33" h. (ILLUS.) **800**

Poplar Raised-back Dry Sink

Poplar, a raised back w/a narrow rectangular top over a row of three small drawers w/porcelain knobs above a wide board back & long well over a pair of paneled cupboard doors w/original cast-iron latches, square nail construction, refinished, ca. 1875-84, 19 x 48", 45" h. (ILLUS.) **900**

Garden & Lawn

Cast iron unless otherwise noted.

Garden suite: settee, armchair & rocker w/arms; wicker, each piece w/a slightly arched crestrail over a loose diamond lattice-woven back, tapering flat wooden open arms, tightly woven seat insert, diamond lattice front stretcher, old paint, needs some restoration, early 20th c., settee 56" l., 36" h., the set (ILLUS. below)... **600**

Gothic-style Garden Bench

Settee, the undulating backrail centered by a large, high central panel cast w/ornate Gothic detail & flanked by back panels of ornate Gothic arches, downscrolled arms over leafy scrolls, seat composed of long round bars, Gothic arch ends, old surface, ca. 1870, 60" l., 36" h. (ILLUS.) ... **3,500**

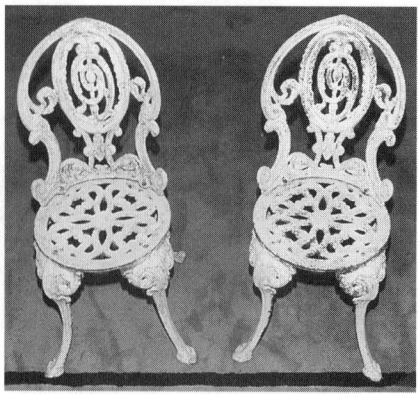

Scroll-cast Garden Side Chairs

Side chairs, a peaked oblong back pierced w/scrolls & an oval central panel w/ribbons & scrolls above the pierced round seat, outswept cabriole front legs w/scroll-cast knees & small paw feet, old white paint, ca. 1875, 34" h., pr. (ILLUS.)...... **600**

Hall Racks & Trees

Hall rack, Arts & Crafts style, wrought steel, four-sided w/a slender square rod forming each corner, joined at the top by gently arched crestrails over wider flat rails supporting long upright S-scroll hooks over another rail w/short hooks, each side of the lower frame enclosing four horizontal square rods w/the center two on each side joined by three thin spindles, two drip pans in base, unmarked, 21" sq., 75" h. **863**

Hall rack, Mission-style (Arts & Crafts movement), oak, a tall slender tapering square post topped by copper-finished cast-iron hooks, on a crossed shoe foot base, early 20th c., 24" sq., 72" h. **316**

Old Wicker Garden Furniture

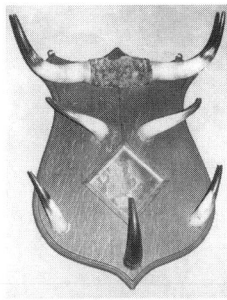

Oak Hall Rack with Steer Horns

Hall rack, oak & steer horn, a large shield-shaped oak plaque mounted at the top w/large longhorn steer horns over another pair of smaller horns over a small diamond-shaped mirror above three lower upturned horns, original finish, late 19th c., 30" w. at horns, 36" h. (ILLUS.) **350**

Carved Golden Oak Hall Rack

Hall rack, Victorian Golden Oak, wall-mounted, wide flat upper & lower quarter-sawn oak rails w/ornate leafy scroll carving joined to slender ring-turned side stiles w/knob finials & mounted w/three double brass hooks on each side, a central rectangular beveled mirror joined by short carved rails to the side stiles, refinished, ca. 1890, 44" l., 36" h. (ILLUS.) **650**

Ornate Late Victorian Hall Tree

Hall tree, late Victorian, mahogany, the tall, wide squared back w/a narrow deep flaring crestrail above a beaded band over a wide section centered by a panel w/carved tight looping scrolls flanked by small open panels w/spindled insets all above a wide rectangular beveled mirror flanked by narrow stiles mounted w/brass hooks above two narrow open slots over a large double panel w/each side carved w/a large seated winged griffin, scrolled open arms flanking the upholstered fixed seat, bobbin-turned front legs & square back legs joined by box stretchers, original dark finish, ca. 1880, 18 x 40", 7' 6" h. (ILLUS.) **2,000**

Massive Golden Oak Hall Tree

Hall tree, Victorian Golden Oak, quarter-sawn oak, massive size w/the tall back topped by a carved fanned crest over scrolls & flanked by scrolled corner ears above a wide half-round frame enclosing a large oval beveled mirror flanked by pairs of triple hooks above a wide central panel w/ornate leafy scrolls & a half-round horizontal column above the shaped flat arms on ring-turned columnar arm supports & front legs flanking the wide lift seat above a deep apron w/serpentine rim, squatty bun feet, refinished, ca. 1890s, 20 x 40", 7' h. (ILLUS.) **3,500**

Hall tree, Victorian Golden Oak, quarter-sawn oak, the carved crest w/shell detail above the rectangular frame enclosing a beveled mirror & mounted w/four double coat hooks, the wide upright back panel centered by an oval panel w/carved leaf sprig above the open curved arms, one mounted w/a metal band for supporting umbrellas, hinged rectangular seat over

Golden Oak Hall Tree

a storage compartment, S-scroll front legs & lower metal band at side, original finish, ca. 1900, 18 x 30", 82" h. (ILLUS.).. **1,100**

Oak Hall Tree with Mirror over Roundel

Hall tree, Victorian Golden Oak, quarter-sawn oak, the tall back w/a serpentine crestrail decorated w/carved scrolls above flat stiles flanking the large rectangular beveled mirror & mounted w/four double coat hooks on pointed brass mounts, the lower back w/a wide central panel carved w/spiky scrolls above an arched panel centered by a large roundel, arched open arms flanking the lift seat w/a deep apron decorated w/a band of wood buttons & scalloped apron & flanked by heavy square legs w/wood buttons above bun feet, refinished, ca. 1900, 18 x 30", 7' h. (ILLUS.)...................... **1,450**

Impressive Golden Oak Hall Tree

Hall tree, Victorian Golden Oak, quarter-sawn oak, the tall back w/an arched crestrail centered w/a pointed scroll-carved finial & a wide band of raised scrolls above a tall rectangular beveled mirror w/scalloped top flanked by side columns on leaf scrolls, mounted w/four cast-brass coat hooks above a plain back panel flanked by shaped flat open arms over the rectangular hinged lift seat over a deep well & apron w/a serpentine edge, shaped arm supports form the front legs, refinished, ca. 1900, 20 x 28", 7' h. (ILLUS.)... **1,600**

Oak Hall Tree with Glass Panel

Hall tree, Victorian Golden Oak, the tall back composed of a diamond-shaped beveled glass panel within a wide flat frame w/scroll-carved rounded sections at each point, flanked by flattened stiles mounted w/four replaced cast-brass double hooks & joined by a flat vase-form panel joined by four shaped braces to the stiles, low open arms on S-scroll arm supports above the rectangular lift-seat over a deep apron w/scalloped edge, refinished, 1890s, 18 x 30", 6' 6" h. (ILLUS.) **1,250**

Fine Renaissance Revival Hall Tree

Hall tree, Victorian Renaissance Revival style, walnut, the tall back w/a large peaked crest centered by a large carved palmette & florettes raised on a row of bobbin spindles above a crestrail flanked by short rows of spindles & above a pierce-carved narrow panel of leaves flanked by pointed & blocked finials above the half-round columns flanking a tall rectangular mirror w/narrow raised burl panels at the top & base, the columns flanked by shaped sides w/carved oblong burl panels & fitted w/small coat hooks, the lower section w/a small rectangular white marble shelf over a small drawer w/a raised burl panel flanked by curved rails forming umbrella holders, scallop-cut lower sides above the bottom shelf w/two brass drip trays centered by a baluster- and ring-turned center post, small turned front feet, refinished, ca. 1875, 16 x 38", 99" h. (ILLUS.) **2,800**

Hall tree, Victorian Renaissance Revival substyle, walnut & burl walnut, the arched crestrail centered by a projecting crown-form center crest carved w/ornate scrolls above a burl panel flanked by roundels & small projecting corner ears, raised above a tall frame w/narrow burl panels enclosing an arched tall mirror, tall slender outside free-standing columns mounted w/coat pegs, U-form umbrella racks at the lower sides above a rectangular white marble shelf above a deep arched apron w/burl trim flanked by

Walnut Renaissance Revival Hall Tree

the round metal umbrella drip trays in heavy round frames, refinished, ca. 1870s, 18 x 46", 7' 6" h. (ILLUS.) **4,400**

Renaissance Revival Hall Tree

Hall tree, Victorian Renaissance Revival substyle, walnut & burl walnut, the tall back w/a large pedimented crest centered by a large carved cartouche medallion w/pointed finial & suspended drops flanked by delicate pierce-carved devices & burl panels above the tall arch-topped rectangular mirror flanked by burl pilasters each mounted w/three brass coat hooks above a burl base panel centered by a raised diamond & flanked by round finials & C-form umbrella holders flanking a rectangular white marble shelf over a narrow burl-trimmed drawer hanging above an open lower platform w/metal shell-form drip trays at each round end, ca. 1870s, 54" w., 8' 4" h. (ILLUS.).... **5,264**

Highboys & Lowboys

Highboys

Chippendale "Bonnet-top" Highboy

Chippendale "bonnet-top" highboy, walnut, two-part construction: the upper section w/a high broken-scroll crest centered by tall urn-form finials & flanked by matching corner finials above a row of three deep drawers, the outside two w/incurved top edges & the center one w/fan carving, all above three long graduated drawers w/brass butterfly pulls; the lower section w/a mid-molding above a long shallow drawer over a row of three drawers each w/fan carving, scalloped apron on cabriole legs ending in claw-and-ball feet, old refinish, replaced finials, considerable restoration, late 18th c., 21 x 42", 84" h. (ILLUS.).. **9,500**

Quality Chippendale Revival Highboy

Chippendale Revival "bonnet-top" highboy, mahogany, two-part construction: the upper section w/a high broken-scroll crest w/molded cornice & roundels centering a scroll-cut panel supporting an urn-form finial w/a tall spiral-turned top, all above a flared cornice above a stack of five long graduated drawers w/pierced brass butterfly pulls; the lower section w/a deep mid-molding above a long shallow drawer over a row of two shallow drawers flanking one deep drawer, scroll-cut apron, cabriole legs ending in claw-and-ball feet, original dark finish & hardware, late 19th - early 20th c., 22 x 40", 84" h. (ILLUS.) **1,600**

Connecticut Queen Anne Highboy

Queen Anne "bonnet-top" highboy, cherry, two-part construction: the upper section w/a broken-scroll crest w/three tall slender urn-form finials above a deep fan-carved drawer flanked by short drawers above a stack of four long graduated drawers w/pierced butterfly brasses; the lower section w/a mid-molding over a long narrow drawer over a fan-carved center drawer flanked by smaller drawers, scalloped apron, simple cabriole legs ending in raised pad feet, Connecticut, late 18th c., some original brasses, old refinish, some reconstruction, 22 x 40", 7' h. (ILLUS.) **9,500**

Queen Anne "flat-top" highboy, maple & poplar, two-part construction: the upper section w/a rectangular top above a deep double-cove molding over a stack of five long graduated thumb-molded drawers w/butterfly brasses & keyhole escutcheons; the lower case w/a mid-molding over a small central drawer flanked by deep drawers all w/pulls above a deeply scalloped & arched apron w/turned drops, on simple cabriole legs ending in pad feet, recent red paint, replaced brasses, Massachusetts, last half 18th c., 18 1/2 x 36", 69 1/2" h. (minor imperfections)... **5,463**

William & Mary "flat-top" highboy, tiger stripe maple, two-part construction: the upper section w/a rectangular top & coved cornice above a case w/a pair of drawers over three long graduated drawers all w/small butterfly pulls & keyhole escutcheons; the lower case w/a mid-molding over a pair of deep drawers centering a shallow drawer above the arched & scalloped apron, raised on six trumpet-form turned legs joined by flat scalloped stretchers resting on turnip feet, replaced brasses, refinished, Massachusetts, ca. 1730, 19 1/2 x 37", 62 1/4" h. (restored).. **12,650**

Lowboys

Chippendale Revival Carved Lowboy

Chippendale Revival lowboy, mahogany, the rectangular top w/a gadrooned edge above a case w/a long drawer centered by a large carved shell over two small drawers on each side flanking an arched central kneehole opening, the front corners carved w/reeded quarter-round column, cabriole legs w/shell-carved knees & ending in claw-and-ball feet, in the Newport, Rhode Island style, refinished, original butterfly brasses, late 19th c., 18 x 36", 30" h. (ILLUS.).............................. **1,500**

William & Mary-Style Lowboy

William & Mary-Style lowboy, cherry & mahogany, the rectangular top w/molded edge overhanging a case w/a pair of deep drawers flanking a shallow center drawer, deeply scalloped apron raised on four trumpet-form legs resting on a serpentine cross-stretcher on turned turnip feet, original brass teardrop pulls, original finish, ca. 1880, 20 x 30", 30" h. (ILLUS.)..... **600**

Ice Boxes

Fine Golden Oak Ice Box

Victorian Golden Oak, a rectangular top w/a deep flaring cornice above a two-panel upper door decorated w/carved scrolls above a tall double-paneled bottom drawer w/matching carving, original hardware, metal nameplate on the front, scroll-decorated apron & block feet, tin-lined, refinished, early 20th c., 18 x 24", 40" h. (ILLUS.) **650**

Love Seats, Sofas & Settees

Norwegian-American Country Daybed

Daybed, Classical country-style, walnut, sleigh bed-style, the upright outward scrolled ends w/a plain rail over a carved shaped rail continuing down to outswept wide legs, a deep flat frame enclosing slats, Norwegian-American, original worn finish, ca. 1860, missing cushion, 28 x 80", 30" h. (ILLUS.) **450**

Classical Country-style Daybed

Daybed, Classical country-style, walnut, the scroll-carved serpentine crestrail above a solid back panel flanked by outscrolled end arms above the lift-top board seat pulling forward to form a double bed, outswept flat legs w/front center block supports, original finish, New England, ca. 1840-60, 28 x 80", 33" h. (ILLUS.) **1,100**

Classical Carved Mahogany Daybed

Daybed, Classical style, mahogany, upright tall ends topped by heavy scroll- and leaf-carved round rails w/florette-carved ends raised on heavy turned & carved posts centered by a central veneered panel, flat rails, raised on heavy carved gourd-form feet, refinished, ca. 1835, 75" l., 32" h. (ILLUS.) **900**

Unusual Victorian Daybed

Daybed, Victorian Renaissance Revival, walnut, the back w/a pair of short scroll-framed hinged end panels pierced w/quatrefoils flanked by matching serpentine end arms w/similar pierced panels all above the deep rectangular rails w/raised panels & center roundels, back panels open allowing the framework to expand to form a full bed, refinished, ca. 1870, 32 x 76" l. closed, 32" h. (ILLUS.) **700**

Stickley Bros. Mission Oak Love Seat

Love seat, Mission-style (Arts & Crafts movement), oak, the two-part back w/two gently arched crestrails over two cross slats joined by slender square stiles, flat tapering & gently curved arms, front square legs continue up to form arm supports, new tan leather seat cushion, wide seatrail & a flat front stretcher, fine original finish, unmarked Stickley Brothers, early 20th c., 23 x 44", 37 1/2" h. (ILLUS.) **1,265**

Medallion-back Rococo Love Seat

Love seat, Victorian Rococo style, walnut, medallion-back style, the back w/a large central oval upholstered panel w/a fruit-carved crest flanked by arched & rounded crestrails w/fruit-carved crests, low outswept upholstered arms w/S-scroll leaf-carved arm supports flanking the upholstered spring seat, serpentine molded seatrail, simple demi-cabriole legs on casters, ca. 1860, refinished & reupholstered, 60" l., 36" h. (ILLUS.) **1,400**

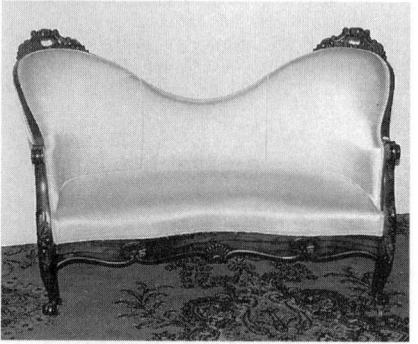

Double-back Rococo Love Seat

Love seat, Victorian Rococo substyle, rosewood, the undulating upholstered back w/high arched ends topped w/scroll-carved crests continuing down & around to form short closed arms on incurved arm supports flanking the upholstered seat, serpentine seatrail w/shell carvings & molded edge, on demi-cabriole front legs w/carved knees & scrolled feet on casters, refinished, new upholstery, ca. 1860, 56" l., 36" h. (ILLUS.) **800**

Federal Revival Upholstered Recamier

Recamier, Federal Revival style, mahogany, a downswept upholstered back at one end backing a high out-scrolled deep upholstered arm w/molded arm supports, a short arm rest & spindle at the lower end of the back panels, rectangular upholstered seat w/a deep apron, raised on ring- and rod-turned tapering legs on casters, late 19th - early 20th c., new upholstery, 50" l., 36" h. (ILLUS.) **1,500**

Recamier, Victorian Rococo style, rosewood, a high rounded crestrail w/floral-carved crest at one end, sloping down to form a long rail over a low upholstered back, the other end curving down to form an upholstered arm w/incurved arm support, long upholstered seat on a serpentine seatrail w/floral-carved trim, demi-cabriole legs on casters, original finish, newer upholstery, ca. 1860, 60" l., 34" h. (ILLUS. below) **2,000**

Victorian Rococo Recamier

Recamier, Victorian Rococo substyle, walnut, the high arched & rounded back w/a scroll-carved crestrail w/a pierced hand grip continuing down to form a short padded & closed side arm & a long low padded back rail, long oval upholstered seat on a finger-carved serpentine seatrail, raised on demi-cabriole legs w/porcelain casters, early reupholstery, ca. 1860, 24 x 68", 36" h. (ILLUS.) **950**

Early Classical Revival Settee

Fine Victorian Rococo Recamier

Settee, Classical Revival, mahogany, the crestrail w/a long flat center section flanked by downswept pierced & scroll-carved ends above the serpentine upholstered back flanked by deep upholstered S-scroll arms w/leaf-carved arm supports, upholstered spring seat w/two bolsters, flat seatrail w/veneered panels, on outswept carved paw feet, old refinish, newer upholstery, late 19th - early 20th c., 70" l., 36" h. (ILLUS.) **1,200**

Deep Classical Revival Settee

Settee, Classical Revival, mahogany, the high crestrail w/a long flat scroll- and shell-carved center flanked by serpentine scroll-carved ends above the tufted upholstered back flanked by deep solid wood S-scroll sides w/scroll-carved arm supports, flat molded seatrail below the deep upholstered seat, scroll-carved front feet w/paws & half-balls on casters, refinished, ca. 1900, later upholstery, 62" l., 36" h. (ILLUS.) **1,600**

Settee, Federal country-style, painted & decorated, the long wide flat crestail w/rounded ends raised on numerous turned spindles & flanked by S-scroll arms on two turned spindles & turned, canted arm supports, long plank seat raised on eight knob- and rod-turned legs joined by turned box stretchers, original copper & silver stenciled morning glories w/black, red & white h.p. detail on the crestrail, yellow & dark brown line borders on a light brown ground, Pennsylvania, first half 19th c., 84" l., 35" h. (edge wear) **1,540**

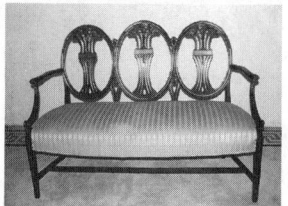

Federal Revival Triple-back Settee

Settee, Federal Revival style, mahogany, triple-back form, the back composed of three oval sections enclosing pierced vase-form splats topped w/a carved urn & swags, shaped slender open arms on incurved arm supports above the wide over-upholstered seat, raised on square

tapering legs joined by a long H-stretcher, late 19th c., reupholstered in the 1920s, original finish, 22 x 58", 40" h. (ILLUS.) **1,600**

Stickley Mission Oak Settee

Settee, Mission-style (Arts & Crafts movement), oak, the long flat crestrail above twelve vertical slats between the square stiles & tapering flat arms over corbels, long cushion seat, square stile legs & wide seatrail, L. & J. G. Stickley, refinished, early 20th c., 64" l., 36" h. (ILLUS.).. **1,600**

Scandinavian-American Settee

Settee, Scandinavian-American country-style, painted pine, mortise & tenon construction, the wide scallop-cut crestrail above three rectangular panels w/slender spindles, high outscrolled end arms w/turned top rails over curved lower rails, the long rectangular hinged seat above a deep well, short square stile legs, original grey paint, ca. 1870, 21 x 80", 36" h. (ILLUS.) **1,200**

Ornately Carved Rococo Settee

Settee, Victorian Rococo style, walnut, asymmetrical chair-back style, one end w/a high simple rounded crestrail over the upholstered back continuing down to form a short upholstered arm & incurved arm support, the low center of the back ornately pierce-carved w/large leafy scrolls continuing up & around an upholstered balloon back w/a padded open arm & incurved arm support, wide serpentine spring seat on a scroll-carved seatrail w/a pierce-carved central section, demi-cabriole front legs, ca. 1860, refinished, 70" l., 36" h. (ILLUS.) **2,400**

Country Windsor Painted Settee

Settee, Windsor country-style, a long flat crestrail above a two-section back w/numerous simple spindles centered by a knob- and baluster-turned spindle & end stiles, shaped arms over a spindle & canted turned arm support, long plank seat raised on eight turned legs joined by double flat stretchers at the front, old black repaint, early 19th c., 72" l., 36" h. (ILLUS.) **600**

Settee, Windsor style, a rod-turned long crestrail above the spindled back centered by a heavier bamboo-turned spindle, bamboo-turned arms over two small spindles & a canted bamboo-turned arm support, long shaped plank seat, on eight canted bamboo-turned legs joined by turned H-stretchers, old black paint w/yellow striping, New England, early 19th c., imperfections, 73 1/2" l., 34 1/2" h. (ILLUS. below) **3,450**

Settees, Victorian Rococo, mahogany, a long oval upholstered back w/a low arched pierced & floral-carved crest above open padded arms w/molded

incurved arm supports, a long upholstered seat w/a serpentine seatrail carved w/scrolls in the center, raised on demi-cabriole front legs on casters, newer velvet upholstery, refinished, ca. 1865, 60" l., 38" h., pr. **3,600**

Settle, Mission-style (Arts & Crafts movement), oak, cube-style, wide flat even crestrail & arm rails above wide vertical panels, long brown leather seat cushion, wide flat seatrail, good original condition & original upholstery, L. & J.G. Stickley label, 27 x 72", 28" h. **3,450**

Classical Mahogany Scroll-arm Sofa

Sofa, Classical, mahogany & mahogany veneer, the long straight round crestrail ending in leaf-carved downturned scroll ends above the long low upholstered back flanked by outswept S-scroll upholstered arms w/leaf- and scroll-carved arm supports, a long straight rounded seatrail raised on carved cornucopia brackets over the paw feet, original finish, old but not original upholstery, ca. 1830, 76" l., 36" h. (ILLUS.) **2,400**

Scrolled Mahogany Classical Sofa

Early New England Windsor Settee

Sofa, Classical, mahogany & mahogany veneer, the wide scrolled crestrail center raised above the narrower ends of the rail above the upholstered back flanked by S-scrolled arms w/veneered arm supports w/roundels continuing down to form the flat seatrail raised on C-scroll veneered feet on casters, old refinish, ca. 1830-40, 80" l., 36" h. (ILLUS.) **1,200**

Sofa, Classical, mahogany, the central flat crestrail w/a leaf-carved top flanked by fluted S-scrolls above the long upholstered back flanked by widely outswept S-scroll arms w/bolsters & scrolled arm supports continuing to form the gently rounded seatrail carved w/roundels, raised on cornucopia-topped paw feet on casters, refinished, ca. 1840, 80" l., 34" h. (ILLUS. below)................................... **2,000**

Classical Sofa with Decorative Arms

Sofa, Classical, mahogany, the wide gently arched central crestrail topped by a heavy rounded rail w/down-curled carved ends over upward curved rails to the padded, upholstered arms w/curved pads & curved carved facings above incurved arm supports enclosing bolsters, long spring cushion seat, w/a carved & stepped seatrail raised on carved cornucopias on outswept paw feet on casters, ca. 1830s, old but not original

upholstery, original dark finish, 84" l., 34" h. (ILLUS. below, bottom) **2,200**

Heavy, Boxy Classical Sofa

Sofa, Classical, mahogany, the wide mahogany-veneered flat crestrail slightly rolled & flanked by shorter S-scrolls at the ends above the rounded upholstered arms over solid wood sides flanking the upholstered back, arm supports carved at the top w/rounded leaves over a flat panel flanking the upholstered spring seat, flat veneered seatrail, heavy leaf-carved paw front feet, old upholstery, refinished, ca. 1835-40, 84" l., 36" h. (ILLUS.) **900**

Classical Revival Mahogany Sofa

Sofa, Classical Revival style, mahogany, the raised round rod crestbar w/carved curled-under ends above the shaped crestrail above the outscrolled rolled arms w/swan head carving above the long upholstered seat w/bolsters, ogee seatrail

Ornately Carved Classical Sofa

raised on winged paw front legs on casters, original finish, ca. 1910, later upholstery, 68" l. (ILLUS.) **1,600**

Classical-Victorian Transitional Sofa

Sofa, Classical-Victorian transitional style, mahogany, the wide serpentine crestrail w/a long central scroll-carved crest & beaded edge trim above the undulating upholstered back flanked by heavy outswept arms w/wide scroll-carved arm supports above the long spring seat, the serpentine seatrail w/scrolls carved at the center & a bead-carved edge, florette-carved blocks at the top of the outswept scroll-carved legs on casters, original dark finish, ca. 1850, 80" l., 36" h. (ILLUS.) **750**

Sofa, Federal Revival style, mahogany, the long flat crestrail carved w/sheaves of wheat & cornucopias above the upholstered back flanked by outswept arms w/reeded arm supports continuing below the long cushion seat, on outswept fluted legs w/carved paw feet, refinished, new upholstery, late 19th - early 20th c., 80" l., 36" h. **2,400**

Sofa, Louis XV Revival style, carved fruitwood, the narrow crestrail ornately pierce-carved w/scrolls above the deep upholstered back & continuing down to form the outscrolled upholstered arms, three-cushion seat above a three-section serpentine seatrail further pierce-carved w/scrolls between the four demi-cabriole

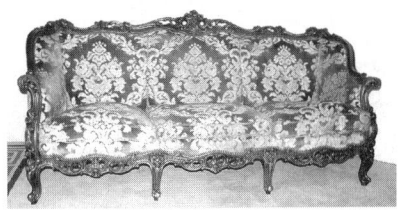

Louis XV Revival Carved Sofa

front legs w/scroll feet, probably Europe, ca. 1920s, 84" l., 40" h. (ILLUS.).. **1,250**

Sofa, Louis XV Revival-style sofa, carved fruitwood, the three-section upholstered back w/an arched central section w/a narrow scroll-carved crestrail continuing to form dividers between the sections & a continual crestrail curved up & around to form deep upholstered sides w/ornate scroll-carved arm supports, long cushion seat over a deep apron w/a serpentine scroll-carved seatrail on four scroll-carved demi-cabriole front legs, recent upholstery, ca. 1920s, 80" l., 38" h. (ILLUS. below) **1,000**

Louis XV-Style Upholstered Sofa

Sofa, Louis XV-Style, carved mahogany, triple-back style, the oblong upholstered center medallion enclosed by narrow pierce-carved molding continuing around the arched serpentine upholstered side panels, serpentine arm rails continuing to incurved front arm support, three-

Fruitwood Louis XV Revival Sofa

cushion seat, serpentine apron w/a scroll-carved serpentine seatrail, on serpentine front legs ending in scroll feet, original finish & upholstery, ca. 1920s, 76" l., 36" h. (ILLUS.) **800**

Victorian Baroque Style Long Sofa

Sofa, Victorian Baroque-Style, rosewood, the long crestrail composed of three large arched & scroll-carved crests above the long rectangular upholstered back flanked by baluster-turned stiles w/small urn finials above the open padded arms ending in large ball grips above baluster-turned arm supports, a flat seatrail above four shot block- and ring-turned front legs joined by long scroll-carved stretchers, original casters, refinished, second half 19th c., 84" l., 48" h. (ILLUS.) **1,500**

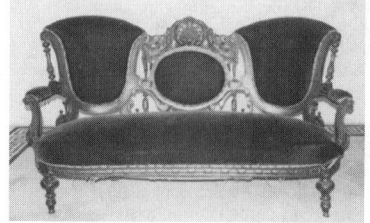

Unique Renaissance Revival Sofa

Sofa, Victorian Renaissance Revival style, walnut, the triple-section back composed of two large U-form upholstered panels flanking a smaller upholstered oval center panel framed by pierced scroll and shell carving, padded open arms w/rolled arm supports above the long oval upholstered seat on a conforming molded seatrail, tapering knob- and ring-turned front legs, original finish, ca. 1875, later velvet upholstery, 68" l. (ILLUS.) **1,400**

Ornate Baudouine Rococo Sofa

Sofa, Victorian Rococo style, carved & laminated rosewood, triple-back style, the ornate back w/a high chair back at each end centered by a lower center section, each section w/a wide ornately pierced-carved crestrail featuring scrolls & flowers all above tufted upholstered back panels, padded open end arms above the long upholstered spring seat w/a serpentine scroll-carved seatrail, molded demi-cabriole front legs on casters, Charles Baudouine, New York City, ca. 1855, refinished, new upholstery, 78" l., 44" h. (ILLUS.) **9,500**

Simple Victorian Rococo Sofa

Sofa, Victorian Rococo style, carved mahogany, the arched & serpentine crestrail w/a carved center crest & rounded corners continuing down around the upholstered back to the padded closed arms w/molded curved arm supports flanking the long upholstered seat w/a serpentine seatrail raised on demi-cabriole front legs on casters, old upholstery, ca. 1860, 66" l. (ILLUS.)... **950**

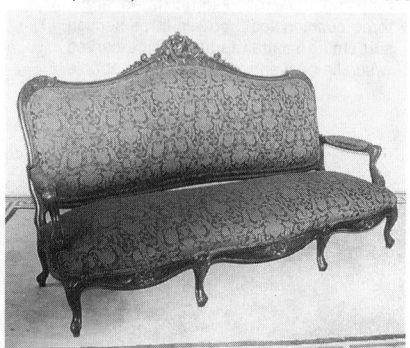

Rococo Sofa with Restrained Design

Sofa, Victorian Rococo style, rosewood, the long serpentine crestrail w/a high shell- and scroll-carved central crest over the long upholstered back w/rounded corners, padded open arms w/incurved arm supports flanking the long upholstered spring seat, serpentine shell-carved seatrail on four short demi-cabriole legs, refinished, new upholstered, ca. 1860-70, 76" l., 44" h. (ILLUS.) **950**

Mirrors

Tall Delicate Adam-Style Mirror

Adam-Style wall mirror, gilt gesso, oval, the tall delicate openwork best composed of a central urn issuing flower stems & leafy scrolls draping down the sides halfway down the central oval beaded mirror frame, further floral stems & leaves flanking the base drop, original surface, early 20th c., 20" w., 48" h. (ILLUS.) **1,000**

Unusual Figural Carved Wall Mirror

Baroque Revival wall mirror, carved pine, a large ornately carved winged dragon supports a large crescent moon-shaped mirror w/a large upright winged mermaid wrapped around the top, her tail w/flowers enclosing one side of the mirror, her large winged body w/her arms wide apart, original finish, Europe, last quarter 19th c., 24" w., 38" h. (ILLUS.) **2,500**

Chippendale Mahogany Wall Mirror

Chippendale wall mirror, mahogany, the high arched & scroll-cut crest w/corner ears above a narrow rectangular molding enclosing the rectangular mirror, scroll-carved pendent base, America or England, late 18th c., refinished, 20 x 40" (ILLUS.).. **650**

Chippendale wall mirror, mahogany, the thin wood scrolling pierced crest w/a composition bird applied at the center above the mirror plate enclosed by a molded & parcel-gilt surround over the similarly scrolling pendent, old refinish, New England, probably Boston, 1800-40, 33" h. (imperfections)....................................... **489**

Fine Classical Girandole Mirror

Classical girandole wall mirror, giltwood, a round coved & reeded frame enclosing a convex mirror flanked by candlearms & topped by a large spread-winged eagle on rockwork finial flanked by scrolling leaf & blossom brackets, scrolling leaf & blossom base drop, original finish, ca. 1830, 22" w., 38" h. (ILLUS.) **2,000**

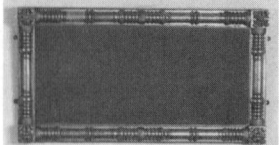

Giltwood Classical Overmantel Mirror

Classical overmantel mirror, gilt gesso & wood, a long rectangular frame decorated w/half-round ring- and rod-turned columns w/corner blocks decorated w/molded florettes, New England, ca. 1825-30, minor imperfections, 25 3/4 x 49 3/4" (ILLUS.).... **2,185**

Fine Classical Shaving Mirror

Classical shaving mirror, mahogany & mahogany veneer, table-top, a flat crest cornice raised on half-round columnar supports flanking the swiveling rectangular mirror w/rounded frame, above a rectangular top w/rounded front corners over two ogee-fronted drawers w/an ivory keyhole or tiny knob, original finish, ca. 1840, 10 x 16", 28" h. (ILLUS.)................................. **350**

Fine Classical Giltwood Wall Mirror

Classical wall mirror, giltwood, the long rectangular frame w/leafy scroll-carved corner brackets at the top & bottom, the frame w/half-round ring- and baluster-turned spindles, an upper reverse-paint-ed tablet w/a scene of sailing ships above the original rectangular mirror plate, original surface, ca. 1830, 22 x 38" (ILLUS.)....... **800**

Decorative Classical Wall Mirror

Classical wall mirror, mahogany & mahogany veneer, the overhanging cornice w/acorn spherules above the frieze w/applied scrolling botanical forms & a central brass boss above the two mirror plates enclosed in reeded narrow frames flanked by split-baluster ring-turned rope-carved engaged columns, original surface, New York State, probably Utica, 1825-35, very minor losses, 37 1/2" h. (ILLUS.).. **920**

Fine Empire Revival Cheval Mirror

Empire Revival cheval mirror, ormolu-mounted mahogany, a long oval narrow frame w/ormolu mounts enclosing a beveled mirror swiveling between tall square uprights w/urn-form finials & swelled scroll base bracket all decorated w/ormolu mounts, the uprights also w/heavy scrolled inner brackets w/ormolu mounts resting on the heavy bottom cross stretcher w/long ornate ormolu mounts, raised on heavy rectangular blocks raised on bun feet on casters, original finish, ca. 1880, 36" w., 6' 10" h. (ILLUS.) **3,000-3,500**

Girandole Wall Mirror with Eagle Crest

Federal girandole wall mirror, giltwood & gesso, the crest w/a large carved spread-winged eagle flanked by scrolled foliate devices above the concave molded round frame w/applied balls & reeded ebonized inner liner surrounding the convex mirror, all on a foliate pendant, America or England, ca. 1830, regilding, imperfections, 25" w., 43" h. (ILLUS.) **1,093**

Federal Bow-front Shaving Mirror

Federal shaving mirror, inlaid mahogany, bow-front table-top style, a rectangular mirror in line-inlaid frame swiveling between S-scroll uprights on a rectangular top w/a bowed form over a row of three small drawers w/tiny ivory pulls, serpentine apron & small French feet, original finish, early 19th c., 10 x 18", 18" h. (ILLUS.) **450**

Federal Transitional Wall Mirror

Federal transitional-style wall mirror, carved walnut, a spread-winged eagle finial perched on a plume above a high arched & pierce-carved leafy scroll crest atop the oval molded frame set w/gilded wood buttons, a pierced leaf-carved band at the bottom, original finish, ca. 1840, 24 x 38" (ILLUS.) **1,000**

Fine Decorated Federal Wall Mirror

Federal wall mirror, giltwood & églomisé, the molded stepped cornice w/applied balls above an églomisé panel painted w/a scene of a horse & cart passing a lake surrounded by a stenciled leaf border on a red field above the rectangular mirror all flanked by rope-twist molded pilasters & molded base, Massachusetts, ca. 1805-15, very minor imperfections, 16 1/4" w. at top, 28 1/4" h. (ILLUS.)...................................... **2,530**

Federal wall mirror, giltwood & white pine, the oval giltwood frame supports a tall central finial composed of neoclassical elements & a carved pineapple-form finial issuing gilded floral & foliate designs cascading down & flanking the mirror also decorated w/similar devices in the bottom pendant, all original, white pine backboard, probably American, 1780-1800, 14 1/2 x 37" (imperfections)........... **24,150**

Federal Mahogany Wall Mirror

Federal wall mirror, mahogany, a flaring deep crestrail w/blocked ends above a central burl veneer panel flanked by blocks w/roundels above reeded panels over leaf-carved & rope twist pilasters flanking the two-section mirror, corner blocks at bottom w/roundels, original finish, ca. 1820, 18 x 42" (ILLUS.) **600**

Unique Victorian Oak Cheval Mirror

Late Victorian cheval mirror, oak, three-part, the tall frame w/a high crest centered by a large leaf- and scroll-carved medallion above a frieze band w/further carved scrolls & a beaded band above reeded stiles flanking a tall rectangular central mirror & w/a hinged swing-out rectangular mirror at each side, on a high trestle base w/carved & stepped legs on casters, original dark finish, ca. 1895, open 52" w. overall, 80" h. (ILLUS.) **2,000**

Louis XVI-Style Gilt Wall Mirror

Louis XVI-Style wall mirror, gilt gesso, a narrow scroll-molded outer frame topped by a crest, floral & fruit swags below reclining putti flanking a central flower-filled urn, the oval mirror overlaid w/a narrow inner oval band joined w/molded brackets to the outer frame, original finish, early 20th c., 36" w. (ILLUS.)............................ **2,000**
Mission-style (Arts & Crafts movement) hall mirror, oak, long rectangular form w/flat rails w/double brass coat hooks at each corner, narrow vertical end panels

Mission Oak Hall Mirror with Hooks

w/raised panels flanking the long rectangular mirror, early 20th c., 20 x 42" (ILLUS.).. **201**

Early Neoclassical Wall Mirror

Neoclassical wall mirror, gilt gesso & walnut veneer, the high arched cresting of an urn of flowers flanked by flowering vines above the arched glass mirror tablet & tasseled cording & a rectangular mirror below bordered by walnut veneer & gesso beading, Northern Europe, late 18th c., old regilding, imperfections, 13 3/4" w., 33" h. (ILLUS.) **1,955**

Ornate Neoclassical-Style Mirror

Neoclassical-Style wall mirror, carved mahogany, an oval frame carved w/clustered, wrapped reeds w/a pair of figural carved kissing birds at the top above a floral-carved swag, suspended on a long forked branch w/a large bow at the top, further floral-carved swags along the lower frame, ca. 1920s, 22 x 40" (ILLUS.).......... **850**

Queen Anne wall mirror, walnut veneer & giltwood, the crest w/an arched center above the central gilt carved leafage & the two-part mirror plate enclosed in a parcel-gilt liner & walnut molded frame, old refinish, some regilding, England, 1730-70, 35 3/4" h. (imperfections) **1,035**

Ornate Rococo Revival Wall Mirror

Rococo Revival wall mirror, gilt gesso, the cartouche-form mirror in a conforming wide molded border w/an outer framework composed of bold ornate pierced leafy scrolls w/a fanned crest, ca. 1900, 16 x 24" (ILLUS.) **450**

Ornate Rococo-Style Wall Mirror

Rococo-Style wall mirror, giltwood, the oblong frame composed of ornate pierced leafy scrolls w/pointed leafy scroll designs at the top & bottom, enclosing an oval mirror w/a beaded edging, late 19th c., 24 x 36" (ILLUS.) **800**

Tramp art wall mirror, chip-carved wood, the ornate shaped mirror frame w/an oblong top center finial above an arched crestrail & serpentine sides w/three-blossom floral clusters projecting at the bottom corners, all composed of thin

Unique Tramp Art Mirror

laminated sawtooth-carved layers, rectangular mirror, old finish, ca. 1890-1910, 29 x 47" (ILLUS.).............................. **5,290**

Fine Victorian Aesthetic Hall Mirror

Victorian Aesthetic Movement hall mirror, walnut, the flat flaring crestrail above S-scroll reeded brackets flanking a frieze band w/bold relief-carved florettes over a beaded band, the side rails mounted w/six ornate scrolled brass hooks flanking the round beveled mirror surrounded by bold scroll carving at each corner of the inner frame, molded flat base rail w/gadrooning, refinished, ca. 1885, 30 x 36" (ILLUS.) **1,100**

Aesthetic Movement Pier Mirror

Victorian Aesthetic Movement pier mirror, oak w/walnut finish, the high crown crest w/an arched rail over a flared molding over a band of carved leafage above a band of carved balls flanked by rounded ears over a flaring crestrail above molded brackets flanking a frieze band inset w/three small diamond-shaped beveled mirrors above the tall rectangular beveled mirror flanked by baluster- and rod-turned side columns ending in blocks flanking the molded bottom rail, original finish, ca 1880-1890, 22" w., 4' h. (ILLUS.) **450**

Renaissance Overmantel Mirror

Victorian Renaissance Revival overmantel mirror, walnut & burl walnut, the stepped crestrail centered by a large medallion cartouche w/a carved palmette & roundel above a narrow frieze band & another band w/two small raised burl panels flanked by carved palmettes above the frame sides composed of two half-round carved & reeded columns flanking the rectangular mirror w/notched interior frame corners, the blocked base w/carved decoration & small burl panels, original finish, ca. 1875, 36 x 70" (ILLUS.) **1,500**

Fine Renaissance Pier Mirror

Victorian Renaissance Revival pier mirror, walnut & burl walnut, the ornate blocked crestrail centered w/an arched block w/a carved palmette above a drop palmette flanked by low scrolls & carved palmette corner finials above blocks flanking a burl frieze band w/gilt incised lines, the long rectangular mirror w/arched framing at the top flanked by slender sides w/blocked panels & raised burl panels, a narrow stepped & blocked base, ca. 1875, 30" w., 96" h. (ILLUS.)...... **1,500**

Victorian Rococo Overmantel Mirror

Victorian Rococo substyle overmantel mirror, gilt gesso, the arched crestrail topped by an elaborate pierce-carved crest w/a central large leaf surrounded by scrolls & lattice above a continuous border w/an egg-and-scroll design around a plain inner band framing the conforming beveled mirror, the bottom corners w/large leafy scrolls, original finish, ca. 1865-85, 28" w., 72" h. (ILLUS.) **1,200**

Parlor Suites

Chair from Karpen Parlor Suite

Unique Upholstered Art Nouveau Parlor Suite

Art Nouveau: love seat & side chair; carved mahogany, each w/an ornately carved heavy framework, the back crest carved w/a standing Art Nouveau maiden w/long swirling hair & wearing a diaphanous gown surrounded by swirling vines & flowers which continue down the sides of the frame, a wide upholstered seat over a heavy seatrail w/further serpentine carving & thick short stylized cabriole front legs on casters, by the Karpen Brothers, Chicago, ca. 1890-1900, original finish, side chair 25" w., 43" h., 2 pcs. (ILLUS. of side chair) **4,600**

Art Nouveau: love seat, tall-back armchair, low-back armchair & four sides chairs; mahogany, the side chairs & tall armchair w/an upturned oblong upholstered back crest raised on a pierced-carved splat flanked by long curved stiles & shaped arms over the upholstered seat w/serpentine seatrail on slender front cabriole legs, the love seat w/a matching all-wood back w/central splat & shaped arms over the upholstered seat, the low-back armchair w/a barrel-shaped upholstered back w/a U-form bottom frame & pierced side slats under the arms, upholstered seat & matching legs, original finish, ca. 1910, love seat 60" l., 40" h., the set (ILLUS. above) **2,000**

Classical Revival Parlor Suite

Classical Revival: sofa, two armchairs, a lady's chair & a rocking chair w/arms; a heavy arched crestrail w/an ornate scroll-carved crest & arched scroll-carved lower panel above the wide upholstered back w/boldly carved stiles, heavy scrolled open arms on incurved arm supports flanking the upholstered spring seat, serpentine seatrail, heavy cabriole legs ending in paw feet on casters, original finish, original upholstery, ca. 1890, sofa 54" l., the set (ILLUS.)... **1,000**

Late Victorian Mahogany Parlor Suite

Unique Late Victorian Parlor Suite

Late Victorian: settee, armchair & side chair; mahogany, each piece w/a wide back rail w/serpentine & scroll-trimmed outline raised above a band of tall turned & tapering spindles, heavy shaped & forked carved arms projecting from the stiles w/no arm supports, wide over-upholstered spring seat, slightly serpentine narrow seatrail, square tapering & slightly outswept front legs on casters, original finish, ca. 1900, ca. 1920s upholstery, settee 56" l., 36" h., the set (ILLUS bottom previous page.) **600**

Late Victorian: settee & two armchairs; walnut, unique novelty style, the settee w/a double-chair back w/each section composed of a flat upholstered crestrail over a narrow row of stick-and-ball spindles on the rail over a double-lobed upholstered panel centered by a small splat, the backrail curving around to form the arms over another double-lobed upholstered panel, rounded overstuffed upholstered seat w/projecting blocked sections, molded conforming seatrail w/four baluster- and ring-turned front legs, matching armchairs, ca. 1890, settee 66" l., 32" h. (ILLUS. above) **1,000**

Late Victorian Rococo Revival: settee, armchair & lady's chair; giltwood, each w/an ornately carved gilded frame, the crestrail centered by a large shell flanked by putti flanked by ornate carved scrolling above the curved tufted upholstered back, the upholstered seat over a serpentine wide seatrail centered by a large carved shell, heavy scroll-carved cabriole front legs w/shell-carved knees, the armchair & settee w/upholstered rolled arms w/ornate C-scroll arm supports, the lady's chair w/half-arms, Karpen Brothers, Chicago, ca. 1890s, old upholstery, original metal casters, settee 68" l., 40" h., the set **8,000**

Late Victorian Rococo Revival: sofa & armchair; carved mahogany, each w/a heavy ornately carved crestrail centered by a large carved shell flanked by figural putti & flanked by further scroll carving curving down to the rolled upholstered closed arms w/bold C-scroll-carved arm supports, tufted upholstered backs & wide over-upholstered seats w/a wide serpentine seatrail carved w/a long central shell flanked by scrolls, boldly carved

Karpen Rococo Revival Parlor Suite

short cabriole front legs, original dark finish, Karpen Brothers, Chicago, Illinois, ca. 1890s, ca. 1920s upholstery, sofa 70" l., 42" h., 2 pcs. (ILLUS.) **6,500**

Louis XV Revival Parlor Suite

Louis XV Revival: love seat, two armchairs & four side chairs; mahogany, each back w/a serpentine scroll-carved crestrail w/incurved ears continuing down to form the squared serpentine upholstered back raised above the over-upholstered seat, the padded open arms w/incurved arm supports, serpentine carved seatrail & simple cabriole front legs, ca. 1900, love seat 60" l., 38" h., the set (ILLUS.) **1,500**

Victorian Eastlake Sofa & Armchair

Victorian Eastlake substyle: sofa & armchair; walnut, each w/an angular stepped

& pierced crestrail, the sofa w/two tufted upholstered panels separated by a scroll-carved panel w/short turned spindles, padded arms on angular blocked arm supports, gently curved seatrail w/angular short center drop, ring-turned tapering front legs on casters, original finish, ca. 1880s, sofa 60" l., 2 pcs. (ILLUS.) **1,000**

Renaissance Love Seat & Side Chair

Victorian Renaissance Revival: love seat & two side chairs; walnut & burl walnut, the love seat w/a double-panel back w/two arched & peaked crestrails joined at the center w/a shell- and swag-carved crest above a burl block & a central pierced & carved splat, the top corners w/shaped ears above the incurved back stiles over the deep curved upholstered arms w/incurved arm supports, long upholstered spring seat w/a gently curved seatrail centered by a narrow burl panel & small drop, on knob- and ring-turned front legs on casters, matching side chairs, old refinish, ca. 1875, later upholstery, love seat 60" l., 36" h. (ILLUS. of part)... **1,000**

Fine Renaissance Revival Armchair

Victorian Renaissance Revival: sofa & armchair; upholstered walnut, each crestrail w/a pedimented crest over a round wreath enclosing a carved female face, oblong upholstered back panels flanked by block- and spindle-turned stiles above upholstered arms w/carved incurved arm supports, deep cushion rounded seat w/wide seatrail centered by carved top,

tapering ring-turned front legs on casters, original dark finish, early 20th c. upholstery, ca. 1875, sofa 80" l., 45" h., 2 pcs. (ILLUS. of armchair) **2,900**

Renaissance Revival Sofa from Suite

Victorian Renaissance Revival: sofa & armchair; walnut, the triple-back sofa w/tufted upholstered back panels below curved crestrails, the center section w/a tall crown-form crest w/a carved classical mask, each section separated by a ring-, rod- and block-turned column w/pointed finial, upholstered closed arms w/curved & carved arm rests, a triple cushion seat on the sofa above a seatrail w/three burl panels above roundel drops, tapering ring-turned front legs on casters, matching armchair, ca. 1875, velvet upholstery ca. 1920, sofa 45" h., 80" l., the set (ILLUS. of sofa) **2,900**

Choice Renaissance Revival Suite

Victorian Renaissance Revival: sofa & two armchairs; carved walnut & burl walnut, the triple-back sofa w/a wide arched upholstered center panel w/an arched crestrail w/a scroll- and bar-carved finial centered by a face of a classical woman, the lower curved side panels divided from the center section by large ornate turned urns, curved padded open arms above the upholstered spring seat, three-section seatrail w/burl panels, raised on trumpet-form turned legs on casters, matching upholstered armchairs, original finish, old upholstery, ca. 1875, sofa 80" l., 44" h., 3 pcs. (ILLUS.) **11,000**

Renaissance Revival Parlor Suite

Victorian Renaissance Revival: sofa, two armchairs, four side chairs; walnut & burl walnut; the sofa & armchairs w/peaked wide crestrails above upholstered back panels above padded open arms on incurved arm supports over upholstered spring seats, narrow seatrails w/a central peak, ring- and rod-turned front legs, each side chair w/a peaked & pierce-carved crest over a pierced vasiform splat over curved skirt guards flanking the upholstered spring seat, ring- and rod-turned front legs, original finish, ca. 1875-80, sofa 62" l., the set (ILLUS.) **1,200**

Belter "Rosalie" Parlor Suite

Victorian Rococo: gentleman's armchair & two side chairs; carved & laminated rosewood, each w/a tall upholstered balloon back w/an ornately floral-carved crestrail continuing to the molded back framework above the upholstered seat, shaped & molded open arms on the armchair, serpentine front seatrail w/floral carving, raised on demi-cabriole front legs & canted rear legs all on casters, "Rosalie" patt., John Henry Belter, New York, New York, ca. 1855, armchair 44" h., the set (ILLUS.) **9,750**

Victorian Rococo Parlor Suite

Victorian Rococo: sofa & armchair; carved walnut, the medallion-back sofa w/an arched grape-carved crest flanked by arched & rounded side rails continuing to low padded closed arms w/incurved molded arm supports, long seat w/gently swelled front on a conforming seatrail, molded demi-cabriole legs on casters, matching balloon-back open-arm armchair, original finish, old reupholstery, ca. 1865, settee 5" l., 2 pcs. (ILLUS.) **1,200**

Victorian Rococo: sofa, armchair & two side chairs; carved & laminated rosewood, each piece w/an ornately pierce-carved crestrail, a central pointed & floral-carved cartouche flanked by beaded serpentine rails over pierced scroll carving continuing down & around the back, the chairs w/waisted upholstered balloon

Meeks Stanton Hall Parlor Suite

back, padded & upholstered arms w/incurved arm supports, wide upholstered seats w/serpentine seatrails w/floral carved center reserves, demi-cabriole front legs, J. & J. Meeks Stanton Hall patt., ca. 1855, original finish, old but not original upholstery, sofa 66" l., 48" h., the set (ILLUS.) **15,000**

Sofa From Meeks "Hawkins" Suite

Victorian Rococo: sofa, two armchairs & two side chairs; carved & laminated rosewood, the back w/ornate pierce-carved crestrails w/the arched middle centered by a pointed floral-carved medallion flanked by ornate scrolling grapevines continuing down the sides of the back, the chairs w/tufted upholstered back panels & the sofa w/a continuous tufted upholstered back, padded & upholstered arms w/incurved arm supports, over-upholstered spring seat, serpentine seatrails carved w/central medallions, demi-cabriole front legs on casters, Hawkins patt., by J. & J. Meeks, New York, New York, ca. 1855, refinished, new brocade upholstery, the set (ILLUS. of sofa) **45,000**

Screens

Firescreen, Victorian Renaissance Revival, carved oak, a large square frame w/carved continuous bands of bellflowers, the top w/an ornate pierce-carved crest of two dolphins flanking a large palmette, raised on a trestle base w/outswept legs carved w/lions' heads & ending in paw feet, joined by a ring- and

Oak Renaissance Revival Firescreen

rod-turned stretcher, original finish, no material in the frame, ca. 1880, 12 x 30", 42" h. (ILLUS.)... **750**

Ornate Victorian Rococo Firescreen

Firescreen, Victorian Rococo substyle, carved walnut, a large horizontal rectangular molded frame w/an arched & pierce-carved scrolling top crest & corner finials suspended between columnar stiles topped w/carved pineapple finials & raised on pairs of boldly carved C-scroll legs w/beaded trim, refinished, no fabric insert, ca. 1860, 18 x 38", 36" h. (ILLUS.)..... **850**

Rare Art Deco Iron Firescreen

Firescreen, wrought iron, Art Deco style, a high arched form w/a wide band of fanned ribs alternating w/tiny tight scrolls above a central full-relief sailing ship facing frontward & flanked on one side by palm leaves & pineapples & on the other side w/large grape leaves & clusters, a narrow looped base band on shoe feet, by Tacconi Paulin, impressed twice w/his name & "1937-1938," 61" w., 51 1/2" h. (ILLUS.)... **12,650**

Victorian Aesthetic Firescreen

Firescreen, Victorian Aesthetic Movement substyle, walnut & glass, the rectangular wood framework w/an arched crest highlighted w/gilt incised lines & scrolls & w/a wide base band w/further gilt incised decoration, swiveling between slender reeded uprights w/gilt trim & turned finials, on outscrolled legs on shaped shoe feet, the framework enclosing a large blue & white etched glass panel w/Neoclassical designs, ca. 1875, original finish, 26" w., 44" h. (ILLUS.) **850**

Victorian Needlepoint Firescreen

Firescreen, Victorian Elizabethan Revival substyle, mahogany & mahogany veneer, a large pierced & scroll-carved crest flanked by small urn finials on a flat veneered crestrail above the tall spool-turned supports flanking the large rectangular needlepoint panel w/a colorful parrot & flowers, raised on a trestle-form base w/spool-turned cross-stretcher connecting the scrolled outswept legs on casters, original finish, minor damage to needlepoint, ca. 1850-70, 18 x 24", 45" h. (ILLUS.)... **750**

Arts & Crafts Three-fold Screen

Folding screen, three-fold, Arts & Crafts style, a simple oak frame w/three rails at the top above color lithographed rectangular panels showing medieval scenes & poems above long dark blue fiberboard panels, original worn finish, ca. 1910, overall 45" w., 64" h. (ILLUS.) **400**

Fine Renaissance Revival Screen

Folding screen, two-fold, Victorian Renaissance Revival style, carved walnut, the tall ornately pierce-carved frame w/a top central cartouche above scrolls & a band of pointed flowerheads, continuous bands of stylized blossoms & leaves down the sides & scrolls at the bottom, raised on a pair of large scrolls & carved paw feet, original velvet fabric & hanging tapestry panels, original dark finish, ca. 1880, overall 44" w., 80" h. (ILLUS.) **1,100**

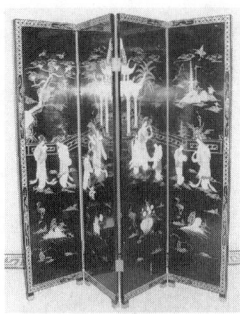

Oriental Lacquer Landscape Screen

Folding screen, four-fold, inlaid lacquer, the four panels depicting a continuous Chinese landscape composed of inlaid figures, buildings & accents w/gilt detailing, inlaid border band, China, ca. 1920s, open 60" w., 5' 10" h. (ILLUS.) **500**

English Queen Anne Pole Screen

Pole screen, Queen Anne style, mahogany, a tall slender pole w/small turned finial above a rectangular framed pictorial needlework w/a parcel-gilt surround, the pole atop a tripod base w/cabriole legs ending in arris pad feet, old refinish, England, 1750-70, wear, losses to textile, 55 1/2" h. (ILLUS.).. **5,750**

Secretaries

Unusual Arts & Crafts Secretary

Arts & Crafts secretary-bookcase, oak, a rectangular top w/a flaring cornice highlighted by a band of diamonds above a pair of geometrically glazed cupboard doors w/clear panes accented by green slag diamond-shaped panes, raised on incurved sides above the rectangular top over a pair of small drawers flanking the kneehole opening, large half-round cutouts at the lower sides & arched base cut-out, front stile legs w/through-tenon construction, original finish, probably English, early 20th c., 18 1/2 x 32", 5' 1/4" h. (ILLUS.) **2,310**

Chippendale Revival Secretary

Chippendale Revival secretary-bookcase, mahogany & mahogany veneer, two-part construction: the upper section w/a broken-scroll pediment centered by a turned urn & flame center finial over a frieze molding above a pair of tall glazed cupboard doors w/geometric grillwork; the lower section w/a wide hinged slant front opening to an interior fitted w/pigeonholes & curve-fronted drawers centered by a shell-carved prospect door, all above a case w/four long double-serpentine front drawers w/simple bail pulls, molded base on short cabriole legs w/claw-and-ball feet, original finish, ca. 1920s, 21 x 40", 90" h. (ILLUS.) **1,200**

Chippendale secretary-bookcase, cherry, two-part construction: the upper section w/a broken-scroll pediment centering a raised spiral-twist finial & flanked by two matching corner finials above a pair of fielded raised panel cupboard doors flanked by reeded pilasters, the interior w/concave shells over three serpentine shelves divided by a cyma-curved vertical board; the lower section w/a hinged slant front opening to a desk interior of valanced compartments & small drawers flanking a prospect door & columns w/a valanced compartment & two small drawers, all above four long

Fine Chippendale Secretary-Bookcase

graduated cockbeaded drawers on a molded base w/scroll-cut tall bracket feet, old replaced butterfly pulls & keyhole escutcheons, refinished, imperfections, Springfield - Longmeadow, Massachusetts, ca. 1780, 20 3/4 x 38", 7' 2 1/2" h. (ILLUS.) **79,500**

Country Chippendale secretary, two-piece, curly maple, pine secondary wood, w/mellow finish & broad striping, high bracket feet & deeply scalloped base w/four dovetailed graduated drawers, fitted interior of desk includes seven drawers & eight pigeonholes w/small door at center, two-door top w/two interior shelves & a broken arch top w/urn-shaped center finial, figure on top matches base but is an old marriage, restorations w/replacements to facings on feet, 19 1/2 x 42", 85" h. **3,250**

Unusual Secretary-Bookcase

Early 20th century secretary-bookcase, mahogany veneer, a long rectangular top above a dentil-carved cornice above the three-section case, each side w/a tall glazed cupboard door topped by a glazed panel w/ornate scrolling latticework flanking the center section w/a pair of small mirrored doors above an open mirror-backed shelf over the fold-down slant front w/applied scroll carving opening to a fitted interior all above stepped-out section w/a long flat-fronted drawer over three bow-fronted drawers all w/stamped brass & bail pulls, molded conforming base on four square tapering feet, original dark finish, ca. 1900, 20 x 60", 72" h. (ILLUS.) **2,800**

Federal Revival Mahogany Secretary

Federal Revival secretary-bookcase, mahogany & mahogany veneer, two-part construction: the upper section w/a flat rectangular top above a row of three round-fronted drawers over a pair of glazed cupboard doors w/geometric grillwork flanking a narrow center panel carved w/a grotesque mask above a cabochon over an acanthus leaf; the lower section w/a hinged slant lid carved w/scrolling stylized serpents & opening to a fitted interior above two long drawers w/brass bails flanked by carved scrolls & above a gently scalloped apron, raised on carved knob- and baluster-turned legs on casters, original hardware & worn finish, ca. 1900, 20 x 38", 60" h. (ILLUS.).. **1,400**

Federal secretary, mahogany & tiger stripe maple veneer, two-part construction: the upper short section w/a rectangular top w/molded edge above a narrow tiger stripe frieze divided into three panels by cross-banded veneer over two rectangular reeded sliding doors opening to a valanced compartment over two drawers flanking a prospect door w/inlaid oval which opens to reveal two document drawers; the lower section w/a narrow inlaid foldout writing surface above a case w/a long cockbeaded tiger stripe drawer above two slightly shorter matching lower drawers flanked by similarly veneered bottle drawers, on reeded baluster-turned legs w/peg feet, replaced round

brass pulls, old refinish, Vermont, 1815-20, 21 x 40 1/2", 46" h. (imperfections)...... **3,738**

Federal secretary-bookcase, cherry, two-part construction: the upper section w/a rectangular top & coved cornice over a pair of tall paneled doors opening to three shelves over small drawers; the lower section w/a hinged slant front opening to an interior fitted w/valanced open compartments over small drawers & a center prospect door opening to a valanced drawer, the lower case w/three long graduated cockbeaded drawers w/bail pulls above a base molding, raised on ogee bracket feet, New England, early 19th c., 21 1/2 x 44", 84 1/2" h. (refinished, replaced brasses, restoration, repairs)......... **6,325**

Fine Federal Secretary-Bookcase

Federal secretary-bookcase, inlaid mahogany & mahogany veneer, two-part construction: the upper section w/a rectangular top w/narrow cornice over a raised molding over a pair of geometrically-glazed cupboard doors over a pair of narrow drawers w/banded line inlay; the lower section w/a hinged fold-out writing shelf above a pair of support slides flanking a long drawer w/banded line inlay over two more long drawers w/matching inlay, scalloped apron & tall French feet, old replaced oval brasses, old filled-in age splits on sides, minor veneer & beading restorations, old alterations to interior top areas, early 19th c., 17 1/2 x 35", 57" h. (ILLUS.) **2,530**

Federal secretary-bookcase, mahogany & mahogany veneer, two-part construction: the upper section w/a rectangular top w/a deep flaring coved cornice above a pair of tall paneled doors opening to two adjustable scratch-beaded shelves; the lower stepped-out section w/a bowfront top over a conforming case of four long cockbeaded graduated drawers w/oval pulls, the top drawer fitted w/a felt-lined sliding writing surface opening to a cavity, molded base on tall scroll-cut bracket feet, old surface, Massachusetts, 1800-10, lower case 33 5/8 x 34 1/2" (replaced brasses, very minor imperfections) **29,900**

Federal-Style Secretary-Bookcase

Federal-Style country secretary-book-case, cherry, two-part construction: the upper section w/a rectangular top w/a narrow molded cornice over a pair of tall diamond-glazed doors opening to shelves; the stepped-out lower section w/a fold-out writing surface above an apron w/a single long drawer w/brass pulls, on slender ring- and rod-turned tapering legs, old refinish, mid-19th c., 23 x 36", 5' 4" h. (ILLUS.)............................... **650**

Ornate Late Victorian Secretary

Late Victorian secretary-bookcase, flame cherry & birch, side-by-side style, the left side w/a tall bookcase section w/a serpentine crestrail w/a pierced center opening & carved leafy scrolls above a pair of tall glazed cupboard doors each w/a frosted clear smaller upper pane w/Gothic arch grillwork above long glazed panels w/scroll-trimmed framing, the right side w/a serpentine crestrail over an asymmetrical beveled mirror over a shelf w/a small handkerchief drawer & pierced scroll trim above a hinged slant front decorated w/an ornate scroll-carved panel opening to a fitted interior above a stack of three graduated drawers w/stamped brass pulls, serpentine aprons & bracket feet, old refinish, ca. 1890s, 18 x 48", 5' 6" h. (ILLUS.)... **2,200**

Aesthetic Cylinder-front Secretary

Victorian Aesthetic Movement "cylinder-front" secretary-bookcase, walnut & burl walnut, two-part construction: the upper section w/a very high stepped cornice w/a pierce-carved crest over a pierced panel carved w/crosses above three burl panels carved w/stylized leafy vines above the flaring cornice over a pair of tall single-pane glazed doors w/small upper corner brackets; the lower case w/a cylinder front w/two burled panels opening to a fitted interior w/pull-out writing surface above a pair of line-incised & burl-trimmed drawers over a small paneled square door beside two small drawers w/incised lines & burl trim, stamped brass pulls, deep molded base, refinished, ca. 1880s, 20 x 40", 8' 2" h. (ILLUS.)... **2,800**

Ornate Aesthetic Secretary-Bookcase

Victorian Aesthetic Movement secretary-bookcase, walnut, the tall case w/a projecting central section, the top sides w/paneled back rails & spindled supports flanking the taller central section w/a rectangular leaf-carved cornice enclosing a hidden drawer above an open compartment framed at the front by an oval railing enclosing short spindles & backed by a rectangular mirror above a large glazed door w/gilt initials over a fold-down writing surface opening to a fitted interior above a stack of three burl-trimmed drawers, the side sections each w/a low top storage section w/three glass beveled panes above tall glazed cupboard doors w/long vertical half-moon molding w/lattice and vine-carved corner sections, each opening to four shelves, a deep stepped & molded flat base, original finish, ca. 1880s, 20 x 72", 6' 6" h. (ILLUS.)... **7,500**

Fine Victorian Country-style Secretary

Victorian country-style secretary-bookcase, feather-grain walnut, two-part construction: the upper section w/a rectangular top w/an arched scroll-carved crest on the deep coved cornice above a pair of 6-pane glazed cupboard doors w/Gothic arches at the top above a scalloped band over the recessed pie shelf; the lower section w/a hinged slant top opening to a fitted interior above a scallop-cut border band over two long, deep drawers w/carved nut & leaf pulls flanked by beveled front corners w/quarter-round drops at the top & bottom, scalloped apron & bracket feet, old refinish, ca. 1870, 24 x 44", 90" h. (ILLUS.).................... **2,000**

Eastlake "Cylinder-front" Secretary

Victorian Eastlake "cylinder-front" secretary-bookcase, walnut & burl walnut, two-part construction: the upper section w/a rectangular top & upright front cre-

strail w/a low arched center above scroll carving & spaced blocks above a frieze band decorated w/a long narrow raised burl band over a pair of glazed cupboard doors opening to three wooden shelves; the lower section w/a two-panel burled cylinder front opening to a fitted interior above a long line-incised & burl projecting drawer w/stamped brass pulls above two smaller drawers beside a small paneled cupboard door, narrow shaped apron w/pierced panels, refinished, ca. 1880, 22 x 42", 7' 8" h. (ILLUS.) **2,600**

Tall Eastlake "Cylinder-front" Secretary

Victorian Eastlake substyle "cylinder-front" secretary-bookcase, walnut & burl walnut, two-part construction: the upper section w/a high stepped crestrail carved w/trefoil finials above blocked panels of trefoils & a central arch over a deep flaring cornice & a sawtooth-cut frieze band above a pair of tall single-pane glazed doors opening to shelves; the lower section w/a narrow notch-cut band above the burl-paneled cylinder front opening to a fitted interior w/a pull-out writing surface above a case w/a long burl-trimmed line-incised drawer w/stamped brass pulls above two short drawers beside an arched burl-paneled cupboard door, blocked & notched side stiles, deep base band, original hardware, refinished, ca. 1885, 26 x 36", 9' h. (ILLUS.).. **2,500**

Secretary-bookcase in Golden Oak

Victorian Golden Oak secretary-bookcase, quarter-sawn oak, the low crestrail w/an arched scroll-carved center above a long narrow shelf raised on scroll-carved supports & a shelf backed by a large oval beveled mirror, the case w/a tall bow-fronted glazed cupboard door opening to shelves on the left & a mirror-backed small open compartment on the right above a small drawer over a hinged flat fall-front panel w/arched scroll carving opening to a fitted interior over an ogee-fronted drawer over two flat-fronted drawers all w/simple brass bail pulls, molded base on cabriole front legs w/paw feet, refinished, ca. 1900, 18 x 42", 6' h. (ILLUS.) **1,600**

Golden Oak Secretary-Bookcase

Victorian Golden Oak secretary-bookcase, quarter-sawn oak, the rectangular top w/a broken-scroll back crest centered by a palm-carved finial above low galleried ends over a pair of tall geometrically-leaded glass doors w/stained glass inserts above the hinged flat fall-front opening to a fitted interior, over a single long drawer over a pair of flat doors all w/simple turned wood knobs, slightly scalloped & scroll-cut apron, short cabriole front legs w/paw feet, original finish, ca. 1900, 18 x 36", 80" h. (ILLUS.) .. **1,500**

Victorian Golden Oak secretary-bookcase, side-by-side style, a high top crest w/scroll-cut sides & a flat crestrail centered by a scroll-carved finial over a narrow half-round shelf on slender spindle supports above an oval beveled mirror above the rectangular top, the left side of the case w/a tall glazed cupboard door w/a scroll-carved top opening to three wood shelves, the right side w/a rectangular mirrored door w/scroll-carved corner above a wide hinged fall front w/oval carved detail & opening to a fitted interior above a single drawer

Oak Side-by-Side Secretary-Bookcase

w/stamped brass pulls over a small paneled cupboard door, scalloped apron & simple stile feet, refinished, ca. 1900, 18 x 40", 5' 8" h. (ILLUS.) **1,200**

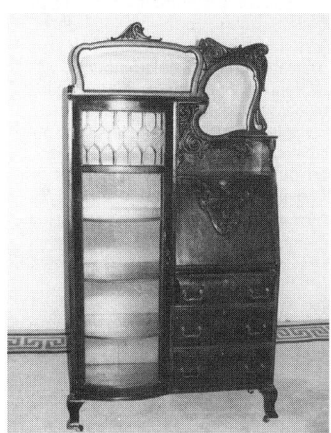

Two-mirrored Oak Secretary-Bookcase

Victorian Golden Oak secretary-bookcase, the two-part ornate crest w/a long beveled mirror w/a rounded & scroll-carved crest beside an ornate scroll-carved crest over an asymmetrical beveled mirror, the taller left side w/a tall curved-front glazed cupboard door w/a geometrically-leaded top panel opening to bowed shelves, the shorter right side w/an ornately-carved panel & small shelf below the mirror & above a hinged slant front w/an ornate scroll-carved panel opening to fitted interior all above a round-fronted drawer over two flat-fronted drawers all w/simple bail pulls, simple short cabriole front legs on casters, original dark finish, ca. 1890s, 18 x 40", 5' 10" h. (ILLUS.) **2,000**

Burl-trimmed "Cylinder-front" Secretary

Victorian Renaissance Revival "cylinder-front" secretary-bookcase, walnut & burl walnut, two-part construction: the upper section w/a high arched & molded cornice centered by a scroll-carved crown-form crest & flanked by trefoil corner finials above a deep flaring cornice over a pair of tall burl-trimmed glazed cupboard doors opening to three shelves; the lower section w/a thin pull-out drawer over the paneled & burled cylinder front opening to a fitted interior w/pull-out writing surface, the lower case w/a single long burl-paneled drawer w/black teardrop pulls over the set-back raised burl paneled lower doors, deep molded flat base, refinished, ca. 1875, 24 x 42", 8' 2" h. (ILLUS.) **3,800**

Ornate Rococo Secretary-Bookcase

Victorian Rococo "cylinder-front" secretary-bookcase, carved & laminated rosewood, two-part construction: the upper section w/a high scroll-carved crest w/a central turned urn finial on the molded cornice over a frieze band above a pair of glazed doors w/ornate scroll-carved latticework opening to shelves; the lower section w/a wide solid roll-front opening to a fitted interior above a single long drawer w/wooden knobs, raised on pierced & carved curved end supports joined at the back by arched brackets & a molded rail w/a high pierced scroll-carved crest, slender ring-turned front supports, all on molded rails raised on half-round disk feet, cleaned original finish, attributed to Meeks of New York, ca. 1855-65, 20 x 40", 6' 8" h. (ILLUS.) **3,800**

Elaborate Rococo Secretary-Bookcase

Victorian Rococo secretary-bookcase, carved mahogany, two-part construction: the upper section w/a high arched scroll-carved cornice centered by a figural bust of Shakespeare above a scroll-carved frieze band above a pair of tall cupboard doors w/large oval mirror panels framed by ornate carved scrolls over a long narrow scroll-carved drawer; the stepped-out lower section w/a white marble top w/a serpentine front above a long scroll-carved fold-down drawer front revealing the writing surface & interior storage, two cupboard doors below w/large round raised panels surrounding large blossom-form panels & w/carved scrolls in each corner w/further scroll-carving down the side stiles, flat blocked base, original finish, possibly by Mitchells and Rammelsberg of Cincinnati, ca. 1850s, 24 x 55", 8' 9" h. (ILLUS.) **8,000**

Secretary in Ornate Converted Case

Victorian Rococo secretary-bookcase, carved rosewood, early conversion from an upright piano or organ, the tall case w/a high peaked & scalloped ornately scroll-carved pediment w/central cartouche, upright end scrolls & a pair of lattice-carved frieze bands over gadrooned end cornices above spiral-twist turned side columns flanking delicate latticework grill panels flanking a central pair of glazed doors w/Gothic arch muntins, a curved hinged lift-lid opens to a converted desk section w/a row of drawers over a pull-out writing surface between carved rolled ends supported on heavy scroll-carved base supports flanking the central long rectangular base panel, case ca. 1855, probably converted ca. 1900, 26 x 48", 6' 4" h. (ILLUS.).. **3,400**

Rare Victorian Rococo Secretary

Victorian Rococo secretary-bookcase, carved rosewood, three-part construction: the upper section w/an ornately pierce-carved scrolling & scalloped crestrail on the deep stepped & flaring cornice over a single wide 2-pane glazed cupboard door w/scrolling grillwork across the top, maple interior w/adjustable shelves; the middle section w/a hinged paneled fall front decorated w/ornate carved scrolls & flanked by large leafy scrolls, opening to a fitted interior; the bottom section w/a rectangular top w/molded serpentine edges above a conforming apron w/a single long drawer w/ornate carved scrolls & a scrolled apron, raised on tall slender cabriole legs w/carved knees, original finish, ca. 1850s, 24 x 38", 90" h. (ILLUS.).................. **4,500**

Shelves

Floor Shelves with Display Rails

Floor shelves, painted pine, a narrow rectangular top on tall tapering scallop-cut sides flanking two boxed shelves w/crosspieces & incised plate grooves for displaying pewter above two lower, wider open shelves, original red paint w/original bluish green on the shelves, Pennsylvania, late 18th c., surface imperfections, top 8 3/8 x 43", 72" h. (ILLUS.) **13,800**

Primitive Painted Pine Shelves

Floor shelves, painted pine, a rectangular top w/molded cornice above three long shelves on a flat base, square nail construction w/later nails on backboards, old red repaint, edge damage, 19th c., 9 1/2 x 29 1/2", 39 3/4" h. (ILLUS.)................. **468**

Ornately Carved Rococo Shelves

Hanging corner shelves, Victorian Rococo, carved mahogany, three quarter-round graduated shelves between delicately pierced & carved shaped sides w/tightly scrolling leafy vines w/blossoms & fruit, original finish, ca. 1850-70, 14 x 18", 44" h. (ILLUS.) **2,400**

Wall shelf, painted poplar & cherry, a single narrow shelf flanked by tall narrow shaped cyma-curved sides & a tall flat backboard, old red surface, New England, early 19th c., 4 3/4 x 18", 14 3/4" h. (minor surface imperfections) **1,035**

Fine Bird-carved Victorian Shelf

Wall shelf, Victorian, carved walnut, a deep half-round shelf w/rounded edges supported on an ornately carved bracket featuring long curled leaves over a full-figure spread-winged realistic grouse, original finish, ca. 1870s, shelf 8 x 8", 14" h. (ILLUS.) **800**

Ornate Victorian Wall Shelf with Mirror

Wall shelf, Victorian Rococo, walnut, a tall scroll-cut top crest w/attached roundels & a small oval mirror above a hinged lid on a shallow box w/raised oval bands enclosing oval ebonized decal reserves, matching scrolling base bracket & backboard, original finish, ca. 1860-80, 7 x 14", 26" h. (ILLUS.) **300**

Wall shelves, mahogany, whale-end style, four narrow open shelves flanked by gently shaped, tapering sides, New

England, early 19th c., old refinish, 32 1/2" w., 31 1/2" h. **1,380**

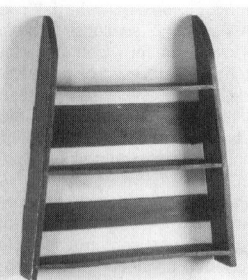

New England Painted Wall Shelves

Wall shelves, painted pine, three graduated open shelves backed by back slats between canted wide sides w/rounded top corners, red paint, New England, 19th c., 25 1/4" w., 28 1/2" h. (ILLUS.) **978**

Renaissance Revival Wall Shelves

Wall shelves, Victorian Renaissance Revival, carved walnut, the rectangular top w/a high scalloped crestrail centered by a center shell flanked by incised latticework lines, four scroll-carved corner finials above corner slats carved w/raised blocks & incised diamonds & enclosing two open shelves above the base shelf enclosed by a scalloped apron matching the crestrail, original dark finish, ca. 1875-85, 12 x 24", 36" h. (ILLUS.) **800**

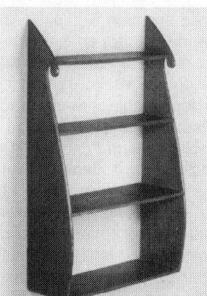

Classic Early Whale-end Shelves

Wall shelves, walnut, whale-end style, four tiers of open graduated shelves between scroll-topped swelling sides, New England, 19th c., minor wear, 7 1/2 x 19", 30" h. (ILLUS.)... **1,725**

Sideboards

Signed Classical Mahogany Sideboard

Classical sideboard, mahogany & mahogany veneer, a tall slat back crest flanked by columnar ends above the rectangular top over a case w/a single long round-fronted drawer over a pair of paneled cupboard doors centered by a stack of three graduated drawers w/original round brass ring pulls, free-standing columns at the sides above the heavy carved paw front feet, on wooden casters, signed "W.J. Underhill, New York," ca. 1840, refinished, 24 x 60", 60" h. (ILLUS.)............... **2,500**

Colonial Revival sideboard, mahogany veneer, the long rectangular top w/a bowed central section topped by a low crestrail arched & shell-carved at the center, the conforming case w/a pair of large flat end cupboard doors w/raised rectangular bands & leaf-carved drops flanking a long shallow bowed drawer over a deep long bowed drawer over a scalloped, scroll-carved apron, raised on pairs of cabriole legs at each end w/shell- and scroll-carved trim & ending in claw-and-ball feet, ca. 1920s, 24 x 64", 44" h. (ILLUS. below) **800**

Empire Revival Tall Sideboard

Empire Revival sideboard, mahogany & mahogany veneer, a rectangular top w/a narrow cornice above a pair of cupboard doors w/raised geometric molding flanked by narrow paneled sides above a tall open compartment centered by a beveled mirror flanked by wide quarter-round columnar supports, the projecting lower case w/a white marble top over a pair of drawers w/silver metal button pulls over a pair of paneled lower doors flanked by narrow long panels, raised on carved paw front feet, refinished, ca. 1880, 20 x 40", 6' 4" h. (ILLUS.) **1,250**

Fine Colonial Revival Sideboard

Very Rare Federal Inlaid Sideboard

Federal "serpentine-front" sideboard, inlaid mahogany, the rectangular top w/serpentine front w/stringing in outline & a molded edge above a conforming case w/a center compartment w/an oval-inlaid door opening to three small fitted veneered drawers flanked by two deep drawers w/oval band inlay further flanked by two larger end cupboard doors w/central shell inlays & oval band inlay, the sections divided by rectangular line inlays & tall slender square tapering legs w/inlaid banding & bellflowers & spade feet, the central arched apron w/inlaid corner brackets, replaced oval brasses, old refinish, minor veneer loss, one repaired leg, attributed to John Shaw, Annapolis, Maryland, ca. 1787, 24 1/4 x 71 3/4", 38" h. (ILLUS. above) ... **74,000**

Federal sideboard, mahogany & mahogany veneer, the tall broken-scroll backboard w/central brass urn & eagle finial & flanked by low spindled end galleries on the rectangular top above a case w/a long central drawer flanked by shorter drawers, all separated by reeded stiles, four paneled cupboard doors below over a flat apron, raised on ring- and rod-turned legs on brass casters, New England, ca. 1820, replaced eagle & shield embossed brasses, refinished, restoration, 23 1/4 x 72", 55" h. **2,990**

Late Victorian Rococo Revival Server

Late Victorian Rococo Revival server, mahogany, a low arched molded back crest w/a shell-carved crest over a long raised panel above the rectangular top w/molded edges & rounded corners over a single long drawer w/a narrow raised panel curving at the bottom above the scroll-carved serpentine apron, scroll-carved corner brackets above the tall slender cabriole legs ending in scroll & peg feet & joined by a shaped medial shelf, cast brass pulls, original finish, ca. 1900, 20 x 42", 44" h. (ILLUS.) **650**

Fine Late Victorian Walnut Sideboard

Late Victorian sideboard, walnut & burl walnut, the tall superstructure w/a wide flat back crest arched in the center over ornate carved leafy scrolls & w/urn finials at each corner above a long shelf incurved at the center & raised on four reeded columns backed by a large rectangular beveled center mirror flanked by vertical oval beveled mirrors framed w/ornate scrolls, all on the rectangular red marble top w/rounded front corners above a case w/a row of three drawers over two longer drawers over a pair of wide flat cupboard doors w/matching scroll-carved designs at one side, thin beaded bands between the doors & on the outer edges, molded base on heavy knob feet on casters, round pierced-brass pulls, refinished, ca. 1890, 22 x 52", 76" h. (ILLUS.)............................. **2,200**

Harvey Ellis-designed Mission Server

Mission-style (Arts & Crafts movement) server, oak, a long & low backboard w/rounded corners above the rectangular top overhanging a case w/a deep central drawer flanked on each side by two small drawers over a long bottom drawer, all w/copper rectangular bail pulls, arched front apron, raised on square stile legs joined by a medial shelf, designed by Harvey Ellis for Gustav Stickley, early 20th c. (ILLUS.)... **9,775**

Mission-style (Arts & Crafts movement) sideboard, oak, the high backsplash w/a gently arched crest above a narrow shelf over a high plate rail, on a rectangular top overhanging the case w/corbels at each corner, the case w/narrow short drawers flanking a long central drawer over a pair of paneled cupboard doors flanking another long drawer above an arched opening, a long drawer across the bottom above the gently arched apron, paneled sides w/arched base openings, hammered copper pulls, knobs & strap hinges, good original finish & condition, branded Limbert mark, 23 x 60", 51" h. **5,463**

Large Stickley Brothers Oak Sideboard

Mission-style (Arts & Crafts movement) sideboard, oak, the tall superstructure w/an open crestrail joining four posts above a long rectangular shelf supported by four square posts joined by arched braces above two back panels flanking a large rectangular beveled mirror, the rectangular top overhanging a case w/four heavy stiles forming legs dividing the facade, a long recessed central drawer over a pair of double-panel recessed cupboard doors all flanked by small projecting drawers over paneled cupboard doors, arched central apron, rectangular copper bail pulls w/one bail missing, good original medium finish, unmarked Stickley Brothers, 37 x 72", overall 63 1/2" h. (ILLUS.).. **4,025**

Aesthetic Movement Cherry Sideboard

Victorian Aesthetic Movement sideboard, cherry, the tall superstructure w/a rectangular top w/a three-quarters gallery flanked by low bands of spindles at the sides & front & capped w/two turned finials raised on arched supports w/slender knob-, ring- and baluster-turned spindles above a long open shelf w/low spindled rails at the ends & a spindled arch at the top of each end, the shelf backed by a large rectangular beveled mirror, all raised on plain square supports & a raised paneled back above the long rectangular top w/molded edges, the lower case w/a long drawer beside a shorter drawer over a long carved & paneled door at one end & a shorter matching door at the other end flanking a central stack of three drawers w/a longer drawer at the base, molded base rail on short turned feet, stamped brass pulls, original finish, ca. 1880s, 22 x 54", 6' 4" h. (ILLUS.)............................ **1,600**

Victorian Aesthetic Movement sideboard, mahogany, the tall superstructure w/an upright cabinet on one end w/a low ball-and-stick gallery over a single beveled glass door beside a stepped-down rectangular top over an open compartment w/a full shelf & half-shelf supported by a block- and ring-turned corner post raised on slender turned columns above the rectangular top backed by a large

Victorian Aesthetic Sideboard

rectangular beveled mirror, the lower case w/a long drawer over a pair of cupboard doors w/panels carved in low-relief w/dead fish & game trophies above a long bottom drawer, the other side w/two small drawers over a similar paneled & carved door, flat molded base, original round ring brass pulls, original finish, ca. 1880, 20 x 42", 84" h. (ILLUS.).................. **2,600**

Ornate Baroque-Style Sideboard

Victorian Baroque Revival sideboard, carved oak, two-part construction: the upper section w/a rectangular blocked top fitted w/a high arched & scrolling pierce-carved crest w/a central cartouche flanked by small turned corner finials above the deep flaring cornice w/a scroll-carved frieze band over a pair of tall cupboard doors w/rounded panels w/raised molding enclosing ornately carved game trophies flanked by pierce-carved scrolling brackets & two small shelves above a recessed paneled compartment flanked by ornately carved brackets; the lower section w/a wide rectangular top w/a molded edge over a pair of narrow paneled drawers carved

w/grapevines above a pair of paneled cupboard doors w/raised molding enclosing finely carved clusters of fruits, three slender turned columns resting on projecting blocks separate & flank the doors, on compressed bun feet, refinished, Europe, late 19th c., 24 x 60", 9' h. (ILLUS.) **5,500**

European Baroque-Style Sideboard

Victorian Baroque Revival sideboard, walnut, the superstructure w/a tall arched beveled central mirror w/a forked crest centered by a large urn-form finial, the scalloped sides w/urn-topped turned colonettes flanked by two small graduated shelves above two small handkerchief drawers on the rectangular top inset w/red marble, the lower case w/a long paneled drawer centered by a large raised diamond above a pair of arch-paneled cupboard doors w/corner floral carving & enclosing ornate carved scrolls, flanked at the sides by large spiral-turned columns on blocks flanking a long narrow base drawer above the deep stepped & flaring blocked base, on large compressed bun feet, Europe, last quarter 19th c. (ILLUS.)... **1,760**

Victorian Cottage Painted Sideboard

Victorian cottage-style sideboard, painted & decorated pine, the tall back crest
w/an arched top over a painted burl panel
over a narrow shelf on shaped brackets
over a larger rectangular painted burl
panel above the rectangular top w/mold-
ed edges over a case w/a pair of burl-
painted drawers w/porcelain knobs over
a pair of paneled cupboard doors
w/painted burl panels, flat molded base,
half-round turned spindle drops under
top corners, overall oak wood graining,
shelved interior, ca. 1875, 18 x 42",
64" h. (ILLUS.).. **1,000**

Victorian Golden Oak sideboard, oak, the
tall superstructure w/a high serpentine
front crestrail decorated w/elaborate
carved scrolls & a center cartouche
above a gadroon-carved frieze band over
four slender spiral-twist columns separat-
ing the beveled glass doors, raised on
baluster- and ring-turned supports above
the rectangular top backed by a large
rectangular beveled mirror, the case w/a
pair of round-fronted drawers w/pierced
brass & bail pulls over a pair of paneled
doors centered by ornate leafy scroll
carving & flanked by half-round turned
spindles & spiral-twist columns at the outside edges all above a long drawer
across the bottom, carved paw front feet,
original hardware & finish, 22 x 54", over-
all 84" h. **4,500**

Oak Sideboard with Leaded Glass

Victorian Golden Oak sideboard, quarter-
sawn oak, the rectangular top w/a wide
bowed center section & a long arched
crestrail over the conforming case
w/small leaded glass windows at the front
sides & ends flanking a pair of large
bowed & leaded glass doors each centered by a large fleur-de-lis design above
a long deep bowed lower drawer all
flanked by a short drawer over a deep
drawer at each end, gently arched apron,
raised on square legs ending in large
paw feet on casters, refinished, early
20th c., 20 x 56", 4' h. (ILLUS.) **1,800**

Victorian Golden Oak sideboard, quarter-
sawn oak, the superstructure w/a flat crestrail centered by a scroll-carved crest
above a rectangular shelf w/a bowed
center section above two small cupboard
doors w/clear glass fronts composed of

Unique Golden Oak Sideboard

beveled glass segments flanking a longer bowed door w/a plain glass front, all
raised on curved leg-form supports
w/paw feet flanking a long narrow beveled mirror above the rectangular top
w/molded edges, the lower case w/a pair
of narrow rounded drawers w/pairs of
ring pulls above a pair of plain bowed
cupboard doors flanking a long rectangular bowed door fitted w/a mirror, all above
a deep long bottom drawer, raised on cabriole front legs w/paw feet on casters,
original finish, ca. 1900, 20 x 45", 6' h.
(ILLUS.).. **2,200**

Nicely Carved Golden Oak Sideboard

Victorian Golden Oak sideboard, quarter-
sawn oak, the superstructure w/a long
narrow crest w/a deep carved frieze supported on figural griffin-carved supports
above a long rectangular beveled mirror,
the rectangular top w/molded edges
above a case w/a pair of long gadroon-
carved drawers w/carved lion mask pulls
above a pair of raised panel end doors
flanking an ornately scroll-carved center
door above a long bottom drawer all
flanked by reeded & blocked pilasters at
the sides, base molding above short front
cabriole legs w/paw feet, refinished, ca.
1895, 20 x 56", 5' 4" h. (ILLUS.) **2,800**

Sideboard with Leaded Glass Door

Victorian Golden Oak sideboard, the superstructure w/a flat crestrail centered by a small carved peaked crest above an oblong mirror w/scroll-carved upper corner panels & flanked by pierced arched sides supporting a small shaped shelf, resting on a rectangular top above a pair of round-fronted drawers w/brass bail pulls & keyhole escutcheons over a central arched leaded glass door w/scroll-carved trim flanked by carved stylized lion pilasters & a curve-fronted door at each end above the long, deep round-fronted bottom drawer, raised on flat legs ending in paw feet, refinished, ca. 1900, 20 x 42", 4' h. (ILLUS.) **1,750-2,000**

Golden Oak Sideboard with Mirrors

Victorian Golden Oak sideboard, the tall superstructure w/an arched & scalloped cornice w/rounded scroll-carved corners above an oblong mirror framed by large scrolls & a beaded band above the deeply scalloped open shelf supported by flat uprights w/bold scroll-carved tops & bases & centered by narrow upright beveled mirrors, also supporting a narrow lower shelf below a large scalloped rectangular beveled mirror, all resting on a rectangular top w/a bowed front above a conforming case w/a pair of drawers over a single long drawer flanked by serpentine side rails above a pair of cupboard doors carved w/a large central oval w/beaded border & flanked by large & small scrolls, narrow rounded base rail flanked by small scrolls, raised on short shaped front feet, refinished, ca. 1900, 20 1/2 x 44", 6' 8" h. (ILLUS.) **2,000**

Fine Carved Renaissance Sideboard

Victorian Renaissance Revival sideboard, carved walnut, the tall superstructure w/an arched & scrolled cartouche-carved pediment above a large panel carved in bold relief w/a game bird above a long rectangular shelf w/rounded corners flanked by angled & burl-veneered brackets & supported by ornate carved scrolls & bold blocked brackets centered by large rectangular burled panels & flanked by scroll-carved sides, the half-round salmon pink marble top w/a wide flattened front section above a conforming case, the case w/a long central drawer w/a raised burl panel above a wide paneled door carved in bold relief w/game bird trophies flanked by blocked

& burled stiles, the curved sides each w/a tall paneled door w/large carved fruit clusters, deep molded base, refinished, ca. 1870s, 22 x 58", overall 96" h. (ILLUS.).. **8,500**

Chestnut & Walnut Victorian Sideboard

Victorian Renaissance Revival sideboard, chestnut & walnut, the tall superstructure w/a high arched & scroll-carved pediment centered by a large scroll-carved cartouche above a high panel w/incurved sides decorated w/tapering curved raised walnut panels flanking a large carved fruit-laden branch above a long narrow shelf w/shaped brackets & supports over a large rectangular panel centered by a large oval w/raised molded edges framed by raised walnut corner panels all within scroll-carved serpentine sides, on a rectangular white marble top w/molded edges over a case w/a pair of drawers w/walnut banding & leaf-carved pulls over a medial band & a pair of tall cupboard doors w/central ovals & walnut corner panels, deep molded base & rounded front corners, original finish, ca. 1865, 23 x 44", 84" h . (ILLUS.).................. **3,000**

Outstanding Victorian Sideboard

Victorian Renaissance Revival sideboard, walnut & burl walnut, the superstructure w/a high arched crestrail centered by a large fanned cartouche-carved crest flanked by carved grapevines above an incised band & burl panels above a molded rail over a scroll-trimmed burl framework enclosing a large arch-topped mirror flanked by carved colonettes & scroll-trimmed small candle shelves over carved block panels, the half-round white marble top w/molded edge & two front projections above a conforming case w/a pair of center drawers w/raised burl panels flanked by rounded side drawers above a pair of flat central cupboard doors w/arched raised panels enclosing burl & large carved grape clusters, matching curved end doors, deep molded base, original finish, ca. 1865, 24 x 74", 8' 2" h. (ILLUS.)........................... **8,500**

Renaissance Revival Sideboard

Victorian Renaissance Revival sideboard, walnut, the tall superstructure w/a high arched crest boldly carved w/leafy fruits & nuts above scroll-cut sides flanking a central panel w/an arched molding above a ring & roundel all above a narrow shaped shelf on scroll-cut brackets above a large oval mirror, the rectangular white marble top w/molded edges above a case w/a pair of drawers w/leaf-carved pulls over a pair of doors w/oval panels centered by carved fruit clusters & w/raised triangular panels in each corner, scroll-cut apron & bracket feet on casters, refinished, ca. 1860, 22 x 42", 6' 8" h. (ILLUS.)........................... **2,400**

Victorian Rococo sideboard, carved walnut, the superstructure w/a wide arched & scrolled pediment centered by a carved urn of grapes & fruits above a wide pierce-carved panel w/further carved grapevines & clusters & scroll-carved corners above a long rectangular shelf supported on tall scroll-carved brackets centered by a long rectangular molded panel centered by a carved boar head

Fine Victorian Rococo Sideboard

mask, the outside edges ornately pierce-carved w/bold scrolls terminating in small lion heads, all on the half-round top w/a wide flat center section, the conforming lower case w/a pair of shallow paneled drawers w/carved pulls over two cupboard doors w/large oval panels centered by large carved fruit & flower clusters, the curved sides each w/a swing-out tray above another cupboard door w/matching oval panels & carved clusters, deep stepped & molded base, attributed to Alexander Roux, New York City, ca. 1855, similar to one in the Samuel Clemens Home, Hartford, Connecticut, 22 x 70", overall 84" h. (ILLUS.) **7,500**

Finely Carved Rococo Sideboard

Victorian Rococo sideboard, chestnut, the tall superstructure w/an arched & stepped crestrail over a panel centered by a large relief-carved cluster of fruits & nuts above two long narrow tiered half-round open shelves supported by fruit-carved scrolling uprights, the shaped outside edges carved w/bold C-scrolls & fruit, all resting on a half-round white marble top w/a flat projecting center section above a conforming case w/a pair of paneled central drawers flanked by curved end drawers, two flat paneled

front doors w/carved fruit clusters & corner roundels w/plain curved & paneled end doors, conforming molded flat base, attributed to Alexander Roux, New York City, ca. 1855-60, original finish, 22 x 70", 6' 2" h. (ILLUS.) **5,500**

Victorian Transitional Small Server

Victorian Transitional-style server, mahogany & mahogany veneer, a high shaped splashback w/central carved scrolls above the rectangular top above a pair of deep ogee-front drawers w/leaf-carved pulls above a pair of inset arch-paneled cupboard doors w/scrolls at the top & in the center of the panel & flanked by cyma-curved side stiles, S-scroll bracket front feet, ca. 1845-50, 20 x 38", 44" h. (ILLUS.) **650**

Stands

Bookstand, Gothic Revival style, oak, a top V-trough w/an arched crest w/Gothic cut-outs above a lower open shelf all flanked by wide sides w/cut-out hand holds at the top & rounded Gothic arch cut-outs at the sides, the lower sides tapering to flared Gothic arch legs joined by a vertical Gothic pierce-carved stretcher w/keyed through-tenon construction, attributed to Rose Valley, early 20th c., 8 1/4 x 23 3/4", 32 1/2" h............................... **518**

Unusual Mission-style Bookstand

Bookstand, Mission-style (Arts & Crafts movement), quarter-sawn oak, the tall rectangular framework w/four open shelves topped by four curved supports below a center post supporting an electric light socket w/curved braces supporting an oak-framed pyramidal shade w/leaded glass paneled sides w/floral designs in red & green on a caramel slag ground, ca. 1915-20, 14 x 22", 60" h. (ILLUS.)............................ **1,200**

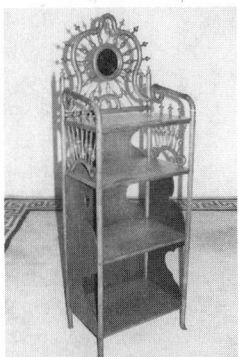

Victorian Stick-and-Ball Bookstand

Bookstand, Victorian stick-and-ball-style, oak & maple, the high arched & shaped bentwood crest accented w/a pinwheel design of slender spindles centering a small round mirror, bentwood side framing w/flaring spindles flanking the two upper shelves & shaped board sides & backs on the two lower shelves, refinished, late 19th c., 16 x 21", 44" h. (ILLUS.)...................................... **450**

Candlestand, Chippendale country-style, cherry, a nearly square thin tray top raised on a slender ring-turned column on a tripod base w/flattened cabriole legs ending in snake feet, probably Connecticut, late 18th c., old refinish, 15 1/2 x 15 3/4", 25 3/4" h. (imperfections)...................................... **2,875**

Candlestand, Chippendale country-style, cherry, a rectangular top on a block support w/a small drawer raised on a heavy baluster- and ring-turned post on a tripod base w/flattened cabriole legs ending in pad feet, old refinish, Connecticut, late 18th c., 16 3/4 x 18 1/4", 25 1/2" h. (minor imperfections)...................................... **1,265**

Candlestand, Chippendale country-style, cherry & birch, a small square top raised on a slender columnar post over a tripod base w/flattened cabriole legs ending in pad feet, probably Connecticut, late 18th c., old refinish, 12" w., 25 3/4" h. (minor imperfections)...................................... **1,955**

Candlestand, Chippendale country-style, mahogany, an oval top tilting above a slender columnar post above a tripod base w/flattened cabriole legs ending in pad feet, New England, late 18th c., 17 3/8 x 23 1/2", 28 3/4" h. (minor repairs)...................................... **1,380**

Candlestand, Chippendale-Style, walnut, high tripod base w/cabriole legs & padded snake feet, urn-turned column has incised line detail, dished tilt top w/molded edge, 20th c., 27" h. **220**

Candlestand, Classical country-style, tiger stripe maple, the rectangular top w/shaped corners tilting above a baluster- and ring-turned standard on a tripod base w/S-scroll outswept legs, refinished, New England, ca. 1820-30, 15 3/4 x 21 3/4", 28 3/4" h. (top slightly warped, repairs)................................ **863**

Candlestand, early American country-style, cherry, a square top w/applied edge molding raised on a slender turned columnar pedestal above a cross-form base w/shaped flat feet, old refinish, possibly Connecticut, late 18th - early 19th c., 14 1/2" sq., 27" h. (minor imperfections)................................ **1,495**

Candlestand, early American country-style, painted cherry, primitive design w/a small square top raised on a slender simply turned post above a heavy cross base w/four curved & tapering feet, brown paint over earlier paints, New England, early 19th c., 10" w., 27 1/2" h. **5,750**

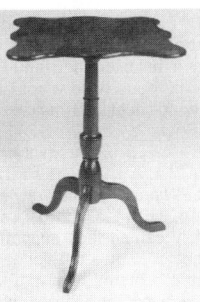

Federal Cherry Candlestand

Candlestand, Federal, cherry, a squared top w/deeply serpentine edges tilting above an urn- and ring-turned pedestal on a tripod base w/flattened cabriole legs, old refinish, New England, late 18th - early 19th c., minor imperfections, 23 1/2" w., 26" h. (ILLUS.) **748**

Candlestand, Federal country-style, butternut & maple, a rectangular top w/canted corners above a vase- and ring-turned pedestal on a tripod base w/flattened cabriole legs ending in pad feet, old red-stained surface, probably Connecticut, ca. 1810-20, 15 1/2 x 19 3/4", 28 1/2" h. (minor repair)................................ **2,070**

Candlestand, Federal country-style, cherry, the round fixed top raised on a vase-turned pedestal on a tripod base w/spider legs, old refinish, ca. 1820, 14" d., 31" h. (ILLUS. top next page) **350**

Candlestand, Federal, decorated mahogany, the round dished top tilting above a slender columnar post on a tripod base w/spider legs ending in spade feet, old black-painted surface w/19th c. stenciled

Federal Country-style Candlestand

floral & butterfly decoration on the top, foliate decoration & striping on the legs,
probably New England, ca. 1790-1805,
16" d., 28 3/4" h. **4,600**

Candlestand, Federal, mahogany, a large
oval top tilting above a baluster- and ring-
turned pedestal on a tripod base w/three
slender outswept spider legs ending in
spade feet, possibly Salem, Massachusetts, 1790-1810, 16 3/4 x 25 3/4", 29" h.
(refinished) **2,875**

Candlestand, Federal, wavy birch, the
square diagonally-placed top w/notched
corners on a baluster- and ring-turned
pedestal on a tripod base w/spider legs
ending in spade feet, old mellow color,
New   England, ca.   1790-1810,
17 3/4 x 18 1/4", 28 1/2" h. (minor imper-
fections)... **2,185**

Candlestand, Windsor country-style, ad-
justable-type, painted, three simple
turned widely canted legs supporting a
thick disk centered by a tall slender post
w/a round top centered by a ring-turned
post fitted w/a two-arm adjustable bar
w/a candle socket at each end, New England, early 19th c., old red stain, 14" d.,
33 1/2" h. (restoration) **1,725**

Canterbury (music stand), Federal style,
mahogany, four block- and ring-turned
posts w/knob finials joined by two rails &
enclosing   five   concave   dividers
w/pierced center splat above a single
drawer, on four caster feet, old refinish,
probably Massachusetts, early 19th c.,
14 x 19", 17 1/4" h. **1,725**

Mission Copper-topped Drink Stand

Drink stand, Mission-style (Arts & Crafts
movement), oak, a round copper top
above a deep slightly canted apron
w/arched lower rim, on four slender
square canted legs, fine original finish,
Quaint metal tag of the Stickley Brothers,
18" d., 27 3/4" h. (ILLUS.) **2,990**

Onyx & Brass Victorian Fern Stand

Fern stand, late Victorian, brass & onyx, an
onyx diamond-form top shelf set in a
pierced brass frame raised on four spiral-
twist supports w/onyx disk finials above a
matching lower onyx shelf raised on slender outswept tapering legs w/scroll tips
on flat disks, original finish, ca. 1890,
16 x 20", 32" h. (ILLUS.) **450**

Federal-Style Fern Stands

Fern stands, Federal-Style, mahogany-
stained hardwood, an octagonal open
top w/molded edges above the basket
holder w/caned panel sides, raised on
square blocks atop tall slender reeded tapering legs joined by an arched cross-
stretcher w/center button finial, small button feet, worn original finish, early 20th c.,
12" w., 34" h., pr. (ILLUS.) **750**

Hall stands, Renaissance-Style, decorated
pine, each carved as two putti, one sitting
on the shoulders of the other & holding
onto a twist-turned flaring pedestal supporting the round top w/a deep scalloped
& shell-carved apron, the lower putto
climbing on a large seashell above a
ringed round base w/projecting paw feet,

Figural Hall Stand with Putti

faux grained to resemble mahogany, original finish, Europe, ca. 1860-70, 18" d., 38" h., pr. (ILLUS. of one) **6,200**

Kettle stand, Chippendale style, mahogany, a small square tray top above an apron w/a narrow candle slide, raised on molded slender Marlborough legs joined by a thin medial cross-stretcher centered by a small shelf, old refinish, England, late 18th c., 11 3/4" w., 28 3/4" h. (restored) **1,035**

Early Country-style Light Stand

Light stand, early American country-style, turned & painted wood, the shaped adjustable double candleholder arm mounted on a spiral-turned shaft w/a circular dished adjustable top below on a turned post & circular platform & a tripod base of canted swelled turned legs, original reddish brown paint, possibly Connecticut, 18th c., shaft repaired, 12 1/4" d., 42" h. (ILLUS.) **3,738**

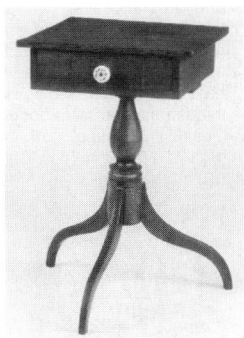

Federal Country-style Light Stand

Light stand, Federal country-style, cherry, a square top above a dovetailed frame & drawer on a baluster- and ring-turned pedestal on a tripod base w/spider legs, old finish, New England, ca. 1820-30, minor imperfections, 16 1/4 x 17 1/2", 27" h. (ILLUS.) **748**

Arts & Crafts Oak Magazine Stand

Magazine stand, Arts & Crafts style, oak, a deep three-quarters gallery w/incurved side rails on the rectangular top shelf above three lower open shelves flanked by sides composed of slats, medium finish, early 20th c., 11 1/2 x 18 1/2", 39" h. (ILLUS.) **1,035**

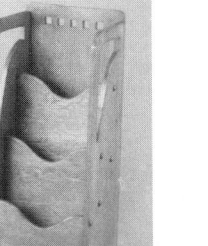

Lakeside Crafts Oak Magazine Stand

Magazine stand, Arts & Crafts style, oak, the tall narrow back w/a row of small squares cut-out near the top & flanked by sides w/large curved cut-outs at the top flanking three tiered magazine slots w/down-curved fronts, arched bootjack side bases, Lakeside Crafters, early 20th c., 9 3/4 x 14 1/4", 38 1/2" h. (ILLUS.).......... **575**

Unmarked G. Stickley Magazine Stand

Magazine stand, Mission-style (Arts & Crafts movement), oak, a square top above three open shelves flanked by solid paneled sides, new dark finish, unmarked Gustav Stickley, 15 1/4" w., 35" h. (ILLUS.)... **2,300**

Unusual Eastlake Magazine Stand

Magazine stand, Victorian Eastlake style, walnut, the top composed of three deeply scalloped upright panels forming deep storage slots, the outside faces ornately incised w/scrolling band w/ebonized trim & a center roundel, raised on a U-form support joining a central post w/urn finial raised on four flat S-scroll legs w/line-incised decoration & ebonized trim, original finish, ca. 1880s, 12 x 18", 28" h. (ILLUS.).. **450**

Magazine stand, walnut, the ends carved as a standing bird w/the spread wings forming the ends of the two compartments & the curved neck & head flanking the high arched & scroll-carved central handle panel, the side panels pierced & carved w/scrolls & a central rim

Unique 1920s Figural Magazine Stand

shell design, original finish, ca. 1920s, 14 x 18", 20" h. (ILLUS.) **400**

Gustav Stickley Mission Music Stand

Music stand, Mission-style (Arts & Crafts movement), oak, four open rectangular shelves each w/a low three-quarters gallery supported by four square stile legs, shallow arched base aprons, refinished, good condition w/four small brad holes, partial paper label of Gustav Stickley, Model No. 670, 15 x 22", 39 1/4" h. (ILLUS.)....................................... **4,313**

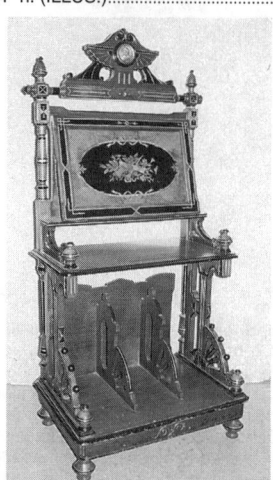

Unique Renaissance Music Stand

Music stand, Victorian Renaissance Revival style, walnut, ebonized wood & inlay, the top crestrail w/a high scrolled & spread-wing form crest centered by a bronze portrait medallion above ebonized brackets & a burl gilt-line incised rail supported between block- and ring-turned stiles w/turned pointed finials & ebonized trim flanking a large rectangular music storage compartment w/a fall front decorated w/a central oval ebonized panel inlaid w/delicate flowers & musical trophies & enclosed by a burl panel further bordered by an ebonized & gilt line border, all above a wide rectangular projecting shelf w/low shaped sides & front corner finials supported by brackets & cut-out sides w/large quarter-round wheel-form brackets w/knobs at the front & two additional matching brackets serving as dividers on the lower shelf, low platform base raised on short turned legs, original surface, ca. 1875, 16 x 24", 42" h. (ILLUS.) **3,000**

Ornate Victorian Rococo Music Stand

Music stand, Victorian Rococo style, walnut, the top rectangular shelf w/a low pierced scroll-carved gallery & four ring- and knob-turned corner finials, supported on four slender turned spindles & pierce-carved sides slats above a wider middle shelf w/two turned finials at the front corners & also supported by matching spindles & side slats above the wider bottom shelf w/corner finials & w/three tall vertical scroll-cut slats forming divisions on the shelf, the bottom shelf w/molded edges above a single long drawer w/scroll-carved pulls & a molded base band raised on disk feet on casters, refinished, ca. 1860-70, 15 x 22", 34" h. (ILLUS) **650**

Renaissance Revival Nightstand

Nightstand, Victorian Renaissance Revival style, a rectangular white marble top w/molded edges above a case w/round-ed corners w/a small drawer w/a raised oval band & carved leaf & nut pull over a mid-molding & a paneled door w/a raised arched band centered by a carved leaf sprig & a turned wood pull, molded base on thin bun feet on casters, refinished, ca. 1865-70, 16 x 18", 30" h. (ILLUS.) **800**

Fine Renaissance Revival Nightstand

Nightstand, Victorian Renaissance Revival style, walnut & burl walnut, a rectangular top w/a deep molded border above a case w/a drawer decorated w/a raised burl panel & scroll-carved pull flanked by diamond-and-button side blocks over a wide molded medial band above a single paneled cupboard door w/a central raised burl cartouche-form panel & flanked by carved leaf drops & narrow burl side panels, molded base on a blocked & carved apron, refinished, ca. 1875, 16 x 18", 30" h. (ILLUS.) **650**

Renaissance Revival Nightstand

Nightstand, Victorian Renaissance Revival style, walnut & burl walnut, the rectangular white marble top w/molded edges above a case w/rounded front corners flanking a single drawer w/burl panels flanking a roundel w/wooden knob, a medial molding above the conforming lower case w/a paneled door centered by a raised burl panel w/a carved floral cluster & wooden knob, deep molded base on rounded thin block feet, refinished, ca. 1875, 16 x 18", 30" h. (ILLUS.)...................... **900**

Louis XV-Style Inlaid Nightstands

Nightstands, Louis XV-Style, inlaid mahogany, the rectangular top w/a serpentine front & low carved gallery above a deep case w/two drawers w/small ring pulls & veneered in a continuous design form a central oval w/flowers within a larger shield-form inlaid panel, side stiles w/carved flowers & ribbon-tied reeds above the simple cabriole legs w/scroll feet flanking the deep serpentine apron, original finish, early 20th c., 15 x 20", 28" h., pr. (ILLUS.)... **900**

Nightstands, Renaissance-Style, walnut, the superstructure w/a small scroll-carved crest flanked by turned finial on the narrow flared cornice above a narrow scroll-carved panel above a large square panel centered by a small shaped shelf & bracket flanked by slender colonettes at the sides, resting on a rectangular black marble top above a single paneled & scroll-carved drawer over a tall paneled & scroll-carved door flanked by slender turned colonettes, molded & blocked

European Renaissance-Style Stands

base on bun feet, original finish, Europe, last quarter 19th c., 16 x 20", 46" h., pair (ILLUS.).. **1,800**

Carved Rococo-Style Night Stand

Nightstands, Rococo-Style, mahogany, an oval top w/molded edges above a deep oval case w/two bowed drawers decorated w/ornate scroll carving & brass ring pulls above a serpentine scroll-carved apron, raised on slender cabriole legs ending in scroll-and-peg feet, refinished, ca. 1920s, 15 x 22", 30" h., pr. (ILLUS. of one)....................................... **1,200**

Victorian Neoclassical Stands

Pedestal stands, Victorian Neoclassical style, giltwood, round marble-inset top w/a molded edge above a beaded apron supported on four slender incurved legs topped w/ scroll medallions joined by open swags surrounding a central reeded post, the legs joined by a medial ring stretcher & ending in hoof feet, on a round molded platform base, ca. 1870, 15" d., 42" h., pr. (ILLUS.) **3,500**

Late Victorian Picture Easel-stand

Picture easel-stand, Victorian Aesthetic Movement style, cherry, the arched crest carved w/a grotesque face above open quarter-round panels w/three turned spindles each, all atop slender reeded slightly tapering stiles & a center support stile, the lower narrow support shelf w/a scroll-cut border, a flat carved cross stretcher near the bottom, hinged rear support leg, refinished, ca. 1890, 22" w., 62" h. (ILLUS.) **375**

Aesthetic Movement Picture Stand

Picture easel-stand, Victorian Aesthetic Movement style, ebonized cherry, the tall back decorated w/a crestrail carved w/small scallops between a center palmette & upright carved corner ears over a pierced & carved square panel w/a wide carved arch over a pierce-carved urn of delicate flowers above a lower rail carved w/tiny spindles, all raised on three square uprights above a lower rail over a hinge-fronted folio compartment carved w/square panels carved w/geometric designs, ring-turned front legs & hinged slender rear support legs, the front legs joined by small turned & angled spindles joining a rectangular center drop panel carved w/large quatrefoils, original finish, ca. 1880, 24" w., 6' h. (ILLUS.) **2,600**

Art Nouveau Figural Plant Stand

Plant stand, Art Nouveau style, carved mahogany, a round top w/a carved & molded border raised on a figural pedestal carved as a standing Art Nouveau maiden w/her arms up supporting a flower bud on her head, her body entwined by a vine, on a quadripartite platform w/reeded feet, original finish, early 20th c., 12" d., 28" h. (ILLUS.) **650**

Carved Figural Stand

Plant stand, Baroque Revival style, pine, a round top supported by a large carved figure of a bearded man (Atlas?) nude except for swagged drapery, the body twisted w/arms up & out straining to support the top, standing on a rockwork base, original finish, Europe, late 19th c., 16" d., 34" h. (ILLUS.) **3,500**

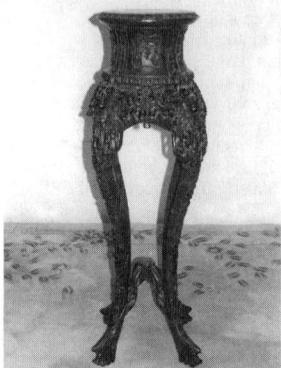

Carved Oriental Plant Stand

Plant stand, carved hardwood, a round top w/egg-and-dart border above waisted cylindrical sides carved w/vertical bands & panels w/carved fruit above a pierce-carved rounded shoulder w/blossoms & scrolls tapering to four serpentine legs w/ornate carved band & stepped feet, joined by a small arched cross-stretcher, probably China, ca. 1900, 16" d., 36" h. (ILLUS.) **450**

Early 20th Century Plant Stand

Plant stand, early 20th century, mahogany, a rounded top raised on a short baluster-turned support on a small round disk raised on a tall flaring turned central pedestal flanked by four long C-scroll brackets all on a cross-form base raised on flared block feet, refinished, first quarter 20th c., 15" d., 40" h. (ILLUS.) **450**

Plant stand, figural, carved mahogany, the round top w/a molded edge & tapering base resting atop the head of a scantily clad classical maiden w/one hand at the

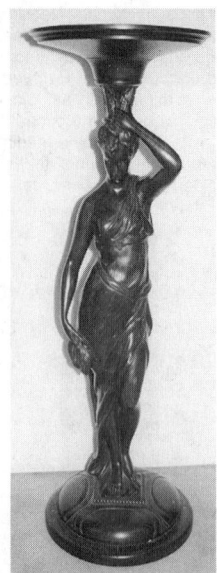

Fine Carved Figural Plant Stand

top of her head & the other at her side, standing on a domed lobe-carved base w/a round border, refinished, ca. 1900, 14" d., 36" h. (ILLUS.) **1,250**

Late Victorian Fancy Plant Stand

Plant stand, late Victorian, mahogany, a rectangular top w/a deep stepped border & coved apron raised on four spiral-turned supports framing a small shelf w/arched rails & tiny turned spindles on two sides, further raised on four taller spiral-turned supports above the lower shelf w/low gallery sides, on turned tapering legs ending in outswept brass ball-and-claw feet w/glass balls, original finish, ca. 1890, 13 x 18", 36" h. (ILLUS.) **500**

Decorative Mahogany Plant Stand

Plant stand, mahogany, a tapering open spiral-twist pedestal supporting a round top w/a rope twist border, raised on a small round platform w/rope twist border & three scroll feet, refinished, ca. 1900, 12" d., 34" h. (ILLUS.) **700**

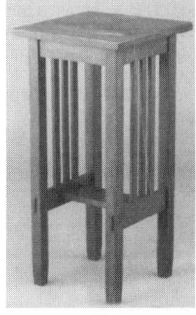

Stickley Brothers Mission Plant Stand

Plant stand, Mission-style (Arts & Crafts movement), oak, a square top overhanging a narrow apron & four stile legs w/three slender square spindles on two sides joined to lower rails connected w/a flat stretcher, mortised legs, good original finish & condition, Quaint metal tag of Stickley Brothers, early 20th c., 17" w., 34 1/2" h. (ILLUS.) **1,610**

Simple Mission Oak Plant Stand

Plant stand, Mission-style (Arts & Crafts movement), oak, four slender square legs joined at the top w/slender rails above a square shelf & w/a matching shelf & rails at the bottom, original finish, early 20th c., 12" w., 28" h. (ILLUS.) **144**

Plant stand, painted pine, country-style corner-type, a graduated tier of five curved open shelves supported by two side & a center board, old brown refinish, mixture of square & round nails, 19th c., 51" w. at base, 47 1/2" h. (splits, edge damage) **220**

Ornately Carved Chinese Plant Stand

Plant stand, pierce-carved teak or rosewood, the round marble-inset top w/a flat pierce-carved border above the deep floral-carved apron raised on ornately carved legs joined by a round medial shelf & ending in paw feet, original finish, China, late 19th c., 18" d., 30" h. (ILLUS.)...... **450**

Fine Aesthetic Movement Plant Stand

Plant stand, Victorian Aesthetic Movement style, cherry, a square white marble top above a deep stepped & flaring cornice above the heavy square pedestal carved w/raised bands flanking a wide band of boldly carved florettes above tall panels carved on each side w/a large realistic sunflower, square base w/gadrooned edge above scalloped & pierced aprons & small bracket feet, refinished, ca. 1880, 16" w., 36" h. (ILLUS.) **850**

Aesthetic Movement Plant Stand

Plant stand, Victorian Aesthetic Movement style, mahogany, the square top w/a scroll-carved narrow apron, raised on a ring- and rod-turned pedestal w/carved bands of flowerheads, on a square platform w/narrow shaped apron raised on cast-metal paw feet, refinished, late 19th c., 14" w., 38" h. (ILLUS.) **650**

Golden Oak Turned Plant Stand

Plant stand, Victorian Golden Oak, a bulbous baluster-turned pedestal supporting a stepped round top, on a round platform base raised on four paw-and-bun feet, refinished, ca. 1900, 14" d., 32" h. (ILLUS.) **550**

Plant stand, Victorian Renaissance Revival style, ebonized wood w/gilt trim, the rectangular top w/cut corners & beveled edges incised w/a scalloped design, raised on a central block flanked by long scalloped & scroll-carved curved brackets above a tall turned urn-form pedestal flanked by tall slender leaf- and scroll-carved brackets above the round base w/four projecting feet, ca. 1875, 12 x 18", 32" h. **1,200**

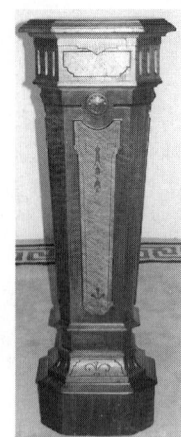

Fine Renaissance Revival Plant Stand

Plant stand, Victorian Renaissance Revival style, figured walnut & maple, the hexagonal top w/molded edges above a deep conforming apron w/burl panels alternating w/incised bands all above a gently tapering paneled pedestal w/a rosette above a long light burl incised panel on the wider sides & resting on a conforming flared line-incised foot on a deep plinth base, refinished, ca. 1880, 14" w., 40" h. (ILLUS.)... **750**

Renaissance Revival Plant Stand

Plant stand, Victorian Renaissance Revival style, walnut, the round dished top inset w/marble above a molded apron w/carved rounded drops, raised on a ring-turned pedestal centering four square-carved uprights w/flame-form carved finials & carved tassels all above four arched legs ending in hoof feet, ca. 1870s, 15" d., 30" h. (ILLUS.)........................... **900**

Plant stand, Victorian Renaissance Revival substyle, carved walnut, the round white marble top w/molded edge on a deep ringed apron raised on a slender columnar pedestal flanked by tall pierced S-scrolls continuing to the scrolled &

Renaissance Marble-top Plant Stand

outswept lower legs, refinished, ca. 1865, 13" d., 32" h. (ILLUS.) **650**

Plant stands, Victorian Eastlake style, cherry, a square white marble top above a flared cornice & dentil molding over an apron of panels incised w/scrolled decoration, raised on four slender square legs joined by a small square medial shelf w/a low spindled gallery, small scroll feet, refinished, ca. 1880, 12" w., 34" h., pr. **800**

Sewing stand, Federal Revival style, inlaid rosewood, a rectangular top flanked by wide drop-leaves each w/corners inlaid w/delicate leafy scrolls above a case w/two small drawers w/small brass knobs & inlaid w/further delicate scrolls w/the side stiles also inlaid, a cloth sewing bag suspended below, raised on legs w/three turned knobs above a slender tapering rod above a knob- and peg-foot on a caster, refinished, late 19th - early 20th c., 16 x 18" closed, 28" h. **1,800**

Sewing stand, Federal style, mahogany, a rectangular top opening to a deep cloth-lined well raised on four slender square supports raised on an arched center platform issuing four downswept reeded legs ending in brass caps on casters, old refinish, ca. 1820s, 15 x 24", 28" h. **1,200**

Sewing stand, Victorian Rococo style, rosewood, the rectangular top w/wide coved edges opening to storage compartments, the front w/a single narrow drawer above the deep arched & scroll-carved apron, raised on simple molded cabriole legs, refinished, ca. 1855, 18 x 22", 30" h. **800**

Shaving stand, Victorian Eastlake style, cherry, a tall upright rectangular frame w/a leaf-carved crest enclosing a tall beveled swiveling mirror over the rectangular top w/molded edges, the case w/two small drawers, one w/a rectangular brass pull, a brass towel bar at the side, raised on slender square legs framing an open three-quarters lower shelf w/a low pierced back crest over the bottom full-width shelf w/matching gallery, refinished, ca. 1880, 16 x 20, overall 72" h. **1,200**

Renaissance Revival Shaving Stand

Shaving stand, Victorian Renaissance Revival style, walnut, a high arched & scroll-carved crest above an arched rectangular mirror frame swiveling between slender uprights w/small side knobs & carved scroll trim, above the rectangular top w/molded edges over a single paneled drawer w/center roundel over two small square drawers flanking an arched center recess supported on a tall tapering paneled pedestal w/a paneled knobbed block raised on a base w/four long outswept C-scroll legs centered by a turned base drop, original finish, ca. 1870, 16" sq., overall 70" h. (ILLUS.) **2,200**

Victorian Rococo Shaving Stand

Shaving stand, Victorian Rococo style, walnut, the rectangular top set w/a small oval-framed mirror w/scroll-carved crest swiveling between scroll- and leaf-carved uprights, the shallow case w/two narrow drawers w/line-incised decoration & small knobs & turned corner drops, raised on a slender reeded columnar pedestal on a tripod base w/flared serpentine legs set w/tiny urn finials, on small brass casters, ca. 1860, 16" w., 5' 8" h. (ILLUS.)... **1,650**

Ornate Carved Telephone Stand

Telephone stand, Rococo-Style, carved walnut, a rounded arch-topped telephone compartment w/a shell-carved crest & side scrolls over tiny leaf-carved side drawers, the paneled door carved w/a tall basket of flowers over looping scrolls, the rectangular stand top w/serpentine molded edges over a single deep drawer paneled & scroll-carved w/a large central carved scroll cartouche & arched apron, raised on ornate front cabriole legs carved at the top w/figural putti, slender tapering turned back legs joined w/an arched & scrolled stretcher & serpentine side stretchers, refinished, ca. 1930, 16 x 22", 48" h. (ILLUS.).............................. **2,400**

Arts & Crafts Oak Umbrella Stand

Umbrella stand, Arts & Crafts style, oak, wide tapering board ends w/heart-shaped cut-outs & a narrow flat crest flanking two flat top raised boards joined by four small cross braces forming umbrella compartments, the rectangular base inset w/a long tin liner above a low peaked apron, low arched base cut-out, liner w/medallion mark of Goodyers, refinished, early 20th c., 11 x 30 3/4", 37" h. (ILLUS.) **748**

Washstand, Classical country-style, tiger stripe maple, the nearly square top w/a high backsplash w/stepped, scroll-cut sides & a small quarter round shelf in each corner, the top w/large bowl cut-out & two smaller cut-outs at the back, raised on four ring- and baluster-turned supports above a medial shelf over a shallow drawer, raised on baluster- and knob-turned legs w/knob feet, New England, ca. 1825, old refinish, 16 3/4 x 17", 36 1/2" h. (minor imperfections)... **978**

Classical Marble-topped Washstand

Washstand, Classical style, mahogany, a high arched & scroll-cut backsplash flanked by short tapering side galleries on the rectangular white marble top, the flat apron supported at the front by heavy S-scroll supports & at the back by slender turned columns, a wide medial shelf over a single deep ogee-front drawer, on scrolled shoe feet on original wood casters, refinished, ca. 1840, 18 x 28", 40" h. (ILLUS.).. **1,400**

Washstand, Classical style, walnut & walnut veneer, a rectangular white marble top w/a high scroll-carved three-quarters gallery above a single long drawer w/round brass pulls raised on slender ring-, baluster- and rod-turned supports above a medial shelf w/bowed front on short baluster-turned legs w/knob feet, old refinish, probably Maryland, 1830s (replaced pull, minor imperfections).......... **1,610**

Federal Country-style Washstand

Washstand, Federal country-style, pine, the square top w/a high three-quarters gallery w/shaped sides & a cut-out bowl hole in the center above a narrow apron raised on ring- and baluster-turned supports on blocks flanking a medial shelf raised on baluster- and ring-turned legs w/knob feet, refinished, first half 19th c., 18" sq., 38" h. (ILLUS.) **450**

Federal Washstand with Base Drawer

Washstand, Federal style, mahogany, a high arched backsplash w/rounded sides above the rectangular top over a scalloped valance raised on slender ropetwist supports above a medial shelf over a single narrow drawer, raised on ropetwist legs ending in brass paw feet, original hardware, refinished, ca. 1820, 16 x 20", 34" h. (ILLUS.) **450**

Washstand, Federal style, mahogany & mahogany veneer, corner-style, the high scalloped splashback above a quarter-round top w/a large center bowl cut-out

Federal Corner-style Washstand

flanked by small cut-outs above a narrow scalloped apron, raised on slender square supports above a medial shelf over a curve-fronted drawer w/a scalloped apron, raised on three outswept legs joined by a flattened T-form stretcher, old refinish, ca. 1810, 16 x 22", 40" h. (ILLUS.) **450**

Federal Mahogany Washstand

Washstand, Federal style, mahogany, the high three-quarters gallery w/scalloped, stepped sides above a rectangular top above a single paneled door over a small drawer w/ring pull, ring pulls at the top of the paneled sides, ring- and baluster-turned legs on knob feet, old refinish, ca. 1820, period but perhaps not original hardware, 18 x 22", 38" h. (ILLUS.) **450**

Washstand, late Victorian, mahogany veneer, a long towel rod between tall slender S-scroll uprights over the rectangular top w/a bowed & molded front over a conforming case w/two long drawers over a pair of plain cupboard doors, bowed apron w/carved central scrolls, angled

Simple Late Victorian Washstand

front corners continuing to from short S-scroll legs on casters, original pierced brass hardware, refinished, ca. 1910, 18 x 32", overall 50" h. (ILLUS.) **450**

Fine Golden Oak Washstand

Washstand, Victorian Golden Oak style, the superstructure w/a tall rectangular mirror frame w/arched scroll-carved crest & base enclosing a mirror swiveling between tall S-scroll uprights joined by short towel bars to shorter S-scroll uprights all above a backsplash carved w/scrolls over a rectangular top w/a serpentine front above a long serpentine-front drawer over two long flat drawers all beside a/lower side section w/a rectangular top w/serpentine edges over a paneled, scroll-carved cupboard door, shaped apron on short curved front legs on casters, original pierced brass pulls, original finish, ca. 1900, 22 x 42", 66" h. (ILLUS.) **900**

Renaissance Washstand with Shelf

Washstand, Victorian Renaissance Revival style, rosewood, the rectangular white marble top above a single narrow drawer supported by ring- and knob-turned columns above a medial shelf w/molded edges over a small paneled cupboard door, small turned & tapering feet, original finish, ca. 1875, 16 x 18", 32" h. (ILLUS.) **1,400**

Signed Renaissance Washstand

Washstand, Victorian Renaissance Revival style, walnut & burl walnut, a tall ornate backboard w/a half-round ball-trimmed finial over a large lily-form carving flanked by bold quarter-round arches flanking carved scrolls & raised burl panels centered by a large roundel, the rectangular white marble top w/ovolo corners above a conforming case w/three long burl-veneered drawers w/pairs of leaf-carved pulls & long slender raised keyhole escutcheons, deep molded base w/ovolo front corners mounted w/turned finials, signed "Mead & Co.,

Cincinnati," ca. 1870, refinished, 18 x 36", 44" h. (ILLUS.).............................. **1,000**

Signed Victorian Walnut Washstand

Washstand, Victorian Renaissance Revival style, walnut & burl walnut, the rectangular white marble top w/a serpentine splashback & molded edges, on a case w/a single drawer w/raised burl panels & T-form drop pulls flanked by ring-turned quarter-round corners above blocked & carved edges flanking the single door w/an arched central panel w/a raised fruit-carved central reserve & shaped burl panels at the top corners, deep molded base w/rounded corners, stenciled label in drawer for Mitchell & Rammelsberg Co., Cincinnati, Ohio, refinished, ca. 1875, 16 x 20", 36" h. (ILLUS.)................... **1,900**

Small Renaissance Washstand

Washstand, Victorian Renaissance Revival style, walnut, the square white marble top w/molded edges above a single drawer w/raised oval panel & grape-carved pull flanked by rounded corners over a mid-molding above the tall cupboard door w/arched raised panel flanked by scroll-carved angled corner brackets, deep molded base w/rounded corners, old refinish, ca. 1870, 18" w., 28" h. (ILLUS.).. **1,200**

Delicate Federal Mahogany Workstand

Workstand, Federal style, mahogany & maple veneer, the thin rectangular top w/ovolo corners above a pair of shallow drawers w/maple veneer cross-banding & small round lion head brass pulls, the top of the legs turned w/rings above the slender tapering reeded lower legs ending in swelled feet, old surface, North Shore, Massachusetts, ca. 1800, minor imperfections, overall 15 1/8 x 20 1/2", 29 1/4" h. (ILLUS.)....................................... **6,325**

Classical two-drawer stand, cherry, a rectangular top w/a bowed front above a conforming case w/two dovetailed curved-front burled drawers each w/two turned wood knobs & flanked by burl side panels, on ring- and knob-turned legs w/a long central spiral-turned section, knob & peg feet, old refinishing, early 19th c., 21 1/2 x 21 3/4", 30" h. (piece repair at one top corner, evidence of old tacked-on covering) **880**

Federal country-style one-drawer stand, birch & maple, a square top overhanging an apron w/a single drawer, raised on square tapering legs, New England, early 19th c., refinished, 17 1/2" w., 27 3/4" h. **546**

Federal country-style one-drawer stand, curly maple, one-board rectangular scrubbed top above an apron w/a single drawer w/a tiny original brass knob, raised on slender tapering turned legs w/ring-turned segments at the top & base above the knob-and-peg feet, original finish, early 19th c., 17 1/2 x 22", 28 1/2" h. (small split in rear apron)............................ **1,540**

Federal country-style one-drawer stand, maple, a rectangular top widely overhanging an apron w/a single deep drawer w/a large old round brass pull, on slender square tapering legs, old refinish, New England, ca. 1800-10, 17 3/4 x 18 1/2", 27" h. (minor imperfections)............................ **488**

Federal country-style one-drawer stand, painted pine, the nearly square top overhanging an apron w/a single drawer, raised on slender square tapering legs, old brown & black grained paint, early 19th c., 18 1/4 x 19 3/4", 26" h. (imperfections) **374**

Federal county-style one-drawer stand, painted & decorated pine, the rectangular top overhanging a case w/a single drawer, raised on tall square tapering legs, the top in yellow paint outlined w/black striping above a similarly decorated drawer, old replaced pulls, New England, early 19th c., 16 1/2 x 18 3/4", 27 1/2" h. (surface imperfections) **1,955**

Federal two-drawer stand, tiger stripe maple, the rectangular top above an apron w/two narrow graduated drawers w/opalescent glass pulls, raised on square tapering legs, New England, 1800-10, 15 3/4 x 20", 29 1/2" h. (refinished, minor repairs) **1,955**

Federal Country One-drawer Stand

Federal country-style one-drawer stand, maple & tiger stripe maple, rectangular top overhanging an apron w/a single drawer w/a porcelain pull, on slender ring-, knob- and baluster-turned legs w/knob feet, old refinish, first half 19th c., 18 x 22", 30" h. (ILLUS.) **400**

Federal-Style Two-drawer Stand

Federal-Style two-drawer stand, mahogany, w/ovolo corners above ring-turned stiles flanking two narrow drawers w/small metal pulls, raised on slender tapering reeded legs ending in knob- and peg-feet, refinished, ca. 1920, 16 x 20", 30" h. (ILLUS.) **500**

Stools

Footstool, country-style, painted & upholstered, the rectangular top w/green-fringed shirred wool upholstery w/tan, red & blue foliate & leaf designs on a brown wool ground, over a red & black grain-painted square on simple short carved legs, New England, second quarter 19th c., 9 x 13", 8" h. (losses to textile & fringe) **1,265**

Square Chippendale-Style Footstool

Footstool, Chippendale-Style, mahogany, the rectangular upholstered top on a flat frame w/turned drop pendants in the center of each side, on cabriole legs w/leaf-carved knees & ending in claw-and-ball feet, original finish, late 19th c., 16" w., 15" h. (ILLUS.) **450**

Fine Chippendale-Style Footstool

Footstool, Chippendale-Style, rectangular top w/new upholstery above a narrow gadroon-carved apron & large cabriole legs w/finely scroll-carved knees & ending in claw-and-ball feet, refinished, late 19th c., 14 x 20", 15" h. (ILLUS.) **700**

Classical Footstool with Scrolled Base

Footstool, Classical, mahogany, the deep square upholstered top above a frame raised on double S-scroll side legs centered by a pierced fanned design & decorated w/carved leaves, original finish & worn upholstery, attributed to Boston, ca. 1830, 18" w., 16" h. (ILLUS.) **1,000**

Georgian-Style Rosewood Footstool

Footstool, Georgian-Style, rosewood, the square top w/an upholstered pad above a narrow arched apron w/scroll-and-button carved corners raised on cabriole legs w/scroll feet, original finish, England, second half 19th c., 12" w., 16" h. (ILLUS.)........ **200**

Gustav Stickley Mission Footstool

Footstool, Mission-style (Arts & Crafts movement), oak, the rectangular woven rush top framed by four slender square legs w/single wide flat side stretchers & double narrow end stretchers, branded mark of Gustav Stickley, 15 1/2 x 19 1/2", 17 1/2" h. (ILLUS.).............. **403**

Footstool, Mission-style (Arts & Crafts movement), the rectangular leather-upholstered top continuing down the deep aprons & trimmed w/tack trim, on square legs, decal mark of Quaker Mission Craft, 15 x 18", 16 1/2" h. (new brown leather top).. **104**

Eastlake Lift-top Oak Footstool

Footstool, Victorian Eastlake, oak, the rectangular upholstered top opening to a storage well decorated on the outside w/angular line-incised decoration, on four slender square legs joined by wide rails pierced w/small spindles alternating w/square blocks carved w/scrolls or flowerheads, brass turned-out foot caps, refinished, new upholstery, ca. 1885, 10 x 22", 18" h. (ILLUS.) **350**

All-original Eastlake Footstool

Footstool, Victorian Eastlake, walnut, the deep rectangular upholstered top on a frame w/incised lines & ring-incised corner blocks raised on pairs of large C-scroll uprights centered by two small spindles on shoe feet, the sides joined by a pair of slender upper round stretchers & a lower flat stretcher, original finish & upholstery, ca. 1885, 13 x 18", 17" h. (ILLUS.).. **350**

Unique Renaissance Revival Stool

Footstool, Victorian Renaissance Revival, cast iron, a rectangular upholstered top on the cast-iron frame molded w/stylized scrolls & geometric designs on canted cabriole legs, original gilt surface on metal, cover replaced w/period fabric, ca. 1875, 12 x 18", 12" h. (ILLUS.) **400**

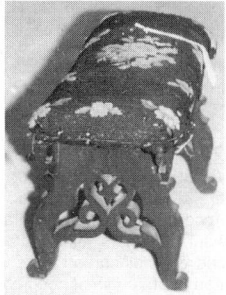

Small Victorian Rococo Footstool

Footstool, Victorian Rococo, a small rectangular upholstered top raised on pierced & scroll-carved bracket legs, old needlepoint fabric, original finish, ca. 1860-70, 8 x 16", 11" h. (ILLUS.) **200**

Rose-carved Rococo Footstool

Footstool, Victorian Rococo, walnut, a deep square upholstered top above a narrow dash-carved band over the serpentine apron carved w/bold rose clusters, demi-cabriole legs w/leaf-carved knees, old refinish, newer upholstery, ca. 1865, 18" w., 15" h. (ILLUS.) **450**

Rococo Footstool with Deep Sides

Footstool, Victorian Rococo, walnut, the deep round upholstered top above a deep apron w/delicate scroll-incised panels alternating w/bold scroll- and fruit-carved panels above each of the carved & pointed short legs, original needlepoint & beadwork upholstery, refinished, ca. 1860-70, 14" d., 16" h. (ILLUS.) **750**

Ornately Carved Rococo Footstool

Footstool, Victorian Rococo, walnut, the rectangular shallow upholstered top above pierced scroll-carved side braces & downswept stretchers joining the ornate pierced & scroll-carved ends, tiny brass button feet, original needlepoint upholstery, original finish, ca. 1860, 10 x 20", 15" h. (ILLUS.) **350**

One of Two Iron Rococo Footstools

Footstools, Victorian Rococo, cast iron, a rectangular upholstered top w/serpentine sides above a conforming cast-iron framework w/pierced sides & ornate cast leafy scroll trim on short scroll legs, frame painted white, new upholstery, ca. 1860, 12 x 16", 10" h., pr. (ILLUS. of one) **500**

Decorative Renaissance Organ Stool

Organ stool, Victorian Renaissance Revival, walnut, round upholstered adjustable seat on a metal screw mechanism above a turned & gilt line-incised pedestal flanked by three angular incised brackets on the tripartite base w/carved paw feet, replaced top upholstery, ca. 1875, 16" d., 20" h. (ILLUS.) **1,400**

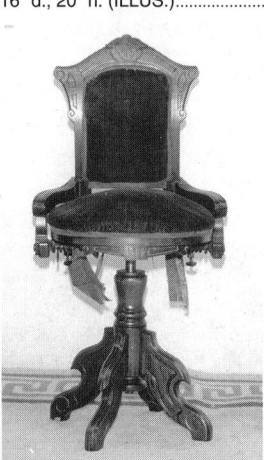

Renaissance Revival Stool with Back

Organ stool, Victorian Renaissance Revival, walnut, the upright back w/an arched & flared carved & burl-paneled crestrail & frame enclosing an upholstered panel, low skirt guards on the round upholstered adjustable seat w/a metal screw mechanism in the center column of the base above four flattened, incised scroll-carved legs, original finish & old upholstery, ca. 1870s, 15 x 18", 34" h. (ILLUS.).. **800**

Rococo Stool Attributed to Belter

Organ stool, Victorian Rococo, carved rosewood, a trilobed upholstered seat on a conforming deep apron ornately carved w/large florals, adjusting on a metal screw mechanism above an acanthus leaf-carved pedestal on a tripod base w/angled curved legs ending in S-scroll feet, original finish & upholstery, attributed to John Belter, New York, New York, ca. 1855, 14" w., 22" h. (ILLUS.) **3,500**

Rococo Organ Stool Attributed to Roux

Organ stool, Victorian Rococo, rosewood, the high upholstered square seat w/a serpentine scroll- and cartouche-carved apron above a metal screw mechanism on the ring-turned center post above a beaded disk over the long downswept S-scroll carved legs, attributed to Alexander Roux, New York, New York, old refinish, 16" w., 20" h. (ILLUS.)............. **2,500**

Rococo Organ Stool with Oval Back

Organ stool, Victorian Rococo, rosewood, the oval upright back w/a pierced & scroll-carved crest continuing down to form the frame for the tufted upholstered panel above a round deep seat over a conforming apron w/a shell-carved front boss, adjusting on a metal screw mechanism on a bold ring-turned pedestal above the four outswept cartouche-carved legs w/scroll feet, original finish, ca. 1860, late upholstery, 16 x 18", 36" h. (ILLUS.) **1,200**

Golden Oak Adjustable Piano Stool

Piano stool, Victorian Golden Oak, the tall gently flared back w/a wide shaped crestrail w/corner scrolls on ring-turned stiles flanking five slender spindles all above the round adjustable seat, the seat platform raised on four ring- and knob-turned canted legs joined by ring-turned stretchers to a center ring-turned post, the legs ending in brass paws w/glass balls, original finish, ca. 1890s, seat 14" d., 36" h. (ILLUS.)...................................... **300**

Piano stool, Federal, mahogany, the round upholstered adjustable seat on a conforming seatrail raised on four tapering reeded & ring-turned legs joined by a flat cross-stretcher centered by a large screw-turned post for adjusting the seat, possibly Massachusetts, ca. 1815-20, 13" d., 20" h. (minor imperfections) **690**

Tables

Rare G. Stickley "Celadine" Tea Table

Arts & Crafts tea table, oak, "Celadine" style, the rounded four-lobed top raised on four slender flat & shaped legs w/small top cut-outs each joined by a through keyed tenon cross-stretcher, Gustave Stickley, Model No. 27 (ILLUS.)..................................... **11,500**

Arts & Crafts telephone table, hardwood, a square top slightly overhanging a narrow apron & a high square open shelf joining the four slender slightly tapering square legs, stained green, 16" w., 30" h. **144**

Unique Baroque Revival Side Table

Baroque Revival side table, walnut, the octagonal top w/a line-inlaid border raised on four tall finely-carved standing egrets resting on figural carved rams' heads on a scalloped cross-form platform w/center finial & raised on curved blocked & reeded feet, original finish, ca. 1920, 20" w., 30" h. (ILLUS.) **2,400**

Carved & Decorated Chinese Table

Chinese work table, painted hardwood, Ming-Style, rectangular top above a front w/a pair of two-panel doors w/the top panel carved w/stylized flowers & the bottom panel w/painted flowers, floral-carved brackets down the sides & a carved apron at the bottom, the sides w/plain panels, original work paint, China, 19th c., 24 x 42", 30" h. (ILLUS.).......... **1,600**

Simple Chinese Work Table

Chinese work table, teak-like wood, Ming-Style, a thick rectangular plank top w/scrolled corner brackets above a case w/a pair of drawers w/bronze pulls above a band of three recessed panels, on square legs joined by high side stretchers, pegged & mortise-and-tenon construction, old rubbed finish, China, 19th c., 18 x 36", 32" h. (ILLUS.) **1,200**

Chippendale Country Tea Table

Chippendale country-style tea table, cherry, the large round top tilting above a birdcage mechanism above the heavy ring- and knob-turned pedestal on a tripod base w/flattened cabriole legs ending in arris pad feet, early reddish brown surface, Connecticut River Valley, late 18th c., imperfections, 35" d., 29 1/2" h. (ILLUS.) **1,265**

Chippendale tea table, mahogany, the wide squared top w/serpentine edges tilting above a turned pedestal w/urn shaping on a tripod base w/cabriole legs ending in arris pad feet, old surface, North Shore, Massachusetts, late 18th c., 33" w., 28 1/2" h. (minor repair to a foot) ... **2,070**

Chippendale tea table, mahogany, the wide squared top w/serpentine edges tilting above a columnar pedestal on a tripod base w/cabriole legs ending in pad feet, Massachusetts, ca. 1770-80, 31" w., 28 1/4" h. (old refinish, minor imperfections) **2,875**

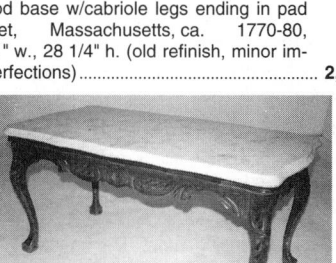

Chippendale-Style Coffee Table

Chippendale-Style coffee table, carved mahogany, the rectangular white marble top w/molded serpentine edges above the leafy scroll-carved apron, raised on cabriole legs w/leaf-carved knees & ending in claw-and-ball feet, original finish, ca. 1920-40, 18 x 32", 18" h. (ILLUS.) **450**

Chippendale-Style Dining Table

Chippendale-Style dining table, mahogany, extension-type, the oval top w/a bold gadrooned edge on an apron supported by large cabriole legs w/ornate scroll-carved knees & claw-and-ball feet, original metal casters, refinished, England, 19th c., w/two wide leaves, 48 x 60", 30" h. (ILLUS.) **1,800**

Fine Chippendale-Style Library Table

Chippendale-Style library table, mahogany, a rectangular top w/a molded edge above a deep scalloped apron carved w/leafy scrolls, cabriole legs w/a lion head carved at each knee above leafy scrolls & ending in paw feet, original finish, late 19th c., 24 x 48", 30" h. (ILLUS.).. **1,800**

Chippendale-Style Inlaid Side Table

Chippendale-Style side table, inlaid mahogany, the round top w/a piecrust rim centered by a large marquetry inlay design of flowers & leaves, the apron carved w/scroll cartouches, raised on slender cabriole legs w/shell-carved knees & ending in paw feet, joined by slender scroll cross-stretchers w/a central urn finial, original finish, ca. 1920s, 20" d., 30" h. (ILLUS.) **800**

Chippendale-Style Oak Side Table

Chippendale-Style side table, oak, the large round top w/a molded edge raised on a baluster-turned & acanthus leaf-carved pedestal on four splayed cabriole legs ending in bold paw feet, refinished, ca. 1900, 22" d., 30" h. (ILLUS.).. **450**

Simple Chippendale-Style Tea Table

Chippendale-Style tea table, mahogany & mahogany veneer, the round top w/a piecrust rim tilting above a slender reeded pedestal on a tripod base w/outswept cabriole legs ending in claw-and-ball feet, original finish, ca. 1920s, 22" d., 30" h. (ILLUS.).. **400**

Chippendale-Style Tea Table

Chippendale-Style tea table, mahogany, stationary octagonal top w/a scalloped & curved low pierced gallery above a curved & scalloped leaf-carved apron, raised on a leaf-carved pedestal on a tripod base w/cabriole legs w/carved knees & ending in raised pad feet, original finish, ca. 1920s, 24" w., 30" h. (ILLUS.) **450**

Fine Chippendale-Style Tea Table

Chippendale-Style tea table, mahogany, the large round top w/a piecrust rim tilting above a baluster- and ring-turned pedestal on a tripod base w/cabriole legs ending in elongated claw-and-ball feet, 24" d., early 20th c. (ILLUS.) **700**

Classical Mahogany Breakfast Table

Classical breakfast table, mahogany & mahogany veneer, a wide rectangular top flanked by two wide drop leaves w/rounded corners, a single long working drawer at one end & a faux drawer at the other, raised on a heavy double-knob turned & acanthus-carved pedestal above four outswept acanthus leaf-carved legs ending in paw feet on casters, original lion head brasses, old refinish, probably New York, ca. 1830-40, imperfections, 26 1/2 x 40 1/2", 28 3/4" h. (ILLUS.).. **920**

Classical Mahogany Console Table

Classical console table, mahogany & mahogany veneer, a rectangular black marble top above a deep ogee apron raised on heavy C-scroll forked supports on a serpentine-fronted platform backed by a rectangular mirror, raised on heavy C-scroll front feet, original finish, ca. 1840, 20 x 38", 34" h. (ILLUS.) **1,600**

Classical country-style breakfast table, painted & decorated, the rectangular top flanked by two hinged rectangular drop leaves above the apron, raised on a heavy square tapering pedestal on a platform base w/incurved sides raised on ball feet on casters, old wood grained painted finish simulating mahogany in red & gold tones, Maine, 1830-40, 19 1/2 x 40 1/4", 29" h. (minor imperfections)............................. **920**

Classical Games Table on Columns

Classical games table, mahogany & mahogany veneer, a rectangular fold-over top w/rounded corners above a concave mahogany veneered apron, raised on two large columnar legs on heavy shoe feet w/scrolled ends & joined by a round cross stretcher, Boston, ca. 1840, refinished, 19 x 38", 30" h. (ILLUS.) **1,600**

Games Table with Fancy Carved Base

Classical games table, mahogany & mahogany veneer, the rectangular fold-over top w/rounded corners above a conforming apron, raised on a turned & acanthus leaf-carved pedestal above four outswept leaf-carved legs ending in paw feet, original finish, ca. 1830-40, 19 x 38", 30" h. (ILLUS.).............................. **1,400**

Quervelle-type Classical Games Table

Classical games table, mahogany, the rectangular fold-over top w/rounded cor-

ners above a rounded apron w/leaf-carved reserves at each corner & at the center of the front, four bold leaf-and-fruit-carved S-scroll supports joined on a platform plinth & centered by a large carved pineapple, raised on four outswept leaf-carved paw feet on original metal casters, original finish, attributed to Anthony Quervelle, Philadelphia, ca. 1830, 24 x 48", 30" h. (ILLUS.) **6,000**

Fine Boston Classical Games Table

Classical games table, mahogany, the rectangular fold-over top w/rounded & reeded edges above a plain apron, raised on a heavy spiral-turned center knob above a deep round platform issuing arched & reeded outswept legs ending in brass paws on casters, Boston, ca. 1820s, old refinish, 19 x 38", 30" h. (ILLUS.) **2,700**

Quervelle-style Classical Pier Table

Classical pier table, mahogany & mahogany veneer, a rectangular white marble top above a flat apron w/a gadrooned border raised at the front on two columns w/brass capitals & base rings & backed by half-round columns flanking a large rectangular mirror w/the original stenciled border all above the lower platform w/a carved gadroon edge, round gadrooned gilt cuffs above the front paw feet, original finish, attributed to Anthony Quervelle of Philadelphia, ca. 1830, 18 x 44", 38" h. (ILLUS.) **3,000**

Classical Revival Center Table

Classical Revival center table, mahogany & mahogany veneer, round top w/a veneered apron, raised on a squared pedestal w/beveled corners above four outswept scroll-carved legs ending in paw feet, refinished, late 19th c., 32" d., 30" h. (ILLUS.) **650**

Large Classical Revival Dining Table

Classical Revival dining table, mahogany, extension-type, the round top w/deep apron raised on a very large bulbous & ring-turned post issuing four large squared outswept scroll-carved legs ending in large paw feet, original finish, w/six leaves, ca. 1890, 56" d., 30" h. (ILLUS.).... **2,400**

Classical Revival Oak Lamp Table

Classical Revival lamp table, oak & quarter-sawn oak veneer, the round top raised on a heavy squared baluster-form pedestal w/a stepped square base resting on a squared platform on C-scroll feet, refinished, ca. 1910, 20" d., 30" h. (ILLUS.) **350**

Classical Revival 1920s Work Table

Classical Revival work table, mahogany, a rectangular top w/ovolo corners above a case w/ring-turned projecting corners flanking three shallow drawers w/turned wood knobs, raised on a double lyre-form base on outswept legs w/paw feet, original finish, ca. 1920s, 16 x 22", 30" h. (ILLUS.) **700**

Classical Mahogany Work Table

Classical work table, mahogany, a rectangular top above a case w/three long graduated drawers w/replaced round brass pulls, on ring-turned & reeded legs on turned feet w/brass-cap casters, refinished, ca. 1830s, 16 x 22", 30" h. (ILLUS.) **750**

Large Classical Work Table

Classical work table, mahogany & mahogany veneer, the rectangular top w/rounded corners above a deep case w/three round-fronted drawers w/ring pulls flanked by rounded front corners, raised on a short pedestal & square plinth above a long platform w/incurved sides raised on outswept C-scroll legs on casters, refinished, ca. 1830s, 16 x 22", 30" h. (ILLUS.) 1,000

Classical Three-drawer Work Table

Classical work table, mahogany, the rectangular top above a deep case w/a projecting drawer above two recessed drawers flanked by half-round ring-turned columns w/acanthus carving, on ring-turned & spiral-turned legs ending in small knob feet, original brasses, refinished, ca. 1830, 16 x 18", 30" h. (ILLUS.) 700

Classical-Style Work Table

Classical-Style work table, mahogany & mahogany veneer, the square top w/gadroon-carved edges flanked by wide drop leaves w/similarly carved edges above a case w/a pair of slightly rounded drawers w/small brass knobs flanked by leaf-carved panels, raised on a turned, tapering leaf-carved pedestal raised on four outswept legs w/leaf-carved inner tips & paw-carved feet, original finish, ca. 1890s, 16" w. closed, 30" h. (ILLUS.) 750

Classical-Style Work Table

Classical-Style work table, mahogany, the square top flanked by wide hinged drop leaves above the deep case w/three drawers w/floral-carved pulls flanked by acanthus leaf & rod-turned pilasters, raised on an acanthus leaf-carved pedestal on a cross-form platform raised on paw feet, original finish, ca. 1920s, 16" sq. plus leaves, 30" h. (ILLUS.) 850

Colonial Revival Mahogany End Table

Colonial Revival end table, mahogany & mahogany veneer, a rectangular top w/molded edges & carved projecting corner stiles flanking a bow-front case w/three narrow graduated drawers w/ornate brass pulls, raised on simple cabriole legs w/leaf-carved knees ending in peg feet, early 20th c., 15 x 22", 30" h. (ILLUS.) 800

Colonial Revival Oak Lamp Table

Colonial Revival lamp table, oak, a four-lobed top overhanging a deep apron w/arched base raised on four ring-turned reeded legs joined by a medial four-lobed shelf, on baluster- and knob-turned feet, original finish, ca. 1890s, 20" w., 30" h. (ILLUS.) 400

Colonial Revival Oak Library Table

Colonial Revival library table, oak, the rectangular top w/rounded corners above an apron w/a single long drawer above cabriole legs ending in paw feet joined by a lower medial shelf w/incurved sides, ca. 1900, refinished, replaced hardware, 26 x 48", 30" h. (ILLUS.) 500

Square Oak Extension Dining Table

Early 20th century dining table, oak, expandable-type, the wide square top divided at the center & raised on a heavy ring-turned divided column surrounded by four smaller ring- and baluster-turned columns resting on knobs & issuing heavy outswept legs ending in paw feet on casters, w/four leaves, original finish, ca. 1900, 48" w., 30" h. (ILLUS.) 1,200

Early 20th Century Oak Dining Table

Early 20th century dining table, quarter-sawn oak, round top above a plain apron, raised on a heavy turned pedestal w/four projecting heavy scroll legs, on casters, refinished, ca. 1910, 48" d., 30" h. (ILLUS.) 1,200

Early American country-style work table, painted pine & maple, a wide long two-board scrubbed top w/breadboard ends overhanging a red-painted apron on block and turned columnar legs ending in casters, original red paint, New England, 19th c., 31 3/4 x 72 14", 28 1/2" h. 2,185

Early American tavern table, painted, a wide rectangular top widely overhanging the apron raised on four slender baluster- and ring-turned legs joined by worn box stretchers, flattened knob feet, old black repaint, possibly Connecticut, second half 18th c. (imperfections) 4,025

Early American tavern table, painted cherry, oval top overhanging a deep apron raised on four ring- and bobbin-turned legs joined by box stretchers, on small turned feet, repainted orange, New England, 18th c., 21 x 27 1/4", 25" h. (imperfections) 3,680

Early American work table, cherry, a rectangular three-board pin top w/breadboard ends & applied moldings above the apron w/a long deep dovetailed drawer w/divided interior & original shaped pull, old finish, on square tapering legs, Pennsylvania, early, 36 1/4 x 55", 29" h. (edge chips on base, old insect damage on interior aprons, small old top patch) 1,265

Federal Mahogany Breakfast Table

Federal breakfast table, mahogany & mahogany veneer, a rectangular top flanked by two wide drop leaves w/rounded corners, recessed veneered panels on the apron, on ring-turned & reeded tapering legs w/ball feet, old refinish, Massachusetts or New Hampshire area, 1815-20, minor surface mars on top, closed 20 1/4 x 38 1/2", 28 1/4" h. (ILLUS.) 805

Federal breakfast table, mahogany & mahogany veneer, rectangular top flanked by two wide drop leaves w/rounded corners, flat recessed paneled & veneered apron raised on ring-turned & reeded legs ending in ball feet, old refinish, Massachusetts or New Hampshire area, 1815-20, open 38 1/2 x 50 3/4", 28 1/4" h. (minor surface mars on top) 805

Federal card table, mahogany & bird's-eye maple veneer, the rectangular hinged top leaf w/gently arched front folding over a conforming top w/both edged in crossbanded veneers above a three-panel apron w/a central inlaid oval patera flanked by rectangular inlaid dies, on slender tapering reeded & ring-turned legs ending in turned peg feet, old color, Boston area, 1790-1810, open 17 5/8 x 37 1/2", 31" h. (imperfections) **7,475**

Federal card table, mahogany & mahogany veneer, a rectangular hinged top w/wide notched corners folding over a conforming top on the conforming apron w/a central oval inlay, on square tapering string-inlaid legs topped by rectangular inlaid dies & ending in double-tapering square feet w/cuff inlays, Boston, ca. 1800, closed 17 1/2 x 36", 29 1/2" h. (old refinish, minor surface imperfections) **6,900**

Federal country-style card table, painted birch & pine, the rectangular fold-over top above a deep apron w/a single long drawer w/simple turned wood knob, on tall slender square tapering legs, original red paint, New Hampshire or northeastern Massachusetts, ca. 1800-10, 17 1/2 x 35 1/2", 28 3/4" h. (imperfections) **1,495**

Country Federal Pembroke Table

Federal country-style Pembroke table, inlaid cherry, a rectangular top flanked by narrow drop leaves w/wide notched corners, the apron w/inlaid banding raised on slender square tapering legs, refinished, probably Connecticut River Valley, early 19th c., minor restoration, 18 x 36 1/4", 28 1/2" h. (ILLUS.) **1,840**

Federal country-style work table, maple, the square top overhanging a deep apron

Federal Country-style Work Table

w/two deep drawers w/original fiery opalescent lacy glass pulls, paneled sides, raised on ring-, knob- and spiral-turned legs w/knob & peg feet, old refinish, ca. 1840, 18" sq., 30" h. (ILLUS.) **450**

Fine Boston Federal Games Table

Federal games table, mahogany & flame birch veneer, the fold-over top w/boldly scalloped serpentine edges on a conforming skirt veneered w/flame birch above rosewood veneer banding, raised on a turned & reeded four-pillar standard

Federal Revival Dining Table

on a rectangular platform w/beaded edges supported by four outswept legs carved & applied w/leafage & teardrops & ending in brass paw feet on casters, Boston area, 1815-25, some sun bleaching, 19 1/2 x 36 1/2", 28 1/2" h. (ILLUS.) **4,025**

Federal Pembroke table, inlaid mahogany, the rectangular top w/rounded molded ends flanked by two half-round drop leaves above the conforming apron w/a working drawer at one end & a faux drawer at the other end each outlined w/string inlay, on square tapering legs ending in cuffed square feet, old refinish, original bail brasses, New England, late 18th c., open 31 1/2 x 38 1/4", 28" h. **5,750**

Federal Revival dining table, mahogany, the rectangular top w/rounded corners raised on two ring- and-baluster-turned pedestal above tripod bases w/outswept legs, refinished, early 20th c., 36 x 72", 30" h. (ILLUS., bottom previous page) **600**

Fancy Federal Revival Games Table

Federal Revival games table, inlaid rosewood, mahogany & maple, the fold-over rectangular top inlaid w/a central checkerboard design flanked by inlaid floral panels, turning to open above an apron inlaid w/banded inlay, on tall square tapering legs w/line inlay, original finish, early 20th c., 18 x 36", 30" h. (ILLUS.) **750**

Federal Revival Mahogany Side Table

Federal Revival side table, mahogany, the rectangular top flanked by drop leaves w/notched, rounded edges, the apron

w/a single end drawer w/brass bail pulls flanked by reeded blocks above curved brackets, raised on slender tapering ring-turned & reeded legs ending in tall curved brass feet, original finish, late 19th c., open 28 x 40", 30" h. (ILLUS.) **750**

Lovely Federal Serving Table

Federal serving table, mahogany & bird's-eye maple veneer, the rectangular top w/a bowed front ending in blocked ends above a single bird's-eye maple veneered long drawer outlined in crossbanded mahogany veneer, raised on ring-turned & reeded tall slender tapering legs ending in swelled peg feet, replaced brass pulls, refinished, probably New Hampshire, 1795-1805, imperfections, 18 1/4 x 27", 29 1/8" h. (ILLUS.) **9,200**

Federal sewing table, mahogany & mahogany veneer, a rectangular top w/ovolo corners & gently bowed front w/reeded edge above a short case w/two narrow bowed drawers w/two simple turned wood knobs & a bag frame suspending a pleated fabric work bag, the top ovolo corners above slender reeded & ring-turned legs ending in original metal casters, old refinish, Salem, Massachusetts, 1800-10, 15 7/8 x 19 5/8", 28 5/8" h. (bag replaced, minor imperfections) **9,200**

Delicate Federal Work Table

Federal work table, mahogany, a rectangular top slightly overhanging a case w/two cockbeaded narrow drawers w/turned wooden knobs, raised on slender tapering ring- and baluster-turned legs w/knob feet, old refinish, northern New England, early 19th c., minor imperfections, 15 3/4 x 18", 28 1/4" h. (ILLUS.) **2,415**

Delicate Federal-Style Side Table

Federal-Style side table, mahogany & mahogany veneer, the delicate superstructure w/a narrow rectangular top w/low serpentine gallery raised on end crossform supports & a solid back w/fine crock-grain veneer above the small rectangular top w/molded edges above a case w/a pair of cross-banded drawers over a long drawer all w/small round brass pulls, the case w/bail end handles, raised on ring-turned & reeded slender legs w/tapering outswept feet, original finish, ca. 1910, 15 x 22", 42" h. (ILLUS.)..... **650**

Fine Georgian-Style Dining Table

Georgian-Style dining table, mahogany, extension-type, the large oval table w/a gadrooned edge above four large cabriole legs w/bold leaf-carved knees & ending in large claw-and-ball feet, England, mid-19th c., original finish, opened &

closed by means of a spiral rod, 48 x 72", 30" h. (ILLUS.).. **1,500**

Hutch (or chair) table, cherry, the large oval top tilting above a deep compartment w/a hinged top, shaped lower sides supported on heavy shoe feet, New England, second half 18th c., old refinish, 35 x 40 1/4", 27" h. (alterations).................. **4,025**

Hutch (or chair) table, country-style, painted pine, rectangular three-board top w/rounded corners, pegs hold top to base, rectangular base w/deep apron forming a lift-lid compartment seat, bootjack ends, old dry red surface, early, 35 x 62 1/2", 30 3/4" h. **2,970**

Early Painted Hutch Table

Hutch (or chair) table, early American, painted pine, the large round top tilting above tapering square uprights over the wide plank seat on square legs joined by slender square stretchers, New England, late 18th c., refinished base, repairs, 49 1/2" d., 26 1/2" h. (ILLUS.) **3,738**

Country Pine Hutch Table

Hutch (or chair) table, early American, pine, the wide rectangular top tilting above shaped end uprights above a wide plank seat, original finish, late 19th c., 48 x 56", 29" h. (ILLUS.) **650**

Long Jacobean Revival Dining Table

Jacobean Revival dining table, mahogany, refectory-style, the rectangular top w/end leaves that drop down & tuck under the top, the apron w/a notched band & scrolled corner brackets, raised on large bulbous ring-turned legs on blocks above bun feet, joined by a long flattened stretcher w/U-form ends, original finish, early 20th c., open 48 x 100", 30" h. (ILLUS., bottom previous page) **750**

Early Jacobean Revival Sofa Table

Jacobean Revival sofa table, mahogany veneer, the long rectangular top above a spoon-carved apron raised on a squared blocked pedestal above a trestle base w/four-part shoe feet, early 20th c., 30 x 72", 30" h. (ILLUS.)................................ **950**

Fine Late Victorian Library Table

Late Victorian library table, mahogany, the rectangular top w/a molded gadroon-carved border above an apron of large ball drops joined by slender spiral-turned rails, raised on heavy canted spiral-twist legs ending in brass claw-and-ball feet & joined by spiral-turned end stretchers & double spiral-turned cross stretchers, original dark finish, late 19th c., 24 x 48", 30" h. (ILLUS.)... **600**

Late Victorian Oak Lobed Table

Late Victorian parlor table, oak, the four-lobed top raised on four canted bobbin-turned legs joined by a square medial shelf, original finish, ca. 1900, 20" w., 30" h. (ILLUS.) **300**

Late Victorian Oak Parlor Table

Late Victorian parlor table, quarter-sawn oak, a square top w/carved corners raised on four canted ring-turned & reeded legs w/bulbous center knobs joined by aprons w/a central palmette leaf carved panel flanked by ring-turned rails & a squared, shaped medial shelf joined to the legs w/iron scrolled mounts, the legs ending in brass claw-and-ball feet w/glass balls, original finish, ca. 1900, 20" w., 30" h. (ILLUS.).................................... **400**

Louis XV-Style Inlaid Side Table

Louis XV-Style side table, marquetry-inlaid mahogany, the oval top w/low scroll-carved end crests, decorated around the top w/delicate floral & scroll marquetry, the serpentine apron carved w/shallow florals, raised on simple cabriole legs w/carved knees & ending in scroll & peg feet, original finish, ca. 1920s, 16 x 24", 30" h. (ILLUS.) **500**

Fancy Louis XVI-Style Coffee Table

Louis XVI-Style coffee table, inlaid mahogany & mixed woods, the rectangular top w/an ornate inlaid diamond design w/inlaid borders & a low pierced brass gallery & edging w/end handles, raised on four square outswept S-scroll legs joined by a slender incurved cross-stretcher, brass cap casters, refinished, ca. 1920s, 20 x 30", 18" h. (ILLUS.) **400**

Louis XVI-Style Curio Table

Louis XVI-Style curio table, giltwood, the oval top w/a flat rim enclosing glass & opening to a shallow display compartment, a line-incised & beaded apron w/florette-carved blocks above the slender reeded tapering legs w/peg feet joined by a curved cross stretcher w/a central medallion, original paint, ca. 1920s, 18 x 34", 30" h. (ILLUS.) **600**

Mission-style (Arts & Crafts movement) dining table, oak, split-pedestal type, round divided top raised on four heavy square legs joined to a central square pedestal w/mortised arched stretchers, original finish & condition, branded mark of Gustav Stickley, w/three leaves, 48" d., 28 1/2" h. (two boards cupped slightly & need regluing, spots of wear, typical finish loss to base) **7,475**

Mission-style (Arts & Crafts movement) director's table, large rectangular top widely overhanging a deep apron & trestle base w/heavy square & slightly canted legs w/pegged construction on long shoe feet, good new finish, unmarked Gustav Stickley, Model No. 631, 48 1/4 x 96", 29 1/4" h. (separations in top)................... **11,500**

Unusual Mission Oak Dressing Table

Mission-style (Arts & Crafts movement) dressing table, oak, the tall superstructure composed of an upright rectangular mirror flanked by two swing-out rectangular mirrors above the rectangular top slightly overhanging a case w/a long central drawer above a kneehole opening flanked by pairs of small drawers all w/wooden knobs, raised on slender square legs joined by flat stretchers on three sides, Quaint decal mark of Stickley Brothers, Model No. 9035, original finish w/staining on top, early 20th c., 20 x 44", overall 55" h. (ILLUS.) **2,185**

Unusual Mission Oak Lamp Table

Mission-style (Arts & Crafts movement) lamp table, oak, the square top w/rounded corners on cross-stretchers above the flat gently tapering sides w/large oblong cut-outs enclosing a round lower shelf, notched base apron, good refinished condition, unmarked Limbert Furniture Co., 20" w., 29 1/2" h. (ILLUS.) **4,313**

Mission-style (Arts & Crafts movement) library table, oak, the long oval top overhanging wide cross-braces mortised through four flat gently tapering legs centered by an oval medial shelf over boxed cross stretchers w/slat cut-outs, original finish, branded Limbert mark, 36 1/4 x 47 1/2", 28 1/2" h. (one inch cut off legs) **7,475**

L. & J.G. Stickley Signed Library Table

Mission-style (Arts & Crafts movement) library table, quarter sawn oak, the rectangular top widely overhanging an apron centered by a long drawer w/copper pull, on heavy square legs joined by flat end stretchers & a medial shelf, L. & J.G. Stickley label, pegged construction, original worn finish, early 20th c., 30 x 48", 30" h. (ILLUS.)... **950**

Mission-style (Arts & Crafts movement) side table, oak, "mousehole" style trestle-type, a wide rectangular top overhanging the trestle base w/a sideways stretcher mortised through the plank sides w/keyed through-tenons & round cut-out openings at the bottom, original finish on base, top refinished, branded mark of L. & J.G. Stickley, 32 x 48", 28 3/4" h. **2,645**

L. & J.G. Stickley Mission Tea Table

Mission-style (Arts & Crafts movement) tea table, oak, the round top on square legs joined by an inset round lower shelf on cross-stretchers, good original finish & condition w/some wear on top, L. & J.G. Stickley Model No. 608, Handcraft mark, 24" d., 23 3/4" h. (ILLUS.) **4,025**

Unique Stacked Book End Table

Modern-style end table, painted gesso on wood, carved to resemble a stack of colorful large books set at various angles, ca. 1950s-60s, 16" w., 24" h. (ILLUS.)... **350**

Modernist Design Dressing Table

Modernist dressing table & stool, steel, the table w/a round mirror raised on slender scroll supports above a scrolled crest over the rectangular clear glass top, bowed scrolled metal legs w/arched openings, short round stool w/straight bar round frame w/cushion seat & low back w/openwork bar crestrail, original surface, ca. 1950s, table 16 x 40", 52" h., 2 pcs. (ILLUS.).. **250**

Country Queen Anne Dressing Table

Queen Anne country-style dressing table, hard pine, the rectangular top above an apron w/a pair of deep drawers centering a small drawer all w/replaced teardrop pulls, slightly serpentine apron, on simple cabriole legs ending in square pad feet, old refinish, possibly New Jersey, ca. 1740-60, imperfections, 21 x 29 1/2", 27 1/2" h. (ILLUS.) **4,025**

Small Queen Anne Dining Table

Queen Anne dining table, maple, a rectangular top w/rounded ends flanked by half-round drop leaves above a deep apron w/serpentine ends, cabriole legs ending in pad feet on casters, two legs form swing-out supports, old refinish, New England, 18th c., repairs, open 44 3/4 x 45", 28" h. (ILLUS.) **3,738**

Queen Anne dining table, sycamore, a narrow rectangular top w/curved ends flanked by wide half-round drop leaves above the shaped apron, raised on nearly straight cabriole legs ending in pad feet, old refinish, New England, ca. 1740-60, open 38 x 38", 27 1/4" h. (imperfections) **3,335**

Rare Queen Anne Dressing Table

Queen Anne dressing table, tiger stripe maple, rectangular top w/molded edges & notched corners above a case w/a long drawer over a pair of deep square drawers flanking a shallower central drawer above a scalloped & scroll-cut apron, butterfly pulls & keyhole escutcheons, cabriole legs ending in paneled pad feet, old refinish, replaced brasses, Delaware Valley, 1710-20, repairs, 20 x 35", 28" h. (ILLUS.) **20,700**

Queen Anne dressing table, walnut, a rectangular top w/molded edges overhanging a deep case w/a single long,

narrow drawer w/butterfly pulls & a keyhole escutcheon above a row of three deep drawers w/the central one carved w/an arched panel, valanced front apron w/two drops, cabriole legs ending in pad feet on platforms, old replaced brasses, old refinish, mid-18th c., 17 x 30 1/8", 30 3/4" h. (top reset, other imperfections & restoration)... **14,950**

Queen Anne tea table, mahogany, a rectangular tray-top w/molded edges above the flat sides over shallow serpentine aprons raised on slender nearly straight cabriole legs ending in raised pad feet, old refinish, 18th c., 19 1/8 x 28 1/4", 27 3/4" h. (repairs).. **6,325**

Queen Anne-Style Small Lamp Table

Queen Anne-Style lamp table, mahogany & mahogany veneer, a square top above a case w/two shallow drawers over two small square drawers flanking an arched opening, on simple cabriole legs ending in pad feet, original finish, ca. 1920s, 16" w., 30" h. (ILLUS.) **350**

Fine Rococo Revival Coffee Table

Rococo Revival coffee table, walnut, the rectangular top inset w/marble & trimmed w/a gadroon-carved border above a serpentine scroll-carved apron raised on cabriole legs w/large grape cluster-carved knees & scroll feet, joined by a serpentine cross-stretcher centered by a carved berry cluster, refinished, early 20th c., 18 x 30", 18" h. (ILLUS. bottom previous page).. **1,200**

Ornate European Console Table

Rococo-Style console table, giltwood, a large squared mirror w/a double-arch top within a narrow ribbon-twist framework w/high ribbon loop crests, resting on a D-form white marble top w/molded edge resting on a narrow apron supported by a single large winged caryatid tapering to a cabriole leg w/scroll foot, Europe, mid-19th c., 16 x 40", 6' 8" h. (ILLUS.).............. **2,400**

Lovely Rococo-Style Dressing Table

Rococo-Style dressing table, mahogany & mahogany veneer, the superstructure w/a tall oblong mirror frame mounted at the top center w/a small oval porcelain plaque & surrounding a beveled mirror swiveling between scrolled uprights resting on stacks of two small handkerchief drawers on the rectangular top above a long bow-fronted drawer w/oval painted porcelain plaques at the brass pulls & centered by a small oval mirror, a serpentine & scroll-carved apron, on simple cabriole legs w/carved knees & feet, refinished, ca. 1900, 22 x 42", overall 64" h. (ILLUS.).. **1,000**

Unusual Italian Rococo-Style Table

Rococo-Style side table, carved fruitwood, the rectangular dished top w/serpentine sides & ornate scroll-carved ends over a scroll-carved apron, bold swag- and leaf-carved cabriole legs each headed by a figural putto head & tapering inward to support a small turtle-top medial shelf, inwardly scrolled feet, original finish, Italy, late 19th c., 17 x 26", 30" h. (ILLUS.)............. **900**

Ornate Rococo-Style Oak Side Table

Rococo-Style side table, oak, the square top w/molded serpentine edges above an ornately scroll-carved apron on slender cabriole legs w/boldly scroll-carved knees & ending in tiny scroll feet on pegs, original finish, late 19th c., 16" w., 30" h. (ILLUS.).. **650**

Rococo-Style side table, painted pine, a wide scrubbed rectangular top raised on red-painted cross-legs joined by a long high flat stretcher, old surface, New England, early 19th c., 29 x 60", 28" h. (minor surface imperfections).. **4,600**

Tavern table, painted pine, the large rectangular scrubbed pine top w/breadboard ends overhangs a deep apron w/a single drawer above black baluster- and ring-turned legs joined by square box stretchers, on turned shaded feet, the base w/early red paint, New England, 18th c., 28 1/4 x 51 1/4", 26" h. (drawer pulls missing, imperfections)................................. **5,175**

Victorian Aesthetic Movement dining table, walnut, extension-type, the wide square top w/molded edges & rounded corners above a deep conforming apron w/line-incised burl corner panels & a repeating wave-like carved border design, raised on a hexagonal central pedestal & four heavy turned columns each joined by a high scallop- & scroll-carved bracket topped by a large roundel, heavy arched square feet w/carved sunflowers & incised geometric lines, refinished, ca. 1885, w/six leaves, 52" w., 30" h. (ILLUS. bottom of page)....... **3,800**

Decorative Aesthetic Movement Table

Victorian Aesthetic Movement parlor table, carved mahogany, the rectangular top slightly overhanging a deep apron pierce-carved w/a continuous band of large wheel-form devices, raised on trumpet- and ring-turned supports above a wide medial shelf w/pairs of small turned spindles above oval medallions pierce-carved w/geometric designs, on short legs w/claw-and-ball feet on casters, original finish, ca. 1885, 20 x 40", 30" h. (ILLUS.)... **950**

Victorian Aesthetic Movement parlor table, walnut & burl walnut, a rectangular

Marble-topped Aesthetic Parlor Table

pink marble top above a deep blocked apron w/leaf-carved panels flanking a central burl panel over a scroll-cut drop, raised on four curved flat supports & a slender central turned post all joined by wide cross-stretchers w/each section pierce-carved w/a large scrolled quatrefoil between incised rails, line-incised outswept scroll legs on casters, refinished, ca. 1885, 22 x 32", 30" h. (ILLUS.)... **1,400**

Asymmetrical Aesthetic Table

Unique Aesthetic Carved Dining Table

Victorian Aesthetic Movement parlor table, walnut & burl walnut, rectangular top w/molded edge above an apron w/a long drawer w/incised floral bands & a brass pull flanked by pierced corner brackets above an asymmetrical lower section w/medial shelf flanked by brass rods above a shallow carved drawer w/brass pull beside a high rounded arch opening w/a small stick-and-ball front gallery & a high end rail above pierce-carved leaves over an arched spindled opening, a long bottom shelf above a narrow shaped apron, on brass claw-and-ball feet, refinished, ca. 1885, 20 x 40", 30" h. (ILLUS. previous page)........ **800**

Carved Baroque-Style Console Table

Victorian Baroque Revival console table, quarter-sawn oak, the rectangular top w/molded edge raised on an apron w/a long deep drawer w/two leafy scroll-carved rectangular panels flanking a large central shield device w/a rampant lion, raised on four heavy square scale-carved legs on end stretchers joined by a stretcher shelf, front scroll feet, original finish, ca. 1880, 18 x 44", 38" h. (ILLUS.)..... **950**

Victorian Baroque Revival Dining Table

Victorian Baroque Revival dining table, oak, expandable, the divided round top w/a deep apron decorated w/applied leaf carving & a beaded lower edge raised on five heavy ring-turned & tapering block supports w/carved leafy scroll decoration raised on a heavy H-form flattened stretcher w/arched & scroll-carved crests, each corner resting on a heavy carved paw foot, original finish, ca. 1895, w/five leaves, 48" d., 30" h. (ILLUS.).......... **3,000**

Victorian Baroque Revival library table, carved oak, the rectangular top w/angled corners & stepped edges above a deep gadroon-carved apron w/the corners carved w/lion masks w/brass rings above drop blocks w/turned drop finials, triple-

Baroque Revival Library Table

arch ends on lower apron raised on pairs of heavy turned & tapering legs w/ga-drooned tops, legs resting on a heavy squared leaf-carved trestle base w/out-swept dolphin-carved feet at the ends, late 19th c., original finish, 22 x 42", 30" h. (ILLUS.) **1,000**

Elaborately Carved Oak Library Table

Victorian Baroque Revival library table, quarter-sawn oak, the wide rectangular top w/chamfered corners decorated around the border w/a wide leafy scroll band & slash-carved edge above the deep apron w/the long sides carved w/two panels each w/a grotesque mask framed by leafy scrolls, florette-carved corner blocks, raised on large nude figur-al caryatid supports over lion-form legs ending in paws, the legs joined by end stretchers connected by a wide medial shelf w/a slash-cut border, refinished, at-tributed to R.S. Horner, New York City, ca. 1880s, 30 x 44", 36" h. (ILLUS.) **10,000**

Baroque Table with Carved Griffins

Victorian Baroque-Style dining table, oak, extension-type, the wide round top above a deep apron carved w/a continu-ous band of scrolled leaves raised on four reeded central columns below heavy square forked brackets arching over large boldly carved figural winged griffins, on a raised cross-stretcher w/shoe feet & a central turned drop pendant above an acorn-form center finial, refinished, last quarter 19th c., w/six leaves, 60" d., 30" h. (ILLUS.).. **7,500**

Eastlake Country-style Oak Table

Victorian Eastlake country-style parlor table, oak, a rectangular top w/molded edges above an apron w/wide angled fan-carved corners flanked by angular corner brackets above reeded block-, knob- and ring-turned legs joined by a medial shelf, refinished, ca. 1890, 20 x 36", 30" h. (ILLUS.)................................ **400**

Eastlake Marble-topped Parlor Table

Victorian Eastlake parlor table, walnut, the white rectangular molded top w/molded edges above a flat apron w/incised bands of flowerheads & angled carved drop corners, raised on four flat scallop-carved & line-incised outswept legs joined by short flat double stretchers to a ring-turned central post, on casters, refinished, ca. 1880, 20 x 30", 30" h. (ILLUS.)... **600**

Victorian Elizabethan Revival dressing table, rosewood, the large cartouche-shaped mirror frame enclosing a conforming mirror & swiveling between figural caryatid-carved uprights above a low pierced Gothic arch back gallery on the rectangular white marble top w/molded serpentine sides, the serpentine apron w/a single long drawer w/central small carved shell & flanked by small corner

Rare Elizabethan Revival Table

drops, raised at each end by pairs of spiral-twist legs on arched, scroll-cut shoe feet joined by a spiral-turned cross-stretcher, original finish, on metal casters, ca. 1855, 18 x 34", overall 56" h. (ILLUS.)... **3,000**

Large Square Oak Dining Table

Victorian Golden Oak dining table, oak, extension-type, wide square top above a deep concave apron raised on four heavy reeded knob-and-baluster-turned legs, w/four leaves, refinished, ca. 1900, 52" w., 30" h. (ILLUS.)................................ **1,100**

Oak Dining Table with Dolphins

Victorian Golden Oak dining table, quarter-sawn oak, expandable, the divided square top over a deep flat apron w/incised bands & carved scrolls at each corner, raised on four heavy ring-, reeded baluster- and block-turned legs & a pair of slender ring- and baluster-turned inner supports, the legs joined by heavy carved stretchers topped by a high rounded panel flanked by carved figural dolphins, refinished, w/six leaves, ca. 1910, 54" w. closed, 30" h. (ILLUS.) **3,300**

Scroll-carved Oak Library Table

Victorian Golden Oak library table, the rectangular top w/slightly serpentine edges carved around the border w/a wide band of leafy scrolls, the serpentine apron w/a single long drawer further carved w/scrolls & spade-form pulls, raised on spiral-twist legs above paw feet joined by spiral-twist stretchers, refinished, ca. 1890, 24 x 48", 30" h. (ILLUS.) **850**

Golden Oak Square Side Table

Victorian Golden Oak side table, the square top w/a slightly serpentine edge above a narrow apron, raised on four slightly canted sausage-turned legs joined by a squared serpentine medial rail & ending in brass claw & glass ball feet, original finish, ca. 1900, 22" w., 30" h. (ILLUS.) **300**

Victorian Dining Table with Ornate Legs

Victorian Renaissance Revival dining table, mahogany, expandable, the round divided top w/a deep apron carved w/scroll trim, raised on a heavy octagonal split pedestal w/half-round knob-turned spindles on panels alternating w/heavy S-scroll outswept legs carved w/beads, panels & roundels, on casters, original finish, w/six leaves, ca. 1875, 48" d., 30" h. (ILLUS.) **1,800-2,000**

Renaissance Revival Dining Table

Victorian Renaissance Revival dining table, walnut & burl walnut, expandable, the divided square top w/rounded corners above a deep apron w/burl trim & burl end panels, raised on a heavy octagonal central post w/burl trim surrounded by four heavy scroll-cut outswept legs w/burl roundels & panels, on casters, refinished, closed 50" w., 30" h. (ILLUS.) **3,500**

Victorian Tilt-top Games Table

Victorian Renaissance Revival games table, walnut, burl walnut & maple, the rounded dished top w/a wide molded border around walnut burl panels centered by a diamond-shaped inlaid checkerboard, tilting & pivoting above a slender turned pedestal on a tripod base w/outswept scroll-cut legs mounted w/roundels, ca. 1875, refinished, 22" d., 30" h. (ILLUS.) **450**

Renaissance Revival Library Table

Victorian Renaissance Revival library table, walnut & burl walnut, partner's-style, the rectangular leather-covered top w/rounded ends & blocked corners above a deep burl-trimmed apron w/pairs of drawers on each side separated by blocks, the wide end supports ornately pierce-carved w/scrolls enclosing pairs of palmette leaves above the blocked shoe feet joined by a rectangular cross-stretcher centered by carved leafy scrolls & a turned finial, on casters, refinished, ca. 1875, 28 x 52", 30" h. (ILLUS.) **1,800**

Inlaid Renaissance Revival Table

Victorian Renaissance Revival parlor table, inlaid & burl walnut, the rectangular top w/pointed ends formed by a wide raised molding enclosing a top surface ornately inlaid w/a central rectangular panel w/flowers flanked by ornate scroll clusters, the deep apron w/raised burl panels & corner blocks raised on forked side supports on reeded, turned & tapering legs & angular, incurved end supports all joined by a cross-stretcher centered by a turned finial, on original porcelain casters, original finish, ca. 1875, 22 x 36", 30" h. (ILLUS.) **1,500**

Ornate Renaissance Revival Table

Victorian Renaissance Revival parlor table, inlaid, gilt-incised & ebonized rosewood, the rectangular top w/wide rounded ends centered by an oblong satinwood-inlaid floral reserve surrounded by a wide band of inlaid burl, the raised molded edges w/an ebonized band raised on a conforming apron w/gilt line-incised central panels, raised on four knob- and ring-turned reeded & ebonized tapering legs joined by a flattened trestle-form stretcher w/gilt line incising & centered by an ebonized & gilt-trimmed carved central urn finial, original brass casters, original finish, ca. 1875, 22 x 36", 30" h. (ILLUS.) **2,500**

Rococo & Renaissance Parlor Tables

Victorian Renaissance Revival parlor table, rosewood, oval white marble top w/molded edge above a serpentine apron carved w/panels & roundels w/half-round turned corner drops, raised on a turned center column surrounded by four large C-scroll supports ending in small turned finials & raised on a cross-form stretcher w/carved scroll terminals above the turned bell-form feet, refinished, ca. 1860, 21 x 36", 30" h. (ILLUS. right with turtletop table) **1,500**

Marble-topped Renaissance Table

Victorian Renaissance Revival parlor table, walnut, oval white marble top w/molded edge above a serpentine apron carved w/panels & center roundels & w/half-round ring-turned spindle drops at the corners, raised on four ring-turned column supports above widely outswept double-C-scroll legs joined by a center post w/tall ring-turned finial, on casters, refinished, ca. 1870s, 20 x 30", 30" h. (ILLUS.) **800**

Round Marble-topped Parlor Table

Victorian Renaissance Revival parlor table, walnut, the round white marble top w/molded edge on a deep serpentine apron carved w/raised burl panels & central oval medallions w/half-round spindle drops at each corner, raised on four inset columnar turned supports joined to a center post flanked by long projecting S-scroll legs ending in paw feet on casters, a large urn-form finial at the center of the base, attributed to Thomas Brooks, New York City, ca. 1870 (ILLUS.) **2,296**

Renaissance Revival Oval Side Table

Victorian Renaissance Revival side table, walnut & burl walnut, the oval white marble top w/molded edges above a deep molded apron, raised on a short heavy baluster-turned post w/a beaded band above four scroll-carved supports above arched & flaring flat legs w/curved raised burl panels & centering a turned bowl-form finial, original casters, original finish, ca. 1870, 16 x 22", 30" h. (ILLUS.) **500**

Inlaid Renaissance Revival Side Table

Victorian Renaissance Revival side table, walnut, the oval top w/a wide beveled rim decorated w/an ebonized background centering a large ornate inlaid scrolling cartouche, raised on four inset carved angular supports around a turned central post, squared angled legs w/turned finials, original finish, ca. 1870s, 15 x 20", 30" h. (ILLUS.) **1,200**

Fine Carved Rococo Console Table

Victorian Rococo console table, mahogany, the half-round white marble top w/serpentine molded edges above a conforming scalloped apron carved w/panels of flowering branches centering a shell, raised on scroll-and-flower-carved front cabriole legs joined to a large carved shell at the center back w/slender serpentine stretchers, the back w/molded incurved sides & a large central oval mirror, ca. 1860, refinished, possibly French, 20 x 40", 36" h. (ILLUS.) **1,600**

Victorian Rococo Dining Table

Victorian Rococo dining table, carved walnut, divided expandable top, the round top w/molded edges & deep apron raised on four baluster-turned & scroll-carved legs & long carved scrolling supports tapering toward the top center & joined by a heavy leaf-carved cross-stretcher centered by a heavy center post w/an acanthus leaf-carved band, five original leaves w/case, original dark finish, ca. 1860, 60" d. closed, 30" h. (ILLUS.) **7,000**

Walnut Rococo Dining Table

Victorian Rococo dining table, walnut & burl walnut, extension-type, the round top above a deep burled apron raised on four heavy cabriole legs w/fruit-carved knees & scroll feet & casters, supported in the center by a ring-, rod- and knob-turned column, refinished, w/six leaves, ca. 1860, 52" d., 30" h. (ILLUS.).... **1,500**

Rococo "Duchesse" Dressing Table

Victorian Rococo dressing table, mahogany, "duchesse" style, the large serpentine-sided squared frame w/an arched scroll- and leaf-carved crest enclosing a large mirror swiveling between tall slender carved dolphin-form uprights on the rectangular white marble top w/serpentine sides & front above a conforming scroll-carved apron enclosing a drawer & raised on four heavy cabriole legs w/scroll feet joined by a incurved medial shelf w/a low serpentine back crest, original finish, ca. 1855, 18 x 44", overall 80" h. (ILLUS.) **2,500**

Victorian Rococo Mahogany Table

Victorian Rococo parlor table, mahogany, the oblong top w/serpentine molded edges above a conforming deep apron w/large shell-carved design flanked by C-scrolls at the center sides, raised on incurved cabriole legs w/ornate scroll carving, joined by serpentine cross stretchers w/a floral-carved center finial, old refinish, ca. 1850-60, 18 x 45", 34" h. (ILLUS.) **1,500**

Rosewood & Marble Rococo Table

Victorian Rococo parlor table, rosewood, the oblong white marble top w/notched corners above a deep conforming apron w/molded edges & center scroll-carved drops, raised on four tall slender leaf-carved S-scrolls centered by a leaf-carved knob-and-rod-turned column all on a cross-form base w/molded edges & thin bun feet, original finish, ca. 1860, 22 x 38", 30" h. (ILLUS.) **2,400**

Extraordinary Meeks Parlor Table

Victorian Rococo "turtle-top" parlor table, carved & laminated rosewood, the white marble "turtle top" on a conforming molded frame w/a deep serpentine apron ornately pierce-carved w/continuous tight scrolls between scrolled corner brackets above the cabriole legs ornately carved w/florals & C-scrolls & ending in scroll-and-peg feet on casters, the legs joined by an arched & scroll-carved cross-stretcher centered by a large urn of fruits over a turned drop, original finish, attributed to Meeks of New York City, ca. 1855, 22x 42", 30" h. (ILLUS.).................. **35,000**

Extremely Ornate Rococo Parlor Table

Victorian Rococo "turtle-top" parlor table, giltwood, the white marble "turtle-top" above a very ornate conforming apron composed of a large leafy scroll-carved medallion in the center of each side framed by further scrolls & joining the large cabriole legs w/medallion-carved knees & inward-scroll feet, joined by an ornate scroll-and-leaf-carved cross stretcher w/a very high floral-and-leaf-carved center ornament, ca. 1855-60, 30 x 52", 30" h. (ILLUS.).............................. **3,000**

Rococo "Turtle-top" Parlor Table

Victorian Rococo "turtle-top" parlor table, mahogany, the white marble "turtle-top" above a conforming apron w/serpentine edges & central carved scrolls w/short rounded corner posts w/drops, raised on a squared baluster-form central pedestal & post w/ball drop framed by

four long outswept scroll-carved legs on casters, old refinish, ca. 1860, 22 x 36", 30" h. (ILLUS.).. **1,600**

Victorian Rococo "turtle-top" parlor table, walnut, the white marble "turtle-top" above a conforming apron w/flower-and-leaf-carved center reserve raised on four tall flattened S-scroll supports on a flattened cross-form stretcher w/a turned center bowl finial, raised on small S-scroll feet, refinished, ca. 1860, 18 x 28", 30" h. (ILLUS. left with Renaissance Revival parlor table)... **800**

Rare William & Mary Dining Table

William & Mary dining table, tiger stripe maple & maple, gate-leg type, a narrow rectangular top w/rounded ends flanked by wide half-round drop leaves above an apron w/a single end drawer, on block-, baluster- and ring-turned legs, two swinging out to support the leaves, on button feet, old refinish, replaced drawer pull, base w/early maple color, New England, 1730-50, imperfections, 37 3/8 x 45 1/2", 29" h. (ILLUS.)... **14,950**

Very Rare Small William & Mary Table

William & Mary tavern table, cherry, the rectangular top w/molded edges overhanging an apron w/a single end drawer, raised on block-, ring- and baluster-turned legs joined by molded box stretchers, turned knob feet, old surface, Connecticut, 1730-50, minor imperfections, 15 1/2 x 24", 24 1/2" h. (ILLUS.).............. **19,550**

Wardrobes & Armoires

Fancy Burled Victorian Armoire

Armoire, late Victorian, walnut & Circassian walnut veneer, the high serpentine crestail carved w/bold leafy scrolls at the top & rounded ends w/further carved leafy band in the frieze above a pair of tall paneled cupboard doors featuring fancy burl veneer & flanked by burl veneer side bands, the base w/a pair of raised panel burled drawers w/pierced brass pulls, deep molded base, demountable, refinished, ca. 1875-95, 20 x 48", 8' h. (ILLUS.) **2,400**

Ornate Louis XV-Style Armoire

Armoire, Louis XV-Style, walnut, demountable, the arched & bead-trimmed crestrail centered by a large pierce-carved crest over a narrow scroll-carved frieze band over a pair of tall two-panel doors w/a winged cupid head at the top center & flanked by putto heads at each corner, each door w/scroll-carved trim, a single

long narrow drawer at the base w/three brass pulls flanked by large scroll-carved corner blocks ending in scroll feet, original finish, France, late 19th c., 21 x 60", 92" h. (ILLUS.) **6,500**

Narrow Aesthetic Movement Armoire

Armoire, Victorian Aesthetic Movement style, walnut & burl walnut, a high upright crestrail composed of roundels over carved points w/roundel-topped corner blocks, a deep stepped & flaring cornice above a single tall burl paneled door flanked by reeded pilasters w/small florette-carved panels, a narrow burl veneered bottom drawer w/brass bar & ring pulls, deep front molding, paneled sides, opens to a single top shelf, refinished, original hardware, last quarter 19th c., 20 x 38", 7' 6" h. (ILLUS.) **2,800**

Fine Aesthetic Movement Armoire

Armoire, Victorian Aesthetic Movement style, walnut & burl walnut, the rectangular top w/a high stepped front crest w/a geometric band above panels of bold scroll & leaf carving above a frieze band w/burl panels & leaf-carved blocks over a pair of tall panels & finely burled doors flanked by narrow side burl bands, two burled drawers at the bottom w/stamped brass pulls, molded flat base on thin block feet, refinished, demountable, ca. 1880s, 20 x 46", 8' h. (ILLUS.) **2,800**

Victorian Aesthetic Walnut Armoire

Armoire, Victorian Aesthetic Movement, walnut & burl walnut, demountable, the very high front crestrail centered by a flat-topped section w/a narrow scalloped burl band above a curved carved band of stylized florals & scrolls over a long burl C-scroll all flanked by high S-scroll ends enclosing further stylized florals, above a stepped & flared cornice over a frieze band w/a narrow burl panel flanked by carved bands of stylized flowers & leaves over the tall doors w/beveled mirrors framed by raised burl panels alternating w/panels of stylized flower & leaf bands, two drawers at the bottom w/raised burl panels & stamped brass pulls, deep molded base on thin block feet, original hardware, ca. 1885, 20 x 56", 96" h. (ILLUS.) **2,500**

Fine Victorian Rococo Armoire

Armoire, Victorian Rococo style, rosewood, demountable, the high arched broken-scroll crest w/a large central urn-form finial & matching corner finials above a wide frieze carved w/large leafy scrolls centered by a cartouche, a pair of tall cupboard doors w/arched & molding-framed mirrors above a molding above a pair of base drawers w/carved pulls, molded base, interior w/an open compartment on one side & shelves on the other, original finish, ca. 1860, 21 x 60", 108" h. (ILLUS.) **3,500**

Victorian Rococo Armoire

Armoire, Victorian Rococo substyle, walnut w/faux rosewood graining, demountable, the rectangular top w/a wide arched front & deep ogee cornice over a large central frieze panel w/ornate carved leafy scrolls over a pair of tall arch-paneled doors w/brass pulls above a pair of bottom drawers w/carved trim, scallop-carved apron, bracket feet, refinished, ca. 1860, 16 x 45", 7' 6" h. (ILLUS.) **2,400**

Fine Painted Pennsylvania Kas

Kas (a version of the Netherlands Kast or wardrobe), painted & decorated, the rectangular top w/a deep flaring molded cornice above a frieze band above a single central double-paneled door above base moldings & a pair of drawers w/butterfly brasses & keyhole escutcheons, molded base on bracket feet, Pennsylvania, late 18th - early 19th c. (ILLUS.)........ **11,500**

Country Kas with Original Paint

Kas (a version of the Netherlands Kast or wardrobe), painted pine, rectangular top w/flared cornice above a pair of tall double raised-panel doors w/a long panel over a shorter panel, a pair of false drawer fronts at the bottom above the molded base w/scroll-cut bracket feet, original salmon red paint w/black trim, pegged construction, mid-19th c., 19 1/2 x 46", 6' 4" h. (ILLUS.)... **1,200**

Art Deco Mahogany Wardrobe

Wardrobe, Art Deco, mahogany, demountable, the arched central crestrail above an arched long door w/a beveled mirror flanked by flat-topped side front panels

w/applied carving, step-out front base w/small bun feet, bird's-eye maple interior, refinished, early 20th c., 22 x 48", 84" h. (ILLUS.) **1,600**

Classical Wardrobe with Gothic Doors

Wardrobe, Classical style, mahogany & crotch-grain mahogany veneer, demountable, the rectangular top w/a very widely flaring stepped cornice above a wide frieze band above a pair of Gothic arch-paneled doors over an ogee base on heavy C-scroll front feet, interior w/drawers & shelves, original finish, ca. 1830, 24 x 66", 90" h. (ILLUS.) **3,500**

Classic Wardrobe with Paneled Doors

Wardrobe, Classical style, walnut, demountable, the rectangular top w/a very deep, stepped cornice w/rounded corners above a pair of tall cupboard doors w/arched panels w/carved ribbon molding, an ogee base band on ogee bracket feet, open interior, old refinish, ca. 1840s, 22 x 60", 90" h. (ILLUS.) **2,800**

European Country Pine Wardrobe

Wardrobe, country-style, scrubbed pine, one-piece construction, the rectangular top w/a narrow flared cornice above a beaded frieze band over wide paneled center door flanked by a pair of narrow paneled doors above a molding & two long paneled drawers, molded base on bun feet, open interior, Europe, late 19th c., 20 x 66", 84" h. (ILLUS.) **1,400**

Ornate Late Victorian Walnut Wardrobe

Wardrobe, late Victorian, walnut & burl walnut, a very high front crestrail w/serpentine outline & carved w/large scrolls & blossom-form designs above a molded flaring cornice over a pair of tall paneled doors w/arched tops in an elaborate burl design, doors flanked by half-round columns, slightly stepped-out base section w/serpentine front enclosing a pair of drawers w/stamped brass pulls, serpentine apron & scroll-carved knob front feet on casters, original hardware, refinished, ca. 1890, 24 x 56", 100" h. (ILLUS.) **3,500**

Fine Victorian Baroque Wardrobe

Wardrobe, Victorian Baroque-style, walnut & Circassian walnut, the rectangular top w/a wide flaring cornice above a wide frieze band ornately carved w/a central shell flanked by long flowering leafy scrolls between scallop-carved corner blocks, a molding above a pair of tall mirrored doors w/rounded burl molding around the mirrors topped by pairs of scrolls, the doors flanked by three full-length spiral-turned columns between carved blocks & burl panels, a lower mid-molding over a pair of paneled base drawers w/pierced brass pulls, molded base on casters, original finish & hardware, ca. 1890, 22 x 58", 96" h. (ILLUS.) **4,000**

Victorian Country-style Wardrobe

Wardrobe, Victorian country-style, butternut, one-piece construction, the arched & scalloped front crestrail centered by a small paneled drawer above the deep ogee cornice over a molding & a pair of tall paneled doors w/scalloped inner borders, quarter-round ring-and-rod-turned posts at each front corner, a lower molding over a pair of deep bottom drawers w/wooden knobs, base molding over the scalloped apron & bracket feet, refinished, ca. 1875, 21 x 52", 88" h. (ILLUS.) **1,800**

Single-door Golden Oak Wardrobe

Wardrobe, Victorian Golden Oak style, a rectangular top w/a high arched & scroll-carved crest on a rounded rail flanked by scrolls & above an arched frieze panel, a tall single door w/carved scrolls above the beveled mirror front, wide side stiles w/scroll-carved drops at the tops, a small projecting shelf below the door & over a long round-fronted bottom drawer w/bail pulls & carved scrolls at each end, beaded base band above the narrow serpentine apron w/shaped block feet on casters, refinished, ca. 1900, 22 x 36", 7' 4" h. (ILLUS.) **1,800**

Large Golden Oak Wardrobe

Wardrobe, Victorian Golden Oak style, a rectangular top w/a wide down-curved cornice w/carved corners & a beaded edge above a cabinet w/a tall narrow mirrored cupboard door on the left & a pair of small scroll-carved doors over a grouping of six drawers featuring scroll-carved panels on the right, all above a single long panel-carved drawer across the bottom, quarter-round slender columns down the front corners, deep molded base, original brasses, refinished, ca. 1900, 22 x 52", 72" h. (ILLUS.) **2,800**

Oak Wardrobe with a High Crest

Wardrobe, Victorian Golden Oak style, a tall scalloped & scroll-carved front crest above a bead-carved flaring cornice above a scroll-carved frieze band over a pair of tall paneled cupboard doors w/carved scrolls across the top, a pair of flat drawers at the base w/original stamped brass hardware, refinished, ca. 1900, 18 x 48", 7' 10" h. (ILLUS.) **1,800**

High-crested Golden Oak Wardrobe

Wardrobe, Victorian Golden Oak style, demountable, the high crestrail w/a scroll-carved top over a plain bar, a wide frieze w/serpentine scrolls above a flaring stepped cornice over a long low rounded bar frieze above a pair of tall doors w/long leafy scrolls above tall beveled mirrors w/shaped tops flanked by spiral-twist bars w/knob ends down the sides, a pair of line-incised drawers w/simple bail pulls, serpentine apron & bracket feet on casters, original finish, ca. 1890s, 21 x 42", 8' 2" h. (ILLUS.)............................ **2,000**

Fine Victorian Golden Oak Wardrobe

Wardrobe, Victorian Golden Oak style, demountable, the high front crest w/a scalloped, scroll-carved top centered by a large shell carving over a frieze band w/further scroll carving over a flared cornice above a frieze band trimmed in scroll carving over a pair of tall cupboard doors w/rectangular panels w/rounded corners & scroll-carved trim, a pair of drawers w/stamped brass pulls at the base above the serpentine apron & scroll-carved feet, refinished, ca., 1900, 20 x 48", 8' h. (ILLUS.)................................. **2,500**

Nice Golden Oak One-door Wardrobe

Wardrobe, Victorian Golden Oak style, de-mountable, the rounded top w/a molded

crestrail centered by scroll carving above the single arched door w/a large oval beveled mirror, the projecting base w/a deep curved-front drawer, on short front cabriole legs w/paw feet, bird's-eye maple interior, original hardware, ca. 1900, 22 x 36", 80" h. (ILLUS.) **2,200**

Elaborate Golden Oak Wardrobe

Wardrobe, Victorian Golden Oak style, quarter-sawn oak, demountable, the rectangular top w/a deep flaring cornice above a wide scroll-carved frieze band above a molding over a pair of recessed tall doors w/rectangular mirrors w/shaped tops trimmed w/scrolls & sepa-rated by a center stile carved w/scroll re-verse, the doors flanked by three-quarter round columns resting on a narrow pro-jecting serpentine shelf above a conform-ing bottom case w/a pair of drawers over a single long drawer all w/pierced brass pulls & also flanked by shorter columns, molded base band on paw feet, original finish, ca. 1900, 22 x 60", 90" h. (ILLUS.).. **5,500**

Fancy Golden Oak Wardrobe

Wardrobe, Victorian Golden Oak style, the high arched top crestrail decorated w/ornate scroll carving & a central flowerhead & rounded corners above a pair of tall paneled cupboard doors w/scroll-carved trim flanked by corner columns & centered by a small vertical rectangular beveled mirror above a flat serpentine panel, a bow-fronted base w/two drawers w/pierced-brass pulls flanked by leaf-carved feet, original dark finish, ca. 1900, 22 x 48", 7' 10" h. (ILLUS.).......................... **2,800**

Double-door Golden Oak Wardrobe

Wardrobe, Victorian Golden Oak style, the rectangular top w/a wide flaring cornice above a narrow rectangular frieze panel composed of heavy half-round molding over a case w/two tall narrow mirrored doors w/scalloped tops & an applied molded bar centered by a narrow rectangular mirrored door w/heavy molding over a stack of five small bow-fronted drawers , half-round rod- and ring-turned colonettes down the sides above the stepped-out serpentine lower section w/a pair of deep serpentine drawers, heavy carved paw front feet, original stamped brass hardware, refinished, ca. 1895, 21 x 60", 88" h. (ILLUS.)............................ **2,600**

Simple Renaissance Wardrobe

Wardrobe, Victorian Renaissance Revival country-style, walnut & burl walnut, the rectangular top w/a plain flaring cornice above a narrow molding over a pair of tall cupboard doors w/arched tops & raised burl long panels centered by a burl roundel, a mid-molding above a pair of bottom paneled drawers w/leaf-carved pulls, deep molded base, refinished, ca. 1875, 18 x 44", 84" h. (ILLUS.) **1,500**

Victorian Rococo Rosewood Wardrobe

Wardrobe, Victorian Rococo style, rosewood, demountable, the rectangular top w/a flaring molded cornice centered by double arches & a cartouche finial above a stepped-out wider flaring cornice above a pair of large two-panel cupboard doors trimmed w/half-round projections at the top, center & bottom, each framing a carved florette, a pair of paneled small drawers w/simple bail pulls at the base, beveled corners at the front, deep molded flat base, open interior, refinished, ca. 1860, 20 x 58", 90" h. (ILLUS.) **3,800**

Victorian Rococo Walnut Wardrobe

Wardrobe, Victorian Rococo style, walnut, demountable, the high arched & scroll-carved front cornice w/a pair of lobed center cut-outs over a molded cornice above a pair of tall arch-paneled doors w/scroll-carved top corners, narrow beveled front corners w/small carved scrolls, two drawers at the bottom w/leaf-carved pulls, serpentine apron & bracket feet, paneled sides, original finish, ca. 1850-70, 20 x 54", 8' h. (ILLUS.) **3,500**

Whatnots & Etageres

Ornate Late Victorian Etagere

Etagere, late Victorian style, mahogany, an arched & scroll-pierced crestrail w/scrolled ears above the top rectangular shelf w/a low knob gallery on each end above a pierced scroll-carved front center drop above two smaller tiered shelves backed by two beveled mirrors & flanked by stick-and-ball side supports, over boldly scrolled & pierced brackets & stick-and-ball rods connecting to another two-tiered shelf backed w/beveled mirrors all above a tall open compartment w/stick-and-ball supports on the left beside a squared mirrored door, molded base on short carved cabriole legs, refinished, ca. 1890, 16 x 30", 72" h. (ILLUS.) **1,600**

Elaborate Brass & Onyx Etagere

Etagere, Rococo Revival style, brass & onyx, the delicate brass framework topped by a high pierced scrolling brass crest above a narrow white onyx shelf above incurved leafy scroll sides flanking a large half-round beveled mirror above a serpentine onyx shelf raised on slender ornate figural griffin-shaped front supports continuing to slender curved brass legs, the side stiles composed of rods mounted w/cylindrical sections of onyx, a pair of small quarter-round onyx medial shelves above a lower serpentine shelf composed of quarter-round end sections flanking a central mirror section, ca. 1885, 38" w., 4' 6" h. (ILLUS.) **3,080**

Renaissance Revival Etagere

Etagere, Victorian Renaissance Revival style, walnut & burl walnut, the tall back w/a large boldly scroll-carved pediment center w/a large cartouche finial over a smaller cartouche flanked by pierced leaf-carved panels & small pointed raised burl panels, above a tall round-topped mirror flanked by wide scalloped sides set on each side w/quarter-round graduated shelves backed by oblong mirrors, the lowest shelves on carved & curved brackets flanked by raised burl panels above the half-round white marble shelf w/a flat projecting center section above a conforming apron trimmed w/raised burl panels & a central roundel, molded base on short turned front legs, ca. 1870, 50" w., 7' 10" h. (ILLUS.) **3,920**

Etagere, Victorian Renaissance Revival style, walnut & burl walnut, the top w/a high arched crestrail centered by a tall carved & pointed crest w/the carved head of Robin Hood above pierced open scrolls above a flat crestrail over a frieze

Fine Renaissance Revival Etagere

band centered by a palmette carving & raised burl panels w/leafy C-scrolls at each side above the tall oblong mirror flanked by wide tapering sides w/cut-out oblong openings & three shaped graduated shelves on each side above closed side panels & a band w/raised burl panels above a serpentine white marble shelf w/block projections above a deep conforming plinth base w/a center drawer, refinished, ca. 1865-75, 18 x 46", 8' 2" h. (ILLUS.) **4,500**

Rosewood Rococo Etagere

Etagere, Victorian Rococo style, carved rosewood, a high arched upright framework w/ornately pierce-carved scrolls & medallions enclosing a mirror above the half-round white marble top w/flattened center front above a conforming case w/two quarter-round mirror-backed shelves on each side centered by two mirror-backed shelves, two wide front pilasters heavily carved w/blossoms & scrolls, scroll-carved borders & brackets,

flat base, original dark finish, probably Philadelphia, ca. 1855-60, 22 x 48", 84" h. (ILLUS.) **3,600**

Fine Labeled Rococo Etagere

Etagere, Victorian Rococo style, carved rosewood, the superstructure w/a deeply scalloped crestrail centered by an arched floral-carved crest & quarter-round side panels above a high arched central mirror flanked on each side by a graduated tier of three quarter-round open shelves backed by mirrors & supported on delicate ring-turned spindles, above the projecting white marble top w/rounded ends & wide projecting serpentine center section above a conforming case, the central serpentine drawer w/carved pull above a mirrored cupboard door w/arched & pierced top flanked by two serpentine quarter-round shelves & serpentine molded sides, serpentine gently scalloped apron on turned knob feet, labeled by Henry Iden, New York City, ca. 1855, refinished, 22 x 60", 102" h. (ILLUS.) **12,000**

Rare Belter Rosewood Etagere

Etagere, Victorian Rococo style, pierced & carved rosewood, the very high peaked cornice pierce-carved overall w/scrolls & grapevines above a tall lobe-topped mirror in a molded frame flanked on each side by a tier of four quarter-round graduated shelves backed by a mirror & supported on delicate scroll-carved uprights, all above the wide white marble base w/a serpentine front above a deep molding w/scroll-carved trim, on casters, original finish, attributed to Belter of New York City, ca. 1855, 16 x 60", 80" h. (ILLUS.).. **35,000**

Fine Walnut Rococo Etagere

Etagere, Victorian Rococo style, walnut, the tall arched & pierce-carved crest composed of leafy vines & fruit above an arched, molded cornice over a scroll-carved frieze band above two tall mirrors each w/oblong borders w/outset rounded corners, the mirrors flanked on each side by a tier of four graduated open shelves w/scrolled-carved brackets & asymmetrical pierced designs, the top two each backed by a small rectangular mirror enclosed by lobed molding, the center bottom w/a rectangular white marble shelf w/a serpentine front above a single conforming drawer w/carved pull over a scalloped apron, small feet, original finish, ca. 1860, 20 x 50", 90" h. (ILLUS.).. **6,500**

Etagere, Victorian Rococo substyle, carved rosewood, the shaped top w/a high arch-centered rail w/a shell-carved recess topped by three urn-turned finials & pierced scrolling bands all raised on very slender ring-turned supports backed by a large arched central mirror flanked by narrow arched side mirrors behind the shaped open shelves & projecting turned side posts enclosing small mirrors, all above the wide serpentine-topped lower section w/a wide shell-carved apron supported on four leafy scroll-carved C-

Fabulous Rococo Rosewood Etagere

scrolls on turned columnar supports flanking raised side shelves & a mirrored back, inset serpentine lower shelf w/scroll-carved trim, on button feet, original finish, attributed to Thomas Brooks of New York, ca. 1850-60, 24 x 62", 9' 6" h. (ILLUS.).. **17,000**

Very Tall Rococo Etagere

Etagere, Victorian Rococo substyle, walnut, the very tall superstructure w/a high arched molded crestrail w/pierced scrolls & a turned center finial along the top & enclosing an arched pierced-carved panel trimmed w/small raised burl panels all above the tall rectangular mirror w/rounded top corners flanked by pierced scroll-carved sides w/slender turned spindles & two small open shelves on each side, the lower shelves w/slender turned spindle supports above small oblong mirrors, all on a half-round white marble top over a conforming deep apron w/a central drawer w/leaf-carved pull raised on turned & tapering front supports & S-scroll side supports above a medial shelf w/incurved sides backed by an arched pierce-carved crest, on small peg feet, ca. 1855-70, 38" w., 7' 1" h. (ILLUS.).. **2,520**

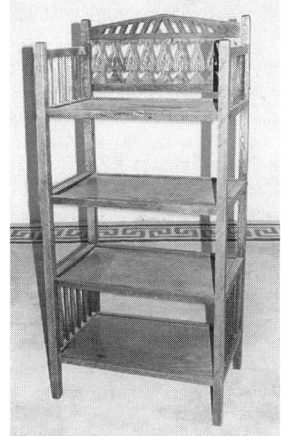

Simple Arts & Crafts Oak Whatnot

Whatnot, Arts & Crafts style, oak, the top crestrail w/a peaked slot-pierced band over a wide band pierce-carved w/spearpoint devices, the top rectangular shelf flanked by rectangular spindled sides & raised on four slender square legs joined by three lower shelves w/spindle sides on the bottom shelf, ca. 1910, refinished, 14 x 20", 40" h. (ILLUS.)................................ **225**

Late Victorian Mirrored Whatnot

Whatnot, late Victorian, mahogany, a large round beveled mirror w/a small scroll-carved crest at the top flanked by small oblong open shelves on incurved supports above a wide oblong shelf raised on slender squared supports above a narrow vertical rectangular beveled mirror above a small open shelf on a forked bracket backed by a smaller mirror, the half-round bottom shelf w/a serpentine front, raised on simple slender cabriole front legs & straight rear legs, refinished, ca. 1910, 14 x 24", 54" h. (ILLUS.)... **600**

GAMES & GAME BOARDS

The following listings cover Early Age American Games for the years 1744-1930. All prices are for games in very good condition. Very good condition is defined as still a collectible game, but shows strong signs of use and deterioration. A game in this condition is still considered collectible in pre-1970 games. The outside box corners have heavy wear, the edges are worn and one or two edges are torn. The box top has minor pen or pencil marks with some fading. The aprons have bowing and wear. Inside of the box is characterized by warped build ups, heavy stress at folds of the board, if this is a card game there are slight creases on the cards. The components of a game considered to be in very good condition are: if the die-cuts are punched, the implements show wear and there may be slight tears in the instructions. Some minor implements can be missing and still be considered in very good condition.

"Bicycle - The Race," board-type, published by JWS&S, New York, designed in England by "JAP," box cover shows high-wheel racers, w/game box & box, late 19th c.. **$358**

Chess set, Oriental carved pieces in black & lacquered case w/checkerboard top, natural & dark red stained, some damage & loose pieces, 16" l., the set ....

Columbia - Land of the West, board-type, color lithographed images of American states & cities & events in American history, ca. 1850, framed & glazed, 23 x 28".. **1,380**

Dominoes set, chip carved box w/two lidded compartments holds dice, & thirty-one bone dominoes (& five wood replacements), box decorated w/leaves, roping & geometric designs, 8" l. **220**

Game board, pine, Parcheesi game painted red, yellow & black, 19th c., 24 x 24" sq.... **3,737**

Game board, painted wood, double-sided, one side w/a green & red checkerboard w/comb-grained borders, the reverse w/a black-painted game on a comb-grained field, America, 19th c., 16 1/4 x 16 1/2" (minor paint wear) **690**

Game board, painted & decorated wood, double-sided, the front w/a Parcheesi game w/areas of wood graining in black, brown & red paint on a green ground, the back w/a game board in black on a red ground, late 19th - early 20th c., 22 1/2 x 22 3/4" (crack, minor paint wear & loss) **3,680**

Game board, painted & decorated wood, the game board face drawn on a polychrome decorated clock face, late 19th - early 20th c., 12 x 12" (paint wear, minor cracks) 115

"Game of Messenger Boy," graphic, J. H. Singer, New York, 8 x 14" 225

Goblin Ten Pins, featuring ten lithographed paper-on-wood figures of men including a chef, a banjo player, a policeman & a dandy, w/separate heads that plug into the body & two bases, in original box w/paper label, Ives, ca. 1890, 8" h. (one figure redone) 575

"Rainbow Fishing Game," board-type, includes two fishing rods & colorful die cut cardboard fish, ca. 1932, Milton Bradley, box 13 x 16" (split at one corner of box) 29

Mechanical Soccer Game

Soccer game, tin & lithographed paper, a metal-framed soccer playing field w/goals at each end, players in slots controlled by levels at ends, w/two wood balls, original box, possibly made in Germany, 7 1/2 x 13 1/2" (ILLUS.) 595

"Train Express" Dominoes, complete set of wooden dominoes w/embossed image of train & coal car on each game piece, in original tin box w/original paper label decorated w/1880s graphics of the Double 9 Express train passing through the countryside, Embossing Co., USA, 13" (box has slight edge wear) 201

GLASS

ALSO SEE: Antique Trader Books Pressed Glass & Bottles Price Guide, 2nd Edition *and* American & European Decorative and Art Glass Price Guide, 2nd Edition.

Alexandrite

Inspired by the gemstone of the same name, Alexandrite is a decorative glass shading from yellow-green to rose to blue. It was produced by Thomas Webb & Sons and Stevens & Williams of England in the late 19th century. The Moser firm of Karlsbad, Bohemia made a similar line.

Finger bowl & underplate, rounded bowl w/squared top on a matching underplate, shading from amber to rose w/lovely blue rims, bowl 5" d., plate 6" d., the set **$2,200**

Finger bowl & underplate, the wide stepped bowl w/an upright crimped & swirled rim, shading violet blue to amber, w/matching round crimped underplate, Webb, underplate 6" d., 2 pcs. **1,176**

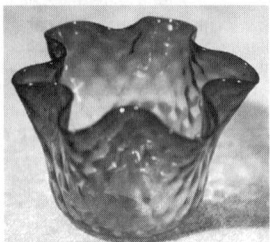

Rare Webb Alexandrite Nut Dish

Nut dish, round w/deeply ruffled & flared upright sides, Honeycomb patt., Thomas Webb & Sons, 3" d. (ILLUS.) **750-950**

Toothpick holder, a small applied amber foot below the tall cylindrical cupped body w/an optic herringbone design, 3 1/4" h. **1,100**

Vase, 4 7/8" h., jack-in-the-pulpit-form, blue foot, possibly Webb **1,073**

Amberina

Amberina was developed in the late 1880s by the New England Glass Company and a pressed version was made by Hobbs, Brockunier & Company (under license from the former). A similar ware, called Rose Amber, was made by the Mt. Washington Glass Works. Amberina-Rose Amber shades from amber to deep red or fuchsia and cut and plated (lined with creamy white) examples were also made. The Libbey Glass Company briefly revived blown Amberina, using modern shapes, in 1917.

Amberina Label

Amberina Swirl Pitcher & Tumbler

Pitcher, Swirl patt., bulbous ovoid body tapering to a wide cylindrical neck w/a pinched spout, applied amber handle, deep color, attributed to the Mt. Washington Glass Co. (ILLUS. right) **$750-1,000**

1.

2.

3.

4.

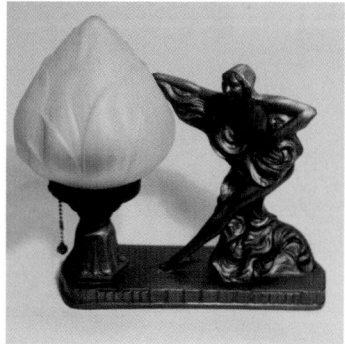

5.

1. Elaborate Victorian cherry fireplace mantel with original finish, ca. 1890, 60" wide, 96" high, **$3,600**.
Courtesy of Mark Moran.

2. Stamped metal Pepsi-Cola bottle carrier with original paint, 8 1/2 x 10 1/2", **$95**.
Courtesy of Mark Moran and Mom's Antique Mall

3. Art Nouveau-style double inkstand in cast spelter with a gold-painted finish and milk glass inserts, 6 3/4" long, **$145**.
Courtesy of Mark Moran and G. & V. Kranz

4. Large carved pine eagle architectural element, mid-19th century, 36" wide, 40" high, **$10,000**.
Courtesy of Mark Moran

5. Art Deco figural table lamp in cast spelter with a bronzed finish and a frosted flame-shaped shade, 12" long, 11" high, **$165**.
Courtesy of Mark Moran and J. Kruesel

1. A 1942 copy of the "Aircraft Spotters' Guide, Part 1," **$50**.

Courtesy of James Trautman

2. An early copy of "Air Stories" pulp magazine from spring 1937, **$25**.

Courtesy of James Trautman

3. Cast-iron and stamped steel building-form bank marked "Twelfth Street Bank,"
2 1/4 x 3 3/4", **$125**.   Courtesy of Mark Moran and Mom's Antique Mall

4. Cast-iron lion bank with old gold and red paint, 6 1/4" long, 5 1/4" high, **$185**.

Courtesy of Mark Moran and J. Kruesel

5. House-form tin razor blade bank marked "Dull House – Home for Aged Blades,"
2 1/4" long, **$125-$150**.   Courtesy of Deborah Gillham

1. Ceramic plaid horse figural child's toothbrush holder marked "Made in Japan," 5"
long, **$85-$95**.
Courtesy of Deborah Gillham
2. Bust of Abraham Lincoln on a cast-iron book end with a gold-painted finish, 5 5/8 x
7 1/4". The pair, **$95**.
Courtesy of Mark Moran
3. Painted box with original deep red paint with a spread-winged eagle and owner's
name on the lid and the front decorated with a pair of birds and cornucopias, found in
Vermont, 19th century, 4 5/8 x 9", 4 3/4" high, **$12,100**.

Courtesy of Garth's Auctions, Delaware, Ohio
4. Ornately carved mahogany Oriental frame suspending a bronze gong, original finish,
late 19th century, 20 x 48", 44" high, **$1,200**.
Courtesy of Mark Moran
5. Finely painted German bride's box, ca. 1850-60, 10 x 18", 8" high, **$950**.

Courtesy of Mark Moran and Greg Kowles

1.

2.

3.

4.

5.

1. Wind-up tin toy with Popeye dancing while Olive Oyl plays the concertina; various cartoon characters around the base, made by Marx, 3 1/2 x 5 1/2", 8 1/2" high, near mint, **$2,650**. *Courtesy of Mark Moran and R. & K. Townsend*

2. A key-wind tin Dick Tracy Squad Car No. 1, made by Marx; rubber wheels and working emergency light, 11" long, **$165**. *Courtesy of Mark Moran and R. & K. Townsend*

3. Modern ceramic Budweiser steins. Left to right: No. CS12 Blue Delft, colored, **$250**; No. CS12 Blue Delft, colored, **$276**; No. CS12 Blue Delft, 1976 wording, **$100**; No. CS12 Blue Delft, colored, **$151**. *Courtesy of Peter J. Kroll, Glasses, Mugs & Steins, Sun Prairie, Wisconsin*

4. Lithographed tin toffee tin in the form of a leather valise, made for Edmondsons Red Seal Toffee, England, 3 3/4 x 9 5/8", 8" high, **$445**.

Courtesy of Mark Moran and R. & K. Townsend

5. Lithographed tin chocolate tin in the form of a German inn, made by Heinrich Haeberlein, Nuremberg, Germany, 3 1/8 x 8", 5 5/8" high, **$225**.

Courtesy of Mark Moran and R. & K. Townsend

1. Interior view of a porcelain compote showing the American-painted decoration of a cluster of pink and white morning glories, with the rim and foot decorated with bands of conventional pink butterflies, burnished gold rim and foot, initialed and dated by the artist in 1881; Charles Field Haviland blank, 8 7/8" diameter, 4 1/4" high, **$200**.

Courtesy of Dorothy Kamm, Port St. Lucie, Florida

2. A pair of Old Paris porcelain urns converted to electric lamps, the urns dating to around 1830, bases 12" high, the pair, **$1,344**.

Courtesy of Charlton Hall Galleries, Columbia, South Carolina

3. A ceramic figural pepper shaker decorated in color with blue Willow pattern trim, unmarked, from Scotland, 5 1/4" high, **$250-$275**.   Courtesy of Jeff Siptak, Nashville, Tennessee

4. An American-painted porcelain bonbon box decorated on the cover with a conventional design of three intertwined peacocks against a baby blue ground, burnished gold rims and feet, opal luster interior, blank marked by T.&V. Limoges, France, ca. 1892-1907, 6" diameter, 3 1/2" high, **$95**.   Courtesy of Dorothy Kamm, Port St. Lucie, Florida

5. A colorful, stylized landscape with a dancing Art Deco lady on a pottery tile by Longwy of France, ca. 1930, 8" square, **$395**.   Courtesy of Temple's Antiques, Eden Prairie, Minnesota

1. Rare ceramic child's feeding dish in the form of a clown, made by California Cleminsons, ca. 1955, **$125-$175**.

Courtesy of Deborah Gillham

2. A colorful molded chalkware fish-shaped child's toothbrush holder made by Miller Studio, ca. 1965; brushes go through the fins, 7" high, **$20-$30**.

Courtesy of Deborah Gillham

3. A stamped tin lithographed child's 11-piece coffee set on tray, early 20th century, tray 6 1/4 x 9", coffeepot 3 1/2" high, the set, **$195**.

Courtesy of Mark Moran and Mom's Antique Mall

4. A colorfully litho-graphed tin rattle featuring a clown face, used during a circus performance, 1940s, **$10**.

Courtesy of Jim Trautman

5. A Noritake porcelain dresser box in the form of an Art Deco lady, 3 1/4" diameter, 5 1/2" high, **$1,075**.

Courtesy of Tim Trapani, West Hempstead, New York.

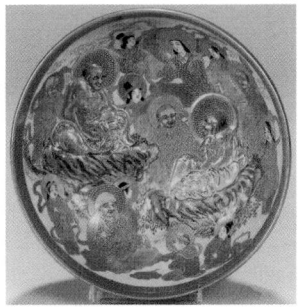

1. A rare English "skeleton" clock signed by Blackhurst, ca. 1855, **$3,740.**

Courtesy of York Town Auction, York, Pennsylvania

2. A rare carved and painted Wood Duck drake decoy by Elmer Crowell, **$24,750.**

Courtesy of Guyette & Schmidt, West Farmington, Maine

3. A group of antique clocks (left to right): black marble temple-form mantel clock with line-incised decoration and porcelain dial, ca. 1880, 6 x 8", 10" high, **$400;** triple-decker Classical-style mantel clock with mahogany veneered case with half-round columns flanking the door featuring a reverse-painted panel of flowers, ca. 1830-40, 30" high, **$450;** Federal Revival beehive-form mantel clock with inlaid mahogany case and silvered metal dial, sold by Baily, Banks & Biddle, Philadelphia, ca. 1910, 7 x 11", 15" high, **$400.**

Courtesy of Mark Moran

4. Japanese Satsuma pottery bowl, 9 5/8" diameter, decorated in relief with figures of male and female disciples of Buddha, signed by Hododa, Shimazu Mon, Meiji period, **$2,240.**

Courtesy of Charlton Hall Galleries, Columbia, South Carolina

5. A figural Lone Ranger on Silver child's toothbrush holder of a molded composition material with a wire brush holder, **$80-$100.**

Courtesy of Deborah Gillham

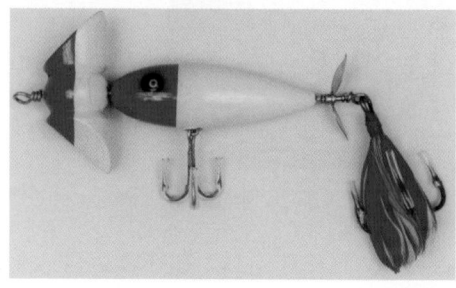

1. A large Ideals Publication book titled The Circus featuring a photo of Emmett Kelly and other clowns on the cover, 1961, **$25.**
Courtesy of Jim Trautman

2. A colorfully painted cast-iron doorstop in the form of a flower-filled pot, marked by Hubley, original paint, 7 1/4" high, **$55.**
Courtesy of Mark Moran and Mom's Antique Mall

3. This lithographed steel Marx dollhouse dates from the Cold War era, circa 1960, and features a bomb shelter in place of a garage, **$200.**
Courtesy of Jim Trautman

4. An unused 1950 George Lawrence, Portland, Oregon, size 15 Tillamook Model leather-trimmed split-willow creel, **$9,020.**
Courtesy of Lang Sporting Collectibles, Inc., Raymond, Maine

5. A painted wooden "Truck-Oreno" fishing lure by the South Bend Fishing Tackle Company, **$2,970.**
Courtesy of Lang Sporting Collectibles, Inc.,

1. This Barbie wearing a "Theatre Date" outfit was made for the Japanese market, **$1,600**.

2. A #1 Ponytail Barbie with box and pedestal stand, **$4,700**.

3. A Twist N' Turn Barbie, near mint in box, **$425**.

4. A solid-dome J.D. Kestner, Germany, 15" baby doll, **$450**.

5. A bisque-headed musical violin player in 18th-century costume, late 19th century, 15", **$950**.

1.

2.

3.

4.

5.

1. Late Victorian Golden Oak gentleman's dresser/wardrobe with a long mirrored door, original brass hardware, refinished, ca. 1900, 22 x 52", 72" high, **$2,800**.

2. Classical Revival tall-poster bed in carved and figured mahogany, ca. 1900, 58 x 80", 80" high, **$3,000**.

3. An ornately carved and gilded three-piece parlor suite made by the Karpen Furniture Company, Chicago, ca. 1890s, the set, **$8,000**.

4. Victorian Renaissance Revival ebonized wood plant stand with gilt trim, 12 x 18", 32" high, **$1,200**.

5. Carved walnut Victorian Renaissance Revival parlor chair attributed to John Jelliff of Newark, New Jersey, ca. 1875, original finish, newer upholstery, 36" high, **$400**.

Photos this page courtesy of Mark Moran

1. An unusual late Victoria pierced and floral-cast cast-iron picture frame,
7 x 10 1/4", **$300.**   Courtesy of Mark Moran and J. Kruesel
2. American-painted porcelain belt buckle brooch beautifully decorated with a portrait
of a lady in 18th-century costume, gold-plated bezel, ca. 1900-1917, 1 7/8 x 2 3/8",
$175.   Courtesy of Dorothy Kamm, Port St. Lucie, Florida
3. A chrome-plated figural car hood ornament in the form of a nude woman with blue
plastic wings, 9 1/2" long, 8 1/4" high, **$135.**   Courtesy of Mark Moran and G. & V. Kranz
4. An early 20th century cast-iron card tray decorated with three kittens, marked by
Bradley & Hubbard, Model 1640, 5 1/2 x 7", **$295.**   Courtesy of Mark Moran and R. & K. Townsend
5. Copper Revere Ware teakettle with Bakelite handle and bird whistle spout, marked
on the bottom "Revere Solid Copper – Rome, N.Y.," early 20th century, 7 1/4" diameter, 7 1/2" high, **$100.**   Courtesy of Mark Moran and C. Williams

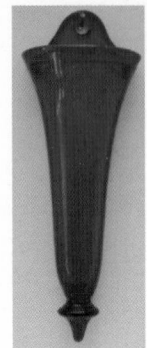

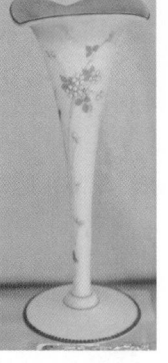

1. Deep red slender conical glass wall pocket, Style No. 320, by Tiffin Glass Company, 9 1/8" long, **$150-$185.** Courtesy of Bobbie Zucker Bryson, Tuckahoe, New York

2. Lily-form Burmese vase decorated with delicate forget-me-nots, Mt. Washington Glass Company, 8" high, **$1,200.**

Courtesy of Louis St. Aubin, Jr. Brookside Antiques, New Bedford, Massachusetts

3. Group of three Gold Ruby blown glass vases by Gundersen-Pairpoint. Left to right: footed banjo-form vase, **$400-$600;** chalice-form vase with a "controlled-bubble" clear connector in base, **$300-$400;** footed fan-form vase with applied clear swan handles, **$400-$600.** Courtesy of Louis St. Aubin, Jr. Brookside Antiques, New Bedford, Massachusetts

4. One of a pair of Mary Gregory-style kerosene lamps in black amethyst decorated in white enamel with a child in a garden, with original chimney and early shade, 18 1/2", the facing pair, **$895.** Courtesy of Temple's Antiques, Eden Prairie, Minnesota

5. Mold-blown Amberina vase with applied amber rigaree around the neck, **$750-$950.** Courtesy of Louis St. Aubin, Jr. Brookside Antiques, New Bedford, Massachusetts

1. A cast spelter lady's shoe-form pincushion, silvered finish, early 20th century, some damage to heel, 5 1/2" long, **$85.** Courtesy of Mark Moran and R. & K. Townsend

2. The March 1962 issue of "Space Magazine" with a cover photo of John Glenn, fair condition, **$30.** Courtesy of Jim Trautman

3. Collectible felt pennant for "Hollywood California," showing Grauman's Chinese Theatre, late 1940s, 26" long, **$50.** Courtesy of Jim Trautman

4. A cardboard advertising poster for "Swift's Premium Ham" showing Jack Sprat and his wife, designed by Maxfield Parrish, **$3,100.** Courtesy of William Morford Antiques, Cazenovia, New York

5. A Polyphon disc music box with six bells in a walnut case with original label, plays 8" discs, case 10 x 10", 5" high, **$1,760.** Courtesy of Alderfer Auction Company, Hatfield, Pennsylvania

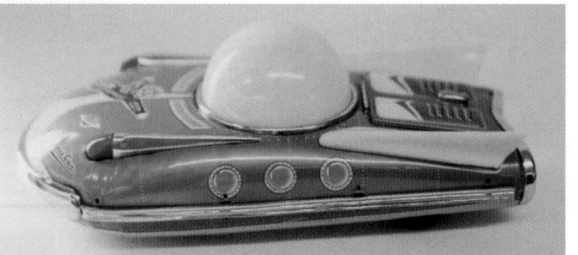

1. An early turned wood and cast-iron smoking stand with cups for matches, cigarettes and cigars on a scroll-pierced base with a thin brass striker on the top front, late 19th to early 20th century, 8" wide, 5 1/2" high, **$78**.   Courtesy of Mark Moran and C. Williams

2. An unusual footed cornucopia-shaped silver plate cigarette lighter, 5" long, **$19**.

Courtesy of Mark Moran and Mom's Antique Mall

3. Lithographed tin battery-operated 1950s "Universe Car" with a light-up dome light, 10" long, **$225**.   Courtesy of Mark Moran and Mom's Antique Mall

4. Part of a set of cardboard trading cards featuring space exploration scenes, information on the reverse, Popsicle premiums, early 1960s, 2 1/4 x 4", each card **$4**.

Courtesy of Jim Trautman

5. Cast-iron toy ice truck made by Arcade, with original red paint and white rubber tires, 6 3/4" long, **$425**.   Courtesy of Mark Moran and R. & K. Townsend

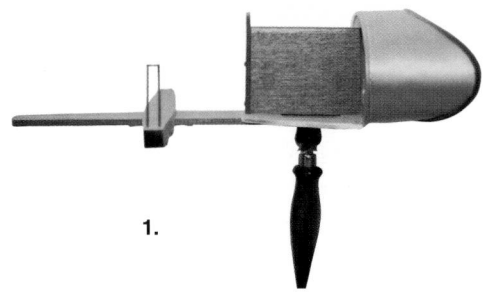

1.

2.

3.

4.

5.

1. A hand-held maple and aluminum stereo viewer by Underwood & Underwood, New York, patented in 1901, **$100**.
Courtesy of Jim Trautman

2. A gilt-bronze figure of an Art Nouveau woman adjusting her sandal, Agathon Leonard and cast by Susse Freres, Paris, ca. 1900, 20 7/8" high, **$5,000**.
Courtesy of Gene Harris Antique Auction Center, Marshalltown, Iowa

3. A cast-metal Tootsie Toy bus with original orange paint, 3 1/2" long, **$245**.
Courtesy of Mark Moran and R. & K. Townsend

4. An architectural parlor stove in the form of a three-story home with mansard roof, marked "Co-operative Stove Co.," **$5,600**.
Courtesy of Jackson's Auctioneers & Appraisers, Cedar Falls, Iowa

5. Domed copper tin-lined food mold decorated on the top with fruit and leaves, 7 1/2" diameter, 4 1/4" high, **$85**.
Courtesy of Mark Moran and C. Williams

1.

2.

3.

5.

4.

1. An elaborate cast-iron double inkwell and stand with clear mold-blown wells, original gilt finish, late 19th century, 4 1/4 x 6 3/4", 6" high, **$325**.

Courtesy of Mark Maron and C. Williams

2. A cast spelter souvenir plate with scenes of the St. Louis World's Fair of 1904, silvered finish, 7" diameter, **$49**.

Courtesy of Mark Moran

3. A fancy silver plate inkstand with two square glass wells with silver hinged caps resting in a dished tray with stamped scroll and floral rim decoration and a central compartment for stamps, made by the Derby Silver Company, Model No. 1745, late 19th century, 4 3/4 x 8 1/4", **$265**.

Courtesy of Mark Moran and C. Williams

4. An early hand-forged iron candle lantern with three glass panels and a conical top with vent holes and a ring handle, early 19th century, 13" high, **$300-$500**.

Courtesy of Mark Moran

5. A rare early movie poster for the "Life and Adventures of Buffalo Bill...," colorful images, produced by the Riverside Printing Company, Milwaukee, Wisconsin, early 20th century, 29 x 43", **$1,815**.

Courtesy of Past Tyme Pleasures Auction, San Ramon California

Pitcher, 6" h., cylindrical body in a diamond optic design, tapering slightly at the shoulder below the widely flaring & tightly crimped neck, smooth applied amber handle, New England Glass Co. **750-950**

Pitcher, 8" h., square top on a squatty bulbous body, Inverted Thumbprint patt., applied clear ropetwist around neck & forming the handle, late 19th c. **392**

Tumbler, Swirl patt., cylindrical, deep color, attributed to the Mt. Washington Glass Co. (ILLUS. left with pitcher) **90-125**

Bulbous Amberina Vase with Rigaree

Vase, bulbous base tapering to a tricorner neck trimmed w/a band of amber rigaree, deep color (ILLUS.) **750-950**

Small Amberina Vase

Vase, miniature, 3 1/2" h., spherical body in Inverted Thumbprint patt., short flaring ruffled neck trimmed w/a band of amber rigaree (ILLUS.) **550-750**

Animals

Americans evidently like to collect glass animals. For the past sixty years, American glass manufacturers have turned out a wide variety of animals to please the buying public. Some were produced for long periods and some were later reproduced by other companies, while others were made for only a short period of time and are rare. We have not included late productions in our listings and have attempted to date the productions where possible. Evelyn Zemel's book, American Glass Animals A to Z, *will be helpful to the novice collector. Another helpful book is* Glass Animals of the Depression Era *by Lee Garmon and Dick Spencer (Collector Books, 1993).*

Asiatic Pheasant, clear, Heisey Glass Co., 7 1/2" l., 10 1/2" h. **$465**

Barnyard Rooster, black, Dalzell/Viking Glass Co. reissue of Paden City Glass Co., 8 3/4" h. **550**

Bird, light blue, Paden City Glass Co., 5" h. **185**

Borzoi, clear, large, New Martinsville Glass Mfg. Co. **70**

Boxer dog, lying down, clear, American Glass Co., 3 7/8" h. **85**

Boxer dog, sitting, clear, American Glass Co., 4 3/4" h. **85**

Cat, light blue, Fostoria Glass Co., 3 1/4" h. **30**

Cat, dark medium blue, No. 1322, 1960s, Viking Glass Co., 8" h. **45**

Chanticleer, clear, Fostoria Glass Co., 10 1/4" h. **240**

"Chessie" cat, milk glass & black satin finish, Tiffin Glass Company **350**

Dog, dark medium blue, No. 1323, 1960s, Viking Glass Co., 8" h. **50**

Dragon Swan, clear, Paden City Glass Co., 9 3/4" h. **175**

Elephant book end, clear, No. 237, New Martinsville Glass Co., 5 1/2" h. **85**

Elephant w/long trunk extended (Mama), clear, Heisey Glass Co., 1944-55, 6 1/2" l., 4" h. **520**

Elephant w/trunk raised (Baby), clear, Heisey Glass Co., 1944-53, 5" l., 4 1/2" h. **310**

Fawn, w/flower floater & sockets for three candles, citron green, Tiffin Glass Co., ca. late 1940s, 14 1/2" l., fawn 10" h., ... **325**

Fawn, w/flower floater & sockets for three candles, copen blue, Tiffin Glass Co., ca. late 1940s, 14 1/2" l., fawn 10" h. **500**

Fighting Rooster, clear, Heisey Glass Co., 1940-46, 7 1/2" h. **145**

Fish book end, clear, A.H. Heisey & Co., 1942-52, 6 1/2" h. **185**

Fish candleholder, clear, A.H. Heisey & Co., 1941-58, 5" h. **200**

Frog, covered dish, green, 1969, Erskine Glass Co. **130**

Heisey Giraffe

Giraffe, clear, A.H. Heisey & Co., 1942-52, 3" l., 10 3/4" h. (ILLUS.) **300**

Goose, wings down, clear, A.H. Heisey & Co., 1947-55, 4 1/2" l., 4 1/2" h. (small bubble in neck) **565**

Goose, wings half up, clear, A.H. Heisey & Co., 1947-55, 5 1/2" l., 5" h. **130**

Goose, wings half up, clear w/Charleton roses decoration, A.H. Heisey & Co., 1947-55, 5 1/2" l., 5" h. **100**

Goose, pale blue, Paden City Glass
Co., ca. 1940, 5" h............................. 125
Goose, wings up, clear, A.H. Heisey & Co.,
1942-53, 7 1/2" l., 6 1/2" h............................. 130
Goose (The Fat Goose), clear & frosted,
Duncan & Miller Glass Co., 6" l., 6 1/2" h...... 225

Heisey Balking Colt

Horse, colt, balking, clear, A.H. Heisey &
Co., 1941-45, 3 1/2" h. (ILLUS.).................... 275
Horse, Plug (Sparky), clear, A.H. Heisey &
Co., 1941-46, 3 1/2" l., 4 1/4" h. 125
Horse, colt, standing, clear, A.H. Heisey &
Co., 1940-52, 5" h. 120
Horse Head book ends, A. H. Heisey Co.,
1937-55, clear, 6 7/8" h., pr. 375
Horse, Head Up, clear, New Martinsville
Glass Co., 8" h... 95
Mama Bear, clear, No. 488, New Martins-
ville Glass Co., 6" l., 4" h. 145
Mama Pig, w/three nursing piglets attached
on each side, clear, No. 1, limited edition
of approximately 200, New Martinsville
Glass Co., 6" l., 3" h. 950
Marmota Sentinel (Woodchuck), caramel
slag, Imperial Glass Co., 4" h. 55
"Oscar," 1991 Heisey Club souvenir, sap-
phire blue opalescent frosted, Fenton Art
Glass Co. 45
"Oscar," 1994 Heisey Club souvenir, frost-
ed green, Fenton Art Glass Co........................ 40
Papa Bear, clear, No. 489, New Martinsville
Glass Co., 6 1/2" l., 4" h. 175
Papa Bear, clear, No. 489, New Martinsville
Glass Co., satin finish, 6 1/2" l., 4" h. 225
Pelican, clear, No. 761, New Martinsville
Glass Co., 8" h. 90
Penguin, amber, No. 1319, 1960s, Viking
Glass Co., 7" h.. 20
Plug Horse, clear, A. H. Heisey & Co.,
clear, 1941-46, 4" l., 4" h. 160
Polar Bear, clear, Fostoria Glass Co.,
4 5/8" h.. 80
Polar Bear on ice, clear, No. 611, Paden
City Glass Co., 4 1/2" h.................................... 75
Police Dog (German Shepherd), clear, No.
733, New Martinsville Glass Co., 5" h............. 70
Porpoise on wave, clear, No. 766, New
Martinsville Glass Co., 6" h............................ 500
Rabbit, large mama, clear, No. 764, New
Martinsville Glass Co., 2 1/2" h. 325
Ringneck Pheasant, clear, Heisey Glass
Co., 1942-53, 12" l., 5" h. 175
Rooster (Chanticleer), pale blue, Paden
City Glass Co., 9 1/2" h. 200
Rooster Head Stopper, clear, A.H. Heisey
& Co., 4 1/2" h.. 65
Rooster with Crooked Tail, clear, No. 668,
New Martinsville Glass Co., 8" h...................... 95

Scottie Dog book ends, Cambridge Glass
Co., 6 1/2" h., pr. 210
Small Cat, black satin, No. 9446, Tiffin
Glass Company... 285
Sparrow, clear, A.H. Heisey & Co., 1942-
45, 4" l., 2 1/4" h.. 125
Squirrel, clear, No. 674, New Martinsville
Glass Co., 4 1/2" h. (no base)......................... 50
Squirrel on curved log, clear, No. 677,
Paden City Glass Co., 5 1/2" h. 60
Swordfish, blue opalescent, Duncan & Mill-
er Glass Co., 5" h.. 500
Swordfish, clear, Duncan & Miller Glass
Co., 5" h... 275
Tiger, Head Up, clear, New Martinsville
Glass Co., 6 1/2" h... 150
Wolfhound, black, No. 716, Dalzell/Viking
Glass Co. reissue of New Martinsville
Glass Co., 7" h.. 450
Wolfhound, clear, No. 716, New Martins-
ville Glass Co., 7" h.. 90

Bohemian

*Numerous types of glass were made in the once-inde-
pendent country of Bohemia and fine colored, cut and
engraved glass was turned out. Flashed and other inexpensive wares also were made; many of these, including
amber- and ruby-shaded glass, were exported to the
United States during the 19th and 20th centuries. One
favorite pattern in the late 19th and early 20th centuries
was Deer & Castle. Another was Deer and Pine Tree.*

Flashed & Cut Bohemian Candelabra

Candelabra, green flashed & cut slender
baluster-form shaft supporting a three-
branch clear glass candlearm, each arm
ending in a green-flashed & cut bobeche
hung w/faceted clear prisms, clear tulip-
form sockets, late 19th - early 20th c.,
21 3/8" h., pr. (ILLUS.).............................. $1,840
Decanter w/stopper, ruby cut to clear,
elongated body w/castle, cartouche &
animal decorations, ca. 1900, 16" h.............. 123
Decanters w/original stoppers, flashed,
amber cut to clear w/circles, cylindrical
body cut w/flutes & fruiting grapevines,
double spout & bulbous spire stopper cut
w/further circles, late 19th c., 14" h., pr. 863
Ewer, a cushion foot supporting a tall
baluster-form body w/a wide arched
spout, light orange w/overall mica flecks,
applied dark green glass handle
continuing as a snake down around the

Ornate Bohemian Ewer

body, gilt squiggles on the body & gilt scales & facial details on the snake, flake at handle, some gilt wear, late 19th c., 12 3/4" h. (ILLUS.) **358**

Bohemian Cut Overlay Mug

Mug, cut overlay, slightly tapering cylindrical body in cobalt blue cut to clear w/tall baluster-form panels & roundels, applied blue handle, metal rim band, gilt trim, early 20th c., 5 1/2" h. (ILLUS.) **403**

Bohemian Fine Cut Overlay Vases

Vase, 16 1/2" h., cut overlay, tall slender goblet-form body above a ringed pedestal & flaring foot, white cut to dark blue w/quatrefoils & spearpoint arches all trimmed in gold, 19th c. (ILLUS. center) ... **1,150**

Vases, 10" h., cut-overlay, squat baluster form w/slight everted lip to a spreading foot, gold enameled trim, white cut to cranberry, late 19th c., pr. **633**

Vases, 16" h., cut overlay, footed bulbous ovoid body tapering to a tall flaring six-lobed neck, white cut to dark blue w/diamond devices & spearpoint panels, overall gilt dot decoration, late 19th c., pr. (ILLUS. right & left) **2,070**

Bryce

From its factory in Mt. Pleasant, Pennsylvania, Bryce produced lines of hand-crafted, mouth-blown glass until it became a part of Lenox circa 1965. Bryce produced a diverse number of stemware lines including many that incorporated two colors and exaggerated shaped stems. Colors include milk glass, Amberina, ruby, dark green, amethyst, light blue, cobalt blue, amber and others. Today it operates as Lenox Crystal.

Basket, No. 1, rimmed edge, arched handle, 6" h. **$42**

Basket, No. 3, rimmed edge, arched handle, 10" h. 48

Bell, No. 1, dinner, twisted rope handle 38

Bowl, finger, Aquarius, Flame/ruby 32

Bowl, fruit, El Rancho, amber 14

Candy jar, cov., low, no stem, "Turnabout," El Rancho, pink 36

Candy jar, cov., stemmed, El Rancho, blue 38

Cocktail, liquor contour, clear bowl & foot w/light blue marble stem 19

Goblet, water, amethyst bowl, clear foot & stem, inverted cone stem, No. 894 34

Goblet, water, Aquarius, blue bowl, cut stem, No. 961 28

Goblet, water, Aquarius, ruby bowl, cut stem, No. 961 32

Goblet, water, Carnation No. 366 plate etching 24

Goblet, water, clear w/green twist stem, No. 325 34

Goblet, water, El Rancho, amber 12

Goblet, water, El Rancho, amethyst 14

Goblet, water, El Rancho, Flame/ruby 26

Goblet, water, El Rancho, milk glass 14

Goblet, water, Laurel cut, two wafer stem, clear, No. 575 16

Pitcher, El Rancho, blue 62

Pitcher, El Rancho, Flame/ruby 84

Plate, El Rancho, Flame/ruby 27

Plate, 8" d., Kingsley floral spray cut No. 298 22

Plate, 8 1/4" d., Aquarius, amber 20

Salt & pepper shakers, El Rancho, Flame/ruby, pr. 38

Sherbet/champagne, Aquarius, dark green bowl & foot, clear block stem 26

Sherbet/champagne, Delhi, chartreuse bowl, clear stem & foot, bulging ribbed stem 22

Sherbet/champagne, Delhi, dark green bowl, clear stem & foot, bulging ribbed stem 32

Teapot, cov., 56 oz. 110

Tumbler, Carousel No. 603, Amberina striped 36

Tumbler, flat, El Rancho, amber 9

Tumbler, flat, El Rancho, smoke 12

Tumbler, footed, El Rancho, smoke 12

Tumbler, highball, Turkey Eagle applied blue medallion, 5 1/4" h. 22

Tumbler, iced tea, Aquarius, blue bowl, cut stem, No. 961 22

Tumbler, iced tea, El Rancho, Flame/ruby 22

Tumbler, juice, El Rancho, Flame/ruby 16

Tumbler, Old Fashion, Indian Head applied amber medallion 18

Vase, 6" h., El Rancho, crimped top, milk glass 22

Vase, 15" h., El Rancho, crimped top, milk
glass... **36**
Vase, "toddy," El Rancho, milk glass................... **28**
Wine, amethyst bowl, colorless foot & stem,
four disk stem, No. 657..................................... **32**
Wine, Aquarius, blue bowl, cut stem, No.
961 .... **24**
Wine, ruby bowl, clear foot & stem, three
knop & three wafer stem, No. 625 .... **38**

Burmese

*Burmese is a single-layer glass that shades from pink
to pale yellow. It was patented by Frederick S. Shirley
and made by the Mt. Washington Glass Co. A license to
produce the glass in England was granted to Thomas
Webb & Sons, which called its articles Queen's Burmese. Gundersen Burmese was made briefly about the
middle of the 20th century, and the Pairpoint Company
is making limited quantities at the present time.*

Bowl, 4" d., 3 1/4" h., spherical body w/hex-
agonal-shaped rim, enameled red ber-
ries & green leaves, satin finish, un-
signed Webb.. **$325**
Bowl, 4 1/4" d., 3 1/8" h., squatty bulbous
body w/an upright short six-sided neck,
decorated w/lavender five-petal blossoms w/green & brown leaves, satin fin-
ish, unsigned Webb.. **395**
Bowl, 4 1/4" d., 3 1/2" h., scalloped rim,
pedestal base, polished pontil, satin fin-
ish... **330**
Bowl, 4 1/2" d., 2 1/2" h., short cylindrical
form w/a high widely flaring crimped &
ruffled rim, decorated w/flowers, buds &
leaves **550**

Mt. Washington Burmese Bowl

Bowl, 4 3/4" d., 2 1/8" h., squatty bulbous
form w/incurved scalloped rim, satin fin-
ish, Mt. Washington Glass Co. (ILLUS.) **350**
Bowl, 8" d., 4 1/4" h., squatty bulbous body
tapering to a widely flaring four-lobed
rolled & crimped rim, attributed to the Mt.
Washington Glass Co. **275**
Bowls, 5 3/4" d., 3 1/4" h., butterfly rim folds
tapering to short cylindrical base, interior
decorated w/orange flowers & gold
leaves, silver-plated footed frame tapering to twining calla lilies to form handle,
calla lily handles on matching spoons,
Thos. Webb & Sons Patented, pr. (one
bowl slightly darker)..................................... **1,675**
Finger bowl, nine-crimp top, satin finish,
Mt. Washington Glass Co., 4 3/8" d.,
2 1/4" h. **225**

Burmese Finger Bowl

Finger bowl, wide squatty bulbous body
w/incurved crimped rim, satin finish, Mt.
Washington Glass Co., 4 1/2" d., 2" h.
(ILLUS.).. **350**
Ice cream dish, individual, ruffled rim, Mt.
Washington Glass Co., 4 3/4" w. **220**
Rose bowl, miniature, spherical body w/an
eight-crimp rim, satin finish, unsigned
Webb, 2 3/8" d., 2 1/8" h. (ILLUS. right) **225**
Rose bowl, spherical w/eight-crimp rim,
decorated w/pink, green & blue maiden-
hair fern & outlined in gold, satin finish,
unsigned Webb, 2 3/8" d., 2 1/4" h............... **375**

Two Miniature Burmese Rose Bowls

Rose bowl, miniature, spherical w/an eight-
crimp rim, satin finish decorated w/enam-
eled lavender five-petal flowers w/green
& brown leaves, attributed to Thomas
Webb, 2 3/8" d., 2 3/8" h. (ILLUS. left).......... **335**

Webb Burmese Rose Bowl

Rose bowl, spherical w/eight-crimp rim,
satin finish, Thomas Webb & Sons, 3" d.,
3" h. (ILLUS.) **225**
Rose bowl, bulbous base tapering to a hex-
agonal rim, decorated w/lavender five-
petal flowers & green & brown leaves,
satin finish, unsigned Webb, 3" d.,
3 1/4" h... **295**
Rose bowl, spherical, six-crimp rim, deco-
rated w/bronze & gold-tinted chrysanthemums & leaves all outlined in gold, un-
signed Webb, 3 3/8" d., 3 3/8" h. **650**
Toothpick holder, cylindrical w/tricornered
rim, Mt. Washington Glass Co. **245**

Toothpick holder, Diamond Quilted patt., satin finish, Mt. Washington Glass Co. . **275-350**

Toothpick holder, footed ovoid body w/a short cylindrical neck, decorated w/lavender blossoms & green & brown leaves, satin finish, attributed to Webb, 2 1/4" d., 3" h. **350**

Toothpick holder, waisted cylindrical form, polished pontil, satin finish, 2 1/2" h. **250**

Toothpick holder, bulbous ovoid body tapering to a short six-sided neck, satin finish, 2 1/2" d., 2 1/2" h. **195**

Toothpick holder, bulbous squatty base w/a flaring squared neck, decorated w/lavender blossoms & green & brown leaves, satin finish, attributed to Webb, 2 1/2" d., 2 7/8" h. **325**

Vase, 3 1/4" h., miniature, cylindrical w/five-point crimped rim, marked "Thomas Webb and Sons" **303**

Vase, 3 1/4" h., miniature, ruffled top, decorated w/wild roses, glossy finish, signed Webb **375**

Vase, 3 1/4" h., 3 1/2" d., miniature, a footed squatty bulbous body tapering to a narrow neck below a widely flaring fluted rim w/pointed fluting, decorated w/enameled oak leaves & acorns, satin finish **325**

Decorated Webb Burmese Vase

Vase, 3 1/2" h., 3" d., miniature, bulbous ovoid body tapering to a short cylindrical neck, decorated w/narrow black bands flanking a band of small blue flowers w/red centers & green leaves, glossy finish, Thomas Webb & Sons, unsigned (ILLUS.) **350**

Vase, 3 5/8" h., 3" d., miniature, squatty bulbous base w/a slightly flaring tall cylindrical neck topped by a fluted & crimped rim, glossy finish, unsigned Webb **195**

Vase, 3 5/8" h., 3 3/8" d., miniature, spherical body w/a short six-sided neck, decorated w/green ivy leaves in two shades of green & tan, satin finish, unsigned Webb **395**

Small Ruffled Rim Burmese Vase

Vase, 3 7/8" h., 2 7/8" d., squatty bulbous base below a cylindrical neck w/widely flaring ruffled & crimped rim, satin finish, Thomas Webb & Sons, unsigned (ILLUS.)... **250**

Vase, 4" h., 2 3/4" d., bulbous body tapering to a flaring neck w/crimped rim, decorated w/blue & white flowers & brown leaves, satin finish, unsigned Webb **375**

Vase, 4" h., 2 7/8" d., conical body w/flaring ruffled rim, satin finish w/peach striped effect in glass, unsigned Webb **250**

Burmese Vase Attributed to Webb

Vase, 4" h., 2 7/8" d., squatty bulbous base tapering to flared rim w/folded over ruffles, unsigned Webb (ILLUS.) **225**

Vase, 4 1/4" h., short body w/ruffled rim & applied ruffled foot, satin finish...................... **220**

Vase, 4 1/4" h., 2 1/2" d., ovoid body w/a four-petal shaped rim, enameled w/coral flower buds & green leaves, satin finish, unsigned Webb.. **425**

Vase, 4 1/2" h., footed baluster-form w/deeply ruffled rim, decorated w/flowers & foliage **300**

Vase, 5" h., bud, bottle-form, footed spherical body w/a tall slender "stick" neck, the body enameled w/dotted daisy-like blossoms & leaves w/gilt trim, the branches & tracery encircling the body, Mt. Washington Glass Co. **2,860**

Vase, 5" h., urn-form w/applied handles, Mt. Washington Glass Co...................................... **350**

Vase, 7 1/4" h., classic baluster-shape urn-form, the bulbous ovoid body raised on a short pedestal foot, wide cylindrical neck w/flaring rim flanked by slender angled handles down to the shoulder, Mt. Washington Glass Co. **900**

Burmese Jack-in-the-Pulpit Vase

Vase, 7 1/4" h., 3 1/2" d., jack-in-the-pulpit style, crimped & upturned rim on a slender trumpet-form body on a disk foot, satin finish, Mt. Washington Glass Co. (ILLUS.) 375

Vase, 8" h., double gourd-shaped, decorated w/peach-colored roses & turquoise-colored forget-me-not blossoms, Mt. Washington Glass Co. 1,250

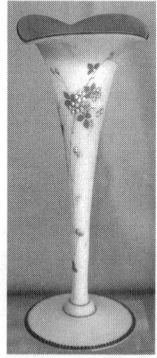

Decorated Burmese Lily Vase

Vase, 8" h., lily-type, tall slender body w/flaring tri-lobed rim, round disk foot, the sides enameled w/delicate forget-me-nots, satin finish, Mt. Washington Glass Co. (ILLUS.) 1,200

Vase, 8 1/4" h., 4" d., footed bottle-form w/tall cylindrical neck, decorated w/green & brown leaves & red flower buds, satin finish, unsigned Webb 750

Vase, 8 3/4" h., cylindrical slightly waisted form w/a flaring ruffled rim, glossy finish 385

Vase, 10 1/4" h., stick-type w/rounded bulbous base & slender neck, decorated w/raised gold flower & vine decoration, satin finish, unmarked Webb 1,100

Vase, 10 1/4" h., trumpet-form body w/a gently ruffled rim, raised on a ringed pedestal on a disk foot, Bryden-Pairpoint 250

Vase, 12 1/2" h., bulbous base w/long "stick" neck, clear applied handles at the base of the neck, decorated overall w/dainty blossoms, shadow foliage & fragile gold branches 2,500

Vase, 12 1/2" h., slender trumpet form w/jack-in-the-pulpit rim, satin finish 750

Vase, 14 1/2" h., trumpet form w/jack-in-the-pulpit tightly crimped rim, glossy finish, Mt. Washington Glass Co. 950

Vase, 23 1/2" h., trumpet-form, footed slender body w/a tricorner rim 1,500

Vases, 6 1/2" h., two-handled, footed rare ginkgo leaf decoration, Mt. Washington Glass Co., pr. 2,100

Cambridge

Cambridge Glass operated from 1902 until 1954 in Cambridge, Ohio. Early wares included numerous pressed glass patterns in imitation of cut glass, often clear and bearing an impressed mark of "NEAR CUT" in the inside center of the object. Later products included color, stylized shapes, animals and hand-cut and decorated

tableware. Particularly popular with collectors today are the Statuesque line, popularly called Nude Stems, and a pink opaque color called Crown Tuscan. When marked, which is infrequently, the Cambridge mark is the letter "C" in a triangle. Other authors have been wise to remind us not to confuse this 20th century company with the earlier New England Glass Company of Cambridge, Massachusetts, at times called "Cambridge Glass."

NEAR CUT   TUSCAN

Cambridge Marks

Etched Rose Point Pattern

Ashtray, clear, 4 1/2" $59

Bell, clear 175

Bowl, 13" d., 12" l., No. 3400/1, clear 110

Butter dish, cov., round, clear, 5 1/2" 200

Cake plate, handled, No. 3500, clear, 13 1/2" d. 80

Cake plate, handled, No. 3900, clear, 14" d. 95

Candlestick, single-light, No. 3400, clear, 5 1/4" h. 45

Candlestick, single-light, No. 3900, clear, 4 1/2" h. 40

Candlestick, two-light, No. 3400, clear 59

Candy dish, cov., No. 3500/57, clear 125

Celery tray, No. 3500, clear, 11 1/2" l. 75

Champagne, No. 3121, clear 35

Rose Point Cocktail and Sherbet

Cocktail, No. 3500, clear, 3 oz. (ILLUS. right) 40

Cordial, No. 3106, clear 250

Cordial, No. 3500, clear, 5 1/2" h. 82

Cordial, No. 7966, clear 175

Cup & saucer, No. 3400, clear 48

Cup & saucer, No. 3900, clear 45

Decanter w/stopper, No. 1320, clear 410

Goblet, No. 3121, water, clear, 8 3/4" h. 50

Lamp globe, hurricane-type, clear, 6" h. 190

Mayonnaise bowl, ladle & underplate, No. 3400, clear, the set 80

Nappy, No. 3500, 6 3/4" d. 39

Oyster cocktail, No. 3121, clear 65

Pitcher, 7" h., No. 3400, clear 420

Pitcher, 8" h., No. 3400, Doulton-style, clear 350

Plate, 8 1/2" d., No. 3500, clear 27

Plate, 9 1/2" d., No. 3400, clear 48
Plate, 10 1/4" d., No. 3400, clear 160
Plate, 10 1/2" d., No. 3900, clear 174
Relish dish, No. 3400, clear, 8" 56
Relish dish, two-part, No. 3400/1093, clear 85
Relish dish, two-part, No. 3500, clear,
    8 1/2" 48
Salt & pepper shakers, No. 3400, clear, pr. 75
Sherbet, No. 3500, clear, tall 7 oz. (ILLUS.
    left) 30
Tumbler, flat, No. 3400, clear, 2" h. 100
Tumbler, flat, No. 3400, clear, 4" h. 68
Tumbler, footed, clear, 7" h. 35
Tumbler, iced tea, clear, 7 1/2" h. 50
Tumbler, No. 497, clear, 8 oz. 125
Tumbler, No. 3400/38, clear, 12 oz. 85
Vase, bud, 8 1/2" h., clear 75
Wine, clear, 5 7/8" h. 94
Wine, clear, 6 1/4" h. 115

Miscellaneous Patterns

Almond dish, individual, etched Cleo patt.,
    pink, 2 1/2" 85
Ashtray, etched Minerva patt., clear 55
Ashtray, pressed Caprice patt., clear, 4" 10
Ashtray, Silhouette line, Royal Blue bowl on
    clear Nude Lady stem 350
Ashtray/match holder, pressed Caprice
    patt., Moonlight (light blue) 20
Basket, footed, two-handled, etched Diane
    patt., Crystal, 6" h. 30
Basket, Janice patt., ruby w/clear handle 195
Basket, reeded handle, No. 3500/52, clear,
    6" h. 550
Bonbon, footed, two handled, etched Can-
    dlelight patt., Crystal 42
Bonbon, pressed Caprice patt., clear, 6" 20
Bowl, 5" sq., jelly, two-handled, pressed
    Caprice patt., No. 151, clear 15
Bowl, 7 1/2" d., footed, Azurite 45
Bowl, 9" d., four-footed, pressed Caprice
    patt., Moonlight 135
Bowl, 10" d., etched Chantilly patt., three-
    part, on silvered metal base, clear 89
Bowl, 10" d., shallow, four-footed, pressed
    Caprice patt., clear 45
Bowl, 10 1/2" d., No. 1359, clear 125
Bowl, 11" d., etched Apple Blossom patt.,
    low footed, gold-encrusted, Mandarin
    Gold (light yellow) 150
Bowl, 11" d., four-footed, No. 3400/45,
    clear 118
Bowl, 11" d., No. 3400/48, clear 135
Bowl, 12" d., etched Chantilly patt., Martha
    line blank, four-footed, clear 275
Bowl, 12" d., etched Wildflower patt., No.
    3400/4, four-footed, flared, gold-encrust-
    ed clear 125
Bowl, 12" d., pressed Caprice patt., pink 75
Bowl, 12" l., etched Wildflower patt., ob-
    long, fancy edge, No. 3900/160, clear 125
Bowl, 12" l., four-footed, oblong, fancy rim,
    No. 3400/160, clear 150
Bowl, 12 1/2" d., 5 1/2" h., crimped rim,
    footed, pressed Caprice patt., Moonlight,
    No. 61 145
Bowl, salad, 13 1/2" d., Caprice patt., No.
    82, Moonlight 325
Bowl, etched Diane patt., four-footed,
    square, clear 75

Bowl, etched Diane patt., Tally-Ho line,
    clear 155
Butter dish, cov., etched Diane patt., clear 195
Butter dish, cov., etched Wildflower patt.,
    No. 3400/52, clear 195
Candelabra, three-light, No. 1338, clear, pr. 200
Candleholder, Martha Washington line,
    Ebony (black), 4" h. 35
Candlestick, three-light, Cambridge Arms
    patt., clear, 5 1/4" h. 65
Candlestick, three-light, pressed Caprice
    patt., clear 42
Candlestick, three-light, pressed Caprice
    patt., clear, 6" h. 40
Candlestick, two-light, etched Wildflower
    patt., No. 647, clear 55
Candlestick, two-light, keyhole stem, gold-
    encrusted, No. 3400/647, clear, 6" h. 95
Candlesticks, etched Diane patt., Martha
    line blank, No. 497, clear, pr. 350
Candlesticks, figural dolphin stem, domed
    base, clear, 8 1/4" h., pr. 140
Candlesticks, Gadroon (No. 3500) line,
    molded ram's heads on the socket, Am-
    ber, 4 1/2" h., pr. 155
Candlesticks, Martha line blank, No. 497,
    w/prisms, clear, 7 1/2" h., pr. 550
Candlesticks, one-light, etched Apple Blos-
    som patt., Topaz, pr. 65
Candlesticks, three-light, pressed Caprice
    patt., No. 1338, Mandarin Gold, 6" h., pr. 135
Candlesticks, two-light, etched Portia patt.,
    cornucopia-stem, Mandarin Gold, pr. 235
Candlesticks, two-light, etched Wildflower
    patt., fleur-de-lis stem, No. 3400/647,
    gold-encrusted clear, 6" h., pr. 125
Candlesticks, two-light, keyhole stem,
    gold-encrusted, No. 3400/647, clear,
    6" h., pr. 150
Candlesticks, pressed Caprice patt., No.
    67, Moonlight, 2 1/2" h., pr. 75
Candlesticks, three-light, pressed Caprice
    patt., clear, 6" h., pr. 85
Candlesticks, pressed Caprice patt., No.
    69, Moonlight, 7" h., pr. 160
Candy box, cov., etched Chantilly patt.,
    footed, clear 135
Candy box, cov., etched Wildflower patt.,
    No. 3900/165, clear 100
Candy dish, cov., three-footed, pressed
    Caprice patt., clear 50
Candy dish, cov., etched Diane patt., clear 130
Center bowl, Gadroon (No. 3400) line, foot-
    ed, scalloped rim, ram's head handles,
    Amber, 9" d. 135
Cigarette box, cov., footed, etched Gloria
    patt., gold encrusted Crown Tuscan 220
Cigarette urn, etched Diane patt., clear 38
Claret, pressed Caprice patt., Moonlight,
    No. 5, 4 1/2 oz. 210
Claret, Statuesque line, Carmen (bright red)
    bowl, clear Nude Lady stem, 7 5/8" h. 275
Claret, pressed Caprice patt., Moonlight, Al-
    pine etching 185
Cocktail, blown Caprice patt., No. 301,
    Moonlight, 3 oz. 45
Cocktail, etched Portia patt., No. 3121,
    clear, 3 oz. 122
Cocktail, Mt. Vernon line, footed, clear, No.
    26, 3 1/2 oz. 10

Statuesque Line Cocktail

Cocktail, Statuesque line, Mandarin Gold
bowl, clear Nude Lady stem (ILLUS.).............. **80**
Cocktail, Statuesque (No. 3011) line, Ame-
thyst bowl, clear Nude Lady stem, 4 1/2
oz., 6 1/2" h... **110**
Cocktail, Statuesque (No. 3011) line, Emer-
ald (light green) bowl, clear Nude Lady
stem, 4 1/2 oz., 6 1/2" h................................ **110**
Cocktail icer, etched Diane patt., clear............ **78**
Cocktail & icer, No. 3600, clear, 2 pcs. **110**
Cocktail & icer, No. 968, clear, 2 pcs. **110**
Cocktail shaker, No. 3400/175, clear **200**
Cocktail shaker, No. 98, clear....................... **210**
Comport, two-handled, Mt. Vernon line,
Emerald green... **65**
Compote, blown, No. 3121 stem, clear,
5 3/8" h. **175**

Compote on Chrome Nude Lady Base

Compote, open, chrome Farberware Nude
Lady stem w/Amethyst bowl insert
(ILLUS.).. **62**
Compote, open, 7" d., low, footed, pressed
Caprice patt., clear **25**
Compote, open, 8" d., Mt. Vernon line, clear....... **25**
Compote, open, Statuesque line, Cobalt,
clear Nude Lady stem.................................... **425**
Console bowl, etched Apple Blossom patt.,
rolled edge, Gold Krystol, 12 1/2" d.............. **125**
Cordial, etched Chantilly patt., No. 3625,
clear, 1 oz. **75**
Cordial, etched Diane patt., clear........................ **45**
Cordial, etched Portia patt., No. 3130,
clear, 1 oz. **75**

Cordial, Line 1341, mushroom-style, Am-
ber.. **10**
Cordial, Line 1341, mushroom-style, Car-
men (bright red) **25**
Cordial, Line No. 3500, Carmen **90**
Cordial, Mt. Vernon line, footed, clear, 1 oz. **22**
Cordial, No. 3121, clear, 1 oz.............................. **93**
Cordial, pressed Cambridge Square patt.,
clear, 2 1/8" h.. **32**
Cordial, pressed Caprice patt., Moonlight,
4 1/2" h.. **125**
Cordial, pressed Pristine patt., No. 1936,
clear, 4 1/2" h.. **55**
Cordial, Tally-Ho line, Forest green, 5" h. **80**
Creamer & sugar bowl, English Hobnail
patt., clear, pr.. **38**
Crown Tuscan candy dish, cov., shell-
shaped, gold decoration, 6" w......................... **70**
Crown Tuscan candy dish, cov., three-
part... **95**
Crown Tuscan cigarette box, cov..................... **65**
Crown Tuscan cocktail, topaz bowl
w/Nude Lady stem, 6 1/2" h.......................... **150**
Crown Tuscan compote, 6" d., Nude Lady
stem, gold-encrusted **200**

Crown Tuscan Plate

Crown Tuscan plate, 7" d. (ILLUS.) **45**
Crown Tuscan plate, 8" d., pressed Ca-
price patt. **35**
Crown Tuscan plate, torte, 14" d...................... **125**
Crown Tuscan urn, cov., 8" h........................... **150**
Crown Tuscan vase, 10" h., Sea Shell
patt., pedestal base... **50**
Cruet w/original stopper, No. 3900/100,
clear, 6 oz. **145**
Cruet w/original stopper, pressed Caprice
patt., oil, No. 101, clear, 3 oz........................... **50**
Cruet w/original stopper & metal holder,
No. 3400 line, oil, Emerald.............................. **40**
Cup, pressed Caprice patt., No. 17, clear........... **15**
Cup & saucer, demitasse, No. 3400 line,
clear... **15**
Cup & saucer, Mt. Vernon line, clear **15**
Cup & saucer, pressed Caprice patt.,
Moonlight... **55**
Cup & saucer, pressed Cascade patt.,
clear... **22**
Cup & saucer, Tally-Ho line, Royal (cobalt
blue)... **70**
Decanter w/stopper, etched Portia patt.,
No. 1321, clear, 28 oz. **325**
Decanter w/stopper, etched Portia patt.,
No. 3400/92, clear, 32 oz............................... **375**
Decanter w/stopper, No. 1372, cut neck &
stopper, clear **1,950**

Figural flower frog/holder, "Draped Lady," clear, 13" h. 125

Figure flower frog/holder, "Bashful Charlotte," Emerald, 13" h. 295

Figure flower holder, "Draped Lady," Emerald, 8 1/2" h. 295

Figure flower holder, "Draped Lady," Ritz Blue, 8 1/2" h. 325

Goblet, etched Apple Blossom patt., clear, 9 oz. 20

Goblet, etched Candlelight patt., clear, 6 1/4" h. 58

Goblet, etched Diane patt., No. 3122, clear, 9 oz. 30

Goblet, etched Diane patt., Regency line, clear 65

Goblet, etched Elaine patt., water, clear 30

Goblet, Mt. Vernon line, clear, 10 oz. 15

Goblet, Mt. Vernon line, clear, 12 oz. 12

Goblet, Statuesque line, banquet-size, Emerald bowl, clear Nude Lady stem, 10" h. 375

Goblet, Statuesque line, table-size, Carmen bowl, clear Nude Lady stem, 9 1/2" h. 275

Goblet, water, Cambridge Square patt., clear, 5" h. 26

Goblet, water, Gadroon (No. 3500 line), Royal, 8 3/8" h. 49

Goblet, water, hand blown Caprice patt., clear, 5 7/8" h. 38

Goblet, water, pressed Caprice patt., clear, 6 3/4" h. 30

Goblet, water, pressed Caprice patt., Moonlight, 6 1/2" h. 48

Goblet, water, pressed Caprice patt., No. 200, clear, 9 oz. 16

Goblet, water, pressed Cascade patt., clear, 5 1/2" h. 18

Honey jar, No. 3500/139, clear........................ 500

Ice bucket, etched Candlelight patt., No. 3900, clear.. 135

Lamp, table model, etched Diane patt., gold-encrusted, slender ovoid body, metal fittings, Carmen, 14 1/2" h. 625

Martini pitcher, etched Diane patt., clear, 60 oz. 1,995

Mayonnaise bowl & ladle, etched Portia patt., 2 pcs. 40

Mayonnaise set: bowl, underplate & ladle; etched Wildflower patt., No. 3900/129, gold-encrusted clear, the set 125

Model of a swan, Crown Tuscan, 6" h............. 150

Model of a swan, Emerald, No. 1040, 3" l............. 50

Mug, Mt. Vernon line, stein-type, No. 84, Amber, 14 oz. 38

Nut dish, low, divided, pressed Caprice patt., Moonlight, No. 94, 7 1/2" d..................... 52

Nut dish, pressed Caprice patt., yellow 38

Parfait, pressed Caprice patt., Moonlight, 6 1/2" h. 154

Pitcher, Caprice patt., ball-shaped, Moonlight, 80 oz. 360

Pitcher, etched Apple Blossom patt., ball-shaped, clear, 80 oz. 175

Pitcher, etched Cleo patt., No. 955, Amber, 62 oz. 275

Pitcher, etched Diane patt., ball-shaped, clear 295

Pitcher, etched Elaine patt., jug-form, clear 295

Pitcher, etched Portia patt., ball-shaped, gold-encrusted, Mandarin Gold..................... 185

Pitcher, pressed Caprice patt., ball-shaped, No. 183, clear, 80 oz....................................... 150

Pitcher, pressed Caprice patt., Moonlight, 32 oz. 400

Plate, 6 1/2" d., bread & butter, etched Portia patt., clear... 9

Plate, 7" d., etched Cleo patt., Decagon line, Moonlight.. 20

Plate, 7" d., pressed Caprice patt., clear............. 15

Plate, 8" d., No. 739 line, Mandarin Gold............. 11

Plate, 8" d., pressed Caprice patt., clear............. 15

Plate, 8 1/2" d., Everglade patt., clear 36

Plate, 9" d., pressed Caprice patt., clear (slight wear)... 20

Plate, 10" d., two-handled, etched Martha patt., clear.. 22

Plate, 10 1/2" d., dinner, etched Portia patt., clear.. 80

Plate, 11" d., three-footed, pressed Caprice patt., clear.. 35

Plate, 14" d., four-footed, pressed Caprice patt., Moonlight, No. 28 110

Plate, 14" d., three-footed, pressed Caprice patt., clear.. 40

Plate, 11", cabaret, pressed Caprice patt., Moonlight... 75

Platter, 13 1/2" l., etched Apple Blossom patt., rectangular w/tab handles, Mandarin Gold... 110

Relish dish, divided, pressed Caprice patt., clear, 6" l... 45

Relish dish, three-part, etched Candlelight patt., No. 3400, clear, 8"............................ 38

Relish dish, two-part, etched Diane patt., clear, 6" l... 27

Relish dish, three-part, No. 3400 line, Emerald, 7" l... 28

Relish dish, three-part, No. 3900/125, gold-encrusted, clear, 9" d. 65

Relish dish, three-part, pressed Caprice patt., No. 124, clear, 8" l................................. 25

Relish dish, five part, clear 375

Relish dish, etched Elaine patt., No. 3500/67, clear, 6 pcs. 250

Caprice Rose Bowl

Rose bowl, pressed Caprice patt., Moonlight, large (ILLUS.) 150-210

Rose bowl & flower frog, pressed Caprice patt., footed, No. 235, Moonlight, 6" d., 2 pcs. 450

Salt dip, No. 3400 line, Amethyst 15

Salt & pepper shakers, etched Elaine patt., clear, pr. (one glass lid)................................. 40

Salt & pepper shakers, footed, etched Chantilly patt., clear, pr................................... 55

Salt & pepper shakers w/glass tops, etched Gloria patt., tall, Mandarin Gold, pr. 120

Salt shaker w/original chrome top, No. 3400 line, Cobalt.. 30

Salt shaker w/original top, etched Apple Blossom patt., Moonlight.............................. 130

Salt shaker w/original top, etched Wildflower patt., No. 3900/1177, clear 20

Salt shaker w/original top, pressed Caprice patt., Moonlight, No. 96........................... 50

Saucer, pressed Caprice patt., No. 17, clear......... 5

Sherbet, blown Caprice patt., tall, No. 300, clear, 6 oz. 14

Sherbet, etched Apple Blossom patt., Mandarin Gold, tall, No. 3130, 6 oz....................... 25

Sherbet, Mt. Vernon line, clear, 6 1/2 oz............. 10

Sherbet, No. 3500, clear, tall 24

Sherbet, pressed Caprice patt., Moonlight, 4 1/2" h. 45

Sherbet, pressed Caprice patt., No. 301, clear, 4 1/4" h. 15

Sherbet, pressed Caprice patt., No. 301, clear, 5 3/4" h. 20

Sherbet, etched Elaine patt., clear, No. 3035 20

Smoke set, pressed Caprice patt., Moonlight, shell-footed, six pieces in original box, the set 110

Sugar bowl, individual, pressed Caprice patt., clear... 15

Sugar bowl, pressed Caprice patt., clear, No. 38, medium....................................... 12

Sugar bowl, pressed Caprice patt., clear, No. 41, large.. 15

Sugar sifter w/lid, etched Cleo patt., footed, Moonlight, 6 3/4" h. 1,500

Tray, for individual creamer & sugar bowl, pressed Caprice patt., clear 20

Tray, oval, pressed Caprice patt., clear, 9" l. 22

Tray, wafer, etched Cleo patt., Emerald........... 365

Tumbler, etched Apple Blossom patt., footed, No. 3135, clear, 12 oz. 22

Tumbler, etched Apple Blossom patt., No. 3130, footed, Mandarin Gold, 12 oz. 40

Tumbler, etched Cleo patt., Amber, 8 oz........... 22

Tumbler, etched Portia patt., footed, No. 3077, clear, 12 oz. 25

Tumbler, footed, Caprice patt., No. 300, Moonlight, 10 oz. 50

Tumbler, footed, Caprice patt., No. 300, Moonlight, 12 oz. 50

Tumbler, footed, Caprice patt., No. 300, Moonlight, 5 oz...................................... 240

Tumbler, footed, Caprice patt., No. 310, Moonlight, 5 oz...................................... 140

Tumbler, footed, pressed Caprice patt., No. 10, Moonlight, 10 oz. 50

Tumbler, footed, pressed Caprice patt., No. 180, Moonlight, 5 oz.............................. 65

Tumbler, footed, pressed Caprice patt., No. 184, Moonlight, 12 oz............................ 60

Tumbler, footed, pressed Caprice patt., No. 184, pink, 12 oz.................................. 50

Tumbler, footed, pressed Cascade patt., clear, 5 1/8" h. 20

Tumbler, iced tea, Caprice patt., No. 300, clear, 6 1/8" h. 36

Tumbler, iced tea, etched Elaine patt., clear, 12 oz. 35

Tumbler, juice, Cambridge Square patt., clear, 4" h.. 15

Tumbler, Old Fashion, pressed Caprice patt., Moonlight, No. 310, 7 oz. 130

Tumbler, pressed Caprice patt., No. 184, Moonlight, 12 oz. 60

Tumbler, Square Line, No. 3797, clear.............. 15

Tumbler, iced tea, pressed Caprice patt., flat, Moonlight.. 115

Tumbler, iced tea, pressed Caprice patt., No. 310, clear, 5 1/4" h. 115

Vase, 6" h., etched Apple Blossom patt., No. 1308, Emerald 600

Vase, bud, 6" h., pressed Caprice patt., Moonlight.. 150

Vase, 6 1/2" h., etched Wildflower patt., globe-shaped, No. 3400/103, Mandarin Gold 375

Vase, 8" h., flip, No. 3500/139, clear............... 125

Vase, 8 1/2" h., ball-shaped, pressed Caprice patt., three ring, Moonlight 450

Vase, 9" h., etched Candlelight patt., keyhole shape, clear...................................... 74

Vase, 11" h., etched Cleo patt., Emerald 130

Vase, bud, Statuesque line, Amber, clear Nude Lady stem 775

Vegetable bowl, cov., etched Cleo patt., Amber, 9"... 190

Water set: Doulton-style 80 oz. pitcher & five flat tumblers; No. 3400, Cobalt (dark blue), the set 275

Water set: pitcher & four tumblers; Gyro Optic line, Amber, the set......................... 68

Water tray, etched Cleo patt., Amber............... 225

Wine, Caprice patt., No. 300, clear, 4 1/2" h......... 44

Wine, Caprice patt., No. 301, clear, 5 5/8" h........ 30

Wine, pressed Caprice patt., clear..................... 38

Wine, Tally-Ho line, No. 1420, clear, 4 1/2" h. 60

Carnival

Earlier called Taffeta glass, the Carnival glass now being collected was introduced early in the 20th century. Its producers gave it an iridescence that attempted to imitate that of some Tiffany glass. Collectors will find available books by leading authorities Donald E. Moore, Sherman Hand, Marion T. Hartung, Rose M. Presznick, and Bill Edwards.

Acanthus (Imperial)

Bowl, 7" d., marigold $55

Bowl, 7 3/4" d., marigold.................................... 48

Bowl, 7 3/4" d., smoky 50

Bowl, 8" to 9" d., green 82

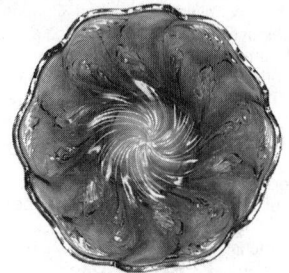

Acanthus Bowl

Bowl, 8" to 9" d., marigold (ILLUS.) 106
Bowl, 8" to 9" d., purple.............................. 200
Bowl, 9" d., ice cream shape, marigold.............. 50
Bowl, 8" to 9" d., smoky 99
Plate, 9" to 10" d., marigold 295
Plate, chop, marigold.. 350
Plate, chop, smoky... 450

Amaryllis (Dugan)
Compote, marigold... 325
Compote, purple 300-325

Apple Blossom Twigs
Banana boat-shaped bowl, purple, ruffled..... 190
Bowl, three-in-one edge, peach opalescent 225
Bowl, 8" to 9" d., blue, ice cream shape,
  Basketweave exterior.................................... 200
Bowl, 8" to 9" d., marigold 55-75
Bowl, 8" to 9" d., peach opalescent 170
Bowl, 8" to 9" d., purple.............................. 230-250
Bowl, 8 1/2" d., peach opalescent, ice
  cream shape.. 175-200
Bowl, 9" d., white, ice cream shape.................. 170
Bowl, peach opalescent, low, ruffled 145
Plate, 9" d., blue 450
Plate, 9" d., marigold... 100
Plate, 9" d., marigold, ruffled 92
Plate, 9" d., peach opalescent.................... 400-450
Plate, 9" d., purple...................................... 300-350
Plate, 9" d., purple, flat, smooth edge.............. 750
Plate, 9" d., white... 268
Plate, 9" d., white, ruffled, ... 200-225

Apple Tree
Pitcher, water, marigold............................. 200-225
Pitcher, water, white.................................... 465-475
Tumbler, blue 85
Tumbler, marigold... 41
Water set: pitcher & 4 tumblers; marigold, 5
  pcs... 375
Water set: pitcher & 4 tumblers; white, 5
  pcs... 1,000-1,500

April Showers (Fenton)
Vase, teal.. 225
Vase, white.. 200
Vase, 7 1/2" h., purple 55
Vase, 8" h., green... 70
Vase, 8" h., marigold... 45
Vase, 9" h., blue, pie crust edge 80
Vase, 9 3/4" h., green, Peacock Tail interior....... 95
Vase, 10" h., blue 50

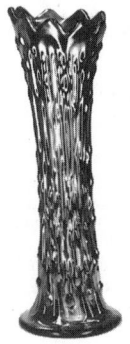

April Showers Vase

Vase, 10" h., purple (ILLUS.) 48
Vase, 10" h., teal 70
Vase, 10 1/2" h., purple, Peacock Tail interi-
  or.. 75-80
Vase, 11" h., blue 80-90
Vase, 11" h., green, Peacock Tail interior........... 90
Vase, 11" h., purple, Peacock Tail interior.......... 70
Vase, 11" h., ribbon candy rim, purple.............. 175
Vase, 11 1/2" h., green, Peacock Tail interi-
  or... 150
Vase, 11 1/2" h., marigold.................................... 57
Vase, 12" h., blue 57
Vase, 12" h., green 65
Vase, 12" h., marigold, Peacock Tail interior....... 40
Vase, 12" h., purple, Peacock Tail interior.......... 90
Vase, 12" h., vaseline.. 175
Vase, 13" h., green 35
Vase, 13 1/2" h., marigold.................................... 46
Vase, purple opalescent............................... 700-750

Australian
Bowl, 9" to 10" d., Emu, marigold 175
Bowl, 9" to 10" d., Emu, purple.......................... 600
Bowl, 9" to 10" d., Kangaroo, black ame-
  thyst.. 650
Bowl, 9" to 10" d., Kangaroo, purple........... 250-275
Bowl, 9" to 10" d., Kingfisher, purple......... 150-200
Bowl, 9" to 10" d., Kiwi, marigold, ruffled... 240-250
Bowl, 9" to 10" d., Kookaburra, purple 188
Bowl, 9" to 10" d., Magpie, marigold.................. 185
Bowl, 9" to 10" d., Swan, marigold.................... 138

Australian Swan Bowl

Bowl, 9" to 10" d., Swan, purple (ILLUS.).. 140-150
Bowl, 9" to 10" d., Thunderbird, marigold 215
Bowl, 11" d., Kookaburra, marigold, ice
  cream shape... 185-200
Compote, Butterflies & Waratah, marigold....... 200
Sauce dish, Kangaroo, purple............................ 57
Sauce dish, Magpie, purple............................... 300

Beaded Bull's Eye (Imperial)
Vase, 5 1/4" h., green... 325
Vase, 7" to 12" h., marigold................................. 65
Vase, 7" to 12" h., purple 148

Beaded Cable (Northwood)
Candy dish, marigold..................................... 40-45
Candy dish, purple... 65
Rose bowl, aqua.. 345
Rose bowl, aqua opalescent............................. 400
Rose bowl, blue... 275
Rose bowl, green 100-125
Rose bowl, ice blue... 850
Rose bowl, ice green...................................... 1,800
Rose bowl, lavender 375
Rose bowl, marigold.. 125
Rose bowl, white... 500

Beaded Shell (Dugan or Diamond Glass Co.)

Butter dish, cov., purple 160
Creamer, purple 64
Mug, blue 140-150
Mug, marigold 105-115

Beaded Shell Mug

Mug, purple (ILLUS.) 50
Mug, white 700
Sauce dish, purple 42
Spooner, footed, marigold 40
Sugar bowl, cov., marigold 55
Tumbler, blue 190-225
Tumbler, lavender 80
Tumbler, marigold 55-65
Tumbler, purple 75-80

Beauty Bud Vase

Marigold, 8" h. 40
Marigold, 9 1/2" h. 35
Purple, 6 1/2" h. 88
Purple, 8" h. 40

Bird with Grapes

Wall vase, marigold, 7 1/2" w., 8" h. 86

Blackberry Bramble

Compote, green, ruffled, ... 63
Compote, marigold, ruffled 50-60
Compote, olive green, ruffled 80
Compote, purple, ruffled 43
Compote, purple, ruffled, sq. 78

Blackberry (Fenton)

Basket, blue 65-75
Basket, green 155
Basket, marigold 45
Basket, purple 115
Basket, red 250-375
Bowl, 8" to 9" d., green, ruffled 95

Blackberry Plate

Plate, marigold, openwork rim (ILLUS.) 500-525

Blackberry Miniature Compote

Blackberry Miniature Compote

Blue (ILLUS.) 75-85
Green 200-350
Marigold 85
Purple 75

Blackberry Spray

Bonbon, marigold 29
Bowl, 7" d., marigold 25
Compote, 5 1/2" d., green 45
Compote, 5 1/2" d., marigold 38
Hat shape, amber 99
Hat shape, amber, jack-in-the-pulpit, crimped rim 145
Hat shape, Amberina 350
Hat shape, Amberina opalescent, ruffled 725
Hat shape, aqua 88
Hat shape, aqua, jack-in-the-pulpit, crimped rim 105
Hat shape, blue 48
Hat shape, blue, jack-in-the-pulpit, crimped rim 63
Hat shape, green 120
Hat shape, green, jack-in-the-pulpit, crimped rim 200-225
Hat shape, ice green opalescent 300-350
Hat shape, jack-in-the-pulpit, crimped rim, red 407
Hat shape, marigold 38
Hat shape, milk white w/marigold overlay 165
Hat shape, purple 53
Hat shape, red 277
Hat shape, red opalescent 675
Hat shape, red slag 550-575
Hat shape, vaseline 71
Hat shape, vaseline, jack-in-the-pulpit, crimped rim 70-75
Hat shape, vaseline w/marigold overlay 60

Blackberry Wreath (Millersburg)

Bowl, 5" d., green 80-100
Bowl, 5" d., marigold 35
Bowl, 5" d., marigold, ruffled 80
Bowl, 5" d., marigold variant, fluted 100
Bowl, 5" d., purple 63
Bowl, 5" d., purple, candy ribbon edge 100
Bowl, 5" d., purple variant, ice cream shape, fluted 200-215
Bowl, 6" d., green, three-in-one edge 124
Bowl, 6" d., marigold, ruffled 63
Bowl, 6" d., purple, three-in-one edge 137
Bowl, 7" d., marigold 60-70
Bowl, 7" d., purple 85
Bowl, 7" d., three-in-one edge, purple 78
Bowl, 7 1/2" d., clambroth, three-in-one edge 75

Bowl, 7 1/2" d., purple, ruffled........................... 100
Bowl, 8" d., green, ruffled 59
Bowl, 8" d., marigold, three-in-one edge........... 103
Bowl, 8" to 9" d., green 197
Bowl, 8" to 9" d., marigold 88
Bowl, 8" to 9" d., purple............................. 100-115
Bowl, 8 1/2" d., ice cream shape, green 65
Bowl, 9" d., green, crimped rim................. 125-175
Bowl, 9" d., three-in-one edge, green............... 165
Bowl, 9" d., three-in-one edge, purple.............. 113
Bowl, 10" d., blue 925-1,500
Bowl, 10" d., green 100-120
Bowl, 10" d., green, ice cream shape............... 245
Bowl, 10" d., marigold 125-150
Bowl, blue, ice cream, large 750
Bowl, green, ice cream, large 80-100
Bowl, marigold, ice cream, large 65-70
Bowl, purple, ice cream, large 213
Bowl, marigold, triangular, large...................... 110
Plate, 6" to 7 1/2" d., marigold........................... 750

Bouquet
Pitcher, water, blue.. 525
Pitcher, water, marigold..................................... 200
Tumbler, blue 63
Tumbler, marigold.. 41

Broken Arches (Imperial)
Punch cup, marigold.. 25
Punch cup, purple 45

Broken Arches Punch Set

Punch set: bowl, base & 6 cups, marigold,
8 pcs. (ILLUS.) 437
Punch set: bowl, base & 6 cups; purple, 8
pcs... 725

Butterfly & Berry (Fenton)
Berry set: master bowl & 5 sauce dishes;
marigold, 6 pcs.. 150-250
Bowl, 8" to 9" d., blue, master berry, four-
footed... 175-200
Bowl, 8" to 9" d., green, master berry, four-
footed... 230-250
Bowl, 8" to 9" d., marigold, master berry,
four-footed... 65
Bowl, 8" to 9" d., purple, master berry, four-
footed... 165-275
Bowl, 8" to 9" d., white, master berry, four-
footed... 500-750
Butter dish, cov., blue.. 250
Butter dish, cov., green................... 750-1,000
Butter dish, cov., marigold................................ 160
Creamer, marigold 75-85
Hatpin holder, blue 1,900
Hatpin holder, marigold.................................. 1,600
Pitcher, water, green... 595

Butterfly & Berry Pitcher

Pitcher, water, marigold (ILLUS.).............. 240-275
Sauce dish, blue... 50-75
Sauce dish, green....................................... 100-125
Sauce dish, marigold... 30
Sauce dish, purple... 65-85
Spooner, marigold... 50
Spooner, purple... 140
Sugar bowl, cov., marigold................................. 75
Table set, marigold, 4 pcs......................... 350-400
Tumbler, blue... 45-60
Tumbler, green 150
Tumbler, marigold.. 30-40
Tumbler, purple... 125-150
Vase, 6" to 10" h., amber........................... 150-175
Vase, 6" to 10" h., blue................................. 75-85
Vase, 6" to 10" h., green........................... 155-165
Vase, 6" to 10" h., marigold......................... 40-50
Vase, 6" to 10" h., purple........................... 125-150
Water set: pitcher & 6 tumblers; marigold, 7
pcs... 450-500
Water set: pitcher & 6 tumblers; purple, 7
pcs.. 1,050

Butterfly & Fern (Fenton)
Pitcher, water, blue 538
Pitcher, water, green.. 510
Pitcher, water, marigold............................... 275-300
Pitcher, water, purple.................................... 350-400
Tumbler, blue... 55-60
Tumbler, green 110
Tumbler, marigold.. 38
Tumbler, pastel marigold..................................... 35
Tumbler, purple.. 45-50
Water set: pitcher & 6 tumblers; purple, 7
pcs.. 620

Captive Rose
Bonbon, blue, two-handled, 7 1/2" d............. 80-90
Bonbon, green, two-handled, 7 1/2" d. 75
Bowl, 8" d., blue, three-in-one edge 108
Bowl, 8" d., purple, three-in-one edge............... 106
Bowl, 8" to 9" d., blue.. 102
Bowl, 8" to 9" d., green 75
Bowl, 8" to 9" d., marigold 90-95
Bowl, 8" to 9" d., purple 65
Bowl, 8" to 9" d., blue, candy ribbon edge........... 75
Bowl, 8" to 9" d., green, candy ribbon edge...... 122
Bowl, 8" to 9" d., marigold, candy ribbon
edge.. 60

Captive Rose Bowl

Bowl, 8" to 9" d., purple, candy ribbon edge
(ILLUS.).. 121
Compote, blue... 75
Compote, green.. 58
Compote, ice blue..................................... 125-150
Compote, marigold..................................... 70-80
Compote, purple.. 100
Compote, purple, candy ribbon edge 130
Compote, white.. 149
Plate, 7" d., blue... 250
Plate, 7" d., purple... 250
Plate, 9" d., blue... 200
Plate, 9" d., green.. 500
Plate, 9" d., marigold.. 450
Plate, 9" d., purple..................................... 525-575

Caroline
Basket w/applied handle, peach opalescent..... 450
Bowl, 7" sq., peach opalescent............................. 83
Bowl, 8" d., peach opalescent, handgrip,
ruffled... 130-135
Bowl, 8" to 9" d., peach opalescent 77
Bowl, 8" to 9" w., peach opalescent, tricor-
nered 100
Bowl, 9" d., peach opalescent, pie crust
edge, shallow 65
Bowl, 9" d., peach opalescent, ruffled 139
Bowl, 9" sq., peach opalescent................... 100-115
Bowl, peach opalescent, fluted edge, one
side up.. 180
Plate, w/handgrip, peach opalescent................. 125

Chatelaine
Pitcher, purple.. 2,500

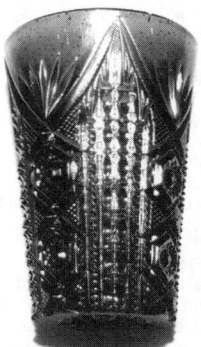

Chatelaine Tumbler

Tumbler, purple (ILLUS.)........................... 200-225

Cherry (Dugan)
Bowl, 5" d., purple, Jeweled Heart exterior.......... 63
Bowl, 6" d., purple.. 85-100
Bowl, 6" d., purple, Jeweled Heart exterior.......... 75

Bowl, 7" d., peach opalescent, three-foot-
ed, crimped rim... 185-200
Bowl, 8" d., purple, ruffled 173
Bowl, 8" to 9" d., marigold, three-footed 75
Bowl, 8" to 9" d., peach opalescent, three-
footed 175
Bowl, 8" to 9" d., purple, three-footed......... 160-175
Bowl, 10" d., purple, Jeweled Heart exterior.... 220-
250
Plate, 6" d., purple, ruffled 275
Plate, 6 1/2" d., purple, candy ribbon edge....... 330
Plate, 6 1/2" d., purple, ruffled, Jeweled
Heart exterior 225
Sauce dish, purple... 75
Sauce dish, purple, Jeweled Heart exterior........ 60

Cherry or Cherry Circles (Fenton)
Bonbon, two-handled, blue............................. 60-65
Bonbon, two-handled, green 120
Bonbon, two-handled, marigold.................... 55-65
Bonbon, two-handled, purple 75-100
Bowl, 5" d., blue, fluted....................................... 33
Bowl, 6" d., marigold, ruffled............................... 38
Bowl, 7" d., marigold, three-footed 40
Compote, marigold.. 50
Plate, 5" d., white... 160
Plate, 6" d., purple... 275

Christmas Compote
Marigold 3,250
Purple 2,800-3,000

Cobblestones Bowl (Imperial)
Green, 9" d.. 96
Marigold, 7" d.. 81
Marigold, 9" d., Arcs patt. exterior 110
Marigold, ruffled.. 150
Purple, 9" d.. 350

Coin Spot (Dugan)
Compote, 7" d., ice green 300
Compote, 7" d., marigold...................................... 20
Compote, 7" d., peach opalescent 75
Compote, 7" d., peach opalescent, fluted 100
Compote, 7" d., purple, fluted............................ 150
Green, enameled 2,700
Plate, 9" d., purple... 45

Comet or Ribbon Tie (Fenton)
Bowl, 8" d., green, ice cream shape.................. 125
Bowl, 8" to 9" d., blue... 65
Bowl, 8" to 9" d., lavender, candy ribbon
edge... 88

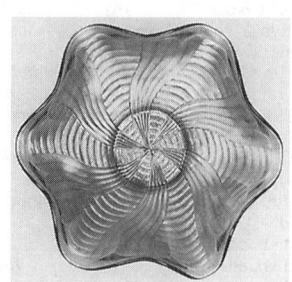

Comet Bowl

Bowl, 8" to 9" d., marigold (ILLUS.)..................... 60
Bowl, 8" to 9" d., purple 65

Bowl, 9" d., blue w/electric iridescence, three-in-one edge **175-200**
Bowl, green, candy ribbon edge **95**
Bowl, green, ruffled **125**
Plate, 9" d., blue, ruffled **250-300**
Plate, 9" d., marigold, ruffled **142**
Plate, 9" d., purple, ruffled **190**

Concave Diamond - See Diamond Concave Pattern

Concord (Fenton)
Bowl, ruffled, purple **400**
Bowl, 8 1/2" d., marigold, piecrust rim **125**
Bowl, 9" d., blue, ruffled **363**
Bowl, 9" d., green, three-in-one edge **800**
Bowl, green **325**
Bowl, ice cream shape, green **475**

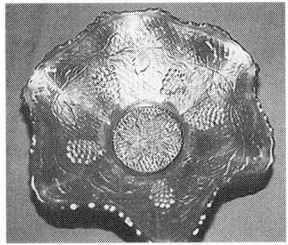

Concord Bowl

Bowl, marigold (ILLUS.) **102**
Bowl, marigold, ruffled **310**
Bowl, marigold, three-in-one edge **300**
Bowl, purple **163**
Bowl, purple, three-in-one edge **425-500**
Plate, green **3,500-5,000**
Plate, marigold **1,250-2,000**
Plate, purple **1,100**

Constellation (Dugan)
Compote, clambroth **150**
Compote, marigold **85**
Compote, purple **310**
Compote, white **95-125**

Coral (Fenton)
Bowl, 8" to 9" d., green, collared base **170**
Bowl, 8" to 9" d., marigold, collared base **335**
Plate, 9" d., marigold **1,150**

Corinth (Westmoreland)
Bowl, 7" d., purple, shallow **35**
Bowl, milk white w/marigold overlay **98**
Bowl, teal blue, flat, round **60**
Dish, banana, amber **34**
Dish, banana, marigold **35**
Dish, banana, purple **39**
Vase, 7 1/2" h., peach opalescent, jack-in-the-pulpit **105**
Vase, 7 1/2" h., smoke **28**
Vase, 7 1/2" h., teal blue **63**
Vase, 8" h., purple, jack-in-the-pulpit **48**
Vase, 8 1/2" h., purple **27**
Vase, 8 1/2" h., teal blue **50**
Vase, 8 3/4" h., lavender **20**
Vase, 9" h., blue opalescent **275**
Vase, 9 1/4" h., purple, jack-in-the-pulpit **65-70**
Vase, 9 1/2" h., teal blue, jack-in-the-pulpit **135**

Vase, 9 3/4" h., purple **40**
Vase, marigold, small **25**

Corn Bottle
Green **250**
Marigold **275**

Corn Bottle

Smoky (ILLUS.) **275**

Cosmos

Cosmos Bowl

Bowl, 9" d., green (ILLUS.) **50**

Crab Claw (Imperial)
Bowl, 4 1/2" d., green **25**
Bowl, 10" d., purple **100**
Bowl, fruit, w/base, marigold **90**
Cruet, marigold, no stopper **400-425**
Cruet, marigold, w/original stopper **798**
Tumbler, marigold **65**

Crackle
Bowl, 7 1/2" d., marigold **18**
Candlesticks, marigold, 7" h., pr. **30**
Candy jar, cov., marigold **25**
Plate, chop, 12" d., marigold **45**
Rose bowl, marigold, low **28**
Tumbler, marigold, dome-footed **12**
Vase, marigold, fan-shaped **24**
Wall pocket, marigold **28**
Water set: pitcher & 6 footed tumblers; marigold, 7 pcs. **150-175**

Crucifix
Candlesticks, marigold, pr. **1,250**

Daisies & Drape Vase (Northwood)
Aqua opalescent **575-600**
Cobalt blue **900**
Ice blue **2,500**

Marigold **613**
Purple **1,100**
White **287**

Daisy Cut Bell

Daisy Cut Bell

Marigold (ILLUS.) **425**

Daisy Squares
Compote, green **625**
Compote, marigold **400**

Daisy Wreath (Westmoreland)
Bowl, 8" to 9" d., blue opalescent **300**
Bowl, 8" to 9" d., milk white w/marigold
   overlay **188**
Bowl, 8" to 9" d., moonstone **200-220**
Bowl, 8" to 9" d., peach opalescent **100-125**

Dandelion, Paneled (Fenton)
Pitcher, water, blue **500**
Pitcher, water, green **713**
Pitcher, water, marigold **448**
Pitcher, water, purple **725**
Tumbler, blue **40**
Tumbler, green **70**
Tumbler, marigold **50**
Tumbler, purple **65**
Water set: pitcher & 5 tumblers; blue,
   6 pcs. **700-750**

Diamond Concave or Concave Diamond (Fenton)
Pitcher w/cover, vaseline **750**
Tumbler, celeste blue **55**
Tumbler, vaseline **146**

Diamond Lace (Imperial)
Bowl, 8" to 9" d., marigold **55**
Bowl, 8" to 9" d., purple **70**

Diamond Lace Pitcher

Pitcher, water, purple (ILLUS.) **400**
Sauce dish, green, 5" d. **40**
Sauce dish, marigold, 5" d. **20-25**
Sauce dish, purple, 5" d. **35-40**
Tumbler, purple **75**

Diamond & Rib Vase (Fenton)
Vase, 6" to 12", aqua **40**
Vase, 6" to 12", blue **50**
Vase, 6" to 12", green **45-65**
Vase, 6" to 12", ice green **80**
Vase, 6" to 12", marigold **43**
Vase, 6" to 12", purple **55-75**
Vase, 6" to 12", white **45**
Vase, 13" to 20", blue **71**
Vase, 13" to 20", green **945**
Vase, 13" to 20", marigold **125**
Vase, 13" to 20", purple **343**

Diamond Ring (Imperial)
Bowl, 8" to 9" d., marigold **40-45**
Bowl, 8" to 9" d., purple **200**

Diamond Ring Bowl

Bowl, 8" to 9" d., smoky (ILLUS.) **40-45**
Rose bowl, marigold **400**

Diamond & Sunburst
Decanter w/stopper, purple **200**
Wine, lavender **70**
Wine, marigold **30**
Wine, purple **65**

Diamonds (Millersburg)
Pitcher, water, green **350**
Pitcher, water, marigold **175-200**
Punch bowl & base, green, 2 pcs. **2,000-3,000**
Tumbler, green **55**
Tumbler, marigold **45**
Tumbler, purple **65-70**
Water set: pitcher & 4 tumblers; marigold,
   5 pcs. **355-375**
Water set: pitcher & 6 tumblers; purple,
   7 pcs. **550-600**

Diving Dolphins Footed Bowl (Sowerby)
Marigold, embossed scroll interior **110**

Dogwood Sprays
Bowl, purple, tricornered **200**
Bowl, 8" to 9" d., marigold, dome-footed **34**
Bowl, 8" to 9" d., peach opalescent, dome-
   footed **150**
Bowl, 8" to 9" d., purple, dome-footed **174**
Bowl, blue opalescent **300**

Double Dutch Bowl
Marigold, 8" to 9" d., footed **46**
Smoky, 8" to 9" d., footed **70**

Double Star or Buzz Saw (Cambridge)
Cruet w/stopper, green, small, 4"..................... 500
Cruet w/stopper, green, large, 6" 350-400
Cruet w/stopper, marigold, large, 6" 400
Pitcher, water, green................................... 275-300
Pitcher, water, marigold............................. 875-885
Tumbler, green... 55
Tumbler, marigold.. 275
Tumbler, purple.. 115
Water set: pitcher & 4 tumblers; green,
   5 pcs. 500

Double Stem Rose
Bowl, 7" d., marigold, dome-footed...................... 98
Bowl, 8" to 9" d., aqua, dome-footed 450
Bowl, 8" to 9" d., blue, dome-footed 225
Bowl, 8" to 9" d., celeste blue,
   dome-footed... 575-600
Bowl, 8" to 9" d., lavender, dome-footed... 175-200
Bowl, 8" to 9" d., marigold, dome-footed.......... 150
Bowl, 8" to 9" d., peach opalescent, dome-
   footed.. 130
Bowl, 8" to 9" d., purple, dome-footed.............. 100
Bowl, 8" to 9" d., white, dome-footed................ 125
Bowl, 10" d., peach opalescent 175
Plate, marigold, dome-footed 80
Plate, white, dome-footed 175

Drapery (Northwood)
Candy dish, tricornered, ice blue 175-225
Candy dish, tricornered, marigold........................ 70
Candy dish, tricornered, purple................. 100-150
Candy dish, tricornered, white........................... 125
Rose bowl, aqua opalescent 325-350
Rose bowl, blue 375
Rose bowl, blue w/electric iridescence 650
Rose bowl, ice blue 650
Rose bowl, marigold 100-225
Rose bowl, purple 225-250
Rose bowl, white 250-300
Shade (gas), marigold.. 60
Vase, 3 3/4" h., marigold................................... 145
Vase, 7" to 10", aqua opalescent....................... 575
Vase, 7" to 10", blue.. 200
Vase, 7" to 10", ice blue 425
Vase, 7" to 10", ice green............................ 200-250
Vase, 7" to 10", marigold................................ 90-100
Vase, 7" to 10", purple...................................... 110
Vase, 7" to 10", white.. 150

Estate (Westmoreland)
Creamer, blue opalescent, souvenir 150
Creamer, peach opalescent 60
Creamer, peach opalescent, souvenir................. 75
Mug, marigold 71
Sugar bowl, marigold.. 55
Sugar bowl, marigold, souvenir...................... 45-50
Sugar bowl, peach opalescent........................... 75
Sugar bowl, peach opalescent, souvenir............ 40

Fan (Dugan)
Bowl, 6" d., peach opalescent, footed 63
Creamer, peach opalescent 55
Sauceboat, peach opalescent 125
Sugar bowl, cov., square 95

Fanciful (Dugan)
Bowl, 8" to 9" d., blue, ruffled............................. 165
Bowl, 8" to 9" d., marigold............................... 50-75
Bowl, 8" to 9" d., marigold, piecrust rim 100-125
Bowl, 8" to 9" d., peach opalescent 200-225

Fanciful Bowl

Bowl, 8" to 9" d., purple, ruffled (ILLUS.).......... 115
Bowl, 8" to 9" d., white, ruffled.......................... 155
Bowl, 9" d., white, three-in-one edge 225
Bowl, 10" d., white, ruffled................................. 165
Bowl, peach opalescent, ice cream shape........ 127
Bowl, purple, ice cream shape 255
Bowl, white, ice cream shape 190
Plate, 9" d., blue... 298
Plate, 9" d., marigold 110
Plate, 9" d., peach opalescent 275-300
Plate, 9" d., purple..................................... 200-250
Plate, 9" d., white....................................... 200-250
Plate, 9 1/2" d., white, ruffled 140

Fantail
Bowl, ice cream shape, blue (buffed point) 270
Bowl, 9" d., blue, footed.............................. 185-200
Bowl, 9" d., blue, shallow, footed, w/Butter-
   fly & Berry exterior.. 175
Bowl, 9" d., marigold, footed 90
Bowl, 9" d., marigold, ice cream shape,
   w/Butterfly & Berry exterior........................... 163
Bowl, blue, low, ruffled, footed 285-300

Feather & Heart
Pitcher, water, green.................................. 400-500
Tumbler, green 225
Tumbler, marigold 70

Feather & Heart Tumbler

Tumbler, purple (ILLUS.)................................... 125
Water set: pitcher & 4 tumblers; purple, 5
   pcs. 975

Feather Stitch Bowl
Aqua 200-225
Green 60
Marigold 125

Feathered Serpent
Bowl, 8" to 9" d., purple 75-95
Bowl, 9" d., blue, ice cream shape 175
Bowl, 10" d., blue, ruffled 93

Bowl, 10" d., green, fluted 110
Bowl, 10" d., marigold 80
Bowl, 10" d., purple, flared 105
Sauce dish, blue 34
Sauce dish, green 30
Sauce dish, marigold 20

Fern
Compote, purple, w/Daisy & Plume exterior
  (Northwood) **100-125**
Dish, hat-shaped, marigold (Fenton) 34

Field Flower (Imperial)
Pitcher, water, amber 425
Pitcher, water, green 250-300
Pitcher, water, marigold 230
Pitcher, water, purple 425-500
Tumbler, blue 85
Tumbler, green 70
Tumbler, marigold 25-35
Tumbler, purple 95
Water set: pitcher & 1 tumbler; green,
  2 pcs. 300-350
Water set: pitcher & 1 tumbler; marigold,
  2 pcs. 250-275

Field Thistle (English)
Bowl, 10" d., marigold 50
Compote, marigold 210
Plate, 6" d., marigold 255
Plate, 9" d., marigold 375
Spooner, marigold 73
Vase, 7" h., marigold 65
Water set: pitcher & 6 tumblers; marigold,
  7 pcs. 500-600

File & Fan
Compote, blue opalescent 250
Compote, milk white w/marigold overlay 200
Compote, peach opalescent 140

File (Imperial)
Bowl, 8" d., marigold 40
Spooner, marigold 60
Sugar bowl, marigold 115
Vase, marigold 315
Water set: pitcher & 3 tumblers; marigold, 4
  pcs. 950

Fine Rib (Northwood & Fenton)
Bowl, 7" d., white 33
Bowl, master berry, 9" d., marigold 35
Compote, green, ruffled 45
Vase, 5 1/2" h., footed, jack-in-the-pulpit,
  blue 175
Vase, 6 1/2" to 12" h., aqua 75

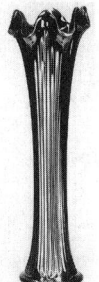

Large Fine Rib Vase

Vase, 6 1/2" to 12" h., blue (ILLUS.) 48
Vase, 6 1/2" to 12" h., green 60
Vase, 6 1/2" to 12" h., ice blue 210
Vase, 6 1/2" to 12" h., marigold 32
Vase, 6 1/2" to 12", purple 55-75
Vase, 6 1/2" to 12", red (Fenton) 313
Vase, 6 1/2" to 12", vaseline (Fenton) **75-100**
Vase, 14" to 17", blue 60-80
Vase, 14" to 17", marigold 50-75
Vase, 14" to 17", purple 80-100

Finecut & Roses (Northwood)
Candy dish, amber, three-footed 55
Candy dish, aqua opalescent,
  three-footed **400-425**
Candy dish, blue w/electric iridescence,
  three-footed 68
Candy dish, green, three-footed 130-150
Candy dish, ice blue, three-footed 275-300
Candy dish, marigold, three-footed 75
Candy dish, pastel marigold, three-footed 95
Candy dish, purple, three-footed 70-85
Rose bowl, aqua opalescent 1,650
Rose bowl/whimsey, lavender, straight top 650

Fishscale & Beads
Banana boat, peach opalescent, 7" l. 75
Bonbon, marigold, 6" 30
Bowl, 6 1/2" d., purple, ruffled & crimped
  edge 88
Bowl, 7" d., marigold 30
Bowl, 7" d., purple, candy ribbon edge 40
Card tray, peach opalescent, 4 x 7" 70
Plate, 6" d., peach opalescent 125-150
Plate, 7" d., marigold 95-125
Plate, 7" d., peach opalescent, ruffled rim . 125-150
Plate, 7" d., purple 413
Plate, 7" d., white 125
Plate, 7 1/2" d., marigold 75

Fleur De Lis (Millersburg)
Bowl, 8" to 9" d., marigold, dome-footed 200

Fleur De Lis Bowl

Bowl, 8" to 9" d., purple, dome-footed
  (ILLUS.) **275-300**
Bowl, 10" d., green 250-300
Bowl, 10" d., marigold 210
Bowl, 10" d., purple 450-500
Bowl, marigold, dome-footed, ruffled 150-250
Bowl, purple, dome-footed 425
Bowl, marigold, tricornered, footed 300
Bowl, purple, dome-footed, ruffled 425
Bowl, purple, tricornered, footed 650
Bowl, three-in-one edge, green 525

Floral & Grape (Dugan or Diamond Glass Co.)

Pitcher, water, blue..................................... 300-350
Pitcher, water, dark marigold............................ 250
Pitcher, water, marigold................................... 180
Pitcher, water, purple....................................... 233
Pitcher, water, white... 475
Tumbler, blue 35-40
Tumbler, purple.. 27
Tumbler, white.. 80
Tumblers, purple, set of 4 180
Water set: pitcher & 4 tumblers; blue, 5 pcs...... 450

Floral & Wheat Compote (Dugan)

Blue 50
Marigold 37
Peach opalescent 80
White 205

Flowers & Beads

Card tray, purple, tricornered, 7" w.................. 125
Plate, 7 1/2" w., peach opalescent, six-sid-
ed 75-100
Plate, purple, flat.. 55

Flowers & Frames

Bowl, 7" d., peach opalescent.................... 100-175

Flowers & Frames Bowl

Bowl, 7" d., purple, dome-footed (ILLUS.) 350
Bowl, 9" d., green, dome-footed 275
Bowl, 9" d., peach opalescent, dome-footed
.... 150-200
Bowl, peach opalescent, tricornered............... 150
Bowl, purple, tricornered, dome-footed 200-250

Flute & Cane

Compote, marigold, 6 1/2" d., 6" h.................... 100
Goblet, marigold... 65
Pitcher, marigold.. 225
Pitcher, milk, marigold...................................... 160

Flute (Imperial)

Berry set: master bowl & 6 sauce dishes;
marigold, 7 pcs.. 135
Bowl, 8" d., teal green 200
Bowl, 8" to 9" d., marigold 31
Butter dish, cov., marigold............................ 95-125
Celery vase, purple, 5 1/2" 400
Compote, green 25
Compote, marigold, 11" d., 7" h. 100
Creamer, green, breakfast size 50
Creamer, marigold, breakfast size 50
Creamer, purple, breakfast size..................... 65-70

Creamer & open sugar bowl, purple,
breakfast size, pr. 100-115

Flute Matchbox Holder

Matchbox holder, purple (ILLUS.) 900
Pitcher, water, marigold..................................... 275
Pitcher, water, purple... 575
Punch cup, marigold... 37
Punch set: bowl, base & 5 cups; marigold,
7 pcs.. 495
Sauce dish, marigold....................................... 15-20
Sauce dish, purple 40-45
Sugar bowl, open, purple, breakfast size........... 60
Toothpick holder, blue 225
Toothpick holder, green....................................... 50
Toothpick holder, lavender.......................... 75-100
Toothpick holder, marigold............................ 65-75
Toothpick holder, purple 55
Toothpick holder, vaseline 200-250
Tumbler, marigold 40
Tumbler, purple.. 90
Vase, 9" h., marigold... 30
Vase, 13" h., green 150
Vase, 13" h., marigold, funeral........................... 275

Flute (Northwood)

Pitcher, milk, marigold... 20
Salt dip, marigold, master size 51
Salt dip, vaseline, master size............................. 95
Toothpick holder, purple 80
Tumbler, marigold 48

Formal

Hatpin holder, marigold 675
Hatpin holder, purple.. 925
Vase, marigold, jack-in-the-pulpit 310
Vase, purple, jack-in-the-pulpit 738

Four Seventy Four (Imperial)

Compote, marigold.. 185
Goblet, water, marigold 50-55
Pitcher, milk, green 365-400
Pitcher, milk, marigold 155

Four Seventy Four Pitcher

Pitcher, water, green (ILLUS.) **400-450**
Pitcher, water, marigold **175-225**
Pitcher, water, purple, mid-size **3,000**
Punch bowl & base, marigold, 2 pcs. 168
Punch cup, green 40
Punch cup, marigold **20-25**
Punch set: bowl, base & 6 cups; marigold,
   8 pcs. 375

Frosted Block
Bowl, 8" to 9" d., clambroth, scalloped &
   fluted 35
Bowl, clambroth, square 35
Bowl, marigold, square 45
Compote, clambroth 100
Creamer, marigold 35
Nut dish, clambroth 41
Nut dish, white 75
Pitcher, milk, clambroth 48
Pitcher, milk, marigold 43
Plate, 7" sq., clambroth 175
Plate, 7 3/4" sq., smoky 140
Plate, 9" d., clambroth 125
Plate, 9" d., marigold 55
Plate, 9" d., white 70
Relish, marigold 44
Rose bowl, clambroth 70
Rose bowl, marigold 35
Rose bowl, white 48
Vase, clambroth 175
Vase, 6" h., marigold 55

Fruit Salad
Punch bowl, marigold (no base) 135
Punch bowl & base, purple, 2 pcs. 650
Punch cup, marigold 28
Punch cup, peach opalescent **75-100**

Garland Rose Bowl (Fenton)

Garland Rose Bowl

Blue (ILLUS.) **185**
Green **195**
Marigold **55**

God & Home
Pitcher, blue **2,000-2,250**
Tumbler, blue **225-250**

God & Home Water Set

Water set: pitcher & 6 tumblers; blue, 7 pcs.
   (ILLUS.) **3,800**

Golden Harvest or Harvest Time (U.S. Glass)
Decanter w/stopper, marigold 100
Wine, marigold 8
Wine, purple 75
Wine set: decanter & 6 wines; marigold, 7
   pcs. 200-225

Grape Arbor (Northwood)
Bowl, 10" d., purple, footed (Dugan) **350-375**
Hat shape, blue 87
Hat shape, ice green 350
Hat shape, marigold **75-100**
Hat shape, purple 195
Hat shape, white 100

Grape Arbor Pitcher

Pitcher, tankard, ice blue (ILLUS.) **1,500**
Pitcher, tankard, marigold 80
Pitcher, tankard, purple 400
Tumbler, blue **175-225**
Tumbler, blue w/electric iridescence 200
Tumbler, ice blue 250
Tumbler, ice green **375-400**
Tumbler, marigold **45-55**
Tumbler, pastel marigold 40
Tumbler, purple 63
Tumbler, white 125
Water set: tankard pitcher & 4 tumblers;
   marigold, 5 pcs. **525-550**
Water set: tankard pitcher & 4 tumblers;
   purple, 5 pcs. 800
Water set: tankard pitcher & 4 tumblers;
   white, 5 pcs. **1,000-1,050**

Water set: tankard pitcher & 6 tumblers; ice
blue, 7 pcs. 3,000-3,500

Grape & Cable (Northwood)
Banana boat, banded rim, stippled, aqua......... 575
Banana boat, blue 425-500
Banana boat, blue, banded rim 550-600
Banana boat, blue, banded rim,
stippled 1,000-1,200
Banana boat, green 300
Banana boat, green, banded rim, stippled 550-600
Banana boat, green, stippled..................... 300-325
Banana boat, ice blue.. 700
Banana boat, ice green 750
Banana boat, marigold 150-200
Banana boat, marigold, stippled 200-250
Banana boat, purple.. 335
Berry set: master bowl & 4 sauce dishes;
purple, 5 pcs. 375
Bonbon, two-handled, blue 148
Bonbon, two-handled, green 75-100
Bonbon, two-handled, horehound.................... 375
Bonbon, two-handled, marigold 75
Bonbon, two-handled, purple...................... 75-100
Bonbon, two-handled, stippled, blue 175-200
Bonbon, two-handled, stippled, green 165
Bonbon, two-handled, stippled, marigold 60-70
Bonbon, two-handled, white 500-550
Bowl, 5" d., blue (Fenton) 60
Bowl, 5" d., green.. 60
Bowl, 5" d., marigold... 30
Bowl, 5" d., purple... 60
Bowl, 6" d., three-in-one edge, marigold
variant... 160
Bowl, 6 1/2" d., Amberina (Fenton)................... 650
Bowl, 6 1/2" d., marigold.................................... 38
Bowl, 7" d., ice cream shape, marigold
(Fenton) 35
Bowl, 7" d., ice cream shape, milk white
w/marigold overlay (Fenton) 250
Bowl, 7" d., ice cream shape, purple (Fen-
ton).. 55
Bowl, 7" d., ice cream shape, vaseline
(Fenton) 45
Bowl, 7" d., ruffled, green (Fenton) 58
Bowl, 7" d., ruffled, marigold 25
Bowl, 7" d., ruffled, red.................................... 613
Bowl, 7" d., spatula-footed, green (Fenton) 85
Bowl, 7 1/2" d., ball-footed, aqua (Fenton) 80-85
Bowl, 7 1/2" d., ball-footed, blue (Fenton).... 75-100
Bowl, 7 1/2" d., ball-footed, marigold (Fen-
ton).. 55
Bowl, 7 1/2" d., ball-footed, purple (Fenton) 89
Bowl, 7 1/2" d., ball-footed, red (Fenton) 575
Bowl, 7 1/2" d., ruffled, green................................ 85
Bowl, 7 1/2" d., ruffled, red 800-825
Bowl, 7 1/2" d., ruffled, vaseline, ... 100
Bowl, 7 1/2" d., spatula-footed, green
(Northwood).. 100
Bowl, 7 1/2" d., spatula-footed, purple
(Northwood).. 63
Bowl, 8" d., ice cream shape, footed, blue
(Fenton).. 60-65
Bowl, 8" d., ruffled, green 65
Bowl, 8" d., ruffled, red (Fenton)...................... 800
Bowl, 8" to 9" d., ball-footed, celeste blue
(Fenton).. 1,200
Bowl, 8" to 9" d., ball-footed, green (Fenton)....... 76
Bowl, 8" to 9" d., ball-footed, pastel mari-
gold (Fenton) 55

Bowl, 8" to 9" d., piecrust rim, aqua opales-
cent (Northwood).. 3,450
Bowl, 8" to 9" d., piecrust rim, blue,
stippled.. 375-425
Bowl, 8" to 9" d., piecrust rim, blue w/elec-
tric iridescence.. 300-350
Bowl, 8" to 9" d., piecrust rim, green 100-110
Bowl, 8" to 9" d., piecrust rim, green, Bas-
ketweave exterior 250-300
Bowl, 8" to 9" d., piecrust rim, ice blue.......... 1,150
Bowl, 8" to 9" d., piecrust rim, marigold 85
Bowl, 8" to 9" d., piecrust rim, marigold,
Basketweave exterior 40-45
Bowl, 8" to 9" d., piecrust rim, marigold,
stippled.. 185
Bowl, 8" to 9" d., piecrust rim, pastel mari-
gold... 85-90
Bowl, 8" to 9" d., piecrust rim, purple 275
Bowl, 8" to 9" d., piecrust rim, purple, Bas-
ketweave exterior 150-175
Bowl, 8" to 9" d., spatula-footed, blue
(Northwood).. 250
Bowl, 8" to 9" d., spatula-footed, green
(Northwood).. 90
Bowl, 8" to 9" d., spatula-footed, lavender........ 250
Bowl, 8" to 9" d., spatula-footed, marigold
(Northwood).. 65
Bowl, 8" to 9" d., spatula-footed, ruffled,
purple (Northwood) 85-90
Bowl, 8" to 9" d., stippled, blue.......................... 388
Bowl, 8" to 9" d., stippled, green, ruffled........... 275
Bowl, 8" to 9" d., stippled, marigold, ruffled,
Basketweave exterior 300
Bowl, 8 1/2" d., scalloped, marigold 85
Bowl, 8 1/2" d., scalloped, purple (North-
wood).. 95
Bowl, 8 12" d., ruffled, stippled, green 270
Bowl, 9" d., Basketweave exterior, green............ 60
Bowl, 9" d., ruffled, Basketweave exterior,
marigold 40
Bowl, berry, 9" d., clambroth.............................. 88
Bowl, berry, 9" d., green................................... 188
Bowl, berry, 9" d., ice green............................... 838
Bowl, berry, 9" d., marigold............................... 135
Bowl, berry, 9" d., purple..................................... 80
Bowl, 10" d., ruffled, stippled, Basketweave
exterior, marigold 225
Bowl, 10 1/2" d., ruffled, Basketweave exte-
rior, marigold 70
Bowl, 10 1/2" d., ruffled, Basketweave exte-
rior, purple 125
Bowl, 10 1/2" d., ruffled, white 150
Bowl, orange, 10 1/2" d., blue, footed 475
Bowl, orange, 10 1/2" d., blue, footed, Per-
sian Medallion interior (Fenton) 350
Bowl, orange, 10 1/2" d., blue w/electric iri-
descence, footed, stippled (Northwood)......... 650
Bowl, orange, 10 1/2" d., green, footed 325
Bowl, orange, 10 1/2" d., green, footed,
Persian Medallion interior (Fenton)............... 350
Bowl, orange, 10 1/2" d., ice green, footed ... 1,050
Bowl, orange, 10 1/2" d., marigold, banded 413
Bowl, orange, 10 1/2" d., marigold, footed 188
Bowl, orange, 10 1/2" d., marigold, footed,
Persian Medallion interior (Fenton) 125-150
Bowl, orange, 10 1/2" d., marigold, footed,
stippled... 400
Bowl, orange, 10 1/2" d., purple, footed........... 450

Bowl, orange, 10 1/2" d., purple, footed, Persian Medallion interior (Fenton)............... **388**
Bowl, orange, 10 1/2" d., white, footed........... **1,538**
Bowl, 11" d., ice cream shape, blue............... **1,200**
Bowl, 11" d., ice cream shape, green............... **517**
Bowl, 11" d., ice cream shape, green, Basketweave exterior... **750**
Bowl, 11" d., ice cream shape, ice blue **2,425**
Bowl, 11" d., ice cream shape, ice green...... **1,350**
Bowl, 11" d., ice cream shape, marigold........... **325**
Bowl, 11" d., ice cream shape, purple...... **350-400**
Bowl, 11" d., ice cream shape, purple, Basketweave exterior... **400**
Bowl, 11" d., ice cream shape, white................ **375**
Bowl, 11" d., ice cream shape, white, Basketweave exterior.................................... **300-325**
Bowl, 11" d., ruffled, green **195**
Bowl, fruit, blue.. **438**
Bowl, fruit, green **488**
Bowl, fruit, purple **750**
Bowl, spatula-footed, ruffled, marigold (Fenton).. **30**
Breakfast set: individual size creamer & sugar bowl; green, pr. **172**
Breakfast set: individual size creamer & sugar bowl; marigold, pr. **140**
Breakfast set: individual size creamer & sugar bowl; purple, pr. **188**
Butter dish, cov., amber............................... **115**
Butter dish, cov., blue.................................... **350**
Butter dish, cov., green............................ **200-250**
Butter dish, cov., ice blue **350**
Butter dish, cov., marigold **125-150**
Butter dish, cov., purple............................ **150-225**
Candle lamp, green **1,000**
Candle lamp, marigold................................. **1,100**
Candle lamp, purple.. **850**
Candle lamp shade, green **575**
Candle lamp shade, marigold........................ **750**
Candlestick, green **135**
Candlestick, marigold **75**
Candlestick, purple **115**
Candlesticks, green, pr. **223**
Candlesticks, purple, pr. **225-250**
Centerpiece bowl, marigold **250-300**
Centerpiece bowl, purple........................ **375-425**
Cologne bottle w/stopper, green............. **250-275**
Cologne bottle w/stopper, ice blue **725-775**
Cologne bottle w/stopper, marigold **185**
Cologne bottle w/stopper, purple................... **325**
Cologne bottle w/stopper, white **625-650**
Compote, cov., purple, large...................... **550-600**
Compote, cov., purple, small **375**
Compote, open, green, large................. **925-1,100**
Compote, open, marigold, large....................... **425**
Compote, open, purple, large **475**
Compote, open, purple, small.................... **275-300**
Cracker jar, cov., marigold............................. **450**
Cracker jar, cov., purple **375-425**
Creamer, green **125**
Creamer, marigold **75-80**
Creamer, purple **95**
Creamer, green, individual size **75-80**
Creamer, marigold, individual size **65**
Creamer, purple, individual size **75-85**
Cup & saucer, purple **250-300**
Cuspidor, purple.................................... **3,000-4,000**

Grape & Cable Whiskey Decanter

Decanter w/stopper, whiskey, marigold (ILLUS.).. **175**
Dresser set, purple, 7 pcs............................. **1,500**
Dresser tray, green............................... **250-275**
Dresser tray, ice blue **1,500**
Dresser tray, marigold..................................... **200**
Dresser tray, purple.. **225**
Fernery, purple... **725-775**
Hat shape, green **75**
Hat shape, marigold **55**
Hat shape, purple **50-60**
Hatpin holder, marigold **300-375**
Hatpin holder, purple................................. **300-350**
Humidor, cov., marigold **300**
Humidor, cov., purple **550-600**
Nappy, green, single handle **80**
Nappy, marigold, single handle **50-60**
Pin tray, green... **350**
Pin tray, ice blue **900-950**
Pin tray, marigold **125-175**
Pitcher, tankard, 9 3/4" h., green..................... **1,500**
Pitcher, water, 8 1/4" h., green......................... **475**
Pitcher, water, 8 1/4" h., marigold.................... **275**
Pitcher, water, 8 1/4" h., purple.................. **185-275**
Pitcher, tankard, 9 3/4" h., ice green............. **8,000**
Pitcher, smoky **800**
Plate, 5" to 6" d., marigold, two sides up........... **125**
Plate, 5" to 6" d., purple (Northwood) **125**
Plate, 8" d., clambroth................................. **125-150**
Plate, 8" d., marigold, flat, spatula-footed **175**
Plate, 8" d., marigold, footed.............................. **95**
Plate, 8" d., purple...................................... **200-225**
Plate, 9" d., Basketweave exterior, green.......... **350**
Plate, 9" d., Basketweave exterior, marigold....... **98**
Plate, 9" d., Basketweave exterior, purple **160**
Plate, 9" d., blue, spatula-footed **145-150**
Plate, 9" d., blue, stippled................................ **1,200**
Plate, 9" d., clambroth..................................... **165**
Plate, 9" d., green **400**
Plate, 9" d., green, spatula-footed...................... **143**
Plate, 9" d., ice green, spatula-footed......... **850-875**
Plate, 9" d., marigold, spatula-footed............ **95-115**
Plate, 9" d., purple... **198**
Plate, 9" d., purple, spatula-footed...................... **112**
Plate, 9" d., stippled, green **725**
Plate, 9" d., stippled, marigold **700**
Plate, 9" d., stippled, marigold, variant....... **175-300**
Plate, 9" d., stippled, purple.............................. **450**
Plate, 9" d., stippled, sapphire blue...... **3,300-3,500**
Powder jar, cov., green **335**
Powder jar, cov., marigold **175**
Powder jar, cov., purple **155**

Punch bowl & base, horehound, 11" d., 2
pcs.. **2,450**
Punch bowl & base, purple, 14" d., 2 pcs....... **575**
Punch bowl & base, marigold, 17" d., 2
pcs.. **1,000**
Punch cup, marigold **28**
Punch cup, purple **25-30**
Punch set: 11" bowl, base & 6 cups; purple,
8 pcs. **688**
Punch set: 14" bowl, base & 6 cups; purple,
8 pcs. **1,375**

Grape & Cable Punch Set

Punch set, 14" bowl, base & 6 cups; white,
8 pcs. (ILLUS.) **5,500**
Punch set, master: 17" bowl, base & 6
cups; purple, 8 pcs. **3,200**
Punch set, master: 17" bowl, base & 8
cups; marigold, 10 pcs............................ **2,450**
Sauce dish, green **25**
Sauce dish, marigold **45**
Sauce dish, purple.. **25-30**
Sherbet or individual ice cream dish,
marigold.. **30**
Sherbet or individual ice cream dish, pur-
ple **55-65**
Sherbet or individual ice cream dish,
white... **160-170**
Spooner, green **100**
Spooner, marigold **68**
Spooner, purple **85**
Sugar bowl, cov., marigold **85**
Sugar bowl, cov., purple............................ **145-175**
Sugar bowl, individual size, purple **60-70**
Sweetmeat jar, cov., purple **198**
Table set: cov. sugar bowl, creamer, cov.
butter dish & spooner; green, 4 pcs.............. **450**
Tumbler, green.. **55-65**
Tumbler, ice green...................................... **375-400**
Tumbler, marigold... **50-75**
Tumbler, purple.. **40**
Water set: pitcher & 6 tumblers; purple, 7
pcs. **600**
Whiskey set: whiskey decanter w/stopper
& 6 shot glasses; marigold, 7 pcs. **1,100**
Whiskey shot glass, marigold **125-150**
Whiskey shot glass, purple............................. **175**

Grape & Gothic Arches (Northwood)
Berry set: master bowl & 4 sauce dishes;
blue, 5 pcs. **225-250**
Berry set: master bowl & 6 sauce dishes;
marigold, 7 pcs....................................... **130-140**
Bowl, master berry, blue **90**
Bowl, master berry, marigold **40-45**
Butter dish, cov., blue................................. **150-175**
Creamer, blue... **75-80**
Creamer, green **200**
Creamer, marigold **45**
Creamer, purple **85**
Creamer & cov. sugar bowl, marigold, pr. **100**

Pitcher, water, blue **275**
Pitcher, water, marigold.................................... **190**
Sauce dish, aqua **25**
Sauce dish, blue... **40**
Sauce dish, green **35**
Sauce dish, marigold **10-15**
Spooner, blue.. **70-80**
Spooner, green.. **175**
Spooner, marigold **45**
Sugar bowl, cov., blue..................................... **100**
Sugar bowl, cov., green **96**
Sugar bowl, cov., marigold................................. **55**

Grape & Gothic Arches Table Set

Table set, blue, 4 pcs (ILLUS.).................... **400-450**
Tumbler, blue.. **55-65**
Tumbler, green **77**
Tumbler, marigold **37**
Tumbler, pearl pastel milk white **150-175**
Tumbler, purple... **45**
Water set: pitcher & 6 tumblers; green,
7 pcs. **700**

Grape Leaves (Northwood)
Bowl, 8" d., green **75-85**
Bowl, 8" d., green, ribbon candy rim........... **200-250**
Bowl, 9" d., green, ruffled **125**
Bowl, 9" d., marigold **35**
Bowl, 9" d., purple... **125-150**
Bride's basket, w/handle & silver exterior,
purple **250**

Grapevine Lattice
Bowl, 7" d., purple, ruffled **75**
Bowl, 7" d., white, ruffled **50-60**
Bowl, white, fluted.. **85**
Pitcher, water, purple.................................. **700-800**
Plate, 6" to 7" d., marigold **55**

Grapevine Lattice Plate

Plate, 6" to 7" d., purple (ILLUS.) **200-250**
Plate, 6" to 7" d., white **75-85**
Plate, 8" d., white **150**
Tumbler, marigold **20-30**
Tumbler, purple.. **60**

Harvest Flower (Dugan or Diamond Glass)
Tumbler, lime green **395**
Tumbler, marigold **95**

Harvest Time - See Golden Harvest Pattern

Heart & Horseshoe (Fenton's Good Luck)
Bowl, lavender, ruffled w/ribbed exterior 625

Heart & Vine (Fenton)
Bowl, 8" to 9" d., blue 90-100
Bowl, 8" to 9" d., blue, candy ribbon edge 55
Bowl, 8" to 9" d., green 83

Heart & Vine Bowl

Bowl, 8" to 9" d., green, candy ribbon edge
(ILLUS.) 58
Bowl, 8" to 9" d., marigold, candy ribbon
edge 70
Bowl, 8" to 9" d., purple 95
Bowl, 8 1/2" d., purple, candy ribbon edge 100-120
Plate, 9" d., blue 425
Plate, 9" d., marigold 250
Plate, 9" d., purple 395-425

Hearts & Flowers (Northwood)
Bowl, 8" d., white 350-400
Bowl, 8" to 9" d., aqua opalescent 1,700
Bowl, 8" to 9" d., blue 600
Bowl, 8" to 9" d., piecrust rim, blue 900
Bowl, 8" to 9" d., piecrust rim, blue w/elec-
tric iridescence 2,300
Bowl, 8" to 9" d., piecrust rim, green 2,000
Bowl, 8" to 9" d., piecrust rim, ice blue 1,000
Bowl, 8" to 9" d., piecrust rim, ice green 1,000
Bowl, 8" to 9" d., piecrust rim, lime green 2,750
Bowl, 8" to 9" d., piecrust rim, marigold 450-500
Bowl, 8" to 9" d., piecrust rim, purple 700-725
Bowl, 8" to 9" d., ruffled, aqua 1,575
Bowl, 8" to 9" d., ruffled, blue 364
Bowl, 8" to 9" d., ruffled, green 1,275-1,300
Bowl, 8" to 9" d., ruffled, ice blue 367
Bowl, 8" to 9" d., ruffled, ice green 900
Bowl, 8" to 9" d., ruffled, marigold 350-400
Bowl, 8" to 9" d., ruffled, purple 338
Bowl, 8" to 9" d., ruffled, white 200
Compote, 6 3/4" h., aqua opalescent 450-500
Compote, 6 3/4" h., blue 375
Compote, 6 3/4" h., blue opalescent 1,500
Compote, 6 3/4" h., blue w/electric irides-
cence 1,050
Compote, 6 3/4" h., green 1,450
Compote, 6 3/4" h., ice blue 825-900
Compote, 6 3/4" h., ice green 500
Compote, 6 3/4" h., lime green 1,500-2,000
Compote, 6 3/4" h., marigold 325-350
Compote, 6 3/4" h., moonstone 5,000

Compote, 6 3/4" h., pastel marigold 178
Compote, 6 3/4" h., purple 450-500
Compote, 6 3/4" h., Renniger blue 1,750
Compote, 6 3/4" h., white 175-200
Plate, green 2,500
Plate, ice blue 1,100
Plate, lime ice green, ribbed exterior 5,750
Plate, marigold 800-1,000

Hearts & Flowers Plate

Plate, purple (ILLUS.) 900
Plate, white 2,475

Heavy Grape (Dugan, Diamond Glass or Millersburg)
Bowl, 6" d., purple 75
Bowl, 7" d., green, ruffled 35
Bowl, 8" d., marigold 65
Bowl, 9" d., purple 60
Bowl, 10" d., marigold 45
Bowl, master berry, 10" d., peach opales-
cent 550-650
Bowl, master berry, 10" d., purple 205
Bowl, master berry, 10" d., vaseline w/mari-
gold overlay 165
Bowl, 12" d., marigold 140-145
Sauce dish, green, 5" sq. 29

Heavy Iris (Dugan or Diamond Glass)
Pitcher, water, marigold 283
Pitcher, water, peach opalescent 1,000
Pitcher, water, white 1,250
Tumbler, marigold 75
Tumbler, purple 100-125
Tumbler, white 225
Water set: pitcher & 5 tumblers, marigold,
6 pcs. 725-800

Hobnail (Millersburg)

Hobnail Butter Dish

Butter dish, cov., purple (ILLUS.) 625
Cuspidor, green 1,250
Cuspidor, marigold 725-775

Cuspidor, purple 825-875
Rose bowl, marigold 275
Rose bowl, purple 325
Sugar bowl, cov., marigold 300
Vase, 15 1/2" h., marigold, variant.................... 195
Vase, 16" h., purple, variant............................... 245
Vase, 16 3/4" h., marigold, variant..................... 250
Vase, 17" h., green, variant 253

Hobstar Band
Pitcher, marigold.. 175

Hobstar Band Tumbler

Tumbler, marigold (ILLUS.)..................................... 55

Hobstar (Imperial) (CG Issue)
Bowl, 10 3/4" d., marigold..................................... 35
Butter dish, cov., marigold................................... 95
Compote, marigold.. 50
Cracker jar, cov., green 90
Cracker jar, cov., marigold 85
Creamer, green 85
Creamer, marigold 40
Creamer, purple 80
Humidor, cov., marigold 98
Spooner, marigold 35
Sugar bowl, cov., green 70
Sugar bowl, cov., marigold 50

Holly Whirl or Holly Sprig (Millersburg, Fenton & Dugan)
Bowl, 6" w., green, tricornered............................. 85
Bowl, 6" w., marigold, tricornered....................... 295
Bowl, 6" w., purple, tricornered........................... 125
Bowl, 7" d., green... 60
Bowl, 7" d., marigold.. 50
Bowl, 7" d., purple, ruffled 60-70
Bowl, 7" w., tricornered, marigold...................... 180
Bowl, 7 1/2" w., tricornered, purple 98
Bowl, 8" d., ice cream shape, marigold, variant.. 125-150
Bowl, 8" d., ice cream shape, purple 325
Bowl, 8" to 9" d., green 80
Bowl, 8" to 9" d., marigold 75-80
Bowl, 8" w., tricornered, green............................. 97
Bowl, 10" d., ruffled, marigold 55
Bowl, 10" d., ruffled, purple (Millersburg).. 150-200
Bowl, ruffled, green (Millersburg) 250
Card tray, two-handled, green 50-85
Card tray, two-handled, marigold.................. 75-100
Nappy, single handle, peach opalescent (Dugan) 65
Nappy, single handle, purple (Dugan) 75-100
Nappy, tricornered, green (Dugan) 98
Nappy, tricornered, marigold (Millersburg)........... 95

Nappy, tricornered, purple (Dugan) 100-125
Nappy, tricornered, purple (Millersburg) 175-200
Nappy, two-handled, green (Dugan) 85
Nut dish, two-handled, green 100-125
Nut dish, two-handled, marigold 66
Nut dish, two-handled, purple 84
Rose bowl, blue.. 275-300
Sauce dish, green, 6 1/2" d. (Millersburg). 100-125
Sauceboat, peach opalescent (Dugan) 135

Honeycomb
Bonbon, marigold... 29

Honeycomb Rose Bowl

Rose bowl, peach opalescent (ILLUS) 143

Illinois Soldier's & Sailor's Plate
Blue 2,300
Marigold 1,850

Illusion (Fenton)
Bonbon, two-handled, blue 85
Bonbon, two-handled, marigold.................... 50-55

Inverted Coin Dot
Pitcher, marigold.. 195
Tumbler, marigold 80

Inverted Feather (Cambridge)
Compote, jelly, marigold..................................... 80

Inverted Feather Cracker Jar

Cracker jar, cov., green (ILLUS.)...................... 190
Creamer, purple 160
Parfait, marigold... 60

Inverted Strawberry (Cambridge)
Bowl, 8" to 9" d., purple 145
Bowl, master berry, 10" d., purple.............. 235-300
Celery, blue.. 1,200
Compote, souvenir, marigold (minor roughness on edge) 295
Compote, open, green, 5" d., 6" h. 525
Creamer, blue.. 300-400
Creamer, marigold....................................... 150-200

Creamer, purple 270
Cuspidor, green 1,000-1,200
Cuspidor, marigold 875-950
Powder jar, cov., green 225-250
Powder jar, cov., marigold 350
Rose bowl, purple, large (made from master berry).. 1,000
Sauce dish, marigold 65
Sauce dish, purple... 45
Spooner, purple 200-250
Sugar bowl, cov., green 250-300
Table set, purple, 4 pcs. 1,500-2,000
Tumbler, green... 275
Tumbler, marigold.................................... 140-175
Tumbler, purple 200

Inverted Thistle (Cambridge)
Plate, chop, purple 1,750
Tumbler, purple 210

Iris
Compote, blue, 6 3/4" d. 195
Compote, green, 6 3/4" d. 138
Compote, marigold, 6 3/4" d. 50-60
Compote, marigold, etched "Mother, 1909," 6 3/4" d. 75
Compote, purple, 6 3/4" d. 105
Compote, marigold, wide top, 7 1/2" d. 55
Goblet, buttermilk, green 110
Goblet, buttermilk, marigold 60-75
Goblet, buttermilk, purple 60

Jeweled Heart (Dugan or Diamond Glass)
Bowl, 10" d., purple.. 100

Jeweled Heart Pitcher

Pitcher, marigold (ILLUS.)......................... 650-850
Plate, 7" d., ruffled, peach opalescent 100
Sauce dish, peach opalescent 40-45
Sauce dish, purple... 41
Spooner, green 35
Tumbler, marigold... 85

Lattice & Grape (Fenton)
Pitcher, marigold... 95
Pitcher, tankard, blue 650
Pitcher, tankard, marigold 200
Tumbler, blue 45-55
Tumbler, marigold... 30
Tumbler, purple 40
Water set: tankard pitcher & 5 tumblers; marigold, 6 pcs... 225-250
Water set: tankard pitcher & 6 tumblers; blue, 7 pcs. 675-700

Lattice & Poinsettia (Northwood)
Bowl, blue w/electric iridescence...................... 800

Bowl, ice blue 2,100
Bowl, marigold.. 600
Bowl, purple 1,300

Lattice & Points
Hat shape, marigold.. 39
Vase, 3 1/2" h., marigold.................................... 30
Vase, 7 1/2" h., blue w/electric iridescence 200
Vase, 8" h., blue 68
Vase, 8" h., purple.. 45
Vase, 8 1/2" h., marigold.................................... 25
Vase, marigold.. 125
Vase, white 60
Vase, 7" h., purple.. 90

Leaf Chain (Fenton)
Bowl, 6" d., ruffled, red...................................... 613
Bowl, 7" d., aqua... 115-125
Bowl, 7" d., blue 70
Bowl, 7" d., green, ruffled 150
Bowl, 7" d., ice green, ruffled 950
Bowl, 7" d., marigold 60
Bowl, 7" d., white 66
Bowl, 8" d., ice cream shape, blue 120
Bowl, 8" d., ice cream shape, clambroth 160
Bowl, 8" d., ice cream shape, green.......... 145-150
Bowl, 8" d., ice cream shape, white.................. 150
Bowl, 8" to 9" d., blue................................ 100-125
Bowl, 8" to 9" d., clambroth 63
Bowl, 8" to 9" d., green 80
Bowl, 8" to 9" d., light blue 125
Bowl, 8" to 9" d., marigold.......................... 95-100
Bowl, 8" to 9" d., purple 84
Bowl, 8" to 9" d., vaseline.................................. 95
Bowl, 8" to 9" d., white 95-125
Bowl, 8 1/2" d., ice cream shape, marigold........ 45
Bowl, ruffled, purple 213
Plate, 7" to 8" d., blue 130-150
Plate, 7" to 8" d., marigold 125-150
Plate, 9" d., clambroth 125-150
Plate, 9" d., green 195

Leaf Chain Plate

Plate, 9" d., marigold (ILLUS.) 975
Plate, 9" d., pastel marigold 293
Plate, 9" d., purple.. 240
Plate, 9" d., white 225-300

Leaf & Flowers or Leaf & Little Flowers (Millersburg)
Compote, miniature, green 475
Compote, miniature, marigold 350-375
Compote, miniature, purple 400

Leaf Rays Nappy
Marigold 20-30
Peach opalescent 25-50

Purple **55-65**
Purple, spade-shaped, handled......................... **35**
White **85-95**

Leaf Swirl Compote
Amber **87**
Marigold **45**
Purple **60**
Teal blue **150**
Vaseline **74**

Leaf Tiers
Bowl, 8" d., footed, marigold **35**
Pitcher, footed, marigold...................................... **450**
Shade, milk white w/marigold overlay.................. **60**
Spooner, marigold **90**
Tumbler, blue **270**
Tumbler, marigold.. **115**

Lined Lattice Vase
Blue **75**
Marigold **54**
Marigold, 5" h., squatty w/flared rim **240**
Peach opalescent, 6" h.. **150**
Purple, 7 1/2" h.. **75**
White **77**

Little Barrel Perfume

Little Barrel Perfume

Green (ILLUS.) **325**
Marigold **100-150**

Little Fishes (Fenton)

Little Fishes Bowl

Bowl, 6" d., three-footed, marigold.................. **60-65**
Bowl, 6" d., three-footed, purple........................ **175**
Bowl, 8" to 9" d., three-footed, blue **310**
Bowl, 8" to 9" d., three-footed, marigold.............. **88**

Bowl, 10" d., three-footed, blue (ILLUS.) **375**
Bowl, 10" d., three-footed, marigold **130**
Sauce dish, three-footed, blue, 5" d......... **120-125**
Sauce dish, three-footed, marigold, 5" d. **50**
Sauce dish, three-footed, purple, 5" d. **138**

Little Flowers (Fenton)
Bowl, 6" d., blue, ice cream shape **30-40**
Bowl, 6" d., ruffled, blue....................................... **80**
Bowl, 6" d., ruffled, marigold................................ **35**
Bowl, 6 1/2" d., purple.................................... **50-60**
Bowl, 8" to 9" d., blue... **98**
Bowl, 8" to 9" d., marigold.................................... **66**
Bowl, 8" to 9" d., purple **85-100**
Bowl, 10" d., amber **190**
Bowl, 10" d., green **80-100**
Bowl, 10" d., ruffled, marigold **70**
Bowl, 11" d., marigold.. **81**
Sauce dish, amber, 5" d....................................... **65**
Sauce dish, blue, 5" d. **50-85**
Sauce dish, marigold, 5" d................................... **34**
Sauce dish, purple, 5" d. **60-75**

Little Stars Bowl (Millersburg)
Bowl, 7" d., green **185**
Bowl, 7" d., marigold **135-140**
Bowl, 7" d., purple.. **164**
Bowl, 7 1/2" d., marigold, three-in-one edge...... **425**
Bowl, 7 1/2" d., purple, ruffled **200**
Bowl, 8" d., ice cream, green............................. **600**
Bowl, 8" d., ruffled, green **265**
Bowl, 8" d., ruffled, marigold **90**
Bowl, 8" d., ruffled, purple **200**

Loganberry Vase (Imperial)
Amber **440-450**
Green **463**
Marigold **210**
Pastel marigold **350**

Long Thumbprints
Sugar bowl, marigold.. **37**
Vase, 7" h., green... **36**
Vase, 8" h., marigold.. **40**
Vase, 9 1/2" h., purple **64**

Lotus & Grape (Fenton)
Bonbon, two-handled, blue................................. **363**

Lotus & Grape Bonbon

Bonbon, two-handled, celeste blue
(ILLUS.)... **90**
Bonbon, two-handled, green **85**
Bonbon, two-handled, lime green......................... **95**
Bonbon, two-handled, marigold **40**
Bonbon, two-handled, purple **88**
Bonbon, two-handled, red................... **1,450-1,500**
Bonbon, two-handled, teal green............... **225-250**
Bowl, 5" d., celeste blue **1,600**
Bowl, 5" d., footed, blue..................................... **125**
Bowl, 5" d., footed, purple **75**

Bowl, 6" d., footed, blue 65
Bowl, 6" d., footed, green 75
Bowl, 7" d., footed, marigold 41
Bowl, 8" d., ruffled, blue 93
Bowl, 8" to 9" d., blue 93
Bowl, 8" to 9" d., green 115
Bowl, 8" to 9" d., marigold 125
Bowl, 8" to 9" d., purple.................................... 105
Bowl, 9" d., ruffled, blue 80
Bowl, ruffled, blue 150
Plate, 9" d., blue 1,225

Louisa (Westmoreland)

Bowl, 7" d., footed, green 43
Bowl, 7" d., ice cream shape, blue.................. 250
Bowl, 8" to 9" d., three-footed, green.................. 50
Bowl, 8" to 9" d., three-footed, marigold.............. 46
Bowl, 8" to 9" d., three-footed, purple................. 51
Nut bowl, footed, green 60
Nut bowl, footed, purple 55
Plate, 9 1/2" d., footed, aqua..................... 140-150
Plate, 9 1/2" d., footed, marigold...................... 105
Plate, 9 1/2" d., footed, purple........................... 110
Rose bowl, footed, amber................................... 95
Rose bowl, footed, aqua..................................... 79
Rose bowl, footed, blue...................................... 80

Louisa Rose Bowl

Rose bowl, footed, green (ILLUS.) 57
Rose bowl, footed, lavender 110
Rose bowl, footed, marigold 40
Rose bowl, footed, purple 69

Lustre Flute (Northwood)

Hat shape, fluted, purple, 5" d. 59
Nappy, green 45-50
Punch cup, green 25

Many Fruits (Dugan)

Punch bowl, 9 3/4" d., purple 375-450

Many Fruits Punch Bowl & Base

Punch bowl & base, purple, 2 pcs. (ILLUS.)..... 375
Punch bowl & base, white, 2 pcs. 765

Punch cup, blue 30-40
Punch cup, marigold.. 35
Punch cup, purple 30-40
Punch cup, white.. 70
Punch set: bowl, base & 4 cups; marigold,
    6 pcs.. 550-600
Punch set: bowl, base & 6 cups; purple, 8
    pcs... 900-1,000

Many Stars (Millersburg)

Bowl, 7 5/8" d., straight-sided, deep, purple.. 1,400
Bowl, 8" to 9" d., ruffled, green........................... 413
Bowl, 8" to 9" d., ruffled, marigold.................... 418
Bowl, 10" d., ruffled, purple.............................. 450
Bowl, ice cream, 10" d., green................... 775-800
Bowl, ice cream, 10" d., purple.................. 850-900
Bowl, square, crimped edge, purple.............. 3,300
Bowl, three-in-one edge, marigold.................... 700

Marilyn (Millersburg)

Pitcher, water, purple................................. 375-475
Tumbler, green 225
Tumbler, marigold 138
Tumbler, purple... 150-200
Water set: pitcher & 1 tumbler; marigold,
    2 pcs.. 600

Mary Ann Vase (Dugan)

Blue opalescent 250
Marigold 65
Purple 225-275

Memphis (Northwood)

Berry set: master bowl & 5 sauce dishes;
    purple, 6 pcs...................................... 750
Bowl, master berry, marigold............................ 118
Fruit bowl & base, purple, 2 pcs. 400
Punch bowl & base, ice green,
    2 pcs.. 5,000-7,000

Memphis Punch Bowl & Base

Punch bowl & base, purple, 2 pcs. (ILLUS.)...... 625
Punch cup, green.. 35-55
Punch cup, ice green.. 135
Punch cup, marigold.. 20
Punch cup, purple 36
Punch cup, smoky 60
Punch cup, white.. 45
Punch set: bowl, base & 10 cups; purple,
    12 pcs... 950-1,000
Sauce dish, marigold.. 75

Mikado (Fenton)

Compote, 10" d., blue...................................... 500
Compote, 10" d., marigold................................. 140

Millersburg Pipe Humidor - See Pipe Humidor Pattern

Mirrored Lotus
Bowl, 7" d., blue 90
Bowl, 7" d., ruffled, marigold 175
Rose bowl, marigold 450

Morning Glory (Millersburg & Imperial)

Morning Glory Pitcher

Pitcher, tankard, purple (ILLUS.)................. 10,000
Tumbler, purple.. 1,200
Vase, 4" to 10" h., green 79
Vase, 4" to 10" h., marigold 53
Vase, 4" to 10" h., purple.................................... 190
Vase, 4" to 10" h., smoky 110
Vase, 4" to 10" h., white 150
Vase, 10 x 12", funeral, marigold...................... 275
Vase, 12 1/2" h., funeral, purple................. 575-650
Vase, 9 1/2 x 13", purple................................. 345
Vase, 16" h., funeral, green 210
Vase, 18" h., marigold...................................... 200
Vase, miniature, smoky 55

Nautilus (Dugan)
Bowl, footed, purple... 175
Creamer, peach opalescent 170-190
Creamer, purple...................................... 250-300
Creamer & sugar bowl, peach opalescent, pr. 265
Dish, flattened boat shape, peach opalescent, 6 x 7 1/2", 3" h. 260-275
Sugar bowl, open, peach opalescent....... 200-250
Sugar bowl, open, purple........................ 225-300
Vase, marigold, whimsey 200
Vase, purple, whimsey...................................... 300

Nesting Swan (Millersburg)
Bowl, 9" d., green... 524
Bowl, 9" d., marigold.. 450
Bowl, 10" d., green 325-375
Bowl, 10" d., marigold 250
Bowl, 10" d., purple.. 360

Night Stars (Millersburg)
Bonbon, green 475-500
Bonbon, marigold 975

Octagon (Imperial)
Bowl, 8" to 9" d., marigold 30-35
Bowl, 8" to 9" d., pastel marigold........................ 50
Butter dish, cov., marigold.................................. 85

Compote, jelly, marigold....................................... 85
Creamer, marigold.. 60
Creamer, purple... 180-200
Creamer & sugar bowl, marigold variant, pr. 110
Decanter w/stopper, green 500

Octagon Wine Decanter

Decanter w/stopper, marigold (ILLUS.).... 100-125
Goblet, water, marigold 45
Pitcher, milk, marigold 85
Pitcher, milk, purple 250-275
Pitcher, water, 8" h., light blue w/marigold overlay.. 125
Pitcher, water, 8" h., marigold 63
Pitcher, water, 8" h., purple 550-600
Spooner, marigold... 45
Sugar bowl, cov., marigold................................... 50
Toothpick holder, marigold............................... 130
Tumbler, marigold 23
Tumbler, purple.. 125
Vase, 8" h., marigold (minor nick on one tooth on base)... 150
Wine, marigold.. 28
Wine set: decanter & 1 wine; marigold, 2 pcs... 150

Orange Tree Orchard (Fenton)
Pitcher, marigold.. 365
Pitcher, white.. 475
Tumbler, blue.. 50-55
Tumbler, marigold 60
Water set: pitcher & 6 tumblers; blue, 7 pcs....... 675
Water set: pitcher & 6 tumblers; marigold, 7 pcs.. 850-900
Water set: pitcher & 6 tumblers; white, 7 pcs... 1,500

Oriental Poppy (Northwood)
Pitcher, tankard, marigold................................. 265
Pitcher, water, green....................................... 1,250
Pitcher, water, marigold.................................... 372
Pitcher, water, purple............................... 750-850
Pitcher, water, white............................ 1,500-2,000
Tumbler, ice green 275
Tumbler, marigold 30
Tumbler, purple.. 55
Tumbler, white.. 155-165
Water set: pitcher & 5 tumblers, marigold, 6 pcs. 500-600
Water set: pitcher & 6 tumblers, green, 7 pcs. 1,800-2,500

Palm Beach (U.S. Glass Co.)

Bowl, 5" d., marigold, four turned-in sides **80-90**
Rose bowl, marigold w/Goofus finish **213**
Sauce dish, white **70-75**
Sauce dish, white, oval, Gooseberry interi-
or, small **55**
Spooner, white **110**
Sugar bowl, cov., honey amber **158**
Tumbler, amber.. **200**
Tumbler, white..................................... **190-200**
Vase, whimsey, purple... **65**

Paneled Dandelion - See Dandelion, Paneled Pattern

Peach (Northwood)

Bowl, 9" d., white.. **225**
Butter dish, cov., white....................................... **225**

Peach Pitcher

Pitcher, water, blue (ILLUS.)............................ **1,250**
Sauce dish, white **45**
Spooner, white **135-150**
Sugar bowl, cov., white **125-150**
Tumbler, blue **85-100**
Tumbler, blue w/electric iridescence **140-150**
Tumbler, marigold.. **2,100**
Tumbler, white.. **95**

Peacock & Dahlia (Fenton)

Bowl, 6" d., marigold, ice cream shape **80**
Bowl, 6 1/4" d., aqua opalescent....................... **100**
Bowl, 7" d., aqua, ruffled..................................... **115**
Bowl, 7" d., blue, ruffled **100-125**
Bowl, 7" d., marigold... **100**
Bowl, 7" d., purple, ruffled **70-75**
Bowl, 7" d., vaseline, ice cream shape...... **175-200**
Bowl, 7 1/2" d., aqua **125**
Bowl, 7 1/2" d., marigold, ice cream shape,
spatula-footed... **38**
Bowl, 7 1/2" d., purple w/blue base.................. **250**

Peacock & Grape (Fenton)

Bowl, 8"., collared base, amber...................... **120**
Bowl, 8" d., collared base, blue **70-90**
Bowl, 8" d., collared base, ice green, ruffled..... **225**
Bowl, 8" d., collared base, purple........................ **90**
Bowl, 8" d., ice cream shape, green **100-125**
Bowl, 8" d., ice cream shape, marigold..... **100-125**
Bowl, 8" d., ice cream shape, red........ **1,000-1,125**
Bowl, 8" d., spatula-footed, green **125-150**
Bowl, 8" d., spatula-footed, ice green opal-
escent.. **450-500**
Bowl, 8" d., spatula-footed, marigold.................. **55**
Bowl, 8" d., spatula-footed, purple............. **95-125**

Bowl, 8 3/4" d., amber... **160**
Bowl, 9" d., ruffled, collared base, blue.............. **145**
Bowl, 9" d., ruffled, green **100**
Bowl, 9" d., ruffled, marigold................................ **45**
Bowl, 9" d., ruffled, purple **110**
Bowl, 9" d., ruffled, red....................................... **300**
Bowl, Bearded Berry exterior, blue.................... **165**
Bowl, ruffled, spatula-footed, lime green
opalescent **245**
Bowl, footed, ice cream shape, purple **175**
Bowl, ice cream shape, blue **125**
Bowl, three-in-one edge, collared base,
purple **175**
Plate, 9" d., collared base, green **250**
Plate, 9" d., collared base, marigold.................. **275**
Plate, 9" d., collared base, pastel marigold **750**
Plate, 9" d., dark marigold, berry exterior.......... **950**
Plate, 9" d., flat base, marigold.......................... **475**
Plate, 9" d., spatula-footed, emerald
green **1,000-1,500**
Plate, 9" d., spatula-footed, green.............. **175-200**
Plate, 9" d., spatula-footed, marigold......... **300-325**
Plate, 9" d., spatula-footed, purple.............. **375-400**
Plate, footed, green **850**

Peacock Tail (Fenton)

Berry set: 9" d. bowl & four 5" d. bowls;
green, 5 pcs. **150**
Bonbon, two-handled, green **80**

Peacock Tail Bonbon

Bonbon, two-handled, marigold (ILLUS.) **37**
Bonbon, tricornered, marigold............................... **22**
Bonbon, tricornered, purple **35-40**
Bowl, 4" d., marigold **40**
Bowl, 5" d., ruffled, green **20-25**
Bowl, 5" d., ruffled, marigold................................ **24**
Bowl, 6" d., ruffled, marigold **30-35**
Bowl, 6" d., ruffled, purple **40**
Bowl, 7" d., blue, ruffled....................................... **55**
Bowl, 9" d., blue, candy ribbon edge................... **65**
Bowl, 9" d., green **49**
Bowl, 9" d., green, candy ribbon edge **175-200**
Bowl, 9" d., marigold, crimped............................. **50**
Bowl, 9" d., purple, candy ribbon edge **55-65**
Bowl, 9" sq., purple, candy ribbon edge **475**
Bowl, 10" d., green, candy ribbon edge............. **225**
Compote, blue, 6" d., 5" h. **60**
Compote, green, 6" d., 5" h. **65**
Compote, marigold, 6" d., 5" h. **80-90**
Compote, marigold, variant, 6" d., 5" h. **90**
Compote, purple, 6" d., 5" h. **50-60**
Compote, purple, variant, 6" d., 5" h. **165-175**
Plate, 6" d., blue **195-225**
Plate, 6" d., purple, tricornered, Panels ex-
terior **125-150**
Plate, 9" d., marigold **1,250**
Whimsey, green, hat-shaped **60-65**

Peacock & Urn (Millersburg, Fenton & Northwood)

Bowl, 5" d., ice cream shape, blue, stippled..... 155
Bowl, 5 1/2" d., ruffled, blue (Millersburg)...... 1,700
Bowl, 6" d., ice cream, blue w/electric iridescence.. 375
Bowl, 6" d., ice cream shape, green (Millersburg).. 338
Bowl, 6" d., ice cream shape, marigold (Millersburg).. 105
Bowl, 6" d., ice cream shape, purple (Millersburg).. 188
Bowl, 6" d., ice cream shape, purple satin....... 150
Bowl, 6" d., ice cream shape, white.......... 120-150
Bowl, 8" d., ice cream shape, green (Fenton)... 225
Bowl, 8" d., ice cream shape, marigold (Fenton)... 100-125
Bowl, 8" to 9" d., blue (Fenton)................. 240-250
Bowl, 8" to 9" d., green (Millersburg) 375
Bowl, 8" to 9" d., marigold (Fenton) 140-160
Bowl, 8" to 9" d., marigold, ruffled (Millersburg).. 225
Bowl, 8" to 9" d., purple (Fenton) 155
Bowl, 8" to 9" d., white (Fenton) 225-250
Bowl, 8 3/4" d., ice cream shape, purple (Millersburg).. 1,000
Bowl, 9" d., ice cream shape, blue (Fenton)..... 350
Bowl, 9" d., ice cream shape, marigold (Fenton)... 185
Bowl, 9" d., ruffled, blue (Fenton)...................... 135
Bowl, 9" d., ruffled, purple (Fenton) 275-300
Bowl, 9" d., ruffled, white 295
Bowl, 9 1/2" d., berry, purple (Millersburg).. 550-600
Bowl, 10" d., ice cream shape, aqua opalescent (Northwood) 13,300
Bowl, 10" d., ice cream shape, blue (Northwood).. 800
Bowl, 10" d., ice cream shape, cobalt blue, stippled (Northwood) 1,100
Bowl, 10" d., ice cream shape, green (Northwood) 1,500
Bowl, 10" d., ice cream shape, green w/bee (Millersburg).. 900
Bowl, 10" d., ice cream shape, honey amber, stippled (Northwood) 1,400
Bowl, 10" d., ice cream shape, ice blue (Northwood) 842
Bowl, 10" d., ice cream shape, ice green (Northwood) 2,000
Bowl, 10" d., ice cream shape, marigold (Millersburg) 375-425
Bowl, 10" d., ice cream shape, marigold (Northwood) 550
Bowl, 10" d., ice cream shape, marigold, stippled (Northwood) 700
Bowl, 10" d., ice cream shape, pastel marigold (Northwood) 550-600
Bowl, 10" d., ice cream shape, pastel marigold, stippled (Northwood) 438
Bowl, 10" d., ice cream shape, purple (Millersburg) 1,100
Bowl, 10" d., ice cream shape, purple (Northwood) 506
Bowl, 10" d., ice cream shape, white (Northwood).. 438
Bowl, 10" d., ruffled, marigold 145
Bowl, 10" d., ruffled, purple 350-400
Bowl, 10" d., three-in-one edge, purple (Millersburg).. 650-700

Bowl, 10 1/2" d., ruffled, green (Millersburg) 325-350
Bowl, 10 1/2" d., ruffled, marigold (Millersburg) 225-250
Bowl, 10 1/2" d., ruffled, purple (Fenton) ... 275-300
Bowl, 10 1/2" d., ruffled, purple (Millersburg) 300
Bowl, ruffled, Bearded Berry exterior, marigold.. 198
Bowl, ruffled, marigold (Northwood) 245
Bowl, ruffled, white (Fenton) 150-175
Bowl, three-in-one edge, green 375
Compote, 5 1/2" d., 5" h., aqua (Fenton).......... 165
Compote, 5 1/2" d., 5" h., blue (Fenton) 125-150
Compote, 5 1/2" d., 5" h., marigold (Fenton).. 50-60
Compote, 5 1/2" d., 5" h., white (Fenton) 245
Compote, green (Millersburg Giant) 1,500-1,550
Compote, marigold (Millersburg Giant)......... 1,700
Compote, purple (Millersburg Giant) 2,000
Goblet, blue (Fenton) 90
Goblet, marigold (Fenton) 65
Ice cream dish, purple, 5 3/4" d. (Millersburg) 350-400
Ice cream dish, blue w/electric iridescence...... 180
Ice cream dish, green, small (Northwood)........ 950
Ice cream dish, purple, small 95
Plate, 6 1/2" d., green (Millersburg) 1,500

Peacock & Urn Plate

Plate, 6 1/2" d., marigold, Millersburg (ILLUS.)... 1,000
Plate, 6 1/2" d., purple (Millersburg) 1,000-1,200
Plate, 9" d., blue (Fenton).................................. 558
Plate, 9" d., marigold (Fenton) 388
Plate, 9" d., purple (Fenton) 150
Plate, 9" d., white (Fenton) 400-500
Plate, chop, 11" d., marigold (Millersburg)..... 2,200
Plate, chop, 11" d., purple (Millersburg) 750
Plate, chop, 11" d., purple (Northwood) 1,400
Sauce dish, blue (Millersburg) 1,000-1,200
Sauce dish, blue, stippled (Northwood)..... 150-160
Sauce dish, ice green, 6" d. (Northwood) . 375-400
Sauce dish, lavender (Millersburg)................... 100
Sauce dish, marigold (Northwood)...................... 85
Sauce dish, purple (Millersburg)....................... 100
Whimsey sauce dish, purple, 5 1/4" d. 275-300

Perfection (Millersburg)

Pitcher, water, green.............................. 3,900-4,225

Perfection Pitcher

Pitcher, water, purple (ILLUS.) **3,200**
Tumbler, purple **420-475**

Persian Garden (Dugan)
Bowl, 5" d., peach opalescent **40**
Bowl, 5" d., purple **75**
Bowl, 5" d., white **70-80**
Bowl, 6" d., ice cream shape, white **75-80**
Bowl, 10" d., marigold **50**
Bowl, 10" d., ruffled, purple **400-425**
Bowl, 11" d., ice cream shape, peach opal-
escent **155**
Bowl, 11" d., ice cream shape, white **275-325**
Fruit bowl & base, marigold, 2 pcs. **225**
Fruit bowl & base, peach opalescent,
2 pcs. **650**
Fruit bowl & base, purple, 2 pcs. **1,000**
Fruit bowl & base, white, 2 pcs. **725**
Fruit bowl (no base), marigold **125-130**
Fruit bowl (no base), purple **250**
Plate, 6" to 7" d., marigold **35**

Persian Garden Plate

Plate, 6" to 7" d., peach opalescent (ILLUS.)
.... **165-200**
Plate, 6" to 7" d., purple **488**
Plate, 6" to 7" d., white **150-175**
Plate, chop, 11" d., white **700-800**

Petal & Fan (Dugan)
Bowl, 5" d., purple **70**
Bowl, 6" d., ruffled, peach opalescent **70**
Bowl, 6" d., ruffled, purple **80**
Bowl, 10" d., ruffled, peach opalescent **200-250**
Bowl, 10 1/2" d., purple, Jeweled Heart ex-
terior **625**
Bowl, 11" d., fluted, white **450-500**
Bowl, 11" d., peach opalescent **365**

Bowl, 11" d., purple, ruffled **268**
Bowl, 11" d., purple, star-shaped, stippled,
Jeweled Heart exterior **300**
Bowl, 12" d., Jeweled Heart exterior, white **325**
Plate, 6" d., candy ribbon rim, green **225**

Petals (Northwood)
Compote, marigold **60-70**
Compote, purple **69**

Peter Rabbit (Fenton)
Bowl, 8" d., blue **1,000-1,100**
Bowl, 8" d., green **950-1,000**
Bowl, 8" d., marigold **1,500**

Peter Rabbit Plate

Plate, green (ILLUS.) **3,500-4,000**

Pine Cone (Fenton)
Bowl, 5" d., aqua **100-150**

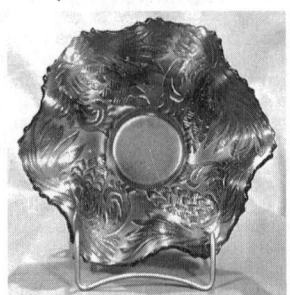

Pine Cone Bowl

Bowl, 5" d., blue (ILLUS.) **45**
Bowl, 5" d., marigold **60-70**
Bowl, 5" d., purple **45**
Bowl, 6" d., blue, ruffled **135**
Bowl, 6" d., marigold **40-50**
Bowl, 6" d., marigold, ruffled **58**
Bowl, 6" d., purple, ruffled **175**
Bowl, 7" d., blue, ruffled **85**
Bowl, 7" d., purple, ruffled **85**
Plate, 6 1/2" d., blue **165**
Plate, 6 1/2" d., green **150-175**
Plate, 6 1/2" d., marigold **80**
Plate, 6 1/2" d., purple **195**
Plate, 7 1/2" d., amber **650-700**
Plate, 7 1/2" d., marigold **125**

Pineapple (Sowerby, England)
Bowl, 6" d., marigold **25**
Compote, marigold **40**
Creamer, marigold, 4 1/2" h. **40-50**
Rose bowl, marigold **60**

Pipe Humidor (Millersburg)

Pipe Humidor

Green (ILLUS.) 6,500
Marigold 5,000

Plaid (Fenton)
Bowl, 8" d., green, deep.................................. 350
Bowl, 8" d., marigold, ice cream shape............. 155
Bowl, 9" d., ruffled, blue............................... 240-275
Bowl, 9" d., ruffled, green 400-450
Bowl, 9" d., ruffled, marigold 155
Bowl, 9" d., ruffled, red................................... 1,750
Bowl, ice cream, 10" d., blue............................. 300
Bowl, ice cream, 10" d., green................... 800-900
Bowl, ice cream, 10" d., purple................... 400-450
Bowl, ice cream, red... 2,450

Plume Panels Vase (Fenton)
Blue 60
Green 70
Marigold 46
Red 1,150-1,175

Pods & Posies or Four Flowers (Dugan)
Bowl, 6" d., peach opalescent............................. 52
Bowl, 8" to 9" d., green 145-155
Bowl, 8" to 9" d., marigold 125
Bowl, 8" to 9" d., purple...................................... 95
Bowl, 10" d., peach opalescent 150-200
Bowl, 10" d., purple.................................... 175-225
Plate, 6" d., peach opalescent............................ 160
Plate, 6" to 7" d., peach opalescent, w/exterior pattern... 125-140
Plate, chop, 11" d., peach opalescent 200
Plate, chop, 11" d., purple..................... 2,275-3,000

Poinsettia & Lattice
Bowl, footed, purple... 475
Bowl, ice blue 2,900

Polo
Ashtray, marigold.. 45-50

Pond Lily
Bonbon, blue.. 70
Bonbon, green 68
Bonbon, marigold 45
Bonbon, purple.. 75
Bonbon, white 95

Pony
Bowl, 8" to 9" d., aqua............................... 450-500
Bowl, 8" to 9" d., ice green 850-875

Pony Bowl

Bowl, 8" to 9" d., marigold (ILLUS.) 85-100
Bowl, 8" to 9" d., purple 250

Poppy (Millersburg)
Compote, green... 592
Compote, green, flared-out salver shape...... 2,800
Compote, purple............................... 1,000-1,150

Poppy (Northwood)
Pickle dish, aqua opalescent 900-950

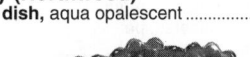

Poppy Pickle Dish

Pickle dish, blue (ILLUS.)................................... 295
Pickle dish, green 200-250
Pickle dish, marigold 100
Pickle dish, purple 200-225
Pickle dish, white 350-400

Poppy Show Vase (Imperial)
Marigold 425

Poppy Show Vase

Purple (ILLUS) 2,750

Primrose Bowl (Millersburg)
Green 83
Marigold 105
Purple 175-200

Prisms
Bonbon, marigold.. 38
Bonbon, purple 55
Compote, two-handled, marigold, 4 1/2" d......... 75
Compote, two-handled, purple, 4 1/2" d. 55

Compote, two-handled, marigold, 7 1/4" d.,
2 1/2" h.. 49
Compote, teal.. 80

Pulled Loop
Vase, 9 1/2" h., peach opalescent........................ 45
Vase, 10" h., peach opalescent............................ 60
Vase, 10" h., purple... 48
Vase, 11" h., aqua... 425
Vase, 11" h., marigold..................................... 35-45
Vase, 11" h., peach opalescent............................ 30
Vase, 11" h., purple... 95
Vase, 12 1/2" h., peach opalescent................... 100
Vase, sapphire.. 350

Puzzle
Bonbon, blue.. 140
Bonbon, marigold... 40
Bonbon, purple, two-handled................................ 70
Bonbon, white.. 113

Raindrops (Dugan)
Bowl, 7" d., turned-up, fluted, peach opal-
escent... 96
Bowl, 9" d., dome-footed, marigold...................... 90
Bowl, 9" d., dome-footed, peach
opalescent.. 90-100

Raindrops Bowl

Bowl, 9" d., dome-footed, peach opalescent, candy ribbon edge (ILLUS.)................. 150
Bowl, 9" d., dome-footed, purple....................... 140

Rambler Rose (Dugan)
Pitcher, water, blue.. 95-125
Tumbler, blue... 65
Tumbler, marigold.. 25
Water set: pitcher & 4 tumblers; blue, 5 pcs...... 450

Raspberry (Northwood)
Pitcher, milk, green.................................... 350-400
Pitcher, milk, marigold.. 208
Pitcher, milk, purple.. 350
Pitcher, milk, white... 1,000
Pitcher, water, green... 350
Pitcher, water, ice blue.................................. 2,100
Pitcher, water, ice green..................... 2,000-2,150
Pitcher, water, marigold............................. 160-175
Pitcher, water, white..................................... 650-700

Raspberry Sauceboat

Sauceboat, purple (ILLUS.)............................... 185
Tumbler, green... 75
Tumbler, green w/marigold overlay................... 125
Tumbler, ice blue... 275-300
Tumbler, ice green....................................... 550-650
Tumbler, marigold.. 45
Tumbler, purple... 75
Water set: pitcher & 4 tumblers; marigold,
5 pcs.. 350-400

Rays & Ribbons (Millersburg)
Bowl, 8" to 9" d., marigold.................................. 85
Bowl, 8" to 9" d., purple..................................... 85
Bowl, 8" to 9" d., purple, ice cream shape......... 250
Bowl, 9" d., marigold, ruffled, three-in-one
edge.. 150-175
Bowl, 10" d., green...................................... 100-120
Bowl, 10" d., marigold..................................... 70-75
Bowl, 10" d., purple.. 80-90
Bowl, 10" sq., green..................................... 200-250
Plate, chop, purple... 2,100

Rising Sun
Pitcher, water, blue.. 1,150
Pitcher, water, marigold, domed base....... 400-425
Pitcher, water, marigold, pedestal base.... 550-650
Tumbler, marigold....................................... 225-250

Robin (Imperial)

Robin Mug

Mug, marigold (ILLUS.).. 43
Pitcher, water, marigold..................................... 310
Tumbler, marigold.. 75
Tumbler, smoky... 500

Rosalind (Millersburg)
Bowl, 9" d., ruffled, green.................................. 350
Bowl, 10" d., marigold................................ 250-275
Bowl, 10" d., purple... 215
Bowl, 10" d., ruffled, aqua................................ 575
Bowl, 10" d., ruffled, green............................... 155
Compote, tall, ruffled, purple, 6" d................. 4,250
Compote, jelly, tall, flared, green.................. 4,250
Plate, 9" d., green... 1,775
Plate, 9" d., purple... 1,700

Rosette
Bowl, 6" d., purple.. 70
Bowl, 7 1/2" d., ruffled, purple............................ 85
Bowl, footed, marigold (Northwood).............. 35-40
Bowl, footed, purple (Northwood)....................... 75

Scale Band
Bowl, 6" d., marigold.. 25
Bowl, 6" d., red, Stippled Rays interior.............. 550
Plate, 6" d., flat, marigold................................... 29
Plate, 7" d., flat, marigold................................... 40

Tumbler, marigold.. 44
Water set: pitcher & 6 tumblers; blue, 7 pcs. 750
Water set: pitcher & 6 tumblers; marigold, 7
pcs.. 175

Scales
Bowl, 6" d., marigold... 20
Bowl, 6" d., peach opalescent.......................... 50-55
Bowl, 7" d., purple... 45
Bowl, 8" to 9" d., milk white w/marigold
overlay.. 150-200
Bowl, 8" to 9" d., peach opalescent 80-100
Bowl, ice cream shape, peach opalescent 65-75
Plate, 6 1/2" d., marigold.................................. 40-45
Plate, 6 1/2" d., purple 57
Plate, 9" d., milk white w/marigold overlay 450

Scotch Thistle Compote
Blue 100-150
Green 100 to150
Purple 85

Scroll Embossed
Bowl, 4" d., marigold... 30
Bowl, 5" d., purple... 80
Bowl, 6 1/2" d., purple, Hobstar exterior 65
Bowl, 8" to 9" d., green 40
Bowl, 8" to 9" d., marigold 30-40
Bowl, 8" to 9" d., purple....................................... 95
Bowl, 9" d., lavender, ruffled 100-125
Compote, green 30-40
Compote, marigold 30
Compote marigold, Easter Star exterior............. 55
Compote, marigold, File exterior 50
Compote, purple 98
Compote, purple, miniature............................... 325
Plate, 9" d., green... 90-100
Plate, 9" d., marigold.. 160
Plate, 9" d., pastel marigold................................. 85
Plate, 9" d., purple... 275-300
Sauce dish, purple, 5 1/2" d................................. 40
Sauce dish, purple, ruffled, 5 3/4" d. 70

Seacoast Pin Tray (Millersburg)
Green 575-600
Marigold 450-500
Purple 525-550

Seaweed (Millersburg)
Bowl, 8 1/2" d., marigold, ice cream shape 265
Bowl, 10" d., marigold, ice cream shape.......... 125
Bowl, 10" d., marigold, ruffled 375
Bowl, 10" d., purple, ruffled 375-425
Lamp, marigold... 275-300

Shell (Imperial)
Bowl, 7 1/2" d., amber.. 190
Bowl, 7 3/4" d., smoky, ruffled 60
Bowl, 8" d., marigold.. 40-45
Bowl, 8" d., purple... 95
Plate, marigold... 350

Shell & Jewel
Creamer, cov., green.. 41
Creamer, cov., marigold....................................... 30
Creamer & cov. sugar bowl, green, pr. 65-75
Sugar bowl, cov., green 65
Sugar bowl, open, green............................... 15-20

Shell & Sand
Bowl, purple.. 225-275
Bowl, 7" d., teal, ruffled 175
Bowl, 8" to 9" d., purple, ruffled 88

Bowl, teal 275
Mug, marigold.. 110

Shell & Sand Plate

Plate, marigold (ILLUS.).................................... 1,400

Single Flower
Basket, handled, ruffled, peach
opalescent 750-1,000
Bowl, 7 1/2" d., peach opalescent, candy
ribbon edge 85-90
Bowl, 8 3/4" d., peach opalescent, ruffled 59
Bowl, 9" d., peach opalescent 55
Bowl, 9" d., peach opalescent, framed, tri-
cornered... 85-95
Bowl, 9" d., peach opalescent, three-in-one
edge.. 135
Bowl, peach opalescent, candy ribbon
edge.. 125-150
Bowl, peach opalescent, framed, candy rib-
bon edge 113
Plate, 7" d., peach opalescent, framed,
crimped rim.. 50-100
Plate, peach opalescent, framed, w/hand
grip.. 90-100

Six Petals (Dugan)
Bowl, 7" d., purple.. 90-100

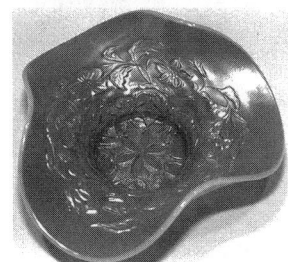

Six Petals Bowl

Bowl, 7" w., peach opalescent, tricornered
(ILLUS.).. 70-80
Bowl, 8" d., peach opalescent 85-95
Bowl, 8" d., purple... 80-90
Bowl, 8" d., white... 100-125
Bowl, 8 1/2" d., ruffled, peach opalescent 50
Bowl, 9" d., dome-footed, peach opalescent.. 55-60
Bowl, black amethyst, ruffled............................... 80

Ski Star (Dugan)
Banana bowl, peach opalescent 170
Basket, peach opalescent.................................... 520
Bowl, 5" d., ruffled, peach opalescent................. 45
Bowl, 5" d., ruffled, purple 75-95
Bowl, 6" d., ruffled, peach opalescent................. 60
Bowl, 10" d., marigold... 62

Bowl, 10" d., peach opalescent 125
Bowl, 10" d., purple...................................... 300-375
Bowl, 11" d., peach opalescent 125-150
Bowl, 11" d., purple...................................... 225-275

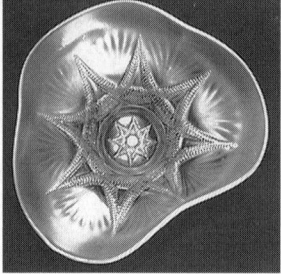

Ski Star Bowl

Bowl, tricornered, dome-footed, peach
opalescent (ILLUS.)............................... 100-125
Plate, 6" d., crimped rim, peach opalescent 175
Plate, 7" d., deep, candy ribbon edge,
peach opalescent... 65
Plate, 8 1/2" d., dome-footed, w/handgrip,
peach opalescent.. 185

Soutache (Dugan)

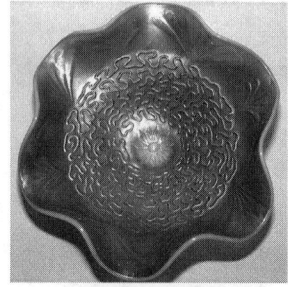

Soutache Bowl

Bowl, 8" d., dome-footed, ruffled, peach
opalescent (ILLUS.).. 93
Bowl, 8" to 9" d., dome-footed, piecrust rim,
peach opalescent... 159
Plate, 9 1/2" d., dome-footed, peach opal-
escent 200-250

Springtime (Northwood)
Bowl, master berry, marigold 125
Butter dish, cov., green...................................... 400

Springtime Butter Dish

Butter dish, cov., marigold (ILLUS.) 250-275
Butter dish, cov., purple.................................... 300
Creamer, marigold.. 125
Pitcher, green.. 950-1,000
Pitcher, marigold.. 300
Sauce dish, 5" d., green...................................... 53
Sauce dish, 5" d., purple..................................... 55
Spooner, green.. 255-275
Spooner, marigold.. 125
Spooner, purple.. 300
Sugar bowl, cov., marigold................................ 235
Sugar bowl, open, green.................................... 165
Tumbler, green 170-175
Tumbler, marigold 65
Tumbler, purple... 95

Star & File (Imperial)
Bowl, 8" sq., marigold 45-55
Bowl, 8" to 9" d., marigold................................. 35
Bowl, two-handled, marigold.............................. 35
Celery vase, two-handled, marigold.............. 55-65
Champagne, marigold 10
Compote, large, marigold.............................. 45-50
Creamer, marigold... 30
Pitcher, water, marigold.............................. 125-150
Plate, 6" d., marigold 125
Rose bowl, marigold 40-50
Sherbet, marigold 25
Sherbet, marigold, w/underplate, tall................ 125
Tumbler, marigold 78
Wine decanter w/stopper, marigold................. 138

Star Medallion
Bowl, 5" sq., marigold 25
Bowl, 8" d., smoky 47
Compote, marigold....................................... 35-40
Goblet, marigold 30
Goblet, smoky 48
Pitcher, milk, clambroth 55-60
Pitcher, milk, marigold 50
Pitcher, milk, purple 58
Pitcher, milk, smoky 80
Plate, 9" to 10" d., clambroth............................. 75
Plate, 9" to 10" d., marigold........................... 25-30
Sherbet, stemmed, marigold............................. 35
Tumbler, marigold 20-25
Vase, smoky.. 100-125

Star of David & Bows (Northwood)

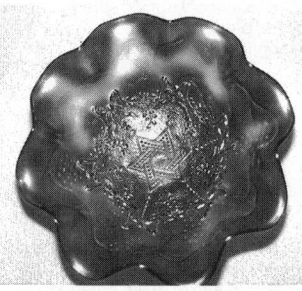

Star of David & Bows Bowl

Bowl, 7" d., dome-footed, marigold (ILLUS.)........ 46
Bowl, 7" d., dome-footed, purple................... 60-65
Bowl, 8" to 9" d., dome-footed, fluted, green........ 95
Bowl, 8" to 9" d., dome-footed, fluted,
purple 90-100

Bowl, Embossed Scroll exterior, purple 98

Stippled Flower (Dugan)
Bowl, 7" d., three sides up, peach opalescent 48
Bowl, 8 1/2" d., stippled, fluted, peach opalescent 70-80
Bowl, 8 1/2" w., tricornered, peach opalescent 68

Stippled Petals
Banana boat, dome-footed, candy ribbon
edge, peach opalescent 100-125
Basket, two sides up, peach
opalescent 135-140
Bowl, 9" d., peach opalescent 30
Bowl, peach opalescent 80-100

Stork & Rushes (Dugan or Diamond Glass Works)
Basket, marigold, handled 125-150
Bowl, marigold, master berry or fruit 55
Butter dish, cov., marigold 135
Creamer, marigold 72
Hat shape, blue 40
Hat shape, marigold 25
Mug, blue 750
Mug, marigold 30-35
Pitcher, water, marigold 375
Punch bowl & base, marigold, 2 pcs. 225
Punch cup, blue 35
Punch cup, marigold 17
Punch cup, purple 20-35
Punch set: bowl, base & 6 cups; marigold,
8 pcs. 300-325
Sauce dish, marigold 38
Spooner, marigold 80
Spooner, purple 90
Tumbler, blue 50-60
Tumbler, marigold 30-35
Vase, marigold 30-35
Water set: pitcher & 1 tumbler; blue,
2 pcs. 450-500
Water set: pitcher & 4 tumblers; marigold, 5
pcs. 513

Strawberry (Fenton)
Bonbon, Amberina 175
Bonbon, two-handled, amber 75-100
Bonbon, two-handled, blue 60-65
Bonbon, two-handled, green 65-75
Bonbon, two-handled, ice green opales-
cent 450-500
Bonbon, two-handled, marigold 31
Bonbon, two-handled, marigold 65
Bonbon, two-handled, purple 85
Bonbon, two-handled, red 350
Bonbon, vaseline w/marigold iridescence,
two-handled 100-125

Strawberry Scroll (Fenton)
Pitcher, water, marigold 1,850-2,000
Tumbler, blue 190
Tumbler, marigold 200-225

Stream of Hearts (Fenton)
Bowl, 9 1/2" d., green 80
Compote, clambroth 25
Compote, marigold 100-120

Sunflower Bowl (Northwood)

Sunflower Bowl

Bowl, 8" d., footed, blue (ILLUS.) 1,200
Bowl, 8" d., footed, blue w/electric irides-
cence 650-700
Bowl, 8" d., footed, green 127
Bowl, 8" d., footed, ice blue 1,275
Bowl, 8" d., footed, lavender 90
Bowl, 8" d., footed, marigold 75
Bowl, 8" d., footed, pastel marigold 300
Bowl, 8" d., footed, purple 165
Bowl, 8" d., footed, purple, Meander exteri-
or 150-160
Bowl 8", footed, emerald green 363

Sunflower Pin Tray (Millersburg)
Green 350
Marigold 450
Purple 500-550

Swan Pastel Novelties (Dugan)
Salt dip, amber 250
Salt dip, celeste blue 40-45
Salt dip, ice blue 33
Salt dip, ice green 45-50
Salt dip, marigold 100-125
Salt dip, peach opalescent 375-450
Salt dip, purple 250-275
Salt dip, teal 350

Swirl Hobnail (Millersburg)
Cuspidor, green 3,000
Cuspidor, marigold 1,000

Swirl Hobnail Cuspidor

Cuspidor, purple (ILLUS.) 895
Rose bowl, marigold 175
Rose bowl, purple 350-400
Vase, green 700
Vase, marigold 350
Vase, 10" h., green 395
Vase, 10" h., purple 285
Vase, 16" h., marigold, variant 450

Swirl Rib
Tumbler, marigold 37

Vase, 8" h., 6" d., smoky 55
Vase, 10" h., purple.. 65

Target Vase (Dugan)
Marigold, 9 1/2" h. 40
Peach opalescent, squatty, 7" h................. 85-100
Peach opalescent, 10" h.................................... 78
Peach opalescent, 11 1/2" h. 55
Purple, 6" h.. 75
Purple, 11" h. 65-75
Vaseline opalescent, 11" h. 400-500
White 10" h... 100-125

Ten Mums (Fenton)

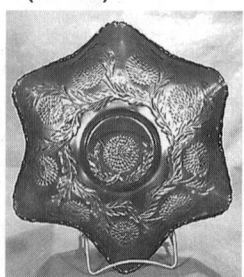

Ten Mums Bowl

Bowl, 10" d., green, footed (ILLUS.) 200

Tree Trunk Vase (Northwood)
Aqua opalescent, 9" to 12" h. 500-600
Blue, 8" to 10" h.. 225
Blue, 12" h.. 160
Blue, 13 1/2" h. 450-525
Blue w/electric iridescence, 10 1/2" h............. 126
Blue w/electric iridescence, 14" h.,
   funeral... 1,375-1,500
Green, 7" h. 45-75
Green, 7 1/2" h., squatty 145
Green, 8" to 11" h... 68
Green, 10" h.. 125-150
Green, 13" h.. 238
Ice blue, 7" h.. 500
Ice green, 7" to 11" h.. 225
Ice green, 11" h.. 285
Marigold, 9" to 10" h.. 43
Marigold, 11" h... 70
Marigold, 12" h... 175
Marigold, 13" h... 145
Marigold, 14" h... 125
Purple, 6" h., squatty 50
Purple, 7" h. 215

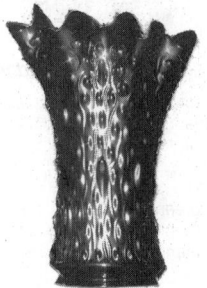

Tree Trunk Vase

Purple, 8" to 11" h. (ILLUS.)........................ 110-120
Purple, 9" to 10" h.. 80
Purple, 11" h... 90
Purple, 12" h., w/elephant foot,
   funeral 2,900-2,975
Purple, 13" h... 275
Purple, 14" h., funeral 1,700
Purple, 22" h., funeral 2,100
White, 9" h.. 165

Twig Vase
Marigold, bud.. 25
Purple, 3 1/2" h. 550-600
Purple, 9 1/2" h. 68

Twins or Horseshoe Curve (Imperial)
Bowl, 5" d., ruffled, smoky.................................... 65
Bowl, 6" d., green 45
Fruit bowl, marigold.. 65
Fruit bowl & base, marigold, 2 pcs................... 108

Two Flowers (Fenton)
Bowl, 6" d., footed, aqua 175
Bowl, 6" d., footed, blue 75
Bowl, 6" d., footed, lime green............................ 175
Bowl, 6" d., footed, marigold............................... 38
Bowl, 6" d., footed, vaseline........................ 100-125
Bowl, 7" to 8" d., footed, blue.................... 85-100
Bowl, 7" to 8" d., footed, green............................ 90
Bowl, 7" to 8" d., footed, marigold................. 60-65
Bowl, 7" to 8" d., footed, purple, fluted.......... 50-60
Bowl, 8" d., marigold, collared base 100-125
Bowl, 8" d., marigold, collared base, ice
   cream shape 133
Bowl, 8 1/2" d., blue, footed 275-300
Bowl, 9" d., footed, black amethyst, ice
   cream shape 375
Bowl, 9" d., footed, blue, ice cream shape 195
Bowl, 9" d., footed, purple, ice cream shape........ 65
Bowl, 10" d., footed, aqua 350-375
Bowl, 10" d., footed, blue 125
Bowl, 10" d., footed, blue, scalloped rim........... 125
Bowl, 10" d., footed, green, scalloped rim......... 95
Bowl, 10" d., footed, marigold............................. 85

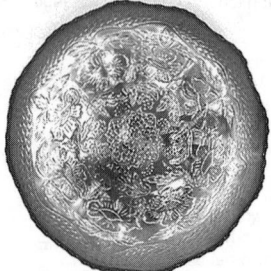

Two Flowers Fruit Bowl

Bowl, 10" d., footed, marigold, scalloped
   rim (ILLUS.)... 60
Bowl, 10" d., footed, purple................................. 525
Bowl, 10 1/2" d., blue, ruffled...................... 125-150
Bowl, 10 1/2" d., marigold, footed, ruffled........... 65
Bowl, 11" d., blue................................... 225-250
Bowl, 11" d., blue, ice cream shape 140-150
Bowl, 11" d., lime green/marigold, ice
   cream shape 175
Bowl, 11" d., marigold.. 115
Bowl, 11" d., purple, footed, ruffled.................... 750

Bowl, 13" d., footed, marigold **75**
Plate, 9" d., footed, marigold **600-650**
Plate, chop, 11 1/2" d., three-foot, marigold .. **1,225**
Rose bowl, three-footed, blue **123**
Rose bowl, three-footed, giant, marigold.. **250-300**
Rose bowl, three-footed, marigold...................... **70**
Rose bowl, three-footed, vaseline **150**

Two Fruits
Banana boat, marigold **90-100**
Bonbon, divided, blue **195**
Bonbon, divided, green....................................... **175**
Bonbon, divided, marigold **85**
Bowl, large, in metal holder, marigold **125-150**

Vineyard
Pitcher, water, marigold...................................... **100**
Pitcher, water, purple **320-350**
Tumbler, marigold... **26**
Tumbler, purple **60-70**
Water set: pitcher & 1 tumbler; marigold,
    2 pcs. **125-175**

Waffle Block
Basket w/tall handle, clambroth, 10" h. **65**
Basket w/tall handle, marigold, 10" h................. **46**
Basket w/tall handle, smoky, 10" h. **73**
Basket w/tall handle, teal, 10" h...................... **120**
Bowl, 7 1/2" sq., marigold.................................... **36**
Creamer, clambroth.. **34**
Pitcher, water, marigold...................................... **103**
Punch set: bowl, base & 6 cups; clambroth,
    8 pcs. **200-225**
Sugar bowl, clambroth... **30**
Tumbler, clambroth **142**
Tumbler, marigold.. **215**

Water Lily (Fenton)
Bonbon, marigold, 7 1/2" d. **25**
Bowl, 5" d., blue **70**
Bowl, 6" d., aqua.. **145**
Bowl, 6" d., blue **83**
Bowl, 6" d., green, footed **150-175**
Bowl, 6" d., ice green opalescent **1,200**
Bowl, 6" d., marigold, footed **44**
Bowl, 6" d., red, footed................................... **1,000**
Bowl, 6" d., red opalescent, footed **1,025-1,050**
Bowl, 6" d., vaseline, footed.............................. **100**
Bowl, 9" d., footed, lavender, ice cream
    shape... **175-200**
Bowl, 9" d., footed, marigold **75**
Bowl, 10" d., footed, blue, fluted................... **95-100**
Bowl, 10" d., footed, marigold **100**

Wild Strawberry (Northwood)
Bowl, 6" d., purple.. **50**
Bowl, 6" d., purple, ruffled **100**
Bowl, 7" d., marigold.. **35**
Bowl, 9" d., green... **85**
Bowl, 10" d., green **200-225**
Bowl, 10" d., ice green **2,500**
Bowl, 10" d., lime green, ruffled...................... **1,400**
Bowl, 10" d., marigold... **110**
Bowl, 10" d., purple....................................... **160-175**
Bowl, 10" d., white.. **195**
Bowl, 10" d., white, ruffled................................. **650**
Plate, 6" to 7" d., w/handgrip, green........... **225-275**
Plate, 6" to 7" d., w/handgrip, marigold............. **155**
Plate, 6" to 7" d., w/handgrip, purple................. **265**

Windflower
Bowl, 8" to 9" d., blue **95**
Bowl, 8" to 9" d., marigold **85**

Bowl, 8" to 9" d., purple **73**
Bowl, ruffled, marigold **15**
Bowl, 8" to 9" d., amber.. **83**
Plate, 8" d., marigold.. **123**
Plate, 9" d., blue... **235**
Plate, 9" d., marigold.. **85**
Sauceboat, ice green **375**
Sauceboat, marigold... **35**
Tumbler, marigold **180-200**

Chrysanthemum Sprig, Blue

The Chrysanthemum Sprig pattern, originally called "Pagoda," was one of several patterns produced by the Northwood Glass Company at the turn of the 20th century in its creamy white Custard glass. A limited amount of this pattern was also produced in a blue opaque color, sometimes erroneously called "blue custard."

The following prices are for pieces that have 85 percent of total gold, with no problems in the glass: chips, nicks or cracks. These pieces must also have excellent fire due to the homogeneous factor of the glass mixture.

Blue Sprig Master Berry Bowl

Bowl, master berry (ILLUS.) **$675**
Butter dish, cov. **1,375**
Celery dish **1,650**
Compote, jelly **550**
Creamer **425**
Cruet w/original stopper, 6 1/2" h................ **1,550**
Pitcher **1,475**

Blue Sprig Salt & Pepper Shakers

**Salt & pepper shakers w/original metal
    tops, pr.** (ILLUS.).. **625**
Sauce dish **255**
Spooner **365**
Tumbler **235**

Consolidated

The Consolidated Lamp and Glass Company of Coraopolis, Pennsylvania was founded in 1894. For a number of years it was noted for its lighting wares but also produced popular lines of pressed and blown tablewares. Highly collectible glass patterns of this early era include the Cone, Cosmos, Florette and Guttate lines.

Lamps and shades continued to be good sellers, but in 1926 a new "art" line of molded decorative wares was introduced. This "Martelé" line was developed as a direct imitation of the fine glasswares being produced by René Lalique of France, and many Consolidated patterns resembled their French counterparts. Other popular lines produced during the 1920s and 1930s were "Dancing Nymph," the delightfully Art Deco "Ruba Rombic," introduced in 1928, and the "Catalonian" line, which debuted in 1927 and imitated 17th century Spanish glass.

Although the factory closed in 1933, it was reopened under new management in 1936 and prospered through the 1940s. It finally closed in 1967. Collectors should note that many later Consolidated patterns closely resemble wares of other competing firms, especially the Phoenix Glass Company. Careful study is needed to determine the maker of pieces from the 1920-40 era.

A book that will be of help to collectors is Phoenix & Consolidated Art Glass, 1926-1980, by Jack D. Wilson (Antique Publications, 1989).

Consolidated Martelé Label

Cone

Cone Pattern Caster Set

Caster set, four Cone patt. shakers w/original metal lids, in green, light blue, darker blue & pink, fitted in a silver plate holder w/rings centered by a figural donkey below an upright loop handle, on a square footed base, 4 1/2" w., 7" h. (ILLUS.).......... **$550**
Cruet w/original stopper, yellow satin **300**
Sugar shaker w/original lid, green opaque..... **200**

Cone Syrup Pitcher

Syrup pitcher w/original top, cased pink (ILLUS.).. **425**

Cosmos

Cosmos Butter Dish

Butter dish, cov., blue band decoration (ILLUS.).. **225-250**
Pitcher, water, h.p. molded flowers on white ground **325**
Syrup pitcher w/original top, pink band decoration.. **300**
Tumbler, pink band decoration............................ **65**

Florette
Pitcher, 6 3/4" h., bulbous w/applied clear handle, cased pink satin.................................... **200**
Syrup pitcher w/original top, pink satin.......... **450**
Toothpick holder, blue opaque satin **140**

Guttate

Guttate Cased Pink Pitcher

Pitcher, 9 1/2" h., cased pink, glossy finish
(ILLUS.)... **325**
Salt & pepper shakers, green & blue, pr. **60**
Syrup pitcher w/original lid, pink cased,
glossy finish, applied clear handle, tall.......... **300**
Toothpick holder, white..................................... **100**

Later Lines

Ruba Rombic Bowl

Bowl, 8 x 9", 3 1/2" h., Ruba Rombic patt.,
oblong w/closed rim, jade green w/slight
opalescence, minor rim nick, ca. 1928
(ILLUS.).. **900**
Candlesticks, Ruba Rombic patt., smoky
topaz, pr. **650**
Creamer & open sugar bowl, Ruba Rom-
bic patt., topaz, 2 1/8" & 3 1/2" h., pr. (mi-
nor neck on both rims)................................. **1,300**
Dinner set: six each of goblets, sherbets,
8 1/2" d. plates & one 12" d. plate; Five
Fruits patt., each w/molded fruit design &
overall purple wash, ca. 1930, the set
(mold imperfections, slight wear to wash)..... **230**

Ruba Rombic Dresser Set

Dresser set: multifaceted oblong tray, a
large toilet bottle w/stopper & smaller
perfume bottle w/stopper; Ruba Rombic
patt., lavender finish cased over colorless, tray 10 1/2 x 11 1/2", toilet bottle
7 3/4" h., the set (ILLUS.)............................ **5,750**
Lamp, table model, Dogwood patt., Martelé
line, brass fittings, baluster-form, tan **125**
Vase, 6" h., Screech Owls patt., Martelé
line, brown decoration on a milk white
ground **100**
Vase, 6" h., Screech Owls patt., Martelé
line, brown owls on green reeds against
a custard satin ground **115**
Vase, 6" h., 4" d., Dragonfly patt., Martelé
line, ovoid w/wide mouth, blue on white
satin ground **115**
Vase, 6" h., 4" d., Dragonfly patt., Martelé
line, ovoid w/wide mouth, green & brown
on white satin ground.. **95**

Vase, 6 1/4" h., Peonies patt., Martelé line,
pink, green & brown on milk white ground........ **80**
Vase, 6 1/2" h., Chickadee patt., wide flattened ovoid form w/rectangular mouth,
stained red birds on ruby leafy branches
against a clear ground.................................... **110**
Vase, 6 1/2" h., Chickadee patt., wide flat-
tened ovoid form w/rectangular mouth,
brick red birds on green leafy branches
against a custard ground................................ **144**

Consolidated "Jonquil" Vase

Vase, 6 1/2" h., Jonquil patt., slender ovoid
body w/flaring mouth, deep rose peach
blossoms w/green stems on a creamy
custard satin ground (ILLUS.) **115**

Rare Ruba Rombic Pattern Vase

Vase, 6 1/2" h., Ruba Rombic patt., angular
tapering cylindrical form, silvery grey, mi-
nor nicks (ILLUS.).. **700**
Vase, 10" h., Love Bird patt., bulbous ovoid
body w/a small short rolled neck, pairs of
salmon-colored birds on a creamy white
ground... **240**
Vase, 10" h., Poppy patt., wide ovoid body
w/wide low flared rim, decorated w/red
poppies on custard ground **275**
Vase, 10 1/2" h., Dogwood patt., dark rosy
peach petals on greenish tan stems on a
creamy custard ground.................................... **420**
Vase, 11" h., pillow-type, Sea Gulls patt.,
blue ground **595**

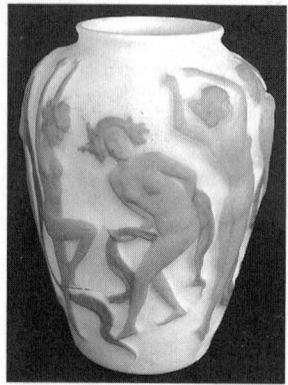

Consolidated "Dancing Girls" Vase

Vase, 11 1/2" h., Dancing Girls patt., tall ovoid body, girls & Pan relief-molded & colored in deep rose & tan on a creamy custard ground (ILLUS.) **525**

Crown Milano

This glass, produced by Mt. Washington Glass Company late in the 19th century, is opal glass decorated by painting and enameling. It appears identical to a ware termed Albertine, also made by Mt. Washington.

Printed Crown Milano Mark

Cracker jar, cov., barrel-shaped creamy satin ground decorated w/stylized scrolling florals trimmed w/fine dotting, silver plate cover w/figural turtle, rim & swing bail handle, silver marked "MW 524," paper label on base w/"Mt. W.G. Co. Crown Milano," 7 1/2" h. **$1,200**

Crown Milano Cracker Jar

Cracker jar, cov., cylindrical, decorated w/pastel pansies outlined w/gold & round panels of swirled spider webbing in gold on a creamy white ground, low domed silver plate cover molded in relief w/embossed florals & a figural butterfly finial, marked w/Crown Milano logo & "534," 4 1/4" d., 5" h. (ILLUS.) **950**

Cracker jar, cov., peach shaded to cream body decorated w/gold flowers & leaves overall, ornate silver plate rim, bail handle & cover, marked "Pairpoint" **950**

Cracker jar, cov., squatty bulbous body in creamy white satin decorated w/gold-outlined exotic blossoms & leaves, silver plate ruffled rim, cover & bail handle, silver marked "MW 4419/C," base w/purple crown mark **1,200**

Cracker jar, cov., squatty melon-ribbed body decorated w/dainty multicolored flowers & ornate gold scrolling, original ornate silver plate cover, rim & bail handle, 5 1/4" d., 5 3/4" h. to top of handle **1,200**

Cracker jar, cov., wide bulbous body decorated w/a creamy tan ground & heavily enameled w/large gilt mums on leafy stems & orange leaves w/acorns, embossed silver plate rim w/ruffled edge, inset domed cover & swing bail handle, signed on the pontil, 7 1/2" d. **896**

Creamer & cov. sugar bowl, each of squatty bulbous form tapering to a narrow neck, the sugar bowl w/small loop shoulder handles & a bulbous domed cover w/knob finial, the creamer w/a high curved spout & applied handle, each decorated w/sprays of blue cornflowers, purple asters, pink & yellow roses & red wild roses on a soft beige ground w/heavy gilt trim, sugar 4 3/4" h., creamer, 4 1/4" h., pr. (hairline in base of sugar) **1,250**

Creamer & cov. sugar bowl, each of squatty bulbous form, the creamer w/silver plate rim & high curved metal spout, the sugar bowl w/small loop silver plate handles, knop finial & marked "M.W. 2039" on lid, each decorated w/blue flowers on pale pinkish yellow background, pr. **800**

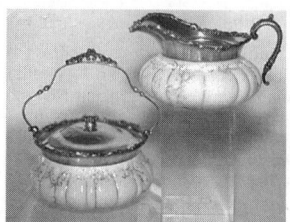

Crown Milano Creamer & Sugar Bowl

Creamer & cov. sugar bowl, squatty bulbous ribbed bodies decorated w/molded scrolls & florals trimmed w/gilt, silver plate scroll-edged rim & handle on creamer & scroll-edged rim, cover & bail handle on sugar, sugar lid incised "M.W. 2040," sugar 6" h., pr. (ILLUS.) **450**

Sweetmeat jar, cov., melon-ribbed, decorated w/h.p. pastel flowers & gold foliage, signed **950**

Sweetmeat jar, cov., squatty bulbous body decorated w/alternating white & pale pink rickrack swirled stripes decorated w/gold autumn flowers, silver plate ruffled rim, bail handle & inset cover w/figural turtle finial, marked "MW 4416," 4 1/2" h. **1,100**

Table set: creamer, open sugar bowl & cov. jam jar; slightly globular lobed form, shaded pink decorated w/gold chrysanthemums, ormolu mounts, signed, 3 pcs... **1,500**

Tumbler, cylindrical, decorated w/heavy gold garlands, flowers, ribbons & bows on a semi-glossy white ground, marked w/red crown & wreath, 2 7/8" d., 3 7/8" h. **550**

Vase, 3 3/4" h., 4 3/8" d., flat-sided body w/flared rim, creamy satin ground decorated w/light peach & light yellow stylized maple leaves in background, light peach, apricot & greenish charcoal five-petal flowers in the center ground & large rust & gold maple leaves & barren branches in the foreground... **650**

Two Decorated Crown Milano Vases

Vase, 4 3/4" h., squatty bulbous body tapering to a short rolled neck flanked by small loop handles, decorated w/gilded wild roses over a peach & amber leafy ground, folded gold rim handles, unsigned Mt. Washington (ILLUS. right) **750**

Bulbous Crown Milano Vase

Vase, 6" h., 5 3/4" d., footed bulbous body lightly molded w/narrow swirled ribs tapering to a short small neck w/four-crimp rim, decorated w/clusters of tiny white & blue flowers on the yellow shaded to creamy white ground, logo signature (ILLUS.) **1,100**

Vase, 7 1/2" h., footed squatty bulbous base tapering sharply to a very tall slightly flaring slender cylindrical neck, sepia wash decorated w/gold grape leaves & vines, unsigned............................... **728**

Vase, 8" h., squared bulbous spherical body w/a short cylindrical neck w/rolled rim flanked by ribbed S-scroll handles, deco-

rated w/gold enameled oak leaves & acorns over a shadowy amber patterned background, stamped mark in blue (ILLUS. left) **1,500**

Vase, 9" h., footed ovoid body tapering to a tiny cylindrical neck, decorated overall w/green leafy maidenhair fern design w/three delicate gold medallions & a scroll-decorated neck, unsigned **650**

Vase, 9 3/4" h., tall tapering cylindrical form w/rounded base & bifurcated rim w/curled-under points, enamel-decorated w/floral bouquets & an elaborate gilt neck border, blue enameled mark on pontil (light enamel wear).............................. **546**

Vase, cov., 10 1/2" h., wide ovoid body w/a small high, domed cover w/a ribbed & pointed finial, the body decorated w/large green & brown ivy leaves & vines w/lighter tan swirled designs on the cover & around the base all on a creamy white ground, unmarked **2,285**

Vase, 11 1/2" h., cream ground decorated w/gold spider mums w/shadow medallions, signed **950**

Vase, 11 3/4" h., footed bulbous base tapering to a long 'stick' neck, decorated w/nine gulls flying over salmon-colored background highlighted w/moon & stars in gold... **3,200**

Daum Nancy

This fine glass, much of it cameo, was made by Auguste and Antonin Daum, who founded a factory in 1875 in Nancy, France. Most of their cameo and enameled glass was made from the 1890s into the early 20th century.

Daum Cameo Landscape Vase

Cameo vase, 8" h., cylindrical body w/shaped lip, grey internally streaked w/lemon yellow, overlaid in orange & cut w/a snowy forest scene, enameled in shades of black & white, signed in gilt, ca. 1900 (ILLUS.).............................. **$4,025**

Cameo vase, 8" h., ringed cushion foot & short waisted pedestal supporting a bulbous ovoid body tapering to a short flaring neck, grey shaded to pale blue & internally streaked w/yellow, overlaid in purple & cut w/crocus blossoms & leafage, signed in cameo "Daum - Nancy" w/a cross of Lorraine, ca. 1900 .... **2,415**

Cameo vase, 8 3/4" h., cushion foot below the bulbous ovoid lower body tapering to a tall swelled cylindrical neck, pale grey ground streaked w/yellow & salmon, overlaid in mottled yellow, butternut, burgundy & green, etched & wheel-carved w/nicotiana & blossom, engraved signature **2,760**

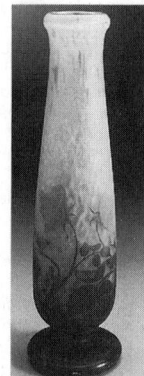

Daum Cameo Vase with Roses

Cameo vase, 13 1/2" h., thick cushion foot below the tall slender swelled cylindrical body tapering to a cupped rim, mottled white, pink & clear overlaid in shades of green & rose & etched w/branching roses, signed, staining (ILLUS.) **11,500**

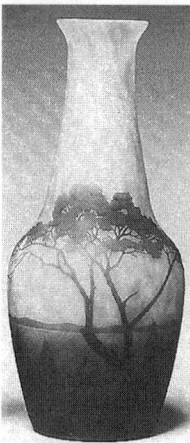

Tall Daum Nancy Cameo Vase

Cameo vase, 16 1/2" h., wide ovoid body tapering to a tall tapering cylindrical neck w/flared rim, grey mottled w/yellow, orange & ochre & overlaid w/brown & cut w/a landscape of sailboats on a lake w/trees in the foreground, signed in cameo, ca. 1910 (ILLUS.) **2,875**

Cameo vase, 17 1/2" h., footed, very tall slender baluster form in mottled white overlaid w/mottled brown & orange & cut w/leaves, signed **1,840**

Large Cameo Vase with Leaves

Cameo vase, 19 3/4" h., cushion foot below the tall slightly flaring cylindrical body w/a bulbed rim, mottled white & blue overlaid w/streaked reddish orange & cut w/leaf & nut clusters, signed, ca. 1900 (ILLUS.)...... **4,600**

Cameo vase, 23 1/2" h., footed bulbous base tapering to a very tall cylindrical neck w/molded rim, mottled blue & white neck shading to mottled purple at the base & overlaid in mottled green, yellow & purple & cut w/flying dragonflies around the sides & base w/ranunculus leaves & blossoms around the base, signed in cameo, ca. 1904 .... **26,450**

Vase, 4" h., miniature, footed squatty bulbous base w/a wide shoulder centering a tall cylindrical neck, etched & enameled w/delicate violets & leaves, signed **1,150**

Vase, 4 3/8" h., square waisted form, frosted ground etched & enameled in lavender, green, yellow & orange w/flowering violets, cameo signature **3,450**

Vase, 4 3/4" h., cushion foot below the bulbous ovoid body tapering to a tall slightly flaring cylindrical neck, grey mottled w/purple & yellow & cut w/delicate stems of small flowers on an acid-textured ground, the foot cut w/"Les Jardies - Emilia - Paris," design enameled w/blue, green, red & gilt, signed in gilt "Daum - Nancy" w/cross of Lorraine, ca. 1900 .... **2,300**

Vase, 4 7/8" h., wide flattened ovoid form w/a flat rim, mottled blue & pumpkin orange ground etched & enameled to depict a snowy Dutch winter landscape scene w/windmills, in white, brown & grisaille, signed **3,450**

Vase, 8" h., "verre parlant," wide squatty bulbous ovoid body w/the wide rounded shoulder centered by a short tapered cylindrical neck w/molded rim, frosted aqua ground enameled in gold around the neck w/dragonflies, the body enameled in light rose & pale green w/water lilies & lily pads w/a gilt enameled inscription in French "Et des roses sortaient des eaux - Et des esprits sortaient des roses. - V. Hugo," signed in gilt, ca. 1895 .... **6,900**

Tall Daum Vase with Fuchsias

Vase, 13 1/8" h., a cushion foot below a bulbed stem continuing to a tall slender trumpet-form body, frosted milky white shading to violet etched w/delicate fuchsia blossoms & foliage, enameled in magenta, lavender & green w/gilt accent, cameo signature (ILLUS.) **6,325**

Fine Acid-etched Daum Vase

Vase, 13 1/4" h., bulbous ovoid body w/a short slightly flaring cylindrical neck, textured clear ground etched w/a stylized jungle scene w/a large gazelle, all enameled in black, signed, ca. 1925 (ILLUS.).. **11,500**
Vase, 13 5/8" h., simple cylindrical form, shaded mottled yellow to dark brown ground, etched w/slender leafy stems up the sides & enameled w/reddish orange blossoms, etched gilt-trimmed scrolls around the base, signed in gilt.................... **5,175**

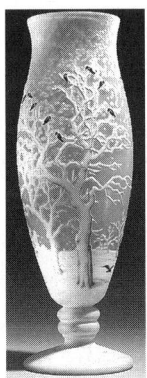

Large Rare Enameled Daum Vase

Vase, 15 7/8" h., disk foot w/double-knop stem in frosted white, the tall baluster-form body in mottled frosted pale blue etched & enameled w/a winter landscape of large snow-covered trees & blackbirds, signed in intaglio, ca. 1910 (ILLUS.) **19,550**
Vase, 21 7/8" h., wide cushion foot supporting a tall cylindrical body w/a slightly flared rim, mottled white to purple ground, the foot & lower body etched & highlighted in gilt w/angular bands & scrolls w/panels of insects & leafage, the body enameled in dark green w/large violet leaves & tall slender stems w/purple violet blossoms, signed in intaglio **23,000**
Vase, 25 1/2" h., spreading square form in mottled blue, purple & green **1,955**

Depression

The phrase "Depression Glass" is used by collectors to denote a specific kind of transparent glass produced primarily as tablewares, in crystal, amber, blue, green, pink, milky-white, etc., during the late 1920s and 1930s when this country was in the midst of a financial depression. Made to sell inexpensively, it was turned out by such producers as Jeannette, Hocking, Westmoreland, Indiana and other glass companies. We compile prices on all the major Depression Glass patterns. Collectors should consult Depression Glass references for information on those patterns and pieces which have been reproduced.

Adam, Jeanette Glass Co., 1932-34 (Process-etched)

Ashtray, green, 4 1/2" sq. $25
Ashtray, pink, 4 1/2" sq. 28
Bowl, dessert, 4 3/4" sq., pink 22
Bowl, cereal, 5 3/4" sq., green.............................. 50
Bowl, cereal, 5 3/4" sq., pink 50
Bowl, nappy, 7 3/4" sq., green.............................. 28
Bowl, nappy, 7 3/4" sq., pink 28
Bowl, cov., 9" sq., green.. 85
Bowl, cov., 9" sq., pink... 75
Bowl, 9" sq., green 42
Bowl, 9" sq., pink 40
Bowl, 10" oval, vegetable, green 40
Butter dish, cov., green....................................... 375
Butter dish, cov., pink.. 95
Butter dish, cov., w/Sierra patt., pink............. **1,600**
Cake plate, footed, green, 10" sq. 38

Cake plate, footed, pink, 10" sq. 35
Candlestick, green, 4" h. 60
Candlestick, pink, 4" h. 50
Candlesticks, Delphite, 4" h., pr. 250
Candy jar, cov., green 125

Adam Candy Jar

Candy jar, cov., pink (ILLUS.) 98
Coaster, green, 3 1/4" sq. 24
Coaster, pink, 3 1/4" sq. 20
Creamer, green 24
Creamer, pink 22
Cup & saucer, green 36
Cup & saucer, pink 34
Cup & saucer, yellow 165
Lamp, green 275
Lamp, pink 250
Pitcher, 8" h., 32 oz., cone-shaped, green 60
Pitcher, 8" h., 32 oz., cone-shaped, pink 48
Pitcher, 32 oz., round base, pink 65
Plate, sherbet, 6" sq., green 12
Plate, sherbet, 6" sq., pink 10
Plate, salad, 7 3/4" sq., green 22
Plate, salad, 7 3/4" sq., pink 20
Plate, dinner, 9" sq., green 35
Plate, dinner, 9" sq., pink 30
Plate, grill, 9" sq., green 28
Plate, grill, 9" sq., pink 25
Plate, salad, round, pink 50
Plate, salad, round, yellow 85
Platter, 11 3/4" l., green 38
Platter, 11 3/4" l., pink 35
Relish dish, two-part, green, 8" sq. 24
Relish dish, two-part, pink, 8" sq. 20
Salt & pepper shakers, footed, green,
    4" h., pr. 120
Salt & pepper shakers, footed, pink, 4" h.,
    pr. 95
Sherbet, green, 3" h. 38
Sherbet, pink, 3" h. 32
Sugar bowl, cov., green 75
Sugar bowl, cov., pink 50
Tumbler, cone-shaped, green, 4 1/2" h.,
    7 oz. 38
Tumbler, cone-shaped, pink, 4 1/2" h.,
    7 oz. 38
Tumbler, iced tea, green, 5 1/2" h., 9 oz. 75
Tumbler, iced tea, pink 5 1/2" h., 9 oz. 80
Vase, 7 1/2" h., green 98
Vase, 7 1/2" h., pink 375

Aunt Polly, U.S. Glass Co., late 1920s (Press-mold)

Bowl, berry, 4 3/4" d., blue 18
Bowl, berry, 4 3/4" d., green 10
Bowl, berry, 4 3/4" d., iridescent 8
Bowl, 4 3/4" d., 2" h., green 20
Bowl, 4 3/4" d., 2" h., iridescent 18
Bowl, 5 1/2" d., single handle, blue 28

Bowl, 5 1/2" d., single handle, green 15
Bowl, 5 1/2" d., single handle, iridescent 12
Bowl, oval, handled pickle, 7 1/4" l., blue 45
Bowl, oval, handled pickle, 7 1/4" l., green 22
Bowl, oval, handled pickle, 7 1/4" l., irides-
    cent 18
Bowl, large berry, 7 7/8" d., blue 50
Bowl, large berry, 7 7/8" d., green 25
Bowl, large berry, 7 7/8" d., iridescent 20
Bowl, oval, 8 3/8" l., blue 135
Bowl, oval, 8 3/8" l., green 60
Bowl, oval, 8 3/8" l., iridescent 50
Butter dish, cov., blue 250
Butter dish, cov., green 250
Butter dish, cov., iridescent 200
Candy dish, footed, two-handled, blue 45
Candy dish, footed, two-handled, green 25
Candy jar, cov., two-handled, green 85
Candy jar, cov., two-handled, iridescent 50
Creamer, blue 50
Creamer, green 25
Creamer, iridescent 20
Pitcher, 8" h., 48 oz., blue 225
Plate, sherbet, 6" d., blue 15
Plate, sherbet, 6" d., green 10
Plate, sherbet, 6" d., iridescent 8
Plate, luncheon, 8" d., blue 24
Salt & pepper shakers, blue, pr. 245
Sherbet, blue 15
Sherbet, green 8
Sherbet, iridescent 6
Sugar bowl, cov., blue 225
Sugar bowl, cov., green 85
Sugar bowl, cov., iridescent 50
Tumbler, water, blue, 3 5/8" h., 8 oz. 35
Vase, 6 1/2" h., blue 58
Vase, 6 1/2" h., green 40
Vase, 6 1/2" h., iridescent 24

Cherry Blossom, Jeannette Glass Co., 1930-38 (Process-etched)

Bowl, berry, 4 3/4" d., Delphite 18
Bowl, berry, 4 3/4" d., green 22
Bowl, berry, 4 3/4" d., pink 24
Bowl, cereal, 5 3/4" d., green 48
Bowl, cereal, 5 3/4" d., pink 60
Bowl, soup, 7 3/4" d., green 90
Bowl, soup, 7 3/4" d., pink 95
Bowl, berry, 8 1/2" d., Delphite 50
Bowl, berry, 8 1/2" d., green 50
Bowl, berry, 8 1/2" d., pink 50
Bowl, berry, 8 1/2" d., yellow 300
Bowl, 9" oval vegetable, Delphite 55
Bowl, 9" oval vegetable, green 50
Bowl, 9" oval vegetable, pink 60
Bowl, two-handled, 9" d., Delphite 40
Bowl, two-handled, 9" d., green 70
Bowl, two-handled, 9" d., Jadite 350
Bowl, two-handled, 9" d., pink 52
Bowl, fruit, three-footed, 10 1/2" d., green 95
Bowl, fruit, three-footed, 10 1/2" d., Jadite 350
Bowl, fruit, three-footed, 10 1/2" d., pink 110
Butter dish, cov., green 115
Butter dish, cov., pink 95
Cake plate, three-footed, green, 10 1/4" d. 42
Cake plate, three-footed, pink, 10 1/4" d. 38
Coaster, green 18
Coaster, pink 20
Creamer, Delphite 24
Creamer, green 24
Creamer, pink 24
Cup, pink 24
Cup & saucer, Delphite 26
Cup & saucer, green 30

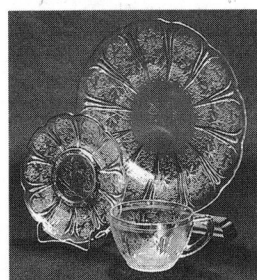

Cherry Blossom Cup & Saucer & Plate

Cup & saucer, pink (ILLUS.) 30
Junior Set, creamer, Delphite 50
Junior Set, creamer, pink 55
Junior Set, cup & saucer, Delphite 50
Junior Set, cup & saucer, pink 56
Junior Set, sugar bowl, Delphite 50
Junior Set, sugar bowl, pink 52
Mug, green, 7 oz. 250
Mug, pink, 7 oz. 325
Pitcher, 6 3/4" h., 36 oz., overall patt., Del-
phite 95
Pitcher, 6 3/4" h., 36 oz., overall patt.,
green 65
Pitcher, 6 3/4" h., 36 oz., overall patt., Ja-
dite 300
Pitcher, 6 3/4" h., 36 oz., overall patt., pink 68
Pitcher, 8" h., 36 oz., footed, cone-shaped,
patt. top, green 60
Pitcher, 8" h., 36 oz., footed, cone-shaped,
patt. top, pink 70
Pitcher, 8" h., 42 oz., patt. top, green 65
Pitcher, 8" h., 42 oz., patt. top, pink 75
Plate, sherbet, 6" d., Delphite 12
Plate, sherbet, 6" d., green 10
Plate, sherbet, 6" d., pink 10
Plate, salad, 7" d., green 26
Plate, salad, 7" d., pink 28
Plate, dinner, 9" d., Delphite 24
Plate, dinner, 9" d., green 28
Plate, dinner, 9" d., pink (ILLUS. with cup &
saucer) 30
Plate, grill, 9" d., green 35
Plate, grill, 9" d., pink 38
Plate, grill, 10" d., green 125
Platter, 9" oval, pink 975
Platter, 11" oval, Delphite 48
Platter, 11" oval, green 58
Platter, 11" oval, pink 65
Platter, 13" oval, green 95
Platter, 13" oval, pink 95
Platter, 13" oval, divided, green 75
Platter, 13" oval, divided, pink 75
Salt & pepper shakers, green, pr. 1,200
Salt & pepper shakers, pink, pr. 1,450
Sandwich tray, handled, Delphite,
10 1/2" d. 35
Sandwich tray, handled, green, 10 1/2" d. 38
Sandwich tray, handled, pink, 10 1/2" d. 45
Sherbet, Delphite 20
Sherbet, green 26
Sherbet, pink 24
Sugar bowl, cov., Delphite 28
Sugar bowl, cov., green 45
Sugar bowl, cov., pink 55
Sugar bowl, open, Delphite 24

Sugar bowl, open, green 22
Sugar bowl, open, pink 20
Tumbler, patt. top, green, 3 1/2" h., 4 oz. 28
Tumbler, patt. top, pink, 3 1/2" h., 4 oz. 24
Tumbler, juice, footed, overall patt., Del-
phite, 3 3/4" h., 4 oz. 28
Tumbler, juice, footed, overall patt., green,
3 3/4" h., 4 oz. 24
Tumbler, juice, footed, overall patt., pink,
3 3/4" h., 4 oz. 20
Tumbler, footed, overall patt., Delphite,
4 1/2" h., 8 oz. 36
Tumbler, footed, overall patt., green,
4 1/2" h., 8 oz. 42
Tumbler, footed, overall patt., pink,
4 1/2" h., 8 oz. 40
Tumbler, patt. top, green, 4 1/4" h., 9 oz. 26
Tumbler, patt. top, pink, 4 1/4" h., 9 oz. 25
Tumbler, footed, overall patt., Delphite,
4 1/2" h., 9 oz. 35
Tumbler, footed, overall patt., green,
4 1/2" h., 9 oz. 42
Tumbler, footed, overall patt., pink,
4 1/2" h., 9 oz. 42
Tumbler, patt. top, green, 5" h., 12 oz. 95
Tumbler, patt. top, pink, 5" h., 12 oz. 110

Columbia, Federal Glass Company, 1938-42 (Press-mold)

Bowl, cereal, 5" d., clear 20
Bowl, soup, 8" d., clear 24
Bowl, salad, 8 1/2" d., clear 20
Bowl, ruffled rim, 10 1/2" d., clear 20
Butter dish, cov., clear 20
Cup & saucer, clear 10
Cup & saucer, pink 35
Plate, bread & butter, 6" d., clear 4
Plate, bread & butter, 6" d., pink 12
Plate, luncheon, 9 1/2" d., clear 10
Plate, luncheon, 9 1/2" d., pink 30
Plate, chop, 11" d., clear 12
Snack plate, handled, clear 20
Snack plate, handled, w/cup, clear 28
Tumbler, juice, 2 7/8" h., 4 oz., clear 20
Tumbler, water, clear, 9 oz. 30

Daisy or Number 620, Indiana Glass Company, 1933-40 (Press-mold)

Bowl, berry, 4 1/2" d., amber 8
Bowl, berry, 4 1/2" d., red 8
Bowl, cream soup, 4 1/2" d., amber 10
Bowl, cream soup, 4 1/2" d., clear 5
Bowl, cream soup, 4 1/2" d., red 10

Daisy Bowl

Bowl, cereal, 6" d., amber (ILLUS.) 25

Bowl, cereal, 6" d., clear 8
Bowl, cereal, 6" d., red 25
Bowl, berry, 7 3/8" d., amber 12
Bowl, berry, 7 3/8" d., clear 6
Bowl, berry, 7 3/8" d., red 12
Bowl, berry, 9 3/8" d., amber 25
Bowl, berry, 9 3/8" d., clear 10
Bowl, berry, 9 3/8" d., red 25
Bowl, 10" oval vegetable, amber 14
Bowl, 10" oval vegetable, clear 6
Bowl, 10" oval vegetable, red 14
Creamer, footed, amber 8
Creamer, footed, clear 4
Creamer, footed, red 8
Cup & saucer, clear 3
Cup & saucer, red 7
Plate, sherbet, 6" d., amber 3
Plate, sherbet, 6" d., clear 1
Plate, sherbet, 6" d., red 3
Plate, salad, 7 3/8" d., amber 5
Plate, salad, 7 3/8" d., clear 2
Plate, salad, 7 3/8" d., red 5
Plate, luncheon, 8 3/8" d., amber 6
Plate, luncheon, 8 3/8" d., clear 3
Plate, luncheon, 8 3/8" d., red 6
Plate, dinner, 9 3/8" d., amber 8
Plate, dinner, 9 3/8" d., clear 4
Plate, dinner, 9 3/8" d., red 8
Plate, grill, 10 3/8" d., amber 6
Plate, grill, 10 3/8" d., clear 3
Plate, grill, 10 3/8" d., red 6
Plate, cake or sandwich, 11 1/2" d., amber 16
Plate, cake or sandwich, 11 1/2" d., clear 8
Plate, cake or sandwich, 11 1/2" d., red 16
Platter, 10 3/4" l., amber 12
Platter, 10 3/4" l., clear 6
Platter, 10 3/4" l., red 12
Relish dish, three-part, amber, 8 3/8" 20
Relish dish, three-part, clear, 8 3/8" 10
Relish dish, three-part, red, 8 3/8" 20
Sherbet, footed, amber 6
Sherbet, footed, clear 3
Sherbet, footed, red 6
Sugar bowl, open, footed, amber 8
Sugar bowl, open, footed, clear 4
Sugar bowl, open, footed, red 8
Tumbler, footed, amber, 9 oz. 14
Tumbler, footed, clear, 9 oz. 6
Tumbler, footed, red, 9 oz. 14
Tumbler, footed, amber, 12 oz. 30
Tumbler, footed, clear, 12 oz. 10
Tumbler, footed, red, 12 oz. 30

Diana, Federal Glass Co., 1937-41 (Press-mold)

Ashtray, clear, 3 1/2" d. 2
Ashtray, pink, 3 1/2" d. 4
Bowl, cereal, 5" d., amber 12
Bowl, cereal, 5" d., clear 4
Bowl, cream soup, 5 1/2" d., amber 18
Bowl, cream soup, 5 1/2" d., clear 5
Bowl, cream soup, 5 1/2" d., pink 20
Bowl, salad, 9" d., amber 18
Bowl, salad, 9" d., clear 10
Bowl, salad, 9" d., pink 24
Bowl, scalloped rim, 12" d., amber 20
Bowl, scalloped rim, 12" d., clear 10
Bowl, scalloped rim, 12" d., pink 30
Candy jar, cov., round, amber 45
Candy jar, cov., round, clear 20

Candy jar, cov., round, pink 50
Coaster, clear, 3 1/2" d. 2
Coaster, pink, 3 1/2" d. 8
Console bowl, amber, 11" d. 24
Console bowl, clear, 11" d. 12
Console bowl, pink, 11" d. 30
Creamer, oval, amber 10
Creamer, oval, clear 5
Creamer, oval, pink 12
Cup & saucer, demitasse, clear 12
Cup & saucer, demitasse, pink 45
Cup & saucer, amber 15
Cup & saucer, clear 5
Cup & saucer, pink 28
Junior set, child's plate, 5 1/2" d., clear 2
Junior set, Child's plate, 5 1/2" d., pink 4
Plate, bread & butter, 6" d., amber 3
Plate, bread & butter, 6" d., clear 1
Plate, bread & butter, 6" d., pink 4
Plate, dinner, 9 1/2" d., amber 10
Plate, dinner, 9 1/2" d., clear 5
Plate, dinner, 9 1/2" d., pink 18
Plate, sandwich, 11 3/4" d., amber 16
Plate, sandwich, 11 3/4" d., clear 6
Plate, sandwich, 11 3/4" d., pink 24
Platter, 12" oval, amber 16
Platter, 12" oval, clear 8
Platter, 12" oval, pink 30
Salt & pepper shakers, amber, pr. 95
Salt & pepper shakers, clear, pr. 24
Salt & pepper shakers, pink, pr. 85
Sherbet, amber 10
Sherbet, clear 3
Sherbet, pink 12
Sugar bowl, open, oval, amber 8
Sugar bowl, open, oval, clear 4
Sugar bowl, open, oval, pink 12
Tumbler, amber, 4 1/8" h., 9 oz. 28
Tumbler, clear, 4 1/8" h., 9 oz. 8
Tumbler, pink, 4 1/8" h., 9 oz. 45

Diana, Federal Glass Co., 1937-41 (Press-mold) - Junior set

Junior set: 6 cups, saucers & plates
    w/round rack; clear, set 120
Junior set: 6 cups, saucers & plates
    w/round rack; pink, set 320

Dogwood or Apple Blossom or Wild Rose, MacBeth-Evans, 1929-32 (Process-etched)

Bowl, cereal, 5 1/2" d., Cremax 6
Bowl, cereal, 5 1/2" d., green 38
Bowl, cereal, 5 1/2" d., Monax 6
Bowl, cereal, 5 1/2" d., pink 30
Bowl, cereal, 5 1/2" d., yellow 60
Bowl, berry, 8 1/2" d., Cremax 35
Bowl, berry, 8 1/2" d., green 120
Bowl, berry, 8 1/2" d., Monax 35
Bowl, berry, 8 1/2" d., pink 65
Bowl, fruit, 10 1/4" d., Cremax 120
Bowl, fruit, 10 1/4" d., green 275
Bowl, fruit, 10 1/4" d., Monax 120
Bowl, fruit, 10 1/4" d., pink 550
Cake plate, heavy solid foot, pink, 11" d. 1,350
Cake plate, heavy solid foot, Cremax, 13" d. ... 185
Cake plate, heavy solid foot, green, 13" d. 145
Cake plate, heavy solid foot, Monax, 13" d. 185
Cake plate, heavy solid foot, pink, 13" d. 150
Coaster, pink, 3 1/4" d. 500

Creamer, thin, green, 2 1/2" h.............................. 45
Creamer, thin, pink, 2 1/2" h................................ 24
Creamer, thick, footed, pink, 3 1/4" h. 24
Cup & saucer, Cremax...................................... 50

Dogwood Cup & Saucer

Cup & saucer, green (ILLUS.)............................. 30
Cup & saucer, Monax... 50
Cup & saucer, pink.. 30
Pitcher, 8" h., 80 oz., American Sweetheart
     style, pink 625
Pitcher, 8" h., 80 oz., decorated, green............ 575
Pitcher, 8" h., 80 oz., decorated, pink 275
Plate, bread & butter, 6" d., Cremax 20
Plate, bread & butter, 6" d., green 10
Plate, bread & butter, 6" d., Monax 20
Plate, bread & butter, 6" d., pink........................ 10
Plate, luncheon, 8" d., clear................................. 5
Plate, luncheon, 8" d., green 10
Plate, luncheon, 8" d., pink 12
Plate, luncheon, 8" d., yellow 60
Plate, dinner, 9 1/4" d., pink............................... 38
Plate, grill, border design, 10 1/2" d., pink........... 28
Plate, grill, overall patt., 10 1/2" d., pink 30
Plate, grill, overall patt. or border design
     only, 10 1/2" d., green............................... 28
Plate, salver, 12" d., Cremax.............................. 18
Plate, salver, 12" d., Monax............................... 18
Plate, salver, 12" d., pink 40
Platter, 12" oval, pink 750
Sherbet, low foot, green.................................... 125
Sherbet, low foot, pink.. 38
Sugar bowl, open, thin, green, 2 1/2" h. 42
Sugar bowl, open, thin, pink, 2 1/2" h. 24
Sugar bowl, open, thick, footed, pink,
     3 1/4" h. 20
Tumbler, decorated, pink, 3 1/2" h., 5 oz......... 350
Tumbler, decorated, green, 4" h., 10 oz. 110
Tumbler, decorated, pink, 4" h., 10 oz. 55
Tumbler, decorated, green, 4 3/4" h., 11 oz. 125
Tumbler, decorated, pink, 4 3/4" h., 11 oz.......... 60
Tumbler, decorated, green, 5" h., 12 oz. 120
Tumbler, decorated, pink, 5" h., 12 oz. 85
Tumbler, molded band, pink 24

Hobnail, Hocking Glass Co., 1934-36 (Press-mold)

Bowl, cereal, 5 1/2" d., clear 5
Bowl, salad, 7" d., clear 6
Creamer, footed, clear.. 3
Cup & saucer, clear 5
Cup & saucer, pink... 8
Decanter w/stopper, clear, 32 oz....................... 26
Decanter w/stopper, clear w/red trim,
     32 oz.. 32
Goblet, water, clear, 10 oz. 6
Goblet, iced tea, clear, 13 oz. 10
Pitcher, milk, 18 oz., clear 18
Pitcher, 67 oz., clear 25

Plate, sherbet, 6" d., clear 2
Plate, sherbet, 6" d., pink...................................... 3
Plate, luncheon, 8 1/2" d., clear............................ 4
Plate, luncheon, 8 1/2" d., clear w/red trim 6
Plate, luncheon, 8 1/2" d., pink 8
Sherbet, clear 3
Sherbet, pink 6
Sugar bowl, open, footed, clear............................ 3
Tumbler, whiskey, clear, 1 1/2 oz. 5
Tumbler, wine, footed, clear, 3 oz. 6
Tumbler, cordial, footed, clear, 5 oz..................... 5
Tumbler, juice, clear, 5 oz.................................... 4
Tumbler, water, clear, 9 oz. 6
Tumbler, water, clear, 10 oz. 6
Tumbler, iced tea, clear, 15 oz............................ 12

Madrid, Federal Glass Co., 1932-39 (Process-etched)

Ashtray, amber, 6" sq. 225
Ashtray, green, 6" sq. 200
Bowl, cream soup, 4 3/4" d., amber 20
Bowl, sauce, 5" d., amber 8
Bowl, sauce, 5" d., blue 35
Bowl, sauce, 5" d., clear 5
Bowl, sauce, 5" d., green 8
Bowl, sauce, 5" d., pink 10
Bowl, soup, 7" d., amber 20
Bowl, soup, 7" d., blue 65
Bowl, soup, 7" d., clear 8
Bowl, soup, 7" d., green 20
Bowl, salad, 8" d., amber 18
Bowl, salad, 8" d., blue 45
Bowl, salad, 8" d., clear 8
Bowl, salad, 8" d., green 16
Bowl, large berry, 9 3/8" d., amber 24
Bowl, large berry, 9 3/8" d., clear 10
Bowl, large berry, 9 3/8" d., pink 20
Bowl, salad, deep, 9 1/2" d., amber 35
Bowl, 10" oval vegetable, amber......................... 24
Bowl, 10" oval vegetable, blue 42
Bowl, 10" oval vegetable, clear 10
Bowl, 10" oval vegetable, green.......................... 24
Bowl, 10" oval vegetable, pink............................ 20
Butter dish, cov., amber 75
Butter dish, cov., clear 35
Butter dish, cov., green 85
Cake plate, amber, 11 1/4" d. 30
Cake plate, clear, 11 1/4" d. 15
Cake plate, pink, 11 1/4" d. 24
Candlesticks, amber, 2 1/4" h., pr...................... 24
Candlesticks, clear, 2 1/4" h., pr. 10
Candlesticks, iridescent, 2 1/4" h., pr................. 28
Candlesticks, pink, 2 1/4" h., pr.......................... 24
Console bowl, flared, amber, 11" d. 24
Console bowl, flared, clear, 11" d. 10
Console bowl, flared, iridescent, 11" d............... 28
Console bowl, flared, pink, 11" d. 20
Cookie jar, cov., amber 52
Cookie jar, cov., clear 20
Cookie jar, cov., pink 30
Creamer, amber 8
Creamer, blue 30
Creamer, clear.. 5
Creamer, green 16
Cup & saucer, amber 9
Cup & saucer, blue 25
Cup & saucer, clear 4
Cup & saucer, green 13
Cup & saucer, pink 13
Gelatin mold, amber, 2 1/8" h............................. 16
Gravy boat & platter, amber...................... 2,800
Hot dish coaster, amber, 5" d............................. 65
Hot dish coaster, clear, 5" d. 25

Hot dish coaster, green, 5" d. 60
Hot dish coaster w/indentation, amber 85
Hot dish coaster w/indentation, clear.............. 35
Hot dish coaster w/indentation, green 75
Jam dish, amber, 7" d. 28
Jam dish, blue, 7" d. 38
Jam dish, clear, 7" d. 12
Jam dish, green, 7" d. 24
Lazy Susan, walnut base w/seven clear hot
   dish coasters 975

Madrid Juice Pitcher

Pitcher, juice, 5 1/2" h., 36 oz., amber
   (ILLUS.) 48
Pitcher, 8" h., 60 oz., square, amber................. 55
Pitcher, 8" h., 60 oz., square, blue................... 195
Pitcher, 8" h., 60 oz., square, clear.................... 28
Pitcher, 8" h., 60 oz., square, green 148
Pitcher, 8" h., 60 oz., square, pink..................... 45
Pitcher, 8 1/2" h., 80 oz., jug-type, amber 75
Pitcher, 8 1/2" h., 80 oz., jug-type, green 225
Pitcher w/ice lip, 8 1/2" h., 80 oz., amber 85
Pitcher w/ice lip, 8 1/2" h., 80 oz., green 250
Plate, sherbet, 6" d., amber.................................. 6
Plate, sherbet, 6" d., blue................................... 12
Plate, sherbet, 6" d., clear.................................... 3
Plate, sherbet, 6" d., green................................... 5
Plate, sherbet, 6" d., pink..................................... 5
Plate, salad, 7 1/2" d., amber............................. 12
Plate, salad, 7 1/2" d., blue................................. 24
Plate, salad, 7 1/2" d., clear................................. 5
Plate, salad, 7 1/2" d., green.............................. 10
Plate, salad, 7 1/2" d., pink................................ 10
Plate, luncheon, 8 7/8" d., amber 8
Plate, luncheon, 8 7/8" d., blue 20
Plate, luncheon, 8 7/8" d., clear 4
Plate, luncheon, 8 7/8" d., green......................... 10
Plate, luncheon, 8 7/8" d., pink 8
Plate, dinner, 10 1/2" d., amber 60
Plate, dinner, 10 1/2" d., blue 85
Plate, dinner, 10 1/2" d., clear 25
Plate, dinner, 10 1/2" d., green 50
Plate, grill, 10 1/2" d., amber 10
Plate, grill, 10 1/2" d., clear 5
Plate, grill, 10 1/2" d., green 16
Platter, 11 1/2" oval, amber................................. 24
Platter, 11 1/2" oval, blue.................................... 30
Platter, 11 1/2" oval, clear................................... 10
Platter, 11 1/2" oval, green.................................. 20
Platter, 11 1/2" oval, pink.................................... 16
Relish plate, amber, 10 1/2" d. 20
Relish plate, clear, 10 1/2" d. 10
Relish plate, green, 10 1/2" d. 18
Relish plate, pink, 10 1/2" d................................. 14
Salt & pepper shakers, flat, amber,
   3 1/2" h., pr. 48
Salt & pepper shakers, flat, clear,
   3 1/2" h., pr. 24
Salt & pepper shakers, flat, green,
   3 1/2" h., pr. 65

Salt & pepper shakers, footed, amber,
   3 1/2" h., pr. 135
Salt & pepper shakers, footed, blue,
   3 1/2" h., pr. 170
Salt & pepper shakers, footed, clear,
   3 1/2" h., pr. 45
Salt & pepper shakers, footed, green,
   3 1/2" h., pr. 145
Sherbet, amber 6
Sherbet, blue 18
Sherbet, clear.. 3
Sherbet, green 12
Sugar bowl, cov., amber 58
Sugar bowl, cov., blue....................................... 230
Sugar bowl, cov., clear 25
Sugar bowl, cov., green 81
Sugar bowl, open, amber 8
Sugar bowl, open, blue 30
Sugar bowl, open, clear 5
Sugar bowl, open, green...................................... 16
Tumbler, juice, amber, 3 7/8" h., 5 oz. 15
Tumbler, juice, blue, 3 7/8" h., 5 oz..................... 40
Tumbler, juice, clear, 3 7/8" h., 5 oz..................... 8
Tumbler, juice, green, 3 7/8" h., 5 oz. 30
Tumbler, footed, amber, 4" h., 5 oz. 28
Tumbler, footed, clear, 4" h., 5 oz. 14
Tumbler, footed, green, 4" h., 5 oz. 40
Tumbler, amber, 4 1/2" h., 9 oz. 16
Tumbler, blue, 4 1/2" h., 9 oz. 35
Tumbler, clear, 4 1/2" h., 9 oz. 8
Tumbler, green, 4 1/2" h., 9 oz. 22
Tumbler, pink, 4 1/2" h., 9 oz. 16
Tumbler, footed, amber, 5 1/4" h., 10 oz. 34
Tumbler, footed, clear, 5 1/4" h., 10 oz. 15
Tumbler, footed, green, 5 1/4" h., 10 oz. 48
Tumbler, amber, 5 1/2" h., 12 oz. 24
Tumbler, blue, 5 1/2" h., 12 oz. 45
Tumbler, clear, 5 1/2" h., 12 oz. 10
Tumbler, green, 5 1/2" h., 12 oz. 28

Normandie or Bouquet & Lattice, Federal Glass Co., 1933-40 (Process-etched)

Bowl, berry, 5" d., amber 8
Bowl, berry, 5" d., pink.. 12
Bowl, berry, 5" d., Sunburst iridescent.................. 4
Bowl, cereal, 6 1/2" d., amber 24
Bowl, cereal, 6 1/2" d., pink 36
Bowl, cereal, 6 1/2" d., Sunburst iridescent........ 12
Bowl, large berry, 8 1/2" d., amber 28
Bowl, large berry, 8 1/2" d., pink 40
Bowl, large berry, 8 1/2" d., Sunburst irides-
   cent 14
Bowl, 10" oval vegetable, amber.......................... 24
Bowl, 10" oval vegetable, pink............................. 45
Bowl, 10" oval vegetable, Sunburst irides-
   cent 14
Creamer, footed, amber....................................... 12
Creamer, footed, pink.. 16
Creamer, footed, Sunburst iridescent.................... 8
Cup & saucer, amber 12
Cup & saucer, pink 18

Normandie Iridescent Cup & Saucer

Cup & saucer, Sunburst iridescent (ILLUS.).......... 7

Pitcher, 8" h., 80 oz., amber 90
Pitcher, 8" h., 80 oz., clear 45
Pitcher, 8" h., 80 oz., pink 185
Plate, sherbet, 6" d., amber 6
Plate, sherbet, 6" d., pink 10
Plate, sherbet, 6" d., Sunburst iridescent 3
Plate, salad, 8" d., amber 18
Plate, salad, 8" d., pink 14
Plate, salad, 8" d., Sunburst iridescent 12
Plate, 9 1/4" d., luncheon, Sunburst irides-
  cent 12
Plate, luncheon, 9 1/4" d., amber 20
Plate, luncheon, 9 1/4" d., pink 16
Plate, dinner, 11" d., amber 45
Plate, dinner, 11" d., pink 120
Plate, dinner, 11" d., Sunburst iridescent 10
Plate, grill, 11" d., amber 18
Plate, grill, 11" d., pink 35
Plate, grill, 11" d., Sunburst iridescent 8
Platter, 11 3/4" oval, amber 32
Platter, 11 3/4" oval, pink 38
Platter, 11 3/4" oval, Sunburst iridescent 14
Salt & pepper shakers, amber, pr. 55
Salt & pepper shakers, pink, pr. 95
Sherbet, amber 6
Sherbet, clear 3
Sherbet, pink 10
Sherbet, Sunburst iridescent 5
Sugar bowl, cov., amber 98
Sugar bowl, cov., pink 175
Sugar bowl, open, amber 12
Sugar bowl, open, pink 16
Sugar bowl, open, Sunburst iridescent 8
Tumbler, juice, amber, 4" h., 5 oz. 45
Tumbler, juice, pink, 4" h., 5 oz. 95
Tumbler, water, amber, 4 1/2" h., 9 oz. 35
Tumbler, water, pink, 4 1/2" h., 9 oz. 75
Tumbler, iced tea, amber, 5" h., 12 oz. 55
Tumbler, iced tea, pink, 5" h., 12 oz. 135

(Old) Florentine or Poppy No. 1, Hazel Atlas Glass Co., 1932-35 (Process-etched)

Ashtray, clear, 5 1/2" 12
Ashtray, green, 5 1/2" 24
Ashtray, pink, 5 1/2" 28
Ashtray, yellow, 5 1/2" 28
Bowl, berry, 5" d., clear 12
Bowl, berry, 5" d., cobalt blue 25
Bowl, berry, 5" d., green 16
Bowl, berry, 5" d., pink 18
Bowl, berry, 5" d., yellow 18
Bowl, cereal, 6" d., clear 15
Bowl, cereal, 6" d., green 30
Bowl, cereal, 6" d., pink 35
Bowl, cereal, 6" d., yellow 32
Bowl, 8 1/2" d., clear 15
Bowl, 8 1/2" d., green 28
Bowl, 8 1/2" d., pink 40
Bowl, 8 1/2" d., yellow 35
Bowl, 9 1/2" oval, cov., vegetable, clear 25
Bowl, 9 1/2" oval, cov., vegetable, green 55
Bowl, 9 1/2" oval, cov., vegetable, pink 75
Bowl, 9 1/2" oval, cov., vegetable, yellow 65
Bowl, 9 1/2" oval vegetable, clear 18
Bowl, 9 1/2" oval vegetable, green 40
Bowl, 9 1/2" oval vegetable, pink 60
Bowl, 9 1/2" oval vegetable, yellow 50
Butter dish, cov., clear 85
Butter dish, cov., green 125
Butter dish, cov., pink 175

Butter dish, cov., yellow 165
Coaster-ashtray, clear, 3 3/4" d. 10
Coaster-ashtray, green, 3 3/4" d. 20
Coaster-ashtray, pink, 3 3/4" d. 26
Coaster-ashtray, yellow, 3 3/4" d. 26
Creamer, plain rim, clear 5
Creamer, plain rim, green 10
Creamer, plain rim, pink 18
Creamer, plain rim, yellow 16
Creamer, ruffled rim, clear 20
Creamer, ruffled rim, cobalt blue 75
Creamer, ruffled rim, green 40
Creamer, ruffled rim, pink 38
Cup & saucer, clear 9
Cup & saucer, green 15
Cup & saucer, pink 18
Cup & saucer, yellow 17
Nut dish, handled, ruffled rim, clear 12
Nut dish, handled, ruffled rim, cobalt blue 60
Nut dish, handled, ruffled rim, green 24
Nut dish, handled, ruffled rim, pink 24
Nut dish, handled, ruffled rim, yellow 22
Pitcher, 6 1/2" h., 36 oz., footed, clear 24
Pitcher, 6 1/2" h., 36 oz., footed, cobalt blue 825
Pitcher, 6 1/2" h., 36 oz., footed, green 45
Pitcher, 6 1/2" h., 36 oz., footed, pink 50
Pitcher, 6 1/2" h., 36 oz., footed, yellow 45

(Old) Florentine Pitcher & Tumbler

Pitcher, 7 1/2" h., 48 oz., clear (ILLUS.) 40
Pitcher, 7 1/2" h., 48 oz., green 85
Pitcher, 7 1/2" h., 48 oz., pink 140
Pitcher, 7 1/2" h., 48 oz., yellow 175
Plate, sherbet, 6" d., clear 5
Plate, sherbet, 6" d., green 10
Plate, sherbet, 6" d., pink 10
Plate, sherbet, 6" d., yellow 8
Plate, salad, 8 1/2" d., clear 6
Plate, salad, 8 1/2" d., green 12
Plate, salad, 8 1/2" d., pink 14
Plate, salad, 8 1/2" d., yellow 14
Plate, dinner, 10" d., clear 10
Plate, dinner, 10" d., green 24
Plate, dinner, 10" d., pink 30
Plate, dinner, 10" d., yellow 28
Plate, grill, 10" d., clear 8
Plate, grill, 10" d., green 16
Plate, grill, 10" d., pink 24
Plate, grill, 10" d., yellow 20
Platter, 11 1/2" oval, clear 12
Platter, 11 1/2" oval, green 24
Platter, 11 1/2" oval, pink 30
Platter, 11 1/2" oval, yellow 28

Salt & pepper shakers, footed, clear, pr. 20
Salt & pepper shakers, footed, green, pr. 45
Salt & pepper shakers, footed, pink, pr. 60
Salt & pepper shakers, footed, yellow, pr. 55
Sherbet, footed, clear, 3 oz. 6
Sherbet, footed, green, 3 oz. 12
Sherbet, footed, pink, 3 oz. 14
Sherbet, footed, yellow, 3 oz. 14
Sugar bowl, cov., clear 15
Sugar bowl, cov., green 35
Sugar bowl, cov., pink 45
Sugar bowl, cov., yellow 40
Sugar bowl, open, clear 5
Sugar bowl, open, green 10
Sugar bowl, open, pink 18
Sugar bowl, open, ruffled rim, clear 20
Sugar bowl, open, ruffled rim, cobalt blue 75
Sugar bowl, open, ruffled rim, green 40
Sugar bowl, open, ruffled rim, pink 38
Sugar bowl, open, yellow 16
Tumbler, footed, clear, 3 1/4" h., 4 oz. 8
Tumbler, footed, green, 3 1/4" h., 4 oz. 18
Tumbler, juice, footed, clear, 3 3/4" h., 5 oz.
   (ILLUS. w/pitcher) 8
Tumbler, juice, footed, green, 3 3/4" h., 5
   oz. 16
Tumbler, juice, footed, pink, 3 3/4" h., 5 oz. 28
Tumbler, juice, footed, yellow, 3 3/4" h., 5
   oz. 24
Tumbler, ribbed, clear, 4" h., 9 oz. 8
Tumbler, ribbed, green, 4" h., 9 oz. 16
Tumbler, ribbed, pink, 4" h., 9 oz. 24
Tumbler, water, footed, clear, 4 3/4" h.,
   10 oz. 10
Tumbler, water, footed, green, 4 3/4" h.,
   10 oz. 20
Tumbler, water, footed, pink, 4 3/4" h.,
   10 oz. 28
Tumbler, water, footed, yellow, 4 3/4" h.,
   10 oz. 26
Tumbler, iced tea, footed, clear, 5 1/4" h.,
   12 oz. 15
Tumbler, iced tea, footed, green, 5 1/4" h.,
   12 oz. 35
Tumbler, iced tea, footed, pink, 5 1/4" h.,
   12 oz. 40
Tumbler, iced tea, footed, yellow, 5 1/4" h.,
   12 oz. 38

Oyster & Pearl, Anchor Hocking Glass Corp., 1938-40 (Press-mold)

Bowl, heart-shaped, w/handle, 5 1/4" w.,
   clear 6
Bowl, heart-shaped, w/handle, 5 1/4" w.,
   pink 14
Bowl, heart-shaped, w/handle, 5 1/4" w.,
   white w/green 8
Bowl, heart-shaped, w/handle, 5 1/4" w.,
   white w/pink 10
Bowl, w/handle, 5 1/2" d., pink 14
Bowl, w/handle, 5 1/2" d., ruby 20
Bowl, handled, 6 1/2" d., clear 10
Bowl, handled, 6 1/2" d., pink 18
Bowl, handled, 6 1/2" d., ruby 24
Bowl, fruit, 10 1/2" d., clear 12
Bowl, fruit, 10 1/2" d., pink 28
Bowl, fruit, 10 1/2" d., ruby 55
Bowl, fruit, 10 1/2" d., white w/green 16
Bowl, fruit, 10 1/2" d., white w/pink 18
Candleholders, clear, 3 1/2" h., pr. 10

Candleholders, pink, 3 1/2" h., pr. 36
Candleholders, ruby, 3 1/2" h., pr. 60
Candleholders, white w/green, 3 1/2" h.,
   pr. 16
Candleholders, white w/pink, 3 1/2" h., pr. 18
Plate, sandwich, 13 1/2" d., clear 12
Plate, sandwich, 13 1/2" d., pink 20
Plate, sandwich, 13 1/2" d., ruby 55
Relish, divided, clear, 10 1/4" oval 14
Relish, divided, pink, 10 1/4" oval 30

Petalware, MacBeth-Evans Glass Co., 1930-40 (Press-mold)

Bowl, cream soup, 4 1/2" d., clear 5
Bowl, cream soup, 4 1/2" d., decorated
   Cremax or Monax 22
Bowl, cream soup, 4 1/2" d., Florette 32
Bowl, cream soup, 4 1/2" d., pink 20
Bowl, cream soup, 4 1/2" d., plain Cremax
   or Monax 14
Bowl, cream soup, 4 1/2" d., Red Trim Flo-
   ral 40
Bowl, cereal, 5 3/4" d., clear 5
Bowl, cereal, 5 3/4" d., decorated Cremax
   or Monax 12
Bowl, cereal, 5 3/4" d., Florette 24
Bowl, cereal, 5 3/4" d., pink 16
Bowl, cereal, 5 3/4" d., plain Cremax or
   Monax 8
Bowl, cereal, 5 3/4" d., Red Trim Floral 32
Bowl, soup, 7" d., decorated Cremax or
   Monax 65
Bowl, soup, 7" d., plain Cremax or Monax 45
Bowl, large berry, 9" d., clear 10
Bowl, large berry, 9" d., cobalt blue 60
Bowl, large berry, 9" d., decorated Cremax
   or Monax 30
Bowl, large berry, 9" d., Florette 45
Bowl, large berry, 9" d., plain Cremax or
   Monax 20
Creamer, footed, clear 3
Creamer, footed, cobalt blue 35
Creamer, footed, decorated Cremax or
   Monax 12
Creamer, footed, Florette 18
Creamer, footed, pink 20
Creamer, footed, plain Cremax or Monax 6
Creamer, footed, Red Trim Floral 28
Cup, decorated Cremax or Monax 10
Cup & saucer, clear 5
Cup & saucer, clear w/platinum trim 6
Cup & saucer, decorated Cremax or Monax 14
Cup & saucer, Florette 20
Cup & saucer, pink 14
Cup & saucer, plain Cremax or Monax 10
Cup & saucer, Red Trim Floral 24
Lamp shade, Monax, 6" h. 10
Lamp shade, Cremax, 9" h. 12
Lamp shade, pink, 10" h. 25
Lamp shade, Monax, 11" h. 18
Lamp shade, pink, 12" h. 30
Mustard jar, w/metal cover, cobalt blue 16
Pitcher, 80 oz., clear w/decorated bands 25
Plate, sherbet, 6" d., clear 2
Plate, sherbet, 6" d., decorated Cremax or
   Monax 5
Plate, sherbet, 6" d., Florette 7
Plate, sherbet, 6" d., pink 8
Plate, sherbet, 6" d., plain Cremax or
   Monax 3

Plate, salad, 8" d., clear 3
Plate, salad, 8" d., clear w/platinum trim 4
Plate, salad, 8" d., decorated Cremax or
    Monax... 8
Plate, salad, 8" d., Florette...................................... 10
Plate, salad, 8" d., pink.. 10
Plate, salad, 8" d., plain Cremax or Monax............ 4
Plate, salad, 8" d., Red Trim Floral........................ 24
Plate, dinner, 9" d., clear.. 5
Plate, dinner, 9" d., decorated Cremax or
    Monax... 20
Plate, dinner, 9" d., Florette 35
Plate, dinner, 9" d., pink 18
Plate, dinner, 9" d., plain Cremax or Monax 12
Plate, salver, 11" d., clear 6
Plate, salver, 11" d., clear w/platinum trim 8
Plate, salver, 11" d., decorated Cremax or
    Monax... 14
Plate, salver, 11" d., Florette 20
Plate, salver, 11" d., pink 15
Plate, salver, 11" d., plain Cremax or Monax....... 10
Plate, salver, 11" d., Red Trim Floral 28
Plate, salver, 12" d., decorated Cremax or
    Monax... 24
Plate, salver, 12" d., Florette 28
Plate, salver, 12" d., plain Cremax or Monax....... 18
Plate, salver, 12" d., Red Trim Floral 36
Platter, 13" oval, clear 10
Platter, 13" oval, decorated Cremax or
    Monax... 25
Platter, 13" oval, Florette 30
Platter, 13" oval, pink 25
Platter, 13" oval, plain Cremax or Monax 18
Sherbet, low foot, clear, 4 1/2" h. 4
Sherbet, low foot, cobalt blue, 4 1/2" h................. 30
Sherbet, low foot, decorated Cremax or
    Monax, 4 1/2" h... 16
Sherbet, low foot, Florette, 4 1/2" h. 24
Sherbet, low foot, pink, 4 1/2" h.............................. 15
Sherbet, low foot, Red Trim Floral, 4 1/2" h. 38
Sugar bowl, open, footed, clear............................... 3
Sugar bowl, open, footed, cobalt blue................... 35
Sugar bowl, open, footed, decorated Cre-
    max or Monax.. 12
Sugar bowl, open, footed, Florette 18
Sugar bowl, open, footed, plain Cremax or
    Monax... 6
Sugar bowl, open, footed, Red Trim Floral 28
Sugar bowl, open, pink... 20
Tidbit server, clear.. 15
Tidbit server, decorated Cremax or Monax 28
Tidbit server, Florette 32
Tidbit server, pink 28
Tidbit server, plain Cremax or Monax 24

Princess, Hocking Glass Co., 1931-35 (Process-etched)

Ashtray, Apricot Yellow, 4 1/2" 110
Ashtray, green, 4 1/2" 75
Ashtray, pink, 4 1/2" 80
Bowl, berry, 4 1/2", Apricot Yellow 50
Bowl, berry, 4 1/2", green... 28
Bowl, berry, 4 1/2", pink... 30
Bowl, berry, 4 1/2", Topaz.. 50
Bowl, cereal, 5", Apricot Yellow.............................. 40
Bowl, cereal, 5", green 35
Bowl, cereal, 5", pink.. 40
Bowl, cereal, 5", pink frosted................................... 35
Bowl, cereal, 5", Topaz... 40
Bowl, salad, 9" octagon, Apricot Yellow............... 145
Bowl, salad, 9" octagon, green................................ 50
Bowl, salad, 9" octagon, pink.................................. 60
Bowl, salad, 9" octagon, Topaz 145
Bowl, 9 1/2" hat shape, Apricot Yellow.............. 150

Bowl, 9 1/2" hat shape, green 55
Bowl, 9 1/2" hat shape, green frosted................. 55
Bowl, 9 1/2" hat shape, pink 65
Bowl, 9 1/2" hat shape, pink frosted.................... 60
Bowl, 9 1/2", hat shape, Topaz 150
Bowl, 10" oval vegetable, Apricot Yellow............. 60
Bowl, 10" oval vegetable, green............................ 40
Bowl, 10" oval vegetable, pink............................... 45
Bowl, 10" oval vegetable, Topaz........................... 60
Butter dish, cov., Apricot Yellow 750
Butter dish, cov., green.. 125
Butter dish, cov., pink 145
Butter dish, cov., Topaz....................................... 750
Cake stand, green, 10"... 45
Cake stand, pink, 10".. 48
Candy jar, cov., green 60
Candy jar, cov., pink 68
Coaster, Apricot Yellow, 4" 120
Coaster, green, 4"... 75
Coaster, pink, 4" 85
Coaster, Topaz, 4 "... 120
Cookie jar, cov., blue.. 950
Cookie jar, cov., green frosted.............................. 50

Princess Green Cookie Jar

Cookie jar, cov., green (ILLUS.) 60
Cookie jar, cov., pink 75
Cookie jar, cov., pink frosted................................ 65
Creamer, oval, Apricot Yellow 18
Creamer, oval, green 14
Creamer, oval, pink 16
Creamer, oval, pink frosted................................... 14
Creamer, oval, Topaz... 18
Cup & saucer, Apricot Yellow 18
Cup & saucer, blue... 200
Cup & saucer, green 23
Cup & saucer, pink 25
Cup & saucer, Topaz.. 20
Pitcher, 6" h., 37 oz., jug-type, Apricot
    Yellow... 700
Pitcher, 6" h., 37 oz., jug-type, green................... 65
Pitcher, 6" h., 37 oz., jug-type, pink...................... 70
Pitcher, 6" h., 37 oz., jug-type, Topaz................. 700
Pitcher, 7 3/8" h., 24 oz., footed, green............... 575
Pitcher, 7 3/8" h., 24 oz., footed, pink 650
Pitcher, 8" h., 60 oz., jug-type, Apricot Yel-
    low.. 120
Pitcher, 8" h., 60 oz., jug-type, green................... 60
Pitcher, 8" h., 60 oz., jug-type, pink...................... 65
Pitcher, 8" h., 60 oz, jug-type,Topaz 120
Plate, sherbet, 5 1/2", Apricot Yellow 8
Plate, sherbet, 5 1/2", blue................................... 175
Plate, sherbet, 5 1/2", green.................................. 10
Plate, sherbet, 5 1/2", pink 10
Plate, sherbet, 5 1/2", Topaz................................. 12
Plate, salad, 8", Apricot Yellow............................. 12
Plate, salad, 8" d., green.. 14

Plate, salad, 8", pink 16
Plate, salad, 8", Topaz 18
Plate, dinner, 9", green 28
Plate, dinner, 9", pink.. 30
Plate, dinner, 9", Topaz.. 16
Plate, grill, 9", Apricot Yellow................................. 8
Plate, grill, 9", blue 175
Plate, grill, 9", green... 14
Plate, grill, 9", pink 16
Plate, grill, 9", Topaz.. 8
Plate, sandwich, 10 1/4", handled, Apricot
  Yellow 175
Plate, sandwich, 10 1/4", handled, green............. 28
Plate, sandwich, 10 1/4", handled, pink............... 30
Plate, sandwich, 10 1/4", handled, Topaz 175
Plate, grill, 10 1/2", closed handles, Apricot
  Yellow 12
Plate, grill, 10 1/2", closed handles, green.......... 14
Plate, grill, 10 1/2", closed handles, pink............ 15
Plate, grill, 10 1/2", closed handles, Topaz 10
Platter, 12" oval, closed handles, Apricot
  Yellow 65
Platter, 12" oval, closed handles, green.............. 28
Platter, 12" oval, closed handles, pink................ 30
Platter, 12" oval, closed handles, Topaz............. 65
Relish, Apricot Yellow, 7 1/2" 245
Relish, green, 7 1/2" 185
Relish, pink, 7 1/2"... 195
Relish, Topaz, 7 1/2" 245
Relish, divided, Apricot Yellow, 7 1/2" 95
Relish, divided, green, 7 1/2" 26
Relish, divided, pink, 7 1/2" 28
Relish, divided, Topaz, 7 1/2" 95
Salt & pepper (or spice) shakers, green,
  5 1/2" h., pr. 50
Salt & pepper shakers, Apricot Yellow,
  4 1/2" h., pr. 85
Salt & pepper shakers, green, 4 1/2" h., pr. 65
Salt & pepper shakers, pink, 4 1/2" h., pr. 70
Salt & pepper shakers, Topaz, 4 1/2" h.,
  pr. 85
Sherbet, footed, Apricot Yellow 35
Sherbet, footed, green 25
Sherbet, footed, pink 25
Sherbet, footed, Topaz 35
Sugar bowl, cov., Apricot Yellow 36
Sugar bowl, cov., green 29
Sugar bowl, cov., Topaz 36
Sugar bowl, open, Apricot Yellow....................... 12
Sugar bowl, open, green...................................... 14
Sugar bowl, open, pink.. 16
Sugar bowl, open, pink frosted 14
Sugar bowl, open, Topaz 18
Tumbler, juice, Apricot Yellow, 3" h., 5 oz. 35
Tumbler, juice, green, 3" h., 5 oz. 33
Tumbler, juice, pink, 3" h., 5 oz. 35
Tumbler, juice, Topaz, 3" h., 5 oz. 35
Tumbler, water, Apricot Yellow, 4" h., 9 oz. 30
Tumbler, water, green, 4" h., 9 oz........................ 28
Tumbler, water, pink, 4" h., 9 oz. 30
Tumbler, water, Topaz, 4" h., 9 oz...................... 30
Tumbler, square footed, green, 4 3/4" h.,
  9 oz. 60
Tumbler, square footed, pink, 4 3/4" h.,
  9 oz. 65
Tumbler, footed, Apricot Yellow, 5 1/4" h.,
  10 oz. 28
Tumbler, footed, green, 5 1/4" h., 10 oz. 32
Tumbler, footed, pink, 5 1/4" h. 10 oz. 35
Tumbler, footed, Apricot Yellow, 6 1/2" h.,
  12 1/2" oz. 165
Tumbler, footed, green, 6 1/2" h., 12 1/2 oz. 98
Tumbler, footed, pink, 6 1/2" h., 12 1/2 oz........ 110
Tumbler, footed, Topaz, 6 1/2" h.,
  12 1/2 oz. 165

Tumbler, iced tea, Apricot Yellow, 5 1/2" h.,
  13 oz. 35
Tumbler, iced tea, green, 5 1/4" h., 13 oz. 45
Tumbler, iced tea, pink, 5 1/4" h., 13 oz. 40
Tumbler, iced tea, Topaz, 5 1/4" h., 13 oz. 35
Vase, 8" h., green.. 45
Vase, 8" h., green frosted 40
Vase, 8" h., pink.. 50
Vase, 8" h., pink frosted 45

Sharon or Cabbage Rose, Federal Glass Co., 1935-39 (Chip-mold)

Bowl, berry, 5" d., amber..................................... 10
Bowl, berry, 5" d., green 18
Bowl, berry, 5" d., pink 15
Bowl, cream soup, 5" d., amber 28
Bowl, cream soup, 5" d., green 58
Bowl, cream soup, 5" d., pink 48
Bowl, cereal, 6" d., amber 24
Bowl, cereal, 6" d., green 28
Bowl, cereal, 6" d., pink 28
Bowl, soup, 7 1/2" d., amber............................... 52
Bowl, soup, 7 1/2" d., pink 55
Bowl, berry, 8 1/2" d., amber 6
Bowl, berry, 8 1/2" d., green 35
Bowl, berry, 8 1/2" d., pink 35
Bowl, 9 1/2" oval vegetable, amber 20
Bowl, 9 1/2" oval vegetable, green 35
Bowl, 9 1/2" oval vegetable, pink 35
Bowl, fruit, 10 1/2" d., amber 24
Bowl, fruit, 10 1/2" d., green 48
Bowl, fruit, 10 1/2" d., pink 50
Butter dish, cov., amber 48
Butter dish, cov., green...................................... 110
Butter dish, cov., pink 65
Cake plate, footed, amber, 11 1/2" d................... 24
Cake plate, footed, clear, 11 1/2" d. 15
Cake plate, footed, green, 11 1/2" d................... 65
Cake plate, footed, pink, 11 1/2" d...................... 45
Candy jar, cov., amber 45
Candy jar, cov., green 165
Candy jar, cov., pink 65
Cheese dish, cov., amber 195
Cheese dish, cov., pink 1,500
Creamer, amber 14
Creamer, green 24
Creamer, pink 20
Cup & saucer, amber 13
Cup & saucer, green 30
Cup & saucer, pink 25
Jam dish, amber, 7 1/2" d., 1 1/2" h. 45
Jam dish, green, 7 1/2" d., 1 1/2" h. 65
Jam dish, pink, 7 1/2" d., 1 1/2" h. 250
Pitcher, 9" h., 80 oz., amber 140
Pitcher, 9" h., 80 oz., green 475
Pitcher, 9" h., 80 oz., pink 175
Pitcher w/ice lip, 9" h., 80 oz., amber 145
Pitcher w/ice lip, 9" h., 80 oz., green................ 450
Pitcher w/ice lip, 9" h., 80 oz., pink 195
Plate, bread & butter, 6" d., amber....................... 5
Plate, bread & butter, 6" d., green...................... 10
Plate, bread & butter, 6" d., pink.......................... 8
Plate, salad, 7 1/2" d., amber.............................. 16
Plate, salad, 7 1/2" d., clear 8
Plate, salad, 7 1/2" d., green 24
Plate, salad, 7 1/2" d., pink 28
Plate, dinner, 9 1/2" d., amber 12
Plate, dinner, 9 1/2" d., green 24
Plate, dinner, 9 1/2" d., pink 24
Platter, 12 1/2" oval, amber 20
Platter, 12 1/2" oval, green................................. 30
Platter, 12 1/2" oval, pink 30
Salt & pepper shakers, amber, pr. 35
Salt & pepper shakers, green, pr. 70

Salt & pepper shakers, pink, pr............................ 60
Sherbet, footed, amber.. 12
Sherbet, footed, green 36
Sherbet, footed, pink 18
Sugar bowl, cov., amber...................................... 39
Sugar bowl, cov., green 64
Sugar bowl, cov., pink 52
Sugar bowl, open, amber...................................... 14
Sugar bowl, open, green...................................... 24
Sugar bowl, open, pink... 20
Tumbler, amber, 4" h., 9 oz. 30
Tumbler, green, 4" h., 9 oz.................................... 75
Tumbler, pink, 4" h., 9 oz. 48

Sharon Tumblers

Tumbler, amber, 5 1/4" h., 12 oz. (ILLUS.
left) 65
Tumbler, green, 5 1/4" h., 12 oz......................... 110
Tumbler, pink, 5 1/4" h., 12 oz............................. 95
Tumbler, footed, amber, 6 1/2" h., 15 oz.
(ILLUS. right) 145
Tumbler, footed, clear, 6 1/2" h., 15 oz. 15
Tumbler, footed, pink, 6 1/2" h., 15 oz. 60

Waterford or Waffle, Hocking Glass Co., 1938-44- (Press-mold)

Ashtray, clear, 4"... 8
Bowl, berry, 4 3/4" d., pink.................................. 18
Bowl, cereal, 5 1/4" d., clear 20
Bowl, cereal, 5 1/4" d., pink................................. 38
Bowl, berry, 8 1/4" d., clear 12
Bowl, berry, 8 1/4" d., pink.................................. 28
Butter dish, cov., clear 30
Butter dish, cov., pink 225
Cake plate, handled, clear, 10 1/4" d. 12
Cake plate, handled, pink, 10 1/4" d.................... 30
Coaster, clear, 4" d.. 4
Creamer, oval, clear.. 5
Creamer, oval, pink.. 14
Creamer, footed, clear (Miss America style)........ 40
Cup & saucer, clear 10
Cup & saucer, pink.. 22
Goblet, amber, 5 1/4" h.. 25
Goblet, clear, 5 1/4" h. 18
Goblet, clear, 5 1/2" h. (Miss America Style) 35
Goblet, pink, 5 1/2" h. (Miss America style)......... 95
Lamp, clear, 4" h. 38
Pitcher, juice, 42 oz., tilt-type, clear.................... 28
Pitcher w/ice lip, 80 oz., clear............................. 40
Pitcher w/ice lip, 80 oz., pink 175
Plate, sherbet, 6" d., clear................................... 3
Plate, sherbet, 6" d., pink 10
Plate, salad, 7 1/2" d., clear 8
Plate, salad, 7 1/2" d., pink.................................. 14
Plate, dinner, 9 5/8" d., clear............................... 14
Plate, dinner, 9 5/8" d., pink................................. 28

Plate, sandwich, 13 3/4" d., clear 14
Plate, sandwich, 13 3/4" d., pink 40
Relish, five-section, clear, 13 3/4" d. 18
Salt & pepper shakers, clear, short, pr.............. 12
Salt & pepper shakers, clear, tall, pr................. 14
Sherbet, footed, clear.. 5
Sherbet, footed, pink... 18
Sugar bowl, cov., oval, clear 15
Sugar bowl, cov., oval, pink 65
Sugar bowl, open, footed, clear (Miss
America style) 40
Tumbler, footed, pink, 3 1/2" h., 5 oz. 110
Tumbler, footed, clear, 5" h., 10 oz. 14
Tumbler, footed, pink, 5" h., 10 oz...................... 28

DeVez & Degué

The Saint-Hilaire, Touvier, de Varreaux and Company of Pantin, France used the name De Vez on their cameo glass early in the 20th century. Some of their examples were marked "Degué," after one of their master glassmakers. Officially the company was named "Cristallerie de Pantin."

Cameo perfume bottle w/stopper, slender
teardrop-form, pink cased to clear & layered in cobalt blue & etched as waterfowl
in a marsh scene, signed "DeVez" in
cameo, base marked "Mignon Paris,"
partial metal mount, 7 1/2" h. (loss to
metal mount) $374
Cameo vase, 14 1/4" h., tall ovoid form, am-
ber overlaid w/purple mottled w/crimson
& cut w/maple leaves, engraved "Degué,"
inscribed "Made in France," ca. 1925 1,150
Cameo vase, 14 1/2" h., ovoid body, yellow
overlaid w/orange & brown & cut w/styl-
ized morning glory vines above a lappet
border, inscribed "Degué - Made in
France," ca. 1925 2,300
Cameo vase, 15 3/8" h., double-gourd body
w/a short flaring neck, mottled lemon yellow overlaid w/reddish orange & dark
purple, cut w/chrysanthemums on long
stems w/large leaves, signed
"Degué," ca. 1925....................................... 1,035

Large Degué Cameo Vase

Cameo vase, 16 5/8" h., tall waisted cylindrical form, grey mottled w/ivory, overlaid
w/red & cut w/a central band of flowerheads growing on straight stems w/long
narrow leaves, signed "Degué - Made in
France," ca. 1925 (ILLUS.) 1,610

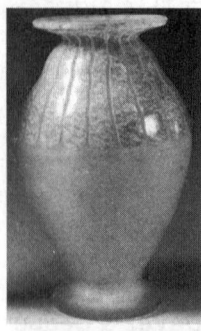

Degué Cameo Vase

Cameo vase, 17" h., ovoid body w/wide flattened rim & cushion foot, frosted grey overlaid w/lavender mottled w/white & cut w/stylized petals around the neck, signed in cameo "Degué," ca. 1925 (ILLUS.)............ **690**

Vase, 9 1/2" h., cylindrical, Art Deco style, grey infused w/blue & acid-etched w/stylized scrolls, signed "Degué," ca. 1920-30..... **690**

Vase, 10 1/4" h., ovoid body molded w/stylized vines, the interior applied w/metallic decoration, acid-etched "Degué," ca. 1925.. **287**

Vase, 17 h., monumental form, Art Deco style, black base, the sides in varied colors w/prominent blues w/yellows, greens & various other tones, signed "Degué"......... **990**

Duncan & Miller

Duncan & Miller Glass Company, a successor firm to George A. Duncan & Sons Company, produced a wide range of pressed wares and novelty pieces during the late 19th century and into the early 20th century. During the Depression era and after, they continued making a wide variety of more modern patterns, including mold-blown types, and also introduced a number of etched and engraved patterns. Many colors, including opalescent hues, were produced during this era, and especially popular today are the graceful swan dishes they produced in the Pall Mall and Sylvan patterns.

The numbers after the pattern name indicate the original factory pattern number. The Duncan factory was closed in 1955. Also see ANIMALS and PATTERN GLASS.

Almond dish, Early American Sandwich patt. (No. 41), clear... **$15**

Ashtray, Canterbury patt. (No. 115), clear, 3".. 12

Ashtray, Early American Sandwich patt. (No. 41), clear, 3" sq................................. 10

Basket, handled, etched First Love patt., 10" oval.. 200

Basket, Early American Sandwich patt., clear, 12".. 250

Basket w/loop handle, Early American Sandwich patt., amber, 6" h. 150

Basket w/loop handle, Early American Sandwich patt., clear, 12"............................... 295

Bonbon, heart-shaped, handled, Early American Sandwich patt., clear, 5"................. 35

Bowl, bouillon, Spiral Flutes patt., pink................. 20

Bowl, cream soup, Spiral Flutes patt., amber.. 25

Bowl, fruit, Canterbury patt. (No. 115), clear......... 8

Bowl, 5" d., Early American Sandwich patt., clear 15

Bowl, 8" d., Spiral Flutes patt., clear.................... 18

Bowl, 9" d., Canterbury patt., clear..................... 30

Bowl, 9" d., tab-handled, Caribbean patt., clear... 75

Bowl, 10" d., flared, etched First Love patt., clear... 85

Bowl, 10 1/2" d., 5" h., crimped rim, etched First Love patt., clear 85

Bowl, 11 1/2" d., fluted, Early American Sandwich patt. 55

Bowl, Canterbury patt., oval, clear..................... 35

Butter dish, w/metal cover, Teardrop patt. (No. 301), clear, 1 lb. 20

Cake salver, pedestal foot, Early American Sandwich patt., clear, 13" d., 5" h................... 83

Candlestick, three-light, Canterbury patt. (No. 115), clear, 6" h. 35

Candlesticks, Canterbury patt., pink opalescent, 3" h., pr................................... 65

Candlesticks, two-light, Canterbury patt., clear, 6" h., pr. 50

Candy dish, cov., Early American Sandwich patt., clear, 6" sq. 425

Candy dish, cov., Canterbury patt. (No. 115), clear, 7" h. 35

Candy dish, cov., footed, Early American Sandwich patt., green, 8" h. 100

Celery dish, etched Beverly patt., amber, 11" l... 15

Champagne, Early American Sandwich patt., clear, 5 1/4" h. 17

Teardrop Champagne

Champagne, Teardrop patt. (No. 301), clear, 5" h., 5 oz. (ILLUS.)................................ 15

Claret, Canterbury patt., clear, 5" h. 20

Coaster, Early American Sandwich patt., clear, 5" d.. 11

Cocktail, Early American Sandwich patt., clear, 3 oz. 16

Cocktail, Teardrop patt., clear, 4 1/2" h., 3 1/2 oz. 15

Cocktail, Caribbean patt., blue, 4 3/4" h., 3 oz. 45

Cocktail shaker, etched First Love patt., clear, 16 oz. 145

Cologne bottle w/original stopper, Hobnail patt., amber, 6 1/2" h., 8 oz. 40

Compote, 5" h., 7" w., Puritan patt., green......... 40

Cordial, etched First Love patt., clear, 3 3/4" h., 1 oz. 85

Cordial, Teardrop patt., clear, 4" h., 1 oz. 40

Cornucopia vase, footed, Three Feathers patt. (No. 117), clear, 8" h. 25

Creamer, Early American Sandwich patt., clear 18

Creamer, Festive patt. (No. 155), aqua 25

Creamer, Teardrop patt., clear............................ 10

Creamer & cov. sugar bowl on tray, Festive patt. (No. 155), aqua, 3 pcs. 85

Creamer & sugar bowl, individual-size, Early American Sandwich patt., clear, pr. 25

Cup, Canterbury patt., clear 10

Cup, Puritan patt., footed, clear 9

Cup & saucer, Canterbury patt., clear 20

Cup & saucer, Early American Sandwich patt., clear 16

Cup & saucer, demitasse, Puritan patt., pink.................. 25

Deviled egg plate, Early American Sandwich patt., clear, 12" d................. 75

Epergne, Early American Sandwich patt., clear.................. 250

Finger bowl & liner, Spiral Flutes patt., amber, 2 pcs. 25

Goblet, Caribbean patt., clear, 4" h., 3 oz. 25

Goblet, etched Buttercup patt., low...................... 20

Goblet, water, Early American Sandwich patt., clear 18

Goblet, water, Spiral Flutes patt., green............... 22

Goblet, Caribbean patt., clear, 3 oz., 4" h. 25

Goblet, Teardrop patt., clear, 4 oz., 5" h. 12

Goblet, juice, footed, etched First Love patt., clear, 4 1/2" h., 5 oz. 24

Goblet, Teardrop patt., clear, 5 3/4" h., 9 oz. 15

Goblet, water, Canterbury patt., clear, 7 1/4" h.................. 17

Goblet, etched First Love patt., clear, 6 3/4" h.................. 45

Ice tub, handled, Spiral Flutes patt., pink............ 52

Lamp, oil-type, Mardi Gras patt. (No. 42), clear........................ 225

Lamp shade, Mardi Gras patt., clear...................... 45

Model of a swan, Pall Mall patt. (No. 30), clear, 5" l.................. 15

Model of a swan, Sylvan patt. (No. 122), pink opalescent, 5 1/2" l. 95

Model of a swan, Pall Mall patt. (No. 30 1/2), clear, 7" l.................. 15

Model of a swan, Pall Mall patt. (No. 30), cranberry stained, 8" l.................. 29

Model of a swan, Pall Mall patt. (No. 30 1/2), clear, 10" l. 40

Nut bowl, Early American Sandwich patt., clear, 11"................. 95

Nut cup, Spiral Flutes patt., amber 12

Oyster cocktail, Early American Sandwich patt., clear 18

Parfait, Spiral Flutes patt., amber...................... 25

Pitcher, Caribbean patt., blue, 16 oz., 4 3/4" h. 275

Pitcher, Iris patt., clear 35

Pitcher w/ice lip, 8" h., Early American Sandwich patt., clear, 80 oz............................ 140

Pitcher w/ice lip, Early American Sandwich patt., clear, 1/2 gal., 8" h............................ 140

Plate, 7" d., Early American Sandwich patt., clear........................ 10

Plate, 7" d., Puritan patt., green............................ 9

Plate, 7" d., Spiral Flutes patt., amber 9

Plate, 7" d., Spiral Flutes patt., pink 9

Plate, 7 1/2" d., Canterbury patt., clear............... 10

Plate, salad, 7 1/2" sq., etched First Love patt., clear 45

Plate, salad, 8" d., Early American Sandwich patt., clear.................. 12

Plate, salad, 8" d., Early American Sandwich patt., green.................. 15

Plate, salad, 8 1/2" d., etched First Love patt., clear........................ 48

Plate, dinner, 9 1/2" d., Early American Sandwich patt., clear 65

Plate, dinner, 10 1/2" d., Puritan patt.,þclear........ 25

Plate, sandwich, 11" d., two-handled, Canterbury patt., clear 22

Plate, cracker, 13" d., Early American Sandwich patt., clear 40

Plate, 14" d., Teardrop patt., clear 35

Plate, chop, 14" d., etched Beverly patt., amber 28

Plate, torte, 14" d., Canterbury patt., clear.......... 25

Plate, torte, 14" d., Teardrop patt., clear 25

Plate, 16" d., Early American Sandwich patt., clear 105

Plate, Lazy Susan, 18" d., Teardrop patt., w/leaf cutting, clear 125

Plateau for cheese plate, Teardrop patt., clear 15

Punch bowl & ladle, Festive patt., clear, 2 pcs. 50

Relish dish, two-part, Teardrop patt., round, clear 8

Relish dish, three-part, Canterbury patt., chartreuse, 8"........................ 25

Relish dish, three-part, Canterbury patt., handled, clear, 9" d. 18

Relish dish, three-part, etched First Love patt., clear, 6 x 10 1/2"........................ 60

Relish dish, five-part, Caribbean patt., clear........ 40

Relish dish, six-part, Teardrop patt., clear.......... 30

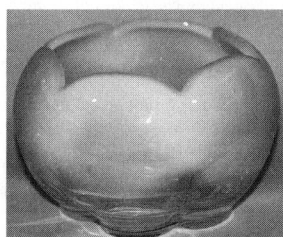

Canterbury Rose Bowl

Rose bowl, Canterbury patt., Jasmine, yellow opalescent (ILLUS.) 110

Salt dip, Early American Sandwich patt., clear........................ 15

Salt & pepper shakers, etched First Love patt., clear, pr........................ 90

Sauce ladle, Festive patt., aqua........................ 40

Saucer, Early American Sandwich patt., clear........................ 5

Sherbet, Early American Sandwich patt., clear, 5 oz........................ 20

Sherbet, Early American Sandwich patt., green 25

Soup plate w/flanged rim, Puritan patt., pink, 8" d........................ 35

Sugar bowl, Early American Sandwich patt., clear, 5 oz........................ 20

Sugar bowl, etched First Love patt., clear 25

Tumbler, Spiral Flutes patt., green, 2 1/2 oz. 12

Tumbler, juice, Canterbury patt., clear,
4 1/4" h. 8
Tumbler, juice, Early American Sandwich
patt., clear, 5 oz. 12
Tumbler, etched Buttercup patt., footed,
12 oz. 25
Tumbler, iced tea, Early American Sand-
wich patt., clear, 12 oz. 18
Tumbler, iced tea, flat, Spiral Flutes patt.,
green.. 75
Tumbler, juice, for ice dish, etched Shirley
patt, pink... 15
Urn, cov., Terrace patt., 5111 1/2, Royal
Blue 200-250
Vase, 4" h., Canterbury patt., clear...................... 17
Vase, 5" h., Canterbury patt., amber................... 25
Vase, 5" h., 6" d., Hobnail patt., pink opales-
cent 65
Vase, 6" h., Canterbury patt. (No. 115),
clear 25
Vase, 8 3/4" h., Spiral Flutes patt., green............ 35
Vase, 9 1/2" h., ruffled rim, Caribbean patt.,
blue 175
Vase/flower arranger, 7" h., Canterbury
patt., clear 40
Vase/flower arranger, 8" h., Canterbury
patt., clear 35
Violet vase, 3" h., Canterbury patt., clear............ 15
Wine, Caribbean patt., blue, 3 oz. 100
Wine, Caribbean patt., clear, 3 oz. 25
Wine, etched First Love patt., clear,
5 1/4" h., 3 oz. 70
Wine, Early American Sandwich patt., clear 20

Durand

Fine decorative glass similar to that made by Tiffany
and other outstanding glasshouses of its day was made
by the Vineland Flint Glass Works Co. in Vineland, New
Jersey, first headed by Victor Durand, Sr., and subse-
quently by his son Victor Durand, Jr., in the 1920s.

Lamp base, "King Tut" patt., small bulbous
base tapering to a tall slender trumpet-
form neck topped by two-socket gilt-metal electric socket fittings, the base raised
on a domed gilt-metal support w/four
thick scroll feet, the lamp in green iridescence w/platinum gold coiled & swirled
decoration, glass 9" h., overall 27" **$550**
Parfait, ribbed footed base & ribbed bowl
w/fluted top, deep shiny rose pink, by
Emil Larsen, 5 3/4" h....................................... 165
Vase, 5" h., ovoid egg-form w/small closed
mouth, overall gold iridescence, signed
on the pontil in aluminum pencil "V - Du-
rand - #20172-S"... 275
Vase, 6 3/16" h., ovoid, amber iridescence
decorated w/heart-shaped leaves & random trailing in pale green, inscribed "Du-
rand - 1968-6," ca. 1920 650
Vase, 6 1/2" h., ovoid beehive-form ribbed
body w/a short wide cylindrical neck,
overall iridescent dark blue, signed in sil-
ver "Durand - 20177-6 1/2".......................... 1,045
Vase, 6 7/8" h., footed squatty bulbous
base w/a wide shoulder centering a tall
trumpet neck w/a widely flaring rim, cobalt blue w/overall strong blue iridescence, shape No. 1730, ca. 1925, pol-
ished pontil (slight wear)................................. 690

Leaf-decorated Durand Vase

Vase, 6 7/8" h., ovoid body w/everted rim,
amber iridescence decorated w/heart-
shaped leafage & trailings in green,
inscribed "Durand - 1710-9," ca. 1920
(ILLUS.).. **1,200**
Vase, 7 1/2" h., simple baluster-form w/a
wide, short flaring neck, gold iridescent
ground w/the exterior covered w/random
gold threading (minimal thread damage)....... 350

Blue Iridescent Durand Vase

Vase, 7 3/4" h., squatty bulbous base tapering to a trumpet-form neck, brilliant silvery blue iridescence, signed "Durand -
1986 - 8," ca. 1925 (ILLUS.)........................... 900

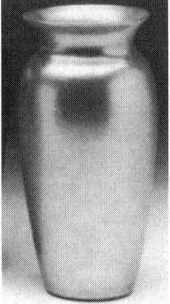

Gold Iridescent Durand Vase

Vase, 8" h., simple baluster-form body
w/flaring rim, overall smooth orangish
gold iridescence, inscribed on base "V.
Durand - 1812-8" (ILLUS.) 600
Vase, 8" h., the wide squatty base centered
by a widely flaring trumpet neck, lightly
molded ribbing, ambergris w/bright blue
iridescent finish highlighted by purplish
green, base signed in silver "V. Durand
1986-8".. 950
Vase, 8" h., 10" d., a squatty wide bulbous
base centered by a short cylindrical neck

w/a bulbed top below the small flattened rim, overall golden iridescence, marked "1977-10" & signed...................................... **1,100**

Vase, 8 1/4" h., "King Tut" patt., wide footed baluster-form body w/a wide short cylindrical neck w/flaring flattened rim, cased amber to opal w/gold iridescent interior, swirling green hooked & coiled decoration on the exterior, unsigned **1,500**

Threaded Durand Vase

Vase, 8 1/2" h., swelled cylindrical body w/a rounded shoulder to the short trumpet neck, ambergris body w/overall lustrous blue iridescent random threading, unsigned (ILLUS.) **650**

Vase, 9 1/4" h., footed ovoid body tapering to a short neck w/wide flattened flaring rim, bright cobalt blue w/iridescent gold heart-leaf & vine decoration, gold iridized interior, base signed.................................... **1,750**

Vase, 9 1/4" h., wide spherical body centered by a tall slender flaring trumpet neck, marigold iridescence decorated overall w/random spider web threading in gold **770**

Vase, 9 1/2" h., footed slender ovoid body w/a short widely flaring neck, overall gold iridescent ground w/large gold pulled feathers extending from the base & edged w/dark green, overall random gold threading, gold iridescent interior............... **1,650**

Vase, 9 5/8" h., shouldered ovoid body, brilliant amber iridescence decorated w/opalescent striated feathering edged in bluish green iridescence, the whole w/applied amber iridescent stringing, inscribed "Durand - 1812-10," ca. 1925 (losses)... **550**

Vase, 11 7/8" h., cylindrical w/squared lip, brilliant amber iridescence decorated w/opalescent heart-shaped leafage & trailings, inscribed "Durand," ca. 1925 .... **750**

Vase, 12" h., a disk foot below a small bulbed segment tapering to a tall slender ovoid body further tapering to a tall trumpet neck, overall dark blue iridescence w/applied amber loop handles from center body to lower bulb, signed "V. Durand 2010-12" (slight annealing cracks at base of handles)...................................... **1,485**

Vase, 12" h., "Moorish" type crackle glass, cushion foot tapering to a trumpet-form

body w/ten molded ribs & overall crackled finish, ambergris w/gold iridescence, silver mark "V. Durand" on base **1,500**

Vase, 12 3/8" h., shouldered ovoid body, brilliant amber iridescence decorated w/opalescent striated feathering edge in blue iridescence, inscribed "Durand," ca. 1925... **1,200**

Durand Vase with Stepped Shoulder

Vase, 13" h., bulbous ovoid body w/a stepped shoulder w/a small mouth, amber w/gold iridescence, polished pontil, unsigned, minor surface wear, Shape No. 1978, ca. 1925... **920**

Vases, 4 1/4" h., ovoid body w/an everted rim, the iridescent gold ground decorated w/an iridescent silvery green wave design, signed, each drilled, pr........................... **300**

Fenton

Fenton Art Glass Company began producing glass at Williamstown, West Virginia, in January 1907. Organized by Frank L. and John W. Fenton, the company began operations in a newly built glass factory with an experienced master glass craftsman, Jacob Rosenthal, as their factory manager. Fenton has produced a wide variety of collectible glassware through the years, including Carnival. Still in production today, its current productions may be found at finer gift shops across the country.

William Heacock's three-volume set on Fenton, published by Antique Publications, is the standard reference in this field.

Fenton Mark

Basket, Rose Burmese, No. 7731 .... **$90**

Basket, Hobnail patt., French Opalescent, 7 1/2" **35**

Bowl, 7" d., Hobnail patt., green opalescent **30-40**

Bowl, 9 3/4" d., fruit, Mandarin Red on black glass stand, No. 846, 2 pcs. **85**

Bowl, 10" d., low sides, Wisteria, stretch finish **80**

Bowl, 10" d., Silver Crest, No. 7221, yellow jonquil decoration w/gold trim on crest edge.. 50
Bowl, 12" d., Silver Crest...................................... 30
Bowl, 14" d., Peach Crest...................................... 60
Cocktail glass, Historic America patt., clear........ 22
Cookie jar, cov., Big Cookies patt., black, handled.. 140
Cruet w/original stopper, Coin Dot patt., No. 418, pink opalescent.................................... 75
Cruet w/original stopper, Dot Optic patt., cobalt blue opalescent.. 95
Cruet w/original stopper, Drape patt., cranberry opalescent.. 100
Cruet w/original stopper, Drape patt., mulberry opalescent 75
Cruet w/original stopper, Fern patt., No. 815, Persian blue opalescent 75

Cranberry Opalescent Fenton Cruet

Cruet w/original stopper, Hobnail patt., cranberry opalescent (ILLUS.)........................... 90
Cruet w/original stopper, Rose Burmese 100
Cruet w/original stopper, Swirl patt., French Opalescent... 75
Epergne, one-lily, Rose Burmese, No. 7202..... 125
Epergne, three-lily, Diamond Lace patt., white opalescent 115
Goblet, Historic America patt., clear 30
Lamp, Gone-with-the-Wind type, Poppy patt., custard, 24" h. 295

Cranberry Opalescent Hobnail Pitcher

Pitcher, footed spherical form, cranberry opalescent Hobnail patt., applied clear handle (ILLUS.)... 115
Plates, 8" d., Silver Crest, set of 8...................... 155
Rose bowl, No. 857, Periwinkle blue................... 48
Vase, 11" h., fan-shaped, Hobnail patt., vaseline opalescent.. 75

Small Hobnail Vase

Vase, 6" h., footed, trumpet-form w/flaring ruffled rim, Hobnail patt., milk glass (ILLUS.)... 15
Vase, 8" h., double crimped rim, Hobnail patt., No. 3958, milk glass................................ 25
Vase, fan-type, dolphin base, Jade green........... 45

Fostoria

Fostoria Glass company, founded in 1887, produced numerous types of fine glassware over the years. Its factory in Moundsville, West Virginia closed in 1986.

Fostoria Label

Appetizer or ice cream set: 10 1/2" oblong tray w/six individual 1 3/4" h. inserts, American patt., amber, the set **$1,100**
Ashtray, individual, Century patt., clear, 2 3/4" 12
Ashtray, American patt., clear, 2 7/8" sq............. 8
Ashtray, American patt., clear, 5" sq................. 100
Ashtray, Coin patt., ruby, 5 1/2" 34
Banana split dish, American patt., clear, 3 1/2" w., 9" l. 1,200
Basket, w/reeded handle, American patt., clear, 7 x 9".. 148
Beer mug, American patt., clear, 12 oz., 4 1/2" h... 88
Bell, American patt., clear 350
Bonbon, three-footed, American patt., clear, 7" d. 15
Bonbon, three-footed, American patt., red, 7" d. 125
Bonbon, three-footed, Colony patt., clear, 7" d. 16
Bottle w/original stopper, cordial, American patt., clear, 9 oz., 7 1/4" h. 110
Bowl, cream soup, Colony patt., clear................. 77
Bowl, almond, 2 1/4" d., footed, Colony patt., clear.. 17
Bowl, 8 1/2" d., three-handled, American patt., clear... 300
Bowl, 8 1/2" d., two-handled, Chintz etching, clear 45
Bowl, 9" d., Century patt., clear............................ 50
Bowl, 9" oval, Coin patt., ruby 55
Bowl, 9 3/8" w., 4" h., Colony patt., clear............. 85
Bowl, salad, 9 3/4" d., Colony patt., clear............ 40

Colony High-footed Bowl

Bowl, 10 1/2" d., high-footed, Colony patt., clear (ILLUS.) 112

Bowl, fruit, 10 1/2" d., three-footed, American patt., clear.................................. 40-45

Bowl, 11" d., footed, rolled edge, Century patt., clear 45

Bowl, 11" tri-cornered, three footed, American patt., clear.................................. 40

Bowl, 12 1/2" oval, 2 7/8" h., No. 2545, Flame patt., Navarre etching, clear.............. 113

Bowl, fruit, low, 14" d., Colony patt., clear 70

Bowl, toddler's, American patt., No. 150, clear 45

Butter dish, cov., Colony patt., No. 2412, clear, 1/4 lb. 50

Butter dish, cov., oblong, American patt., clear, 1/4 lb., 3 1/4 x 7 1/2", 2 1/8" h. 35

Cake plate, handled, Chintz etching, No. 2496, clear, 10" d....................................... 40

Cake plate, handled, Colony patt., clear, 10" d.. 45

Cake plate, three-footed, American patt., clear, 12" d.. 45

Cake salver, American patt., clear, 10" sq. 250

Cake salver, Colony patt., clear, 12" d............... 75

Cake stand, Coin patt., amber.......................... 140

Cake stand, Coin patt., clear, 10" d. 110

Candlestick, Coin patt., ruby, 4 1/2" h. 46

Candlestick, Colony patt., No. 2412, clear, 7" h. 30

Candlestick, two-light, Flame patt., clear 80

Candlestick, Baroque patt., clear w/Lido etching, 4" h. 32

Candlestick, Coronet patt., clear, 4 1/2" h. 20

Candlestick, Chintz etching, clear, 5 1/2" h. 30

Candlestick, Romance etching, clear, 5 1/2" h. 45

Candlestick, Colony patt., No. 2412, clear, 7" h. 30

Baroque Two-light Candlestick

Candlestick, two-light, Baroque patt., clear (ILLUS.)... 24

Candlestick, two-light, Chintz etching, clear....... 38

Candlestick, three-light, Romance etching, clear 65

Candlesticks, Navarre patt., No. 2496, clear, 4" h., pr... 90

Candlesticks, Century patt., clear, 4 1/2" h., pr... 34

Candlesticks, triple-light, Navarre etching, clear, 6 3/4" h., pr................................... 150

Candlesticks, Colony patt., w/eight prisms, clear, 7 1/2" h., pr...................................... 195

Candlesticks, cone-footed, American patt., clear, 15 points, small, pr. 400

Candlesticks, cone-footed, American patt., clear, 16 points, large, pr. 300

Candlesticks, two-light, Romance etching, No. 6023, clear, pr............................... 110

Candy dish, cov., three-part, Chintz etching, clear 165

Candy dish, cov., three-part, Royal etching, amber... 60

Candy dish, cov., Coin patt., ruby, 4 1/4" 42

Candy dish, cov., Coin patt., ruby, 6" 65

Candy dish, cov., American patt., "wedding bowl," milk glass, 8" h.................................. 125

Celery dish, Chintz etching, clear....................... 40

Celery tray, American patt., clear, 10" l. 25

Centerpiece, American patt., clear, shallow, 17" 550

Chamber candles, American patt., clear, pr.. 95

Champagne, Romance etching, clear, 7" h........ 24

Champagne, Chintz etching, clear 20

Champagne, Holly cutting, clear......................... 38

Cheese compote, American patt., clear............ 24

Chintz Cheese & Cracker Set

Cheese & cracker set, Chintz etching, clear, 2 pcs. (ILLUS.)...................................... 70

Cigarette box, cov., American patt., clear.......... 40

Cigarette box, cov., Baroque patt., No. 2496, clear... 50

Claret, American Lady patt., clear, 3 1/2 oz., 4 5/8" h... 18

Claret, American patt., clear, 4 7/8" h., 7 oz........ 63

Cocktail, American Lady patt., cobalt blue, 3 1/2 oz., 4" h... 75

Cocktail, footed, American patt., clear, 3 oz........ 12

Cocktail, American Lady patt., clear, 3 1/2 oz., 4" h. 14

Cocktail, Holly cutting, clear, 3 1/2 oz., 5 1/4" h.. 25

Cocktail, Romance etching, clear, 3 1/2 oz........ 24

Cocktail, Chintz etching, clear, 5" h. 20

Cologne bottle w/original stopper, American patt., clear 100

Compote, 8", Lucere No. 1515, blue milk glass 75

Compote, cov., jelly, Colony patt., clear 45

Compote, cov., 6 1/2" h., Colony patt., clear....... 40

Compote, open, 4 3/8" h., Century patt., clear.. 25

Compote, open, 4 1/2" h., Navarre etching, clear 35

Condiment tray, cloverleaf-shaped, American patt., clear.. 250
Console set: bowl & pr. of double candlesticks; Chintz etching, clear, the set............. 125
Console set: No. 2402 Art Deco-style bowl & pair of candleholders, Ebony, the set.......... 85
Cordial, Colonial Dame patt., clear, 3 1/2" h... 42
Cordial, Colonial Dame patt., green bowl, clear foot & stem, 3 1/2" h....................... 46
Cordial, Mayflower etching, clear, 3 3/4" h........ 44
Cordial, June etching, Topaz, 3 7/8" h. 110
Cordial, Navarre etching, clear, 1 oz., 3 7/8" h.. 65
Cordial, Lido etching, clear, 4" h. 50
Cracker jar, cov., American patt., clear............ 800
Creamer, American patt., clear, medium 15
Creamer, American patt., hexagonal foot, clear 800
Creamer, Chintz etching, clear 20
Creamer, American patt., clear, 4 1/4" h., 9 1/2 oz. 12
Creamer, individual, Century patt., clear, 4 oz.. 9
Creamer, individual, Colony patt., clear, 3 1/4" h., 4 oz. 12
Creamer & cov. sugar bowl, American patt., clear, large, pr. 55
Creamer & open sugar bowl, Colony patt., clear, pr. 22
Creamer & open sugar bowl, Jamestown patt., pink, pr.. 50
Creamer, open sugar bowl & undertray, individual, American patt., clear, the set.......... 45
Creamer, open sugar bowl & undertray, individual size, Century patt., clear, the set.. 40
Creamer & sugar bowl, Coronet patt., clear, pr. 12
Creamer & sugar bowl, footed, Navarre etching, clear, 4 1/4" h., pr. 45
Creamer & sugar bowl, Romance etching, clear, pr. 20
Cruet w/original stopper, American patt., clear, 5 oz. 50
Cruet w/original stopper, Coin patt., clear, 6" h.. 60
Crushed fruit jar, cov., American patt., clear, 10" h. (chip on lid)......................... 1,600
Cup, footed, Colony patt., clear, 6 oz.................... 9
Cup, American patt., clear, 7 oz. 8
Cup, Century patt., clear 17
Cup & saucer, American patt., flared, clear 12
Cup & saucer, Century patt., clear 18
Cup & saucer, Colony patt., clear 15
Cup & saucer, Fairfax patt., orchid 14
Cup & saucer, Kashmir etching, blue.................. 56
Decanter w/original stopper, Coin patt., clear 110
Decanter w/original stopper, American patt., clear, 24 oz., 9 1/4" h. 120
Dresser bowl, oblong, American patt., clear, 1 3/4 x 5" 600
Figure of Madonna, clear, 10" h......................... 55
Figure of Madonna & Child, clear, 13 1/2" h. 95
Finger bowl, Colony patt., clear 75
Finger bowl, American patt., clear, 4 1/2" d. 90
Glove box, cov., American patt., clear (some stretch marks) 600
Goblet, American Lady patt., clear, 10 oz., 6 1/8" h. 24

Goblet, American Lady patt., cobalt blue, 10 oz., 6 1/8" h. 80
Goblet, American patt., clear, 5 1/2" h. 14
Goblet, American patt., clear, 5 1/2" h., 9 oz. 13
Goblet, American patt., clear, 6 7/8" h. 26
Goblet, American patt., hexagonal foot, clear, 10 oz....................................... 15
Goblet, Century patt., clear, 10 1/2 oz., 5 3/4" h. 25
Goblet, Chintz etching, clear, 9 oz...................... 34
Goblet, Colonial Dame patt., clear, 6 1/2" h........ 22
Goblet, Colony patt., clear, 5 1/4" h.................... 20
Goblet, Holly cutting, clear, 10 oz, 8 3/8" h. 40
Goblet, Jamestown patt., blue, 6" h..................... 26
Goblet, Jamestown patt., blue, 9 oz., 4 1/4" h. 26
Goblet, Jamestown patt., clear............................ 15
Goblet, Jamestown patt., green, 6" h.................. 22
Goblet, Jamestown patt., pink, 6" h..................... 26

June Etched Goblet

Goblet, June etching, clear, 8 1/4" h. (ILLUS.).. 46
Goblet, June etching, pink, 8 1/4" h..................... 94
Goblet, Lido etching, clear, 7 1/2" h.................... 28
Goblet, Navarre etching, blue, 10 oz. 45
Goblet, Navarre etching, clear, 7 5/8" oz. 52
Goblet, Navarre etching, pink, 7 5/8" oz. 72
Goblet, Romance etching, clear, 9 oz.................. 28
Goblet, Sunray patt., clear, 5 3/4" h.................... 22
Gravy boat w/undertray, Chintz etching, clear, 2 pcs. 75
Hair receiver, cov., American patt., clear, 3" sq. 725
Hairpin box, cov., American patt., clear, 1 1/2 x 1 2/4", 3 1/2" l. 2,000
Honey jar, cover & spoon, American patt., clear 500
Hurricane lamp, American patt., clear, 8 1/2" h... 325
Ice bowl, Colony patt., footed, clear 200
Ice bucket, Century patt., clear (no handle)........ 65
Ice bucket, Chintz etching, clear........................ 140
Ice bucket, Colony patt., clear........................... 200
Ice dish, American patt., clear............................ 45
Ice dish w/juice tumbler, Hermitage patt., Topaz 45
Ice tub, American patt., clear, 5 5/8" d., 3 3/4" h.. 98
Ice tub, American patt., clear, 6 1/2" d., 4 1/2" h... 65

Ice tub liner, American patt., clear, large............. 95
Jewel box, cov., American patt., clear,
2 1/4 x 5 1/4", 2" h.. 400
Marmalade, cover & spoon, American
patt., clear, the set... 120
Mayonnaise bowl, divided, American patt.,
clear, 3 1/4" d., 6 1/4" h. 20
Mayonnaise bowl, Century patt., clear.............. 35
Mayonnaise bowl, underplate & spoon,
Century patt., clear, 3 pcs. 70
Mayonnaise bowl w/underplate, Colony
patt., clear, 2 pcs. 35
Mayonnaise bowl w/underplate, Ro-
mance etching, clear, 2 pcs. 36
Muffin tray, American patt., clear, 10" l. 36
Mug, Bicentennial, No. 2493/705, clear, 15
oz.. 24
Mustard jar, cov., American patt., clear.............. 40
Mustard jar, cover & spoon, round, Amer-
ican patt., clear (inkwell), the set............... 1,200
Nappy, American patt., flared, green,
4 1/2" d.. 150
Nappy, handled, American patt., clear,
4 1/2" d.. 15
Nappy, handled, Century patt., clear,
4 1/2" d.. 10
Nappy, tri-cornered, handled, American
patt., clear, 5" w. 12
Nappy, American patt., deep, clear, 8" d. 90
Novelty, model of a top hat, American patt.,
clear, 2 1/2" h. 25
Olive dish, American patt., clear, 6" l. 15
Oyster cocktail, American Lady patt., clear,
4 oz., 3 1/2" h.. 14
Oyster cocktail, Colony patt., clear,
3 3/8" h., 4 oz. 20
Oyster cocktail, American patt., clear,
4 1/2 oz.. 13
Parfait, June etching, blue, 5 1/2" h. 94
Party plate, Century patt., clear, 8" d. 24
Pickle dish, Colony patt., clear............................ 25
Pickle dish, American patt., clear, 8" l. 15
Pickle dish, Century patt., clear, 8 3/4" l. 22
Pickle jar w/silverplated lid, cov., Ameri-
can patt., clear, 6" h. 550
Pin tray, oval, American patt., clear,
4 1/2 x 5 1/2".. 138
Pitcher, 6 1/2" h., American patt., clear, 3
pt. 85
Pitcher, American patt., clear, 1 pt...................... 40
Pitcher, milk, Century patt., clear 60
Pitcher, 5 3/8" h., Coin patt., ruby 140
Pitcher, 6 1/2" h., Coin patt., clear 89

Colony Pattern Pitcher

Pitcher, 7 3/4" h., Colony patt., No. 2412,
clear (ILLUS.)... 100
Pitcher, 7 1/2" h., Jamestown patt., pink 160
Pitcher, Jenny Lind patt., milk glass.................... 95
Pitcher, Sunray patt., frosted clear, 2 qt. 75
Pitcher, Vesper etching, No. 5100, footed,
amber.. 310
Pitcher w/ice lip, 8 1/2" h., Colony patt.,
clear, 3 pt... 260
Plate, bread & butter, 6" d., American patt.,
clear... 10
Plate, salad, 7" d., Baroque patt., clear................ 8
Plate, 7 3/8" d., Kashmir etching, blue 38
Plate, 7 1/2" d., Chintz etching, clear................... 17
Plate, 7 1/2" d., Navarre patt., clear..................... 18
Plate, salad, 7 1/2" d., American patt., clear....... 11
Plate, salad, 7 1/2" l., crescent-shaped,
Century patt., clear.. 30
Plate, 8 1/4" d., Jamestown patt., pink 21
Plate, 9" d., Colony patt., clear 25
Plate, 9 1/2" d., Colony patt., clear...................... 27
Plate, dinner, 9 1/2" d., American patt.,
clear... 24
Plate, dinner, 9 1/2" d., Trojan etching, to-
paz... 25
Plate, 12" d., footed, Colony patt., clear............ 125
Plate, torte, 13" d., Colony patt., clear 35
Plate, torte, 13 1/2" oval, American patt.,
clear... 45
Plate, torte, 14" d., American patt., clear 55
Plate, torte, 14" d., Century patt., clear 30
Plate, torte, 14" d., Holly cutting, clear 65
Plate, torte, 15" d., Colony patt., clear................ 60
Plate, dinner, Chintz etching, clear 75
Plate, Holly cutting, clear 25
Plate, Meadow Rose etching, clear 12
Plate, salad, American Lady patt., cobalt
blue.. 15
Plate, sandwich, center handle, Colony
patt., clear... 35
Platter, 10 1/2" l., American patt., clear 60
Platter, 12" l., American patt., clear 65
Pomade or rouge box, cov., American
patt., clear, 2" sq... 395
Puff box, cov., American patt., clear,
1 1/2" d.. 725
Puff box, cov., American patt., clear,
2 1/2" d.. 700
Puff box, cov., American patt., clear, 3" sq....... 225
Puff box, cov., American patt., clear, 4 1/2"
sq. 1,400
Punch bowl, Tom & Jerry-type, pedestal
footed, American patt., clear, 12" d. 235
Punch cup, American patt., clear 8
Relish dish, boat-shaped, handled, divid-
ed, American patt., clear, 12" l. 30
Relish dish, two-part, Colony patt., clear,
7 1/4" 16
Relish dish, two-part, Century patt., clear,
7 3/8" l... 22
Relish dish, two-part, Chintz etching, clear 38
Relish dish, three-part, American patt.,
clear, 9 1/2" l... 45
Relish dish, three-part, two-handled, Colo-
ny patt., clear, 13" 35
Relish dish, three-part, Romance etching,
clear... 45
Relish dish, four-part, rectangular, Ameri-
can patt., clear, 9" l.. 45
Relish dish, four-part, American patt.,
clear, 10" sq.. 190

Ring holder, American patt., clear............. **650-750**
Rose bowl, Baroque patt., topaz........................... **60**

Victoria Pattern Rose Bowl

Rose bowl, Victoria patt., clear w/satin finish (ILLUS.).. **200**
Rose bowl, American patt., clear, 5" d................ **35**

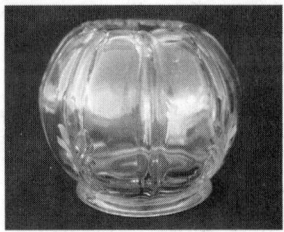

Baroque Rose Bowl

Rose bowl, Baroque patt., blue (ILLUS.)..... **75-100**
Rose bowl, Colony patt., footed, clear.............. **125**
Salt dip w/spoon, American patt., clear, 2 pcs.. **20**
Salt & pepper shakers, Century patt., clear, pr. **20**
Salt & pepper shakers, Coin patt., ruby, pr. **70**
Salt & pepper shakers, Colony patt., clear, 3 5/8" h., pr. **15-20**
Salt & pepper shakers, Coronet patt., footed, clear, pr. **15**
Salt & pepper shakers, Mesa patt., No. 4186, ruby, pr. **28**
Salt & pepper shakers, Navarre etching, clear, 3 1/4" h., pr. **150**
Salt shakers, individual, American patt., clear, 3" h., set of 3............................. **37**
Salver, Century patt., clear, 12 1/4" **90**
Sauce boat & underplate, American patt., clear, 2 pcs. **85**
Sherbet, American Lady patt., clear, 5 1/2 oz., 4 1/8" h... **15**
Sherbet, American Lady patt., cobalt blue, 5 1/2 oz., 4 1/8" h.................................... **60**
Sherbet, American patt., footed, handled, clear, 4 1/2 oz... **145**
Sherbet, American patt., low, flared, clear, 5 oz., 3 1/4" h....................................... **11**
Sherbet, Century patt., clear, 5 1/2 oz., 4 1/4" h. **13**
Sherbet, Chintz etching, clear................................ **21**
Sherbet, Coin patt., clear, 5 1/8" h. **26**
Sherbet, Jamestown patt., amber **9**
Sherbet, Jamestown patt., blue, 6 1/2 oz., 4 1/4" h. **17**
Sherbet, Navarre patt., clear, 6 oz. **24**
Shrimp bowl, American patt., clear, 12 1/4"..... **395**

Spice box, cov., American patt., clear **900**
Spooner, American patt., clear, 3 3/4" h............. **62**

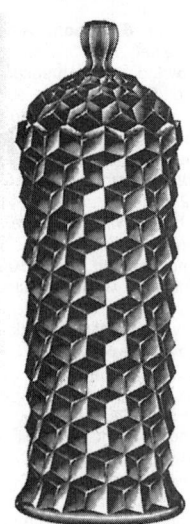

American Pattern Straw Jar

Straw jar, cov., American patt., clear (ILLUS.).. **323**
Sugar bowl, cov., American patt., clear, 5 1/4" h... **60**
Sugar bowl, individual, Baroque patt., Topaz **30**
Sugar bowl, individual, Colony patt., clear.......... **15**
Sugar bowl, individual, Century patt., clear, 3 3/8" h.. **9**
Sugar bowl, American patt., clear, medium........ **15**
Sugar bowl, American patt., hexagonal foot, clear.. **800**
Sugar bowl, Chintz etching, clear......................... **20**
Sugar shaker, American patt., clear, tall **235**
Sundae, American patt., clear, 6 oz., 3 1/8" h.. **12**
Syrup pitcher, cov., American patt., clear, 5 1/4" h.. **120**
Toothpick holder, American patt., clear **24**
Toothpick holder, Priscilla patt., No. 676, clear... **45**
Tray, tidbit, Colony patt., clear w/patterned top **85**
Tray, tidbit, Colony patt., three-toed, clear, 7 1/2" **22**
Tray, muffin, handled, Colony patt., clear, 8 3/8" **45**
Tray, snack, Colony patt., clear, 10 1/2" **40**
Tray, center-handled, Chintz etching, clear, 11" d. **40**
Tray for creamer & sugar bowl, Colony patt., clear... **18**
Trifle bowl, American patt., deep, clear............. **395**
Tumbler, Coin patt., ruby, 9 oz., 4 1/4" h........... **105**
Tumbler, Colony patt., clear, 4" h. **22**
Tumbler, footed, American patt., clear, 9 oz., 4 3/8" h... **15**
Tumbler, footed, Kashmir etching, green, 5" h. **42**
Tumbler, footed, Line 4020, black foot, clear bowl... **32**

American Pattern Iced Tea Tumbler

Tumbler, iced tea, American patt., clear, 12 oz., 5 3/4" h. (ILLUS.) **22**
Tumbler, iced tea, Coin patt., ruby, 5 1/2" h. **95**
Tumbler, iced tea, footed, Colony patt., clear, 12 oz., 5 1/2" h. **26**
Tumbler, iced tea, footed, Holly cutting, clear, 12 oz., 6" h. **18**
Tumbler, iced tea, footed, Jamestown patt., blue **28**
Tumbler, iced tea, June etching, Topaz **58**
Tumbler, Jamestown patt., amber, 12 oz., 5 1/8" **28**
Tumbler, Jamestown patt., amber, 9 oz., 4 1/4" h. **15**
Tumbler, Jamestown patt., green, 5 1/4" h. **28**
Tumbler, juice, footed, American Lady patt., clear, 5 oz., 4 1/8" h. **14**
Tumbler, juice, footed, American Lady patt., cobalt blue, 5 oz., 4 1/8" h. **65**
Tumbler, juice, footed, Jamestown patt., blue **21**
Tumbler, juice, footed, Jamestown patt., smoke, 5 oz., 4 3/4" h. **10**
Tumbler, juice, Jamestown patt., ruby, 4 3/4" h. **22**
Tumbler, juice, Mayflower etching, clear, 4 7/8" h. **19**
Tumbler, whiskey, American patt., clear, 2 oz., 2 1/2" h. **15**
Urn, cov., Colony patt., clear w/patterned base **85**
Vase, sweet pea, 4 1/2" h., American patt., clear **75**

Navarre Etched Vase

Vase, 5" h., Navarre etching, No. 4128, clear (ILLUS.) **125**
Vase, 6" h., American patt., aqua **150**
Vase, 6" h., American patt., peach **150**
Vase, 6" h., handled, Coronet patt., clear............. **45**
Vase, bud, 6" d., Colony patt., clear **20**
Vase, 6 1/2" h., footed, American patt., amber **80**

Vase, 7" h., footed, cupped, Colony patt., clear **60**
Vase, 7 1/2" h., handled, Century patt., clear **95**
Vase, 9 1/2" h., flared rim, American patt., clear **175**
Vase, 10" h., cupped-in top, American patt., clear **250**
Vase, 10" h., straight sides, American patt., clear **95**
Vase, 12" h., Colony patt., clear **275**
Vase, 12" h., straight sides, American patt., clear **150**
Vase, 13" h., Lotus patt., amber **220**
Vase, 14" h., Colony patt., clear **550**
Vase, 18" h., Heirloom patt. No. 5056, blue opalescent **74**
Vase, bud, Coin patt., clear **20**
Vase, bud, Coin patt., ruby **38**
Vase, Coin patt., clear **34**
Vegetable bowl, Century patt., clear, 9 1/2" oval **40**
Water bottle, American patt., clear, 9 1/4" h., 44 oz. **800**
Water carafe, Carmen patt., ca. 1900, clear........ **95**
Water set: pitcher w/ice lip & six flared tumblers; American patt., clear, 7 pcs. **100**
Wedding bowl, American patt., clear, large.. **1,000**
Wine, American Lady patt., clear, 2 1/2 oz. **28**
Wine, American patt., clear, 2 1/2 oz., 4 3/8" h. **15**
Wine, Century patt., clear, 3 1/2 oz., 4 1/2" h. **24**
Wine, Chintz etching, clear.................................... **44**
Wine, Colonial Dame patt., green bowl, clear foot & stem, 4 3/4" h. **36**
Wine, Jamestown patt., amber, 4 oz., 4 5/16" h. **15**
Wine, Jamestown patt., green, 4 5/16" h., 4 oz. **22**
Wine, Jamestown patt., pink, 4 5/16" h., 4 oz. **26**
Wine, June etching, pink, 5 3/8" h....................... **112**
Wine, Navarre etching, clear, 6 1/2" h................. **90**
Wine, Navarre etching, clear, 7 1/4" h................ **150**
Wine, Navarre etching, pink, 6 1/2" h. **82**
Wine, Romance etching, clear, 3 oz. **35**
Wine, Sunray patt., clear, 4 7/8" h. **32**

Fry

Numerous types of glass were made by the H.C. Fry Company, Rochester, Pennsylvania. One of its art lines was called Foval and was blown in 1926-27. Cheaper was its milky-opalescent ovenware (Pearl Oven Ware) made for utilitarian purposes but also now being collected. The company also made fine cut glass.

Collectors of Fry Glass will be interested in the recent publication of a good reference book, The Collector's Encyclopedia of Fry Glassware, *by The H.C. Fry Glass Society (Collector Books, 1990).*

Fry Foval Beverage Set

Beverage set: 10 1/2" h. jug-form pitcher, 6 1/2" h. spherical cov. teapot & six 4 1/2" h. conical tumblers; Foval, each in a white body decorated around the body w/a slender silver overlay scroll & vine design, applied jade green handle on pitcher & teapot, also teapot spout & feet, one tumbler w/overlay loss, nicks to teapot cover, the set (ILLUS.) **$1,500**

Candlesticks, Foval, opalescent wide disc foot w/a blue connector to the tall slender cylindrical white shaft wrapped w/a thin thread of blue below a translucent blue bobeche supporting the pearl white cylindrical socket w/gently flared rim, ca. 1926, one w/faint Fry Shield acid stamp, 10 3/8" h., pr. **345**

Creamer, Foval, creamy opalescent body w/applied green handle...................................... **44**

Cruet w/original stopper, Foval, milky white w/a Delft blue stopper & applied handle, 9 3/4" h. **135**

Pitcher, cov., 11" h., water, Foval, milky white w/Delft blue finial & applied handle, early 20th c. **225**

Fry Foval Footed Vase

Vase, 8 1/2" h., Foval, tall waisted cylindrical body w/flared & ruffled rim, on an applied foot w/a blue applied squared knop (ILLUS.).. **110**

Vase, 12" h., cylindrical, Pearl art line, pulled loopings, pink....................................... **375**

Gallé

Gallé glass was made in Nancy, France, by Emile Gallé, a founder of the Nancy School and a leader in the Art Nouveau movement in France. Much of his glass, both enameled and cameo, is decorated with naturalistic motifs. The finest pieces were made in the last two decades of the 19th century and the opening years of the 20th.

Pieces marked with a star preceding the name were made between 1904, the year of Gallé's death, and 1914.

Cameo vase, 2 1/2" h., miniature, wide pear-shaped body w/short wide cylindrical neck, grey overlaid w/amethyst & etched w/violets, signed in cameo, early 20th c. **$460**

Cameo vase, 2 3/4" h., miniature, shouldered ovoid body in rose & white overlaid w/green & cut w/flowers, signed.................... **863**

Cameo vase, 3 5/8" h., footed wide squared form w/rounded edges & shoulder centering a low molded mouth, yellow & grey overlaid in purple & carved w/clematis, signed in cameo, ca. 1900......... **805**

Cameo vase, 5 3/4" h., spherical body tapering to a tiny neck w/wide deep cupped rim, yellow ground overlaid in pale blue, sea green & aubergine & etched w/a wooded lake scene featuring fir trees & mountains in the distance, signed **3,450**

Cameo vase, 8 3/4" h., pilgrim flask-form, flattened round body tapering to a short narrow neck w/cupped rim, applied small S-scroll handles from rim to shoulder, grey overlaid w/peach, yellow & lime green, cut w/pendent sycamore branches w/leaves & seed pods, signed in cameo w/a star after the name, 1904-10 .... **2,415**

Cameo vase, 8 3/4" h., very wide tapering ovoid body w/a small trumpet-form neck, lemon yellow ground overlaid in teal & plum blue & etched w/a profusion of asters & foliage, cameo signature **4,830**

Cameo vase, 9" h., ovoid body raised on a low flaring foot & w/a short flaring neck, grey shaded orange & mottled w/lemon yellow, overlaid w/brown & cut w/orchids & leaves, signed in cameo, ca. 1900 .... **2,875**

Cameo vase, 10" h., slightly tapering cylindrical form w/a narrow neck below a wide cupped rim, grey shaded w/peach, overlaid w/purple & green & carved w/hydrangea, signed in cameo "Gallé," ca. 1900..... **1,840**

Cameo vase, 11" h., spherical body w/a small trumpet neck, shaded light amber & clear frosted ground overlaid w/dark brown down the neck & shoulders & cut w/pendent grapevine suspending "blown-out" golden grape clusters, signed in cameo **5,750**

Large Gallé Vase with Clematis

Cameo vase, 13 3/8" h., tall tapering cylindrical body w/a narrow wide shoulder centering a low two-lobed pinched-in neck, frosted ground overlaid in lavender & etched w/clematis in bloom, cameo signature (ILLUS.) **1,840**

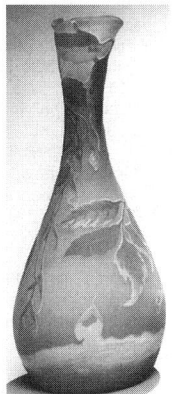

Gallé Cameo Vase with Branches

Cameo vase, 15" h., flat-bottomed ovoid form tapering to a slender trumpet neck w/lobed rim, pink shading to white, overlaid in yellow & green & cut w/leafy branches, signed (ILLUS.) **1,840**

Cameo vase, 18 3/8" h., narrow cushion foot below the tall slender tapering sides, grey opalescent mottled & shaded w/egg yolk yellow, overlaid in blue & deep purple & cut w/clusters of berries pendent from tendrilled leafy vines, signed in cameo, ca. 1900 .... **6,785**

Rare Small Gallé Flacon

Flacon, cov., footed ovoid body tapering to a short cylindrical neck w/low-domed fitted cap, optic-ribbed, the neck in deep lavender shading to pale amethyst & deep amethyst at the base, applied shell-form appliques on the shoulder, the body enameled w/stylized stems, leaves & blossoms in light brown & green, enameled in intaglio "E. Gallé - déposé," 5 1/4" h. (ILLUS.) **5,750**

Vase, 12 1/4" h., bulbous melon-lobed base tapering to a tall very slender waisted neck, pale amber cut w/daisies on an acid-etched ground & enameled yellowish orange, purplish brown, green & gilt, gilt incised signature, ca. 1900 .... **2,587**

Heisey

Numerous types of fine glass were made by A.H. Heisey & Co., Newark, Ohio, from 1895. The company's trademark, an H enclosed within a diamond, has become known to most glass collectors. The company's name and molds were acquired by Imperial Glass Co., Bellaire, Ohio, in 1958, and some pieces have been reissued. The glass listed below consists of miscellaneous pieces and types. Also see ANIMALS and PATTERN GLASS.

Heisey Diamond "H" Mark

Ashtray, Crystolite patt., clear, 3" sq. **$12**
Basket, Lariat patt., footed, clear, 10" **325**
Bowl, cream soup, two-handled, Yeoman patt., Sahara (yellow) **30**
Bowl, 6" d., Empress patt., Sahara **35**
Bowl, jelly, 6 1/2" d., footed, Orchid etching, clear **70**
Bowl, 8" d., Rococo patt., clear **85**
Bowl, 8" d., Twist patt., nasturtium-type, Moongleam (light green) **109**
Bowl, 9" d., Twist patt., floral-type, Moongleam **69**
Bowl, gardenia, 9" d., Queen Anne patt., Orchid etching, clear **60**
Bowl, 10" d., Queen Anne patt., Orchid etching, crimped rim, clear **110**
Bowl, 11" d., floral-style, New Era patt., clear **85**
Bowl, 11" d., floral-type, Minuet etching, clear **125**

Ridgeleigh Floral Bowl

Bowl, 11 1/2" d., oval, floral-type, Ridgeleigh patt., clear (ILLUS.) **65**
Bowl, 13" d., floral-type, shallow, Rose etching, clear **100**
Bowl, 13" l., oval, floral-type, Ipswich patt., clear **36**
Butter dish, cov., Orchid etching, clear **145**
Butter dish, cov., Rose etching, clear **200**
Butter dish, cov., square, Orchid etching, clear **235**

Butter dish, cov., Rose etching, clear, cabachon, 1/4 lb. 375

Cake plate, footed, Rose etching, clear, 15" d. 325

Candleholder, dolphin-footed, Queen Anne patt., No. 1509, clear 45

Candlesticks, one-light, Orchid etching, clear, 3" h., pr. 50

Candlesticks, Pluto patt., No. 114, Moongleam, 3 1/2" h., pr. 60

Candlesticks, two-light, Lariat patt., clear, pr. 80

Candlesticks, two-light, Lariat patt. w/Moonglo cutting, clear, pr. 100

Candlesticks, two-light, No. 301, amber arms, pr. 485

Candlesticks, two-light, Waverly patt., Orchid etching, clear, pr. 120

Candlesticks, three-light, Empress patt., No. 301, Sahara w/clear bobeches, pr. 950

Candlesticks, three-light, Rose etching, clear, pr. 300

Candy box, cov., round, Stanhope patt., clear w/black knob stem on round foot 350

Candy dish, cov., Lariat patt., caramel 75

Candy dish, cov., Rose etching, clear, tall, seahorse finial 250

Candy dish, cov., tall, Plantation patt., clear, 8" h. 400

Candy dish, cov., tall w/seahorse stem, Orchid etching, clear 250

Candy dish, cov., Plantation patt., clear, 5" h. 195

Catsup bottle w/stopper, Old Sandwich patt., clear 70

Celery dish, Plantation patt., clear, 13" l. 50

Celery tray, Empress patt., Sahara 45

Celery tray, Rose etching, Waverly blank, clear, 12" l. 70

Celery tray, New Era patt., clear, 13" l. 40

Celery vase, Fandango patt., clear 85

Champagne, Lariat patt., clear 22

Champagne, saucer-type, Albermarle patt., clear 25

Champagne, saucer-type, Carcassone patt., clear stem w/Sahara bowl, 6 oz. 40

Champagne, saucer-type, Minuet etching, No. 5010, clear, 6 oz. 30

Champagne, saucer-type, Old Dominion patt., Empress etching, clear stem w/Marigold (dark yellow) bowl 30

Champagne, saucer-type, Orchid etching, clear, 6 oz. 45

Champagne, saucer-type, Pied Piper etching, clear 28

Cheese dish, cov., Lariat patt., footed, clear, 5" d. 55

Cigarette box, cov., Lariat patt., clear 55

Cigarette holder, square, footed, Orchid etching, clear 95

Claret, New Era patt., clear, 4 oz. 27

Coaster, Lariat patt., clear 12

Coaster, Plantation patt., clear, 4" d. 50

Cocktail, Carcassone patt., clear stem w/Sahara bowl, 3 oz. 35

Cocktail, figural rooster stem, clear 75

Cocktail, figural sea horse stem, clear 175

Cocktail, Lariat patt. w/Moonglo cutting, clear 32

Cocktail, Minuet etching, No. 5010, clear, 3 1/2 oz. 40

Cocktail, New Era patt., high stem, clear, 3 1/2 oz. 25

Cocktail, Orchid etching, clear, 4 oz. 58

Cocktail, Orchid etching, No. 5025, clear, 4 oz. 58

Cocktail, Rosalie etching, Kenilworth (No. 4092) blank, clear, 3 oz. 18

Cocktail, saucer-type, Old Dominion patt., Empress etching, clear stem w/Marigold bowl 25

Cocktail, Stanhope patt., clear, 3 1/2 oz. 35

Cocktail icer w/insert, Orchid etching, clear 275

Cocktail shaker, cov., Orchid etching, No. 4225, clear, 1 pt. 295

Compote, 6" h., Waverly patt., Orchid etching, clear 50

Compote, 6 1/2" d., Rose etching, Waverly blank, low footed, clear 70

Compote, 7" h., Empress patt., oval, Sahara 110

Compote, 7" h., oval, Rose etching, clear 158

Compote, 7" h., Twist patt., Flamingo (pink) 85

Compote, Charter Oak etching, pink 65

Compote, footed, low, Orchid etching, clear 65

Cordial, New Era patt., clear, 1 oz. 75

Cordial, Rose etching, clear, 1 oz. 200

Cordial, Chintz patt., No. 3389, clear, 1 oz. 120

Cornucopia-vase, Warwick patt., cobalt blue, signed, 5 1/2" h. 225

Creamer, dolphin-footed, Empress patt., Sahara 55

Creamer, Empress patt., pink 55

Creamer, miniature, Sawtooth Band patt., floral etching, ca. 1900 55

Creamer, Ridgeleigh patt., clear 30

Creamer, individual size, Ridgeleigh patt., clear 32

Creamer & open sugar bowl, footed, Plantation patt., clear, pr. 90

Creamer & open sugar bowl, individual size, Rose etching, clear, pr. 90

Creamer & open sugar bowl, individual, oval, Empress patt., Sahara, pr. 90

Heisey Twist Pattern Cruet

Cruet w/original stopper, Twist patt., Moongleam (ILLUS.). 110

Cruet w/stopper, Orchid etching, footed, 3 oz. 200

Cruet w/stopper, Rose etching, clear 225

Cruets, oil, Lariat patt., clear, 6 oz., pr. 115

Cup, Old Sandwich patt., pink 60

Cup, Waverly patt., clear 12

Cup & saucer, Crystolite patt., clear.................... 24
Cup & saucer, Empress patt., Sahara 48
Cup & saucer, footed, Orchid etching, clear....... 60
Cup & saucer, New Era patt., clear.................... 65
Cup & saucer, Rose etching, clear..................... 75
Cup & saucer, Waverly patt., clear..................... 35
Decanter w/sterling stopper, sherry, Or-
  chid etching, clear.. 270
Decanter w/stopper, Old Sandwich patt.,
  cobalt blue, No. 98, 1 pt................................. 625
Decanter w/stopper, sherry, oval, Orchid
  etching, clear.. 260
Decanters w/stoppers, Ridgeleigh patt.,
  clear, 1 pt., pr. 325
Goblet, Albemarle patt., clear 30
Goblet, Carcassone patt., clear stem w/Sa-
  hara bowl, 11 oz. 55
Goblet, Carcassone patt., clear stem w/Sa-
  hara bowl, 11 oz., short 50
Goblet, Empress patt., Sahara, 9 oz. 90
Goblet, Graceful patt., No. 5022, clear................ 25
Goblet, Lariat patt., blown, clear, 10 oz.............. 25
Goblet, Lariat patt. w/Moonglo cutting,
  clear, 10 oz. 35
Goblet, Minuet etching, clear 45
Goblet, Old Dominion patt., Marigold,
  8 3/4" h. 55
Goblet, Orchid etching, clear, tall, 10 oz. 55
Goblet, Orchid etching, low stem, No. 5025,
  clear, 10 oz. 45
Goblet, Rose etching, clear, 9 oz. 60
Goblet, Twist patt., Flamingo, 9 oz. 50
Goblet, Victorian patt., two-ball stem, clear........ 26
Goblets, Victorian patt., clear, 9 oz., set of 8..... 110
Ice tub, Twist patt., Moongleam........................... 95
Jelly dish, two-handled, Plantation patt., Ivy
  etching, 6 1/2" h. 45
Lemon dish, cov., Yeoman patt., round,
  Moongleam, 5" d.. 45
Mayonnaise set, Rose etching, clear, 3
  pcs.. 135
Mustard jar, cover & spoon, Empress
  patt., Sahara.. 140
Nut dish, footed, Empress patt., Sahara............. 35
Nut dish or ashtray, individual size, New
  Era patt., clear... 60
Oil cruet w/original stopper, Victorian
  patt., clear, 3 oz. 75
Oyster cocktail, footed, Ipswich patt., clear....... 12
Parfait, Yeoman patt., clear................................. 9
Pilsner glass, New Era patt., clear, 12 oz.......... 60
Pitcher, blown, w/ice lip, Plantation patt.,
  clear, 1/2 gal. 600
Pitcher, Orchid etching, Donna blank (No.
  3484), clear, 1/2 gal. 625
Pitcher, Rose etching, clear, 76 oz. 660

Heisey Puritan Pitcher

Pitcher, water, Puritan patt., clear, 3 qt.
  (ILLUS.)... 250
Pitcher, Orchid etching, clear............................ 535
Plate, dinner, Orchid etching, clear 180

Plate, 4 3/4" d., Colonial patt., clear...................... 5
Plate, 6" d., Empress patt., Sahara..................... 18
Plate, 6" w., New Era patt., clear......................... 35
Plate, 7" d., Empress patt., Moongleam.............. 18
Plate, 7" d., Empress patt., Sahara..................... 18
Plate, 7" d., Empress patt., Tangerine (deep
  orangish red)... 165
Plate, 7" d., two-handled, Crystolite patt.,
  clear.. 20
Plate, salad, 7" d., Crystolite patt., clear............. 15
Plate, salad, 7" d., Orchid etching, clear............. 25
Plate, 7 1/2" d., Empress patt., Alexandrite
  (lavender).. 90
Plate, 8" d., Fandango patt., clear...................... 50
Plate, 8" d., luncheon, Minuet etching, clear....... 28
Plate, 8" sq., Empress patt., Sahara................... 18
Plate, torte, 14" d., Waverly patt., Rose
  etching, clear.. 85
Plate, center-handled, Orchid etching, clear..... 135
Plate, dinner, Acorn patt., clear 59
Plate, dinner, Lariat patt., clear 115
Plate, dinner, Rose etching, clear 195
Punch bowl, Ridgeleigh patt., clear, 11" d........ 169
Punch cup, Lariat patt., clear 16
Punch cup, Locket & Chain patt., ca. 1900,
  clear.. 45
Punch set: 9 qt. Dr. Johnson punch bowl,
  six cups & ladle; Plantation patt., clear, 8
  pcs.. 1,100
Punch set: 14" d. punch bowl, 21" d. under-
  plate, six punch cups & ladle; Lariat patt.,
  clear, 9 pcs. 190
Punch set: 14" d. punch bowl, 21" d. under-
  plate & eight punch cups; Lariat patt.,
  original hooks, clear, 10 pcs. 225
Relish dish, three-part, New Era patt.,
  clear, 13" l. 40
Relish dish, three-part, Orchid etching, Wa-
  verly blank, clear, 11" l. 75
Relish dish, three-part, Plantation patt.,
  clear, 11" l. 67
Relish dish, three-part, Rose etching, oval,
  clear, 11" l. 80
Relish dish, three-part, Lariat patt., clear,
  12"... 45
Relish dish, three-part, Crystolite patt.,
  clear, 9 1/2" 29
Relish dish, four-part, round, Rose etching,
  Waverly blank, clear, 9" d. 75
Relish dish, four-part, Plantation patt.,
  clear, 8" l. 95
Relish tray, three-part, Crystolite patt.,
  clear, 12" l. 32
Rose bowl, Mermaid etching, clear, 5" d.......... 500

Heisey Pillows Rose Bowl

Rose bowl, pedestal foot, Pillows patt. (No.
  325), clear (ILLUS.)................................. **225-250**

Salt dip, Fandango patt., No. 1201, clear 22
Salt & pepper shakers, Orchid etching,
  clear, pr. 100
Salt & pepper shakers, Rose etching,
  clear, pr. 120
Sandwich server, center-handled, Rose
  etching, Waverly blank, clear, 14" d. 240
Sherbet, blown, Lariat patt., clear, 5 oz. 14
Sherbet, Carcassone patt., clear stem
  w/Sahara bowl, 6 oz. 30
Sherbet, Colonial patt., clear 10
Sherbet, Lariat patt. w/Moonglo cutting,
  clear 20
Sherbet, low, Old Dominion patt., Empress
  etching, clear stem w/Marigold bowl 18
Sherbet, Orchid etching, No. 5025, clear 25
Sherbet, Pied Piper etching, clear 25
Sherbet, Rose etching, clear, 6 oz. 40
Sherbet, Victorian patt., two-ball stem, clear 15
Spooner, large, Greek Key patt., clear 110
Stem, Saturn patt., Zircon (blue green),
  10 oz. 125
Sugar bowl, dolphin-footed, Empress patt.,
  Sahara 40
Sugar bowl, Lariat patt., clear 20
Syrup bottle w/top, Plantation patt., clear 150
Toothpick holder, Continental patt., clear 135
Toothpick holder, Pineapple & Fan patt.,
  green 295
Tray, oval, Ridgeleigh patt., clear, 10 1/2" l. 65
Tumbler, iced tea, footed, Lariat patt.,
  Moonglo cutting, clear, 12 oz. 32
Tumbler, iced tea, Minuet etching, No.
  5010, 12 oz. 60
Tumbler, iced tea, Orchid etching, clear,
  12 oz. 64
Tumbler, iced tea, Orchid etching, No.
  5025, clear, 9 1/2 oz. 80
Tumbler, iced tea, Twentieth Century patt.,
  Dawn (light grey) 60
Tumbler, juice, Carcassone patt., clear
  stem w/Sahara bowl, 5 oz. 35
Tumbler, juice, Ipswich patt., Sahara 75
Tumbler, juice, Plantation patt., footed
  pressed, clear, 5 oz. 65
Tumbler, juice, Provincial patt., footed,
  clear, 5 oz. 18
Tumbler, juice, Twist patt., footed, Flamin-
  go, 5 oz. 29
Tumbler, soda, Ipswich patt., clear, 5 oz. 25
Tumbler, soda, Ipswich patt., clear, 8 oz. 20
Tumbler, toddy, Old Sandwich patt., clear,
  6 1/2 oz. 18
Tumbler, water, Ipswich patt., Sahara 60
Tumbler, Rose etching, juice, footed, clear,
  5 oz. 60
Tumbler, Arch patt., cobalt blue 180
Tumbler, Duquesne patt., Tangerine,
  5 1/4" h. 155
Tumbler, Greek Key patt., flat, clear, 10 oz. 99
Tumbler, Provincial patt., footed, clear,
  8 oz. 24
Tumbler, Saturn patt., flat bottom, Zircon,
  10 oz. 150
Tumblers, iced tea, Lariat patt., Moonglo
  etching, blown, footed, 12 oz., set of six 250
Vase, 4" h., Ivy, No. 4224, clear 125
Vase, 7" h., Lariat patt., footed, clear 45
Vase, 7" h., Warwick patt., Sahara 250
Violet vase, Orchid etching, clear, 4" h. 145

Wine, Albermarle patt., clear, 2 1/2 oz. 25
Wine, Orchid etching, No. 5025, clear, 3 oz. 95
Wine, pressed Lariat patt., clear, 3 1/2 oz. 20

Holly Amber

Holly Amber, originally marketed under the name "Golden Agate," was produced for only a few months in 1903 by the Indiana Tumbler and Goblet Company of Greentown, Indiana. When this factory burned in June 1903 all production of this ware ceased, making it very rare today. The same "Holly" pressed pattern was also produced in clear glass by the Greentown factory. Collectors should note that the St. Clair Glass Company and several other firms have produced some Holly Amber pieces.

Holly Amber Compote

Compote, open, made from two lids
  (ILLUS.) **$800**

Holly Amber Creamer

Creamer (ILLUS.) 550
Pitcher, water 3,200
Sauce dish, round 265

Holly Amber Tumbler with Rim Beads

Tumbler, beads on rim (ILLUS.) 700
Tumbler, plain rim 440
Vase, 6" h. 650

Imperial

Imperial Glass Company, Bellaire, Ohio was organized in 1901 and was in continuous production, except for very brief periods, until its closing in June 1984. It had been a major producer of Carnival Glass early in the 20th century and also produced other types of glass, including an art glass line called "Free Hand Ware" during the 1920s and its "Jewels" about 1916. The company acquired a number of molds of other earlier factories, including the Cambridge and A.H. Heisey Companies, and reissued numerous items through the years. Also see CARNIVAL GLASS.

Candlewick

Ashtray, heart-shaped, clear, 4"........................ **$11**
Ashtray, clear, No. 400/133, 5" d......................... **12**
Ashtray, No. 400/60, clear, 6"............................ **150**
Ashtray, w/embossed eagle center, No. 1776/1, clear, 6 1/2" **70**
Ashtray, No. 400/118, clear **12**
Ashtray set, nested, round, No. 400/450, clear, 3 pcs. **50**
Baked apple dish, No. 400/53X, blue, 6 1/2"... **85**
Baked apple dish, No. 400/53X, clear, 6 1/2"... **25**
Basket, No. 400/40/0, clear, 6 1/2" h. **40**
Basket, No. 400/40/0, clear w/gold beads, 6 1/2" h. **60**
Basket, No. 400/73/0, clear, 11"........................ **255**

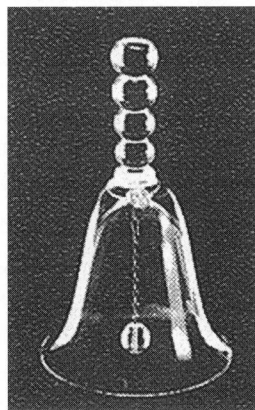

Candlewick Bell

Bell, No. 400/108, clear, 5" h. (ILLUS.) **59**
Bonbon, heart-shaped, handled, clear, 5"........... **24**
Bonbon bowl, handled, No. 400/40H, clear, 5"... **25**
Bonbon bowl, handled, No. 400/51H, clear, 6" **36**
Bonbon bowl, heart-shaped, No. 400/174, clear, 6 1/2".. **22**
Bowl, 5", heart-shaped, clear............................... **18**
Bowl, 5", heart-shaped, No. 400/49H, clear **175**
Bowl, 5" sq., No. 400/231, clear....................... **150**
Bowl, 5 1/2", heart-shaped, No. 500/53H, clear.. **45**
Bowl, cream soup, 5 1/2" d., No. 400/50, clear... **50**
Bowl, 6" d., clear, No. 400/3F **12**
Bowl, 6" h., No. 400/182, three-toed, clear......... **73**

Bowl, 7" sq., No. 400/233, clear......................... **160**
Bowl, 8-8 1/2" d., No. 400/74B, clear **110**
Bowl, 8-8 1/2" d., No. 400/74B, ruby **450**
Bowl, 8 1/2" d., handled, No. 400/72B, clear....... **39**
Bowl, 8 1/2" d., No. 400/69, clear w/cutting......... **55**
Bowl, 9" sq., No. 400/74SC, four-toed, crimped, ribbed, black w/flower..................... **550**
Bowl, 9-10", heart-shaped, No. 400/73H, clear... **105**
Bowl, 10" d., fruit, footed, No. 400/103C, clear... **229**
Bowl, 10-11", No. 400/75F, float-type, clear....... **45**
Bowl, salad, 10" d., No. 400/75B, clear **50**
Bowl, 10 1/2" d., bell-shaped, No. 400/63B, clear... **55**
Bowl, 10 1/2" d., No. 400/63B, clear................... **55**
Bowl, 11" l., oval, divided, No. 400/125A, clear... **550**
Bowl w/underplate, 8" d., two-handled w/10" underplate, bowl No. 400/4272B, underplate No. 400/4272D, clear, the set....... **55**
Butter dish, cov., No. 400/144, clear, 5 1/2" d.. **30**
Butter dish, cov., No. 400/276, clear **140**
Butter dish, cov., round, clear............................. **64**

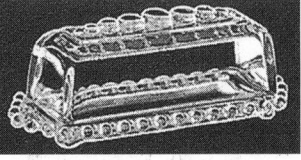

Candlewick Butter Dish

Butter dish, cov., w/beaded top, No. 400/161, clear, 1/4 lb. (ILLUS.) **45**
Butter & jam dish, No. 400/262, three-part, clear, 10 1/2".. **193**
Cake plate, 71 birthday candle holes, clear, 13"... **450**
Cake plate, No. 400/160, clear w/swirl center, 72 candle holes in rim, 13-14" d. **450**
Cake plate, two-handled, clear, 13" d. **75**
Cake stand, No. 400/67D, low-footed, clear, 10" d. **68**
Canape set, plate No. 400/36 & 3 1/2 oz. tumbler, No. 400/142, clear, 2 pcs. **60**
Candle/flower holder, No. 400/40C, clear, 5" h. **47**
Candleholders, No. 400/100, clear, pr. **55**
Candleholders, No. 400/147, clear, pr. **72**
Candleholders, No. 400/207, 4 1/2" h., clear, pr... **260**
Candleholders, No. 400/79R, clear, pr. **35**
Candleholders, No. 400/81, 3 1/2" h., clear, pr.. **112**
Candleholders, No. 400/86, clear, pr. **84**
Candlestick, single light chamberstick w/handle, clear.. **52**
Candlestick, single light, Eagle, clear................. **85**
Candlestick, single light, mushroom form, clear... **28**
Candlestick, three-light, clear **78**
Candy box, cov., No. 400/59, clear, 5 1/2-6 1/2"... **55**
Candy box, cov., No. 400/260, clear, 7"........... **225**
Candy box, cov., three-part, No. 400/110, clear, 7" d.. **172**
Candy dish, No. 400/51C, clear, 6" d. **65**

Celery tray, oval, handled, No. 400/105, clear, 13 1/2" l. 45

Center bowl, No. 100/13B, Viennese Blue, 11" d. 150

Center bowl, No. 400/131B, oval, flat, clear, 14" 450

Champagne/sherbet, No. 3400, saucer-type, clear, 6 oz. 17

Cheese & cracker set, No. 400/88, clear, 10" d., 2 pc. 65

Cigarette box, cov., clear, 3" 45

Coaster, No. 400/78, clear, 4" d. 6

Cocktail, No. 3400, clear, 4 oz. 16

Compote, 4 1/2", clear 26

Compote, 4 1/2" h., No. 400/63B, no bead stem, clear 32

Compote, 5" h., No. 400/220, clear 145

Compote, 5 1/2" h., No. 400/66B, two-bead stem, clear 30

Imperial Compote with Rose Decoration

Compote, 10" h., crimped, three-bead stem, No. 400/103F, clear w/h.p. pink roses & blue ribbons (ILLUS.) **260-400**

Compote, 10" h., fruit, No. 400/103C, clear 275

Compote, 10" h., No. 400/103F, clear w/sterling silver base 325

Compote, 10 1/2" h., No. 400/63B, clear 33

Console bowl, three-toed, No. 400/205, clear, 10" l. 33

Cordial, No. 3400, clear, 1 oz. 48

Cordial, ruby, 4 1/2" h. 95

Cordial decanter, applied handle, No. 400/82, clear etched (top chip) 495

Creamer, clear 16

Creamer, individual, No. 400/96, clear 9

Creamer & sugar bowl, beaded handle, No. 400/30, clear, pr. 20

Creamer & sugar bowl, individual, No. 400/122, clear, pr. 21

Creamer, sugar bowl & undertray, clear, the set 42

Cruet w/original stopper, handled, clear 48

Cruet w/original stopper, No. 400/119, clear 32

Cruet w/original stopper, No. 400/275, clear, 6 oz. 75

Cruet w/original stopper, No. 400/278, handled, clear, 4 oz. 95

Cruet w/original stopper, No. 500/121/O, clear 75

Cup, coffee, No. 400/37, clear 8

Cup, tea, No. 400/35, clear 8

Cup & saucer, demitasse, No. 400/77AD, clear 30

Cup & saucer, No. 400/35, clear 13

Cup & saucer, No. 400/37, clear 14

Decanter w/original stopper, No. 400/163, clear, 26 oz. 875

Epergne set, No. 400/196, clear, 2 pc. 295

Goblet, cocktail, No. 400/190, clear, 3 1/2-4 oz. 19

Goblet, No. 3400, water, black, 7 1/2" h.. 200

Goblet, No. 3400, water, clear, 7 1/2" h.. 25

Goblet, No. 3400, water, ruby, 7 1/2" h.. 118

Goblet, No. 3400, wine, clear, 4 oz. 28

Goblet, No. 400/19, clear, 4 3/4 h. 14

Goblet, No. 400/190, water, clear, 10 oz. 25

Gravy boat, No. 100/169, clear 185

Honey dish, clear, 4 3/4" 119

Hurricane candle lamp, No. 400/79, clear, 2 pcs. 165

Ice tub, No. 400/168, tab-handled, clear, 7" 173

Icer, No. 400/53C, clear, 6" 75

Icer & liner, No. 400/53, clear 135

Jelly/ashtray, No. 400/33, clear, 4" 14

Knife, No. 4000, clear 550

Marmalade set, No. 400/8918, clear, 3 pcs. 110

Mayonnaise bowl & underplate, No. 400/23, clear, 2 pcs. 34

Mayonnaise set: divided bowl & underplate; No. 400/84, clear, 2 pcs. 80

Mint bowl, ring-handled, No. 400/51F, clear, 6" 28

Mustard jar, cov., footed, No. 400/156, clear 45

Mustard jar, cover & spoon, clear, 3 pcs. 70

Nappy, fruit, No. 400/1F, blue, 5" 45

Nappy, handled, No. 400/51, clear, 6" 16

Pastry tray, No. 400/68D, clear, 11 1/2" d. ... 60-70

Pickle/celery dish, No. 400/57, clear, 7 1/2" 32

Pitcher, juice/cocktail, No. 400/19, clear, 40 oz. 325

Plate, 4 1/2" d., No. 400/34, clear 9

Plate, bread & butter, 6" d., two-handled, No. 400/1D, clear 8

Plate, canapé, 6" d., w/off-center indentation, No. 400/36, clear 16

Plate, 7" d., No. 400/52E, two-handled, black 375

Plate, salad, 7" d., No. 400/3D, clear 9

Plate, luncheon, 9" d., No. 400/7D, clear 15

Plate, dinner, 10 1/2" d., No. 400/10D, clear 44

Plate, 11" d., No. 400/145D, two-handled, clear 30

Plate, torte, 12 1/2" d., cupped edge, No. 400/75V, clear 33

Plate, torte, 13", No. 400/75V, rolled edge, clear 58

Plate, 14" d., No. 400/92D, clear 35

Plate, torte, 17" d., clear 34

Plate, torte, 17" d., cupped edge, No. 400/20V, clear 72

Platter, 16" l., oval, two-handled, No. 400/131D, clear 234

Punch set: 13" d. punch bowl, 17" d. cupped-edge underplate, 12 cups & ladle; No. 400/20, clear, 15 pcs. 260

Punch set: punch bowl, ladle, underplate & 12 punch cups; clear, 15 pcs. 190

Relish dish, No. 400/54, clear, 6 1/2" 20

Relish dish, two-part, handled, clear, 6 1/2" 12

Relish dish, two-part, No. 400/84, clear, 6 1/2" 22

Relish dish, two-part, No. 400/234, clear, 7"
sq. 140
Relish dish, two-part, oval, No.400/268,
clear, 8" l. 31
Relish dish, two-part, No. 400/52, clear 25
Relish dish, cov., three-part, rectangular,
No. 400/216, clear, 10" l. 1,250
Relish dish, three-part, three-toed, No.
400/208, clear 127
Relish dish, four-part, No.400/112, clear,
10 1/2" l. 33
Relish tray, three-part, handled, No.
400/213, clear, 10" l. 74
Relish tray, five-part, No. 400/104, clear 65
Relish tray, five-part, five-handled, No.
400/56, clear, 10 1/2" l. 55
Relish tray, five-part, No. 3900/120, clear,
13" 65
Salad fork, No. 400/75, clear 15
Salad serving set, fork & spoon, No. 475,
clear, 9 1/2" l., the set 46
Salt dip, No. 400/61, clear, 2" 12
Salt & pepper shakers, amethyst, pr. 110
Salt & pepper shakers, individual, No.
400/109, clear, pr. 20
Salt & pepper shakers w/chrome tops,
No. 400/190, footed, clear, pr. 100

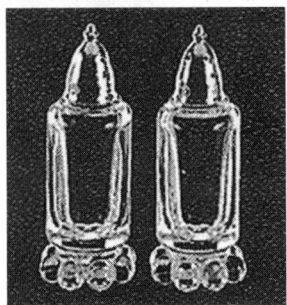

Candlewick No. 400/247 Shakers

Salt & pepper shakers w/chrome tops,
No. 400/247, clear, pr. (ILLUS.) 45
Salt shaker w/chrome top, No. 400/96,
clear 8
Seafood cocktail, No. 400/190, clear,
3 1/2-4 oz. 89
Sherbet, tall, No. 400/190, clear, 5 oz. 18
Sugar bowl, clear 12
Tray, lemon, center-handled, No. 400/221,
clear, 5 3/4" 42
Tray, mint, center-handled, No. 400/149D,
clear, 9" d. 36
Tray, No. 400/159, clear, 9" l. 29
Tray, No. 400/72C, two-handled, crimped,
clear, 10" 30
Tumbler, juice, No. 400/19, clear, 4" h., 5
oz. 15
Tumbler, flat, No. 400/19, clear, 5 1/2" h. 14
Tumbler, iced tea, footed, No. 400/19,
clear, 6" h., 12 oz. 26
Tumbler, iced tea, No. 3400, clear, 6 1/2" h. 28
Tumbler, water, No. 400/19, clear, 10 oz. 15
Tumblers, iced tea, footed, No. 400/19,
clear, 12 oz., set of 6 77
Vase, bud, 7" h., domed foot, No. 400/186,
clear 450

Vase, 8" h., fan-shaped w/beaded handles,
No. 400/87F, blue 121
Vase, 8" h., fluted rim w/beaded handles,
No. 400/87C, clear 44
Vase, 8 1/2" h., No. 400/21, flared rim, clear 413
Vase, two open beaded arms, crimped top,
clear 38
Vegetable bowl, No. 400/69B, clear w/cut-
ting, 8 1/2" d. 55
Wine, No. 3400, clear, 4 oz. 24

Cape Cod

Ashtray, clear 12
Baked apple dish, clear, 5 3/4" 12
Bar bottle, clear 150
Basket, clear, 11" h. 195
Basket, No. 160/73/0, clear 350
Bowl, spider, 4 1/2" d., handled, No.
160/180, clear 25
Bowl, 5" w., heart-shaped, No. 160/49H,
clear 20
Bowl, spider, 6 1/2" d., divided, handled,
No. 160/187, clear 32
Bowl, 8 1/2" d., low, clear 34
Bowl, 11" oval, clear 90
Butter dish, cov., clear, 1/4 lb. 42
Butter dish, cov., round, clear 52
Cake stand, No. 160/103D, clear, 11" d. 115
Cake stand, footed, clear, 12" d. 94
Candlestick, single light, clear, 3" h. 22
Candlestick, single light, clear, 5" h. 24
Candy jar, cov., bamboo handle, clear 74
Center bowl, No. 160/75L, ruffled edge,
clear 65
Cigarette box, cov., clear 38
Cigarette lighter, stemmed, purple slag 40
Coaster, clear, 3" sq. 15
Coaster, No. 160/78, clear 10

Cape Cod Cocktail

Cocktail, No. 1602, clear, 3 1/2 oz. (ILLUS.) 10
Compote, 7" d., No. 160/48B, clear 55
Cookie jar, cov., clear 110
Cordial, clear, 3 3/4" h. 30
Cordial, No. 1602, milk white, 1 1/2 oz. 15
Creamer, clear, 3" sq. 38
Creamer, clear, 4 1/2" h. 10
Creamer & open sugar bowl, No. 160/30,
clear, pr. 24
Cruet w/original stopper, No. 160/119,
amber, 4 oz. 28
Cruet w/original stopper, No. 160/119,
Verde green, 4 oz. 45
Cruet w/original stopper, blown, No.
160/70, clear, 5 oz. 60

Cruet w/original stopper, No. 160/70,
clear, 5 oz. 27
Cruet w/original stopper, No. 160/241,
clear, 6 oz. 55
Cup & saucer, clear 12
Decanter w/original stopper, clear,
8 1/2" h. 124
Decanter w/original stopper, clear,
9 3/4" h. 89
Decanter w/original stopper, ruby-
stained, 9 3/4" h. 119
Decanter w/original stopper, clear, 13" h. 142
Decanter w/original stopper, No. 160/163,
clear, 30 oz. 75
Decanter w/original stopper, square-
shaped, No. 160/212, clear, 24 oz. 80
Decanters w/original stoppers, square-
shaped, clear, in chrome rack w/lock, the
set. 225
Egg cup, No. 160/225, clear 32
Epergne, bowl w/trumpet, clear 175
Goblet, water, clear, 5 1/2" h. 10
Goblet, water, pink, 6 1/4" h. 28
Goblet, water, amber, 6 1/2" h. 10
Goblet, water, clear, 6 1/2" h. 14
Goblet, magnum, No. 160, clear, 14 oz. 28
Goblet, water, No. 1600, clear, 10 oz. 20
Goblet, water, No. 1602, Verde green, 9 oz. 8
Lamp, hurricane-type, clear, 12" h. 96
Mayonnaise bowl, ladle & underplate,
clear, 3 pcs. 36
Mug, clear, 4 3/4" h. 42
Mug, clear, 12 oz. 58
Mustard jar, cover & spoon, clear, 3 pcs. 30
Oyster cocktail, No. 1602, clear 9
Perfume bottle w/original stopper, round,
clear 48
Pitcher, 8 1/2" h., clear. 94
Pitcher, 10" h., clear 240
Pitcher, milk, No. 160/240, clear, 16 oz. 50
Plate, 8 1/2" d., amber 8
Plate, 8 1/2" d., pink 19
Plate, 9" d., clear 26

Cape Cod Dinner Plate

Plate, dinner, 10" d., No. 160/10D, clear
(ILLUS.). 58
Plate, torte, 13 1/2" d., clear 45
Punch bowl & base, clear, 2 pcs. 125
Relish dish, three-part, oval, No. 160/55,
clear, 9 1/2" l. 18
Relish dish, three-part, No. 160/1602, clear 150
Salad serving set: fork & spoon; clear,
9 1/2" l., the set 28
Salt dip, clear, 2 1/4" d. 16
Salt & pepper mill, amber, pr. 55

Salt & pepper shakers w/original tops, in-
dividual, No. 160/251, clear, pr. 20
Salt & pepper shakers w/original tops, in-
dividual, original factory label, No.
160/251, clear, pr. 25
Salt & pepper shakers w/original tops,
Verde green, pr. 40
Salt & pepper shakers w/original tops &
undertray, clear, the set 42
Sherbet, No. 1600, clear, 6 oz. 15
Sherbet, tall, No. 1602, Verde green, 6 oz. 15
Sugar bowl, clear, 4 1/4" h. 10
Tray, for creamer & sugar, No. 160/29,
clear, 7" l. 15
Tumbler, flat, clear, 3 3/4" h., 6 oz. 20
Tumbler, flat, clear, 6 1/2" h., 14 oz. 22
Tumbler, iced tea, flat, clear, 5 1/2" h. 18
Tumbler, iced tea, amber, 6" h. 12
Tumbler, iced tea, clear, 6" h. 16
Tumbler, iced tea, pink, 6" h. 34
Tumbler, juice, footed, No. 1602, clear,
6 oz. 12
Tumbler, juice, footed, No. 1602, Verde
green, 6 oz. 15
Tumbler, juice, No. 1600, clear, 5 1/4" h.,
6 oz. 12
Tumbler, water, footed, No. 1602, clear,
10 oz. 10
Tumbler, water, No. 160, clear, 10 oz. 12
Vegetable bowl, divided, oval, clear, 11" l. 85
Whiskey set w/metal rack, No. 160/260,
clear bottles w/raised letters "Bourbon,"
"Rye" & "Scotch," the set 650
Wine, clear, 4" h. 10

Free-Hand Ware

Candlestick, slender baluster-form stem
w/cushion foot in clear w/white heart &
vine decoration, a tall cylindrical iridescent dark blue socket, original paper la-
bel, 10" h. 440
Vase, 6 1/2" h., Mosaic design, deep cobalt
blue body shaded & swirled w/opal &
lined in iridescent orange 495
Vase, 8" h., small swelled base below the
tall slightly flaring cylindrical body w/a
widely flaring flattened & deeply ruffled
rim, iridescent metallic hues of purple,
green & blue in a wavy random design 130
Vase, 8 1/2" h., cylindrical, iridescent green
heart & vine design on a white ground,
marigold lining w/some wear 385
Vase, 8 1/2" h., decorated w/a dark blue
drapery design on a marigold iridescent
ground 275
Vase, 8 1/2" h., simple cylindrical form, or-
ange iridescent ground decorated w/blue
hanging heart design, cased over white,
rim possibly ground 575
Vase, 8 3/4" h., green heart & vine decora-
tion on opaque white body w/iridescent
lustre overall 690
Vase, 9 1/2" h., bulbous base w/a wide
flared neck, white cased to a cobalt blue
exterior, interior of rim flashed in brilliant
iridescent orange, polished pontil, early
20th c. 575
Vase, 10" h., bulbous ovoid bottom below a
tall trumpet neck, exterior in a mottled taffeta w/amber shoulder band, slate blue
interior 220

Vase, 10" h., Hanging Vine & Heart, white cased w/orange... **450**

Vase, 10" h., tall slender form, iridescent orange exterior w/deep orange throat.............. **210**

Vase, 10 1/2" h., jack-in-the-pulpit-form, wide flared mouth of opaque white w/orange stretch iridescence, raised on an elongated stem w/blue pulled loops, on a blue disk foot w/overall orange & gold iridescence on exterior, polished pontil w/gold foil label, ca. 1925............................ **1,610**

Vase, 10 1/2" h., tall body w/flared rim, a white swagged design on an iridescent ground, stretched multi-hued design at the rim.............. **550**

Vase, 10 3/4" h., very slender baluster-form body w/flaring short neck, overall orange iridescence w/a blue pulled drapery design cased on milk glass................................. **750**

Vase, 11" h., slender swelled cylindrical body w/short rolled neck, overall orange lustre over a milk glass body, ground pontil **110**

Vase, three looped feet, orange w/blue Hanging Vine & Heart **650**

Miscellaneous Patterns & Lines

Animal covered dish, Atterbury lion, purple slag.. **90**

Basket, Daisy patt., marigold carnival, marked "IG" **42**

Basket, Daisy patt., marigold carnival, unmarked.. **48**

Basket w/arched overhead handle, Monticello patt., No. 698, clear, 10" h. **55**

Book end, Cathay line, Lu-tung/Mandarin, No. 5030, jade... **85**

Bowl, pearl amethyst iridescent stretch glass, Iron Cross mark.................................. **100**

Box, cov., model of duck on nest, jade green slag **55**

Candlestick, single light, No. 3130, spiral, green, 3 1/2" h.................................... **24**

Candlestick, single light, Packard patt. No. 320, vaseline, 8 1/2" h. **54**

Candy box, cov., Zodiac patt., No. 619, azure blue, carnival **55**

Compote, No. 3297, shell bowl w/dolphin stem, black w/gold decoration **140**

Creamer & sugar bowl, owl form, red slag, pr. **70**

Cup & saucer, Grape patt., No. 473, rubigold & marigold carnival............................. **62**

Decanter w/original stopper, Grape patt., marigold carnival, marked "IG" **64**

Decanter w/original stopper, Grape patt., marigold carnival, unmarked............................. **95**

Ivy ball, Hobnail patt., No. 742, black.................. **68**

Lamp, Zipper Loop patt., marigold carnival, 8" h... **400**

Paperweight, model of a tiger, Heisey mold, amber & caramel slag **100**

Pitcher, crackle Tree of Life patt., marigold carnival **40**

Pitcher, No. 701, green w/clear reeded applied handle **80**

Pitcher, Windmill patt., marigold carnival, unmarked **70**

Plate, 8" d., Spun patt., reeded, clear **8**

Plate, 8" d., Spun patt., reeded, red **38**

Powder box, cov., Hobnail patt., green opalescent... **35-45**

Molly Rose Bowl with Silver Deposit

Rose bowl, Molly line, black w/silver deposit floral decoration, 5" h. (ILLUS.)............... **40-50**

Tumbler, crackle Tree of Life patt., marigold carnival **8**

Tumbler, Hobnail patt., No. 742, clear **14**

Tumbler, Windmill patt., marigold carnival, unmarked **18**

Vase, Hobnail patt., No. 742, flip, amber............. **38**

Vase, Loganberry patt., ball top, purple carnival **2,200**

Vase, bud, 5" h., Spun patt., reeded, amber........ **28**

Vase, 10" h., Loganberry patt., marigold carnival **240**

Vase, 12" h., Poppy Show patt., Helios green carnival **1,050**

Vase, 12" h., Poppy Show patt., marigold carnival **600**

Vase, fan-shaped, clear **25**

Vase, Peachblow, cased heat sensitive red over white **180**

Wine, Old Williamsburg patt., amber **10**

Wine, Old Williamsburg patt., Azalea **18**

Jack-in-the-Pulpit Vases

Glass vases in varying sizes and resembling in appearance the flower of this name have been popular with collectors since the 19th century. They were produced in various solid colors and in shaded wares.

Cased Deep Rose Jack-in-the-Pulpit

Cased, deep rose pink interior w/an applied clear crimped rim & a small enameled floral cluster, the white exterior enameled w/delicate blue & gold blossoms, cushion foot, 5 1/2" d., 7 1/2" h. (ILLUS.)................ **$175**

Cranberry Shaded Jack-in-the-Pulpit

Cranberry shaded to pink, squatty bulbous base below the tall cylindrical body w/a crimped & ruffled rim, applied clear rim, 4 1/2" d., 7 3/4" h. (ILLUS.) **165**

Maroon & Opalescent Vase

Maroon shading to white opalescent, widely flaring rolled & crimped top w/Hobnail design & back pulled into a point, tapering squatty bulbous body w/overall tiny Diamond Quilted patt. (ILLUS.).............. **110**

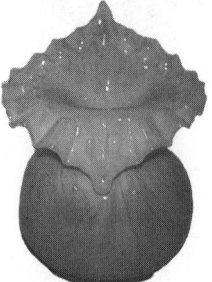

Small Spatter Jack-in-the-Pulpit Vase

Spatter, bulbous ovoid body tapering to a widely flared crimped rim pulled into points at the front & back, deep yellow mottled w/swirled white, 3 1/2" d., 5" h. **85**

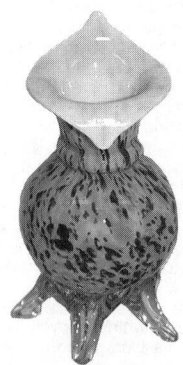

Spatter Jack-in-the-Pulpit with Feet

Spatter, spherical body tapering to a ringed neck w/a flaring rim pulled into points at the back & front, the body in maroon, yellow & blue spatter cased on white, applied clear pointed legs, white interior, 4" d., 8" h. (ILLUS.) **150**

Lalique

Fine glass, which includes numerous extraordinary molded articles, has been made by the glasshouse established by René Lalique early in the 20th century in France. The firm was carried on by his son, Marc, until his death in 1977 and is now headed by Marc's daughter, Marie-Claude. All Lalique glass is marked, usually on, or near, the bottom with either an engraved or molded signature. Unless otherwise noted, we list only those pieces marked "R. Lalique" produced before the death of René Lalique in 1945.

Box, cov., "Deux Sirenes," round amber & clear form molded w/two sirens amid bubbles, the cover molded "R. Lalique," box stenciled "R. Lalique France," 10 1/4" d.. **$3,450**

Box, cov., "Figurines et Voiles," cylindrical w/flat molded cover, clear & frosted, molded on top & base w/bands of diaphanously clad maidens, blue stain, introduced 1929, 4 1/4" d., 2 5/8" h................... **2,070**

Clock, table model, "Marguerites," a narrow rectangular flared foot supporting a narrow upright rectangular frosted glass panel centered by a clock dial framed by molded daisy blossoms, introduced in 1920, 5 3/4" h... **2,530**

Clock, table model, "Naiades," flattened upright squared form in grey molded around the dial on the reverse w/six cavorting water nymphs, inscribed "R. Lalique France," model introduced in 1926, 4 3/8" h... **2,875**

Clock, table model, "Quatre Moineaux du Japon," square flattened frosted clear base w/a round central dial surrounded by four molded plump birds amid dogwood blossoms, wheel-cut "R.Lalique France," the clock dial signed "ATO" & engraved "Made in France," together w/a rectangular metal stand, introduced in 1928, 7 1/4" h.. **2,300**

Decanter w/stopper, "Nippon" patt., clear footed tall flaring cylindrical form w/a tapering shoulder to a small flaring neck, graduated bands of beads around the base of the body & on the acorn-form stopper, introduced in 1930, 9 3/4" h. **809**

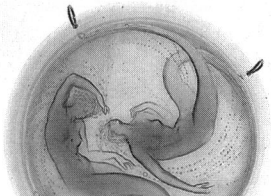

Rare Lalique Plafonnier

Plafonnier, "Deux Sirenes," round shaded reddish amber molded w/two large swirling sirens, molded "R. Lalique," introduced in 1921, 15 1/2" d. (ILLUS.) **24,150**

Vase, 6 1/8" h., "Esterel," sharply tapering wide ovoid body w/a wide shoulder centered by a short cylindrical neck, deep amber molded w/large heavily veined leaves in clear & frosted, introduced in 1923 .... **2,300**

Vase, 6 1/4" h., "Raisins," slightly swelled cylindrical form molded in high relief w/overall scrolling grapevines, frosted clear, inscribed "R. LALIQUE - FRANCE," introduced in 1928 .... **690**

Vase, 6 1/2" h., "Lievres," small foot below the wide squatty bulbous body w/a small flaring cylindrical neck, frosted opalescent molded in low relief w/a band of leaping jack rabbits among spiraling vines, molded "R. LALIQUE," introduced in 1923 .... **1,840**

Vase, 6 5/8" h., "Ormeaux," flat-bottomed spherical form tapering to a small trumpet neck, clear & frosted, molded in relief w/overall overlapping large pointed veined leaves, green stain, introduced in 1926 .... **1,495**

Vase, 7 7/8" h., "Tourbillons," bulbous ovoid form in pale yellow deeply molded overall w/curling thorny branches, model introduced in 1926, inscribed "R. LALIQUE - FRANCE" **10,350**

Vase, 8 1/8" h., "Guirlandes," flaring ovoid form w/a widely flaring cupped rim, clear & frosted opalescent molded w/interlacing bands, introduced in 1935 .... **2,760**

Vase, 8 1/4" h., "Domrémy," wide ovoid green body tapering to a short wide rolled neck, molded in relief w/large round thistle heads & molded tall thistle stems, white stain, introduced in 1926 .... **6,038**

Vase, 9 1/4" h., "Poissons," footed spherical body w/a small short cylindrical neck w/flattened rim, frosted opalescent molded in low-relief w/tropical fish in repeat, molded "R. LALIQUE," introduced in 1921 .... **1,380**

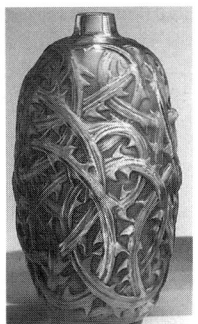

Green-stained "Ronces" Lalique Vase

Vase, 9 1/4" h., "Ronces," footed tall slender swelled cylindrical body w/a tiny cylindrical neck, clear & frosted molded overall in bold relief w/thorny branches, green stain, introduced in 1921 (ILLUS.)... **2,415**

Vase, 10 1/4" h., "Sauterelles," wide bulbous ovoid body tapering slightly to a wide molded mouth, clear & frosted molded w/large grasshoppers on long blades of grass, blue & green stains, introduced in 1912 .... **6,900**

Vase, 11 1/4" h., "Camargue," grey slightly flaring cylindrical form molded around the sides w/four irregular medallions centered by a rearing steed amid swirling clouds of dust, frosted ground, introduced in 1942, acid-stamped "R. LALIQUE - FRANCE" **4,312**

Vase, 12 1/4" h., "Quatre Groupes de Lézards," footed very tall slender tapering ovoid body w/a tiny mouth w/flattened rim, clear & frosted molded w/four narrow vertical bands of climbing lizards alternating w/wider plain bands, brown stain, introduced in 1912 .... **4,600**

Vase, 13" h., "Nanking," spherical form composed of overall facets of molded concentric triangles, clear & frosted w/green stain, introduced in 1925 .... **8,050**

Libbey

In 1878, William L. Libbey obtained a lease on the New England Glass Company of Cambridge, Massachusetts, changing the name to the New England Glass Works, W.L. Libbey and Son, Proprietors. After his death in 1883, his son, Edward D. Libbey, continued to operate the company at Cambridge until 1888 when the factory was closed. Edward Libbey moved to Toledo, Ohio, and set up the company subsequently known as Libbey Glass Co. During the 1880s, the firm's master technician, Joseph Locke, developed the now much desired colored art glass lines of Agata, Amberina, Peach Blow and Pomona. Renowned for its Cut Glass of the Brilliant Period (see CUT GLASS), the company continues in operation today as Libbey Glassware, a division of Owens-Illinois, Inc.

Maize sugar shaker w/original metal lid, yellow leaves, 5 3/4" h. **$413**

Maize sugar shaker w/original top, creamy opaque w/yellow husks & gold trim **350-400**

Libbey Maize Tumbler

Maize tumbler, creamy opaque w/blue husks (ILLUS.) 225
Maize tumbler, creamy opaque w/green husks trimmed in gold 150
Sherbet, Silhouette patt., clear bowl, black figural squirrel stem, signed, 4" h. 145
Sherbet, Silhouette patt., clear bowl, opalescent figural squirrel stem, 4" h. 110

Libbey Silhouette Sherry

Sherry, Silhouette patt., clear bowl, opalescent figural monkey stem (ILLUS.) **95-125**

Loetz

Iridescent glass, some of it somewhat resembling that of Tiffany and other contemporary glasshouses, was produced by the Bohemian firm of J. Loetz Witwe of Klostermule and is referred to as Loetz. Some cameo pieces were also made. Not all pieces are marked.

Loetz Mark

Vase, 3 3/4" h., miniature, a squatty bulbous base centering a wide cylindrical neck w/flared rim, iridescent green decorated overall w/heavy sterling silver overlay in vining leaf & blossom design.............. **$770**

Two Fine Loetz Vases

Vase, 4 1/8" h., bulbous ovoid form w/deeply pinched-in sides below the wide flaring mouth, amber ground decorated w/iridescent silver sweeping swirls, engraved "Loetz Austria" (ILLUS. right) 920
Vase, 5" h., bulbous dimpled form, variegated iridescent coloring on the exterior in violet & gold oil spots & swirls on an amber ground 88

Rare Small Loetz Silver Overlay Vase

Vase, 5" h., bulbous ovoid body w/three side dimples tapering to a small trumpet neck, yellow w/purple & green iridescent trailings & bluish gold oil spots, overlaid around the neck & shoulder w/silver stylized flowers on whiplash vines, signed in enamel "800 - M.692" (ILLUS.) **4,025**
Vase, 5 1/8" h., footed spherical body w/a flaring cylindrical neck, applied scrolled loop handles from side of neck to shoulder, iridescent pale green ground decorated w/an iridescent blue oil spot design, silver overlay cast in a scrolling foliate design in bands down the sides & the handles encased in silver (ILLUS. left)............ **2,530**
Vase, 5 1/4" h., ribbed tree trunk form w/pinched collar opening to a flared top, green w/bluish gold iridescence................... 248
Vase, 5 3/4" h., a wide squatty bulbous base w/a flattened shoulder centering a wide swelled cylindrical neck w/flared rim, yellow iridescent ground w/overall King Tut looping design w/silvery blue iridescence... 1,430
Vase, 8 1/2" h., cylindrical w/a tricorner rolled rim, iridescent green w/blue controlled wavy threading extending up from the base 193
Vase, 8 1/2" h., tall wide twisted cylindrical form resembling a tree trunk, a formosa finish of iridescent light blue random threading covering the iridescent green ground... 633
Vase, 9 1/2" h., trumpet-form w/a bulbous neck & a flaring rim, iridescent bluish gold base & gold top.. 275

Vase, 10" h., rose water sprinkler-form, dimpled bulbous base & tall neck w/jack-in-the-pulpit rim, overall oil spot gold papillon iridescent finish, polished pontil, late 19th - early 20th c. 690

Milk Glass

Opaque white glass, or "opal," has been called "milk-white glass" perhaps to distinguish it from transparent or "clear-white glass." Resembling fine white porcelain, it was viewed as an inexpensive substitute. Opacity is obtained by adding bone ash or oxide of tin to clear molten glass. By the addition of various coloring agents, the opaque mixture can be turned into blue milk glass, or pink, yellow, green, caramel, even black milk glass. Collectors of milk glass now accept not only the white variety but virtually any opaque color and color mixtures, including slag or marbled glass. It has been made in numerous forms and shapes in this country and abroad from about the first quarter of the 19th century. Many of the items listed here were also made in colored opaque glass which collectors call blue or green or black "milk glass." It is still being produced, and there are many reproductions of earlier pieces. Pieces are all-white unless otherwise noted. Also see HISTORICAL, PATTERN GLASS and WESTMORELAND.

Animal covered dish, Baboon on Fleur-de-lis base, attributed to Flaccus, 6 1/2" l. **$600**
Animal covered dish, "British Lion" on base, 6 1/4" l. 250
Animal covered dish, Chick emerging from egg on basket base 80
Animal covered dish, Dog on wide rib base, half white & half blue, Westmoreland Specialty Company, 5 1/2" l. 55
Animal covered dish, Duck w/blue head, Atterbury, marked "Pat. March 15, 1887," 11" l. (no eyes, several minor rim checks) 550
Animal covered dish, Fish, Entwined Fish, ruby eyes, round lattice-edged base, Atterbury, ca. 1889, 6" d. 225
Animal covered dish, Fish on Skiff, attributed to Westmoreland, 7 1/2" l. 43
Animal covered dish, Hen on Sleigh, Westmoreland Specialty 90
Animal covered dish, Rabbit, marked "Portieux," France, 7" l. 375
Animal covered dish, Rabbit on Egg, small rabbit on textured egg w/pedestal base, Vallerysthal, 5 1/4" l., 5" h. 190
Animal covered dish, Swan w/closed neck on basketweave base, Westmoreland Specialty Company, 5 1/2" l., 4 3/4" h. 75
Animal covered dish, Wooly Lamb on Bo Peep base, Flaccus, 6 1/8" l., 3 3/4" h. 350
Bowl, 6" d., 2 1/2" h., Blackberry patt. 35
Covered dish, Car, Vallerysthal, 5 1/2" l., 4 3/4" h. 500
Covered dish, Crate with straps, Vallerysthal, France, 5 1/2" l., 4" w. 135
Covered dish, Moses in Bulrushes, excellent, 5 1/2" l. 150-200
Epergne-compote, Tree of Life patt. bowl, figural Enfant Samuel pedestal base............ 310
Jar, cov., tall Owl, Atterbury, 7" h. 125-130
Jar, cov., tall Owl, Atterbury, blue opaque, 7" h. 350

Lamp, miniature, oil-type, Columbus bust w/beard base, 4 3/4" h. **1,250**
Models of dogs, Mantel Dogs, recumbent animal on an oval serrated base, attributed to England, 7" l., 5" h., pr. **1,700**
Mug, "Tavern Scene" patt. 35
Plate, 5 1/2" d., Woof Woof 45
Plate, 6" d., Dog and Cats, w/inscription "He's All Right," open leaf border, Gillinder, trace of paint on edge, good............... 175
Plate, 7 1/2" d., Three Owls patt., looped border halfway around plate, Westmoreland Specialty Company, ca. 1901 48
Shaker w/original top, figural Columbus bust, beardless 450
Sugar shaker w/original top, Melligo patt., decorated.. 85

Mt. Washington

A wide diversity of glass was made by the Mt. Washington Glass Company of New Bedford, Massachusetts, between 1869 and 1900. It was succeeded in 1900 by the Pairpoint Corporation. Miscellaneous types are listed below.

Leaf-decorated Crown Milano Jar

Cracker jar, cov., barrel-shaped, yellow to peach background decorated w/copper-colored outlined leaves & shaded white blossoms, resilvered rim, cover & bail handle, unmarked (ILLUS.)......................... **$950**
Cracker jar, cov., exterior decorated w/acorns & oak leaves on a pale pink shading to pale yellow ground, white interior, silver plate rim, cover & bail handle, cover marked "No. 4404/a"............................ 900

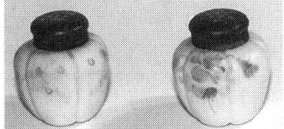

Small Lobed Salt & Pepper Shakers

Salt & pepper shakers w/original metal lids, bulbous lobed form, each h.p. w/purple violets & green leaves & tiny dot flowers, pr. (ILLUS.).. 200

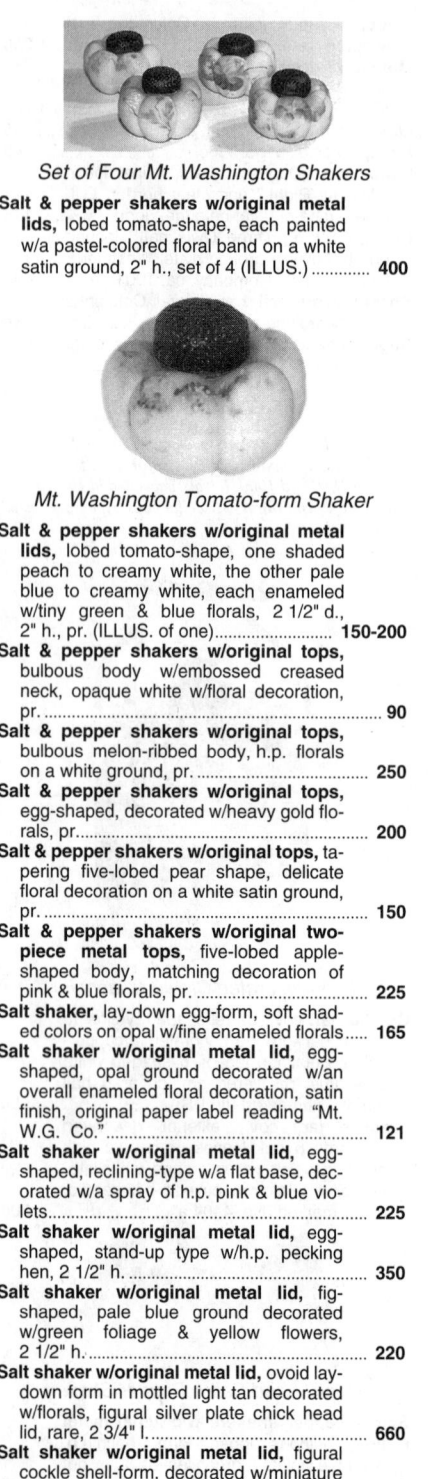

Set of Four Mt. Washington Shakers

Salt & pepper shakers w/original metal lids, lobed tomato-shape, each painted w/a pastel-colored floral band on a white satin ground, 2" h., set of 4 (ILLUS.) **400**

Mt. Washington Tomato-form Shaker

Salt & pepper shakers w/original metal lids, lobed tomato-shape, one shaded peach to creamy white, the other pale blue to creamy white, each enameled w/tiny green & blue florals, 2 1/2" d., 2" h., pr. (ILLUS. of one) **150-200**

Salt & pepper shakers w/original tops, bulbous body w/embossed creased neck, opaque white w/floral decoration, pr. **90**

Salt & pepper shakers w/original tops, bulbous melon-ribbed body, h.p. florals on a white ground, pr. **250**

Salt & pepper shakers w/original tops, egg-shaped, decorated w/heavy gold florals, pr. **200**

Salt & pepper shakers w/original tops, tapering five-lobed pear shape, delicate floral decoration on a white satin ground, pr. **150**

Salt & pepper shakers w/original two-piece metal tops, five-lobed apple-shaped body, matching decoration of pink & blue florals, pr. **225**

Salt shaker, lay-down egg-form, soft shaded colors on opal w/fine enameled florals **165**

Salt shaker w/original metal lid, egg-shaped, opal ground decorated w/an overall enameled floral decoration, satin finish, original paper label reading "Mt. W.G. Co." **121**

Salt shaker w/original metal lid, egg-shaped, reclining-type w/a flat base, decorated w/a spray of h.p. pink & blue violets **225**

Salt shaker w/original metal lid, egg-shaped, stand-up type w/h.p. pecking hen, 2 1/2" h. **350**

Salt shaker w/original metal lid, fig-shaped, pale blue ground decorated w/green foliage & yellow flowers, 2 1/2" h. **220**

Salt shaker w/original metal lid, ovoid lay-down form in mottled light tan decorated w/florals, figural silver plate chick head lid, rare, 2 3/4" l. **660**

Salt shaker w/original metal lid, figural cockle shell-form, decorated w/miniature yellow roses, 3" d. **1,760**

Salt shaker w/original top, egg-shaped, h.p. orchid decoration **150**

Salt shaker w/original top, egg-shaped, reclining-type, h.p. floral decoration on a white satin ground **100**

Salt shaker w/original top, egg-shaped, reclining-type w/a flat base, decorated w/pink apple blossoms on a white satin ground **150**

Sugar shaker w/original metal lid, egg-shaped, opal ground decorated w/green ferns **330**

Sugar shaker w/original metal lid, egg-shaped, shaded peach to pale yellow ground enameled w/floral decoration **578**

Sugar shaker w/original metal lid, lobed tomato-form opal body decorated w/enameled florals **440**

Sugar shaker w/original metal top, egg-shaped, satiny white ground decorated w/purple violets **450**

Sugar shaker w/original metal top, squatty lobed tomato-shape, creamy ground enameled w/delicate blue & yellow blossoms on leafy green stems, original embossed metal lid **258**

Sugar shaker w/original metal top, tomato-shaped, yellow ground w/enameled floral decoration **450**

Sugar shaker w/original metal top, egg-shaped, light shaded blue to cream ground delicately enameled w/pink blossoms w/yellow centers on green leafy stems, 4 1/2" h. **291**

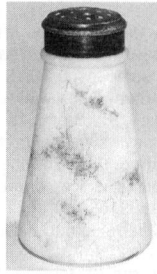

Mt. Washington Sugar Shaker

Sugar shaker w/original metal top, simple tapering cylindrical shape w/ringed flange at neck, satiny white ground h.p. w/delicate blue blossoms & lacy green leafy stems, 5" h. (ILLUS.) **400**

Sugar shaker w/original top, egg-shaped, white opal ground decorated w/h.p. maidenhair ferns **300-375**

Fine Decorated Napoli Vase

Vase, 5" h., 6" d., "Napoli," globular w/widely flaring rim, colorless crystal dimpled bowl w/molded swirls, decorated w/gold floral tracery, green blossoms on rim, marked "Napoli 837" (ILLUS.).................... **1,500**

Muller Freres

The Muller Brothers made acid-etched cameo and other fine glass at Luneville, France, starting in 1910 and until the outbreak of World War II in Europe.

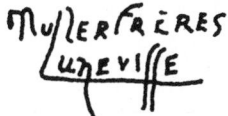

Muller Freres Mark

Cameo vase, 7" h., 8 1/2" d., a cased dark blue short wide neck w/a jagged edge over the wide bulbous textured crystal body w/a central ridge, decorated w/a band of iridescent aqua swimming fish & a band of dark blue bubble designs around the base, signed in cameo........... **$4,070**

Cameo vase, 10" h., a disk foot & short knopped pedestal supporting a large round pillow-form flattened vase tapering to a small trumpet neck, grey infused w/purple & green on a mottled orange & blue pedestal, overlaid in bluish green & cut w/fruit blossoms & vines, signed........... **2,128**

Cameo vase, 10 1/2" h., ovoid form, grey infused w/creamy opalescence, overlaid in amber, moss green & charcoal, cut w/a mountainous landscape, signed in cameo **6,900**

Center bowl, wide low form w/incurved sides, grey w/interior mottling in cobalt blue, green, pink, amber & yellow, signed on the side, 7 3/4" h. **476**

Nakara

Like Kelva, Nakara was made early in this century by the C.F. Monroe Company. For details see WAVE CREST.

Box w/hinged cover, green satin ground w/portrait of woman on cover, raised beading at border, original lining, 4 1/2" d. **$750**

Box w/hinged cover, Octagonal mold, footed, green ground decorated w/large pink rose, 4 1/2" w. **550**

Box w/hinged cover, Octagonal mold, plum ground w/Kate Greenaway tea party scene, 4 1/2" w. **750**

Box w/hinged cover, Bishop's Hat mold, blue ground w/florals, 5" w. **650**

Box w/hinged cover, oval, light green w/pink roses & crown in center of lid, 5 1/2" l. **475**

Box w/hinged cover, Bishop's Hat mold, the top decorated w/a large portrait reserve featuring the bust of Queen Louise framed by a deep pink ground w/scrolls & blossoms of white beading, deep pink

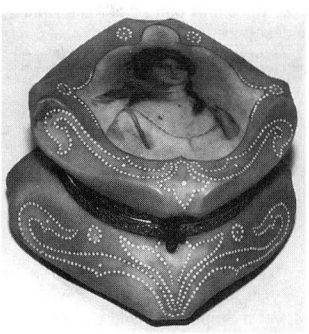

Rare Nakara Portrait Box

base w/matching white beading, 5 3/4" w., 4 1/4" h. (ILLUS.) **1,050**

Box w/hinged cover, Octagonal mold, shaded pale peach to brown ground decorated w/h.p. yellow flowers w/pink centers, 6 1/4" d., 4 1/2" h. **975**

Box w/hinged cover, Rococo mold, decorated overall w/dainty beaded flowers, 8" d. **1,200**

Humidor, cov., base decorated w/h.p. enameled florals & "Tobacco" in gold, 7" w., 7" h. **750**

Pin tray, Bishop's Hat mold, yellow ground decorated w/delicate pink flowers, 4" w. **350**

Pin tray, decorated w/delicate roses, 4 1/2" d. **350**

Pin tray, Bishop's Hat mold, pink & white flowers on green ground, 5 1/2" w. **450**

Nash

A. Douglas Nash, a former employee of Louis Comfort Tiffany, purchased Tiffany's Corona Works in December 1928 and began his own operation there. For a brief period Nash produced some outstanding glasswares, but the factory closed in March of 1931 and Nash then became associated with Libbey Glass of Toledo, Ohio. This quality glass is quite scarce.

Bowl, small, raised Maize patt. in gold iridescent w/blue highlights, signed **$175**

Bowl, 4 1/2" d., 4 1/2" h., blue ground w/silver mottling decorated w/red pulled-up stripes **175**

Compote, open, 3 1/4 x 6 1/4", low, footed, scalloped top & ribbed body, overall gold iridescence, signed **550**

Cordials, Chintz patt., red w/overall silver decoration, signed, set of 6 .... **950**

Nut bowl, ruffled rim, iridescent gold w/blue highlights, 3" d., 2 3/8" h. **125**

Vase, 5 1/4" h., Chintz patt., flared rim on oval body of colorless glass internally decorated by orange stripes alternating yellow-amber pulled threading **173**

Vase, 5 1/2" h., Chintz patt., bulbous body tapering to cylindrical neck, red w/overall silver decoration, signed & numbered........... **750**

Vase, 7" h., 4" d., flared square shape, overall gold iridescence, signed **290**

Vase, 8 1/2" h., Chintz patt., dark blue w/silvery iridescence **575**

Small Iridescent Nash Vases

Vases, 4 1/4" h., tapering ovoid body w/indented panels around the base & interior ribbing on the short, flaring rim, applied to a disk foot, overall gold iridescence, signed "Nash 544," pr. (ILLUS.) **900**

New Martinsville

The New Martinsville Glass Mfg. Co. opened in New Martinsville, West Virginia, in 1901 and during its first period of production came out with a number of colored opaque pressed glass patterns. Also developed was an art glass line named "Muranese," which collectors refer to as "New Martinsville Peach Blow." The factory burned in 1907 but reopened later that year and began focusing on production of various clear pressed glass patterns, many of which were then decorated with gold or ruby staining or enameled decoration. After going through receivership in 1937, the factory again changed the focus of its production to more contemporary glass lines and figural animals. The firm was purchased in 1944 by The Viking Glass Company (later Dalzell-Viking).

Butter dish, cov., Old Glory patt. (No. 719 Line), clear w/gold decoration **$100**

No. 10/4 Candleholders

Candleholder, No. 10/4, blue (ILLUS. left) **35**
Candleholder, No. 10/4, jade green (ILLUS. right) **45**
Candleholder, No. 10/4, light green (ILLUS. center) **35**

Covered Candy Jar

Candy jar, cov., clear w/h.p. orange decoration & gold trim (ILLUS.) **52**

New Martinsville Console Bowl

Console bowl, blue w/black base (ILLUS.) **65**
Creamer, Carnation patt. (No. 88 Line), clear w/ruby-stain & gold decoration **125**

No. 35 Creamer & Sugar Bowl

Creamer & sugar bowl, No. 35 (Statesman), jade green, pr. (ILLUS.) **60**
Creamer & sugar bowl w/tray, individual, Janice patt. (No. 45 Line), light blue, the set **60**
Creamer & sugar bowl w/tray, Janice patt. (No. 45 Line), light blue, the set **75**
Cruet set: oil & vinegar cruets w/original tops & tray; Janice patt (No. 45 Line), light blue, the set **75**
Cruet w/original stopper, Celtic patt. (No. 100 Line), clear w/gold decoration **175**

No. 34 Cup & Saucer

Cup & saucer, No. 34 (Addie), jade green & black, pr. (ILLUS.) **20**

Modernistic Candy Box

Candy box, cov., Modernistic patt. (No. 33 Line), blue, satin finish (ILLUS.) **125**

Satin-finished Dresser Set

Dresser set: two perfume bottles w/original stoppers & powder box on rectangular tray; blue, satin finish, the set (ILLUS.) **250**

Hand-painted Dresser Set

Dresser set: two perfume bottles w/original stoppers & powder box on rectangular tray; green w/h.p. floral decoration, the set (ILLUS.) **325**

Flowering Vine Miniature Night Lamp

Night lamp, miniature, Flowering Vine patt., opaque green (ILLUS.) **300**
Night lamp, miniature, Iris patt., opaque pink **400**

Moondrops Relish Tray

Relish tray, three-part, handled, Moondrops patt. (No. 37 Line), cobalt blue (ILLUS.) **75**

Salt & pepper shakers w/original tops, Janice patt. (No. 45 Line), light blue, pr........ **110**

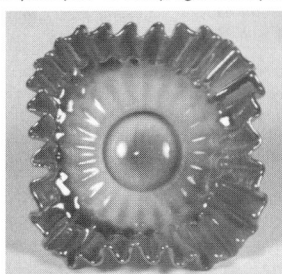

Muranese Sauce Dish

Sauce dish, Muranese, square, crimped rim (ILLUS.) **145**
Shade, gas, Muranese **125**

Moondrops Handled Tumblers

Tumbler, handled, Moondrops patt. (No. 37 Line), amber w/simulated cut decoration, 2 oz. (ILLUS. left) **18**
Tumbler, handled, Moondrops patt. (No. 37 Line), green, 2 oz. (ILLUS. right) **15**

Satin-finished Vase

Vase, Modernistic patt. (No. 33 Line), pink, satin finish (ILLUS.) **85**

Northwood

Harry Northwood (1860-1919) was born in England, the son of noted glass artist John Northwood. Brought up in the glass business, Harry immigrated to the United States in 1881 and shortly thereafter became manager of the La Belle Glass Company, Bridgeport, Ohio. Here he was responsible for many innovations in colored and blown glass. After leaving La Belle in 1887 he opened The Northwood Glass Company in Martins Ferry, Ohio, in 1888. The company moved to Ellwood City, Pennsylvania, in 1892 and Northwood moved again to take over a glass plant in Indiana, Pennsylvania, in 1896. One of his major lines made at the Indiana, Pennsylvania, plant was Custard glass (which he called "ivory"). It was made in several patterns, and some pieces were marked on the base with "Northwood" in script.

Harry and his family moved back to England in 1899 but returned to the U.S. in 1902 at which time he opened another glass factory, in Wheeling, West Virginia. Here he was able to put his full talents to work; under his guidance the firm manufactured many notable glass lines including opalescent wares, colored and clear pressed tablewares, various novelties and, probably best known of all, Carnival glass. Around 1906 Harry introduced his famous "N"-in-circle trade-mark, which can be found on the base of many, but not all, pieces made at his factory. The factory closed in 1925.

In this listing we are including only the clear and colored tablewares produced at Northwood factories. Dr. James Measell, Marietta, Ohio

Almond Dish

Almond dish, cov., low-sided round ribbed dish w/low domed cover w/knob finial, Chinese Coral, Wheeling, West Virginia factory (ILLUS.) **$90**

Grape Frieze Bonbon

Bonbon, low round dish w/applied loop handle on one side, Grape Frieze patt., "Verre D'or" decoration on dark amethyst, Wheeling, West Virginia factory (ILLUS.) 90

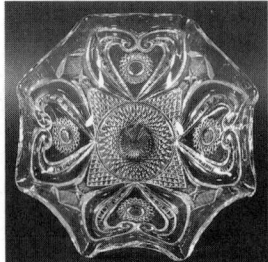

Valentine (No. 14) Bowl

Bowl, octagonal lobed sides, Valentine (No. 14) patt., Wheeling, West Virginia factory (ILLUS.) 30

Cashews Bowl

Bowl, 8" d., Cashews patt., crimped rim, clear opalescent, Wheeling, West Virginia factory (ILLUS.) 35
Celery vase, Chrysanthemum Swirl patt., cranberry opalescent, satin finish, Martins Ferry, Ohio factory 165

Belladonna Blue Creamer

Creamer, Belladonna (No.31) patt., blue w/h.p. decoration, Wheeling, West Virginia factory (ILLUS.) 90
Creamer, child's size, Belladonna (No. 31) patt., clear, Wheeling, West Virginia factory 45

Grape & Leaf Decorated Creamer

Creamer, Grape and Leaf patt., opaque white w/h.p. decoration, Indiana, Pennsylvania factory (ILLUS.) 125

Four-footed Square Hobnail Creamer

Creamer, Hobnail, four-footed, amber, La
Belle Co., Bridgeport, Ohio (ILLUS.) **100**
Creamer, Memphis patt., clear w/gold trim,
Wheeling, West Virginia factory **40**

Mikado (Flower & Bud) Creamer

Creamer, Mikado (Flower & Bud) patt.,
clear w/gold & enameled trim, Wheeling,
West Virginia factory (ILLUS.) **125**

Panelled Holly Opalescent Creamer

Creamer, Panelled Holly patt., white opalescent w/enameled decoration, Wheel-
ing, West Virginia factory (ILLUS.) **60-70**

Carnelian (Everglades) Cruet

Cruet w/original stopper, Carnelian (Everglades) patt., canary opalescent, Wheel-
ing, West Virginia factory (ILLUS.) **700**
Cruet w/original stopper, Diadem (Sun-
burst on Shield) patt., blue opalescent,
Wheeling, West Virginia factory **850**

Encore (Jewel & Flower) Cruet

Cruet w/original stopper, Encore (Jewel &
Flower) patt., blue opalescent, Wheeling,
West Virginia factory (ILLUS.) **750**

Paneled Sprig Cruet & Shakers

Cruet w/original stopper, Paneled Sprig
patt., milk white w/color trim, Ellwood
City, Pennsylvania factory (ILLUS. center, w/Paneled Sprig salt & pepper shak-
ers) **300**

Teardrop Flower Cruet

Cruet w/original stopper, Teardrop Flower
patt., amethyst, Wheeling, West Virginia
factory (ILLUS.) **750**

Grape & Leaf Cruet

Cruet w/replaced stopper, Grape & Leaf patt., cased opaque green, Ellwood City, Pennsylvania factory (ILLUS.) **100**

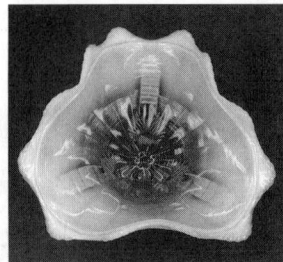

Fluted Scrolls Dish

Dish, Fluted Scrolls patt., tricornered, ruffled edge, three-footed, canary opalescent, Ellwood City, Pennsylvania factory, 7" w. (ILLUS.) **42**

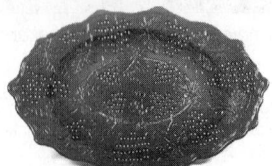

Grape & Cable Blue Dresser Tray

Dresser tray, oval, Grape & Cable patt., cobalt blue, Wheeling, West Virginia factory (ILLUS.) **250**

Southern Gardens Fruit Dish

Fruit dish, Southern Gardens patt., Verre d'Or treatment, blue w/gold decoration,

Wheeling, West Virginia factory, 10" d. (ILLUS.) **325**

Kerosene Lamp w/Grape Decoration

Lamp, hand-type, kerosene, globular font w/molded ribs on a flaring foot w/finger grip handle & interior grape pattern, clear, Wheeling, West Virginia factory (ILLUS.) **175**

Decorated Northwood Pitcher w/Label

Pitcher, bulbous panelled shape, green w/h.p. grapevine decoration & gold trim, original Northwood label on the base, Wheeling, West Virginia factory (ILLUS.) **475**

Clear Decorated Northwood Pitcher

Pitcher, tankard, panelled, clear w/h.p. floral decoration & gold trim, Wheeling, West Virginia factory (ILLUS.) **160**

Decorated Green Tankard Pitcher

Pitcher, tankard, panelled, dark green w/h.p. floral decoration & gold trim, Wheeling, West Virginia factory (ILLUS.) **175**

Green Intaglio Water Pitcher

Pitcher, water, Intaglio patt., green w/gold decoration, Indiana, Pennsylvania factory (ILLUS.)...................................... **165**

Salt & pepper shakers w/original tops, Paneled Sprig patt., milk white w/color trim, Indiana, Pennsylvania factory, pr. (ILLUS. w/Paneled Sprig cruet)..................... **150**

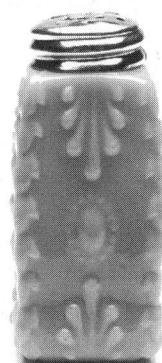

Opaque Green Cactus Salt Shaker

Salt shaker w/original top, Cactus patt., opaque green, Ellwood City, Pennsylvania factory (ILLUS.) **85**

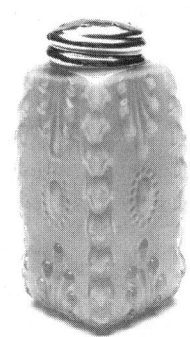

Opaque Pink Cactus Salt Shaker

Salt shaker w/original top, Cactus patt., opaque pink, Ellwood City, Pennsylvania factory (ILLUS.)... **90**

Ribbed Opal Lattice Salt Shaker

Salt shaker w/original top, Ribbed Opal Lattice patt., cranberry, Martins Ferry, Ohio factory (ILLUS.) **60-75**

Decorated Singing Birds Sauce Dish

Sauce dish, Singing Birds patt., clear w/blue decoration, Wheeling, West Virginia factory (ILLUS.) **40**

Northwood Sherbet & Underplate

Sherbet & underplate, No. 685 sherbet & No. 729 underplate, jade green, Wheeling, West Virginia factory, 2 pcs. (ILLUS.)..... **100**

Northwood No. 722 Snack Set

Snack set: cup & underplate; No. 722, Chinese Coral, Wheeling, West Virginia factory, 2 pcs. (ILLUS.) **95**

Panelled Sprig Granite Ware Sugar

Sugar bowl, cov., Panelled Sprig patt., Granite Ware (rough speckled white surface) w/gold decoration, Ellwood City, Pennsylvania factory (ILLUS.) **175**

Sugar bowl, cov., Peach patt., clear w/gold & red trim, Wheeling, West Virginia factory **75**

Aurora Pattern Rubina Sugar Shaker

Sugar shaker w/original top, Aurora patt., rubina, Martins Ferry, Ohio factory (ILLUS.).. **250**

Sugar shaker w/original top, Chrysanthemum Swirl patt., blue opalescent, Martins Ferry, Ohio factory.. **225**

Netted Oak Green Sugar Shaker

Sugar shaker w/original top, Netted Oak patt., light green, Indiana, Pennsylvania factory (ILLUS.)... **165**

Spanish Lace Sugar Shaker

Sugar shaker w/original top, Spanish Lace patt., cranberry opalescent, Ellwood City, Pennsylvania factory (ILLUS.)...... **435**

Beaded Star & Mums Sweets Dish

Sweets dish, Beaded Star and Mums patt., Verre d'Or treatment, green w/gold decoration, Wheeling, West Virginia factory, 6" d. (ILLUS.) **210**

Garden Mums Sweets Dish

Sweets dish, Garden Mums patt., Verre D'or decoration on green, Wheeling, West Virginia factory, 6" d. (ILLUS.) **185**

Ribbons & Overlapping Squares Sweets Dish

Sweets dish, Ribbons & Overlapping Squares patt., "Verre d'or" decoration on blue, Wheeling, West Virginia factory, 6" d. (ILLUS.) **175**

Pink Grape & Leaf Syrup Jug

Syrup jug w/original top, Grape and Leaf patt., opaque pink w/crystal handle, Indiana, Pennsylvania factory (ILLUS.) **400**

Quilted Phlox Syrup Pitcher

Syrup jug w/original top, Quilted Phlox patt., opaque green, Ellwood City, Pennsylvania factory (ILLUS.) **275-300**

Opalescent Stripe Syrup Jug

Syrup jug w/original top, Stripe patt., cranberry opalescent , Martins Ferry, Ohio factory (ILLUS.) **250**

Memphis Tumbler

Tumbler, Memphis patt., green w/gold rim, Wheeling, West Virginia factory (ILLUS.) **38**
Tumbler, Oriental Poppy patt., green w/gold trim, Wheeling, West Virginia factory **30**

Beads & Bark Vase

Vase, Beads & Bark patt., "Mosaic" (slag) glass, Wheeling, West Virginia factory (ILLUS.) **60-70**

Rosita Amber Twisted Vase

Vase, No. 727, twisted, Rosita Amber, Wheeling, West Virginia factory (ILLUS.) **65**

Opaline

Also called opal glass (once a name applied to milk-white glass), opaline is a fairly opaque glass with a color resembling the opal; however, pieces in such colors as blue, pink, green and others also are referred to now as opaline glass. Many of the objects were decorated.

Cache pot, cov., flared rim, blue w/gilded flowerheads & vines, late 19th c., 7" h. **$230**
Powder box, cov., cranberry dots encircled w/enameled foliage & gold trimmed cut top & base, Bohemia, 4" d., 2 1/4" h. **330**
Vase, 28 1/2" h., footed baluster-form w/tall trumpet neck, the body & neck painted w/a continuous scene of putti in various pursuits among clouds, birds & beds of flowers, the low domed round foot decorated w/rose-color leaf-tips & raised on a square gilt-bronze base w/bracket feet, France, late 19th c. **6,325**
Vases, 14" h., Neoclassical form in blue w/gilt decoration, France, 19th c., pr. **460**

Pairpoint

Originally organized in New Bedford, Massachusetts, in 1880 as the Pairpoint Manufacturing Company on land adjacent to the famed Mount Washington Glass Company, this company first manufactured silver and plated wares. In 1894, the two famous factories merged as the Pairpoint Corporation and enjoyed great success for more than forty years. The company was sold in 1939 to a group of local businessmen and eventually bought out by one of the group who turned the management over to Robert M. Gundersen. Subsequently, it operated as the Gundersen Glass Works until 1952 when, after Gundersen's death, the name was changed to Gundersen-Pairpoint. The factory closed in 1956. Subsequently, Robert Bryden took charge of this glassworks, at first producing glass for Pairpoint abroad and eventually, in 1970, beginning glass production in Sagamore, Massachusetts. Today the Pairpoint Crystal Glass Company is owned by Robert and June Bancroft. They continue to manufacture fine quality blown and pressed glass.

Atomizer, bulbous base tapering to a cylindrical neck, embossed swirl design, h.p. lily of the valley & scrolling decoration on white ground, signed "2341," 6" h. **$375**

Box w/hinged cover, border of aqua & white scrolls surrounding vines of wild roses on cover, aqua base decorated w/wild roses, raised on a gilt-metal frame marked "Pairpoint," 4 1/4 x 6 3/4", 4" h. **750**
Castor set: two square cruets w/original square cut stoppers, one square mustard jar w/original silver plate top & circular handle & a silver plate holder w/ornate handle marked "Hartford," clear w/cut & etched overall floral designs, the set............. **175**
Center bowl, clear "controlled" bubble bowl w/applied ruby pedestal base, 12" d. **275**

Pairpoint Engraved Covered Compote

Compote, cov., 8 3/4" d., 13" h., clear deep rounded bowl on a knop stem & round foot, domed cover w/knop finial encasing a white rose & green leaves, the sides engraved w/a rosebush on trellis design, leafy floral bands on cover & foot, Sagamore (ILLUS.) **750**
Compote, cov., 9", ruby w/clear "controlled" bubble knob finial **225**
Compote, open, 5" h., ruby bowl w/clear "controlled" bubble knob pedestal base......... **135**
Compote, open, 7 1/2" d., 4" h., amethyst decorated w/engraved grape design.............. **225**
Compotes, open, 8" d., 7" h., a wide shallow round canary yellow bowl on a tall applied clear baluster-form stem w/a large clear "controlled bubble" knob, applied clear foot, pr. **413**

Rare Pairpoint Flambo Console Set

Console set: footed center bowl & pair of tall candlesticks; Flambo color, deep tomato red bowl & candlestick stems & sockets, each on a clear "controlled bubble" stem knop on a black foot, decorated overall w/silver overlay, the set (ILLUS.)... **3,500-5,000**
Cornucopia-vase, ruby w/clear "controlled bubble" ball connector, 9" h............................ **150**

Cracker jar, cov., milk white w/h.p. blue Delft scenic decoration, silver-plate rim, cover & handle, 5 3/4" h. **550**

Pitcher, 12" h., green body & foot w/clear applied handle & "controlled bubble" knop stem **155**

Plates, 8" d., Tavern line (clear glass w/thousands of bubbles), clear w/galleon decoration, set of 12.................................... **2,400**

Tumbler, Tavern line, barrel-shaped, clear w/h.p. black enameled galleon under full sail & rim trim.. **275**

Gundersen Gold Ruby Vases

Vase, chalice-form w/clear "controlled bubble" connector in pedestal base, rare Gold Ruby by Gundersen-Pairpoint (ILLUS. center).. **300-400**

Vase, footed banjo-form w/taller slender flaring neck, rare Gold Ruby, Gundersen-Pairpoint (ILLUS. left)............................. **400-600**

Vase, footed fanned form w/applied clear swan rim handles, rare Gold Ruby by Gundersen-Pairpoint (ILLUS. right) **400-600**

Pairpoint Tavern Line Vase

Vase, 6" h., Tavern line, ovoid body tapering to a short flaring neck, decorated in black & colors w/a sailing galleon on a wavy sea & enameled rings, signed "D1507" (ILLUS.) **325**

Vase, 9 1/2" h., trumpet-form clear bowl cut in floral decoration w/Aurora (golden amber) applied rim, knob stem & an applied base rim.. **285**

Vase, 11" h., ruby cornucopia-shaped body w/clear "controlled bubble" connector & applied ruby pedestal base **185**

Vase, 11 3/4" h., tall ruby trumpet-form bowl raised on a ruby ringed stem centered by a clear "controlled bubble" knob connector, ruby disk foot, polished pontil, 20th c. **230**

Vase, 12" h., trumpet-shaped green body, clear "controlled bubble" ball connector & green foot... **150**

Vase, 12" h., 6 1/4" d., a large trumpet-form bowl in canary yellow engraved w/a vin-

tage grape design, on a clear applied ringed tall stem w/a large clear "controlled bubble" central knob, applied clear foot w/engraved dots, early 20th c. **503**

Vase, 13" h., 6 1/2" d., cobalt blue trumpet-shaped body & pedestal foot w/clear "controlled bubble" ball connector **425**

Vases, 8 3/4" h., cornucopia shape, ruby w/clear "controlled bubble" knob base, pr...... **300**

Vases, 12" h., ruby body & foot, clear "controlled bubble" ball connector, pr. **450**

Pate de Verre

Pate de Verre, or "paste of glass," was molded by very few artisans. In the pate de verre technique, powdered glass is mixed with a liquid to make a paste which is then placed in a mold and baked at a high temperature. These articles have a finely pitted or matte finish and are easily distinguished from blown glass. Duplicate pieces are possible with this technique.

Bowl, 11" d., footed deep rounded sides w/a wide rolled rim, cast w/bands of colors including orange, purple, light blue, dark blue & white, the interior molded w/purple arches & shafts w/yellow spearpoint heads, by Henri Cros, ca. 1900, unsigned... **$8,625**

Pate de Verre Bowl/Vase

Bowl-vase, deep ovoid form w/a wide flat mouth, shades of blue, turquoise, black & pale yellow, molded around the sides w/three stylized petals & scrolled handles, signed in the mold "G. Argy-Rousseau," ca. 1924, 4" h. (ILLUS.) **4,600**

Pate de Verre Butterfly Bowl/Vase

Bowl-vase, deep rounded form w/wide flat mouth, grey molded in low-relief w/three swallowtail butterflies in deep blue tinged w/green, molded mark of G. Argy-Rousseau, ca. 1915, 3 1/8" h. (ILLUS.) **7,475**

Flower & Foliage Pate de Verre Box

Box, cov., round short cylindrical form, muted purple, molded on the flat cover w/a central red flower w/amber & purple leaves forming a border on the cover & around the sides, G. Argy-Rousseau, ca. 1923, 5 1/4" d. (ILLUS.) **4,313**

Unusual Pate de Verre Coupe

Coupe, "Coupe sur pied aux anses," a round foot issuing large tapering incurled horns flanking a wide deep rounded bowl, large molded blossoms on the sides of the bowl, overall mottled amber, brown & black, G. Argy-Rousseau, ca. 1927, overall 8" w., 4" h. **5,750**

Lamp base, "The Garden of The Hesperides," ovoid body w/a mottled yellow & brown ground overlaid on the upper half w/a continuous scene of a stylized classical maiden in orange & black plucking yellow apples from brown trees, the lower half w/mottled black & brown band w/incised angular scrolls, patinated metal scroll-pierced footed base & domed cap for electric fitting, by G. Argy-Rousseau, 27 3/4" h. **5,175**

Night light, "Dune Flowers," a spherical shade in shades of purple, magenta, cobalt blue, jade & raspberry molded w/swelled block bands under pendent half-round dark blossoms, signed "G Argy-Rousseau - France," set on a round hand-hammered wrought-iron ring w/curled upright bar supports above the thin disk foot, base signed "France 106," ca. 1925, 8 1/4" h. **5,750**

Pendant, frosted clear disk decorated w/red flowers w/dark green & blue centers, Argy-Rousseau, 2" d. **1,265**

Vase, 5 1/2" h., broad ovoid form w/a wide flat mouth, mottled frosted white ground molded around the upper half w/brown twigs & large reddish orange blossoms w/dark centers, G. Argy-Rousseau, ca. 1920 .... **7,475**

Vase, 5 1/2" h., "Crabes et Algues," bulbous ovoid form w/a wide flat rim, dark rusty red rim band above the streaked frosted clear & brown ground, molded on the shoulder w/a large brown crab, G. Argy-Rousseau, ca. 1920 .... **5,750**

Vase, 5 3/4" h., wide flat-bottomed ovoid form tapering to a small trumpet neck, streaked frosted white & purple ground molded around the shoulder w/a dark mottled ground band & large scarab beetles in brown & green, G. Argy-Rousseau, ca. 1923 .... **7,475**

Wolves in the Snow Vase

Vase, 9 1/2" h., "Les Loups dans la neige," simple ovoid body, boldly molded around the rim & lower half w/tiered undulating bands of white against a streaked white & purple ground molded w/a band of dark purple walking wolves, G. Argy-Rousseau, ca. 1926 (ILLUS.) **43,125**

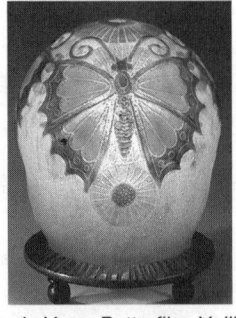

Pate de Verre Butterflies Veilleuse

Veilleuse (night light), "Papillons," large bulbous ovoid domed shade in grey molded in low relief w/three stylized butterflies lighting on blossoms in shades of crimson, black, purple & green, simple round wrought-iron footed base, shade by G. Argy-Rousseau, ca. 1924, 5 3/8" h. (ILLUS.) **12,650**

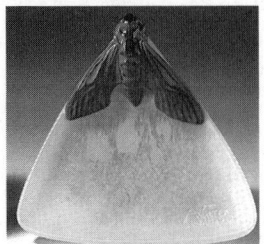

Pate de Verre Vide Poche with Moth

Vide poche (figural dish), triangular, deep
yellow mottled w/orange & molded at one
corner with a large dark moth, A. Walter,
Nancy, ca. 1925, 6 3/8" w., 2" h. (ILLUS.).. **4,945**

Pattern

*Though it has never been ascertained whether glass
was first pressed in the United States or abroad, the
development of the glass pressing machine revolution-
ized the glass industry in the United States, and this
country receives the credit for improving the method to
make this process feasible. The first wares pressed were
probably small flat plates of the type now referred to as
"lacy," the intricacy of the design concealing flaws.*

*In 1827, both the New England Glass Co., Cam-
bridge, Mass., and Bakewell & Co., Pittsburgh, took out
patents for pressing glass furniture knobs; soon other
pieces followed. This early pressed glass contained red
lead, which made it clear and resonant when tapped
(flint.) Made primarily in clear, it is rarer in blue, amethyst, olive green and yellow.*

*By the 1840s, early simple patterns such as Ashburton,
Argus and Excelsior appeared. Ribbed Bellflower seems to
have been one of the earliest patterns to have had complete
sets. By the 1860s, a wide range of patterns was available.*

*In 1864, William Leighton of Hobbs, Brockunier &
Co., Wheeling, West Virginia, developed a formula for
"soda lime" glass that did not require the expensive red
lead for clarity. Although "soda lime" glass did not
have the brilliance of the earlier flint glass, the formula
came into widespread use because glass could be produced cheaply.*

*An asterisk (*) indicates a piece which has been repro-
duced.*

Actress

Bowl, 6" d., flat.. **$45**
Bowl, 6" d., footed... **50**
Bowl, 7" d., footed... **60**
Bowl, 8" d., Adelaide Neilson........................ **65**
Bowl, cov. **110**

Actress Bread Tray

Bread tray, Miss Neilson, 12 1/2" l.
(ILLUS.).. **110**
Butter dish, cov., Fanny Davenport & Miss
Neilson.. **175**
Cake stand, Maude Granger & Annie Pix-
ley, 10" d., 7" h... **295**
Cake stand, frosted stem **150-165**
Celery vase, Pinafore scene............................ **210**
Champagne, rare.. **250**

Cheese dish, cov., "Lone Fisherman" on
cover, "The Two Dromios" on underplate...... **350**
Cologne bottle w/original stopper, 11" h........... **90**
Compote, cov., 6" d., 10" h.................................. **100**
Compote, cov., 7" d., 8 1/2" h., frosted.............. **165**
Compote, cov., 8" d., 12" h.................................. **230**
Compote, cov., 10" d., 14 1/2" h., Fanny
Davenport & Maggie Mitchell **200**
Compote, open, 6" d., 3" h.................................. **55**
Compote, open, 6" d., 11" h................................ **100**
Compote, open, 7" d., 7" h., Maggie Mitch-
ell & Fanny Davenport..................................... **110**
Compote, open, 7" d., 7" h., Miss Neilson......... **150**
Compote, open, 8" d., 5" h. **50**
Compote, open, 10" d., 6" h. **80**
Compote, open, 10" d., 9" h. **100**
Creamer, clear... **75**
Creamer, frosted.. **100**
Creamer, Miss Neilson & Fanny Davenport...... **125**
Dresser box, cov. 3 1/2" d. **60**
Dresser box, cov., footed, 2 1/2 x 6" oval **75**
Egg cup **70**
Goblet, clear bowl, frosted stem **110**
Goblet, Lotta Crabtree & Kate Claxton **95**
Marmalade jar, cov., Maude Granger & An-
nie Pixley **118**
Mug, Pinafore scene... **50**
*Pickle dish, Kate Claxton, "Love's Re-
quest is Pickles," 5 1/4 x 9 1/2"....................... **65**
Pitcher, milk, 6 1/4" h... **350**
Pitcher, water, 9" h., Miss Neilson & Maggie
Mitchell.. **285**
Platter, 7 x 11 1/2", Pinafore scene **75**
*Relish, Miss Neilson, 5 x 8"............................... **40**
Relish, Maude Granger, 5 x 9" **85**
Sauce dish, flat, 4 1/2" d. **15**
Sauce dish, Maggie Mitchell & Fanny Dav-
enport, footed, 4 1/2" d., 2 1/4" h. **24**
Sauce dish, 5" d., footed **28**
Spooner, Mary Anderson & Maude Granger....... **95**
Sugar bowl, cov., Lotta Crabtree & Kate
Claxton **130**

Art (Job's Tears)

Banana stand **100**
Basket, fruit... **165**
Bowl, 5 7/8" d. **38**
Bowl, 7" d., flared rim, footed............................. **45**
Bowl, 8" sq., shallow **50**
Bowl, 8 1/2" d., flat... **45**
Bowl, 9 3/4" d. **55**
Bowl, 6 x 10", teardrop-pulled form **70**
Bowl, triangular **45**
Butter dish, cov., clear **75**
Butter dish, cov., ruby-stained **145**
Cake stand, 9" d. **95**
Cake stand, 10 1/2" d. **100**
Celery vase **85**
Compote, cov., 6" d., 10" h. **80**
Compote, cov., 7" d **85**
Compote, cov., 8" d., high stand........................ **95**
Compote, cov., 9" d.. **115**
Compote, true open, jelly, 5" d. **38**
Compote, true open, 7" d................................... **70**
Compote, true open, 8" d., high stand **70**
Compote, true open, 9" d., 7 1/4" h.................... **85**
Compote, true open, flaring belled scal-
loped rim, 10" d., 9" h. **95**
Cracker jar, cov., 7" d., 8" h. to top of finial....... **150**
Creamer **60**

Cruet w/original stopper, clear 88
Cruet w/original stopper, ruby-stained........... 175
Goblet 75
Mug 50
Pitcher, milk, clear 100
Pitcher, milk, ruby-stained............................... 150
Pitcher, water, bulbous, short, squat............... 145
Pitcher, water, applied handle, bulbous,
 9 1/2" h... 250
Punch cup 20
Relish, rectangular, clear, 4 1/4 x 7 3/4" 40
Relish, rectangular, clear, 6 1/2 x 8 1/2" 40
Relish, rectangular, ruby-stained,
 4 1/4 x 7 3/4" 65
Salt shaker w/original top 45
Sauce dish, flat or footed, each........................ 22
Sauce dish, pulled teardrop shape..................... 24
Spooner 70
Sugar bowl, cov., frosted diamonds 65
Sugar bowl, cov., plain 65
Tumbler 75

Bellflower

Bottle, clambroth, 8 3/4" h............................... 295
Bowl, cov., 9" d.. 195
Bowl, 6" d., 1 3/4" h., single vine 150
Bowl, 7 1/2" d., 2" h.. 400
Bowl, 7 1/2" d., 5" h., single vine 150
Bowl, 8" d., 2" h., round, single vine, scallop
 & point rim, plain polished base 180
Bowl, 8 1/2" d., 4 3/4" h., scalloped rim............ 110
Bowl, cov., 8" d., 9" h., unpatterned low
 foot, hexagonal acorn finial, wafer con-
 struction... 475
Bowl, 9" l., 6" w. oval, rayed base 275
Butter dish, cov. 167
Cake stand, short stem, domed foot, single
 vine, 8 3/4" d., 3" h., 2" h. standard 5,600
Castor bottle w/original stopper 75
Castor set, 4-bottle, w/pewter stand................. 400
Castor set, 5-bottle, single vine, w/pewter
 stand... 558
Celery vase, single vine, banded unpat-
 terned scallop & point rim, single step
 foot base w/32 raised rays & center cir-
 cle, 8" h. (small spots of wear on high
 points of rim).. 425
Celery vase, w/cut bellflowers 313
Champagne, fine rib, double vine, w/cut
 bellflowers, 5" h.. 450
Champagne, straight sides, single vine,
 plain stem, rayed base, 5" h. 125
Champagne, barrel-shaped, fine rib, knob
 stem, plain base, 5 1/4" h................................. 140
Champagne, barrel-shaped, fine rib, single
 vine, knob stem, rayed base, 5 1/4" h.............. 96
Cologne bottle w/stopper, clambroth 500
Cologne bottle w/stopper, clear variant......... 350
Compote, cov., 8 3/4" d., fine rib, single
 vine, low stand 350
Compote, open, 6 1/2" d., single vine, high
 stand... 200
Compote, open, 6 1/2" d., single vine, low
 stand... 135
Compote, open, 7" d., high stand...................... 200
Compote, open, 8 1/2" d., single vine, low
 stand, scalloped rim 185
Compote, open, 9" d., single vine, high
 stand, scalloped rim 300

Compote, cov., 8" d., 8" h., fine rib, single
 vine.. 500
Compote, open, 4 1/2" d., low stand, scal-
 loped rim 87
Compote, open, 7" d., low stand, scalloped
 rim... 150
Compote, open, 7" d., 5" h., fine rib, double
 vine.. 90-100
Compote, open, 8" d., high stand, scal-
 loped rim 250
Compote, open, 8" d., low stand, scalloped
 rim... 175
Compote, open, 8" d., 5" h., coarse rib, sin-
 gle vine, low foot w/scallop rim........................ 250
Compote, open, 9 1/2" d., 8 1/2" h., single
 vine, scalloped rim 342
Creamer, fine rib, double vine, applied han-
 dle 150-200
Creamer, fine rib, single vine, applied han-
 dle 325
Decanter w/bar lip, double vine, qt. 208
Decanter w/bar lip, w/stopper, cut shoul-
 der, single vine... 550
Decanter w/bar lip, double vine, pt. 225
Decanter w/bar lip, fine rib, single vine, pt. 218
Decanter w/bar lip, patent stopper, double
 vine, qt. 385
Decanter w/bar lip, single vine, qt. 225
Decanter w/original stopper, cut shoulder,
 pt. (large chip off ground end of stopper
 where it fits into neck)...................................... 800
Decanter w/original stopper, cut shoulder,
 qt. 950
Egg cup, coarse rib 45
Egg cup, cov., w/shield..................................... 450
Egg cup, double vine, w/cut bellflowers............. 75
Egg cup, fine rib, single vine.............................. 45
Goblet, barrel-shaped, coarse rib, single
 vine... 40-45
Goblet, barrel-shaped, fine rib, single vine,
 knob stem 55-60
Goblet, barrel-shaped, fine rib, single vine,
 knob stem, rayed base...................................... 56
*Goblet, barrel-shaped, fine rib, single vine,
 plain stem 35
Goblet, coarse rib, single vine, flared top 60
Goblet, fine rib, double vine, w/cut bellflow-
 ers.. 425
Goblet, single vine, rayed base........................... 55
Goblet, fine rib, single vine, w/cut bellflow-
 ers, 5 1/2" h. 2,050
Goblet, single vine, w/loops, 5 1/2" h.
 (some mold roughness & tiny flakes on
 ribs).. 228
Honey dish, cov., single vine 82
Honey dish, scalloped rim, star base, 3" d. 100
Honey dish, rayed center, 3 1/4" d...................... 23
Honey dish, ringed center, 3 1/2" d..................... 23
Lamp, kerosene-type, font for suspension
 or bracket lamp, single vine, pattern on
 top of font, plain ribbing on lower section,
 10-petal rosette under base, brass collar,
 side oil filler hole w/brass collar & cap 1,200
Lamp, whale oil, brass stem, clambroth
 pressed square base, single vine, 9" h.
 (small chip on ring under font)........................ 375
Lamp, whale oil, pattern on inside of font,
 top of ribs scalloped, scalloped base,
 9" h. (replaced collar, hard to see internal
 line under collar, probably factory flaw) 650

Lamp, kerosene-type, clear font, brass stem w/engraved decoration & marble base, flint, 11" h. 275
Pitcher, cider, double vine................................. 230
Pitcher, double vine, straight sides, 1 pt., 6 1/4" h. **1,800**
Pitcher, milk, double vine, 7" h. **2,000**
Pitcher, milk, single vine, 7 1/2" h. **1,750**
Pitcher, water, 8 3/4" h., coarse rib, double vine... 463
Pitcher, water, single vine 295
Plate, 6" d., fine rib, single vine......................... 100
Plate, 10 1/2" d., double vine............................ 150
Salt dip, cov., master size, footed, beaded rim, fine rib, single vine 250
Salt dip, open, master size, footed, scalloped rim, single vine 66
Sauce dish, double vine 24
Sauce dish, single vine 24
Spooner, low foot, double vine 145
Spooner, scalloped rim, single vine..................... 66
Spooner, single vine, scalloped rim, cobalt blue **7,000**
Sugar bowl, cov., double vine 137
Sugar bowl, cov., single vine............................. 300
Sugar bowl, cov., octagonal, domed lid, 8" h. **1,450**
Sugar bowl, open, coarse rib, double vine........ 60
Sugar bowl, open, coarse rib, single vine 60
Sweetmeat, cov., high stand, single vine, 6" d., overall 8 1/2" h. **1,000**
Syrup pitcher w/original top, applied handle, fine rib, single vine, clear **1,700**
Syrup pitcher w/original top, applied handle, fine rib, single vine, fiery opalescent... **3,500**
Syrup pitcher w/original top, applied handle, pale green 525
Syrup pitcher w/original top, applied hollow handle, milk glass (handle base curl gone).. 600
Syrup pitcher w/original top, solid handle, milk glass **2,000**
Tumbler, bar, fine rib, single vine..................... 110
Tumbler, coarse rib, double vine....................... 150
*Tumbler, fine rib, single vine 125
Tumbler, fine rib, single vine, plain rim band........ 90
Tumbler, fine rib, single vine, w/cut bellflowers 150
Tumbler, whiskey, handled 250
Tumbler, whiskey, single vine 135
Tumbler, fine rib, double vine, w/cut bellflowers, 3 1/2" h. 400
Tumbler, water, coarse rib, single vine, factory polished table ring, 3 1/2" h. 100
Tumbler, fine rib, double vine, 4 7/8" h. 275
Tumbler, footed, single step foot, 64 rays under base w/large center circle, double vine, 4 7/8" h. (two small bruises on edge of foot & one underneath)............................... 450
Wine, barrel-shaped, fine rib, double vine, w/cut bellflowers.................................... 325
Wine, fine rib, single vine, straight sides, plain stem, rayed base.. 95

Block & Fan

Bowl, berry, 8" d., flat base 40
Bowl, 4 1/2 x 6 1/2", rectangle, flat base............. 35
Bowl, 7 1/2" d., round w/flat base........................ 40
Bowl, berry, 8" d., footed 45

Bowl, 9" l., 5" w., oval.. 40
Bowl, 9 3/4" d. 48
Bowl, 10" l., 6" w., rectangular........................... 40
Bowl, 5 x 12", rectangular 45
Butter dish, cov. 80
Cake stand, 9" to 10" d. 85
Carafe, water 80
Celery vase 40
Compote, open, 7" d., high stand 70
Compote, open, 8" d., high stand 75
Cracker jar, cov. 85
Creamer 45
Cruet w/original stopper, small, 6" h. 50
Cruet w/original stopper, medium 60
Cruet w/original stopper, large 70
Finger or waste bowl 60
Goblet, clear 80
Goblet, ruby-stained.. 110
Ice bucket 85
Pitcher, milk.. 35
Pitcher, water, clear 80
Pitcher, water, ruby-stained............................... 325
Plate, 7" d. 30
Plate, 10" d. 40
Rose bowl, 4 1/2" d... 50
Salt & pepper shakers w/original tops, pr........ 70
Sauce dish, flat or footed, clear 20
Sauce dish, flat or footed, ruby-stained............. 28
Spooner, clear.. 40
Sugar bowl, cov. 60
Sugar shaker w/original top 70
Syrup pitcher w/original top, 7" h..................... 155
Tray, ice cream, 8" x 13 1/2"............................... 75
Tumbler, clear... 30
Wine, clear.. 55
Wine, ruby-stained.. 75

Broken Column (Irish Column, Notched Rib or Bamboo)

Banana stand 175
Bowl, 7 1/2" d., clear.. 65
Bowl, berry, 6" d., clear....................................... 45
Bowl, berry, 6" d., ruby-stained notches 65
Bowl, cov., 6" d. 135
Bowl, berry, 6 1/2" d., clear................................. 50
Bowl, 7" d. 60
*Bowl, 8" d. 70
*Bowl, 8 1/2" d 75
Bowl, 9" d. 80
Bowl, cov., vegetable 95
Butter dish, cov. 140
Cake stand, 9"... 110
Cake stand, 10" d. 140
Carafe, water 145
Celery tray, 5 x 10", ruby-stained notches 95
Celery vase, clear.. 90
Celery vase, ruby-stained notches 155
Compote, cov., 5 1/2" d., high stand, clear....... 95
Compote, cov., 6 1/2" d., high stand, clear 145
Compote, open, 11" d., shallow scalloped rim, clear 155
Compote, cov., 5" d., high stand, clear 105
Compote, cov., 5" d., high stand, ruby-stained notches.. 225
Compote, cov., 7 1/2" d., high stand 195
Compote, cov., 8" d., high stand 175
Compote, cov., 8" d., high stand, ruby-stained notches.. 525
Compote, open, jelly, ruby-stained notches...... 195
Compote, open, 5" d., low stand, flared rim........ 75
Compote, open, 5" d., low stand, ruby-stained notches.. 135

Compote, open, 5" d., 6" h. 65
Compote, open, 6" d., high stand......................... 60
Compote, open, 7" d., low stand 80
Compote, open, 8" d., high stand, ruby-
 stained notches... 250
Compote, open, 8" d., low stand 90
Compote, open, 9" d., high stand, clear.............. 75
Compote, open, 9" d., high stand, ruby-
 stained notches... 175
Compote, open, 10" d., low stand...................... 110
Cracker jar, cov... 120
*Creamer, clear 110
Creamer, ruby-stained notches 250
Cruet w/original stopper, clear 125
Cruet w/original stopper, ruby-stained
 notches.. 525
*Goblet, clear 85
Goblet, ruby-stained notches............................. 250
Marmalade jar w/original cover 125
Pickle castor, cov., clear, original ornate
 frame.. 238
Pickle castor, ruby-stained, w/frame &
 tongs.. 413
*Pitcher, water, clear... 135
Pitcher, water, ruby-stained notches............... 450
Plate, 5" d. 32
Plate, 6" d. 35
Plate, 7" d. 45
Plate, 7" d., ruby-stained notches...................... 95
*Plate, 8" d., clear.. 50
Plate, 8" d., ruby-stained notches...................... 75
Punch cup, blue.. 95
Punch cup, clear... 25
Punch cup, ruby-stained notches....................... 60
Relish, 3 3/4 x 5", clear 30
Relish, 3 3/4 x 5", green...................................... 85
Relish, 6 1/2" l. 35
Relish, clear, 9" l., 6" w. 45
Relish, ruby-stained notches............................... 95
Salt shaker w/original top, clear....................... 85
Salt shaker w/original top, ruby-stained
 notches.. 125
*Sauce dish, clear, 3 1/2" d., 4" d. &
 4 1/2" d., each 20
Sauce dish, ruby-stained notches, 4 1/2" d. 30
*Spooner, clear 65
Spooner, ruby-stained notches 125
*Sugar bowl, cov., clear 135
Sugar bowl, cov., ruby-stained notches............ 150
Sugar shaker w/metal top, clear...................... 110
Sugar shaker w/metal top, ruby-stained
 notches.. 495
Syrup pitcher w/metal top, clear 150
Syrup pitcher w/metal top, w/red notches 405
Tumbler, ruby-stained notches........................... 85
*Wine 85

Canadian

Bowl, cov., w/a flanged rim, rare 150
Bowl, 6" d., handled.. 28
Bowl, berry, 7" d., 4 1/2" h., footed 69
Bowl, 8" d., handled.. 45
Bowl, 9 1/2" d. 55
Butter dish, cov. 75
Compote, cov., 6" d., low stand........................... 95
Compote, cov., 6" d., 9" h. 105
Compote, cov., 7" d., low stand......................... 115
Compote, cov., 7" d., 11" h. 125
Compote, cov., 8" d., low stand......................... 125
Compote, cov., 8" d., 11" h. 145
Creamer 85

Canadian Goblet

Goblet (ILLUS.).. 65
Honey dish, flat, 3 1/2" d...................................... 25
Pitcher, milk, 8" h.. 125
Pitcher, water.. 150
Plate, 6" d., handled 40
Plate, 7" d., handled 45
Plate, 8" d., handled 55
Plate, 9" d... 60
Sauce dish, flat or footed, each 25
Spooner 75
Sugar bowl, cov... 135
Wine 45

Classic

Bowl, cov., 6 1/2" d., collared base.................... 173
Bowl, cov., 6 1/2" d., open log feet.................... 180
Bowl, cov., 7" hexagon, open log feet............... 175
Bowl, cov., 7 1/2" d., 8" h., open log feet........... 250
Bowl, cov., 9" d., open log feet.......................... 350
Bowl, cov., 12 1/2" d., collared base 325
Bowl, cov., 8" hexagon, open log feet............... 200
Butter dish, cov., collared base......................... 200
Butter dish, cov., open log feet......................... 250
Celery vase, collared base 145
Celery vase, open log feet 175
Compote, open, 8 1/2" d., 8" h., scalloped
 edge, collared base, etched 50
Creamer, collared base 125
Creamer, open log feet 175
Goblet 295
Marmalade jar, cov., open log feet................... 600
Pitcher, milk, 8 1/2" h., open log feet 525
Pitcher, water, 9 1/2" h., collared base 263
Pitcher, water, 9 1/2" h., open log fee.............. 425
Plate, 10" d., "Blaine" or "Hendricks," signed
 "Jacobus," each 250
Plate, 10" d., "Cleveland"................................... 250
Plate, 10" d., "Logan"... 350
Plate, 10" d., "Warrior"....................................... 150
Plate, 10" d., "Warrior," signed "Jacobus".......... 185
Sauce dish, open log feet 40
Spooner, collared base 155
Spooner, open log feet 185
Sugar bowl, cov., collared base........................ 175
Sugar bowl, cov., open log feet 200

Cut Log

Bowl, 6 1/2" d., footed or flat............................ 30-40
Bowl, 7" d., footed or flat 50-60
Bowl, 8" d., scalloped rim, flat base.................... 55
Bowl, master berry or fruit, 8" d., footed 65

Bowl, 9 1/2" d., footed or flat............................ 75-85
Butter dish, cov. 85
Cake stand, 9 1/4" d., high stand........................ 85
Cake stand, 10 1/2" d., high stand.................... 125
Celery tray 30
Celery vase 75
Compote, cov., jelly, 5 1/2" d., high stand 65
Compote, cov., 7 1/4" d., high stand 85
Compote, cov., 8" d., high stand 95
Compote, open, jelly, scalloped rim, 5" d. 40
*Compote, open, 6" d., scalloped rim, high
    stand... 40
Compote, open, 7 1/2" d., scalloped rim,
    high stand 45
Compote, open, 8" d., scalloped rim, high
    stand... 75
*Compote, open, 9" d., scalloped rim, high
    stand... 85
Compote, open, 9 3/4" d., scalloped rim,
    high stand 165
Compote, open, 10 3/4" d., scalloped rim,
    high stand 185
Creamer 60
Creamer, individual size.. 25
Cruet w/original stopper, small, 3 3/4" h. 45
Cruet w/original stopper, 4" h............................. 65
Cruet w/original stopper, large, 5" h.................. 75

Cut Log Goblet

Goblet (ILLUS.) 80
Honey dish, cov., square 110
Mug, 3 1/4" h. 25
Olive dish, handled, 5" d. 30
Pitcher, helmet shaped w/design on handle..... 125
Pitcher, water, tankard, clear................................ 80
Pitcher, water, tankard, ruby-stained................ 240
Relish, boat-shaped, 9 1/4" l................................ 30
Salt dip, master size, scarce................................ 85
Salt shaker w/original tin top 40
Sauce dish, flat or footed, smooth or scal-
    loped edge, each 25
Spooner 60
Sugar bowl, cov.. 80
Sugar bowl, cov., individual size.......................... 55
Tumbler, juice... 40
Tumbler, water.. 75
Vase, 15" h., swung-type 50
Vase, 16" h., swung-type 55
Vase, 18" h., swung-type 60
Wine 20

Fleur-De-Lis and Drape (Fleur-de-Lis and Tassel)

Bottle, water, clear... 65
Bottle, water, emerald green............................. 115

Bottle, water, milk white...................................... 250
Bowl, berry, 6" d., clear.. 25
Bowl, berry, 6" d., emerald green 45
Bowl, berry, 6" d., milk white............................... 100
Bowl, berry, 8" d., clear.. 35
Bowl, berry, 8" d., emerald green 50
Bowl, berry, 8" d., milk white...................... 100-125
Butter dish, cov., clear, flat................................... 55
Butter dish, cov., emerald green, flat 75
Butter dish, cov., milk white, flat....................... 175
Butter dish, cov., clear, footed, flanged rim....... 65
Butter dish, cov., emerald green, footed,
    flanged rim... 85
Butter dish, cov., milk white, footed,
    flanged rim... 200
Cake stand, clear, high stand, 9" d. 55
Cake stand, emerald green, high stand,
    9" d. 75
Cake stand, milk white, high stand, 9" d........... 100
Cake stand, clear, high stand, 10" d. 60
Cake stand, emerald green, high stand,
    10" d. 80
Cake stand, milk white, high stand, 10" d. 110
Celery tray, clear, oval.. 35
Celery tray, emerald green, oval 45
Celery vase, clear.. 45
Celery vase, emerald green 55
Celery vase, milk white... 90
Champagne, clear.. 40
Champagne, green 50
Claret, clear 35
Claret, emerald green 50
Compote, cov., clear, 5" d., high stand............... 35
Compote, cov., emerald green, 5" d., high
    stand... 55
Compote, cov., milk white, 5" d., high stand....... 75
Compote, cov., clear, 6" d., high stand............... 45
Compote, cov., emerald green, 6" d., high
    stand... 65
Compote, cov., milk white, 6" d., high stand....... 75
Compote, cov., clear, 7" d., high stand............... 55
Compote, cov., emerald green, 7" d., high
    stand... 75
Compote, cov., milk white, 7" d., high stand....... 85
Compote, cov., clear, 8" d., high stand............... 65
Compote, cov., emerald green, 8" d., high
    stand... 85
Compote, cov., milk white, 8" d., high stand....... 95
Compote, cov., clear, 5" d., low stand 30
Compote, cov., emerald green, 5" d., low
    stand... 50
Compote, cov., milk white, 5" d., low stand........ 75
Compote, cov., clear, 6" d., low stand 60
Compote, cov., emerald green, 6" d., low
    stand... 60
Compote, cov., milk white, 6" d., low stand........ 80
Compote, cov., clear, 8" d., low stand 60
Compote, cov., emerald green, 8" d., low
    stand... 80
Compote, cov., milk white, 8" d., low stand........ 85
Cordial, clear.. 35
Cordial, emerald green.. 45
Creamer, clear.. 30
Creamer, green... 45
Cruet w/original stopper, clear............................ 55
Cruet w/original stopper, emerald green........... 85
Cruet w/original stopper, milk white................. 110
Custard cup, clear 15
Custard cup, emerald green 25
Custard cup, milk white... 30

Custard cup & saucer, clear.............................. 25
Custard cup & saucer, emerald green............... 35
Custard cup & saucer, milk white....................... 40
Custard cup & saucer, ruby-stained 55
Finger bowl, clear... 35
Finger bowl, emerald green................................. 45
Goblet, clear 35
Goblet, emerald green 55
Goblet, milk white.. 50-60
Honey dish, cov., clear, square, ribbed lid 50
Honey dish, cov., emerald green, square,
ribbed lid.. 65
Honey dish, clear, flat, 3 1/2" d. 15
Honey dish, emerald green, flat, 3 1/2" d. 20
Honey dish, milk white, flat, 3 1/2" d. 25
Honey dish, clear, footed, 3 1/2" d. 15
Honey dish, emerald green, footed,
3 1/2" d... 20
Honey dish, milk white, footed, 3 1/2" d. 30
Lamp, finger-type, clear 95
Lamp, kerosene-type, clear, tall pedestal,
7 1/2" h.. 100
Lamp, kerosene-type, clear, tall pedestal,
8 1/2" h.. 110
Lamp, kerosene-type, clear, tall pedestal,
9 1/2" h.. 125
Mustard jar, cov., clear, handled......................... 35
Mustard jar, cov., emerald green, handled 50
Mustard jar, milk white, handled 55
Pickle dish, clear, boat-shaped........................... 18
Pickle dish, emerald green, boat-shaped............ 24
Pickle dish, milk white, boat-shaped................... 30
Pitcher, milk, clear, 1 qt. 50
Pitcher, milk, emerald green, 1 qt. 75
Pitcher, water, clear, 1/2 gal. 60
Pitcher, water, emerald green, 1/2 gal. 85
Plate, 6" d., clear 15
Plate, 6" d., emerald green 25
Plate, 7" d., clear 20
Plate, 7" d., emerald green 30
Plate, 8" d., clear 25
Plate, 8" d., emerald green 35
Plate, 9" d., clear 30
Plate, 9" d., emerald green 40
Plate, 10" d., clear 35
Plate, 10" d., emerald green................................ 45
Relish dish, clear, flat, oblong, 8" l. 25
Relish dish, emerald green, flat, oblong,
8" l. 35
Relish dish, milk white, flat, oblong, 8" l. 45
Salt shaker w/original top, clear.......................... 25
Salt shaker w/original top, emerald green........ 40
Sauce dish, clear, 3 1/2" d., flat, ... 8
Sauce dish, emerald green, 3 1/2" d., flat, ... 12
Sauce dish, clear, flat, 4" d. 10
Sauce dish, clear, footed, 4" d. 12
Sauce dish, emerald green, flat, 4" d. 14
Sauce dish, emerald green, footed, 4" d. 16
Sauce dish, milk white, flat, 4" d. 15
Sauce dish, clear, flat, 4 1/2" d. 10
Sauce dish, clear, footed, 4 1/2" d. 12
Sauce dish, emerald green, footed,
4 1/2" d.. 16
Sauce dish, milk white, flat, 4 1/2" d.................... 15
Sauce dish, milk white, footed, 4 1/2" d. 18
Spooner, clear 28
Spooner, emerald green...................................... 45
Sugar bowl, cov., clear.. 35
Sugar bowl, cov., emerald green......................... 60

Sugar shaker w/original top, clear 45
Sugar shaker w/original top, emerald
green 90
Syrup pitcher w/original top, clear.................... 55
Syrup pitcher w/original top, emerald
green 135
Tray, water, clear, 11 1/2" d. 55
Tray, water, emerald green, 11 1/2" d. 85
Tray, water, milk white, 11 1/2" d. 90
Tumbler, water, clear, flat 25
Tumbler, water, emerald green, flat 35
Wine, clear 28
Wine, emerald green 35
Wine, milk white 45

Plume

Bowl, cov., 8" d. 60
Bowl, open, 6" d. 24
Bowl, open, 7" d., flat, scalloped rim 30
Bowl, open, 8" d., shallow 30
Bowl, open, 9" d. 40
Butter dish, cov., clear.. 55
Butter dish, cov., ruby-stained........................... 135
Cake stand, 9" d., high stand 75
Cake stand, 10" d... 75
Celery vase, clear, horizontal plumes................. 45
Celery vase, clear, vertical plumes...................... 65
Celery vase, ruby-stained & engraved................ 95
Compote, cov., 7" d., high stand 75

Plume Open Compote

Compote, open, 7" d., high stand (ILLUS.) 40
Compote, cov., 8" d., high stand 85
Compote, cov., 9" d., high stand.......................... 95
Compote, open, 9" d., high stand 55
Compote, cov., 6 1/2" d., 12" h. 60
Compote, open, 8" d., high stand 40
Creamer, applied handle, clear 45
Creamer, ruby-stained 95
Finger or waste bowl 45
*Goblet, clear 40
Goblet, engraved.. 50
Goblet, ruby-stained & engraved 100
Lamp, kerosene-type 95
Pitcher, water, bulbous, clear, engraved 100
Pitcher, water, bulbous, clear, plain 80
Pitcher, water, bulbous, ruby-stained......... 200-250
Pitcher, water, tankard, blown, clear................... 50
Relish 22
Sauce dish, flat or footed, clear 15
Sauce dish, ruby-stained..................................... 20
Spooner, clear, engraved..................................... 55
Spooner, clear, plain.. 40
Spooner, ruby-stained 85
Sugar bowl, cov., clear.. 55
Sugar bowl, cov., ruby-stained 115
Tray, water, 13" d.. 55
Tumbler, blown 30

Tumbler, pressed, clear 60
Tumbler, ruby-stained 75

Roman Rosette

Bowl, 5" d. 25
Bowl, 6" d. 30
Bowl, 7" d. 30
Bowl, 6 1/4 x 9 1/2" oval 40
Bread platter, 9 x 11" 35
Butter dish, cov., flanged base, clear 65
Butter dish, cov., ruby-stained 105
Butter dish, cov., two-handled base, clear 95
Cake stand, 9" to 10" d. 85
Castor set, two shakers in handled holder,
   the set 50
Celery vase, clear 60
Celery vase, ruby-stained 120
Compote, cov., 5" d. 70
Compote, open, jelly, 5" d. 25
Compote, cov., 6" d., high stand 70
Compote, open, 8" d., high stand 45
Compote, open, 7" d., high stand 40
Compote, open, 9" d., high stand 55
Cordial 95

Roman Rosette Creamer

Creamer, clear (ILLUS.) 30
Creamer, ruby-stained 46
*Goblet 50
Honey dish, cov., square 75
Mug, large, barrel-shaped 48
Mug, small, barrel-shaped, clear 35
Mug, small, barrel-shaped, ruby-stained 55
Mug, tapering sides, 3" h. 16
Pitcher, milk 85
Pitcher, water 100
Plate, 7 1/4" d. 45
Relish, 3 1/2 x 8 1/2" 25
Salt & pepper shakers w/original tops, on
   original glass stand w/handle, set 50
Salt & pepper shakers w/original tops,
   ruby-stained, pr. 90
Salt shaker w/original top 24
Sauce dish, 4 1/4" d. 18
Sauce dish, 5 1/4" d. 20
Spooner, clear 30
Spooner, ruby-stained 65
Sugar bowl, cov. 50
Tumbler, clear 60
Tumbler, ruby-stained 75
Vegetable dish, oval, 6 1/2 x 61/2" 40
Vegetable dish, oval, 5 x 7 1/4" 35
Vegetable dish, oval, 4 x 8 1/2" 38
Wine, clear 75
Wine, ruby-stained 100

Royal Crystal

Banana stand, clear 125

Banana stand, ruby-stained 450
Bowl, rectangular, flat, 4 1/2 x 7", clear 25
Bowl, rectangular, flat, 4 1/2 x 7", ruby-
   stained 45
Bowl, rectangular, flat, 5 1/4 x 8 1/4", clear 30
Bowl, rectangular, flat, 5 1/4 x 8 1/4", ruby-
   stained 55
Bowl, round, flat, 5" d., flared sides, clear 20
Bowl, round, flat, 5" d., flared sides, ruby-
   stained 35
Bowl, round, flat, 5" d., straight sides, clear 20
Bowl, round, flat, 5" d., straight sides, ruby-
   stained 35
Bowl, round, flat, 6" d., flared sides, clear 25
Bowl, round, flat, 6" d., flared sides, ruby-
   stained 40
Bowl, round, flat, 6" d., straight sides, clear 25
Bowl, round, flat, 6" d., straight sides, ruby-
   stained 40
Bowl, round, flat, 7" d., flared sides, clear 30
Bowl, round, flat, 7" d., flared sides, ruby-
   stained 45
Bowl, round, flat, 7" d., straight sides, clear 30
Bowl, round, flat, 7" d., straight sides, ruby-
   stained 45
Bowl, round, flat, 8" d., flared sides, clear 35
Bowl, round, flat, 8" d., flared sides, ruby-
   stained 50
Bowl, round, flat, 8" d., straight sides, clear 35
Bowl, round, flat, 8" d., straight sides, ruby-
   stained 50
Bowl, square, 7 1/2" w., 3 3/4" h., clear 30
Bowl, square, 7 1/2" w., 3 3/4" h., ruby-
   stained 45
Bowl, triangular, handled, 6" l., clear 25
Bowl, triangular, handled, 6" l., ruby-stained 35
Bread plate, round, clear, 10" d. 35
Bread plate, round, ruby-stained, 10" d. 75
Butter dish, cov., clear, 6 1/2" h. 55
Butter dish, cov., ruby-stained, 6 1/2" h. 145
Cake stand, high standard, clear, 9" d. 55
Cake stand, high standard, ruby-stained,
   9" d. 225
Cake stand, high standard, clear, 10" d. 60
Cake stand, high standard, ruby-stained,
   10" d. 250
Carafe, clear, 5 pt. 65
Carafe, ruby-stained, 5 pt. 155
Celery vase, clear, 6 1/2" h. 65
Celery vase, ruby-stained, 6 1/2" h. 155
Cologne bottle w/original stopper, clear,
   4 oz. 65
Cologne bottle w/original stopper, ruby-
   stained, 4 oz. 175
Compote, open, 6" h., high standard, clear 25
Compote, open, 6" h., high standard, ruby-
   stained 70
Compote, open, 7" d., high standard, clear 30
Compote, open, 7" d., high standard, ruby-
   stained 75
Compote, open, 9 1/2" d., flared rim, high-
   stand, clear 75
Cracker jar, cov., clear 75
Cracker jar, cov., ruby-stained 325
Creamer, 5 1/4" h., clear 40
Creamer, 5 1/4" h., ruby-stained 65
Cruet w/original stopper, 5 oz., clear 45
Cruet w/original stopper, 5 oz., ruby-
   stained 165
Cruet w/original stopper, 8 oz., clear 55
Cruet w/original stopper, 8 oz., ruby-
   stained 195

Dish, flat, handled, 4" d., clear 25
Dish, flat, handled, 4" d., ruby-stained................. 45
Dish, flat, handled, 4 1/2" d., clear 25
Dish, flat, handled, 4 1/2" d., ruby-stained 45
Dish, flat, handled, 5" d., clear 30
Dish, flat, handled, 5" d., ruby-stained................. 55
Goblet, 6 1/4" h., 1/2 pt., clear 45
Goblet, 6 1/4" h., 1/2 pt., ruby-stained................. 95
Pitcher, bulbous, milk, 1 qt., clear........................ 95

Royal Crystal Ruby-stained Pitcher

Pitcher, bulbous, milk, 1 qt., ruby-stained........ 275
Pitcher, bulbous, water, 1/2 gal., clear............. 125
Pitcher, bulbous, water, 1/2 gal., ruby-
stained... 295
Pitcher, tankard, water, 9 1/2" h., 1/2 gal.,
clear 100
Pitcher, tankard, water, 9 1/2" h., 1/2 gal.,
ruby-stained.. 275
Plate, 6" d., clear 20
Plate, 6" d., ruby-stained...................................... 35
Salt shaker w/original top, clear....................... 30
Salt shaker w/original top, ruby-stained 75
Sauce dish, flat, 4" d., clear 15
Sauce dish, flat, 4" d., ruby-stained..................... 25
Sauce dish, footed, 4" d., clear 20
Sauce dish, footed, 4" d., ruby-stained 30
Sauce dish, flat, 4 1/2" d., clear 15
Sauce dish, flat, 4 1/2" d., ruby-stained 25
Sauce dish, footed, 4 1/2" d., clear...................... 20
Sauce dish, footed, 4 1/2" d., ruby-stained 30
Spoonholder, clear 45
Spoonholder, ruby-stained 60
Sugar bowl, cov., 7 1/2" h., clear 55
Sugar bowl, cov., 7 1/2" h., ruby-stained............. 95
Sugar bowl, open, individual size, clear 35
Sugar bowl, open, individual size, ruby-
stained... 65
Syrup pitcher w/original metal top, 6" h.,
clear 95
Syrup pitcher w/original metal top, 6" h.,
ruby-stained.. 350
Toothpick holder, clear.. 45
Toothpick holder, ruby-stained 175
Tumbler, water, 4" h., 1/3 pt., clear...................... 30
Tumbler, water, 4" h., 1/3 pt., ruby-stained 45
Wine, 4" h., clear 30
Wine, 4" h., ruby-stained...................................... 65

Peach Blow

Several types of glass lumped together by collectors as Peach Blow were produced by half a dozen glasshouses. Hobbs, Brockunier & Co., Wheeling, West Virginia, made Peach Blow as a plated ware that shaded from red at the top to yellow at the bottom and is referred to as Wheeling Peach Blow. Mt. Washington Glass Works produced an homogeneous Peach Blow shading from a rose color at the top to pale blue in the lower portion. The New England Glass Works' Peach

Blow, called Wild Rose, shaded from rose at the top to white. Gundersen-Pairpoint Co. also reproduced some of the Mt. Washington Peach Blow in the early 1950s and some glass of a somewhat similar type was made by Steuben Glass Works, Thomas Webb & Sons and Stevens & Williams of England. New England Peach Blow is one-layered glass and the English is two-layered.

Another single-layered shaded art glass was produced early in the 20th century by the New Martinsville Glass Mfg. Co. Originally called "Muranese," collectors today refer to it as "New Martinsville Peach Blow."

New England

Peach Blow Darner & Pear

Darner, ball-shaped w/handle, deep rose
pink shaded to white, glossy finish,
2 1/4" d., 6" l. (ILLUS., left) **$135**
Model of a pear, deep pink shaded to white,
glossy finish, 3" d., 5" l. (ILLUS., right) 135
Tumbler, cylindrical, glossy finish, 3 3/4" h. 101

Webb

Small Decorated Peach Blow Bowl

Bowl, 3 7/8" d., 2 5/8" h., small gilt footring
below the wide squatty rounded body w/a
wide incurved rim, decorated around the
sides w/heavy gold prunus blossoms on
branches, gold pine needles, satin finish,
glossy white interior (ILLUS.) 365
Bowl, 4" d., 2 1/2" h., squatty bulbous
shape, decorated w/heavy gold prunus &
pine needles & a gold butterfly in flight,
creamy white lining, satin finish 300
Vase, 3 1/4" h., 2 3/4" d., round short pedestal base below the bulbous nearly
spherical body tapering to a short, wide
rolled mouth, heavy gold decoration of
flowers w/a butterfly on the reverse, gold
rim trim, creamy white lining, satin finish...... 325
Vase, 5" h., 3 1/2" d., ovoid body tapering to
a short cylindrical neck, heavy gold decoration of prunus blossoms, branches &
bee in flight, creamy white lining.................... 245
Vase, 5" h., 3 1/2" d., ovoid body tapering to
a short flared neck, enameled w/two-col-

ored birds, white flowers & gold foliage, creamy white lining, propeller mark **495**

Silver- and Gold-decorated Vase

Vase, 5 1/8" h., 3 1/4" d., baluster-form, decorated w/gold & silver florals & leaves, creamy white interior (ILLUS.) **295**

Vase, 5 1/8" h., 3 1/4" d., ovoid body tapering to a cylindrical neck w/flaring rim, overall decoration of silver flowers & heavy gold leaves, creamy white lining, glossy finish **295**

Vase, 6 1/2" h., 3 5/8" d., squatty bulbous body tapering to a cylindrical neck, decorated w/gold branches, prunus blossoms & a small butterfly, propeller mark **345**

Vase, 7 1/2" h., 3 5/8" d., bulbous body tapering to a tall "stick" neck w/short flaring rim, decorated w/heavy gold florals & foliage, glossy finish **325**

Vase, 7 1/2" h., 4" d., squatty bulbous body tapering to a cylindrical neck, decorated w/heavy gold prunus blossoms, branches & pine needles, creamy white lining, glossy finish **325**

Wheeling

Vase, 7 3/4" h., "Morgan Vase," slender ovoid shouldered body w/slender cylindrical ringed neck w/flared rim, satin finish (no stand) **805**

Vase, 7 3/4" h., "Morgan Vase," slender ovoid shouldered body w/slender cylindrical ringed neck w/flared rim, glossy finish (no stand) **950**

Vase, 8" h., bottle-form, spherical body w/a tall slender "stick" neck, satin finish **825**

Wheeling Peach Blow Bottle Vase

Vase, 9 1/4" h., bottle-form, bulbous base tapering to a slender "stick" neck, glossy finish (ILLUS.) **985**

Vase, 10 5/8" h., bottle-shaped, spherical footed base tapering to a tall "stick" neck **978**

Vase, 11" h., stick-type **1,200**

Pillar-Molded

This heavily ribbed glassware was produced by blowing glass into full-sized ribbed molds and then finishing it by hand. The technique evolved from earlier "pattern moulding" used on glass since ancient times but in pillar-molded glass the ribs are very heavy and prominent. Most examples found in this country were produced in the Pittsburgh, Pennsylvania area from around 1850 to 1870, but similar English-made wares made before and after this period are also available. Most American items were made from clear flint glass and colored examples or pieces with colored strands in the ribs are rare and highly prized. Some collectors refer to this as "steamboat" glass believing that it was made to be used on American riverboats, but most likely it was used anywhere that a sturdy, relatively inexpensive glassware was needed, such as taverns and hotels.

Celery vase, eight-rib, a deeply waisted bowl w/a flaring slightly scalloped rim, on an applied squatty knopped stem & disk foot, clear, 9 1/8" h. **$220**

Celery vase, eight-rib, baluster stem, round base, pronounced scallop rim, 11 3/8" h. (some pot stones) **550**

Celery vases, eight-rib, tall wasted tulip-form bowls w/swirled ribs, on tall applied knopped stem w/disk foot, clear, 10" h., pr. **523**

Compote, open, 7" d., 6 1/2" h., eight-rib, a deep flaring bell-form bowl on an applied tall stem & disk foot, clear, mid-19th c. **358**

Pomona

First produced by the New England Glass Company under a patent received by Joseph Locke in 1885, Pomona has a frosted ground on clear glass decorated with mineral stains, most frequently amber-yellow, sometimes pale blue. Some pieces bore smooth etched floral decorations highlighted with staining. Two types of Pomona were made. The first Locke patent covered a technique whereby the piece was first covered with an acid-resistant coating which was then needle-carved with thousands of minute criss-crossing lines. The piece was then dipped into acid which cut into the etched lines giving the finished piece a notable "brilliance."

A cheaper method, covered by a second Locke patent on June 15, 1886, was accomplished by rolling the glass piece in particles of acid-resistant material which were picked up by it. The glass was then etched by acid which attacked areas not protected by the resistant particles. A favorite design on Pomona was the cornflower.

Bowl, 4" d., crimped & folded rim, 2nd patent **$60**

Bowl, 5 1/4" d., 2 1/2" h., round, satin finish w/clear ruffled rim w/copper hue, a band of pale blue cornflowers around sides of body, 2nd patent **193**

Bowl, 10" d., blue cornflower decoration, 2nd patent **250**

Pomona Creamer & Sugar Bowl

Creamer & open sugar bowl, squatty bulbous body w/Inverted Thumbprint patt., flaring ruffled amber rim & applied amber handles, 1st patent, pr. (ILLUS.) **600**

Finger bowl & underplate, 3" d. bowl w/ruffled rim, 4 1/2" d. underplate; blue cornflower decoration, 2nd patent, 2 pcs. **100**

Finger bowls, amber-stained, 1st patent, 4 1/2" d., pr. **345**

Punch cup, blue cornflower decoration, 2nd patent... **125**

Punch cup, blueberry decoration w/honey amber stain on rim, leaves & handle, 1st patent, 2 5/8" d., 2 3/4" h................................ **175**

Toothpick holder, applied rigaree band around the neck, 2nd patent **225**

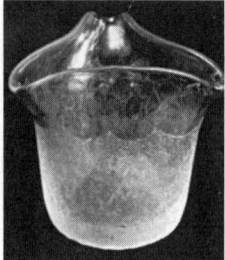

Pomona Toothpick Holder

Toothpick holder, cylindrical base w/tricorner top, 1st patent (ILLUS.).................... **225-275**

Tumblers, cylindrical, decorated w/blue cornflowers, honey amber leaves & honey amber tops, 2nd patent, 2 1/2" d., 3 5/8" h., 4 pcs. **540**

Vase, 3" h., 6" w., fan-shaped w/ruffled rim, blue cornflower decoration, 1st patent **275**

Vase, 5 1/2" h., ruffled rim, clear applied base, blue cornflower decoration, 1st patent... **220**

Quezal

In 1901, Martin Bach and Thomas Johnson, who had worked for Louis Tiffany, opened a competing glassworks in Brooklyn, New York. The Quezal Art Glass and Decorating Co. produced wares closely resembling those of Tiffany until the plant's closing in 1925.

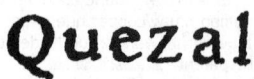

Quezal Mark

Center bowl, deep flaring wide-ribbed bowl on a ribbed funnel base, blue shading to purple w/overall golden iridescence, signed, ca. 1900, 13 1/8" d. **$1,200**

Compote, open, 5 1/4" d., 4 1/2" h., a disk foot & short ringed pedestal in bluish gold iridescence supporting a wide squatty bulbous bowl tapering below the wide flaring rim, bowl w/marigold iridescent exterior & gold iridescent interior, signed **550**

Rare Quezal Decanter

Decanter w/original pointed mushroom stopper, bulbous base tapering to a tall "stick" neck w/flared rim, green & gold double-hooked feather designs on green, gold iridescent neck & stopper, designed by Martin Bach, signed, 11 1/2" h. (ILLUS.)... **4,750**

Lamp, table model, two-light, the baluster-form body in cased white decorated w/feathered trailings in blue & iridescent silver & in iridescent gold, w/reeded & foliate-cast metal mounts, two curving arms fitted w/a pair of paneled opalescent floriform shades w/iridescent gold interiors & gold feathering on the exterior, each side signed, ca. 1925, overall 25 3/4" h... **750**

Plate, 6 1/2" d., gold iridescence w/purple highlights... **225**

Taster, squared sides w/pinched dimples, gold iridescent interior & exterior, signed "Quezal" on base, 2 3/4" h. **175**

Bulbous Quezal Pulled-Feather Vase

Vase, bulbous ovoid body tapering to a short rolled neck, bold gold pulled-feather & scroll designs on a dark colored ground w/white around the shoulder & neck, gold iridescent interior (ILLUS.) **2,800**

Vase, floriform, a decorated cushion foot supporting a slender stem to the widely flaring ruffled top, iridescent gold ground decorated w/white pulled-feather design ... **2,750**

Vase, 3 3/4" h., miniature, bulbous squatty form, overall gold iridescence, signed **440**

Vase, 4" h., simple ovoid form w/flaring trumpet neck, green pulled-feathers extending down from the gold iridescent pulled upper band all on an opal ground, signed "Quezal H 319" **2,915**

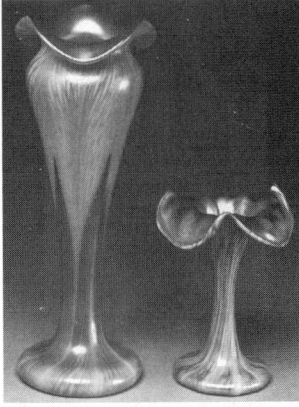

Quezal Floriform Vases

Vase, 4 1/4" h., floriform, cushion foot below tapering to a slender ribbed body w/a trefoil floriform lip, white w/green trailings & pink & amber iridescence, signed "Quezal - 167" centering a "T" (ILLUS. right) **920**

Vase, 4 1/2" h., ruffled rim, gold iridescent pulled-feather decoration, signed **550**

Short and Tall Quezal Vases

Vase, 5 1/8" h., wide ovoid body tapering to a tiny short neck, deep reddish amber w/silvery blue & gold iridescence, overlaid w/silver depictions of flowers & wispy foliage, signed "Quezal - D1150" (ILLUS. left) **1,380**

Vase, 6" h., "Agate," ovoid body tapering to a tall trumpet neck, opaque greyish brown w/agate-like streaks of amber, blue, aqua, green & black at the rim, signed on the base **2,500**

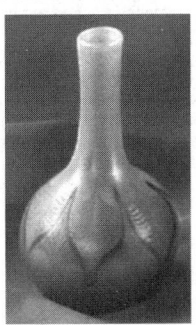

Fine Pulled-Feather Quezal Vase

Vase, 6" h., bottle-form, spherical base tapering to a tall slender "stick" neck, yellow opal ground in iridescent gold w/a pulled-feather band around the base trimmed in dark green, signed on the pontil (ILLUS.) **2,090**

Vase, 6" h., floriform, a round thin cushion foot tapering to a short slender stem supporting the cupped bowl w/a high wide six-lobe flaring rim, green pulled-feather design from the foot up halfway on the opal body, gold iridescent interior, signed "Quezal 8" **3,080**

Vase, 6" h., ruffled rim on a flared body, opal white w/five pulled green & gold lustre feathers, interior w/gold iridescence w/stretching at rim, polished pontil, inscribed & gilded "Quezal L617" (light wear) **1,840**

Vase, 6 3/16" h., floriform body on a low domed foot, opalescent decorated w/pulled green feathering w/amber iridescent interior, inscribed "Quezal - R - 858," ca. 1900 .... **1,500**

Vase, 6 1/4" h., bulbous ovoid body w/a rounded shoulder to the cylindrical neck w/a flared ruffled rim, amber iridescent ground overlaid around the neck & shoulder w/stylized interlacing sterling silver design, inscribed mark, ca. 1920 .... **1,500**

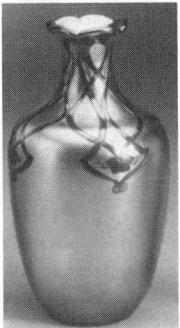

Quezal Vase with Silver Overlay

Vase, 6 1/2" h., ovoid body w/a broad shoulder tapering to a short cylindrical neck w/a flaring crimped rim, amber w/gold iridescence, overlaid around the neck & shoulder w/silver Art Nouveau floral & vine designs, glass stressed at rim silver attachment, signed "Quezal - D 1193" (ILLUS.) **1,035**

Vase, 7 1/2" h., floriform, the opalescent sides decorated w/green striated feathering, the foot further decorated w/amber iridescent feathering, the interior in amber iridescence, inscribed "Quezal," ca. 1925.. **1,550**

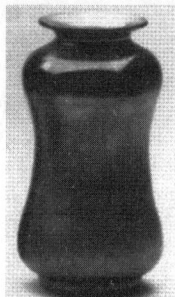

Blue Iridescent Quezal Vase

Vase, 8" h., footed double-bulbed cylindrical body w/a short flaring neck, blue iridescent exterior, signed (ILLUS.) **750**

Vase, 8" h., ovoid body w/a slender neck w/everted rim, overall gold iridescence, signed **483**

Vase, 8" h., swelled cylindrical shouldered body tapering to a trumpet-form neck, silvery & bluish green gold iridescent finish, signed on base **750**

Vase, 8" h., tall ovoid body w/a short flaring neck, overall gold iridescence, signed **578**

Vase, 8 1/4" h., floriform, slender baluster-form body w/a trefoil lip & cushion foot, white w/green pulled-leaf decoration & gold trailings w/pink iridescence, very small internal crack under foot, signed "Quezal - 794" surrounding an "O" (ILLUS. left with small floriform vase) **1,035**

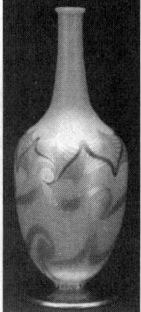

Fine Decorated Quezal Vase

Vase, 9" h., footed ovoid body tapering to a slender "stick" neck, Egyptian Revival style w/a creamy white body decorated w/a green zigzag shoulder design above

gold iridescent double hooked & pulled-feather design, by Martin Bach, foot inscribed "Quezal N.Y." (ILLUS.) **4,000**

Vase, 9 3/8" h., slender footed ovoid body w/constricting neck & flaring lip, amber iridescence shading to yellow & violet, pontil signed, ca. 1920 .... **750**

Vase, 9 1/2" h., flared rounded base tapering gently to a tall cylindrical body w/a flat rim, amber w/golden crimson iridescence, signed "Quezal - D1203" (ILLUS. right with silver-decorated vase) **546**

Vase, 9 3/4" h., a cushion foot supporting a slender trumpet-form body w/a widely flaring & ruffled rim, opaque white ground decorated on the exterior w/green & gold pulled-feather designs & a band of gold iridescent hearts around the neck, etched "Quezal 6" **2,750**

Vase, 9 7/8" h., bulbous ovoid base tapering to a tall slender & slightly flaring "stick" neck, amber iridescence overlaid in sterling silver & cut w/blossoms, leaves & whiplash strapwork, signed on pontil, ca. 1910 .... **1,600**

Vase, 10 1/2" h., baluster-form w/a cushion foot, the rounded shoulder w/a small widely flaring trumpet neck, overall blue iridescence, signed **1,210**

Vase, 10 3/4" h., jack-in-the-pulpit-form, green pulled-feather design tipped in iridescent gold stretch from base to top, iridescent gold interior............................... **3,300**

Vase, 12 1/4" h., jack-in-the-pulpit form w/cushion foot, slender cylindrical body & wide rolled rim, purplish blue shading to golden iridescence, silver feathering on the foot extending into the body, signed.... **2,750**

Vase, 12 3/4" h., bulbous cushion foot tapering to a tall slightly flaring cylindrical body w/a widely flaring six-ruffle rim, overall gold iridescence, signed.................. **1,568**

Vase, 12 3/4" h., tall baluster-form body swelled at the top & w/a short cylindrical neck, opalescent decorated w/pulled green & gold iridescent leafage & applied w/reeded gold medallions w/tendrils down the sides, unsigned, ca. 1910 .... **4,500**

Vase, 13 1/8" h., jack-in-the-pulpit form, the widely flaring ruffled rim above a slender stem & bulbous base in opalescent decorated w/finely pulled feathering in mint green & amber iridescence, the interior in amber iridescence, signed, ca. 1920 .... **5,750**

Vase, 13 1/2" h., jack-in-the-pulpit form, widely flaring top above a slender stem & squatty bulbous base, overall amber iridescence w/the top tinged w/rings of pink & green, signed "Quezal - G646," ca. 1920... **5,750**

Vase, 16" h., jack-in-the-pulpit form, the broad undulating mouth w/crackled gold iridescence, issuing from a slender stem & bulbous cushion foot, elaborately decorated w/gold & green pulled-feather & swirled designs, signed "Quezal M 702".... **6,500**

Rose Bowls

These decorative small bowls were widely popular in the late 19th and early 20th centuries. Produced in various types of glass, they are most common in satin glass or spatter glass. They are generally a spherical shape with an incurved crimped rim, but ovoid or egg-shaped examples were also popular.

Their name derives from their reported use, to hold dried rose petal potpourri or small fresh-cut roses.

Miniature Amethyst Rose Bowl

Amethyst, miniature, six-crimp rim, enameled w/white & rust blossoms & green leaves, 2" h. (ILLUS.) $250

Two Intaglio Engraved Rose Bowls

Amethyst, six-crimp rim, deep color w/intaglio floral engraving, attributed to Moser, ca. 1910, 2 1/2" h. (ILLUS. right).. **300-350**

Two "Jewell" Glass Rose Bowls

Blue, eight-crimp rim, threaded body w/overall thumbprints, Stevens & Williams "Jewell" glass, 2 1/4" h. (ILLUS. right).. **125-175**

Reproduction Maize Rose Bowl

Cased, golden amber cased in white, Libbey's Maize patt. reproduced by L.G. Wright Glass Co., ca. 1970, 4 1/2" h. (ILLUS.) **85-125**

Two Thomas Webb Satin Rose Bowls

Cased satin, eight-crimp rim, blue shaded to pale blue, decorated w/heavy gilt prunus blossoms, decorated by Jules Barbe for Thomas Webb & Sons, 2 1/4" h. (ILLUS. left) **250-325**

Floral Embossed Rose Bowl

Cased satin, eight-crimp rim, dark green shaded to pale green, Floral Embossed patt., ca. 1890s, 3 1/2" h. (ILLUS.) **125-175**
Cased satin, eight-crimp rim, deep red shaded to soft orange, decorated w/heavy gold prunus blossoms, a butterfly on the reverse, decorated by Jules Barbe for Thomas Webb & Sons, 3" h. (ILLUS. right with blue bowl).................... **400-600**

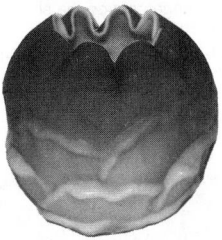

Cabbage Pattern Satin Rose Bowl

Cased satin, eight-crimp rim, deep rose pink shaded to creamy white, Cabbage patt., white lining, 4 1/2" d., 4 1/2" h. (ILLUS.)... **165**

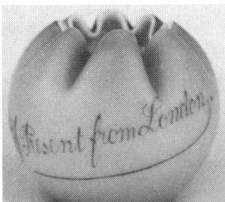

Souvenir Satin Rose Bowl

Cased satin, eight-crimp rim, peach shaded to creamy white, inscribed in yellow enamel "A Present from London," marked on base "Made in Bohemia," 3 1/2" h. (ILLUS.)...................................... **125-175**

Mother-of-Pearl Satin Rose Bowl

Cased satin, eight-crimp rim, shaded blue mother-of-pearl Diamond Quilted patt., probably Webb, 3 3/4" h. (ILLUS.)......... **275-325**

Shell & Seaweed Pattern Rose Bowl

Cased satin, eight-crimp rim, Shell & Seaweed molded patt., deep pink shaded to pale pink, enameled around the top w/orange leaves & white blossoms, orange dots on the shells, ca. 1880s, 5" h. (ILLUS.).............................. **125-175**

Cased satin, eight-crimp rim, spherical, shadow dark brown to cream enameled w/gold foliage w/a butterfly on the reverse, attributed to Webb, 3 1/4" d., 3" h..... **468**

Box-pleated Satin Rose Bowl

Cased satin, six-crimp box-pleated rim, brown shaded to creamy white, Stevens & Williams, 4 3/4" h. (ILLUS.) **200-250**

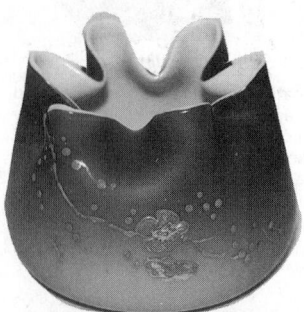

Plum Satin with Prunus Rose Bowl

Cased satin, six-crimp rim, miniature, plum shaded to light plum, heavy gilt prunus blossoms decoration, creamy lining, Thomas Webb, 3 1/2" d., 2 1/2" h. (ILLUS.)........ **245**

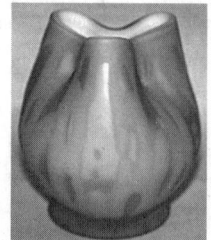

Mother-of-Pearl Stripe Rose Bowl

Cased satin, three-crimp rim, miniature, green mother-of-pearl Stripe patt., Thomas Webb, 2 1/2" h. (ILLUS.) **150-200**

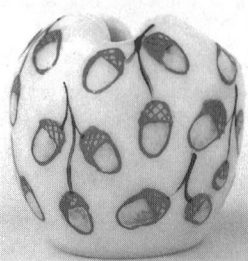

Satin Rose Bowl with Acorns

Creamy white, four-crimp rim, miniature, satin ground decorated overall w/orange acorns on green stems, 2 3/4" h. (ILLUS.).. **85-110**

Decorated Satin Rose Bowl

Creamy white, three-crimp rim, footed satin decorated w/light green & brown ginkgo branches, Thomas Webb, 2 3/4" h. (ILLUS.).. **225-275**

Miniature Rose Bowl with Daisies

Crown Milano, eight-crimp rim, miniature, pale blue shaded to creamy white, boldly enameled w/large yellow & purple daisies w/green leafy stems, 2 3/4" h. (ILLUS.) **400**

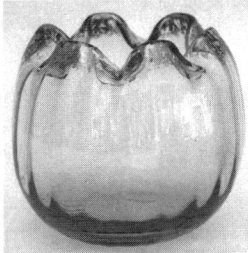

Pale Green Decorated Rose Bowl

Green, six-crimp rim, miniature, pale optic-ribbed form w/gilt decoration around the rim, 2" h. (ILLUS.) **75-100**

Green shaded to clear, miniature, six-crimp rim, intaglio etched w/a large blossom, attributed to Moser, ca. 1910, 2" h. (ILLUS. left w/amethyst intaglio bowl) ... **250-300**

Olive green, eight-crimp rim, threaded body w/overall thumbprints, Stevens & Williams "Jewell" glass, 2 1/4" h. (ILLUS. left w/blue "Jewell" bowl).............................. **125-175**

Porcelain Souvenir Rose Bowl

Porcelain, six-crimp rim, miniature, souvenir-type, cobalt blue ground w/a round gold-trimmed reserve w/a color transfer scene of the "National Cash Register Co., Dayton, Ohio," 2" h. (ILLUS.) **35-55**

Satin glass, spherical melon-lobed form w/an eight-crimp rim, decorated w/enameled stylized flowers & scattered gold scrolls, 4 1/2" d., 3 1/2" h................................ **193**

Spangled Glass Rose Bowl

Spangled, eight-crimp rim, reddish orange cased in white spatter w/silver mica flecks throughout, 3 1/2" h. (ILLUS.) **100-150**

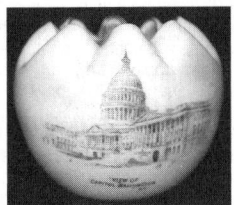

White Satin Souvenir Rose Bowl

White, eight-crimp rim, souvenir-type, satin ground decorated w/a black transfer of the U.S. Capitol, made in Austria, 4 1/2" d., 3 3/4" h. (ILLUS.)..................... **100-150**

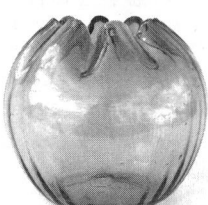

Yellowish Green Optic Ribbed Bowl

Yellowish green, eight-crimp rim, optic ribbed design, 5" h. (ILLUS.) **45-50**

Rubina Verde

This decorative glass, popular in the late 19th and early 20th centuries, shades from ruby or deep cranberry to green or greenish-yellow.

Bowl, 4 1/2" d., 2 3/4" h., Inverted Thumbprint patt., attributed to Hobbs, Brockunier **$138**

Cheese dish, cov., the domed mold-blown Coin Spot shaded cover sitting on a round pressed green Daisy & Button patt. base, overall 7" d.. **275**

Creamer, square top & squatty bulbous body, Inverted Thumbprint patt., applied clear green handle, 5" h. **146**

Decanter w/original stopper, spherical Inverted Thumbprint patt. body tapering to a cylindrical neck w/tricorner rim, applied yellow reeded handle & facet-cut stopper, 9 1/2" h... **385**

Pitcher, 7 1/4" h., spherical w/cylindrical neck, Inverted Thumbprint patt., applied greenish yellow handle, attributed to Hobbs, Brockunier... **275**

Fine Rubina Verde Pitcher

Pitcher, 8 1/2" h., spherical base w/a tall wide cylindrical neck w/flared & lightly scalloped rim w/pinched spout, optic ribbed design, applied angular reeded green handle, sand bruise on interior (ILLUS.) **385**

Vase, 12" h., jack-in-the-pulpit-form, the tall widely flaring blossom-form top in deep cranberry w/the wide rim pulled into long points, the back petal turned up, tapering to a slender stem w/the lower half in green on a green foot...................................... **275**

Schneider

This ware is made in France at Cristallerie Schneider, established in 1913 near Paris by Ernest and Charles Schneider. Some pieces of cameo were marked "Le Verre Francais" and others were signed "Charder."

Schneider Mark

Fine Schneider Cameo Ewer

Cameo ewer, bulbous cylindrical body tapering sharply to a tall slender neck w/a cupped rim & high arched spout, grey shading to lemon yellow, internally mottled & streaked w/amethyst, overlaid w/orange & cut w/arbutus berries & leaves, enameled in shades of brown & green, signed, ca. 1924, 10 3/4" h. (ILLUS.) **$5,750**

Schneider Poppy Cameo Vase

Cameo vase, 9" h., a dark purple round cushion foot & knopped stem supporting a wide bulbous ovoid body tapering to a molded mouth, deep golden yellow overlaid w/dark reddish orange & wheel-carved w/large stylized poppy blossoms w/angular spiraling stems, signed in intaglio, ca. 1925 (ILLUS.) **5,750**

Large Schneider Centerpiece

Centerpiece, small ovoid center pedestal supporting a wide rounded & gently dished form, mottled blue, turquoise, tangerine & burgundy, signed, ca. 1925, 15" d. (ILLUS.) **1,495**

Vase, 9 3/4" h., tapering ovoid body w/a wide dished rim, grey mottled w/orange shading to pink & cobalt blue, blown into a wrought-iron mount w/alternating straight rods & small circles on a circular hammered foot, glass signed, ca. 1925..... **2,875**

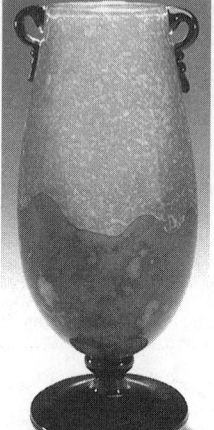

Large Schneider Vase

Vase, 12" h., an aubergine disk foot & shoulder knopped stem supporting a tall ovoid internally decorated body in mottled rose red & yellow, the lower body w/a casing of deeper red & mottled grey, small aubergine loop handles at the flat rim, engraved signature (ILLUS.)............... **2,530**

Vase, 14 1/4" h., swelled cylindrical form w/a flattened shoulder centering a cupped neck decorated w/three bosses

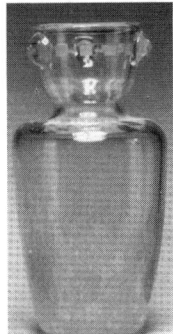

Shaded Clear Etched Schneider Vase

alternating w/three etched squares & two rectangles, clear shading to tangerine at the base w/captive bubbles of various sizes, signed, ca. 1925 (ILLUS.) **1,725**

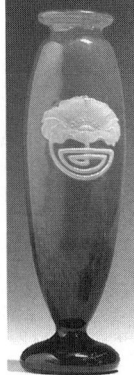

Schneider Vase with Applied Poppy

Vase, 15" h., cushion foot supporting a tall slender ovoid body w/a short flattened flaring neck, red internally shaded w/mottled amethyst at the base, overlaid w/a stylized orange poppy blossom w/an ideogram-form stem, the petals finely wheel-carved, signed in intaglio, ca. 1925 (ILLUS.) **6,325**

Silver Deposit - Silver Overlay

Silver Deposit and Silver Overlay have been made commercially since the last quarter of the 19th century. Silver is deposited on the glass by various means, most commonly by utilizing an electric current. The glass was very popular during the first three decades of this century, and some pieces are still being produced. During the late 1970s, silver commanded exceptionally high prices and this was reflected in a surge of interest in silver overlay glass, especially in pieces marked "Sterling" or "925" on the heavy silver overlay.

Cigar box, cov., rectangular, black amethyst glass, the cover w/silver overlay scene of goose in flight over lake, foliate silver border on cover & base, red enam-

el trim, acid-stamped marks of the Rockwell Silver Co., ca. 1925, 3 1/2 x 4 3/4", 1 7/8" h. (loss to enamel) **$173**
Pitcher, 9 1/4" h., tapering clear body bound w/sterling silver grapevine overlay, ca. 1900 .... **476**

Mexican Silver Overlaid Shakers

Salt & pepper shakers w/tray, tapering cylindrical clear glass shakers overlaid w/sterling floral vines, on small dished rectangular silver tray, marked "Taxco Mexico," tray 2 3/4 x 5 1/8", shakers 2 1/2" h., the set (ILLUS.) **35**
Vase, 8" h., fan-shaped, the widely flaring flattened black opaque top decorated w/silver overlay in a floral design within geometric panels, on a short baluster stem & disk foot w/silver rim band, maker's mark "Rockwell - no.1371B," ca. 1930 .... **259**
Vase, 10" h., green vase-form body overlaid in sterling silver floral & vine designs, ca. 1900 .... **672**
Vase, 10 1/4" h., Art Nouveau style, green body, overlaid w/gently scrolling florals & vine designs, ca. 1900 .... **560**

Smith Brothers

Originally established as a decorating department of the Mt. Washington Glass Company in the 1870s, the firm later was an independent business in New Bedford, Massachusetts. Beautifully decorated opal white glass was its hallmark, but it also did glass cutting. Some examples carry its lion-in-the-shield mark.

Smith Brothers Mark

Cracker jar, cov., melon-lobed body in almond decorated around the middle w/a raised gold floral design, silver plate rim & puffy cover w/embossed floral designs, bail handle, cover stamped "405," body inscribed "ROS [over] DTB" **$303**
Cracker jar, cov., melon-ribbed body, decorated w/h.p. daisies, silver plate cover, signed **375**

Sweetmeat jar, cov., melon-ribbed body, beige satin ground enameled w/h.p. white daisies w/yellow centers & green leaves, ornate silver plate handled cover w/crown-shaped finial, red rampant lion mark, 8" d., 4 3/4" h. 450

Smith Double Pilgrim Vase

Vase, 7 1/4" h., 8" w., double pilgrim-style, two flattened round vases joined at the side & at the short cylindrical neck, creamy white ground decorated w/lavender wisteria blossoms traced in gold, gold beading at the top (ILLUS.) 1,500

Cylindrical Stork-decorated Vases

Vases, 4 1/4" h., 2 1/4" d., plain cylindrical form, h.p. w/facing standing storks in black, white & brown w/red legs & beaks, standing amid grasses, pale blue background, pr. (ILLUS.) 250-300

Stevens & Williams

This long-established English glasshouse has turned out a wide variety of artistic glasswares through the years. Fine satin glass pieces and items with applied decoration (sometimes referred to as "Matsu-No-Ke") are especially sought after today. The following represents a cross-section of its wares.

Basket, rounded blue cased in white body trimmed w/an amber band on the ruffled rim & an applied amber loop handle, applied w/an oak leaf in cranberry swirled in amber, white & cranberry spots on applied clear rosette, 10" h. (rough spot on leaf) $165

Bottle w/original stopper, footed tall tapering conical body w/greenish amber foot & body, the body applied w/tiers of crystal shells giving a Christmas tree effect, the tall matching stopper topped by an applied crystal figural peacock, 5" d., 11" h. (ILLUS. top of column) 500

Tree-form Appliqued Bottle & Stopper

Cracker jar, cov., cranberry w/a frost surface decorated w/a white overall arboresque design, hammered metal Moorish design rim, cover & bail handle, overall 8" h. 248

Intaglio-cut Finger Bowl & Underplate

Finger bowl & underplate, crystal cased in dark green & intaglio-cut w/wide grapevines, seven grape clusters on the bowl & vines & leaves on the underplate, the round bowl w/tapering rounded sides, plate 6 1/2" d., bowl 4 3/4" d., 2 1/2" h., 2 pcs. (ILLUS.) 265

Stevens & Williams Striped Tumbler

Tumbler, slightly flared cylindrical form, alternating wide vertical stripes of opaque white & chartreuse green & thin clear stripes, wide silver rim band, 3" d., 4 7/8" h. (ILLUS.) **100-125**

Rare Mother-of-Pearl Satin Vase

Vase, 5 3/8" h., 5 1/4" d., wide bulbous ovoid body w/a wide shoulder to the short widely flaring neck w/a flattened rim, mother-of-pearl satin Pompeian Swirl patt. in pale greenish yellow shading to deep red, white interior (ILLUS.) **750**

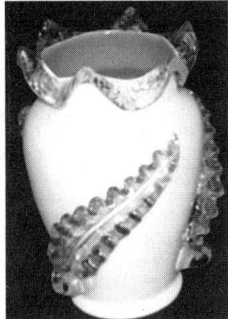

Stevens & Williams Appliqued Vase

Vase, 7 1/2" h., 4 1/2" d., footed ovoid body in opaque creamy white tapering to a flattened shaped rim applied w/a band of amber scallops, the body applied w/three large shaded green, amber & cranberry leaves curving up around the sides, deep rose interior (ILLUS.) **225**

Decorated Stevens & Williams Vase

Vase, 10 1/2" h., slender baluster-form body w/a flaring cupped rim w/a flat edge, creamy satin ground finely decorated w/a tall branch of green leaves & soft pink blossoms & a large blue & rose perched bird, all trimmed w/gold, thin gold lancet bands around the rim & base (ILLUS.) .. **425-450**

Vase, 12 1/2" h., bulbous ovoid base tapering to a tall slender cylindrical neck, deep orange mother-of-pearl satin Swirl patt. **952**

Tiffany

This glassware, covering a wide diversity of types, was produced in glasshouses operated by Louis Comfort Tiffany, America's outstanding glass designer of the Art Nouveau period, from the last quarter of the 19th century until the early 1930s. Tiffany revived early techniques and devised many new ones.

Bowl, 4 1/2" d., 2 1/2" h., squatty bulbous form w/deeply ruffled & pinched rim, overall gold iridescence, signed on base "L.C.T." **$288**

Bowl, 6 1/4" d., 2 1/4" h., round shallow form w/pinched ruffled rim, applied ribbed disk base, amber iridescent glass, early 20th c., inscribed "L.C.T. Favrile" (wear) **460**

Bowl, 6 1/4" d., 2 5/8" h., paperweight-type, wide squatty bulbous form tapering slightly to a wide flared rim, clear w/green leaves spread out from the base, signed "L.C. Tiffany - Favrile 3432D" **798**

Bowl, 8" d., 3 1/2" h., scalloped rim w/ribbed & tapered sides, overall gold iridescence, signed **990**

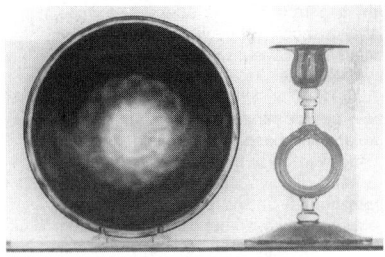

Tiffany Bowl & Candlestick

Bowl, 8 1/4" d., 2 1/8" h., wide rounded sides w/a pattern-molded honeycomb design, overall blue iridescence, etched signature & paper label, minor wear (ILLUS. left) **523**

Candlesticks, a spiral-ribbed shaft & wide flared foot supporting a ribbed wide cupped socket, amber w/overall gold iridescence, signed, 5" h., pr. **1,380**

Candlesticks, pastel green w/ribbed opalescent socket on a clear shaft above a ribbed opalescent white ring above another clear knob & the slightly domed ribbed foot, signed "L.C.T. Favrile - 1850" & paper label, 7 1/4" h., pr. (ILLUS. of one, w/bowl) **935**

Compote, open, 5" h., a small rounded bowl w/a widely flaring flattened rim, raised on a slender stem on a round foot, overall iridescent blue w/silver shadings, inscribed "L.C. Tiffany Favrile - 1838," ca. 1892 862

Compote, open, 6" d., the ruffled-edge tray top on an inverted baluster-form stem & a slightly domed round foot, grey w/amber, pink & blue iridescence, signed "L.C.T. - 4475," ca. 1920 977

Compote, open, 6" d., 3 3/4" h., wide shallow ten-ribbed swirled bowl w/gently scalloped rim raised on a waisted pedestal & domed disk foot, amber w/overall gold iridescence, signed "5 - L.C.T. Favrile" 1,093

Compote, open, 6 1/2" h., plain stem & disk foot supporting a bulbous ribbed bowl w/a wide cupped neck w/a wide flattened flaring rim, overall peacock blue iridescence, signed "LCT - Tiffany - Favrile - #3360" 2,860

Compote, open, 9" h., the shallow wide dish tapered slightly to a wide flattened rim, raised on a slender swelled stem on a domed foot, iridescent amber, signed "L.C. Tiffany - Favrile - 3919H," ca. 1913 1,955

Compote, open, 9" d., 3" h., the rounded bowl w/a widely flaring flattened rim, raised on a wide short pedestal base, blue w/strong blue lustre & stretched iridescence around the rim, base signed "L.C. Tiffany Inc. Favrile X" (very light center wear) 805

Dish, round footed form w/low incurved sides w/a scalloped rim, overall blue iridescence, signed, 6" d. 660

Dish, ruffled rim on a small bowl, amber w/overall gold iridescence, signed, 3" d. 230

Dish, a narrow footring supports a wide, shallow bowl, w/deeply fluted, swirled & incurved sides, vivid iridescent gold w/blue, violet orange highlights, signed "L.C.T.," 3" d., 1" h. 165

Finger bowl, deep flaring bell-form tapering to a small base, overall golden iridescence w/reddish highlights, signed, 3" d., 2 1/2" h. 248

Finger bowl & undertray, deep form set in a dished tray of amber glass, the interiors w/iridescent gold lustre, early 20th c., both inscribed "L.C.T." around the polished pontils, bowl 4 3/4" d., 2" h., plate 5 3/4" d. 288

Flower bowl & frog, deep wide round bowl centered by a wide upright cylinder w/a double band of flower frog rings, bright iridescent blue decorated on the interior w/green heart-shaped leaves & tendrils, bowl inscribed "L.C. Tiffany - Favrile - 3595 L," front inscribed "L.C. Tiffany - Favrile - 3596," ca. 1917, 10" d. 1,840

Flower frog, short cylindrical form w/an eight-loop rim, overall gold iridescence, signed "6 LC Tiffany Favrile," 3 1/2" d., 2 3/4" h. 330

Goblet, flared pedestal foot supporting a wide swelled cylindrical bowl decorated around the base w/a band of gold threading & pulled prunts, amber w/overall gold iridescence, original paper label, 5 1/8" h. 863

Urn, a round flaring foot supporting a deep widely flaring body w/a flattened shoulder centered by a short rolled neck, small tightly scrolled shoulder handles, vivid iridescent blue w/violet & green highlights, signed "L.C. Tiffany - Favrile - 1064," 5 1/2" d., 4" h. 990

Vase, miniature, 2 1/2" h., a simple rounded cup-form w/a wide flat mouth, vivid iridescent gold & light blue w/violet & orange highlights & a band of narrow hooked & pulled decoration around the middle, signed "L.C.T." 242

Vase, 4 1/4" h., floriform, a widely flaring five-lobed ruffled rim above the bulbous ovoid body tapering to a short stem & disk foot, gold w/gold stretched iridescence, signed "L.C. Tiffany - Favrile - 8651 D," ca. 1910 1,265

Vase, 4 1/4" h., ovoid tapering to a tiny flared neck, cased iridescent turquoise blue lined in white, signed "6467 N.L.C. Tiffany Favrile" 1,760

Vase, 4 1/4" h., swollen cylindrical body w/a short cylindrical neck in bright iridescent amber, the pinched surface w/a random pattern of attenuated drips & tendrils, two continuing to form short vestigial feet, inscribed "L.C. Tiffany, Favrile - 542 C," ca. 1908 1,840

Vase, 4 1/2" h., wide squatty bulbous form tapering toward base, the wide rim pinched into a tricorn opening, overall gold iridescence, inscribed "L.C. Tiffany - Favrile 3517D" (minor surface abrasions) 690

Vase, 4 1/2" h., 5 1/2" d., wide-mouthed urn-form body of amber w/two applied scrolling shell handles & overall gold iridescence, footed base, signed "L.C. Tiffany - Favrile X239" on pontil 1,610

Vase, 4 3/4" h., simple ovoid form tapering to a small trumpet neck, iridescent blue ground decorated around the shoulder & body w/silver pulled-feather designs, engraved "L.C.T. D2686" 3,220

Vase, 5" h., wide baluster-form body w/a flaring mouth, intaglio-carved, iridescent amber cased over white decorated w/elaborate ribboning each enclosing an intaglio-carved butterfly or flower inscribed "Tiffany - Favrile - T 4961," original paper label, ca. 1903 2,000

Vase, 5 1/2" h., wide bulbous ovoid body w/the shoulder centered by a wide thin cylindrical neck, overall gold iridescence decorated w/green stems & lily pads descending from the shoulder, signed "5431-C L.C. Tiffany Favrile" 1,760

Vase, 6 1/4" h., flora-form, opal & crystal round foot below a short slender stem & a slender ovoid bowl w/green pulled feathers tapering to a tricorner opal rim, signed "1026G LC Tiffany Favrile" 3,300

Vase, 6 1/2" h., a small cushion foot supporting an ovoid body w/a flattened shoulder centered by a tall cylindrical neck, delicate swirled design in gold iridescence w/orange & violet highlights, signed "L.C. Tiffany - Favrile - 1145-9359L" 880

Tiffany Oriental Poppy Vase

Vase, 6 1/2" h., Oriental Poppy line, gently flaring trumpet form w/white opalescent ribs & applied foot w/lilac tinge, etched signature partly obscured by old paper label, also w/an embossed paper label, very tiny piece of frit near base (ILLUS.) **358**

Vase, 8 1/2" h., ovoid body w/short flared rim, amber decorated w/brown hearts & vine on an iridescent gold surface, ca. 1907, signed "L.C.T. 840 B" around a reinforced button pontil (minor wear) **1,955**

Vase, 8 1/2" h., simple ovoid body tapering to a short neck w/rolled rim, experimental design in amber w/iridescent pulled-feather decoration, the feather tips reserved, late 19th-early 20th c. **1,035**

Vase, 8 3/4" h., ovoid body tapering to a short trumpet-form neck, amber iridescent decorated w/darker amber vines & wheel-carved w/green heart-form leaves, signed "L. C. Tiffany - Favrile 5674H," ca. 1913.. **3,737**

Vase, 9" h., a small flared foot below the tall flaring cylindrical body w/a wide slightly angled shoulder centered by a low rolled rim, amber w/pink & blue iridescence & green trailing vines & heart-shaped leaves in a band below the shoulder, signed "L.C. Tiffany - Favrile 387T," ca. 1925.. **1,725**

Vase, 9" h., disk foot below the tall slender tapering ovoid ribbed body w/a small partially ruffled mouth, overall blue iridescence, signed "X191 L.C. Tiffany - Favrile".. **1,540**

Vase, 10 1/8" h., bud-type, slender trumpet-form body in amber decorated w/five elongated green leaves on an iridescent gold ground, disk foot signed "3232 J L.C.Tiffany - Favrile," ca. 1915 (interior staining)... **863**

Vase, 10 1/4" h., stick-type, a conical bottom tapering sharply to a tall slightly flaring cylindrical neck, the upper body in dark gold iridescence w/a band of dark green pulled up pointed leaves around the base, signed "L.C. Tiffany - Favrile - 436J".. **1,210**

Vase, 11" h., floriform, the bulbous bowl w/a high flaring & deeply ruffled rim & tapering at the bottom to a slender knopped stem w/a domed round foot, iridescent amber, inscribed "L.C.T. - 3689 B," ca. 1907 .... **2,300**

Vase, 13" h., a slightly domed round foot centered by a short baluster-form stem

supporting a tall, slender trumpet-form bowl w/gently fluted rim, pink to white opalescence w/gold iridescent highlights, signed "L.C.T. - Favrile - 1888" **990**

Vase, 13" h., 5 " d., floriform, a disk foot below the tall slender swelled stem supporting a swelled ribbed bowl w/a wide flaring, ruffled & twisted rim, overall reddish gold iridescence, signed "165-D L.C. Tiffany - Favrile" **4,950**

Vase, 13 1/4" h., blossom-form w/bulbous bowl w/closed rim decorated w/intaglio-carved leaves above a band of large white petals over green leaves issuing from the tall slender pale green stem, raised on a domed folded round foot w/further green leaves in the clear ground, signed "L.C.T. W 7809," ca. 1905... **25,850**

Vase, 18 7/8" h., jack-in-the-pulpit-form, a thick cushion foot below the very tall slender stem topped by a widely flaring crimped & upturned rim, overall gold iridescence, signed "7793C L.C. Tiffany - Favrile" **11,500**

Fine Tiffany Wine Set

Wine set: decanter w/original stopper & six wine glasses; overall gold iridescence, the decanter w/a squatty bulbous base tapering sharply to a tall slender neck w/flared rim fitted w/a tall mushroom stopper, wine glasses w/tall cylindrical bowls on a tall slender stem, all engraved w/a grapevine design, the set (ILLUS. of part) **3,000-4,000**

Val St. Lambert

This Belgian glassworks was founded in 1790. Items listed here represent a sampling of its numerous and varied lines.

Val St. Lambert Mark

Bowl-vase, bulbous body tapering slightly to a wide flaring & ruffled rim, finely decorated in blue & white monochrome w/a scene of two young Dutch boys blowing pipe smoke towards a puppy, frosted satin ground, smoke becomes visible when held to light, ground pontil, 6" h. **$224**

Cameo box, cov., low wide round cylindrical form w/fitted flat cover & faceted button finial, clear layered in lavender & etched as flowering wisteria vines on a frosted & textured ground, ca. 1920, 6 1/2" d., 3 3/4" h. **863**

Cameo box, cov., low wide round cylindrical form w/fitted flat cover & faceted button finial, clear layered in lavender & etched as flowering wisteria vines on a frosted & textured ground, ca. 1920, 9" d., 4" h. **978**

Val St. Lambert Engraved Vase

Vase, 8 1/2" h., footed bulbous ovoid body tapering to a short flared neck, heavy colorless crystal enclosed w/a large single perfect rose on leafy stem at the center, base signed "VSG C. Graffart - Piece Unique 1949," attributed to Charles Graffart (ILLUS.) **347**

Venetian

Venetian glass has been made for six centuries on the island of Murano, where it continues to be produced. The skilled glass artisans developed numerous techniques, subsequently imitated elsewhere.

Finger bowls & underplates, each in gold-flecked clear glass, the deep round bowls w/flared rims & applied scrolling decoration above the fluted bottom, plain dished underplates, ten bowls & eight underplates, early 20th c., plates 7 1/4" d., bowls 4 5/8" d., 2 1/2" h., the set (ILLUS. bottom of page) **$448**

Stemware set: ten wine glasses & seven champagnes; each in a gold flecked clear w/an optic swirled design & slender teardrop strands extending up around the bowls from the double-knop stem on a round foot, early 20th c., 6 5/8" & 10" h., the set (ILLUS. bottom of page) **1,680**

Vase, 8 3/4" h., "losanghe," swelled cylindrical form w/a wide flat rim, clear decorated w/a spiral grid of squares in white & caramel w/aubergine strips, Archimede Seguso, ca. 1956, unsigned **2,875**

Vase, 8 7/8" h., "tutti frutti," flaring cylindrical form w/pinched rim, clear cased over a layer of multi-colored glass canes comprising latticinio, millefiori, zanfirico, cane pieces & other broken pieces of glass, over a burst silver foil layer, further cased over deep turquoise blue, unsigned, remains of paper label of A.V.E.M., ca. 1955 .... **632**

Vase, 10 1/2" h., domed foot on a gently flaring cylindrical body w/a rounded bottom, bowl overlaid in gold foil & further decorated w/random applied dark spots,

Venetian Gold-flecked Finger Bowls

Gold-flecked Venetian Stemware Set

deep purple foot, unsigned Fratelli Toso, ca. 1950s **2,990**

Vase, 10 1/2" h., "scavo," blown & applied irregular bottle form w/applied figure of a nude woman carrying a basket of fruit, the reverse w/two fish, heavily textured glass, designed by Napoleone Martinuzzi for Cenedese, ca. 1953-58, unsigned **3,450**

Vase, 10 1/2" h., "sommerso," thick slightly flared heavily swirl-ribbed squared form, pale amber cased over cranberry, Archimede Seguso, ca. 1960, unsigned **460**

Vase, 10 5/8" h., "piume," slender teardrop bottle-form w/ovoid body & tall slender neck, clear cased over peach, internally decorated in filigree feathers in white, black, periwinkle blue & yellow, Archimede Seguso, designed circa 1956 .. **4,025**

Venini

Founded by former lawyer Paolo Venini in 1925, this Venetian glasshouse soon developed a reputation for its fine quality decorative glass and tablewares. Several noted designers have worked for the firm over the years and their unique pieces in the modern spirit, made using traditional techniques, are increasingly popular with collectors today. The factory continues in operation.

Clock, table model, in blue w/green inclusions, acid-stamped "Venini - Murano - Made in Italy," ca. 1950s, 6 1/4 x 6 3/8", 6" h. **$402**

Decanter w/stopper, "sommerso inciso," tall slender slightly tapering triangular form w/a short neck & tall pointed & ribbed stopper, brilliant turquoise blue, acid-stamped "VENINI - MURANO - ITALIA," designed by Paolo Venini, ca. 1956, 14 3/4" h. **575**

Model of a fish, shown lying flat, the body blown in lavender cased in clear, decorated w/applied canes in yellow & mustard yellow, applied turquoise eye, inscribed "venini - italia," designed by Ken Scott, ca. 1951, 19 1/2" l. **1,840**

Models of chickens, a hen & a rooster w/angled cornucopia-shaped bodies in opaque white w/polychrome applied bands, applied small black wings, white legs w/yellow feet, red combs & yellow beaks, designed by Fulvio Bianconi, acid-stamped "venini murano ITALIA," ca. 1950s, 7 1/2" h. (rooster's first comb removed, possibly done at the factory), pr. **2,860**

Vase, 3" h., "fazzoletto" handkerchief-style, rounded flaring upright pulled & ruffled sides composed of orange & green "zanfirico" canes, paper label & acid-stamped mark "venini murano ITALIA," designed by Fulvio Bianconi, ca. 1950s **121**

Vase, 5 1/2" h., "zanfirico fazzeletto," a handkerchief-style piece w/a rounded bottom & wide, upright folded & ruffled sides in clear enclosing vertical "zanfirico" canes in white & creamy yellow & aubergine, acid-stamped "VENINI - MURANO - ITALIA," designed by Fulvio Bianconi, designed ca. 1949 .... **2,875**

Vase, 9" h., "a canne," simple conical form w/angled rim, clear fused w/pale amber, blue, violet, teal & red stripes, acid-stamped "venini - murano - ITALIA," designed by Paolo Venini, ca. 1954 .... **2,875**

Vase, 9" h., "inciso sommerso," simple tall flaring cylindrical form, clear cased over green, acid-stamped "VENINI - ITALIA - MURANO," designed by Paolo Venini, ca. 1956 .... **690**

Venini Bianconi-designed Vase

Vase, 9" h., "Pezzato Americano," flaring cylindrical body w/undulating rim, clear w/green, black, yellow & straw yellow in an overall patchwork design, acid-stamped "venini - murano - ITALIA," designed by Fulvio Bianconi, ca. 1950s (ILLUS.) **6,600**

Vase, 9 1/2" h., "fasce verticale," cylindrical dimpled form in clear fused w/vertical stripes in shades of pale amber, red, green & cobalt blue, acid-stamped "venini - murano - ITALIA," designed by Fulvio Bianconi, ca. 1952 .... **7,475**

Venini "Incalmo" Cylindrical Vase

Vase, 9 7/8" h., "incalmo," simple cylindrical form w/six rows of fused black & red on white alternating murrine w/transparent green bands above & blue below, base stamped "Venini Murano Italia," w/square numbered paper label, designed by Riccardo Licata, 1953-56 (ILLUS.) **7,188**

Vase, 10 1/2" h., "fazzoletto" (handkerchief) style, upright randomly pulled & ruffled sides composed of a vertical arrangement of pink & white "zanfirico" & "reticello" canes, acid-stamped "venini - murano - ITALIA," designed by Fulvio Bianconi, 1948 .... **3,450**

Vase, 10 1/2" h., "veronese," simple baluster-form w/short knopped pedestal & a small flared neck, brilliant ruby red, designed by Napoleone Martinuzzi, ca. 1925, unsigned.. **690**

Vase, 11" h., figural, blown in the form of a nude female torso w/the arms stretched upwards, olive amber, designed by Fulvio Bianconi, ca. 1950, signed "venini - murano - ITALIA".. **6,325**

Vase, 14 1/4" h., "Tessuto," tall ovoid bottle form w/rounded shoulder to slender cylindrical neck, black & turquoise blue vertical fused canes, polished pontil w/foil label marked "Venini S.A. Murano," design attributed to Carlo Scarpa, mid-20th c., light abrasions **1,955**

Vase, 14 3/4" h., tall slender amphora-form w/funnel foot & flaring neck flanked by applied long C-scroll handles, clear, designed by Napoleone Martinuzzi, ca. 1925, unsigned.. **690**

Wall Pocket Vases

Aladdin Alacite, conical w/scrolled handles & end finial, ribbed design on base, beaded rim, 8 1/2" l. **$150-175**

Amethyst, satin finish, wide form w/finial, Tiffin Glass Co., 10 x 10"........................ **250-300**

Black, tapered horizontal ribs, 7 1/2" l...... **100-135**

Canary yellow, Daisy & Button patt. canoe shape, hole in each end, 12" l. **65-85**

Cobalt blue, w/metal holders, ruffled rim, 4 1/4" h... **12-15**

Crystal, conical shape, painted medium blue w/cornucopia of multicolored flowers, 5 3/4 x 8 1/2" **95-125**

Crystal, slender conical form, Beaded Grape patt., U.S. Glass Co., 10" l. **65-85**

Crystal, vertical ribs w/flower basket painted on front & red painted trim, 6" h............ **25-35**

Crystal, w/flashed-on green, ribbed conical form w/pointed end finial, Anniversary patt., No. 2930, by Jeannette Glass Co., 3 1/2 x 6 1/2"... **20-30**

Crystal, w/flashed-on yellow, ribbed conical form w/pointed end finial, Anniversary patt., No. 2930, by Jeannette Glass Co., 3 1/2 x 6 1/2"... **20-30**

Green, glass & metal, bottle shape w/painted flowers, 9 1/2" l. **20-25**

Green, slender conical form, Beaded Grape patt., U.S. Glass Co., 6" l. **50-75**

Green, slender conical form, Beaded Grape patt., U.S. Glass Co., 8" l. **75-95**

Marigold, w/crackle finish, scalloped edge, Jeannette Glass Company, ca. 1920s, 7 1/4" h. **35-50**

Peacock blue, Style No. 1881, Fostoria Glass Co., 3 x 8 1/4" **95-125**

White milk glass, whiskbroom shape, blue foil label "Imperial U.S.A., Genuine Milk Glass," & embossed "IG," 8" l. **40-50**

White milk glass, zig-zag molded design, h.p. green w/black applied trim, 4 3/4 x 6 1/8" **40-50**

Wave Crest

Now much sought after, Wave Crest was produced by the C.F. Monroe Co., Meriden, Connecticut, in the late 19th and early 20th centuries from opaque white glass blown into molds.

It was then hand-decorated in enamels and metal trim was often added. Boudoir accessories such as jewel boxes, hair receivers, etc., were predominant.

WAVE CREST WARE
Wave Crest Mark

Small Wave Crest Box

Box w/hinged lid, Egg Crate mold, lid decorated w/central floral decoration of pink & maroon flowers & green leaves on a shaded light green ground, 3" d., 2 1/2" h. (ILLUS.).............................. **$225**

Box w/hinged lid, Helmschmied Swirl mold, dainty flowers on the top, 3" d., 3" h. **248**

Box w/hinged lid, Hexagonal mold, applied pink ceramic flowers surrounded by green leaves on a light green ground, 4 1/2" d.. **1,250**

Box w/hinged lid, Helmschmied Swirl mold, h.p. floral decoration on a creamy white ground, 4 1/2" d., 3" h. **425**

Box w/hinged lid, Helmschmied Swirl mold, pale blue ground w/h.p. flowers, 4 1/2" d., 3" h. **350**

Box w/hinged lid, Shell mold, blue w/pink flowers on cover, 4 1/2" d., 3" h. **375**

Box w/hinged lid, Egg Crate mold, pink ground decorated w/clusters of blue flowers, raised gold borders surround floral groupings, wide gilt-metal mountings, 4 1/2 x 4 3/4"... **550**

Box w/hinged lid, Egg Crate mold, decorated w/yellow & purple flowers, 5" sq............... **430**

Box w/hinged lid, Helmschmied Swirl mold, decorated w/delicate flowers on the lid & sides, 6" d., 5" h. **400**

Box w/hinged lid, Egg Crate mold, decorated w/two classical women, 6" d., 6" h. **950**

Box w/hinged lid, Egg Crate mold, creamy ground w/lovely h.p. pink flowers, 6 1/2" w. **495**

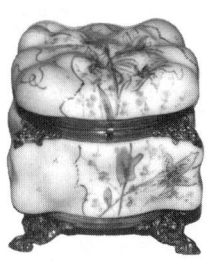

Large Egg Crate Wave Crest Box

Box w/hinged lid, Egg Crate mold, yellow lilies on a white ground w/light blue panels, all trimmed w/lavender & gold enamel, 6 3/4" w., 6 1/2" h. (ILLUS.) **1,750**

Box w/hinged lid, Egg Crate mold, decorated w/mauve to purple floral clusters, green ribbons w/enameled white dots & outlined in gold, 7" sq. **750**

Baroque Shell Wave Crest Box

Box w/hinged lid, Baroque Shell mold, top decorated w/blue, purple & grey flowers, green leaves & pink trim on a creamy white ground, 7" d., 4" h. (ILLUS.) **750**

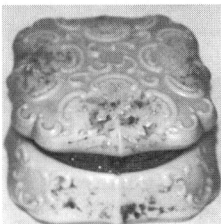

Scroll-molded Large Wave Crest Box

Box w/hinged lid, squared shape w/overall delicate molded scrolls highlighted w/pastel blue & pink blossoms & green leaves, delicately embossed metal fittings, unlined, unsigned, 7" w., 4" h. (ILLUS.) **750**

Box w/hinged lid, Embossed Rococo mold, decorated w/pink & white florals, 7 1/4" d., 5 1/2" h. **750**

Box w/hinged lid, Helmschmied Swirl mold, decorated w/h.p. florals, 8" d. **495**

Cigar humidor, cov., decorated w/sprays of blue flowers on front, back & lid, tan & white background, relief-molded shell lid, "Cigars" written in gold script on front, label w/red banner mark, mint condition, 6" h. **1,650**

Cologne bottle w/atomizer, squatty bulbous body, h.p. yellow floral decoration & enameled white dots on a white opal ground, nickel plate atomizer dated "1889" w/rubber bulb **275**

Cracker jar, cov., barrel-shaped, satin finish w/fern decoration on a pale yellow ground, silver plate rim, cover & bail handle, overall 10 1/2" h. **280**

Cracker jar, cov., Egg Crate mold, colorful floral decoration, silver plate rim, cover & twisted bail handle, 7 3/4" w., 5" h. **450**

Cracker jar, cov., squared form w/raised scrolls around the edges, decorated w/colored florals, silver plate rim, cover & bail handle, glass 4 3/4" w., 5 3/4" h. **248**

Cracker jar, cov., Tulip mold, decorated w/pink apple blossoms front & back, cream shading to blue ground **350**

Wave Crest Cracker Jar

Cracker jar, cov., barrel-shaped, panels of yellow flowers w/pink centers & green leaves decorate a soft pink ground, resilvered rim, cover & bail handle, unmarked, 5 1/2" d., 7 1/4" h. (ILLUS.) **350**

Cracker jar, cov., barrel-shaped w/embossed scrolling, h.p. pink, blue & yellow pansies on a creamy white ground, resilvered cover, rim & bail handle, 5 3/4" d., 7 3/4" h. **295**

Cracker jar, cov., Egg Crate mold, decorated w/h.p. lavender, green & tan florals on a white shaded to pale blue ground, 5" d., 9" h. **650**

Cracker jar, cov., barrel-shaped w/large embossed leaf design, shaded yellow to white ground, decorated w/h.p. ferns, silver plate rim, cover & bail handle, overall 10 1/2" h. **280**

Ewers, bulbous rounded melon-lobed body decorated w/yellow florals, top fitted w/tall metal arching forked spout & a large S-scroll handle, raised on tapering pedestal above a flaring scroll-molded cast-metal footed base w/grotesque masks at each corner, pr. **500**

Ferner, Egg Crate mold, decorated w/light pink spider mums, no liner, 7" sq. **375**

Ferner, Egg Crate mold, decorated w/yellow wild roses, metal twisted rope rim, 7" sq. **650**

Ferner, low cylindrical body on a narrow footed ring base w/gilt-metal rim insert, light overall scrolling w/h.p. green & brown fern leaves on a shaded yellow ground **650**

Glove box w/hinged cover, pink w/blue floral decoration, 4 x 8 1/2"...................... **1,200**

Humidor w/hinged metal cover, cylindrical body w/scroll-embossed domed cover, floral decoration on a blue & cream ground, "Tobacco" across the front, 5 1/4" h.. **750**

Humidor w/original brass cover, bulbous tapering cylindrical body decorated w/enameled house & bridge scene, cover w/finial & tapering base........................ **750**

Jardiniere, wide bulbous smooth body w/a wide short cylindrical neck, decorated w/large clusters of chrysanthemums around the body, gilt lacy lancets around the neck, 14" d., 10" h................................. **950**

Match holder, decorated w/flowers & beading on the top & bottom, on four gilt-metal ornate feet... **195**

Mirror tray, embossed scrolls, decorated w/dainty blue flowers on a creamy white ground, ornate gilt-metal frame, 5 1/4" d. .. **1,200**

Photo receiver, Egg Crate mold, the body decorated w/clusters of pink & blue flowers & light green foliage on a creamy white ground, ornate gilt-metal rim **425**

Photo receiver, Egg Crate mold, upright rectangular form, floral decoration on a creamy white ground w/gilt-metal rim & gilt-metal footed base................................. **525**

Ring box, cov., green ground decorated w/a transfer-printed color portrait of a lady on the cover w/a white background, 2" d., 2 1/2" h..................................... **960**

Salt dip, Tulip mold, h.p. floral decoration **165**

Salt & pepper shakers w/original tops, embossed scrolling design, pink ground w/front & back blue floral decoration, pr. **250**

Salt & pepper shakers w/original tops, Erie Twist mold, decorated w/peach & blue forget-me-nots & daisies, pr................. **175**

Syrup pitcher w/original hinged top, Helmschmied Swirl mold, white & beige swirls highlighted w/lavender & gold florals **295**

Syrup pitcher w/original hinged top, paneled cylindrical body w/tapering shoulder, lacy transfer decoration & h.p. pink daisy-like flowers **165**

Syrup pitcher w/original hinged top, Ribbed Skirt mold, h.p. blue florals, tall......... **165**

Toothpick holder, cylindrical w/molded designs & decorated w/florals, signed, 1 1/2" h... **138**

Toothpick holder, h.p. yellow daisies, footed gilt-metal frame, signed.......................... **275**

Vase, 5 3/4" h., slender baluster-form w/ovoid body & tall slender flaring cylindrical neck, fitted w/a gilt-metal rim & shoulder bands, joined by openwork scrolling handles raised on a short pedestal above domed scroll-cast metal base, decorated w/delicate florals on the front.. **428**

Vase, 6 1/2" h., footed, cylindrical body, embossed scrolling, beaded rim, decorated w/pink flowers.................................... **325**

Vase, 9" h., 1 1/4" rim d., squatty bulbous body tapering to a tall cylindrical neck, decorated w/shaded pink to burgundy

mums, deep green enameled swags & a deep green enameled rim w/white dotting, footed gilt-metal base............................ **750**

Vase, 9" h., pink shading to burgundy w/h.p. floral decoration & raised gold beading **2,200**

Vase, 12 1/2" h., 4 3/4" d., cylindrical body w/brass collar, decorated w/pink wild roses on light blue ground, ornate metal feet.. **1,500**

Vase, 13 1/2" h., footed, burnt orange ground decorated w/large purple orchids on the front & back, signed........................ **1,500**

Westmoreland

Westmoreland Specialty Company was founded in East Liverpool, Ohio, in 1889 and relocated in 1890 to Grapeville, Pennsylvania, where it remained until its closing in 1985.

During its early years Westmoreland specialized in glass food containers and novelties but by the turn of the 20th century it had a large line of milk white items and clear tableware patterns. In 1925 the company name was shortened to The Westmoreland Glass Company. It was during that decade that more colored glasswares entered its line-up. When Victorian-style milk glass again became popular in the 1940s and 1950s, Westmoreland produced extensive amounts in several patterns that closely resemble late 19th century wares. These and the figural animal dishes in milk white and colors are widely collected today, but buyers should not confuse them for the antique originals. Watch for Westmoreland's "WG" mark on some pieces. A majority of our listings are products from the 1940s through the 1970s. Earlier pieces will be indicated.

Animal covered dish, Camel, amber satin, Humphrey **$48**

Animal covered dish, Duck, rimmed base, blue milk glass **50**

Animal covered dish, Duck, ruby carnival **65**

Animal covered dish, Eagle, two-part, w/added eyes, milk white **85**

Animal covered dish, Hen on Nest, looking left, green slag **65**

Animal covered dish, Hen on Nest, looking left, milk white, red decoration........................ **38**

Animal covered dish, Mother Eagle w/chicks, milk white.. **85**

Animal covered dish, Rabbit, ruby carnival........ **50**

Ashtray, Beaded Grape patt., milk white............. **10**

Ashtray, square, Paneled Grape patt., milk white, large.. **19**

Paneled Grape Banana Bowl

Banana bowl, bell-footed, Paneled Grape patt., No. 47, milk white, 12" (ILLUS.)............ **125**

Lotus Single Candlestick

Compote, cov., 5" h., square, low footed,
Old Quilt patt., milk white.................................... 22

Compote, cov., 7" h., footed, Paneled
Grape patt., milk white 33

Compote, open, 4 1/2" d., 6" h., ruffled rim,
Paneled Grape patt., milk white w/pansy
decoration No. 34 30

Compote, open, 9" sq., footed, Paneled
Grape patt., milk white.. 40

Compote, open, 6" d., Della Robbia patt.,
clear w/colored staining...................................... 30

Compote, open, footed, crimped & ruffled,
Waterford patt., No. 32, clear w/ruby
stain 119

Console set: bowl & pr. of candlesticks;
Thousand Eye patt., clear, 3 pcs. 145

Cordial, footed, Waterford patt., No. 5, clear
w/ruby stain, 1 oz. 49

Cordial, English Hobnail, square base,
clear, 3 3/4" h. 20

Creamer, Paneled Grape patt., milk white,
6 1/2 oz. 13

Creamer & cov. sugar bowl, Paneled
Grape patt., milk white, pr. 45

Creamer & open sugar bowl, Della Robbia
patt., clear w/colored staining, pr. 35

Creamer & open sugar bowl, individual,
Paneled Grape patt., milk white, pr. 25

Creamer & open sugar bowl, Maple Leaf
(Bramble) patt., milk white, pr. 28

Creamer & sugar bowl, American Hobnail
patt., milk white, pr. 26

Creamer & sugar bowl, Thousand Eye
patt., clear, pr. 110

Cruets, English Hobnail patt., milk white,
6 1/2" h., set of 2 50

Cruets w/original stopper, Paneled Grape
patt., milk white, pr. 38

Cup, Paneled Grape patt., milk white 8

Cup & saucer, American Hobnail patt., milk
white... 18

Cup & saucer, Beaded Edge patt., milk
white.. 12

Cup & saucer, English Hobnail patt., milk
white.. 16

Cups & saucers, English Hobnail patt., milk
white, 8 sets.. 65

Decanter w/stopper, American Hobnail,
milk white... 42

Egg cup, American Hobnail, clear, 4 1/2" h......... 42

Fairy lamp, two-part, Thousand Eye patt.,
Brandywine blue 28

Flowerpot, Paneled Grape patt., milk white,
4 1/4" h. 30

Fruit cocktail w/underplate, Paneled
Grape patt., milk white, 3 1/2", 2 pcs............... 18

Goblet, American Hobnail patt., clear, 6" h. 16

Goblet, American Hobnail patt., milk white,
6" h. 9

Goblet, Beaded Grape patt., round, footed,
clear, 8 oz. 24

Goblet, Della Robbia patt., stained dark col-
ors, 6" h. 48

Goblet, English Hobnail patt., round base,
clear, 6" h. (ILLUS. top next column)............... 14

Goblet, English Hobnail patt., square base,
clear, 6" h. 15

Goblet, Paneled Grape patt., clear, 6" h. 19

Goblet, Paneled Grape patt., ruby, 6" h. 29

Goblet, water, footed, Beaded Grape patt.,
milk white, 9 oz. 11

English Hobnail Goblet

Goblet, water, Paneled Grape patt., No. 14,
milk white, 8 oz. 14

Goblet, wine, Della Robbia patt., milk white,
4 3/4" h. 16

Goblet, wine, Della Robbia patt., stained
dark colors, 4 3/4" h. 52

Goblet, wine, Paneled Grape patt., clear,
4" h. 18

Goblet, wine, Paneled Grape patt., milk
white 20

Goblet, wine, Paneled Grape patt., ruby,
4" h. 29

Goblets, stemmed, Paneled Grape patt.,
milk white, set of 8.. 80

Gravy boat & liner, Paneled Grape patt.,
milk white.. 40

Ivy ball vase, footed, cupped rim, Paneled
Grape patt., milk white.. 38

Jardiniere, Paneled Grape patt., milk white,
5" h. 18

Jardiniere, Paneled Grape patt., milk white,
6 1/2" h. 20

Marmalade dish w/ladle, cov., English
Hobnail patt., milk white, 5 1/2", 2 pcs............ 25

Mayonnaise dish, underplate & ladle,
Paneled Grape patt., milk white, 3 pcs. 28

Mint compote, flat, footed, Waterford patt.,
No. 19, clear w/ruby stain, 5 1/2" d. 59

Mint compote, footed, crimped rim, Water-
ford patt., No. 34, clear w/ruby stain 49

Model of butterfly, No. 2, green satin, small....... 18

Model of owl, on two stacked books, cobalt
carnival, 3 1/2" h... 26

Model of owl w/glass eyes, dark blue,
5 1/2" h.. 35

Model of Pouter Pigeon, apricot mist,
2 1/2" h... 35

Model of Pouter Pigeon, clear, 2 1/2" h. 25

Model of sleigh, milk white w/holly decora-
tion, No. 1872.. 30

Model of slipper, grandma's, blue satin
w/white decoration 18

Nappy, round, Paneled Grape patt., milk
white, 4 1/2" d. 9

Nappy, round, handled, Paneled Grape
patt., milk white, 5" d. 14

Novelty, model of a straw hat, milk white
w/decoration, 4 1/2" 38

Novelty, model of a top hat, English Hobnail
patt., milk white, 3" h.. 10

Pickle dish, Paneled Grape patt., oval, milk
white, 8" l... 13

Pitcher, 7 1/4" h., American Hobnail, milk
white 68

Rocker Pattern Covered Pitcher

Paneled Grape Milk Glass Vase

GRANITEWARE

This is a name given to metal (customarily iron) kitchenware covered with an enamel coating. Featured at the 1876 Philadelphia Centennial Exposition, it became quite popular for it was lightweight, attractive, and easy to clean. Although it was made in huge quantities and is still produced, it has caught the attention of a younger generation of collectors and prices have steadily risen over the past few years. There continues to be a constant demand for the wide variety of these utilitarian articles turned out earlier in this century and rare forms now command high prices.

Blue & Grey Splatter

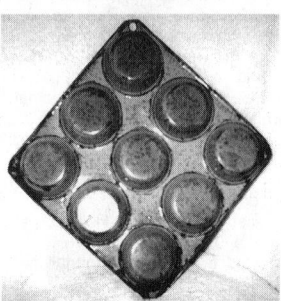

Blue & Grey Splatter Muffin Pan

Muffin pan, hangs in triangle, 9 cups, 10" x 10" **$50**

Blue & White Chicken Wire

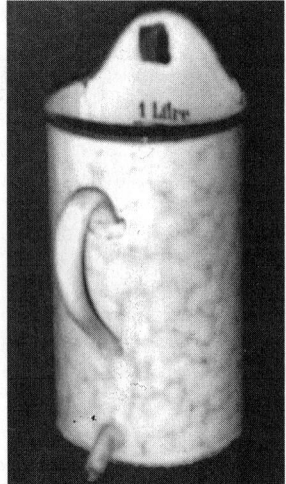

Blue & White Nasal Irrigator

Nasal irrigator, cobalt trim, 7" **80**

Blue & White Mottled

Blue & White Mottled Coffeepot

Coffeepot, w/riveted attachment for lid, cobalt trim, 7" h. (ILLUS.) **45**

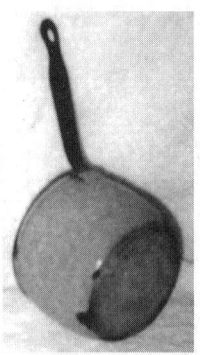

Blue & White Mottled Dipper

Dipper, cobalt rim & handle, rivet handle, 3" h., 4" d. (ILLUS.) **60**

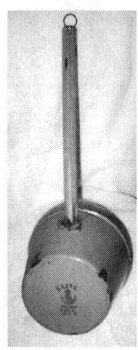

"Elite, Austria" Mottled Dipper

Dipper, w/riveted handle w/seam & ring to hang it, "Elite, Austria," 18" l., 6" dipper (ILLUS.) **80**

Blue & White Mottled Spoon

Spoon, black handle, white interior, 13" l. **30**

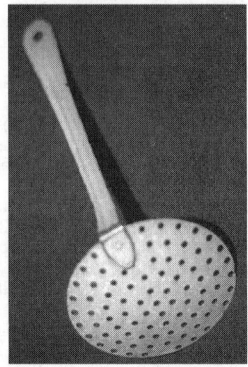

Blue & White Mottled Strainer

Strainer, rivet handle, bent at angle, 9" handle, 5" d. **40**

White Interior Mottled Strainer

Strainer, white interior, 14" l. **50**

Blue & White Swirl

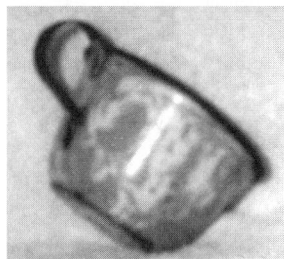

Blue & White Swirl Cup

Cup, white interior, rivet handle, black rim & handle, 2" h. (ILLUS.) **70**

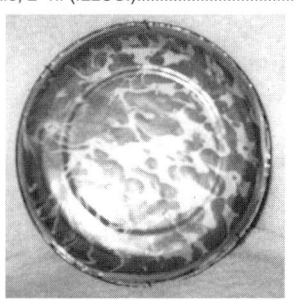

Blue & White Swirl Plate

Plate, white interior, black rim, 9" d. **60**

Brown & Tan Mottled

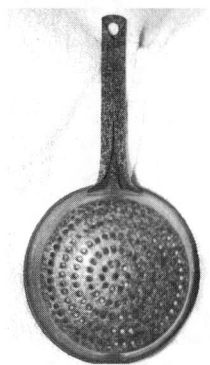

Brown & Tan Mottled Strainer

Strainer, seam handle, 7" handle, 6" d. **35**

Brown & White Mottled

Brown & White Mottled Funnel

Funnel, closed seam, 5" h. (ILLUS.).................... **65**

Brown & White Splatter

Brown & White Splatter Pressure Cooker

Pressure cooker, Burpee pressure cooker, 12" d., 12" h.. **60**

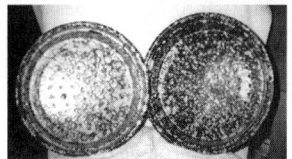

Brown & White Splatter Strainer

Strainer, 10" d. (ILLUS.) **40**

Brown & White Swirl

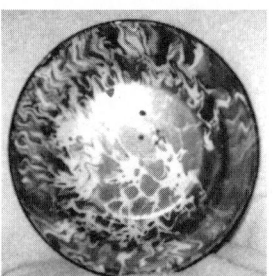

Brown & White Swirl Plate

Plate, 8" d., black rim (ILLUS.).............................. **60**

Chrysolite & White Swirl

Chrysolite & White Mug

Mug, black rim, white interior, rivet handle, 2" (ILLUS.) **100**

Cobalt Blue & White Splatter

Strainer, 10" d. **40**

Green & White Mottled

Green & White Mottled Lunch Pail

Lunch pail, inside tray, wire handle, 6" h. (ILLUS.) **50**

Green & White Mottled Plate

Plate, unusual color, cobalt rim, 9" d. (ILLUS.) **70**

Green & White Relish

Green & White Relish Coffee/Teapot

Coffee/Teapot, cov., wood handle w/rivets, white interior, lid missing, 6" h. (ILLUS.).......... **45**

Green & White Swirl

Bowl set, all white interior, black rim, 6" d., set of 3 .... **100**

Grey

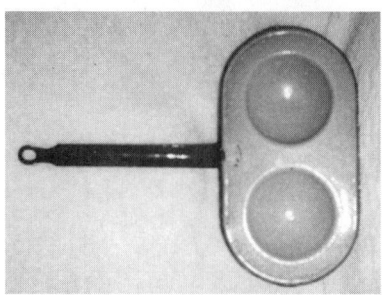

Grey Egg Poacher

Egg poacher, egg holder, red & brown handle & reverse side, 6" handle, 8" across (ILLUS.)... **80**
Flat skimmers, rivet handle, stamped "Agate nickel steelware," 12" handle, 6" d., each **70**

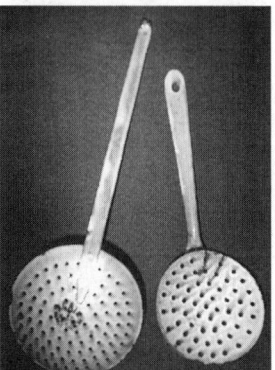

Grey Flat Skimmers

Flat skimmers, w/rivet handle, 10" handle, 5" d., each (ILLUS.).. **40**

Grey Gravy Strainer

Gravy strainer, rivet handle, screen, 5" handle, 7" d.. **70**

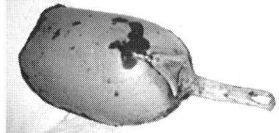

Grey Scoop

Scoop, w/3-rivet triangle handle, 12" l. (ILLUS.)... **40**

Grey Splatter

Grey Splatter Skillet

Skillet, w/pocket seam handle, 21" l. (ILLUS.)... **40**

Grey & White Swirl

Grey & White Swirl Coffeepot

Coffeepot, cov., rivet hinge, 9" h. (ILLUS.) **30**

Miscellaneous

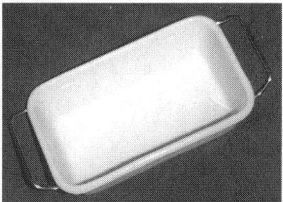

Yellow Cake Pan

Cake pan, yellow, in wire holder, ca. 1950s, 9" x 5" (ILLUS.)... **30**

White & Blue Child's Cup

Child's cup, white w/blue rim, black riveted handle, 2" h. (ILLUS.) **45**

White & Black Creamer

Creamer, white, w/black rim, unusual shape, 2" h., 4" d. base (ILLUS.)...................... **50**

White & Blue Mug

Mug, white w/dark blue almost black rim & handle, 3" h. (ILLUS.)... **35**

White & Black Nasal Irrigator

Nasal irrigator, white, w/labels, black rim, 8" l. (ILLUS.) **50**

White & Black Plate

Plate, 8" d., old white w/black rim, two Dutch children kissing (ILLUS.).................................... **35**

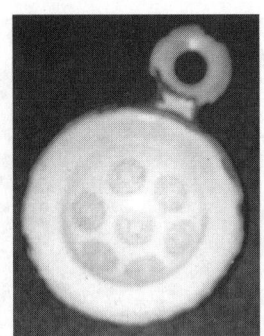

White Tea Strainer

Tea strainer, white, 4" d. (ILLUS.) **25**

Robin's-egg Blue Tub

Tub, oblong, robin's-egg blue, w/label, black trim, 16" across, 20" l. (ILLUS.)........................ **40**

Red & White Splatter

Red & White Splatter Pan

Pan, oblong, black trim, 12" x 12" (ILLUS.).......... **50**

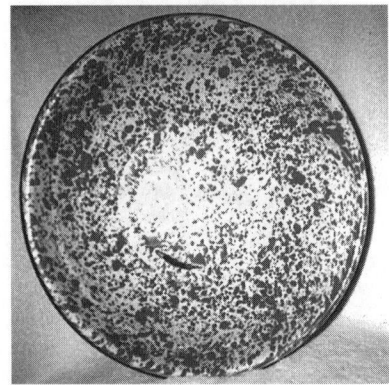

Red & White Splatter Wash Basin

Wash basin, 14" d. (ILLUS.) **70**

Red & White Swirl

Red & White Swirl Bowl Set

Bowl set, all white interior, black rim, 6" d.
each, set of 3 (ILLUS.).................................... **100**

Red & White Swirl Platter

Platter, w/cobalt rim, 18" d. (ILLUS.) **70**

Red & Yellow Swirl

Red & Yellow Swirl Coffeepot

Coffeepot, cov., 9" (ILLUS.)................................. **40**
Cup, yellow interior, 3" h. (ILLUS.) **40**

Yellow & Orange Swirl

Yellow & Orange Swirl Mug

Mug, w/black rim, 3" h. (ILLUS.)........................... **35**

Yellow & White Swirl

Bowl set, all white interior, black rim, 6" d. each,
the set **100**
Mug, w/white interior, 4" h. **35**

ICART PRINTS

"Coursing II" Etching

Coursing II, etching, embossed windmill
mark in lower margin, "1929" copyright,
16 1/2 x 26 1/4" (ILLUS.)........................... **$1,430**
Love's Blossom, 1937, 17 x 25".................... **3,080**
Sleeping Beauty, 1927,15 1/2 x 19 1/2"
oval **1,502**
Sofa (The), 1937, 17 x 26 1/4" **3,920**
Thoroughbreds, 1938, 18 7/8 x 35 1/8" **6,160**

INDIAN ARTIFACTS & JEWELRY

Baby carrier, Ute or Paiute wicker basket
w/indigo cloth trim, w/Native-manufac-
tured cloth doll wearing frilled lace bon-
net, 18" h. **$165**
Container, "Niagara Falls," Iroquois, rectangular shape tapering out at bottom,
leather w/green floral beaded designs &
white folky bird on front, "Box" on lid,
5 1/2" l. **110**
Jar, San Ildefonso black on blackware by
Marie & Julian Martinez, flaring underside, painted above flaring shoulder w/re-
peated negative feather patt., signed on
bottom "Marie & Julian," ca. 1940,
2 3/4" h. (scratch on side) **935**
Kachina, White Buffalo kachina w/white
body & two black marks on face, arms,
legs & body, white fur, black horns, white

leather kilt, leather straps w/shells & bells, figure holds rattle & bow, wooden base, 25 1/2" h. (minor edge damage).......... **440**

Navaho Rug

Rug, Navaho, early Crystal area, serrate linear diamond design in hand-carded tans, red, natural & some blue yarn outlining, 3'9" x 6'3" (ILLUS.) **770**

Klagetoh Sunrise Design Rug

Rug, Navaho, Klagetoh area, Klagetoh sunrise design w/terraced & serrate elements, carded grey/tan, double dye red & natural, 3' x 5'5" (ILLUS.)........ **880**

Rug, Navaho regional rug, probably Ganado, w/two large stepped diamonds in charcoal & carded grey on a natural carded ground w/double dye red accents & border, 3'7" x 5'6" (stains) **550**

Rug, Navaho, regional, Shiprock area w/expanding terraced diamonds in browns, greys & black on soft blush background, visible spirit line, 2' x 2'2"................................ **303**

Rug, Navaho, regional w/banded serrate diamonds in rows throughout central design area in natural, dark red & black on carded grey ground, white border, 1930s, 4'3" x 6'8" **1,210**

Rug, Navaho, West Reservation Storm patt., w/central field & four sacred mountain blocks at corners, crab motifs at ends, fine weave & intricate Tees Nos Pas border in red, dark brown, golden tan on natural white & carded tan background, 4'6" x 7'6".. **825**

Rug, Navaho, West reservation-type design of stepped terraces & serrate elements in russet browns, carded grey/tan & natural surrounded by dark red border w/black crosses, 4'11" x 6'4" (color runs & some stains, edge damage) **495**

Rug, Navaho, Wide Ruins area, early example w/vegetable dye in golds & sagebrush pink w/aniline black in bands w/in-

termittent stepped diamonds, 3' x 4'9" (minor edge damage & light stains)............... **275**

Weaving, Navaho Yei, w/two female yei figures holding bows & arrows, centered w/a cornstalk & surrounded by the Rainbow God, bright polychrome hand-carded yarn on creamy white ground, 2'6" x 3'4" **550**

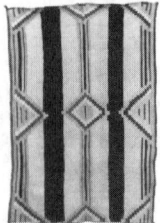

Navaho Chief Pattern Weaving

Woven panel, Third Phase Navaho Chief patt., finely woven blanket/rug weight, dark black/brown w/carded grey, natural & faded aniline red, corner tassels, early 1900s, repaired spots, 3'10" x 5'6" (ILLUS.).. **880**

JEWELRY

American Painted Porcelain

American painted porcelain jewelry comprises a unique category. While the metallic settings and porcelain medallions were inexpensive, the painted decoration was a work of fine art. The finished piece possessed greater intrinsic value than costume jewelry of the same period because it was a one-of-a-kind creation, but one that was not as expensive as real gold and sterling silver settings and precious and semi-precious jewels. Note that signatures are rare, backstamps lacking.

Dorothy Kamm

Bar pin, decorated w/pink roses & greenery, brass-plated bezel, ca. 1880s, 7/16 x 1 1/2" **$30**

Bar pin, decorated w/pink roses on a pale green ground, burnished gold tips & brass-plated bezel, ca. 1900-1915, 2 5/8" w. **50**

Belt Buckle Brooch with Portrait

Belt buckle brooch, oval, decorated w/a profile of a woman wearing a pink top & white shawl, pink roses in her curly brown hair, black choker at her neck, burned gold rim, gold-plated bezel, signed "M.e.M.," 1900-17, 1 7/8 x 2 3/8" (ILLUS.) **175**

Belt Buckle Brooch with Pansy

Belt buckle brooch, oval, decorated w/a white pansy, accented w/white enamel, on a burnished gold ground, gold-plated bezel, 1900-17, 1 11/16 x 2 1/4" (ILLUS.) **75**

Art Nouveau Florals on Belt Brooch

Belt buckle brooch, oval, decorated w/an Art Nouveau-style water lily design outlined w/raised paste, petals filled in w/lavender enamel, burnished green & gold background, gold-plated bezel, 1900-17, 1 7/8 x 2 5/8" (ILLUS.) **110**

Bachelor Buttons on Belt Brooch

Belt buckle brooch, oval, decorated w/blue bachelor buttons & greenery on a polychrome ground, irregular burnished gold border outlined in black, gold-plate bezel, 1900-17, 1 7/8 x 2 5/8" (ILLUS.) **95**

Belt buckle brooch, oval, decorated w/roses & greenery on a polychrome ground, burnished gold scalloped border outlined in black, gold-plated bezel, 1900-17, 1 15/16 x 2 11/16" **115**

Brooch, decorated w/violets on a light yellow brown ground w/raised paste scrolled border covered w/burnished gold & burnished gold rims, gold-plated bezel, ca. 1890-1920, 1 1/2" d. **45**

Brooch, diamond-shaped, decorated w/a water lily & waterscape w/white enamel highlights, sky & clouds in background, burnished gold rim, gold-plated bezel, ca. 1930s-1940s, 7/8" sq. **35**

Heart-shaped Brooch with Roses

Brooch, heart-shaped, decorated w/a pink & a ruby rose w/leaves on a polychrome ground, white enamel accents, burnished gold rim, gold-plated bezel, 7/8 x 7/8" (ILLUS.) **30**

Brooch, horseshoe shape, decorated w/pink & ruby roses on a green & yellow ground, white enamel highlights & burnished gold tips, ca. 1880s-1915, 1 1/4 x 1 1/2" **75**

Forget-me-nots on Long Oval Brooch

Brooch, long oval, decorated w/forget-me-nots & leaves on a pastel polychrome ground, white enamel highlights, burnished gold rim, gold-plated bezel, 1 x 1 3/4" **45**

Brooch, lozenge shape, decorated w/forget-me-nots on a pink & pale yellow ground w/white enamel highlights & burnished gold rim, brass-plated bezel, ca. 1890-1920, 7/8 x 1 5/8" **35**

Brooch, oval, decorated w/a conventional-style Colonial dame in light blue & yellow w/opal lustre background & burnished gold rim, brass-plated bezel, ca. 1915-25, 1 5/8 x 2 1/8" **60**

Brooch, oval, decorated w/a conventional-style lavender iris & green leaves outlined in black on a yellow lustre ground w/white enamel highlights on petal edges & yellow enamel highlights on flower centers, burnished gold rim, gold-plated bezel, ca. 1900-20, 1 5/8 x 2 1/8" **75**

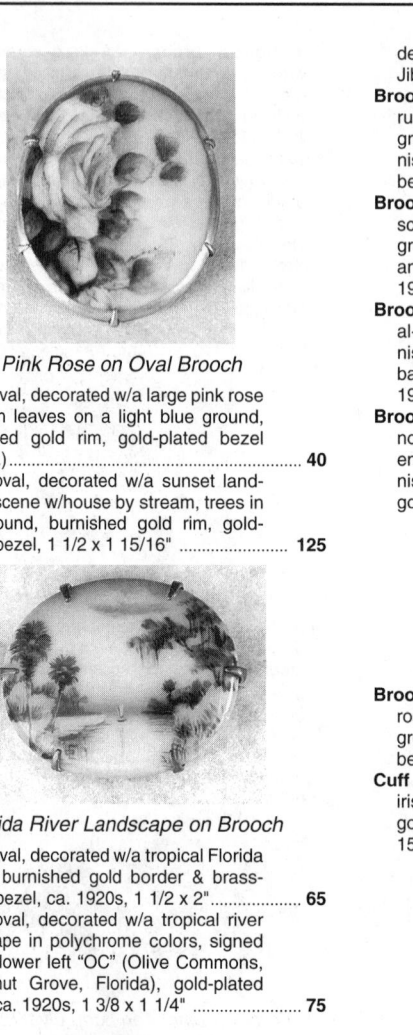

Pink Rose on Oval Brooch

Brooch, oval, decorated w/a large pink rose & green leaves on a light blue ground, burnished gold rim, gold-plated bezel (ILLUS.)... **40**

Brooch, oval, decorated w/a sunset landscape scene w/house by stream, trees in background, burnished gold rim, gold-plated bezel, 1 1/2 x 1 15/16" **125**

Florida River Landscape on Brooch

Brooch, oval, decorated w/a tropical Florida scene, burnished gold border & brass-plated bezel, ca. 1920s, 1 1/2 x 2".................. **65**

Brooch, oval, decorated w/a tropical river landscape in polychrome colors, signed on the lower left "OC" (Olive Commons, Cocoanut Grove, Florida), gold-plated bezel, ca. 1920s, 1 3/8 x 1 1/4" **75**

Art Nouveau Maiden on Brooch

Brooch, oval, decorated w/an Art Nouveau maiden's portrait surrounded by forget-me-nots on an ivory ground, white enamel highlights, framed by burnished gold raised paste scrolls & dots, gold-plated bezel, 1 1/4 x 1 5/8" (ILLUS.)............................ **80**

Brooch, oval, decorated w/forget-me-nots on a pale yellow center w/pale blue bor-

der, gold-plated bezel, signed "A. Jibbing," ca. 1900-20, 1 3/8 x 1 1/2" **75**

Brooch, oval, decorated w/pink & white & ruby roses & green leaves on a rich blue ground w/white enamel highlights, burnished gold border & rim, gold-plated bezel, ca. 1940s, 1 1/2 x 2" **65**

Brooch, rectangular, decorated w/a tropical scene of palm tree in white on a platinum ground, painted by Olive Commons, Miami, Florida, sterling silver bezel, ca. 1920s-1940s, 3/4 x 1" **80**

Brooch, round, decorated w/a conventional-style trillium w/raised paste & burnished gold pistols & burnished gold background, brass-plated bezel, ca. 1910-15, 1 9/16" d.. **35**

Brooches, oval, decorated w/forget-me-nots on a pale pink & blue ground w/white enamel highlights on petal edges, burnished gold rims, gold-plated bezels, gold wear, ca. 1900-20, 13/16 x 1", pr............. **70**

Brooches with Pink & Ruby Roses

Brooches, round, decorated w/pink & ruby roses & green leaves on a polychrome ground, burnished gold rim, gold-plated bezel, 7 /8" d., pr. (ILLUS.) **70**

Cuff pin, rectangular, decorated w/a purple iris outlined & bordered in burnished gold, brass-plated bezel, ca. 1900-15, 1/4 x 1 1/6".. **15**

Cuff Pins with Forget-me-nots

Cuff pins, rectangular, decorated w/forget-me-nots on a burnished gold ground, gold-plated bezel, ca. 1900-15, 1/4 x 1", pr. (ILLUS.).. **45**

Flapper pin, oval, decorated w/a stylized, elegant red-haired woman wearing blue dress & fur stole, pink flower & large comb in her hair, white ground w/burnished gold border, gold-plated bezel, ca. 1922-30, 1 11/16 x 2 1/8" **85**

Flapper pin, oval, decorated w/bust of stylized red-haired flapper on a pastel polychrome ground, burnished gold rim & brass-plated bezel, ca. 1924-28, 1 5/8 x 2 1/8".. **75**

Pendant, decorated w/a purple pansy w/white enamel center accents & burnished gold border, gold-plated bezel, ca. 1880s-1914, 1" d. **50**

Pendant, oval, decorated w/forget-me-nots on a pastel polychrome ground w/white enamel highlights & burnished gold rim, gold-plated bezel, ca. 1900-25, 1 1/4 x 1 3/4" **65**

Scarf pin, medallion-shaped, decorated w/violets, brass-plated bezel & shank, ca. 1880-1920, medallion 1 1/4" d., shank 3" l. **50**

Shirtwaist Button with Clover Leaf

Shirtwaist button, oval w/shank, decorated w/a three-leaf clover in green on a yellow & brown ground, burnished gold rim, 7/8 x 1 1/16" (ILLUS.) **20**

Shirtwaist Button with Flower

Shirtwaist button, round w/eye, decorated w/a conventional stylized long blossom flanked by pointed oval leaves in pale yellow, dark blue & black on a burnished gold ground, 1 1/16" d. (ILLUS.) **30**

Unusual Portrait Shirtwaist Button

Shirtwaist button, round w/shank, decorated w/the bust portrait of a young blonde-haired girl, wearing a pale blue dress, against a shaded yellow to black ground, 1 3/8" d. (ILLUS.) **80**

Shirtwaist buttons, heart-shaped, decorated w/pink roses, raised paste scrolled border covered w/burnished gold, ca. 1890-1910, 1 1/8 x 1 3/16", pr. **75**

Shirtwaist Buttons with Pinwheels

Shirtwaist buttons, round, each decorated w/a geometric pinwheel design in light blue, black & gold trimmed w/burnished gold dots & a center turquoise "jewel," on a burnished gold ground, two 1" d., three 7/8" d., the set (ILLUS.) **115**

Shirtwaist set: oval brooch & pr. of oval cuff links; decorated w/blue forget-me-nots on an ivory background w/white enamel highlights, brass-plated mounts, ca. 1900-10, brooch w/burnished gold free-form border & rim, 1 3/8 x 1 3/4", cuff links w/burnished gold rims, 13/16 x 1 1/16", the set **250**

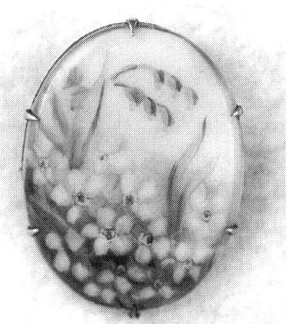

Brooch from Shirtwaist Set

Shirtwaist set: oval brooch & two round buttons w/shank; each decorated w/forget-me-nots & greenery on a pastel polychrome ground, burnished gold rim, gold-plated bezel, brooch 1 1/4 x 1 3/4", buttons 15/16" d., the set (ILLUS. of brooch) **90**

Shirtwaist set: oval cuff links & three round buttons w/shanks; decorated w/clusters of violets on pale yellow ground, burnished gold rim, gold-plated bezel on cuff links, ca. 1900-15, cuff links 3/4 x 1 1/4", buttons 1 1/4" d., the set **175**

Watch chatelaine, oval, decorated w/a woman wearing a rose-colored bodice, light shading to dark warm green ground, set in gold-plated rim w/twisted gold edge, ca. 1880s, 1 1/8 x 1 3/8" **125**

Antique (1800-1920)

Cameo Etruscan Revival Bar Pin

Bar pin, hardstone cameo, Etruscan Revival-style, a sardonyx cameo depicting the profile of a classical figure in an oval ropetwist frame, set within a bar pin decorated w/beads & wiretwist, applied florette terminals, 14k gold mount (ILLUS.) **294**

Silver & Marcasite Bar Pin

Bar pin, marcasite & sterling silver, slender almond shape of hand-hammered silver decorated w/wiretwist centering an oval faceted marcasite, hallmark for Fahrner, ca. 1908 (ILLUS.) **764**

Bar pin, moonstone & diamond, the knife-edge bar surmounted by a carved moon-face moonstone & diamond-set crescent flanked by rose-cut diamond stars, silver-topped gold mount, Edwardian..................... **999**

Bracelet, bi-color gold (14k) & moonstone, chain-type, composed of three sections of trillion-shaped moonstones set in a bow style, each design highlighted by two square-cut sapphires & a single-cut diamond melée, alternating w/rose-colored & green geometric-shaped links, 7 1/2" l... **1,116**

Gold Bracelet with Emeralds & Pearls

Bracelet, emerald, pearl & gold, 18k yellow gold bangle w/filigree gold work containing three emerald-cut emeralds, four pearls, surrounded by rose-cut diamonds

& accented with eleven small round-cut emeralds, ca. 1890 (ILLUS.)....................... **5,573**

Bracelet, garnet, bangle-type, a wide hinged & tapering form centering one large rose-cut & ten pear-shaped garnets set as a florette, set overall w/pavé bead-set round rose-cut garnets, 14k gold mount, Victorian... **1,763**

Bracelet, gold (14k) & seed pearl, the top of the hinged bangle decorated w/chased leaf & flowerhead designs set w/split pearls & seed pearls **499**

Bracelet, gold (15k), bypass bangle-type, hinged band entwined by a chased & engraved snake w/red stone eyes, ball terminals accented by applied wiretwist decoration, Victorian, 6" l. **323**

Bracelet, gold mesh, slide-type, a wide mesh band surmounted by an oval medallion slide engraved & decorated w/black enamel, the terminal w/similar decoration, name engraved on back, Victorian (ILLUS. below)....................................... **764**

Bracelet, sterling silver, link-type, composed of six round medallions depicting the profiles of classical figures, the clasp w/geometric designs, Shiebler mark, ca. 1900, 7 1/2" l. **470**

Bracelets, gold (14k) & enamel, flat bangle decorated overall w/black tracery enamel in a floral vine design, inscribed "H.E. Roth - July 27, 1871," pr................................. **823**

Amethyst & Diamond Circle Brooch

Brooch, amethyst & diamond, circle-form, designed w/eight bezel-set round faceted amethysts spaced between sixteen bead-set old European-cut diamonds, platinum-topped 14k yellow gold mount w/millegrain accents, partial number on back, Edwardian (ILLUS.) **1,645**

Brooch, pearl, diamond & gold, model of a bee, the body set w/a mabe pearl & a bezel-set rose-cut diamond, the wings set w/ten bead-set old mine-cut diamonds,

Victorian Gold Mesh Slide Bracelet

green stone eyes, 14k yellow gold & silver mount **1,175**

Brooch, plique-à-jour & diamond, set throughout w/rose-cut diamonds in a floral & vine design, decorated w/cobalt blue plique-à-jour enamel w/white enamel accents, ruby & pearl highlights, 14k gold mount (minor enamel imperfections).. **1,880**

Plique-à-jour & Sapphire Brooch

Brooch, plique-à-jour & green sapphire, circular form centering a bezel-set green sapphire within a green plique-a-jour lily pad design decorated w/wiretwist, 18k gold mount, designed by Louis Comfort Tiffany, marked by Tiffany & Co., one bead detached, minor loss to plique, ca. 1910 (ILLUS.) **4,113**

Reverse-painted Crystal Brooch

Brooch, reverse-painted crystal, round crystal reverse-painted w/a shore bird on grass on a mother-of-pearl background, within a diamond & millegrain 14k gold-topped platinum mount, Edwardian (ILLUS.) **2,585**

Sterling Art Nouveau Bust Brooch

Brooch, sterling silver, Art Nouveau style, depicting a bust of a maiden w/flowing openwork hair, stamped "127" (ILLUS.)........ **235**

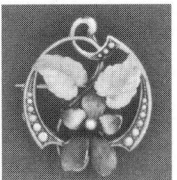

Victorian Flower Brooch/Pendant

Brooch/pendant, pearl, enamel & gold,14k yellow gold open-work form set w/14 seed pearls centered by an enameled lavender pansy & green & leaf form centered w/a seed pearl, ca. 1880 (ILLUS.)........ **252**

Cameo brooch, carved shell, depicting seated Cupid w/his net, bow & quiver of arrows, 14k gold frame, w/a Trefry & Partridge box **411**

Memorial Cameo Brooch

Cameo brooch, carved shell, memorial portrait of women in Victorian dress standing by monument, mounted in revolving gold frame w/beveled glazed compartment on reverse, ca. 1900 (ILLUS.).............................. **280**

Hardstone African Woman Cameo

Cameo brooch, hardstone, a profile bust of an African woman wearing a 14k gold diadem & rose-cut diamond earrings & choker, 10k gold mount (ILLUS.) **2,585**

Chain, gold (18k) & enamel, composed of 51 shaped hollow gold links w/polychrome floral & foliate champlevé enamel decoration, Swiss, ca. 1840, 54" l. (some enamel wear) **3,290**

Cross pendant, diamond, enamel & gold, the cross set w/23 old mine-cut diamonds in a 14k gold mount outlined w/black enamel, suspended by a fine gold chain ... **1,175**

French Diamond Cross Pendant

Cross pendant, diamond, scrolling cross set throughout w/old mine- and rose-cut diamonds, similarly set bail, French assay marks & maker's mark, silver-topped 18k gold mount (ILLUS.)............................. **1,528**

Crucifix, diamond, enamel & 14k pink gold, engraved floral-form medallions on each cross-point, body of Christ in relief on blue enamel cross, & 16 round diamonds, Russian, ca. 1900........................... **1,344**

Cuff links, crystal round tops reverse-painted w/horseheads, 18k gold round mount, pr. **529**

Earrings, diamond, designed as a flower-head, set throughout w/38 old mine-cut diamonds, silver-topped gold mounting, pr. **1,998**

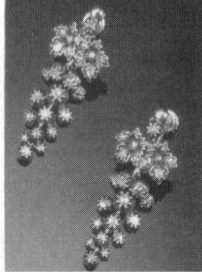

Diamond Grape Cluster Earrings

Earrings, diamond, designed as leaves suspending flexibly-set grape cluster set throughout w/rose-cut diamonds, silver-topped 14k gold mounts, replaced findings, pr. (ILLUS.)... **823**

Earrings, diamond, foliate tops suspending a leaf pendant, set throughout w/fifty-four old mine-cut diamonds, silver-topped gold mounting, pr. (later findings) **1,175**

Earrings, diamond & pearl, each set w/a cluster of five pear-shaped rose-cut diamonds, approx. total weight 4.06 cts., suspending a detachable teardrop-shape white pearl measuring approx. 15.79 x 12.85 mm, platinum mount, pr. **9,400**

Earrings, diamond & silver, flower-form, designed as pansies, the center set w/an old mine-cut diamond, surrounded by six collet-set diamond melée & pave old mine-cut diamond petals, silver mounts, pr. **4,113**

French Gold & Pearl Earrings

Earrings, gold (18k) & pearl, Art Nouveau style, long slender openwork floral & foliate design mount suspending a baroque freshwater pearl, French hallmarks, boxed, pr. (ILLUS.)................................... **1,880**

Earrings, platinum, diamond & sapphire pendant earrings w/rose cut diamond set floral design w/sapphire links holding scrolling diamond set pendant attached to sapphire set circle ending in diamond set link, ca. 1910, 1 1/7" l. **1,456**

Lavaliere, angel skin coral, delicate oval trace links joined by a button-shaped coral element suspending two cone-shaped coral drops accented by seed pearls, Edwardian, 14 1/4" l. **353**

Lavaliere, emerald, pearl & diamond, the fine curb-link platinum chain suspending a scrolling openwork pendant centering a bezel-set rectangular-cut emerald & set throughout w/old mine-cut diamonds, teardrop-shape pearl terminal, millegrain accents, platinum-topped 14k gold mount, Edwardian, 18 1/2" l. (chain later).. **1,880**

Carnelian & Micromosaic Locket

Locket, carnelian, micromosaic & gold, an oval carnelian surmounted by a fine micromosaic depicting a woman holding a flower, the frame decorated w/four pearls & wiretwist, verso w/a glass locket compartment, pearl-set bail, initial mark of Edwin Streeter & Co. (ILLUS.) **764**

Pearl & Gold Heart Locket

Locket, pearl & gold (14k), heart-shape pavé-set w/pearls, opens to reveal two round picture compartments, suspended by a seed pearl & trace link chain, Edwardian, overall 28" l. (ILLUS.) **823**

Fine Arts & Crafts Jeweled Necklace

Necklace, aquamarine, pearl & gold, Arts & Crafts style, centering a large oval aquamarine framed by cabochon aquamarines & seed pearls, suspended from a fine triple curb link 14k gold chain highlighted by bezel-set rectangular-cut aquamarines, pearls & fancy links, 18" l. (ILLUS. of part).. **5,875**

Necklace, coral & gold, the 14k gold festoon chains set w/oval coral beads, suspending in the center a carved coral theatrical mask & an ovoid bead pendant, inscribed on the back "Eighth," stamped "R.W. Edwards"... **1,058**

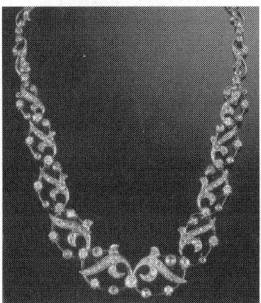

Fine Antique Diamond Necklace

Necklace, diamond, consisting of graduated foliate links set w/cushion-shape old mine- and rose-cut diamonds, detaches to become a bracelet, French hallmarks, silver-topped 18k gold mount, 15 1/4" l. (ILLUS.)... **8,225**

Necklace, diamond, seed pearl & gold,14k yellow gold slide w/two black onyx stones, two small diamonds & four seed pearls, chain ending in tassels, ca. 1871, 32" l... **1,400**

Necklace, gold,14k yellow gold engraved floral designs attached w/floral-design links that meet in central medallion of engraved filigree flowers, ca. 1900 .... **952**

Necklace, gold (18k) & enamel, composed of six rectangular polychrome enamel hollow plaques depicting Meso-American deities alternating w/black & white enamel florets, floral links & ball spacers, 36" l. (enamel wear, dents to ball spacers) **1,528**

Edwardian Opal & Diamond Necklace

Necklace, opal & diamond, festoon-style, fancy platinum open & navette-shaped diamond links supporting a platinum-topped gold festoon drop set w/pear-shaped opals surrounded by old European-cut diamonds & a diamond bow swag design of later origin, mark of J. E. Caldwell & Co., Edwardian, 16 3/4" l. (ILLUS.).. **3,760**

Pearl, Diamond & Platinum Necklace

Necklace, seed pearl, diamond & platinum, the delicate pearl mesh chain set w/four openwork plaques suspending an extension chain, a bezel-set old European-cut diamond weighing approx. .75 cts., a round white pearl & an openwork circular brooch centering a cream-colored pearl measuring approx. 8.6 mm, set throughout w/old European- and mine-cut diamonds & seed pearls, millegrain accents, elements detachable, Edwardian, 22 1/4" l. (ILLUS. of part)............................. **9,988**

Necklace, shell, silver & pearl, composed of small half-shells each centered by a button pearl, spaced by silver florets, suspending a similarly designed removable pendant cross, stamped "TTJ & Son - Sydney," Australia, ca. 1890, 18" l.............. **1,763**

French Diamond & Opal Pendant

Pendant, diamond & opal, the peacock form centered by a circular-cut opal, set throughout w/seven old mine-cut & 60 rose-cut diamonds, platinum-topped 18k gold mount, French guarantee & import stamps (ILLUS.).. **2,233**

Moonstone & Diamond Pendant

Pendant, moonstone & diamond, a rose-cut diamond crown suspending a detachable large pear-shaped moonstone w/diamond bail, silver-topped gold mount w/millegrain accents, Edwardian (ILLUS.)... **2,468**

George IV Pendant on Chain

Pendant on chain, diamond, emerald, pearl & gold,14k gold, round w/leaf-shaped scrolling designs set w/ten rose-cut diamonds, three emeralds & a natural pearl, George IV, ca. 1820 (ILLUS.).............. **532**

Pendant/brooch, diamond & enamel, star-shaped, set w/a cushion-shape old mine-cut diamond weighing approx. .47 cts., further set w/12 old mine-cut & 24 rose-cut diamonds, black enamel frame & 18k gold mount, French import mark................ **1,763**

Fine Edwardian Diamond Brooch

Pendant/brooch, diamond & platinum, the bow-form three-pendant scrolling brooch centering a bezel-set old European-cut diamond weighing approx. 1.02 cts., set throughout w/old mine-cut diamonds, platinum-topped 14k gold mount, Edwardian... **6,463**

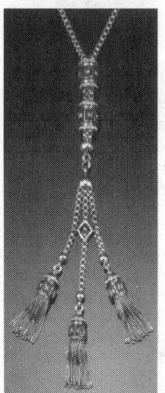

Russian Diamond & Enamel Necklace

Pendant/necklace, diamond & enamel, slide-type, the ribbed 14k gold curb link chain supporting two hexagonal blue enamel-decorated 18k bi-color gold slides set w/rose-cut diamonds, all suspending a triple curb-link chain pendant w/conforming hexagonal terminals & foxtail fringe, Russian assay mark, Victorian, 20" l. (ILLUS.).. **2,820**

Pin, gem-set, figural bird perched on a branch, set throughout w/rose-cut diamonds, cabochon red stone eyes, two pearl accents, silver & gold mounting, English registry number................................... **646**

Pin, reverse-painted crystal, two diamond-shaped sections each reverse-painted w/an image of a swan swimming in a lake amid cattails, the reverse w/a pierced cattail design, platinum mount, mark of Marcus & Co., Edwardian............................ **3,408**

Silver & Plique-à-Jour Art Nouveau Pin

Pin, sterling silver, plique-à-jour & chalcedony, Art Nouveau style, the openwork curvilinear form decorated w/green plique-à-jour enamel & a bezel-set oval green chalcedony, hallmark for Fahrner, ca. 1901 (ILLUS.).. **881**

Pins, gem-stone & enamel, model of a beetle-like insect, one w/a green guilloché enamel body & cabochon red stone eyes, other w/a red enamel body & rose-cut diamond eyes, wings set w/seed pearls, 14k gold mount, Edwardian, pr. (some pearls missing)... **764**

Ring, amethyst & diamond, intaglio-type, prong-set faceted oval amethyst carved w/a flower inset w/gold & rose-cut diamonds, chased & engraved shoulders, Victorian, 14k gold mount, size 4 1/2 .... **206**

Arts & Crafts Garnet & Pearl Ring

Ring, demantoid garnet & pearl, Arts & Crafts style, centering a circular-cut bezel-set green demantoid garnet flanked by seed pearls, the shoulders accented by gold & foliate designs, 14k gold mount, hallmark "MR" for Margaret Rogers, size 6 3/4 (ILLUS.)............................... **3,290**

Ring, diamond, bezel-set w/one old European & two old mine-cut diamonds in a vertical mount, approx. total weight .67 cts., within a scalloped frame highlighted by 22 single-cut diamonds, millegrain accents, diamond-set split shoulders, platinum-topped 18k gold mount, ca. 1910, size 7 1/2 (ILLUS.)...................................... **1,410**

Ring, diamond & gold, prong-set .91 ct. old European-cut diamond solitaire in a 14k mount, size 13 1/4 .... **1,293**

Ring, diamond & platinum, set w/one old mine & two old European-cut diamonds, approx. total 1 ct., foliate openwork chased & engraved shoulders, gallery & shank, platinum mount, Edwardian, size 7 1/4 .... **999**

Ring, diamond, set w/an old European-cut diamond weighing approx. .58 cts., 14k gold mount, size 5 .... **470**

Fine Antique Emerald & Diamond Ring

Ring, emerald & diamond, centering an emerald-cut emerald measuring approx. 9.36 x 8.14 x 5.13 mm & weighing approx. 2.87 cts., flanked by old mine-cut diamonds, approx. total weight .92 cts., 18k yellow gold mount, England, size 5 (ILLUS.)... **8,225**

Ring, pearl & diamond, set w/one white & one pink pearl highlighted by 11 old mine-cut diamonds in a navette mount w/millegrain accents, openwork gallery, platinum-topped 14k gold mount, pearls probably natural, Edwardian, size 7 3/4 .... **558**

Ring, sapphire & diamond, set w/an old European-cut diamond weighing approx. .20 cts. & a circular cut sapphire, the scrolling shoulders highlighted by ten old mine-cut diamonds, platinum-topped 14k gold mount, size 5 1/2 .... **529**

Sets

Brooch, earrings & necklace, carved coral, the brooch designed as a cluster of roses & leaves, matching earrings w/a spray of five-petal flowers & leaves, together w/a coral bead necklace, the set........ **441**

Necklace & brooch, platinum, seed pearl & diamond, the delicate pearl mesh chain set w/four openwork plaques suspending an extension chain, a bezel-set old European-cut diamond weighing approx. .75 cts., a round white pearl & an openwork circular brooch centering a cream-colored pearl measuring approx. 8.6 mm, set throughout w/old European-cut & mine-cut diamonds & seed pearls, millegrain accent, elements detachable, Edwardian, 22 1/4" l... **9,988**

Rare Pearl Necklace & Brooch Set

Necklace & brooch, seed pearl, necklace composed of links formed by concentric circles of seed pearls within crimped gold mountings w/closed backs, matching brooch, in a fitted Tiffany & Co. box, nearly identical to a set once owned by Mary Todd Lincoln, the set (ILLUS.) **11,163**

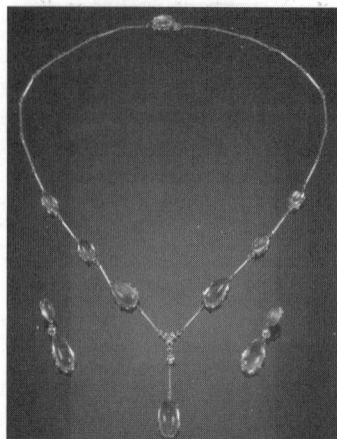

Moonstone & Platinum Jewelry Set

Necklace & earrings, moonstone & platinum, the necklace w/graduated oval moonstones joined by baton links, suspending a diamond & moonstone drop supported by a trefoil diamond melée cluster, matching drop earrings, necklace 15 1/4" l., the set (ILLUS.) **2,468**

Pearl & Diamond Necklace from a Set

Necklace & earrings, pearl & diamond, set w/fifteen natural baroque pearls alternating w/fifteen old mine-cut diamonds suspending a teardrop-shaped pearl joined by eight quatrefoil links, completed by a natural pearl & four old mine-cut diamond clasp, silver-topped 14k gold mount, matching earrings, necklace 14 1/2" l., spacers added later, one pearl earring drilled, the set (ILLUS. of necklace) **7,638**

Modern (1920-1960s)

Bar pin, diamond, Art Deco style, set w/a straight row of 17 old mine-cut diamonds, approx. total weight 2.75 cts., engraved gallery, silver-topped 14k gold mount **1,528**

Bracelet, carved citrine, onyx & diamond, Art Deco style, set w/four large intaglio citrines carved w/images of the four seasons, joined by flexible links set w/onyx & single-cut & old European-cut diamonds, platinum mount, 7" l. **8,519**

Bracelet, crystal & gold, Art Deco style, designed w/three oval carved crystal plaques centered by diamond melée spaced by pierced & millegrained shaped 14k white gold links, 7 3/4" l. (ILLUS. bottom, upper).. **764**

Bracelet, diamond & gold, Art Deco style, 18k white gold w/213 marquise & round-cut diamonds, 6 1/2" l. **2,240**

Bracelet, diamond & platinum, Art Deco style, the geometric rectangular links set w/approx. 171 single-cut & old European-cut diamonds, French hallmarks, 6 3/4" l. **6,169**

Bracelet, diamond & sapphire, Art Deco style, narrow band set w/a line of circular-cut diamonds accented w/four French-cut sapphires & single-cut diamonds bordered by calibre-cut sapphires, approx. total weight 2.78 cts., platinum mount w/foliate-engraved edge & millegrain accents, signed by Tiffany & Co., 7" l. **10,575**

Bracelet, diamond, sapphire & platinum, Art Deco style, flexible rectangular plaques set w/three marquise-cut & six triangular-cut diamonds flanked by calibré-cut sapphires, the bracelet set throughout w/transitional & single-cut diamonds, joined by hinges set w/onyx button termi-

Crystal & White Gold Bracelet

Outstanding Art Deco Bracelet

Silver & Enamel Art Deco Bracelet

nals, millegrain accents, applied plaque w/store mark of Bert H. Satz, New York City, 7 1/8" l. (ILLUS. bottom previous page, lower).. **19,975**

Bracelet, sapphire, diamond & platinum, Art Deco style, w/43 French-cut sapphires & 282 round diamonds on platinum, 7 1/2" l. **3,136**

Bracelet, silver & enamel, Art Deco style, composed of ten hinged plaques decorated w/purple guilloché & black enamel in an alternating eight-pointed star & geometric line design, stamped w/number 18, 7" l. (ILLUS. top of page) **499**

Banded Bakelite Brooch

Brooch, Bakelite, designed w/lozenge-shaped sections of black, orange, green & red, ca. 1930s (ILLUS.)............................... **646**

Brooch, crystal & gem-set, Art Deco style, flower basket shape bezel-set w/eight multi-colored stones including topaz, amethyst, beryl & kunzite cut in round, cushion & pear shapes, carved crystal basket, onyx & single- and rose-cut diamond highlights, millegrain accent, platinum mount, French platinum & gold standard guarantee stamps **6,463**

Diamond & Gold Art Deco Brooch

Brooch, diamond & gold, Art Deco style, oblong openwork plaque set w/33 transitional and circular-cut diamonds, millegrain accents, chased & engraved edge, 18k white gold mount (ILLUS.)......... **1,293**

Brooch, diamond, onyx & platinum, Art Deco style, oblong openwork form centered by an old European-cut diamond weighing approx. .91 cts., set throughout w/77 old European- and mine-cut diamonds, accented by calibré-cut onyx forming an ellipse, millegrain accents, signed "G & C & Co.," boxed (ILLUS.)...... **3,878**

Dress clips, platinum & diamond, Art Deco, two detachable triangular clips set throughout w/128 round brilliant, transitional & baguette-cut diamonds, approx. total weight 3.02 cts., w/10k white gold & diamond frame attachment, pr. **4,818**

Earrings, diamond, sapphire & 18k yellow gold, Art Deco style, each diamond-set floral form bearing diamond-set pendant ending w/center blue sapphire surrounded by diamonds, ca. 1920.............................. **784**

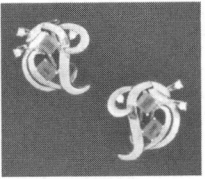

Gold & Emerald Earrings

Earrings, emerald, diamond & gold,14k yellow gold leaf scroll forms centered w/two emerald cut emeralds & three small round diamonds, ca. 1940, pr. (ILLUS.) **1,456**

Necklace, diamond, Art Deco riviere-style, composed of 73 graduated old European-cut & transitional-cut diamonds from approximately .15 to 1.50 cts., set in millegrained bezels, approx. total weight 3.3 cts., 16" l. **44,650**

Necklace, platinum, diamond & gem-set, charm-type, Art Deco-style, the delicate platinum links suspending six single-cut pavé diamond charms including a monkey, dachshund, bulldog w/ruby collar & eye, swordfish w/blue enamel fin, pair of lovebirds w/ruby eyes & a rabbit in a black enamel hat, heart-form jump rings, 14" l... **2,938**

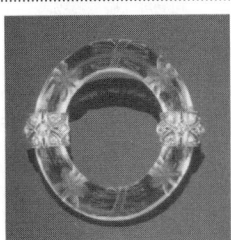

Tiffany Crystal & Diamond Circle Pin

Outstanding Diamond Brooch

Pin, crystal & diamond, Art Deco style, circular ring, etched crystal w/floral designs intersected by two platinum plaques set w/transitional-cut diamonds, millegrain accents, signed by Tiffany & Co., 14k yellow gold findings (ILLUS.) **3,055**

Ring, diamond, Art Deco style, centering a bead-set old European-cut diamond weighing approx. .64 cts., set within a lozenge-shaped openwork mount highlighted by six old European-cut diamonds, approx. total weight .17 cts., millegrain accents, 14k white gold mount, size 6 1/2............. **764**

Ring, jadeite jade & diamond, Art Deco style, centering an oval jade stone, the split shoulders each set w/three bullet-shaped diamond baguettes, platinum mount, Trefry & Partridge box, size 6......... **1,763**

Art Deco Sapphire & Diamond Ring

Ring, sapphire, diamond & platinum, Art Deco style, a cabochon sapphire measuring approx. 12.7 x 10.71 x 7.95 mm, the millegrain accented openwork shoulders set w/old mine- and single-cut diamonds, approx. total weight .80 cts., platinum mount, size 5 3/4.............................. **3,055**

Extraordinary Art Deco Tiffany Ring

Ring, sapphire, diamond & platinum, Art Deco style, centering a prong-set cushion-cut sapphire weighing 3.07 cts., flanked by diamond trillions, approx. total weight 1.20 cts., shoulders accented by 16 circular-cut diamonds & incised foliate designs, millegrain accents, pierced gallery, platinum mount, signed by Tiffany & Co., size 7 (ILLUS.) **25,850**

Rare Art Deco Ring/Watch

Ring/watch, ruby & platinum, Art Deco style, barrel-shaped form centered by a rose gold colored dial w/Arabic numerals & blue-steeled hands highlighted by a curved crest of French-cut calibré rubies set in rose gold, wide grooved shank, within a platinum shell mount, size 8 (ILLUS.) **881**

Sets

Bracelet & earrings, sterling silver, the bracelet w/nineteen flexible foliate plaques, matching earrings, stamped "Margo de Taxco," Mexico, 20th c., bracelet 16 1/4" l., the set **353**

Brooch & earrings, sterling silver, brooch designed as a pair of large leaves suspending a cluster of grapes, matching earrings, Georg Jensen, Nos. 217B & 40, 20th c., the set **499**

KITCHENWARES

Coffee Mills

Box Mills

Box mill, advertising mill w/colorful litho printing made for Hoffmann's Old Time Coffee, based on Arcade's Telephone Mill **$1,300**

Box mill, iron mill w/tin drawer w/wood front, based on 1885 patent by the founders of Arcade, New Model made by New Union **225**

English "Cannon" Coffee Mill

Box mill, iron w/raised brass hopper, emblem on front marked "Cannon," England (ILLUS.).. **150**

Parker National No. 430 Coffee Mill

Box mill, w/decorative iron top & hopper cover, machine-made dovetails on box & drawer, partial paper label, Parker National No. 430(ILLUS.) **150**

Box mill, wooden, w/decorative iron top & pivoting lid embossed "IXL, Arcade Mfg. Co.," side crank, Home Coffee Mill No. 777, 11" h. **500**

Box mill, wooden, w/raised Britannia hopper, Peck, Stow & Wilcox American No. 1006 .... **200**

Primitive coffee mills

Box mill, w/brass hopper, decorative paint & Moravian base, signed "IFM" **180**

Box mill, w/raised pewter hopper, signed "G. Selsor, #2," ca. 1870 .... **200**

Wall mill, cast iron, decorative, based on Ami Clark's 1833 patent, adjusting thumbscrew in back, two-sided grinding burr design **800**

Parker Union No. 20 Coffee Mill

Side mill, iron w/double gears behind wood back, Parker Union No. 20 (ILLUS.) **150**

Wilson's Best Coffee Mill

Side mill, w/tin hopper & lid, wood backing board, decorative adjusting screw behind the board, brass emblem marked "Increase Wilson's Best Quality, New London," based on 1818 patent (ILLUS.) **150**

Side mill, w/wood backing, brass emblem embossed w/the script logo "PS&W" for Peck, Stow & Wilcox, American **140**

Upright mills

Upright mill, cast iron, iron cup could be used to catch the ground coffee or as a hopper cover to protect coffee beans when not in use, "Clawson & Clark's Double Grinding Mill, Pat. Sept. 28, '86" embossed on 6" wheel **1,050**

Lane Brothers No. 13 Swift Mill

Upright mill, cast iron, No. 13 Swift Mill, double 11 1/2" wheels w/"spiderweb" spoke design, pivoting hopper cover, rectangular tin catch can, faded red paint w/decals & gold striping, complete & original, Lane Brothers (ILLUS.) **850**

Upright mill, cast iron, w/17" wheels, pivoting cover on hopper, original red paint, decals & pin striping, 1898 patent date marked on grinding burrs, Enterprise #7 .. **1,400**

Upright mill, cast iron, w/nickel-plated brass hopper, 10 3/4" wheels, Enterprise No. 4 .... **1,500**

Upright mill, Landers, Frary & Clark No. 11 Crown Coffee Mill, approx. 12" h. **325**

Upright mill, w/sliding hopper cover & flower decals, 10 3/4" wheels, Charles Parker No. 3000 .... **1,500**

Miscellaneous

Box mill, child's, A.C. Williams Daisy No. 867, 2 1-2 x 2 1/2" base, same size as Arcade's Little Tot, but metal castings are different **150**

Box mill, child's, w/bronzed iron parts, Arcade Mfg. Co.'s "Our Baby" No. 1, first made in 1897, patented grind adjustment nut, very efficient, 4 x 4" base **250**

Clamp-on coffee mill, blue, clamp-on grinder for table or shelf, made by Landers, Frary & Clark for Simmons Hardware Co. Koffee Krusher No. 10 .... **150**

Spong No. 2 Coffee Mill

Iron mill, wall or shelf-type w/open hopper, black w/gold trim, decal & embossed lettering, cylindrical metal catch cup, Spong No. 2, England, new condition (ILLUS.)........ **100**

Wall-mounted mill, cast iron, "Old 74" made by Edward Cornwall of Connecticut in the 1830s **300**

Kitchen Utensils

Aebleskiver pan, cast iron, Griswold #32 .... **50**

Apple corer, tin, T-handle, handmade, 5" **15**

Apple corer, tin & wood, "Boye Pat No. 1206403 Made in USA" **15**

Apple corer, tin & wood, "Vantage Apple Corer Pat Apl'd For R.M.S. Co," 6 1/2" **50**

Apple peeler, cast iron, "F.W. Hudsons Improved Apple Parer Leominster, Mass Pat Dec. 2, 1862"... **175**

Apple peeler, cast iron, Goodell, 1898................. **55**

Apple peeler, cast iron, "Lockey & Howland, Pat Dec 5, 1856"................................... **65**

Apple peeler, cast iron, "Manfu'd by Goodell Co, Antrim, H. Pat Mar 18, 1884," vertical arc shape **200**

Apple peeler, "Nonpareil Parer, Patented May 6, 1858 J.L. Haven & Co. Cin. O".... **1,000 +**

Apple peeler, "Patd Oct. 5, 1880," unmarked Peck, Stow & Wilcox........................ **275**

Apple segmenter, cast iron, "R. Buchi Chicago Pat'd Aug 28, 1923"............................. **100**

Apple segmenter, cast iron, "Tollman Mfg Co, Mt. Joy, Pa Pat Apld Apple Cutter"........... **20**

Biscuit cutter, tin, Jenny Wren advertising on strap handle **15**

Biscuit cutter, tin, Rumfordþadvertising, 3 1/2".. **15**

Butter paddle, wood, early, 10" **25**

Can opener, cast iron, "Duket Mfg. Co. Toledo, Ohio, Patd. 8-11-25," 6 1/4" **20**

Can opener, steel, Sieger, 5 1/2" **15**

Can opener & jar opener combination tool, tin, "Distributed By C.S. Ripley & Co Cleveland, Ohio," 8 1/4".................................... **25**

Cherry pitter, cast iron, "Enterprise Cherry Stoner Pat Appl'd For No 12," 13" **125**

Cherry pitter, cast iron, "The Boss Raisin Seeder, Pat. Pdg., " 11 3/4" **150**

Cherry pitter, glass & tin, "Krasco Cherry and Olive Pitter, Pat. App For, Chicago, Ill," paper label, 9"... **30**

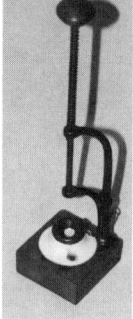

Wood, Porcelain & Iron Cherry Pitter

Cherry pitter, wood, porcelain & cast iron, unmarked, 10 1/2" (ILLUS.) **125**

Chocolate grater, tin, "Edgar Pat Nov. 10, 1890," 8 1/2"... **300**

Churn, "Dazey Churn & Mfg. Co. St. Louis, Mo.," 1 qt... **1,850**

Churn, "Dazey Churn No. 40, Patented Feb. 14, 22," **120**

Churn, glass base, "1 qt" embossed on jar, top cast-iron frame & gears **325**

Churn, tin & cast iron, "Home Butter Merger, Patd. Sept. 14, 1909"................................ **300**

Cookie cutter, tin, eagle, scalloped-edge tail & wings, 6" h. (very light rust) **165**

Tin Elephant Cookie Cutter

Cookie cutter, tin, elephant, w/ strap handle, 4 5/8" l. (ILLUS.)..................................... **55**

Cookie cutter, tin, early handmade heart in hand design, 3 x 4" **350**

Cookie cutter, tin, early handmade horse w/rider, spot-soldered, 5 x 6 1/2" **275**

Cookie cutter, tin, early handmade pig, spot-soldered, 3 x 4" **45**

Roller-type Cookie Cutter

Cookie cutter, tin & wood, roller cutter w/six designs, 9" (ILLUS.)...................................... **65**

Cornstick pan, cast iron & yellow enamel, Griswold... **150**

Egg beater, cast iron, "Cyclone Pat. 6-25-1901 Reissue 8-26-1902," 11 1/2"................... **85**

Egg beater, cast iron, "Dover Egg Beater U.S.A.," 10 3/4"... **40**

Egg beater, cast iron, "Holt's Patented Flared Dasher Egg Beater N.Y. U.S.A.," 10 1/2".. **45**

Egg beater, cast iron, "Perfection Pat'd Feb. 22, 1898 Albany N.Y.," 10 1/4" **350**

R.P. Scott & Co. Eggbeater

Egg beater, cast iron, "R.P. Scott & Co. Newark N.J. Patented," 10 1/2" (ILLUS.)... **1,250**

Egg beater, steel, "Ladd Beater July 7, 1908 Oct. 18, 1921," 11 1/2" 25

Egg beater, steel w/red plastic handle, "Dazey, Reg U.S. Pat. Off.," 12 1/2" 30

Egg beater, tin, base marked "Made In United States of America A&J," top marked "Full Vision Beater Set," 7 1/2" 40

Egg beater, tin, Betty Taplin model w/red plastic cup, 6 oz., 6" 50

Egg separator, plastic, blue, advertising, marked "Charles Chips"............ 10

Egg Baking Powder Egg Separator

Egg separator, tin, advertising "Egg Baking Powder" (ILLUS.)............ 150

Egg separator, tin, advertising, marked "Use Puritan Fadeless Dyes - None Better"............ 25

Flour sifter, tin & wood, "Duplex Sifter 5 cup, Pat. Nov. 1917 & 1922, Mfg. by Ullrich Tinware Co." 30

Flour sifter, wood, stenciled "Blood's Sifter Pat Sept 17, 1861"............ 375

Funnel, tin, advertising, marked "Forbes' Quality Coffee," 3" 50

Ice cream freezer, glass, "Dazey Ice Cream Freezer, Whip, Eggbeater, Butter Churn, Mold, Dazey Churn Mfg. Co. St. Louis, Mo," 11" 950

Ice shaver, cast iron, "The Griswold Mfg Co. Classic Ice Shredder No 2 Erie PA USA" 300

Jar lid reformer, cast iron, "The Eakin Mfg Co. Salem, Ohio," 7" 40

Jar lid reformer, tin, unmarked, 7 1/2"............ 20

Jar lifter, wire, unmarked, 8 1/2" 30

Jar opener, cast iron, "Mfd by Hoffman Hinge & Fdry Co. Cleveland, O," 8"............ 30

Jar opener, tin, "Perfect, Pat Pending," 7 1/4"............ 15

Jar opener, tin, "The Turney Mfg. Co. Detroit, Mich Pat Oct 31, 1905"............ 30

Jar opener & jar lifter combination tool, tin, Hotong, 10" 25

Juicer, tin w/wall mount, "Dazey Churn & Mfg Co, St. Louis, MO" 40

Knife sharpener, cast iron, "Dazey Sharpit, Dazey Churn & Mfg. Co. St. Louis, Mo.," 5 1/2"............ 25

Mixer, stainless steel, "Japan Bicor Battery Power," 9" 15

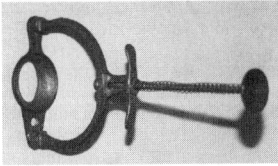

Iron Perfection Nut Cracker

Nut cracker, cast iron, clamp-style for attaching to table edge, clamp-form cracker, marked "Perfection Nut Cracker - Made in Waco, Texas - Patented 1914," 6 x 6 1/2" (ILLUS.)............ 69

Nutmeg grater, japanned tin, paper label reading "The Rapid Nutmeg Grater," 6"........ 250

Nutmeg grater, tin, coffin-style, 5"............ 15

Nutmeg grater, tin, "MTE Co.," 4 1/4"............ 75

Nutmeg grater, tin, "The Boye Nutmeg Grater Pat Apl'd For," 6"............ 85

Nutmeg grater, tin, wire & cast iron, referred to as wire loop handle grater, "Pat US Mar 25 84, Aug 4 96," 7" 150

Nutmeg grater, wood, tin & cast iron, "Edgar Mfg. Co. Pat. Aug 18, 91," 7" 95

Pastry mixer, tin, "Lambert Patent 486255"........ 20

Peach Stoner

Peach stoner, cast iron, "Rollman Mfg. Co. Pat Pend Mount Joy PA U.S.A.," 8 3/4" (ILLUS.)............ 250

Pie crimper, wood, hand-turned maple, 5 1/2" 25

Wire Pie Lifter

Pie lifter, wire, unmarked, 19" (ILLUS.) 50

Pot scraper, graniteware, advertising, marked "Penn Stoves"............ 150

Pot scraper, graniteware, advertising, marked "Red Wing Flour"............ 650

Pot scraper, steel, advertising-type, marked "Case Tractors" 95

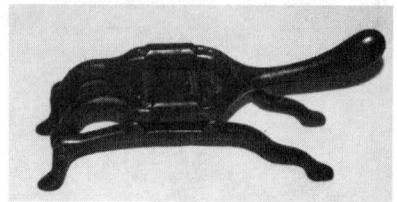

Raisin Seeder

Raisin seeder, cast iron, four leg base, "Pat'd May 7, 95," 6" (ILLUS.) **500**

Raisin seeder, cast iron w/tin tray, "EZY Raisin Seeder, Pat May 21, 1895" **250**

Rolling pin, stoneware, white w/blue bands, 8" l. plus handles **275**

Rolling pin, stoneware, white w/brown bands, advertising, marked "Bryant & Yeldell Clayton, Illinois," 8" l. plus handles... **550**

Rolling pin, tin w/wood handles, unmarked **300**

Skillet, cast iron, large emblem, no heat ring, Griswold #2 .... **350**

Skillet, cast iron, large emblem w/smoke ring, Griswold #14.. **200**

Skillet, cast iron & red enamel, Griswold #5 .... **40**

Spatula, tin w/steel handle, heart cut-out in tin base, Rumford advertising, 11 1/2" **50**

Spoon, tin w/steel handle, advertising, marked "Kitchen Bouquet Inc." on handle along w/measurements for 1/2 teaspoon, 1 teaspoon & 1/2 tablespoon, 11 1/2" l. **20**

Spoon rest, tin, advertising, marked "The Big Store - McCammon Investment Co. Props.".. **65**

Sugar nippers, cast iron, scissors-shaped, 9 1/2"... **150**

Tea strainer, plastic, red, advertising, marked "Humpty Dumpty" **10**

Tea strainer, tin, advertising-type, marked "Royal Crest Dairy".. **25**

Blue Willow Porcelain Toaster

Toaster, porcelain, Blue Willow, by Toastrite, central heating panel, on four feet, used only as exhibition piece at its introduction in 1928 (ILLUS.)............................. **2,301**

Whisk, tin w/steel handle, advertising, marked "Couch & Son" on handle, 9 1/2" **20**

Whisk, wood & wire, "March 24, 1868," 9 1/4"... **20**

Napkin Dolls

Until the 1990s, napkin dolls were a rather obscure collectible, coveted by only a few savvy individuals who appreciated their charm and beauty. Today, however, these late 1940s and 1950s icons of post-war America are a hot commodity.

Ranging from the individualistic pieces made in ceramics classes to jeweled Japanese models and the wide variety of wooden examples, these figures are no longer mistaken as planters or miniature dress forms. Of course, as their popularity has risen, so have prices, putting smiles on the faces of collectors who got in on the ground floor and stretching the pocketbooks of those looking to start their own collection.

Bobbie Zucker Bryson is co-author, with Deborah Gillham and Ellen Bercovici, of the pictorial price guide Collectibles For The Kitchen, Bath & Beyond - Second Edition, *published by Krause Publications. It covers a broad range of collectibles including napkin dolls, stringholders, pie birds, figural egg timers, razor blade banks, whimsical whistle milk cups and laundry sprinkler bottles. Bryson can be contacted via e-mail at Napkindoll aol.com.*

Bisque, figure of lady in pink layered skirt, bell sleeves w/gold trim & yellow hat, golden hair & expressively painted eyes, ink-marked "Japan," 9" h. **75-85**

Ceramic, bartender, black & white, holding tray w/indentation for candle, "Gold Viking - Made in Japan" sticker, 8 3/4" h.;matching 3 1/4" h. shakers, $20.00-25.00; the set $125.00-150.00; holder alone... **85-100**

Ceramic, figure of angel, blue & white, holding a bouquet, slits in shoulders for wings & in rear, "Japan" paper label, 5 3/8" h.. **100-115**

Ceramic, figure of angel holding a Christmas tree, yellow, wings in back & candleholder in halo, marked "Kreiss & Company," 11" h. **90-110**

Ceramic, figure of Art Deco-looking woman w/black hair, wearing white dress w/pink scalloped trim, holding oblong tray attached at waist, 10 3/4" h. **75-85**

Ceramic, figure of genie, white w/gold trim, holding a lantern, wearing tag, "Genie At Your Service," Enesco, 8" h. **100-135**

Ceramic, figure of girl in yellow dress decorated w/red roses, black hat tied under chin, short white gloves, marked "Sunbonnet Miss - Holt Howard 1958," 5" h. **125-150**

Ceramic, figure of Oriental woman in beige w/gold yoke across shoulders, carrying salt & pepper shaker buckets on her hips, candleholder in her coolie hat, toothpick holes below her waist & back, paper label on bottom w/"Hachiya Brothers, No. 81435, Made in Japan," 10 1/4" h. **125-150**

Ceramic, figure of peasant woman, yellow dress w/puffy sleeves & flowers on front of dress, holding toothpick holder bowl on head, blue jeweled eyes, ink-marked "Japan," 9 1/4" h... **60-75**

Ceramic, figure of Spanish dancer, gold & white, holding tambourine, marked "#460

California Originals USA," ca. 1950s, 13" h. $135.00; 15" h. $135.0-150.00; 8 3/4" h. **85**

Napkin Doll with Blue Hat & Bowl

Ceramic, figure of woman, blonde, wearing dress w/pink & maroon flowers & green leaves, holding blue bowl & wearing blue hat, marked "Helen Lewis," 9 1/2" h. (ILLUS.) **95-135**

Ceramic, figure of woman holding a muff, green & jewel-decorated, hat masks candleholder, marked "Kreiss and Co.," 10 1/4" h. **95-110**

Ceramic, figure of woman in pink carrying a ceramic basket of fruit w/toothpick holes, yellow, 10 1/2" h. **100-135**

Ceramic, figure of woman in pink holding yellow toothpick tray, painted flowers on bottom of skirt, made in Japan, 9 3/4" h. ... **75-95**

Ceramic, figure of woman in pink skirt, white & black top, one hand holding a toothpick tray on head, 8 1/2" h. **95-110**

Ceramic, figure of woman in white dress w/blue & gold trim, carrying tray w/sugar & creamer, 9" h. **125-140**

Ceramic, figure of woman on base, black hair, white dress, molded pink lustre apron, one arm holding toothpick bowl on her head, by Marcia of California, 13" h. **125-150**

Napkin Doll with Toothpick Holder

Ceramic, figure of woman, pink dress w/puffy sleeves & flowers on front, holding toothpick holder bowl on head, blue jeweled eyes, ink-marked "Japan," 8 1/2" h. (ILLUS.) **65-85**

Ceramic, figure of woman, pink & white lustre dress, flowers on front, holding a pink bird on outstretched hand & a toothpick tray on her head w/other hand, 9 1/2" h. ... **75-95**

Ceramic, figure of woman w/braids, wearing kitchen mitts & holding turkey on tray w/toothpick holes, yellow & white, 9 3/4" h.; matching 3 3/8" shakers $25.00-35.00; set: $100.00-135.00; holder alone **75-95**

Ceramic, figure of young girl, aquamarine & white dress w/black bodice & black bows on front & back of skirt, large pockets for napkins, marked "3475" on bottom, 7 7/8" h. **75-95**

Ceramic, figure of young girl, pink & white dress w/black bodice & black bows on front & back of skirt, large pockets for napkins, marked "3475" on bottom, 7 7/8" h. **75-95**

Ceramic, girl w/brown hair, wearing low-cut light blue Colonial-style dress w/bell sleeves, slits in back only, handmade, 7 3/4" h. **75-95**

Ceramic, white figure of woman holding a pitcher, corsage of lavender roses w/green leaves on her shoulder & on the pitcher, gold trim, handmade, 11" h. **95-115**

Ceramic, young woman in turquoise draped dress w/matching scarf & hat on her head, holding a white fan, slits in back only, handmade, 6 1/4" h. **50-65**

Ceramic & metal, half figure of Santa Claus, holding a gift in one hand & a Christmas stocking w/toothpick holes in the other, 7" h. **150-175**

Ceramic, metal & wood, half figure of Mexican woman w/yellow blouse & hat w/red trim, multicolor striped scarf on shoulder, wooden base w/wire napkin holder, 9" h. **150-185**

Ceramic, metal & wood, half figure of milk maid, carrying buckets across shoulders, "Davar Originals" sticker, 6" h. **95-110**

Chalkware, figure of woman w/beige lace skirt & fitted jacket, candleholder in hat, 13" h. **95-125**

Metal, wiry figure of woman w/gold skirt, gold wrist bands, necklace & hoop earrings, 8 1/2" h. **135-175**

Wood, Black native woman, multi-colored, w/basket of fruit on head, movable arms, 6 3/4" h. **65-85**

Wood, figure of woman in maroon & beige dress w/black & beige flowers, wearing a small saucer-shaped black hat, 6 1/2" h. **50-60**

Wood, red umbrella w/white polka dots, maroon base w/white & yellow flowers & green leaves, light brown hooked handle, 8 3/8" h. **25-35**

Wood & wire, figure of person wearing wide-brimmed hat, wires for arms, Finland, 10 1/4" h. **40-50**

Reamers

Ceramic, figure of woman's head w/black hair, sitting in white lustre saucer, 3 1/4" h. **325-400**

Ceramic, red & cream, Hall China, 6" h. **500-600**

rose, yellow w/green leaves & handle, marked "Germany," ..." h. **225-300**

...ic, saucer shape, rough orange fin-ish, white interior, green handle, Czecho-slovakia, 2 1/4" h. **40-50**

Two German Reamers

Ceramic, two-piece chick, yellow w/maroon crown & wings, Germany, 3 1/2" h. (ILLUS. right) **225-250**

Two-piece Chick Reamer

Ceramic, two-piece, chick, yellow w/orange crown, bill & feet, green tail & wings, white cone, marked "Sarsasparilla, W.N.Y. (c) 1984, Deco Designs, #970," 3 1/2" h. (ILLUS.) **50-60**

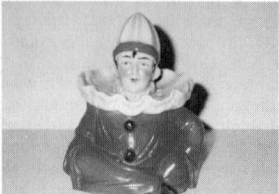

Clown Reamer

Ceramic, two-piece, clown, sitting cross-legged, orange suit w/white ruffled collar & cone, German, 5" h. (ILLUS.) **275-300**
Ceramic, two-piece, clown, yellow body w/maroon buttons & collar, cone hat, 6" h. **85-100**

Cream Pitcher Reamer

Ceramic, two-piece, cream pitcher w/multi-colored floral design, marked "Universal Cambridge Ovenproof Made in USA," 9" h. (ILLUS.) **135-165**

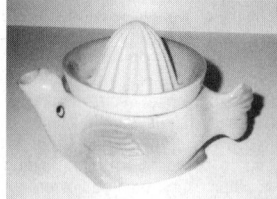

Duck & Pig Reamers

Ceramic, two-piece, duck, California Classics, ca. 1989, 3 1/4" h. (ILLUS. left).. **20-25**
Ceramic, two-piece, elephant, yellow w/black trim & white cone, Goebel, Germany, 4 1/8" h. (ILLUS. left with chick).. **250-275**

Fish Reamer

Ceramic, two-piece, fish, orange & white, marked "Jager," 3 1/4" h. (ILLUS.) **175-200**
Ceramic, two-piece, pig, California Classics, ca. 1989, 3 1/4" h. (ILLUS. right w/duck,) **20-25**
Ceramic, two-piece, pitcher w/clown head top, bottom decorated w/yellow & purple flowers, yellow cone, lustre trim, marked "Made in Japan," 6" h. **75-95**
Ceramic, two-piece, pitcher, white w/yellow plaid design, marked "Japan" on bottom, 7" h. **55-65**

Roly-poly Man Reamer

Ceramic, two-piece, roly-poly man holding a top hat that acts as the spout, white w/black trim, 4 3/4" h. (ILLUS.) **275-300**
Ceramic, two-piece, smiling face, ruffled top, yellow w/orange & black trim, marked "Carltonware," 3 3/4" h. **95-125**
Ceramic, two-piece, teapot shape, yellow w/purple flowers & green leaves, top in-verts into a lid, 6" h. **100-125**

Ceramic, two-piece, yellow bear, marked
"Foreign," 4 1/2" h...................................... **325-400**

Red Wing Reamer

Ceramic, yellow, Red Wing USA, 6 3/4" h.
(ILLUS.).. **115-125**

Two Jenny Reamers

Glass, aquamarine Jenny, loop handle,
5 1/2" d. (ILLUS. left)................................ **125-135**
Glass, clear, w/square loop handle, em-
bossed "Balencia" on front, 6" d............. **185-225**
Glass, crystal Jenny, loop handle, 5 1/2" d.
(ILLUS. right)... **125-135**
Glass, crystal, saucer-type w/small loop
handle, Cambridge Glass Company,
4 1/8" d... **15-20**
Glass, custard-colored milk glass, saucer-
type on base w/loop handle, McKee
Glass Company, 5 1/2" d. **30-35**

Fry Glass Reamer

Glass, green, double-ribbed w/loop handle,
Fry, 6 1/4" d. (ILLUS.) **30-40**
Glass, green opaque glass, long pointed
cone, embossed "Saunders," 6 1/8" d
.... **1,400-1,600**
Glass, green, ribbed w/loop handle, Anchor
Hocking Glass Company, 6" d.................... **20-25**

Blue Glass Reamer

Glass, light blue, saucer-type w/seed dam &
tab handle, 4 3/4" d. (ILLUS.)................. **100-120**

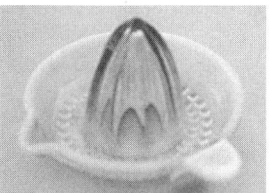

Opalescent Hobnail Reamer

Glass, light blue & white opalescent
hobnail, saucer-type w/tab handle, 4" d.
(ILLUS.).. **150-165**
Glass, opalescent white, embossed
"SUNKIST" & marked "Pat. No. 18764
Made in USA," McKee Glass Co., 6" d.. **125-150**
Glass, opaque pink, embossed "SUNKIST"
& marked "Pat. No. 18764 Made in USA,"
McKee Glass Co., 6" d. **175-225**
Glass, pink, one-piece w/tab handle, Jean-
nette Glass Company, 5 7/8" d. **40-50**
Glass, two-piece, crystal, Westmoreland
Glass Company, 4 5/8" h. **60-70**

Frosted Crystal Reamer

Glass, two-piece, frosted crystal, decorated
w/"Baby's Orange," 4 1/4" h. (ILLUS.) **65-75**
Glass, two-piece, pink two-cup measure,
Hazel Atlas Glass Company, 5 3/8" h.... **140-160**
Glass & metal, hinged black metal w/clear
glass insert, marked "Williams," 7 3/4" l. ... **50-75**

Silver-trimmed Reamer

Glass & silver, pressed glass w/embossed
silver trim on base, loop handle, France,
3 1/4" d. (ILLUS.)... **85-100**
Gold plated, three-piece cocktail shaker,
marked "Made in Italy," 9" h. **75-100**

Metal, one-piece w/levered handle, marked "Super Juicer," 6" h. **15-20**

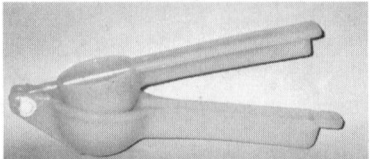

Plastic Handled Reamer

Plastic, yellow, 8" l. (ILLUS.).............................. **8-12**

Plastic & Bakelite Reamer

Plastic & Bakelite, green w/tab handle, marked "Pressitor, Brev. Dep." on handle & "Brev Suisse" on base, 5 3/4" d. (ILLUS.)... **40-50**

Silver Plate Reamer

Silver plate, marked "CS Co 2," 6 5/8" h. **75-100**

Embossed Silver Plate Reamer

Silver plate, saucer-type, decoratively embossed, 4 3/4" d. (ILLUS.)....................... **135-150**

Salt & Pepper Shakers

Birthday set, ceramic, miniature, image of card w/"Happy Birthday!" in red, w/black line drawings of smiling faces & image of wrapped gift w/pink ribbon & bow, Arcadia Ceramic Company, USA (ILLUS. left, below)... **35**

Fishing set, ceramic, miniature, image of goldfish w/open mouth & image of green wiggly worm, Arcadia Ceramic Company, USA (ILLUS. center, w/other miniatures, below)... **35**

Green Pepper Salt & Pepper Shakers

Green peppers, ceramic, Rosemeade, USA (ILLUS.) **45**

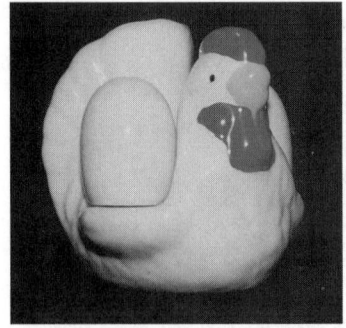

Hen & Eggs Shaker Set

Hen & eggs, ceramic, white egg shakers sit on wings of white hen w/red comb & wattle, yellow beak, black eyes, tail acts as napkin holder, China (ILLUS.)............................ **8**

Laundry set, ceramic, miniature, image of wash tub w/wringer & image of ironing

Miniature Salt & Pepper Sets

board w/shirt draped over it & iron sitting to the side, Arcadia Ceramic Company, USA (ILLUS. right, w/other miniatures) **35**

Submarine Sandwich Set

Submarine sandwiches, ceramic, large sandwich w/applied red pepper forming handle of lid holds condiments, smaller sandwiches are salt & pepper shakers, Japan (ILLUS.) **22**

Tea Serving Accessories

People around the world have been drinking tea for centuries, and the art of brewing the perfect cup has long been considered an art form. Tea balls, or infusers as they're sometimes called, were used to hold loose tea and hung into the pot or cup to properly steep. Most of the pieces came with a bottom or tray to catch the residual drips of water and tea. When tea bags came into common use and the potential of tea stains persisted, the decorative tea strainer was put into service as an acceptable receptacle even at the most elegant tables.

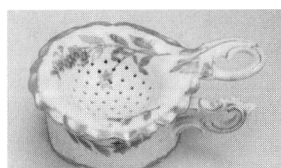

Strainer with Floral Decoration

Bisque, two-piece tea strainer, cream w/purple flowers, green leaves & gold trim, handle on bottom half & flower inside bottom, marked "6677" w/crossed-arrows logo, 1 3/4" h., 5 7/8" l. (ILLUS.) **75-100**

Figures of Kneeling Asian Man

Ceramic, figure of kneeling Asian man, orange w/beige lustre head, marked "Made in Japan," 3" h. (ILLUS. right) **100-125**

Ceramic, figure of kneeling Asian man, orange w/beige lustre head, stamped "Goldcastle, Made in Japan" w/pagoda logo on screw-off top of head, 4" h. (ILLUS. left) **85-125**

Models of Cat & Pig

Ceramic, model of cat, yellow w/brown nose, eyelashes & whiskers, sitting on green basketweave tray, "Quality Product Japan" sticker, 3" h. (ILLUS. right, w/pig) **55-65**

Ceramic, model of duck, white w/yellow beak, orange trim, sitting on oblong tray, ca. 1934, 3 1/4" h. **95-125**

Models of Fish

Ceramic, model of fish, white & orange w/yellow fin & tail & grey scales, marked "DRGM" on screw-off top of head & "8899" on side, ca. 1932, 3" h. (ILLUS. left) **95-125**

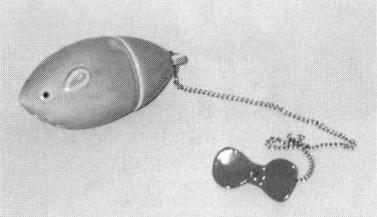

Model of Green Mouse

Ceramic, model of green mouse, "Sigma" label & marked "Made in Japan," 3 1/2" l. (ILLUS.) **75-95**

Ceramic, model of pig, pink w/large green bow on head, heavy black eyelashes, sitting on green basketweave tray, "Quality Product Japan" sticker, 3" h. (ILLUS. left, w/cat) **55-65**

Ceramic, "Tillie the Tea Strainer," model of fish, white w/brown eyes & lashes, pink cheeks & mouth, ca. 1952, 2" h. Add $10.00 to 15.00 if complete w/tray. (ILLUS. right w/other fish) **25-35**

Seated Asian Figure

Ceramic, two-piece figure of cross-legged Asian man, incised "Germany, D.R.C.M." on screw-off top of head, ca. 1933, 3 3/4" h. (ILLUS.) **85-125**

Oriental Ceramic Figures

Ceramic, two-piece figure of kneeling Asian man, white w/red collar & red & green trim, ca. 1933, 4" h. (ILLUS. right) **85-125**

Figure of Kneeling Boy in Green Suit

Ceramic, two-piece figure of kneeling boy in green suit, yellow & light green ruffled collar, 2 3/4" h. (ILLUS.) **75-85**
Ceramic, two-piece figure of kneeling boy, yellow & green ruffled collar & yellow cuffs, incised "Germany D.R.G.M." on screw-off top of head, 4" h. **125-175**
Ceramic, two-piece figure of kneeling Oriental man, white w/yellow collar & red, blue & yellow trim, stamped "Germany" on bottom & incised "Germany, D.R.C.M." on screw-off top of head, ca. 1933, 4" h. (ILLUS. left, w/other kneeling Asian man).. **85-125**

Figure of Standing Asian Man

Ceramic, two-piece full figure of standing Asian man, incised "Germany, D.R.C.M." on screw-off top of head, ca. 1933, 3 3/4" h. (ILLUS.).. **85-125**

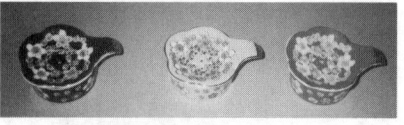

Two English Tea Strainers

Ceramic, two-piece strainer hooks over small round bowl, white & pink roses & multicolored bouquet, gold trim, marked "Derby Crown, Royal Crown Derby English Bone China, Derby Posies XXXIII," newer vintage, 1 1/4" h., 5" l. (ILLUS. right) **10-20**
Ceramic, two-piece strainer hooks over small round bowl, white & pink roses, white & orange flowers & green leaves, gold trim, marked w/crown logo, "Royal Park Fine Earthenware Staffordshire England," newer vintage, 1 1/4" h., 5" l. (ILLUS. left, w/other English strainer) **10-20**

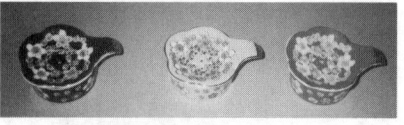

Floral Decorated Tea Strainers

Ceramic, two-piece tea strainer, black w/pink & white flowers & green leaves, 1 3/8" h., 3 7/8" l. (ILLUS. left)...................... **5-10**
Ceramic, two-piece tea strainer, red w/pink & white flowers & green leaves, 1 3/8" h., 3 7/8" l. (ILLUS. right, w/floral decorated strainers) **5-10**

Strainer with Landscape Scene

Ceramic, two-piece tea strainer, white, round bottom w/pink & green highlights, yellow top w/landscape image of house & tree, marked "Hand Painted Nippon" on bottom & "H813" under top, 1 5/8" h., 5 1/8" l. (ILLUS.) **35-55**

Black & White Strainer w/Floral Trim

Ceramic, two-piece tea strainer, white w/black band trim, pink & yellow flowers, heart-shaped hole in handle, marked "Nagoya SNB Nippon," 1 5/8" h., 5 3/8" l. (ILLUS.) **30-40**

Ornate Tea Strainer

Ceramic, two-piece tea strainer, white w/blue, green & red design w/heavy gold decorations, marked "Made in Japan," 1 5/8" h., 5 3/4" l. (ILLUS.) **35-55**

Strainer with Gold Trim

Ceramic, two-piece tea strainer, white w/gold outlined roses & leaves, gold trim, marked "Handpainted Japan," 1 3/4" h., 6 1/4" l. (ILLUS.) **35-55**

Nippon Tea Strainer

Ceramic, two-piece tea strainer, white w/gold roses & leaves & gold trim, marked "Hand Painted Nippon," 1 3/4" h., 6 1/8" l. **50-60**

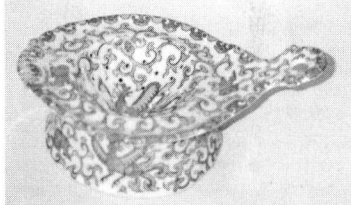

Phoenix Dragon Design Strainer

Ceramic, two-piece tea strainer, white w/green Phoenix Dragon design, bottom marked w/Oriental characters, 1 1/2" h., 6" l. (ILLUS.) **85-125**

White & Maroon Tea Strainer

Ceramic, two-piece tea strainer, white w/maroon & gold scalloped design trim, 1 5/8" h., 6 1/4" l. (ILLUS.) **25-35**

Strainer Decorated with Poppies

Ceramic, two-piece tea strainer, white w/red poppies, green leaves & gold trim,

marked "Made in Japan," 1" h, 6" l.
(ILLUS.).. **35-55**
Ceramic, two-piece tea strainer, yellow
w/pink & white flowers & green leaves,
1 3/8" h., 3 7/8" l. (ILLUS. center w/black
& red floral strainers)..................................... **5-10**

LIGHTING DEVICES

Also see Antique Trader Lamps & Lighting Price
Guide.

Early Non-Electric Lamps & Lighting

Aladdin® Mantle Lamps

*The Mantle Lamp Company of America, creator of
the world famous Aladdin lamp, was founded in Chicago
in 1908. Like several of its competitors, the Aladdin cou-
pled the round wick technology with a mantle to produce
a bright incandescent light comparable to the illumination provided by a 60 to 75 watt bulb. Through aggres-
sive national advertising and an intensive dealer
network, the Aladdin lamp quickly overcame its competitors to become the standard lighting fixture in the rural
American home.*

*From the company's origin until 1926, Aladdin lamps
were produced in table, hanging, and wall bracket
styles, made mostly of brass and finished in either satin
brass or nickel plate. With the purchase of an Indiana
glass plant in the mid-1920s, the Mantle Lamp Company
began to make its own glass shades and chimneys in
addition to the manufacture of glass lamp bases. Glass
shades, both plain and decorated with reverse painting,
were made in a variety of styles. Later, colorful parchment shades were produced in a myriad of colors and
with decorations ranging from large, gaudy flowers in
the early 1930s to delicate florals and intricate geometrics, sometimes with flocking, from the mid-1930s
through the post-war years.*

*Aladdin kerosene lamps are probably best known for
the colorful glass bases made from the late 1920s to the
early 1950s. The earliest glass lamps were vase lamps
that consisted of a glass vase finished in different colors
that had a drop-in brass kerosene font. Later, seventeen
different glass patterns were produced and most patterns
were offered in a variety of different glass colors. Crystal
glass lamp bases commonly came in clear, green, or
amber colors, but for a few years crystal bases were produced in ruby red and cobalt blue. The latter two colors
are especially prized by collectors. A translucent to
opaque glass called moonstone was produced during the
1930s and was available in white, green, rose and, for one
pattern in the late 1930s, yellow. A few styles had white
moonstone fonts attached to a black stem and foot. Other
lamps had a moonstone font mounted on a metallic base.*

*An ivory to white glass called Alacite is unique to the
Aladdin lamp. The late 1930s glass formula contained
uranium oxide, and the ivory to marble-like appearance
sometimes leads to its confusion with the Crown Tuscan
glass of Cambridge. With the commencement of the Manhattan Project, this compound was placed on the
restricted list and, as a consequence, the glass formula
was changed. Early Alacite lamp bases will glow under a
blacklight, whereas later ones will not. The later Alacite
lamps also tend toward a white color rather than ivory.*

*Aladdin kerosene lamps are still being made today.
The Mantle Lamp Company left Chicago in 1948 and
was absorbed into Aladdin Industries, Inc. In April 1999,
the Aladdin Mantle Lamp Company was formed in
Clarksville, Tenn. The new limited partnership produces
kerosene lighting for domestic and foreign markets and
supplies/accessories for older lamps.*

*Aladdin kerosene lamps and their related accessories
have been avidly collected over the last thirty years. As a
consequence, prices have risen steadily even for the
common lamps. Expectedly, condition of the lamp or
shade is a very important consideration in determination
of value. Glass damage, electrification, or missing parts
can seriously depreciate value. By comparison, lamps in
mint, unused condition and in the original carton fetch
premium prices.*

—Thomas W. Small

A

Aladdin Hanging Lamp

Hanging lamp, decorated w/h.p. roses on
ball shade, Model No. 6 (ILLUS.)... **$4,000-5,000**

Aladdin Student Lamp

Student lamp, original w/functional tank,
unelectrified, Model No. 4 (ILLUS.) . **7,500-8,500**

Aladdin Table Lamp, Model No. 8

Table lamp, brass finish, No. 8 flame
spreader & No. 401 shade, Model No. 8
(ILLUS.)... **450-550**
Table lamp, nickel finish, No. 10 flame
spreader, Model No. 10 .... **450-550**
Table lamp, nickel plated, No. 6 flame
spreader, Model No. 6 .... **80-100**

Aladdin Table Lamp, Model No. 1

Table lamp, nickel plated w/embossed
foot, 1/2 qt. font, Model No. 1 (ILLUS.) . **600-700**
Vase lamp, blue variegated, gold foot edge,
three feet, 10 1/4" h................................. **600-700**
Vase lamp, green w/dark green foot edge,
model No. 12, six feet, 10 1/4" h. **250-300**
Vase lamp, variegated green, gold foot
edge, three feet, 10 1/4" h....................... **300-350**

Aladdin Vase Lamp

Vase lamp, variegated peach, gold foot
edge, three feet, 10 1/4" h. (ILLUS.) **300-350**

B

*The following pattern glass names are from J.W.
Courter reference books on Aladdin lamps.*

Table lamp, Beehive patt., clear, Model B **100-125**
Table lamp, Beehive patt., green or amber
crystal... **125-175**
Table lamp, Cathedral patt., green or am-
ber crystal **150-200**
Table lamp, Cathedral patt., rose moon-
stone.. **450-500**
Table lamp, Cathedral patt., white moon-
stone.. **400-500**
Table lamp, Corinthian patt., amber or
green crystal... **125-150**
Table lamp, Corinthian patt., clear.............. **80-100**
Table lamp, Corinthian patt., white moon-
stone font w/green, rose or black foot.... **350-450**
Table lamp, Diamond Quilted patt., green
moonstone... **350-400**
Table lamp, Lincoln Drape patt., short, am-
ber or ruby crystal w/metal collar at font
top.. **100-125**
Table lamp, Lincoln Drape patt., short, ruby
crystal, raised glass collar at font top. **900-1,000**
Table lamp, Lincoln Drape patt., tall, cobalt
blue, foot top w/circular ring............. **1,300-1,500**
Table lamp, Lincoln Drape patt., tall, cobalt
blue, scalloped ring on foot top **1,900-2,100**
Table lamp, Lincoln Drape patt., tall, ruby
crystal, lower value for light ruby, higher
for dark... **850-1,100**
Table lamp, Lincoln Drape patt., tall, slightly
tapered stem, Alacite............................. **150-200**

Aladdin Table Lamp, Orientale Pattern

Table lamp, Orientale patt., ivory, green, or
bronze enamel, metallic finish (ILLUS.). **150-175**
Table lamp, Queen patt., green, white, or
rose moonstone on metallic foot............ **250-350**
Table lamp, Simplicity patt., Alacite, green
or white enamel **150-175**
Table lamp, Simplicity patt., rose enamel.. **175-200**
Table lamp, Solitaire patt., white moon-
stone... **2,800-3,000**
Table lamp, Venetian patt., clear, fused
stem-foot/bowl, Model A......................... **350-400**
Table lamp, Venetian patt., green or peach
enamel **125-150**
Table lamp, Venetian patt., white enamel. **100-125**
Table lamp, Vertique patt., green moon-
stone.. **350-400**

Aladdin Mantles

Table lamp, Vertique patt., yellow moonstone 500-600
Table lamp, Victoria patt., ceramic w/floral decoration & gold bands 600-650
Table lamp, Washington Drape patt., clear crystal, plain stem, w/or without oil fill 75-100
Table lamp, Washington Drape patt., clear, green, or amber w/open, thick round stem 100-150
Table lamp, Washington Drape patt., green or amber crystal, plain stem 100-150

Miscellaneous

Aladdin Lamp Chimneys

Chimneys, boxed, each (ILLUS.) 100-125
Mantles, boxed, each (ILLUS. center w/other mantles) 5-15
Mantles, boxed, each (ILLUS. left, w/other mantles) 75-100
Mantles, boxed, each (ILLUS. right, w/other mantles) 40-50

Aladdin Matchholder

Matchholder, copper w/accessories & instruction booklet (ILLUS.) 100-150

Other matchholders, each 25-40
Shades, floral, No. 601F roses 600-700
Shades, green cased, No. 202 artichoke, No. 204 eight panel, each 900-1,100
Shades, plain, No. 201, No. 301, No. 401, No. 501 (for Model No. 11), No. 601, each 100-125
Shades, plain, opal No. 205 w/fire polished bottom rim 400-500
Shades, reverse painted, No. 601 Log Cabin, No. 616 Gristmill, No. 620 Windmill, each 350-400
Shades, reverse painted, No. 616F poppies, No. 620F roses, each 800-1,000
Shades, Whip-O-Lite parchment, floral, geometric, or scenic, 14" h., each 150-200
Wicks, boxed, mounted, each 40-50
Wicks, boxed, No. 11 & No. 12, each 10-15
Wicks, boxed, No. 6, mounted, ech) 20-25

Fairy Lamps

These are candle burning night lights of the Victorian era. Best known are the Clarke Fairy Lamps made in England, but they were also made by other firms. They were produced in two sizes, each with a base and a shade. Fairy Pyramid lamps usually have a clear glass base and are approximately 2 7/8" d. and 3 1/4" h. The Fairy Lamps are usually at least 4" d. and 5" h. when assembled. These may or may not have an additional saucer or bottom holder to match the shade in addition to the clear base.

Amber Embossed Fairy Lamp

Amber embossed shade, fairy-size, embossed overall w/crosses surrounded by diamonds, rests on the smooth shoulder of a matching swirl-molded lamp cup w/two rows of applied & tooled petals around the rim, cup marked "Rd 176239," 4 3/4" d., 4 1/4" h. (ILLUS.) **250**

Amber Ribbed Fairy Lamp

Amber ribbed shade, fairy-size, on the smooth shoulder of a matching handled cylindrical base w/a flared, ribbed rim & foot, 4 1/4" w., 5" h. (ILLUS.) **150**

Amethyst Diamonds Fairy Lamp

Amethyst Four-in-One Diamonds patt. shade, pyramid-size, in a clear Clarke Fairy Pyramid swirl design lamp cup, 2 3/4" d., 3 5/8" h. (ILLUS.) **200**

Baccarat-signed Blue Fairy Lamp

Baccarat blue Pinwheel patt. shade, fairy-size, in a matching scalloped upwardly flared base marked "Baccarat Déposé," 5 1/2" d., 4" h. (ILLUS.) **350**

Blue Cased & Embossed Fairy Lamp

Blue cased in white shade, overall embossed reverse drape patt. in a clear Clarke lamp cup base, 4" d., 4 1/2" h. (ILLUS.) **200**

Decorated Blue Fairy Lamp

Blue decorated shade, fairy-size, blue ground decorated w/pink flower & green leaves, resting on the smooth shoulder of the matching lamp cup, 3 1/3" d., 4 1/2" h. (ILLUS.) **250**

Frosted Blue Petal-form Fairy Lamp

Blue frosted satin shade, an inward-crimped shade w/five applied clear frosted petals around the sides, on a matching pedestal base w/five applied frosted clear leaf-form feet & three upturned leaves, 9 1/2" h. (ILLUS.) **500**

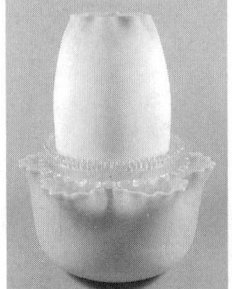

Shaded Blue Satin Fairy Lamp

Blue shaded satin shade, fairy-size, blue shaded to white cased in creamy white, w/a crimped upper rim, in a clear Clarke Fairy lamp cup resting on six rounded scallops on the upright rim of the matching bowl-shaped base, 5 1/8" d., 5 5/8" h. (ILLUS.) **500**

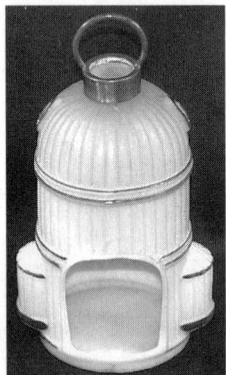

Figural Birdcage Fairy Lamp

Blue shading to white figural shade, a ribbed satin finish figural birdcage trimmed w/gold bands & protruding feeders, brass fitting w/finger ring at top opening, 4 1/4" w., 6" h. (ILLUS.) **250**

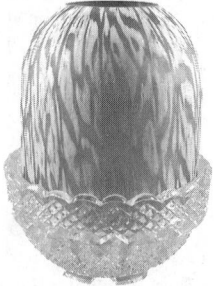

Blue & White Spatter Pyramid Lamp

Blue & white spatter shade, pyramid-size, blue ground w/white swirled spatter in the arabesque design, in a clear Clarke Fairy Pyramid lamp cup, 3" d., 3 1/2" h. (ILLUS.) **200**

Brass Jeweled Filigree Fairy Lamp

Brass jeweled filigree shade, fairy-size, the dome set w/eight large colored jewels in individual filigree frames alternating w/eight smaller jewels, on a four-footed brass base w/integral candle cup, 3 1/2" d., 4 1/4" h. (ILLUS.) **250**

Decorated Burmese & Ceramic Lamp

Burmese decorated shade, fairy-size, satin finish, decorated in the woodbine design, on a creamware flower bowl base decorated w/polychrome flowers & signed "Taylor, Tunnicliffe & Co.," the shade atop an integral lamp cup w/ribbed shoulder marked "S. Clarke's Patent Trade Mark Fairy" inside candle depression, 7 1/2" d., 6" h. (ILLUS.) **1,000**

Decorated Burmese Shade & Base

Burmese decorated shade, fairy-size, satin finish, decorated w/red forget-me-not-like flowers & green leaves, in a clear Clarke lamp cup marked "S. Clarke Trade Mark Fairy" on a matching Burmese quatrefoil base w/unrefired Burmese foot, 5 3/4" w., 5 3/4" h. (ILLUS.) **2,500**

Rare Decorated Burmese Epergne

Burmese decorated shades, epergne-style, fairy-size, three satin finish shades decorated in a prunus design, on clear Clarke lamp cups in matching Burmese bowls on crystal supporting arms w/three crystal fronds w/applied tooled leaves, a central elevated satin finish decorated Burmese bowl w/crystal support arm w/applied leaves, all on a mirrored plateau base, 12" d., 11" h. (ILLUS.) **6,500**

Undecorated Burmese Fairy Lamp

Burmese shade, plain satin finish shade on a Clarke Burmese lamp cup (ILLUS.)............ **350**

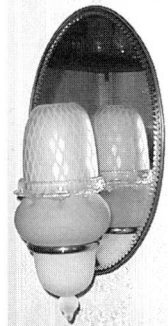

Satin Fairy Lamp on Mirrored Plaque

Butterscotch mother-of-pearl satin shade, fairy-size, Diamond Quilted patt., in a clear Clarke lamp cup resting on a similarly colored satin bowl shading to opaque w/a crimped top edge & opaque

finial on the bottom, in a brass supporting ring attached to an oval mirrored wall plaque, 9" w., 13" h. (ILLUS.) **800**

Cameo Shade on Creamware Base

Cameo glass shade, fairy-size, three-color cameo in pink cut to white cut to a frosted yellow ground w/a design of a flowering cherry branch, resting on the ribbed shoulder of a creamware lamp cup marked "S. Clarke's Patent Trade Mark Fairy," in a Tapestry Ware flower bowl base marked by Taylor, Tunnicliffe & Co., 7 1/2" d., 6" h. (ILLUS.) **2,000**

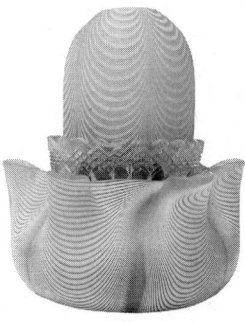

Citron Verre Moiré Nailsea-style Lamp

Citron green & white Verre Moiré Nailsea-type shade, pyramid-size, citron ground w/overall white loopings, in a Clarke Fairy Pyramid lamp cup, set in a matching upright curved bowl w/six outward drawn loops, 4 1/2" d., 5 1/2" h. (ILLUS.) **500**

Clear Cricklite & Crystal Epergne

Clear Clarke Cricklite shade, epergne-style, in a brass ring embossed "Clarke Cricklite" in a clear Clarke Cricklite lamp cup w/original hand-stitched silk bead-trimmed shade, raised on a cut crystal standard above two cut crystal bud vases on a brass frame w/a footed base, 9" w., 19" h. (ILLUS.)... **1,500**

Clarke Fairy Lamps on Silver Column

Clear Clarke Cricklite shades, epergne-style, five shades in clear Clarke lamp cups on the arms of an ormolu frame attached to a tall weighted silver plated classic Corinthian column base, each glass shade w/the original yellowish gold fabric & blue wooden-beaded shade, 17" w., 31" h. (ILLUS.) **2,000**

Cranberry Spangled Shade on Base

Cranberry silver-spangled shade, pyramid-size, threaded on the exterior in green glass, on a signed Taylor, Tunnic-liffe & Co. creamware flower bowl base decorated w/polychrome flowers, an integral lamp cup w/ribbed shoulder marked "S. Clarke's Patent Trade Mark Fairy" inside candle depression, 5 7/8" d., 5" h. (ILLUS.)... **750**

Dark Blue Drapery Fairy Lamp

Dark blue cased Drapery patt. shade, fairy-size, cased in white, in a clear Clarke lamp cup resting on the rim of the matching quatrefoil base w/an opaque foot, 5 1/2" w., 6" h. (ILLUS.)...................... **1,000**

Figural Bisque Castle Fairy Lamp

Figural bisque lamp, modeled as a tall castle w/a red-painted shingled roof, white walls & a green base w/a covered arch gate, 4 3/4" w., 8 1/4" h. (ILLUS.) **500**

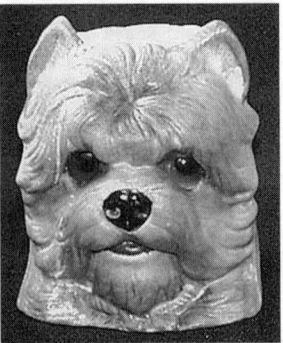

Bisque Terrier Head Fairy Lamp

Figural bisque shade, model of a brown Terrier head w/transparent amber eyes & a blue rope around the front of the neck, rear impressed w/a stylized fleur-de-lis design, 4" w., 4 1/4" h. (ILLUS.)..................... **350**

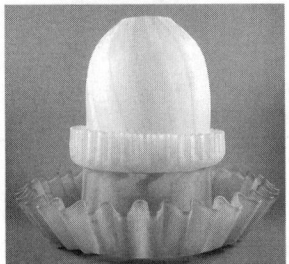

Frosted Yellow, Clear & White Lamp

Frosted yellow, clear & white Cleveland Swirl patt. shade, fairy-size, resting in a matching lamp cup w/a crimped rim & in a matching saucer base w/upturned flar-

ing & crimped rim acid-marked "Clarke
Patent Fairy," 6 1/2" d., 6 1/4" h. (ILLUS.)..... **750**

Gold Satin Swirl Pattern Fairy Lamp

Gold mother-of-pearl satin shade, fairy-
size, Swirl patt., cased in creamy white
w/an inwardly crimped top rim, in a clear
Clarke Trade Mark Fairy lamp cup, 4" d.,
4 1/3" h. (ILLUS.) **250**

Swirled Pink & White Spatter Lamp

**Pink & white spatter Reverse Swirl patt.
shade,** fairy-size, stripes of white & pink
in a matching base w/a row of applied
clear icicles around the lamp cup rim &
another row on the bottom forming feet,
3 1/4" d., 4" h. (ILLUS.).................................. **250**

Lithophane Paneled Fairy Lamp

Porcelain lithophane shade, domed
shade w/two lithophane panels known as
"Little Miss Muffet," one panel depicting a
girl scared by a frog in her dish, the other
showing a child in the woods w/a rabbit,

four notched air vents on the bottom rim,
in a low matching saucer base w/integral
candleholder, 4" d., 4 1/4" h. (ILLUS.) **600**

Rainbow Mother-of-Pearl Satin Lamp

Rainbow mother-of-pearl satin shade,
fairy-size, Diamond Quilted patt., cased
in white & w/a crimped upper rim, resting
on a clear Clarke lamp cup atop the star-
form center post of the matching shallow
base w/a flaring crimped rim, 7 3/4" d.,
7 1/2" h. (ILLUS.)... **5,000**

Red Satin Ribbon Shade on Base

Red satin mother-of-pearl shade, fairy-
size, red cased in white w/a Ribbon patt.,
crimped rim & scalloped & flared base
rim, resting in a tricorner green-striped
pond lily base w/recessed center,
5 1/2" w., 4 3/4" h. (ILLUS.) **750**

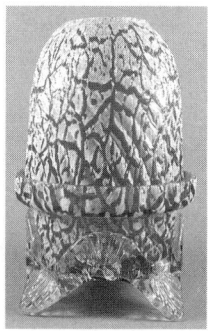

Red & White "Cracked Ice" Fairy

Red & white "cracked ice" shade, fairy-
size, a red ground w/an overall mottled
white casing, in a matching smooth-
shouldered lamp cup w/applied tooled
clear feet, 6" d., 5 1/4" h. (ILLUS.).................. **350**

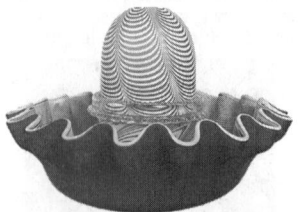

Red Nailsea-style Fairy Lamp

Red & white Nailsea-style shade, fairy-size, deep red ground w/overall white loopings in a clear Clarke lamp cup resting on the center post of a deep red bowl base lined in white & w/a flaring ruffled rim, 9 1/2" d., 5 1/4" h. (ILLUS.) **650**

Flame-shaped Ruby Red Fairy Lamp

Ruby red flame-molded shade, pyramid-size, on a clear Clarke Fairy Pyramid lamp cup, 2 3/4" d., 3 3/4" h. (ILLUS.).......... **150**

Silver-spangled Blue-threaded Lamp

Silver-spangled blue-threaded shade, pyramid-size, silver spangled ground w/random blue threading & a molded swirl design, in a clear Clarke Fairy Pyramid lamp cup, 3" d., 3 1/2" h. (ILLUS.).......... **250**

Green Threaded Spangled Fairy Lamp

Spangled glass shade, pyramid-size, green w/silver mica spangles & threaded around the sides in green glass, resting in a clear Clarke lamp cup, 3" d., 3 1/2" h. (ILLUS.)... **250**

Red & Yellow Spatter Fairy Lamp

Spatter glass shade, fairy-size, mottled brown & white w/white casing & cased on the exterior w/a clear reverse swirl design, in a matching smooth-shouldered lamp cup, 3 3/4" d., 4 1/2" h. (ILLUS.) **300**

Christmas Tree-decorated Lamp

White decorated shade, fairy-size, decorated w/two Christmas trees trimmed w/transparent jeweled ornaments, resting on a Clarke glazed creamware base w/gold trim, base marked "Taylor, Tunnicliffe & Co.," 4 1/4" d., 5" h. (ILLUS.).............. **350**

Yellow Appliqued Glass Fairy Lamp

Yellow appliqued shade, fairy-size, the yellow ground decorated w/five rows of clear tooled applied clear leaves, resting on the ribbed inner shoulder of the integral lamp cup of the pressed clear Clarke base in the diamond & star design, 7" d., 5" h. (ILLUS.)..................................... **500**

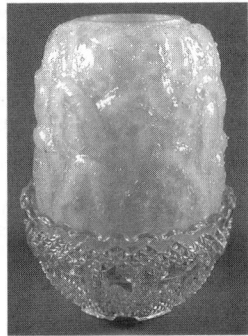

Yellow Cased Petal-embossed Lamp

Yellow cased in clear shade, pyramid-size, w/an overall molded petal design, on a clear Clarke lamp cup, 3" d., 3 1/2" h. (ILLUS.) **150**

Yellow Satin Fairy Lamp Epergne

Yellow satin shade, epergne-style, fairy-size, a single cased satin shade in a clear Clarke fairy lamp cup resting on the upright ribbon rim of a matching yellow satin base w/four frosted, applied feet, the base straddles an ormolu frame which attaches to a scalloped, beveled & notched mirror plateau & also supports six rings each holding a matching bulbous satin bud vase w/a flared, scalloped rim & applied opaque berry prunts, 10 1/4" w., 6 3/4" h. (ILLUS.).. **2,000**

Yellow Satin Air-trap Pattern Lamp

Yellow satin shade, fairy-size, produced w/an air-trapped ribbon swirl design, resting on the smooth shoulder of a matching lamp cup, 3" d., 5" h. (ILLUS.)........................ **250**

Miniature Lamps

Our listings are generally arranged numerically according to the numbers assigned to the various miniature lamps pictured in Frank R. & Ruth E. Smith's book Miniature Lamps, *now referred to as Smith's Book I, and Ruth Smith's sequel,* Miniature Lamps II. *All references are to Smith's Book I unless otherwise noted. Lamps are glass unless otherwise noted.*

Banquet lamp, white opaque font, stem & ball shade, all w/blue transfer & white enamel floral decoration, brass connector, square brass foot, overall 17" h. (missing burner, connector rod replaced)...... **330**

Milk glass, base & ball-shaped shade w/embossed scroll & floral design, maroon flowers w/yellow centers, leaves & scrolls in dark green, light green band at bottom of shade & below collar of base, overall 7 7/8" h. (normal roughness on bottom of shade).. **523**

Clear, "Little Beauty" finger-type, applied handle, embossed name on side, clear glass chimney, Nutmeg burner, 6 1/4" h., No. 16 (slight chip on chimney base).............. **95**

Clear, "Nutmeg" lamp, embossed "Nutmeg" on font, clear chimney, narrow brass band forms removable handle, Nutmeg burner, 2 3/4" h., No. 29.................................. **77**

Cobalt blue, "Nutmeg" lamp, embossed "Nutmeg" on font, clear chimney, narrow brass band forms removable handle, Nutmeg burner, 2 3/4" h., No. 29.................... **61**

Green, "Nutmeg" lamp, embossed "Nutmeg" on font, clear chimney, narrow brass band forms removable handle, Nutmeg burner, 2 3/4" h., No. 29.................. **228**

Amber, ribbed low cylindrical font w/an attached cylindrical basketweave pattern match holder w/ring handle to the side, ribbed conical matching shade, clear chimney, Hornet burner, 8" h., No. 52 .... **252**

Embossed blue milk glass, w/brass hanger & nickel reflector, Nutmeg burner, 3" h. to top of collar, No. 56 .... **100**

Beaded Heart & Cosmos Lamps

Green, Beaded Heart patt., hearts around font raised on pedestal w/round domed foot, collar w/split & piece missing, no chimney or shade, 5" h., No. 109 (ILLUS. left, w/Cosmos lamp)....................................... **850**

Clear, Beaded Heart patt., Acorn burner, 5 1/2" h., No. 109.............................. **80**

Green, Beaded Heart patt., Acorn burner, 5 1/2" h., No. 109.............................. **206**

Amber Daisy with Bull's-eye Lamp

Amber, Daisy with Large Bull's-eye patt., octagonal stem, no chimney or shade, 4 3/4" h., No. 112 (ILLUS.)............................. **160**

Amber, Fish-scale patt., Nutmeg burner, 5" h., No. 116................................. **50**

Blue, Fish-scale patt., Nutmeg burner, 5" h., No. 116................................. **202**

Clear, Fish-scale patt., Nutmeg burner, 5" h., No. 116................................. **87**

Green, Fish-scale patt., Nutmeg burner, 5" h., No. 116................................. **80**

Vaseline, Fish-scale patt., Nutmeg burner, 5" h., No. 116................................. **175**

Clear, "waffle" bulbous tapering font, raised on a slender brass pedestal base w/a flaring foot, cranberry chimney, Acorn burner, 8 1/4" h., No. 117 .... **90**

Clear, Greek Key patt., paneled rounded font w/band of design on a paneled stem & square foot w/further design, w/insert collar, no chimney, 3 1/2" h., No. 167 .... **110**

Clear, stem lamp w/swirl pattern, brass insert in glass collar, top of collar marked "Patented Sep. 19 & Nov. 14, 1911," Acorn burner, 4 7/8" to top of font, 5 1/8" to top of collar, Book II, No. 179...................... **41**

Milk glass, w/wide embossed ribs, painted blue shading to white, Nutmeg burner, 7" h., No. 189 .... **89**

Milk glass, paneled bulbous base & domical shade "Sunflower" lamp, multicolored decorations, Nutmeg burner, 8" h., No. 206.. **352**

Milk glass, w/embossed Maltese Cross, blue paint, Hornet burner, Eagle Glass & Mfg. Co., Wellsburg, W.Va., ca. 1894, 9 1/2" h., No. 214.................................... **60**

Blue opaque, w/swirl-ribbed band on base & globe-chimney, Hornet burner, 7 3/4" h., No. 215.................................... **400**

Milk glass, called the "Nellie Bly" lamp, milk glass base & clear shade w/upper part of shade painted white to resemble frosting, upper part of both base & shade w/orange ground, floral sprays in white, yellow & green, Hornet burner, 9" h., No. 219 .... **53**

Milk glass, base & ball-shaped shade embossed w/fleur-de-lis & other designs, Acorn burner, clear glass chimney, 7" h., No. 228 (normal roughness on top & bottom edges of shade) **66**

Milk glass, bell-shaped base w/globe-chimney shade w/embossed scroll leaf design, trimmed in blue w/blue flowers, Nutmeg burner, 8 3/4" h., No. 240...................... **272**

Amethyst Opalescent Miniature Lamp

Amethyst opalescent, embossed overlapping leaves pattern w/gold trim, Hornet burner, 9" h., No. 257 (ILLUS.) **231**

Cobalt blue, embossed overlapping leaves pattern w/gold trim, Hornet burner, 9" h., No. 257.. **350**

Cased pink, Cosmos patt., domed shade w/embossed flowers & matching rounded base, no color trim, burner cover & shade spider missing, normal mold roughness, overall 6 1/4" h., No. 286 (ILLUS. right with Beaded Heart lamp).............. **160**

Cased yellow, Cosmos patt., base & umbrella shade w/pink-stained band & colored florals, Nutmeg burner, 7 1/2" h., No. 286 .... **417**

Sylvan Pattern Miniature Lamp

Milk glass, Sylvan patt., ribbed shade & paneled, rounded font on foot, undecorated, Westmoreland Specialty Company, 8 1/4" h., No. 296 (ILLUS.) **60**

Milk glass, ribbed panel pattern, green decoration, Nutmeg burner, 8" h., No. 311 .... **253**

Milk glass, orange ground fading to yellow, blue flowers & green leaves in fired-on paint, Nutmeg burner, 8 3/4" h., No. 314 ..... **284**

Milk glass, painted blue around top of shade & base, blue & green floral decorations, Nutmeg burner, 8 1/4" h., No. 315 .... **189**

Cased pink, melon-ribbed, glossy finish, Nutmeg burner, 7" h., No. 390....................... **407**

Yellow satin, footed bulbous shouldered base & globe-chimney shade w/embossed pansy pattern, Nutmeg burner, 8 3/4" h., No. 398... **670**

Banquet lamp, white metal w/brass finish, filigree font holder, solid textured stem & ornate foot, ring attached to hold cranberry Hobbs Optic shade, overall 16 1/2" h., Book II, No. 422 (electrified through font, wear to brass finish, shade ring loose, hard-to-see chip on interior rim of shade)..... **143**

Ceramic base, "stein" lamp, cylindrical base w/applied handle, round milk glass shade, horse head decoration, drop-in brass font flashed black w/copper highlights, Hornet burner, Handel Ware, 11" h., Book II, No. 444 .... **2,310**

Amber, pedestal base w/flaring tulip-form shade w/Stars & Bars embossed design, clear chimney, Nutmeg burner, L.G. Wright Glass Company, 8" h., No. 482 .... **135**

Amberina, pedestal base w/flaring tulip-form shade w/Stars & Bars embossed design, clear chimney, Nutmeg burner, L.G. Wright Glass Company, 8" h., No. 482 .... **155**

White bisque, figural Skeleton bust lamp, blue & orchid trim, green glass eyes, foreign burner, possibly German, No. 490 ..... **4,400**

Clear, w/purplish opal swirl, Nutmeg burner, 6 1/2" h., No. 512.. **760**

Greenish gold, Tiffany lamp, twist design base w/flaring foot & cupped top, matching chimney, flaring ruffled shade marked

"The Twilight," Nutmeg burner, base & shade signed "L.C.T.," 12 3/4" h., No. 586 .... **2,750**

Red satin, Artichoke patt., base only w/burner & chimney, 3 1/4" h., Book I, Fig. III **2,200**

Blue satin, Artichoke patt., Nutmeg burner, 8" h., Book I, Figure III..................................... **935**

Milk glass, Artichoke patt., w/green & yellow paint, Nutmeg burner, 8" h., Book I, Figure III... **275**

Kerosene Lamps & Related Lighting

Kerosene lamps were used from about 1860 until replaced by electric lighting when it became available. In cities and towns this was generally from about 1900 until 1920. Rural electrification occurred in the 1930s or later.

Today, kerosene lamps are sought after for their appearance and function. Some owners light them occasionally, while a few enjoy them every night. Certainly experimenting with the lamps can add another dimension to collecting. Try placing lamps strategically—not just to illuminate a room but to create dramatic shadows.

If a hanging lamp is the only source of illumination in a room, patterns of light and shadow and perhaps colors will be splayed out on the ceilings and walls. The flickering of an open flame will create shadows in motion which can give a favorite piece of folk art or furnishings, such as a clock or collectible, a different nighttime look. Natural wood finishes which can look flat under incandescent light will glow with a warm sheen to create the mood of a century ago. Most examples shown here are ones that would have been relatively inexpensive when they were made and are compatible with country furnishings. There was tremendous competition and production in the kerosene lamp business. This led to the creation of an astounding variety of lamps and accessories. Because electric lighting was not perfect, kerosene lamps were preserved for emergencies. Thus Americans are blessed with a good supply and an appreciation that will ensure a continuing demand.

—Catherine Thuro

Photographs by Catherine M.V. Thuro.

Note: Lamps do not include burner & chimney, unless otherwise noted. Pricing information provided by Dennis Hearn and Antique Trader Price Guide editors.

Evaluating Early Lighting: Here are some important factors to consider when evaluating early glass lamps. First, look for mold marks. Three mold marks indicate production before 1880. Next, check the metal collar of the lamp: a grey petrified-looking cement is a good indication of age. Then check the bottom of the base - it should show dull, uneven wear. Finally, any markings, such as patent dates, can provide a good indication of age and add to the value.

Collectors should also take note of lamp patterns currently being reproduced. These include: Sweetheart, Bullseye Fine Detail, Princess Feather, Daisy, Shield & Star, Prince Edward, Coolidge Drape and Heart & Star.

Finally, remember that prices vary greatly depending on geographic region and marketplace. Expect to pay less at flea markets and auctions and more in repu-

table shops and shows. With the advent of the Internet and auction sites, prices can vary greatly. Excellent buys can be found when posted by inexperienced sellers but be sure to ask questions before bidding. Expect to pay a premium from reputable and experienced sellers as they attract more buyers and will guarantee the quality and authenticity of pieces they sell. - Dennis Hearn.

Pre-Kerosene Lamps

Various Pre-Kerosene Lamps

Hand lamp, pressed waffle design, flared font w/applied handle, burning fluid burner, ca. 1850 (ILLUS. right) **$300-325**
Table lamp, free-blown squatty round font above a flared columnar standard, w/whale oil burner, ca. 1850 (ILLUS. left) .... **250 -275**
Table lamp, pressed Star-and-Punty patt., slightly flared font w/smooth domed top, w/burning fluid burner, ca. 1850 (ILLUS. center) **325-350**

Kerosene Lamps

Hand lamp, blue opalescent blown glass, Sheldon Swirl patt., footed **550-650**
Hand lamp, blue blown glass, Whirlpool patt., footed **250-300**
Hand lamp, clear blown glass, Bull's-eye patt. **125-150**

Polka Dot Pattern Kerosene Hand Lamp

Hand lamp, opalescent blown Polka Dot patt. w/cranberry or ruby dots, clear pressed handle & round patterned base, unusual crimped chimney (ILLUS.) .... **900 and up**

Various Quartered Block Table Lamps

Hand lamp, flat base, clear pressed glass, Quartered Block patt., w/handle, flat bottom, kerosene slip or prong burner & "pie crust" chimney, ca. 1890 (ILLUS. center) **125-150**
Hand lamp, footed, clear pressed glass, Quartered Block patt., one-piece, kerosene slip or prong burner & "pie crust" chimney, ca. 1880s (ILLUS. right) **125-175**

Ribbed Pattern Kerosene Lamps

Hand lamp, clear blown glass rounded ribbed font tapering into flared foot, ca. 1860s (ILLUS. center front with other ribbed lamps) **100-125**
Hand lamp, clear blown glass rounded ribbed font w/applied handle, ca. 1860s (ILLUS. right front with other ribbed lamps) **150-175**
Hand lamp, clear blown glass rounded, ribbed font w/applied handle, ca.1860s (ILLUS. left front with other ribbed lamps) **100-125**

Atterbury & Co. Kerosene Hand Lamp

Hand lamp, footed, clear blown glass ribbed Atterbury Filley patt. font w/patent-dated pressed handle & base, ca. late 1860s-1870s (ILLUS.) **75-100**

Adams & Co. Kerosene Hand Lamp

Hand lamp, footed, pressed opaque white glass, flared foot below tapered font w/drip-trough & clear shoulder, Collins burner & milk glass Sun chimney, rare combination, Adams & Company, 1870s (ILLUS.) **1,200-1,500**

Kerosene Lamps

Hand lamp, tin & glass, painted tin w/handle & removable glass font, w/Columbia burner & chimney combination, font & holder marked "Bradley's Security Factory Lamp" (ILLUS. left, front) **250-300**

Adjustable Hanging Kerosene Lamp

Hanging lamp, elaborate cast-iron adjustable arms, delicate open design & original finish, the arms support fonts w/a frosted Star design & Vienna shades, ca. 1870s-80s (ILLUS.) **1,500-2,000**

Mechanical lamp, Wanzer Mechanical lamp, metal base w/forced draft for operation even without a chimney, complete w/key, combination 5" d. shade holder & opalescent Hobnail shade (ILLUS. far right with kerosene lamps), lamp base only **550-650**

Mechanical lamp shade, 5" d. opalescent Hobnail patt. (ILLUS. with lamp) .... **150 and up**

Mechanical lamp shade holder, for Wanzer Mechanical lamp, 5" d. (ILLUS. with lamp) **50**

Kerosene Parlor Lamp

Parlor lamp, milk glass, low rounded shade tapering to slightly flaring rim above squatty pear-shaped base, both decorated w/raised & painted flowers, ca. 1880s-1890s (ILLUS.) .... **325 and up**

Parlor Vase Lamp

Parlor vase lamp, white glass ball shade w/original h.p. roses & leaves, matching red-painted vase holder & gold-plated metal parts (ILLUS.) .... **375 and up**

Student Lamp

Student lamp, all-original Leader student lamp w/rectangular burner & chimney & milk glass Vienna shade, nickel-plated brass, ca. 1880 (ILLUS.)................... **750 and up**

Student lamp, brass & glass, Manhattan Brass Co., original nickel-plate base & cased green glass shade (ILLUS. center back w/kerosene lamps)................... **450 and up**

Corn Table Lamp

Table lamp, clear blown, Corn design patented by Daniel Ashworth, base marked w/1873 patent date, La Belle Glass Company, Bridgeport, Ohio (ILLUS.)....... **250 and up**

Table lamp, clear blown glass, Corn-in-Shield patt., Oval Band patt. base ... **250 and up**

Eyewinker Table Lamp

Table lamp, clear blown glass, Eyewinker patt. round font w/Bubble base, Dalzell,

Gilmore & Leighton Company (ILLUS.)..................................... **125-150**

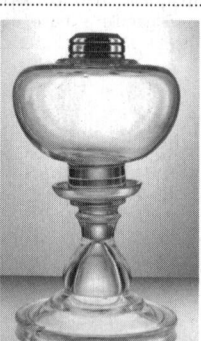

Ewing Patent Table Lamp

Table lamp, clear blown glass font above Ewing patent drip catcher above clear glass plain stem on round base, ca. 1870s (ILLUS.).. **150-225**

Gaiety Table Lamp

Table lamp, clear blown glass, Gaiety patt., ribbed font decorated w/opalescent feathered design, rounded pressed base, slip burner w/special crimped top (ILLUS.)... **425-500**

Table lamp, clear blown glass, McKee Tulip patt.. **300 and up**

Blown Glass Table Lamps

Table lamp, clear blown glass, plain design, rounded font w/brass stem & square marble base, ca. 1860s (ILLUS. of three w/chimneys & burners), lamp only, each **90-150**

Table lamp, clear blown glass, rounded ribbed font, columnar standard w/flared ribbed base, ca. 1850s-1870s (ILLUS. back left with other ribbed lamps) **125-150**

Table lamp, clear blown glass, rounded ribbed font on a free-form, knopped round base, ca. 1860s-1880s (ILLUS. back right with other ribbed lamps) **125-175**

Table lamp, clear blown glass, Wild Rose patt., Riverside patented collar **250-300**

Bull's-eye & Fleur-de-Lis Table Lamp

Table lamp, clear pressed glass, Bull's-eye & Fleur-de-lis patt. font tapering to a paneled stem & scalloped base, 1860s (ILLUS.) **150-200**

Table lamp, clear pressed glass, Chadwick patt., w/milk glass base **225-325**

Daisy & Button Table Lamp

Table lamp, clear pressed glass, Daisy and Button patt. font, plain shoulder & pressed six-sided base, ca. 1890s (ILLUS.) **125-150**

Table lamp, clear pressed glass, Moon and Crescents patt. **350-450**

Table lamp, clear pressed glass, Quartered Block patt., w/handle, footed, kerosene burner & "pie crust" chimney, ca. 1880s (ILLUS. left with other Quartered Block lamps) **150-200**

Sawtooth Table Lamp

Table lamp, clear pressed glass, Sawtooth patt., large round font, brass connector & pressed opaque white glass Baroque base, lip burner & tall chimney (ILLUS.) **300-350**

Veronica Table lamp

Table lamp, clear pressed glass, Veronica patt. (on inside of font), rounded font tapering to brass stem on a marble base, Hobbs, Brockunier & Company, ca. mid-1860s - mid-1870s (ILLUS.) **150-200**

Snowflake Pattern Table Lamp

Table lamp, cranberry or ruby blown opalescent glass Snowflake patt., square font, metal screw connector w/glass sleeve, clear pressed base, Hobbs, Brockunier & Company (ILLUS.) ..... **750 and up**

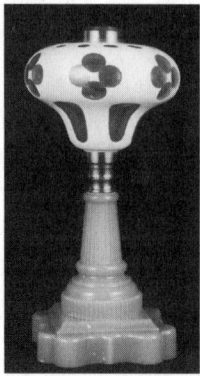

Cut-overlay Table Lamp

Table lamp, cut-overlay, inverted pear font in white cut to green, tapering brass connector, green alabaster Baroque base (ILLUS.) .... **1,800 and up**

Figural Table Lamp

Table lamp, figural, angular frosted & clear glass font w/star- and cross-like designs, above spelter fisherwoman holding spear w/a basket full of fish at her feet, all on tiered square metal base, Bradley & Hubbard Mfg., ca. 1888 (ILLUS.) **250-300**

Table lamp, figural, clear blown glass font & spelter figure of Mary & her lamb **125-225**

Empress Eugenie Table Lamp

Table lamp, figural, clear frosted glass font w/Greek Key design above spelter bust of Empress Eugenie (wife of Napoleon III), soapstone base, ca. 1870s (ILLUS.) **175-225**

Table lamp, green blown glass, Vera patt. **175-225**

Table lamp, marigold Carnival blown glass, Zipper Loop patt. **750-850**

Table lamp, Ripley Wedding Lamp, two matching blue Ripley patented fonts flanking toothpick holder on an alabaster glass base .... **1,800 and up**

Other Kerosene Lamps

Banquet & Gone-with-the Wind Lamps

Banquet lamp, a domed open-topped blue opaque shade w/a brass crown resting in a deep pierced brass ring suspending prisms & raised on a burner above an Acanthus Leaf patt. onion-form font on a brass ring connection to a tall baluster-form Acanthus Leaf patt. standard set on a domed pierced brass footed base, w/chimney, Consolidated Lamp & Glass Co., late 19th c., overall 26 1/2" h. (ILLUS. center) **495**

Consolidated Pink Banquet Lamp

Banquet lamp, a large cased pink glass ball shade above a squared squatty cased pink font w/molded scrolls above a connector ring & a tall slender baluster-shaped matching pedestal on a domed pierced brass footed base, Consolidated Lamp & Glass Company, ca. 1900, overall 25" h. (ILLUS.) **606**

Porcelain & Glass Banquet Lamps

Banquet lamp, a white milk glass ball shade decorated in blue w/a Dutch Delft-style landscape, raised on a brass foreign burner above the porcelain base w/an onion-form font ornately molded w/scrolls & applied flowers above a slender matching scroll-molded shaft & domed scroll-molded three-footed base, base marked "Germany - RW - Rudolstadt," early 20th c., overall 21 1/2" h. (ILLUS. left).. **358**

Large & Small Banquet Lamps

Banquet lamp, cast- and wrought-iron tripod base w/scrolled trim & pierced knop supporting a bulbous brass font & burner, a ball-shaped pink cased glass shade, Plumb & Atwood Victor burner, overall 18 1/2" h. (ILLUS. right) **220**

Banquet lamp, composite-type, black round stepped ceramic foot w/a brass domed top & slender brass standard supporting a squatty rounded clear glass font cut w/thumbprints, brass Hink's Duplex Patent burner, rounded open-topped clear glass shade cut w/strawberry diamonds & fans, clear chimney, base stamped "Veritas Lamp Works," late 19th c., overall 22 1/2" h. **209**

Banquet lamp, pressed clear glass, a brass Duplex double wick burner on the half-round font w/an overall diamond design above a tall slender diamond design standard w/brass screw connectors above the deep round diamond design

foot, late 19th-early 20th c., overall 24" h. (ILLUS. right with Delft-style banquet lamp)... **413**

Fostoria Colony Pattern Banquet Lamp

Banquet lamp, pressed clear glass, Fostoria's Cascade or Colony patt., the domed swirled ribbed foot supporting a tall swirled rib baluster-form standard below a ball connector & a half-round swirled font, two-section w/screw connectors, Stern Bro's New York double wick burner, overall 20 1/2" h. (ILLUS.)......................... **550**

Large Group of Cut-overlay Lamps

Cut-overlay table lamp, inverted bell-form font, cobalt blue cut to white cut to clear, cut w/slash, punty & oval designs, a brass connector to the tall waisted matching cut standard on a square stepped marble base w/gilt-metal trim, minor imperfections, possibly Boston & Sandwich Glass Co., ca. 1860-80, 16 1/4" h. (ILLUS. front row, far left with the large group) **9,775**

Cut-overlay table lamp, inverted bell-form glass font, cobalt blue cut to white cut to clear, cut w/oval designs, on a brass connector to the tall slender waisted matching cut standard on a stepped marble base w/gilt-metal trim, minor imperfections, possibly Boston & Sandwich Glass Co., ca. 1860-80, 16 1/2" h. (ILLUS. front row, far right with the large group) **12,650**

Cut-overlay table lamp, inverted bell-form glass font, transparent teal blue cut to clear, cut w/slashes, punties & ovals, on a brass connector raised on a similar cut overlay tall waisted standard on a square stepped marble base w/gilt-metal trim, minor wear, possibly New England, ca. 1860-80, 16 1/8" h. (ILLUS. back row, far left with large group) **4,025**

Cut-overlay table lamp, inverted pear-shaped font, transparent amethyst glass cut to clear w/quatrefoil, oval & punty designs, raised on a flared fluted columnar brass standard & square stepped marble base w/brass trim, minor wear, possibly Boston & Sandwich Glass Co., ca. 1860-80, 10 5/8" h. (ILLUS. center, front row with large grouping) **2,530**

Cut-overlay table lamp, inverted pear-shaped glass font, cranberry cut to white cut to clear, cut ovals & punty designs, raised on a flared fluted brass columnar standard & a square stepped marble base w/brass trim, imperfections, possibly New England, ca. 1860-80, 13 1/2" h. (ILLUS. back row, second from right with large group) **1,955**

Cut-overlay table lamp, inverted pear-shaped glass font, cranberry cut to white cut to clear, w/quatrefoils, stars & ovals, raised on a flared brass fluted columnar standard on a square stepped marble base w/brass trim, very minor wear, possibly Boston & Sandwich Glass Co., ca. 1860-80, 12 1/2" h. (ILLUS. back row, second from left with large group) **2,070**

Cut-overlay table lamp, squatty inverted pear-shaped glass font, white cut to transparent green w/gilt outlines on font, cut w/punty & oval designs, on a brass connector w/suspended leaves over a similar tall waisted overlay standard on a square stepped marble base w/gilt-metal trim, minor imperfections, possibly Boston & Sandwich Glass Co., ca. 1860-80, 16 1/4" h. (ILLUS. back row, far right with large group) **6,900**

Cut-overlay table lamps, tall ovoid font, cobalt blue cut to white cut to clear, cut w/slash, punty & oval designs, raised on a flared fluted columnar brass standard & square stepped marble base w/brass trim, minor imperfections, possibly Boston & Sandwich Glass Co., ca. 1860-80, 11 3/4" h., pr. (ILLUS. front row, second from left & right with the large group) **4,025**

Finger lamp, pressed glass cranberry opalescent Coin Spot patt., footed bulbous font w/clear applied side handle, w/old burner, ca. 1900, 3 1/2" h............................... **715**

Finger lamp, pressed glass Emma patt., squatty bell-shaped font in a clear opalescent Coin Spot patt., applied clear side handle, w/burner, ca. 1900, 3 1/4" h............. **275**

Finger lamp, pressed squared blue opalescent Hobb's Snowflake patt. font, applied blue loop handle, w/burner & ribbed edge chimney, Hobbs, Brockunier & Co., ca. 1890, font 3" h., overall 9 1/2" h. **770**

Finger lamp, pressed squared cranberry opalescent Hobb's Snowflake patt. font, applied clear loop handle, w/burner & ribbed edge chimney, Hobbs, Brockunier & Co., ca. 1890, font 3" h., overall 9 1/2" h. **990**

Gone-with-the-Wind table lamp, a large ball shade molded in relief w/a band of large elephant heads w/the trunks hanging down & painted in shades of dark brown & mottled yellow & orange, a wide scrolled metal collar to the waisted bulbous font molded w/matching elephant heads & similar paint, on a domed

pierced cast-metal footed base, Bradley & Hubbard, ca. 1900, 26" h. **4,200**

Two Gone-with-the-Wind Floral Lamps

Gone-with-the-Wind table lamp, a large milk glass ball shade decorated w/oversized wild rose blossoms in pink & red w/green leaves against a shaded pink & red background, above a scalloped flaring brass collar & a squatty bulbous matching font, raised on a pierced brass domed & footed base, no chimney, electrified, ca. 1900, 22" h. (ILLUS. left)........ **413**

Gone-with-the-Wind table lamp, a large milk white ball shade decorated w/large pink & white rose blossoms & green leaves against a shaded dark to light green ground, above a wide scalloped brass collar & bulbous tapering ovoid matching font, raised on a pierced & domed cast-brass footed base, ca. 1900, overall 23" h. (ILLUS. right with two other Gone-with-the-Wind lamps, below) **231**

Gone-with-the-Wind table lamp, a milk glass ball globe shade painted w/a scene of dogs playing in a garden w/tall green trees & blue skies w/white clouds in the background, a brass burner & collar on the oblong milk glass lower globe decorated w/a full color lakeside landscape, on a domed brass base w/thick curved corner feet, both shade & base signed "Baccarat," France, late 19th c., 18" h. **1,848**

Three Gone-with-the-Wind Lamps

Gone-with-the-Wind table lamp, a milk white ball shade decorated w/large pink & red roses w/green leaves against a shaded pink to white ground, above a wide brass collar w/burner above the bulbous matching font, raised on a pierced brass domed & footed base, ca. 1900, overall 23" h. (ILLUS. left) **248**

Gone-with-the-Wind table lamp, a milk white globe shade w/molded poppy blossoms & leaves alternating w/smooth panels hand-decorated w/stylized four-petal blossoms, overall purple & pink background shading, above a wide scrolled brass collar above the matching tapering ovoid glass font on a pierced, high four-footed metal base, electrified, no chimney, ca. 1900, overall 22" h. (ILLUS. right with wild rose lamp).............................. **413**

Gone-with-the-Wind table lamp, Artichoke patt., mold-blown frosted clear ball shade on a shade ring w/burner above the matching inverted pear-shaped font on a squared pierced metal base w/chimney, overall 16" h. (ILLUS. left with banquet lamp).. **264**

Gone-with-the-Wind kerosene table lamp, Artichoke patt., mold-blown red satin ball shade on a shade ring w/burner above the matching inverted pear-shaped font on a squared pierced metal base w/chimney, overall 16" h. (ILLUS. right with banquet lamp) **495**

Gone-with-the-Wind table lamp, large frosted clear molded Grape patt. ball shade above a wide scrolled brass collar above the matching bulbous, tapering font, on a scroll-pierced domed & footed brass foot, w/chimney, overall 24" h. (ILLUS. center with rose-decorated lamps) **468**

Cranberry Opalescent Parlor Lamp

Hanging parlor lamp, a domed open-topped cranberry opalescent Hobnail patt. shade, fitted in a pierced brass shade ring hung w/prisms above a large bulbous brass font w/a scrolled brass frame, suspended on chains above an upper ring w/prisms & the ceiling plate w/smoke bell (ILLUS.)................................ **3,250**

Two Kerosene Hanging Parlor Lamps

Hanging parlor lamp, domical 13 1/2" d. blue opaque glass shade in a wide brass shade ring & a brass crown, above a bulbous embossed brass font & scrolling brass frame, suspended by four chains joined to an upper ring suspended w/glass prisms, further prisms around shade ring, ca. 1890 (ILLUS. left).................. **825**

Hanging parlor lamp, domical 13 1/2" d. deep cranberry Hobnail patt. shade, in a stamped brass shade ring & w/a brass crown above a bulbous brass font w/scrolling brass frame, suspended on chains below an upper ring & ceiling plate, clear prisms around the shade ring, w/brass smoke bell, ca. 1890 (ILLUS. right with blue opaque shaded lamp) **770**

Organ floor lamp, a milk glass ball shade painted w/large deep red & white blossoms & green leaves against a shaded dark green to yellow ground, on a burner above an ornately pierced bulbous brass font holder raised on a slender brass standard which continues down through the center of three rounded brass shelves flanked by four slender legs ending in pad feet, ca. 1890, overall 64" h. **575**

Table lamp, blown glass Hobb's Snowflake patt., the squatty squared cranberry opalescent font raised on a clear glass connector sleeve on the clear stem w/round scalloped foot, Hobbs, Brockunier & Co., ca. 1890, crack in connector sleeve, w/burner, 9" h... **523**

Table lamp, blown glass squared cranberry opalescent Seaweed patt. font, raised on a clear ringed glass pedestal on a square foot, w/old burner, ca. 1890, 9" h............... **1,430**

Table lamp, clear blown glass, plain design, w/appropriate burner & chimney combinations, add to the lamp value **250-375**

Table lamp, clear opalescent glass squatty bulbous Coin Spot font raised on a clear glass pressed Inverted Thumbprint & Fan pedestal base, 8 1/2" h.................................... **220**

Table lamp, pressed blue glass "match holder" base lamp, squatty bulbous ringed font raised on a tapering cylindrical standard above the squared foot w/a pair of shallow indentations on the top to hold matches, ca. 1890, 7 1/2" h. (minor roughness on base corners, minor flakes under base) **275**

Coolidge Drape & Eason Lamps

Table lamp, pressed glass Coolidge Drape patt., scalloped pedestal base, cobalt blue, flat chip & flake under base, ca. 1900, 9" h. (ILLUS. left) **198**

Table lamp, pressed glass Eason patt., a bulbous cranberry opalescent Coin Dot patt. font above a clear ribbed standard & ribbed domed foot, w/burner, 9 1/2" h. (ILLUS. right with Coolidge Drape lamp) **385**

Two Riverside Glass Table Lamps

Table lamp, pressed glass Fern patt., the squatty bulbous green patterned font w/shell-form leaf clusters raised on a tall slender clear glass pedestal w/round foot w/embossed beading underneath, Riverside Glass Co., ca. 1900, 10" h. (ILLUS. left) **138**

Table lamp, pressed glass Panel patt., a short wide cylindrical green font raised on a tall slender clear glass pedestal w/round foot, Riverside Glass Co., ca. 1900, 7 1/2" h. (ILLUS. right with Fern lamp) **138**

Victorian Kerosene Wall Sconces

Wall sconces, a cast-brass Neoclassical design w/an ornate cartouche-form wall plate supporting a scrolled griffin-mounted swing arm w/a tall oblong font supporting a burner & ring fitted w/a white opalescent Hobnail patt., flaring & ruffled crown-style shade, overall 15" h., pr. (ILLUS.) **385**

Lamps, Miscellaneous

Argand lamp, brass, two-arm model, the acanthus leaf finial above a fluted reservoir flanked by foliate & scroll buttresses, overhanging prisms above a fluted stem flanked by two arms terminating in electrified candle sockets w/added plaques w/"B. Gardiner - N. York," & frosted & etched tulip-shaped shades, over outscrolling leaves w/hanging pendent

prisms above a foliate & turned shaft on a square metal base, first half 19th c., 24 1/2" h. **2,115**

Fluid burning lamp, blown glass, "sparking" lamp, a waisted cylindrical font w/applied loop handle, cobalt blue, w/original brass collar & camphene burner, mid-19th c., 3 3/4" h. **1,760**

Fluid burning lamp, blown & pressed glass, a cobalt blue blown font w/sixteen ribs swirled to the right, a rolled mouth & angled wide shoulder above tapering cylindrical sides, attached w/a wafer to a lacy glass cup plate foot No. R-54, Boston & Sandwich Glass Co., ca. 1828-35, slight refracting half-inch line on rim of font, 7" h. **11,000**

Fluid burning lamp, blown & pressed glass, a spherical blown font attached w/wafers to a tall pressed square scrolled standard & paw foot lion head base, possibly Boston & Sandwich Glass Co., late 1820s, 8 1/4" h. **1,100**

Bennington Flint Enamel Lamp

Fluid burning lamp, flint enamel lamp, w/square stepped base, paneled baluster stem in olive, replaced copper front w/prism ring & prisms, Bennington, 14 1/2" h. (ILLUS. of base & font) **2,530**

Large Group of Glass Fluid Lamps

Fluid burning lamp, pressed flint glass, Acanthus Leaf patt. font, blue leaf-molded font on a clambroth vasiform standard w/four leaves above the tiered beaded square base, sand finish, New England Glass Co. or Boston & Sandwich Glass Co., mid-19th c., imperfections, 10 1/4" h. (ILLUS. far right with large group) **1,150**

Fluid burning lamp, pressed flint glass, Bigler patt. font on an octagonal concave paneled standard & square base, deep amethyst, possibly Boston & Sandwich

Glass Co., ca. 1840-60, imperfections, w/whale oil burner, 9 1/2" h. (ILLUS. fourth from left with large group) **2,185**

Fluid burning lamp, pressed flint glass, Bigler patt. font on an octagonal concave paneled standard & square base, amethyst, possibly Boston & Sandwich Glass Co., ca. 1840-60, minor imperfections, 9 1/2" h. (ILLUS. fifth from left with large group) **2,185**

Fluid burning lamp, pressed flint glass, Three-Printie Block patt. font, on a knop above a paneled hexagonal base, canary yellow, probably New England, mid-19th c., minor imperfections, 8" h. (ILLUS. third from left with Acanthus Leaf lamp group) **374**

Fluid burning lamp, pressed flint glass, Waisted Loop patt. font, on a pressed square monument base, canary yellow, possibly Boston & Sandwich Glass Co., ca. 1840-60, minor chips on base, 10 1/2" h. (ILLUS. fifth from right with Acanthus Leaf lamp group) **2,990**

Fluid burning lamps, pressed flint glass, Bigler patt. font on an octagonal concave paneled standard & square base, sapphire blue, possibly Boston & Sandwich Glass Co., ca. 1840-60, 9 3/4" h., pr. (ILLUS. far left with Acanthus Leaf lamp group) **4,600**

Fluid burning lamps, pressed flint glass, Loop patt. font, on a hexagonal standard & tiered hexagonal base, canary yellow, probably New England, mid-19th c., minor imperfections, 8" & 8 1/2" h., 2 pcs. (ILLUS. second from right with Acanthus Leaf lamp group) **805**

Fluid burning lamps, pressed flint glass, tapering Loop patt. font raised on a waisted paneled standard on a round foot, dark sapphire blue, original pewter collar & camphene burner, 9" h., pr. (usual mold roughness, small open bubble on base of one) **7,150**

Electric Lamps & Lighting

Handel Lamps

The Handel Company of Meriden, Connecticut (1885-1936) began as a glass and lamp shade decorating company. Following World War I it became a major producer of decorative lamps that have become very collectible today.

Handel Boudoir Lamp

Boudoir lamp, 7" d. reverse-painted floral shade in pinks & greens, on original green-painted base, shade & base signed, interior rim chip, 14" h. (ILLUS.).... **2,300**

Boudoir lamp, 6" w. bell-shaped bent-glass six-paneled shade w/a flat drop rim, the upper panels in striated yellow & deep red slag glass overlaid w/filigree of palm trees, the pale yellow border panels w/a looping metal filigree, on a slender paneled Handel base w/a hexagonal foot **2,464**

Boudoir lamp, 7" d. domical reverse- and obverse-painted shade, decorated w/a winter landscape of a group of four tall bare trees above snowy ground w/a cluster of shrubbery beyond, against a pale yellow sky, in shades of dark brown, black & white, on a signed Handel tree trunk base, shade signed "Handel 5624 R.D." **3,640**

Boudoir lamp, 7" d. domical reverse-painted shade decorated w/a snowy winter landscape w/a cluster of leafless trees in the foreground & further trees in the distance, in brown, rust, green, white & pale orange, raised on a signed tree trunk base, shade ring signed "Handel 5624" **3,360**

Handel Desk Lamp

Desk lamp, 6" d. six-sided fluted slag glass shade w/metal overlaid rectilinear design & interlocking circles at border, adjustable bronzed metal base, original patina, lightly cleaned shade, base & shade signed, very good condition, 14" h. (ILLUS.) **2,300**

Handel Desk Lamp with Etched Shade

Desk lamp, 12" w. etched glass shade, shade signed & numbered, bronzed metal base w/original patina, shade cracked w/minor chip, 16 1/2" h. (ILLUS.) **575**

Floor lamp, 10" d. domical reverse-painted shade decorated in the "Oriental Pheasant" patt., a long-tailed exotic bird flying among dark purple foliage & large bluish purple & yellow blossoms all against a deep reddish orange ground, shade suspended from a high looped harp on a tall slender standard w/three outswept feet, shade signed "Handel 7009".................... **12,320**

Handel Hydrangea Floor Lamp Shade

Floor lamp, 16" d. domical reverse-painted shade in the "Hydrangea" patt., decorated w/large clusters of deep rose, pink & lavender blossoms among light yellow & brown leaves against a mottled yellow ground, shade signed "Handel 6739," on a tall slender Handel standard on a tripod base w/cabriole legs ending in scroll feet (ILLUS. of the shade)................................ **17,920**

Floor lamp, 22" w. eight-panel bent caramel slag glass shade, each tapering panel overlaid w/a metal graduated block-style filigree above a dark gold slag border band w/further lattice filigree & small painted green diamonds, signed, on a tall bronzed metal standard w/a domed four-buttress foot... **6,720**

Handel Spherical Peacock Hall Light

Hall light, 10" d. spherical painted shade decorated w/a colorful stylized design of a peacock perched on brown branches w/red & yellow blossoms & green leaves, against a textured tan ground, a pierced

scrolled hanger & bell-shaped cap at the top & metal drop & tassel at the bottom, shade signed "Handel 7257" (ILLUS.) **6,664**

Table lamp, 12" d. domical mushroom-shaped painted shade w/the upper portion in pale pink above a wide scalloped border band in light green, the section separated w/delicate white enameled leafy scrolls w/small pink blossoms w/jeweled centers, raised on a bronzed metal slender base w/four pierced & scroll-cast openings above the flaring, round scroll-cast foot, shade signed "Handel Co. 2583" **1,288**

Table lamp, 15" d. domical reverse-painted shade, decorated w/a winter landscape, a pair of tall bare trees beside a curving lakeside bank covered in snow, a thick forest of trees in the background under the pale yellow sky w/small tan clouds, on bronzed metal slender ribbed Handel base w/a round ribbed foot, shade signed "Handel 5624 R.C." **4,032**

Table lamp, 15" d. domical reverse-painted shade, "Tropical Sunset" patt., a continuous scene of a tropical inlet framed by grasses & tall palm trees w/a sailboat in the distance under a full moon, in shades of dark & lighter brown, dark blue, peach w/a pale cream moon & stars, signed "Handel 6971A," on a slender ribbed bronzed metal standard w/a flaring ribbed round foot **5,600**

Table lamp, 16" d. domical reverse-painted shade, decorated w/a rare design of large leafy vines in shades of orange, brown & blue w/clusters of white & pale yellow blossoms against a light green ground, shade signed "Handel 7131," on a slender Handel bronzed-metal ring-turned base **7,840**

Table lamp, 18" d. domical reverse-painted shade decorated w/large yellow daffodils & long green leaves & stems against a background w/clusters of black leaves & small reddish orange blossoms divided by thin yellow striping & a pale yellow ground, heavy baluster-form Handel base w/a stepped, round foot, shade signed "Handel P.R. #7122" **16,800**

Table lamp, 18" d. domical reverse-painted shade in the "Exotic Bird" patt., large spread-winged deep reddish orange & purple exotic birds perched among golden flowering leafy branches, all against a black ground, shade signed "Handel 7026 Bedigie," on a tall three-legged bronzed metal base w/a short upper urn suspending amber glass teardrops & ending in a round foot w/a lappet rim band.. **22,400**

Table lamp, 18" d. domical reverse-painted shade in the "Floral & Exotic Bird" patt., decorated w/a wide border band of flying dark blue & red exotic birds among clusters of red & pink blossoms & green & yellow leaves all on a black ground, the upper side w/radiating bands of pale yellow separated by narrow black stripes, raised on a gilt-metal slender ring-turned

base, shade signed "Handel 6930 Bed-
igie" **6,720**

Table lamp, 18" d. domical reverse-painted
shade, "Love Bird" patt., decorated w/a
repeating design of a love bird perched
among large pink, red & yellow blossom
clusters w/reddish leaves against a background of tall slender black leafy trees
w/a dark violet-colored background,
shade signed "Handel 7127 S.," on a
large bronzed metal ribbed urn-form
base w/square foot, signed w/felt tab **42,000**

Handel Slag Glass Lamp with Overlay

Table lamp, 19 1/2" d. domical paneled
leaded glass shade, composed of geometric tile & grapevine border metal filigree overlay over eight striated green
slag glass bent panels & a drop apron,
marked w/Handel tag, on a two-socket
ribbed baluster-form bronze metal
tagged Handel base, one cracked apron
panel, joinery, 22 3/4" h. (ILLUS.) **1,955**

Table lamp, 20" d. wide conical leaded
glass shade w/a drop apron, composed
of radiating small squares of green slag
glass, raised on a very tall, slender
bronzed metal signed Handel base w/a
round foot **6,440**

Table lamp, 20" w. domical six-panel shade
w/tapering panels of caramel slag glass
overlaid w/metal filigree in a design of
leafy rose vines highlighted in pale yellow
& green paint, on a slender bronzed metal baluster-form signed Handel base,
shade signed on ring **5,040**

Pairpoint Lamps

"Puffy" Rose Boudoir Lamp

Boudoir lamp, 5" d. "Puffy" bonnet-shaped
reverse-painted shade in the Four Color
Rose patt., four large rose blossoms in
pink, red, yellow & accented white w/dark
green leaves around the border, on a
slender signed Pairpoint bronzed metal
base w/lily pad leaves around the bottom .. **8,960**

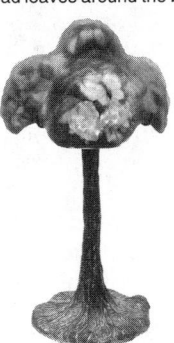

Rare Lilac Puffy

Boudoir lamp, 5" d. "Puffy" domed & lobed
reverse-painted Lilac patt. shade, each
lobe w/a cluster of lilac blossoms in purple, deep rose or pink, some w/a yellow
butterfly, against a ground of mottled
dark green & yellow leaves, on a Pair-
point tree trunk base **24,080**

Boudoir lamp, 5" d. "Puffy" pointed domical
reverse-painted Pansy patt. shade, the
overall large blossoms painted in yellow
& red & deep red on a dark green leafy
ground, raised on a signed base w/a
shade ring supported on a slender baluster-form standard above the domed
round foot, rare **16,800**

Table lamp, 8" d. "Puffy" reverse-painted
Lilac patt. shade, deep purple & deep red
clusters of blossoms w/colorful butterflies
against a ground of mottled green & yellow leaves, on a gilt-bronze Pairpoint tree
trunk base **39,200**

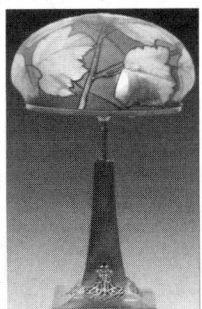

Reverse-painted Pairpoint Lamp

Table lamp, 10" d. domed mushroom-
shaped reverse- and obverse-painted
shade, decorated on the interior & exteri-
or w/overall large yellow, green & white
mottled maple leaves & dark brown
branches against a dark brick red
ground, raised on a ring above the gilt-

metal square tapering standard w/pierced loop reserves near the rectangular foot (ILLUS.) **2,240**

"Puffy" Azalea Lamp

Table lamp, 10" d. "Puffy" reverse-painted Azalea patt. shade, overall large reddish orange & yellow-streaked blossoms & dark green mottled leaves against a black ground, raised on a gilt-metal base w/the shade ring supported by outswept blossom-cast arms issuing from the top of a pyramidal base on small square feet (ILLUS.)... **38,640**

Pairpoint Apple Tree "Puffy"

Table lamp, 12" d. "Puffy" reverse-painted Apple Tree patt. closed-top shade, the deep domical form brightly painted w/large red & yellow apples & green leaves alternating w/large pink & yellow apple blossoms w/large colorful butterflies, raised on a bronzed metal tree trunk signed base, shade signed (ILLUS.) **65,520**

Garden of Allah Lamp

Table lamp, 18" d. reverse-painted "Carlisle" shade decorated in the Garden of Allah patt., a continuous desert landscape w/Arabs on camels by palm trees & the pyramids in the background against an orange sky, on a ribbed baluster-form bronzed metal Pairpoint base w/a squared foot (ILLUS.) **4,480**
Table lamp, 20" d. domical reverse-painted "Berkley" shade, decorated w/an autumnal landscape w/large clusters of leafy trees in wide meadows, in shades of dark & light green, orange, yellow, dark & light grey & blue, on a gilt-metal slender urnform Pairpoint base w/slender loop shoulder handles & a square notched foot (ILLUS.)...................................... **3,640**

Tiffany Lamps
Boudoir lamp, 7" d. sharply conical Favrile glass shade w/knobbed finial, in iridescent white w/stripes of small gold iridescent dots up the sides, raised on a slender signed Tiffany bronze base w/a domed, paneled foot highlighted in each panel w/a band of gold dots, shade signed "L.C.T. Favrile," 14 1/2" h. **3,080**
Chandelier, "Rhododendron," 28" conical open-topped leaded shade w/a border band of large clusters of red & pink blossoms framed by mottled green leaves, on a background of graduated blocks of white to deep red & purple mottled glass, signed.. **53,200**

Tiffany Linenfold Desk Lamp

Desk lamp, "Linenfold," 7" d. paneled shade w/each section composed of an amber linenfold panel below a small horizontal matching panel, supported in an arched harp above a slender standard on a domed paneled round base w/small knob feet, shade signed, base signed "Tiffany Studios - New York - 424" (ILLUS.).. **5,645**
Floor lamp, 10" d. domical damascene swirled green & gold banded shade suspended from a long S-scroll counter-balance arm above the tall slender knopped bronze standard raised on five tall slender outswept legs w/spearpoint flat feet, shade & base signed **11,200**

Floor lamp, "Curtain Border," 25" d. domical leaded glass shade, the upper section w/radiating blocks of mottled yellow glass above a drop border of small arches above a band of narrow deep mottled amber panels, raised on a tall slender Tiffany ribbed bronze standard w/a wide & deep round footed base cast w/ribbed leaf devices, shade & base signed **72,800**

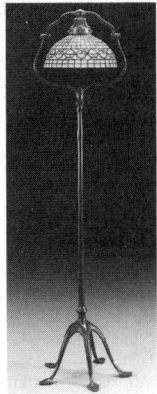

Vine Border Floor Lamp

Floor lamp, "Vine Border," 12" d. leaded glass shade composed of bands of mottled yellow tiles flanking a band of mottled yellow leafy vine, on a bronze harp standard floor base w/five tall legs w/pad feet, base stamped "TIFFANY STUDIOS - NEW YORK - 423 H," shade stamped "TIFFANY STUDIOS - NEW YORK" w/an indistinct number, ca. 1910, 4' 10" h. (ILLUS.) **12,925**

Rare Grueby-Tiffany Table Lamp

Table lamp, "Acorn," a 12" d. domical leaded glass shade w/radiating blocks of striated green & yellow glass & a wide band w/a vine w/yellow stylized acorns, raised on a fitting w/cylindrical font inset into a Grueby pottery base w/a cylindrical neck above a squatty bulbous body, the lower body molded w/wide leaves alternating w/thin stems topped by yellow buds, complete w/four original paper labels on

the base, shade & base signed, overall 16" h. (ILLUS.) **37,375**

Tiffany Autumn Poppy Lamp

Table lamp, "Autumn Poppy," 20" d. domical leaded glass shade composed of large poppy blossoms & buds in shades of crimson red & orange striated, mottled & textured glass, bronze round filigree poppy seed pods scattered among leaves & flowers, raised on a bronze slender reeded Tiffany standard w/a deep rounded foot w/cast ribbed pods raised on scroll feet, base marked "Tiffany Studios Provenance - 363" (ILLUS.)... **81,200**

Table lamp, "Dichroic Dragonfly," 20" d. conical leaded glass shade w/large overlapping dragonflies in rare blue opalescent mottled & striated glass & green eyes & bodies against a ground of dichroic amber to orangish red narrow panels fitted w/large amber "jewels," raised on a gilt "Four Virtues" bronze Tiffany base, shade signed "Tiffany Studios 1495-6," base signed "Tiffany Studios 557" **56,000**

Tiffany Lily Lamp

Table lamp, "Lily," twelve-light, a signed bronze lily pad base issuing a cluster of twelve upright slender stems w/arched tops ending in sockets each fitted w/a signed trumpet-form gold iridescent Tiffany shade (ILLUS.) **21,280**

Pine Needle Table Lamp

Table lamp, "Pine Needle," 12" d. domical bent green slag glass shade w/overall pine needle metal filigree, shade signed, raised on a wide bulbous baluster-form signed Tiffany bronze base (ILLUS.) **12,320**

Tiffany Poppy Lamp

Table lamp, "Poppy," 16" d. conical leaded glass shade, undulating band of large reddish orange poppy blossoms, some w/filigree centers & mixed w/striated purple & green poppy buds all against a striated yellow & orange ground w/a lower band of large curved striated green & blue leaves, a border band w/two narrow golden orange bands centered by a striated blue band, shade signed "Tiffany Studios - New York - 1461," raised on a slender reeded bronze standard w/a wide domed & reeded base on tab feet, base signed "Tiffany Studios - New York - 362 - 9175" (ILLUS.) **72,800**

Table lamp, "Wisteria," 18 1/4" d. leaded glass shade composed of openwork branches at the top center suspending mottled green leaves above long mottled

Rare Tiffany Wisteria Lamp

dark purple blossoms ending in an uneven border, bronze tree trunk base, rounded underside of fitter stamped "7001," top of base stamped "10117 - TIFFANY STUDIOS - NEW YORK - 10117," ca. 1910, 26 3/4" h. (ILLUS.) **270,000**

Lamps, Miscellaneous

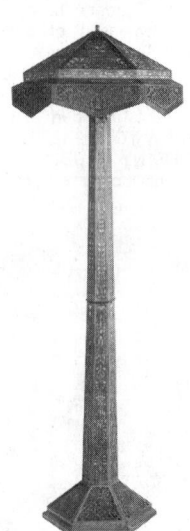

Slag Glass & Filigree Lamp

Art Nouveau floor lamp, slag glass & brass filigree, a 21" w. six-sided pyramidal shade w/a deep apron of pointed panels, overall delicate pierced floral & scroll filigree w/caramel slag inserts in the upper shade & reddish slag panels in the apron, raised on a very tall, slender & slightly tapering matching hexagonal standard w/filigree over slag glass & set on a wide matching pyramidal foot, one cracked glass panel in center section, unsigned, early 20th c., 70" h. (ILLUS.) **3,450**

Stickley Brothers Table Lamp

Arts & Crafts table lamp, hammered copper hexagonal base & shade w/an x design over amber glass, good original patina, unsigned, Stickley Brothers, one replaced pane, three replaced sockets, very good condition, 20" d. x 26" h., (ILLUS.)............................. **4,888**

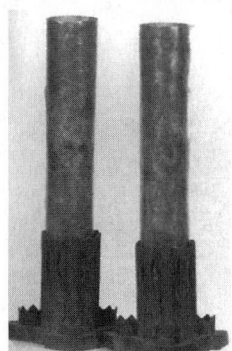

Arts & Crafts Table Lamps

Arts & Crafts table lamps, bronze base w/original patina supporting a mica-inset shade, very good condition, some distress to mica, 12" h., pr. (ILLUS.)................. **575**
Astral-style table lamp, brass, marble & glass, a small square white marble base supports w/tall slender reeded brass standard below a compressed brass font fitted w/an electric socket & shade ring, a frosted clear ball shade w/a Greek Key design, a "Cornelius, Philad."-style emblem tag, the font hung w/cut glass prisms, second quarter 20th c., 28" h. **220**
Boch Freres table lamp, a deep round brass base supporting a wide bulbous ovoid pottery vase incised & painted w/an Art Deco design of gazelles in shades of blue & black against a crackled creamy white ground w/blue & green stylized leaves around the top & base, fitted w/a brass collar & electric fittings w/a tall silk shade, ca. 1930s, base 9" h. **920**
Bradley & Hubbard table lamp, 6" w. six-paneled bent-glass shade w/green slag

Bradley & Hubbard Aladdin Lamp

upper panels under a block design metal filigree above the caramel panel border band w/scrolling tulip-style designs in filigree, raised on a gilt-metal Aladdin lamp-style base w/ornate cast designs & a large stepped, round foot (ILLUS.) **2,800**

Czech Art Deco Lamp

Czechoslovakian table lamp, 14" d. sharply pointed conical reverse-painted glass shade, decorated w/an Art Deco design of large diamonds & triangles enclosing radiating designs in yellow & green against a deep reddish orange ground, the spherical footed base w/matching large diamond reserves against the deep reddish orange ground, signed, ca. 1930 (ILLUS.) **2,912**
Duffner & Kimberly floor lamp, 27" d. domical bell-shaped leaded glass shade, composed of large wisteria blossom clusters in mottled purple & white on dark green & brown leafy stems against a mottled white & pale greenish yellow ground, the tapering center top w/an ornate gilt-metal scrolling cap, raised on a tall slender bronzed-metal Duffner & Kimberly base w/a lappet-cast band on the round foot **67,200**

Daffner & Kimberly Lamp

Duffner & Kimberly table lamp, 14" d. domical leaded glass shade in an Art Nouveau style design w/the scalloped border w/scrolled & curved slag glass segments arranged to resemble a stylized owl face, border in shades of deep purple, white, yellow & light & dark green, the upper shade composed of curved overlapping scallops in white & green striated slag glass, on a bronzed metal Duffner base w/a slender square standard w/small loop handles above the flaring squared foot (ILLUS.) **7,280**

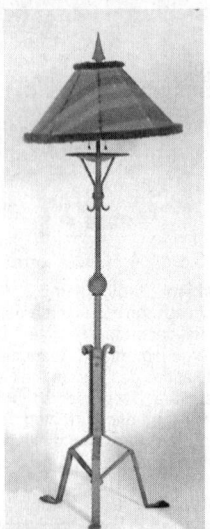

Early Electric Wrought-Iron Floor Lamp

Floor lamps, wrought iron, an arrow-shaped finial on a slender shaft w/two sockets above a disk w/wrought scrolls, raised on an angular wrought-iron tripod base, woven striped paneled shade, scattered corrosion, early 20th c., 4' 8" h., pr. (ILLUS. of one) **805**

Heintz Art Metal Lamp

Heintz Art Metal Shops table lamp, sterling on bronze, floral design, original patina, very good condition, signature plate missing from bottom, liner gone from shade, 11" w., 11" h. (ILLUS.) **978**

Reverse-painted Jefferson Lamp

Jefferson table lamp, 13" w. hexagonal flat-topped reverse-painted shade painted w/a continuous stylized landscape w/large feathery trees in brown & deep rose in the foreground & lower trees & water below w/low distant hills in dark brown all against a cream & yellow sky w/streaked blue clouds, on a slender paneled bronzed metal baluster shaft above a high domed paneled foot (ILLUS.)... **1,680**

Leaded glass table lamp, 18" d. bell-shaped leaded shade composed of mottled red, pink & yellow overlapping scale-like segments extending down to the deep drop border composed of stylized leaves & fruits in greens, reds, pinks & blues, attributed to Duffner & Kimberly, on a tall slender ribbed bronzed metal standard w/a stepped round foot **5,600**

Marble floor lamp, a deep octagonal red marble base striated w/white supporting a tall red marble columnar standard trimmed w/ormolu swags & leaves & supporting a decorative ormolu urn at the top

Marble Floor Lamp

below the electric fitting w/two sockets, fitted w/a domical silk & lace-trimmed shade, traces of original gilding on metal, early 20th c., overall 69" h. (ILLUS.)........... **1,980**

Moe Bridges boudoir lamp, 8" d. domical reverse-painted shade decorated w/a continuous landscape featuring large trees & grass in the foreground w/a silhouetted village & trees in the distance, done in shades of dark purple against a deep red sky, on a slender painted metal urn-form handled base painted black w/a pointed arch shoulder band in deep yellow, 14" h. **460**

Moe Bridges Table Lamp

Moe Bridges table lamp, reverse painted shade w/boats at sea on a bronzed metal base, original patina, 18" d., stands 24" h., w/secured crack, shade good condition (ILLUS.).. **1,150**

Mosaic Lamp Company of Chicago table lamp, 18" domical leaded glass shade in the Cherry Tree patt., composed of clusters of deep pink cherries on brown

Mosaic Lamp Co. Table Lamp

branches w/green leaves against a mottled greenish yellow ground, raised on a Chicago Mosaic tree trunk base (ILLUS.).. **2,240**

Chicago Mosaic Table Lamp

Mosaic Lamp Company of Chicago table lamp, 18" d. domical leaded glass shade, composed of a border band of large deep rose four-petal blossoms centered in leaf clusters against a caramel slag ground, the upper side w/bands of alternating narrow green slag & larger caramel slag, on a tall slender bronzed metal baluster-form standard on a round foot (ILLUS.)... **3,360**

Mosaic Lamp Company of Chicago table lamp, 18" d. umbrella-form leaded glass shade, the wide flaring top composed of a honeycomb design in caramel slag, a narrow green slag band above the deep drop border composed of a band of five-petal pink blossoms & green slag leaves on a caramel slag ground, raised on a tree trunk bronzed metal base **2,800**

Muller Freres boudoir lamp, cameo glass, the tall pagoda shaped glass shade in yellow overlaid w/red & deep purple & cameo cut w/a landscape of tall trees & grass by a body of orange water, w/a slender tapering cylindrical matching glass base on a hammered iron foot, cameo signature, France, early 20th c., overall 15 1/2" h... **3,910**

Muller Freres Art Deco Table Lamp

Muller Freres table lamp, Art Deco style, a 9 1/2" d. rounded, paneled & pointed etched clear molded shade w/rosette & geometric skyscraper-influenced designs, on a wrought-iron base w/angular bars & conical foot, shade signed "Muller Freres - Luneville," France, ca. 1930, several minute rim nicks, 19 1/4" h. (ILLUS.) **1,093**

Phoenix Table Lamp with Landscapes

Phoenix table lamp, 18" d. domical reverse-painted shade, decorated w/a crude stylized landscape w/a roadway through fields & a rail fence w/a farmhouse & trees in the distance, in shades of dark brown, medium brown, frosted white, pale yellow & orange, on a tapering cylindrical reverse-painted glass base decorated w/landscape scenes & framed by gilt-metal filigree bands above the egg-and-dart band foot (ILLUS.) **1,176**

Pittsburgh table lamp, 16" d. domical acid-etched glass shade, decorated w/radiating bands of alternating chain pendants & graduated leafy wreaths in tan against an

Pittsburgh Acid-etched Lamp

opal white ground, a narrow border band of small tan circles (ILLUS.) **952**

Pittsburgh table lamp, 16" d. domical reverse- and obverse-painted shade, decorated w/a continuous summer landscape w/tall leafy trees flanking a stream against a deep orange sky w/small yellow clouds, the trees in dark & light green & yellow, on a patinated metal Pittsburgh base w/a central slender shaft flanked by three C-scroll bottom braces on a tripartite platform foot w/cast border band **2,464**

Simple Slag Glass Lamp

Slag glass table lamp, domical six-panel slag glass shade, each panel in caramel & white slag w/a half-round spiderweb metal filigree along the bottom edge of each panel, raised on a ribbed bronzed metal base w/flaring round foot, ca. 1920, 18 1/2" h. (ILLUS.) **460**

Slag glass table lamp, 20" w. flattened domical shade composed of six wide tapering caramel slag upper panels & a wide drop apron band of deep red slag glass, delicate stylized floral metal filigree overlay forming bands across the top and around the apron of the shade, raised on a bronzed metal classical-style urn-form base w/a round paneled foot **896**

Fine Suess Table Lamp

Suess table lamp, 18" d. widely flaring conical leaded glass shade w/a flat drop apron, decorated around the top w/large oblong stylized geometric deep burgundy blossoms w/yellow centers above a swagged vine of dark green leaves & yellow dots all on a background of mottled white & white & green slag, the drop apron w/half-round matching blossoms & leaf sprigs w/green slag swags, raised on a slender bronzed metal standard w/a wide disk foot (ILLUS.)................................. **4,480**

Suess table lamp, 20" d. domical leaded glass shade, the top w/radiating squares of caramel slag above two narrow green slag border bands flanking a wider band of stylized spearpoint dark green leaves against a pinkish tan slag ground, on a very slender bronzed metal standard w/a wide thin round foot.................................... **3,640**

Wilkinson Floral-bordered Table Lamp

Wilkinson table lamp, 19" d. domical leaded glass shade w/the upper shade composed of green & yellow striated slag blocks above the deep border band composed of large stylized blossoms in deep orange, pink & maroon w/green slag leaves, on a tall slender bronzed metal tree trunk-style standard w/four knobs on the round disk foot (ILLUS.)........................ **4,760**

Wilkinson table lamp, 20" d. domical bent-panel slag glass shade, composed of eight bent tapering caramel slag glass panels overlaid w/a bronzed metal fish scale filigree above a dark green slag glass border band w/a stylized leafy vine filigree overlay, raised on a bronzed metal tall slender ringed standard on a round loop-cast foot.. **3,360**

Impressive Williamson Floor Lamp

Williamson floor lamp, 24" d. domical leaded glass shade, composed of leafy rose branches descending from the top center & ending in large pink, deep red, golden yellow & deep orange blossoms against a background of caramel slag segments, raised on a tall slender reeded & leaf-cast bronze standard above three bent animal legs ending in paws resting on a tripartite foot, overall 70" h. (ILLUS. of shade)....................................... **30,800**

Lanterns

Arts & Crafts lantern, hanging-type, exterior in wrought iron w/two tiered roof cages of textured glass, three original sockets, lower hinged cover is missing, good condition, 16" w., 16" h. **150**

Arts & Crafts Lanterns

Arts & Crafts lanterns, very unusual two-light exterior sconces w/a copper frame having Greek Key design supporting two six-sided shades w/a metal overlay & a Scottish Rose design in green & red jeweled glass, one replaced pane, three replaced sockets, worn original patina, needs wiring, one shade damaged, overall very good condition, 13 x 20", 17" h., pr. (ILLUS.)... **1,955**

Barn lantern, oak or ash & pine w/glass, the upright pegged wooden framework enclosing glass sides & door, original dark finish, wire bail handle & wrought-iron hardware, early, 14 1/2" h.............................. **578**

Barn lantern, pine & glass, an upright dark-stained pine frame, enclosed glass sides & door, chamfered corners on frame, wire bail handle, copper deflector at top, various nails including some worn, crack in door glass, splits in frame, late, 14" h. (ILLUS. top next page) **248**

Early Barn Lantern

Punched Tin Candle Lantern

Candle lantern, punched tin, rectangular shape w/pointed top, tin candle socket & ring handle, door w/chained latch, stylized designs on top, sides embellished w/rayed circle designs, 11 3/8" h. (ILLUS.) **825**

C.M. Hall Lamp Co. Carriage Lantern

Carriage lamp, nickel-plated brass, carbide, cylinder base, bracket attachment, faceted glass inserts, one red, one blue, on either side, "Solar" model, made by C.M. Hall Lamp Co. of Kenosha, Wisconsin, 7" h. (ILLUS.) **115**

Carriage lamp, nickel-plated brass, carbide, orb base, bracket attachment, faceted glass inserts, one red, one blue, on either side, "Solar" model, made by Badger Brass Mfg. Co. of Kenosha, Wisconsin, 7 3/4" h. **142**

Dark lantern, tin & glass, a domed pierced foot & short shaft supporting the font & burner enclosed by a round clear lens w/hinged lens cover, large vent knob at the top, painted black, marked "T.E. Bladon & Sons," early 20th c., 8" h. (ILLUS. top next column) **165**

Early Dark Lantern with Lens Cover

Old Super Baby Kerosene Lantern

Kerosene lantern, tin, "Super Baby - Feuer," No. 175, Germany, early 20th c., 7 1/2" h. (ILLUS.) **165**

LIPSTICK HOLDER LADIES

Collecting items for the woman's vanity has gained much popularity in recent times. There has always been a need to organize all her paraphernalia, whether it be jewelry, perfume, hair accessories or makeup. Everyone knows that the right color lipstick is essential to the outfit one wears. Where do we keep all these different shades of lipstick? In the 1940s through the 1960s the lipstick "lady" seemed to be the answer. What a cute way to have your lipsticks right at hand. These adorable ladies, usually made from some type of ceramic material, seem to have gotten the job done well. Keeping them within reach at your dressing table kept them readily available.

Lipstick ladies are not easy to find. Because of their fragile nature, many were relegated to the trash can after use or damage.

Two Girls Lipstick Holder

Figure group, two girls standing back to back, one wearing a pink party dress, the other blue jeans, stump-form brown holders (ILLUS.) **$100**

Figure of a girl, brown hair pulled up at top, short torso on wide domed pale blue skirt w/lipstick holders, by Josef Originals **50**

Figure of a lady, "Miss Pretty Face," brown hair w/large pink blossom, hands together near face, ruffled blue & white gown w/large pink blossoms forming the lipstick compartments **65**

Angel Lipstick Holder

Figure of angel, seated atop a round lobed & footed pink box, gold hair & trim, Josef Originals (ILLUS.) **75**

Geisha Girl Lipstick Holder

Figure of Geisha girl, standing wearing a long blue robe, on an oblong, scalloped base w/a large round framed mirror at her side, gold trim on base (ILLUS.) **65**

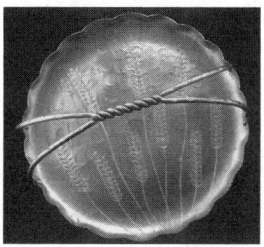

Girl Holding Flowers

Figure of girl, standing holding bouquet of colored flowers, wearing flaring white dress w/gold trim w/lipstick holes & a white bonnet (ILLUS.) **75**

Figure of girl, standing, wearing a long-sleeved & widely flaring green skirt w/applied roses on bodice **55**

Lady Curtseying Lipstick Holder

Figure of lady, curtseying, wearing a widely flaring all-white dress & hat, holder holes at the back (ILLUS.) **50**

Figure of lady, seated beside round mirror w/holders in front, wearing a real lace gown & holding lipstick, base & mirror frame in yellow w/gold trim **55**

Lady in 18th Century Style Gown

Figure of lady, standing holding edge of her 18th c. style pink gown, gold trim (ILLUS.) **75**

Figures of girls, holding glasses, mirror & fan, each **75**

METALS
Aluminum

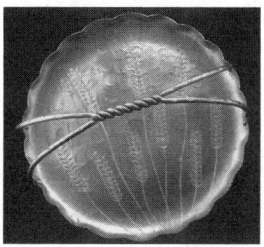

Basket with Wheat Design

Basket, flat round form w/upturned fluted rim, double handle w/twist design, wheat decoration, Milcraft, 14" d. (ILLUS.).............. **$14**

Aluminum Beverage Server & Stand

Beverage server, cover & stand, tapering cylindrical body w/wide upturned loop side handle & spigot near the base, low domed cover w/large loop handle, on a separate ring base w/twisted strap angled legs curving in to support a center burner, Buenilum, overall 20" h. (ILLUS.)........ **95**

Bowl, hammered, looped handle, Buenilum, 6" d. **8**

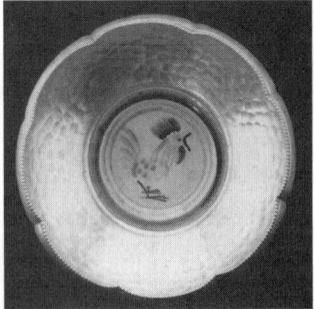

Aluminum Bowl with Pottery Insert

Bowl, lightly scalloped cupped rim w/hammered design, small yellow & tan pottery insert in center decorated w/a crowing rooster, Modern Hand Made #147, 7 1/2" d. (ILLUS.) **35-50**

Aluminum Covered Casserole

Casserole, cov., hammered, footed ring-style caddy, vegetables & wheat decoration, ridged fan-shaped handles & cover finial, Pyrex glass insert, Crown, 8 1/2" d. (ILLUS.)... **25**

Hammered Aluminum Coaster Set

Coaster set, hammered, four coasters w/stamped bamboo motif, the rectangular holder w/four short feet, fluted rim & indents for coasters, Everlast, 4 x 6 3/4", the set (ILLUS.)... **13**

Aluminum Cocktail Shaker

Cocktail shaker, cov., chrysanthemum decoration, pouring spout on shoulder, handle w/decorative leaf, Continental #530, 12" h. (ILLUS.) **50-75**

Bullet-shaped Pencil Sharpener

Pencil sharpener, cast, in the shape of a bullet, 5/8 x 1 3/8" (ILLUS.)................................ **45**

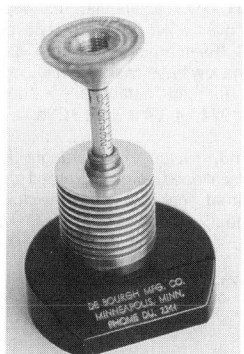

Aluminum Advertising Postage Scale

Postage scale, Art Deco style w/"De Bourgh Mfg. Co. - Minneapolis, Minn." & phone number printed in gold on black Bakelite base, top unscrews to reveal graded spring-loaded column, 2 5/8 x 3", 4 1/8" h. (ILLUS.) **95**

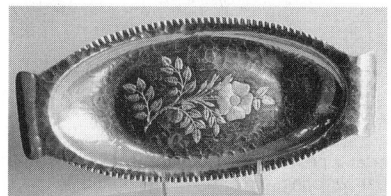

Hammered Aluminum Tray

Tray, hammered, w/rolled handle, serrated rim, stamped wild rose decoration, style 1071, Continental Silver Co., 6 1/4 x 13 1/2" (ILLUS.) **12**

Brass

Cast Brass "Operative" Badge

Badge, cast, circle stamped w/"American Protective League" at outer rim, surrounding inner rim stamped w/"Auxiliary to U.S. Dept of Justice," which surrounds the number "106" in the middle, all topped by banner stamped "Operative" topped by spread-winged eagle, 1 3/8 x 2 3/8" (ILLUS.) **145**

Plated Brass Peace Officer's Badge

Badge, plated, star shape printed w/"Peace Officer" that sits inside ring printed w/"Minnesota Public Safety Commission," 2 1/4" d. (ILLUS.) **185**

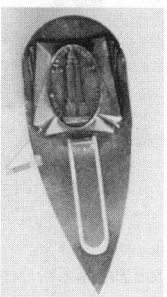

Plated Brass Souvenir Bookmark

Bookmark, plated, teardrop-shape souvenir of the Empire State Building w/image of building in oval above page clip, 1 1/2 x 3 3/4" (ILLUS.) **35**

Brass Cachepot

Cachepot, rounded tapering paneled shape w/ring handles attached to four /lion head decorations, short scroll feet, late 19th c., 11 3/4" d., 10 h. (ILLUS.) **448**

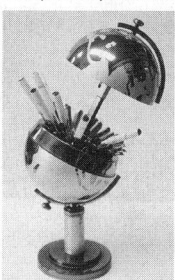

Elaborate Brass Cigarette Dispenser

Cigarette dispenser, two concentric circles form base, w/a shaft connected to a globe that holds cigarettes, top part of globe pulls open & retracts to close, cigarettes pop out when globe is opened, when open 4 1/4 x 6 1/2", 11 1/4" h. (ILLUS.) **150**

Plated Brass Corkscrew

Corkscrew, plated, retractable, in the shape of a beer bottle w/Anheuser Busch label, when open measures 5/8 x 2 1/2 x 2 3/4" (ILLUS.) **75**

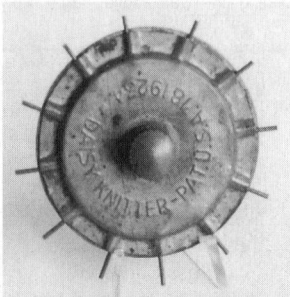

Stamped Brass Daisy Knitter

Daisy knitter, stamped, w/retractable spokes, patent number stamped in circle around center knob, 5/8 x 1 7/8" (ILLUS.) **25**

Brass Jewelry Box with Jewels

Jewelry box, cov., rectangular, flat-topped domed cover w/Art Nouveau-style cast scrolls & inset amethyst-colored glass jewels, the low base cast w/fern leaves & beading, marked "Latauska - Patented July 28, 1924," 4 3/4 x 6 1/2", 2" h. (ILLUS.) **129**

Kettle stand, rectangular, wrought iron frame w/scalloped apron w/pierced top & sides, front cabriole legs w/clover-shaped feet, side handles, 13 x 17 1/2", 13" h. **413**

Brass Mortar & Pestle

Mortar & pestle, footed short bell-form mortar w/flaring rim, matching ring-turned pestle, mortar 5" d., 3 1/2" h. (ILLUS.) **110**

Brass Art Deco Perfumer

Perfumer, footed, tapering cone shape w/raised Art Deco design, wide flaring stopper, black glass insert, marked on bottom "Apollo 3197," 5 1/2' h. (ILLUS.) **100**

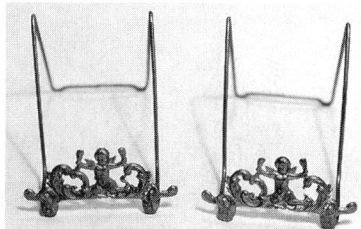

Miniature Picture Easels

Picture easels, miniature, cast-brass & iron, gold-tone finish, decorated w/cherubs & C-scrolls, one marked on back "Howell" & one marked "H," 3 3/4 x 4 x 5 3/4", the pr. (ILLUS.) **100**

Brass Smoking Accessories

Smoking set, three pieces w/raised square design on rims, set includes 11 1/4" d. tray, match holder & 11 1/4" h. cigarette holder, Bradley & Hubbard, the set (ILLUS.) **350**

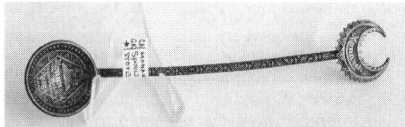

Cast Brass Advertising Spoon

Spoon, cast, in stylized Arabic motif, w/long handle w/crescent-shaped end stamped "Monarch," advertising Monarch Ranges of Keewaskum, Wisconsin, in bowl w/picture of range in diamond within border, 1 1/4 x 6 3/8" (ILLUS.) **125**

Roycroft Brass Bud Vase

Vase, bud-type, trapezoid base holding curved arm ending in open circle that holds glass vial-like vase, maker's mark on bottom, Roycroft, 7 1/4" h. (ILLUS.)......... **395**

Hammered Brass Trench Art Vase

Vase, Trench art-type, hammered, domed foot below swelled cylindrical body w/flaring ruffled rim, overall hand-hammered background w/embossed bow & roses, ca. 1917, 4 1/2" d., 11 1/2" h. (ILLUS.).. **135**
Whale oil lamps, ring-turned inverted acorn-form fonts w/burners on a baluster- and knob-turned standard on a domed round foot, 8 1/2" h., pr..................................... **715**
Whale oil lamps, turned brass w/stepped ring bases, inverted beehive stems, small fonts w/burners, 8 1/2" h., the pr.................... **715**

Bronze

Ashtray, floor model, gold finish, flared base supporting long shaft holding bowl-shape tray w/hinged top & match holder, marked on base, Tiffany Studios, New York, No. 1649, 9 x 28" **2,995**

Bronzed Baby Shoes

Baby shoes, high-button, worn-looking, 2 1/2 x 4", 6 1/2" l., the pr. (ILLUS.)................ **35**
Book ends, cast, copper finish, flat base merging into upright embossed w/heads of Abraham Lincoln & George Washington in profile, 4" h., the pr. **195**
Book ends, cast, silver finish, stepped base, arched open Moorish-style upright w/figure of knight in armor holding a shield standing between pillars w/background of embossed vining leaves, marked on reverse "Travelers Convention, Palm Beach, Florida, 1931 - patent pending," 3 x 4 1/2", 8" h., the pr. **250**

Louis XV-style Chandelier with Putto

Chandelier, Louis XV-style, nine-light, gilt-bronze, a scroll-cast ceiling plate suspending a long central rod flanked by three long scrolled supports each issuing three short scrolled arms ending in light sockets, a figure of a putto at the center above leafy swags, early 20th c., 36" h. (ILLUS.) **10,800**

Decorative Cast Bronze Owl

Figure of owl, cast, hollow, some engraved design, Oriental lettering on back, 4 3/4" h. (ILLUS.) **300**

Oriental-style Bronze Heater

Heater, cov., Oriental-style, high tripod base w/raised lizards, incised water buffalo, bats, trees, double-ring handles in mythical trunks on the hexagonal bowl, pierced detail on the lid w/raised birds & foo dog finial, chocolate brown patina (ILLUS.) **330**

Early Meiji Bronze Incense Burner

Incense burner, in the form of a seated shishi w/ball, Japanese, early Meiji period, 9 1/4" h. (ILLUS.) **448**

Medallion, commemorative, honoring labor, rectangular, w/embossed scene of classically garbed woman w/arm around boy & pointing to distant industrial scene and the word "Labor" radiating from it, 2 x 2 1/4" **75**

Medallion, commemorative, in honor of James J. Hill, front shows embossed bust of Hill under "Memorial" w/his name underneath, reverse marked "Sept. 16, 1838 to May 29, 1916 - One of the world's greatest builders," 3 1/8" d. **65**

Paperweight, tapered rectangular base embossed "Metro Goldwyn Mayer Lion - The Greatest Star on the Screen," holds model of roaring MGM lion, 2 3/8 x 3 1/8", 5" l. **285**

Plate, gilt finish, dished form w/wide flat Greek key & shell border w/green enamel ovals in the center of the shells, marked "Louis Tiffany Furnaces, Inc. 309," 8 1/4" d. (minor wear) **165**

Posnet (footed cooking pot), three short canted legs support the wide slightly flaring cylindrical pot w/a long straight handle extending from the rim, marked by Taylor of Richmond, Virginia, early 19th c., overall 20" l., 6" h. **4,200**

Japanese Bronze Sensor

Sensor, cov., dome-shaped & pierced-work lid w/foo lion finial, ovoid-shaped body decorated w/cartouche w/figures of birds in foliage, serpent handles, molded circular base decorated w/elephant heads, Japanese, 19th c., 49" h. (ILLUS.) **2,576**

Vase, club form w/two handles on neck, melon ribbed body, 19th c., Japanese, 8 1/4" h. (ILLUS. right, w/poppy & foliage vase) **138**

Vase, cylindrical w/raised rim & base w/relief designs & good patina, mark for Shoyeido, Japan, ca. 1800, 12 1/2" h. **165**

Vase, tall cylindrical oval form cast around the sides w/relief figures of men on horseback, four small figures form the feet, cast signature on the base, removable tin liner, China, 19th c., 15" h. **385**

Japanese Bronze Vases

Vase, w/poppy & foliage design in relief, signature chop on base, patina w/red, Japanese, 8 1/2" h. (ILLUS. left) **275**

Chrome

Chrome-plated Ashtray

Ashtray, plated, ridged round base w/indents for cigarettes, w/image of Australia embossed in center, topped w/streamlined model of submarine, 5 1/2 x 7 3/4", 2 3/4" h. (ILLUS.) **50**

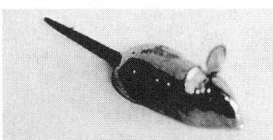

Chrome-plated Decorative Mouse

Figure of mouse, plated, streamlined design w/tail straight out behind, ears upright, 3 1/4" l. (ILLUS.) **22**

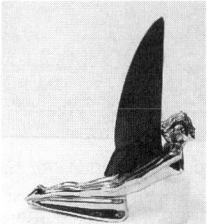

Chrome Hood Ornament

Hood ornament, stylized figure of nude woman w/flowing hair and arms clasped at sides, w/blue translucent plastic wings, style number 511, 4 1/2 x 8 1/4 x 9 1/2" (ILLUS.) **135**

Chrome-plated Iron

Iron, plated, w/wooden handle, made by Diamond Iron Lamp Manufacturing Co., 1936, 6 1/4" l. (ILLUS.) **50**

Copper

Covered Elephant Box

Box, cov., plated, stylized figure of tusked trumpeting elephant, top heavily hand-decorated, made in India, 3 x 3 3/4", 6 3/4" l. (ILLUS.) **145**

Hammered-copper Candleholder

Candleholder, hammered, Arts & Crafts style, footed domed base w/short standard holding bowl-shaped socket w/slightly curved bobêche, applied hammered-brass strap handle, 4 1/2" h. (ILLUS.) **295**

Gustav Stickley Copper Coal Scuttle

Coal scuttle, flared base, rolled rim, strap swivel handle, Gustav Stickley, 24" h. (ILLUS.) **10,925**

Hammered-copper Mold

Food mold, hand-hammered, tin-lined, decorated w/design of fruit & leaves, ring for hanging, 4 1/4 x 7 1/2" (ILLUS.) **85**

Dirk Van Erp Jardiniere

Jardiniere, hammered, Arts & Crafts style, bulbous shape, Dirk Van Erp, early 20th c. (ILLUS.) **7,475**

Hammered Copper Jardiniere

Jardiniere, hammered, Arts & Crafts style, squat bulbous shape w/red blush patina, Dirk Van Erp, early 20th c. (ILLUS.) **37,375**

Copper Dirk Van Erp Table Lamp

Lamp, hammered, Arts & Crafts style, table model, bulbous base w/conical shade held by four metal supports ending in metal squat round finial, early Dirk Van Erp, early 20th c. (ILLUS.) **48,875**

Minnow bucket, cov., deep oval form w/iron end rim handles, w/a matching oval lift-out insert pierced overall w/small holes & w/a hinged flat lid, brass overlaid initials on the outer top rim, signed "R.W.J. Davison," England, late 19th-early 20th c., 8 1/2 x 15", 9 1/2" h. **275**

Teakettle, cov., dovetailed construction, wide flat bottom & swelled cylindrical sides below a flat shoulder centered by a short cylindrical neck w/a fitted domed cover w/acorn finial, long angled goose-neck spout, high swing bail & wood handle, signed inside lid "Maurice Cohen & Co. London," 12" h. (dents) **165**

Copper Teakettle

Teakettle, cov., marked "Britton" on applied strap swivel handle, knob handle on cover, old solder repairs to handle, spout & base, 9 1/2 x 12 3/4", 12" h. (ILLUS.) **225**

Revere Ware Copper Teakettle

Teakettle, Revere Ware, w/applied black Bakelite handle and bird whistle spout, marked on bottom "Revere Solid Copper - Rome, N.Y.," 7 1/4 x 7 1/2" (ILLUS.) **100**

Copper Strap-on Water Bottle

Water bottle, strap-on type, wide oval shallow gently arched shape w/small brass spout & screw-on cap, one strap guide missing, 8 x 12", 3" h. (ILLUS.) **79**

Iron

Aebleskiver pan, Griswold #32............................ **50**

Apple peeler, cast, "F.W. Hudsons Improved Apple Parer Leominster, Mass Pat Dec. 2, 1862"... **175**

Apple peeler, cast, Goodell, 1898 .... **55**

Apple peeler, cast, "Lockey & Howland, Pat Dec 5, 1856"... **65**

Apple peeler, cast, "Manfu'd by Goodell Co, Antrim, H. Pat Mar 18, 1884," vertical arc shape **200**

Apple peeler, cast, "Patd Oct. 5, 1880," unmarked Peck, Stow & Wilcox........................ **275**

Apple peeler, "Nonpareil Parer, Patented May 6, 1858 J.L. Haven & Co. Cin. O".... **1,000 +**

Apple segmenter, cast, "R. Buchi Chicago Pat'd Aug 28, 1923"................................... **100**

Apple segmenter, cast, "Tollman Mfg Co, Mt. Joy, Pa Pat Apld Apple Cutter".................. **20**

Star-shaped Architectural Brace

Architectural brace, cast, in form of five-pointed star w/hole in center, repainted, 9 1/4 x 9 3/4" (ILLUS.) **65**

Cast-iron Bill Hook

Bill hook, cast, pointed shield form w/pierced leaf & scroll design, 3 1/2 x 6" (ILLUS.)... **11**

Cast-iron Bison Book End

Book ends, cast, antiqued bronze finish, model of bison on rock, marked "COPR 1930 American Bison - 924," 5 1/2 x 5 3/4", pr. (ILLUS. of one) **115**

Cast-iron Book End with Chariot Race

Book ends, cast, antiqued copper finish, high-relief design of Roman chariot race, marked "695," 5 1/4 x 6 1/4", pr. (ILLUS. of one) **115**

Rare Cast-iron Dove-shaped Box

Box, cov., cast, in shape of a sitting dove, ca. 1840, rare, 3 x 7", 4" h. (ILLUS.).. **1,200**

Can opener, cast, "Duket Mfg. Co. Toledo, Ohio, Patd. 8-11-25," 6 1/4"............................. **20**

Hand-forged Candle Lantern

Candle lantern, hand-forged, flat front, half-round back, punched vents in conical top w/applied carrying handle, ca. 1850, 6 x 7 1/2", 14 1/4" h. (ILLUS.)a **350**

Candle Lantern with Fluted Reflector

Candle lantern, hand-forged, w/fluted reflector & pitcher handle, ca. 1820, 5 x 7", 9 1/4" h. (ILLUS.) **250-350**

Cats Card Tray

Card tray, in the form of three grey & white cats, marked on back "B&H" and style number 1640, made by Bradley & Hubbard, 5 1/2 x 7" (ILLUS.) **295**

Cherry pitter, cast, "Enterprise Cherry Stoner Pat Appl'd For No 12," 13" **125**

Cherry pitter, cast, "The Boss Raisin Seeder, Pat. Pdg.," 11 3/4" **150**

Sheet Iron Christmas Light

Christmas light, soldered sheet iron, star-shaped, w/opaque white glass inserts (one missing) & hole in hinged back for bulb, ca. 1930, 4 1/2 x 12 1/4 x 12 1/2" (ILLUS.) **150-200**

Clock, cast, gilt finish, travel size, Art Nouveau w/rococo influence, swirling leafy openwork decoration, on four ornate flared feet, 2 x 3 3/4", 5 1/4" h. **395**

Wrought-iron Cowbell

Cowbell, wrought, w/leather collar, strap handle, 2 x 4", 9" h. (ILLUS.) **25**

Dark Lantern Used by James Garfield

Dark lantern, hand-forged, w/red glass panes, burned whale oil, 1835, carried by future President James A. Garfield at the age of 16 on an Erie Canal tow boat, 2 3/4 x 3 1/2", 5 3/4" h. (ILLUS.) **1,200**

Cast-iron Door Knocker

Door knocker, cast, in the form of a basket of flowers w/ribbon garland, original worn paint, 2 3/4 x 4" (ILLUS.) **65**

Door knocker, cast, large tall grotesque face w/tall pointed scroll top ears & crest & scalloped leaves below the chin, large ring knocker fitted in the mouth, old cream paint over earlier green, late 19th-early 20th c., 8 1/2" w., 21" h. **633**

Cast-iron Vase of Flowers Doorstop

Doorstop, cast, black triangular stepped base holding white handled vase of flowers in polychrome decoration of yellow, white, green, peach & black, 10" h. (ILLUS.) **145**

Cast-iron Carriage Doorstop

Doorstop, cast, image of enclosed coach pulled by two horses, w/driver in front and trumpeter standing at back, English, 3 1/2 x 13", 7 1/2" h. (ILLUS.)......................... **350**

Cast-iron Spiral Envelope Holder

Envelope holder, cast, spiral holder w/two feet at each end, marked "K Diamond," 3 x 3 1/2", 3" h. (ILLUS.).................................... **48**

Cast-iron Flag Stand

Flag stand, cast, base w/four ball-and-claw feet, embossed w/stars and "Loyalty," "Fraternity," "Charity" and "WRC," 3 1/2 x 6 1/4" (ILLUS.) **35**

Cast-iron Two-piece Fluter

Fluter iron, cast, two-piece, rectangular footed base w/fluting grooves & hand-held roller, painted & plated, marked "American Machine Co. Philadelphia, Pa.," late 19th c.-early 20th c., base 3 3/4", the set (ILLUS.) **165**

Miniature Souvenir Frying Pan

Frying pan, cast, miniature, w/polychrome painted image of Statue of Liberty and sailing ships, souvenir of Galesville, Wisconsin, made by John Wright of Wrightsville, Pennsylvania, w/original box, pan measures 3 1/4 x 4 3/4" (ILLUS.) **25**

Hitching post, cast, in the form of a tapered tree trunk w/grapevines & stars, a ring near the top, 70" l. (overall pitting, base chipped) **605**

Hitching post finial, cast, in form of horse-head, old dark surface w/good detail, acanthus leaves around base, horse's mouth holds hitching ring, 13" h..................... **440**

Ice shaver, cast, "The Griswold Mfg Co Classic Ice Shredder No 2 Erie PA USA"...... **300**

Cast-iron Lawn Sprinkler

Lawn sprinkler w/copper tubing, cast, Rain King model D, various patent numbers, Sunbeam Corp., Chicago, 4 1/2 x 7 1/2", 9 1/2" h. (ILLUS.)... **55**

English Mailbox on Base

Mailbox on base, cast, oblong base has shaped corners & holes for mounting to floor, round column w/leaf designs & urn-shaped detail below octagonal box w/re-lief designs of horns on either end & a man on horseback w/horn, peaked roof w/scale designs, crown finial, late white enameling, areas of rust, English, 11 1/2 x 16 1/2", 46" h. (ILLUS.) **358**

Cast-iron Match Holder

Match holder, cast, hanging, flat rectangular back, top features openwork design w/middle peak flanked by two pillars, holder in form of leering face, 2 x 3 1/2", 7 1/4" h. (ILLUS.) **125**

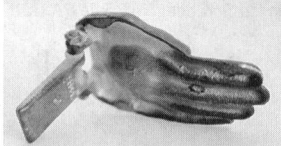

Cast-iron Hand

Model of hand, cast, life-size form of human hand hinged at wrist, marked twice on reverse w/style numbers Y1657 & Y1658, exact use unknown but may be a lodge piece or door knocker, 1 1/2 x 4 3/8", 7" l. (ILLUS.) **850**

Cast-iron Horse & Carriage

Model of horse & carriage, cast, flat design w/wire support, polychrome painted finish in white, black & red, early 20th c., 11 1/4" l., 5" H. (ILLUS.) **69**

Iron Perfection Nut Cracker

Nut cracker, cast, clamp-style for attaching to table edge, clamp-form cracker, marked "Perfection Nut Cracker - Made in Waco, Texas - Patented 1914," 6 x 6 1/2" (ILLUS.)... **69**

Home Nut Cracker

Nut cracker, cast, handle embossed w/"Home Nut Cracker," patented 1915, 4 x 11 1/2" (ILLUS.)... **69**

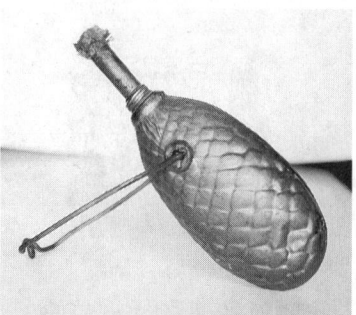

Parade or Campaign Torch

Parade or campaign torch, wrought, in the form of a pineapple, w/wick protruding from tube in top, wire handle, old gold painted surface, burned kerosene or whale oil, c. 1880, 3 x 3 1/4", fully extended 9 3/4" l. (ILLUS.) **350**

Rollman Peach Stoner

Peach stoner, cast, "Rollman Mfg. Co. Pat Pend Mount Joy PA U.S.A.," 8 3/4" (ILLUS.)... **250**

Two-arm Plant Holder

Plant holder, cast, Victorian, decorated w/tendrils & scrolls & stylized leaf motif, two pierced circular holders, ca. 1880, 5 1/2 x 10 x 15" (ILLUS.).......................... **300-400**

Cast-iron Plant Holder

Plant holder, cast, Victorian, four-arm holder w/pierced base & circular arms w/C-scrolls, ca. 1880, 17 x 18", 6 1/2" h. (ILLUS.) **300-500**

Miniature Cast-iron Sad Iron

Sad iron, miniature, double-pointed base marked "Dover USA," iron uprights w/turned wood handle, 1 1/2 x 3 1/4", 2 1/8" h. (ILLUS.) **69**

Toy Cast-iron Iron & Trivet

Sad iron & trivet, cast, toy size, pointed iron w/upright handle on pierced three-footed trivet w/end handle, 3 3/4" l., pr. (ILLUS.) **32**
Shooting gallery target, cast leaping mountain goat, rare large size, old, worn white paint, 8 3/4" l. **149**
Shooting gallery target, cast running lion, rare large size, white paint hides possible damage to lower jaw & tail, 12 1/2" l. **220**

Cast-iron Griswold Skillet

Skillet, cast, Griswold trademark & "Model 0 - No. 562 - Made in Erie, Pa.," 5" w., 6 3/4" l. (ILLUS.) **85**

Skillet, cast, large emblem, no heat ring, Griswold #2 .... **350**
Skillet, cast, large emblem w/smoke ring, Griswold #14 .... **200**
Sugar nippers, cast, scissors-shaped, 9 1/2" **150**

Cast-Iron Sugar Nippers

Sugar nippers, cast, stamped leaf designs at rivet, handle stamped "B. Smith," minor edge damage to one end and short split in spring, 9 1/2" l. (ILLUS.) **275**
Teakettle, cov., cast, deep squared body w/side flanges & a paneled spout, bail handle & a tin cover, marked "Troy, NY," old black repaint, 19th c., 9" l., 5 1/4" h. plus handle **83**

Wrought- Iron Hanging Utensil Rack

Utensil rack, wrought, hanging style, stepped crest w/scrolled rods & center rod w/twisted detail, five hooks on rod w/diamond-shaped ends, 21 1/4" l., 13" h. (ILLUS.) **495**

Pewter

Baptismal bowl, round domed foot tapering to a pedestal supporting a deep wide round bowl w/flattened flaring rim, Roswell Gleason, Dorchester, Massachusetts, 1822-71, 8 1/8" d., 5" h. **1,265**
Basin, round w/deep slightly flaring sides & wide flat bottom, eagle touch of Thomas Danforth III, Stepney, Connecticut & Philadelphia, 1777-1818, 12" d. (light pitting).. **1,155**

Shallow Pewter Basin

Basin, shallow, partial Love touchmark & faint "London" (Jacobs #207, in or near Philadelphia, last half of the 18th c. or early 19th c.), American (ILLUS.) **350**

Candlesticks, round foot tapering up to a ringed, tall waisted stem supporting a tall inverted bell-form socket w/wide rim, beaded detail, w/push-ups, unmarked, probably American, 19th c., 10" h., pr. **385**

Chalices, round foot & ringed stem below the tall slightly flaring bell-form cylindrical cup, Leonard, Reed & Barton, Taunton, Massachusetts, 1835-40, 7" h., pr. (polished) **385**

Large Pewter Charger

Charger, faint touchmarks on back, front rim also has touchmarks of rooster-like bird and "Ø" repeated four times, hanger added, 20 1/4" d. (ILLUS.) **110**

Charger, "London" mark w/sailing ship touch w/"United States of America, Flourish, Maxwell," Scottish, made for American trade, 16 5/8" d. **495**

Charger, Love touchmark w/double "London" marks, late 18th or early 19th c., 13" d. **440**

Charger, round w/flanged slightly rolled rim w/tooled line, partial angel touch mark & "G.N.K.," 15 3/8" d. **330**

Charger, round w/wide flanged rim, John Danforth, Norwich, Connecticut, 1773-95, 12 1/8" d. (knife scratches & minor dents) **1,265**

Pewter Charger

Charger, Scottish, made for the American trade w/sailing ship touchmark & "Success to the United States," also partial Graham & Wardrop touchmark (Glasgow, 1776-1806, Cotterell #1943), 16 1/2" d. (ILLUS.) **440**

Tall Pewter Coffeepot

Coffeepot, bulbous body w/tooled lines & stepped dome lid w/wooden wafer finial, black paint on finial & handle, touchmark "F. Porter Westbrook No. 1," (Freeman Porter, Westbrook, Maine, ca. 1835-1860), 11 1/4" h. (ILLUS.) **358**

Coffeepot, cov., tall lighthouse-form, hinged domed cover w/wafer finial, tapering body, stepped base, paneled spout, scrolled ear handle, touch mark for "Sellow & Co. Cincinnati," 11" h. (minor wear & finial bent) **413**

Dish, round shallow form w/wide flanged rim, eagle touch of James Porter, Connecticut valley, 1795-1803 & Baltimore, Maryland, 1803, 13" d. (areas of pitting) **330**

Dish, round shallow form w/wide flanged rim, Samuel Danforth, Hartford, Connecticut, 1795-1816, 13 1/8" d. (pitting) **413**

Flagon, cov., ringed base & slightly tapering cylindrical body w/a stepped dome cover w/thumbrest, S-scroll handle, arched rim spout, eagle touch of Boardman & Co., New York, New York, 1825-27, 7 3/4" h. .. **2,860**

Flagon, cov., tall slightly tapering cylindrical body w/a flaring ringed base, hinged pointed pagoda cover w/pointed finial, wide rim spout, C-form handle, lion touch of Thomas D. Boardman, Hartford, Connecticut, 1830+, 11 1/2" h. (base slightly battered) **440**

Flagon, cov., tall slightly tapering cylindrical body w/a flaring ringed base & rings below the flaring rim, domed cover w/knob finial, S-scroll handle w/thumbrest, wide rim spout, Israel Trask, Beverly, Massachusetts, 1807-56, 12 1/4" h. **1,100**

Pewter Lamp

Lamp, round base, acorn font w/burning fluid burners & snuffer caps, touchmark for "Capen & Molineax, NY," (1848-1854), 9 1/4" h. (ILLUS.) **413**

Pewter Three-rabbit Chocolate Mold

Mold, chocolate, in the form of three upright rabbits, hinged at feet, closed measures 3 x 13", 8 1/2" h. (ILLUS.)............................... **395**

Four-egg Pewter Chocolate Mold

Mold, chocolate, in the shape of four Easter eggs decorated w/lambs, rabbits & chicks, hinged down middle of mold, closed measures 3 x 8 1/4", 10 1/2" h. (ILLUS.) **395**

Pewter Masonic Ice Cream Mold

Mold, ice cream, in the form of Masonic symbol, marked "948 1/2 E&G Co. NY," closed measures 1 x 4 1/2 x 5 1/2" (ILLUS.)... **70**

Pewter Owl Ice Cream Mold

Mold, ice cream, in the shape of an owl, hinged at side, marked "175," closed measures 2 x 3 3/8", 4 1/4" h. (ILLUS.) **145**

Plate, round, partial touch marks for Thomas Danford (Taunton, Massachusetts & Norwich, Connecticut, 1727-1773), J# 110, 9" d.. **248**

Plate, round w/deep center well & flanged rim, William Calder, Providence, Rhode Island, 1817-56, 11 3/8" d. (light overall pitting)... **358**

Plate, round w/flanged rim, Boardman & Co., New York, New York, 1805-50, 9 3/8" d. (scratches, some battering) **215**

Plate, round w/flanged rim, eagle touch of Thomas Danforth III, Stepney or Rocky Hill, Connecticut & Philadelphia, 1777-1818, 7 7/8" d. (minor wear & battering)....... **385**

Plate, round w/flanged rim, Joseph Danforth, Middletown, Connecticut, 1780-88, 7 7/8" d. (some wear & pitting)...................... **440**

Tankard, cov., cylindrical w/flared ringed base, hinged stepped domed cover, S-scroll handle w/pierced thumbpiece, interior touch of H.A. and Sons, w/letter to Charles Montgomery, 6 7/8" h. (minor dents) **1,705**

Teapot, cov., flaring ringed foot below the spherical body tapering to a flaring neck, hinged domed cover, D-form scroll handle, swan's-neck spout, George Richardson, Sr., Boston, Massachusetts, 1818-28, Cranston, Rhode Island, 1828-45, 8" h. (pitting)...................................... **330**

Teapot, cov., footed half-round lower body w/a short waisted & widely flaring neck, domed cover w/disk finial, ornate C-scroll handle & swan's-neck spout, Boardman & Hart, New York, 1828-53, 7 1/2" h. (minor dents).. **358**

Teapot, cov., footed squatty bulbous body w/wide center band tapering to a low flaring neck, hinged domed cover w/disk finial, pointed scroll black-painted metal handle, swan's-neck spout, Josiah Danforth, Middletown, Connecticut, 1825-37, 6 3/4" h. (worn handle paint) **385**

Allen Porter Pewter Tall Teapot

Teapot, cov., footed tall baluster-form body w/a high domed cover & disk finial, high C-scroll black-painted handle, tall swan's-neck spout, Allen Porter, Westbrook, Maine, 1830-40, 12 1/4" h. (ILLUS.).. **413**

Teapot, cov., squatty pear shape w/a hinged stepped & pointed domed cover w/wooden disk finial, paneled swan's-neck spout, arched black-painted C-scroll handle, Roswell Gleason, Dorchester, Massachusetts, 1822-71, 6 3/4" h. (split in finial, flake in handle) **825**

Teapot, cov., tall baluster-form body w/tooled ring base & wide raised band around the middle, domed cover w/small wood wafer finial, ornate C-scroll black-painted metal handle, swan's-neck spout, eagle touch of Ashbil Griswold, Meriden, Connecticut, 1802-42, 10" h. (minor dents & pitting) **578**

Teapot, cov., wide flaring foot below the wide half-round lower body & wide tapering shoulder to a short flaring neck, domed cover w/disk finial, high C-scroll black handle, swan's-neck spout, Sellew & Co., Cincinnati, Ohio, 1830-60, 71/2" h. (small dent, tiny paint flake on handle).......... **303**

Sheffield Plate

Sheffield Plate Meat Cover

Meat cover, dome-shaped body w/engraved coat of arms and Greek Key design at base, beaded base rim, cornucopia & beaded handle at top, made by Henry Wilkinson & Co., England, ca. 1838, 11 x 14 x 18" (ILLUS.).......................... **672**

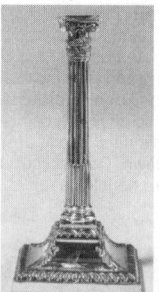

Sheffield Plate Taperstick

Taperstick, Corinthian column form on rectangular gadrooned base, crested, w/pseudo-hallmarks, made by Thomas Law, Sheffield, ca. 1765-70, 6 1/2" h. (ILLUS.).. **480**

Vegetable dishes, cov., rectangular body w/highly decorative trim & lid handle, ca. 1830, 9 x 12 1/4", 6 1/2" h., pr. **308**

Sheffield Plate Wine Cooler

Wine coolers, classical urn-form, fitted w/handles, decorated w/gadroon, shells, floral bands & acanthus leaf designs, 19th c., pr. (ILLUS. of one).......................... **1,904**

Silver

American (Sterling & Coin)

Sterling Silver Baby Rattle

Baby rattle, w/embossed cat heads on both sides & mother-of-pearl handle also used for teething, marked "Gorham Sterling - N236," engraved "MAS," 3 3/4" l. (ILLUS.).. **195**

Sterling Baby's Cup

Baby's cup, model of a rabbit dressed in suit making up the handle, marked "S&B Sterling 719," 2 1/2 x 2 3/4 x 4" (ILLUS.)....... **135**

Coin Silver Footed Basket

Basket, coin silver, oblong footed basket on oval rimmed base, hand-hammered decoration of fruit & flowers, swivel handle divided at top, 3 1/4 x 4 x 5 1/2" (ILLUS.).. **1,100**

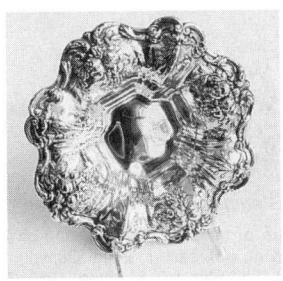

Sterling Francis I Pattern Bowl

Bowl, Francis I patt., flat quatrefoil bottom flaring out to form sides w/scalloped rims, heavily embossed w/fruit & scroll decoration, Reed & Barton, 8 1/2" d. (ILLUS.) **595**

Sterling Oblong Bowl

Bowl, oblong, center engraved "KTV - Oct. 28 - 1879-'04," sides decorated w/deep relief flowers & scrolls, marked "Sterling" w/a sword in a wreath and the number "1148 1/2," 5 5/8 x 7 1/4" (ILLUS.) **245**

Hand-hammered Oval Bowl

Bowl, oval, hand-hammered surface, deep, flaring bowl on short base, marked "F.S. Co. - Sterling - Y-3," 3 1/4 x 5 5/8", 3 1/4 h. (ILLUS.) **125**

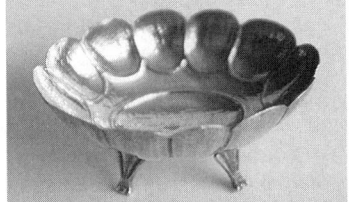

Hand-hammered Sterling Bowl

Bowl, oval, hand-hammered surface, flaring sides made up of petal sections, paw feet, indistinct maker's mark, 2 x 3 1/2 x 4 3/4" (ILLUS.) **95**

Sterling Bowl with Decorated Rim

Bowl, round, concentric sides, rim decorated w/flowers & scrolls & leaves, marked "Gorham Sterling - 109," 5 1/2" d. (ILLUS.) **75**

Sterling Bowl by Gorham

Bowl, round, flat bottom, flaring rim w/scalloped edge decorated w/stylized scrolls, marked "Gorham Sterling - 739," 6 1/4" d. (ILLUS.) **75**

Decorated Silver Box

Box, cov., cylindrical, w/embossed decoration of daisy-type flowers & leaves covering base & lid, marked on bottom "Theo B. Starr," 2 1/4" d., 3 3/8" h. (ILLUS.) **450**

Tiffany Sterling Covered Butter Dish

Butter dish, cov., round body w/chased floral design on upper section, raised on shell feet, the domed lid w/floral finial & chased work design similar to body, Tiffany & Co., ca. 1855, 5 3/4" d., 5 3/8" h. (ILLUS.) **784**

Sterling Covered Butter Dish & Tray

Butter dish & tray, cov., rim of round tray, sides of dish & center of domed lid covered w/heavily embossed flower & fruit decoration, the lid topped w/figure of resting cow, the dish w/two upright tab handles, marked "S. Kirk & Son - 11 ounces," 7 1/2" d., 4" h. (ILLUS.) **2,495**

Sterling Christmas Ornament

Christmas ornament, in the form of an angel w/hands clamped in front, 3/4 x 1/12", 3 7/8" h. (ILLUS.).................. **62**

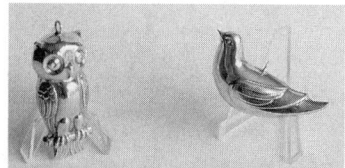

Sterling Christmas Ornaments

Christmas ornaments, in the shape of a dove & an owl, each marked "Copyright RMTRUSH Sterling" & dated 1972 & 1974 respectively, each 1 x 2 3/4", each (ILLUS.)... **65**

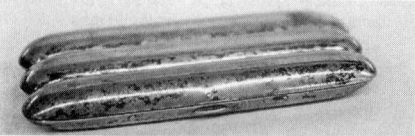

Silver Cigar Case

Cigar case, rectangular hinged three-section style, 2 5/8 x 5 1/2" (ILLUS.) **69**

Tiffany Sterling Cigarette Lighter

Cigarette lighter, unadorned cylinder shape rests on slightly flared base, Tiffany & Co., 2 3/4" h. (ILLUS.) **145**

Coffeepot, cov., coin, footed tapering cylindrical body w/a stepped domed hinged cover w/berry finial & chased floral & foliate band, the body w/a central reserve depicting a country fishing scene surrounded by C-scrolls, floral & foliate designs, a crab stock handle w/acorns & oak leaves, ribbed swan's-neck spout, monogrammed, Obadiah Rich, Boston, ca. 1830, 10" h. (minor dent) **1,725**

Sterling Demitasse Cup & Saucer

Demitasse set: 12 cups w/inserts & saucers, both cups & saucers w/pierced-design rims, Steuben Aurene glass inserts for cups, applied handles, 2 1/8 x 3 3/4", the set (ILLUS. of one cup w/insert & saucer) **6,500**

Medal Honoring Charles Lindbergh

Medal, round, honoring Charles Lindbergh, one side w/embossed bust of Lindbergh in headgear, w/goggles hanging around neck, around rim "Charles A. Lindbergh," marked on edge "Medallic Art Co., .999+ pure silver," reverse w/images of eagle & angels, 2 7/8" d. (ILLUS.) **165**

Sterling Silver Schnauzer

Model of Schnauzer, standing dog w/mouth open slightly, 2 1/4 x 6 x 7" (ILLUS.).............. **375**
Pitcher, coin, classical-style, round domed foot & short pedestal below the wide bulbous body w/a stepped shoulder & high, wide arched spout, large S-scroll handle, original presentation inscription dated 1836, marked by Jones, Lows & Ball of Boston, 10 7/8" h. **853**
Pitcher, coin, presentation-type, graceful form w/scrolled handle, round stepped base, inscribed "Ohio State Board of Agriculture Premium," maker's mark "Blynn & Baldwin," 8 1/4" h. **303**
Pitcher, water, classical form w/floral & vine decoration & "R" on side, ca. 1930, 9" h. **420**

"Normandic" Pattern Water Pitcher

Pitcher, water, footed ovoid body chased w/a band of floral clusters around the shoulder, a wide arched spout & C-scroll handle., in the "Normandic" patt. by Wallace Silversmiths, four-pint capacity, engraved "R" on front (ILLUS.)........................... **896**
Pitcher, water, Neoclassic form w/paneled body & garland decoration, ca. 1930, 9" h. **420**
Punch ladle, "Tomato Vine" patt., w/heart form bowl and monogram "JBH," Tiffany & Co., ca. 1872, 11 1/2" l. **672**

Salt & Pepper Shaker Arches

Salt & pepper shakers, in the form of Japanese arches decorated w/lily pad medallions on cross bars, each column resting on six-sided stepped base, 2 3/8" h., pr. (ILLUS.)... **135**

Lantern-style Salt & Pepper Shakers

Salt & pepper shakers, in the form of Japanese lanterns on six-sided base, w/original lined box, 3 1/4" h., pr. (ILLUS.) **145**

Pagoda Salt & Pepper Shakers

Salt & pepper shakers, in the form of Japanese pagodas, 1 1/4 x 1 1/2", 3 1/4" h., pr. (ILLUS.)... **125**
Serving spoon, coin, coffin-end handle, mark attributed to William Holmes, Jr., Boston, 1742-1825, 9 1/4" l. **55**

Sterling Silver Spoon

Spoon, pierced bowl w/shell motif & decorated w/scrolls, marked on back of handle "Sterling," 4 1/2" l. (ILLUS.).......................... **65**

Tankard, cov., coin, ringed baluster form, applied double-scroll handle, domed lid w/pierced shell & scroll thumbpiece, marked twice on base "A UNDERHILL" in rectangle for Andrew Underhill, New York, ca. 1780, 8 1/2" h. **24,900**

Tazza, wide shallow dished top w/a piercedwork rim divided by floral designs & surrounding an etched bouquet in vases, monogrammed in the center, raised on a simple flaring round pedestal base, Woodside Sterling Company, ca. 1910, 9" d., 4 1/2" h. **179**

Sterling Silver Coffee & Tea Service

Tea & coffee service: cov. teapot, cov. coffeepot, creamer, cov. sugar & waste bowl; sterling, patt. #1103/87 by Dominick & Haff, early 20th c., the set (ILLUS.)...... **784**

Pierced Sterling Tea Strainer

Tea strainer, w/pierced handle & stylized floral pattern, mark of Frank M. Whiting Co. & "Sterling - 5005," 5 1/4" l. (ILLUS.) **125**

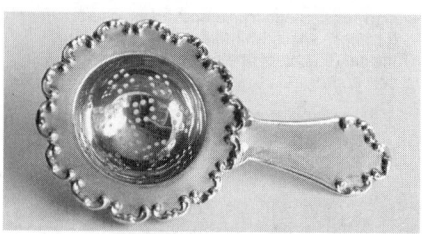

Sterling Silver Tea Strainer

Tea strainer, w/scalloped bowl decorated w/C-scrolls, 4 3/4" l. (ILLUS.) **125**

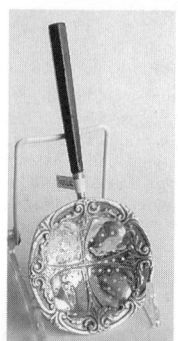

Wooden-handled Sterling Tea Strainer

Tea strainer, w/wooden handle, bowl decorated w/stylized C-scrolls & leaves, 6 3/4" l. (ILLUS.).. **175**

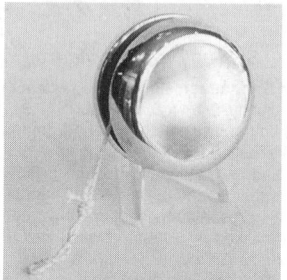

Tiffany Sterling Yo-yo

Yo-yo, sterling, unadorned, made by Tiffany & Co., w/cloth pouch, 2 1/4" d. (ILLUS.)........ **295**

English & Others

Coin Silver Ashtray

Ashtray, composed of three hammered Peruvian coins joined at base, w/tiny full-bodied llamas as feet, applied leaf forms for holding cigarettes, 2 x 4" (ILLUS.) **125**

Oval Silver Basket

Basket, oval, flaring pierced basketweave sides, decorated w/garland swags & scrollwork, lion heads at sides w/rings in mouths form handles, indistinct hallmark, 2 1/2 x 3 1/8 x 5 1/2" (ILLUS.) **345**

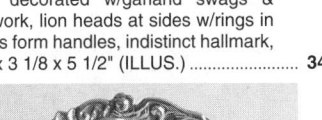

English Silver Bowl

Bowl, round, w/elaborate raised design of scrolls, flowers & leaves along flaring sides, marked "WC" & hallmarks for London, England, 4 3/4" d. (ILLUS.) **155**

Turtle Covered Box

Box, cov., in the form of a turtle poking its head out of its shell, indistinct mark on bottom, 3 1/4" l. (ILLUS.) **165**

Sterling Silver Egg-shaped Box

Box, egg-shaped, two piece, Mexican sterling, 1 3/4 x 3 1/2" (ILLUS.) **79**

Russian Embossed Cigarette Case

Cigarette case, rectangular, heavily embossed design of bears in woods, amethyst glass bead in clasp of lid, gold applied charm reading "From Momma 1-1-1917," hallmarked "84" & engraved "1914 Misha," Imperial-era Russia, 1/2 x 3 3/8 x 4 3/8" (ILLUS.) **395**

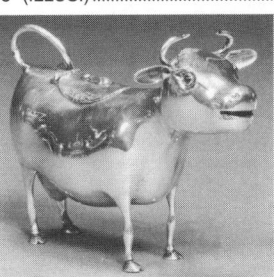

Dutch Silver Cream Pitcher

Creamer, cov., figure of cow w/red glass eyes, handle formed by tail raised to brush off the fly applied to the cover, open mouth pours cream, Dutch, ca. 1900, 4" h., 5 1/2" l. (ILLUS.) **1,120**

Rare German Silver Cow Creamer

Creamer, cov., figure of cow w/red glass eyes, handle formed by tail raised to brush off the fly applied to the cover, open mouth pours cream, German, ca. 1900, , rare, 3 1/4" h., 4 1/2" l. (ILLUS.) **1,232**

English Sterling Silver Creamer

swelled plain boat-shape
arched spout & reeded rim,
ed strap handle, engraved
m w/a cartouche & mono-
Ann & William Bateman,
London, ca. 1801, 4 7/8" h. (ILLUS.)............ **336**

Prussian Silver Cup with Cover

Cup, cov., cylindrical body engraved w/leaf
& scroll decoration inset w/coins, ball-
shaped feet, the dome-shaped cover
w/bust finial of William I, Prussian, dated
1885, 8 1/4" h. (ILLUS.)................................... **448**

Shell-form Sterling Silver Dish

Dish, shell-form, top ending in handle, decorated w/heavily chased floral and foliate
body, made in Sheffield, England, dated
1889, 2 1/2 x 2 x 11" (ILLUS.) **616**

Russian Carte-de-Visite Picture Frame

Frame, for carte-de-visite picture, Art Nouveau style, hallmarked "84," Imperial-era
Russia, 3 1/4 x 5 5/8" (ILLUS.)....................... **295**

Mexican Silver Jewelry Box

Jewelry box, figural, in the shape of a
dome-top trunk w/a hinged cover,
marked "Clavel Sterling - 0.950," Mexico,
2 x 2 1/2" (ILLUS.).. **395**

Heart-shaped Sterling Silver Mirror

Mirror, heart-shaped pierced frame ornately decorated w/birds, flowers, garlands &
scrollwork, beveled mirror, purple velvet
backing, 10 3/4 x 13 1/2" (ILLUS.) **2,495**

Mexican Sterling Pitcher

Pitcher, fluted body flaring out to shoulder,
flaring rim w/shallow spout, round
stepped base, ring handle, marked "Ster-
ling - 553," Mexican, 6" h. (ILLUS.) **185**

Figural Sterling Salt & Pepper Shakers

Salt & pepper shakers, figures of a fisherman w/accordion & a fishwife holding a
fish, Denmark, 2 5/8" h., pr. (ILLUS.) **165**

English Silver Teaspoon

Teaspoon, trowel-shaped bowl pierced
w/diamond-shaped holes along rim, bowl
& handle decorated w/scrolls, leaves &
shell motif, made by John Betteridge, En-
gland, c. 1820, 3 1/4" l. (ILLUS.) **195**

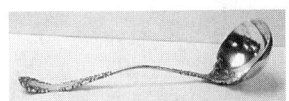

English Sterling Silver Tray

Tray, footed shell-shaped tray w/elaborate
scrollwork & engraved but indistinct ini-
tials, English, 9 1/2 x 16" (ILLUS.) **995**
Wine bottle coasters, a turned wood base
surrounded by low upright sides bright-
cut engraved & pierced w/a lion crest
centered by paterae alternating w/fes-
toons, all centered by two scroll borders
w/beaded rims, Hester Bateman, Lon-
don, 1804, 5" d., pr. **1,560**

Silver Plate (Flatware)

*The following is a selection of popular silver plate
flatware from the turn of the 19th century. The pattern
name is followed by the maker and model number in
parentheses, which is followed by the date the pattern
was introduced.*

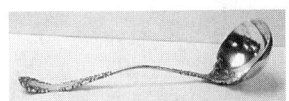

Large Silver Plate Ladle

Ladle, Yale I patt., curved handle decorated
w/flowers & scrollwork, Wm. Rogers,
1894 patent, 12 1/2" l. (ILLUS.) **78**

Assyrian Head (Rogers Bros. 1847) - 1886
Nut cracker **125**
Pickle tongs **75**
Sugar tongs **65**
Teaspoon **24**

Floral (R. Wallace 1835) - 1902
Bonbon spoon **75**
Cake server **55**
Cake serving fork, individual **55**
Food pusher **55**
Sugar tongs **65**

Moselle (American Silver Co.) - 1906
Cake serving fork, individual **195**
Cheese scoop **200**
Ice cream fork **250**
Lettuce fork **275**
Sugar shell **65**
Tomato server **350**

Raphael (Rogers & Hamilton) - 1896
Berry spoon **75**
Butter, individual **25**
Citrus fruit spoon **35**
Ice cream fork **45**
Seafood cocktail fork **38**
Sugar shell **35**

Silver Plate (Hollowware)

Silver Plate Base or Holder

Base or holder, probably for decorative
glass, top missing, circular stepped base
is decorated w/applied figures of boy &
begging dog & cylindrical shaft of holder
w/flaring base, made by Aurora Silver
Plate   Co.,   style   number   029,
3 1/4 x 5 1/4" (ILLUS.) **295**

Pierced-design Basket

Basket, pierced base & swivel strap handle
w/applied flower decoration, style number   1728,   made   by   Meriden,
7 3/4 x 9 1/2 x 9 3/4" (ILLUS.) **245**

Swivel-handle Basket

Basket, round, w/swivel openwork decorated handle, repoussé grape vine decoration, made by Simpson, Hall, Miller & Co., 5 x 6" (ILLUS.) **195**

Silver Plate Engraved Baton Head

Baton head, round, engraved "Nancy Ruth Heverly - Center Point, Iowa - 1937" in diamond border, 2" d. (ILLUS.) **28**

Biscuit Warmer & Tray

Biscuit warmer & tray, cov., footed biscuit warmer has raised repeating design around top & bottom, narrow ribbed rims on lid & tray, lid w/decorated knob handle & tray w/decorative handles applied to raised rim, faint marks on bottom, 7 x 7 1/4 x 10 3/4" (ILLUS.) **400**

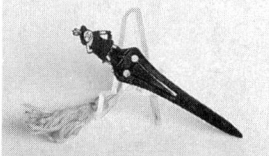

Scotsman Bookmark

Bookmark, shaft tapering to point, topped w/figure of Scotsman in tam & kilt, enamel detail, attached tassel, 3" l. (ILLUS.) **25**

Reed & Barton Footed Bowl

Bowl, deep oval shape w/scalloped rim & flat bottom on ball feet, sides decorated w/embossed flowers & figures of two girls, flowers embossed on ends to form handles, marked "708" on bottom, Reed & Barton, 3 1/2 x 4 x 6 3/4" (ILLUS.) **495**

Silver Plate Inscribed Bowl

Bowl, footed deep gently flared form inscribed "25 Years of Service - Northwest Orient Airlines," 6" w., 3 1/4" h. (ILLUS.) **42**

Art Nouveau-style Covered Box

Box, cov., Art Nouveau-style, footed, decorated w/roses, marked on bottom "92 DL," possibly a hair receiver, 2 3/4 x 2 3/4 x 3 1/2" (ILLUS.) **165**

Fancy Silver Plate Butter Dish

Butter dish, cov., spherical form w/ribbed dome top supported in circular ring raised on three cabriole paw-foot legs w/lion heads at top, front of top rolls back to reveal interior, marked "Trademark 1883 - Rogers Silver Co.," missing glass liner, 5 1/2" d., 4 1/2" h. (ILLUS.) **75**

Candelabra, a square stepped base & slender flaring squared column w/urn-form top socket inset w/two serpentine arms ending in urn-form sockets & centered by a third socket, marked "W.H. & S.B.," late 19th-early 20th c., pr. **605**

Silver Plate Card Tray

Card tray, four-lobed squared-shape tray decorated w/engraved flowers & insects, attached to round base by three legs & two applied leaf & flower supports, maker's name indistinct, 5 7/8 x 6 1/4" (ILLUS.) **175**

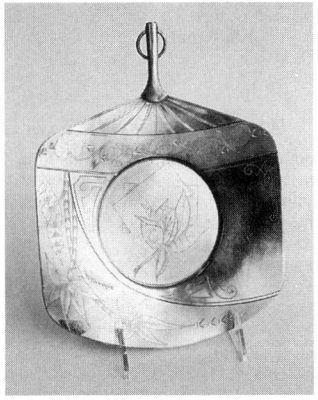

Footed Card Tray

Card tray, in the shape of an Oriental fan w/handle, decorated w/engraved shapes of lily pads & assorted flora, on three turtle-shaped feet, marked "3518," 8 x 10" (ILLUS.) **365**

Girl Figure with Clock

Clock, figural, in form of bonneted girl holding folds of cloak open, w/clock set in folds on one side, 2 1/2 x 7 x 7" (ILLUS.) **795**

Wilcox Cocktail Pitcher

Cocktail pitcher, cov., domed base & body decorated w/embossed scrollwork, flowers & leaves, short spout, decorated handle, style number N59, Wilcox, in the Paisley design, 12 1/2" h. (ILLUS.) **225**

Covered Coffee Container with Spoon

Coffee container, cov., rolled foot, hand-hammered & pierced decoration above pierced letters spelling "COFFEE," blue glass liner, spoon attaches to holder, 3 7/8 x 5 1/2" (ILLUS.) **35**

Floral-decorated Coffeepot

Coffeepot, cov., domed ringed base raised on applied leaf-style feet, lower pot w/engraved flowers, upper part, spout & handle w/raised flowers & leaves, pierced finial on flat lid, style number 2902, Simpson, Hall, Miller & Co., 11" h. (ILLUS.) **245**

Reed & Barton Footed Coffeepot

Coffeepot, cov., on outward curving legs decorated w/flower & leaves, bottom of pot decorated w/stylized birds, flowers & leaves, hinged domed lid w/knob handle, decorative thumbpiece on pot handle, style number 2962, Reed & Barton, 5 1/2 x 9 x 13 1/4" (ILLUS.) **225**

Plated Collar and Cuff Box

Collar & cuff box, cov., square, applied openwork fern, scrollwork & shield design on sides and extending to feet, top engraved "Collars and Cuffs," 6 3/4" (ILLUS.) **900**

Plated Compote with Squirrel

Compote, deep rounded bowl w/figure of squirrel sitting on a branch eating an acorn applied to rim, on a slender pedestal w/domed foot, marked "Sheffield USA," 6" d., 9" h. (ILLUS.)............................. **325**

American Silver Compote

Compote, engraved line decoration & initials of newlyweds & dated 1869, shaped rim & base on short foot, handles decorated w/lions' heads, marked on bottom "Rogers Smith & Co., New Haven, Conn. No. 1299," 9 x 13 1/2", 6" h. (ILLUS.) **2,950**

Silver Plate Creamer & Sugar

Creamer & open sugar, slightly tapering lobed oval classical shape w/overall hammered finish, delicate scroll handles, each 5 1/4" wide, 3 1/2" h., pr. (ILLUS.) **42**

Silver Plate Ewer-form Cup

Cup, ewer form w/handle, bulbous lower part on rolled base & engraved "Florence '88," slightly flaring top third w/embossed birds & floral design, made by Meriden Co., style number 151, 2 1/2 x 3 1/2" (ILLUS.) **35**

Abstract Design Dish

Dish, abstract shape decorated w/molded flowers, bee & cicada, style number 524M, Simpson, Hall, Miller & Co., 4 1/2 x 6 1/4 x 7 1/2" (ILLUS.) **325**

Silver Plate Egg Cup

Egg cup, figural egg form, two-part, divided at center & engraved w/flowers, a figural chick & wishbone at the sides, chick head finial (ILLUS.) **179**

Silver Plate Epergne

Epergne, in the form of a palm tree w/sinuous trunk and six palm fronds, w/a fox running at the circular, ringed base, topped w/a cranberry glass trumpet-shaped flower, 6 1/2" h. (ILLUS.) **1,495**

Reed & Barton Goblet

Goblet, round stepped ringed base w/baluster-shape stem, decorated w/stylized flowers, scrolls & fans, style number 4702, Reed & Barton, 7" h. (ILLUS.) **65**

Victorian Silver Plate Hairbrush

Hairbrush, tapering oval head decorated w/repoussé flowers & plants, swirl pattern on handle, Victorian, 3" w., 10" l. (ILLUS.) **18**

Art Nouveau Jewelry Box

Jewelry box, cov., Art Nouveau-style, decorated w/embossed decoration of maiden w/flowing hair standing next to a large rose, velvet lining, marked "Mermod and Jackson Jewelry Co. - Derby Silver Co. - 3464," 3 x 6 1/2 x 7" (ILLUS.) **595**

Singing Bird Knife Rest

Knife rest, in the form of a singing bird perched on ball end of knife rest attached to scroll support that sits on round base w/floral detail, 2 x 2 3/4", 5" l. (ILLUS.) **235**

Squirrel Knife Rest

Knife rest, rod supported at two ends by figures of squirrels holding acorns, bottom marked "Reed & Barton," style number 90, 1 3/4 x 1 7/8", 4 1/4" l. (ILLUS.) **245**

Bud Vase/Napkin Ring

Napkin ring, Egyptian Revival style, ring engraved w/floral decoration and applied busts of Egyptian-style women on either side, their arms elongated to form feet of napkin ring, a trumpet form bud base mounted on top of ring, 5 5/8" h. (ILLUS.)..... **495**

Nut or Candy Dish

Nut or candy dish, oval petal design, style number 839, Pairpoint, 5 x 8 3/4" (ILLUS.)... **32**

Leprechaun Paperweight

Paperweight, round domed base decorated in stylized oak leaves, acorns & flowers holds mushroom on which hatted leprechaun sits, marked "Reed & Barton," 3" h. (ILLUS.).. **250**

Silver Plate Pipe Holder

Pipe holder, holder sits on flaring rimmed base decorated w/applied leaves & flowers, two flowers applied to edge of holder to keep pipe in place, marked "Warranted," indistinct style number, 2 1/2 x 2 1/2 x 3 1/2" (ILLUS.)........................ **295**

Silver Plate Salt Cellar

Salt cellar, in the form of a dolphin carrying a shell on its back, rimmed base w/design depicting ocean waves, handle in the form of a ribbed leaf, 2 x 2 3/4 x 4 1/2" (ILLUS.)................................ **275**

Silver Plate Salt Dispenser

Salt dispenser, footed urn form, engraved "Salt" on front, w/special spring-loaded plunger for dispensing salt through bottom, marked "Rasnik Co.," 3 1/2" h. (ILLUS.) **49**

Serving dish, cov., double, a rectangular two-section dish w/a flanged rim w/gadrooned borders & shells & foliage, raised on curved paw feet, turned faux ivory end handles, removable wells w/domed rectangular covers, crown mark w/"C.S.C." & stars, late 19th-early 20th c., 12 1/2 x 20 1/2", 7 1/4" h. **248**

Owl Smoking Accessory

Smoking accessory, consisting of figure of owl on branch attached to three hollow tree stumps w/removable inserts for holding cigarettes, matches & ashes, 5 x 7 x 7 1/2" (ILLUS.)............................ **750**

Four-prong Plated Spool Holder

Spool holder, rounded triangular footed base w/ raised rim ornately decorated, center holds four knobbed prongs for spools, Meriden, No. 2110, 2 1/8 x 5" (ILLUS.)... **145**

Silver Plate Spoon Holder

Spoon holder, narrow oblong shape w/pierced leafy scroll sections at each end, upright angled strap handles, 1 3/4 x 8", 3" h. (ILLUS.) **35**

Silver Plate Stamp Box

Stamp box, cov., rectangular, embossed "U.S. Mail" on top, w/floral design border and sides, 5/8 x 1 3/4 x 2" (ILLUS.).............. **125**

Cufflink Box

Stud box, cov., round, footed, decorated w/applied flowers, silver stud on lid, marked on bottom "W.B. Mfg. Co. - No. 2503," 2 1/4 b 3" (ILLUS.) **145**

Silver Plate Tea & Coffee Set

Tea & coffee set: cov. teapot, cov. coffeepot, cov. hot water kettle, milk pitcher, cov. sugar, creamer, waste bowl & tray; a classical form paneled body w/etched floral design, tray w/double handles, Barbour Silver Co., patt. #5314, ca. 1895, the set (ILLUS.).................. **952**

Souvenir Toothpick Holder

Toothpick holder, figural, in the form of a cherub on pierced floral base, carrying an egg-shaped holder w/pierced floral-decorated edge, front of holder engraved "Souvenir of Spokane, Wash.," 2 1/8 x 3 1/2" (ILLUS.) **175**

Monkey Toothpick Holder

Toothpick holder, figural, round stepped base holds figure of monkey holding staff and carrying on its back a basket w/basketweave decoration & rope twist rim, Meriden & Co., 3 1/3" h. (ILLUS.) **550**

Pan-Pacific Expo Tray

Tray, commemorating the 1915 Pan-Pacific Expo in San Francisco, raised rim embossed "San Francisco - 1915" & center embossed w/image of North & South America and ships sailing through Panama Canal, 1/2" deep, 5" d. (ILLUS.) **55**

Tin & Tole

Chocolate grater, tin, "Edgar Pat Nov. 10, 1890," 8 1/2" **300**

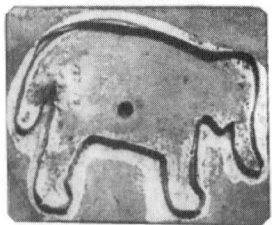

Tin Elephant Cookie Cutter

Cookie cutter, tin, elephant, w/ strap handle, 4 5/8" l. (ILLUS.) **55**
Apple corer, tin, T-handle, handmade, 5" **15**
Apple corer, tin & wood, "Boye Pat No. 1206403 Made in USA" **15**

Football Arena Advertising Ashtray

Ashtray, in the form of a football arena w/printed details of field surrounded by bleachers full of fans, advertising Chesterfield cigarettes, "They Satisfy" in red letters in center, 5 3/8 x 6 1/4" (ILLUS.) **65**

Tin Armored Car Still Bank

Bank, still, in the form of an armored car in red, black & silver-grey, w/plastic wheels, windup alarm sounds when back door is opened, made in Japan, 4 x 4 1/2", 9 3/4" l. (ILLUS.) **145**
Biscuit cutter, tin, Jenny Wren advertising on strap handle **15**
Biscuit cutter, tin, Rumfordþadvertising, 3 1/2" **15**

Toleware Box

Box, cov., tole, painted & polychrome-decorated, lion head handle on domed lid appears to be original, Pennsylvania, first quarter 19th c., 6 x 7 1/2 x 10" (ILLUS.) ... **1,080**
Can opener & jar opener combination tool, tin, "Distributed By C.S. Ripley & Co Cleveland, Ohio," 8 1/4" **25**

Tole Hanging Candle Box

Candle box, tole, cylindrical body w/two tabs for hanging, old red & yellow grained paint w/red, white, yellow & black floral decoration, 14 3/8" l. (ILLUS.) **908**
Candle lantern, punched-tin Paul Revere-style, cylindrical w/pierced design circles & rays on the hinged door, overall piercing around the sides, a tall conical cap w/pierced design & vent holes, large strap ring handle at top, 19th c. (light pitting overall, a small hole) **275**
Candle lantern, tin & glass, a tin framework w/glass sides & door w/wire protectors, pyramidal top pierced w/stars & circles, large strap ring handle, stamped "Parker's Patent - 1855 - Proctersville, VT," mid-19th c., 15 3/4" h. **523**

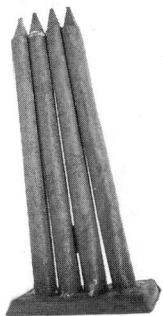

Tin Candle Mold

Candle mold, tin, four-tube, on rectangular foot, base handle missing, base 2 1/4 x 5 1/2, 11" h. (ILLUS.) **129**

Candle sconces, tin, crimped tombstone crest w/molded edges, back w/rectangular mirror, semicircular base w/three candle holders, 17 1/2" h. (minor rust), pr.......... **825**

Tin Candle Sconce

Candle sconces, tin, round, crimped reflectors & crimped-edge pans, reflectors w/concentric crimped circles & small center mirrors, minor resoldering, 8 3/4" h., pr. (ILLUS. of one) **2,310**

Tin Miniature Suitcase Container

Candy container, tin, miniature model of suitcase in gold decorated w/red & pink Teenie Weenie comic characters, 1922, near mint, 1 1/4 x 3 1/2 x 5" (ILLUS.)............. **295**

Victorian Coal Hod

Coal hod, cov., tole, Oriental decoration including Japanese woman & crane, flowers, etc., original black paint & faint decoration, domed lid w/embossed ray tole designs and ring handle, side handles are attached to Minerva heads, short cast-iron feet have animal faces, complete w/lift-out insert, Victorian, 20" h. (ILLUS.) **220**

Coffeepot, cov., tin, flaring cylindrical foot below the flaring cylindrical lower body & tapering cylindrical upper body, punched overall w/fine wrigglework including an urn of tulips & other flowers on each side

Tole Coffeepot & Document Boxes

& four bands of entwining lines, domed cover w/brass finial, angled swan's-neck spout, strap handle w/grip, first half 19th c., 11 1/4" h. (dents & resolder)................. **1,595**

Coffeepot, cov., tole, tapering sides w/gooseneck spout, strap handle, domed cover, w/worn dark japanning w/a white circle on each side w/strong folk-style yellow, red & green flowers including tulips, yellow stylized foliage border around short flaring base, 10 1/4" h. (ILLUS. left, bottom previous page) **1,210**

Large Tin Cookie Cutter

Cookie cutter, tin, bakery-type, w/outline of man in flat-top hat, large oval handle, 7 5/8" l. (ILLUS.) **220**

Creamer, cov., tole, cylindrical body tapering from base, short spout, strap handle, worn japanning w/yellow lines & red & green rose-like flowers, 4 1/4" h. (ILLUS. top right, w/other various toleware)............... **330**

Document box, tole, cov., rectangluar, dark japanning w/white swags on front & sides & strong full-petaled red & yellow flowers & green leaves, yellow designs on domed lid w/brass bail handle, oval escutcheons, tin hasp, 3 5/8 x 4 3/4 x 8 1/4" **440**

Document box, cov., tole, rectangular, dark japanning w/bright green foliage & red flowers & berries on front, yellow scrollwork & stripes on domed lid w/tin hasp & wire bale handle, 5 5/8 x 6 1/2 x 9 3/8" (ILLUS. right with coffeepot & other document box).. **440**

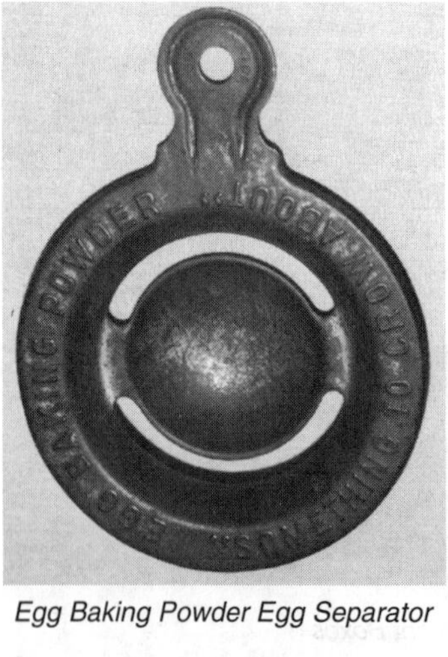

Egg Baking Powder Egg Separator

Egg separator, tin, advertising "Egg Baking Powder" (ILLUS.).. **150**

Egg separator, tin, advertising, marked "Use Puritan Fadeless Dyes - None Better"... **25**

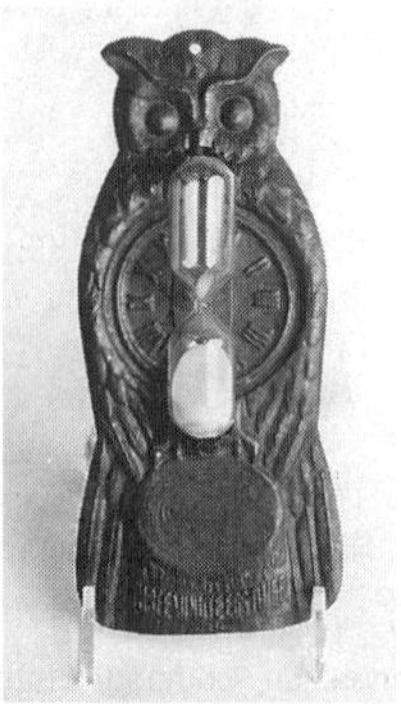

Tin Owl Egg Timer

Egg timer, stamped, three-minute egg timer glass vial attached to the form of an owl perched on a stump w/a clock design on its chest & "Three Minute Egg Timer" embossed at the bottom, 6 1/2" h. (ILLUS.) **145**

Flour sifter, tin & wood, "Duplex Sifter 5 cup, Pat. Nov. 1917 & 1922, Mfg. by Ullrich Tinware Co." **30**

Food mold, tin, deep heart-shaped form w/the flat top pierced w/stylized leafy stems & small blossoms, small strap handle at the top, on three small feet, 4 1/2" l., 3 1/8" h. (small old soldered repair)... **385**

Tin Headlamp

Headlamp, tin, rectangular, w/punched holes around base, large round glass pane, nickel-plated burner, flattened dome chimney, for traction engine (trolley or tram), burned kerosene, ca. 1900, 24" h. (ILLUS.) **1,200**

Jardinieres, tole, serpentine shapes w/lionhead handles & paw feet, decorated w/floral design swags, 9 x 14 1/2", 9" h., pr. **448**

Match holder, pressed tin, backplate w/scalloped border shows image of build-

Pressed-tin Match Holder

ing in circle below banner w/"Carnegie Library - Newton, Kansas," square holder for matches attached to front w/"Matches" embossed on it, decorative leaf borders at corners of both pieces, 3 1/4 x 5" (ILLUS.) 125

Mug, tole, very slightly tapering cylinder shape w/rolled rim at base & strap handle, w/original floral decoration in red, yellow & & brown on a ground of very worn brown japanning, 5 3/4" h. (ILLUS. right with sugar bowl) 385

Tin Minstrel Noise Maker

Noise maker, tin, drumhead-like piece w/handle, decorated w/figures of dancing black minstrels within decorative border, original paint in reds, blues & yellows & original printed design, noise is produced when ball at end of shaft fastened to handle is swung against it, made in Germany, 6 1/2" l. 245

Nutmeg grater, tin, "The Boye Nutmeg Grater Pat Apl'd For," 6" 85

Tin Oil Lamp

Oil lamp, tin, w/ lidded opening on top, strap handle, & straight spout where wick end comes out, 1 3/4 x 2", 5 1/2" l. (ILLUS.) 85

Pencil sharpener, plated tin, in the form of an alarm clock w/printed dial, made in Germany, 1/2 x 1 1/8 x 1 3/4" 65

Pencil sharpener, tin, model of a table radio, w/peeling paint, made in Germany, 1/2 x 1 1/8 x 1 3/8" 55

Spoon rest, tin, advertising, marked "The Big Store - McCammon Investment Co. Props." 65

Tole Sugar Bowl & Mug

Sugar bowl, cov., tin, tapered body w/slightly flaring base, w/original floral decoration in red, yellow & green on a very worn dark ground, 3 3/4" h. (ILLUS. left) 385

Sugar container, cov., tole, cylindrical, tapering to short base, worn japanned ground w/large red fruit & green leaf design, lid w/finial, red & yellow leaves on bare tin, 3 1/2 x 4" (ILLUS. bottom left, w/other various toleware) 550

Tea caddy, cov., tole, cylindrical, black ground w/red acorn-like designs & yellow & green flourishes, 6" h. (some wear)........... 495

Tea caddy, cov., tole, cylindrical, red ground w/pinkish white band at top, w/red, yellow & green flowers, 4 1/8" h. (ILLUS. top left, w/other various toleware).. 495

Various Toleware Pieces

Tea caddy, tole, cylinder body, cone-shape neck, dark japanned ground w/design of a red ball shape w/copper-colored feathering, 6 3/4" h. (ILLUS. second from right, w/other various toleware) 358

Tinder box, cov., tin, low cylindrical form w/the top half lifting off, flat top centered by a candle socket, finger ring on base half, interior damper lid w/flint & oversized striker, 19th c., 4" d. 413

Tray, tole, octagonal, sides w/ivory band of red fruit & flowers & green leaves & yellow flourishes, dark decorated border around rim, center w/traces of red crystallization, 5 3/4 x 8 1/2" (some wear, over varnish has yellowed)............................ 220

Tray, tole, oval, dark japanned ground w/yellow wavy line & red & yellow center design, 6 7/8" l. (ILLUS. bottom right, w/other various toleware) 1,760

Tray, tole, rounded oblong apple tray, black japanned ground w/red & yellow rim design & center rectangle decorated w/red, yellow & green floral design, 8 1/2 x 13 1/4" (minor wear)........................... 770

MILITARIA & WARTIME MEMORABILIA

Civil War (1861-65)

Civil War-era Artillery Drum

Artillery drum, w/original decoration of eagle w/shield, holding a banner in its beak w/"Reg. U.S., Artillery," stars & yellow rays over its head, all on a thin red ground, old dark patina on unpainted side & brass tacks (two missing), old ropes are threaded through the hoops & several leather tabs remain, original interior paper label for "C&F Soistmann, No. 458, Philadelphia, PA.," minor stitched repair to one area of cord, includes snare cords on bottom, stenciled "C.D." next to them, three sticks, 17" d., 15 5/8" h. (ILLUS.).. $11,555

Cartridge box w/cross belt & plates, dark leather w/tin liners remaining & a brass "U.S." oval plate on front & eagle plate on belt, 8" w., 7" h. (short splits in strap) 665

Collection of Captain John A. Sloan, Co. B, 27th Regt., North Carolina, Guilford Greys, includes ambrotype of Sloan in uniform w/star belt plate, noncommissioned officer's sword & Hardee hat on

table w/infantry & "G.G." insignias, 2 3/4 x 3 1/4"; documents, most in dark brown ink, including personal letters, journals from early 1860s & during war, court martial w/"Head Quarters, Army of Northern Virginia" letterhead; & oval cloth eagle hat insignia w/gold thread, the group 5,225

Group of images: seven cartes-de-visite & one tintype, all identified in old brown ink, some from the 77th U.S. Infantry, grouped in Victorian frame, 17 x 17 1/2" (some stains, frame chipped on one corner) 605

Musician's sword w/scabbard, partial stamped signature for Ames Mfg., Chicopee, Massachusetts, w/"1862," 28" blade w/brass hilt, leather scabbard w/brass tips, 35 1/4" l................................... 413

Officer's sword belt plate, rectangular cast-brass eagle plate w/applied nickel silver wreath, section of the original belt remaining, 19 1/2" l. 330

Copper Civil War Powder Flask

Powder flask, copper, w/embossed decoration of flags, cannon, swords & rifles, pistols & shot, 6 1/4" h. (ILLUS.)..................... 120

MOLDS - CANDY, FOOD & MISCELLANEOUS

Also see BUTTER MOLDS & STAMPS and METALS

Candle mold, floor-model, tin & cherry, 36 long tin candle tubes mounted w/an open dovetailed wood framed w/bootjack ends, old varnished surface, 7 x 18 1/4", 15" h. $1,210

Cross & Flowers Chocolate Mold

Chocolate, cross w/flowers, tin, two-piece, 3 1/4 x 5" (ILLUS.) **35**

Small Pipe Chocolate Mold

Chocolate, pipe, tin, two-piece, 1 5/8 x 3 1/2" (ILLUS.) **25**

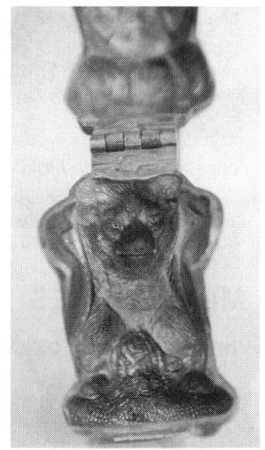

Pewter Airplane Ice Cream Mold

Ice cream, airplane, pewter, hinged, No. 1132, closed 4 1/2 x 5" (ILLUS.) **125**

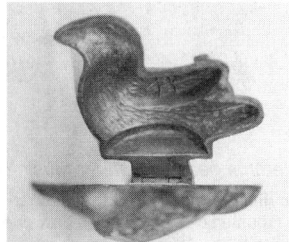

Pewter Bear Ice Cream Mold

Ice cream, bear, pewter, hinged, marked "E & Co." w/indistinct number, closed 2 1/4 x 4 1/4" (ILLUS.) **175**

Perched Bird Ice Cream Mold

Ice cream, bird, pewter, perched bird, hinged, closed 3 1/2 x 3 3/4" (ILLUS.).............. **75**

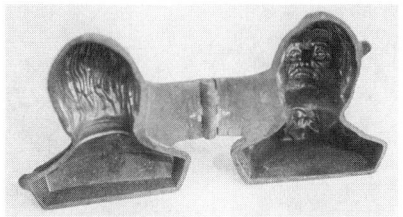

Lincoln Bust Ice Cream Mold

Ice cream, bust of Lincoln, pewter, hinged, marked "E & Co. - 1177," closed 3 3/4 x 4 1/4" (ILLUS.) **185**

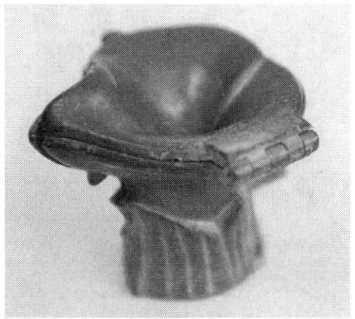

Calla Lily Ice Cream Mold

Ice cream, calla lily, pewter, double hinged, marked "Patent Applied For - 210," closed 3 x 4" (ILLUS.)..................................... **155**

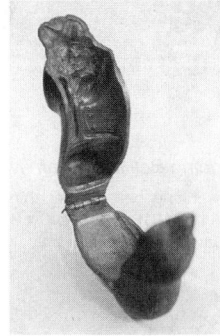

Cat in Shoe Ice Cream Mold

Ice cream, cat in shoe, pewter, hinged, 2 x 4 3/4" (ILLUS.)... **165**

Standing Elephant Ice Cream Mold

Ice cream, elephant, pewter, standing animal, hinged, marked "E & Co. - 656," closed 3 1/4 x 4 1/2" (ILLUS.) **150**

Grape Cluster Ice Cream Mold

Ice cream, grape cluster, pewter, hinged, closed 3 1/2 x 5" (ILLUS.) **62**

Pewter Touring Car Ice Cream Mold

Ice cream, touring car, pewter, hinged, marked "E & Co. - 1143," closed 3 x 5" (ILLUS.) **225**

Wedding Bell Ice Cream Mold

Ice cream, wedding bell, pewter, hinged, marked "NY - 1019," closed 3 x 3 3/4" (ILLUS.) **125**

Ice Cream Mold with Wedding Couple

Ice cream, wedding couple, pewter, hinged, plain lower half w/crimped rim, No. 468, 4 x 4 1/4" (ILLUS.) **125**

Witch on Broomstick Ice Cream Mold

Ice cream, witch on broomstick, pewter, marked "NY 1153," 4 3/4 x 5 1/2" (ILLUS.) **495**

Zeppelin Ice Cream Mold

Ice cream, zeppelin, pewter, hinged, marked "E & Co. - 1140," closed 2 1/2 x 6" (ILLUS.) **185**

MUSIC BOXES

Cylinder Music Boxes

Interchangeable Cylinder Music Box

Swiss cylinder music box, in mahogany case mounted on stand w/fitted drawer & cabriole legs, 18" cylinder plays six tunes, w/tune indicator, safety check lever, stop/start & slow/fast levers & zither attachment, Swiss, late 19th c., 26 x 48", 43" h. (ILLUS.) **$4,025**

Disk Music Boxes

Polyphon Floor Model Music Box

Polyphon disk music box, floor model, coin-operated player, encased in walnut w/gallery top, single glass door flanked by carved columns, original finish, plays 24 1/2" disks, 54" h. (ILLUS.).................... **11,550**

Polyphon 8"-Disk Music Box

Polyphon disk music box, w/six bells, walnut case w/original full-color label on inside of lid, plays 8" disks, 10" sq., 5" h. (ILLUS.)... **1,760**

Regina disk music box, brass mechanism w/duplex combs, in mahogany case w/raised panel top, moulded base resting on small bun feet, on stand, w/approximately 95 15 1/2" disks, ca. 1900, 9 1/2" h., 31 1/2" h. w/stand **5,152**

Regina Corona Home Music Box

Regina disk music box, Corona / model No. 35, w/gilt gallery, mah case w/twist columns on either siuᴄ bowed glass-front door over a single drawer, w/shelf below, on cabriole legs, double combs, piano sounding, plays 15 1/2" disks, 18 x 21", 60" h., refinished (ILLUS.).. **17,050**

Console Regina Phone Music Box

Regina disk music box, mahogany floor case w/columns decorated w/lion heads & claws, serpentine front & sides, casters supporting two hinged doors below two sliding bowed doors, hinged, paneled lift lid, turntable w/short bed plate & double combs, plays 15 1/2" disks, 21 x 24", 51" h., refinished (ILLUS.)........................... **9,900**

Symphonion Disk Music Box

Symphonion disk music box, carved mahogany case, includes six disks w/various tunes, ca. 1895 (ILLUS.)...................... **4,480**

Symphonion Disk Music Box

Symphonion disk music box, in four-column mahogany tabletop case w/hinged paneled lid containing glass-enclosed Symphonion print of children w/instruments, acorn feet, comes with seven 12" disks, 16 x 20", 11" h. (ILLUS.) **3,190**

Symphonion Upright Music Box

Symphonion disk music box, No. 130, upright walnut case w/original top gallery, coin-operated, original condition, by "Symphonion Musikwerke - Leipzig," 120-tooth complex combs & ten saucer bells, plays 21 1/4" disks, 81" h. (ILLUS.).. **6,392**

OLYMPIC COLLECTIBLES

1928 Art Deco Style Ashtray

Ashtray, 1928, Amsterdam, Summer, commemorative, Art Deco style, heavy glass, amber color, "Olympiade Amsterdam 1928" around top, decorative ashtray, rare, approx. 6 1/2" octagonal, 2 1/2" h. (ILLUS.) **$220**

1932 Olympic Stadium Staff Badge

Badge, 1932, Los Angeles, Summer, Olympic Stadium staff badge, orange & white celluloid, approx. 3 1/2" (ILLUS.) **574**

Badge, 1936, Berlin, Summer, Oberleitung Leichtathletik - Track & Field head leader badge, silvered AE, by Lauer, rings over Brandenburg Gate, inscribed "Oberleitung," w/orange ribbon & "Leichtathletik" bar, very rare, approx. 1 1/2 x 1 3/4" **2,005**

Encampment Badge, 1936 Olympics

Badge, 1936, Berlin, Summer, official German Sports Federation Encampment badge, second week of the games, silvered AE, w/red rosette, official English guide pg. 65, scarce, approx. 1 1/2", silvering lightly worn (ILLUS.) **275**

Badge, 1936, Berlin, Summer, worn by pre-Berlin Olympic winners, silvered, winner w/wreath, color rings & Brandenburg Gate in background, two white bars below, approx. 1 x 1 1/2" (replacement pin on back) **145**

1940 Helsinki Badge

Badge, 1940, Helsinki (canceled), Winter, Polish official's badge, silvered, enameled in red & white, Olympic rings above Polish eagle, "19-40" below, toned, approx. 1/2 x 3/4" (ILLUS.) **200**

XII Olympiad Tokyo 1940 Badge

Badge, 1940, Tokyo (canceled), Summer, XII Olympiad, silvered & color enameled, on green moire rosette, badge was mounted w/a semihard rubber on reverse, closure still there, approx. 2 1/2" (ILLUS.) **2,200**

1956 Radio-TV Badge

Badge, 1956, Cortina D'Ampezzo, Winter, radio-TV badge, goldplated, multicolor, rare, approx. 1 1/2 x 1 3/4" (ILLUS.) **1,300**

1964 Equestrian Competitor's Badge

Badge, 1964, Tokyo, Summer, Equestrian competitor's badge, goldplated, partially enameled, with dark brown ribbon, belonged to a future gold medal winner in two Olympic Games, approx. 1 1/2 x 2 1/2" (ILLUS.) **525**

Equestrian First Place Badge, 1976

Badge, 1976, Montreal, Summer, equestrian first place badge for the winning horse Mehmed awarded in dressage team competition, red silk, w/Montreal logo in center, w/long red-ivory-red ribbons inscribed in gold in French & English "Games of the XXI Olympiad Montreal 1976. Team Competition 1st Gold," light spots on ribbons, approx. 6 1/2" (ILLUS.).. **1,300**

1936 American Olympic Fund Reflector

Bicycle reflector, 1936, Berlin, Summer, American Olympic Fund, bicycle reflector, aluminum, background reflective red, w/original envelope, approx. 3 1/2" (ILLUS.) **180**

Book, 1936, Garmisch Winter & Berlin Summer Games, report of the Norwegian Olympic Committee 1932-1936 & July 1935 to June 1936, paper covers, 116 pp., three photographic plates of which two show Norwegian winners in Garmisch: Sonja Henie, I. Ballangrud, O. Hagen, Birger Ruud, etc., in Norwegian, approx. 6 1/4 x 9" (light marginal browning, small tears) **193**

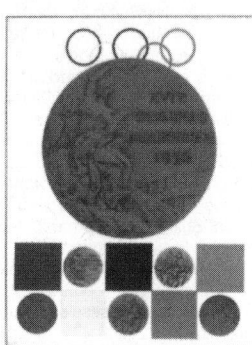

"The Games of the Sixteenth Olympiad"

Book, 1956, Melbourne, Summer, "The Games of the Sixteenth Olympiad Melbourne 1956," souvenir of the Argus & Australian Ltd., under the authority of the Organizing Committee, Melbourne, 61 pp., profusely illus., includes events, records, story of the Olympic Games since 1896, etc., stiff color covers, approx. 9 1/4 x 11 3/4" (ILLUS.) **100**

Commemorative 1956 Olympic Bracelet

Bracelet, 1956, Cortina D'Ampezzo, Winter, commemorative Olympic bracelet, gilt, color enameled, views of different Olympic venues linked by color Olympic rings, approx. 8 1/2" l. (ILLUS.) **200**

1936 Brochure, "By Air to Olympia"

Brochure, 1936, Berlin, Summer, "By Air to Olympia," published by German Lufthansa Airline, fold-out brochure in 16 sections, each section illustrated, in English, advertising to go to winter Olympic games in Garmisch & summer games in Berlin, color covers, approx. 4 1/4 x 9 1/2" (ILLUS.) **150**

Brochure, 1936, Garmisch-Partenkirchen, Winter, Messerli, Fr.-M. Rapport sur la Participation Suisse aux IC(mes) Jeux Olympiques d'Hiver, report on the Swiss participation in the IVth Olympic Winter Games, in French, 6 pp., report was presented at the Swiss NOC session, March 7, 1936 in Aarau **150**

Daily official program, 1904, St. Louis, No. 171, Tuesday, November 15, 1904, 17 pp., 2-page map in center of exhibition grounds w/Athletic Field of Olympic Games & Olympian Way, association football (soccer) played at the stadium, first day, at 2:30 p.m. railway stop Nr. 6 at stadium: "Olympian Games," color cover is shown as 1904 poster in IOC poster book, approx. 6 x 9 1/4" **400**

Daily official program, 1912, Stockholm, Summer, July 11, 64 pp., in Swedish &

English, finals in 10000 meters (Kohlemainen, Finland); 200 meters (Craig, USA); pole jump (Babcock, USA); also wrestling & modern pentathlon, incl. abbreviated rules, approx. 5 3/4 x 8 3/4" (light crease, light browning) **150**

Daily official program, 1912, Stockholm, Summer, July 12, 64 pp., in Swedish & English, finals in discus (Taipale, Finland); 110 meter hurdles (Kelly, USA); modern pentathlon, wrestling, approx. 5 3/4 x 8 3/4" (light browning) **150**

Daily official program, 1912, Stockholm, Summer, July 13, 56 pp., in Swedish & English, finals in 400 meters (Reidpath, USA); long jump (Gutterson, USA); equestrian, wrestling, approx. 5 3/4 x 8 3/4" (light browning) **165**

Daily official program, 1912, Stockholm, Summer, marathon day, July 14, 40 pp., in Swedish & English, marathon (McArthur, South Africa); decathlon w/Jim Thorpe in the participant's list, wrestling, approx. 5 3/4 x 8 3/4" **165**

Daily official program, 1924, Paris, Summer, July 7, 15 pp., in French, 100 meter (Abrahams, Great Britain), 400 meter hurdles (Taylor, USA), etc.; javelin thrower on cover, approx. 8 3/4 x 10 3/4" (partially scored in pencil) **175**

Daily official program, 1924, Paris, Summer, July 9, 15 pp., in French, finals in 200 meters (Scholz, USA); 110 meter hurdles (Kinsey, USA); 3000 meter steeplechase (Ritola, Finland); includes list of all athletics participants, javelin thrower on cover, approx. 8 3/4 x 10 3/4" (partially scored in pencil) **200**

Daily official program, 1926, Berlin, Summer, August 6, 64 pp., finals in javelin (Stoeck, Germany); 1500 meters (Loveland, New Zealand); soccer, hockey, handball, polo, approx. 6 x 8 3/4" **100**

Daily official program, 1936, Berlin, Summer, August 13, 72 pp., soccer standing 3rd & 4th place, swimming, equestrian, hockey, rowing, boxing, etc., approx. 6 x 8 3/4" (creases on cover) **100**

Daily official program, 1936, Berlin, Summer, August 15, 56 pp., hockey finals (India-Germany 8:1); soccer (Italy-Austria 2:1); fencing, sabre individual (Kabos, Hungary); swimming women, 400 meter freestyle (Mastenbroek, Holland), etc., approx. 6 x 8 3/4" **110**

Daily official program, 1936, Berlin, Summer, August 4, 48 pp., Jesse Owens wins 200 meters; fencing, soccer & polo, approx. 6 x 8 3/4" **100**

Daily official program, 1936, Berlin, Summer, August 4, 48 pp., Jesse Owens wins long jump; Mauermayer, Germany, wins discus; 400 meter hurdles (Hardin, USA, Loaring, Canada, 2nd); 800 meters (Woodruff, USA); 100 meters women (Helen Stephens, USA); also polo, hockey, soccer, etc., approx. 6 x 8 3/4" **110**

Daily official program, 1936, Berlin, Summer, August 7, 64 pp., finals in 5000 meters (G. Hoeckert, Finland); 400

meters (Archie Williams, USA); cycling, hockey, shooting, polo, etc., approx. 6 x 8 3/4".. **100**

Daily official program, 1936, Berlin, Summer, August 8, 72 pp., decathlon (Morris, USA); shooting, soccer, basketball, hockey, polo, canoeing, cycling, approx. 6 x 8 3/4".. **100**

Daily official program, 1936, Berlin, Summer, August 9, 56 pp., marathon (K. Son, Korea); also finals in woman's high jump, 4 x 100m relay; swimming 100m freestyle (Csik, Hungary); wrestling, pictorial covers w/ancient Greek marathon runner, approx. 6 x 8 3/4" (a few results penciled in) **100**

Daily official program, 1936, Garmisch-Partenkirchen, Winter, opening ceremony, Feb. 6, 32 pp. illus., color chart of flags of participating nations; ice hockey, complete program, daily program Feb. 7...... **225**

Daily official program, 1948, London, Summer, complete set of 8, July 30 & 31, August 2-7, four w/scores noted, approx. 7 3/4 x 10 3/4", 8 pieces **375**

Daily official program, 1948, London, Summer, July 29, opening ceremony, 25 pp., illus., incl. torch relay account w/map, description of venues, history of the Olympic Games, color covers, approx. 8 1/2 x 10 3/4" (crease, four punch holes at one).. **90**

1936 Berlin Diploma

Diploma, 1936, Berlin, Summer, official A. Hitler ink-signed diploma for the First Class Olympic Games decoration, red & black legend, large embossed Third Reich government eagle on lower left, diploma is scarcer than the decoration, Hitler's signature is not often found, comes w/accompanying letter, September 8, 1936, on official stationery, rare set, light soiling, approx. 8 1/4 x 11 3/4", 2 pcs. (ILLUS.) **2,400**

Letter, January 13, 1914, Summer, handwritten, by Pierre de Coubertin, on official stationery of the 20th anniversary celebration of the restoration of the Olympic Games & the IOC Congress in Paris in June 1914, w/color rings in upper left (Olympic rings were introduced at the 1914 celebration; the stationery is probably the first time that the Olympic rings were used officially), Coubertin asks for the speedy writing of the text for the Olympic Hymn which will be composed by Gustave Doret, approx. 8 1/2 x 10 1/2", folded twice (light browning, 1" tear at center gold at right) **1,600**

Map, 1936, Garmisch-Partenkirchen, Winter, official map of downhill ski & shalom events, men & women, multicolor, scarce, approx. 11 1/2 x 17 1/2" **170**

Medal, 1904 Louisiana Purchase Expo

Medal, 1904, St. Louis, Summer, award medal, goldplated AE, of Louisiana Purchase Exposition, this is the first of the gold medals seen goldplated, light wear on high points, approx. 2 3/4" (ILLUS.)......... **275**

1908 Gold Medal, Team Swimming

Medal, 1908, London, Summer, first place winner's medal awarded for 200 meter team swimming, gold, hallmarked 15 karat, by Lindberg/MacKennal, two females crowning winner, reverse w/St. George killing dragon, "Winner 200 Metres Team Swimming" engraved on edge (only in the 1900, 1904, 1908 & 1912 Olympic Games were actual gold medals awarded to the winners), approx. 1 1/4", almost 1 oz. (ILLUS.)... **5,500**

1912 Olympic Yachting Badge

Medal, 1912, Stockholm, Summer, Olympic yachting event participant's badge, silver, blue & white enamel, rare, about 3/4" (ILLUS.).. **250**

Medal, 1920, Antwerp, participation medal, bronze, by P. Theunis, Nike standing before tripod crowning victorious athletes, reverse w/Flying Victory crowning charioteer in biga, approx. 2 1/2" 360

Medal, 1920, Antwerp, VIIth Olympiad archery championship medal, AE, bow & arrow in laurel wreath, reverse w/6-line legend, toned, approx. 1 x 1 1/2" 175

1924 French Olympics Gold Medal

Medal, 1924, Paris, Summer, French Republic Olympic games gold award medal, goldplated AE, by Desaide/Bertrand, laureated bust of French Republic, reverse panel over palm & laurel branches, Olympic legend at right in original box, scarce, approx. 2 1/2" (ILLUS.) 670

Medal, 1924, Paris, Summer, Portuguese NOC badge, white enamel, buttonhole closure on back, rare, approx. 1 x 1 1/2" 300

1936 Gold First Place Winner's Medal

Medal, 1936, Berlin, Summer, gold first place winner's medal, goldplated silver, by Cassioli, Victory seated above stadium, reverse w/winner carried by jubilant athletes, approx. 2 1/4" (ILLUS.) 3,800

Medal, 1936, Berlin, Summer, merit medal, silvered, Olympic rings above eagle w/spread wings & "19-36," reverse legend over oak sprig, mottled, in original (soiled) presentation case 125

Medal, 1936, Berlin, Summer, participation medal, cast AE, by Placzek, five athletes, reverse w/Olympic bell, seldom seen, approx. 2 3/4" (casting flaws) 440

Medal, 1936, Berlin, Summer, participation medal, cast bronze, by O. Placzek, five athletes representing the five continents, pulling the ropes of the Olympic bell, reverse w/Olympic bell embossed w/German eagle holding Olympic rings, within five concentric circles, in original box, toned, approx. 2 3/4" 325

Medal, 1936, Garmisch-Partenkirchen, Winter, third place winner's medal, bronze, by R. Klein, Victory w/laurel wreath in triga to left, bobsled, ski, hockey stick & skate below, reverse w/large Olympic rings surrounded by "IV Olym-

pische Winterspiele 1936," this is the largest winner's medal, very rare, approx. 4" 15,500

Official 1964 Gold Medal

Medal, 1964, Innsbruck, Winter, official gold medal, gold "900," by Welz, view of Innsbruck, reverse w/official logo, P-I fields, approx. 2 oz., light handling, approx. 2 1/4" (ILLUS.) 750

1964 Bronze Medal for Water Polo

Medal, 1964, Tokyo, Summer, bronze third place winner's medal awarded for water polo, bronze, by Toshikaka Koshiba, Victory seated above stadium, reverse w/winner carried by jubilant athletes, w/moire ribbon in white & Olympic colors, approx. 2 1/2" (ILLUS.) 3,750

1964 Gold Medal Awarded for Fencing

Medal, 1964, Tokyo, Summer, gold first place winner's medal awarded for fencing, goldplated silver, by Toshikaka Koshiba, Victory seated above stadium, reverse w/winner carried by jubilant athletes, w/multicolor ribbon, in lacquered box, hinges loose, approx. 2 1/2" (ILLUS.) 5,200

Medals, 1924, Paris, Summer, French Republic Olympic Games gold award medal, AW, by R. Benard, city view of Paris over French legend in three lines, reverse w/Victory w/laurel wreaths crowning victorious athletes, approx. 2 1/4" each, pr. 405

Medals, 1936, Berlin, Summer, group of four participation medals w/casting flaw at top, cast AE, by Placzek, five athletes, reverse w/Olympic bell, patina: dark brown (two), greenish brown & light brown, approx. 2 3/4" each, 4 pcs. 800

Official torch, 1936, Berlin, Summer, steel, made by Krupp Factory, designed by Carl Diem, carried during the first torch relay from Olympia, Greece to Berlin, a distance of 1,906 mi. in 12 days, approx. 10 3/4" h. **4,000**

Pass booklet, 1936, Berlin, Summer, swimming season, contains two tickets, August 11, springboard diving (R. Degener, USA) & August 12, still attached, 400m freestyle (Jack Medica, USA), approx. 5 1/2 x 2 1/2" **220**

1932 Hungarian Team Pin

Pin, 1932, Los Angeles, Summer, team pin, Hungarian, multicolor enamel, Hungarian shield over globe w/the Americas, beautiful pin, approx. 1" (ILLUS.)............................ **325**

Pin, 1936, Garmisch-Partenkirchen, Winter, commemorative pin, silvered, Olympic rings over legend, Alps in back, approx. 1 1/2 x 1 3/4" **100**

1952 American Team Patch Helsinki

Patch, 1952, Helsinki, Summer, American team patch, multicolor, scarce, approx. 2 1/4 x 3" (ILLUS.)...................................... **120**

Photo album, 1936, Garmisch-Partenkirchen, Winter, bobsled photo album of a German participant, bronze medal winner in Lake Placid, 1932, vellum-style covers w/"Bob" in gold lettering, contains 29 stiff pages w/44 b&w photos, bobsled event, opening ceremony, an accident, the bobsled team, etc., album is missing tying cord, rare documentation, album approx. 11 3/4 x 8 1/2", photos ranging in size from approx. 3 1/2 x 2 1/2" to full-page 7 x 8 1/2" **600**

1956 Kenyan Team Pin

Pin, 1956, Melbourne, Summer, Kenyan team pin, multicolor, rare, approx. 3/4 x 7/8" (ILLUS.) **242**

1956 Argentine Team Pin

Pin, 1956, Melbourne, Summer, Argentine team pin, multicolor enamel, buttonhole closure, rare, approx. 7/8 x 1" (ILLUS.) **200**

1928 Uruguayan Soccer Team Pin

Pin, 1928, St. Moritz, Summer, Uruguayan soccer team member pin presented to gold medal winning team members, silvered, enameled in color, flag behind soccer ball encircled by "Campeones Olimpicos 1924/1928," very scarce, approx. 1/2" (ILLUS.) **360**

1960 Austrian Team Pin

Pin, 1960, Rome, Summer, Austrian team pin, goldplated, approx. 1 x 1 3/4", gold plating lightly worn (ILLUS.) **160**

Gold Merit Pin for Boxing Gold Medalist

Pin, 1960, Rome, Summer, gold merit pin for a boxing gold medal winner, 18 karat gold "750," female w/palm branch surrounded by ribbon, in presentation box, 4.5 grams, approx. 3/4 x 3/4" (ILLUS.) **198**

1964 Austrian Team Pin

Pin, 1964, Innsbruck, Winter, Austrian team pin, gilt, multicolor enamel, beautiful, approx. 1 1/2 x 1 1/4" (ILLUS.) **235**

1964 French Team Pin

Pin, 1964, Innsbruck, Winter, French team pin, multicolor, scarce, approx. 3/4 x 1" (ILLUS.) **418**

1960 Hong Kong & Israel Team Pins

Pins, 1960, Rome, Summer, Hong Kong & Israel team pins, multicolor, approx. 3/4" & 1/2 x 5/8" (ILLUS.), 2 pcs. **120**

1964 Japanese Rowing Plaque

Plaque, 1964, Tokyo, Summer, official Japanese Rowing Association plaque, goldplated AE, rower over color enameled rings, reverse w/Japanese legend, approx. 2 x 2" (ILLUS.) **105**

Small Size Official Poster, 1936

Poster, 1936, Berlin, Summer, small size official poster, stiff paper, multicolor offset printing, by Frantz Wuerbel, winner's bust over Brandenburg Gate, approx. 7 1/4 x 11 1/2" (ILLUS.) **400**

1936 Commemorative Poster Plaque

Poster plaque, 1936, Berlin, Summer, commemorative official Berlin poster plaque, lithographed iron, by Wuerbel, in color, four small holes in corners, as made, approx. 14 x 21 1/2" (ILLUS.)............................. **100**

Press news, 1936, Winter, Feb. 16, Ski Stadium; honored guests attending special ski jump event incl. Hitler, Goebbels, Goering, IOC President Baillet-Latour, etc.; total visitors in Garmisch: 1 million during games; second page w/results of Canada-Hungary Ice Hockey game, honored guests: Baillet-Latour, Count Bonacossa, 2 pcs. **105**

1936 Olympics Winner's Ring

Ring, 1936, Berlin, Summer, silver & brown precious stone Olympic winner's presentation ring, set w/silver Reich Sport eagle & Olympic rings, three oak leaves on either side, presented together w/an award document (not included) to German medal winners deemed true Aryan athletes, extremely rare, approx. 3/4 x 1" (ILLUS.) .. **2,000**

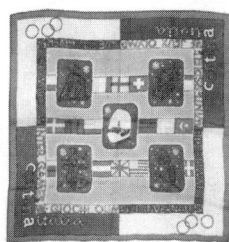

1956 Commemorative Olympics Scarf

Scarf, 1956, Cortina D'Ampezzo, Winter, commemorative Olympic Winter Events scarf, multicolor silk, view of Cortina surrounded by skier, bobsled, skater & ski jumper, approx. 19 1/4" sq. (ILLUS.)............. **126**

Kiel Olympia 1936 Spoon

Spoon, 1936, Berlin, Summer, Commemorative Kiel Olympics, goldplated AE, "Olympia 1936" & Olympic rings inside spoon, ornate handle topped w/color enamel Kiel city shield, attractive & scarce, light wear to gold plating, approx. 4 1/2" (ILLUS.) **150**

Telegram to Discus Event Winner, 1936

Telegram, 1936, Berlin, Summer, official telegram congratulating Gisela Mauermayer for winning the discus event, Aug. 4, 1936, multicolor, winner's head, reverse w/Olympic bell in gold, green & blue, approx. 8 1/2 x 12" (ILLUS.) **225**

Ticket, 1900, Paris, Summer, blue ticket to the World's Exposition, one franc (the 1900 Olympic Games were held in conjunction w/the World's Fair), approx. 3 x 2" **75**

Ticket, 1900, Paris, Summer, light blue & brown ticket to the World's Exposition, one franc, approx. 3 x 2" **93**

Ticket, 1904, St. Louis, Summer, day 219 (August 6), approx. 2 3/4 x 1" (light crease) **110**

Ticket, 1904, St. Louis, Summer, day 262 (September 18), approx. 2 3/4 x 1" (light marginal browning).. **100**

Ticket, 1904, St. Louis, Summer, day 263 (September 19), men's archery, Double American Round (Bryant, USA) & Women's Archery Double, Columbia Round (Howell, USA), light marginal browning **175**

Ticket, 1912, Stockholm, Summer, July 8, Olympic Stadium, section A, price 10 kronor, light green, 800 meters (Melvin Sheppard, USA), 10,000 meters (Johan Kolehmainen, Finland), etc., approx. 4 3/4 x 3" (light crease).................................... **238**

Ticket, 1928, Amsterdam, Olympic Art Competition, valid May 12-August 12, 1928, Stedelijk Museum, scarce, approx. 4 x 2 1/2" (evidence of mounting on back)... **93**

Ticket, 1928, Amsterdam, Summer, opening ceremony, July 28, 1928, Olympisch Stadion, scarce ticket, price ƒ1.25, ocher, approx. 4 1/2 x 2 1/2" (paper loss at one corner)... **88**

Ticket, 1928, Amsterdam, Summer, soccer, Olympisch Stadion, Marathon Tribune, price ƒ4.-, yellow, approx. 4 1/2 x 2 1/2" **100**

Ticket, 1928, Amsterdam, Summer, Soccer, Olympisch Stadion, price ƒ 1.-, approx. 4 1/2 x 2 1/2" (creases) **88**

Ticket, 1928, Amsterdam, Summer, trio of soccer tickets, Olympisch Stadion, Zijvak (2x), teal, Marathon Tribune, yellow, approx. 4 1/2 x 2 1/2", 3 pieces 165

Ticket, 1932, Los Angeles, Summer, August 7, 6:00 p.m., Olympic Auditorium, price $2.00, approx. 4 1/2 x 2 1/2" 60

Ticket, 1932, Los Angeles, Summer, closing ceremony, August 14, 1:00 p.m., Olympic Stadium, $2.00, brown & yellow, approx. 4 1/2 x 2 1/2" 132

Ticket, 1936, Berlin, Summer, fencing participant, August 7, 9:00 & 15.00 h., Tennis Stadion (Reichssportfeld), price RM 4.-, scarce ticket for a participant, approx. 4 1/2 x 2 1/2" (crease).................................... 175

Ticket, 1936, Berlin, Summer, soccer, August 13, 16.00 uhr, Olympia Stadion, price RM 6.25.-, approx. (light creases).......... 70

Ticket, 1952, Oslo, Winter, speed skating, men, 500 meters, Feb. 16, 15.00 h, Bislett Stadium, standing room, K. Henry USA won gold metal...................................... 100

Ticket, 1956, Melbourne, Summer, final U.S. Olympic tryouts, June 29 & 30, Los Angeles Coliseum, price $5.00, approx. 2 1/2 x 3 1/2" 52

Ticket, 1956, Melbourne, Summer, equestrian games, Olympic Grand Prix jumping competition, 2nd round & closing ceremony, June 17, 4:00 p.m., Olympic Stadium, price kr. 20.-, blue, scarce, approx. 4 3/4 x 3" 165

Ticket, 1984, Sarajevo, Winter, full ice hockey, Feb. 13, 17.00 h, Zetra, price din. 750, color, approx. 7 1/4 x 2 1/2"............. 90

Tickets, 1952, Helsinki, Summer, basketball, July 30; bicycling, July 29; gymnastics, July 20; kayak, July 28; venue map of event on back, approx. 4 1/2 x 3 1/2", group of four tickets....................................... 125

Tickets, 1992, Albertville, Winter, opening ceremony rehearsal invitation, Feb. 6, 17:00 h, blue; & opening ceremony, Feb. 8, 17: h, red, full tickets, approx. 8 1/2 x 2 3/4", two pieces 100

Tickets, 1992, Albertville, Winter, trio of tickets: cross country skiing, relay 4x5 km women, Feb. 17; & relay 4x10 km men, Feb. 18, both in Les Saisies; & Nordic combines - cross country skiing, 3x10 km Feb. 18, Courchevel, approx. 6 1/2 x 2 1/2", 3 pieces 90

1936 Olympic Village Welcome Address

Welcome address, 1936, Berlin, Summer, w/gold laurel branch & color rings for English speaking competitors arriving at the Olympic Village, stiff paper, welcome words by V. Blomberg & Dr. Lewald, Organizing Committee President, aerial view of Olympic Village above, scarce, light marginal browning, approx. 8 3/4 x 13 1/4" (ILLUS.).................................. 225

PENNANTS

All are felt unless otherwise noted.

Alaska Hi-Way Milepost Pennant

Alaska Hi-Way, milepost sign showing the distances to places along the highway, dark blue ground w/lettering in white & sign in white, pink, green & yellow, pink streamers, 1950, 17" l. (ILLUS.) $12

Arizona - Grand Canyon Pennant

Arizona - Grand Canyon State, dark red ground w/white lettering & shading pink, red & pale blue canyon vignette, gold border & streamers, late 1940s-early 1950s, 25" l. (ILLUS.) 12

Beatles, images of each band member w/words "Yeah, Yeah, Yeah," wearing collarless jackets, 1964, 21" l. 425

Benson's Animal Park Pennant

Benson's Animal Park, Hudson, N.H., red ground w/lettering in red, blue & yellow, color image of tiger & gorilla at one end, gold edging & white streamers, 1978, 26" l. (ILLUS.)... 10

Boise, Idaho, blue ground w/white lettering, scenes of pine trees, mountains & lake in color, green streamers, 1940s, 26" l. 20

Bonneville Dam, blue ground w/white lettering, multi-colored scene of the dam & surrounding area, dark blue streamers, 1930s, 29" l. 25

Captain Marvel, blue ground w/portrait of Captain Marvel in dark red & white, copyright by Fawcett Publications, mid-1940s, 14 1/2" l. 140

Chicago Bears, dark blue w/orange design, football player in leather helmet w/ball running toward viewer, opposing players in pursuit, bear cub above the Bears kicking a football, 1930, 11 1/2 x 27" 65

Chicago, Illinois, bright green ground w/white letters, colored picture of the Merchandise Mart Building in left corner, 1950, 15" l. 8

Chicago, Illinois - Museum of Science & Industry, blue ground w/white letters, colorful scene of U.S. Navy ships & the capture of the German submarine U505 during World War II, dark gold border, gold streamers, 1950s, 26" l. 25

Daytona Beach, Florida, black ground w/white lettering, designs matching illustrated Daytona Beach pennant, 1960, 26 1/2" l. 15

Daytona Beach Pennant

Daytona Beach, Florida, red ground w/yellow edging, white, blue & yellow designs of alligator, race car, surfer & beach, 1960, 26 1/2" l. (ILLUS.) 15

Destruction Bay Lodge - Mile 1083 - Yukon, dark blue ground w/yellowish-gold lettering, map & river running length, shows Alaska, White Horse, B.C., Destruction Bay & Fort Nelson, yellow streamers, 1950, 17" l. 10

Detroit, Michigan - 200th Birthday, purple ground w/white letters, portrait of Ottawa Indian chief & Cadillac, founder of the city, both shown riding in a Cadillac auto w/license plate reading "1701-1951," green streamers, 1951, 26" l. 50

Early Disneyland Pennant

Disneyland, dark blue ground w/gold wording & scene of Sleeping Beauty's castle, gold border & streamers, 1955, early park item, 26" l. (ILLUS.) 100

Disneyland, orange ground, scene of Main Street, w/Mickey & Minnie Mouse, 1982, 29" l. 5

Edaville R.R., red & white ground w/a dark train engine, inscribed "The Famous Historic Narrow Gauge Steam Powered Edaville R.R. - South Carver, Massachusetts," further inscription below, 1970s, 25" l. 8

Fontana Dam, North Carolina, dark green w/white border, image of the dam, red streamers, 1950s, 26" l. 8

Golden Gate Bridge, dark green ground w/the bridge on the left w/a surfaced submarine passing under it, 1945, 26" l. 45

Hanna, Alberta Pennant

Hanna, Alberta, "No. 9 Highway Jubilee Service," dark blue ground w/pink & blue lettering, picture of five cattle at one end, 1950, 17 1/2" l. (ILLUS.) 10

Early Hollywood Pennant

Hollywood, California, black ground w/bright pink letters, color vignette of Grauman's Chinese Theatre, yellow border & black streamers, late 1940s, 26" l. (ILLUS.) 50

Hopalong Cassidy, black ground w/white lettering, rope script lettering & white trim, black streamers, late 1940s-early 1950s, 28" l. 125

Indianapolis 500 Race, red border around green, shows a car w/driver & co-driver & inscribed "Indianapolis - 500 Mile Auto Race," a second version has a gold border around red, both issued in 1914, the date noted on the tip of the pennant, either version 250

Jackie Robinson, green ground w/white letters, Brooklyn Dodgers team name & large image of Robinson holding a bat, his name & first base position on the uniform (after 1948 he played third base), issued in his first year in the major leagues, very rare, 1947 500

John Glenn, red, white & blue w/3" photo of Glenn & inscription "Feb. 20, 1962 - 1st US Orbital Flight - Friendship 7," 1962, 17 1/2" l. 40

Krak-R-Krik Pennant

Krak-R-Krik - Mile 987 - Alaska Hi-way, dark blue ground w/white & shaded pink & yellow letters, golden bust picture of mountain sheep at one end, red streamers, 1950, 17" l. (ILLUS.) **10**

Mickey Mouse Toytown, Christmas pennant featuring Mickey, Donald Duck, Pluto & Santa Claus singing Christmas carols, reads "Welcome to Toytown," 1930s **500**

Negro League Baseball, series featuring the various teams including the Newark Eagles, New York Cuban Stars, Baltimore Elite Giants, Homestead Grays, Philadelphia Stars, each features the team name & scene of a catcher standing & batter swinging, different colors, 1930s, rare, 26" l., each.................................. **200**

Nevada - Free State, dark orange w/purple lettering, manufactured by Angelus Souvenirs, California, 1915, 23" l. **35**

![New Mexico Pennant with Chief Head]

New Mexico Pennant with Chief Head

New Mexico, dark blue ground w/white lettering & color profile portrait of a Native American chief, a popular design in the 1940s & '50s, gold border & blue streamers, 1952, 25" l. (ILLUS.).................................... **15**

New York Giants, dark blue ground w/scene of a large football player w/ball & other players in background, 1950s, 12 x 29 1/2".. **60**

Pennsylvania Turnpike, purple w/white lettering w/scene of the Kittatinny Tunnel, 1952, 27" l. **13**

Philadelphia Centennial Exhibition, swallow-tail linen pennant w/38 stars & "1776" in one corner & "1876" in the other, American eagle & flag in center w/"Centennial" across the bottom, 1876, 18 x 24" **225**

Philadelphia, Pennsylvania, blue ground, features scenes of the Betsy Ross House & the Liberty Bell, yellow streamers, 1950s, 12" l. **10**

Portland, Oregon - City of Roses, purple ground w/large painted rose at left, one bloom open & a second smaller bloom about to bud, yellow streamers, 1930s, 25 3/4" l. **20**

San Francisco, California, light green ground w/white lettering, multi-colored scenes w/the Cliff House, Golden Gate Bridge, China Town & Seal Rocks, no streamers, 1930s, 26" l. **45**

Santa's Workshop Pennant

Santa's Workshop - North Pole on Whiteface Mt., N.Y., dark blue ground w/white lettering & red Santa w/reindeer, gold border sleeve top holds a pencil, early 1950s, 8 1/2" l. (ILLUS.).................................... **30**

Saskatchewan Grey Cup Champs - 1989 - Rough Riders, green & white w/grey & white lettering, large helmet on the left, small Canadian Football League logo helmet in the corner, 26" l. **15**

Sea World, dark blue w/red lettering, killer whale flying through air on left, waves in the background & viewing tower w/American flag, 1980, 26" l. **3**

Snowqualmie Falls, Washington, dark brown w/multicolored graphics of the falls, small white border strip, bright red streamers, late 1940s, 26" l. **12**

Soviet All-Stars, red w/white lettering, title w/crossed hockey sticks & puck on the left & initials "CCCP," 1950s, 29" l. **250**

State of Washington, black ground w/white letters, pictures totem pole, Narrows Bridge, Mt. Rainier & other sights, 1950s, 26 1/2" l.. **20**

Statue of Liberty, black ground w/color illustration of the Statue w/clouds in background, late 1930s-early 1940s, 29 1/2" l........ **22**

Sunset Carson - Republic Pictures - Hollywood, California, black ground w/a multi-colored portrait of Sunset Carson on the left, black streamers, 1940s, 26" l........ **40**

Syracuse, New York Memorial Arena

Syracuse, N.Y. - Onondaga County War Memorial, dark green ground w/white letters & white, green & pink vignette of the memorial arena at the left end, gold streamers, 1950, 25" l. (ILLUS.) **30**

Universal Studios, California, black ground w/scenes of Universal Studios including colored tour bus, camera crews, street scene, Battlestar Galactica, etc., 1980, 26" l. **8**

University of Alabama Pennant

University of Alabama, crimson red ground w/white lettering, large seal of the University w/school symbol & the year of founding, 1831, streamers w/a white border, 1940s, 26" l. (ILLUS.)................................. **40**

Early Virginia Souvenir Pennant

Virginia, dark red ground w/white lettering & white & pink scenic vignette at one end, gold border & white streamers, 1940s, 25" l. (ILLUS.)... **15**

Watino Bridge Opening Pennant

Watino Bridge - Official Opening - June 15th, 1955, red ground w/white lettering & scene of new bridge, purple streamers, 17" l. (ILLUS.)... **8**
Whitehorse, Yukon, white w/black letters, design of a rearing horse above "Alaska Hy-Way," pink streamers, 1945, 9 1/4" l. **10**

PERFUME, SCENT & COLOGNE BOTTLES

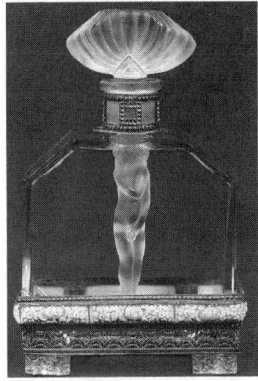

Austrian Glass Perfume Bottle

Austrian glass, clear bottle & stopper, frosted stopper molded w/finely detailed nude, angular bottle encased in metal & decorated w/jade glass panels of flowers w/glass feet, metal signed "Austria," Hoffman, 6 15/16" l. (ILLUS.) **$3,300**
Baccarat glass, clear bottle & inner stopper w/hat overcap, molded woman's head & hat, red enamel decoration & label, empty, bottom signed "Baccarat," sits in red silk vanity stand w/mirror, Bacc. #782, 1939, very rare, Suzy Escarlate de Suzy, 4 1/2" h. **880**

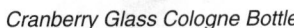

Cranberry Glass Cologne Bottle

Blown glass, cranberry, ovoid body on circular base, cylindrical neck w/fluted flared rim, decorated w/small blue & white daisy-like flowers w/yellow centers, gold leaves, gold trim around base & rim, clear glass ball stopper, 7 1/4" h. (ILLUS.).. **165**

Cranberry Ribbed Cologne Bottle

Blown glass, cranberry, slightly ribbed bulbous base w/long neck ending in flared rim, w/clear wafer foot & clear cut stopper, 7 1/4" h. (ILLUS.)...................................... **135**
Brass & red Bakelite, unique design, includes paper "how to operate" instructions, original box w/satin ribbon, back of box marked "Patent Pending," signed "DeVilbiss," rare, 1 7/8" l.ɒ **220**
Bristol glass, bulbous base w/gold-outlined panels, cylindrical body ending in short neck, turquoise blue decorated w/gold & white flowers on body, band of pink & blue flowers around top rim of body, gold ball stopper, 6 1/2" h. (ILLUS.) **135**

Turquoise Bristol Glass Perfume Bottle

Ceramic, figural Bambi perfume lamp, re-
wired, green & brown w/pink flowers, well
for perfume in back, signed "Goebel V,"
impressed "Dis 160" on bottom, "Disney"
on side, 6 1/2" (tight hairline at base) **110**

Ceramic Figural Perfume Bottle

Ceramic, figural perfume bottle, woman
w/brown hair in blue lustre dress w/pink
ribbon & yellow rose, cork stopper &
glass dauber, unsigned, probably of Ger-
man origin, 5" h. (ILLUS.) **132**

Miniature Metalwork Bottle

Czechoslovakian glass, miniature clear
bottle & metal cap w/glass dauber, front
covered w/metalwork, parts enameled &
decorated w/turquoise glass stones, un-
signed, 2 1/4" l.(ILLUS.) **132**

Czechoslovakian glass, blue bottle
w/clear stopper, oblong bottle w/steps &
vertical facets, stopper intaglio cut
w/maiden standing on flower, w/dauber,
bottom signed "Czechoslovakia" in circle
& w/fragment of silver label, 8 1/8" l. **1,540**
Czechoslovakian glass, cinnamon bottle &
stopper, bottle highly faceted w/twelve
points, stopper molded as a flower
wreath w/dauber, bottom signed "Czechoslovakia" in a line, very rare color & de-
sign, 6 15/16" l. **1,045**
Czechoslovakian glass, clear blue bottle &
stopper, bell- shaped, well cut w/stylized
flowers, stopper cut w/star design, un-
signed, 4 5/8" h. **55**
Czechoslovakian glass, clear bottle &
green stopper, hexagonal shape, stopper
in stylized prism design, tiny dauber, bottom signed "Czechoslovakia" in oval,
4 1/4" h. **99**

Russian Enamel & Gold Scent Bottle

Enamel, gold & diamond, round base
w/gold-decorated rim, body flares from
base to gold neck & stopper topped w/di-
amond, Russian, 3" h. (ILLUS.) **3,000**
Etched glass, black enameled cov. powder
box, heavy etching & gold enameled,
signed "DeVilbiss," superb condition,
about 2 1/4" d. **297**
Lalique glass, clear bottle & stopper, con-
centric rings, label on bottom, signed "R.
Lalique," in blue box, Worth Imprudence,
2 7/8" h. **495**
Lalique glass, clear bottle & stopper, front
of both molded w/leaves & berries designs, recesses enameled black, bottom
signed "R. Lalique - Utt #ML-13," ex-
tremely rare, 3 3/8" l. **2,860**
Lalique glass, cylindrical bottle w/metal
pump atomizer attachment, figures of
classical maidens, amber patina, bottom
signed "R. Lalique," Maison Lalique, 5" l. **605**

My Jerrycan Metal Bottle

Metal, bottle & stopper, gas can-shaped, bottom signed "Marc Fael Paris," Marc Fael My Jerrycan, rare box, ca. 1940s 1 15/16" h. (ILLUS.) **242**

Metal, collar & atomizer, interior black enamel, exterior green orange & yellow enameled leaves, original ball (hardened), bottom signed "DeVilbiss," 9 1/2" h. **770**

Le Narcisse Bleu Bottle & Box

Molded glass, clear bottle & stopper, hexagonal shape w/molded design of stylized flowers on front & stopper w/recessed blue enamel, empty, dark blue & gold label, box blue with white blossoms, Mury Le Narcisse Bleu, 2 3/8" h. (ILLUS.) **275**

Molded glass, clear bottle w/brass cap, open blossom mold w/gold label, in box decorated w/Art Deco floral bouquet, Bourjois Jasmin, 3 3/8" h. **143**

D'Orsay Le Lys Glass Box & Cover

Molded glass, clear & frosted box & cover, molded w/flowers & signed "D'Orsay," brown patina in recesses, D'Orsay Le Lys, 3 15/16" h. (ILLUS.) **242**

Molded glass, frosted w/metal atomizer attachment, design of leaves & berries in the French Art Deco style, new ball & tassel, unsigned, DeV #VS-501, 1928, "DeVilbiss," 6 1/2" h. **413**

Molded glass, light amber ginger jar & cover w/atomizer insert, exterior etched w/pine needle design in gold, bottom signed "DeVilbiss" in acid, DeV #S800-6, 1937 DeVilbiss, about 6 1/3" h. (bruise to glass well) **413**

White Lace-covered Perfume Bottle

Metal Perfume Lamp With Glass Panels

Metal, perfume lamp w/two glass panels in enameled blue inside & gold birds outside, original writing, perfume burner complete w/amber finial, DeV #BQ-4, 1926, DeVilbiss, 8 1/2" h., small chip on inside of one panel (ILLUS.) **440**

Blue Glass Perfume Bottle

Molded glass, blue w/frosted glass stopper, cork-lined stopper, silver label on front, in star-form box, Bourjois Evening in Paris, empty, almost 3" h. (ILLUS.) **77**

Molded glass, clear apothecary-shaped bottle, clear stopper, intact antique label on front bottom signed "Guerlain Paris France," Guerlain Eau de Cologne **358**

Molded glass, clear bottle & frosted glass stopper, bottle cushion-shaped, stopper is kneeling nude woman, empty, figure is thought to be Isadora Duncan, Eroy Adorée, 4 1/2" h. **176**

Molded glass, clear bottle, obelisk-shape, metal atomizer attachment, names in white enamel, Christian Dior Diorling, 6 15/16" h. **55**

Molded glass, opaque white, gold metal stopper w/long dauber, covered in black lace held in place by a gold metal spring, in black purse, Marcel Rochas "Femme," about 2 1/2" h., empty, small tear on one side (ILLUS.)... **77**

Pressed glass, clear bottle & stopper, oval shaped, empty, label around neck, black & gold box decorated w/colorful chopsticks, Merle Norman Jolly Sin, ca. 1950s, 2 3/8" h. **143**

Pressed glass, clear bottle w/gold ribbed cap, full gold label w/pair of lovebirds, bottom signed "Bourjois Paris," silver coffret lined in white satin, ca. 1950s, scarce, bottle 4 1/2" h. **66**

Ahmed Soliman Glass Bottle

Pressed glass, clear bottle w/metal cap w/green stone finial, enameled w/Egyptian figure on front, empty, Ahmed Soliman, 4 1/2" (ILLUS.).. **605**

Pressed glass, clear, cologne bottle w/orange cap, mini w/orange cap, both w/labels & full, in celluloid box w/original Bourjois price tags marked "$1.00 plus tax," Bourjois "On the Wind," large bottle is 4" h., small bottle almost 2" h., the set **55**

Clear Hexagonal Perfume Bottle

Pressed glass, clear, hexagonal w/metal shaker top, beautifully enameled w/roses & leaves in Art Nouveau style, bottom

signed "DeVilbiss Toledo" in the mold, probably pre-1920s, DeVilbiss, 4" h. (ILLUS.)... **66**

Pressed glass, clear pyramid shaped bottle w/frosted crystal Pharaoh's head stopper, empty, two labels on front, bottom, label marked "Bichara, Parfumeur Syrien," shows Bichara chasing a maiden w/inscription "Comment Bichara saisit La Fortune ("How Bichara seized Fortune"), Syriana, Bacc. #236, 1913, 4" h. **4,125**

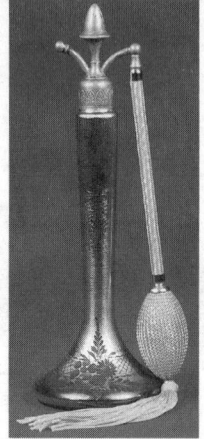

Steuben Blue Glass Bottle w/Atomizer

Steuben glass, blue Aurene w/metal atomizer, acorn finial, shading from iridescent turquoise to royal blue top to bottom, wheel-carved flowers, new ball & tassel, bottom signed "DeVilbiss," gold enamel, rare, 9 7/8" (ILLUS.)................................... **1,100**

Steuben glass, translucent & opalescent w/jade green glass stopper, melon shape w/eight lobes, long neck, stopper w/lobes & long dauber, unsigned, 4 1/2" h. **495**

POLITICAL & CAMPAIGN ITEMS

Campaign

Rare Political Fraktur

Fraktur, 1848 campaign, pen & ink & watercolor on paper, decorated at the top w/two large facing parrots flanking a band reading "Berks County 1848," a lower inscription in German referring to the birds & "I am for Gen. Scott," stylized floral borders, done in yellow, blue, orange & green, stains & some damage, molded frame in old black, minor wear, Pennsylvania, 9 7/8 x 11 3/4" (ILLUS.) **$2,295**

Handkerchief, 1880 campaign, red w/black images of General Winfield S. Hancock & Hon. William H. English for Democratic President & Vice-President in 1880, 18 x 24" **200-250**

Handkerchief, 1888 campaign, red ground, black on natural printed portraits of Grover Cleveland & Allen G. Thurman in bordered ovals, banners w/"For President - Grover Cleveland of New York" beneath Cleveland's picture, 22 x 23" **110**

Hanging sign, 1940 campaign, silk, "Wendell Wilkie for President," 5 x 7" **15-20**

Harrison & Morton Kerchief

Kerchief, 1888 campaign, cotton printed w/picture of spread-winged eagle guarding a next of eaglets in center surrounded by "Harrison & Morton" & "Protection," w/ "1888" in left top corner, "1892" in right top corner, "Civil Service Reform" in lower left corner & "Reduction of Surplus" in lower right corner, all within a star & chain border, within another band of darker color, framed & glazed, 25 x 27" (ILLUS.) **546**

Medal, 1900 campaign, eagle, mechanical, McKinley-Roosevelt.. **72**

1868 Presidential Campaign Pennant

Pennant, 1868 campaign, cotton, Grant & Colfax, w/depiction of candidates in corner & "Grant & Colfax," pennant bordered in stars & zigzag design, framed & glazed, 25" l. (ILLUS.).................................... **805**

Pinback button, 1956 campaign, Adlai Stevenson & Estes Kefauver, "Students for - Stevenson - Kefauver," bands of red, white & blue, 1" d. **88**

Presidential election atlas, 1952 campaign, features photos of Eisenhower, Nixon, Stevenson & Sparkman, includes 39 maps showing electoral votes, framed, 9 1/4 x 11 1/2" **20-25**

Watch chain button, 1888 campaign, portrait of Grover Cleveland on obverse & Allen Granberry Thurman on reverse, gilt metal frame w/eagle finial, loop for suspension, 1" h. **143**

Non-Campaign

Book end, pot metal, bust image of President Lincoln, signed "Abraham Lincoln" across bust, 7 1/2" h. **$50-75**

Bronze image, Gerald R. Ford, from term as Vice-President (inaugurated December 6, 1973), 2 3/4" d. **20-25**

Cup & saucer, demitasse, white w/gold trim on edges & inside of cup, featuring image of President William McKinley, 2 1/2" **35-50**

Matchbox cover, metal w/celluloid overlay, images of FDR, Churchill & Stalin on one side & General Montgomery, Alexander & Eisenhower on the other, side reads, "Souvenir of the World War, Martyn Defries & Co. Ltd., [Green Man] Plumstead, SE18 & Branches, Licensed Caterers," marked "British Made" & "Copyright," 1 3/4 x 2 1/4" **100-125**

Print, Garfield (James), Lincoln (Abraham) & McKinley (William) w/"In Memoriam" & "God's Will, Not Ours be Done," ca. 1901 .... **85**

Abraham Lincoln Colored Engraving

Print, hand-colored engraving of "Abraham Lincoln," shown standing beside a table wearing formal attire, published by Rudolf Lesch, New York, minor margin stains, short tears in lower margin, later molded frame, 23 1/2 x 30 3/4" (ILLUS.) **275**

Print, signing of the Declaration of Independence w/images of John Hancock, George Washington & Thomas Jefferson, framed, 15 x 19".............................. **125-150**

POP CULTURE COLLECTIBLES

Male Pop Singers

In the 1920s and '30s there were crooners. In the postwar world and through the 1960s there were the male pop singers who become know as song stylists, standards singers, rendition singers and even lounge lizards. Their earthly domains were the cocktail lounge (and the ever-popular cocktail party), the supper club and the TV variety show – their Valhalla was Las Vegas.

This price guide section covers male popular singers of the postwar years 1945-1969. This was the golden age of the male vocalists – between the eclipse of the big bands and before rock redefined popular music. Though these vocalists continued in popularity with their generation, their milieu had faded by the 1970s. The appearance of teen singing idols in the late 1950s-early 1960s (Elvis, Ricky Nelson, Fabian) shifted the definition of the male singer towards a younger crowd and a newer beat. Prices are for items in very good to excellent condition.

We are concerned here with men who had careers strictly as singers (though a few were songwriters and some branched out into successful acting careers). Included also are a few performers from before the war whose popularity continued for years after (e.g. Louis Armstrong, Bing Crosby) as well as 1940s singers who started with the big bands.

With the rebirth of the cocktail culture craze, new interest in these performers is starting to appear. Obviously Sinatra is the king of this genre, but the multitude of other male singers offers numerous items as well. Of interest to collectors are vinyl recordings (45, 33 1/3 & 78 rpm), sheet music, autographs/photos and a few other oddities. Most of this musical genre has been re-released on CD.

Al Martino recording, 45 rpm, promotion, "If You Must Leave My Life/Wake Up To Me Gentle".. **$4-6**
Al Martino recording, LP, "Daddy's Little Girl" (ST-2733), Capitol Records.................... **3-8**

Al Martino Recording

Al Martino recording, LP, "I Love You More/Tears and Roses," Capitol Records (ILLUS.).. **3-8**
Al Martino sheet music, "The Girl I Left in Rome"... **4-6**
Andy Williams recording, LP, "Call Me Irresponsible," Columbia CS8971 .... **4-8**
Andy Williams sheet music, "Hawaiian Wedding Song".. **5-15**
Bing Crosby magazine cover, cover photo, Photoplay Magazine, March 1947 (ILLUS. next column) **10-20**
Bing Crosby recording, "Family Christmas Favorites," Decca DL34487, 1957 .... **5-10**

Bing Crosby Magazine Cover

Bing Crosby sheet music, "If You Please" from Dixie.. **5-10**

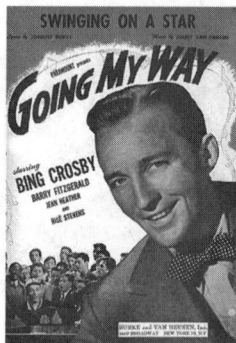

Bing Crosby Sheet Music

Bing Crosby sheet music, "Swingin' On A Star" (ILLUS.).. **5-10**
Bobby Vinton advertisement, promotional, "Blue Velvet," 1960s, 15 1/4" x 11" **10-15**
Bobby Vinton recording, 45 rpm, "Mr. Lonely," Epic Records, picture sleeve......... **8-12**
Bobby Vinton sheet music, "Blue on Blue" **4-8**
Bobby Vinton trade card, photos, 1960s...... **5-10**
Cab Calloway program, "Hello Dolly" playbill, w/Pearl Bailey, 1968 .... **10-20**
Cab Calloway recording, "Sings Hi-Di-Hi-Di-Ho," LP, Premier PM2013, hi-fi............. **10-20**
Cab Calloway recording, "Take the A Train/Chattanooga Choo Choo," 45 rpm record, Okeh label.................................... **5-10**
Dean Martin photograph, publicity photo w/Jerry Lewis, autographed, 8" x 10"........ **25-50**
Dean Martin recording, "Change of Heart," 78 rpm, Capitol CL14523 .... **10-25**
Dean Martin recording, "Dino Latino," LP, Reprise R-6054.................................... **15-25**
Dean Martin recording, "Dream With Dean," LP, Reprise R-6123 .... **15-25**
Dean Martin sheet music, "Angel Baby," 1950s **10-15**
Dick Jurgens recording, "At The Aragon Ballroom," LP, Columbia Records **4-8**
Dick Jurgens sheet music, "Elmer's Tune" **3-5**
Dick Jurgens sheet music, "You Call Everybody Darling," 1946 .... **3-5**

Eddie Fisher magazine cover, "Confidential Magazine," photo on cover, Sept. 1956 .... **10-12**

Eddie Fisher recording, "Christmas with Eddie Fisher," LP, 8 songs, LPM, 10" **10-15**

Eddie Fisher sheet music, "Dungaree Doll," 1955 .... **5-10**

Englebert Humperdinck program, 1977 Tour, 20 pgs. **10-20**

Englebert Humperdinck recording, "Englebert," LP, Parrot PAS71026 .... **5-15**

Englebert Humperdinck recording, "Release Me," reel to reel tape, Parrot PRX79012 .... **3-6**

Fats Waller recording, "Fats Waller Plays and Sings" LP, Jazztone Records **30-40**

Fats Waller recording, "Fats Waller Plays and Sings," LP, RCA Victor LPT-1001, 1954 .... **10-15**

Fats Waller recording, "Two Sleepy People/The Minor Drag," 78 rpm, RCA Victor #20-1583 .... **10-20**

Fats Waller Song Book Folio

Fats Waller sheet music, "Original Conceptions," song book folio, 10 songs (ILLUS.) **10-15**

Frank Sinatra recording, "Ring-A-Ding-Ding," LP Reprise R1001 .... **10-15**

Frank Sinatra recording, "Sings for Only the Lonely," LP, Capitol 1053, 1958 .... **10-20**

Frank Sinatra sheet music, "All or Nothing At All" w/Harry James **5-10**

Harry Belafonte photo, singing at NYC Civil Rights rally, early 1960s **10-20**

Harry Belafonte postcard, photo, black & white, 1960s, 3 1/2" x 5 1/2" **4-8**

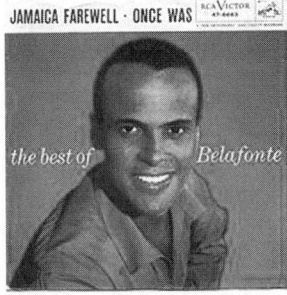

Harry Belafonte Recording

Harry Belafonte recording, "Jamaica Farewell/Once Was," 45 rpm, RCA #6663, picture sleeve, 1955 (ILLUS.) **15-25**

Harry Belafonte recording, "Shenandoah/Scarlet Ribbons/Man Smart/Jerry," 45 EP, RCA EPA-412 .... **10-20**

Jerry Vale recording, "Girl Meets Boy," LP, Philips B07105 .... **10-15**

Jerry Vale Recording

Jerry Vale recording, "There Goes My Heart," LP, Columbia CL2387 (ILLUS.) **5-15**

Jerry Vale sheet music, "Can't You See I'm Sorry" **4-8**

John Gary recording, "That's the Way it Was," LP, RCA Victor LSP 4233, 1969 ..... **10-15**

John Gary Recording

John Gary recording, "The John Gary Christmas Album," LP, RCA Victor LSP2940 (ILLUS.) **5-15**

John Gary sheet music, "How Many Teardrops?" **4-8**

AT THE MARDI GRAS

Johnnie Johnston Sheet Music

Johnnie Johnston sheet music, "At the Mardi Gras," 1943 (ILLUS.) **5-10**

Johnnie Johnston sheet music, "Autumn Serenade," 1945 4-8
Johnnie Ray recording, "Live at the London Palladium," LP, Philips BBR8001, 10" 10-20
Johnnie Ray recording, "Mr. Cry," Sunset 5125 10-15
Johnnie Ray recording, "Walkin' My Baby Back Home," 78 rpm, Columbia C1943 5-10

Johnnie Ray Sheet Music

Johnnie Ray sheet music, "Please Mr. Sun," 1951 (ILLUS.) 4-8
Johnny Mathis recording, "Greatest Hits," LP, Columbia Records 5-10
Johnny Mathis recording, "Johnny's Mood," LP, Columbia COL1526 5-10

Johnny Mathis Sheet Music

Johnny Mathis sheet music, "My Love for You" (ILLUS.) 5-10
Louis Armstrong article, Life Magazine, April 15,1966 4-8

Louis Armstrong Hot Five Recording

Louis Armstrong recording, "Hot Jazz Classics," w/His Hot Five, 78 rpm album (ILLUS.) 15-20

Louis Armstrong recording, w/Danny Kaye, LP 33 1/3, The 5 Pennies 5-10
Louis Armstrong recording, w/Ella Fitzgerald, album, 10" 10-15

Louis Armstrong Sheet Music

Louis Armstrong sheet music, "Hello Dolly!" (ILLUS.) 5-10
Mel Torme recording, "I Can't Give You Anything But Love," 78 rpm, Musicraft Label 5-10
Mel Torme recording, "Swings Shubert Alley," LP, Verve Records, rare 10-25

Torme "Dance, Ballerina, Dance" Sheet Music

Mel Torme sheet music, "Dance, Ballerina, Dance" (ILLUS.) 5-10

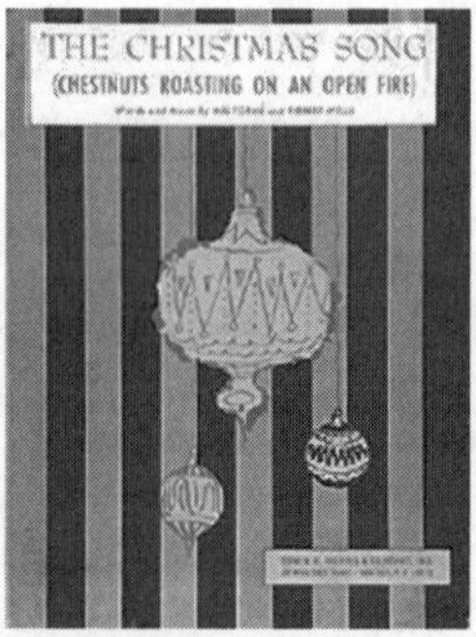

Mel Torme Christmas Sheet Music

Mel Torme sheet music, "The Christmas Song," 1946 (ILLUS.) 3-5
Nat King Cole recording, "Mona Lisa/Too Young," 45 rpm, Capitol Records 10-12

Nat King Cole recording, "Sings For Two in Love," record, Capitol 420, 10" **10-15**

Nat King Cole sheet music, "Unforgettable" **4-8**

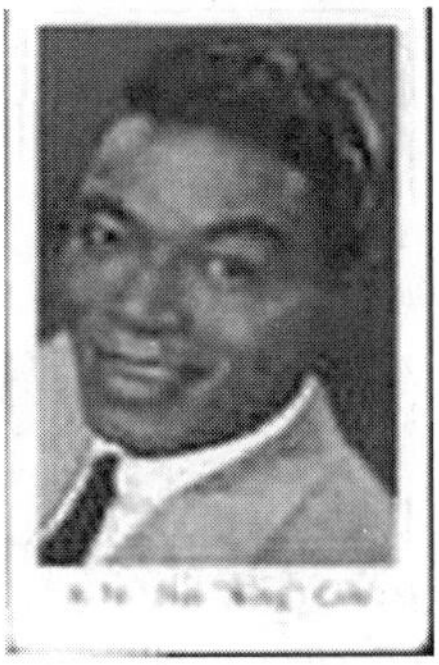

Nat King Cole Trading Card

Nat King Cole trading card, color, 1950s (ILLUS.) **3-6**

Pat Boone book, Twixt Twelve and Twenty, hardbound, 1959 .... **4-8**

Pat Boone recording, "Stardust," KP, HiFi, Dot DLP3118 .... **10-20**

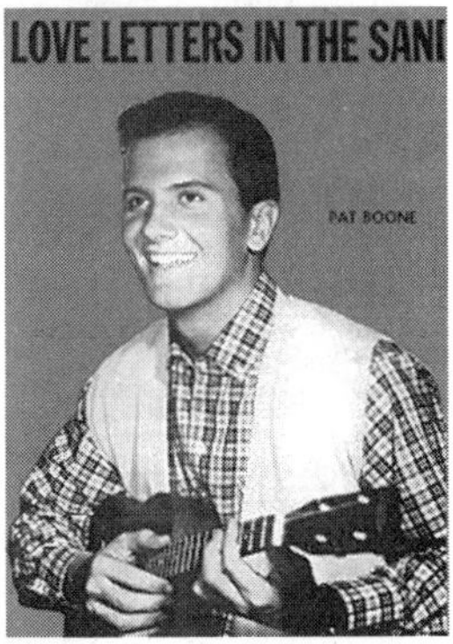

Pat Boone Sheet Music

Pat Boone sheet music, "Love Letters in the Sand" (ILLUS.) **4-8**

Perry Como recording, "Merry Christmas Music," LP, Camden CAS660, 1961 .... **5-15**

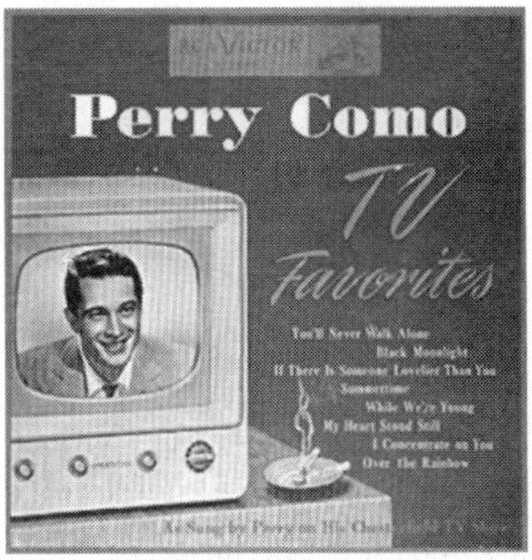

Perry Como Recording

Perry Como recording, "TV Favorites," LP, 8 songs, RCA LPM 3013 10" (ILLUS.) **25-50**

Perry Como sheet music, "Hot Diggity," mid-50s **4-8**

Robert Goulet recording, "The Girl That I Marry," 45 rpm, Columbia Picture, sleeve **3-6**

Robert Goulet recording, "Woman, Woman," LP, Columbia CS9695 .... **5-15**

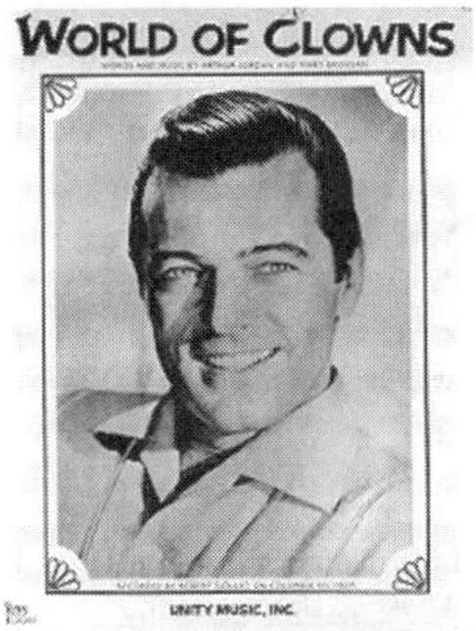

Robert Goulet Sheet Music

Robert Goulet sheet music, "World of Clowns" (ILLUS.) **5-10**

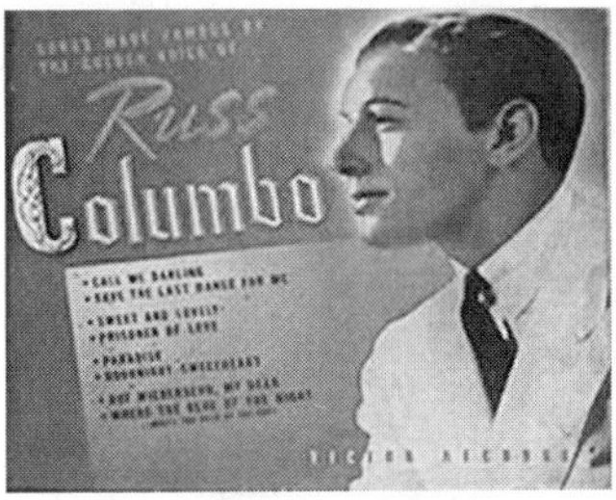

Russ Columbo Recording

Russ Columbo recording, 78 rpm album, 4 records, Victor P95 (ILLUS.) **10-20**

Russ Columbo sheet music, "Make Love the King," 1932 .... **10-15**

Russ Morgan recording, "Forever and Ever," 78 rpm, Decca 24569 .... **3-5**

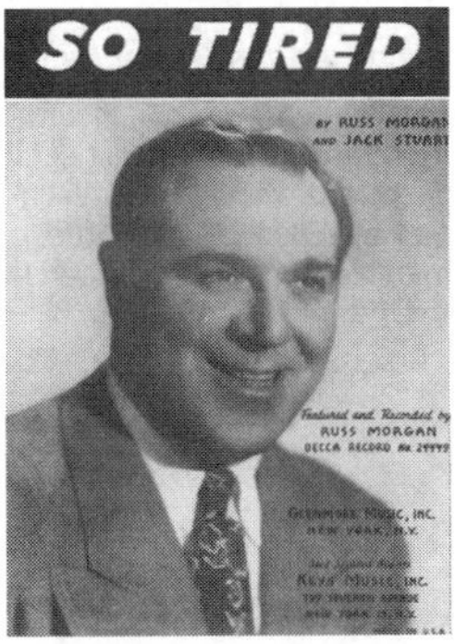

Russ Morgan Sheet Music

Russ Morgan sheet music, "So Tired," 1943 (ILLUS.) **3-6**

Sergio Franchi recording, "Do I Hear A Waltz?" soundtrack LP, Columbia KOS 2770, 1965 .... **5-10**

Sergio Franchi Recording

Sergio Franchi recording, "From Sergio With Love," LP, RCA Victor LPM3654 (ILLUS.)... **5-15**
Tom Jones recording, "It's Not Unusual," LP, Parrot PAS71004 .... **10-20**
Tom Jones recording, "What's New Pussycat?" 45 rpm, Parrot 9765, picture sleeve **5-10**
Tom Jones sheet music, "With These Hands".. **3-5**
Tony Bennett concert handbill, face shot, 1995, Denver, Colorado, 11" x 17" **10-15**
Tony Bennett recording, "Close Your Eyes," 78 rpm, Columbia Records CO 52876, 1953.. **4-8**
Tony Bennett recording, "Who Can I Turn To?," LP, Columbia CS9085...................... **10-20**

Tony Bennett Sheet Music

Tony Bennett sheet music, "I Left My Heart in San Francisco," 1950s (ILLUS.)....... **4-8**
Tony Martin photo, movie still, "Let's Be Happy," w/Vera Ellen, 8" x 10" **10-15**
Tony Martin recording, "At the Desert Inn," LP, RCA LSP2146, 1960............................ **15-25**

Tony Martin Sheet Music

Tony Martin sheet music, "Fools Rush In" (ILLUS.)... **4-8**
Vic Damone magazine cover, Song Hits Magazine, March 1954................................. **5-10**

Vic Damone Photograph

Vic Damone photograph, autographed, 8" x 10" (ILLUS.)..................................... **5-10**
Vic Damone recording, "Angela Mia," 33 1/3 LP, Columbia CL1088, Hi-Fi, 1957...... **15-25**
Vic Damone sheet music, "April in Portugal," 1953... **2-4**

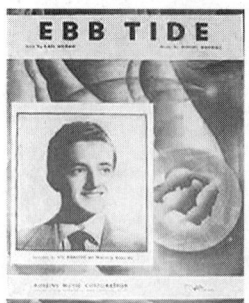

Vic Damone Sheet Music

Vic Damone sheet music, "Ebb Tide," 1953 (ILLUS.).. **4-8**

PURSES & BAGS

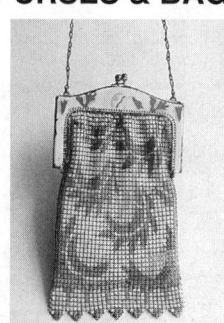

Enameled Mesh Handbag

Enameled mesh, white metal mesh & frame w/enameled design in blue & green & yellow floral design, scalloped bottom border, swing chain, 4 x 6 1/2" not including chain (ILLUS.) **$325**

Mesh Handbag with Bold Floral Design

Enameled mesh, white metal mesh w/bold enameled floral design in blue & yellow & red on black background, decorative black frame w/Art Deco-style clasp, swing chain, 5 1/2 x 6 1/2" not including chain (ILLUS.) **275**

Black Flower-decorated Mesh Purse

Enameled mesh, white metal mesh w/enameled design in green & rust & pale blue, scalloped bottom border, black frame decorated under clasp w/painted basket of flowers & at corners w/single pink flowers, swing chain, 4 x 6 3/4" not including chain (ILLUS.) **325**

Mesh Handbag with Abstract Design

Enameled mesh, white metal mesh w/enameled abstract design in blue & green & beige, scalloped bottom border, decorated brass frame & clasp, marked "Whiting & Davis," swing chain, 4 x 6 3/4" not including chain (ILLUS.) **195**

Mandalian Handbag with Fringe Border

Enameled mesh, white metal mesh w/enameled design in tan, green, yellow & black, M-shaped bottom border w/chain-link fringe, metal floral-design frame tapers to clasp, marked "Mandalian Mfg. Co.," swing chain, 3 1/2 x 8" not including chain (ILLUS.) **195**

Mesh Handbag with Art Deco Clasp

Enameled mesh, white metal mesh w/enameled design in blue & beige geometric design, blue frame w/Art Deco-style clasp, marked "Whiting & Davis," swing chain, 5 1/2 x 7" not including chain (ILLUS.) **325**

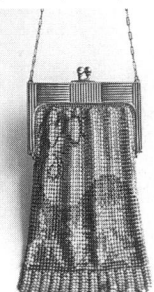

Mesh Handbag in Bold Art Deco Style

Enameled mesh, white metal mesh w/enameled design in yellow & pale green & charcoal, scalloped bottom border, bold Art Deco-style silver frame, swing chain, 5 x 7 3/4" not including chain (ILLUS.) **295**

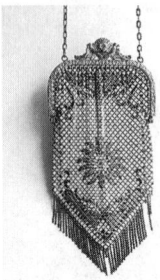

Mandalian Mfg. Mesh Handbag

Enameled mesh, white metal mesh w/enameled floral design in pale & dark greens & taupe, gold-tone frame w/bird & flower-motif clasp, bottom border fringed in V shape, marked "Mandalian Mfg. Co.," swing chain, 3 1/2 x 7 1/4" without chain (ILLUS.) **225**

Mesh Bag with Bold Florals

Enameled mesh, white metal mesh w/enameled floral design in red, green, black & beige, bottom border w/eight red beads suspended at regular intervals, metal frame w/pierced scrollwork & flower design, marked "Mandalian Mfg. Co.," swing chain, 3 3/4 x 8" without chain (ILLUS.) **295**

Black & White Mesh Handbag

Enameled mesh, white metal mesh w/enameled geometric design in black & white, scalloped bottom border, frame features clasp w/two blue glass beads, marked inside "patent applied for," swing chain, 5 x 6 1/2" not including chain (ILLUS.) **135**

Fringed Mesh Bag with Bead Border

Enameled mesh, white metal mesh w/enameled geometric design in rust & blue-green & beige, scalloped bottom border w/silver beads on fringe, silver metal frame w/clasp featuring pierced design of birds & flowers, marked "Mandalian Mfg. Co.," swing chain, 5 x 8 1/2" not including chain (ILLUS.) **295**

Fringed Mesh Handbag

Enameled mesh, white metal mesh w/enameled geometric & floral design in orange & black & beige, Victorian-style frame, chain-link fringe at bottom tapers to V shape, swing chain, 3 3/4 x 6 3/4" not including chain (ILLUS.) **195**

Whiting & Davis Scalloped Mesh Bag

Enameled mesh, white metal mesh w/enameled scroll design in tan & yellow & purple, scalloped bottom border, frame decorated w/painted Art Deco-style design, marked "Whiting & Davis," swing chain, 5 3/4 x 6 3/4" without chain (ILLUS.) **295**

Enameled mesh, yellow ground decorated w/multicolored triangular designs & triangular notched fringe, gold frame & bar & ring link chain handle, Whiting & Davis, 5 x 9 1/2" **350**

Lucite, gold confetti oval form sides, clear top w/rhinestone trim, clear carved swing handle, bead trim around top & bottom rim, 3 1/2 x 10" **500**

Lucite, tortoise triangular form w/black frame & handle, Patricia of Miami, 1950s, 4 x 8" **200**

Sterling silver, octagon-shaped body w/large center compartment & fitted powder compartments, small chain handle, Eastwood-Park Co., ca. 1925, 8 1/2" l. **123**

RADIO & TELEVISION MEMORABILIA

Addams Family Haunted House Kit

Addams Family model kit, Addams Family Haunted House, Aurora, 1965 (ILLUS.)... **$300-750**

Addams Family model kit, Addams Family Haunted House, Polar Lights, Aurora reissue, glow version, 1995 .... **20-35**

Addams Family puzzle, jigsaw-type, Addams Family "Mystery Jigsaw Puzzle," Milton Bradley, 1965.. **40-60**

Adventures of Robin Hood playset, based on British TV series, Marx, No. 4722, 1956.. **200-1,300**

Banana Splits model kit, Banana Buggy (from Banana Splits TV show), 1/25 scale, yellow, Aurora, 1969.................... **250-400**

Banana Splits puzzle, jigsaw-type, frame tray-type, Whitman, 1969 .... **20-40**

Banana Splits puzzle, jigsaw-type, shows group skiing, Whitman, 1970, 100 pieces, 14 x 18"... **15-25**

Mad Lab Bart'nstein Kit

Bart Simpson model kit, Bart'nstein, Bart Simpson as Frankenstein, limited edition, Mad Lab, resin kits sculpted by Michael Parks, 1990s-present, 9" h. (ILLUS.) **50-100**

Aurora Batman Kit

Batman model kit, Batman, w/tree, bats & owl, 1/8 scale, painted by Evan Stuart, 1964 (ILLUS.)... **100-300**

Aurora Batmobile Kit

Batman model kit, Batmobile, 1/32 scale, Aurora, 1966 (ILLUS.) **100-275**

Beany & Cecil puzzle, jigsaw-type, wooden frame tray-type, Playskool, 1961 .... **35-55**

Dark Shadows model kit, Barnabas, MPC, plastic kits, 1968 .... **100-350**

Dark Shadows model kit, Barnabas Vampire Van, MPC, plastic kits, late 1960s **75-225**

Dark Shadows model kit, Werewolf, MPC, plastic kits, 1969 .... **75-275**

Screamin' Productions Elvira Kit

Elvira model kit, 1/4 scale w/mini poster, Screamin' Productions, large vinyl kits, 1988 (ILLUS.)... **60-100**

Elvira model kit, Elvira bust, w/Bio-matched glass eyes, by Lil' Monsters, life-size, 1990s.. **150-175**

Elvira model kit, Elvira, Mistress of the Dark '58 Thunderbird with painted Elvira figure, limited edition of 10,000, together w/certificate of authenticity, Rev-

Revell/Monogram Elvira Figure

ell/Monogram, plastic kits (ILLUS. of
Elvira figure shown by certificate)............. **25-45**

Monogram Elvira's Macabre Mobile Kit

Elvira model kit, Elvira's Macabre Mobile,
Monogram (most re-issued Aurora),
1988 (ILLUS.)... **20-40**

Farrah Fawcett Jigsaw Puzzle

Farrah Fawcett puzzle, jigsaw-type, Farrah
Fawcett photo, 200 pieces, Pro Arts,
1977 (ILLUS.)... **12-30**

Fat Albert Round Jigsaw Puzzle

Fat Albert puzzle, jigsaw-type, Fat Albert
round puzzle, baseball scene, 125 piec-
es, Whitman, 1974, 20" d. (ILLUS.)............ **15-25**
Flipper model kit, based on dolphin TV se-
ries, Revell, plastic kits, 1965 .... **75-150**

Aurora Incredible Hulk Kit

Incredible Hulk (The) model kit, 1/12
scale, Aurora, 1966 (ILLUS.)................... **75-250**

George Jetson Tumbler

Jetsons tumbler, clear glass w/color imag-
es from "The Jetsons" TV show & "1990
Hanna-Barbera Productions" near base
(ILLUS.).. **30**
Johnny Tremain Revolutionary War set,
based on TV series, Marx, No. 3402,
1957.. **450-2,100**
Jungle Jim playset, based on TV series,
Marx., No. 3706, 1957 .... **400-1,500**
Land of the Giants model kit, w/giant
snake, 1/48 scale, Aurora, 1968 .... **150-350**

AMT Kenworth Truck Tractor Kit

Movin' On model kit, from NBC TV
series, 1/25 scale Kenworth truck tractor,
AMT & AMT/Ertl, plastic kits (ILLUS.).......... **8-20**
Munsters (The) model kit, "Dragula" car,
AMT & AMT/Ertl - Plastic Kits, 1965 .... **50-225**
Munsters (The) model kit, living room
scene, Aurora, 1964, rare **400-900**

Polar Lights Munsters Living Room Kit

Munsters (The) model kit, living room
scene, Polar Lights, Aurora reissue,
1997 (ILLUS.) **15-25**

AMT Munster Koach Kit

Munsters (The) model kit, Munster Koach,
1964, AMT & AMT/Ertl - Plastic Kits
(ILLUS.) **50-175**
Munsters (The) model kit, Munster Koach
& Dragula, reissued in one package,
AMT & AMT/Ertl - Plastic Kits, 1991 .... **35-50**
Penguin (Batman villain) model kit, w/um-
brellas, 1/12 scale, Aurora, 1967 .... **250-500**
Rin Tin Tin playset, based on TV series,
Marx, No. 3628, 1956 .... **200-900**
Scooby-Doo vehicle, airplane, Scooby-
Doo Bump & Go Airplane, Boley, 1998,
boxed **15-20**
Scooby-Doo vehicle, friction-powered,
Scooby-Doo on Ski Vacation, Boley,
1998, boxed **15-20**
Sons of Liberty playset, based on TV se-
ries, Marx, No. 4170, 1950s **50-350**
12 O'Clock High model kit, B17 Bomber
Formation, w/three planes, Aurora,
1965 .... **100-250**
Untouchables playset, based on TV se-
ries, Marx, No. 4676, 1961 .... **300-700**

RADIOS & ACCESSORIES

Addison, Model 2A, white Bakelite case **$550**
Admiral,   Model   4-A-15,   AM/FM
console, ca. 1948 .... **40**
Admiral, Model 5M21, Bakelite, ra-
dio/phono, large **55**
Admiral, Model 5X12, plastic, tabletop, late
1940s **35**
Admiral, Model 6P32, leatherette, portable,
1940s **35**

Admiral, Model AZ593, "farm" set, portable,
takes 6-volt battery, ca. 1938 .... **35**
Air Castle, Model 5012, wooden, tombstone-shaped, tabletop, 1930s **85**
Air Castle, Model 935, Bakelite, tabletop,
1940s **45**
Air King, Model 5000, leatherette, portable,
1940s **45**
Air King, Model 66, Bakelite, "skyscraper"
w/clock, white, 1933 .... **4,500**
Air King, Model A-600, Catalin, green &
yellow, 1947 .... **1,200**
Arvin, Model 441-T, metal, Hopalong
Cassidy tabletop **750**
Arvin, Model 532, Catalin set, yellow &
brown, 1930s **2,000**
Arvin, Model 850T, painted plastic, 1950s **435**
Atwater Kent, Kiel table model w/six legs,
top exposes radio inside **350**
Atwater Kent, Model 10, breadboard style,
exposed controls & tubes **1,250**
Atwater Kent, Model 20C, wooden, table-
top, wide, 1920s **75**
Atwater Kent, Model 441, metal, tabletop,
late 1920s **85**
Belmont, Model 6D120, Bakelite, stream-
lined style, ca. 1940s **155**
Bendix, Model 0526C, Catalin, green
w/black trim **850**
Bendix, Model 0626A, painted Bakelite,
white **55**
Bendix, Model 301, wooden, tabletop, ca.
1949 .... **35**
Capehart, Model T-522, plastic, tabletop,
1950s **25**
Colonial New World Globe, Bakelite, novel-
ty radio, 1930s **850**
Crosley, Model 56TU, painted Bakelite,
tabletop, ca. 1940s **65**
Crosley, Model 66CS, wooden, ra-
dio/phone console, 1940s **35**
Crosley, Model 9-113, plastic, tabletop,
1949 .... **20**
Crosley, Model 9-205M, radio/phono con-
sole, 1950 .... **35**
Crosley, Pup, metal set w/tube in top **250**
Detrola, Model 576-1-6, wooden, miniature
console-shaped tabletop **75**
DeWald, Model A-501, Catalin, brown body,
late 1930s **650**

Emerson "Baby" Model

Emerson, "Baby" model, one-tube, 1920s,
complete (ILLUS.) **650**
Emerson, Model 520, Catalin, tabletop,
brown **145**

Emerson, Model 539, wooden, tabletop, mid-1940s 20

Emerson, Model 575, plastic, portable, ca. 1950 20

FADA, Model 1001, wooden, tabletop, ca. 1949 35

FADA, Model 5F-50, Catalin, tabletop, yellow body, small 1,000

FADA Model 711 Radio

FADA, Model 711, gold Catalin case, round dial (ILLUS.) 350

FADA, Model 845, plastic, "Cloud," tabletop 150

FADA, Model P-100, alligator leather, portable, 1940s 35

FADA, Model P80, portable, late 1940s 75

General Electric, Model 410, wooden, AM/FM, tabletop 25

General Electric, Model 511, plastic, clock radio, ca. 1950 35

General Electric, Model 670, plastic, portable, 1950s 20

Motorola, Model 58R11, plastic, tabletop, ca. 1947 35

Motorola, Model 5A7, plastic, portable, w/flip-up cover 30

Motorola, Model 67F14, wooden, radio/phono console, large 75

Motorola, Model 85F21, console radio w/phonograph, ca. 1948 40

RCA, Aeriola Junior, one-tube set, usually marked "Westinghouse," 1920s 175

RCA, Model 2R51, plastic, portable, mid-1950s 25

RCA, Model 66X11, plastic, tabletop w/Chinese-style grille, 1948 75

RCA, Radiola 18, wooden, wide, late 1920s 65

Sparton, Model 10BW76, console radio w/pull-out phono, 1940s 55

Sparton, Model 132, plastic, oval-shaped, ca. 1950 95

Sparton, Model 301, portable w/handle on top, ca. 1950 25

Sparton, Model 5AW06, Bakelite, mid-1940s 35

Standard, Model SR-H437, chrome & black, pocket-size 75

Stewart Warner, Model A6S, Dionne Quints novelty radio 750

Zenith, Model 7H820, plastic, tabletop, three-band, large, ca. 1949 45

Zenith, Model 8H023, plastic, tabletop, three-band, mid-1940s 55

Zenith, Model H725, Bakelite, tabletop w/handle, 1950 35

RECORDS
Children's

45 RPM - Bonus Play

In the early days of sound recording, the few 78s with "kiddie" themes were recorded vaudeville acts with children or child-like characters. Records aimed specifically at the children's market arrived in earnest in the postwar years. In the late 1940s and early '50s, 78s were the standard, and children's records came in album sets. With the introduction of 45s, 10" records and the LP, 78s gradually became extinct. Children's 45 record players helped create a thriving market for 45s. By the early '60s children's LPs had become equally popular.Today, 78s from the late '40s-50s are scarce; 45s from the 1950s are easier to find. Collectors search for scarce 78s and 45s in the original picture sleeves. Peter Pan Records, Cricket Records and Little Golden Records are most often found. Themes include nursery rhymes and songs, marching and play records, cowboy and space themes and, of course, licensed cartoon characters. All records originally came with illustrated picture sleeves, and some records were made of colored vinyl. The children's 33 1/3 LP record joined 45s in popularity by the early '60s. Collections of TV themes, soundtracks from children's movies, TV shows and educational records helped carry children's records through the rest of the 20th century. Numerous popular adult singers, television and film stars made recordings for children, Patti Page's recording of "How Much is That Doggie in the Window?" being one of the most memorable.Records listed below are from the postwar years of 1945-1965. Prices are based on condition and whether the record has a picture sleeve. 45 RPM size - some are 45 RPM and some play at 78 RPM; Bonus Play size - 7" - usually play at 78 RPM; 10" size - smaller than LP - usually play at 78 RPM; LP size - 12" - usually play at 33 1/3 RPM.

"A Toot and A Whistle ..."

"A Toot and A Whistle, A Plunk and A Boom," Disney, yellow vinyl, Little Golden Records (ILLUS.) $5-10

"Andy Panda Polka/Chilly Willy the Penguin," Cricket Records 5-10

"Bimbo/Punchy the Clown"

"**Bimbo/Punchy the Clown,**" yellow vinyl, copyright 1953, Cricket Records (ILLUS.)...... **3-5**

"Cinderella"

"**Cinderella,**" back of sleeve has paper doll cutouts, Star-Brite Records (ILLUS.).......... **10-12**

"**Cinderella Work Song,**" yellow vinyl, copyright 1950 Walt Disney Prod., Little Golden Records... **5-10**

"De Camptown Races/Clementine"

"**De Camptown Races/Clementine,**" yellow vinyl, copyright 1949, Little Golden Records (ILLUS.).. **3-5**

"**Dennis Day Sings Johnny Appleseed/Romper Room Dooby Song,**" Cricket Records **10-12**

"**Doing the Hokey Pokey/Dilly Dally Song,**" copyright 1953, Pickwick Sales Corp. **3-5**

"**Donald Duck's Singing Lesson/Pluto the Pup,**" yellow vinyl, Little Golden Records... **5-10**

"**Fiddle Dee Dee/Pease Porridge Hot,**" red vinyl, copyright 1949, Record Guild of America **4-8**

"**Five Little Firemen/Flute Dance,**" yellow vinyl, Little Golden Records **4-8**

"Foghorn Leghorn/Henery Hawk"

"**Foghorn Leghorn/Henery Hawk,**" yellow vinyl, Little Golden Records (ILLUS.).......... **5-10**

"**Frosty the Snowman,**" yellow vinyl, copyright 1951, Little Golden Records **3-5**

"Happy Birthday to You/For He's a Jolly Good Fellow"

"**Happy Birthday to You/For He's a Jolly Good Fellow,**" Peter Pan Records (ILLUS.)... **3-5**

"**Hi Hi, Hi Ho/Looby Lou,**" Jack & Jill Records.. **3-5**

"**I Saw Mommy Kissing Santa Claus,**" red vinyl, Record Guild of America.................... **5-10**

"It's a Small World"

"**It's a Small World,**" Disney, copyright 1963, Disneyland Records (ILLUS.)............. **5-10**

"Jack and the Beanstalk"

"**Jack and the Beanstalk/Turkey in the Straw,**" Cricket Records (ILLUS.).................. **3-5**

"Johnny Appleseed"

"Me and My Teddy Bear"

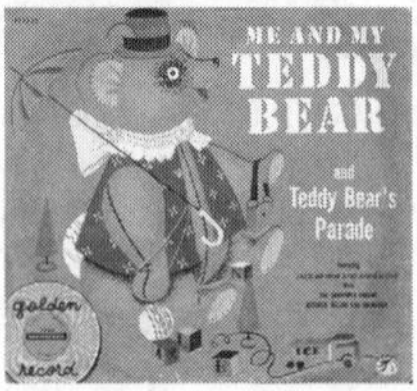

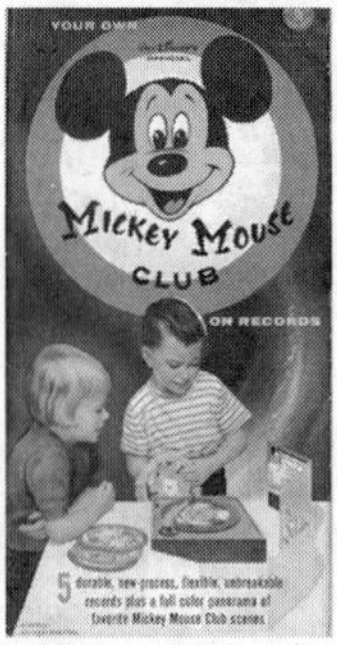

"Mickey Mouse Club on Record"

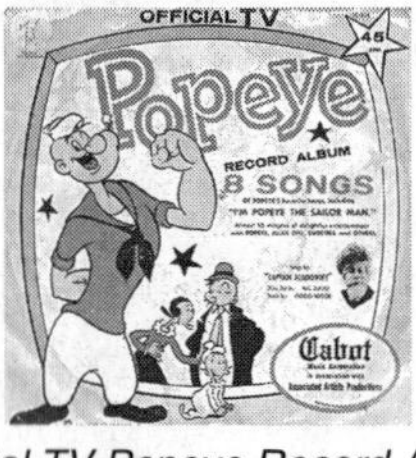

"Official TV Popeye Record Album"

"Rover the Strongman"

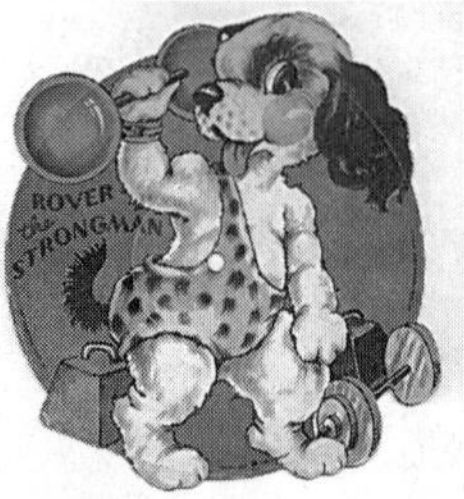

"The Syncopated Clock"

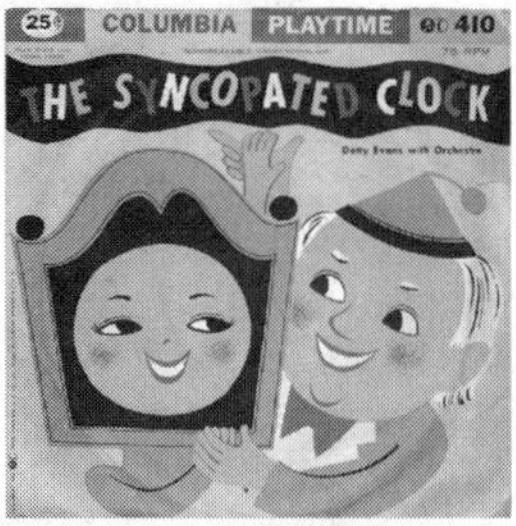

Woody Woodpecker Song Record

"The Woody Woodpecker Song/Wood-pecker Dance," yellow vinyl, Little Golden Records (ILLUS.) **5-10**
"Tina the Ballerina," yellow vinyl, Peter Pan Records... **4-8**

"Volare/Little Star"

"Volare/Little Star," Little Golden Records (ILLUS.).. **3-5**
"Who's Afraid of the Big Bad Wolf?," copyright 1954, red vinyl, Peter Pan Records.. **4-8**
"Willipus Wallipus/Jolly Tunes," Cricket Records... **4-6**
"Wynken, Blynken, Nod/Storm in the Bathtub," yellow vinyl, Little Golden Records... **4-8**

78 RPMs

Vintage kiddie records in this listing refer to 78 rpm discs. Some may have also appeared in 45 and/or 33 1/3 rpm format, but each listing here is for 78 rpm only. The era of 78s was from 1894 to the mid-1960s. As a general rule, any children's record issued from the 1940s and later should have its original picture sleeve or album cover in order to have any value. It is the beautiful designs and colors that attract collectors. Post-World War II loose records have little or no collector value. Pre-World War II loose records generally can be found for $10 or less. The exception would be "picture" discs (Vogue types) where the sleeve, if it exists at all, is not as important as the record itself with its vivid graphics.

Another rule of thumb which helps establish value is the content. "Character" related record subjects, be they fictional or real, will be more valuable than "generic" fairy tales, fables, nursery rhymes or educational material. Famous characters from comic books, movies, cartoons, TV and radio will usually attract more buyers, and thus have greater value. Almost all generic kiddie records in their original sleeves can be found for

under $10 (with the exception of picture discs). Ninety percent of character-related children's 78s will go for $5-$15, but a small percentage will be higher, including a select few which can cost as much as $1,000-$3,000.

Note: some dates given are "guesstimates."

Picture Discs

"A Holiday Greeting to You," Voco, No. 224, 1947, w/mailer envelope add $20...... **15-20**
"Cinderella," Playola, No. 102, very small 4" d. records, three in an album, 1948, the set.. **80-150**
"Home On the Range/The Cowboy," Playsong, No. WW-31/32, 1948 .... **8-15**
"How to Catch," Sight N' Sound, no number, rare H.O. Oats send-away premium, 1952.. **50-75**
"It's Fun To Whistle," Disney item, Wheaties box cut-out, no number, 1952......... **4-8**
"Jack and Jill," Pix, No. 108, 1941............... **40-60**
"Jacob's Dream/Joseph & His Brothers," Standard Publishing, No. RO-771/712, 1948.. **8-12**
"Kitty Cat/Ten Little Indians," Voco, No. 507/607, 1948.. **6-10**
"Lazy Jack/Wolf Wolf," Story Book, no number, Walt Kelly art, 1949...................... **25-45**
"Little White Duck/Three Little Kittens," Record Guild-Picture Play, No. PP-8, very rare, 1948.. **50-75**
"Noah's Ark," Magic Talking Books, No. T-4, book w/cover as a record, 1955 .... **10-15**
"Pinocchio/Snoopy Sniffer," Toy Toon, No. P-18, 1950.. **6-10**
"Rock-a-by-Baby/Peter Peter Pumpkin Eater," Record Guild of America, No. 5002P, 1948, w/color sleeve add another $10... **8-15**
"Sleepy Time/Time To Get Up," Pat, No. 6-A-1/2, rare, 1948.................................... **80-120**
"Song & Story Book #1," Kiddie Rekord Co., No. 1001-1006, rare set of six, ca. 1928, the set **200-300**
"Superman, the Magic Ring," Musette, no number, comic book w/two records, 1947 **75-100**
"The Tiger," Talking Books, no number, record attached to die-cut backing, 1919 **60-100**

Trial of "Bumble" the Bee Record

"The Trial of 'Bumble' the Bee," Vogue, No. R-746, 1947 (ILLUS.) **50-75**

The Whistler & His Dog Picture Disc

"The Whistler and His Dog," Red Raven, No. M-29, 1956 (ILLUS.) **25-45**

"Winnie the Pooh, Christopher Robin Songs," Victor, No. 221, 1934, very rare, one of a set of three (ILLUS.) **200-300**

"Your Trip to Disneyland," Mattel, no number, five records in folder to be cut out, 1955, the set **75-125**

Regular (Non-Picture Disc) Records

"A Child's Introduction to The Orchestra," Golden Record Chest, No. GRC-1, 1954, eight records in a box-carrying case, the set **15-25**

"Aesop's Fables," Merry-Go-Round, No. TP-6, 1950 .... **2-4**

"Aladdin's Lamp," Little Folks Favorites, No. LF-1-2, narrated by BeBe Daniels, 1948 .... **25-30**

"Alice In Wonderland," Adventure, No. A-5, 1947 .... **3-5**

"Animal Fair," Columbia Playtime, No. PV-378, narrated by Arthur Godfrey, 1951 .... **3-4**

"Animal Polka/Little Sir Echo," Animal, No. 168, 1953 .... **3-4**

"Billy Goats Gruff," Mercury Childcraft, No. MC-14, narrated by Boris Karloff, 1951 .... **10-15**

"Birthstone," March, no number, 1956, ring & record set **3-4**

"Celeste," Coral, No. 2300, narrated by Victor Jory, 1949 .... **7-12**

"Cinderella/Ugly Duckling," Jack and Jill, No. J-11, 1955 .... **2-3**

"Clap Hands/Up! Up! Up!," Pram, No. 5, 1949 .... **2-3**

"Dick Tracy in Catch That Thief," Durotone, No. R-111, 1930s, records came w/film strips & projector, the set **5-10**

"Do My Dolly Do/The Little Red Playhouse," Cricket, No. C-57, 1953 .... **2-3**

"Franz Schubert," Magic-Tone, No. M-15, 1949 .... **5-10**

"Freedom Songs," Melodee, No. MA-26, 1946 .... **5-10**

"Frosty The Snowman/Santa Gets Your Letter," Columbia, No. MJV-75, by Gene Autry, 1950 .... **4-6**

"Funnybone Alley," Disc, No. 606, narrated by Pete Seeger, 1948 .... **25-35**

"Goldilocks & The Three Bears," Peter Pan, No. 119 A/B, 1946 .... **2-3**

"Grimm's Fairy Tales, Vol. I," Black and White, No. BW50, 1950 .... **4-8**

"Grow Grow/Swim Swim," Cub, No. 4, narrated by Woody Guthrie, 1950 .... **20-30**

"Hansel & Gretel," Barker, no number, 1955, record comes w/cardboard record player **40-60**

"Hillbilly Songs," Caravan, No. C-19, 1949 ...... **4-5**

"Homerun Mickey/The Detective," Talkie-Jektor, No. 10A-1, from Disney's Silly Symphonies, 1930s **6-12**

"Hopalong Cassidy & The Big Ranch Fire," Capitol, No. CAS-3024, 1949 .... **25-35**

"Howdy Doody & The Air-O-Doodle," RCA Victor, No. 397, 1950 .... **20-25**

"I Like People/Yankee Doodle Dandy," Big Golden Record, No. BR-9, by Jimmy Durante, 1952 .... **10-15**

"I Want A Doll House/Playing To," Plasco, No. 4-Mar, 1955, record came w/dollhouse furniture **2-3**

"It's A Small World," Disneyland Little Gem, No. LG-775, 1964 .... **5-10**

"King Thrushbeard," Bel-Tone, No. BT-3, 1949 .... **3-6**

"Let's Go To The Zoo," Mayfair, No. K-103, 1950 .... **3-5**

"Lion and Mouse/Frog and Ox," Lionel, No. 114, 1965 .... **3-5**

"Lionel Lion/Thank You," Color Tunes, No. 112/113, 1956 .... **2-3**

"Little Black Sambo," Musette Musical Radio Script, No. 76512/3, 1941 .... **80-100**

"Little Orley, Adventures with Bubble Gum, etc." Decca, No. CUS-7, narrated by Uncle Lumpy, 1947 .... **25-35**

"London Bridge," Little Wonder, No. 793, 1918, one-side 5" d. record **4-8**

"London Bridge/Three Blind Mice," Golden, No. R-363, 1957 .... **2-3**

"Mighty Mouse," Peter Pan, No. 528, 1959.. **10-20**

"Mother Goose Songs #1, 2," Edison, No. 51251, 1920s **15-25**

"Myrtle the Turtle," Musette Listen Look Picture Book, No. LL-5, 1941, book & record **8-15**

"Oh Susanna/If All The Seas," Bingola, No. 622, 1920s **6-8**

"Percy The Seal/The Elephant Who Forgot," Admiral, No. K-202, 1950, narrated by Arnold Stang **8-12**

"Petrouchka," Kiddie Land, No. KL-12, 1954 .... **3-5**

"Pied Piper of Hamelin," Carnival, No. 102-3, 1956, records come w/special record player **1-2**

"Pinocchio," RCA Victor, No. P-18, w/original die-cut cover, 1940 .... **100-125**

"Rip Van Winkle," MGM, No. 46-A, narrated by Lionel Barrymore, 1949 .... **15-20**

"Robin Hood," Musicraft, No. RR-6, 1947 .... **5-8**

"Rumplestiltskin," Star Bright Classics, No. R-414, 1949, record in folder w/paper doll punch-outs **8-12**

"Silent Night/Adeste Fideles," Rocking Horse, No. 218/219, 1947 .... **2-3**

"Sing-A-Song of Presidents," Records of Knowledge, No. ROK-2, 1954 .... **5-8**

"Song Book No. 1," La Velle Bobolink, No. 550/551, 1922, two records in illustrated book **65-90**

"Space Trip (with Foodini & Pinhead)," Jim Dandy, No. 12, 1953 .... **20-25**

"Sparky and The Talking Train," Capitol, No. BC-66, three-record album, 1947 .... **40-75**

Tom Corbett Record Sleeve

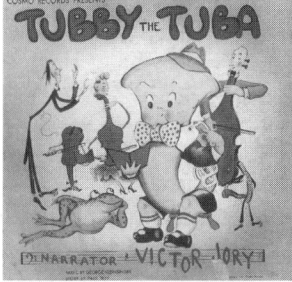

Tubby The Tuba Record Sleeve

Disney Mouseketunes 45 RPM Record

78s/78 Album Sets/10" Records

"Margaret O'Brien Stories for Children,"
album set, Capitol Records, the set............ 20-25
"Nursery Rhymes," two record set, copy-
right 1948, Capitol Records .... 10-15'
"On Lemmer Lemmer Street," an Old
Dutch Song, Children's Record Guild.......... 5-10
"Pee-Wee the Piccolo," album set, RCA
Victor Records... 10-15
"Rusty in Orchestraville," album set, Cap-
itol Records... 15-20
"Sheep and the Pig Who Set Up House-
keeping," RCA Victor Records.................. 10-12
"Smokey Joe Cowboy Songs," red vinyl,
Peter Pan Records 10-12
"Songs That Children Love," Peter Pan
Records.. 10-15
"Story of Peter Rabbit," Children's Record
Guild... 5-10
"The Barber of Seville," red vinyl, Mercury
Childcraft Records...................................... 10-15
"The Big Record of Merry-Go-Rhymes,"
copyright 1949, Peter Pan Records........... 10-12
"The Chugging Freight Engine," copy-
right 1949, Children's Record Guild............. 5-10
"Toy Symphony," by Joseph Haydn, copy-
right 1948, Young People's Records........... 5-10
"Uncle Don's Musical Stories," copyright
1949, Varsity Records................................. 10-12
"Uncle Mac's Nursery Rhymes," RCA
Victor Records... 10-12
"When the Husband Kept House," RCA
Victor Records... 10-12

LP Records
"Dr. Seuss Presents Yertle the Turtle and
Other Stories," RCA Camden Records.... 10-15
"Fun in Shariland with Shari Lewis and
Lambchop," RCA Camden Records........ 10-20
"Six Complete Stories from Deputy
Dawg," RCA Camden Records 10-20
"Song Hits from The Wizard of Oz/Dis-
ney's Pinocchio," RCA Records.............. 10-15
"Soundtrack from The Wizard of Oz,"
MGM Records 20-25

SCIENTIFIC INSTRUMENTS

Burglar Alarm Telegraph

Burglar alarm telegraph, marked "E.
Holmes - Burglar Alarm Telegraph," on
stepped rectangular wood base, 1853
(ILLUS.).. **$3,921**

Enigma Cipher Machine

Cipher machine, Enigma cipher machine of
World War II fame, metal, 10-rotor, 1935
(ILLUS.) **52,275**

Brass Microscope from 1780

Microscope, brass, by "J. Simons, London," on wood base w/shallow drawer for
attachments, English, 1780 (ILLUS.) **2,875**
Microscope, brass & steel, w/an 8x eye-
piece & single-power lens, Spencer Lens
Company, w/mahogany case, 14 1/4" h....... **105**

George Adams Microscope

Microscope, cuff-type microscope, signed
"Geo. Adams," w/attachments & original
box, English, 1750 (ILLUS.)........................ **7,670**
Microscope, w/telescoping viewer & tri-fo-
cal lenses, Bausch & Lomb Optical
Co., ca. 1900, 13" h. **140**

Edison Stock Ticker

Stock ticker, marked "Mfg. by T.A. Edison, Inc. - 12942" on inner workings, round black base marked "Tikkerdiens - Amsterdam" (ILLUS.) **5,114**

Surveyor's level, lacquered brass, marked "C.L. Berger & Sons, Boston Mass - 31217" on base, in fitted wood case, ca. 1920 .... **840**

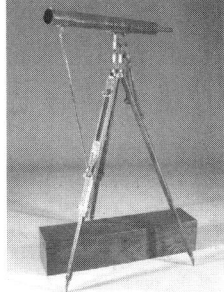

English Brass Telescope on Tripod

Telescope, brass, on adjustable oak tripod stand, long brass case w/various adjusting mechanisms, w/original fitted mahogany case, made by J.H. Steward Ltd. of London, ca. 1900, 46" l. (ILLUS.) **1,792**

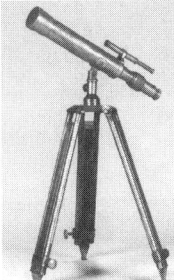

Brass Telescope on Tripod

Telescope, brass, on expandable tripod base, made by Thomas J. Evans, English, ca. 1900, 24 1/2" h. (ILLUS.) **560**

Barometers

Barometers, those famous weather indicators, were first invented around 1643 when Torrecelli introduced the mercury barometer.

There are two basic types of barometers: mercury and aneroid. Mercury barometers are either a stick-type or wheel (banjo)-type. The stick-type has mercury in a glass tube about 29 1/2" long which is either exposed or hidden in the case. Aneroid barometers didn't come on the scene until the 1840s, and their invention is attributed to M. Vidi. They work by measuring variations in air pressure using metal concentric circles (bellows).

Other forms of barometer include the Laboratory (Kew or Fortin), pocket altimeters, which come in all sizes, the Admiral Fitzroy and barographs, which are recording barometers.

Aneroid & Assorted Types

Barograph Barometer & Case

Barograph, instrument enclosed in glass case, a recording barometer w/eight-day clock (ILLUS.) **750**

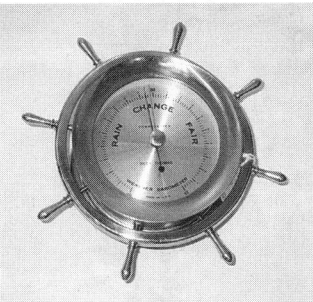

Seth Thomas Brass Barometer

Brass, model of a ship's wheel, Seth Thomas, American (ILLUS.) **150**

Brass Pocket-type Barometer

Brass, pocket-type (altimeter), round w/top ring handle, made in England for Andrew J. Lloyd & Co., Boston, beveled glass front, 2 1/2" d. (ILLUS.) **150**

Bonschur & Holmes Barometer

Brass, round frame w/silvered metal dial, 5" d. beveled glass cover w/mercury half-round thermometer, by Bonschur & Holmes, Philadelphia, Pennsylvania (ILLUS.) **225**

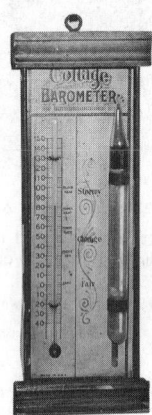

Cottage Barometer

Cottage barometer, long dial w/wood board at top & base, advertising giveaway (ILLUS.) **65**

Nautical-style Oak Barometer

English, nautical-style, round carved oak case, dial signed "John Lilley & Son, Ltd. - Wilson & Gillie," English, 8" d. (ILLUS.) **75**

German-made Pocket Barometer

Pocket barometer, round silvered metal case w/ring handle, fitted in hinged leather case, w/instructions, made in Germany (ILLUS.) **145**

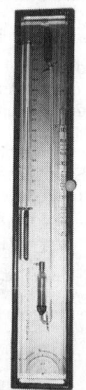

Sympiesometer Barometer

Sympiesometer, narrow case enclosing long metal silvered dial, signed "North" (ILLUS.) **3,000**

Stick-type

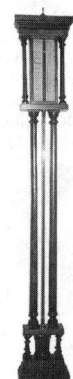

McKay Barometer in Fancy Case

American, McKay, New York, New York, rectangular pediment above dial flanked by colonettes over tall open columns flanking the tube, small spindles & blocked base, double vernier (ILLUS.) **2,450**

Wheel or Banjo-type

English Dolland Barometer

English, mahogany case w/broken-scroll pediment, made by Dolland, ca. 1840 (ILLUS.) **4,000**

Crichton Bros. Barometer

English, stepped cornice above tall narrow case, beveled glass, double vernier, Crichton Bros., London, 19th c. (ILLUS.)... **2,400**

Gimballed Walker Barometer

English, Walker, very slender mahogany case, gimballed in wall bracket (ILLUS.).... **3,700**

Henry Green Wheel Barometer

American, slender upper case w/broken-scroll pediment above dials & center small round mirror over large round lower dial, Henry Green, United States, base 8" d. (ILLUS.) **1,500**

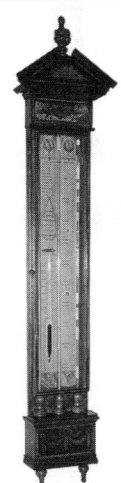

Dutch Contra Walnut Barometer

Dutch, walnut case w/high pediment centered by a turned finial, long glass-covered case w/decorated insets, Contra model, thermometer mercury tube (ILLUS.).. **4,500**

English, mahogany banjo-form case, a small broken pediment above a panel w/a blossom inlay above the temperature gauge flanked by shell inlay, the round barometer at the bottom w/siphon tube mechanism, the faced signed "Pozzi & Co.," the rounded base drop w/an inlaid blossom, England, early 19th c., 38 3/8" h. **1,610**

G. Croce English Barometer

English, mahogany case w/broken-scroll pediment over swelled back over the large round dial, G. Croce, England, early 1820s, case 8" d. (ILLUS.) **850**

Martinelli & Son Barometer

English, mahogany case w/broken-scroll pediment w/tiny brass finial over small dials & a large round dial at the bottom, Martinelli & Son, King St., England, wheel w/five functions, base 10" d. (ILLUS.) **1,250**

SEWING ADJUNCTS

With sewing tools and accessories so popular, collectors in the United States, Canada and England actively search for these small antiques. The wide variety available gives buyers a good selection from which to choose - and allows for plenty of different price ranges too. Be cautious of reproductions - Victorian and Georgian style sterling thimbles and needlecases marked "Thailand" are found frequently, and new pewter thimble holders are sometimes sold as old. A good reference book on sewing tools and accessories is Gay Ann Rogers' An Illustrated History of Needlework Tools, which can be found in many bookstores. All items listed below are in good condition, with minor wear and no missing parts.

Bodkin, brass, English, 1880s **$15**
Bodkin, sterling silver, plain w/no design, American, 1920s **45**
Bodkin (ribbon threader), bone, English, 1880s **30**
Crochet hook, bone w/turned end, American, late 19th c. **15**
Crochet hook, brass, decorative w/sliding hooks to protect point, English, 1870s **48**
Crochet hook, carved mother-of-pearl handle, English, 1890s **38**
Crochet hook, wood, fancy turnings & extra long, American, late 19th c. **25**
Darner, wood ball in socket design, Shaker-made, American, late 19th c. **225**
Darner, wood, double-ended glove-type, floral decoration, American, 1920s **155**
Darner, wood w/metal clip to hold fabric, American, 1920s **15**
Darner, wood w/swirled enamel paint design, American, 1920s **35**
Emery, double-ended barrel-form, Scottish Mauchline ware, 1860s **145**
Emery, model of a strawberry w/sterling silver top, English, 1920s **125**
Emery, velvet, model of a strawberry, American, 1940s **18**
Emery, velvet, model of a strawberry w/h.p. seeds, American, 1860s **145**
Hem measure, sterling silver in the Art Nouveau style, American, ca. 1900 .... **155**
Knitting gauge (to measure knitting needles), steel bell-shaped, English, ca. 1900 .... **24**
Knitting needle guards, ivory carved in the form of boots, English, 1860s **275**
Knitting needle guards, turned wood, no design, English, 1880s **185**
Knitting needles, metal, American, early 20th c., pr. **10**
Lace bobbin, bone, spiral saying, Honiton, English, 1850s **155**
Lace bobbin, wood, no design, English, 1850s **35**
Lace bobbin, wood w/pewter butterfly inlay, English, 1840s **135**
Lace bobbin, wood w/pewter rings, English, 1840s **65**
Lacemaker's lap pillow & bobbins, Belgium, 1850s, the set **795**
Nanny pin, goldstone, complete w/needle cylinder, English, 1890s **245**
Needle case, beadwork on bone, flat style, English, 1840s **150**
Needle case, brass, cylindrical mitrailleuse, w/Sears advertising, 1920s **45**
Needle case, carved ivory in the form of an umbrella w/a built-in Stanhope, English, 1860s **175**
Needle case, carved ivory w/Chinese figures, Chinese Export, 1850s **145**
Needle case, plastic, early pink & cream model of an umbrella, English, 1920s **75**
Needle case, sterling silver w/bright-cut decoration, English, 1800-1810 .... **185**
Needlebook, red velvet w/flannel pages, American, 1880s **55**
Needlebook, tooled leather cover w/flannel pages, American, 1880s **60**
Needlework clamp, carved ivory, originally from a Chinese workbox, 1840s **385**

Pin disc, advertising-type, advertising Prudential, w/picture of mother holding child, American, 1940s.. 18

Pin disc, carved bone decoration, English, 1850s... 125

Pin disc, glass w/hand-painted butterfly, English, 1850s, rare 225

Pin disc, ivory, carved w/a pinwheel decoration, French Dieppe work, 1830s................ 155

Pin disc, silver plate, pierced decoration, from a chatelaine, American, 1890s................ 95

Pincushion, brass, model of a Victorian chair, English, 1880s...................................... 145

Camel Pincushion

Pincushion, camel in gold-tone spelter, back of resting camel holds cushion, marked "U.S.A.," 3 1/8" l. (ILLUS.)................ 145

Cat Pincushion

Pincushion, cat figure in gold-tone spelter, back of sitting cat holds cushion, marked "U.S.A.," 4" l. (ILLUS.)..................................... 165

Pincushion, ceramic, model of a dog, Japan, 1950s, 2" h....................................... 18

Pincushion, fabric, model of a female leg, American, 1880s... 85

Pincushion, pierced bone in flat bellows form, English, 1840s 225

Pincushion, Scottish Mauchline ware, flat heart-shape w/seaweed decoration, 1860s... 195

Pincushion, Scottish Tartanware, cylindrical, 1860s.. 150

Woman's Alligator Slipper Pincushion

Pincushion, slipper, spelter w/silver finish, in the form of a woman's alligator shoe, cushion is inset in the shoe, 5 1/2" l., damage to heel (ILLUS.) 85

Pincushion, Tunbridgeware, model of a teapot, English, 1850s 195

Pincushion, velvet, model of a carrot, American, 1940s.. 65

Pincushion clamp, steel w/netting hook, English, 1860s 175

Pinholder, flat rectangular form, showing Victorian children playing, 1870s.................... 35

Scissors, silver plate, figural blade in form of the Salem Witch, Germany, early 20th c., rare 395

Scissors, silver plate, figural stork-form, Germany, early 20th c. 49

Scissors, steel, buttonhole-type, American, 1880s, extra large.. 55

Scissors, sterling silver, scroll-decorated handles, American, late 19th c., 5" l. 95

Scissors, white metal, figural stork-form, American, 1920s... 25

Scissors sheath, woven sweet grass, American, early 20th c.. 35

Sewing bird, brass, patent-dated 1853 on wings, w/two pincushions, American, late 19th c.. 325

Sewing set: ivory box w/a pencil, stiletto, bodkin, thimble, scissors & needle case; French, 1860s, the set.................................. 725

Sewing set: red leather case w/gold thimble, stiletto, scissors, bodkin & needlecase; Europe, 1840-50, the set...................... 675

Silk winder, carved bone, snowflake-form, English, 1860s 65

Silk winder, mother-of-pearl, pillow-form, English, 1850s 85

Silk winder, Tartanware, English, 1850s........... 155

Stiletto, metal blade w/carved mother-of-pearl handle, English, 1920s 75

Stiletto, metal blade w/sterling silver handle w/floral design, w/guide, 1880s..................... 85

Stiletto, metal blade w/sterling silver handle w/simple line decoration, no guide, ca. 1910.. 65

Tape measure, brass & copper, model of a coffee grinder, Germany, 1890s 245

Tape measure, brass, model of an alarm clock, Germany, 1890s.................................. 195

Tape measure, carved vegetable ivory, urnform w/wood turner, English, 1850s 145

Tape measure, celluloid, model of a cottage, English, 1920s 145

Tape measure, ceramic, figural clown 60

Tape measure, model of a black cat on short pedestal, Germany, 1920s.................... 295

Tape measure, model of a pansy, Germany, 1920s... 155

Tape measure, plastic, model of a fish, Japan, 1930s.. 145

Tape measure, plastic, model of an apple, American, 1950s... 45

Rare Turtle Tape Measure

Tape measure, plated brass, model of a turtle, embossed shell design on the back w/wording "Pull my head but not my leg," pull head to reveal tape, 1 3/8 x 2 1/8" (ILLUS.)... 295

Tape measure, silver plate, model of a pig, tail winds up tape, American, late 19th c. 255

Tape measure, souvenir-type, spring-wound, from Niagara Falls, American, 1930s.. 40

Tape measure, Tunbridgeware, silk tape, English, 1840s... 235

Tape measure, wood, model of a barrel w/bone turner, English, 1850s........................ 145

Tatting shuttle, bone incised w/flowers, English, 1870s... 85

Tatting shuttle, bone, no design, American, 1850s.. 38

Tatting shuttle, horn inlaid w/mother-of-pearl flowers, English, 1860s...................... 195

Tatting shuttle, sterling silver, Greek key design, American, 1920s.............................. 145

Tatting shuttle, whale baleen, undecorated, American, 1850s................................... 30

Thimble, 14k gold, plain band, marked, American, 1920s.. 175

Thimble, gold-plated, three incised lines around band, American, 1910s.................. 95

Thimble, silver w/coral cabochons set around border, Europe, 1870s..................... 185

Thimble, sterling silver, eight-panel band w/alternating design of flowers & Xs, American, 1880s.. 48

Thimble, sterling silver, incised florals around band, American, 1920s.................... 45

Thimble, sterling silver w/enameled band of flowers, Europe, 1910s.............................. 135

Thimble, sterling w/steel, Dorcas by Charles Horner, plain, English, late 19th c. 85

SHEET MUSIC
Location

In the category of sheet music there are many different smaller groupings from which a collector can choose. In fact, the subject is almost too broad to not specialize. Sheet music with a location in the title is only one of many ways to go. One might try to find an example from all the fifty states of the Union, while another might amass songs that feature his or her hometown or state. It's a fun, rather plentiful way to gather the music of old. (Listed at the end of each item will be special categories and cover artists that effect value.)

"A Latin from Manhattan," 1932, by Al Dubin & Harry Warren, from the movie "The Jolson Story," Al Jolson $6

"A Little Rendezvous in Honolulu," 1936, by Edgar Leslie & Joe Burke 4

"A-M-E-R-I-C-A," 1917, by Mae Greene & Billy Lang, Patriotic & WWI 15

"Ain't You Coming Back to Old New Hampshire Molly," 1906, by Robert Roden & J. Fred Helf.. 10

"Alabama Jubilee," 1915, by Jack Yellen & Geo. L. Cobb, photo of Elizabeth Murray (Dixie) 10

"All I Owe Iowa," 1945, by Richard Rodgers & Oscar Hammerstein II, from the movie "State Fair" 5

"Along the Road to Singapore," 1915, by Richard W. Pascoe, Hans Von Holstein & Alma M. Sanders.. 5

"Along the Santa Fe Trail," 1940, by Dubin, Coolidge & Grosz, from the movie of the same name... 5

"Alpine Valley by Engelmann & Brehm," 1909, cover artist: Pfeiffer................................ 15

"Alsacian Railroad Gallops by Guignard," 1845, pre-1900 & Transportation......... 60

"America Forever!," 1917, by E.T. Paull, cover artist E.T. Paull, lithograph: S. Hoen & March 35

"An Old Fashioned Garden in Virginia," 1915, by Marion Sunshine & Henry I. Marshall, cover artist: Starmer 10

"Annapolis," The Midshipman's March, 1933, by W.J. Francis Jr., Zoe Elliot & Maurice La Farge, March & Patriotic............... 15

"April in Paris," 1932, by E.Y. Harburg & Vernon Duke 2

"April in Portugal," 1953, by Jimmy Kennedy & Paul Ferras 1

"Are You From Dixie?"

"Are You From Dixie?," 1915, by Jack Yellen & George L. Cobb, cover artist: Starmer & Dixie (ILLUS.).................................. 25

"Arizona March," by Smith & E.T. Paull, cover artist: E.T. Paull & March 35

"Arkansas Traveler," 1941, by Newt Martin, photo of Patsy Montana 4

"Atlanta, Ga.," 1945, by Sunny Skylar & Arte Sheftel... 5

"Back to the Caroline You Love," 1914, by Grant Clark & Jean Schwartz........................ 5

"Ballad of Savannah"

"Ballad of Savannah," 1969, by Roy Blackburn (ILLUS.) 3
"Barcelona Tango," 1914, by Jones, cover artist: Pfeiffer 10
"Basin Street Blues," 1933, by Spencer Williams, photo of Phil Harris (Blues) 5
"Be Good to California, Mr. Wilson, California Was Good to You," 1916, by Andrew B. Sterling & Robert A. Keiser, photo President Woodrow Wilson, cover artist: Starmer & Presidents 35
"Beale St. Blues," 1916, by W.C. Handy, Blues 10
"Beautiful Ohio," 1917, by Ballard MacDonald & Mary Earl, cover artist: Barbelle 8
"Belle of Idaho," 1910, by Rosenberg, cover artist: Pfeiffer 12
"Bethlehem," 1889, by C. Whitney Coombs, pre-1900 15
"Blue Ridge Mountain Cottage," 1929, by Al Sherman & Al Lewis 4
"By The Shawnee River," 1915, by H.W. Mayddleton 500
"California, Here I Come," 1924, by Al Jolson, B.G. DeSylva & Joseph Meyer, from the movie "The Al Jolson Story" 700

"Capitol City March"

"Capitol City March," 1911, by Harry J. Lincoln, Capitol Building on cover, Patriotic & March (ILLUS.) 12
"Carolina Mammy," 1923, by Billy James, photo Aunt Jemima, cover artist: JVR & Black, Black Face 30
"Carry Me Back to Old Virginny," 1906, by James Bland, Black, Black Face & Dixie 25
"Chattanooga Choo Choo," 1941, by Mack Gordon & Harry Warren, from the movie "Sun Valley Serenade," photo Sonja Henie 15
"Cincinnati," 1916, by Matthew Ott, cover artist: E.S. Fisher 8
"Cross the Great Divide I'll Wait For You," 1913, by Lewis & Meyer, cover artist: Pfeiffer (ILLUS.) 10
"Cuban Moon," 1920, by McKiernan & Spencer 3
"Dallas Blues," 1912, by Wand, Blues 7
"Dear Old Portland Town," 1916, by Henry L. Stone 5
"Did Your Mother Come From Ireland," 1936, by Jimmy Kennedy & Michael Carr, photo: Kate Smith on cover, cover artist: Immy & Irish 15
"Dixie, I Wish I Was in Dixie's Land," 1860, by Dan Emmett, pre-1900 & Dixie 20
"Down Georgia Way," 1913, by Geo. B. Norton & J.F. Barrie, cover artist: Starmer & Dixie 10
"Down in Borneo Isle," 1917, by Henry Creamer & Turner Layton 2
"Dreamy Hawaii," 1921, by Ray Sherwood & F.W. Vandersloot 5
"Egypt," 1903, by Clare Kummer 3
"El Paso," 1921, by Eugene West & Clarence Senna 5
"Everything is Peaches Down in Georgia," 1918, by Grant Clark, Milton Ager & Geo. W. Meyer, small war edition 10
"Fifth Ave.," 1936, Joseph M. Daly 3

"Florida"

"Florida," 1925, by Abel Green & Jesse Greer (ILLUS.) 5
"Forty Five Minutes From Broadway," 1933, by George M. Cohan, from the movie "Yankee Doodle Dandy," George M. Cohan 10
"From Galilee A Mother Came," 1929, by J. Sheldon Tyler & Geoffrey O'Hara 5
"Galveston," 1968, by Webb, photo of Glen Campbell 3
"Georgia on My Mind," 1941, by Stuart Correll & Hoagy Carmichael 4
"Glory of Jamestown," 1907, by James W. Casey, March & Indian 25

"Goodbye France"

"Goodbye France," 1918, by Irving Berlin, cover artist: Barbelle, WWI & Irving Berlin (ILLUS.) 15
"Greenwich Village Sue," 1920, by A. Swanstorm & Carey Morgan 5

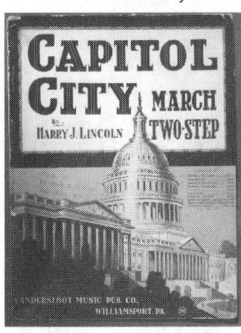

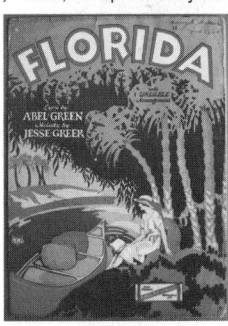

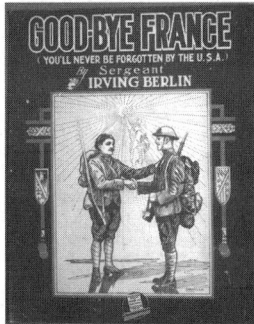

"Home in Pasadena"

"Ireland, My Ireland"

"Kentucky Lullaby"

"Memphis, Tennessee"

"Mississippi Moon"

"Old Virginia Moon"

"San Fernando Valley"

"She's the Sunshine ..."

"Sidewalks of New York"

"Ten Little Fingers & Ten Little Toes ..."

"The Madagascar Mangle"

"The Yellow Rose of Texas"

"There's a Cradle in Caroline!"

"Walkin' to Missouri"

"When It's Springtime in the Rockies"

"When That Midnight Choo-Choo ..."

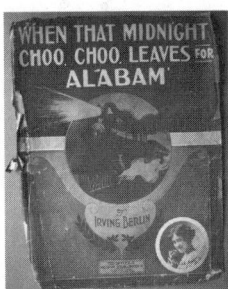

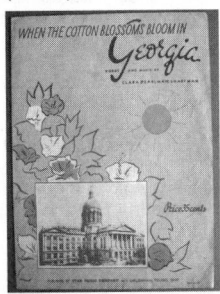

"When That Midnight Choo-Choo Leaves for Alabam'," 1912, by Irving Berlin, cover artist: Pfeiffer, Irving Berlin & Transportation (ILLUS.) 6

"When the Cotton Blossoms Bloom ..."

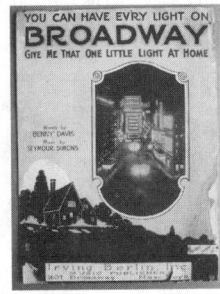

"When the Cotton Blossoms Bloom in Georgia," 1948, by Clara Sharfman, cover shows Capitol Building in Atlanta (ILLUS.) 6

"When the Sun Goes Down in Jersey (Life Begins on Old Broadway)," 1915, by W.L. Beardsley & Ben Deely, cover artist: Dunk 10

"When You Dream of Old New Hampshire, I Dream of Tennessee," 1916, Jack Murphy & George Cobb 5

"Where Rolls the Oregon," 1916, by MacBoyle & Costa, cover artist: Barbelle 7

"Why Do They All Take the Night Boat to Albany?," 1918, by Al Jolson (Al Jolson) 9

"Wyoming," 1920, by Gene Williams, cover artist: Starmer 4

"You Brought Ireland Right Over to Me," 1917, by Brennan & Ball, Irish 10

"You Can Have Ev'ry Light ..."

"You Can Have Ev'ry Light on Broadway Give Me That One Little Light at Home," 1922, by Benny Davis & Seymour Simons, cover artist: R.S. (ILLUS.) 8

SIGNS & SIGNBOARDS

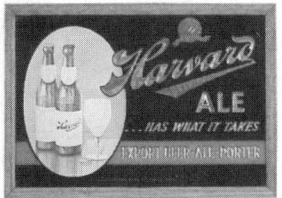

Harvard Ale Sign

Ale, "Harvard Ale," rectangular, reverse-painting on glass w/cardboard backing, easel-back, cardboard images of bottles & glass on left, right side w/"Harvard Ale ... Has What it Takes" below logo, red band at bottom reads "Export Beer - Ale - Porter," cardboard images appear faded, 13 x 19" (ILLUS.) **$88**

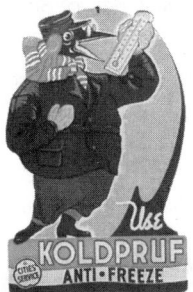

Cities Service Anti-Freeze Sign

Anti-freeze, "Cities Service," double-sided, die-cut cardboard, comical image of penguin dressed in winter clothing holding thermometer, marked at bottom "Use Cities Service Koldpruf Anti-Freeze," tiny nicks & flecks, 11 1/2 x 18" (ILLUS.) **231**

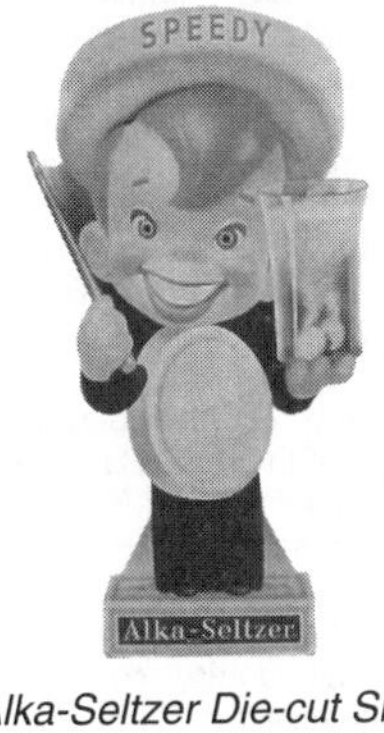

Alka-Seltzer Die-cut Sign

Antacid, "Alka-Seltzer," die-cut cardboard, easel-back, features "Speedy" holding glass & stick, minor soiling & overall wear, area behind stick reinforced, light creases at top areas, edge wear, 21 3/4 x 39 3/4" (ILLUS.) **132**

Auto service, "Ford," rectangular tin, thick tacker-style, blue top w/white letters reading "Service Station - Ford - Sales Agency," white arrow at bottom w/blue letters reading "Schenck Manufacturing & Supply Co. - Parkers Landing, PA.," minor bends at some corners, scratches, 11 5/8 x 35 1/2" **798**

Nash Service Sign

Auto service, "Nash," shield-shaped porcelain, double-sided, shades of blue & white, marked "Authorized - Nash - Service," chips at mounting hole, edge & field, 22 x 36" (ILLUS.).................... **2,640**

Auto service, "Pontiac," rectangular porcelain, black & white, reads "Oakland - Sales - Service - Pontiac," 23 3/4 x 35 1/2" (minor edge wear, scratches & small chips)................................ **633**

Willys-Overland Whippet Sign

Automobile, "Whippet Automobile," tin, red w/embossed gold letters reading "Dollar for Dollar Value - Whippet - Product of - Willys-Overland Company," by M.C.A. Sign Company, Massillon, Ohio, wood frame, ca. 1920s, 15 x 25" (ILLUS.) **125-150**

Automobile club, "National Automobile Club," double-sided porcelain, white w/shield form, eagle on globe w/image of United States, stars & stripes w/"National Automobile Club" at top below black letters reading "OFFICIAL," Balto Enamel Mfg. information on lower right corner, 18 x 21" (minor edge & mount hole chips & wear) **292**

Automotive, "National Refining Co.," two-sided lithographed tin, curb-type on signed iron base, figure of boy wearing black & white checked knee pants & red stockings holding rectangular black sign

National Refining Company Sign

w/red border & yellow border w/black letters reading "En-Ar-Co Motor Oil - En-Ar-Co Gear Compound - White Rose Gasoline - National Light Kerosene," litho by Mathews Ind. Inc., Detroit, Michigan, ca. 1917, 27 3/4 x 45" (ILLUS.) **2,500-3,500**

Automotive products, "Bowes Seal Fast Auto Products," rectangular porcelain, flange-type, white w/black & white lettering, reading "For Smoother Motoring - Bowes Seal Fast - Auto Products," large red seal at bottom, 14 x 19 1/2" (couple small edge & flange chips).............................. **275**

Mica Axle Grease Sign

Axle grease, "Mica Axle Grease," (Standard Oil), cardboard, rectangular, blue, yellow & green, image of hand holding magnifying glass over grease gun, can at bottom pops back to allow the display of a one pound can, marked "Mica Axle Grease - The Mica Fills the Pores - Wheels Turn Easier," some warping, minor edge wear, missing top right corner, 14 x 17" (ILLUS.)... **171**

Anheuser-Busch Malt Nutrine Sign

Baby formula, "Malt Nutrine," rectangular, self-framed tin w/cardboard back, depicts a stork carrying in its beak two bottles tied together & flying over a man w/a raised whip in a carriage pulled by a racing white horse, titled "A Hurry Call," frame marked "Malt Nutrine," Anheuser-Busch Brewing Company, St. Louis, Missouri, ca. 1915, 7 1/2 x 12 1/2" (ILLUS.).. **250-350**

Malt Nutrine Sign "Coming Events... "

Baby formula, "Malt Nutrine," rectangular, self-framed tin w/cardboard back, scene of a doctor dressed in black, carrying his bag & an umbrella up the lane towards a house in the distance, his shadow cast in the form of a stork, titled "Coming Events....," Anheuser-Busch Brewing Company, St. Louis, Missouri, ca. 1915, 7 1/2 x 12 1/2" (ILLUS.) **250-350**

Exide Battery Sign

Battery, "Exide Batteries," flange-type tin, die-cut battery-form, black & red, marked "Exide" on front & side, date coded 5-53, rust, wear & paint flakes on outer edge, bend w/paint flake on upper terminal, 19 1/2 x 26" (ILLUS.)..................................... **358**

Majestic Batteries Sign

Battery, "Majestic Batteries," rectangular tin, embossed, dark blue w/logo at center in yellow & red w/"Majestic" in white, "Sales and Service" above & "Batteries" below, minor surface scratches & edge wear, 19 1/2 x 26" (ILLUS.)............................ **440**

Red Seal Dry Battery Sign

Battery, "Red Seal Dry Battery," curved die-cut porcelain, red, white & blue battery-form reading "Guaranteed for all Open Circuit Work - Red Seal Dry Battery - A Battery Suitable For Every Use," chips, scratches & wear, 14 1/2 x 34 1/4" (ILLUS.).. **798**

Berghoff Beer Sign

Beer, "Berghoff Beer," rectangular tin, cardboard backing, string-hung, snowy scene w/two hunting dogs, one brown & white, the other black & white, soiling & wear, minor subtle bends, 13 x 21" (ILLUS.) **72**

Pabst Blue Ribbon Beer Sign, Ca. 1938

Beer, "Pabst Blue Ribbon Beer," rectangular cardboard, scene of African-American in waiter's uniform, one hand holding a tray of bottles & glasses, reads "Quality - Yes - Suh-h," ca. 1938, Pabst Brewing Company, Milwaukee, Wisconsin, 24 x 34" (ILLUS.)..................................... **300-375**

Pabst Blue Ribbon Beer Sign, Ca. 1933

Beer, "Pabst Blue Ribbon Beer," rectangular cardboard, smiling elderly gentleman pouring beer from a bottle into a glass, reads "Pabst Blue Ribbon - The Beer of Quality," ca. 1933, Pabst Brewing Company, Milwaukee, Wisconsin, 20 x 25 1/2" (ILLUS.).............................. **300-375**

Feigenspan Quality Brews Sign

Brewery, "Feigenspan Quality Brews," reverse-painting on glass, "P.O.N." (Pride of Newark), in large gold letters, framed, minor wear to reverse detail, some flaking, 13 x 16" (ILLUS.) **88**

Brewing, "Bartholomay Brew. Co., Rochester, N.Y.," chromolithograph shows girl in thin white dress w/pink sash riding a wheel w/wings, silver w/gesso flowers period frame, ca. 1890, 35 x 45 1/2" (scrapes, stains, chip at top, minor chips to frame).. **330**

Trailways Bus Depot Sign

Bus depot, "Trailways," rectangular, double-sided porcelain, white w/red letters at top reading "Bus Depot," above black image of map of the United States w/yellow banner w/red letters reading "Trailways"

& "National - System" in yellow letters, small chips overall, 18 1/4 x 22" (ILLUS.)...... **688**

Packard Cable Sign

Cable, "Packard Cable," rectangular paper, lake scene of young girl dressed in red sitting on post w/attached cable marked "Tie To Packard Cable," wood frame, ca. 1900, 18 1/2 x 25 1/2" (ILLUS.).............. **350-425**

Kodak Film Sign

Camera film, "Kodak Film," rectangular porcelain, double-sided, both sides w/Art Deco style image of film roll & product box in yellow w/red letters, dark blue background bordered by a wide black & two narrow yellow bands, white lettering at top reading "Developing & Printing," minor to moderate surface wear & scratches, edge wear & chips, reverse w/lower field chips, 14 x 20" (ILLUS.) **660**

Wrigley's Gum Sign

Chewing gum, "Wrigley's Gum," rectangular tin w/cardboard easel-back, colorful lithograph by American Can Company shows packages of four different gum flavors on black background, marked "Wrigley's" in red letters & "Delicious Lasting Flavors" in white letters, ca. 1920s, 6 7/8 x 11" (ILLUS.)................................. **325-400**

Wrigley's P.K. Gum Trolley Sign

Chewing gum, "Wrigley's P.K. Gum," rectangular cardboard, trolley-type, black background w/hand open & holding three packages of gum, yellow, white & black lettering reading "Wrigley's P.K. New Handy Pack - 3 Packs 5¢ - Sugar Coated Chewing Sweet Peppermint Flavor," wood frame, ca. 1928, 11 3/4 x 22" (ILLUS.) **650-750**

Devlish Good Cigar Sign

Cigars, "Devlish Good Cigars," rectangular tin, chain-hung embossed display, blue w/center image of box of cigars, lid depicts three babies smoking cigars, reading "The Devlish Good - Cigar - None Better - 5 Cents," red flames above large black letters, wear, flecks & soiling, light bend at top center, 10 x 13 3/4" (ILLUS.) **171**

Hoffmanettes Cigars Sign

Cigars, "Hoffmanettes Cigars," rectangular cardboard, scene of two men leaning out of a window to see a man standing below & smoking a cigarette, reads "'It's up to you' - Smoke - Hoffmanettes 5¢ Cigar - The Hilson Co. Makers - New York," wood frame, ca. 1900, 15 1/2 x 21 1/2" (ILLUS.) **350-425**

Cocoa, "Van Houten's Cocoa," chromolithograph on cardboard shows young peasant girl w/basket, in original gilt frame w/label, 31 x 45 1/2" (margin tears, small hole, areas of flaking) **660**

Coffee, "Chase & Sanborn Coffee," rectangular paper, scene of four older men sitting around an old round heating stove, dog lying nearby, the shopkeeper in the background, titled "An Old Fashioned New England Grocery" & "Compliments of Chase & Sanborn," signed mat & wood frame, Chase & Sanborn, Boston, Massachusetts, ca. 1897, 22 1/2 x 24 1/2" **550-700**

Dale Brothers Coffee Sign

Coffee, "Dale Brothers Coffee," rectangular porcelain, white w/red letters reading "Dale Bros. Coffee," image of friar holding coffee cup on left side, minor edge chips, corner bends, surface scratches & wear, 14 x 42" (ILLUS.) **358**

Ken-L-Ration Dog Food Sign

Dog food, "Ken-L-Ration Dog Food," rectangular tin, blue base w/white & yellow letters reading "Feed Your Dog the Best - Ken-L-Ration - Ken-L-Biskit - Ken-L-Meal," top w/die-cut dog head logo in yellow w/black nose & eyes, red tongue, minor scratches, 14 x 21" (ILLUS.) **330**

Broadies' Drug Store Sign

Drugstore, "Broadies' Drug Store," rectangular, reverse-painting on glass, gold leaf on glue chip glass, scroll decoration, copper frame, ca. 1890, 17 1/2 x 25 1/2" (ILLUS.) **900-1,300**

Rose Exterminator Co. Die-cut Sign

Exterminator, "Rose Exterminator Co.," die-cut porcelain, black, white & flesh-tone figural "spraying man," minor edge chips, 10 3/4" h. (ILLUS.) **358**

Clear Quill Flour Sign

Flour, "Clear Quill Flour," self-framed tin, w/cardboard back, blue w/image of white quill pen over table holding loaf of bread & slices on plate w/white flour sack at left marked w/red letters "Union Mill Company - Clear Quill - Fancy Patent - Warranted Waterloo, Iowa - 49 lbs.," red & white letters read "Clear Quill Fancy Patent Flour - Often Buttered - Never Bettered," ca. 1890, 14 1/2 x 20 1/2" (ILLUS.) **700-900**

Stanley Garage Door Holders Sign

Garage door holders, "Stanley Garage Door Holders," rectangular tin, lithographed image of garage w/double doors open, right side w/blue letters on yellow background reading "Stanley Garage Door Holders" w/red letters near bottom reading "Hold Your Garage Doors Open!," by H.D. Beach, ca. late 1900-1920s, slots at bottom held brackets that displayed the product, minor bends, wrinkles, dings, dents & scratches, 26 1/4 x 34" (ILLUS.)...................................... **853**

Conoco Gasoline Sign

Gasoline, "Conoco Gasoline," round, double-sided porcelain, yellow w/"Minute Man" in center, top marked "Conoco" in black letters, "Gasoline" in red letters at bottom, crazing, chips, wear & overall scratches, 25 1/4" d. (ILLUS.) **880**

Gasoline, "Pure Oil Company," flange-type tin, one-sided, round, blue w/white letters reading "Energee - True Gasoline - The Pure Oil Co." 17 1/2 x 20" **330**

Dead Shot Gunpowder Sign

Gunpowder, "Dead Shot Gunpowder," rectangular paper, bird falling to the ground w/"Dead Shot" above & "American Powder Mills - Boston - Chicago - St. Louis" below, wood frame marked "Gunpowder," ca. 1910, 25 x 31" (ILLUS.).. **1,200-1,800**

Wildroot Hair Cream-Oil Sign

Hair cream-oil, "Wildroot Hair Cream-Oil," die-cut cardboard, easel-back display shows illustration of Al Capp Dick Tracy-like character Fearless Fosdick w/smoking gun & removing his hat, saying "Fearless Fosdick Says - Get Wildroot Cream-Oil Charlie!," letters above gun read

"Grooms the Hair - Relieves Dryness - Removes Loose Dandruff," center of sign flanked by die-cut red, white & blue striped barber poles, letters on globes reading "Time For A Haircut" & "Best Haircut in Town" & dated "1954" at bottom left, minor edge & surface wear, 30 x 30 1/4" (ILLUS.)...................................... **248**

E.D. Pinaud's Hair Dressing Sign

Hair dressing, "E.D. Pinaud's Eau de Quinine," rectangular tin, bottle in center flanked by embossed florals, w/"Use Only The Genuine - E.D. Pinaud's" above & "Eau de Quinine - An Ideal Hairdressing" below, wood frame, ca. 1900, 17 1/2 x 23" (ILLUS.)............................... **225-275**

Lucky Tiger Hair Oil Sign

Hair oil, "Lucky Tiger," rectangular cardboard, easel-back, center w/image of blonde woman & head of tiger & bottle containing green liquid in lower right corner, top reading "Lucky Tiger - For Hair and Scalp - With Oil or Without," minor wear, 22 x 33 1/2" (ILLUS.)............................ **550**

Arden Ice Cream Sign

Ice cream, "Arden Ice Cream," bevel-edged Masonite w/original yellowed surface varnish, center oval w/milkman logo at top w/banner reading "We Serve Delicious," red oval center w/"Arden - Fine - Ice Cream - for Vital Energy" & banner at bottom marked "A Nutritional Vital Energy Food," minor edge & surface wear, 7 1/4 x 12" (ILLUS.)....................................... **176**

Ice cream, "Eskimo Pie," rectangular porcelain, white w/blue letters, 6 1/2 x 36" (minor edge chips, soiling & wear)..................... **215**

City of New York Insurance Co. Sign

Insurance, "City of New York Insurance Company," rectangular, reverse-painted glass w/"City of New York - Insurance Company - Fire" above & below oval sepia scene of New York City flanked by embossed brass scrolls, wood frame, ca. 1920s, 21 1/2 x 30" (ILLUS.).................. **425-500**

Cetacolor Sign

Laundry product, "Cetacolor," rectangular, lithographed fabric in wood frame, oval on left side depicts a woman wearing a red & white striped blouse, one side faded flanked by black letters reading "Result Without Using Cetacolor," the other side bright w/"Result With Using Cetacolor," white & green lettering on right side reading "Not a Soap - Cetacolor - Prevents Wash Goods from Fading. - 10¢ Package.," by Acme Sign Printing Co., Dayton, Ohio, ca. 1890, 25 x 37" (ILLUS.).. **375-450**

Quaker Maid Milk Sign

Milk, "Quaker Maid Milk," die-cut porcelain, red w/pretty milkmaid & blue banner reading "First in Quality" in center, wear, edge & mount hole chips, 24 x 41" (ILLUS.) **633**

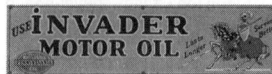

Invader Motor Oil Sign

Motor oil, "Invader Motor Oil," rectangular tin, yellow w/black, white & red image of knight on horseback on the right flanked by black letters reading "Lasts Longer - Serves Better," large black letters on left read "Use Invader Motor Oil" above red seal marked "100% Pure Pennsylvania Oil," touch-up repair lower left corner, wear, light bends, 9 x 26" (ILLUS.)............... **440**

Ring-Free Motor Oil Sign

Motor Oil, "Macmillan Ring-Free Motor Oil," die-cut embossed tin, the rectangular blue base w/image of a hand holding the die-cut can in red, white & blue, marked "Ring-Free - Motor Oil," white letters on bottom of sign reading "Raise Your Car's Standard of Living," minor edge & surface wear, 27 1/4 x 34" (ILLUS.)................... **281**

Goodyear Motorcycle Tires Sign

Motorcycle tires, "Good Year," porcelain, flange-type, rectangular base in blue & red w/"Good [logo] Year" in yellow, "Made in USA" at base of flange, black & white die-cut image of rider on motorcycle at top, same image on both sides, minor field, edge & flange chips & wear, 19 x 24" (ILLUS.) **8,250**

Coles Nerve Tonic Sign

Nerve/blood tonic, "Coles Peruvian Bark and Wild Cherry Bitters," porcelain on metal, blue w/white letters reading "No

More Malaria - Coles Peruvian Bark and Wild Cherry Bitters Will Cure You - The Best Nerve and Blood Tonic" & in upper left corner "Cure Debility " & lower right corner "Cure Dyspepsia," framed, ca. 1880, 7 1/2 x 17 1/2" (ILLUS.)............... **700-900**

Nesbitt's Orange Drink Sign

Orange drink, "Nesbitt's Orange Drink," rectangular cardboard, colorful scene of girl in white bathing suit relaxing near swimming pool, orange trees in background, a table nearby w/bowl of oranges & bottle, the chair's blue tented cover marked in white & orange letters reading "Drink Nesbitt's California Orange," original Nesbitt frame, ca. 1955, 28 1/2 x 39" (ILLUS.).. **350-450**

OshKosh Overalls Sign

Overalls, "OshKosh Overalls," rectangular cardboard, top w/wide red band marked in white & yellow "OshKosh B'gosh - Union Made - The World's Best Overall," center section light background w/four men of different sizes pictured wearing overalls indicated for "Fat - or Thin - Short - or Tall," the men in middle holding yellow sign marked "OshKosh B'Gosh Fits 'Em All," bottom marked "Always Buy Your Correct Size," ca. 1930, 13 1/2 x 14 1/2" (ILLUS.)....................... **175-250**

Houbigant Perfume Sign

Perfume, "Houbigant Parfums," rectangular, paper on cardboard, scene of young woman standing at an open window & holding & smelling blossoms on vine beside the window shutter, mat marked "Parfums Houbigant - Paris," ornate frame, ca. 1920s, 16 1/2 x 20 1/2" (ILLUS.) **250-325**

Sunray D-X Petroleum Products Sign

Petroleum products, "Sunray D-X Petroleum Products," octagonal porcelain, yellow sunrays on orange w/D-X logo near bottom, white letters on black at bottom reading "Petroleum Products," missing top grommet, 9 x 9" (ILLUS.) **1,320**

Raytheon Radio Tubes Sign

Radio tubes, "Raytheon Radio Tubes," flange-type tin, rectangular, red, white & blue lettering reading "Radio Service - We use and recommend Raytheon Radio Tubes - For Better Reception," tube & box pictured on left, 1934 date on tube box, background yellow/tan from paper staining, some paper marks visible, nicks & scratches, paint loss at flange edge area, 14 x 18" (ILLUS.) **270**

Chicago & Alton Railroad Sign

Railroad, "Chicago & Alton Railroad," rectangular, paper & cardboard w/hand-colored photographs, the center shows an engine & freight car w/"Chicago & Alton R.R. - 'The Only Way,'" in white letters below & w/a photograph on the left of a passenger car interior & on the right an interior photograph of the dining car, wood frame, ca. 1910, 15 x 39" (ILLUS.) **635-775**

Grand Trunk Pacific Railway Photo

Railroad, "Grand Trunk Pacific Railway," duo-tone photograph titled "Moose Lake British Columbia," signed mat & frame, ca. 1900, 28 1/2 x 35" (ILLUS.) .. **650-750**

Refrigerator, "Dry-Kold Refrigerator Company," rectangular porcelain, white w/black oval in center bordered by icicles & w/white lettering w/icicle decoration reading "The 'Dry-Kold' - Refrigerator Company - Niles - Michigan," 11 3/4 x 22" (minor scratches, bottom edge cut down from larger unknown size)...... **138**

Rye, chromolithograph for "Brookfield Rye," w/scene of girl holding a bottle, bright colors & fine detail, made by Meek Co., Coshocton, Ohio, 23 x 33" **2,750**

Rye, chromolithograph on canvas advertising "Old Overholt Rye," scene of fly fisherman in a stream, copyright by the company in 1913, signed in the plate by "R. Bohune," original frame, 20 1/2 x 33" **495**

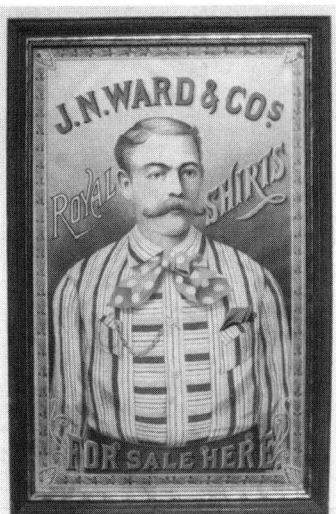

J.N. Ward & Co. Shirt Sign

Shirts, "J.N. Ward & Co. Shirts," rectangular, lithographed paper on cardboard, depicts man wearing blue & white striped shirt, blue & white polka dot tie, red & white letters read "J.N. Ward & Cos. Royal Shirts - For Sale Here," wood frame, litho by J.W. Frank & Sons, Peoria, Illinois, ca. 1880, 14 x 21" (ILLUS.) **475-650**

Red Goose Embossed Celluloid Sign

Shoes, "Red Goose Shoes," embossed die-cut w/molded celluloid goose body, easel-back, marked "Red Goose Shoes," flanked by running schoolgirl & schoolboy w/books, marked at the bottom "They're Half the Fun of Having Feet," ca. 1910, Friedman-Shelby Shoes, 11 x 13 1/2" (ILLUS.)............................ **900-1,300**

Wolverine Soap Chips Sign

Soap, "Wolverine Soap Chips," rectangular, colorful lithographed display of various products surrounding red center marked "Not Kept in Stores - But Sold - Direct to Consumers - By Our Own Canvassing Agents" & marked at bottom "Agents - Wanted," Terriff & Co., Portland, Michigan, litho by Calvert Litho Company, Detroit, Michigan, wood frame, ca. 1900, 28 1/2 x 34" (ILLUS.) **750-1,100**

7Up Bottle Sign

Soft drink, "7Up," embossed tin bottle-form, dated "7-62" at bottom, minor edge wear, 13 x 44 1/2" (ILLUS.)...................................... **413**

Cherry Blush Sign

Soft drink, "Cherry Blush," rectangular tin w/cardboard back, black w/bunch of cherries & leaves & "Cherry Blush" in white outlined in red in center, red lettering above w/"Drink" & green lettering at bottom reading "Cherries Only Rival," ca. 1900, 6 1/4 x 9" (ILLUS.) **650-800**

Cleo Cola Sign

Soft drink, "Cleo Cola," embossed rectangular tin, green & black w/tiled effect border, image of Cleopatra on right & reading "Genuine Cleo Cola - 12 ounces for 5 cents," soiling, nicks & scratches, 12 1/2 x 27 3/8" (ILLUS.)................................. **358**

Dad's Root Beer Sign

Soft drink, "Dad's Root Beer," rectangular tin, black & yellow w/embossed lettering in black outlined in red, "Have A Dad's Old Fashioned Root Beer ....It's Delicious," ca. 1950s, 19 x 27" (ILLUS.)... **225-300**

Pepsi-Cola Sign

Soft drink, "Pepsi-Cola," die-cut tin bottle cap-shaped sign w/red, white & blue double dot logo, minor surface scratches, 13 1/4 x 13 7/8" (ILLUS.)................................. **385**

Squirt Sign

Soft drink, "Squirt," rectangular tin, flange-type, double-sided, both sides yellow & display waving blue flag reading "Drink Squirt - It's Tart-Sweet," dated 1941 at bottom, minor wear & scratches (ILLUS.)..... **385**

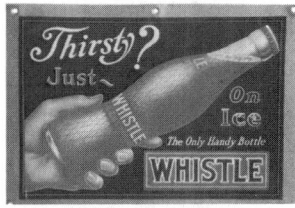

Whistle Soda Sign

Soft drink, "Whistle," rectangular embossed tin lithograph by American Art Works, black ground w/gold-colored border, w/"Thirsty? Just ~ [above image of hand holding orange bottle marked "Whistle"] On Ice - The Only Handy Bottle," w/"Whistle" again in orange box in lower right corner, 6 3/4 x 9 3/4" (ILLUS.)..... **715**

Campbell's Soups Sign

Soup, "Campbell's Soups," rectangular tin, red top w/white & yellow letters reading "Campbell's Soups - M'm! M'm! Good!," white center w/various soups listed & image of Campbell Kid on left, yellow band at bottom w/red letters reading "Ready in a Jiffy," light wear, scratches & rubs, 11 1/2 x 17 1/2" (ILLUS.)................................. **165**

A.C. Spark Plugs Sign

Spark plugs, "A.C. Spark Plugs," embossed tin, self-framed rectangular, blue & yellow w/large red circle in center w/spark plug flanked by the letters "A - C," tan band at bottom w/black letters reading "Spark Plugs" & dated "11-41" at bottom left, nicks & scratches, factory flaw at right side top to bottom in blue to tan, 9 x 18" (ILLUS.) **275**

Spark plugs, "Champion Spark Plugs," rectangular tin, flange-type, black, red & white, white & black letters reading "Dependable - Champion - Spark Plug Service," ca. 1950-60s, 23 3/4 x 35 1/2" (light nicks & scratches) **149**

International Stock Food Co. Sign

Stock food, "International Stock Food Company," rectangular paper, scene of pacer horse "Dan Patch" & jockey, information on horse at lower left, marked at bottom "Dan Patch 1:55 - Owned by International Stock Food Co., Minneapolis, Minn.," wood frame, ca. 1910, 20 x 27 1/2" (ILLUS.)... **225-325**

Garland Stoves Sign

Stove, "Garland Stoves," square tin, curved corner-type, porcelain on tin, white w/black logo printed "Garland Stoves and Ranges" w/banner at bottom marked "'The World's Best,'" B.S. Co., State St., Chicago, Illinois, 24 x 24" (ILLUS.).. **1,300-1,750**

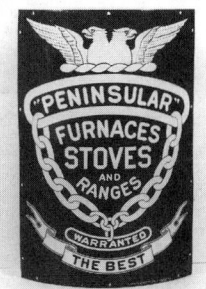

Peninsular Stoves Sign

Stove, "Peninsular," rectangular tin, curved corner-type, porcelain on tin, black w/white image of double eagle heads & wings over shield-shape formed w/bars & chain links reading "'Peninsular' - Furnaces - Stoves and Ranges" w/"Warranted - The Best" on banner at the bottom, made by B.S. Co., State St., Chicago, Illinois, ca. 1890, 18 x 24" (ILLUS.) **1,300-1,750**

Fisk Tires & Auto Supplies Sign

Tires, "Fisk Tires," flange-type porcelain, rectangular, red & black w/white letters reading "Gasoline - Fisk Tires - Auto Supplies," early Ingram-Richardson sign w/volcano-style mount holes, scattered edge chips & field scratches, 18 x 24 1/4" (ILLUS.) **1,018**

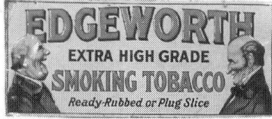

OK Tires Die-cut Sign

Tires, "OK Tires," die-cut Masonite, figural logo of boy saluting, chest marked "OK," red, white & black, minor wear, thin paint & soiling, 16 x 25 1/4" (ILLUS.) **121**

Edgeworth Smoking Tobacco Sign

Tobacco, "Edgeworth Smoking Tobacco," rectangular tin, yellow w/red & black letters reading "Edgeworth - Extra High Grade - Smoking tobacco - Ready-Rubbed or Plug Slice," the lower corners depicting a laughing balding man, overall light wear, scratches, rust pitting & flecks, two nail holes added at top, 11 1/4 x 27 1/4" (ILLUS.) **369**

Tobacco, "Hi-Plane Tobacco," embossed rectangular tin, green w/red & white vest pocket tin w/airplane on left & reading "Hi-Plane Tobacco - for Pipe and Cigarettes - 10¢" in black & white letters, 11 3/4 x 35 1/4" (minor high point wear & scratches) **215**

Mohawk Tool Works Sign

Tool works, "Mohawk Tool Works," cast brass w/raised detailed logo in center w/"Arrowsharp Axes & Knives - Est. 1893 - Troy, N.Y.," leather-look background, 10 x 16" (ILLUS.) **853**

Hickman-Ebbert Company Sign

Wagon, "Hickman-Ebbert Co.," rectangular tin, self-framed colorful lithographed scene depicting girl picking apples & a boy loading them onto a horse-drawn green wagon w/red wheels, titled "In The Shade Of The Old Apple Tree," upper left corner reads "Best at the Price - The Ebbert - Owensboro, KY - Always the Same," litho by Charles W. Shonk, frame marked "The Hickman-Ebbert Co. - Owensboro, Kentucky," ca. 1906, 25 1/2 x 37 1/2" (ILLUS.) **1,200-1,800**

Standard Distilling Company Sign

Whiskey, "Hanover Pure Rye," round, reverse-painted convex glass front w/ornate openwork gold metal frame, image of brown horse head in center flanked by grain wreath & encircled by dark blue border w/"Standard Distilling Co. - Cincinnati, Ohio" in gold letters, further encircled by wide white border w/gold leaf letters reading "Hanover - Pure Rye," ca. 1890, 24" d. (ILLUS.) **850-1,100**

Whiskey, "Lakeside Club Bouquet - Wm. Drueke Company, Grand Rapids, Mich.," milk glass panel on black wooden frame, 18 1/2 x 21 1/2".. **3,300**

Solona White Port Wine Sign

Wine, "Solona White Port Wine," rectangular paper, scene of woman in green dress w/her arm on the shoulder of a dark-haired man in dark suit, white shirt & bow tie, the couple seated at a table trimmed w/pink flowers, two glasses & wine bottle, wood frame, ca. 1900, 16 x 18" (ILLUS.) **175-225**

Wiper blades, "Trico Wiper Blades," circular, aluminum, flange-type, black & yellow w/white, black & yellow letters reading "Replace Your - Trico Wiper Blades - Once A Year," 18 x 19 3/4" (fading & wear)... **165**

Oshkosh Work Clothes Sign

Work clothing, "OshKosh Work Clothes," tin, red & yellow w/embossed white & yellow letters reading "OshKosh B'gosh - Union Made - Work Clothes," ca. 1930s, 9 1/4 x 13 1/2" (ILLUS.) **100-150**

SODA FOUNTAIN COLLECTIBLES

The neighborhood ice cream parlor and drugstore fountain are pretty much a thing of the past as fast-food chains have sprung up across the country. Memories of the slower-paced lifestyle represented by the rapidly disappearing local soda fountain have spurred the interest of many collectors today. Anything relating to the soda fountains of old and the delicious concoctions they dispensed are much sought-after.

Duffy's Pure Malted Milk Container

Counter container, "Duffy's Pure Malted Milk," enameled tin, cylindrical w/a tall tapering domed cover, creamy white ground w/blue wording on the front, some chips on cover, base & edges, some cracking of enameling, a few scuffs & soiling, 6" d., 10" h. (ILLUS.) **$138**

Pepsi-Cola Mechanical Display Unit

Counter display figure, "Pepsi-Cola," electric mechanical group in plastic & metal, a model of a monkey & a large Pepsi can spin in a circle when plugged in, on a cluster of purple & white flowers on the round platform base w/an oval Pepsi-Cola logo, some scratches, soiling, wear, 26" d., 37" h. (ILLUS.)................................. **1,210**

Pepsi Mechanical Display with a Seal

Counter display figure, "Pepsi-Cola," plastic & rubber composite, a white shaped plastic oblong platform base trimmed w/Pepsi-Cola logos supports a heavy rubber composite model of a black seal balancing a red, white & blue ball on its nose, seal moves back & forth when activated, two stress cracks in base, 37 x 40", 39" h. (ILLUS.).............................. **1,843**

Early Moxie Horsemobile Model

Countertop display, "Drink Moxie," molded chalkware model of an early Moxie Horsemobile w/advertising panels at each side, tiny flecks on fender tips, scattered wear on base, early 20th c., 4 x 8", 9 3/4" h. (ILLUS.) **1,540**

Carnation Malted Milk Dispenser

Dispenser, "Carnation Malted Milk," cylindrical porcelain body w/a domed & peaked aluminum lid, red & white background w/white & green wording above & below a cluster of large red, white & green carnations, small chips on reverse bottom, very minor edge chips hidden by lid, 8 1/2" h. (ILLUS.) **413**

Dispenser, "Thompson's Malted Milk," cylindrical body w/a white ground & red, blue & grey wording on one side, a coat-of-arms style logo on the other side, aluminum peaked lid, 5 5/8" d., 9 1/2" h. (minor surface wear, scattered rim chips, two small base chips)..................................... **231**

Pepsi-Cola Tin Door Handle

Door handle, "Pepsi-Cola," painted tin, squared tab ends w/mounting holes & arched handle, dark blue ground w/wavy white bands on each tab, top reads "Enjoy - Pepsi-Cola" & bottom reads "Bigger - Better" in red & white, very minor surface wear, yellowing to white, 2 3/4 x 12" (ILLUS.).. **490**

Door push, "Golden Bridge Root Beer," embossed tin, long rectangular form, dark gold ground w/a color image of a large bottle below the word "Remember" in red, 3 3/4 x 11 3/4" (minor scattered wear & scratches) **94**

Door push, "Hires Root Beer," tin, long narrow rectangular, dark gold ground w/a large color bottle of the product, red & black wording at top & bottom reads "Finer Flavor because of Real Root Juices - Ice Cold," 3 1/2 x 11 1/2" (very minor bend at bottom, light scratches at bottom center) **187**

Door push, "Pepsi-Cola," raised tin, long narrow rectangular form w/a dark blue ground & white wording centered by a wavy white center band w/the old fashioned red Pepsi-Cola logo & "5¢" in a red dot, wording reads "Come In For That Big, Big Bottle of..." & "Buy It By The Carton Too!," 2 3/4 x 10" (minor edge & surface wear, yellowing to the white)................. **550**

Early Pepsi-Cola Hand Fan

Fan, "Pepsi-Cola," die-cut cardboard hand-type, the wide arched blade printed in color on one side w/a wide wavy white center band flanked by dark blue bands, the old fashioned red Pepsi-Cola logo in the center, "Drink" in white at the top w/"12 ounce Bottle - 5¢" w/a small bottle of the soda in the lower band, the reverse w/blue, red & pink comic figures of Pepsi policemen, Pepsi & Peter, pouring a bottle of Pepsi & saying in red "Plenty! - Plenty! - Plenty!" & "Good! - Good! - Good!," white background, dated 1940, w/wooden flat handle, very minor soiling & wear, light creases, 7 3/4 x 12" (ILLUS.) **105**

Old Soda Fountain Stools

Fountain stools, black metal pedestal bases & silvered metal round seat frames w/upholstered seats, ca. 1930s, some overall wear, 12 1/2" d., 19" h., set of 3 (ILLUS.) **66**

Glass, "Allen's Red Tame Cherry," tall waisted clear glass form w/white wording (ILLUS. second from left with Cascade tumbler) **25**

Group of Early Soda Fountain Glasses

Glass, "Cascade Ginger Ale," clear cylindrical glass printed in white w/"Cascade Ginger Ale - There's A Toast in Every Glass" (ILLUS. far left) **35**

Glass, "Moxie," clear cylindrical glass w/white wording, reads "Drink Moxie Nerve Food" (ILLUS. second from right)....... **165**

Glass, "Moxie," swelled tapering glass design w/white wording, reads "Drink Moxie" (ILLUS. far right)... **45**

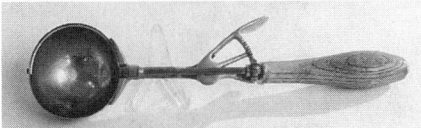

Gilchrist No. 31 Ice Cream Scoop

Ice cream scoop, Gilchrist Model 31, plated brass w/wooden handle, early 20th c., 11 1/4" l. (ILLUS.) **75**

Hendlers Ice Cream Menu Board

Menu board, "Hendlers Ice Cream," cardboard, chain-hung, top reads "Serving Hendlers Ice Cream - 'The Velvet Kind,'" flavors listed below on paper inserts, framed under glass, 10 x 20" (ILLUS.).......... **176**

Squirt Menu Chalkboard

Menu board, "Squirt," embossed tin w/chalkboard, top w/message in circle reading "Switch to Squirt - Never an After-Thirst," flanked by Squirt boy & bottle, bottom dated 1950, white stains to chalkboard, minor bends & wrinkles, 19 1/2 x 27 1/2" (ILLUS.) **165**

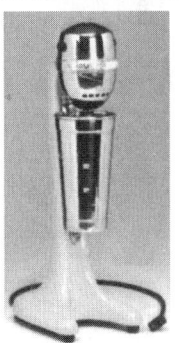

Old Hamilton Beach Shake Mixer

Milk shake mixer, "Hamilton Beach Model 33," electric, single head, light green porcelain base w/chrome top & canister, some soiling & scuffs, 18" h. (ILLUS.) **154**

Service pin, "7Up," enameled gold-filled metal, an oblong frame of gilt laurel leaves surrounding a green, red & gold bottle of 7Up featuring the Bubble girl above a small black square w/a gold "5," for five years of service, 1/2 x 3/4" (very minor wear) **160**

Whirla-Whip Sign

Sign, "Whirla-Whip," die-cut Masonite, red & white tub filled w/swirled soft-serve ice cream & a red spoon, tub reads "Whirla-Whip Treats - in - a - Tub," minor surface & edge wear, 20 1/2 x 24" (ILLUS.) 110

Rare Fan-Taz Syrup Dispenser

Syrup dispenser, "Fan-Taz," large ceramic model of a baseball on a round base, orange & black wording w/a tan baseball bat, ca. 1900, 16" h. (ILLUS.) .... **$8,000+**

Cherry Smash Syrup Dispenser

Syrup dispenser, "Fowler's Cherry Smash," glass & chrome, the tapering cylindrical cranberry red glass container printed w/white wording, flat metal cover, base & spigot, bowl 7 1/2 x 9", overall 17" h. (ILLUS.).. 633

Hires Root Beer Syrup Dispenser

Syrup dispenser, Hires Root Beer Munimaker, on rectangular base w/plate reading "Hires" on front & sides, ovoid dispenser handle reads "Drink Hires - It is pure" in red (ILLUS.) **8,000**

SONJA HENIE MEMORABILIA

Sonja Henie was born in Oslo, Norway in 1910. The Henie family, wealthy fur merchants, could well afford expensive training for their daughter, who showed dancing talents at an early age. Sonja saw her older brother, Leif, skate at Frogner Rink in Oslo and she then begged for her own ice skates. Santa obliged. She went on to win the Norwegian Championship at age 10, the beginning of her incredible career.

She won ten World Championships consecutively from 1927 to 1937. During the period she also won three Olympic Gold medals.

In 1936 Sonja arrived in Hollywood and, after a skating exhibition, was signed to a contract with 20th Century Fox. Her first film, "One In A Million," was a box office smash. Ten more movies followed. Sonja teamed up with Arthur Wirz, and the dynamic duo then produced the "Hollywood Ice Revue," which appeared in many major cities during the 1940s and 1950s.

When she married her third husband, Niels Onstad, they established the Henie-Onstad Art Center in Norway and presented it to her homeland. Sonja died of leukemia in 1969, but the memory of her dimpled smile and golden hair live on in the hearts of collectors around the world.

Royal Crown Cola Ad with Sonja Henie

Advertisements, various magazine full-page ads for products such as Royal Crown Cola, Trimz Wallpaper, Adys, Kool-Ade, Drene, Lux & Quaker Puffed Wheat, each (ILLUS. of one)...................... **$9-12**
Book, "Story of Sonja Henie," by Charles Hoff, written in Norwegian, Oslo, 1937 ...... **50-65**
Book, "XIII Olympic Winter Games - Lake Placid - 1980" produced by the Ice Skating Institute of America, photos of Sonja Henie supplied by contributor Ann J. Bates, 9 x 11 1/2" **25-35**

Various Books About Sonja Henie

Books, various titles including "Wings On My Feet," Prentice-Hall, 1940; "Mitt livs eventyr," 1938 & 1953; "Som i en Drom," by Alf G. Andersen, 1985; "Queen of Ice - Queen of Shadows," by Raymond Straight & Leif Henie, 1985; "Figure Skating to Fancy Skating - Memoirs of the Life of Sonja Henie," by Michale Kirby, 2000; "The Sports 100 - The 100 Greatest Athletes of the 20th Century," The Associated Press; "100 Most Important Women of the 20th Century," Ladies' Home Journal, each (ILLUS. of various titles) **35-75**

Catalog, Sotheby's, New York, sale catalog for June 7, 1994, several pages featuring jewelry owned by Sonja Henie **18**

Sonja Henie Coloring Book

Coloring book, full-color cover image of Sonja in skating outfit, No. 3476, Merrill Publishing Company, 1939, 10 1/2 x 15 1/4" (ILLUS.) **75-125**

Sonja Henie Dolls

Doll, Arranbee Doll (R&B), hard plastic w/jointed arms & legs, original wine-colored velvet outfit w/white trim & white muff, 1945, sold in lobby of her ice shows, 13" h. (ILLUS. center) **100**

Doll, celluloid & felt, head & skates of celluloid, body & ice outfit in felt, ca. 1930s, 6 1/2" h. (ILLUS. left with other dolls) **35**

Doll, composition, blonde mohair wig, brown sleep eyes, Madame Alexander, mint w/original truck w/complete wardrobe, 14" h., the group **1,800**

1930s Alexander Sonja Henie Doll

Doll, composition, Madame Alexander, blonde mohair wig, open-close eyes, green velvet dress, brown skates w/one blade broken, late 1930s, 18" h. (ILLUS.) **375**

Doll, composition, Madame Alexander, original clothes, hair in original set, tag & original skates, in original box, 21" h. **1,800**

Early Mme. Alexander Sonja Henie

Doll, composition, Madame Alexander "Tiny Betty" Sonja Henie model, first Sonja Henie doll by Madame Alexander, in original skating outfit, mint in box, 1936, from collection of Barbara Jo McKeon (ILLUS.) **1,000**

Doll, composition, marked on back "Wendy Ann - Madame Alexander - New York," original clothes, mint in box, 14" h. **500-800**

Large Alexander Sonja Henie Doll

Doll, composition w/blonde hair, Madame Alexander, wearing original white outfit & ice skates, 18" h. (ILLUS.)...................... **600-800**

Doll, hard plastic, hazel sleep eyes, blonde mohair wig, jointed arms & head, wearing pink white-trimmed dress & white skates w/metal blades, sold in the lobby of her ice shows, 7 1/2" h. (ILLUS. right with other dolls) **25-35**

Plastic Sonja Henie Souvenir Doll

Doll, hard plastic, large blonde wig, molded skates, pink outfit w/Center Theatre ribbon, white feathers in hair, jointed arms & legs, sold in the lobby of her ice shows, 9" h. (ILLUS.).. **50**

Alexander Vinyl Head Sonja Henie Doll

Doll, vinyl head & hard plastic body, Madame Alexander "Madeline" model, original pink outfit & white skates, 1951, 18" h. (ILLUS.).. **595**

Simplicity Doll Dress Pattern

Doll dress pattern, Simplicity No. 2936 (ILLUS.).. **15**

Doll ice skates, oil cloth or canvas w/paper soles & metal blades, white, vintage, 2" l., 2 1/4" h., pr. **20**

Doll outfit, girdle, Madame Alexander, for 14" doll, 1940 .... **15**

Doll outfit, negligee panties, Madame Alexander, for 14" h. doll, 1940................................ **11**

Doll outfit, wooden skis, leatherette boots & ski poles, for a Madame Alexander doll, the group.. **35**

Norwegian Carved Sonja Henie

Figure, hand-carved wooden figure of Sonja Henie on skis w/poles, wool hat, sweater & mittens, Norwegian, 8 1/2" h. (ILLUS.).. **200**

Figurine, ceramic, marked "H-S 9088," purchased in Germany in 1955, 8 3/4" h............. **150**

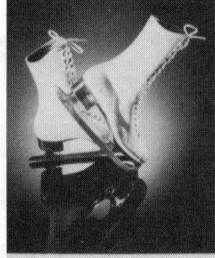

Henie Skates in the Smithsonian

Ice skates, personally owned & worn by Sonja Henie, Stanzione boots, New York City, Strauss blades (St. Paul, Minnesota), Henie signature on each boot, property of the Smithsonian Institution, Washington, D.C. (ILLUS.) **5,000**

Jacket, woman's, endorsed by Sonja Henie, from her Knitwear line, wool & part wool in red & black w/12 black glass buttons, 32" w. shoulders, 29-30" waist, overall 21" l., 1940s... **158**

Lobby Card from "Thin Ice"

Lobby cards, displayed in movie theatres, from her various films, each (ILLUS. of one from "Thin Ice," 1937)............................ **15-30**

Magazine, "Blades - Skating's Most Exciting News Magazine," October-November 1993, Sonja Henie cover story **8**

Magazine, "Doll Reader - Collector's Guide to Dolls and Miniatures," April-May 1979 issue, cover story on Sonja Henie **10**

Various Magazines Featuring Henie

Magazines, various titles from the 1930s through the 1950s, each (ILLUS. of a variety)... **20-40**

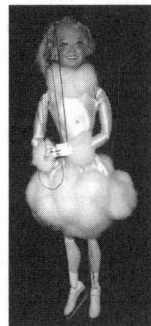

Sonja Henie Marionette

Marionette, figure of Sonja Henie in skating costume, courtesy of Frances Defoe, World, Olympic & Pairs Ice Skating Champion, 19" h. (ILLUS.) **1,500**

Movie lobby card, "Sun Valley Serenade," title card, cardboard, 11 x 14"............................ **52**

Movie videos, copies of eleven of her films including "Queen of the Ice," American version, "Queen of the Ice," Norwegian version, "The Immortals," "Reflections on Ice" & "A Diary of Women's Figure Skating," VHS, each... **12-30**

New Sonja Henie Paper Dolls Set

Paper dolls set, "Sonja Henie Paper Dolls by Ton Tierney," two dolls & 23 costumes, new, 12 1/2 x 13" (ILLUS.)................... **15**

Sonja Henie Paper Dolls Set

Paper dolls set, "Sonja Henie Paper Dolls," three dolls plus costumes, uncut very good condition, No. 3475, Merrill Publishing Co., 1939, 11 x 13" (ILLUS.) **175-200**

Passport, personal passport of Sonja Henie issued in 1957 & signed by Henie in three places **465**

Sonja Henie Ice Revue Felt Pennant

Pennants, felt, "Sonja Henie Ice Revue," red w/white letters & gold ties, sold in lobbies of the shows, each 8 x 26 1/2", each (ILLUS. of one) **26-50**

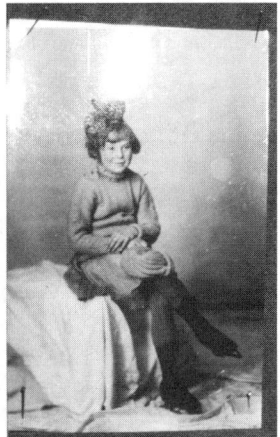

Early Photo of Sonja Henie

Photograph, black & white portrait of Sonja Henie at age 6 wearing her first pair of skates, 4 x 6 1/4" (ILLUS.).......................... **15-20**

Photograph, Sonja accepting First Prize from Salchow, President of the ISU in 1934... **20-30**

Sonja Henie 1929 Photo

Photograph, Sonja Henie in 1929, shown winning her 5th title in the Norwegian Championship, 6 1/2 x 8 1/2" (ILLUS.)....... **20-30**

Photograph, Sonja & her husband, Niels Onstad (left), with architects of the Henie-Onstad Art Center w/model of the center, 5 x 7"... **20-30**

Sonja & Husband, Niels Onstad

Photograph, Sonja & her new husband, Niels Ostand, after their honeymoon, contributor Ann J. Bates owns the mink

jacket shown here, which is currently at the Olympic Museum in Lake Placid, New York, 8 1/4 x 10" (ILLUS.).................. **20-30**

Photograph, Sonja in a skating outfit posed in front of the Model B-1950 Zamboni machine built specially for her, 8 1/4 x 10".. **20-30**

1928 Photo of Sonja Henie

Photograph, Sonja in St. Moritz, Switzerland in 1928, at the time of her first Olympic victory, 5 1/2 x 8 1/4" (ILLUS.) **15-20**

Photograph, Sonja in the Trophy Room of her Henie-Onstad Museum in Oslo, Norway, during its opening in 1968 (ILLUS. below).. **20-30**

Photograph, Sonja meeting King Olav & Queen Maud of Norway at her Ice Show in Oslo, August 1953 .... **20-30**

Photograph, Sonja on the podium at the 1936 Olympics, accepting gold medal w/other medal winners flanking her........... **20-30**

Photograph, Sonja with the King of Norway at the opening of the Henie-Onstad Art Center in Oslo in October 1968, 7 x 9 3/4".. **20-30**

Sonja Henie in Her Museum

Studio Color Photo of Sonja Henie

Photograph, studio colored picture of Sonja Henie in Norwegian costume, on card stock, 11 x 14" (ILLUS.)................................... **100**

Pin, figure of Sonja Henie wearing a red, white & blue skirt, metal inset w/rhinestones, her name near the base, 2" h. **30**

Pinback button, picture of Sonja Henie w/attached tiny silver skates, pin 1 3/4" d., skates 2 1/4" l..................................... **45**

Sheet of U.S. Postage Stamps

Postage stamps, U.S. 10¢ stamp sheet showing various movie actors, Sonja Henie in the upper right, the sheet of 12 (ILLUS.).. **15**

Modern Sonja Henie Postcard

Postcards, contemporary cards sold through the World Figure Skating Hall of Fame Museum, Colorado Springs, Colorado, each (ILLUS. of one)................................... **3**

Poster, color photo of Sonja on skates in a leap, dark blue ground, white wording at

Photo Poster of Sonja Henie

bottom reads "Sonja Henie and her 1950 Hollywood Ice Revue" (ILLUS.)........................ **20**

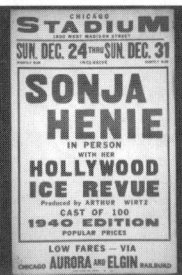

1940 Hollywood Ice Revue Poster

Poster, "Hollywood Ice Revue," 1940 appearance in Chicago, red & green lettering on white, issued by the Chicago, Aurora and Elgin Railroad, 22 x 14" (ILLUS.)... **200**

Swedish Color Print of Sonja Henie

Print, Swedish color print based on movie poster, matted, 8 x 10" (ILLUS.) **15**

Hollywood Ice Revue Programs

Programs, "Hollywood Ice Revue," various editions, 1937-1953, each (ILLUS. of various copies) **15-50**

Programs, various productions at the Center Theatre of Rockefeller Center, New York City, produced by Sonja Henie & Arthur Wirtz, each (ILLUS. of various examples, bottom of page) **25-40**

Refrigerator magnet, picture of Sonja Henie **5**

Modern Sculpture of Sonja Henie

Sculpture, custom-made impressionistic papier-maché figure of Sonja in a stag jump (ILLUS.) **300**

Sonja Henie Sheet Music

Sheet music, various illustrated covers featuring songs from her movies, each 9 1/2 x 12 1/2", each (ILLUS. of group) **10-20**

Sonja Henie Pleasure Skates in Box

Skates, "Sonja Henie Pleasure Skates by Nestor Johnson," sold by Sears, 1939, near mint in box (ILLUS.) **100-125**

Skating bonnet, red wool, Sonja Henie label, 5 x 6" w/13" l. straps **35**

Souvenir pin, 1952 Sonja Henie Ice Revue pin **16-25**

Souvenir pin, Lake Placid Sonja Henie skating pin **30**

Various Sonja Henie Ice Show Pins

Center Theatre Ice Show Programs

Souvenir pins, sold in the lobby of her ice shows, various designs, mostly metal (ILLUS. of varied group) **10-45**

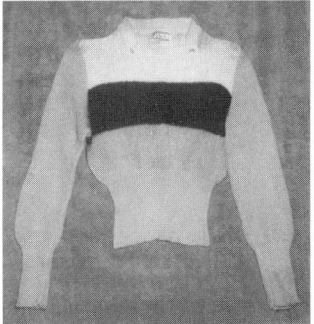

Sonja Henie Child's Sweater

Sweater, child's size, yellow, black & light blue wool, endorsed by Sonja Henie, rare (ILLUS.) **35-45**

"My Lucky Star" Theatre Poster

Theater poster, "My Lucky Star," darker purplish blue & white w/yellow title, framed 13 x 16" (ILLUS.).................................... **75**

Tickets, Sonja Henie Hollywood Ice Revue, various performances from 1945 through 1951, the group.. **35**

Various Sonja Henie Trading Cards

Trading cards, cardboard, various types including tobacco cards, coffee cards, Aviatik cards & weight machine movie cards, each (ILLUS. of a variety) **10-18**

Wristwatch, child's, blue band & face, tin frame w/cardboard face, made in Japan, late 1940s **25**

SPACE AGE COLLECTIBLES

Although fiction novels about space exploration have been around since the 19th century, and such space fantasies as "Flash Gordon" and "Buck Rogers" were popular in the 1930s, the modern Space Age started after World War II. There have been dozens of space science fiction movies and television shows produced since the early 1950s, when Russia and the United States were locked in the "Space Race." Our listings include items from the Space Race era as well as items produced as tie-ins to all the movies, TV shows and works of fiction released since the early 1950s. These listings are arranged alphabetically by the name of the character, show or movie.

Space Fantasy Items

Alien action figure, Alien Queen, Kenner, 1993, 6" h. **$8-15**

Alien Action Figure

Alien action figure, articulated figure w/movable jaws, clear head dome, 1979, 18" h. (ILLUS.) **250-500**

Alien action figure, Bull Alien, Kenner, 1994, 4" h. **10-20**

Alien action figure, Flying Alien Queen, Kenner, 1993, 7" h. **8-15**

Alien action figure, fully posable, Real Action Series, Takara, Japan, 1996, 12" h. . **75-125**

Alien action figure, Gorilla Alien, soft vinyl head, squirts water, claws grasp, Kenner, 1992, 5 1/5" h... **10-20**

Alien action figure, Killer Crab Alien w/dual launching chest busters, Kenner, 4" h. **4-8**

Alien action figure, King Alien, deluxe Alien leader, Kenner, 6 1/2" h. **9-20**

Alien action figure, Mantis Alien, Kenner, 1994, 5 1/2" h... **5-10**

Alien action figure, Night Cougar Alien, Kenner, 1994.. **4-8**

Alien action figure, Panther Alien w/flying attack parasite, Kenner, 5 1/2" h. **4-8**

Alien action figure, Queen Face Hugger, Kenner, 2" h.. **5-10**

Rhino Alien Action Figure

Alien action figure, Rhino Alien, Kenner, 4" h. (ILLUS.).. **7-15**

Scorpion Alien Action Figure

Alien action figure, Scorpion Alien, Kenner, 1992, 5 1/2" h. (ILLUS.) **7-15**

Snake Alien Bendee Figure

Alien action figure, Snake Alien, bendee, Kenner, 15 1/2" l. (ILLUS.) **5-10**
Alien action figure, Swarm Alien, electronic, laser eyes, Kenner, 6 1/2" h. **10-20**
Alien action figure, Warrior Alien from Aliens vs. Predator two-pack, Kenner, 1994, 5" h... **10-25**
Alien action figure, Wild Boar Alien w/hidden power attack spikes, Kenner, 1994, 6" h.. **4-8**
Alien collectors case, Operation Aliens, holds 12 figures, Kenner **12-20**
Alien costume, "Alien 3," ten-piece latex full body suit, Distortions.................... **1,200-1,400**
Alien costume, black & white, Ben Cooper **50-100**
Alien game, board-type, Kenner, 1979 .... **65-95**
Alien game, computer-type, Commodore, 1985 .... **20-35**

Alien game, "Operation Aliens," British only.. **20-40**
Alien model kit, 1979, MPC, plastic kits, 1960s-present... **25-100**

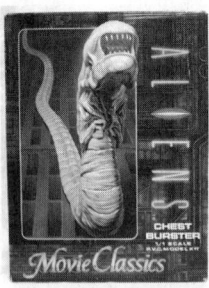

Halcyon Alien Chestburster Kit

Alien model kit, Alien Chestburster, 1/1 scale, tan vinyl, Halcyon, 1992, 10" h. (ILLUS.)... **100-135**
Alien model kit, Alien, completed model sold boxed, Kenner mold, Hobby, Tsukuda, vinyl kits (Japanese), 1980s-present. **90-130**

Halcyon Alien 3 Dog Burster Kit

Alien model kit, Alien Dog Burster, Alien 3, 1/1 scale, tan vinyl, Halcyon, 1990s, 12" h. (ILLUS.) **100-150**
Alien model kit, Alien Facehugger, tan vinyl, 1992, life-size, Halcyon, 1990s, 50" l... **200-250**
Alien model kit, Alien Facehugger with Fetus, vinyl, Halcyon, 46" h.......................... **50-115**
Alien model kit, Alien Queen black vinyl, 1992, Halcyon, 1990s, 14" h. **100-150**
Alien model kit, Alien Queen Chestburster, tan vinyl, Halcyon, 1990s, 10 1/2" **125-175**
Alien model kit, Alien Queen Facehugger w/Fetus, vinyl, Halcyon, 1990s, 46" h. **50-115**

Mad Lab Alien Kit

Alien model kit, Alien, "Tiny Terrors" running alien, unmarked, Mad Lab, resin kits sculpted by Michael Parks, 1990s-present, 4 1/2" h. (ILLUS.)............................ **15-35**
Alien model kit, Alien, Tsukuda reissue, black vinyl, Halcyon, 1990s, 16".............. **85-195**
Alien model kit, Alien Warrior, Aliens, base & egg, plastic, Halcyon, 1990s, 9" **30-90**

Halcyon Attacking Alien Kit

Alien model kit, Attacking Alien w/base, Halcyon, 1990s, 1/9 scale (ILLUS.) **25-40**
Alien model kit, plastic, MPC, 1979............ **25-100**
Alien movie viewer, hand-turned, w/"Alien Terror" film cartridge, Kenner.................. **100-150**
Alien playset, w/Queen Alien, Kenner, hive is 11 1/2" h. **15-25**
Alien replica, "Facehugger," foam latex, life-size, Distortions **80-120**
Alien target set, "Blaster Target," tall outline target of alien, HG Toys, 1979, 33" h.. **175-250**
Alien target set, "Chase Target," HG Toys, 1979, target 12 x 18 3/4" **125-200**

Revell Astronaut in Space Kit

Astronaut Model kit, Astronaut in Space, Revell, plastic kits, 1968-present, frequently reissued (ILLUS.)............................. **5-10**
Buck Rogers action figure, Buck, Mego, 1979, 4" h... **30-70**
Buck Rogers figure, articulated plastic w/removable clothes, Mego, 1979, 12" h.... **40-90**
Buck Rogers flying saucer, printed paper plates w/metal rim, S.P. Co., 6" d., each **400-600**
Buck Rogers playset, "Buck Rogers Spaceport," Mego, 1979......................... **125-200**
Buck Rogers rocket ship, tinplate toy w/clockwork motor, lithographed designs & image of two passengers in window, in original box decorated w/image of rocket blasting off and two people waving goodbye, w/"Buck Rogers 25th Century

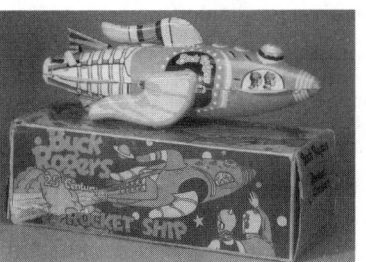

Buck Rogers Rocket Ship

Rocket Ship," by Marx for Daisey, 12" l. (ILLUS.).. **1,495**
Buck Rogers toy, windup tin, "Buck Rogers Space Ship," Marx, 1934, 12" **400-800**

Chewbacca Promotional Mask

"Chewbacca" mask, promotional mask of character from Star Wars movies, full headpiece covered in hair/fur, open mouth (ILLUS.) **259**
Lost in Space costume, silver space suit w/show logo, Ben Cooper, 1965............. **125-225**
Lost in Space game, board-type, Milton Bradley, 1965.. **50-100**
Lost in Space model kit, Cyclops w/rock, 1/42 scale, Aurora, 1966 .... **200-800**
Lost in Space model kit, Jupiter II w/wind-up motor, Marusan, 1966.................... **500-1,000**

Lost in Space Robot Model Kit

Lost in Space model kit, robot shooting lightning bolt, Aurora, 1968, 6" h. (ILLUS.).. **400-800**

Lost in Space model kit, w/chariot, deluxe
edition, Aurora, 1966-67 .... **600-1,200**
Lost in Space robot, windup plastic, Masu-
daya, 1985, 4" h. **25-40**
Lost in Space toy, battery-operated, Lost in
Space robot, plastic, made in various col-
ors, Remco, 1966, 12" h., each **400-800**

Lost in Space Battery-operated Robot

Lost in Space toy, battery-operated, Lost in
Space robot, plastic w/wired control box,
Toy Island, 1998, 10 1/4" h. (ILLUS.) **25-45**
Lost in Space toy set, signal ray gun hel-
met & gun set, Remco, 1966 .... **500-800**
Lost in Space View-Master reel set, GAF,
1968, set of 3 .... **45-70**
Outer Limits model kit, Sixth Toe, "Tiny
Terrors," Mad Lab, resin kits sculpted by
Michael Parks, 1993 .... **15-25**
Rocketship X-M movie poster, 1950, star-
ring Lloyd Bridges & Osa Massen, each
w/a color photo scene from the movie,
each 27 x 41", each **500**

Four Cards from Rare Star Trek Set

Star Trek cards, set of 72 cards by Leaf,
rare, write-ups on back don't correspond
to black & white images on front, 1967
(ILLUS. of four) **3,202**
Star Trek comic book artwork, original
cover artwork for Star Trek Comic Book
No. 1 April 1980, Marvel Comics Group,
by Leialoha, pen & ink w/brush on paper,
signed by artist in lower left corner, w/im-
ages of Kirk & Spock dominating images

Star Trek Comic Book Artwork

of spaceship & other characters, 10 x 15"
(ILLUS.) **460**

Cover Artwork for Star Trek Book

Star Trek cover painting for book, original
cover painting for first Star Trek paperback book from Bantam Books, oil &
mixed media on illustration board by
James Bama, Kirk & Spock in foreground
w/other characters & spaceship circling
planet in background, matted & framed,
1967, 16 x 17" (ILLUS.) **8,625**

Star Trek Dolls

Star Trek doll, Capt. Kirk w/accessories,
removable clothes, Mego, 1974, 8" h.
(ILLUS. left) **30-75**
Star Trek doll, Mr. Spock w/accessories,
removable clothes, Mego, 1974, 8" h.
(ILLUS. right) **30-75**

Star Trek dolls, "Barbie & Ken Star Trek Giftset" in window box, Mattel, 1996, the set.. **10-30**

Star Trek game, board-type, Hasbro, 1974... **35-75**

Star Trek Game

Star Trek game, "Star Trek the Role Playing Game," Fasa, 1983 (ILLUS.)................ **20-45**

Star Trek lunch box w/thermos, metal, dome top, 1968, Aladdin **920**

Star Trek model kit, Galileo 7 Shuttlecraft, 1/35 scale, AMT & AMT/Ertl, plastic kits, 1974... **50-100**

Mr. Spock Model Kit

Star Trek model kit, Mr. Spock, 1/12 scale, painted by Evan Stuart, AMT, 1968 (ILLUS.).. **60-120**

Star Trek model kit, Mr. Spock, shooting three-headed monster, 1/12 scale, AMT & AMT/Ertl - Plastic Kits, 1967 .... **40-125**

Star Trek model kit, Star Trek The Motion Picture, Klingon Cruiser, AMT & AMT/Ertl - Plastic Kits, 1984.. **10-20**

Star Trek model kit, USS Enterprise, 18" h. w/lights, AMT & AMT/Ertl - Plastic Kits, 1966... **75-200**

AMT Enterprise Command Bridge Kit

Star Trek model kit, USS Enterprise Command Bridge, 1/32 scale, AMT & AMT/Ertl - Plastic Kits, 1975 (ILLUS.)........ **20-50**

Star Trek puzzle, jigsaw-type, frame tray-type, Spock & Kirk on bridge, Whitman, 1970s **15-35**

Star Trek toy, Star Globe, USS Enterprise 1701 w/lights & glitter, limited edition, Willits Designs, 1992 .... **40-80**

Star Wars, jigsaw-type, 500 pieces, Kenner, 1970s, 15 x 18"................................... **10-15**

Star Wars action figure, Luke Skywalker, 1st series card w/twelve figures shown on back, Kenner, 1978 .... **40-350**

Star Wars action figure, Luke Skywalker, Hoth Battle Gear (Empire Strikes Back), Kenner, 1981... **20-75**

Star Wars action figure, Luke Skywalker, X-Wing Pilot, Kenner, 1978-79................... **30-50**

Star Wars Comic Book Artwork

Star Wars comic book artwork, original cover artwork for Star Wars No. 35 May 1989 Marvel Comics Group, by Carmine Infantino & Bob Wiacek, pen & ink w/brush on paper, signed by Bob Wiacek in lower left corner, w/original logos intact, one of only two covers that ever showed entire cast of main characters, 10 x 15" (ILLUS.) **1,495**

Star Wars doll, Boba Fett, boxed, Kenner, 1980, 12" h. **125-400**

Star Wars game, "Battle at Sarlacc's Pit" (Return of the Jedi), w/figures, Parker Bros., 1983 .... **15-30**

Star Wars model kit, Darth Vader Tie-fighter, MPC/Ertl, MPC, plastic kits, 1989 reissue **8-15**

Star Wars model kit, Darth Vader w/glowing light saber, MPC/Ertl, MPC, plastic kits, 1989 reissue, 11 1/2" h. **8-15**

Star Wars toy, AT-AT walker, large plastic vehicle, boxed, Kenner, 1979-80........... **100-200**

Star Wars Ewok Paploo

Star Wars toy, plush, Ewok, Paploo w/cowl, Kenner, 1983, 4" h. (ILLUS.)........................ **25-50**

Star Wars Ewok Princess Kneesa

Star Wars toy, plush, Ewok, Princess Kneesa w/cowl, Kenner, 1983, 4" h. (ILLUS.).. **20-45**

Tom Corbett, Space Cadet coloring book, Saalfield, 1950s.................................. **25-50**

Tom Corbett, Space Cadet rifle, official Tom Corbett Sparkling Space Gun, plastic & metal, Marx, 1950s, 21" l.............. **100-200**

Tom Corbett, Space Cadet View-Master reel set, Sawyer, 1950s, set of 3............... **25-50**

Twiki (Buck Rogers TV) action figure, Mego, 1979.. **25-50**

Space Race Items

Advertisement, comic book ad for the American Body Building Club promoted becoming "Astronaut Tough," early 1960s.. **40**

Space Model Kits Advertisement

Advertisement, from "American Modeler" magazine, April 1959, full-page ad for Monogram Space Age Hobby Kits, black & white photos & artwork promoting Willy Ley Space Models (ILLUS.) **25**

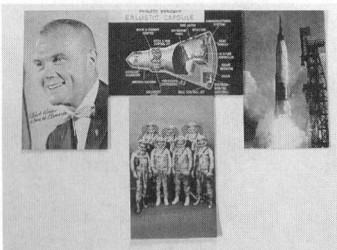

Space Age Arcade Picture Cards

Arcade picture cards, black & white photos of the original seven astronauts, satellites & space rockets, information on the back of each, sold in arcade machines, early 1960s, 3 1/2 x 5 1/2", each (ILLUS. of several) **5**

"Across the Space Frontier" Book

Book, "Across the Space Frontier," by Dr. Werner von Braun, Dr. Willy Ley, Dr. Fred Whipple, Dr. Joseph Kaplan, Dr. Heinz Haber & Oscar Schachter, edited by Cornelius Ryan, full-color illustrations by Chesley Bonestell, Fred Fruman & Ron Klep, used by Disney for Tomorrowland segments on 1950s TV show, 150 pages of artwork & photos, Viking Press, 1952, complete w/dust jacket, 8 1/4 x 11" (ILLUS.)... **400**

"Army Missiles - Rockets" Book

Book, "Army Missiles - Rockets," issued by the Department of the Army, features every missile in the Army arsenal in 1958, 1958, paperback, 45 pp. (ILLUS.) **10**

"Destination Space" Paperback Book

Book, "Destination Space," by John Russell, Jr., dust jacket art of Jupiter C rocket used to launch first U.S. satellite, Popular Mechanics Press of Chicago, 1959, paperback, 6 1/2 x 9 1/2" (ILLUS.) 12

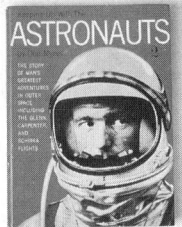

"Keeping Up With the Astronauts" Book

Book, "Keeping Up With the Astronauts," by Don Myrus, red background cover w/white & black type & black & white photo of an astronaut in space suit, includes material on American astronauts & early Russian cosmonauts, Rutledge Books, 1963, hardcover, 8 3/4 x 11" (ILLUS.) 12

Book, "Project Space," by Judith Viorst, covers the story of U.S. space exploration up to 1962, Washington Square Press, New York, New York 8

Book, "Rocket Manual for Amateurs," by Captain Bertrand R. Brinley, Project Officer, 1st US Army Amateur Rocket Program, foreword by Dr. Willy Ley, Ballantine Books, 1960, rare paperback 40

Book, "Satellite - From Satellites to Space Platforms - To the Moon and Beyond - Man's Greatest Adventure," by Erik Bergaust & William Beller, painting of earth & orbiting satellite on the cover, Bantam, 1957, paperback 10

Book, "Satellites, Rockets and Outer Space," by Dr. Willy Ley, illustrations by Chesley Bonestell, Signet Paperback, 1955 edition 50

Book, "Seeing the Earth From Space," by Irving Adler, material on ongoing satellite research, published right after launch of Sputnik, Signet Paperback Books, 1957 15

Book, "The Birth of the Missile - The Secrets of Peenemunde," Otto Merk & Ernest Kleer, introduction by Werner von Braun, translated by T. Schoeters, story of the development of the V-1 & V-2 rockets in Germany, E.P. Dutton and Company, 1963, 150 photos & illustrations, dust jacket 75

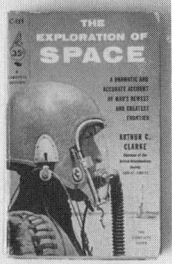

"The Exploration of Space" Paperback

Book, "The Exploration of Space," by Arthur C. Clarke, Chairman of the British Interplanetary Society, full of illustrations & color photos, Harper Publishing, Cardinal Edition, 1952, paperback (ILLUS.) 30

Book, "We Seven - The Original 7 Astronauts," authored by the original seven Mercury astronauts, Cardinal Books, 1963, paperback.. 8

Cape Kennedy Action Play Set

Cape Kennedy Action Play Set, w/metal carry-all case, Marx, No. 4625, 1968 (ILLUS.)... **50-150**

Lionel Missile Age Equipment Catalog

Catalog, Lionel Trains, "Lionel 'Missile Age' Equipment," cover art of trains & rockets in shades of black, grey & sepia, 1959 (ILLUS.)... 60

Revell Challenger Space Shuttle Kit

Challenger Space Shuttle model kit, 1/72 scale, Revell, plastic kits, 1982 (ILLUS.) ... **20-45**

"Space Man" Comic Book

Comic book, "Space Man," Dell Comics, No. 9, July 1972, color cover art, fair condition (ILLUS.) **6**

Friendship 7 model kit, Everything is "Go," Friendship 7 Mercury rocket, Revell, plastic kits, 1962 .... **25-75**

I.G.Y. Satellite Base playset, Marx, No. 4800, 1959... **300-1,000**

Keychain, gilt metal, in the form of the Mercury 7 capsule, issued by the AMVETS, early 1960s **4**

1952 "Collier's" Magazine on Space

Magazine, "Collier's," March 22, 1952, "Man Will Conquer Space Soon" cover story by top scientists including Werner von Braun, 15-page feature, artwork by Chesley Bonestel, material from the book "Across the Space Frontier," 10 1/2 x 13 1/2" (ILLUS.)..................................... **50**

Magazine, "Countdown - An Insider's Story of Our Men in Space - The Race to the Moon: Who Will be America's Astronauts of the Future?," by Alvin B. Webb, Jr., UPI Bureau Chief for Cape Canaveral, history of rockets & future space probes, back cover w/photo of seven new astronauts, MACO Magazines of New York, 1962 .... **10**

Magazine, "Life," September 24, 1965, cover photo of the coastline of Baja, California, taken by Gemini 5, inside feature w/other views from 100 miles up.......................... **5**

"National Geographic" Mercury Issue

Magazine, "National Geographic," July 1960, color cover art of Mercury capsule & 41-page story on the Mercury space program, fair condition (ILLUS.) **5**

"Popular Science" 1947 Issue

Magazine, "Popular Science," March 1947, cover story "Going Up for Keeps," cover art of rocket blasting off, very early material ahead of its time, 6 3/4 x 9 1/2" (ILLUS.).. **45**

1962 "Space World" Magazine

Magazine, "Space World," March 1962, color cover photo of John Glenn, cover feature "Astronaut's Report - 'How We Trained for Orbital Flight,'" Spaceways Publishing, New York, New York, fair condition (ILLUS.)... **30**

Magazine, "Time," July 25, 1969, first man on the moon issue w/photo cover...................... **7**

Magazine advertisement, full-page, promoting membership in the Science Program Book Club, lists various promotional items you receive including an 11 x 17" flight map & log book, appeared in various magazines, 1962... **45**

Northrop Snark Missile Model Kit

Model kit, Northrop Snark missile kit, unassembled in large box, Lindberg Models, 1950s, box 17 1/2" l. (ILLUS.) **100**

Revell Redstone Rocket Kit

Model kit, U.S. Army Redstone Chrysler rocket, scaled from official blueprints, includes portable launch pad, mobile radar van & three-man crew, late 1950s, Revell, boxed (ILLUS.) **80**

Model kit, Vanguard rocket w/satellite, plastic, rocket model opens to show inner workings, Renwal, late 1950s, boxed **220**

Operation Moon Base playset, Marx, No. 4654, 1962 .... **150-550**

Pennant, felt, black & white photo of John Glenn against a red, white & blue ground, commemorates the first U.S. orbital flight, 17 1/2" l. **45**

Photograph, color portrait of the crew of Apollo 11, actually autographed by each crew member, Armstrong, Aldrin & Collins **1,100**

Pinback button, Apollo 8 commemorative showing the three astronauts & "Welcome Back to Earth," flight on December 27, 1968, 1 3/4" d. **50**

Pinback photo button, black & white picture of Alan Shepard, first American in space, issued for his flight May 5, 1961, 1 3/4" d. **30**

Plaque, metal, replica of plaque left on moon on July 20, 1969, including the original inscription & names of astronauts & President Nixon, 6 x 8" **7**

Melamine Apollo Flights Plate

Plate, Melamine Texas Wear, commemorating the Apollo flights through Apollo 17, color insignia of each flight around a color center moon scene, 1979, 10" d. (ILLUS.) **25**

Postcard, commemorating Alexei Leonov's space walk, 1966 .... **50**

Project Mercury Cape Canaveral playset, Marx, No. 4524, 1959 .... **100-500**

Astronauts of Apollo 11 Jigsaw Puzzle

Puzzle, jigsaw-type, "Astronauts of Apollo 11 - 'First On the Moon,'" artwork of the astronauts & moon on the box cover, 500 pieces, Milton Bradley, 1969, box 11 x 16" (ILLUS.) **60**

Rex Mars Planet Patrol playset, Marx, No. 7040, 1958 .... **125-450**

Rings, plastic flicker-type, issued to commemorate the Apollo Space Program, each features an astronaut, the space launch or Eagle module, came in a set of 12, each ring **35**

Sculpture, "Shepard's Surprise Moon Shot," by J. Anderson Luster, shows golfing on the moon **900**

Kennedy Space Center Booklet

Souvenir booklet, "Kennedy Space Center," color cover photo of spaceman in space suit w/visitors, information on touring the center, inside back cover lists all manned missions before the shuttle program, 1978 (ILLUS.) **4**

Space suit, Apollo Moon Program training suit including helmet, boots & gloves, only used on testing on earth, the set **7,000**

Spoons, commemorative, Apollo Missions sets issued for Mission 8 & ll, handle depicts space capsule in orbit, portraits of various astronauts in each bowl, each **25**

Stamp album, postal commemorative honoring Alan Shepard & America's space achievements, limited edition including First Day Covers w/stamps issued by other nations honoring the life of Alan Shepard, 650 issued, Kenmore Stamp Company, 1971 .... **250**

Space Travel Golden Stamp Book

Stamp book, "Space Travel - A Golden Stamp Book," stamps of rockets, spaceports, satellites, planetary exploration, etc., 36 stamps in original sheet, Golden Press, New York, 1959, 48 pp., 8 1/2 X 11" (ILLUS.).. **12**

Trading cards, "Astronauts," cardboard w/color front images of space exploration, information on the back, Topps, 1963, set of 55, 2 1/2 x 3 1/2", each card.......... **7**

Topps 1958 Space Cards

Trading cards, "Space Cards," cardboard w/color images, information on the back, Topps, 1958, set of 88, each card (ILLUS. of several) **6**

Space Exploration Trading Cards

Trading cards, space exploration scenes, cardboard, color front illustrations, information on the back, Popsicle premiums, 1960s, 2 1/2 x 4", each (ILLUS. of two) **4**

SPORTS MEMORABILIA
Also see BASEBALL MEMORABILIA

Basketball

Basketball, George Mikan game-used model, Official Rawlings ABA model w/red, white & blue bands, stamped facsimile signature of Mikan, overall excellent **$3,580**

Rare Mint ABA Official Basketball

Basketball, original red, white & blue Official Rawlings ABA ball stamped "Mike Storen," fifth of the seven ABA Commissioners, in original box & wrapped in its plastic bag, gem mint condition (ILLUS.). **$3,436**

Rare Michael Jordan Rookie Card

Basketball card, Michael Jordan, 1986 Fleer #57, Jordan rookie card, gem mint condition (ILLUS.)...................................... **10,189**

Game ring, Magic Johnson's 1990 NBA All-Star game ring, polished steel alloy w/rectangular beveled setting w/an amethyst-colored stone, bands flanking the stone above & below w/raised silver wording against a black ground reading "NBA - All-Star," one side w/the year date over the logo of the Miami team, other side w//his name above the official NBA logo **10,928**

Game ring, Rick Barry's 1970 ABA All-Star ring, 10k gold w/a large round center blue gemstone, one side w/a red, white & blue-enameled basketball & the other side w/a figure of a ball player, cast inscription around the center stone **4,071**

Jersey, game-worn by David Johnson of the Anderson Duffy Packers of the National Basketball League, 1947-48 &

Rare, Early Basketball Jersey

1949-50, maroon w/blue & white letters & number, some light wear, size 40 (ILLUS.) 3,450

Program, 1929 American Basketball League World Series, Cleveland Rosenblums vs Fort Wayne, Cleveland Hall of Fame center Joe Lapchick on the cover, white w/black lettering, unscored, eight pages (light creasing & discoloration, slight tear restoration) 1,180

Billiard Collectibles

Advertising, "Burrowes Billiard and Pool Tables," The Saturday Evening Post, half page black & white ad, 1910s, 5" x 12"........... 10

Advertising, Carrom-Archarena Co., "The Tuilleries," third page black & white ad, 1903, 4" x 7" 10

Advertising, E.T. Burrowes Co., Ladies' Home Journal, November 1901, "Home Entertaining," black & white ad, 2" x 7" 10

Advertising, Kimberly-Clark Corp., "A Billiard Table Is King To Your Eyes," full page color ad, 1936, 11" x 14" 20

Advertising, "Lucky Strike," Will Hoppe, full color ad, 7" x 10" 20

Advertising, Palmolive Soap, full page color ad, 1930, 10" x 14" 20

Advertising, Popular Science Monthly, "Billiards by Wire," featuring Charles Peterson, full color full page article, 1938 20

Advertising, The Brunswick-Balke-Collender Co., The Geographic, "Teaching Young America To Shoot," full page ad, 1914, 6" x 10" 10

Advertising, The Brunswick-Balke-Collender Co., The Saturday Evening Post, "Billiards - A Gentleman's Game," full page black & white ad, 1924, 11" x 14" 20

Advertising, The Bryant Heater & Mfg. Co., The Saturday Evening Post, "Where The Pup is Furnace Man," full page black & white ad, 1928, 11" x 14"................................ 15

Artwork, Harper's Weekly, February 18, 1882, "The Billiard Match Between Slosson And Vignaux - Cheering The Victor," half page 25

Artwork, Harper's Weekly, March 21, 1868, "Billiard Room in Ludlow Street Jail," third page, 5" x 16" 20

Artwork, Harper's Weekly, March 31, 1866, "The Game of Billiards," full page front cover, 11" x 16"................................ 40

Harper's Blackville Billiard Club

Artwork, Harper's Weekly, March 31, 1883, "The Blackville Billiard Club," full page, 11" x 16".. 40

Artwork, Harper's Weekly, November 28, 1885, "The Billiard Tournament At Chicago - November 15-21," half page, 8" x 10".. 25

Artwork, The Daily Graphic, November 19, 1875, "Billiard Problems Illustrated," full column w/six shot diagrams of match w/Garnier, Rudolph, Dion & Sexton 25

Artwork, The Graphic, May 15, 1920, "The Billiard Battle: As Seen by Will Owen," full page illustration, 8" x 10" 20

Artwork, The Graphic, "The Old Antagonists," half page from British newspaper, 1872, 6" x 9" 25

Artwork, The Illustrated London News, January 9, 1909, "A '100 Up' And Down: Billiards on a Liner; On a Table That Levels Itself Mechanically," full page cover illustration, 12" x 17" 35

Artwork, The Illustrated London News, July 12, 1873, "Preparing For The Camp at Wimbledon," half page....................................... 25

Artwork, The Saturday Evening Post, full page color cover w/cue stick & eight ball 40

Autograph, "Boston Shorty Signed Banquet Ticket," to BCA Hall of Fame Banquet, signed July 1999 at induction.................. 40

Autograph, brochure, "Trick Fancy Shots," small black & white by Charles Ursetti, original promoter of "ABC's Wide World of Sports" billiard tournaments in 1970s, contains several shot diagrams & photos of top 1970s players, signed by author on front cover, 1978, 8" x 10"................................. 15

Autograph, card, "Willie Mosconi Signed Index Card," written & dated 12/27/55 by Willi Mosconi, excellent condition 40

Autograph, dollar bill, "Steve Mizerak Signed Dollar Bill," new bill, signed by Billiard Hall of Famer Steve Mizerak, 1999 45

Autograph, letter, "Willie Hoppe Signed Letter," typewritten to a Mr. Valper & hand signed by Willie Hoppe, April 15, 1940, very good condition 350

Autograph, phonecard, "Club Friends Phonecard," phone time no longer active, one of the only American billiard phone cards known to exist 5

Autograph, phonecard, "Rack-Em-Up Phonecard," phone time no longer active, one of the only American billiard phonecards known to exist 5

Autograph, photo, "Babe Cranfield," black & white, inducted into BCA Hall of Fame 1997, 8" x 10"...................................... 35

Autograph, photo, "Steve Mizerak Signed Photo," black & white signed by "The Miz" July 2000, Kansas BCA trade show, 8" x 10" 25

Autograph, pool ball, "Irving Crane Signed Photo," old clay, signed by BCA Hall of Famer 1999 50

Autograph, print, "Buddy Hall Signed Print," by Birkbeck Twins, July 2000 at BCA trade show Kansas City, Missouri, Buddy Hall was inducted into BCA Hall of Fame July 2000, 22" x 28" 50

Billiard ball, "Bud Light Pool Ball," recent, solid blue w/Budweiser logo 15

Billiard ball, "Budweiser Pool Ball," recent, solid red, w/Budweiser logo 15

Billiard ball, "Jeanette Lee 'Black Widow' Pool Ball," laser engraved w/signature & logo of Jeanette Lee, known as "The Black Widow" 15

Billiard ball, "McDermott Cue Ball," w/McDermott logo etched in green, collector cue ball 15

Billiard ball, "McDermott Eight Ball," w/McDermott logo etched, collector eight ball 15

Billiard ball, "McDermott Nine Ball," w/McDermott logo etched, collector nine ball 15

Billiard ball, "Olde English 800 Pool Ball," promotional cue ball w/Olde English 800 logo 15

"Playboy Bunny Logo Cue Ball"

Billiard ball, "Playboy Bunny Logo Cue Ball," recent, w/Playboy bunny logo (ILLUS.) 20

Billiard ball, "Playboy Bunny Logo Eight Ball," recent, w/small black bunny logo where the eight should be 30

Billiard balls, "Harley-Davidson Three Ball Set," novelty set w/Harley-Davidson cue ball, eight ball & nine ball, cardboard box 35

"Brunswick-Balke-Collender Clik Chalk"

Billiard chalk, "Brunswick-Balke-Collender Clik Chalk," hard to find, unused in excellent condition, 1940s, three cubes (ILLUS.) 15

Billiard chalk, "Player's Choice Chalk," recent, w/pictures of Nick Varner, Loree Jon Jones, Oliver Ortmann & Efren Reyes on each side, three pcs 15

Billiard Silk

Billiard silk, embroidered design on black background, 2" x 3" (ILLUS.) 15

Book, "Billiards and Snooker: The Postcard Album," Roger Lee, softcover with photos of 120 billiard and snooker postcards, a must for any fan of the game, 1997 12

Book, "Billiards and Snooker," Walter Lindrum, 1937 150

Book, "Billiards - How To Play And Win," Melbourne Inman, 1924 20

Book, "Billiards Simplified," Burroughs & Watts, 1889 100

Book, "How To Play Snooker," Stanley Newman, first edition, 1936 45

Book, "Hustlers, Beats and Others," Ned Polsky, hard to find, 1969, softcover 40

Book, "The Art of Practical Billiards," Maj. Gen. A.W. Drayson, second edition, 1912 50

Book, "The Billiard Book," Captain Crawley, first edition, 1866 175

Book, "The Modern Guide To Pocket Billiards," Luther Lassiter, 1964 30

Book, "Willie's Game," Willie Mosconi, first edition, hardcover, great reading on greatest pool player of all time, book sold out soon after it came out and is now very hard to find, 1993 30

Books, "History of Pool, Billiards & Snooker," William Hendricks, Craven A405, softcover, 1974 15

Cue stick, "Brunswick Master Stroke Cue stick," excellent example, probably made during war, has plastic joint, leather wrap, 1940s, 18 oz 300

Daguerreotype, rare, features two men holding cue sticks, mid-19th c., 2" oval 250

Letter, "The J.M. Brunswick & Balke Co.," original handwritten from Cincinnati office to Chicago office, written by Leo Schmidt 30

Lobby cards, "The Color of Money," French color, 1986, 8" x 10", set of 12 150

Movie photo, "Beach Blanket Bingo," original black & white, 1965, 8" x 10" 20

Movie photo, "Cloportes," original black & white, 8" x 10" 20

Movie photo, "Never So Few," original color, 1959, 8" x 10" 20

Movie photo, "The Hustler," original black & white, 1961, 8" x 10" 20

Movie photo, "The Hustler," original black & white, 1961, 8" x 10" **20**
Movie photo, "The Hustler," original black & white, 1961, 8" x 10" **20**
Movie photo, "Untitled," original black & white, 1947, 8" x 10" **20**
Movie poster, "The Color of Money," rare original from Japan, 1986, 22" x 30".............. **250**

"The Hustler" British Poster

Movie poster, "The Hustler," British Crown, extremely rare, film originally received an "X" rating when released in Britain in 1961, poster printed with "X" rating on it, before movie came out rating was changed, all posters destroyed, only known surviving example, 1961 (ILLUS.) **900**

"The Hustler" Japanese Poster

Movie poster, "The Hustler," Japanese two sheet, very rare, 1961, 46" x 22" (ILLUS.) **850**

"The Hustler" Italian Poster

Movie poster, "The Hustler," Lo Spaccone, original Photobusta Italian poster, fea-

tures Paul Newman & Jackie Gleason by pool table holding cue sticks, one of best images in series, excellent condition, 1961 (ILLUS.)... **400**

Italian "The Hustler" Poster

Movie poster, "The Hustler," original La Candina from Italy, yellow background, 1961, 13" x 27" (ILLUS.) **450**
Movie soundtrack, "The Color of Money," original album, 1986... **20**

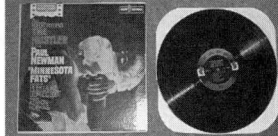

Hustler Original Movie Soundtrack

Movie soundtrack, "The Hustler," original album, extremely rare, only a handful have surfaced over past ten years, 1961 (ILLUS.).. **100**
Movie still, "A Bedtime Story," original black & white, 1933, 8" x 10" **25**
Movie still, "Fools For Luck," original black & white, 1928, 8" x 10" **25**
Movie still, "Fools For Luck," original black & white, 1928, 8" x 10" **25**
Movie still, "Good Girls Go To Paris," original black & white, 1942 .... **25**
Movie still, "Lonely Are The Brave," original black & white, 1962, 8" x 10"........................... **20**
Movie still, "Lorraine Day," original black & white, 1940s, 8" x 10" **20**
Movie still, "Mister Cory," original color, 1957, 8" x 10".. **20**
Movie still, "Sleuth," original black & white, 8" x 10"... **20**

Joe Camel Porcelain Plate

Plate, "Joe Camel Porcelain Plate," limited edition, never used, original box, 8" d. (ILLUS.) 25
Print, color, Neve Campbell, 8" x 10" 20
Trade card, S. Cohen & Co., small French, color w/advertising on back, 1890s, 2" x 3" 50
Videotape, "The Hustler," extremely hard to find, 1961 20

Football

Football, Gale Sayers record-breaking six touchdown game-used ball, faded signatures of Chicago Bears team members on three sides, also inscribed w/final score of the game & the date "Dec 12, 1965" 2,195
Football cards, 1957 Topps complete set of 154 plus checklist card, cards vary from excellent to near mint, the set............ 1,321

Complete Ticket to Super Bowl I

Game ticket, 1967 Super Bowl I, January 15, 1967, complete ticket, Green Bay Packers vs the Kansas City Chiefs, excellent to mint, beware of reproductions (ILLUS.) 3,215

Extremely Rare Super Bowl II Ticket

Game ticket, 1968 Super Bowl II, January 14, 1968, complete ticket for President's Box, Green Bay Packers vs the Oakland Raiders, last game coached by Vince Lombardi, near mint (ILLUS.) 17,022
Helmet, Barry Sanders game-worn model, grey w/blue Detroit Lions logo & blue face guard, signed by Sanders, 1990s 5,032
Helmet, Ed Sprinkle Chicago Bears game-used model, black hard plastic shell &

leather-cushioned inside, Wilson Sporting Goods, 1950s 1,814

Early Spalding Leather Helmet

Helmet, Spalding black leather Model J, black leather cap w/heavy cotton padding, original chin strap, minimal use, ca. 1900 (ILLUS.) 1,648
Helmet, Spalding "White Turtle Front" helmet, white leather suede w/company logo on the forehead, original chin strap, size 7 1/4, only known example (some interior leather cracking, minor exterior wear) 1,682
Jersey, Joe Montana San Francisco 49ers game-worn model, white nylon w/red lettering & numbers on the front & back, signed by Montana on the front hand warmer, size 46, ca. 1990 5,299
Program, 1911 University of Michigan vs Pennsylvania, cream w/wording in rectangular golden border band framing a sketch of a male cheerleader, 32 pp., near mint 991

1934 NFL Championship Program

Program, 1934 NFL Championship Game, between the New York Giants & Chicago Bears, known as the "Sneakers Game," white w/blue type & a photo of player Ken Strong, very minor creases, slight trace of center fold (ILLUS.) 1,938
Souvenir spoon, sterling silver, 1893 Princeton vs Yale championship, commemorates the Princeton Tigers National Championship against Yale, tiger head & laurel leaves on handle w/the words to a popular cheer, the bowl embossed inside w/"Champions - 1893 - 6-0," reverse of bowl cast as a football, near mint (ILLUS. front & back) 665

Early Football Championship Spoon

STEREOSCOPES & STEREO VIEWS

Hand stereoscope viewers with an adjustable slide may be found at $30.00 to $50.00 each in good condition. Elaborate table models are priced much higher. Prices of view cards depend on the subject material and range from less than $1.00 to $10.00 or more.

Stereo Views

Alaska Gold Rush, "Golden Stairs - Chilkoot Pass," part of a series, No. 9191 .... **$20**

Alaska Gold Rush, part of a series, scene of men panning for gold, water spraying to rinse the gold **40**

American views, part of series, including Central Park in New York & Prospect Park, Brooklyn, unknown maker, poor quality, each **2**

Ashville, North Carolina, scene of mountain ox hauling timber, when flipped over there is a view of Arch Rock from Land, Mackinac Island, Michigan, maker unknown **2**

Return of the Unknown Soldier

"Back in Home Land!," photo view of the return of the World War I Unknown Soldier to Washington, D.C., Keystone View Company (ILLUS.) **50**

Boston, Massachusetts, view of swan boats on a lake in the public gardens, World Series Stereoviews **2**

Boy playing w/Lionel toy train sets, No. P-21329, Keystone View Company **50**

Christmas scene, Santa Claus w/toys coming down the chimney, No. 11434, Keystone View Company **45**

Civil War view, Captain Custer with Confederate Prisoner, Matthew Brady, photographer **950**

Wedding Night Scene

Comic domestic scene, "Alone! At Last Alone," bride & groom in their bedroom on their wedding night, No. 11447, B.W. Kilburn, Littleton, New Hampshire, 1897 (ILLUS.) **5**

Coney Island, "Brilliant Luna Park at Night - Coney Island, New York," Underwood & Underwood, early 20th c. **100**

Cutting Sugar Cane in Cuba

Cutting sugar cane, part of the Picturesque Cuba series, Stereoscopic Gems, 1900 (ILLUS.) **3**

Dome of the U.S. Capitol at Night

Dazzling Dome of the Capitol on a Rainy Night, Washington, D.C. view No. 32229, Keystone View Company, 1920s (ILLUS.) **10**

Domestic comic view, four women sitting in a parlor & having tea, caption reads "Say Girls, Antoinette is Engaged," 1899, Underwood & Underwood **3**

Fjords of Norway, "Poetry of Light," sun setting on a fjord, ships shown, B.W. Kilburn, Littleton, New Hampshire **10**

Gems of German Life, man standing in open window smoking a pipe & with a tankard of beer on the window ledge **2**

Graf Zeppelin over Egypt, shows the desert & the Pyramids, Keystone View Company, early 20th c. **35**

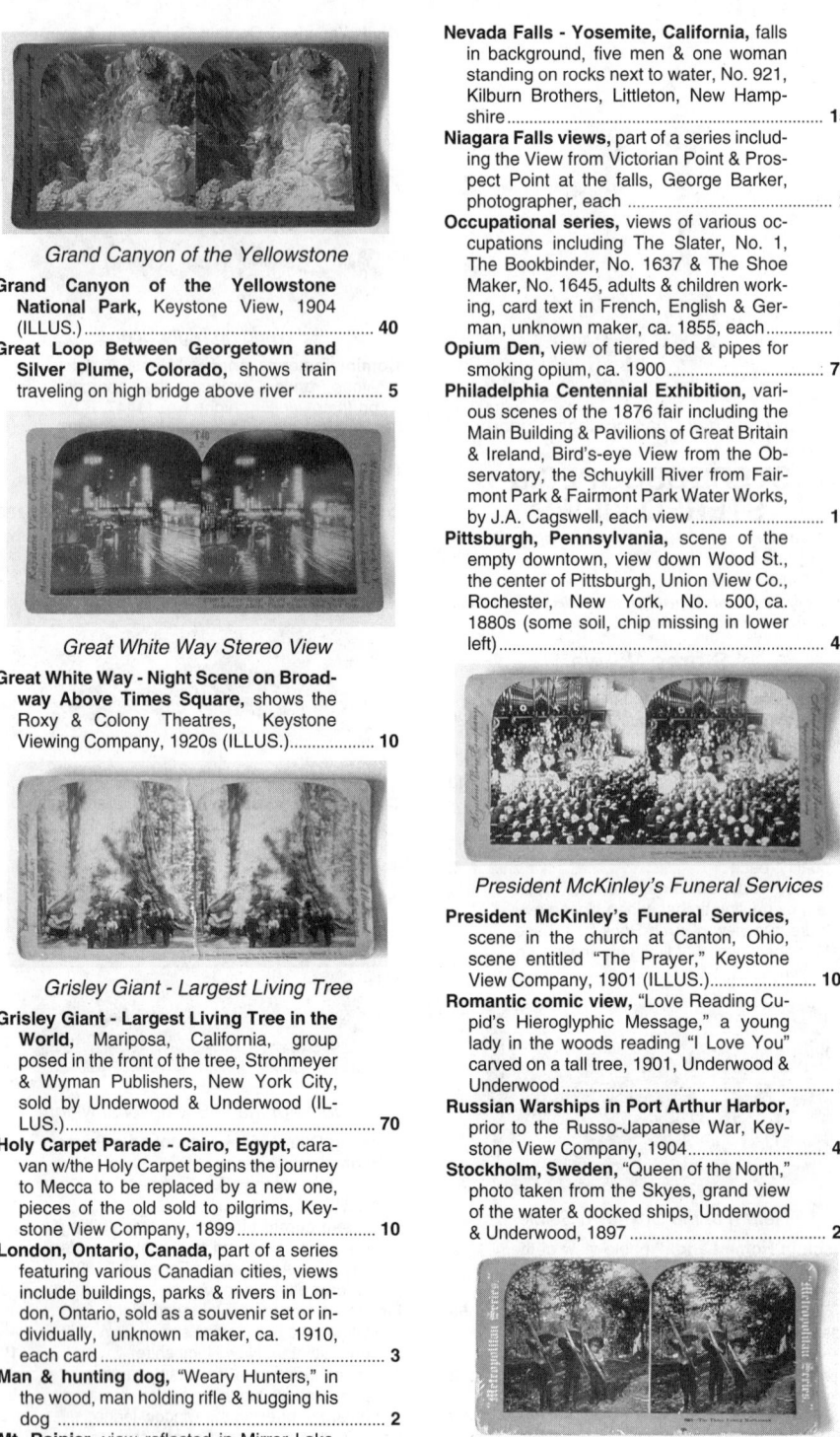

Grand Canyon of the Yellowstone

Great White Way Stereo View

Grisley Giant - Largest Living Tree

President McKinley's Funeral Services

Three Young Marksmen View

Three Young Marksmen, three little boys w/bows & arrows, No. 803, Metropolitan Series, 1890 (ILLUS.) **3**

Tower of London Stereo View

Tower of London, the castle & Tower w/a tree-lined street w/horse-drawn carriages, Underwood & Underwood, 1910 (ILLUS.)...................................... **5**

U.S. Navy Warship Bancroft - New York Harbor, scene of annual naval review, Underwood & Underwood, 1893...................... **15**

United States historic sites, series includes views of graves of soldiers at Arlington National Cemetery, Tomb of Late President McKinley, Red Room in the White House, White House Grounds & Mt. Vernon, ca. 1920, each.................... **5**

Watkin's Pacific Railroad - Lick House Entrance - San Francisco, California, shows single rail track along water, mountains in background **5**

World War I German Troops

World War I German troops, lined up for review in 1914, Keystone View Company, Card #3 in a set of 500 covering the history of the war, set came in leatherbound volumes, single card (ILLUS.) **50**

World War I Troops in France

World War I troops, shown leaving a French town, Underwood & Underwood (ILLUS.)... **50**

Stereoscopes

Hand-held, maple w/aluminum hood & metal slide, slight padding around eye view-

Hand-held Stereoscope

ing area, Underwood & Underwood, New York, patented in 1901 (ILLUS.) **100**

Victorian Stereoscope

Table model, wood, Victorian (ILLUS.)......... **1,300**

TEXTILES

Coverlets

Homespun counterpane, overall design formed from pulled loops in the weft, pine trees & fleur-de-lys-type designs around a central star w/diamond center, natural tan, edges w/decorative loops, 84 x 100" (light stain) **$110**

Coverlet in Diamond Grid Pattern

Jacquard, summer/winter two-piece, in tomato red, navy blue & dark olive green on
natural in Diamond Grid patt., w/flowers
& bird borders, corner blocks signed "F.
Yearous, Loudonville, Ohio 1852,"
73 x 90" (ILLUS.) 1,265

Jacquard, two-piece double-weave in navy
blue & natural, bands of leaves & stars
w/two pheasant borders & tulip borders,
eagle corner block dated "1844" for Samuel Graham (1805-1871 New Castle, Indiana), one end turned over, 72 x 86".......... 440

Jacquard, two-piece double-weave in navy
blue & natural, rose medallions surrounded by stars, "Pyna Rosc Wove in Logan
Co. Ohio by W. Buechel 1847," missing
fringe, ends bound over, 72 x 80" 248

Summer/winter coverlet, woven, two-
piece, navy blue & white w/pine tree borders, 70 x 79" (wear & small stains)............. 220

Linens & Needlework

Early American Flag

American flag, wool w/thirteen white linen
stars handstitched to both sides of blue
field, red & white stripes sewn on a trea-
dle machine, brass grommets w/"1884"
patent dates, light black lettering along
the end, 36 x 62", some holes (ILLUS.)..... 1,155

Blanket, early wool blanket w/yellow & red
floral crewelwork embroidery along both
sides & a large flower at each end,
69 x 76" (light staining & some holes
w/moth damage) 248

Blanket, wool, blue & natural plaid, two
pieces sewn together w/additional piece
to go between the bed posts, 95" sq............ 303

Confederate First National Flag

Confederate flag, First National flag w/one
white stripe flanked by two red stripes, &
seven stars appliquéd to a blue ground in
corner on one side, w/the blue cut away
to show the stars on the reverse, w/doc-

ument that identified the flag as "General
Braggs Head Quarters flag" (ILLUS.)....... 17,600

Family register, silk embroidery on linen,
an upper border band of large rose blossoms & leaves above the sewn inscription "Register of Richard Wilcox family"
above a row of three large pots overflowing w/flowers above name & date registers, a landscape w/a three-story Federal
house in the lower left & a large weeping
willow tree above a monument in the lower right, possibly Connecticut, ca. 1825,
18 x 19 1/2" 8,050

Show towel, rectangular, petit point detail in
blue & burgundy floss on white, stylized
design of three flowering trees across top
w/birds perched in branches, larger birds
in between, "M.H.L.H. - 1864" in panel
below trees border design underneath,
fringed bottom, framed, 17 x 21 1/2"
(light stains, minor edge wear, frame re-
painted) 248

19th-century South Carolina State Flag

South Carolina state flag, made after
South Carolina seceded from the Union,
w/palmetto tree flanked by letters S & C
at its base, crescent moon in upper left
corner, grey ground, white trim, mounted
w/tack to black board & framed, 19th c.,
23 x 30", tearing & holes (ILLUS.) 3,024

Quilts

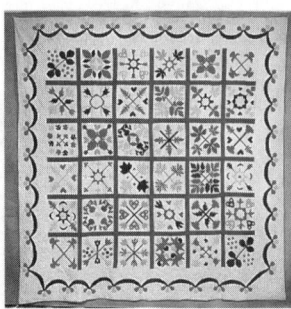

Album Quilt

Album quilt, square, worked in red, green,
yellow & blue-green in various floral &
leaf designs, w/scalloped ribbon border,
red rim, York County, Pennsylvania
(ILLUS.)... 7,920

Appliquéd, slate blue turkey tracks on white
ground, feathered bands w/flowers,
leaves w/berries & compass stars in corners, 84" sq. (small tear & bleach stain)........ 440

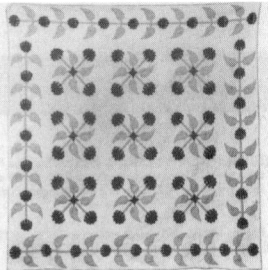

Appliquéd Poppy & Medallions Quilt

Appliquéd poppy & medallions, handsewn, w/diagonal lines & princess feather quilting, border in red & tan on white ground w/tan edging, pencil lines remain, 79 x 82" (ILLUS.) **1,045**

Tulips Quilt

Appliquéd tulips, green, red & orange three-flower tulips on white ground, handsewn, teal blue edging, princess feather quilting, made by Cora Mack, Marion, Ohio, ca. 1870, 66 x 82" (ILLUS.)... **770**

Crib Quilt

Crib quilt, basket of flowers resembling poppies in red, yellow & green calico on white square, yellow sawtooth border w/green corners & white border w/green edging, border w/quilted double wavy lines, handsewn, attributed to Philadelphia, 40 1/2 x 42", minor rust spots, sewn to stretcher (ILLUS.)...................................... **935**

Pieced Irish Chain patt., navy blue & pink calicos on white ground, white has quilted sunflowers between chain & feathered border, 90" sq. (minor stains, pink has wear, especially the binding).................. **413**

Pieced Lone Star patt., red, pink, gold & teal blue w/pink stripe, handsewn w/meandering quilted border, pencil marks remain, 82" sq. (light stains).............................. **589**

Pieced sampler quilt, w/different squares of calico fabrics on blue grid, square designs include school house, fan, bow tie, pinwheels, etc., handsewn, 68 x 81".............. **715**

Samplers

Alphabet, silk on linen, rectangular needlework sampler w/alphabet & date of 1802 among designs of house, trees, animals & figure of woman or girl, & "Elizabeth Lawrence, born January 21 1791," American, 9 x 18 3/4" (some discoloration & darkening).. **2,700**

Religious Verse Sampler

Religious verse, needlework sampler on homespun, religious verse among trees filled w/birds, a brick house, figures of people & animals, baskets of flowers, butterflies, peacocks, crowns, in colorful strawberry border on light tan background, signed "Hannah Munro her work Aged 8 years," in old frame w/gilt liner, 20 1/2" sq., stains (ILLUS.) **1,980**

TOBACCIANA

Devil Head Bronze Ashtray

Ashtray, bronze, head of a leering devil w/mouth wide open, 4 1/4 x 5", 2 3/4" h. (ILLUS.)... **$69**

Cast-Iron Ashtray with Indian Chief

Ashtray, cast iron, round dished form w/a high-relief face of a Native American chief at the top rim flanked by tomahawks, center embossed "1750 Fort Ligonier," appears unused, 4 1/2 x 5 1/2" (ILLUS.).. **149**

Figural Advertising Ashtray

Ashtray, cast spelter & steel, rectangular base w/rounded corners & incurved ringed sides, a platform at the top back w/a figural man of iron shoveling coal, embossed on front edge "Iron Fireman," by Advance Products, Cleveland, Ohio, 4 1/4 x 6 3/4", 4 1/2" h. (ILLUS.) **75**

Early China Cigar Ashtray

Ashtray, "Foster-Hilson Company - Makers - The Hoffman House Bouquet Cigar - New York," white china w/brown wording & a color picture of a cigar, china mark of the Marx & Gutherz Company of Carlsbad, Austria, ca. 1900, minute age crack, 6" d. (ILLUS.)... **259**

Mobil Flying Pegasus Ashtray

Ashtray, "Mobil Gasoline," Art Deco design, a figural cast-metal flying red Pegasus logo rising from one end of the flaring round black glass tray base, some paint wear on Pegasus, 5" d. (ILLUS.).................... **138**

Ashtray with Figural Borzoi

Ashtray, spelter, rectangular dished tray w/a figural reclining borzoi dog across the back, bronzed finish, early 20th c., 4 3/4 x 5 1/2", 3" h. (ILLUS.)............................ **25**

Tin Coal Scuttle Ashtray

Ashtray, tin, model of a coal scuttle, wire bail handle, 3 x 3 3/4", 3" h. (ILLUS.)............... **16**

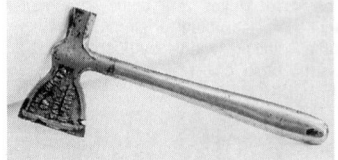

Silvered Cast-Iron Cigar Box Opener

Cigar box opener, silvered cast iron, model of a hatchet, the black embossed "Compliments of Savill & Rafferty," 2 3/4 x 6 1/2" (ILLUS.) **69**

Cigar case, carved ebony & silver inlay, rectangular w/rounded corners, ebony carved in relief w/mythological scene of putti & a ram at play, silver inlay leafy border, English, ca. 1870, 3 1/2 x 5 1/2" **224**

Cigar cutter, "Grand Republic 5¢ Cigar," pocket-sized, nickel silver w/gold finish, flat rectangular form w/insert hole for tip & push cutting blade, 1 x 2" **55**

Tenorio Counter-top Cigar Cutter

Cigar cutter & matchbox holder, "Tenorio 5¢ Cigar," nickel-plated metal, countertop design w/oval leaf-embossed base band below ribbed sides around cutter & flanged matchbox holder on one side, finish wear & slight rust on bottom, 3 x 5 x 5" (ILLUS.) **77**

Small Advertising Cigar Lighter

Cigar lighter, stamped brass & Bakelite, marked "Fresh Havana Blended Cigars Direct From Factory to Smoker - What Edwin Makes Make Edwin," Edwin Cigar Company, New York, New York, 1 3/4" h. (ILLUS.)... **24**

Cigar lighter, "White Owl Cigars," pocket-type w/flip-up top, black enameled ground w/a white owl perched on a brown cigar on the sides, excellent condition, 1/2 x 1 1/2" **143**

Unique Figural Cigar & Match Holder

Cigar & match holder, figural cast metal, the cylindrical holder at the back cast as a cluster of upright cigars, two crossed pipes for holding matches at the front, painted in brown, red, black & white, good original paint, 5" w., 5" h. (ILLUS.)........... **83**

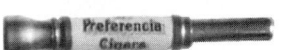

La Preferencia Cigar Piercer

Cigar piercer, "La Preferencia Cigars," nickel plated metal & celluloid, central celluloid section w/black wording, early 20th c., 3/8 x 2 3/4" (ILLUS.).............................. **83**

Aluminum Pocket Cigar Case

Cigar pocket case, "Rogert J. - Clear Havana Filler - 5¢ Cigar - 'Are Really Excellent,'" aluminum oblong form molded to hold three cigars, ca. 1930s, 2 1/2 x 5" (ILLUS.)... **44**

Cigar pocket pouch, "Bohemian Club - Havana Cigars - Compliments of Dwight J. Russell," red leather w/gold lettering & brass corner trim, unused, 3 x 5"..................... **66**

Amoco Motor Oil Cigarette Lighter

Cigarette lighter, "Amoco 300 Motor Oil," metal, can-shaped, printed in red, white & blue on a silver & white ground, w/original blue box, 2" h. (ILLUS.)............................... **77**

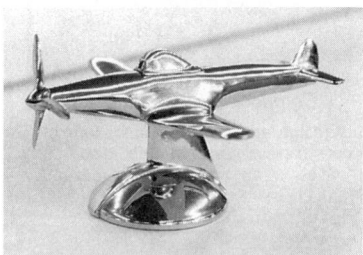

Fighter Plane Cigarette Lighter

Cigarette lighter, chrome-plate, model of a World War II fighter plane, top open when propeller is spun, marked "Negbauer NY USA - Patent Pending," 6 1/2 x 6 1/2", 3 1/2" h. (ILLUS.).. **195**

Harley Davidson Cigarette Lighter

Cigarette lighter, "Harley Davidson - of Long Beach," silvered metal, Japanese "slimline" design, decorated w/an enameled sketch of a man & woman in tan, red, black & white riding a black mortorcycle, wording in red, in original box, very minor wear, design of shop owner's business card on the reverse, 1 7/8 x 2 1/8" (ILLUS.)... **220**

Mohawk Gasoline Cigarette Lighter

Cigarette lighter, "Mohawk Gasoline," steel rectangular table model by Zippo, red Mohawk logo on the side, on a narrow stepped base, minor overall wear, 3 3/8" h. (ILLUS.) **231**

Cornucopia Cigarette Lighter

Cigarette lighter, silver plate, in the form of a cornucopia w/bands of embossed fruit & leaves, on an oval base w/rim design, 5" l. (ILLUS.) **19**

Spelter Camel Cigarette Lighter

Cigarette lighter, spelter, model of a recumbent camel, howdah lifts off back to expose lighter, 3" l., 2" h. (ILLUS.) **26**

Trumpeting Elephant Cigarette Lighter

Cigarette lighter, spelter, model of an elephant w/trunk raised, lighter on its back, 2 1/2" l., 2" h. (ILLUS.)` **25**

Simple Steel Cigarette Lighter

Cigarette lighter, steel, Art Deco style, marked "Imco - SOLO - Made in U.S.A. - Patent Pending," 1 1/2 x 2 1/4" (ILLUS.) **6**

Texaco-Firestone Cigarette Lighter

Cigarette lighter, "Texaco - Firestone," Japanese "slimline" style in silvered metal w/white, red & silver advertising on each side, distributor's name & address on each side w/the Texaco logo on one side & the Firestone logo on the other, from Great Falls, Montana, made by Nationwide, 1 7/8 x 2 1/8" (ILLUS.) **176**

Cigarette pack, "One-Eleven American Cigarettes," full pack decorated w/a large round bust portrait of a Native American chief in color against a red ground, cream ground on the pack, American Tobacco Company, 2 x 2 3/4" **66**

Decorative Early Cigarette Stand

Cigarette stand, cast iron & wood, a round metal base w/ornate pierced scroll-cast legs & apron, fitted w/three turned wood chalice-form holders, the larger for cigarettes & the two smaller for used & unused matches, late 19th-early 20th c., 8" w., 5 1/2" h. (ILLUS.) **78**

Jose Vila Cigars Counter Pad

Counter felt pad, "Jose Vila Havana Cigars," rectangular cloth in bright gold printed in large red letters & centered by an outline-sketched bust of a 17th c. cavalier, unused, minute moth hole, bright colors, 7 1/4 x 11" (ILLUS.) **55**

Dice shaker, "Smoke Banner Cigars," a nickel-plated small metal cylinder holding five miniature bone die & a small round metal token, 3/4 x 1 1/4" **160**

Brass Airedale Matchbox Holder

Matchbox holder, brass, a stylized Art Deco Airedale dog standing on top of rectangular holder w/open sides & ends, 1 5/8 x 2 1/2 x 2 3/4" (ILLUS.) **60**

Merriam & Co. Bulldog Paperweight

Paperweight, "John W. Merriam & Co. Bulldog Segars," cast hollow spelter model of a standing bulldog w/stamped writing on back, small hole in bottom side, 2 x 3 x 4" (ILLUS. of two views) **110**

Admiration Cigars Salt & Pepper

Salt & pepper shakers, "Admiration Cigars," figural porcelain, each molded as the smiling man's rounded face w/a cigar in his mouth, one in white, other in brown, advertising labels on the base, new in the box, 2 1/2 x 2 3/4" (ILLUS. tops & bases)...... **132**

Stickpin, "Rosa Cigars," a cast-metal figural cigar embossed w/the word "Rosa" & painted to resemble a lit cigar, on a long pin, appears unused, ca. 1910-15, 1 1/2" l. **77**

Saboroso Cigar Store Tape Measure

Tape measure, "Saboroso Cigar Store," round celluloid, decorated on one side w/black wording on cream reading "Compliments Saboroso Cigar Store - Chestnut & 4th Sts. - Philadelphia," the other side w/a square logo in blue, white gold & red reading "Smoke Vetterlein Bros. Saboroso Philadelphia Cigars," 1/2 x 1 3/4" (ILLUS. of front & back) **44**

Early Cast-iron Tobacco Cutter

Tobacco cutter, cast iron, long handle on blade mechanism, narrow rectangular base, arched frame cast w/scrolls, base cast w/raised name "Superb," late 19th c., 4 1/4 x 18", 7 1/4" h. (ILLUS.) **60**

TOYS

Home-made Airplane Toy

Airplane, sheet steel, home-made single engine model of the Spirit of St. Louis, later silver & red paint, rubber tires, 22 3/8" l., 7" h. (ILLUS.) **$275**

Marx Steel Auto Service Station Island

Auto service station island, pressed steel, battery-operated, flat curved rectangular base w/tall square gas tank w/light-up globe, tall air pump, flattened oil & grease rack & "In" & "Out" signs, painted red, white, black & yellow, Marx, 3 x 9 1/2", 5 7/8" h. (ILLUS.) **450**

Tootsie Toy Touring Car

Automobile, cast spelter, touring car w/original green paint & metal wheels, Tootsie Toy, 2 1/4" l. (ILLUS.) **45**

Friction-powered Touring Car

Automobile, friction-powered, tin, early open touring car w/a driver, painted in dark green & orange, 4 1/2" l. (ILLUS.) **150**

Art Deco Pressed Steel Auto

Automobile, pressed steel, sleek Art Deco coupe, original orange paint, white vulcanized rubber tires, missing battery-powered headlights, ca. 1930s, 8 3/4" l. (ILLUS.) **195**

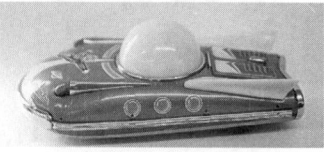

Battery-operated Universe Car

Battery-operated, automobile, stamped steel & plastic, futuristic "Universe Car," space ship design in blue & red w/yellow plastic fins, white light-up dome on top, 5 1/4 x 10", 4" h. (ILLUS.) **225**

"Blushing Frankenstein" Battery Toy

Battery-operated, "Blushing Frankenstein," plastic figure w/shirt & pants, on tin base, Rosko, 1960s, 13" h. (ILLUS.) **175-350**

"Hootin Hollow Haunted House"

Battery-operated, "Hootin Hollow Haunted House," Marx (ILLUS.) **1,540**
Battery-operated, "Mighty King Kong," tin, Marx **200-350**

Battery-operated Stagecoach Toy

Battery-operated, stagecoach & driver, pressed steel, pulled by two brown horses, coach in red w/figures in color, 3 3/4 x 13", 6 1/4" h. (ILLUS.) **250**

Walking Frankenstein Toy

Battery-operated, walking Frankenstein, tin, Marx, 1963, 12 1/2" h. (ILLUS.)... **1,000-1,600**

Marx Battleship Friction Toy

Battleship, friction-operated, tin, painted grey & black w/yellow & red on top, marked "U.S.S. Washington" on stern, Marx, 14 1/2" l. (ILLUS.) **295**

Tootsie Toy Metal Bus

Bus, cast spelter, orange body & silver metal wheels, Tootsie Toy, 3 1/2" l. (ILLUS.) **245**

Spring-loaded Toy Cannon

Cannon, tin, spring-loaded, red barrel w/soldier wearing helmet in red, blue & white, large green wheels, some paint wear, 6 1/2" l. (ILLUS.) **145**

Early Cast-iron Cart & Cow

Cart & cow, cast iron, two-wheeled cart w/open sides painted red & pulled by a silver-painted cow, original paint, 3 1/4 x 6 3/4", 3" h. (ILLUS.) **265**

Early Steel Toy Cash Register

Cash register, pressed steel, black case w/silver keys, marked on bottom "Durable Toy Novelty Co. - New York - Cleveland - Patent Applied For - No. 37," drawer opens & keys work, slight rust, 4 1/2 x 5", 4 3/4" h. (ILLUS.) **27**

Victorian Clockwork Locomotive

Clockwork locomotive, painted tin, early locomotive w/four small pierced front wheels & two large rear wheels, closed cab w/pointed arch windows, bell, smokestack & cowcatcher, worn black, gold & red paint w/faint stenciled "Union" on side, last quarter 19th c. (ILLUS.) **2,475**

Clockwork ocean liner, lithographed tinplate, two funnels, white superstructure, black & red hull, keywind through on funnel, Arnold Co. (Nuremburg, Germany), 13" l. **460**

Sleek Art Deco Toy Coaster Wagon

Coaster wagon, toy-size, pressed steel, sleek Art Deco body w/original worn red paint & decals, marked "Comet," steel handle, black rubber tires, ca. 1930s, 7 1/2" l. (ILLUS.) **55**

Miniature Stamped Tin Combine

Combine, stamped tin, miniature, printed in red & yellow & marked "Co-Op Combine 12" on the side, rubber wheels, 5 1/2" l., 1 3/4" h. (ILLUS.) 115

Fire hook & ladder truck, cast iron, three-horse team & driver, white-painted body w/iron wheels, Wilkins Co., 25" l. (paint wear) 546

Steel Hook & Ladder Fire Truck

Hook & ladder fire truck, pressed steel, red body & steel ladder, small firemen at the sides, removable telescoping ladders, 11 1/2" l. (ILLUS.) 145

Horse & bell toy, tin horse w/original yellow & orange paint, on cast-iron wheels w/hearts, 7" l. (some wear) 275

Model kit, 20 Million Miles to Earth, "Tiny Terrors" Ymir holding Dumbo, Mad Lab, resin kits sculpted by Michael Parks, 1990s-present 20-40

Model kit, 20 Million Miles to Earth, Ymir, resin, Billiken, 1980s 550-650

Aurora Alfred E. Neuman Kit

Model kit, Alfred E. Neuman (MAD Magazine), w/optional signs & arms, Aurora, 1965 (ILLUS.) 75-175

Model kit, Allosaurus, 1/13 scale, Monogram (re-issues from Aurora's Prehistoric Scenes line), 1979 & 1987 25-35

Model kit, Allosaurus, No. 736, 1/13 scale, green & yellow, Aurora, 1971 90-125

Model kit, American Mastodon skeleton, Palmer, plastic kits, late 1950s, 10" h. 20-40

Model kit, Angel Fink, Revell, plastic kits, Custom Monsters Series, designed by Ed "Big Daddy" Roth, 1965 50-175

Model kit, Ankylosaurus, 1/13 scale, Monogram (re-issues from Aurora's Prehistoric Scenes line), 1979 & 1987 20-30

Model kit, Anzio Beach, World War II diorama, 1/8 scale, Aurora, 1968 10-50

Model kit, Apatosaurus, 1/30 scale, Horizon, vinyl kits, 1980s-90s 35-45

Model kit, Armored Dinosaur (Ankylosaurus), No. 744, 1/13 scale, orange, Aurora, 1971 90-125

Model kit, Army Men series, most in green, Marx, paintable plastic figures, 1960s-70s, about 6" h., each 2-4

Model kit, Baragon, vinyl, Billiken, 1980s-present 75-100

Hawk Beach Bunny Catchin' Rays Kit

Model kit, Beach Bunny Catchin' Rays, painted by Evan Stuart, Hawk, Silly Surfers, 1964 (ILLUS.) 35-70

Billiken Beast from 20,000 Fathoms Kit

Model kit, Beast from 20,000 Fathoms, red or green vinyl, Billiken, 1980s (ILLUS.).. 350-500

Model kit, Bert's Bucket, Lindberg, plastic kits - Lindy Loonys, "The Hep Model in the 'Square' Box," 1965 35-80

Aurora Big Horn Sheep Kit

Model kit, big horn sheep, 1/12 scale, Aurora, 1963 (ILLUS.) 25-60

Model kit, Big Wheeler, Lindberg, plastic kits - Lindy Loonys, "The Hep Model in the 'Square' Box," 1965 35-80

Model kit, Bigfoot, 1/7 scale, AMT & AMT/Ertl, plastic kits, 1978 20-45

Model kit, Birthday Bird, Revell, plastic kits, Dr. Seuss Series, 1960 50-175

Model kit, Black Knight of Nurnberg — 1580, 1/8 scale, Aurora, 1956 30-60

Aurora Caballero Kit

Model kit, Caballero, 1/8 scale, Aurora, 1957 (ILLUS.) **35-95**

Marx Campus Cuties Figures

Model kit, Campus Cuties series, fleshtone, Marx, paintable plastic figures, 1960s-70s, 6" h., each (ILLUS. of two) **3-5**

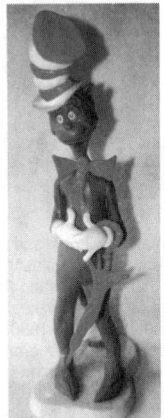

Revell Cat in the Hat Kit

Model kit, Cat in the Hat, Revell, plastic kits, Dr. Seuss Series, 1959 (ILLUS.) **50-150**
Model kit, Cat in the Hat with Thing 1 and Thing 2, Revell, plastic kits, Dr. Seuss Series, 1960 .... **125-300**

Aurora Cro-Magnon Man Kit

Model kit, Cro-Magnon Man, No. 730, 1/13 scale, tan, Aurora, 1971 (ILLUS.) **20-30**

Aurora Cro-Magnon Woman Kit

Model kit, Cro-Magnon Woman, No. 731, 1/13 scale, tan, Aurora, 1971 (ILLUS.) **30-40**
Model kit, Cryptkeeper, w/book, real hair, 1/4 scale, Screamin' Productions, large vinyl kits, 1980s-90s, 14" h. **50-85**

Aurora Customizing Monster Kit

Model kit, Customizing Monster Kit, Aurora, 1964 (ILLUS.) **60-240**
Model kit, Dr. Phibes bust, painted by Joe Fex, maker unknown, resin, small, 1990s .. **50-75**
Model kit, Dr. Seuss Zoo Set, Revell, plastic kits, Dr. Seuss Series, includes Gowdy, Tingo & Norval, 1960, the set ... **250-600**
Model kit, Drag Hag, Hawk, Weird-ohs, designed by Bill Campbell, 1963 .... **40-90**

AMT/Ertl Gigantics Tarantula Kit

Model kit, Gigantics, Mantis, Scorpion or Tarantula Diorams (Fundimensions reissue), 1996, AMT/Ertl (ILLUS. of Tarantula) **8-15**

Aurora Gladiator Kit

Model kit, Gladiator, Adventure series, 1/8 scale, Aurora, 1964 (ILLUS.) **50-120**

Monster Studio Set

Model kit, Monster Studio set, six figures w/paints, Marx molds, by Uncle Milton, Marx, paintable plastic figures, 1991, the set (ILLUS.).. **40-80**

Mad Lab Morlock Kit

Model kit, Morlock, from The Time Machine, "Tiny Terrors," painted by Joe Fex, Mad Lab, resin kits sculpted by Michael Parks, 1990s-present (ILLUS.).................... **15-35**

Model kit, Mother's Worry, Revell, plastic kits, Custom Monsters Series, designed by Ed "Big Daddy" Roth, 1963 .... **30-80**

Model kit, Mr. Gasser, first kit released in Ed Roth series, Revell, plastic kits, Custom Monsters Series, designed by Ed "Big Daddy" Roth, 1963.............................. **50-150**

Model kit, Napoleon, Airfix, plastic kits (Britain/France), 1978 .... **5-10**

Aurora Neanderthal Man Kit

Model kit, Neanderthal Man, No. 729, 1/13 scale, tan, Aurora, 1971 (ILLUS.) **20-30**

Model kit, Night Crawler Wolf Man Car, MPC, plastic kits, 1971 .... **45-125**

Marx Caveman Figure

Model kit, Prehistoric Times series, large cavemen, Marx, paintable plastic figures, 1960s-70s, about 5-6" h., each (ILLUS.)..... **5-10**

Model kit, Protoceratops, 1/8 scale, Pyro, plastic kits, late 1950s-late 1960s.............. **20-40**

Model kit, Pteranodon, Monogram (re-issues from Aurora's Prehistoric Scenes line),1987.. **30-40**

Model kit, Quick Snap Dinos, tiny 1/100 versions of Aurora kits, Revell, plastic kits, 1994, each.. **4-8**

Model kit, Rat Fink, Revell, plastic kits, Custom Monsters Series, designed by Ed "Big Daddy" Roth, 1963...................... **60-140**

Model kit, Rat Patrol, 1/87 scale, Aurora, 1967.. **20-70**

Aurora Red Knight of Vienna Kit

Model kit, Red Knight of Vienna (The), 1/8
scale, Aurora, 1957 (ILLUS.) **30-60**

Revell/Monogram Kothoga Monster Kit

Model kit, Relic, Kothoga monster from the
film, limited edition of 5,000, vinyl, Rev-
ell/Monogram, plastic kits, 1997 (ILLUS.).. **20-35**
Model kit, Road Hog, Lindberg, plastic kits,
Lindy Loonys, "The Hep Model in the
'Square' Box," 1965 .... **35-80**

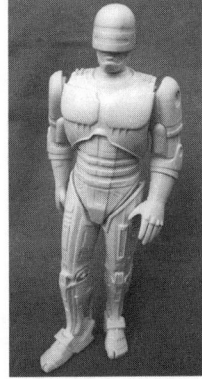

Horizon Robocop 3 Figure

Model kit, Robocop 3, 1/6 scale, Horizon,
vinyl kits, 1989 (ILLUS. of figure) **25-45**

Aurora Humorous Vampire Kit

Model kit, Vampire, humorous design by
William Castle, painted by Evan Stuart,
Aurora, 1966 (ILLUS.) **50-150**

Aurora Vampirella Kit

Model kit, Vampirella, w/optional poses,
Monster Scenes series, painted by Evan
Stuart, Aurora, 1971 (ILLUS.).................... **75-200**
Model kit, Velociraptor pack, six different,
1 1/2 to 2", Tamiya, plastic kits (Japa-
nese), 1994 .... **15-25**
Model kit, Vincent Price bust on pedestal,
by Steve West, resin, 1990s **65-75**

Aurora Woolly Mammoth Kit

Model kit, Woolly Mammoth, No. 743, 1/13
scale, green & cream, painted by Evan
Stuart, Aurora, 1971, 18" l. (ILLUS.) **90-125**
Model kit, Yeti, half human adult w/optional
bodies, 1/8 scale, factory paint, limited
edition, X-Plus, 1988 .... **150-200**
Model kit, Yeti, half human child
w/rabbit, 1/8 scale, factory paint, limited
edition, X-Plus, 1988 .... **75-100**

Military Police Motorcycle Toy

Motorcycle, friction-powered, pressed tin, marked "Military Police," in red, blue, white & yellow, rubber wheels, probably made in Japan, 3 1/2" l. (ILLUS.) **85**

U.S. Zone Germany Motorcycle Toy

Motorcycle, pressed steel, key-wind, woman stunt rider in grey, brown & tan on a red motorcycle, goes in circles & tilts back & forth, marked "Made in U.S. Zone Germany - Patent Applied For," 7" l. (ILLUS.) **295**

Motorcycle & Rider

Motorcycle, w/rider, battery-operated, tin, Modern Toys, 12" l. (ILLUS.) **770**

Early Elephant Penny Toy

Penny toy, elephant w/rider on rectangular platform w/wheels, stamped tin w/old worn red & yellow paint, flywheel-powered, 3 x 4 3/4" (ILLUS.) **295**

Penny Toy Touring Car

Penny toy, touring car, tin w/metal wheels, painted yellow & black w/white wheels, missing driver & steering wheel, 1 3/4 x 3 3/8" (ILLUS.) **195**

Playset, American Airlines International Jet Port Marx, No. 4810, 1962 .... **125-400**

Army Training Center Headquarters

Playset, Army Training Center, Marx, No. 4102, 1955 (ILLUS. of one building) **150-450**

Playset, Bar-M Ranch, Marx, No. 3956 .... **75-250**

Playset, Battle of Iwo Jima, Marx, No. 4147, 1964 .... **100-500**

Playset, Battle of the Blue and Gray, Deluxe Civil War Centennial Edition, Marx, No. 4744, 1963 .... **300-1,250**

Playset, Battle of the Little Big Horn, Marx, No. 4679, 1962 .... **150-350**

Playset, Ben Hur, based on the movie, Marx, No. 4696, 1959 .... **200-750**

Playset, Big Top Circus, Marx, No. 4310, 1952 .... **100-600**

Playset, Boys Camp, Marx, No. 4103, 1956.... **150-700**

Playset, Cattle Drive, Marx, No. 3983, 1970 .... **75-300**

Playset, D.E.W. (Distant Early Warning) Line Set, Marx, No. 4802, w/atomic bomb rack, 1958 .... **300-900**

Playset, Desert Fox, Marx, No. 4177, 1966 .... **125-500**

Playset, Dollhouse w/bomb shelter inside, Marx, 1958-59 .... **75-150**

Playset, Fort Pitt, Marx, No. 3741, 1959 ...... **90-400**

Playset, Fort York, Canada, Marx, No. 3640, 1958-59, sold only in Canada **1,000-1,500**

Playset, Freight Terminal, Marx, No. 5220, 1955 .... **90-200**

Playset, Knights and Vikings, Marx, No. 4743, 1970 .... **75-250**

Lazy-Day Farm Set

Playset, Lazy-Day Farm, Marx, No. 3948, 1950s (ILLUS.) **100-425**

Playset, Little Red School House, Marx, No. 3381, 1956 .... **100-450**

Playset, Navarone Mountain Battleground, Marx, No. 3412, 1976 .... **30-150**

Playset, Pet Shop, Marx, No. 4210, 1953 ... **50-300**

Playset, Sears Store, Marx, No. 5490,
1961 .... **400-1,900**
Playset, Service Station, Marx, No. 3495 .... **30-100**
Playset, Strategic Air Command, Marx, No.
6013, 1960.. **225-800**
Playset, Ward's Service Station, Marx, No.
3488, 1959.. **100-500**
Pull toy, buckboard & horse, steel, yellow
wheels & horse frame, 19th c., 28" l. **259**

Steel Butterfly Pull Toy

Pull toy, butterfly, steel, printed design on
embossed body & wings, butterfly flaps
wings when pulled, handle & antennae
missing, 5" w., 9" l. (ILLUS.) **55**
Pull toy, cow on wheels, brown felt-covered
body w/glass eyes, black-painted nostrils
& mouth, fur tip on tail, wooden hooves
attached to tin wheels, early 20th c.,
11 1/2" l., 8 1/2" h. **230**

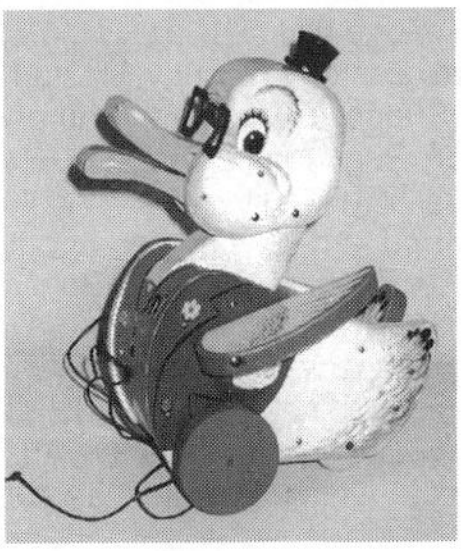

"Dr. Doodle" Pull Toy

Pull toy, "Dr. Doodle," Fisher-Price #132,
1957 (ILLUS.) **143**

Kiddies Play Pump

Pump, "Kiddies Play Pump," tin w/two small
tin buckets, decorated w/children wearing fire hats, Ohio Art No. 262, 1950s, to-
gether w/original box (ILLUS.) **143**

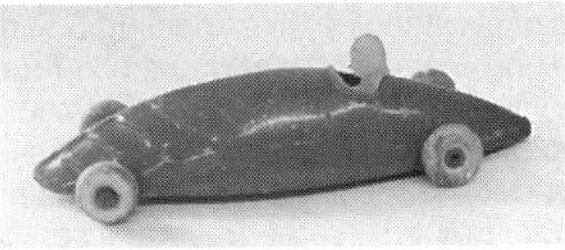

Bullet-shaped Art Deco Racer

Race car, cast spelter, spring-powered,
sleak bullet-shaped Art Deco body, silhouetted driver, vulcanized white rubber
tires, ca. 1930s, 7 1/4" l. (ILLUS.).................. **145**

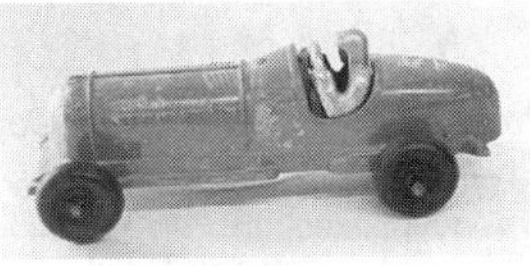

Kiddie Toy Race Car

Race car, cast spelter w/cast-iron driver,
sleak green-painted body w/silver driver
& black rubber tires, Kiddie Toy, worn
paint, 7" l. (ILLUS.)... **60**

"Atom Jet" Racer

Racing car, "Atom Jet" (ILLUS.)..................... **1,320**

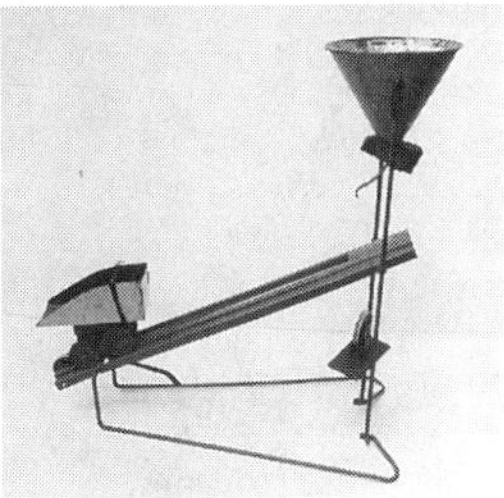

Early Steel Sand Toy

Sand toy, steel, "Sandy Andy," composed
of a funnel & wheeled cart on slanted
stand, Wolverine Supply and Manufacturing Company, Pittsburgh, ca. 1910,
6 1/2 x 13", 13 1/2" h. (ILLUS.) **115**

Toy-size Cast-iron Scales

Scales, cast iron, original worn red paint,
w/holders for weights, No. 244, weights
missing, 3 1/4" x 5 1/2", 3 1/4" h. (ILLUS.)........ **20**

Friction-type School Bus Toy

School bus, friction-type, pressed steel,
yellow w/red trim, rubber wheels, 7" l.
(ILLUS.).. **125**

Pressed Steel Yellow Taxi Cab

Taxi cab, pressed steel, friction-powered, yellow body marked on side "Yellow Cab," panel on truck readers "Stop - Go," black rubber tires, 6 3/4" l. (ILLUS.)................. **25**

Cracker Jack Prize Toy Top

Top, miniature, tin, Cracker Jack prize, advertising on the top, in red, white & blue w/wooden peg handle,1 3/8" d. (ILLUS.) **29**

Toy soldier, Auburn, hard rubber, soldier w/bugle, 1930s... **5-10**

Barclay Anti-aircraft Gunner

Toy soldier, Barclay, cast-metal, anti-aircraft gunner, 1930s (ILLUS.) **10-18**

Toy soldier, Barclay, cast-metal, cannon, 1930s, 3" l. (ILLUS.right, w/motor unit vehicle) **10-15**

Barclay Motor Unit Vehicle & Cannon

Toy soldier, Barclay, cast-metal, Motor Unit Vehicle, 1930s, 3" l. (ILLUS. left, w/cannon)... **10-15**

Toy soldier, Barclay, cast-metal, soldier w/dog, 1930s... **40-60**

Toy soldier, Barclay, cast-metal, soldier w/range finder, early version w/helmet attached w/a pin, 1930s................................. **10-18**

Toy soldier, Britains, cast-metal, 25-pound howitzer cannon, 1950s............................. **35-60**

Toy soldier, Britains, cast-metal, sound locator & operator, 1930s-40s **50-100**

Toy soldier, Comet of England, World War II soldier crawling.. **8-15**

Toy soldier, Courtenay-Greenhill, Jean, Sieur De L'Isle, position Z-17, reeling from blow to head, mace fallen from right hand, signed Peter & Gilly Greenhill **425**

Toy soldier, Courtenay-Greenhill, Joan of Arc, bareheaded, in full armor, mounted on white horse under whose belly is inscribed "La Pucelle" ("The Maid") & carrying her personally designed three-tailed banner **700**

Toy soldier, Courtenay-Greenhill, John De Weston, position 7, advancing w/sword in right hand, signed Peter Greenhill **325**

Toy soldier, Courtenay-Greenhill, Sir Walter Woodland, Banner Bearer of the Black Prince, position Z-5, sword in right hand, banner in left, movable visor, signed Peter Greenhill **650**

Toy soldier, Elastolin, cast-metal, figure of Hitler, 1930s... **150-300**

Toy soldier, Elastolin, cast-metal, German soldier kneeling firing rifle, 1930s, 2 3/4" h. **35-60**

Toy soldier, Tradition, Potsdamer Grenadiers, 1750, elite guard to King Frederick, studio-painted, 90mm, pr., a few chips **200**

Toy soldiers, Auburn, soldiers, vehicle, truck & tank, 1950s, boxed sets, each....... **10-20**

Toy soldiers, Authenticast, Set No. 541, Scottish Infantry, 1914, standing in khaki service dress, pith helmets & kilts, w/standing officer holding binoculars & pointing, original box, set of 7 (some chips, tip of one rifle missing)....................... **130**

Toy soldiers, Baston & Trophy, Baston Set No. A-5, Sudan & Boer War Campaign, The Suffolk Regiment, in action in foreign service dress, 1900, standing firing, loading & at port arms, w/bugler & officer, original box; Trophy, Sudan & Boer War Campaign, Naval Landing Party Sailors, standing at ease w/Gatling gun, in wrong Trophy box, both sets **170**

Toy soldiers, Britains, cast-metal, Australian's Battle Dress World War II set, 1950s.. **130-150**

Toy soldiers, Britains, Display Set No. 55F, Animals & Trees, Farm Series, comprised of stable boy, dog, large tree, shire horse, cart horse, foal, colt, light horse & small trees, original display box w/color-illustrated lid, set of 10 (chips, slight damage to base of large tree, box fraying, glue repairs) **250**

Toy soldiers, Britains, Set No. 109, Royal Dublin Fusiliers, marching at the trail in khaki service dress & pith helmets, ca. 1910, original printer's box w/regimental battle honors, set of 8, some chips, glue repairs to box lid **650**

Toy soldiers, Britains, Set No. 10W, British Infantry of the Line, "W" Series, small scale, marching at the slope in review order, ca. 1925, original box, set of 6.............. **90**

TToy soldiers, Britains, Set No. 1325, The Gordon Highlanders Firing from Three Positions, in tropical service dress, comprised of six standing, five kneeling & five lying firing, variation from usual six, four & six, ca. 1940, original display box w/"Types of the British Army" black & silver Art Deco label, set of 16 (some chips, crease in box tray, some fraying to lid) **600**

Toy soldiers, Britains, Set No. 133, Russian Infantry, pre-war, marching at the trail in green uniforms, blanket rolls & flat top caps, w/officer holding sword, ca. 1935, original "United Sates of Soviet Russia" Whisstock box, set of 8, a few chips **550**

Toy soldiers, Britains, Set No. 1349, The Royal Canadian Mounted Police, mounted at the gallop in summer dress, w/officer, original box, set of 5 (some chips, box has some fraying) **200**

Toy soldiers, Britains, Set No. 136, Imperial Russian Cossacks, mounted at the gallop w/lances & slung rifles, w/officer holding sword, three black & one brown horse instead of usual two & two, original box, set of 5 .... **130**

Toy soldiers, Britains, Set No. 1620, Royal Marine Light Infantry, marching at the slope in review order w/officer, issued only 1938-41, original "Types of the Royal Navy" box, rare, set of 8, a few chips **700**

Toy soldiers, Britains, Set No. 1723, Royal Army Medical Corps Unit in Battledress, comprised of stretcher bearers w/stretchers & wounded man & nurses, original box, set of 9 (noticeable chips, tie-in card not original) **90**

Toy soldiers, Britains, Set No. 17F, Farm Display, pre-war, Farm Series, comprised of bull, pigs, piglets, donkey, goat, drover & boy w/stick, ca. 1930, original box, set of 13 (noticeable chips on several farm animals, glue repairs on box, dirt & water stains) **160**

Toy soldiers, Britains, Set No. 1893, Indian Army Service Corps, marching at the trail in khaki service dress & turbans, w/mule, mule handler & British officer in battledress, original box, set of 7 (chips, dirt stains on box lid, tie-in card not original) **200**

Toy soldiers, Britains, Set No. 216, Argentine Infantry, marching at the slope in review order, issued post-war only 1946-1949, ca. 1946, original "Types of the Argentine Army" printer's box, set of 8 (chips, noticeable on one soldier's face) **250**

Toy soldiers, Britains, Set No. 225, The King's African Rifles, marching at the slope in khaki service dress & red fezes, set of 8 (a few chips) **120**

Toy soldiers, Britains, Set No. 26, Boer Infantry, marching at the slope in khaki uniforms & black Montana hats, first version, oval bases, w/officer, rare, ca. 1900, original printer's box, set of 8, some chips **1,700**

Toy soldiers, Britains, Set No. 28, Royal Artillery Mountain Gun, comprised of six marching gunners, four mules carrying parts of howitzer & mounted officer, original box, set of 12 (chips, one gunner's face retouched, box lid stained & has glue repairs, tie-in card not original) **150**

Toy soldiers, Britains, Set No. 33, 16th/5th Lancers, mounted at the halt in review order, w/officer turned in the saddle, original illustrated box, set of 5 (some chips mainly on horses' legs) **170**

Toy soldiers, Grey Iron, cast-metal, soldier w/radio & aerial, 1930s, the set **100-250**

Toy soldiers, Heinrich?, British Camel Corps/Sudan Campaign, comprising 11

troopers w/sabers & a bugler in red tunics & white pith helmets mounted on camels, German-made, small scale/25mm, original box, set of 12 (chips & some wear on troopers, side & end panels missing on box) **100**

"French Infantry Marching No. 177"

Toy soldiers, Heyde Miniatures, cast-metal, "French Infantry Marching No. 177," comprising general, officer, standard bearer, drummer & 41 infantrymen, in maker's box, Heyde (box taped, lid incomplete); a partial set of the same comprising general, two officers, standard bearer, drummer & 18 infantrymen & 16 mounted French cavalry (possibly not Heyde), comprising general, two officers, bugler & 12 cavalrymen (ILLUS.) **1,035**

Toy soldiers, Imperial, Set No. 6, Auckland Rifle Volunteers, standing firing in green uniforms & caps, w/bugler, set of 6 .... **100**

Toy soldiers, Imperial, Set No. 7, South Australian Scottish Infantry, 1903, marching at the slope in scarlet tunics, Gordon tartan kilts & white pith helmets, w/officer, set of 6 .... **100**

Toy soldiers, Imperial, Set No. 9, 3rd Battalion Victorian Infantry Brigade/Boer War Period, 1899, attaching w/fixed bayonets in khaki uniforms & spiked pith helmets, w/officer pointing sword, set of 6 .... **100**

Toy soldiers, London Toys of Canada, cast-metal, soldier, two cannons & a Hurricane aircraft, 1939, boxed set **100-200**

Toy soldiers, Mignot, Ancient Egyptian War Chariot, comprised of chariot drawn by two-horse team, w/driver, original plain cardboard box, as issued by factory, reinforcement to yoke to prevent sagging, set of 5 .... **225**

Toy soldiers, Mignot, Band of the French Alpine Chasseurs, 1890-1914, marching in summer white uniforms w/full instrumentation & band director, original box, set of 12 .... **375**

Toy soldiers, Mignot, French Army Staff Car, World War I, 195, comprised of staff car w/driver & two officer passengers including one reading map, in horizon blue uniforms, original box, set of 4 .... **325**

Toy soldiers, Mignot, French Army Work Party/Corvees, 1914, comprised of soldiers in fatigue uniforms w/various implements & carrying sacks, bundle of straw

& mess tins, ca. 1950, original box, set of 12, a few chips, end splits in box lid **325**

Toy soldiers, Mignot, French Napoleonic Valaisan Battalion, 1810, marching at the slope in red & white uniforms & plumed shakos, w/officer, drummer & standard bearer, original box, set of 12 .... **325**

Toy soldiers, Mignot, French Turcos, 1890-1910, assaulting w/fixed bayonets in light blue uniforms trimmed in yellow & turbans, w/officer, bugler & standard bearer, original box, set of 12 (a few chips, water stains on box & fraying on lid)............ **180**

Toy soldiers, Mignot, Italian Light Infantry, 1810, marching at the slope in green uniforms faced in blue & plumed shakos, w/officer, drummer & standard bearer, original box, set of 12 .... **275**

Toy soldiers, Stadden, various military units, comprised of a French Napoleonic drum major of the Imperial Guard, 1812; Austrian Cuirassier, 1915; Prussian Chasseur, 1813; soldier of Congress's Own Canadian Regiment, 1777; trooper of the 9th Queen's Royal Lancers, 1890; studio-painted, 54mm, set of 5, a few chips **350**

Toy soldiers, The Soldier Shop, Indian & Sudan Campaigns, Connoisseur figures of British Military Units, comprised of officer & enlisted men of the Gordon & Seaforth Highlanders, Northwest Frontier, 1898, professionally painted by Kurt Stackhouse; & an officer & troops of the 21st Lancers, Sudan, 1898, professionally painted by G. Wilson; all mounted on wooden bases, 54 mm, set of 5 .... **250**

Early Cast-Iron Tractor Toy

Tractor, cast iron, red chassis & driver, large green painted wheels, 5 3/4" l. (ILLUS.).. **190**

Cast-iron Toy Tractor

Tractor, cast iron, red painted body & driver, silver wheels & front-end loader, marked "Patent Applied For," 3 1/4" l. (ILLUS.).. **155**

Train engine & tender, Lionel O-gauge, steam engine NO. 224 & tender 2466W, in boxes, 2 pcs.. **115**

Train set: Lionel Standard gauge, electric engine No. 8E, Pullman car No. 309, Mail car No. 310 & Observation cars No. 312; in brown & tan, the set **403**

Mack Hollywood Film Ad Truck

Truck, B Mack Hollywood film ad, six-wheels, red, Smith Miller (ILLUS.).............. **1,843**

Arcade Heinz Delivery Truck

Truck, cast iron, delivery truck, silvered railing on open bed, red body w/white vulcanized rubber tires, Heinz company logo on railing, marked "82274 - Made in USA," original paint, Arcade, 4 7/8" l. (ILLUS.).. **350**

Arcade Cast-iron Ice Truck

Truck, cast iron, open bed embossed "Ice," original worn red paint, white rubber tires, Arcade, 6 3/4" l. (ILLUS.) **425**

Barclay Beer Delivery Truck

Truck, cast spelter, beer delivery truck, high open bed embossed "Beer," cab w/open windows, white vulcanized rubber tires, Barclay, worn paint, 3 7/8" l. (ILLUS.)............. **55**

Truck, delivery truck, pressed steel, green w/high back sides printed w/color advertising for "Curtiss Baby Ruth Candy" above "Railway Express Agency," Buddy L, 22" l. **575**

Truck, pick-up, cast iron, Model A Ford, red w/nickeled metal wheels, Arcade, 8 1/4" l. **230**

Courtland Ice Cream Delivery Truck

Truck, pressed steel, ice cream delivery-type w/open bed & closed cab, white, red & black body w/"Ice Cream" in red, yellow interior to bed, black rubber wheels, Courtland, near mint, 8 5/8" l. (ILLUS.)......... **125**

Midgetoy Boxed Vehicle Set

Vehicle set, cast spelter, includes two tanks, military truck & assault craft, two trailers, two jets, emergency car, tanker truck, Jeep, space ship, pick-up truck, futuristic car & convertible car, Midgetoy, new in box, box 10 x 14" (ILLUS.) **275**

Windup Bunny on Tricycle

Windup celluloid & tin bunny on tricycle, white rabbit w/red coat on red & blue tricycle w/domed bell on back, Japan, 4 3/4" h. (ILLUS.) **95**

Windup Tin Model T Touring Car

Windup tin automobile, Ford Model T 1915 rag-top touring car, red & black, Banda Baby, Japan, 1950s, some wear & minor rust, 7 1/2" l. (ILLUS.) **195**

Sleek Marx Windup Automobile

Windup tin automobile, long sleek red body w/looped metal front & rear bumpers, Marx, 1930s (ILLUS.) **500**

Windup Tin Dog Jumping Rope

Windup tin dog, jumps robe, tan dog wearing blue shorts & black & yellow striped shirt, marked "Made in Japan" w/patent number, 5 1/2" h. (ILLUS.) **65**

"Fishing Monkey on Whales"

Windup tin "Fishing Monkey on Whales," TPS (ILLUS.) **440**

Early Jazzbo Jim Windup Tin Toy

Windup tin "Jazzbo Jim," stereotypical black man wearing gaudy red, blue, black & white suit & cap standing on a plain red roof of a cabin decorated w/scenes of blacks against a yellow ground, marked "Jazzbo Jim - The Dancer on the Roof - Patented October 21, 1921 - Copyrighted," excellent condition, 3 1/2 x 5 1/2", 10" h. (ILLUS.) **850**

Marx Motorcycle Cop Windup Variation

Windup tin motorcycle, police officer in white & red uniform on a yellow cycle, black & white windup button on side, L. Marx, ca. 1930s (ILLUS.) **220**

Windup Tin Pelican Toy

Windup tin pelican, hopping action, painted blue, white, red, yellow & tan, key in back, J. Chein & Co., 5" h. (ILLUS.) **50**

Windup Tin Steam Roller

Windup tin steam roller, chrome-plated, ca. 1930s, 5 x 11", 7 1/2" h. (ILLUS.) **795**

Windup Tin Zilotone Toy

Windup tin Zilotone, clown standing on mechanism playing curved xylophone keyboard, w/seven metal disks, Wolverine, 1930s (ILLUS.) **413**

Early Cast-iron Zeppelin Toy

Zeppelin, cast iron, bullet-shaped body on metal wheels, worn original orange paint, minor damage on underside, 6" l. (ILLUS.) **75**

TRADE CARDS

For a picture of life in the 19th century, there is nothing better than Victorian trade cards. From fashions to medicine, cleaning products to pianos, animals to tobacco ... it's all there plus much more. Brought to you in vivid colors, trade cards fall into many collectible categories. This makes them some of the most searched for paper items in the antiques world. Values given are only for cards in very fine condition. Cards with major flaws such as torn corners will only bring one third or less of the listed price.

Acorn Stoves and Ranges, die-cut acorn w/range illustration **$18**

Austen's Forest Flower Cologne

Austen's Forest Flower Cologne, cherub w/flowers.. **8**

Ayer's Cherry Pectoral

Ayer's Cherry Pectoral, little girls w/medicine bottle (ILLUS.) **15**

Ayer's Sarsaparilla

Ayer's Sarsaparilla, women & children (ILLUS.)... **8**

Besse Baker Co.

Besse Baker Co., Clothiers-Hatters-Furnishers, Spring of 1895 fashions, featuring children (ILLUS.) 5

Boston Baked Beans, Uncle Sam feeding Indian.. 50

Candy, "Heide's Licorice Pastilles - Mint - and Assorted JuJubes - Are The Best - 5¢ Boxed," a color scene of a cute young boy holding up packages of the candy w/an open crate behind him, printed across the top "Pan American Exposition - This pretty little boy insists that...," w/further advertising down the side & at the bottom, a Sarah Bernhardt testimonial on the reverse, 1901, bright colors, 3 1/2 x 5 1/2" 77

Chase & Sanborn's Coffee, die-cut folder of tea cup, Columbian Exposition, 1893 20

Coon Skin Cigars Trade Card

Cigars, "I Toot My Horn - For de - Coon Skin Cigars," rectangular, a grotesque color caricature of a black musician playing a long slender horn, ca. 1880s, 1 3/4 x 3 1/2" (ILLUS.) 44

Cigar Trade Card with Bathing Beauty

Cigars, "T.R. Keating Cigars," die-cut cardboard, cut to resemble an open seashell w/a colorful bathing beauty in the lower half & advertising in the upper half, 4 1/4 x 6" (ILLUS.).. 149

Colgate & Co., soap, newsboy rests in alley........ 15

Columbus Buggy Co., die-cut............................. 30

Corset Clasps, celluloid 25

Davis Sewing Machine, angel over sewing machine 15

DeLaval Separator, die-cut woman & cow 50

Die-cut, boot stock card in shape of woman's high-top shoe... 15

Dr. Jayne's Expectorant

Dr. Jayne's Expectorant, "The Gipsy Fortune Teller," the 18th card in series (ILLUS.)... 18

Dr. Morse's Indian Root Pills, 1883 calendar... 35

Dr. Thomas' Electric Oil

Dr. Thomas' Electric Oil (ILLUS.)....................... 10

Edwin Burt Fine Shoes, man in lady's shoe holding American flag 6

Elf & pansy, stock card 15

Globe Evaporated Milk Trade Card

Evaporated milk, "Globe Evaporated Milk," color image of a young boy dressed as Uncle Sam & standing on a can of the product holding out a white banner, black & red wording, reads at top "I Am the Weather Man - Watch My Flag" above lists of colors & the weather they predict, at center left is "Globe Label Indicates - Highest Quality - Absolute Purity - Perfect Sterlization - Perfection in Canned Milk," further advertising at bottom, 3 1/2 x 6" (ILLUS.) 44

Fairbank Corned Beef, Lion Brand, lion in derby 40

Fan Shaped Die-Cut

Fan shaped, die-cut, A. Stowell & Co., Rich Clocks, Bronzes, Fancy Goods on back, dated 1874 (ILLUS.) 8

Fisk, Clark & Flaggs Gloves, two gentlemen, gold background 8

Five Puppies

Five puppies, one food dish, "Where is Mother," on back "Beautiful Pictures given away free with 10 Paper Rags of the Celebrated 'Newsboy' Plug Tobacco," copyright 1892 (ILLUS.) 7

Four-In-Hand Coach, Studebaker Bros. Mfg. Co., large size 65

Genuine Frank Coffee, elves on coffee grinder, Germany 30

Gold Dust Washing Powder, die-cut, showing the Gold Dust Twins in washtub 40

Great Atlantic & Pacific Tea Co., die-cut teacup & saucer 12

Great Atlantic & Pacific Tea Co., ice fishing scene, big fish, many men 25

Griffin & Skelley Co. Raisin Packers, California 60

Gum, "Beeman's Pepsin Chewing Gum," color image of a young girl dressed as an elderly lady w/bonnet & holding knitting

Beeman's Gum Trade Card

seated on a package of gum, titled at bottom "Playing Grandma," 3 1/2 x 5 1/2" (ILLUS.) 33

Harry Clinton Tobacco Dealer, children holding long cigar, man smoking 12

Heinz Apple Butter, die-cut pickle 35

Henderson's School Shoes

Henderson's School Shoes, school scene (ILLUS.) 20

Hold Fast Tobacco, 3-fold metamorphic, dog bites thief on ankle 40

Huyler's Cocoa, die-cut, cocoa bean shape 12

J.&P. Coats

J.&P. Coats, man & woman fishing, thread boxes, 1880 calendar on back (ILLUS.) 15

J.&P. Coats

J.&P. Coats, "We Never Fade," black boy
riding spool of thread (ILLUS.)........................... 12

James C. Davis & Son Soap Makers

James C. Davis & Son Soap Makers, Boston, Pure Coin (ILLUS.) 4

Jas. S. Kirk & Co. Soap Makers

Jas. S. Kirk & Co. Soap Makers, "Columbia" (ILLUS.) 10
"Jolly Nigger," toy savings bank 700

Jordan Marsh & Co.

Jordan Marsh & Co., Boston................................ 25
Kendall's French Laundry Soap, die-cut
frog on rock w/"Clean Up" written on
throat.. 20
Kerr's Thread, New York Stock Exchange 25

Large Clark & Morgan Candies

Large Clark & Morgan Candies, little girl
holding basket & flowers (ILLUS.) 5
Lion Coffee, die-cut of Mother Goose................. 15

Lydia Pinkham's Vegetable Compound

Lydia Pinkham's Vegetable Compound,
country snow scene (ILLUS.) 5
Mallory Line, rates for shipping oranges............ 45

Colorful Horlick's Trade Card

Malted milk, "Horlick's Malted Milk," die-cut
stand-up type w/a full color image of a
milkmaid holding a package of the
product & standing beside a cow, 4 x 5"
(ILLUS.)... 77
Mapl-Flake, "Um-Um, but it's good!" 20

Marks Adjustable Chair

Merrick Thread Co.

Mrs. Winslow's Soothing Syrup

Pearline

Pears Transparent Soap

Santa & Christmas Tree Image

Miller's Crown Dressing Trade Card

Shoe polish, "Frank Miller's Crown Dressing for Ladies & Children's Shoes - Will Not Injure the Finest Leather," die-cut cardboard model of a lady's shoe w/lady & children inside, near mint, 5 x 7 1/2" (ILLUS.) 55

Babbitts Soap Powder Trade Card

Soap powder, "Babbitts Soap Powder," color scene of Uncle Sam with two bearded men putting bags of gold on a large balance scale w/a large box of the product on the other scale pan, nice landscape background, great color, 4 x 5 1/2" (ILLUS.) 121

Soft drink, "Hires Rootbeer (sic)," rectangular color bust portrait of a pretty blonde late Victorian lady w/a pink rose in her hair & holding a bouquet of pink & red roses all against a pale blue ground, black wording reads "Put Roses in Your Cheeks - Drink Hires Rootbeer," 3 x 5" (minor edge & corner wear, slightly warped) 33

Solar Tip Shoes, wise man, foolish man story 15

Story & Clark Organ, "The First Lesson," mom holds child on stool while father watches 15

Ten's Oyster House & Dining Room

Ten's Oyster House & Dining Room w/Bowling Alley, stock card, featuring a scantily clad Carrie Perkins (ILLUS.) 6

The Renowned Two Headed Lady, 8th Wonder of the World, Millie Christine 100

Thompson's Eye Water, large eye w/lady inside 15

Tobacco, "Day & Night Tobacco," risque color cartoon of a young woman w/her long dress caught on a rail fence & an elderly farmer on the other side of the fence unhooking the skirt & peeking underneath, advertising on the rails of the fence, 3 1/2 x 5 3/4" 83

Tobacco, "Lorillard's '49' Cut Plug," a color scene of early gold miners sluicing, pro-

duced in San Francisco, bright colors, 3 1/4 x 4 1/2" 253

Trick dog bank, clown holds hoop, barrel, dog 6,000

Victorian bedroom & parlor, stock card 35

White Sewing Machines

White Sewing Machines, Medieval couple carving on tree (ILLUS.) 5

Willimantic Thread "Jumbo Must Go," featuring Jumbo the elephant 20

Woolson Spice, Lion Coffee, Cinderella w/story on back side 20

TRAVEL MAPS

Alabama, issued by the state, Governor George Wallace & wife Lureen on the front, 1967 .... $8

Arkansas, Conoco Gasoline, Continental soldier logo & views of gas stations, 1920s.. 25

Caverns of Luray, Virginia Booklet

Caverns of Luray, Virginia, "The Beautiful Caverns of Luray, Virginia - Souvenir Booklet," features Virginia in the Shenandoah Valley, back notes distances to other points on the East Coast, in mailer, 1939, 5 x 7 1/2" (ILLUS.) 25

Colorado, Conoco Gasoline, Continental soldier logo, view of gas station w/car & factories & oil derricks, 1920s 25

Shell Expo 67 Road & Fair Map

Expo 67, Shell map of the 1967 World's Fair in Montreal, Quebec, multi-colored w/some displays of the fair on the front, bilingual text, road map of area & the Expo grounds, 1967, 3 1/2 x 6 1/2" (ILLUS.) **3**

Gilmore Oil Company of California, each map features the Gilmore red lion logo, covered the states of California, Washington & Oregon, rare, 1930s, each **75**

Illinois, plain color, issued by the Division of Highways, front featured a bust of Lincoln, notes Henry Horner as Governor, 1939 .... **25**

Map of Korea & Japan

Korea - Japan, issued by the Department of the Army - Military Sea Transportation Service (MSTS), blue & white photo of Liberty Ship on the front, back w/history of the MSTS, 1949, 4 1/4 x 6" (ILLUS.) **12**

Chevron Map of Maine

Maine, Chevron Gasoline, color cartoon cover of station attendant & man in car, early 1960s, 4 1/2 x 9" (ILLUS.) **4**

Wartime Map of the World

Map of the World, "Follow the War with Hagstrom's Map of The World - and Detail Maps of Europe, Mediterranean, North Africa, Pacific, Aleutians," color front images of various tanks, ships & planes, information on bombing ranges & main routes, also an ad for buying War Bonds, 1943, 8 x 10" (ILLUS.) **35**

Michigan to Walt Disney World Map

Michigan (and Chicago Area) to Walt Disney World on Interstate 75, Gulf Gasoline, map features Gulf service centers along the route, picture of Walt Disney World on the front, descriptions of each section of the park inside, 1972, 3 1/2 x 7" (ILLUS.) **15**

Map of Montreal from Eaton's

Montreal, "Eaton's of Canada welcomes you to Montreal," color photo of the city from Mt. Royal, city map inside also includes directory of Eaton's, formerly Canada's largest retailer, now out of business, back text in French, 1950s, 3 1/2 x 8 1/2" (ILLUS.) **10**

Natural Bridge of Virginia - U.S. 11 Map

Natural Bridge of Virginia - U.S. 11, cover w/black & white photo of the Natural Bridge, background in pale green & white, notes "Hotel and Cottages - Accommodations for Every Class of Tourist," 1939, 4 x 9" (ILLUS.) **20**

New Jersey Bicentennial Map

New Jersey, 1776-1976 Official Bicentennial Map & Guide, front w/color scenes of the Revolutionary War, includes a chart of 200 years of New Jersey history, 4 1/2 x 9" (ILLUS.) **5**

New Jersey, Esso Gasoline, cover features scene of family in a convertible, station attendant wiping the windshield, back w/ad for Esso credit card, 1970, 4 x 8 1/2" **2**

New Jersey Turnpike, printed on a 6 1/2" tall glass drinking tumbler w/the map running the length of the side, blue & orange, sold in restaurant shops along the Turnpike, 1950s **20**

Texaco New York State Map

New York - Host State for the World's Fair, Texaco, front w/colorful painted scene of the fair, ad & Texaco logo at the bottom, promotion of Texaco exhibit at the fair on the back & ad for applying for a Texaco credit card, 1964-65 (ILLUS.)........... **10**

New York Thruway Map

New York Thruway, color aerial view of a section of the highway along the Hudson River, back features a welcome from Governor Nelson Rockefeller, 12th edition, 4 1/2 x 9" (ILLUS.) **2**

New York World's Fair & City Map

New York World's Fair and Metropolitan New York City, Atlantic-Imperial Gasoline, cover in color w/logo & auto at gas station, inside is a full map of the 1964-65 New York World's Fair as well as New York City, 4 1/2 x 9" (ILLUS.) **10**

Northern Ontario, Centennial Issue - 1867-1967, Department of Highways, Ontario, front cover art shows a Hudson Bay trapper looking down on the highway & mountains, back lists newspapers & area radio & police services, 4 1/2 x 10" **4**

Ohio, Shell Gasoline w/plain cover showing Shell logo in the front panel, inside includes information on various speed limits & hand & arm signals, shows paintings of autos of the late 1940s & early 1950s, 4 1/2 x 9" **8**

Pennsylvania, Esso Gasoline, one of a series of pictorial maps, pictures various sites in the state, 1954.......................... **5**

Pennsylvania, Delaware, Maryland, Virginia & West Virginia, from Gulf Gasoline, cover scene of cars on highway & pulling into Gulf station, information on credit card use & motor laws of the various states, 1965, 4 1/2 x 9" **3**

Shell License Plate-type, one features a woman in an open convertible w/a terrier dog, at the top of the map is the name of the state, at bottom are the license plates of every state & the Shell logo, a second version features a man & woman in a convertible, bright colors of strong yellow, red & blue, 1932-33, each.................................. **55**

Shell Road Maps, date at top w/state covered below, features a scene of a Shell station in the center, the remainder features five period cars, a wooden speed boat & aircraft, multi-colored, 1929, each...... **125**

Gray Line Tours - Southern California

Southern California, The Gray Line Sightseeing, includes various cities in the region & Gray Line tours available, 1974, 4 x 9" (ILLUS.)... **15**

The Milepost Book - Alaska & Yukon

The Milepost - Alaska & Yukon Travel Guide, features all routes by land, sea & air, large booklet w/extensive maps of the region, mile by mile notations, 156 pp., 1961, 5 1/4 x 9" (ILLUS.)..................................... **6**

United States, from the American Automobile Association, bland painted cover scene of mountains, trees & sailboats, ad inside for Quaker State Motor Oil, back lists services of the AAA, 1969, 4 1/2 x 9" **2**

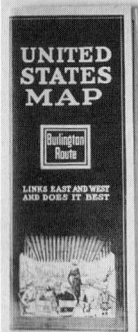

United States Map - Burlington Route

United States, from the Burlington Route Railroad, black & white cover w/sketch of tourists overlooking a panoramic scene, map features sights from Chicago to the Pacific Northwest, 1920s, 4 x 9 1/2" (ILLUS.).. **30**

Picture Map of the United States

United States, "Picture Map of the United States," distributed by Esso Standard Oil Company, front & back features painted color scenes around the U.S., the inside highway map covers the U.S. & features painting of each key area & its products & famous historical events, early 1950s, 4 1/2 x 9" (ILLUS.)... **30**

TRAYS - SERVING & CHANGE

7-20-4 Cigar Change Tray

Change, "7-20-4 Cigar," lithographed tin in wood-grained brown & gold, rectangular w/rounded corners, good color, 4 1/2 x 6 1/2" (ILLUS.) **$33**

Antikamnia Tablets Change Tray

Change, "Antikamnia Tablets," rectangular, metal, red & gold, image of woman sitting in chair, lettering near her reads "Feeling is a Sense - Feeling Pain is Nonsense - No Matter When or Where - Antikamnia Tablets - Two Every Three Hours," border marked "Insomnia and Nervousness

- Pain, Fever, La Grippe," Antikamnia Chemical Company, St. Louis, Missouri, souvenir of 1904 St. Louis World's Fair, by American Can Co., New York & Chicago, Illinois, 3 1/4 x 4 3/4" (ILLUS.) **125-175**

Carnation Chewing Gum Change Tray

Change, "Carnation Chewing Gum," round, metal, yellow & green w/pink carnation flowers & white package in center, red letters read "Dorne's Carnation Chewing Gum" w/black letters at bottom reading "Chew Dorne's Carnation Gum" & "Taste The Smell" in red letters in the top & bottom border, ca. 1900, 4 1/4" d. (ILLUS.) **200-275**

City & Suburban Homes Change Tray

Change, "City and Suburban Homes Co.," round, metal w/scalloped rim, image of three white horseheads in center, border reads "City and Suburban Homes Co., Ltd. - Real Estate - Loans - Renting Agents - Fire Insurance - 35 and 37 State St., Detroit," litho by H.D. Beach Co., Coshocton, Ohio, ca. 1910, 4 1/4" d. (ILLUS.) **100-150**

DeLaval Separators Change Tray

Change, "DeLaval Cream Separators," round, metal, scene of woman in long red dress & white apron at separator, young child near doorway, gold lettering on border reads "DeLaval Cream Separators - The World's Standard," ca. 1906, 4 1/4" d. (ILLUS.) **275-325**

Donaldson's Glass Block Store Tray

Change, "Donaldson's Glass Block Store - Minneapolis, Minn.," oval, woodgrained border w/gold lettering, color center scene of the Rock of Gibraltar w/further advertising, 4 x 6" (ILLUS.) **49**

Fairy Soap Change Tray

Change, "Fairy Soap," round, lithographed tin, red shading to yellow background w/little girl in red coat & frilly black hat sitting on white oval bar of soap marked "Fairy," black border marked w/yellow letters reading "Fairy Soap - 'Have you a little Fairy in your home?,'" N.K. Fairbank Co., Chicago, Illinois, litho by Passaic Metalware Co., Passaic, New Jersey, ca. 1910, 4 1/2" d. (ILLUS.) **100-175**

Fraternal Life Insurance Change Tray

Change, "Fraternal Life & Accident Insurance Company," rectangular, metal, center scene of large building, scalloped &

ruffled blue border reads at the top "Fraternal Life and Accident Insurance - Reserve Deposited with the State of Iowa" & at the bottom "Home of the Brotherhood of American Yeomen, Des Moines, Iowa," ca. 1920, 3 1/4 x 5" (ILLUS.)......... **65-100**

Frost Wire Fence Co. Change Tray

Change, "Frost Wire Fence Co.," round, metal w/scalloped rim, lithographed metal, center w/three white horseheads, the border marked "Compliments of The Frost Wire Fence Co. - Cleveland, O.," litho by H.D. Beach Co., Coshocton, Ohio, ca. 1910, 4 1/4" d. (ILLUS.).......... **125-175**

Globe-Wernicke Bookcases Tray

Change, "Globe-Wernicke Bookcases," round, lithographed metal, scene of woman seated on a rug & holding a book near a man standing before a bookcase, the border reading "Globe-Wernicke - Sectional Bookcases - The Orleans Furniture & Undertaking Co. - Licensed Embalmers - Orleans, Ind.," litho by Charles Shonk Co., Chicago, Illinois, ca. 1915, 4 1/2" d. (ILLUS.) **125-175**

Change, Globe-Wernicke, round, center w/chromolithographic image of man & woman arranging a bookcase, w/"Globe-Wernicke Sectional Bookcase" & "The Peck-Leach Furniture Co. - Taunton, Mass." on raised rim, 4 1/4" d. (ILLUS.) **230**

Grain Belt Beer Change Tray

Change, "Grain Belt Beer," round, metal, red & yellow logo in center below "A Barley Malt Product" w/"'The Minneapolis Beer'" below, Grain Belt Brewery, Minneapolis, Minnesota, ca. 1920, 4 1/8" d. (ILLUS.).. **75-125**

Gypsy Hosiery Change Tray

Change, "Gypsy Hosiery," round, lithographed tin, center oval w/gypsy girl in red surrounded by scene of tents & horses, top marked "Gypsy Hosiery" & bottom "E. J. Schroeder, Breese, Illinois," Hargadine-McKittrick Co., litho by H.D. Beach Co., Coshocton, Ohio, ca. 1910, 6" d. (ILLUS.).. **75-125**

Change, "Heptol Splits - for Health's Sake," black border w/gold wording, color center scene of a cowboy riding a bucking bronco, dated 1904, based on artwork by Charles Russell, 4 3/16" d. (scattered stains, overall normal checking, some wear).. **200-275**

Hyroler Whiskey Change Tray

Change, "Hyroler Whiskey," lithographed in shades of brown with a center scene of a well-dressed gentleman in top hat & tails, wording around border reads "Hyroler Whiskey - Louis J. Adler & Co.," 4 1/4" d. (ILLUS.) **53**

King's Pure Malt Change Tray

Change, "King's Pure Malt," oval, center w/black background & image of uniformed maid holding tray w/a glass & bottle, marked in top border "King's" & the bottom w/medals & banner reading "Panama - Pacific - Medal of Award - International Exposition," ca. 1915, 4 1/4 x 6" (ILLUS.) **100-175**

King's Pure Malt Change Tray

Change, "King's Pure Malt," oval, lithographed metal, shows bottle in center marked "Pure Malt," border marked "King's - Strengthening - Healthful - Good For Insomnia," litho by American Art Works, Coshocton, Ohio, ca. 1910, 4 3/8 x 6" (ILLUS.) **125-175**

La Primadora Cigar Glass Change Tray

Change, "La Primadora" cigars, heavy clear glass over a color label w/the bust of a pretty dark-haired woman framed by gold wording & scrolls, 6" d. (ILLUS.) **175**

Change, "Lakeside Club Bouquet," round, whiskey from Grand Rapids, Michigan, shows young couple w/older gentleman seated at table, 4 1/4" d. (edge has minor wear).. **110**

Lehnert's Beer Change Tray

Change, "Lehnert's Beer," round, lithographed metal, image of stag w/large antlers, border w/"Drink Lehnert's Beer - Made in Catasauqua, PA," litho by American Art Works, Coshocton, Ohio, ca. 1910, 4 1/4" d. (ILLUS.).......................... **125-175**

Lily Beer Change Tray

Change, "Lily Beer," rectangular, metal, table set w/snack food, bottle of beer & full glass below "Lily - A Beverage" flanked by white calla lily, border reads "Pure As It's (sic) Name - In A Class By Itself! - Heathful and Refreshing - Bottled Only By Rock Island Brewing Co. - Rock Island, Illinois," ca. 1915, 4 1/2 x 6 1/2" (ILLUS.) **175-275**

Miller High Life Beer Change Tray

Change, "Miller High Life Beer," rectangular, metal, center blue w/stars & Miller girl sitting on crescent moon, holding glass, marked "Miller - High Life - The Champagne of Bottle Beer," goldtone border, ca. 1960s, 4 1/2 x 6 1/2" (ILLUS.).. **35-65**

Change, "Mokaine Liqueurs," lithographed tin, rectangular w/flanged rim & rounded corners, center color scene of a seated fat man at an outside cafe table looking over at a parrot on perch, titled below "'What Heat' - Try Mokaine and Soda," brown panels w/white wording on each rim flange & small images of the product in each corner, produced in France for the American market, light wear, 3 3/4 x 4" **56**

Monticello Whiskey Change Tray

Change, "Monticello Whiskey," oval, lithographed metal, fox hunt scene w/large building in background, gold border marked "Monticello - It's All Whiskey," litho by Charles Shonk Co., Chicago, Illinois, ca. 1915, 4 3/8 x 6 1/8" (ILLUS.)...................................... **225-275**

National Cigar Stands Change Tray

Change, "National Cigar Stands Co.," round, metal, center w/young girl wearing red sleeveless one-shouldered gown, holding daisies & w/a wreath of daisies in her dark upswept hair, the border designed w/various cigar band seals, marked at the top "Our Brands" & at the bottom "National Cigar Stands Co.," ca. 1910, 6" d. (ILLUS.) **75-125**

Quick Meal Ranges Change Tray

Change, "Quick Meal Ranges," oval, lithographed metal, scene of young chicks near an empty shell, red border reading

"'Quick Meal' Ranges - Made in St. Louis, Mo.," litho by Ohio Art Company, Bryan, Ohio, ca. 1900, 3 1/4 x 4 1/4" (ILLUS.) **150-200**

Change, "Red Raven Splits - Ask the Man," red border band w/gold wording, color center scene w/a large red raven serving another red bird all against a black background, celebrating the 1904 St. Louis World's Fair, appears to be unused, minor rim scuffs, 4" d. **55**

Change, "Red Raven Splits - 'For High Livers' Livers,'" center scene of a large red raven beside a small bottle of the product, a dark green border band w/gold lettering, 4 1/4" d. (minor crazing) **58**

Red Raven Splits Change Tray

Change, "Red Raven Splits," rectangular w/rounded corners, color center scene of a pretty woman wearing a low-cut black dress, large hat w/red feather & black gloves, one arm around a large red raven, a large bottle of the product to her right, wide green border w/gold rim band, minor edge dings, 4 x 6" (ILLUS.).................... **44**

Sears, Roebuck and Co. Change Tray

Change, "Sears, Roebuck and Co.," oval, metal, scene of factory w/waist-length image of woman holding scales on right, marked at top "Sears, Roebuck and Co. - Chicago" & at the bottom "Originators of the Guarantee that Stands the Test in the Scales of Justice," ca. 1920, 4 3/8 x 6" (ILLUS.)... **125-175**

Sen-Sen Aluminum Change Tray

Change, "Sen-Sen Chewing Gum," rectangular, aluminum w/scalloped rim, center w/embossed ribbon-tied package marked "Sen-Sen - 5¢," ca. 1910, 3 1/4 x 4 1/4" (ILLUS.) **65-100**

Slade's Products Change Tray

Change, "Slade's Products," round w/flanged rim, printed in deep orange on white, center reads "Don't Take Chances - All Slade's Products - Are Sure Winners," four border panels each showing a racing horse w/the name of a different food product, appears unused, 4 1/4" d. (ILLUS.) **55**

Stollwerck Chocolate & Cocoa Tray

Change, "Stollwerck Chocolate & Cocoa," round, lithographed metal, gold & red, marked "Stollwerck" in center w/"Gold Brand" above & "Chocolate & Cocoa" below, scrolled border, litho by Kaufmann & Strauss Co., New York, ca. 1910, 5" d. (ILLUS.) **75-125**

Tech Beer Change Tray

Change, "Tech Beer," rectangular w/rounded corners, black ground w/thin red rim band, a large color picture of a bottle of beer in the center, the name in red at the

top & "'None Better'" in small white letters under the bottle, dated 1913, few minor edge chips, 4 1/2 x 6 1/2" (ILLUS.) **44**

The Davenport Co. Change Tray

Change, "The Davenport Company," round, lithographed metal, center w/bust portrait of lady on red background flanked by Art Deco floral designs, brown border w/yellow letters reading "Compliments of The Davenport Co.," litho by Meek & Co., ca. 1903, 4 1/4" d. (ILLUS.) **75-125**

Welsbach Mantles Change Tray

Change, "Welsbach Mantles," round, lithographed tin, center w/shield form, eagle & banner marked "Welsbach Quality" above red scroll marked in yellow "All mantles are not Welsbachs. See that the mantle you buy has the Shield of Quality on the box," yellow decorated border, litho by Meek & Beech Co., Coshocton, Ohio, ca. 1900, 4 1/4" d. (ILLUS.) **125-175**

White Rock Table Water Change Tray

Change, "White Rock Table Water," round, lithographed metal, scene w/woman kneeling on rock over water, yellow border w/red & black lettering reads "White

Rock - The World's Best Table Water," litho by Charles Shonk Co., Chicago, Illinois, ca. 1900, 4 3/8" d. (ILLUS.) **225-300**

Orange-Julep Serving Tray

Serving, "Drink Orange-Julep," rectangular w/rounded corners, a large color center scene of a 1920s bathing beauty sitting holding an umbrella & holding a glass of the soda, black border band w/orange wording, a few minor white spots, 10 1/2 x 13 1/4" (ILLUS.) **358**

Edelweiss Beer Serving Tray

Serving, "Edelweiss Beer," center color bust portrait of a pretty young red-headed girl wearing a white & red shawl against a black ground, the border band w/edelweiss blossoms, dated 1913, backside repainted, 13" d. (ILLUS.) **154**

Haines-CeBrook Ice Cream Serving Tray

Serving, "Haines-CeBrook Ice Cream - 'The Better Kind,'" rectangular w/rounded corners, red border band w/gold trim, half-length portrait of a smiling young woman eating ice cream, wearing a red tam hat

& black dress fading into the black background, minor scrapes & blemishes, 10 1/2 x 15 1/4" (ILLUS.) **182**

Hires Serving Tray with Pretty Girls

Serving, "Hires Root Beer," oval lithographed metal, center color scene w/bust portraits of two pretty young women drinking from large glass w/straws, border band printed w/repeating word "Hires," the center scene includes "Drink Hires" at the right end, based on artwork by Harry Morse Meyers, ca. 1915, professionally restored, 19 1/2 x 23 1/2" (ILLUS.) **1,100**

Early Hires Serving Tray with Hires Boy

Serving, "Hires Root Beer," oval lithographed tin, wide wood-grained border band around a center color image of the Hires boy holding a mug of root beer & laughing & pointing, white wording reads "Say Hires," some professional paint-in, ca. 1907, 20 x 24" (ILLUS.) **1,540**
Serving, "Jacob Ruppert Beer Ale," oval lithographed metal, black & yellow border bands around a green board background w/the wording in yellow above two hands holding up large mugs of beer, ca. 1939, 10 3/4 x 14 1/2" (overall scuffs & soiling) **39**

NuGrape Soda Serving Tray

Serving, "NuGrape Soda," rectangular w/rounded corners, beautiful young woman holding bottle, the top & bottom borders reading "A Flavor You Can't Forget," light wear & scratches, 10 1/2 x 13 1/4" (ILLUS.) **121**

Serving, "Rainier Pale Beer," ceramic glazed base w/tin plate surround, open D-form side handles, snowy scene w/evergreens & mountain in background, top marked "Compliments - Of - The - Season," light surface scratches, one handle loose, 9 1/4" d. plus handles **99**

TRUNKS

Oak Immigrant's Trunk

Dome-top, oak, immigrant's trunk, w/ornate wrought-iron strap hinges, corner braces, handles at sides & keyplate, wooden pegged & dovetailed construction, carved design in top depicts a cornucopia spilling fruit, base retains original wooden rollers, four feet & scalloped apron, original lock & key, lidded till inside, original finish, northern European, ca. 1840, 22 x 50", 30" h. (ILLUS.)............................ **$1,500**

Oak Dome-top Trunk

Dome-top, oak, w/pierced strap iron fitting & hinges, original lock & key, dovetailed & pegged construction, till inside, original finish, ca. 1800, 24 x 40", 22" h. (ILLUS.)..... **950**

Hand-painted Pine Trunk

Dome-top, pine, h.p. scroll banding on sides in pale gold, stenciled ivy borders in green & orange-red on lid around central panel w/dark green ground & floral

decoration in shades of green & gold rimmed w/orange/red decoration, original lock, ca. 1850-60, 14 x 20", 12" h. (ILLUS.)... **400**

Dated Immigrant's Trunk

Dome-top, pine immigrant's trunk, dovetailed & pegged construction, open interior w/till on one end, painted in green w/initials & date of 1841 painted on front in yellow, original lock & key, wrought-iron fittings & handles on sides, northern European, 24 x 60", 24" h. (ILLUS.).............. **950**

Inscribed Immigrant's Trunk

Dome-top, pine, immigrant's trunk, w/traces of original paint decoration, till compartment inside, name & inscription painted on front, dated 1856, northern European, 20 x 36", 20" h. (ILLUS.) **400**

Small Dome-top Trunk

Dome-top, pine, w/original sponge-grained painted surface, dovetailed construction, original hardware, ca. 1860, 14 x 22", 12" h. (ILLUS.) **250**

Stained Pine Immigrant's Trunk

Dome-top, stained pine, immigrant's trunk, dovetailed construction, w/carved floral motifs on lid and front, molded base, open interior, wrought-iron hinges, handles on sides, hasp & keyplate, original lock & key, northern European, ca. 1830s, 20 x 40", 18" h. (ILLUS.).................... **650**

Sponge-decorated Country Trunk

Flat-top, country grain-painted trunk, probably pine, w/original sponge-decorated surface, hinged lid, open interior, recessed panels on front & sides, turned legs, ca. 1840, 22 x 44", 28" h. (ILLUS.)....... **400**

Louis Vuitton Trunk

Flat-top, Louis Vuitton, traditional "LV"-monogrammed canvas trimmed in leather & wood slat bound, fitted tufted interior, w/original label, numbered 206534, ca. 1900, 13 x 21 x 44" (ILLUS.).. **1,008**

Carpenter's Trunk

Flat-top, pine, carpenter's tool trunk, w/ornate copper brackets nailed to corners & raised panels on top, cast-iron handles at sides, interior has shelves & recessed areas for holding tools, ca. 1890, 20 x 36", 20" h., hasp missing from lock, refinished (ILLUS.) **450**

Paint-decorated Pine Trunk

Flat-top, pine, immigrant's trunk, dovetailed construction, bold painting on all sides w/bone inlay escutcheon, high bracket

base, interior w/lift-lid till, European, ca. 1850s, 20 x 48", 22" h. (ILLUS.) **650**

Painted Immigrant's Trunk

Flat-top, pine, immigrant's trunk, painted except for lid, w/applied carving & molding to front, iron hinges, side handles & hasp, roller base, open interior, northern European, 21 x 44", 20" h. (ILLUS.).............. **400**

WATCHES

Pocket watch, hunting case, 18k yellow gold, B Lever set, white face w/black Roman numerals, seconds hand, stem wind, size 18, monogrammed inside case cover w/"Frank Snowden 1881," marked "three-fourths plate, works - Amn Watch Co.; adjusted; Waltham Mass.; Ser. # 1144912" & "#19950 - 18K," American Watch Co., ca. 1877 .... **$616**

Canadian Gold-filled Pocket Watch

Pocket watch, hunting case, Crown Watch Co., Canada, gold-filled case w/engraved shield on the front, case marked inside "Guaranteed 20 Years - Philadelphia Watch Company 8373761," works marked "Crown Watch Co. Patented 17 Jewels," ca. 1915, near mint (ILLUS.)............ **448**

Fine Elgin Solid Gold Pocket Watch

Pocket watch, hunting case, Elgin National Watch Co., 14k gold highly engraved case, case marked "Guaranteed 14k 585 Fine - The KWC Co. 5625549," works marked "Elgin National Watch Co. USA 18658911," 17 jewels, adjusted double roller, ca. 1915, near mint (ILLUS.)............... **840**

Lady's Elgin Gold-filled Watch

Pocket watch, hunting case, lady's gold-filled pendant-type, the front applied w/a four-color engraving of a bird on a limb, the reverse w/floral engraving surrounding a center shield-shaped medallion, case marked inside "2094881" & engraved w/inscription dated 1892, works marked "Elgin Natl. Watch Co. 6277676," seconds hand, 17 jewels, engraved bezel, near mint (ILLUS.).................................. **420**

Man's Waltham Gold Pocket Watch

Pocket watch, hunting case, man's, 14k gold w/scalloped case w/applied four-color gold floral design, inside of case marked "899954 - Fahys 14k Monarch," works marked "American Waltham Watch Co. Safety Carrel 5197900," 15 jewels, seconds hand, ca. 1890 (ILLUS.)..... **420**

Solid Gold Waltham Lady's Watch

Pocket watch, hunting case, Waltham, lady's pendant-type, 14k gold w/applied three-color gold engraving w/floral design on front & deer on reverse, 17 jewels, seconds hand, ca. 1904, near mint (ILLUS.).. **504**

Pocket watch, open-faced, Elgin, gold face, case marked "14K #21424," engraved "May 31, 1914," works marked "serial #16842679," back of case monogrammed, seconds hand, 17 jewels, ca. 1911.. **252**

Howard Chronometer Railroad Watch

Pocket watch, open-faced, Howard Watch Co. chronometer railroad model, gold-filled case, case marked "Howard Watch Co. Keystone Extra 312614 Boston," works marked "E. Howard Watch Co. Boston USA 978164 Adjusted," 17 jewels, near mint (ILLUS.).................................... **840**

Pocket watch, open-faced, Waltham, case marked "Roy 14K 585/1000 fine," works marked "19 jewels AWWCO Waltham Mass. Riverside Adjusted ser. #23006721," winding stem contains blue sapphire **252**

WEATHERVANES

Initial Banner Weathervane

Banner, copper banner weathervane w/initials "ECL" on banner, w/directionals & pole, traces of gilt, American, 19th c., banner 29 1/2 x 72", approx. 12' h. overall, repairs & imperfections (ILLUS.) **$575**

Copper & Zinc Bull Weathervane

Bull, molded sheet copper body & cast-zinc head, w/traces of gilding & underpaint, mounted on rod w/base, American, 19th c., 17" h., 26" l. (ILLUS.).............................. **4,312**

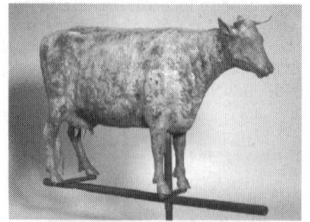

Cow Weathervane

Cow, molded copper, standing cow w/weathered gilt surface, American, late 19th c., 8" l., 21" h. (ILLUS.) **13,800**

Fish Weathervane

Fish, copper fish w/molded sheet metal fins, possibly J.W. Fiske, New York, second half 19th c., retains some original gilding & weathered verdigris, mounted on rod & black metal stand, 30" h., 8" l. (ILLUS.) ... **10,925**

Galloping Horse Weathervane

Horse, Black Hawk, copper molded galloping horse weathervane, allover verdigris, traces of gilt, American, late 19th c., 33" l., 18 1/2" h., minor imperfections (ILLUS.) **6,555**

Running Stag Weathervane

Stag, gilded copper swell-bodied form w/cast-zinc head & antlers, front legs tucked & rear legs extended as if running, w/original directionals, remains of old gilding, late 19th c., on modern rod & base, overall 23 1/2" h. (ILLUS.) **6,900**

Leaping Stag Weathervane

Stag, molded copper, figure of stag leaping over log, attributed to Harris & Co., Boston, on cast-iron stand w/cardinals, late 19th c., 26" h., 29 1/2" l., overall 69" h., repair to antlers, minor seam imperfections (ILLUS.) **16,100**

Sulky & Driver Weathervane

Sulky & driver, molded copper, four-wheeled sulky, one horse & driver w/whip on rectangular wooden base, attributed to J.W. Fiske, Boston, late 19th c., 19 1/2" h., 50" l. (ILLUS.) **17,250**

WESTERN CHARACTER COLLECTIBLES

Buffalo Bill Advertising Poster

Buffalo Bill poster, stone litho poster advertising "Life and Adventures of Buffalo Bill - Actual Scenes in Moving Pictures by Cody Himself," w/full-color busts of four Native American chiefs in full regalia surrounded by scenes of a camp w/teepees, braves in full headdress riding horses and tribe members dancing around a campfire, all in a Native American-motif border of red, blue & black, Riverside Printing Co., Milwaukee, 29 x 43" (ILLUS.) **$1,815**

Gene Autry Doll by Terri Lee

Gene Autry doll, hard plastic head w/painted blue eyes, feathered brow, painted upper lashes, accented nostrils, open-closed mouth w/white space for teeth, lightly molded & brush-stroked hair, five-piece hard plastic body wearing gold satin shirt w/silver piping, denim jeans, & brown & white cowboy boots, marked "Terri Lee / Pat. Pending" on back, "Gene Autry" on tag on shirt, 16" h., light wear to finger tips & toes, jeans may not be original, left snap broken (ILLUS.) **1,700**

"Blazing Guns" Poster

Hoot Gibson, Ken Maynard movie poster for the Monogram movie "Blazing Guns," full-color poster w/top panel of two Western characters peeking out from behind the slats of a fence w/guns drawn, the bottom w/three Western characters, two talking to each other, the other cocking the trigger of his gun, middle panel w/"Ken Maynard - Hoot Gibson" in heavy lettering (ILLUS.) **210**

Lone Ranger Safety Scout Badge

Lone Ranger badge, blue & silver, image of Lone Ranger & Silver in center w/"Lone Ranger - Safety Scout - Silvercup" around rim, 1935, 14/16" (ILLUS.) **125-225**

Lone Ranger Bandanna

Lone Ranger bandanna, cloth, red & white, 1948-1950, 7 1/4 x 21 1/4" (ILLUS.).......... **75-95**

Bond Bread Bakers Blotter

Lone Ranger blotter, rectangular, depicts Lone Ranger & Silver on left side w/"The Lone Ranger Says Let Safety Be Your Rule For the Honor of Your School - Always Be Careful!," Bond Bread Bakers, 1938, 3 3/4 x 8 10/16" (ILLUS.) **55-85**

Advertisement for Bubble Gum

Lone Ranger bubble gum advertisement, yellow & white w/black & red lettering, image of box filled w/packages of bubble gum at top, 12 x 13 1/4" (ILLUS.) **25-45**

Lone Ranger Lantern

Lone Ranger "Chuck Wagon Lantern," R.E. Deitz Co., Syracuse, New York, 1945, 4 11/16 x 8 1/2" (ILLUS.).............. **150-225**

Lone Ranger Comics

Lone Ranger comic books, Whitman Comics, 1950s, published by Western Publishing Co., Inc., North Road, Poughkeepsie, New York, each (ILLUS. of edition #19 & #20)... **15-35**

Lone Ranger Deputy Badge & Brochure

Lone Ranger deputy badge, gold color, together w/four-fold club brochure, 1951 (ILLUS.)... **125-155**

Official Lone Ranger First Aid Kit

Lone Ranger First Aid Kit, official kit manufactured by The American White Cross Labs, Inc., New Rochelle, New York, 1938, 4 x 4" (ILLUS.).................................... **75-95**

Lone Ranger Game

Lone Ranger game, board-type, "Hi Yooooo Silver!," Parker Brothers, Inc., 1938 (ILLUS.)... **75-125**

"The Legend of the Lone Ranger" Game

Lone Ranger game, board-type, "The Legend of the Lone Ranger," 1980, Milton Bradley Co. (ILLUS.).................................. **55-95**

Lone Ranger Comic Game

Lone Ranger game, "The Lone Ranger Comic Game," Mattel, 1971, w/original card (ILLUS.) **35-75**

Lone Ranger Guns & Holster Set

Lone Ranger gun & holster set, double, official outfit w/original box (ILLUS.)....... **150-225**

Lone Ranger Harmonica

Lone Ranger harmonica, Magnus Harmonica Corporation, Newark 5, New Jersey, 1947, 1 2/16 x 4 2/16" (ILLUS.) **55-120**

Lone Ranger Lunch Box

Lone Ranger lunch box, metal, colorful scene of Lone Ranger & Tonto on horseback, 1946, 6 5/16 x 8 9/16" (ILLUS.) ... **350-550**

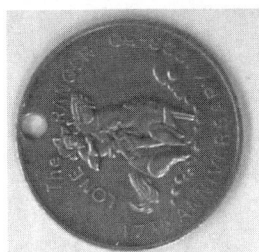

Lone Ranger Anniversary Medal

Lone Ranger medal, round, image of Lone Ranger & Silver in center, embossed "The Lone Ranger 17th Anniversary 1933-1950," 1 3/16" d. (ILLUS.) **125-175**

Lone Ranger Pedometer

Lone Ranger pedometer, official item, 1947, 2 1/2" d. (ILLUS.) **45-85**
Lone Ranger pin, gold & blue, head of Lone Ranger shown above V, "Lone Ranger Victory Corps" in circular border, 1942, 13/16 x 1/2" **75-105**

Lone Ranger Pinback Button

Lone Ranger pinback button, beige w/center red circle depicting Lone Ranger on Silver, "The Lone Ranger - Sunday Herald and Examiner" around border, 15/16" (ILLUS.) **35-65**
Lone Ranger pinback button, light blue background showing Lone Ranger wearing a red shirt, 1950, 1 1/8 x 1 1/2".............. **35-55**

Lone Ranger Pocket Knife

Lone Ranger pocket knife, w/rawhide thong, Camillus Cutlery Co., Camillus, New York, w/original card, 1947, card 3 1/2 x 4 14/16" (ILLUS.)............................ **55-95**

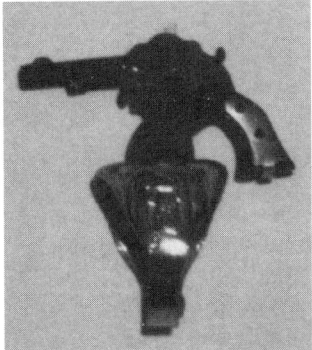

Lone Ranger Six Gun Ring

Lone Ranger ring, gold w/pearl-handled gun on top, saddles imprinted on sides of ring, horseshoes on stand of gun, top of ring w/symbols of star, bullet & various emblems, cereal give-away, 1948, 1 1/2 x 1 1/2" (ILLUS.) **150-175**

Lone Ranger Rocking Horse

Lone Ranger rocking horse, white horse w/red & yellow saddle, yellow rockers, Lone Ranger pictured on one side, Tonto on other, Lone Ranger, Inc., 1940, 2' h. (ILLUS.).. **325-575**

Lone Ranger Safety Club Badges Set

Lone Ranger Safety Club badges, red or black lettering on silver, 1955, 1 1/4 x 1 1/2", each $35.00, card w/complete set of 12 (ILLUS.)............................ **150-225**

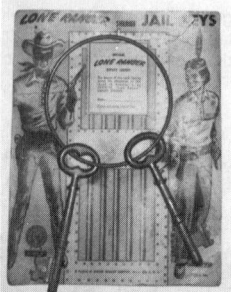

Lone Ranger Sheriff Jail Keys

Lone Ranger "Sheriff Jail Keys," two keys on metal ring on original card, Esquire Novelty Company, Jersey City 5, New Jersey, 1945, card 7 x 9" (ILLUS.)............. **55-95**

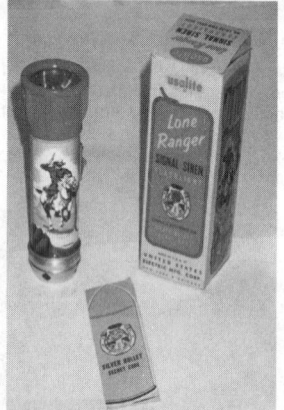

Lone Ranger Signal Siren Flashlight

Lone Ranger Signal Siren flashlight, complete w/Morse and Silver Bullet Secret Code, United States Electric Mfg. Corp., New York - Chicago, Usalite R, w/original box (ILLUS.) **95-150**
Lone Ranger soap, Castile Soap by Kerk Guild, 1939, box size 1 3/4 x 4 1/2"............ **50-75**

Lone Ranger Tumbler

Lone Ranger tumbler, clear w/frosted image of Lone Ranger on Silver, narrow red band at top & bottom, Anchor Hocking, 1938, 5 5/16" h. (ILLUS.) **75**
Fort Apache playset, Marx, No. 6063, 1965... **125-575**
Johnny Ringo Western Frontier Set, Marx, No. 4784, 1959 .... **1,300-2,700**
Roy Rogers Rodeo Ranch playset, Marx, No. 3979, 1952 .... **100-350**
Tales of Wells Fargo playset, Marx, No. 4260, 1950s... **200-750**

Aurora Tonto Kit

Tonto model kit, 1/10 scale, w/eight page comic book, Aurora, 1974 (ILLUS.)........... **15-35**
Western Mining Town playset, Marx, No. 4265, 1950s.. **175-600**

WHISTLES

Whistle with Bird Decoration

Bird-decorated whistle, spelter, pipe-shaped, w/molded figure of dove perched on rock or tree trunk base, whistle stem protruding from base at an angle, traces of original paint, 4" l. (ILLUS.) **$25**

Copper & Brass Bosun's Whistle

Bosun's whistle, brass & copper, copper mouth tube w/brass ball end & hanging

chain, marked "Made in England," early
20th c., 4 3/4" l. (ILLUS. with chain) **45**

Novelty Bird Whistle

Novelty whistle, stamped brass, an oblong
well at the bottom to hold water, a rubber
tube was inserted & when blown made
the figural bird at the top warble & flutter
its beak & tail, 2 3/4 x 4 1/4" (ILLUS.) **55**

Marked Police Whistle

Police whistle, German silver, standard design marked "Signal," 2 1/4" l., w/chain
(ILLUS.) **16**

Plated Referee's Whistle

Referee's whistle, plated brass, marked
"Biffar - Chicago," 2 1/4" l. (ILLUS.) **22**

WOOD SCULPTURES

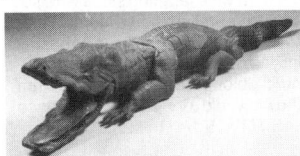

Carved Wooden Alligator

Alligator, carved & painted figure of alligator w/patterned body, hinged jaw opens
to reveal red-painted tongue & rows of
teeth, small section of back covered
w/painted canvas, Noah Weiss, Ameri-
can, late 19th c., 95" l. (ILLUS.) **$13,800**

Carved Figure of Calliope

Calliope, painted, parcel-gilt & carved figure
of Calliope, Muse of epic poetry, in classical attire & wearing breast plate & helmet, holding lyre in left hand, right arm
extended, 19th c., 49 1/2" h. (ILLUS.) **9,200**

Cigar Store Indian Shading Eyes

Cigar store Indian, carved & painted full-
length figure of Indian chief w/feathered
headdress & costume, raising one hand
to shield eyes, the other hand holding tobacco leaves, one foot raised, American,
third quarter 19th c., on rectangular base,
71" h. (ILLUS.) **14,950**

Cigar Store Indian on Pedestal

Cigar store Indian, pine, full-length carved
& painted figure of Indian chief wearing
feathered headdress & red & yellow costume w/brown cloak, carrying blocks of
tobacco & cigars, mounted on a wooden
base on black-painted wooden pedestal,
probably New York, third quarter of 19th
c., 58" h., repainted (ILLUS.) **8,400**

Carving of a Farm Laborer

Farm laborer, carved wood figure of man
standing holding shovel, w/hat in hand,
looking down to a plate at his feet that
holds fruit, vegetables & a sheaf of
wheat, executed in the WPA style, un-
signed, 34" h. (ILLUS.) **11,200**

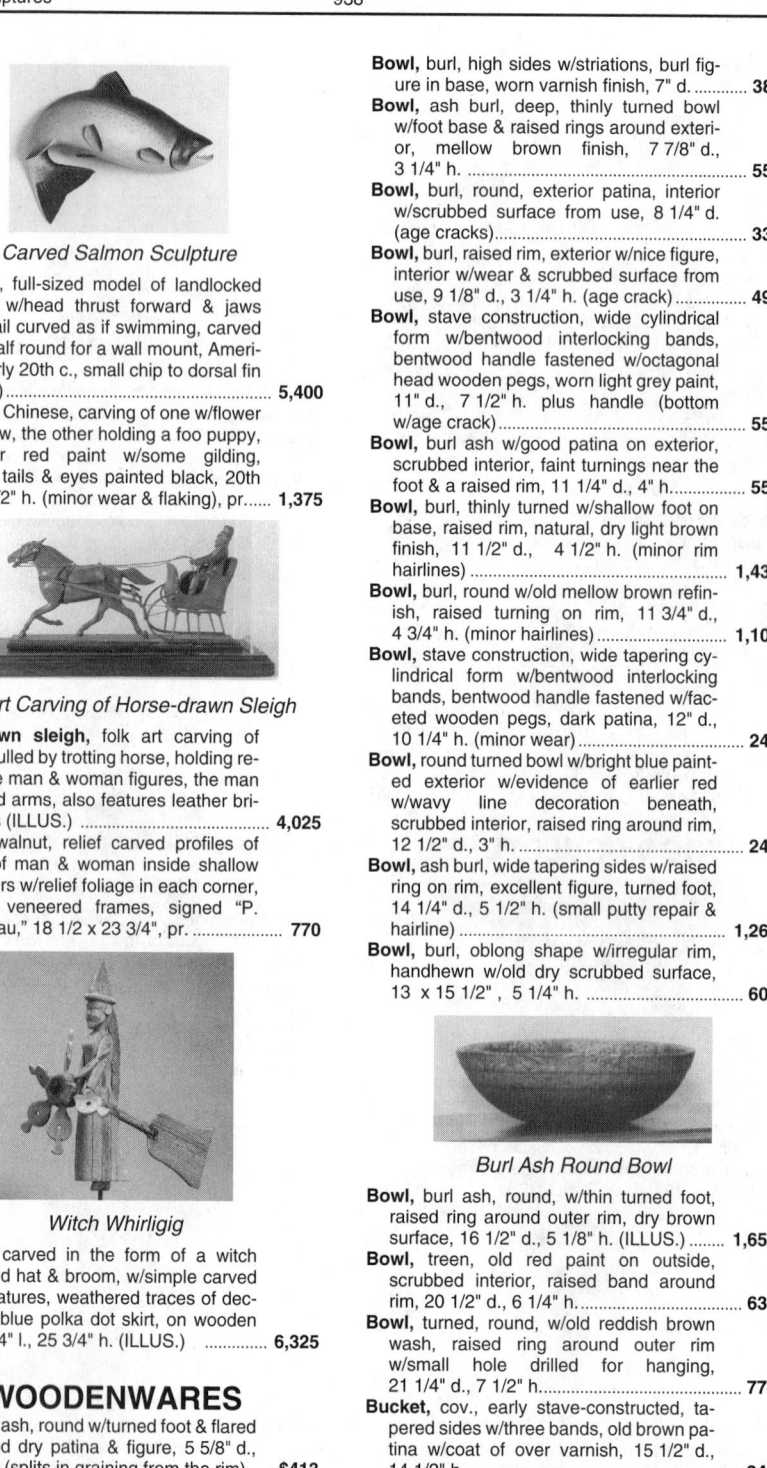

Carved Salmon Sculpture

Fish, pine, full-sized model of landlocked salmon w/head thrust forward & jaws open, tail curved as if swimming, carved in the half round for a wall mount, American, early 20th c., small chip to dorsal fin (ILLUS.) **5,400**

Foo dogs, Chinese, carving of one w/flower in its paw, the other holding a foo puppy, cinnabar red paint w/some gilding, manes, tails & eyes painted black, 20th c., 16 1/2" h. (minor wear & flaking), pr...... **1,375**

Folk Art Carving of Horse-drawn Sleigh

Horse-drawn sleigh, folk art carving of sleigh pulled by trotting horse, holding removable man & woman figures, the man w/jointed arms, also features leather bridle pulls (ILLUS.) **4,025**

Plaques, walnut, relief carved profiles of heads of man & woman inside shallow oval liners w/relief foliage in each corner, molded veneered frames, signed "P. Condesau," 18 1/2 x 23 3/4", pr. **770**

Witch Whirligig

Whirligig, carved in the form of a witch w/pointed hat & broom, w/simple carved facial features, weathered traces of decoration, blue polka dot skirt, on wooden stand, 14" l., 25 3/4" h. (ILLUS.) **6,325**

WOODENWARES

Bowl, burl, ash, round w/turned foot & flared rim, good dry patina & figure, 5 5/8" d., 2 3/8" h. (splits in graining from the rim) **$413**

Bowl, ash burl, deep, thinly turned bowl w/shallow foot & raised ring around rim, 6 5/8" d., 3" h.. **719**

Bowl, burl, high sides w/striations, burl figure in base, worn varnish finish, 7" d. **385**

Bowl, ash burl, deep, thinly turned bowl w/foot base & raised rings around exterior, mellow brown finish, 7 7/8" d., 3 1/4" h. **550**

Bowl, burl, round, exterior patina, interior w/scrubbed surface from use, 8 1/4" d. (age cracks).. **330**

Bowl, burl, raised rim, exterior w/nice figure, interior w/wear & scrubbed surface from use, 9 1/8" d., 3 1/4" h. (age crack) **495**

Bowl, stave construction, wide cylindrical form w/bentwood interlocking bands, bentwood handle fastened w/octagonal head wooden pegs, worn light grey paint, 11" d., 7 1/2" h. plus handle (bottom w/age crack)... **550**

Bowl, burl ash w/good patina on exterior, scrubbed interior, faint turnings near the foot & a raised rim, 11 1/4" d., 4" h................ **550**

Bowl, burl, thinly turned w/shallow foot on base, raised rim, natural, dry light brown finish, 11 1/2" d., 4 1/2" h. (minor rim hairlines) **1,430**

Bowl, burl, round w/old mellow brown refinish, raised turning on rim, 11 3/4" d., 4 3/4" h. (minor hairlines) **1,100**

Bowl, stave construction, wide tapering cylindrical form w/bentwood interlocking bands, bentwood handle fastened w/faceted wooden pegs, dark patina, 12" d., 10 1/4" h. (minor wear).................................... **248**

Bowl, round turned bowl w/bright blue painted exterior w/evidence of earlier red w/wavy line decoration beneath, scrubbed interior, raised ring around rim, 12 1/2" d., 3" h. **248**

Bowl, ash burl, wide tapering sides w/raised ring on rim, excellent figure, turned foot, 14 1/4" d., 5 1/2" h. (small putty repair & hairline) **1,265**

Bowl, burl, oblong shape w/irregular rim, handhewn w/old dry scrubbed surface, 13 x 15 1/2" , 5 1/4" h. **605**

Burl Ash Round Bowl

Bowl, burl ash, round, w/thin turned foot, raised ring around outer rim, dry brown surface, 16 1/2" d., 5 1/8" h. (ILLUS.) **1,650**

Bowl, treen, old red paint on inside, scrubbed interior, raised band around rim, 20 1/2" d., 6 1/4" h..................................... **633**

Bowl, turned, round, w/old reddish brown wash, raised ring around outer rim w/small hole drilled for hanging, 21 1/4" d., 7 1/2" h.. **770**

Bucket, cov., early stave-constructed, tapered sides w/three bands, old brown patina w/coat of over varnish, 15 1/2" d., 14 1/2" h.. **248**

Butter paddle, burl, handle w/beveled edges & stylized bird head hook, good figure & patina, 9" l. (corner has glued repair) **550**

Butter paddle, curly maple, handle w/chamfered edges & square hooked end, copper wire hanger, golden color w/good patina, 9" l. (one corner is glued) **330**

Butter paddle, curly maple, long curved handle w/simple hook end, good curl, natural finish w/soft patina on handle & lightly scrubbed surface on bowl, old tack holes on bowl, 10 1/2" l................................. **248**

Butter paddle, curly maple, stylized horse-head handle, dark patina, 8 1/4" l. **275**

Canteen, stave construction, old bluish green repaint w/iron bands & bail handle, embossed letters "B.L.," 8 1/2" d. (warped sides have pulled away from slot) **303**

Canteen, stave construction w/flat base & arched sides, worn blue repaint, 6 1/2 x 9", 8 1/4" h. (cracks in one stave) **440**

Carrier, cov., hickory & pine bentwood w/brown refinish, arched handle w/pegs, steel tacks, 9 1/2" d., 10 1/2" h. **385**

Wooden Cookie Board

Cookie board, rectangular, w/carved figure of soldier in profile on prancing horse, 4 x 5 1/2" (ILLUS.)............................ **358**

Cricket, walnut, old reddish brown paint w/square nail construction, canted legs w/bootjack cutouts & unusual stepped cutouts on aprons, 6 3/8 x 14 1/2", 5 1/8" h... **330**

Cutlery box, curly maple, rectangular w/sides tapering out toward top, dove-tailed construction, hinged lids on either side of arched handle w/cutout finger space, golden finish, 9 1/2 x 15", 4 1/2" h. (minor restored breaks in base molding).. **2,090**

Dish, burl, striated figure on edges w/burl figure in center, 6" d. (age crack).................. **578**

Pine & Maple Dough Box on Stand

Dough box on stand, pine & maple, country Sheraton, removable work surface top above tapered trough, dovetailed construction, splay-leg base w/pegged construction, turned legs, ca. 1820, 22 x 44", 28" h., refinished (ILLUS.)........................... **700**

Drying rack, folding type, three sections, each having three cross pieces, dry lime green paint over earlier white, 71 1/4" w., 63 1/4" h... **660**

Wooden Firkin

Firkin, stave construction w/sides tapering in at top, round wooden base, multiple bentwood laced bands around top & bottom, 6" d., 6 3/4" h., edge & base damage (ILLUS.)...................................... **413**

Jar, cov., treen, poplar, raised rings on the base & near the top, slightly domed lid & round finial, w/original sponge decoration of arches & earthworm designs in red over mustard (minor chip on finial & hairline in side) **1,760**

Knife box, curly maple, dovetailed w/high, canted sides & a shaped divider w/curved cut-out handle, old mellow finish w/good patina, 8 1/2 x 11 1/4", 7 1/2" h. **1,320**

Kraut cutter, walnut, tombstone-shaped top w/heart cutout & reeding on the edge, stamped star decoration, 6 3/4 x 18 3/4" (age split along edge) **110**

Mortar & pestle, burl, turned ash, roughed out interior, turned wooden pestle shows more wear than mortar, 5" d., 6 1/2" h.......... **220**

Mortar & pestle, burl, turned pestle, 4 1/2" d., 6 1/4" h. (wear & minor edge damage to pestle) **220**

Pantry box, cov., round bentwood, w/iron tacks, wooden pegs around base, in old yellow paint, 7" d., 2 3/4" h. (hairline across lid) **605**

Pipe box, painted pine, hanging-type, tall upright form, carved scroll-shaped backboard & top above a single base drawer, old red painted surface, New England, early 19th c., 3 3/4 x 5 3/4", 19 3/4" h. (surface wear, replaced drawer pull)......... **4,025**

Quilt rack, ash, shaped shoe feet w/two mortised cross members & arched tops on ends, mellow golden brown finish, later wire nails 26" w., 31 1/2" h. **330**

Spice chest, pine, w/four 6" w. drawers on right side & six 3 1/2" w. drawers over one 7" w. drawer on left side, 7 x 13 1/4 x 14 1/2" (open knot hole in backboard, some later nails) **550**

Sugar bucket, cov., tapering cylindrical sides, w/copper tacks & wooden pegs in lid, wire bale & turned wood handle, original red paint, 7 3/4" h. (small split in rim of lid)... **550**

Treenware container, cov., round, w/original brown sponged decoration in the shape of leaves over reddish ground, turned rings at top & bottom, tapered finial, 7 1/2" h. (paint alligatored & varnish darkened).. **715**

Trencher, hewn, old worn tan painted exterior w/scrubbed interior, small hole at one end for hanging, 19 5/8" l. 468

Wall pocket, red-painted & carved w/tombstone-shaped backboard w/hanging hole & applied square mirror flanked by carved candle sockets, w/small open compartment in base, wire nail construction, 9" w., 16 1/2" h. 275

WORLD'S FAIR COLLECTIBLES

There has been great interest in collecting items produced for the great fairs and expositions held through the years. During the 1970s, there was particular interest in items produced for the 1876 Centennial Exhibition and now interest is focusing on those items associated with the 1893 Columbian Exposition. Listed below is a random sampling of prices asked for items produced for the various fairs.

1876 Philadelphia Centennial

Kerchief, fabric, unhemmed design in blue on orange, a large scene of the Memorial Hall Art Gallery in the center w/round vignettes in each corner w/varied scenes at the fair, a large spread-winged American eagle & shield at top center w/a banner in its beak above swags w/"Centennial International" & "Exhibition - Fairmount Park - Philadelphia - 1776-1876" at the bottom center, folded, four tiny tack holes, 26" sq. $184

Kerchief, printed cotton, a large central scene w/a spread-winged American eagle & shield above a large fair building, star border band, titled under building "Memorial Hall Art Gallery Centennial 1776-1876," printed in black & red, unframed, 19 x 25 1/2" (age stains, some purple stains) 83

Needlework picture, a design of an American eagle w/banner & laurel wreath & "United We Stand...1776-1876," worked in shades of green, grey, ivory & lavender on pre-printed punched paper ground, in a Victorian criss-cross walnut frame w/applied leaves at the corners, paper label on the back "From W.R. Reid...Cleveland, O.," 13 5/8 x 26" 193

Paperweight, clear glass, oval w/inset image of Memorial Hall, dated "1776 - 1876," 4 x 5 1/4".............................. 36

1876 Centennial Puzzle Blocks

Puzzle blocks, set of 15 blocks depicting six of the Philadelphia exhibition buildings, in wooden case (ILLUS.)....................... 460

1876 World's Fair Stevengraph

Stevengraph, six-color Stevengraph depicts Centennial Hall of Philadelphia w/industrial scenes, George Washington, spread-winged eagle and elongated flags, w/"Philadelphia International Exhibition" at top, "Centennial - United States - Independence" in banner at bottom, 6 x 10 1/2", minor staining (ILLUS.) 330

Textile, printed silk, decorated in brown w/images of George Washington w/a figure of America in a chariot pulled by leopards, Benjamin Franklin w/Lady Liberty, cherubs, the Liberty Tree, etc., matted & framed, 33 x 35 5/8" (stains, stitched repairs).. 248

Tickets, paper admission tickets for the exhibition, each 2 1/4 x 4", pr. 55

1939-40 New York World's Fair

Considered by many as the last truly great World's Fair, its theme "Building a World for Tomorrow" was changed in 1940 to "For Peace & Freedom" as war clouds loomed. It also commemorated the 150th anniversary of George Washington's inaugural. Dominating a 1,216 acre Art Deco panorama, the stark white 110-foot-tall Trylon and 180-foot-diameter Perisphere were designed by Henry Dreyfus. The 1 1/2 year fair attracted almost 45 million visitors. (Futurama alone drew some 28,000 attendees daily.) This marked the first time that major corporations featured their products and services in separate pavilions. Many visitors got their first glimpse of the latest innovations: air conditioning, television, Kodachrome slides, stereophonic sound and Electro the Robot. Over 4,000 NYWF-related products were licensed worldwide bearing familiar orange and blue colors - a boon to collectors, as many sell for modest sums, though a lot of "green" is needed for rarer items.

Ashtray, white metal tray, NYWF figural diving nude lady w/Egyptian symbols surround 20-25

Bandana, "150th Centennial of First U.S. President," center medallion of George Washington, stylized inset of map of "Little Old New York," red, white, blue, green, 22 1/2" sq. 35-40

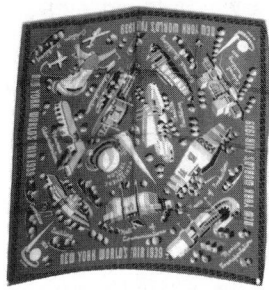

Bandana w/Diorama of NYWF

Bandana, diorama of entire NYWF w/Trylon
& Perisphere in center, stylized cartoon
form, designed by Cordelia Benjamin
(ILLUS.) **25-30**
Bank, figural Remington typewriter penny
bank, white metal, National Products
Corp. **20-25**

Gasoline Promo Banner

Banner, large horizontal cotton banner "Get
There With Richfield/World's Fair Free
Map/Information," blue & white, gasoline
promo (ILLUS.) **200-210**

NYWF Canvas Banner

Banner, large official Trylon & Perisphere
NYWF banner, canvas, orange & blue,
approx. 5' l. x 3' h. (ILLUS.) **200-210**
Cap, child's felt beanie w/Trylon & Peri-
sphere symbols **10-15**
Carpet sweeper, "Thirty Nine" white Trylon
& Perisphere on dark blue background,
Bissell, dark blue background, bright or-
ange handle **50-55**
Cigarette case, red, white, blue, gold, wafer
thin Art Deco metal case w/views of the
Trylon & Perisphere & other pavilions **75-85**
Cigarette dispenser, blue, orange, brown,
Polish pavilion w/NYWF scenes, wooden
handcrafted house, dispenses cigarette
in groove when roof is pushed down **30-35**

Clothing brush & tie rack, Syrocco backed
w/bas relief of Trylon & Perisphere in
clouds, it touts winning gold medal at
Fair, by Redlich **20-25**
First Day Cover, Commemorative NYWF
3¢ stamps on first day cover dated April
1, 1939, autographed by Franklin
Roosevelt, NY State Gov. Herbert Leh-
man & NYC Postmaster Albert Goldman,
without signatures of notables a NYWF
cacheted covers sells in $8-10
range **1,500-1,600**
Newsletter/flyer, black & white, Mimeo
flashes daily newsletter promoting Mim-
eograph Duplicator & Swiss Pavilion
Handout, ea. **10-15**

Trylon & Perisphere Figurals

**Paperweights, thermometers, ashtrays &
banks,** blue & orange plastic & white
metal, Trylon & Perisphere figurals, each
(ILLUS.) **15-20**
Parasol, child's size w/painted pictures of
Trylon & Perisphere plus other pavilions ... **45-50**
Parasol, green, blue & orange, full size
w/scenes of NYWF in each panel,
32" d. **45-50**
Pencil holder, white, plaster model of Ital-
ian Pavilion w/groove for pencils
at base **125-150**
Pinback, black, brown & blue, "Peter &
Penelope/Ice" cartoon of two bunnies
w/cake of ice **30-35**
Pinback, black & white, "Frank Buck's Jun-
gleland" midway attraction bust photo of
Buck in pith helmet **25-30**
Pinback, blue & white, "Little Miss Junket"
photo of young lady in chef's hat promot-
ing package of Junket dessert **12-15**
Pinback, orange & blue, "Dawn of a New
Day/NYWF 1939" flag atop Trylon & Peri-
sphere **15-20**
Pinback, orange & blue, Florida/NYWF,
view of Florida Pavilion **15-20**
Pinback, red, white & blue, "Gas Wonder-
land/NYWF" image of bright red flame **15-20**
Pinback, white, w/brown background,
"Guernsey" bovine bust, w/Trylon & Peri-
sphere **20-25**

Pinbacks & Studpins

Pinbacks/studpins, sampling of NYWF giveaways, the most popular being Futurama button & the figural green Heinz Pickle studpin, each (ILLUS.) **10-12**

Pipe holder, brown, red & blue, Syrocco figural hewn log w/Trylon & Perisphere image, carved out to cradle briar pipe **15**

Pitcher, asymmetrical pottery, orange on white, small Trylon & Perisphere, A.E. Hull **50-55**

Plate, ceramic, blue on white, w/NYWF vignettes, Wedgwood **150-175**

Plate, ceramic, NYWF Trylon & Perisphere w/vignettes of pavilions surround **25-30**

Plate, Syrocco bas-relief plate w/Fair outline, ornate leaf & flower border **25-30**

Multicolored Postcard

Postcard, multicolor, 14-ton Underwood Typewriter Exhibit (ILLUS.) **15-20**

Poster, blue & white, "The World's Fair/Biggest Show of Your Life," transit subway poster, cartoon of NYC Mayor Fiorello LaGuardia conducting band w/baton **85-90**

Poster, cardboard counter display sign, yellow, black & white,"Take a Kodak to the NYWF," young lady in sun hat photographing Trylon & Perisphere **75**

Poster, "Go By All Means/NYWF/1940," fairgoers scurrying by riding bicycles, scooters, pushing baby buggies **75-85**

Poster, multicolor, "Makes You Proud of Your Country/NYWF/1940," waist high image of beaming man, by Howard Scott .. **65-70**

Poster, multicolor, "NYWF Railroads on Parade/To Do Full Honor to America's Railroads," image of streamliner passing vintage 1890s engine, Forbes litho poster, by Leslie Ragan **400-425**

Polish Pavilion Poster

Poster, multicolor, "Polish Pavilion/NYWF," signed "JHR '38" (ILLUS.) **300-325**

Bakelite Table Radio

Radio, Bakelite, RCA, table-type, brown faux wood w/white Trylon & Perisphere mounted on speaker front (ILLUS.) **250-300**

Razor, white plastic, "NYWF/1939/Electrical Products Building" inscription, Remington Electric **40-45**

Robe, terry cloth lounging robe, blue, orange & white w/blue buttons, NYWF symbols & name "Expo Hostess Wang" **40-50**

Metal Serving Tray

Serving tray, orange & blue, metal tray, New York 1939 Art Deco Trylon & Perisphere (ILLUS.) **25-30**

Spoon, sculpted Tiffany limited edition Art Deco silver spoon w/Perisphere as bowl & Trylon as handle, originally sold at $140 .... **250-300**

Spoons, sterling silver w/outline of Manhattan skyline, set of five demitasse spoons w/different pavilions inscribed in bowl, each **20-25**

World's Fair Tapestry

Tapestry, brown, black & white, large horizontal linen rendering of Trylon & Perisphere flanked by Federal & Administration buildings (ILLUS.) **175-185**

George Washington Toby Mug

Toby mug, ceramic figural bust mug, white, George Washington honoring sesquicentennial of his inauguration (ILLUS.) **10-15**

Toy, "Build Your Own Fair Kit," boxed lithographed cardboard cut-out pieces for assembling various pavilions, by Standard Toycraft Products, 10 1/2" h. x 14" w. **75-80**

Arcade Tour Bus Tractor

Toy, cast iron, blue & orange, NYWF Tour Bus Tractor w/box, Arcade (ILLUS.)...... **175-200**

Toy, cast iron, blue, white & orange, Greyhound Bus, w/NYWF logo, Arcade, 10 1/2" l. **175-185**

Toy, cast iron, blue, white & orange, Greyhound Bus, w/NYWF logo, Arcade, 7" l. **130-135**

Toy, cast iron, blue, white & orange, Greyhound Bus, w/NYWF logo, Arcade, 8 1/2" l. **135-150**

Toy, George Washington metamorphic paper toy viewer.. **35-40**

Toy, teardrop shaped futuristic silver bullet cars, General Motors Futurama **150-175**

Walking stick, multicolor, spring-loaded, reveals Tony Sarg's illustrated map of NYWF **30-35**

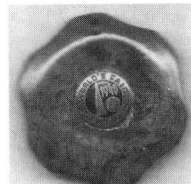

New York World's Fair Watch Fob

Watch fob, plastic made to look like yellow tortoiseshell, rounded six-sided fob, center w/images of Trylon & Perisphere & "1940" within border reading "World's Fair - New York," reverse w/Elks emblem, 1 1/4" d. **17**

WRITING ACCESSORIES

Early writing accessories are popular collectibles and offer a wide variety to select from. A collection may be formed around any one segment —pens, letter openers, lap desks or inkwells, for instance—or the collection may revolve around choice specimens of all types. Material, design and age usually determine the value. Pen collectors like the large fountain pens developed in the 1920s but also look for pens and mechanical pencils that are solid gold or gold-plated. Also see: BOTTLES & FLASKS

Inkwells & Stands

Brass stand, w/candle cup & wafer box, probably 18th c., 5 x 6" **$170**

Brass stand, double-style, figural, an owl in relief, 7 x 13" **230**

Brass well, travel-type, w/single cup in small hinged box covered w/thin green leather, cup w/own extra hinged fitted top...... **125**

Brass well, figural, a grasshopper w/lidded ink cup, finely detailed, marked "BJW" on base, 4" l. **110**

Bronze & art glass well, "Pine-Needle" patt., hingebacked to a larger than usual glass cup, marked "Tiffany Studios, New York" & numbered **550**

Bronze stand, figural, New Orleans Carnival & Parade "King" REX, probably a carnival "favor," gold washed, 8 x 11" **350**

Bronze stand, stylized peacocks or partridges on pedestal stand, hinges back to reveal double white pottery ink cups, 4 x 11 1/2" **750**

Bronze well, round, pinkish sides decorated w/various boats in very high relief & Celtic swirl designs, lid features mythological warrior battling a dragon wearing a high cap & unusual sword, marked "Real Bronze," ca. 1870s, 6" d. **950**

Bronze well, figural, stylized Art Deco pyramid, top 1/3 lifts back exposing glass insert, 4 x 4 x 5" h.. **250**

Bronze well, figural, books lift back to reveal double inkwells, 3 x 7 1/2" **145**

Bronze well, desk-style w/glass cups, elegant & usually undecorative, initialed "B&H" (Bradley & Hubbard) or marked w/an "Aladdin's lamp," 4 x 9" **450**

Bronze well, figural, an Indian maiden, reclining bust, classic Art Deco style, 4 x 9 1/2".. **350**

Bronze well, Harem "houri" (draped female figure w/face covered) of 1920s "Valentino" romantic Arabic styling, enameled, 4 x 9 1/2" **350**

Bronze well, figural, an Art Deco owl, fantail inset w/semi-precious stone inserts, ca. 1900, no mark, 4 1/2 x 10" (ILLUS.)............... **450**

Bronze well, figural, a panther in graceful elongated stalking position, accurate & very realistic portrayal in the "naturalistic" school, hingeback lid revealing double white pottery ink cups, ca. 1903, 4 1/2 x 12" **850**

Cast-iron & Glass Victorian Stand

Cast iron & glass stand, cast-iron frame w/angular design decorated w/Victorian

Aesthetic Movement designs, pair of angled uprights form pen rests above the inset clear pressed glass well w/metal cover, marked on bottom "Patent Nov. 5, 1879," 4 x 4 1/2", 4 1/2" h. (ILLUS.).............. **245**

Cast-iron Stand with Tilting Inkwells

Cast iron & glass stand, cast-iron rectangular frame w/cast florettes at each corner & center of base w/Greek key & line borders, three shaped uprights form pen rests & support two round clear blown glass tilting inkwells, traces of original gilt finish, late 19th c., 4 1/4 x 6", 6 3/4" h. (ILLUS.) **325**

Double Cast-iron & Glass Inkstand

Cast iron & glass stand, double-style, the angular cast-iron frame w/Aesthetic Movement designs & three uprights forming pen rests above two clear pressed glass wells w/metal caps, marked on base "Patent Nov. 5, 1879," 4 x 7", 4 1/2" h. (ILLUS.) **365**

Cast-iron Square Inkstand with Well

Cast iron & glass stand, squared iron base w/rounded corners & a coved border w/cast lines, two scalloped uprights for

pens flank the clear pressed glass well w/hinged metal cover, late 19th c., 3 3/8 x 4 1/2", 4 1/2" h. (ILLUS.) **245**

Ceramic well, square w/h.p. floral design, large cork lid, ca. 1920s, 2" **60**

Copper stand, desk-style w/hingebacked double cup, marked "G. Stickley" **475**

Cut glass well, hobstar & fan patt., 3 1/2" **130**

Enameled metal stand, figural, a deer & elk combination on stand, elk antlers designed to hold quill pen, liftback reveals large glass cup, sponge enameled, German **130**

Enameled metal well, figural, a Bengal tiger head, hingeback, single well, smaller type w/good enamel... **95**

Enameled metal well, figural, a Bengal tiger head, hingeback w/single glass well, larger style (darkened paint)........................... **450**

Glass & metal stand, thin metal butterfly forms pen rest behind floral tray w/clear glass well, thin ramped holder, gold washed... **145**

Glass stand, clear bottle-type, fitted to metallic red tray featuring a tiny, brass housefly, probably Japanese, ca. 1930s **100**

Glass stand, horseshoe backs a single glass lidded well on a wooden base, brass studded horseshoe forms a triple pen rest, "Lucky" message well **190**

Glass stand, figural, an ink bottle, lavender, w/molded pen tray, 3 x 3"................................. **60**

Coral Pink Cut-glass Inkwell

Glass well, coral pink cut-glass faceted round base, flat-topped tapered cylinder hinged top, metal rims where top & base meet, 4" h. (ILLUS.) **295**

Square Amber Inkwell

Glass well, heavy amber glass, square base w/embossed stippled design &

large round indentations on each side, metal neck, hinged top of amber glass, 4" h. (ILLUS.)..................... **295**

Glass well, Sengbusch "globe" of unusual black glass in bottom cup, rotates position to any angle **90**

Glass well, clear bottle w/attached hinged brass lid, low relief, marked "U," 2 1/2" **45**

Glass well, clear well w/removable floral silver cap, marked "Sterling," made through the 1920s, 2 3/4" d. **90**

Metal & glass stand, child's, early Art Nouveau style w/tiny deer against stump, stump hinges back to a very small glass ink cup, France, ca. 1800s, 1 1/8" **325**

Metal stand, figural, a cowboy "Buckaroo" w/bronco rider in full figure, multiple metals including tin shield for the single glass well, 7" h. **80**

Metal well, figural, a cat sitting w/curled-around tail, enameled, single cup **100**

Metal well, figural, a lady waits sadly by a fence, the rail fence hints at a Lincoln Memorial theme as does the great stump concealing the cup, Victorian "message" inkwell, various metals including iron **185**

Metal well, square, holds glass bottle w/hinged top, plain styling, 3" **75**

Metal well, figural, a bulldog head, top of head hinges back to single cup, 3 7/8" d. **95**

Metal well, figural, a camel, reclining w/heavily tasseled saddle & blanket, 6 w., 7" h. **135**

Oak stand, teacher's desk-type, top receptacle above pen rest w/unusually sized glass ink cup, 7 1/2 x 13" **195**

Papier-maché well, box w/tiny legs, white w/gold scrolling & cross-hatching on lid, hingeback lid reveals small double glass cups, ca. 1890 .... **80**

Papier-maché well, box-type, black w/h.p. flowers, hinges back to single glass insert, ca. 1925 .... **75**

Pewter stand, Colonial-style, w/round cup on bottom plate, quill holes in flared lip, 3" (ink stained) **95**

Pewter stand, figural, tree stump w/broken branches, type known as "message" in Victorian era & often presented to one who had lost a family member, w/light sealant to prevent discoloring, 5 x 7" **270**

Pewter well, pewter barrel well w/attached "Mary Poppins"-like enameled female figure wearing black high-crowned hat, colorful enamel, England, ca. 1890s **205**

Porcelain stand, clock w/double porcelain ink cups **130**

Porcelain stand, double, w/gold h.p. scrolls & flowers, marked "M.F. France," ca. 1900 .... **400**

Porcelain well, Pa Carter inkwell, black (slight scuffing) **95**

Porcelain wells, Ma & Pa Carter inkwells, brilliant orange & blue, Carter Inks, the pr. **300**

Pot metal stand, figural, a cannon w/basket inkstand, small snap-lid travel well w/blown glass insert within the basket, ca. 1850-1860 .... **480**

Pot metal well, figural, enameled clown head w/liftback hinge (some paint damage) **110**

Pot metal well, square, floral relief, box w/hingeback to reveal cup **50**

Pottery well, figural, an elephant behind single glass cup in holder, primitive................. **90**

Fine Silver Plate Victorian Inkstand

Silver plate & glass, double-type, a footed rectangular tray base w/a wide gently rolled rim stamped w/ornate leafy scrolls, pen rests at the front edge, holds a pair of square clear glass wells w/hinged scroll-cast domed caps flanking a rectangular stamp box, marked by the Derby Silver Co., No. 1745, late 19th c., 4 3/4 x 8 1/4", 3" h. (ILLUS.) **265**

Silver well, floral footed casket, w/liftback lid revealing double glass cups, ca. 1925, marked "Simmons," 2 x 2 3/4 x 4 3/4"........... **145**

Sterling silver stand, triple pedestal design w/double white glass insert, pinstriped, added copper strips, English hallmarks, 5 x 5 x 5 1/2" h. **190**

Sterling silver well, figural, a dog chomping on unrolled newspaper, ca.1898, 3 x 5 x 9" **375**

Wooden stand, handmade primitive stand w/animal, box-like container for the cup, Amish, 3 1/2 x 4 1/2"......................... **75**

Wooden well, hand-carved figural camel, saddle lifts back to reveal narrow blown glass well brush holder, Syria, probably 1920s... **120**

Wooden well, hand-carved wooden bear on pedestal, small pressed glass ink cup w/wooden acorn cap, Germany (Black Forest-type cottage industry), ca. 1800s **250**

Wrought-iron well, Black man w/straw hat, reclining bust, an advertising symbol known by several names including "Cotton Joe," ca. early 1900s, head lifts back to reveal cup................................. **450**

Wrought-iron well, figural, a ram's head w/curled horns, hinged lid reveals cup, painted, original blackened appearance, 4 1/2 x 6" **95**

Letter Openers

Letter Opener with Seal-form Handle

Bronze, the handle w/a model of a seal, long flat blade, 7" l. (ILLUS.)............................. **55**

Advertising Letter Opener with Knife

Plated bronze, advertising-type, the flattened pointed handle embossed "Broenniman Company Inc. - Flour - Produce Exchange, N.Y.," long silvered blade, handle encloses fold-out knife blade, early 20th c., 9 1/2" l. (ILLUS.) **135**

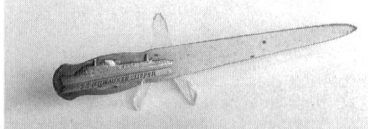

Letter Opener with Ship Decoration

Plated steel, advertising-type, flat gilt handle & blade w/an applied silvered relief of passenger liner stamped in red "SS Milwaukee Clipper," 20th c., 8 3/4" l. (ILLUS.) **58**

Miscellaneous

Patriotic Eagle Inkstand

Desk set: inkstand, blotter & letter rack; cast iron w/bronzed finish, the rectangular stand cast in the middle w/a large spread-winged American eagle & shield above a wreath & flanked by raised square wells w/raised band design, the upright serpentine letter rack w/an openwork eagle design, the roller blotter decorated on top w/small eagles & loops flanking the center knob handle, marked "4964," inkstand, 5 1/2 x 10 1/2", the set (ILLUS. of inkstand).. **345**

Owl on Bough Letter Rack

Letter rack, cast iron w/bronzed finish, undulating Art Nouveau design pierced frame ends centered by a relief-cast owl on pine boughs, telescoping tubing connects the sides, No. 9776, contracted size 6 1/2 x 9 1/2", 4 1/2" h. (ILLUS.) **145**

Bradley & Hubbard Letter Rack

Letter rack, cast spelter w/gilt finish, flat rectangular sides cast in relief w/an overall lacy leaf design within leaf borders, on scroll feet & w/arched scroll loop handles at the top, Bradley & Hubbard, original paper label on bottom, late 19th-early 20th c., 2 1/2 x 6 1/4", 5 1/4" h. (ILLUS.) **345**

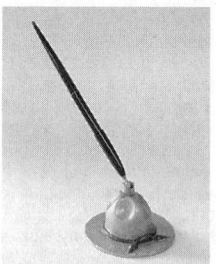

Hat Pen Holder

Pen holder, cast iron, base in the form of a WWI soldier's or Rough Rider's wide-brimmed hat, in original green & silver paint, w/pen holder at top of hat, advertising Channon Emery Stove Co., Quincy, Ill., 3 1/2 x 4" (ILLUS.).. **70**

Victorian Cast-iron Pen Rack

Pen rack, cast iron, arched end uprights w/cast leaf designs, each w/three small scrolls to support pens, joined by a slender crossbar, original black finish, late 19th c., 3 1/4 x 5", 3 1/4" h. (ILLUS.)............... **95**

Index